# Contents at a Glance

# Table of Contents

# PURE

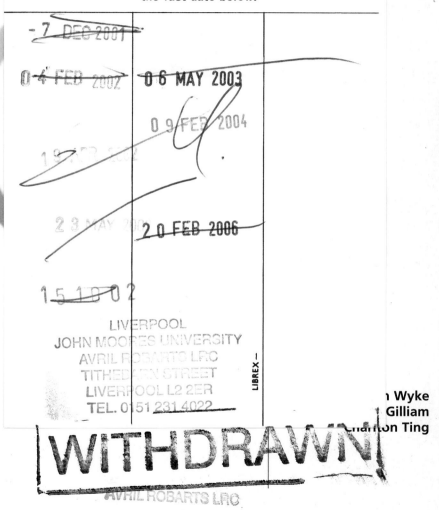

n Wyke
Gilliam
harlton Ting

**SAMS**     20     LIVERPOOL JMU LIBRARY     ndiana 46290

# Pure JavaScript

## Copyright © 1999 by Sams Publishing

International Standard Book Number: 0-672-31547-5

Library of Congress Catalog Card Number: 99-62353

Printed in the United States of America

First Printing: August 1999

01   00                    4

## Trademarks

## Warning and Disclaimer

**ACQUISITIONS EDITOR**
Randi Roger

**DEVELOPMENT EDITOR**
Scott D. Meyers

**MANAGING EDITOR**
Lisa Wilson

**PROJECT EDITOR**
Rebecca Mounts

**COPY EDITOR**
Pat Kinyon

**INDEXER**
Heather Goens

**PROOFREADER**
Cynthia Fields

**TECHNICAL EDITORS**
Andrew Wooldridge
Nate Kassebaum

**INTERIOR DESIGN**
Karen Ruggles

**COVER DESIGN**
Anne Jones

**COPY WRITER**
Eric Borgert

**LAYOUT TECHNICIAN**
Brad Lenser

## 7   CLIENT-SIDE BROWSER SYNTAX                                                457

## PART IV  APPENDIXES  1317

# About the Authors

**R. Allen Wyke**, Practice Manager of System Integration Consultants at Engage Technologies, has developed intranet pages and Internet sites for several leading companies. His writing experience includes co-authoring *The Perl 5 Programmer's Reference*, *The Official Netscape Navigator 4 Book*, as well as contributing to two additional books on HTML (*The HTML 4 Programmer's Reference* and *HTML Publishing for the Internet*, 2nd Edition). He has also worked on another book that contains a section on Internet resources, and is designed for college graduates.

**Jason D. Gilliam**, a software engineer at KOZ.com in the Research Triangle Park, NC, has developed many intranet Web pages and CGI programs as well as numerous C++ GUI applications and database connectivity programs. He holds a bachelor's degree in Computer Engineering from North Carolina State University. When not at work, Jason creates Windows-based audio programs and composes original music using PCs.

**Charlton Ting**, of Vienna, VA, is a software engineer for Lucent Technologies and develops Internet telephony solutions for leading Internet companies. He has created numerous applications and Web sites using Java, JavaScript, CGI, CORBA, and HTML technologies. Charlton holds bachelor's degrees in Computer Engineering and Electrical Engineering from North Carolina State University.

# Dedications

*This one is for my sisters: Sandra, Valerie, and Evelyn. They truly are inspirations in my life and have broadened my visions and provided support well beyond anything I would have ever imagined. I love each of you very much.*
*—R. Allen Wyke*

*I dedicate this book to my wonderful wife, Deena, who is the greatest! Your constant encouragement, love, and support has carried me through the writing of this book. I love you!*
*—Jason D. Gilliam*

*This book is dedicated to my family: John, Alice, Angela, Melissa, and Olivia. Thank you for all your love and support for everything I've done in my life. I love you all very much.*
*—Charlton Ting*

# Acknowledgments

On the publishing side, I would like to thank Bob Kern of TIPS Publishing and my co-authors, Jason and Chuck, for their professionalism, hard work, and overall support in the proposing and writing of this book. I would also like to thank Randi Rogers, who has been nothing short of an absolutely fabulous Acquisitions Editor, and Scott Meyers, who developed the book and kept us focused. Additionally, I would like to thank everyone at Sams who worked on the book and helped make sure it was the best it could be.

I would also like to thank Beth Roach and Dan Peterson for allowing me the flexibility and opportunity to write during all my work and travel. I want to say thanks to little Miss Wendy as well. She has provided a VERY honest perspective on many things as of late and helped keep me in line.

And finally, I would like to thank the "Raccoons." You have made the last six months the happiest of my life.

—R. Allen Wyke


I would like to thank Bob Kern of TIPS Publishing and my co-authors, Allen and Chuck, for their efforts in developing and writing this book. I would also like to thank our Acquisitions Editor, Randi Roger and Development Editor, Scott Meyers, for all of their hard work as well as everyone at Sams who helped make this book possible.

I would also like to thank the "lunch guys" for their open ears and words of encouragement.

—Jason D. Gilliam


I would like to thank Bob Kern of TIPS Publishing for all his hard work in making this book possible. I also want to thank my co-authors, Allen and Jason, for all their hard work, dedication, and encouragement to make this book a success. Additionally I want to thank our Acquisitions Editor Randi Roger, Scott Meyers, and everyone at Sams who worked so hard at making this book possible.

I also want to thank all my friends who provided so much support during the rough times: Mike, Carolyn, Monty, Theresa, John, Blanke, Stacey, the doc (Sunil), and anyone I may have forgotten to mention. You guys are the greatest friends anyone could have.

—Charlton Ting

# Tell Us What You Think!

As the reader of this book, *you* are our most important critic and commentator. We value your opinion and want to know what we're doing right, what we could do better, what areas you'd like to see us publish in, and any other words of wisdom you're willing to pass our way.

You can fax, email, or write me directly to let me know what you did or didn't like about this book—as well as what we can do to make our books stronger.

*Please note that I cannot help you with technical problems related to the topic of this book, and that due to the high volume of mail I receive, I might not be able to reply to every message.*

*When you write, please be sure to include this book's title and authors as well as your name and phone or fax number. I will carefully review your comments and share them with the authors and editors who worked on this book.*

Fax:        317-581-4770

Email:      `internet_sams@mcp.com`

Mail:       Mark Taber
            Associate Publisher
            Sams Publishing
            201 West 103rd Street
            Indianapolis, IN 46290 USA

# Introduction

Welcome to *Pure JavaScript*! This book has been written by JavaScript programmers for JavaScript programmers. It is your complete reference for developing, testing, and deploying JavaScript solutions in pages and on Web sites.

*Pure JavaScript* was not written to teach a person how to program, but rather to provide the details and semantics of the JavaScript language so programmers can exploit it as they see fit. JavaScript has evolved over the past few years and is reaching into new areas, many of which are addressed in this book. The book itself is broken into three main parts, including references on concepts, techniques, and syntax. Each represents a valuable step in learning and using a language.

Part I of the book, "A Programmer's Overview of JavaScript," acts as a bridge for programmers who are currently programming in another language. Many times programmers don't want to buy a beginner's book on JavaScript because they do not need to know how to program, but rather they need specifics about the language. Once they know these specifics and semantics, the syntax is easy. This section provides the necessary information for such a programming migration.

Part II, "Programming in JavaScript," shows you the advantages and strengths of JavaScript. It discusses some of the pros and cons of using the language and the environments in which it is interpreted. Programmers will learn how to use JavaScript in real world instances. They will be introduced to some of the browser issues as well as how to process Web information. Programmers will even be shown how to access Java functions within an applet. After you have completed this section, you will be ready to move forward and start programming. This leads you into the last section of the book.

Part III, "JavaScript Reference by Object," makes up the majority of the book and contains some of the most useful information for current JavaScript programmers—reference material organized by object. Each property, method, and event is discussed in detail under its associated object; and you'll see an example of its use. Each entry also shows the appropriate language version and browser or server support. The section itself is broken into four chapters. The first chapter covers JavaScript standard objects and syntax. The next chapter covers client-side and browser scripting objects. The third chapter covers server-side JavaScript objects (for Netscape Enterprise servers). Finally, we cover JavaScript geared for Microsoft Active Scripting interface.

In addition, several appendixes have been included. Located here are quick reference tables to find browser and version support of the syntax. There is also an appendix, "JavaScript Resources," that includes JavaScript Web resources for additional documentation and help with programming issues that you may come across.

And that covers it! For new JavaScript programmers, welcome to the world of JavaScript. For those of you wanting a good, solid reference for your programming, we hope you find this book to be the most resourceful and current title on the shelves today!

R. Allen Wyke

Jason Gilliam

Charlton Ting

# PART I

# A PROGRAMMER'S OVERVIEW OF JAVASCRIPT

# CHAPTER 1

## What Is JavaScript to a Programmer?

In the beginning, there were Assembly and compiled languages. Later came scripting languages such as sed, awk, and Perl, which many programmers used to perform a variety of tasks. These were followed by, in the late 80s and early 90s, the Internet, which exploded into a technological revolution that allowed anyone with a modem to communicate and retrieve information from around the world. As the Internet grew in number of users, it was obvious that an increase in functionality was needed in the browsers being used and in the data they were rendering.

HTML, even with its advantages, was falling short of providing the control many developers wanted when creating Web pages and applications. This prompted the use of server-side programs to handle some of the page dynamics developers needed from their sites.

These programs helped Web developers by allowing them to increase a site's functionality and to process user-submitted information. However, CGI, or Common Gateway Interface, programs had to generate a response that told the user to resubmit a request when he or she sent incorrect or incomplete information. This led to a lot of back-and-forth data transmission between a browser and a server. But, overall, it was a minor price to pay for the functionality received.

It became increasingly obvious that client-side intelligence was needed to replace some of the CGI functionality and error checking and decreasing the amount of time a user spent connecting to a server. This would also allow the Web site to offload some of its processing load to the browser machine, which meant an increase in the overall performance of a site.

It was partially this lack of client-side functionality and efficiency that helped spawn a new scripting language—one that could be executed within a browser's environment and not on the server. This language could be used to perform some client-side tasks such as form validation and dynamic page content creation—one that would put the programming into HTML publishing. Welcome to the birth of JavaScript.

On December 4, 1995, Netscape and Sun jointly introduced JavaScript 1.0, originally called LiveScript, to the world. This language, unlike its server-based predecessors, could be interpreted within the new Netscape Navigator 2 browsers. As an interpreted language, JavaScript was positioned as a complement to Java and would allow Web developers to create and deploy custom applications across the enterprise and Internet alike. JavaScript gave developers the power to truly program—not just format data with HTML.

In addition to the client-side control developers desired, Netscape implemented server-side JavaScript. This allowed developers to use the same programming language on the server as they did in their pages for browsers. Database connection enhancements were added to the language (called LiveWire) allowing the developer to pull information directly from a database and better maintain user sessions. JavaScript had truly bridged the gap between the simple world of HTML and the more complex CGI programs on the server. It provided a common language for Web developers to design, implement, and deploy solutions across their networks and distributed the overall processing load of their applications.

The next level of acceptance in the world of JavaScript was Microsoft's implementation of the language in its Internet Explorer 3 browser—its interpretation of the language was called JScript. Like Netscape, Microsoft also implemented the language on the server-side (JScript 2.0) that was done in tandem with its ASP, or Active Server Pages, technology.

## JAVASCRIPT VERSUS JSCRIPT, AND WHAT IS ECMASCRIPT?

JScript was based on the published documentation from Netscape, so it should have been the same thing as JavaScript 1.1. However, there were a few "features" that Netscape did not publish, as well as some functionality that was not re-created by Microsoft correctly. The result of this is that there are some discrepancies between JScript 1.0 and JavaScript 1.1 in Microsoft's first generation releases.

Since the release of these initial browsers, JavaScript was submitted and has become a standard, known as ECMAScript 1.0 (ECMA-262), with the European Computer Manufacturers Association (ECMA). Because of this standardization, it is now perceived that JavaScript is Netscape's implementation of ECMAScript and JScript is Microsoft's implementation.

The adoption of ECMAScript 1.0 occurred in June 1997 followed by its adoption by the International Organization for Standardization and International Electrotechnical Commission in April 1998 (ISO/IEC 16262).

**NOTE**

Since ECMAScript was standardized after Netscape's JavaScript, this book will refer to it as JavaScript.

So, what is JavaScript to the programmer? Well, in its purest form it is an object based, cross-platform, loosely-typed, multi-use language that allows a programmer to deploy many types of solutions to many clients. It not only involves adding functionality to Web pages as rendered within a browser, it also allows server-side processing for Netscape and Microsoft Web servers.

JavaScript has also most recently been included in Microsoft's Windows Scripting Host to allow programmers to write scripts to be executed on the operating system itself. This functionality is similar to the old DOS batch files, but gives programmers more functionality and versatility in what they can accomplish. It is this type of advancement that has allowed the language to take hold in the computer world and continue to progress.

In addition to the benefits of these environments where JavaScript can be executed, there are security measures in place to protect end users against malicious code. Even though it is still young in terms of age, JavaScript, in its current version, is very mature and powerful. It is this functionality, ability, and versatility that positions JavaScript as the best solution for programmers.

Now that you've learned about what JavaScript is, you should now dive a little deeper into what it means to a programmer. Being programmers ourselves, we know that a few strategically placed words do not make a language useful. First, you'll look at the object based characteristics of JavaScript.

# Object based Technology

Since you are reading this book, it's assumed that you have programmed in at least one other language before, even if only for one semester in college. Going one step further, I bet the language you programmed in was either C++, Java, or Perl—with Java and C++ being object-oriented (OO). Java specifically is OO by virtue of having all created objects extending from core Java language classes.

For those of you unfamiliar with object-oriented programming (OOP), it is a concept that allows you to create reusable objects or classes in code. An object or class has associated with it various characteristics and functionality that define what kind of properties and states it can take on. Once these are created and defined, it is possible to create new instances—sometimes referred to as a "children"—that inherit the ability to have the same characteristics of their "parent" object.

To give you an example of how this might work, create a vehicle object. Part of the characteristics assigned to this vehicle object are the number of doors, the color, and the type (such as sports car or truck). In addition to these characteristics, define the ability to move or stop the vehicle. The pseudo-code for this type of object might look something like the following:

```
object vehicle(){
  // Characteristics of the vehicle
  num_doors;
  color;
  type;

  // Methods used to move and stop the truck. Note that the move()
  // method takes a direction as a property. This direction could
  // be something like forward, backward, left, or right.
  move(direction);
  stop();
}
```

Now that this vehicle object is defined, it is easy to create new instances of it. A vehicle that is a car with four doors and is red can be easily created. You could also create a vehicle that is a truck with two doors and is black. In addition to creating these instances of the vehicle object, you have also made it possible to program in the ability to change the state of your instance. This is accomplished by specifying whether it is stopped or moving.

As an example in pseudo-code, the following creates a black, two-door truck that is moving forward:

```
// Create the new instance of the vehicle
myTruck = new vehicle();

// Define the type, number of doors and color
myTruck.doors = 2;
myTruck.color = "black";
myTruck.type = "truck";

// Define the "state" of the truck
myTruck.move(forward);
```

The basic process here is to create an instance of the vehicle object and then to assign characteristic values to it. It is these values that make it a unique instance of a vehicle, which you have specified as a truck.

As you can see in this example, the creation of the vehicle object allows you to easily create more vehicles with different characteristics. When programming, this "ease" translates into less code—something all programmers like to hear. Now that this object is defined, it is possible to create new instances that inherit its characteristics without having to redefine them. You are able to capitalize on any overlaps in characteristics within objects by doing this. The idea is to create a general, master object that gives you the ability to then derive child instances from it.

This can also be taken a step further by creating new objects—not instances—that inherit the parent objects' characteristics. Doing so allows you to derive child instances from the child object that you have decided will inherit only certain characteristics. You could define a child object to only pass on the parent object's color characteristic to any child instances of its own. It is the concept of this object orientation that allows you to perform this modular type of programming.

The following pseudo-code example shows how you could create an `airplane` object based on the `vehicle` object:

```
// Create the new object that inherits the vehicle
object airplane(){

  // Inherit the vehicle object
  this = new vehicle();

  // Define the doors property, then assign it to the size
  // property of the plane object
  this.doors = "747";
  this.size = this.doors;

  // Assign the color and type of plane
  this.color = "silver";
  this.type = "American Airlines";

  // Define the "state" of the plane
  this.move(up);

  // Now that the object is created with the values, return the
  // object.
  return this;
}
```

Not all languages support this concept, and there are other languages only based on its concepts. This concept definitely supplies advantages to the language, but it is not required to write good, effective, modular code. JavaScript is a perfect example of how a language has applied some of these concepts, but is not completely OO. It does this by being *object based*.

**NOTE**

Talking about OOP in further detail is beyond the focus of a JavaScript book, but it is worth some investigation if you are a real programming enthusiast. Check out your local bookstore for a selection of titles on this subject. You can also visit Object Central (`http://www.objectcentral.com`) on the Web for reference and links to OOP information.

So how does object based fit into the equation? It is very similar to OO except that it does not have all the functionality or characteristics. There are limited amounts of inheritance, scope, and functionality that you can perform with an object based language. This should not be taken as a mark against JavaScript, because it makes the language easier to learn and maintain for the developer. OOP is no easy beast to tackle and will provide many headaches before it is implemented correctly.

JavaScript also makes up for many of its OO limitations by allowing you to create your own object-like elements, as well as extend the core objects in the language by prototyping new properties. To get an idea of how this is done, take a look at JavaScript object orientation.

# Object Orientation of JavaScript

Before we go into a lot of detail on the object orientation of JavaScript, first look at some differences in the core components and functionality between server-side and client-side JavaScript. Both have objects that are specific to their runtime environment, so object initialization and creation occur at different times. Because of this characteristic, you will look at the language in two parts: client-side and server-side.

Client-side JavaScript is, at its lowest level, several core objects that are created when a page is loaded in the browser. In addition to these core objects, there are also derived objects that are created when certain tags are included on a page. These derived objects inherit some of the various characteristics of their parent object and also allow scripting access to the HTML tag's properties.

Understanding the hierarchy of the JavaScript objects is a very important item if you plan on doing any in-depth programming. You will get a better understanding of how parent and child objects interact as well as how they are referenced. To help with this understanding Figure 1.1 gives a graphical representation of the basic client-side JavaScript hierarchy.

As depicted in this diagram, all client-side objects are derived from either the Window or navigator objects. Considering that this is an object based language, this structure makes complete sense. All objects on a given page are constructed within the browser's window, hence all objects that JavaScript can create are descendants of the Window object. By using the Window object, a programmer is allowed to access the various frames, documents, layers, and forms on a page, as well as many other objects and properties.

The navigator object pertains to elements that are "part" of the browser itself. This specifically refers to the plug-ins installed and the MIME (Multipart Internet Mail Extension) types with which the browser is associated. Using the navigator object allows checking of the browser version, determining the plug-ins installed, and what programs are associated with the various MIME types registered on the system. There is also the ability to access other properties of the browser.

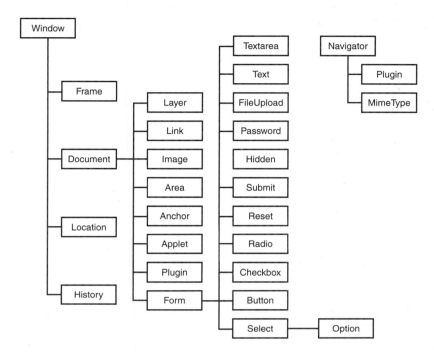

**Figure 1.1**

*Client-side JavaScript object hierarchy.*

Like its client-side, server-side JavaScript has several core objects from which all other objects are derived. The root objects are the `DbPool` and `database` objects from which you can create connections to a database, as well as access cursors, stored procedures, and the result sets you generate. Figure 1.2 shows the specific server-side object hierarchy.

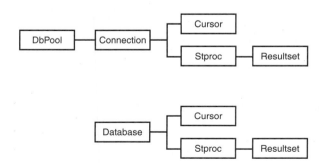

**Figure 1.2**

*Server-side JavaScript object hierarchy.*

**NOTE**

Both of the server-side and client-side JavaScript languages are based on objects. Programmers familiar with Java will find this very similar to the Java language. There are not as many objects/classes in the JavaScript language, but the structure and manner in which you access them are similar.

Because of this object hierarchy, accessing the various objects and elements on a page is done by using the hierarchy itself. If you wanted to access a specific text field in a form on a page, you would do so using the following syntax:

```
window.document.formName.textboxName.value
```

**TIP**

With JavaScript, programmers have the ability to create their own objects or extend the core ones defined by the language. The explanation of how to create your own objects—and some examples—is covered in the section on functions in Chapter 2, "Details of the Language." If you want to learn more about extending the functionality of the existing objects, look up objects with the *prototype* property in the reference section of this book.

Because JavaScript is object based, it automatically provides many advantages to using a modular approach to your programming. By creating your own objects and methods, you are able to better maintain the code with which you are working. You will be creating code that can be reused in other programs, locations, and instances. Why write virtually the same code twice (or many times), when you can create it once and pass the characteristics that differentiate it from other, similar objects?

## Modular Programming

To program in the modular fashion in JavaScript really involves three key things. Using these items in your programming will allow you to create code that can be reused from project to project. These are

- Creating your own objects
- Defining general functions to handle common tasks
- Placing reusable code in external JavaScript source files (commonly *.js or *.mocha files)

**NOTE**

Like any other language, remember that good comments and documentation are often the most beneficial aspects of programming.

Because creating your own objects is discussed in Chapter 2, take a look at defining functions to handle common tasks. As with other programming languages, there are instances where you have to perform certain processes over and over. Many times this might involve a different value of parameters passed, but the processes you go through are the same.

As an example, verify a date entered by a user. This user is suppose to enter the month, date, and year in a form that will be submitted to your Web server for further processing. One of the concerns of the programmer is that he or she needs to have the date in a MM/DD/YYYY format, where the month and date need to be two characters and the year should be four.

To accomplish this task, you can create a single function that pre-pends a `"0"` in front of any single digit passed. This function could simply check to see if the value passed was less than the number 10, and, if so, it would perform the pre-pend. By defining this process in a function, a programmer will be able to use the same function for both the month and date verification. This avoids the trouble of writing a function for each. Even though this is a simple example, it illustrates the benefits of function and code reuse.

Programmers can also modulate their programming techniques by including their code in external JavaScript source files. This allows them to write code once, store it in a single location, and include it on many pages by simply referencing the location of the source file. If the function needs to change, they only have to change it in a single file and not every file that uses it. It is simple things like these that save Web programmers hours or days of work time.

# Security

One of the biggest issues facing Internet development today is security. It is not possible to successfully develop any kind of application, whether it's Web based or based on the Web, and not have to implement some kind of security features. A program's security measures can ultimately determine how valuable the over-all application is to a user. If the code can be tampered with or is subject to destruction from another program, the program will be subject to scrutiny and denial of use.

Since JavaScript is interpreted most often within a browser's environment, a user can be subject to malicious code. Browser's run off the operating system itself, meaning it has access to a user's file system. This makes it feasible that a JavaScript program could take advantage of a hole in the browser's security measures to access the file system. Once a programmer has accomplished this, many things are possible—even access to private documents or the ability to delete them altogether. This leaves a user at the mercy of a hacker.

Providing security for JavaScript scripts is actually twofold. One is that of responsibility, which lies with the programmer. A programmer must ensure the script the user executes is not malicious. The second responsibility falls to the users themselves. Users should make the ultimate decision whether or not to run a script on their systems—this is something that must be implemented in the browser's functionality.

Because of these potentially destructive situations, there are various levels of security that users and programmers can rely on when programming in JavaScript. As discussed, some are the responsibility of the programmer, while others involve measures put in place by the browser that allow the user to control what is executed on his or her system.

## What Security Measures Are in Place?

When JavaScript 1.0 was released in the Navigator 2.0, Internet Explorer 3.0 (JScript 1.0), and Opera 3.0 browsers, the only real security layer was that of a user having the ability to turn JavaScript on or off. The browser itself controlled the runtime environment for the language and any security measures it had in place.

In this model, when JavaScript was enabled, it was up to the browser to protect the user from any harmful code. Originally, this seemed like a thorough plan for implementing security. "Leave it to the experts to protect the users." However, where there is a will there is a way, and the first misuses of JavaScript began to surface.

The primary item that seemed to be a potential problem occurred when frames were used on a Web site. Since frames load separate documents in each of the predefined areas, it is possible to load documents from several different domains and servers to make up the content displayed to the user. The problem arose when a document's JavaScript variables from one server were available for examination and modification on another.

To help protect users from this problem, Navigator 2, Internet Explorer 3, and Opera 3 implemented the *Same Origin Policy*. This prevented JavaScript code that was sent from one server to access properties of a document sent from another server, another port, or another protocol and return that information to its server.

Obviously, this policy does not affect all the elements of a given document, but it does include a core set. At the time of this printing, the document properties that must pass this origin check are in Table 1.1.

*Table 1.1   Document Objects That Must Pass Origin Verification*

| Object | Property/Method |
|--------|-----------------|
| document | Read/Write: anchors, applets, cookie, domain, elements, embeds, forms, lastModified, length, links, referrer, title, URL, each form instance, each Java class available to JavaScript via LiveConnect<br>Write: all other |
| image | lowsrc, src |
| layer | src |
| location | all except location.X and location.Y |
| window | find |

Because it may be desirable for a script to access variables located on a page served from another server within the same domain, there is an exception to this security model. By definition, it would not be possible to access and upload document properties in a frame served from `http://myscripts.purejavascript.com` from another frame that was delivered from `http://mydocs.purejavascript.com`. Even though the domain is the same, the complete URL is not.

To get around this minor situation, programmers can set the `document.domain` property to the suffix of the current domain. This will allow them to access JavaScript properties on pages served from other servers within their domain. Following the example in the last paragraph, using the following line in the code can enable this feature:

```
document.domain = "purejavascript.com";
```

Setting this property will allow you to access the other *sub-domains* within your domain.

When JavaScript 1.1 was released in Navigator 3.0, Netscape implemented a more complete security solution referred to as *data tainting*. In addition to the security model in the first generation JavaScript browsers, data tainting allowed the user and programmer to specify if they wanted scripts to access properties in other documents from other servers. When data tainting is not enabled, which is the default, the user will get a message saying that accessing document properties from other servers is not allowed.

Users can enable tainting if they want scripts on a page to have global access to other scripts and document properties. This is a security risk, but may be necessary within an enterprise environment where other security measures are in place. To enable data tainting, environment variables must be set for the browser running the scripts. Table 1.2 shows how this can be accomplished on the various operating systems.

**Table 1.2    *How to Enable Data Tainting for Your Navigator Browser***

| Operating System | Environment Variable | Notes System |
|---|---|---|
| Windows | NS_ENABLE_TAINT=1 | Set this in the `autoexec.bat` for Window 3.1x, Windows95, or Windows98. For NT, you can set it in the user environment settings or the `autoexec.bat`. |
| UNIX | NS_ENABLE_TAINT=1 | Depending on which shell you are in, you will use some form of *set env* or *env* to set this variable. |
| Macintosh | Remove the two ASCII slash (//) comments before the NS_ENABLE_TAINT | This can be found by editing the resource with type Envi and number 128 in the Navigator application itself. It should be near the end. |
| OS/2 | NS_ENABLE_TAINT=1 | Set this in the `config.sys`. |

Once this variable is set, there are a number of document properties that will be affected. Table 1.3 shows a list of the document objects that are tainted by default.

**Table 1.3 Document Objects That Are Tainted by Default**

| Object | Tainted Property |
|---|---|
| document | cookie, domain, forms, lastModified, links, referrer, title, URL |
| Form | action, name |
| each Form instance | checked, defaultChecked, defaultValue, name, selected, selectedIndex, text, toString, value |
| history | current, next, previous, toString |
| image | name |
| Link | hash, host, hostname, href, pathname, port, protocol, search, toString |
| location | hash, host, hostname, href, pathname, port, protocol, search, toString |
| Option | defaultSelected, selected, text, value |
| Plugin | name |
| window | defaultStatus, name, status |

**TIP**

As a programmer, you can test to see if the user has tainting enabled by using the `navigator.taintEnabled()` method. See this entry in Chapter 7, "Client-Side Browser Syntax," for an example of using this method.

In addition to the user having the ability to specify how he or she wants to handle tainting, a programmer can specify, or *taint*, objects or information that cannot be passed from one script to the next without the user's permission. When this occurs, the browser will pop up a dialog box that allows the user to decide if the information can be passed.

**NOTE**

For more information on data tainting, please see the Client-Side JavaScript Guide on Netscape's DevEdge (`http://developer.netscape.com`) site. There is an entire section ("Using Data Tainting in JavaScript 1.1") in the "JavaScript Security" chapter devoted to security and the concepts of data tainting.

Because data tainting did not provide the true security model JavaScript needed, Netscape removed its functionality in JavaScript 1.2 and replaced it with signed scripts. This is the current and most complete model that has been implemented.

# What Are Signed Scripts?

Signed scripts are a security model that Netscape has implemented to allow a programmer the ability to gain access, after user authorization, to various restricted information. This model, which was based on the signed objects model in Java, uses LiveConnect and the Java Capabilities API to execute its functionality. Using this model gives programmers very defined control over what they can and cannot do on a user's machine.

**TIP**

> More information on the Java Capabilities API can be found on Netscape's DevEdge site at `http://developer.netscape.com/docs/manuals/signedobj/capabilities`.

When using this model, you have the ability to sign external JavaScript source files (called through the SRC attribute of the <SCRIPT> tag), event handlers, and code that is included inline on the page. The actual signing of these scripts is implemented by using Netscape's Page Signer tool, which is available at `http://developer.netscape.com`.

This Page Signer tool allows you to build a JAR (Java Archive) file that includes the programmer's security certificate and code. When the browser encounters a <SCRIPT> tag that has an ARCHIVE attribute set, it will go through the proper verification process before the script is executed. This process involves popping up a Java Security dialog box that gives the user the ability to grant or deny the rights to the script. The following is an example of syntax used on a page that includes a signed script:

```
<SCRIPT SRC="myScripts.js" ARCHIVE="sample.jar"></SCRIPT>
```

If the code is inline, the JAR file will contain only the programmer's certificate. Calling the appropriate JAR file would then look like the following, which does not have the SRC attribute, and it would have the code between the beginning and ending <SCRIPT> tags.

```
<SCRIPT ARCHIVE="sample.jar" ID="pureJS">
// Your code here
</SCRIPT>
```

Even though signed scripts are based on a Java model, there are enough differences in the languages that make it a bit harder to secure JavaScript code. Unlike JavaScript, a Java programmer can protect, make private, or make final variables and methods in their code. This inherently protects them from hackers because these elements cannot be accessed or changed—the Java language defines them as such.

There are some expanded privileges that can be accessed through the netscape. security.PrivilegeManager.enablePrivilege() method, which gives more control on scripts. This Java method allows a programmer to try to enable one of a set of privileges by asking the user to accept or reject his or her access. Like with other signed scripts, this will prompt the user to grant or deny a programmer's request. The following list shows the privileges that a programmer can attempt to access for these purposes.

- `UniversalBrowserAccess` Allows both reading and writing of privileged data in browser.
- `UniversalBrowserRead` Allows the reading of privileged data in browser. This is required when using an `about:` (but not `about:blank`), getting any property of the `history` object, or getting the value of the data property of a `DragDrop` event within your scripts.
- `UniversalBrowserWrite` Allows the writing of privileged data in browser. This is required when setting any property of an `event` object, adding or removing any of the browser's bars (location, menu, status, and so on), as well as using several of the methods and setting some of the properties of the `Window` object within your scripts.
- `UniversalFileRead` Allows the script to read files on the file system of the machine on which it is running. This is required when using a file upload within your scripts.
- `UniversalPreferencesRead` Allows the script to read browser preference settings.
- `UniversalPreferencesWrite` Allows the script to write browser preference settings.
- `UniversalSendMail` Allows the script to send mail under the user's name. This is required when using a `news:` or `mailto:` within your scripts.

JavaScript has quite an extensive list of security measures in place that can be used by the programmer. However, a programmer should use the security measures in a manner that maximizes their effectiveness. If this is not done, the scripts are subject to hacking.

Now that you have an understanding of the security measures in place for JavaScript, take a look at some of the overall advantages of using the language as a means of deploying solutions on the Internet or within an enterprise.

## Advantages of JavaScript

Up to this point, you may not have seen any big reasons where and why JavaScript can help you. It is object based, can be interpreted within a browser, and there are security measures in place—but so is Java. Now that browsers support plug-ins and ActiveX controls, it is possible to design client-side functionality with more common languages like C++ or Visual Basic. So what does JavaScript really give you?

For starters, it is platform independent. This is a major advantage over ActiveX controls and plug-ins because they have to be recompiled and potentially rewritten for the various platforms out there today. Netscape Navigator, for example, runs on nearly 20 platforms and even though most of these are various flavors of UNIX, at its core, you would still have to build a control or plug-in for Windows 16- and 32-bit systems, MacOS, UNIX, and OS/2. Also note that flavors of UNIX can run on several types of processors (MIPS, Intel, and so on), and Windows NT runs on Intel and Alpha machines. This becomes quite an extensive list of components to maintain if you develop in a platform-dependant language.

Another advantage of JavaScript is that both Netscape and Microsoft Web servers have built-in interpreters. Both of these companies have implemented this in a different fashion, but, as a Web developer, you still have the ability to use the same language on the server-side that they do on the client-side. The only real competitor to JavaScript in this aspect is Java with its Java applet and servlet technology.

## Platform Independence

Platform independence is probably the number one reason to use JavaScript within your applications. True, there are some environments that interpret JavaScript a bit differently, but the majority of the language is processed the same. The code is interpreted, so you can write it once and let the execution environment interpret it.

This is a simple fact, but can be a big one in deciding how to implement an application solution. As a programmer, you do not want to have to modify code to work on different operating systems or recompile for different microprocessors. You want to write the code once and be done with it. You want to be able to make changes easily and quickly without having to recompile 10 or 15 times. Lets face it, you want JavaScript.

## Client-Side and Server-Side Versatility

The majority of the discussion to this point has focused on using JavaScript on the client-side. Even with its initial release, JavaScript has also been implemented on the server-side within Netscape Web servers. This server-side code contains many of the same objects and methods as the client-side, but it also has objects specific to the server environment—objects that allow you to connect to, query, and get results from a database. All of this information is collected and processed before the server sends the page back to the requesting browser.

By providing this scripting capability on the server, a programmer can now use the language to dynamically build pages based on the execution of the server-side scripts it contains. Server-side JavaScript also can be used to maintain state for users as they move through a site. This maintaining of state is often implemented as a "shopping cart" on commercial sites. As users shop on a given site, server-side JavaScript can be used to track them and keep selected items in their carts.

Microsoft has also implemented a type of server-side JScript within its Internet Information Server (IIS). Its implementation is used in Active Server Pages (ASP), where the ASP filter parses a site's pages before they are sent back to the requesting browser. As these pages are parsed, the filter executes any server-side JScript that is contained in the ASP content. As with Netscape's implementation, this allows a Web developer to dynamically build the content of a page before it is sent back to the browser.

**NOTE**

Remember that JScript is Microsoft's equivalent to JavaScript.

Because of the functionality of these pages, ASP has given developers the ability to use JScript to call server-side components (such as ActiveX controls), pass the necessary parameters, and write the results to the screen. This allows a Web site to modularize all the functionality of building pages with individual components that are responsible for their specific tasks. JScript is used to handle the requests and results to and from these modules, and then write the results to the page.

# When to Use JavaScript

One of the most important things to know about JavaScript is when to use it. Even though it provides much needed functionality in many scenarios, there are often times it is simply not needed. One reason is the fact that JavaScript is not always interpreted the same or correctly—an important point to remember.

As a programmer, you should be able to write code, no matter how simple or complex, that will be executed correctly. However, there are browsers that have bugs that prevent JavaScript from working the way it was programmed. Before programming in JavaScript, you should first try to understand any documented bugs that exist. Doing so can save you hours of debugging in the long run.

Try to determine if you really need to use JavaScript on a given page as well. Ask yourself if you are using it to add functionality to the page or just make its appearance better. JavaScript can do a lot of neat things to a Web page, but, if it causes your page to break in certain browsers, you should avoid using it. There is a fine line between what you gain in functionality and what you expose as problems, so be sure to test your code with as many browsers on as many platforms as possible.

Depending on programmers' objectives when using JavaScript, they may be able to impose browser requirements. If they have stated that their pages only work in browsers later than Netscape Navigator 4 and Internet Explorer 4, it is safe for them to use JavaScript 1.2 or lower for their scripting needs. This immediately eliminates them from having to support older browsers, which can save many lines of code. Developers might not be able impose these restrictions on a Web site, but it is likely that they can on Web-based applications.

Overall, programmers should be smart about using the language. They need to evaluate what their objectives are and who their audience is. Once these requirements are defined, they can reverse engineer the project to determine what code they need to write. This is often a much easier approach than starting with an idea and trying to make it work in all circumstances.

Now that you've taken a quick look at some of the general items to analyze before using JavaScript, take a look at what you can do with it. The following pages contain some of the common uses of the language, as well as some more complex and specific uses.

## Web Page Enhancements

Web page enhancements were the first real use of JavaScript. Any of you that have been working with the Internet since the release of Netscape Navigator 2 probably remember those annoying scrolling messages in the status bar of the browser window. This was one of the first enhancements done using JavaScript. Even though it became annoying, it definitely caught the eye of users.

Another popular item JavaScript is used for is writing the current date and time to a page. Some sites write the date and time the document was last modified, while others write the current date and time. This is widely used on sites that are news related where the date of the document is very important to readers.

**TIP**

Writing the date and time to a page is a perfect item to modulate. If the code is written as a function, it can be included easily on all your pages and called when needed. If you are using some kind of browser intelligence on the server side, it is possible to include this function based on the browser that is requesting the page. If it can interpret JavaScript, make it part of the page. If it cannot, do not include it.

A final example of using JavaScript to enhance Web pages is to produce rollover buttons. This usually occurs on pages where the linked images change when a user rolls over them. It is also possible to program in a "down" state when a user clicks the image. Even though this is a simple enhancement, it makes a page look and feel more professional. This effect allows a Web site to give the user the same experience as using their favorite application, be it a Web browser, a word processor, or a money manager.

These three implementations of JavaScript to enhance Web pages are pretty simple, but are by no means the limit of what can be done. Many sites have used JavaScript for advertisements, pop-up navigation windows, page redirects, and validating forms. Because the language is executed within the browser's environment and is often used to complement HTML publishing, there is virtually no limit to what can be done.

**TIP**

If you want to use JavaScript to enhance your Web pages, don't make the mistake of trying to think of something cool you can do with the language. You should try to reverse engineer it. Think of something cool for your site, and then figure out how to do implement it in JavaScript.

## Interactive Email

Interactive email is something that has come about with the newest email applications. It wasn't long ago that many of these programs were only able to read text emails. These programs now have the ability to render HTML email within their interface, which extends the formatting options a user can exploit. This not only improves the look and feel of the email, it also improves the readability of it. If a user wants something in italic, you can put it in italic.

Because HTML email has become widely used in the Internet community, more and more email applications are supporting it. In addition to HTML, Netscape Messenger and Microsoft Outlook98 support JavaScript within the body of an email message. This makes it possible for a user to send HTML emails containing JavaScript that is interpreted when the recipient reads the message.

As a programmer, you need to keep in mind an email application is not a browser. Users are very particular about what they experience in their messages, and overuse of JavaScript could lead to annoying your recipients. JavaScript should be used sparingly in emails. It should be reserved for simple page enhancements such as image and link rollovers or calling ads within your message. Anything beyond this could cause problems when the application interprets your scripts.

## Web-Based Applications

Web-based applications are probably the most useful instances of JavaScript. They allow a programmer to set user browser requirements, which in turn gives them a head start on the version of JavaScript they have at their disposal. This also results in limited exposure to browser bugs, since programmers can define which browsers they support.

One of the most common uses of JavaScript within Web-based applications seems to be in controlling forms on a page. This can be anything from checking a user's values before submission, to dynamically adjusting the values based on user-selected data. By implementing JavaScript at this level, a programmer is able to reduce the amount of user error when submitting forms. No more invalid credit card numbers because one digit too many was entered. No more usernames and passwords submitted as email addresses, and no more incomplete forms.

JavaScript is also used in more full-blown Web-based applications. These applications are not necessarily for the common Internet user to experience, but rather are interfaces to enterprise level applications a company might have purchased. Some of the more common are used for reporting or ad delivery and management. Since the content on the application's pages is dynamic and always changing, a developer usually interfaces the application with a database or system process to build the pages on-the-fly. Using JavaScript allows developers to verify items before requests are made, as well as add an appealing look and feel to the application.

## Email and News Filters

Netscape, being the Internet technology pioneer that it is, also allows the creation of email and news filters using JavaScript code. This gives JavaScript developers complete control of how Messenger 4 and later (Netscape's email and news client) handle incoming email messages and news articles. These filters can do anything from automatically filling messages to changing the priorities on them.

**NOTE**

Netscape's news client was called Collabra in all 4.0x versions. In 4.5, the email and news client are together and called Messenger.

The filters will need to be stored in a file named `filters.js`, which is loaded when the application starts. For this file to be loaded, you must reference it in the mail rules file. The location of this rules file is specific, so use Table 1.4 to determine where the file is on your system. Note that `<communicator_install_dir>` should be replaced with the path to the Communicator installation directory.

**Table 1.4 Location of the Mail Rules File for Netscape Mail and News Readers**

| Platform | Filename | Location |
|---|---|---|
| Windows | rules.dat | Located at `<communicator_install_dir>`\Users\`<username>`\Mail\rules.dat |
| UNIX | mailrule | Located at `<username>`/.netscape/mailrule |
| Macintosh | Filter Rules | Located at `System Folder:Preferences:Netscape Users:<username>` |
| OS/2 | rules.dat | Located at `<communicator_install_dir>`\Users\`<username>`\Mail\rules.dat |

**NOTE**

If you do not have a rules file, you can create one in the appropriate location outlined in Table 1.4. This file should simply be a plain text file.

When you reference your `filter.js` file in the filter rules file on your system, you will have to include several lines. They are defined as the following:

- `name="name_of_filter"` Where the *name_of_filter* parameter specifies the name you want to call the filter.
- `enabled="yes_or_no"` Where the *yes_or_no* parameter specifies if you want the filter enabled or not. `Yes` means that it is enabled.
- `type="type_of_filter"` Where *type_of_filter* specifies the type of filter it is. Use `"2"` if it is a mail filter and `"8"` if it is a news filter.
- `scriptName="function_to_call"` Where *function_to_call* is the name of the function in your `filters.js` file that you want to call.

This simple feature, implemented in the Netscape product, allows you to take message filtering in your own hands. This is something that can be very helpful to power users—especially within an enterprise environment.

**TIP**

Want more information on writing these filters? Check out the JavaScript Guide on Netscape's DevEdge site at `http://developer.netscape.com/docs/manuals/communicator/jsguide4`.

# Windows Scripting

Microsoft's Windows Scripting Host comes with Windows98 and Windows2000 and can be installed in Windows95 and NT 4 systems. This scripting host is language independent for ActiveX scripting on Windows 32-bit systems. *Language independent* means that there are a variety of programming languages that can be used in conjunction with the host. The reason it's mentioned in this book is that it natively supports JScript—Microsoft's implementation of ECMAScript.

**NOTE**

In addition to the JScript language, this scripting host also supports Visual Basic Script (VBScript) as well as other third-party languages such as Perl, REXX, TCL, and Python.

Using JScript in the scripting host allows an administrator or user to create scripts that perform various tasks on the operating system. These can be as simple as logon scripts or can be used to call ActiveX controls to perform more complex tasks. If you work in the Microsoft Windows environment, you will find this implementation of JScript can be very helpful.

**TIP**

For more information on the Windows Scripting Host, check out Microsoft's Developer Network site at http://msdn.microsoft.com/scripting and click the link to Windows Scripting.

# Moving On

This chapter covers the overview of the JavaScript language. As you can see, JavaScript is actually a very powerful scripting language that has many advantages. There are security features in place and other implementations of the language that make it worth any programmer's time to learn.

In the next chapter, you will take a look at the details of the language These details will give you, the programmer, an understanding of how the language deals with operators, datatypes, variables, functions, loops, conditionals, as well as how to correctly implement JavaScript within the body of an HTML document.

# CHAPTER 2

## Details of the Language

For experienced programmers to pick up a new language quickly, they look for similarities at the core of the new language and other languages they have used. These similarities generally include operators that make programs think, variables that provide memory, and the ability to apply the same operation to various items. Understanding how to use these core pieces of the language is essential if you want to begin programming in JavaScript.

If you have been programming for a long time, you might be tempted to skip over this chapter. Because JavaScript is still a young scripting language with some wrinkles to be ironed out, it is a good idea to understand these instances for backwards compatibility reasons. Taking a little time to make sure the core elements perform as you are expecting will save a lot of programming time in the future.

## Things to Know about JavaScript Syntax

Before getting too deep into the core elements of the language, there are a few things a programmer should know about JavaScript syntax. Understanding these points will get you up and programming in a more timely fashion.

### The Semicolon

If you have done any programming in C, C++, or Java, even as simple as a *Hello World* program, you already know 75% of all there is to know about the JavaScript semicolon ( ; ). Just like C and C++, the semicolon is placed at the end of a piece of code to signify that the code between the semicolon and the beginning of the line should be executed before moving to the next portion of code. If you forget a semicolon at the end of a line in C++, you get compile errors, but JavaScript doesn't complain. Because JavaScript is a loosely typed language, forgetting a semicolon tells JavaScript to assume you intended for one to appear at the end of the line, and it executes your code accordingly. This does not mean you should not use semicolons! It is good programming practice to always include semicolons at the end of a line of code except when dealing with statements like for, while, and if.

Although it is good programming practice to have only one functional piece of code per line, there are times when it is advantageous to put two independent pieces of code on one line. When this case arises, you must use a semicolon to separate the two pieces of code. In Listing 2.1, a semicolon is used to separate two independent pieces of variable declaration code that are placed on one line. Notice that semicolons were placed at the end of each line though JavaScript would do it for you. The result of executing the code is the phrase, "The sales tax on $5 is $.3," being displayed in the browser.

*Listing 2.1   Using Semicolons*
```
<SCRIPT LANGUAGE="JavaScript">
<!--Hide

// Declare 2 numeric variables on the same line
var fiveDollars = 5; var salesTax = 0.06;

// Compute the sales tax on 5 dollars and use the
// document.write() function to display the result.
document.write('The sales tax on $');
document.write(fiveDollars);
document.write(' is $');
document.write(fiveDollars*salesTax);

// End Hide -->
</SCRIPT>
```

# Using the <SCRIPT> Tag

The first time a programmer works with a new language, he'll want to know the key pieces of syntax needed to start programming. In JavaScript, the HTML <SCRIPT> tag is that key piece. <SCRIPT> tags tell the browser that everything between <SCRIPT> and </SCRIPT> should be interpreted by the interpreter specified in the LANGUAGE attribute. There is no limit to the number of tags that can be used, as long as they are used in pairs.

Notice that the browser interprets the code between the <SCRIPT> tags based on the LANGUAGE attribute. Because there are other scripting languages, like VBScript, it is important that the LANGUAGE attribute be set any time the <SCRIPT> tag is used. To set the attribute to the most current version of JavaScript supported by the browser, use the format <SCRIPT LANGUAGE="JavaScript">. It is also possible to force the interpreter to use different versions of JavaScript (<SCRIPT LANGUAGE="JavaScript1.2">, for example).

**NOTE**

Currently, if the LANGUAGE attribute is left out of the <SCRIPT> tag, Navigator and Internet Explorer will assume the most current version of JavaScript should be used.

## Comments

JavaScript is very generous with its commenting options by providing the /* */ comment tags from C, the // comment tag from C++, and the <!-- tag from HTML. Just as in C and C++, the /* */ enables comments to span multiple lines by just placing comments between the two tags. The // comment tag enables comments to be placed between the // and the end of the line.

As mentioned earlier, JavaScript provides one other comment tag that may not be familiar to you, the HTML <!-- comment. JavaScript interprets this comment the same way it interprets the // characters. You are probably asking yourself, "Why two different comment tags that do the same thing?" Some older browsers that did not understand the <SCRIPT> tags would display all the code between the <SCRIPT> tags as standard HTML text. To prevent this with non-JavaScript–enabled browsers, <!-- is placed on the line directly below the <SCRIPT> tag, and //--> is placed on the line directly above the closing </SCRIPT> tag. This causes non-JavaScript–enabled browsers to treat the code between the tags as HTML comments, but allows browsers with JavaScript interpreters to execute the code. Examples of this style of commenting can be seen in the examples throughout the book.

**NOTE**

The // comment characters have to be placed in front of the HTML --> comment closer because JavaScript will misinterpret --> as a pre-decrement operator.

# Data Types and Variables

Before diving into JavaScript operators, conditionals, and loops, one should understand JavaScript data types and variables. These are building blocks that will be important going forward. Fortunately, JavaScript kept its implementation of data types simple and easy to use, unlike other programming languages. In addition to simple data types, variables are much easier to work with because there are no restrictions on the types of values they can hold.

## Numbers

JavaScript's approach to numbers is different from other languages, because every number is treated as a floating-point number. This does not imply that JavaScript does not support integers, octal, hexadecimal, and so on. These numbers are supported at a high level, but, at the lowest level, JavaScript sees numbers as floating-point numbers. The following sections discuss different formats numbers can have at the higher level.

## Integers

Integers are numbers that contain no fractional parts, can be positive or negative, and can be formatted as a decimal, octal, or hexadecimal in JavaScript. Because integers are actually floating-point numbers in JavaScript, it is possible for the numbers to be very large.

Decimal integers, also referred to as base-10, are probably the most common numerical values programmers use in their code. This type of integer is made up of numbers from 0 to 9 and cannot begin with leading zeros.

Octal integers, also referred to as base-8, are a little different from decimal integers in that they must begin with a leading zero. Each digit following the leading zero can be 0 to 7.

Hexadecimal integers, also referred to as base-16, must begin with 0x or 0X. Each digit following the leading zero can be 0 through 15, but 10 through 15 are represented by the letters a (or A) through f (or F).

## Floating-Point Numbers

Unlike the integer, floating-point numbers can contain fractional parts and can use exponential notation for added precision. Floating-point numbers are made up of a decimal integer followed by a period (.) and the fractional portion of the number.

Exponential notation can be used by adding an e or E to the end of a floating-point number followed by a decimal integer that does not exceed 3 digits. This tells JavaScript to multiply the floating-point number by 10 to the exponent of the number following the e.

## Built-in Values

Because computer programs are often used to solve scientific problems, the programs must know many of the numerical constants that are used in math and science. To make programming easier for you, JavaScript has included some of the more commonly used numerical constants in the Math object, which are shown in Table 2.1.

### Table 2.1  Numerical Constants Provided by JavaScript

| Math Constant | Description |
|---|---|
| Math.E | Base of natural logarithms |
| Math.LN2 | Natural log of 2 |
| Math.LN10 | Natural log of 10 |
| Math.LOG2E | Base 2 log of e |
| Math.LOG10E | Base 10 log of e |
| Math.PI | PiMath.SQRT1_2    Square root of fi |
| Math.SQRT2 | Square root of 2 |

## Special Values

JavaScript also provides some special values that are common in the mathematical world but not so common in the computer world. These special values are available through the Number object, as shown in Table 2.2.

**Table 2.2    Special Numerical Values**

| Number Constant | Description |
| --- | --- |
| Number.MAX_VALUE | Largest representable number |
| Number.MIN_VALUE | Smallest representable number |
| Number.NaN | Not-a-number |
| Number.POSITIVE_INFINITY | Positive infinity |
| Number.NEGATIVE_INFINITY | Negative infinity |

# Strings

Strings provide programs a voice with which to communicate. It would be inconceivable to create a programming language today that did not use strings because they are so important.

## Strings

In the world of C and C++, dealing with strings is like having to go to the doctor—dreaded! Dealing with strings in JavaScript is like going to a big candy store. A string is made up of any number of characters or a lack of characters. Strings are declared by placing the characters that make up the string between a pair of double quotes (" ") or single quotes (' '). What if a string contains double quotes or single quotes? No problem. JavaScript interprets single quotes as part of the string if the single quotes are inside a pair of double quotes. Likewise, double quotes are considered part of the string if they appear between a pair of single quotes. If single quotes are your only option for declaring a string that contains single quotes, or if double quotes must be used to declare a string that contains double quotes, you will you need to use escape sequences (see the next section, "Special Characters").

## Special Characters

Just as in C and C++, escape sequences, which are noted by a backslash character (\), allow special characters, that cannot normally be stored in a string, to be declared. Table 2.3 lists all the possible escape characters.

**Table 2.3    Escape Sequences and Their Associated Characters**

| Escape Sequence | Character |
| --- | --- |
| \b | Backspace |
| \f | Form feed |
| \n | Newline |

*continues*

**Table 2.3    continued**

| Escape Sequence | Character |
|---|---|
| \r | Carriage return |
| \t | Tab |
| \' | Single quote |
| \" | Double quote |
| \\ | Backslash |
| \xxx | Character represented by three octal digits *xxx* (0 to 377) |
| \xx | Character represented by two hexadecimal digits *xx* (00 to FF) |
| \uXXXX | Unicode character represented by four hexadecimal digits. |

# Other

Outside of the world of computers, there are uncertainties and indefinable values that we come in contact with daily. When computer programs are written to simulate the world we live in, they must handle uncertainties and values that have no definition. JavaScript provides some special data types to handle these situations.

## Boolean

The Boolean data type is much simpler than any of the other data types because it has only two possible values: `true` and `false`. Sometimes it is easier to think of true as "on" or "yes" and false as "off" or "no" when working with some expressions that use the Boolean data type. In JavaScript, `true` and `false` are often represented by 1 (`true`) and 0 (`false`).

## null

JavaScript provides the keyword `null` for representing a condition when there is no value. In some languages, `null` and 0 are considered the same value, but JavaScript sees `null` and 0 as two completely different values.

## Undefined Values

At this point, you might be thinking that `undefined` and `null` are essentially the same, but this is not true. In fact, `undefined` is a concept rather than a keyword like the `null` data type. Undefined is equivalent to `NaN` for numbers, the string `undefined` for strings and `false` when dealing with Boolean values.

# What to Know About Variables

Computer programs would not do much if they did not have some type of temporary memory. Variables provide a way for data to be stored during the execution of a program. Some languages, such a C and C++, impose many restrictions on how variables are used, but JavaScript keeps variables simple and easy to use.

## Naming Variables

One of the keys to writing great code is to use variable names that help you, and programmers who modify your code, remember what data is stored in the variable. Before beginning to think of great variable names, remember the following guidelines imposed on variable names by JavaScript:

- The first character of the name must be a letter or an underscore (_).
- All characters following the first character can be letters, underscore, or digits.
- Letters can be either upper- or lowercase. JavaScript does distinguish between the two cases. For example, a variable called jobTitle is different from a variable called JOBtitle.

## Assigning Values

Once the perfect variable name has been derived, it is time to declare that variable and assign it a value. To declare a variable, use the keyword var followed by the variable name. Some programmers like to keep their code compact by declaring multiple variables using the same var statement. When this is the case, the variable names are separated by commas. At this point, the variable is undefined because no value has been assigned to it. Keep in mind that undefined is a special JavaScript value.

Now that the variable is declared, a value can be assigned to it using the assignment operator (=). In many cases, the declaration and assignment steps are performed in one step. If a value is assigned to a variable that has not been declared using the var keyword, JavaScript will automatically create a global variable. Listing 2.3 demonstrates the ways variable declaration and assignment can be performed. The code displays the sentence "James is 49 and 6 feet tall." in the browser window.

*Listing 2.2    Variable Declaration and Assignment*

```
<SCRIPT LANGUAGE='JavaScript'>
<!--

//Variable declaration without assignment
var firstName;

//Variable assignment without declaration
firstName = "James";

//Variable declaration and assignment
var age = 49, height = 6;

//Display the results
document.write(firstName,"  is ",age," and ",height," feet tall.");

//-->
</SCRIPT>
```

**TIP**

Always use the var keyword to declare all variables to prevent variable scope problems.

## Scope

A variable can be either global or local in JavaScript. All variables are global unless they are declared in a function in which case the variable is local to that function. It is possible for two variables with the same name to exist if one is global and the other is local to a function. When accessing the variable from within the function, you are accessing the local variable. If the variable is accessed outside the function, the global variable is used (see Listing 2.3).

### CAUTION

Always use the var keyword to declare local variables in functions. Without var, JavaScript will create a global variable.

*Listing 2.3    Variable Scope Example*

```
<HTML>
<H2><U>Computer monitor specifications</U></H2>

<SCRIPT LANGUAGE="JavaScript">
<!--Hide

//Initialize global variables
color = "green";
var size = 15;

//Declare a monitor specification function
function monitorSpecs()
{
  //Declare and set variables inside function
  color = "purple";
  price = "$300.00";
  var size = 17;
  document.write("The ",size," inch ",color);
  document.write(" monitor is ",price);
}

//Display results of monitorSpec() function
monitorSpecs();

//Display variable values outside of function
document.write("<BR>The ",size," inch ",color);
document.write(" monitor is ",price);

// End Hide -->
</SCRIPT>

</HTML>
```

The results of running this script within the body of an HTML document can be seen in Figure 2.1. The code begins by declaring two global variables, `color` and `size`. The `monitorSpec()` function creates a new variable called `size` that only exists within the scope of the function. Because the function did not specify var, the global variable `color` was changed from green to purple. In addition, a new global variable, `price`, was declared within the function because the word var was not used.

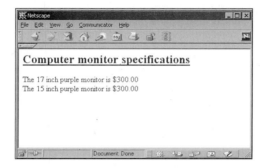

**Figure 2.1**

*The result of executing Listing 2.3.*

## Type Conversion

In languages like C and C++, type conversion is very important and complicated, but, in JavaScript, type conversion is effortless. Unlike other languages, JavaScript allows a variable to hold any data type at any time. This means that a variable can be assigned a string initially and then the same variable can be reassigned to an integer. JavaScript also attempts to perform all necessary type conversions for you, such as strings to numbers and numbers to strings.

## Arrays

Arrays enable programmers to store multiple data, based on a numbered position called an index, into one storage structure. The numbering of the index always starts at 0 and goes up. Also, JavaScript supports having arrays within arrays, called multidimensional arrays.

The implementation of arrays in JavaScript has been changing ever since JavaScript was introduced. The original implementation of arrays in JavaScript 1.0 were not really arrays at all but rather JavaScript objects with multiple property settings. A true Array object was added in JavaScript 1.1, and additional features added in following versions. Today, arrays are very robust and full featured, but, because of their changing past, you should spend some time digging into the history of arrays as they apply to JavaScript versions. You will begin by understanding how arrays work in the last versions of JavaScript and then come back to JavaScript 1.1, since it is no longer the preferred method of creating arrays

## One-Dimensional

To create an instance of an array, you must use the new operator along with the Array object. There are four ways to declare an array. First, an empty array that contains no elements can be created by leaving the constructor parameters empty:

```
var x = new Array();
```

The second way to create an array is to fill in the constructor parameters with the array elements. One of the nice things about JavaScript arrays is that an array can contain elements of various types:

```
var x = new Array("red","yellow","green",1,5,8);
```

The third way to create an array is to fill in the constructor parameter with just the size of the array. This causes the array to be initialized to hold the number of elements specified, but does not specify the actual elements.

```
var x = new Array(6);
```

**NOTE**

The var x = new Array(n); format, described previously, is not recognized by JavaScript 1.2, so the number specified in the constructor parameter is stored as an element in position 0.

The fourth, and quickest, way to create an array is to use the standard array square brackets to fill in the array elements directly:

```
var x = ["red","yellow","green",1,5,8];
```

Once an array has been created, it can be written to and read from by using the [ ] operator. By placing a position number in this operator, the data stored at this index can be accessed and even overwritten.

## String Indexes

So far, you have only accessed elements in arrays via the numerical index, but it is possible to index arrays using strings. To access an element, a string index value is placed into the [ ] operator. Listing 2.4 demonstrates the use of strings as indexes for a clothing store's product quantity array. Figure 2.2 displays the clothing store's current inventory of products.

*Listing 2.4   Using Strings for Array Indexes*

```
<HTML>
<H2><U>Clothing Store Inventory</U></H2>

<SCRIPT LANGUAGE="JavaScript">
<!--Hide
```

```
//Populate an array with product quantities
function populateArray(products)
{
  products["shirts"]=46;
  products["pants"]=23;
  products["hats"]=14;
  products["socks"]=153;
}

//Display product quantities
function displayArray(products)
{
  document.write(products['shirts']," shirts.<BR>");
  document.write(products['pants']," pants.<BR>");
  document.write(products['hats']," hats.<BR>");
  document.write(products['socks']," pairs of socks.");
}

//Create a product quantity array
var productQty = new Array();

//Set product quantities
populateArray(productQty);

//Display the product quantities
displayArray(productQty);

// End Hide -->
</SCRIPT>
</HTML>
```

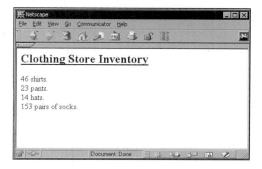

**Figure 2.2**

*The result of executing Listing 2.4.*

## Length

Unlike arrays in C and C++, JavaScript allows the size of an array to change dynamically at any time. For example, it is possible to write directly to a position that was not even declared using the [ ] operator. The length of the array can also be changed by altering the length attribute of the Array object. If the length of an array is originally 10 and is reduced to 5 by changing the value stored in the length attribute, the elements in position 6 through 10 are lost.

One of the advantages to using the Array object is the methods it provides to manipulate and access itself. Table 2.4 lists the methods that are currently available in the Array object. Details of these methods can be found in Chapter 6, "Core Syntax," in the "Array" section.

*Table 2.4   Methods Available in the Array Object*

| Method | Description |
| --- | --- |
| join() | Concatenates all elements into one string |
| reverse() | Reverses the order of the elements in the array |
| sort() | Sorts elements in array |
| concat() | Concatenates an array on to an array |
| slice() | Returns a subsection of the array |
| splice() | Inserts and removes elements from an array |
| push() | Adds elements to the end of an array |
| pop() | Deletes the last element from an array |
| unshift() | Adds elements to the front of an array |
| shift() | Deletes elements from the front of an array |
| toString() | Converts elements to a string |
| toSource() | Converts elements to a string with square brackets |

## Multidimensional

To create multidimensional arrays in JavaScript, the element of an array must be another array. The inner array can be accessed by putting two [ ] operators back to back. Listing 2.5 uses a multidimensional array to hold an inventory list of brake parts. As seen in Figure 2.3 the brake parts list is accessed by using double [ ] operators and displayed in a table.

*Listing 2.5   Using a Multidimensional Array*

```
<HTML>
<H2><U>Brake Parts Inventory List</U></H2>

<SCRIPT LANGUAGE="JavaScript">
<!--Hide

//Display brake part inventory in a table
function displayInventory(table)
{
```

```
document.write("<TABLE BORDER=ON>");
document.write("<TH>Item Number</TH><TH>Item Name</TH>");
document.write("<TH>Model Number</TH><TH>Quantity</TH>");
//Display each part
for(x=1; x<=3; x++)
{
  document.write("<TR><TD>",x,"</TD>");
  //Display all information for each part
  for(y=0; y<=2; y++)
  {
    document.write("<TD>",table[x][y],"</TD>");
  }
  document.write("</TR>");
}
document.write("</TABLE>");
}

//Create a brake parts inventory list using a
//multidimensional array
part1 = new Array("Brake Pads","39D48G",78);
part2 = new Array("Brake Shoes","7D9UK3",45);
part3 = new Array("Rotors","97WOST","14");
brakeParts = new Array("",part1,part2,part3);

//Display the inventory of brake parts
displayInventory(brakeParts);

// End Hide -->
</SCRIPT>
</HTML>
```

**Figure 2.3**

*The result of executing Listing 2.5.*

## Arrays as Objects

Because arrays are essentially JavaScript objects, it is possible to access the elements of arrays as properties if a string index is used. Dot notation is used, rather than the [ ] operators. For example, the clothing store example, in Listing 2.4, could have been created using properties as shown in Listing 2.6. Notice how the [ ] operators and dot notation are used interchangeably when accessing the contents of the array. The result of executing the code is the same as shown in Figure 2.3.

*Listing 2.6   Accessing Array Properties*

```
<HTML>
<H2><U>Clothing Store Inventory</U></H2>

<SCRIPT LANGUAGE="JavaScript">
<!--Hide

//Populate an array with product quantities
function populateArray(products)
{
  products.shirts=46;
  products.pants=23;
  products["hats"]=14;
  products["socks"]=153;
}

//Display product quantities
function displayArray(products)
{
  document.write(products['shirts']," shirts.<BR>");
  document.write(products['pants']," pants.<BR>");
  document.write(products.hats," hats.<BR>");
  document.write(products.socks," pairs of socks.");
}

//Create a product quantity array
var productQty = new Array();

//Set product quantities
populateArray(productQty);

//Display the product quantities
displayArray(productQty);

// End Hide -->
</SCRIPT>
</HTML>
```

## *JavaScript 1.0 Arrays*

As mentioned earlier, JavaScript originally used the Object() constructor to create arrays in JavaScript 1.0. Because the properties of an Object() could be accessed by using the [] operator, it was possible to give the illusion of an array.

To create an array using this concept, a new object is created using the Object() constructor. Once created, elements can be assigned to the object using the [] operators. Because this is just a basic object, the programmer is responsible for keeping track of the length of the array. The easiest way to remember the length is to create a property called length. Unfortunately, properties use the same positions that are accessed by the [] operator, so the length property would actually be array position 0.

Listing 2.7 demonstrates how to create an array representing a toolbox using the Object() constructor. The code displays the sentence, "The toolbox holds: hammer wrench nails" in the browser window.

*Listing 2.7    Creating Arrays in JavaScript 1.0*

```
<SCRIPT LANGUAGE="JavaScript">
<!--Hide

//Create a toolbox array using the Object() constructor
var toolbox = Object();
toolbox.length=3;    //array position zero
toolbox[1]="hammer";
toolbox[2]="wrench";
toolbox[3]="nails";

//Display the items in the toolbox.
document.write("The toolbox holds:  ");
for(x=1; x<=toolbox.length; x++)
{
   document.write(toolbox[x]," ");
}

// End Hide -->
</SCRIPT>
```

# Operators

JavaScript provides most of the common operators that can be found in other programming languages. Due to the JavaScript's way of handling strings, some of these operators are a bit easier to use than in other languages.

## Arithmetic

Just like other programming languages, JavaScript allows many arithmetic operations. These operations include the common addition and subtraction that all programmers use, as well as the less common modulus and incremental.

## NOTE

All the common arithmetic operators will attempt to convert strings to numbers when applicable. If a string cannot be converted to a number, NaN (Not A Number) will be returned.

Those who have programmed in other languages will find that JavaScript is very robust in its support of operators and mathematical functions. This is not only because of the built-in operators, but also because of the access to advanced mathematical operations that are provided through the Math object. The functions of this object are shown in Table 2.5 and are covered in Chapter 6.

**Table 2.5    Advanced Mathematical Methods**

| Method | Description |
| --- | --- |
| Math.abs() | Absolute value |
| Math.acos() | Arc cosine |
| Math.asin() | Arc sine |
| Math.atan() | Arc tangent |
| Math.atan2() | Arc tangent |
| Math.ceil() | Ceiling |
| Math.cos() | Cosine |
| Math.exp() | Natural exponent |
| Math.floor() | Floor |
| Math.log() | Natural logarithm |
| Math.max() | Max |
| Math.min() | Min |
| Math.pow() | Power of |
| Math.random() | Random number |
| Math.round() | Round |
| Math.sin() | Sine |
| Math.sqrt() | Square root |
| Math.tan() | Tangent |

## Addition

The addition operator (+) is, of course, one of the most widely used and common operators. If the values on either side are numerical values, the values are added together. When the values are strings, they are concatenated together. The following line of code

```
var resultOfAdd = 34 + 12;
```

would set the variable *resultOfAdd* equal to 46, while this line of code

```
var resultOfAdd = "a" + "corn";
```

would set the variable *resultOfAdd* equal to the string "acorn".

## Subtraction

The subtraction operator (-) subtracts the number to the right of the operator from the number on the left. When either of the operands are strings, an attempt is made to convert the strings to numbers. For example, the line of code:

```
var resultOfSub = 25 - 102;
```

would result in the value -77 being stored in the variable *resultOfSub*.

## Multiplication

The multiplication operator (*) works the same as it would in any other language by multiplying the left operand by the right operand. The multiplication operator is no different than addition in its efforts to handle strings. If either of the values is a string, an attempt is made to convert the string to a number. For example, the following line of code

```
var resultOfMult = 5 * 7;
```

would result in the value of 35 being stored in the variable *resultOfMult*.

## Division

The division operator (/) is the operator that, although simple, can be confusing when you have been writing code all day and your senses are dulled. You ask yourself, "Which number divides into the other?" Reading the expression from left to right, the left value is divided by the right value. As before, if either of the operands is a string, an attempt is made to convert the string to a number. For example, the following line of code

```
var resultOfDiv = 42 / 7;
```

would result in the value of 6 being stored in the variable *resultOfDiv*.

## Modulus

Although the modulus operator (%) is not used as often as some of the other operators, I am always excited when I do get to use it because it usually means I am performing a neat math trick. This operator starts like the division operator, by dividing the left value by the right, but instead of returning the normal result of division, only the remainder is returned by the operation. Once again, if either value is a string, an attempt is made to convert the string to a number. For example, the following line of code

```
var resultOfMod = 26 % 3;
```

would result in the remainder of 2 being stored in the variable *resultOfMod*.

## Pre-Increment

The pre-increment operator (++) combines two very common steps that programmers use over and over again into one, thus making code more concise and readable. This operator is especially handy when working with for loops. In your code, the pre-increment operator is placed directly before the variable to be incremented. The operation begins by incrementing the variable by 1. The new incremented value is returned by the operation to be used in another expression. If the variable is a string, it is converted to a number. For example, the following segment of code

```
var price = 5
var pricePlusShipping = (++price) + 3;
```

would result in the variable *price* being changed from 5 to 6 dollars, and the value of 9 dollars would be stored in the variable *pricePlusShipping*.

## Post-Increment

The post-increment operator (++) has the same operator as the pre-increment operator but it behaves differently. First, the post-increment operator appears directly after the variable that is to be incremented. The operation begins by incrementing the variable by 1. Unlike the pre-increment operator, the post-increment operator returns the original value before it was incremented. If either of the values is a string, an attempt is made to convert the string to a number. For example, the following segment of code

```
var price = 5
var pricePlusShipping = (price++) + 3;
```

would result in the variable *price* being changed from 5 to 6 dollars, and the value of 8 dollars would be stored in the variable *pricePlusShipping*.

## Pre-Decrement

The pre-decrement operator (--) is very similar to the pre-increment operator in its placement to the left of a variable and its order of execution. But there is one key difference between the operators: the pre-decrement operator decrements the value by 1. Once again, if the variable is a string, it is converted to a number. For example, the following segment of code

```
var price = 20
var priceMinusDiscount = (--price) - 6;
```

would result in the variable *price* being changed from 20 to 19 dollars, and the value of 13 dollars would be stored in the variable *priceMinusDiscount*.

## Post-Decrement

The post-decrement operator (--) is very similar to the post-increment operator in its placement to the right of a variable and its order of execution. But, as the name implies, the post-decrement operator decrements the value by 1. If the variable is a string, it is converted to a number. The following segment of code

```
var price = 20
var priceMinusDiscount = (price--) - 6;
```

would result in the variable *price* being changed from 20 to 19 dollars, and the value of 14 dollars would be stored in the variable *priceMinusDiscount*.

**TIP**

Even though the speed at which modems transfer data is increasing, causing download time to become less of an issue, it is a good idea to keep your code as short as possible without sacrificing clarity. One way to do this is to use the pre/post increment and decrement operators in place of the more traditional addition/subtraction/assignment combination (x=x+1, for example).

## *Unary Negation*

The unary negation operator (-) is usually used when performing a mathematical equation where a number needs to be changed from positive to negative or vice versa. Keep in mind when negating a variable that the contents of the variable do not change, only the value returned is negated. Like all the other operators, if the value is a string, an attempt is made to convert the string to a number. For example, the following segment of code

```
var aNumber = 67;
var resultOfNeg = -aNumber;
```

would result in the value of -67 being stored in the variable *resultOfNeg*.

# String

The addition operator (+) has a special purpose when dealing with strings. If the values on either side of the addition operator are strings, the strings are concatenated together. If only one of the values is a string, the other value is converted to a string and concatenated with the first value. To help understand these various combinations of applying the addition operator to numeric and string values, see Listing 2.8.

*Listing 2.8    Using the Addition Operator on Numeric and String Values*

```
<SCRIPT LANGUAGE="JavaScript">
<!--Hide

// Declare 2 numeric variables and 2 string variables
var sStringVar1 = "Hello";
var sStringVar2 = "World";
var nNumVar1 = 5;
var nNumVar2 = 10;

// Apply the addition operator to create 3 totals
var sStringTotal = sStringVar1 + sStringVar2;
var nNumTotal = nNumVar1 + nNumVar2;
var sStringNumTotal = sStringTotal + nNumTotal;

// Use the document.write() function to write the totals to the page
```

```
// Notice that we even use the addition operator in place of a comma
// to concatenate the results with some text on the page.
document.write("<b>The string total is: </b>"+sStringTotal+"<BR>");
document.write("<b>The numeric total is: </b>",nNumTotal,"<BR>");
document.write("<b>The string + numeric total is: </b>",sStringNumTotal);
// End Hide -->
</SCRIPT>
```

The results of running this script within the body of an HTML document can be seen in Figure 2.4. As can be seen from the figure, when the addition operator is applied to two strings or a string and a numeric value, a concatenation occurs. As expected, when applying this operator to two numeric values, the values are added.

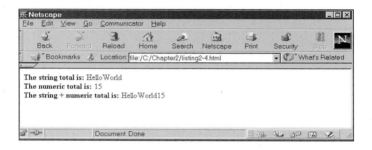

**Figure 2.4**

*The result of executing Listing 2.8.*

# Assignment

What good are variables if data cannot be assigned to them? Like all languages, JavaScript provides assignment operators to allow data to be stored in variables. The basic format of the assignment operator is shown in the following example, where a value of 6 is assigned to the variable x:

```
x = 6;
```

In addition to this one-to-one assignment, this operator can also be stacked to create simultaneous assignments. Simultaneous means that several variables can be assigned at once. This is demonstrated in the following example, where variables x, y, and z all contain the value of 6:

```
x = y = z = 6;
```

Anytime multiple assignment operators occur in the same expression, they are evaluated from right to left. So in the previous example z would be assigned the value 6 first. Once the assignment has been made, y would be assigned the value stored in z and, finally, x would be assigned the value stored in y. The overall effect is that all three variables would be assigned a value of 6.

Because the assignment operator is an operator, like addition (+) or subtraction (-), it can be used within an expression. This enables a programmer to perform an assignment and evaluate a mathematical expression all in one step.

```
y = (x = 3) + 4;
```

In the preceding example, the value 3 is assigned to the variable x, which is then added to the value 4 and assigned to the variable y. Once the expression is fully evaluated, y will contain the value 7. This enables programmers to accomplish three things at once. They are able to assign a value to the x variable, perform an addition, and assign the result to the y variable. Features like this help make JavaScript very versatile and easy to use.

Now that you have looked at how the assignment operator works, look at a more detailed example—one that performs each of the assignments discussed, as well as some more complex ones. Listing 2.9 contains such an example, and Figure 2.5 shows the result.

*Listing 2.9    Use of the Assignment Operators in JavaScript*

```
<SCRIPT LANGUAGE="JavaScript">
<!-- Hide

// Declare variables using single assignment
x = 3;
y = 7;
z = 9;

//Display the values stored in the variables after single assignment
document.write("<U>After single assignment</U><BR>");
document.write("x=",x,"<BR>y=",y,"<BR>z=",z,"<BR>");

//Perform multiple assignment on variables x = y = z = 14;

//Display the values stored in the variables after multiple assignment
document.write("<U>After multiple assignment</U><BR>");
document.write("x=",x,"<BR>y=",y,"<BR>z=",z,"<BR>");

//Perform multiple assignment in one expression
x = (y = 17) + (2 * (z = 2));

//Display the values stored in the variables after multiple assignment
//in one expression.
document.write("<U>After multiple assignment in one expression</U><BR>");
document.write("x=",x,"<BR>y=",y,"<BR>z=",z,"<BR>");

// -->
</SCRIPT>
```

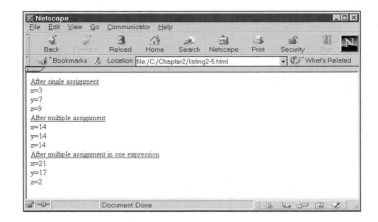

**Figure 2.5**

*The result of executing Listing 2.9.*

In addition to the basic assignment operator, JavaScript also offers a number of advanced assignment operators that extend assignment functionality. These operators combine the functionality of basic assignment and other operators into one functional operator. Table 2.6 shows these advanced assignment operators along with their equivalent operations.

**Table 2.6 Advanced Assignment Operators**

| Operator | Example | Description |
|----------|---------|-------------|
| += | x+=y | x = x + y; |
| -= | x -=y | x = x − y; |
| *= | x*=y | x = x * y; |
| /= | x/=y | x = x / y; |
| %= | x%=y | x = x % y; |
| <<= | x<<=y | x = x << y; |
| >>= | x>>=y | x = x >> y; |
| >>>= | x>>>=y | x = x >>> y; |
| &= | x&=y | x = x & y; |
| ¦= | x¦=y | x = x ¦ y; |
| ^= | x^=y | x = x ^ y; |

All the advanced assignment operators, except for +=, will attempt to convert strings to numbers before performing the operation. If strings are used with the += operator, the left operand is concatenated to the end of the right operand. For example, in Listing 2.10, the string `"lighthouse"` would be assigned to the variable y and the phrase "y= lighthouse" is written to the browser.

*Listing 2.10   Using the Addition Operator to Perform String Concatenation*

```
<SCRIPT LANGUAGE="JavaScript">
<!--Hide

// Declare a string
y = "light";

//Concatenate the string "house" to the
//end of string stored in  the variable y
y += "house";

// Print the output to the screen
document.write("y= ",y);

// End Hide -->
</SCRIPT>
```

So far, you have only considered assignment of values to variables, but what about assigning a reference to a variable? When the assignment operator works on primitive values (numbers, strings, Boolean, null, and undefined), a copy of the value is made. When the assignment operator works on JavaScript objects, references to the objects are copied. To demonstrate this difference, Listing 2.11 creates a variable and an array to hold numbers. The variable is then copied by value to another variable, and the array is copied by reference to another array. To show the difference, the value stored in one of the variables and one of the arrays is changed, and then all the values are displayed in the browser as seen in Figure 2.6.

*Listing 2.11   Assignment by Value Versus by Reference*

```
<SCRIPT LANGUAGE="JavaScript">
<!--Hide

//Declare a variable and an array object
var number1 = 94;
var arrayOfNum1 = new Array(23,86);

//Assign by value
var number2 = number1;

//Assign by reference
var arrayOfNum2 = arrayOfNum1;

//Modify value stored in copied variable and array.
number2 = 29;
arrayOfNum2[1] = 47;

//Display the values stored in each variable and array
```

*continues*

*Listing 2.11    continued*

```
document.write("number1=",number1,"<BR>");
document.write("number2=",number2,"<BR>");
document.write("arrayOfNum1[0]=",arrayOfNum1[0],"<BR>");
document.write("arrayOfNum1[1]=",arrayOfNum1[1],"<BR>");
document.write("arrayOfNum2[0]=",arrayOfNum2[0],"<BR>");
document.write("arrayOfNum2[1]=",arrayOfNum2[1],"<BR>");

// End Hide -->
</SCRIPT>
```

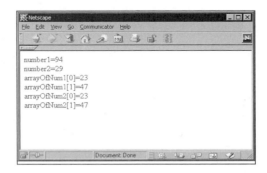

**Figure 2.6**

*The result of executing Listing 2.11.*

# Logical

JavaScript provides three logical operators. Without these operators, programs would be very long and complex. At first glance, most programmers might think that they already know how these operators work, but it is important to dig a little deeper. Not knowing how the logical operator works can lead to what would appear to be random errors that are impossible to locate and correct. So take the time to read the description of each of the logical operators.

**NOTE**

> JavaScript defines `true` as anything other than `0` (zero), `""` (empty string), `null`, undefined, and, of course, `false`.

## Logical AND

The logical AND operator (`&&`) returns `true` if the expression to the left and the expression to the right of the operator evaluate to `true`. If either the left, right, or both expressions evaluate to `false`, the result of the operation is `false`.

Unfortunately, the implementation of the logical AND operator in JavaScript is more complex than what was just mentioned. The AND operation begins by evaluating the left operand. If the left operand evaluates false, the basic logic of the AND operator is complete, so the right operand is never evaluated. But if the left operand evaluates true, the right operand must be evaluated to determine the final result of the AND operation. In either case, the final result returned by the AND operation is actually the result of the last operand to be evaluated.

## *Logical OR*

The logical OR operator (¦¦) returns true if the expression to the left or the expression to the right of the operator evaluates to true. If both the left and the right expressions evaluate to true, the result of the operation is false.

Like the logical AND operator, it is important you understand how JavaScript actually evaluates the logical OR operator. The OR operation begins by evaluating the left operand. If the left operand evaluates true, the basic logic of the OR operator is complete, so the right operand is never evaluated. But if the left operand evaluates false, the right operand must be evaluated to determine the final result of the OR operation. In either case, the final result returned by the OR operation is actually the result of the last operand to be evaluated.

## *Logical NOT*

The logical NOT operator (!) is not as complex as the comparison operators. The result of the expression following the operator is inverted. If the expression evaluates to true, the result of the operation is false. If the expression evaluates to false, the result is true. When the expression evaluates to a non-Boolean value, it is converted to true or false before performing the inversion.

**NOTE**

The result returned from ¦¦ and && operations is not always the Boolean true or false. This is because the final result returned by the logical operators is actually the result of the last operand to be evaluated. There is a bug in the ¦¦ and && operators in Navigator 2 and 3: Rather than returning the result of the left operand, the result is converted to a Boolean value.

# Comparison

JavaScript provides the usual comparison operators found in most languages plus a couple of new ones. Because JavaScript is still evolving, there are some inconsistencies that are still being straightened out in the comparison operator department. For this reason, it is important to understand how these operators work.

## *Equal*

The equal operator (==) compares the value to the left of the operator to the value to the right of the operator. If the values are equal, true is returned from the operation. If the values are not equal, false is returned from the operation.

Originally, JavaScript attempted to convert the operands of the equality operator to the same type before performing a comparison. For example, if the left operand of an equal operator is a number and the right operand is a string, JavaScript would attempt to convert the string to a number, so that two numbers are compared. In an attempt to guess what would be in the then unreleased ECMAScript standard, the decision was made not to do type-conversion on the operands of the equality operator in JavaScript 1.2. When the ECMAScript standard was released, it supported type-conversion, so JavaScript 1.3 came full circle by once again attempting to convert the operands of the equality operator to the same type before performing a comparison.

JavaScript determines which behavior should be used by the <SCRIPT> tag. By setting the LANGUAGE attribute of the <SCRIPT> tag equal to JAVASCRIPT, type-conversion will be used. If the LANGUAGE attribute is set to JAVASCRIPT1.2, no type-conversion will be used. An example of this behavior is demonstrated in the following code:

```
<HTML>
<SCRIPT LANGUAGE="JAVASCRIPT1.3">
// Type-conversion turned on
document.write("The == operator with type-conversion turned on returns: ");
document.write(3=="3");
</SCRIPT>
<SCRIPT LANGUAGE="JAVASCRIPT1.2">
// Type-conversion turned off
document.write("<BR>The == operator with type- ");
document.write("conversion turned off returns: ");
document.write(3=="3");
</SCRIPT>
</HTML>
```

**TIP**

Avoid setting the LANGUAGE attribute to JAVASCRIPT1.2 in your code, because the industry standard is for type-conversion to be used on the operands of the equality operator.

So far you've seen type-conversion used with the equality operators, but you haven't seen how the type-conversion operates. Understanding how type-conversions work for the equality operators will again save time when trying to find bugs. Type-conversion adheres to the following rules:

- rue is converted to the number 1, and false is converted to zero before being compared.
- If either of the operands are NaN, the equality operator returns false.
- null and undefined are equal.
- null and undefined are not equal to 0 (zero), "" , or false.
- If a string and a number are compared, attempt to convert the string to a number and then check for equality.

- If an object and a string are compared, attempt to convert the object to a string and then check for equality.
- If an object and a number are compared, attempt to convert the object to a number and then check for equality.
- If both operands of an equality operation are objects, the addresses of the two objects are checked for equality.

## Not Equal

The not equal operator (!=) compares the value to the left of the operator to the value on the right. If the values are not equal, true is returned from operation. If they are not equal, false is returned. The != operator is victim to the same type-conversion bug as the == operator. Just like the == operator, use the LANGUAGE attribute of the <SCRIPT> tag to force the desired behavior.

## Greater Than

The greater than operator (>) compares the value to the left of the operator to the value on the right. If the value on the left is greater than the value on the right, true is returned from operation. If the value to the left of the operator is less than or equal to the value on the right, false is returned. If either of the values is a string, it is converted to a number before the comparison takes place.

## Less Than

The less than operator (<) compares the value to the left of the operator to the value on the right. If the value on the left is less than the value on the right, true is returned from operation. If the value to the left of the operator is greater than or equal to the value on the right, false is returned. If either of the values is a string, it is converted to a number before the comparison takes place.

## Greater Than or Equal

The greater than or equal operator (>=) compares the value to the left of the operator to the value on the right. If the value on the left is greater than or equal to the value to the right of the operator, true is returned from operation. If the value to the left of the operator is less than the value on the right, false is returned. If either of the values is a string, it is converted to a number before the comparison takes place.

## Less Than or Equal

The less than or equal operator (<=) compares the value to the left of the operator to the value on the right. If the value on the left is less than or equal to the value on the right, true is returned from operation. If the value to the left of the operator is greater than the value on the right, false is returned. If either of the values is a string, it is converted to a number before the comparison takes place.

## Identity

The identity operator (===) compares the value to the left of the operator to the value on the right. If the value on the left is equal to the value on the right side of the operator, `true` is returned from operation. If the values are not equal, `false` is returned. No type-conversion is performed on the operands before the comparison.

### Non-Identity

The non-identity operator (`!==`) compares the value to the left of the operator to the value on the right. If the value on the left is not equal to the value on the right side of the operator, `true` is returned from operation. If the values are equal, `false` is returned. No type-conversion is performed on the operands before the comparison is made.

**NOTE**

The identity and non-identity operators are only available in JavaScript 1.3 and later.

## Conditional

Many programmers are not familiar with the conditional operator (`?:`), even though it exists in numerous languages. Most individuals will use the standard `if` statement rather than the conditional operator, even though they do the same thing. The conditional operator is a little harder to read than the standard `if` statement, but it is much more compact, which is important when download time is a consideration.

The format of the conditional operator can be a bit confusing. An expression that evaluates to a Boolean is always placed to the left of the question mark (`?`). If the expression evaluates to `true`, the value between the question mark and the colon (`:`) is returned from the operation. If the expression evaluates to `false`, the value following the colon is returned. In Listing 2.12, a standard `if` statement is shown, along with same functionality produced by using the conditional operator. Figure 2.7 shows that the same functionality is produced from both the `if` statement and the conditional operator.

*Listing 2.12    The Conditional Operator and `if` Statement Are Compared*

```
<SCRIPT LANGUAGE="JavaScript">
<!--Hide

// Set the mail flag to "YES"
mailFlag = "YES"
var message1;
var message2;

//Standard if statement
if (mailFlag == "YES")
message1 = "You have email!";
else
message1 = "No email.";

//Same statement using conditional operator
message2 = (mailFlag == "YES") ? "You have email!" : "No email.";
```

```
// Print the message to the screen
document.write("The if statement returns: ",message1,"<BR>");
document.write("The conditional operator returns: ",message2);

// End Hide -->
</SCRIPT>
```

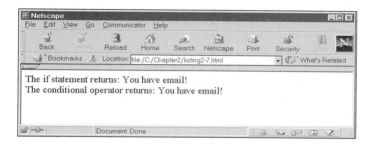

**Figure 2.7**

*The result of executing Listing 2.12.*

# Bitwise

The bitwise operators look similar to the comparison operators, but their functionality is very different. If you have ever worked with truth tables, you might recognize the operators in this section. Bitwise operators in JavaScript only work with integers that are 32 bits in length. If an integer is not 32 bits, it is turned into one because the bitwise operators evaluate numbers at the binary level where everything is ones and zeros. Bitwise operations are not used often in programming, but there are times when the operators are indispensable.

## Bitwise AND

The bitwise AND operator (&) looks at the integer numbers on both sides of the operator as 32-bit binary numbers. The logical AND (&&) operator, discussed earlier in the chapter, individually evaluates each of the 32 bits representing the number to the left of the operator to the corresponding bit of the number to the right of the operator. The 32-bit binary result of logical AND operation is converted to an integer value and returned from the bitwise AND operation.

## Bitwise OR

The bitwise OR operator (¦) looks at the integer numbers on both sides of the operator as 32-bit binary numbers. The logical OR (¦¦) operator, discussed earlier in the chapter, individually evaluates each of the 32 bits representing the number to the left of the operator to the corresponding bit of the number to the right of the operator. The 32-bit binary result of logical OR operation is converted to an integer value and returned from the bitwise OR operation.

## Bitwise XOR (exclusive OR)

The bitwise XOR operator (^) looks at the integer numbers on both sides of the operator as 32-bit binary numbers. Unlike the bitwise OR operator, bitwise XOR uses a special version of the logical OR operator, called exclusive OR, to evaluate each bit of a binary number.

**NOTE**

An exclusive OR operation returns true if either the value to the left or the value to the right of the operator is true, but not both. If both values are false or both values are true, the result of the operation is false.

The exclusive OR individually evaluates each of the 32 bits representing the number to the left of the bitwise XOR operator to the corresponding bit of the number to the right of the operator. The 32-bit binary result of exclusive OR operation is converted to an integer value and returned from the bitwise XOR operation.

## Bitwise NOT

The bitwise NOT operator (~) is simpler than the bitwise AND, OR, and XOR operators. The bitwise NOT operator begins by looking at the number to the right of the operator as a 32-bit binary number. Each bit of the given number is reversed so that all ones become zeros and all zeros become ones. The 32-bit binary result is converted to an integer value and returned from the bitwise NOT operation.

## Shift Left

The shift left operator (<<) looks at the integer to the left of the operator as a 32-bit binary number. All the bits in this number are shifted to the left by the number of positions specified by the integer to the right of the operator. As the bits are shifted to the left, zeros are filled in on the right. Because the number can only be 32 bits long, the extra bits on the left are lost. The 32-bit binary result of shifting operation is converted to an integer value and returned from the shift left operation.

## Shift Right with Sign

The shift right with sign operator (>>) is similar to the shift left operator. The shift right with sign operator looks at the integer to the left of the operator as a 32-bit binary number. All the bits in this number are shifted to the right by the number of positions specified by the integer to the right of the operator. As the bits are shifted to the right, either ones or zeros are filled in on the left. If the original number is positive, ones are added to the left side of the binary number. On the other hand, if the original number is negative, zeros are used. Because the result can only be 32 bits long, the extra bits on the right are lost. The 32-bit binary result of the shifting operation is converted to an integer value and returned from the shift right with sign operation.

## Shift Right Zero Fill

The shift right zero fill operator (>>>) operates just like the shift right with sign operator, except that the binary number is always padded on the left with zeros, regardless
of the sign of the original integer.

# Precedence

JavaScript, like other languages, enables numerous operators to be used in one expression. Because operators can appear just about anywhere within an expression,
JavaScript follows guidelines that determine which operator is evaluated first, second,
third, and so on. Table 2.7 shows the precedence of all the JavaScript operators. The
Read From... column tells what order (left-to-right or right-to-left) operators of equal
precedence are evaluated. It is possible to override the precedence of operators by using
parentheses.

**TIP**

Use parentheses even when precedence is not an issue, just to make your code
more readable.

*Table 2.7    Operator Precedence*

| Precedence | Read From... | Operator | Operator Name |
|---|---|---|---|
| Highest | L to R | . | Object property access |
| | L to R | [ ] | Array index |
| | L to R | ( ) | Function call |
| | R to L | ++ | Pre/Post Increment |
| | R to L | — | Pre/Post Decrement |
| | R to L | - | Negation |
| | R to L | ~ | Bitwise NOT |
| | R to L | ! | Logical NOT |
| | R to L | delete | Undefine a property |
| | R to L | new | Create a new object |
| | R to L | typeof | Return data type |
| | R to L | void | Return undefined value |
| | L to R | *, /, % | Multiplication, division, modulus |
| | L to R | +, - | Addition, Subtraction |
| | L to R | + | String concatenation |
| | L to R | << | Left shift |
| | L to R | >> | Right shift with sign |
| | L to R | >>> | Right shift zero fill |
| | L to R | <, <= | Less than, less than or equal |
| | L to R | >, >= | Greater than, greater than or equal |

*continues*

*Table 2.7  continued*

| Precedence | Read From... | Operator | Operator Name |
|---|---|---|---|
| | L to R | == | Equality |
| | L to R | != | Inequality |
| | L to R | === | Identity |
| | L to R | !== | Non-identity |
| | L to R | & | Bitwise AND |
| | L to R | ^ | Bitwise XOR |
| | L to R | ¦ | Bitwise OR |
| | L to R | && | Logical AND |
| | L to R | ¦¦ | Logical OR |
| | R to L | ?: | Conditional |
| | R to L | = | Assignment |
| | R to L | *=, /= | Assignment plus operation %=, +=, -=, <<=, >>=, >>>=, &=, ^=, ¦= |
| Lowest | L to R | . | Multiple evaluation |

# Loops and Conditionals

Loops and conditionals give programs the power to make decisions and perform tasks multiple times. JavaScript provides the standard conditionals and looping structures that are available in many computer languages. In fact, these structures were patterned after those found in C, C++, and Java, so if you have written code in any of these languages, you will find this section very straightforward.

## Conditionals

Conditional statements enable programs to make decisions based on preset conditions that use the operators discussed earlier in the chapter.

### if

The if statement is by far the most common conditional statement simply because it is simple and easy to use. The format of a simple if statement looks like the following:

```
if (expression)
  statement;
```

If the expression in parentheses evaluates to true, the statement is executed; otherwise, the statement is skipped. The statement to be executed can appear on the same line as the if expression, but the code is usually easier to read if the statement appears on the next line as shown in the preceding pseudo code. If two or more lines of code are to be executed, curly braces {} must be used to designate what code belongs in the if statement.

Use the keyword else to extend the functionality of the basic if statement to provide other alternatives should the initial statement fail. The format of an if...else combination looks like the following:

```
if (expression)
  statement1;
else
  statement2;
```

Now, if the expression evaluates to true, *statement1* is executed, otherwise, *statement2* is executed. Listing 2.13 demonstrates the use of if and else with a hotel occupancy example. When executed, the code returns the message "There are not enough rooms for 5 guests."

*Listing 2.13   Basic* if...else *Structures*

```
<SCRIPT LANGUAGE='JavaScript'>
<!--

//Declare variables
var emptyRooms = 2;   //Two people per room
var numberOfGuests = 5;

if (emptyRooms == 0)
  document.write("There are no rooms available.");
else
{
  if ((emptyRooms*2) >= numberOfGuests)
    document.write("There are enough rooms for ",numberOfGuests," guests.");
  else
document.write("There are not enough rooms for ");
    document.write(numberOfGuests," guests.");
}

//-->
</SCRIPT>
```

Notice how Listing 2.13 used curly brackets {} to nest an if...else structure inside another if...else structure. Nesting gives programs more decision-making power, but this power comes at the cost of readability.

## *else...if*

The else...if phrase is used in place of nested if...else structures to make code more readable. Each else...if phrase is followed by an expression enclosed in parentheses. Use as many else...if statements as needed. Use a final else statement to execute code when all other conditionals evaluate to false. Listing 2.14 has the same functionality as the code in Listing 2.13, but it uses the else...if structure. This code displays the phrase, "There are not enough rooms for 5 guests."

*Listing 2.14   Making Nested* `if...else` *Statements more Readable with the* `else...if` *Phrase*

```
<SCRIPT LANGUAGE='JavaScript'>
<!--

//Declare variables
var emptyRooms = 2;   //Two people per room
var numberOfGuests = 5;

if (emptyRooms == 0)
  document.write("There are no rooms available.");
else if ((emptyRooms*2) >= numberOfGuests)
  document.write("There are enough rooms for ",numberOfGuests," guests.");
else
  document.write("There are not enough rooms for ",numberOfGuests," guests.");

//-->
</SCRIPT>
```

## switch

JavaScript offers the `switch` statement as an alternative to using the `if...else` structure. The `switch` statement is especially useful when testing all the possible results of an expression. The format of a `switch` structure looks like the following:

```
switch (expression)
{
  case label1:
    statement1;
    break;
  case label2:
    statement2;
    break;
  default:
    statement3;
}
```

The `switch` statement begins by evaluating an expression placed between parentheses, much like the `if` statement. The result is compared to labels associated with `case` structures that follow the `switch` statement. If the result is equal to a label, the statement(s) in the corresponding `case` structure are executed. A `default` structure can be used at the end of a `switch` structure to catch results that do not match any of the `case` labels. Listing 2.15 gives an example of the `switch` structure.

*Listing 2.15   Using the* `switch` *Structure*

```
<SCRIPT LANGUAGE='JavaScript'>
<!--

//Declare variables
```

```
var color = "green";

//Display the color of the car based on the variable "color"
switch (color)
{
  case "red":
    document.write("The car is red.");
    break;
  case "blue":
    document.write("The car is blue.");
    break;
  case "green":
    document.write("The car is green.");
    break;
  default:
    document.write("The car is purple.");
}

//-->
</SCRIPT>
```

There are a few key points to note about the format of the `switch` structure in Listing 2.15. First, notice that a colon always follows a label. Secondly, curly brackets {} are used to hold all the `case` structures together, but they are not used within a `case` structure, even when multiple statements are to be executed. Finally, the keyword `break` is used to break out of the entire `switch` statement once a match is found, thus preventing the `default` structure from being executed accidentally. The result of executing the code in Listing 2.15 is shown in Figure 2.8.

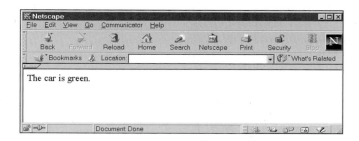

**Figure 2.8**

*The result of executing Listing 2.15.*

# Loops

There are times when the same portion of code needs to be executed many times with slightly different values. Use loops that run until a condition is met to create this functionality.

## *for*

The for loop is a very rigid structure that loops for a preset number of times. JavaScript uses the C and C++ for loop structure. This particular structure is very flexible, which makes this type of loop very useful.

From a very high level, the for loop is made up of two parts: condition and statement. The condition portion of the structure determines how many times the loop repeats, while the statement is what is executed every time the loop occurs.

The condition structure is contained within parentheses and is made up of three parts, each separated by a semicolon (;). The first part of the condition structure initializes a variable to a starting value. In most cases, the variable is declared within this section as well as initialized. The second part is the actual conditional statement that determines how many times the loop with be iterated. The third and final part determines how the variable, which was initialized in the first part, should be changed each time the loop is iterated. It is this third part that gives the for loop its flexibility by causing the variable to be incremented, decremented, factored, or any other adjustment trick you can devise. The format of the for loop looks like the following:

```
for (initialize; condition; adjust)
{
   statement;
}
```

It is important to take time to think about how to implement for loops because it is easy to accidentally create an infinite loop. Specifically, make sure the conditional will catch the adjusted variable at some point. In many cases, it is advantageous to use the variable in the statement portion of the for loop, but take care not to adjust the variable in such a way that an infinite loop is created. Listing 2.16 makes use of the for loop to create a multiplication table as shown in Figure 2.9.

*Listing 2.16   Multiplication Table Using* for *Loop*

```
<SCRIPT LANGUAGE='JavaScript'>
<!--

document.write("<H2>Multiplication table for 4</H2>");

for (var aNum = 0; aNum <= 10; aNum++)
{
   document.write("4 X ",aNum," = ",4*aNum,"<BR>");
}

//-->
</SCRIPT>
```

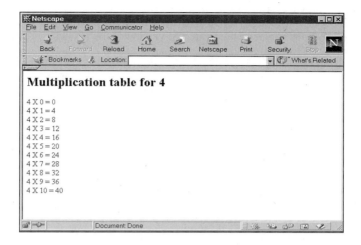

**Figure 2.9**

*Result of executing Listing 2.16.*

## *while*

When the `for` loop is too restrictive for a particular piece of code, consider using the `while` loop. The `while` loop can do everything that the `for` loop can do, but not as cleanly. So why even use the `while` loop? The `while` loop goes beyond the `for` loop's capabilities by not restricting the number of times the loop will execute.

The `while` loop is easy to understand if the phrase "While true, loop" is remembered. This phrase means that while the expression—in parentheses—evaluates to `true`, execute the statements in the loop. Once the last statement in the loop is executed, go back to the top of the loop and evaluate the expression again. When the expression evaluates to `false`, the next line of code following the `while` loop structure is executed. To keep the loop from executing indefinitely, a statement must be included in the loop that modifies a variable that is in the expression. The format of the `while` loop looks like the following:

```
while (expression)
{
  statement;
}
```

Because the expression is evaluated before the loop, it is possible the loop will never be executed should the expression evaluate to `false` the first time. Listing 2.17 simulates an automated traffic light using the `while` loop.

*Listing 2.17    Automated Traffic Light Using* while *Loop*

```
<SCRIPT LANGUAGE='JavaScript'>
<!--

//Declare a variables
var light = "red";            //traffic light
var counter = 1;              //create car traffic
var carsInLine = new Array(); //cars in line

//Make 5 cars go through intersection
while (counter <= 5)
{
  document.write("Car ",counter," approaches intersection.<BR>");
  carsInLine[carsInLine.length++] = counter;

  //When 2 cars are in line light turns green
  if (carsInLine.length == 2)
  {
    light = "green";
    document.write("Traffic light turns ",light,"<BR>");
  }

  //while light is green cars pass through intersection
  while (light == "green")
  {
    document.write("Car ",carsInLine[carsInLine.length-1]);
    carsInLine.length—;
    document.write(" goes through intersection.<BR>");

    //When no cars are in line light turns red
    if (carsInLine.length == 0)
    {
      light = "red";
      document.write("Traffic light turns ",light,"<BR>");
    }
  }
  counter++;    //Next car
}

//-->
</SCRIPT>
```

Listing 2.17 uses two while loops to simulate an automated traffic light. The first while loop could have just as easily been created using a for loop, but the second while loop would have been nearly impossible to implement using a for loop. The while loop handles this type conditional loop with ease. In Figure 2.10, you see that the traffic light automatically turns green when two cars are in line at the intersection. After the two cars go through the intersection, the light turns red.

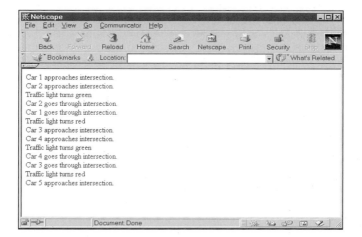

**Figure 2.10**

*Result of executing Listing 2.17.*

## do...while

The do...while loop is simply a variation of the basic while loop that was just discussed. Other than syntax, the only difference between the do...while loop and the while loop is that the do...while loop always executes the loop once before evaluating the expression for the first time. This difference is seen in the following format:

```
do
{
  statement;
}
while (expression);
```

Once the loop has executed for the first time, the expression—in parentheses—is evaluated. If true, the loop is executed again. When the expression evaluates to false, the next line of code following the while structure is executed. As was the case with the while loop, a statement must be included in the loop that modifies a variable in the expression to prevent an infinite loop. Also, notice that a semicolon (;) must be placed after the rightmost parenthesis. Listing 2.18 is the same automated traffic light simulator as shown in Listing 2.17, except do...while loops are used instead of while loops.

*Listing 2.18   Automated Traffic Light Using* do...while *Loop*
```
<SCRIPT LANGUAGE='JavaScript'>
<!--

//Declare variables
var light = "red";              //traffic light
```

*continues*

*Listing 2.18  continued*

```
var counter = 1;                  //create car traffic
var carsInLine = new Array();  //cars in line

//Make 5 cars go through intersection
while (counter <= 5)
{
  document.write("Car ",counter," approaches intersection.<BR>");
  carsInLine[carsInLine.length++] = counter;

  //If light green then execute loop more than once
  do
  {
    //When 2 cars are in line light turns green
    if (carsInLine.length == 2)
    {
      light = "green";
      document.write("Traffic light turns ",light,"<BR>");
    }

    //When no cars are in line light turns red
    if (carsInLine.length == 0)
    {
      light = "red";
      document.write("Traffic light turns ",light,"<BR>");
    }

    //Cars pass through intersection while light is green
    if (light == "green")
    {
      document.write("Car ",carsInLine[carsInLine.length-1]);
      carsInLine.length--;
      document.write(" goes through intersection.<BR>");
    }
  }
  while (light == "green");

  counter++;    //Next car
}

//-->
</SCRIPT>
```

The output generated from running Listing 2.18 is exactly the same as executing Listing 2.17.

## for...in

The for...in loop should not be confused with the for loop because they are quite different. The only similarity is that both iterate through the loop a set number of times, but this is as far as the similarity goes. The `for...in` loop is a special looping construct found only in JavaScript to provide access to all the enumerated properties of a JavaScript object. This includes elements of the `Array` object, since they are stored the same way property names are stored in JavaScript object. The statement(s) in the loop are executed for each property of an object until every property has been accessed. Any parts of an object—such as methods and some properties—that are not enumerated are not accessed by this looping structure. The format of the `for...in` loop looks like the following:

```
for (variable in object)
{
  statement;
}
```

Before the statements in the loop are executed, a property name, of the object specified to the right of the keyword `in`, is assigned to the variable on the left side of the keyword `in`. The variable would then be used within the loop code. This process will continue until all of the properties have been accessed. Unfortunately, the order in which the properties are accessed can vary, so do not assume a particular order. Listing 2.19 shows the properties of a simple HTML button.

*Listing 2.19    Accessing Property Names of the* `Button` *Object*

```
<HTML>

<FORM NAME="aForm">
  <INPUT TYPE="button"
         NAME="Big_Button"
         VALUE="Big Button"
         onClick="alert('The Big Button was pressed!')";
  >
</FORM>

<SCRIPT LANGUAGE='JavaScript'>
<!--

var aProperty;

for (aProperty in document.aForm.Big_Button)
{
  document.write(aProperty,"<BR>");
}

//-->
</SCRIPT>

</HTML>
```

Notice that in Figure 2.11, the name of the properties in the `Big Button` object, rather than the values stored in those properties, was returned.

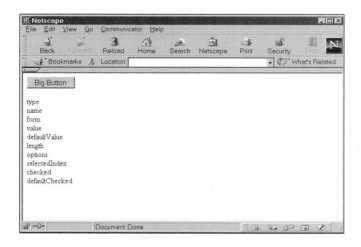

**Figure 2.11**

*The result of executing Listing 2.14.*

## break

The keyword `break` provides a way for JavaScript to exit out of loop structures and `switch` conditionals prematurely. Most of the time, the word `break` appears on a line by itself, but there are times when a label will follow the keyword. When a label is used, JavaScript completely breaks out of the area designated by `label` and proceeds to the code that follows the area.

JavaScript labels can be thought of as placeholders. To label a statement, simply place the label name followed by a colon (`:`) in front of the code that needs to be broken out of during code execution. Labels are useful when working with nested loops, as shown in Listing 2.20.

*Listing 2.20    Using Breaks and Labels*

```
<SCRIPT LANGUAGE='JavaScript'>
<!--

//Create outerloop
forLoop1:
for (var counter1 = 1; counter1 <= 5; counter1++)
{
  //Create innerloop
  for (var counter2 = 1; counter2 <= 5; counter2++)
  {
```

```
  //Display values in counters for both loops
  document.write("Counter1=",counter1);
  document.write(" Counter2=",counter2,"<BR>");

  //Determine when to break out of loop
  if (counter2 == 3)
    break;
  if (counter1 == 3)
    break forLoop1;
  }
}

document.write("All done!");

//-->
</SCRIPT>
```

Notice how the break statement with no label (see Figure 2.12) breaks out of just the innerloop. When the break statement is used with a label, JavaScript knows at what level to break.

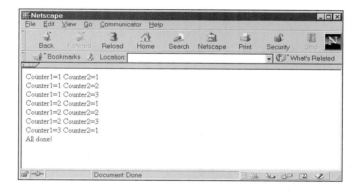

**Figure 2.12**

*Result of executing Listing 2.20.*

## *continue*

Unlike the JavaScript break structure, the continue statement forces the execution of the code to continue at the beginning of the loop. Like the keyword break, the continue keyword usually appears on a line by itself, but there are times when a label will follow the keyword. When a label is used, JavaScript immediately jumps to the beginning of the loop designated by a label and begins executing code.

The beginning of a loop varies depending on the type of loop structure. Table 2.8 shows where each looping structure jumps when a continue structure is encountered.

### Table 2.8 Where the Continue Statement Jumps

| Looping Structure | Continue Jumps To |
| --- | --- |
| `for` | Expression in parentheses following `for` keyword |
| `while` | Expression in parentheses following `while` keyword |
| `do...while` | Expression in parentheses following `while` keyword |
| `for...in` | Next property name in object |

## CAUTION

There is a bug in Navigator 4 that causes the expression in parentheses following the `while` keyword to not get executed when jumped to using a `continue` statement. Instead, execution of code starts at the top of loop after the `continue` statement.

As discussed in the `break` section, JavaScript labels can be thought of as placeholders. To label a statement, simply place the label name followed by a colon (:) in front of the code that code execution needs to continue. Listing 2.21 demonstrates the use of `label` and `continue`.

*Listing 2.21  Using the* `continue` *Statement*

```
<SCRIPT LANGUAGE='JavaScript'>
<!--

//Create outerloop
outerLoop:
  for (var counter1 = 1; counter1 <= 2; counter1++)
  {
    document.write("Top of outerLoop.<BR>");
    //Create innerloop
    innerLoop:
      for (var counter2 = 1; counter2 <= 2; counter2++)
      {
        //Display values stored in counters of both loops
        document.write("Top of innerLoop.<BR>");
        document.write("Counter1=",counter1,"<BR>");
        document.write("Counter2=",counter2,"<BR>");

        //Determine where to continue looping
        if (counter2 == 2)
        {
          document.write("Continue at top of innerLoop.<BR>");
          continue;
        }
        if (counter1 == 2)
        {
          document.write("Continue at top of outerLoop.<BR>");
```

```
                continue outerLoop;
        }
        document.write("Bottom of innerLoop.<BR>");
    }
    document.write("Bottom of outerLoop.<BR>");
}

document.write("All done!");

//-->
</SCRIPT>
```

This example is a bit complicated, so take time to compare Listing 2.21 to the output in Figure 2.13. Notice how the phrase `Bottom of innerLoop.` was not printed after the `Continue at top of innerLoop.` because code execution jumped back to beginning of the intermost loop. When a label was attached to the `continue` keyword, code execution jumped back to the beginning of the loop labeled `outerLoop`.

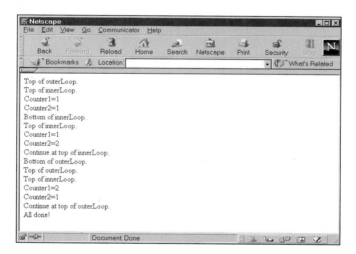

**Figure 2.13**

*Result of executing Listing 2.21.*

## *with*

The object-oriented design of JavaScript quite often requires long lines of code to access properties and methods of objects. JavaScript provides a special `with` statement to help reduce the length of code needed to access these properties and methods. The `with` statement works by placing the repetitive portion of the object's path in parentheses after the `with` keyword. Now, any properties or methods that are used within the with statement will automatically have the repetitive portion of the object's path (located in parentheses) added to the front of the string. Listing 2.22 shows how the with statement can save time when resetting text fields to their default values.

*Listing 2.22    The* with *Statement Reduces Repetitive Code*

```
<HTML>

<!--Create a form that has 3 text fields
    and a reset button-->
<FORM NAME="personalInfoForm">
Name<INPUT TYPE="text" NAME="nameBox"><BR>
Occupation<INPUT TYPE="text" NAME="occupationBox"><BR>
Age<INPUT TYPE="text" NAME="ageBox"><BR>
<INPUT TYPE="button" NAME="ResetButton"
 VALUE="Reset" onClick="ResetFields()">
</FORM>

<SCRIPT LANGUAGE='JavaScript'>
<!--

//Set text field values initially
ResetFields();

//Reset text fields to default values
function ResetFields()
{
  with(document.personalInfoForm)
  {
    nameBox.value="[Enter your name]";
    occupationBox.value="Student";
    ageBox.value="";
  }
}

//-->
</SCRIPT>
```

In Figure 2.14, you see that the text fields contain default data that appear initially as well as any time the Reset button is pressed. To achieve this functionality, the Reset button is connected to a function, called ResetFields(), that assigns default values to the text fields. To reduce repetitive code, the with statement was used in setting the default values, as seen in Listing 2.22.

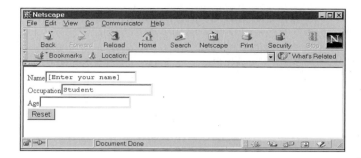

**Figure 2.14**

*Result of executing Listing 2.22.*

# Functions

One of the strengths of JavaScript is that it provides support for functions, which is uncommon among scripting languages. On the other hand, JavaScript functions are not as fully developed as those found in languages like C and C++. The functionality that JavaScript does provide through its functions is more than enough to make Web pages come alive.

## Syntax

The syntax of JavaScript functions is very straightforward. All function declaration must begin with the keyword `function` followed by the name of the function. The name of the function is the name that will be used to call on the function within code. Parentheses are placed after the function name to hold arguments that are to be passed into the function. If more than one argument is to be passed into the function, use commas to separate the arguments. On the other hand, if no arguments need to be passed into the function, leave the space between the parentheses empty. Finally, curly brackets are used to contain the code related to the function. Curly brackets are not optional, they are required in JavaScript, even if the function is only made up of one line of code.

## Call by Value Versus Call by Reference

If you have done programming in C or C++, you are probably familiar with the phrases "call by value" and "call by reference" as related to function arguments. In very basic terms, *call by reference* passes the location of the actual argument to the function, while *call by value* makes a copy of the argument to be used just within the function. JavaScript keeps the functionality of passing arguments simple by just using call by value. Using call by value gives the freedom to manipulate the arguments within the function without fear of changing the argument's values outside the function. Listing 2.23 shows an example of JavaScript call by value.

*Listing 2.23    Call by Value*

```
<SCRIPT LANGUAGE='JavaScript'>
<!--

//Declare variables
var aString = "banana"
var aNumber = 15;

//Function declaration
function test(aString, aNumber)
{
  aString = "orange";
  aNumber = 124;

  //Display values stored in function variables.
  document.write("During function call:<BR>");
  document.write("aStringCopy=",aString,"<BR>");
  document.write("aNumberCopy=",aNumber,"<BR>");
}

//Display variables before function call
document.write("Before function call:<BR>");
document.write("aString=",aString,"<BR>");
document.write("aNumber=",aNumber,"<BR>");

//Call on function
test(aString,aNumber);

//Display variables after function call
document.write("After function call:<BR>");
document.write("aString=",aString,"<BR>");
document.write("aNumber=",aNumber,"<BR>");

//-->
</SCRIPT>
```

In Figure 2.15, you see that the values stored in aString and aNumber appeared to be changed while in the function test. But after exiting the function, the values reverted back to their initial value. What actually happened was that a local copy of the variables was made for use within the function. These new variables even have the same name as the ones that were passed into the function. Once execution of the function was completed, the local variables no longer existed, so final values displayed were of the original variables.

If you need to pass in a large number of arguments but do not want to assign each one to a variable, it is possible to access the arguments as an array. To do this, leave the area in parentheses blank and use the arguments object and the array operator [ ] to access each argument. Listing 2.24 displays the arguments passed into the function using the arguments array as shown in Figure 2.16.

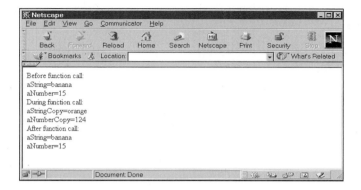

**Figure 2.15**

*Result of executing Listing 2.23.*

*Listing 2.24    Accessing Function Arguments with the* `arguments` *Array*

```
<SCRIPT LANGUAGE="JavaScript1.2">
<!--Hide

//Create a function that displays the arguments it receives.
function displayArguments()
{
  document.write("The following arguments were passed:<BR>");
  for(i=0; i<arguments.length; i++)
  {
    document.write(i," = ",arguments[i],"<BR>");
  }
}

//Pass some arguments into function
displayArguments(34,"hat",-7945,"shoes");

// End Hide -->
</SCRIPT>
```

# Returning Values

What if a value needs to be passed back from a function to be used later in the code? JavaScript provides a `return` statement that can be used in a function to return a value back to the statement that called the function. The value to be returned is simply placed after the keyword `return`. The undefined value is returned from a function if no value is specified after the keyword `return` or if the `return` statement is not used at all.

A value returned from a function can be assigned to a variable or used within an expression. In Listing 2.25, the value returned from the function is used in an expression to write the phrase, "3*5=15" to the browser window.

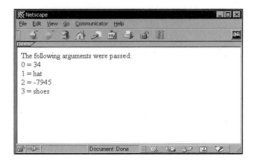

**Figure 2.16**

*Result of executing Listing 2.24.*

*Listing 2.25    Returning a Value from a Function*

```
<SCRIPT LANGUAGE='JavaScript'>
<!--

//Function declaration
function multiplyByFive(aNumber)
{
  return aNumber*5;
}

//Display variables before function call
document.write("3*5=",multiplyByFive(3));

//-->
</SCRIPT>
```

# Functions as Objects

The functions that have been described so far are created statically when the Web page is loaded, but there is also a dynamic function that is not created until it is called, which enables functions to be objects. The syntax for this type of function is more like the declaration of a variable.

```
var varName = new Function(argument1,...,lastArgument);
```

The keyword Function is used to create a new function dynamically from the arguments. All of the arguments must be strings, and the last argument should always contain the functionality of the function. Listing 2.26 shows a simple example of using the Function object. Once again the phrase, "3*5=15" is written to the browser window.

*Listing 2.26    Returning a Value from a Function*

```
<SCRIPT LANGUAGE='JavaScript'>
<!--

//Create the dynamic Function
```

```
var multiplyByFive = new Function("y","return y*5");

document.write("3*5=",multiplyByFive(3));

//-->
</SCRIPT>
```

# Pattern Matching

Two of the most common uses of Web pages today are for gathering and distributing data. These two areas, by nature, use data manipulation to understand what the user needs and then return information tailored to the user's specifications. One of the key tools for processing data is pattern matching. Some scripting languages, such as Perl, are well suited to handle pattern matching, while others provide very little pattern matching capabilities. If you are familiar with Perl, you will probably recognize JavaScript pattern matching because it was based on Perl's implementation of pattern matching. The implementation of pattern matching into JavaScript greatly aids in the processing of data for the Internet.

JavaScript uses the RegExp (short for Regular Expression) object to handle pattern matching. This object holds the pattern definition, as well as provides methods for performing matching. You'll begin by learning how to define patterns and then learn how to use the RegExp objects to test for pattern matches.

## Defining the RegExp Object

The RegExp object can be created in two different ways, which are similar to defining strings. The first way is to use the RegExp constructor and the keyword new:

```
var lastName = new RegExp("Jones");
```

This notation creates a new RegExp object called lastName and assigns the pattern *Jones*. The same functionality could have been accomplished by using a direct assignment:

```
var lastName = /Jones/;
```

To differentiate this notation from that used to define strings, the forward slash character (/) is used to designate the beginning and end of the pattern. Notice that forward slashes were not needed in the RegExp() constructor because this could be distinguished from the String() constructor.

## Defining Patterns

The syntax used to define patterns in JavaScript could be considered a scripting language in itself, because it is so extensive. There are special characters for creating almost any pattern one could imagine, including characters for handling groups, repetition, position, and so on. Table 2.9 shows the special pattern matching characters available in JavaScript.

*Table 2.9  Special Pattern Matching Characters*

| Character | Description |
| --- | --- |
| \w | Match any word character (alphanumeric). |
| \W | Match any non-word character. |
| \s | Match any whitespace character (tab, newline, carriage return, form feed, vertical tab). |
| \S | Match any non-whitespace character. |
| \d | Match any numerical digit. |
| \D | Match any character that is not a number. |
| [\b] | Match a backspace. |
| . | Match any character except a newline. |
| [...] | Match any one character within the brackets. |
| [^...] | Match any one character not within the brackets. |
| [x-y] | Match any character in the range of x to y. |
| [^x-y] | Match any character not in the range of x to y. |
| {x,y} | Match the previous item at least x times but not to exceed y times. |
| {x,} | Match the previous item at least x times. |
| {x} | Match the previous item exactly x times. |
| ? | Match the previous item once or not at all. |
| + | Match the previous item at least once. |
| * | Match the previous item any number of times or not at all. |
| ¦ | Match the expression to the left or the right of the ¦ character. |
| (...) | Group everything inside parentheses into a subpattern. |
| \x | Match the same characters that resulted from the subpattern in group number x. Groups, which are designated with parentheses, are numbered from left to right. |
| ^ | Match the beginning of the string or beginning of a line, in multi-line matches. |
| $ | Match the end of the string or end of a line, in multiline matches. |
| \b | Match the position between a word character and a non-word character. |
| \B | Match the position that is not between a word character and a non-word character. |

These special pattern matching characters are used within the pattern to aid in defining complex patterns. Looking at Table 2.9, you might notice that characters like the asterisk (*), plus sign (+), and backslash (\) hold special meanings that would keep them from being used as a literal. For example, what if you wanted to find all the plus signs (+) in a string. To use a literal plus sign, a backslash (\) must precede the sign. Table 2.10 shows all the characters that require a backslash character to be taken literally within a pattern.

*Table 2.10*  *Literal Characters*

| Character | Description |
| --- | --- |
| \f | Form feed |
| \n | Newline |
| \r | Carriage return |
| \t | Tab |
| \v | Vertical tab |
| \/ | Forward slash (/) |
| \\ | Backward slash (\) |
| \. | Period (.) |
| \* | Asterisk (*) |
| \+ | Plus (+) |
| \? | Question Mark (?) |
| \¦ | Horizontal bar (¦) |
| \( | Left parenthesis ( |
| \) | Right parenthesis ) |
| \[ | Left bracket ([) |
| \] | Right bracket (]) |
| \{ | Left curly brace ({) |
| \} | Right curly brace (}) |
| \xxx | ASCII character represented by the octal number xxx |
| \xHH | ASCII character represented by the hexadecimal number HH |
| \cX | The control character represented by x |

There is one final piece of syntax that JavaScript provides for creating patterns. Unlike the syntax covered so far, these pieces of syntax appear outside the forward slashes that define the pattern. These attributes are shown in Table 2.11.

*Table 2.11*  *Pattern Attributes*

| Character | Description |
| --- | --- |
| g | Global match. Find all possible matches. |
| i | Make matching case-insensitive. |

# Testing for Pattern Matches

Once a pattern has been defined, it can be applied to a string by using special methods that exist in the `RegExp` and `String` objects. The pattern matching methods in the `String` object require `RegExp` objects, as shown in Table 2.12.

*Table 2.12   Pattern Matching Methods in the String Object*

| Method | Description |
|---|---|
| match(*regExpObj*) | Searches for *regExpObj* pattern in string and returns result. |
| replace(*reqExpObj*,*str*) | Replaces all occurrences of the *regExpObj* pattern with *str*. |
| search(*reqExpObj*) | Returns the position of matching *regExpObj* pattern within the string. |
| split(regExpObj,max) | The string is split everywhere there is a matching *regExpObj* pattern up to max splits. The substrings are returned in an array. |

The pattern matching methods in the RegExp object require String objects, as shown in Table 2.13.

*Table 2.13   Pattern Matching Methods in the RegExp Object*

| Method | Description |
|---|---|
| exec(*str*) | Searches for pattern in *str* and returns result |
| test(*str*) | Searches for pattern in *str* and returns true if match found, otherwise false is returned |
| (*str*) | Same as exec(*str*) method |

Listing 2.27 uses the RegExp constructor, special pattern syntax, and the String replace method to successfully modify a string as seen in Figure 2.17.

*Listing 2.27   Using Regular Expressions*

```
<SCRIPT LANGUAGE='JavaScript'>
<!--

//Create a text string
var str = "John traded 5 oranges for 135 grapes.<BR>"

//Create RegExp object
var span3to5 = new RegExp("[3-5]","g");

document.write(str);
document.write("Replace digits 3 to 5 with nines.<BR>");
document.write(str.replace(span3to5,"9"));

//-->
</SCRIPT>
```

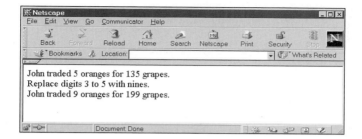

**Figure 2.17**

*Result of executing Listing 2.27.*

# CHAPTER 3

# Server-Side JavaScript

So far, you have taken an in-depth look into the JavaScript language. You have examined some of the functionality JavaScript has and some of its applications. The following chapters will discuss how to approach JavaScript as a programming language, and how to maximize your coding efforts by understanding the environments in which it is interpreted.

In addition to applying JavaScript on the client-side, there is also server-side usage. This feature, which is implemented in Netscape's Enterprise line of servers, allows developers to build robust Web-based applications. The use of these Web-based programs can be limitless, but is most commonly used to maintain user sessions and interact with databases.

In this chapter, you will take a closer look at server-side JavaScript. You'll see how it is different from client-side and learn how to compile and deploy your applications. You will analyze the various uses of the technology and learn how to manage your program with Netscape's JavaScript Application Manager. Overall, this chapter will be a primer for any server-side JavaScript you may be deploying on your site.

## NOTE

As discussed in the first chapter, Microsoft has also implemented a scripting engine in its IIS Web servers. However, its implementation falls within the realm of ASP and is not discussed in this book.

# How Does Server-Side Differ from Client-Side?

Server-side JavaScript is not only different from client-side because of the environment in which it is interpreted, it also has different concepts that are applied. These differences can be placed into two major categories, each of which will be further broken down in this chapter. The initial levels are

- Actual programming differences from client-side
- Compiling your scripts into .web byte code files before they are deployed

As a developer, you should be aware of these two items before you begin writing server-side applications. Server-side is conceptually different from client-side, even though much of the language semantics and syntax are shared.

## Programming Differences

The first item to analyze in server-side JavaScript is the programming differences that occur. Besides the functionality added on the server-side, JavaScript also has some key programming differences. These are

- Scripts to be executed on the server-side are contained between beginning <SERVER> and ending </SERVER> tags.
- There are additional objects, methods, properties, and events that are available on the server-side.
- Not all of the client-side objects, methods, properties, and events are available on the server-side.

Unlike the client-side scripts, which are contained between a beginning <SCRIPT> and ending </SCRIPT> tags, all scripts to be executed on the server-side are contained between a beginning <SERVER> and ending </SERVER> tags. This tells the Enterprise Web server to execute all the code between these tags. As a programmer, this allows you to have client-side code on the same page without it being interpreted by the server.

Server-side JavaScript has additional objects, methods, properties, and events available. Because a Web-based application has to deal with many issues, such as user sessions, server-side JavaScript has objects that deal specifically with user sessions and requests. There are objects for sending mail, opening connections to a database, managing a pool of connections, and handling the returned data. It also incorporates objects for opening, closing, and managing files on your file system. The syntax expansion on the server-side makes server-side JavaScript a rich language for developing the robust applications you need.

The final difference, which is somewhat related to the previous, is the fact that not all client-side objects and any associated properties, methods, and events, are available on the server-side. This is really nothing more than a reflection of the environment in which the scripts are interpreted. For instance, there is no navigator object or any of the Form objects. These are all specific to the client that is interpreting the script.

**NOTE**

Because there are differences in the server-side and client-side implementations, you should refer to Part III, "JavaScript Reference by Object," to determine if the object, method, property, or event you want to use is supported.

## Compiling Your Scripts

Unlike client-side JavaScript, the server-side implementation requires that you compile your scripts into .web files. These files, which are compiled down to byte code, contain all the files necessary for your Web-based application. It would include any .html files that contain your server-side code, as well as any external source JavaScript .js files that you may be using.

Netscape has provided a command-line tool, the JavaScript Application Compiler (jsac), to compile your applications. The minimum requirement for compiling the application is the .html file that contains your code. The tool itself takes a variety of parameters, defined in Table 3.1, to build your .web file.

**NOTE**

In the following table, all the options are listed as -option. The tool also accepts the syntax of /option. In addition, all paths should use a backslash (\) for directory mappings because the forward slash maps to the use of an option.

*Table 3.1    Command-Line Parameters Available to jsac*

| Option | Description |
| --- | --- |
| -a *version* | This option allows you to specify the version of the interpreter against which to compile the application. At the time of this writing, this option has only one value, 1.2, and is used to tell the compiler how to handle comparison operators, which was different in JavaScript 1.2. |
| -c | Verifies the syntax in your script, but does not create a .web file. Do not use this option with the -o option. |
| -d | Displays the JavaScript contents of your files. |
| -f *filelist* | This specifies a text file that contains the name of all the files you want to include in your build. The primary reason for this option is for those operating systems that have a limit to the number of characters you can specify on a single command line. Each filename in the file should be separated by a space. If your filename has a space in it, include the name within quotes. |

*continues*

*Table 3.1  continued*

| Option | Description |
|---|---|
| -h | Displays help for the tool. Do not use with any other options. |
| -i *inputfile* | Specifies the name of a single input .html file. See -f when including multiple files. |
| -l *characterset* | Allows you to specify the character set used when compiling your application. This would be something like iso-8859-1. |
| -o *outputfile* | Specifies the name of the output .web file you are creating. Do not use this with the -c option. |
| -p *path* | Designates the root for any relative path filenames you specify. |
| -r *errorfile* | This option allows you to specify a file to which to have all errors written. |
| -v | Displays verbose information about the execution of the compile. |

Using these options, a typical build of an application might look something like the following. It specifies to display the build process verbose, defines the output file as myApp.web, and gives the filenames of the files to include.

```
jsac -o myApp.web -v index.html results.html jsbeans.js
```

Here is another example that specifies a full path to the input file as well as sets an error file to log any errors during the compilation process.

```
jsac -o myApp.web -v -i /js/myapps/index.html -r /js/logs/myapperror.log
```

As many programmers know, it is very important to know your command-line options. Knowing how to troubleshoot compiling a project can often be just as challenging as creating one.

# Uses of Server-Side JavaScript

Now that you have seen some of the differences of server-side and client-side JavaScript and how to compile your applications, take a look at some of its uses. This section does not try to outline all the uses you may encounter, but rather discusses some of the more common aspects of using server-side JavaScript. These examples use some of the core objects specific to the server-side implementation and should give you a good taste of what you can do with this powerful language.

## USER SESSIONS AND DATABASE ACCESS

An extensive discussion of how to manage user sessions and database connections as various users access your application is beyond the scope of this book. However, there are some items you should be aware of when performing these tasks.

First, you should know how database queries are handled. You should understand how the information is returned from your specific database and how to process the information. Specifically, check the `Connection`, `Cursor`, `database`, `DbPool`, `Resultset`, and `Stproc` entries in Chapter 8, "Netscape's Server-Side Additions," for information on the objects, properties, and methods you have at your disposal.

You should also know how to appropriately manage user connections to your application. It is possible your application will have to manage many connections from many users at the same time. If your sessions and connections get crossed, you may send the wrong information to the wrong user. For information on user sessions, reference the `Lock`, `project`, `request`, and `server` entries in Chapter 8.

Maintaining and managing your user sessions and database connections can be a very important factor and you should take great care when working with them.

# Database Connectivity

One of the major features of server-side JavaScript is its ability to connect to databases. As you know, Netscape has paved the way for the use of standardized technology, and you can expect nothing less when connecting to databases. It provides native-support, industry-leading databases such as DB2, Informix, Oracle, and Sybase databases, as well as access through ODBC for other databases, such as Microsoft's SQL Server.

The functionality server-side JavaScript provides for connecting to databases is done through its LiveWire service. This service provides JavaScript objects you can use to connect to your database. Once connected, you are able to run the SQL statements necessary to perform the operations you want.

**NOTE**

When Netscape released version 2 of Enterprise server, LiveWire was a blanket term for "server-side JavaScript." By the time version 3 of Enterprise server was released, the acceptance of JavaScript as an industry standard had increased. To maintain some consistency across terminology, the term LiveWire has now, starting with version 3 of Enterprise server, been associated with the service that allows developers to write code to interact with databases.

Connections to a database are maintained in a "pool." Before you open a connection to database and have the ability to run queries against it, you must create an instance of the `DbPool` object. Once the instance is created, you can obtain connections from the pool as needed. The pool object itself takes all the parameters necessary to make the connection. It is possible to create a pool without specifying any parameters. However, you must pass the parameters when the first connection is attempted.

The following code is the syntax for creating a `DbPool` object. Each parameter is defined in the bulleted list following the example.

```
var myPool = new DbPool (DBType, DBInstance, UID, PWD, DBName, MaxConn,
➡CommitFlag);
```

- DBType   The type of database it is. Possible values are ORACLE, SYBASE, INFORMIX, DB2, or ODBC.
- DBInstance   This is the instance name of the database. For ODBC it is the DSN entry name.
- UID   The username or ID you want the connections to connect as.
- PWD   The password for the user you are connecting as.
- DBName   The name of the database into which you want to log. For Oracle, DB2, and ODBC connections this should be a blank, " ", string. In Oracle, the name of the database for these connections is set up in the tnsnames.ora file and are defined by the DSN for ODBC connections. DB2 does not have a database name and is referenced only by the DBInstance.
- MaxConn   The maximum number of connections to the pool. This is effectively the number of connections the pool will open to the database.
- CommitFlag   This flag determines if a pending transaction is committed when the connection is released. If it is set to false, the transaction is rolled back. If it is set to true, it is committed.

Because it is possible to create an instance of this object by passing a limited set of these parameters, as well as passing none, you should reference the DbPool entry in Chapter 8 before using this object.

**NOTE**

Version 2 of Enterprise Server only allowed one database connection request.

Once you have created a pool, you can use the connections within that pool as needed. To pull a connection, use the connection() method on your pool. This will return an available connection to use for processing. The syntax and a description of the parameters are as follows:

```
var myConn = myPool.connection(name, timeout);
```

- name   This is a name you can give your connection. Since you actually store the connection in a variable, this name's primary function becomes one for debugging purposes.
- timeout   A numeric value for the number of seconds you give the instance to connect.

After the connection has been made, you are able to perform the necessary processing you require for your application. For more information on the methods available, check entries for the Connection, Cursor, and database objects in Chapter 8.

# Email

Another feature that can be exploited and implemented within server-side JavaScript applications is the capability to send mail. The properties and methods needed to perform these tasks are contained in the SendMail object. Table 3.2 has a list of the properties and methods of this object. Note, however, that a more detailed description of each of the methods and properties is located in Chapter 8.

**Table 3.2 The SendMail Methods and Properties**

| Function or Property | Description |
| --- | --- |
| Bcc | Contains the email address of those users you wish to blind carbon copy |
| Body | Contains the actual body of the message |
| Cc | Contains the email address of those users you wish to carbon copy |
| errorCode() | Returns an integer error code that can be incurred when sending email |
| errorMessage() | Returns a string related to any error messages that can be incurred when sending email |
| Errorsto | Contains the email address to which to send error messages |
| From | Contains the sender's email address |
| Organization | Contains the sender's organization |
| Replyto | Contains the sender's reply to email address |
| send() | Sends the email |
| Smtpserver | Specifics the IP address or hostname of the mail server to send the message |
| Subject | Contains the subject of the email |
| To | Contains the email address of the recipient |

Using the SendMail object is very straightforward. Simply set the same properties contained in the everyday email you send and invoke the send() method. If an error is encountered, it can be analyzed by using the error methods supplied. Listing 3.1 shows an example use of this object to create a page for users to send email. Figure 3.1 shows what is displayed to the user when he or she encounters this page, and Figure 3.2 shows the results of submitting a successful email.

*Listing 3.1    Example of Using the* SendMail *Object*

```
<HTML>
<HEAD>
  <TITLE>Listing 3-1: Using the SendMail object</TITLE>
</HEAD>
<BODY>
<SERVER>

// See if they have submitted or just need the form
if(request.method == "POST"){

  // Create an instance of the SendMail object
  var myMail = new SendMail();

  // Assign the properties their values
```

*continues*

*Listing 3.1    continued*

```
  myMail.To = request.toAddress;
  myMail.From = request.fromAddress;
  myMail.Subject = request.subject;
  myMail.Body = request.body;
  myMail.Smtpserver = "mail.purejavascript.com";
  myMail.Errorsto = "errors@purejavascript.com"

  // Try to send the mail.
  if(!myMail.send()){

    // If there was an error, give the user the e-mail address of who they
    // should contact about the error, as well as the error code and message.
    write("There was an error sending your message. Please send e-mail to ");
    write(myMail.Errorsto + " with the following error message");
    write("Error " + myMail.errorCode() + ": " + myMail.errorMessage());
  }else{

    // If there was not an error, tell the user they were successful.
    write("Your message was sent successfully!");
  }
}else{

  // If this page was called and a form was not submitted, write the
  // email form to the page for the user to use.

  write('<FORM NAME="myForm" METHOD=POST>');
  write('<TABLE BORDER=1><TR><TD>');
  write('<TABLE BORDER=0>');
  write('<TR ALIGN=LEFT VALIGN=TOP>');
  write('<TD><B>To:</B></TD>');
  write('<TD><INPUT TYPE=TEXT NAME="toAddress" SIZE=30></TD>');
  write('</TR>');
  write('<TR ALIGN=LEFT VALIGN=TOP>');
  write('<TD><B>From:</B></TD>');
  write('<TD><INPUT TYPE=TEXT NAME="fromAddress" SIZE=30></TD>');
  write('</TR>');
  write('<TR ALIGN=LEFT VALIGN=TOP>');
  write('<TD><B>Subject:</B></TD>');
  write('<TD><INPUT TYPE=TEXT NAME="subject" SIZE=30></TD>');
  write('</TR>');
  write('<TR ALIGN=LEFT VALIGN=TOP>');
  write('<TD><B>Body:</B></TD>');
write('<TD><TEXTAREA NAME="body" COLS=60 ROWS=10 WRAP=SOFT></TEXTAREA>');
  write('</TD>');
  write('</TR>');
  write('<TR ALIGN=LEFT VALIGN=TOP>');
write('<TD COLSPAN=2 ALIGN=RIGHT><INPUT TYPE=SUBMIT VALUE="Send Mail">');
  write('</TD>');
```

```
    write('</TR>');
    write('</TABLE>');
    write('</TD></TR></TABLE>');
    write('</FORM>');
}
</SERVER>
</BODY>
</HTML>
```

**Figure 3.1**

*Building an email page for your applications.*

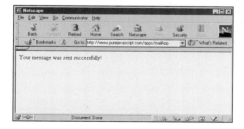

**Figure 3.2**

*The results of submitting an email successfully using the code in Listing 3.1.*

As the example demonstrates, the SendMail object makes it easy to create a page through which users can send mail. In a true, fully developed, Web-based application, a programmer should add code to check for errors in the submission. This would be an appropriate time to use client-side JavaScript to ensure that basic requirements, such as syntactically correct email addresses, are entered.

# Working with Files

The final item to address when programming in server-side JavaScript is the use of the `File` object. This object allows you to perform various tasks, such as reading and writing to a file on your disk.

The `File` object itself has many methods and a `prototype` property that allows a programmer to create new properties and methods of the object. Table 3.3 gives list of the methods accessible and a brief description of each. For a more in depth discussion, please see the entry for the `File` object in Chapter 8.

*Table 3.3* **Methods of the File Object**

| Method | Description |
| --- | --- |
| byteToString() | Converts the byte number passed into its string equivalent |
| clearError() | Clears the `File.eof` and `File.error` error status |
| close() | Closes the file you opened |
| eof() | Returns if you are at the end of the file you have opened |
| error() | Returns the current error |
| exists() | Checks to see if the file you want to process exists |
| flush() | Writes the contents of the current buffer to the file |
| getLength() | Returns the length of the file |
| getPosition() | Returns your current position within a file |
| open() | Opens the file |
| read() | Reads the number of specified characters into a string |
| readByte() | Reads the next byte, or character, in the file |
| readln() | Reads the current line, starting at your current position, into a string |
| setPosition() | Sets your position in a file |
| stringToByte() | Converts the string passed into its byte number equivalent |
| write() | Writes a string to the file you opened |
| writeByte() | Writes a byte of data to a binary file you opened |
| writeln() | Writes a string and a carriage return to the file you opened |

Much like the `SendMail` object, the use of the `File` object is straightforward. The methods provided allow you to perform the various tasks needed on the files in your file system.

Part of the functionality of working with these files allows a programmer to specify how he or she wants to open the file. A file can be opened to read, write, append, or open in binary mode. These options are specified in the `open()` method in the following form. Table 3.4 gives a list and description of these options.

```
myFile.open("option");
```

**Table 3.4    Options of the open() Method**

| Option | Description |
| --- | --- |
| a | This option opens a file for appending. If the file does not exist, it is created. This method always returns `true`. |
| a+ | This option opens a file for reading appending. If the file does not exist, it is created. This method always returns `true`. |
| r | This option opens a file for reading. If the file exists, the method returns `true`, otherwise it returns `false`. |
| r+ | This option opens a file for reading and writing. If the file exists, the method returns `true`, otherwise it returns `false`. Reading and writing start at the beginning of the file. |
| w | This option opens a file for writing. If the file does not exist, it is created. If it does exist, it is overwritten. This method always returns `true`. |
| w+ | This option opens a file for reading and writing. If the file does not exist, it is created. If it does exist, it is overwritten. This method always returns `true`. |
| *optionb* | Appending `b` to the end of any of these options specifies that you wish to perform the operation in binary mode. |

In your applications, you may want to display the contents of a file. This program could be an administration application that reads a file and displays its contents on a page. Listing 3.2 contains an application that displays the contents of a selected log file on the file system.

*Listing 3.2    Using the `File` Object to Display the Contents of a File*

```
<HTML>
<HEAD>
  <TITLE>Listing 3-2: Using the File object</TITLE>
</HEAD>
<BODY>
<SERVER>

// See if they have submitted or just need the form
if(request.method == "POST"){

  // Create an instance of the File object and pass it the file
  // the user specified they wanted to view.
  var myLog = new File(request.file);

  // Try to open the file.
  if(!myLog.open("r")){

    // If there was an error, tell the user.
```

*continues*

*Listing 3.2    continued*

```
    write("There was an error opening the file: " + request.file);
  }else{

    // If there was not an error, then open the file and display it.
    write('<H3>The contents of ' + request.file + ' are as follows:</H3>);
    while(!myLog.eof()){
      write(myLog.readln());
    }
  }
}else{

  // If this page was called then write the select box to the page for
  // the user to use select which log they want to see.

  write('<FORM NAME="myForm" METHOD=POST>');
  write('<SELECT NAME=file>');
  write('<OPTION VALUE="/logs/admin.log">Admin Log</OPTION>');
  write('<OPTION VALUE="/logs/user.log">User Log</OPTION>');
  write('<OPTION VALUE="/logs/error.log">Error Log</OPTION>');
  write('</SELECT>');
  write('<INPUT TYPE=SUBMIT VALUE="View Log">');
  write('</FORM>');
}

</SERVER>
</BODY>
</HTML>
```

In this example, a user has the ability to select a file for viewing. After submitting the request, the example tries to open the file for reading. If it is unsuccessful, an error with the filename is returned to the user. If the file opens, the contents are displayed in the document.

# The JavaScript Application Manager

The JavaScript Application Manager, shown in Figure 3.3, is the program used to manage server-side applications. From within this common interface, you can start, stop, restart, run, debug, modify, and remove applications created for a Web site. It is a cockpit to all the server-side JavaScript applications installed.

This manager is much more than a start and stop location for applications. In fact, it is most useful for verifying current status and information, debugging, and setting configuration options. Once an application has been compiled and added to the JavaScript Application Manager, this interface is used to maintain all aspects of the program—not including the actual coding, of course. However, before you can use the JavaScript Application Manager, you must do a few things.

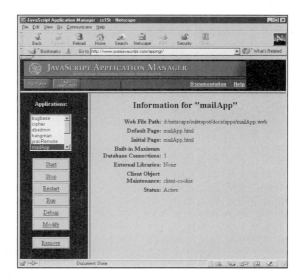

**Figure 3.3**

*Netscape's JavaScript Application Manager.*

## Configuration

Before the JavaScript Application Manager is even available for use, it must be enabled within an instance of Enterprise Server. This can be done easily from the Netscape Server Administration.

Once logged in to the Administration, simply click the button that represents the instance of the Web server on which you wish to enable server-side JavaScript. When you have accessed the administration for this instance, click the Programs button in the menu bar. Next, click the link to "Server Side JavaScript" in the navigation bar to the left of the page. This will take you to the main screen, shown in Figure 3.4.

Once you have access to this page, there are two options:

- Activate the server-side JavaScript environment
- Require a password for access to the JavaScript Application Manager

The first thing you need to select in this screen is to activate the server-side JavaScript environment. Next, consider using the Administration password to access the JavaScript Application Manager. This is highly recommended because it is a major security risk to unprotect applications. Without the password, a person could stop, or even worse, modify the settings for applications.

Once server-side JavaScript is enabled and you have made a decision on whether or not to password protect the application manager, click the OK button. This will take you to the Save And Apply Changes page where you should click Save And Apply to activate these options. An alert box will be displayed confirming a successful or unsuccessful change.

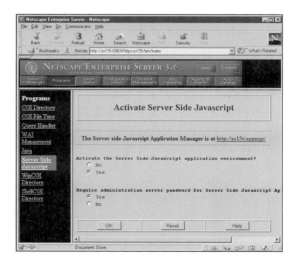

**Figure 3.4**

*Enabling server-side JavaScript through Netscape's Enterprise Administration.*

If problems are encountered here, check the following:

- Are there any NSAPI (Netscape Server Application Programming Interface) plug-ins running that might conflict with server-side JavaScript?
- Is there any kind of third-party software being used to dynamically build the Web pages for this site that may have conflicting or overlapping settings?
- Has someone hand modified the obj.conf file recently?

For the first two, think specifically about those applications or NSAPI plug-ins that parse pages. Consider turning off Parsed HTML if it is enabled. This can be done within the Web server instance's administration by clicking the Content Management menu item and then clicking the Parse HTML link in the navigation.

Finally, if there are still troubles or if the third bullet came into play, consider loading a previous version of the obj.conf file. This can be done by clicking the Server Preferences menu item, and then selecting the Restore Configuration link in the navigation. Check under the obj.conf column and roll it back one version at a time until it works. Note that you are undoing any prior changes of the configuration file. Doing so may break another process while trying to fix the JavaScript Application Manager.

Once a successful saving of the obj.conf file and restarting of the Web server has been accomplished, you will be returned to the Active Server Side JavaScript page. At the top of the page, there will now be a link to the Server Side JavaScript Application Manager. This link will be in the following form, where *machinename* is replaced with the name of your machine.

```
http://machinename/appmgr
```

Now that everything is configured to run the application manager, click the link. This will launch another page and load the JavaScript Application Manager. When on this page, click the Configure item in the menu. This will display a page to set up some defaults when adding new applications and set a couple of preferences.

In setting the default values for new applications added to the JavaScript Application Manager, Table 3.5 defines the options available.

**Table 3.5   Default Application Settings That Can Be Set for the JavaScript Application Manager**

| Setting | Description |
| --- | --- |
| Web File Path | This is the default path to your `.web` file. If you store all your applications in a subdirectory of `/ssjsapps/myprojects`, you should choose this option. |
| Default Page | This option specifies the default page of your application. For practical purposes, you may want to set this to `index.html`. |
| Initial Page | This specifies the initial page of your application. For example, if your application has global settings that are only loaded when the application is first started and you have stored this in a file called `global.html`, you should set this option to this file. |
| Built-In Maximum Database Connections | Those of you who are using databases that charge on a per connection basis will like this feature. It is the default that restricts your applications to a set number of maximum connections. |
| External Libraries | This contains the absolute path to any external libraries that your application may be using. |
| Client Object Maintenance | This default option is used to determine if you are going to maintain user sessions in your application. The possible choices are Client Cookie, Client-URL, Server-IP, Server-Cookie, and Server-URL. |

After specifying the options for the Default Values When Adding Applications section, specify your preferences. Within the Preferences section, there are two items to set:

- *Confirm On*—This option determines if a confirmation dialog box is to pop up before you perform a task. The list of tasks this can be enabled on are Remove, Start, Stop, and/or Restart an application.
- *Debug Output*—This option allows you to choose if you want to do your debugging in the Same Window or Other Window of the application.

Once these settings are completed, click the OK button. This will finish the configuration of the JavaScript Application Manager. Additional help or documentation can be accessed by clicking the links within the user interface.

# Script Management

Managing scripts may be one of the most overlooked aspects of deploying a Web-based application. The mentality seems to be, "it was written to never break," which, as we all know, simply never holds up in the real world. Even applications that worked perfectly for years will eventually hit a bump. It might be after an upgrade to a new server, or maybe a new browser has come out that implements some client-side JavaScript differently than expected. Either way it will happen, so expect it.

The JavaScript Application Manager provides a common location to manage applications as well as perform maintenance on them. The interface to this manager is made up of three main sections: Menu, Controls, and the Information Page. From within these sections, a variety of tasks can be performed.

In the Menu section is the ability to configure the JavaScript Application Manager's defaults and preferences. It is also possible to add applications to be managed, link to online documentation at DevEdge, and launch the help window and documentation.

The Controls section offers the list of applications currently installed. These are located in a scrolling text area at the top of the section. Once an application is selected, any of the options defined in Table 3.6 can be used.

*Table 3.6* *Application Options in the Controls Section*

| Control Option | Description |
| --- | --- |
| Start | Starts the application and makes it available for your users to use. |
| Stop | Stops the application you have selected. |
| Restart | Stops and restarts the application you have selected. |
| Run | Launches a separate window and loads the URL to the application you have selected. This allows you to quickly test your application to ensure it is working properly. |
| Debug | Launches either one or two windows, depending on how you set your preferences, to debug your application. |
| Modify | Allows you to modify any of the settings you have for that application. |
| Remove | Removes the application from your list of managed applications. |

The Controls section really provides the ability to manage applications. It works in conjunction with the Information Page to display the settings as well as the current status of each application.

Any more discussion of the JavaScript Application Manager would include very specific details of the application and is beyond the scope of this book. However, you'll take a closer look at using the Debug feature next because this is a valuable tool for any server-side JavaScript developer.

To launch the Debugging window, select the application to debug, and then click Debug in the Controls section of the user interface. Depending on how the preferences are set, you will see one or two main windows. If there is only one window, it will be split into two frames.

One of these elements is the Trace Information window, seen as a single window in Figure 3.5. As a program runs, the contents of this window will change as JavaScript code is processed within the application. This tool provides a look at the information being passed back and forth. It is possible to see variables being set, as well as objects created and their various states.

**Figure 3.5**

*The Trace Information section is used to display various bits of information about the application being debugged.*

As a programmer, you often will want to know the value of variables you create and return values of methods. Server-side JavaScript makes this possible by using the `debug()` method in scripts to write information to the Trace Information window during runtime. This method is similar to the `write()` server-side method, where a string or variable is passed, and the interpreter writes the data passed to the window. A typical use of this method might look like the following:

```
debug('myFunction entered and was passed: ' + myVar);
```

## NOTE

For more information on using the `debug()` method, see its entry in Chapter 8.

In addition to knowing how to debug applications, it is important to understand the error messages you may run across. There are two main types of errors. One of the types of errors, which is common for syntax mistakes, is your standard server-side JavaScript error. This error will return the object in which the error occurred, the error message, the filename of the application, and the line number.

The second type of errors are those generated by databases. These errors can have several different types of information returned, but usually contain the following:

- *Database/Function*—This error alerts the programmer there was a database error, and it gives the function in which it occurred.
- *LiveWire Services Error*—This error is generated by the LiveWire database connection service, states an error occurred, and gives a message as to why.
- *Vendor Error*—This error is also returned by the LiveWire service, but it reports an error specific to the database to which you are connecting. You will need to know your database error codes to decipher this error.
- *Standard Server-Side JavaScript Error*—This error is the same as the first type, except it is specific to your use of a database connection.

In addition to the Trace Information window, there is a main window, or frame. When debugging an application, this window contains the application itself. The combination of this window and the Trace Information window allows a developer to step through, as a user would, and see what is going on in the background. With the Debug feature of the JavaScript Application Manager, a developer can correct and work through almost any problem he or she may encounter.

# Moving On

This concludes Part I of *Pure JavaScript*. In these three chapters, you have been introduced to the language, seen many of its features, learned its semantics and much of the syntax, and worked with the server-side environment. Part II, "Programming in JavaScript," provides a look at the environments in which JavaScript can be interpreted and into the actual use of the language.

# PART II

# PROGRAMMING IN JAVASCRIPT

# CHAPTER 4

## The JavaScript Runtime Environment

The first three chapters of this book have discussed the semantics of the JavaScript language and Netscape's server-side implementation. The first chapter took a look at how it worked, where it can be interpreted, and some of the features it had to offer. You saw how JavaScript can be used to interact with other objects on a page and what security features are in place.

The second chapter looked specifically at the details of the language. You learned how the operators, data types, variables, loops, conditionals, and functions worked. Even though this might have been a review for programmers experienced with JavaScript, it was a very important step in understanding how the language works and where it fits in to the overall programming equation.

Chapter 3, "Server-Side JavaScript," introduced you to Netscape's server-side implementation in its Enterprise Web servers. It discussed the added objects for processing file system data and database content. With JavaScript's continued growth on the server-side, Chapter 3 provided firsthand exposure to implementing the language to build your pages.

In this chapter, you will look at several aspects of the language. We'll look specifically at how the browsers interpret JavaScript. You'll also deal with some of the issues that surround browsers and how they handle the scripts—issues like bugs and differences in functionality.

Later in the chapter, you will look at how JavaScript can extend a browser's functionality. This is done with some of its object arrays and through the use of LiveConnect. These topics were mentioned in the first chapter, but they warrant a more detailed explanation and examples to help your understanding of the benefits they offer and the functionality they present.

This chapter will point out specific instances of problem areas within a browser's environment and will give you a better understanding of how some of the features work. The examples themselves should greatly help your overall understanding of JavaScript's interpretation within the browser, which will lead to a more efficient JavaScript programming experience.

## Supporting Browsers and Their Issues

Even though JavaScript seems to have been a foundation building block in today's Internet technology, it wasn't always there. It wasn't until the "newest" browsers that its functionality was included. Currently, there are only three browsers that interpret JavaScript: Netscape Navigator, Internet Explorer, and Opera. However, just because they interpret the language does not mean that they do so in the same manner, which is something you will be looking into shortly.

**NOTE**

Because many users use AOL's online service to connect to the Internet, you should know that the AOL browser is actually an Internet Explorer browser with different "chrome."

For those of you familiar with Java, you know that different *JVMs*, or Java Virtual Machines, can interpret the language differently. JavaScript is no different, except that the market is less fragmented. For the most part, browsers do interpret JavaScript the same. The big difference is that they all have different version support, and they have different bugs. Most of the core objects of the language work, it's just *how* they work that makes them unique.

To give you an idea of the versions and support among these browsers, take a look at Table 4.1. It breaks these runtime environments down by browser version and language version.

*Table 4.1   Language Support by Browser Version*

| Browser | Version | Language |
|---|---|---|
| Netscape Navigator | 2.0 | JavaScript 1.0 |
| | 2.02 for OS/2 | JavaScript 1.1 |
| | 3.0 | JavaScript 1.1 |
| | 4.0–4.05 | JavaScript 1.2 |
| | 4.06–4.7 | JavaScript 1.3 |
| | 5.0 | JavaScript 1.4 |
| Microsoft Internet | 3.0 | JScript 1.0 |
| Explorer | 4.0–4.5 | JScript 3.0 |
| | 5.0 | JScript 5.0 |
| Opera | 3.0–3.5 | Javascript 1.1 |

**NOTE**

The jumps in JavaScript versions in Microsoft browsers are due to the fact they have also included interpreters in other products. For instance, some of Microsoft's servers have the JScript 2.0 interpreter.

## JAVASCRIPT 1.1 IN NAVIGATOR 2.02 FOR OS/2?

If you take a second look at the previous table, you will notice that the 2.02 version of Navigator for OS/2 is JavaScript 1.1 compliant. This is because the OS/2 versions of the Navigator browsers were co-developed by engineers from both Netscape and IBM.

Before Navigator was ported to this platform, OS/2 machines only included IBM's Web Explorer browser. Even though this browser had various advancements, it lacked the overall functionality that the newer browsers had. Hence the need for an OS/2 version of Navigator.

The OS/2 version of Navigator was not announced or in beta until the 3.0 version of the browser was already released. Those of you who used the 3.0 browsers heavily might have noticed that they seemed more buggy than the 2.0 versions. Enhancements that were added seemed to make the code more unstable, which prompted the OS/2 version using the more stable 2.0 interface to be built, but included the 3.0 backend. This gave the OS/2 version a 3.0 backend with a 2.0 interface.

Because browser versions are often determined using JavaScript, a OS/2 user with Navigator 2.02 can start the browser with the "-3" option that will tell its user agent string to report that it is a 3.0 browser rather than a 2.02. Because it has the ability to interpret all the JavaScript on the page, this option allows the user to experience all of the enhancements for the 3.0 browsers.

These facts are important for programmers to properly implement features in their scripts. You can now check for the Navigator 2.02 for OS/2 browser and know that it is JavaScript 1.1 compliant— with or without the -3 option.

New browsers are released a couple of times a year, which forces the market to become fragmented in terms of the JavaScript runtime environment with which users will be accessing a site. Extra care needs to be taken in writing scripts so browsers will interpret them correctly. As discussed in Chapter 2, "Details of the Language," most of the version control can be accomplished using the LANGUAGE or TYPE attribute of the <SCRIPT> tag, but not all browsers correctly implement this. As a programmer, you will have to write in code to accommodate these browsers.

The first browser you are going to look at is Netscape's Navigator browser. It was the pioneering browser that first interpreted the language co-developed by Sun and Netscape. It is also the browser that has taken the language beyond the basics of interpreting scripts by adding in the security features and the ability to interact with plug-ins and the Java runtime environment.

# Netscape Navigator

Netscape Navigator (see version 4.5 in Figure 4.1) first included its support for JavaScript in its version 2 browsers. This was a major step for JavaScript because Navigator was by far the most widely-used browser in the world. Web developers could add scripts to their pages and feel very confident that the majority of their visitors would be able to experience their enhancements.

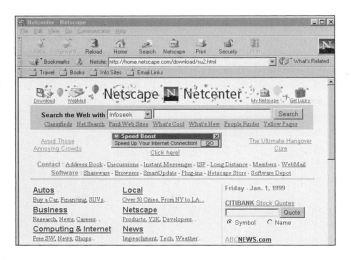

**Figure 4.1**

*Netscape Navigator 4.5 browser.*

Like anything else Netscape has implemented in its browsers, it has continued to expand the language and add to it. With each major release, new functionality and language attributes have been added that keep it ahead of other browsers in terms of support. Table 4.2 outlines the JavaScript support in Navigator browsers and gives you some additional information that was not contained in Table 4.1.

**Table 4.2    JavaScript Language Support by Browser**

| Browser Version | Language Version | Notes |
| --- | --- | --- |
| 2.0 | JavaScript 1.0 | First browser to interpret JavaScript. |
| 2.02 for OS/2 | JavaScript 1.1 | As discussed in previous sidebar, this browser has the 2.0 interface, and it has the 3.0 backend for rendering HTML and interpreting JavaScript. |

| Browser Version | Language Version | Notes |
| --- | --- | --- |
| 3.0 | JavaScript 1.1 | First version to support SRC attribute of <SCRIPT> tag, which can be used to include external JavaScript source. |
| 4.0–4.05 | JavaScript 1.2 | Enhancements for Dynamic HTML and added signed scripts as a model of security. |
| 4.06–4.7 | JavaScript 1.3 | Completes Navigator's support for ECMAScript 1.0, as well as other enhancements expected in ECMAScript 2.0. |
| 5.0 | JavaScript 1.4 | Includes more advanced functions for error checking and control. |

Even though version 2 of the browsers paved the way for JavaScript, there were still some limitations and bugs that exposed the immaturity of the language. Being a new language, it was expected that problems and limitations would arise after developers started programming with it. Future versions of the language either corrected these issues or programmers found ways to program around them.

**NOTE**

The Java programming language has gone through this process of change as well. From Java 1.0 to 1.1, many of the methods in which the language handled events changed. Most recently in Java 1.2, graphical user interface (GUI) enhancements have been added to the core language that were only available as an add-in for 1.1.

JavaScript 1.0 (included in Navigator 2) had a couple of key limitations and bugs that hindered its adoption in some instances. These can be programmed around by careful implementation and watching your code. It is worth stating these here so you can avoid them. They are as follows:

- `window.open()` method not opening URL in window on UNIX and Macintosh platforms.
- `onLoad` event fires when window is resized in Navigator 2 and 3 (JavaScript 1.1) browsers.
- There are no objects for the creation of arrays.
- There is a bug when interpreting scripts located in nested tables.

Those of you who have been programming in the language may know of many other bugs in the browser or differences in its interpretation, but these are four core items of which JavaScript programmers should be aware. If they are not, they will not understand how to avoid problems on their pages and how to code around language

inefficiencies. These problems are easy to code around. However, they are hard to figure out when you are testing your pages.

**NOTE**

> Not every difference is a bug or limitation that spans all platforms of the browser.
> For instance, in JavaScript 1.0 support for the NaN language element is not
> defined, however, it is implemented in the 2.0 UNIX and OS/2 versions of the
> browser. It is recommended that you not use it because Windows and Macintosh
> systems do not support the element.

The window.open() situation arises on the Macintosh and UNIX versions of the
browser when this method is used in conjunction with passing it a URL as the parameter. If you pass the URL as a parameter on these platforms, the browser opens the
window but does not load the URL. However, if you call the window.open() method
again, the URL will be loaded in the window. Listing 4.1 shows you how you can program around this minor situation.

*Listing 4.1    Calling the* window.open() *Method a Second Time for Navigator 2
on UNIX and Macintosh Platforms to Get Around a Bug*

```
<SCRIPT LANGUAGE="JavaScript">
<!-- Hide
function openWin(){
// Determine if the browser is Navigator 2 and if the platform is UNIX
  // or Macintosh
  isMac = (navigator.userAgent.indexOf('Mac') != -1);
  isUnix = (navigator.userAgent.indexOf('X11') != -1);
  isNav2 = ((navigator.userAgent.indexOf('compatible') == -1) &&
            (navigator.appVersion.charAt(0) == "2"));

  // Open the window using default chrome settings
  window.open("http://www.purejavascript.com", "myWin", "");

  // Check to see if the browser needs to have the method called again. If
  // it isNavigator 2 on UNIX or Macintosh, call the
  // window.open() method again.
  if((isMac || isUnix) && isNav2){

    // Open window using default chrome settings
    window.open("http://www.purejavascript.com", "myWin", "");
  }
}
// End hide -->
</SCRIPT>
```

**TIP**

For more information on the `window.open()` method and the parameters that it can accept, see its entry in Chapter 7, "Client-Side Browser Syntax."

A second limitation appearing in Navigator 2 is the fact the `onLoad` event is executed when the browser window is resized. This obviously causes problems when this event is used to initialize variables that change or are modified with user interaction.

As a programmer writing scripts to be compatible with that version of the browser, you should avoid setting any variables with which the user will be interacting using this event. For instance, it would not be a good idea to clear a form using this event, because it is completely possible a given user will resize the browser window after he or she has entered part of their data. Using `onLoad` will cause all the information to be lost if the user resizes the window.

To see an example of this, use the simple example in Listing 4.2. Once you have created this file, load it in a Navigator 2 or 3 browser. Doing so should give you an alert box, shown in Figure 4.2. If you resize the window, you will see it again because the `onLoad` event is fired. In fact, it has been my experience that you will actually see the dialog box twice—another undocumented "feature."

**Figure 4.2**

*Alert box fired by the `onLoad` event in Listing 4.2.*

*Listing 4.2   Example That Shows the `onLoad` Event Firing When Window Is Resized*

```
<HTML>
<HEAD>
  <TITLE>Listing 42: onLoad Event Example</TITLE>
<SCRIPT LANGUAGE="JavaScript">
<!-- Hide
// This function is called by the onLoad event.
function loadDone(){
  alert('Your page has finished loading');
}
// End Hide -->
</SCRIPT>
</HEAD>
<BODY onLoad='loadDone()'>
</BODY>
</HTML>
```

Another item missing from the first release of the language is the fact there is no object for creating arrays. Arrays are commonly used to store information, and almost every language contains a native object for their creation. However, arrays were not introduced until JavaScript 1.1.

Because arrays provide a great amount of functionality to the programmer, you may want to create your own array object to handle your programming needs. This is shown in Listing 4.3. Also in this code listing, you will see how to create an instance of the Array object and populate it.

*Listing 4.3    Creating Your Own* Array *Object*

```
<SCRIPT LANGUAGE="JavaScript">
<!-- Hide
function Array(nSize) {

  // Defining a length property for your array object as the ability to
  // query an array instance you created for its length.
  this.length = nSize;

  // Use a for loop to create the actual array full of nulls.
  for (var i = 1; i <= nSize; i++){
    this[i - 1] = null;
  }
  return this;
}

// Create an instance of your Array object
var myArray = new Array(5);

// Populate the array instance we created
myArray[0] = "This is the first position";
myArray[1] = "This is the second position";
myArray[2] = "This is the third position";
myArray[3] = "This is the fourth position";
myArray[4] = "This is the fifth position";

// End hide -->
</SCRIPT>
```

This function simply creates an array by using a for loop to populate the this property. Notice also the length property included in the Array object. This allows a programmer to find the size of the array.

Note the Array object is named Array. This was done for a couple of reasons, however, doing so will be dependent on a programmer's objective in his or her script. As you saw in Chapter 1, "What Is JavaScript to a Programmer," JavaScript now has a native Array object. By defining the object with the same name, you will override the native Array object. This will work fine as long as you don't plan on using properties other than the length property, which you have defined in your version of the object.

If you have a script that needs access to an array, you have to support Navigator 2 browsers, and you will not need any of the other properties of the native `Array` object, it is recommended that you name your object `Array`. It is best to include it in separate `<SCRIPT>` tags in the `<HEAD>` of your document so that, as time goes on and you no longer have to support the Navigator 2 browser, you will be able to simply remove that entire entry from your page. Because the native `Array` object supports the same syntax for entering values into the array, your code will continue to work.

The final item you need to take a close look into is when JavaScript is executed within table cells. Tables and JavaScript as a whole seem to be a problem with the early versions of Navigator browsers. Not only are there some obvious issues when placing your scripts in cells, there are also some not so obvious issues—ones that really do not have an explanation. Netscape seems to have cleaned up most of these starting with version 4, but versions 2 and 3 seem to have lots of problems.

One of the biggest problems occurs when your scripts appear in nested tables. Listing 4.4 shows a script that is in three tables.

*Listing 4.4    Bugs in JavaScript When Nested in a Table*

```
<HTML>
<HEAD>
    <TITLE>Listing 4.4: JavaScript in Tables</TITLE>
<SCRIPT LANGUAGE="JavaScript">
<!-- Hide

// Declare a global variable
nGlobalCounter = 0;

// End Hide -->
</SCRIPT>
</HEAD>
<BODY>
<TABLE>
  <TR>
    <TD>
      <TABLE>
        <TR>
          <TD>
            <TABLE>
              <TR>
                <TD>
<SCRIPT LANGUAGE="JavaScript">
<!-- Hide

// Create a local variable
var nLocalCounter = 0;

// Increment the global and local counter by 1
```

*continues*

*Listing 4.4    continued*

```
nGlobalCounter += 1;
nLocalCounter += 1;

// Write both the values of the counters to the page.
document.write('<B>The current value of the global counter is: </B>')
document.write(nGlobalCounter);
document.write('<BR><B>The current value of the local counter is: </B>');
document.write(nLocalCounter);

// End Hide -->
</SCRIPT>
                </TD>
              </TR>
            </TABLE>
          </TD>
        </TR>
      </TABLE>
    </TD>
  </TR>
</TABLE>
</BODY>
</HTML>
```

There is some JavaScript in the `<HEAD>` of the document that declares a global variable. Nested within three tables is some additional JavaScript that performs a couple of tasks. First, it declares a local variable and initializes it to 0. Next, both the global and local variables are incremented by one. Finally, the results of these increments are written to the page using the `document.write()` function.

As you can see in Figure 4.3, Navigator 2 throws up an error. Navigator 3, shown in Figure 4.4, displays the JavaScript on the page. Only Navigator 4, shown in Figure 4.5, is able to handle the code correctly.

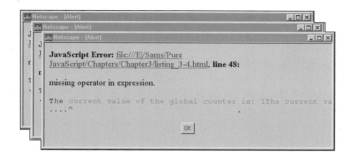

**Figure 4.3**

*Navigator 2 displaying the results of loading the page defined in Listing 4.4.*

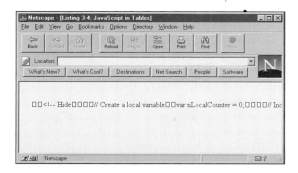

**Figure 4.4**

*Navigator 3 displaying the results of loading the page defined in Listing 4.4.*

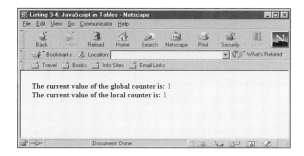

**Figure 4.5**

*Only Navigator 4 displays the results of loading the page defined in Listing 4.4 correctly.*

If you take a closer look at what the JavaScript interpreter is doing in Navigator 2, you will see that the script is actually processed four times. What happens is scripts nested in tables are executed $2^{n-1}$ times, where $n$ represents the number of tables involved. There were three tables in Listing 4.4, so the script was executed $2^2$ times for a total of four.

**NOTE**

Since it is $n-1$, you should see no problems when your scripts are in a single table. However, it has been noticed that if the table cells and rows are not ended correctly and proper HTML syntax is not used, you may see some unusual results in your scripts.

To test the theory of the number of executions in nested tables, the local variable declaration can be removed, which is actually the part that causes the errors in Navigator 2 and 3. Simply write the value of the global variable to the page. Listing 4.5 demonstrates this.

*Listing 4.5    Exposing the Number of Times a Script Is Executed in Nested Tables*

```
<HTML>
<HEAD>
    <TITLE>Listing 4.5: JavaScript in Tables</TITLE>
<SCRIPT LANGUAGE="JavaScript">
<!-- Hide
// Declare a global variable
nGlobalCounter = 0;
// End Hide -->
</SCRIPT>
</HEAD>
<BODY>
<TABLE>
  <TR>
    <TD>
      <TABLE>
        <TR>
          <TD>
            <TABLE>
              <TR>
                <TD>
<SCRIPT LANGUAGE="JavaScript">
<!-- Hide
// Increment the global counter by 1
nGlobalCounter += 1;

// Write both the values of the counters to the page.
document.write('<B>The current value of the global counter is: </B>');
document.write(nGlobalCounter);
// End Hide -->
</SCRIPT>
                </TD>
              </TR>
            </TABLE>
          </TD>
        </TR>
      </TABLE>
    </TD>
  </TR>
</TABLE>
</BODY>
</HTML>
```

The browser should have written the number 1 to the screen, but, as you can see in Figure 4.6, it writes 4. Adding another level of tables will cause it to write 8, and then 16, and so on. This little bug can definitely be a problem to programmers, so it should be avoided if at all possible. This can partially be done by performing some of your calculations in the <HEAD> of the document. In other instances, a JavaScript programmer will simply have to work with the Webmaster to remove the extra layers of tables when executing his or her scripts.

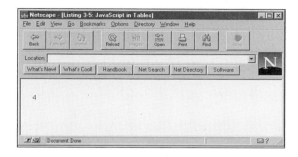

**Figure 4.6**

*Navigator 2 displaying the results of executing Listing 4.5 where JavaScript has been interpreted within three levels of tables.*

There are certainly other bugs programmers will come across the more code they write. These four Navigator-specific bugs should be remembered though, because they seem to be the ones a programmer comes across the most.

**TIP**

Netscape's DevEdge site has more information on JavaScript bugs. It can be accessed at `http://developer.netscape.com/tech/javascript/index.html`, and then follow the link for `Known Bugs`.

# Internet Explorer

Even though Internet Explorer (see version 5.0 in Figure 4.7) was the second browser to follow suit in its support of JavaScript, it seems to have avoided the Navigator problems just discussed. However, JScript does have issues that inhibit its performance and functionality as well.

Because Microsoft did not want to purchase the licensing to JavaScript from Netscape to implement in its Internet Explorer browser, it had to reverse-engineer the scripting language and give it a new name. This led to the birth of JScript.

In the short run, this seemed like a bad thing for JavaScript programmers. Now that there were two versions of the language on the market, how could they be assured their scripts would work in both browsers? Luckily, this version incompatibility only lasted for version 3 of Internet Explorer. By the time version 4 of the browser came out, ECMAScript 1.0 was well on its way to adoption, and Microsoft based its JScript 3.0 on the standard. This refocused and aligned both JavaScript and JScript and reduced the problems of incompatibility between them.

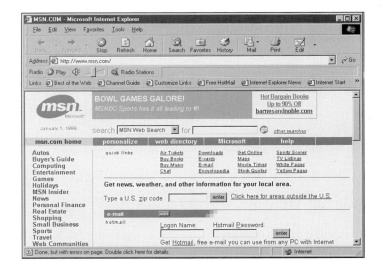

**Figure 4.7**

*Internet Explorer 5 browser.*

Because JScript 3.0 is on track with ECMAScript 1.0, and JScript 5.0 is on track with ECMAScript 2.0, most of the problems a programmer needs to address with JScript are in the 1.0 version itself. In fact, even items that pertain to the browser itself seem to occur mostly in Internet Explorer 3. Three of the biggest issues will be discussed. The first issue, however, seems to be one that Microsoft is notorious for and may be the root of most of the problems you run up against.

- Microsoft provides the ability for users to update their scripting engines without updating the browser. It also distributes different engines with minor updates to the browser.
- No support for the `Image` object on the Windows platform.
- Support for the `SRC` attribute of the `<SCRIPT>` tag was implemented in the 3.02 maintenance release of Internet Explorer and did not fully work.

**NOTE**

Microsoft refers to its interpreter as a *JScript Scripting Engine*. This terminology will be used in this section.

Before taking a look at these problems, take a look at the language itself and its support in the Internet Explorer browsers. Table 4.3 breaks down the browsers that have been released by Microsoft and its JScript support by version. The table also includes some notes that give more information about what the release added to the language.

*Table 4.3* *JScript Language Support by Browser*

| Browser Version | Language Version | Notes |
| --- | --- | --- |
| 3.0 | JScript 1.0 | First Internet Explorer browser to interpret JScript. |
| 4.0–4.5 | JScript 3.0 | Added enhancements for Dynamic HTML and support for ECMAScript 1.0. This is the first version to fully support SRC attribute of <SCRIPT> tag, which can be used to include external JavaScript source. |
| 5.0 | JScript 5.0 | ECMAScript 2.0–compliant. |

**NOTE**

Microsoft appears to have jumped around a bit in its JScript versions. This is because other versions of its scripting interpreter have been implemented in its Web servers and Visual InterDev development environment.

The first thing to address with Internet Explorer browsers is their inconsistency of JavaScript support in version 3. Beginning with version 4, Microsoft heavily integrated its browser into the Windows operating system. In fact, it has been a recent argument in the federal court system that there is no difference at all. Elements of this appeared in Internet Explorer 3, which makes it increasingly apparent that it was the first step to this integration with the operating system.

For users, the integration and segregation of these components of a browser means that they can update certain aspects of their browsers' functionality easily. Web developers, on the other hand, have to bear the responsibility of writing scripts that work with different versions of the Microsoft scripting engines. Because users can upgrade engines, it is very possible they could be using an Internet Explorer 3.02 browser that has either version 1 or version 2 of the JScript engine.

In some of the more recent versions of the engines, Microsoft has provided functions that allow developers to determine what version of the engine users are running. However, using some of these functions causes engines that do not support them to return an error. This puts developers in an impossible situation. They can avoid problems by knowing the version of the engine, but using these functions on old browsers results in errors.

Listing 4.6 includes the Microsoft-specific elements of JScript that a developer can use to determine the version of the scripting engine the user has.

*Listing 4.6    JScript's Elements for Determining Scripting Engine Version Information*

```
<SCRIPT LANGUAGE="JavaScript">
<!-- Hide
// Create a variable to hold all the engine information in a single string
var jscriptVer = ScriptEngine() + " " + ScriptEngineMajorVersion() + "." +
                 ScriptEngineMinorVersion() + " Build " +
                 ScriptEngineBuildVersion();

// Write the string to the user's browser
document.write('<b>You are running:</b> ' + jscriptVer);

// Write each of the individual elements of the engine's version to the
// browser
document.write('<br><br><b>ScriptEngine:</b> ' + ScriptEngine());
document.write('<br><b>ScriptEngineMajorVersion:</b> ');
document.write(ScriptEngineMajorVersion());
document.write('<br><b>ScriptEngineMinorVersion:</b> ');
document.write(ScriptEngineMinorVersion());
document.write('<br><b>ScriptEngineBuildVersion:</b> ');
document.write(ScriptEngineBuildVersion());
// End hide -->
</SCRIPT>
```

**TIP**

> The scripting engine for JScript is contained in the `jscript.dll`. You can check the properties in this DLL file to see what version you have on your machine.

The result of opening Listing 4.6 in an Internet Explorer browser is shown in Figure 4.8. As you can see, this can be very helpful if developers need to know the specific build the user is using when executing their scripts. However, they will have to be careful to avoid versions that do not support these elements.

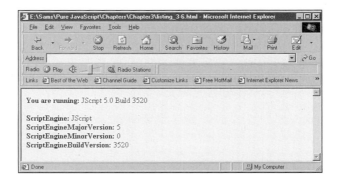

**Figure 4.8**

*Internet Explorer 5 displaying the result of loading Listing 4.6.*

The first version of Internet Explorer for the Macintosh did not include a JScript engine at all. It wasn't until version 3.01 for the Macintosh that JScript was added. This leads directly to a second major issue with JScript—no Image object for Windows platforms with JScript 1.0. Oddly enough, this is something Internet Explorer 3.01 for the Macintosh did have.

The Image object is commonly used for two main purposes. One is to swap images when a user clicks or rolls over an image. The second use of this object is for pre-caching images. Because developers will want to maximize their user's experience when browsing their sites, they may want to take advantage of the support of the Image object in a Macintosh without causing problems for Internet Explorer 3 users on a Windows machine. Listing 4.7 shows how this can be accomplished.

*Listing 4.7   Detecting Internet Explorer 3 Users on a Windows Machine to Avoid Problems with the Lack of an* Image *Object*

```
<HTML>
<HEAD>
  <TITLE>Listing 4.7: Rollovers for Mac IE 3</TITLE>
<SCRIPT LANGUAGE="JavaScript">
<!-- Hide
var isWinIE3 = ((navigator.userAgent.indexOf('Win') != -1) &&
               (navigator.userAgent.indexOf('MSIE') != -1) &&
               (navigator.userAgent.indexOf('3.') != -1));

function imageSwapOut(imgOut){
  if(isWinIE3){
    // Do nothing
  } else {
    var imgOutPath = "http://www.purejavascript.com/images/" + imgOut;
    var myOutImg = new Image ();
    myOutImg.src = imgOutPath;
    document.home.src = myOutImg.src;
  }
}

function imageSwapIn(imgIn){
  if(isWinIE3){
    // Do nothing
  } else {
    var imgInPath = "http://www.purejavascript.com/images/" + imgIn;
    var myInImg = new Image ();
    myInImg.src = imgInPath;
    document.home.src = myInImg.src;
  }
}
// End hide -->
</SCRIPT>
```

*continues*

*Listing 4.7   continued*

```
</HEAD>
<BODY>
<A HREF="http://www.purejavascript.com/home.html"
   onMouseOver='imageSwapIn("homeover.gif")'
   onMouseOut='imageSwapOut("home.gif")'>
  <IMG NAME=home SRC="http://www.purejavascript.com/images/home.gif">
</A>
</BODY>
</HTML>
```

As you can see in the source, the first item the script determines is if a Windows version of Internet Explorer is trying to render the page. If it is, the `isWinIE3` variable is set to `true`. This is used by the two functions that perform the actual image rollovers.

In the body of the page, you will see that an image is placed on the page. Within the `<A>` tag, you have used the `onMouseOut` and `onMouseOver` event handlers to call the appropriate functions. You will also notice that each function takes in a parameter that is the name of the rollover image itself. When the function is called, it evaluates the value of `isWinIE3`, and then either performs nothing or performs the image swapping.

**NOTE**

Use of the `<A>` tag is required to call the `onMouseOut` and `onMouseOver` event handlers in almost all browsers. Beginning with version 4, however, Internet Explorer provides the ability to include this within the `<IMG>` tag, which seems much more appropriate. Code named *Gecko*, Netscape's next generation rendering engine follows the `<IMG>` model as well.

One final issue that you must consider with Internet Explorer browsers is the fact that support for the `SRC` attribute of the `<SCRIPT>` tag was not in the original release of version 3, but was added in the 3.02 maintenance release. As discussed previously, this attribute is a very powerful and helpful item to JavaScript programmers. It allows them to centrally store and manage some of their source code by simply adding a reference to it on the page.

Because Internet Explorer 3.02 does support this attribute, a programmer might feel the urge to use it. Doing so, however, will definitely cause problems on pages rendered by versions prior to 3.02. It is strongly recommended that you set the `LANGUAGE` attribute to `"JavaScript1.1"` when using the `SRC` attribute. Doing so will avoid any Internet Explorer 3 browser from trying to load the external source file, therefore preventing version incompatibility problems. The only exception to this would be if you are in an enterprise environment and are guaranteed that your users have browsers that supported this tag.

## Opera

The Opera browser (see version 3.5 in Figure 4.9) has received a lot of press recently because of its position as an alternative to Navigator and Internet Explorer. The developers at Opera Software have taken on the responsibility of providing a lot of functionality to their users without a lot of unneeded flash. The mail and news functionality is limited, and there is no conference software. It is not bloated with an HTML editor or a Java Virtual Machine. Opera is mostly a pure browser, but it does have support for Navigator plug-ins. This allows its users to gain the needed support to position it as a real alternative.

**NOTE**

Because Opera supports plug-ins, you can install Sun's Java plug-in that will allow the browser to run Java applets. Do note that calling the plug-in to load an applet is different than traditionally using the <APPLET> tag. This means that sites that deploy applets solely by using the <APPLET> tag will not work in Opera.

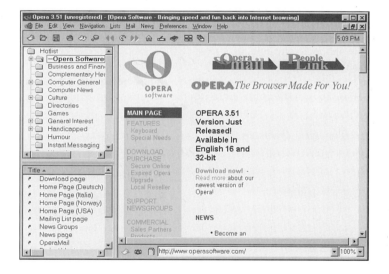

**Figure 4.9**

*The Opera 3.5 browser is available at* http://www.operasoftware.com.

Do not take the lack of other applications in Opera as a lack of functionality. Opera supports many of the newest HTML tags, as well as having an implementation of ECMAScript (it references it as Javascript). It also has a very unique interface allowing its users to open multiple pages within the environment. This feature, which can be seen in Figure 4.5, is very similar to most popular word processing programs. Opera also runs using few system resources, and it runs well on the older i386 computers.

**NOTE**

Even in today's world of free browsers, Opera will cost you $35 to own. However, evaluations are free to download and try.

Opera, as an overall browser, has a lot to offer Internet users today in its compact state. However, as a JavaScript developer, there are items you should watch out for.

- The Opera browser did not support the SRC attribute of the <SCRIPT> tag until version 3.2.
- The Opera browser does not support the LANGUAGE attribute of the <SCRIPT> tag.
- The navigator.appName property returns "Netscape".

The first major item developers should be aware of when creating scripts to be executed in Opera browsers is its lack of support for the SRC attribute of the <SCRIPT> tag. Programmers will not be able to reference external source files that contain functions they wish to use on a given page. This limits overall script control and maintenance for a developer, but this is an item affecting Internet Explorer 3 and Navigator 2 browsers. In the instance of Opera 3.x and 3.1x browsers, you simply have to include all of your code in the body of your <SCRIPT> tags.

The second item programmers must account for in Opera browsers is its lack of support for the LANGUAGE attribute of the <SCRIPT> tag. This can force developers to include code that determines if the browser is an Opera browser before they execute any code in JavaScript 1.2 or 1.3 blocks. Opera should be able to handle JavaScript 1.0 and 1.1, so these two versions are currently the only ones for which a developer needs to check. Listing 4.8 gives an example how to do this.

*Listing 4.8    Checking Opera to Mimic* LANGUAGE *Support*

```
<HTML>
<HEAD>
  <TITLE>Listing 4.8: Checking Opera to mimic LANGUAGE Support</TITLE>
<SCRIPT LANGUAGE="JavaScript">
<!-- Hide
notOpera = !(navigator.userAgent.indexOf('Opera') != -1);
// End hide -->
</SCRIPT>
</HEAD>
<BODY>
<SCRIPT LANGUAGE="JavaScript1.2">
<!-- Hide
if(notOpera){
  // You can execute JavaScript 1.2 specific code here.
}
// End hide -->
</SCRIPT>
</BODY>
</HTML>
```

As you can see in Listing 4.8, the navigator.userAgent property is used to see if the browser loading the page is an Opera browser. If it is, you take its negation and store it in the variable notOpera. The reason you store the negation of this value is to make it easier in the if clauses that you will use later in your code.

Down in the body of the document is another script section that specifies the JavaScript language to be 1.2. Because Opera will ignore this, you have to wrap the entire script in this section in an `if` clause. Because you took the negation of the browser determination, you simply need to check the `notOpera` variable to make sure it is `false`.

The third item that programmers should be aware of is the fact that the `navigator.appName` property returns `"Netscape"`. I am sure that many of you use this property to determine browser version, which means that you should avoid it when checking for Opera browsers. In fact, it's recommended that you use the following code when determining an Opera browser:

```
isOpera = (navigator.userAgent.indexOf('Opera') != -1);
```

This syntax is short, simple, and effective. It will return a `true` or `false` to the `isOpera` variable, which makes it easy to evaluate in an `if` clause. If you are looking for a specific version of Opera, like 3.5 for instance, you simply need to add another condition. Doing so would look like the following:

```
isOpera35 = ((navigator.userAgent.indexOf('Opera') != -1) &&
(navigator.userAgent.indexOf('3.5') != -1));
```

In this script, you not only make sure the browser is an Opera one, you also analyze the `navigator.userAgent` property to see if it is version 3.5. When both of these evaluate to `true`, the `isOpera35` variable will be initialized to `true`. As you can see, using this type of code makes it easy to effectively determine the browser on which your users are interpreting your code.

This concludes the section on support browsers and their issues. The next section of this chapter will dive into the extended functionality of the browsers and the role JavaScript plays in this.

# Other JavaScript Environments

In addition to the core browsers that support JavaScript, applications are now appearing that interpret the language. One such example is Macromedia's Dreamweaver 2.

Dreamweaver 2, an HTML tool created by Macromedia (`http://www.macromedia.com`), also contains a form of a JavaScript interpreter. It has a JavaScript API that allows developers to extend the functionality of the program using HTML, XML, JavaScript, and C. This extended functionality is accomplished by allowing users to write their own objects, behavior actions, commands, property inspectors, and data translators. Readers familiar with Dreamweaver will recognize these terms. If you have not worked with Dreamweaver, understand that the items listed affect the way the tool works, what it can do, and the types of elements it can create.

Dreamweaver supports a Document Object Model (DOM) that interfaces with the JavaScript API, which allows these custom JavaScript functions. Some of these functions are already built into Dreamweaver and can be used in any object, behavior action, command, property inspector, or data translation file.

Going into Dreamweaver's implementation of JavaScript is beyond the scope of this book. It is mentioned here to demonstrate its rapid adoption in tools other than browsers and servers.

# Extended Browser Functionality

In addition to the scripting functionality you can add to Web pages, JavaScript can also be used to extend your browser's functionality. Today's most functional browsers support plug-ins and/or ActiveX controls. These plug-ins are loaded by the browser when it starts and are accessed when called via HTML. tags on a page. Because plug-in instances run as objects within the browser's environment, some core JavaScript objects can be used to access, modify, and control their functionality.

JavaScript also supports interaction with Java applets embedded in a page. This type of interaction can occur in both directions—from the applet to scripts on a page, and from scripts to the applet. The technology behind this is referred to as LiveConnect and will be discussed in more detail later in the chapter.

# Built-In Functions for Control

Not all browsers have the same set of controls for their extended functionality, but there are some common language controls that allow developers to access these various items. These are considered *built-in* control elements in the JavaScript language itself. The control elements to access this functionality include two arrays.

Overall, there are several built-in control functions in the JavaScript language, but the two most commonly used are the applet and plug-in arrays. These two items are arrays containing references to all the applets the browser has loaded on a given page and all the plug-ins the browser has installed. Through these arrays, a developer is able to access and interact with these components.

## Applet Array

The applet array stores references to all the Java applets loaded on a page. This allows a developer to retrieve the total number of applets on a page and to directly interact with them. If the developer is using LiveConnect to interact with the applet, the applet itself can be referenced by its indexed location. The second applet, for instance, could have its information accessed by the following JavaScript code:

```
var myAppletInfo = document.applets[1];
```

This allows developers to store information about this applet in a variable, where they can then parse it and process the information about the applet. The information stored in the `myAppletInfo` example would contain the applet's name, dimensions, and the layout package used to create the applet.

With the increased use of dynamic pages, it is not uncommon for a developer to not know how many applets are on a page. Because this number can vary, a developer might have to include JavaScript code that analyzes the page to see how many applets are on it. Listing 4.9 shows an example of this.

*Listing 4.9    Checking for Java Applets with the* `length` *Property of the Applet Array*

```
<HTML>
<HEAD>
  <TITLE>Listing 4.9: Checking for Java Applets</TITLE>
<SCRIPT LANGUAGE="JavaScript1.1">
<!-- Hide
function checkApplets(){

  // Store the number of applets on the page in a variable
  var numApplets = document.applets.length;

  // If there are no applets on the page, go to the "noapplets"
  // page.
  if(numApplets == 0){
    window.location.href = "http://www.purejavascript.com/noapplets.html";

  // If there is only one applet on the page, go to the
  // "oneapplet" page.
  } else if (numApplets == 1){
    window.location.href = "http://www.purejavascript.com/oneapplet.html";

  // If there are more than two applets on the page, go to the
  // "manyapplets" page.
  } else if (numApplets > 2){
    window.location.href = "http://www.purejavascript.com/manyapplets.html";
  }
}
// End Hide -->
</SCRIPT>
</HEAD>

<BODY onLoad='checkApplets()'>
<CENTER>
<TABLE BORDER=1>
  <TR>
    <TD>
      <APPLET CODE="TestApplet"
        CODEBASE="."
        WIDTH=200
        HEIGHT=35
        NAME="AppletOne"
        MAYSCRIPT>
        This browser is not able to run Java applets
<PARAM NAME="clickurl"
              VALUE="http://www.purejavascript/cgi-bin/redirect.cgi">
```

*continues*

*Listing 4.9    continued*

```
        </APPLET>
      </TD>
    </TR>
    <TR>
      <TD>
        <APPLET CODE="TestApplet"
          CODEBASE="."
          WIDTH=200
          HEIGHT=35
          NAME="AppletTwo">
          This browser is not able to run Java applets
          <PARAM NAME="clickurl"
                VALUE="http://www.purejavascript/cgi-bin/redirect2.cgi">
        </APPLET>
      </TD>
    </TR>
  </TABLE>
</CENTER>
</BODY>
</HTML>
```

As you can see in the listing, once the page has fully loaded, a onLoad event handler is called by the <BODY> tag. This event triggers a function that checks to see how many applets were loaded on the page. Depending on the number of applets loaded, the browser may be redirected to another location. If the number of applets on the page is two, the page does not redirect to another location.

**NOTE**

You are only able to access properties and the results of applet methods after the applet is fully loaded and running. To ensure this, use the onLoad event handler in the <BODY> tag. Note that there are bugs in certain platforms of Navigator browsers that incorrectly fire this event. Be sure to account for these instances.

As you can see, the applet array can be a very helpful resource in accessing the applets on your pages. You should use it with caution, however, because not all browsers that support JavaScript support the ability to run applets.

## Plug-in Array

The plug-in array is the second array that can be used to control elements loaded by an HTML page. Developers commonly determine if a particular plug-in is installed on the user's machine by using this array. Once this has been determined, the developer can then make the appropriate decisions about whether or not to try and load the plug-in.

The actual plug-in array has several properties that can be used to retrieve this information. These include items such as the name of the plug-in, the actual filename, and a description. Listing 4.10 demonstrates the use of the plug-in array by writing the information it can retrieve to the page. Figure 4.10 shows the result of running this in a browser with several plug-ins installed.

*Listing 4.10    Checking the Plug-Ins Array*

```
<HTML>
<HEAD>
  <TITLE>Listing 4.10: Checking the plug-ins Array</TITLE>
</HEAD>
<BODY>
<SCRIPT LANGUAGE="JavaScript">
<!-- Hide

// Store the number of plug-ins in a variable
var numPlugins = navigator.plugins.length;

// Write the title of the page.
if (numPlugins > 0){
  document.write('<H3>The Plug-ins You Have Installed</H3><HR>');
}else{
  document.write('<H3>You have No Plug-ins Installed.</H3>');
}

// Write the various installed plug-in information to the page.
for (i = 0; i < numPlugins; i++){
  currPlugin = navigator.plugins[i];
  document.write('<P><B>Name:</B> ' + currPlugin.name + '<BR>');
  document.write('<B>Filename:</B> ' + currPlugin.filename + '<BR>');
  document.write('<B>Description:</B> ' + currPlugin.description + '<BR>');
}
// End hide -->
</SCRIPT>
</BODY>
</HTML>
```

In the script, you access the total number of plug-ins installed by using the length property of the plug-ins array. Once this has been done, determine the appropriate header to write to the page and run through a for loop writing the plug-ins information as well. This is a fairly simple example, but accessing these properties can be very useful when determining what elements you want your pages to use when loaded by a browser.

# LiveConnect

LiveConnect is a Netscape-specific technology, provided in Netscape Navigator 3 and later browsers, that provides a communication link between JavaScript scripts, Java, and plug-ins. It allows JavaScript to access certain Java core functionality through the Packages object. It can also access specific Java applets through the Applet array and plug-ins through the Plugin array.

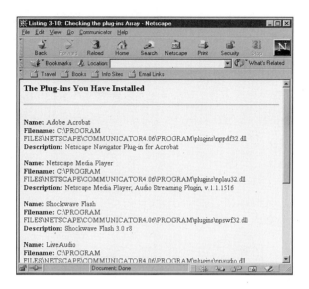

**Figure 4.10**

*The result of running Listing 4.10 in a browser with several plug-ins installed.*

In this section, you'll take a closer look at LiveConnect as it pertains to Java applets. You'll also step through some examples of using LiveConnect to extend the browser's interpretation of scripts and Java.

## LiveConnect in the Enterprise Vision

Netscape has been a pioneer in the world of Internet technology over the last several years. It developed the first truly powerful suite of Internet applications when it released Navigator 2.0, and it has continued to expand on the standards it has developed. In addition to the tools and applications Netscape has released, it has also paved the way for the advancement of various technologies and their interaction with one another. This was first referred to as Netscape ONE technologies, but has since changed to simply Netscape's Internet Technologies.

All of the technologies and products Netscape releases fall into its "Enterprise Vision." This vision is the overall road map that drives the company and products to work together, regardless of platform and operating system. LiveConnect is part of this vision in that it provides developers with a common method to allow interaction with JavaScript and Java applets that are loaded on a given page. By summing the powers of these two technologies, a developer is able to get the benefits of both, individually and collectively.

## Why LiveConnect?

LiveConnect plays a very important role in linking JavaScript and Java together so that each can rely and expand on the functionality the other has to offer. The ability to dynamically change and interact with a Java applet on a page after it is loaded makes it easy for a Web developer to harness the power of Java. This can be done in modular fashion, since it is completely possible that another developer wrote the applet.

On the flip side, LiveConnect allows an applet to access information contained in scripts. Because information can be passed to and from the applets, developers are able to maximize the functionality of their pages when using it. Using LiveConnect within an enterprise gives the developer the ability to exploit these features. Netscape has developed LiveConnect so that it fits nicely within its Enterprise Vision and adds to the mix of technologies that support the "write once, run anywhere" theories.

## LiveConnect Java Examples

What follows are two examples to give you a better understanding of how LiveConnect works within Navigator browsers. The first example will show you how JavaScript can access some of the Java language functionality natively (through the `Packages` object). The second example shows how you can use JavaScript to interact with an applet.

Listing 4.11 uses some of Java's native methods available via the `Packages` object. In this example, a user can type some information in a form text box, and then click the Print button to print his or her text to the Java Console. The `onClick` event is used to pass the text information to a JavaScript function, where it then writes the information. The result of running this example in a browser is shown in Figure 4.11.

*Listing 4.11   Accessing Java Methods Through JavaScript's* `Packages` *Object*

```
<HTML>
<HEAD>
  <TITLE>Listing 4.11: LiveConnect Example #1</TITLE>
<SCRIPT LANGUAGE="JavaScript1.2">
<!-- Hide

//This function takes the text entered in by the user and prints
//it to the Java Console.
function writeToConsole(inText){
  Packages.java.lang.System.out.println(inText);
}
// End Hide -->
</SCRIPT>
</HEAD>

<BODY>
<FORM>
  <INPUT TYPE=TEXT NAME=entered WIDTH="10">
<INPUT TYPE=BUTTON VALUE="Print"
        onClick='writeToConsole(form.entered.value)'>
</FORM>
</BODY>
</HTML>
```

**Figure 4.11**

*Using the* `Packages` *object to access the* `System.out.println()` *method in Java.*

The second example is a little more complex. It takes text entered by the user and passes it to a method within an applet to change the text the applet is displaying. To help you get a full understanding of this example, the listing includes both the applet code and the JavaScript code needed to perform this task. Listing 4.12 shows the Java code necessary, while Listing 4.13 shows the JavaScript.

*Listing 4.12   Java Code Used in the Example*

```
// Imported classes
import java.applet.*;
import java.awt.Graphics;

public class PSLiveConnectExample extends Applet {

  // Initialize an instance of a public string variable
  public String sText;

  // Initial the string itself with a value
  public void init() {
    sText = new String("Pure JavaScript");
  }

  // Draw the string in the applet at this location
  public void paint(Graphics gArea) {
    gArea.drawString(sText, 20, 20);
  }

  // Method used to change the string when passed to the applet
  // from JavaScript.
  public void changeString(String aString) {
```

```
    sText = aString;
    repaint();
  }
}
```

*Listing 4.13    HTML Used to Load the Applet and Change the Text Within It*

```
<HTML>
<HEAD>
  <TITLE>Listing 4.13: LiveConnect Example #2</TITLE>
</HEAD>

<BODY>
<CENTER>
<TABLE BORDER=1>
  <TR>
    <TD ALIGN=CENTER>
      <APPLET
        CODE="PSLiveConnectExample.class"
        CODEBASE="."
        NAME="TextChanger"
        WIDTH=150
        HEIGHT=25
        MAYSCRIPT>
      </APPLET>

      <FORM NAME="inputForm">
<INPUT TYPE="button" VALUE="Change Text"
onClick="document.TextChanger.changeString(document.inputForm.inputText.value)"
>
        <INPUT TYPE="text" SIZE="20" NAME="inputText">
      </FORM>
    </TD>
  </TR>
</TABLE>
</CENTER>
</BODY>
</HTML>
```

As you can see in Listing 4.13, the applet that displays the initial "Pure JavaScript" text is loaded. Once the page has finished loading, the user can enter text into the text box and click the Change Text button to modify the text displayed by the applet. This button directly accesses the changeString() method in the applet to change the text from the default to that entered by the user. Figure 4.12 shows the result of changing this text.

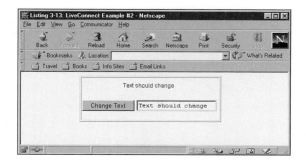

**Figure 4.12**

*Using JavaScript to change the text in a Java applet.*

# Moving On

This chapter reviewed a lot of material. It contained discussions on browser items and objects that extend the functionality of the browser itself. As a serious JavaScript developer, you should have found much of this information very useful, if not immediately applicable in the applications you are now creating.

Chapter 5, "Forms, Cookies, Windows, and Layers," will take you through the maze of information surrounding these topics. You will learn how they fit together, and you can practice their application on the examples detailed in the chapter.

# CHAPTER 5

## Forms, Cookies, Windows, and Layers

JavaScript is very useful for enhancing a Web site. Today's Web pages have become extremely user-interactive, due partly to the use of Common Gateway Interface (CGI). However, CGI is performed on the server-side. JavaScript can be used to perform similar CGI tasks and perform work on the client-side. This client-side programming allows a developer to perform many tasks the user will be able to see and use without having to send a page to the server again. It is this benefit alone that prompts most of the JavaScript programming on the Web today.

Client-side interaction deals mostly with information that users see and transmit. Forms are very popular and abundant on the Internet today. People use them to do things such as place orders online for material goods and submit information to databases. Forms are probably the most common means of client-side interaction in today's Internet world.

Cookies are also becoming increasingly popular. Even though a large percentage of Internet users interact with cookies everyday, not many people know what cookies are or how they are used. Users are not aware cookies are used by sites to save preferences or maintain sessions as they move through sites. In fact, most users do not even know that their browsers are using cookies.

Window manipulation is also a very visible method of client-side interaction. Windows appear to be very basic on the outside, but underlying JavaScript provides a lot of power for configuring and manipulating windows to meet your needs.

Finally there is the concept of dynamically positioning HTML elements within a Web page using JavaScript. This concept would allow developers to move, show, and hide HTML elements in three-dimensional space. Netscape initially tackled positioning with the `<layer>` tag in Netscape Navigator 4, but the advent of Cascading Style Sheets in both Netscape and Internet Explorer is changing the way in which positioning is handled. This area is still in a state of change, with standards being hammered out at this time.

In this chapter, you will take a look at some of the ways JavaScript can be used to perform these client-side tasks. You will learn about how JavaScript works with forms, what cookies are and how they are used, window manipulation, and element positioning. With a solid understanding of these concepts, developers can expand their sites to have no bounds.

# Form Processing

Before JavaScript was developed, most developers used CGI programs to send information from a user's browser to a Web server. This information was transmitted by an HTML form. When using a form, the user would enter his or her information and submit the form to the server. This usually was slow, due to transmission delay back and forth to the server and the fact that the Web server did most of the work with the form, such as parsing information and validation.

JavaScript helps to speed up this process by interacting with the form data, similar to CGI, before it is sent to the server. This saves the Web server work and reduces the amount of time spent transmitting information. Using JavaScript for form processing can be very useful to the developer and time-saving to the user.

**NOTE**

Form processing refers to the ability of Web developers to pass fields of information from the browser to be processed by a server. Once this information is passed to the server, developers can use it as their application sees fit.

Many forms collect user information like names, addresses, or interests. By collecting this information, developers open up a whole new level of possibility in their sites' functionality. They are no longer placing static information out on their site for the world to see, rather, it is a means of communication—communication between users and their sites.

Communication between users and sites is mostly done through forms. When a user fills out an online form and submits it, the information needs to be validated and processed. Without JavaScript, these actions can only be done on the server-side. The validation and processing work can be broken out by using JavaScript. This is where JavaScript's use of form processing really benefits developers.

Accurate processing of forms is dependent on the validity of the information given. It is very easy to input incorrect data into a form and then submit it. When this is done, you generally let the server handle any problems that may occur. These problems can be avoided if JavaScript is used on the client-side to validate the data before it is submitted. JavaScript can check the data content and format before transmitting the data, which, in turn, frees the server from encountering and dealing with these types of problems. The server's only job now is to process the information being sent.

## FORM SUBMISSION 101: *GET* VERSUS *POST*

When creating a form, one of the attributes you must specify within the <FORM> tag is METHOD. This attribute can be set to either GET or POST, both of which can be used as the type of submission for the form. However, their uses differ slightly.

GET, which is the default setting, passes the form values on the URL. This is sent in a single transmission to the URL specified in the ACTION attribute. The following simple form can be used as an example.

```
<FORM ACTION=http://www.purejavascript.com/cgi-bin/sampleform.cgi
    ➥METHOD=GET>
  <SELECT NAME=STATE>
    <OPTION VALUE=NC>North Carolina</OPTION>
    <OPTION VALUE=SC>South Carolina</OPTION>
    <OPTION VALUE=CA>California</OPTION>
  </SELECT>
  <INPUT TYPE="button" VALUE="Submit">
</FORM>
```

When the user selects one of the items from the pull-down menu and clicks the Submit button, the information will be passed on the end of the URL. If the user selected "North Carolina," for instance, the passed information would look like the following:

```
http://www.purejavascript.com/cgi-bin/sampleform.cgi?STATE=NC
```

The POST method, on the other hand, works differently. When POST is used, the browser contacts the URL specified in the ACTION property and sends the data in the body of the HTTP request. For those of you familiar with the HTTP standard, you know that information is passed back to the browser in two main parts: the "head" and the "body." When a browser sends a POST form, it performs a similar task as the server in that it sends the information in the body of the request and not on the URL.

There are different cases for using the two methods. If you are sending large amounts of form information to the server, the POST method should be used. Normally a server will have problems handling large amounts of data using the GET method. The POST method is also useful for keeping your data from being easily seen, because the form information is sent in a data block.

Keep in mind that JavaScript is not a complete substitute for server-side CGI form processing programs. It should be used more as a complement to these CGI programs. By combining the use of JavaScript and CGI, a developer can create a very effective and efficient means of processing forms.

Before programmers can use JavaScript with forms, they need to know how to get and parse forms for information. The next section will take a look at methods of extracting information from forms using JavaScript.

# The Form Array

One of JavaScript's built-in objects used to access components within a page is the Form array. The Form array, which is a property of the document object, is an array containing a list of the forms within a given document. Because it is an array, each form in the document can be referenced by the index number that represents its position in the document.

For instance, if you had a document containing three forms and you wanted to access a property in the second form, you would reference it with the following syntax:

`document.forms[1].property`

In this example, the *document* object refers to the document in which the form is located, and the *property* element refers to the property you are trying to access.

Listing 5.1 is an HTML page that contains two forms. In addition to the forms on this page, two JavaScript functions are included in the <HEAD> portion of the page that show different methods of accessing forms and perform some input validation. Each of the forms contains a text area for the user to insert text, as well as a Submit button. When the user attempts to submit the form, an onClick event is fired and the contents of the form are passed to a JavaScript function for processing.

*Listing 5.1    Using the* Forms *Array to Access Multiple Forms on a Page*

```
<HTML>
<HEAD>
   <TITLE>Listing 5.1: Forms Array Example</TITLE>
<SCRIPT LANGUAGE="JavaScript">
<!-- Hide

// function verifyZip checks for a valid zip code.  If user enters invalid
// zip code, then an alert box is used to inform user. Function
// takes the length as an input parameter
function verifyZip(length){

// Create variable and store the form value for the zip input
  var zipEntry = document.forms[0].zip.value;

// Parse the input for an integer number using 10 as the radix
  var zipNum = parseInt(zipEntry, 10);

// Check to see that the length is 5
  if (document.forms[0].zip.value.length == length){
// verify that the zip is a number
    if(zipNum != 0 && isNaN(zipNum) == false){
      alert(zipEntry + " is a valid zip code");
```

```
    } else {
// Inform the user if the zip is not valid
      alert("Invalid Zip Code Entered. Please Re-enter");
    }
  } else {
    alert("Invalid Zip Code Entered. Please Re-enter");
  }
}

// function myName displays the name the user entered
function myName(){
// Get the form value of the name entered
  var name = document.form2.name.value;
  alert("You Entered: " + name);
}

// End hide -->
</SCRIPT>
</HEAD>
<BODY>
<P>
<CENTER><B>Forms Example</B></CENTER>
<BR><BR><BR>
<TABLE>
<FORM NAME="form1" METHOD=POST>
  <TR>
    <TD ALIGN="right">Enter a 5 Digit Zip Code:</TD>
    <TD ALIGN="left">
      <INPUT TYPE= "TEXT" NAME="zip" SIZE="15">
<INPUT TYPE="BUTTON" NAME="button1"
       VALUE="Verify" onClick="verifyZip(5)">
    </TD>
  </TR>
</FORM>
<FORM NAME="form2" ACTION="" METHOD="post">
  <TR>
    <TD ALIGN="right">Enter Your Name:</TD>
    <TD ALIGN="left">
      <INPUT TYPE="TEXT" NAME="name" SIZE="15">
      <INPUT TYPE="BUTTON" NAME="button2" VALUE="Show Name"
       onClick="myName(this.form)">
    </TD>
  </TR>
</FORM>
</TABLE>
</BODY>
</HTML>
```

In the first form, validation is performed on the input. The user is asked to enter a five-digit zip code. Once entered, the user can push the verify button, which calls the verifyZip function. This function uses the forms array index number to access the user input. Figure 5.1 shows this example of accessing the forms array.

**Figure 5.1**

*Output result for processing the first form.*

**NOTE**

Remember that form indexes are zero indexed and are stored in the array in sequential order. The first form in the document is forms[0], the second form is forms[1], the third form is forms[2], and so on.

Once a script has the input, it can perform checks to make sure it is the correct length and that a numeric value was entered. If the correct information has been entered, a message is displayed informing the user the input was valid. If incorrect information was entered, an error message will be displayed informing the user of an invalid entry.

The second form takes a name as input and passes it to the showName function, which displays the name in a window when the Show Name button is chosen. Notice that the function accesses the form information differently than the first function. Instead of using the forms array, it references the form by its name value.

In this example, the variable *name* is set using the NAME attribute of the <FORM> tag instead of the index number of the Forms array. Either method of accessing a form element is valid. However, if a document contains many forms, it may be easier to use the form NAME instead of counting the Forms array index numbers. Accessing a form through the NAME attribute also tends to make the script easier to understand.

This example demonstrates some uses of combining forms and JavaScript. Another useful function of JavaScript and forms is information manipulation. For instance, if the form processing program on the server-side only processes phone numbers without the hyphen, developers can program their scripts to strip all hyphens out of phone numbers before submission.

## Accessing and Writing Information

Just as the document object contains a forms array, the form object contains an elements array. The elements array works similar to the forms array in that items are indexed in the order they appear, and you can access a specific element by its NAME instead of index number. Listing 5.2 demonstrates the two different ways of accessing form elements.

*Listing 5.2    Using Different Methods of Accessing Form Elements*

```
<HTML>
<HEAD>
<TITLE>Example of Accessing Form Elements</TITLE>

<SCRIPT LANGUAGE="JavaScript">
<!-- Hide

// Function displays the car information entered.
function showCar(){

// Access the car information by using the elements array
  var car = document.car.elements[0].value;
  alert("Your favorite car is: " + car);
}

// Function displays the color information entered
function showColor(){

// Access the color value directly by form name
  var color = document.pref.color.value;
  alert("Your favorite color is: " + color);
}

// End hide-->
</SCRIPT>
</HEAD>
```

*continues*

*Listing 5.2    continued*
```
<BODY>

<FORM NAME="pref" METHOD=POST>
Enter the name of your favorite car:
  <INPUT TYPE="text" NAME="car" SIZE=25>
  <INPUT TYPE="BUTTON" NAME="carButton" VALUE="Show Car"
onClick="showCar(this.form)">
<BR>
Enter your favorite color:
  <INPUT TYPE="text" NAME="color" SIZE=15>
  <INPUT TYPE="BUTTON" NAME="colorButton" VALUE="Show Color"
onClick="showColor(this.form)">
</FORM>

</BODY>
</HTML>
```

The information entered into each text box becomes an element of the form. Using the elements array, a script can access each individual element of the array. As you can see in the showCar function, the car element is referred to by document.pref. elements[0].value. This is accessing the first element of the elements array in this specific form. The button would be the second element and would be referenced by document.pref.elements[1].value and so on for other elements throughout the form.

The showColor function references the color object differently. It references it by the color object name with document.pref.color.value. If you were to use the elements array, this value would be referenced by document.pref.elements[2].value. Referencing by element name is much safer and easier to keep track of, and it can prevent future problems. For example, suppose you have a Web page containing two frames, A and B respectively. Frame A contains a JavaScript program that references elements within frame B using the elements array. If the Web page in frame B were to change but still contain form elements, your JavaScript program in frame A would be accessing incorrect form elements. Another reason for using element names is that if new form elements are inserted in the future, all the element numbering would not have to be changed.

**TIP**

Referencing by elements array can be useful if you want to keep your program generic, but if you want better maintainability and ease of use, referencing by NAME is the preferred choice.

In addition to accessing form elements, you can also write or modify form information. This can be a very useful technique for automatic form correction. Just about any object that carries information within a form can be modified.

Take a look at a simple example of writing information to forms. Listing 5.3 contains a form with one text box with a question and one Submit button. The user is asked to enter the answer to the question. If the answer is correct, an information box appears indicating so. If it is wrong, an alert box will appear informing the user that he or she entered the wrong answer and the correct answer is automatically written to the text box.

*Listing 5.3    Writing Information to JavaScript Forms*

```
<HTML>
<HEAD>
<TITLE>Example of Writing Form Elements</TITLE>

<SCRIPT LANGUAGE="JavaScript">
<!-- Hide

// Function checks to see if the text submitted is the
// correct answer.
function checkText(){

// Perform an equality check to see if the input is correct
  if( document.FormExample3.textbox.value == "Bugs Bunny"){
    alert("You are correct!");
  } else {

// If the original input was incorrect, output the
// correct information and inform the user.
    document.FormExample3.textbox.value = "Bugs Bunny";
    alert("That is incorrect. The correct answer is now in the text box.");
  }
}

// End hide-->
</SCRIPT>
</HEAD>
<BODY>

<FORM NAME="FormExample3" METHOD=POST>
What Loony Tunes Character is gray and has long ears?
  <INPUT TYPE="text" NAME="textbox" SIZE=25>
<INPUT TYPE="BUTTON" NAME="Bugs" VALUE="Submit"
  onClick="checkText(this.form)">
</FORM>
</BODY>
</HTML>
```

Building on the foundation of the code in Listing 5.3, it's possible to create a JavaScript method that creates a customized pull-down menu based on specific user input.

# Form Example

Listing 5.4 presents a sample Web page that allows a user to enter his or her personal information to submit. After all the information is entered and the user clicks the Submit button, all the form data is validated on the client-side before passing the data to the server for further processing.

*Listing 5.4    Example Using a Form for Client-Side Validation*

```
<HTML>
<HEAD>
<TITLE> Form Validation Example </TITLE>
<SCRIPT LANGUAGE="JavaScript">
<!-- Hide


// function checks to see that the personal
// information entered is valid
function validatePersonalInfo(){

 // declare variables to hold input values
  var _first = document.info.fname.value;
  var _last = document.info.lname.value;
  var _street = document.info.street.value;
  var _city = document.info.city.value;
  var _zip = document.info.zip.value;
  var _phone = document.info.phone.value;
  var _email = document.info.email.value;

// verify that the all input fields are filled in
  if(_first.toString() == ""){alert("Please enter a first name.");}
  if(_last.toString() == ""){alert("Please enter a last name.");}
  if(_street.toString() == ""){alert("Please enter your street name.");}
  if(_city.toString() == ""){alert("Please enter your city.");}
  if(_zip.toString() == ""){alert("Please enter your zip.");}
  if(_phone.toString() == ""){alert("Please enter your phone number.");}
  if(_email.toString() == ""){alert("Please enter your email.");}

  else{
     // check that the zip and phone numbers are valid inputs
     var checkZip = checkNum(5);
     var phoneInput = document.info.phone.value;
// initialize variables
     var validPhone = false;
     var validZip = false;

    if(checkZip == true){
       validZip = true;
    }
    else{
```

```
      alert("Invalid Zip Code" + validZip);
    }

    // if the phone number is not valid, then inform user
    if(!checkPhone(phoneInput)){
        alert("Phone number is invalid." + validPhone);
      }
    else{
      validPhone = true;
    }

    if(validZip && validPhone){
      alert("Your form has been verified");
    }
  }
}


// Strips hyphens out of phone number and verifies that
// phone number is valid. Any phone number in the format
// xxxxxxxxxx, xxx-xxx-xxxx, or (xxx)xxx-xxxx will be valid
function checkPhone(str){
  var regexp = /^(\d{10}¦\d{3}-\d{3}-\d{4}¦\(\d{3}\)\d{3}-\d{4})$/;
  return regexp.test(str);
}

// Function checks that the zip code is valid
function checkNum(length){
  var zipEntry = document.info.zip.value;
  var zipNum = parseInt(zipEntry, 10);

  if (document.info.zip.value.length == length){
    if(zipNum != 0 && isNaN(zipNum) == false){
      // Valid Zip code
      return true;
    }
    else {
      // Invalid Zip Code
      return false;
    }
  }
  else {
    //Too Many digits- Invalid
    return false;
  }
}

// End hide-->
```

*continues*

*Listing 5.4    continued*

```
</SCRIPT>
</HEAD>
<BODY>
<P>
<CENTER><B>Form Validation Example</B></CENTER>
<P>This page demonstrates how JavaScript can do form
validation on a Web page.  Using JavaScript to do validation on the client-side
can greatly reduce processing time by
reducing the chance of submitting incorrect forms.

<HR>
<BR>
<B>Personal Information:</B>
<FORM NAME="info"  ACTION="" METHOD="post">
<TABLE>
<TR><TD ALIGN="left">First Name:</TD>
<TD ALIGN="left">
<INPUT TYPE="text" NAME="fname" SIZE=15>
Last Name:
<INPUT TYPE="text" NAME="lname" SIZE=20>
</TD>
</TR>

<BR>
<TR><TD ALIGN="left">Street:</TD>
<TD ALIGN="left">
<INPUT TYPE="text" NAME="street" SIZE=30></TD>
</TR>

<BR>
<TR>
<TD ALIGN="left">City:</TD>
<TD ALIGN="left">
<INPUT TYPE="text" NAME="city" SIZE=15>
State:

<SELECT NAME="state">
<OPTION value=AL>AL
<OPTION value=AK>AK
<OPTION value=AZ>AZ
<OPTION value=AR>AR
<OPTION value=CA>CA
<OPTION value=CO>CO
<OPTION value=CT>CT
<OPTION value=DE>DE
```

```
<OPTION value=FL>FL
<OPTION value=GA>GA
<OPTION value=HI>HI
<OPTION value=ID>ID
<OPTION value=IL>IL
<OPTION value=IN>IN
<OPTION value=IA>IA
<OPTION value=KS>KS
<OPTION value=KY>KY
<OPTION value=LA>LA
<OPTION value=ME>ME
<OPTION value=MD>MD
<OPTION value=MA>MA
<OPTION value=MI>MI
<OPTION value=MN>MN
</SELECT>

Zip:
<INPUT TYPE="text" NAME="zip" SIZE=7>
</TD>
</TR>

<BR>
<TR><TD ALIGN="left">Phone (w/area code):</TD>
<TD ALIGN="left">
<INPUT TYPE="text" NAME="phone" SIZE=20></TD>
</TR>

<BR>
<TR><TD ALIGN="left">Email:</TD>
<TD ALIGN="left">
<INPUT TYPE="text" NAME="email" SIZE=20></TD>
</TR>

<BR>
</TABLE>

<CENTER>
<INPUT TYPE="button" VALUE="Submit" onclick="validatePersonalInfo()">
</CENTER>

</FORM>
</BODY>
</HTML>
```

Figure 5.2 shows how the personal information form looks.

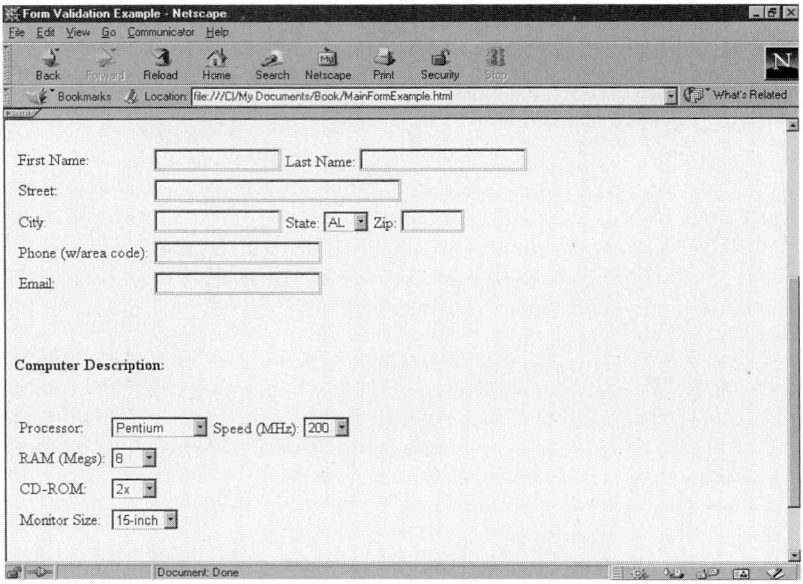

**Figure 5.2**

*Form Validation Example.*

The form begins by validating that all the input fields have been filled. If any of the fields are left empty, an alert box will appear indicating that the field requires input. There are two main inputs that require special validation: the zip code and the phone number.

The first function called is `ValidatePersonalInfo`. This main function checks to see that all the user entries are valid. If so, an alert box is returned indicating that the form has been validated. Before the form can be completely validated, the zip code and phone number must be checked. The zip code verification is performed by the sub-function called `checkNum`. This function takes one parameter—the string length. For the Zip code, the string length must be five digits. If this is found to be true, then the zip code is validated.

The second sub-function called is `checkPhone`. The `checkPhone` function takes the input for the phone number and checks it against three different standard phone number formats. If any are found to be valid, the function returns `true`. After both checks are performed, the form is determined to contain valid information.

# JavaScript and Cookies

A cookie is a small bit of organized information that is stored in a text file on the user's computer by a browser. Cookies are typically used to store information pertinent to a specific site that is currently used and can be reused in the future.

The location of a cookie text file differs according to the browser being used. In Navigator, all cookies are stored in a file named `cookies.txt`. In Internet Explorer, each cookie is stored as its own individual text file in the Cookies folder, which is located by default in the Windows folder.

There are limitations to cookies. The size of a cookie is limited to 4KB kilobytes. Also, browsers only allow for 300 total cookies to be stored on the user's computer. This keeps the size of the `cookies.txt` file or Cookies folder to a 1200KB maximum. In addition, each Web server is only allowed to store a total of 20 cookies. If the 300 total cookies or 20 cookies per Web server limit is exceeded, the least recently used cookie is deleted to accommodate any additional cookies.

Browsers let the user control how cookies are used. In Navigator, under Edit, Preferences, there is an Advanced category. This category gives you the option to accept all cookies, accept cookies that get sent back to the server, or disable cookies. There is also an option to warn you before accepting a cookie. Enabling this option will force the browser to notify you when a cookie requests to be set and inform you of what the cookie contains. Figure 5.3 shows a picture of what a cookie warning would look like.

**Figure 5.3**

*Cookie warning example.*

**NOTE**

When a cookie is first set, it is stored in the browser's memory. It's not until the browser is exited that the cookie gets written to the file.

The `cookie` object is part of the `Document` object. Cookies can be created, set, and modified by setting the appropriate values of the `cookie` property. A cookie has four name attributes: `expires`, `path`, `domain`, and `secure`.

By default, a cookie lasts only during the current browsing session. When the browsing session is over, the cookie is destroyed. For a cookie to last beyond the current browsing session, the `expires` attribute must be set. This attribute specifies the life of a cookie. The value of this attribute can be set to any valid date string. If the `expires` attribute is set, after the current browsing session is over the cookie is written to the cookie text file. If no `expires` attribute is set, the cookie will expire when the user's browsing session ends.

The path attribute specifies the domain associated with the cookie. The level of association begins at the specified path and goes down into any subfolders. So for example, suppose http://www.purejavascript.com/examples/cookie.html was setting a cookie and wanted the cookie to be shared across Web pages on the purejavascript.com domain. To do this, the cookie path attribute needs to be set to "/". This allows the cookie to be accessed from any page on the www. purejavascript.com Web server. If the path was set to "/examples", the cookie would only be valid to pages in the examples folder and its subfolders.

**NOTE**

If the secure attribute is specified, the cookie will be only be transmitted over a secure channel (HTTPS). If secure is not specified, the cookie can be transmitted over any communications channel.

Understanding the cookie attributes is the first step in being able to read and write cookies. Now that you do understand this, look at how to read cookies.

# Reading Cookies

As stated before, cookies are part of the document object. The first thing you have to do is to read the cookie property. This can be done with the following statement:

```
var cookieName = document.cookie;
```

This statement creates the variable cookieName and assigns it the cookie property of the document object. Once you have accessed this property, you must extract the various attributes of the cookie. The cookie property itself returns a string containing all the cookies pertaining to the current document.

Cookies are interpreted in name/value pairs. The string returned from the cookie property contains the list of cookie name/value pairs. To read an individual attribute, you must parse through its string. You can use built-in JavaScript string methods to accomplish this.

Look at the example in Listing 5.5 to see how to read a cookie.

*Listing 5.5   Getting a Cookie Value*
```
<html>
<body>

<script language="JavaScript">
<!-- Hide

// Declare variable to hold all the cookies contained
// in the document.
   var cookies = document.cookie;

// Function that gets a cookie's value by searching
```

```
// for the name of the cookie.
function readCookie(name) {

    // declare variable to set the "name=" value
    var start = cookies.indexOf(name + "=");

    // Det the index if the cookie name is found
    if (start == -1){
            alert("Cookie not found");
    }
    // Get the first character of the cookie
    start = cookies.indexOf("=", start) + 1;

    // Read to the end of the cookie
    var end = cookies.indexOf(";", start);

    if (end == -1){
        end = cookies.length;
    }

    // Get the cookie value, reversing the escaped format by
    // using the unescape method
    var value = unescape(cookies.substring(start, end));

    if(value == null){
        alert("No cookie found");
    }
    else{
      alert("Cookie value is: " + value);
    }

}

// End Hide -->
</script>

</body>
</html>
```

# Writing Cookies

Cookie values can be created, modified, and set. Remember that cookies are read as name/value pairs. Therefore, when you write a cookie, its attributes must be written as a name/value pair.

To set a cookie value, you first create a cookie and assign it a name. Then you must set each individual attribute for the new cookie. Keep in mind that when you set the expires attribute, you must have a valid date string. It is best to use the JavaScript Date methods to create a date string, which can be assigned. Additional cookie attributes can be set similarly. The following is an example of how this is done:

```
document.cookie = "name=" + form.cookie.value + "; expires=" + month;
```

If you want to modify a specific value in the cookie, just set its attributes again. You can delete a cookie's value by modifying that attribute.

# Windows in Action

A window object is used in all your JavaScript programs, whether you specify it or not. The window object is one level higher than the document object in the JavaScript object hierarchy and provides a developer with the ability to manipulate the current window as well as create new window instances.

The ability to create new windows allows developers to add functionality to their sites. Some sites, such as GeoCities (http://www.geocities.com) shown in Figure 5.4, have advertisers create new windows to show their advertisement banners.

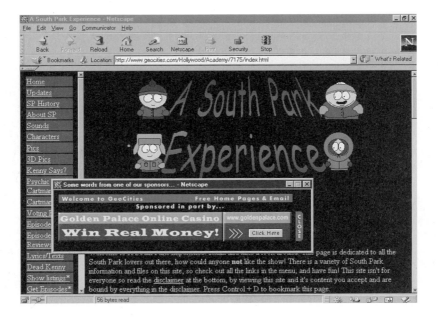

**Figure 5.4**

*Window advertisement banner.*

## The Parent/Child Relationship

Windows use what is described as a parent/child relationship when they are initiated. This means that if window B is created from within window A, window B is considered a child of window A, which is its parent. Any actions performed on the child by its parent must be referenced through its parent. Look at the following code:

```
<html>
<body>

<script language="JavaScript">
<!-- Hide
// Function creates a new window called myChild
// with the index.html file in it
function create(){
   open("index.html", "myChild");
}
// End Hide -->
</script>

<form name="form1">
<input type="button" value="Create Child" onClick='create()'>
</form>
</body>
</html>
```

The function `create` simply creates a new window that would be considered a child of the original window. The name of the child is specified in the second parameter of the `window.open` function, which is `"myChild"`. Any values in the child window are referenced using the name of the parent window. If the child window has a child of its own, this would be considered a grandchild of the parent. For a grandparent to perform actions on its grandchild, it must first reference its immediate parent and then its grandparent. Suppose the grandchild is named Jane, its parent is named Bob, and the grandparent is named Joe. For Jane to be manipulated by Joe's window it must reference the value by:

```
joe.bob.jane.document.form1.textBox.value
```

The parent has total control of its immediate child window and any subsequent child (grandchild) windows. If the parent window is destroyed, all control for the remaining child windows is lost.

A child window can find out who its parent is by using the `opener` method. The `opener` method will tell the child from which window it was created. You use the `opener` method as shown in the following:

```
var name = window.opener.document.name;
```

This will return the name of the parent document to the `name` variable.

You can use multiple instances of `opener` if you have several levels of windows. If a grandchild wanted to reference its grandparent, it could do so by simply adding another level.

```
window.opener.opener.document.form1.textbox.value
```

For a window to refer to its own properties, you can use the window `self` property. Suppose you wanted to set a `textbox` value within a form document in a window. You could refer to the value as shown in the following:

```
self.document.formName.textbox.value = "JavaScript is cool";
```

## Creating Windows

JavaScript provides a built-in method to create new instances of windows. The `open` method can be used to create any primary or secondary window. The following is an example of how `open` can be used.

```
window.open("web.html", "newWin", "resizeable,menubar,toolbar");
```

This creates a window that is resizable, contains a menu bar, and has a toolbar. The `"web.html"` is the file that will open in the newly created window. `"newWin"` represents the name of the window object. Many different features can be added to a window. This example only shows a few. Other features include `outerHeight`, `outerWidth`, `innerHeight`, `innerWidth`, `alwaysRaised`, `alwaysLowered`, `location`, `screenY`, and `screenX`. The features are specified in the parameters of the `open` function.

**NOTE**

Be careful not to include any spaces between window features; this will cause errors to occur in your window creation. Refer to the `windows` object in Chapter 7, "Client-Side Browser Syntax," for more details on other windows properties.

Once you create a new window, you can manipulate it. JavaScript also provides you with the ability to interact between multiple windows. As long as a `window` property is referenced correctly, you can modify objects in other windows. Remember the parent-child relationship when referencing `window` objects.

## Window Limitations

In older versions of JavaScript, windows could only be referenced from the top down. This meant that a parent window would know the properties of its child windows, but not vice versa. In JavaScript version 1.2 and later, this problem is resolved. As mentioned earlier, using the `opener` property will resolve any child/parent referencing conflicts.

## Window Example

The next example shows how you can send information between two windows. It begins with the parent window. Figure 5.5 shows both the parent and child windows open with the parent window on the top.

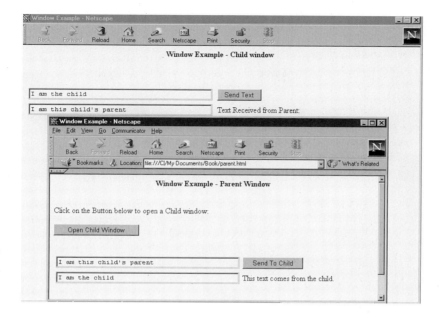

## Figure 5.5

*Example Parent/Child windows.*

Look at the code for the parent window in listing 5-5.

*Listing 5.5 Parent Code for Window Example*

```
<HTML>
<HEAD>
<TITLE> Window Example - Parent</TITLE>
<SCRIPT LANGUAGE="Javascript">
<!-- Hide

// Function creates and opens a new child window
function openWin(){
// Open a new window named "ChildWin"
  childWin=open("child.html", "ChildWin",
"toolbar,scrollbars,menubar,status,innerwidth=250,innerheight=350");
}

// Function sends a value from the parent window to the
// child window.
function sendToChild(){
  childWin.document.childForm.childText.value =
```

*continues*

*Listing 5.5   continued*

```
document.parentForm.parenttext.value;
}


// End Hide-->
</SCRIPT>
</HEAD>

<BODY>
<P>
<CENTER>
<B>Window Example - Parent Window</B>
<BR><BR><BR>
</CENTER>
<FORM NAME="parentForm">
Click on the Button below to open a Child window:
<BR><BR>
<INPUT TYPE="button" NAME="submit" VALUE="Open Child Window"
  onclick="openWin()">
<BR><BR><BR>
<TABLE>
<TR><TD ALIGN=left>
<INPUT TYPE="text" NAME="parenttext" size=45></TD>
<TD ALIGN=left>
<INPUT TYPE="button" NAME="submit" VALUE="Send To Child"
  onclick="sendToChild()">
</TD>
</TR>
<TR><TD ALIGN=left>
<INPUT TYPE="text" NAME="received" size=45></TD>
<TD ALIGN=left>
This text comes from the child.
</TD>
</TR>
</TABLE>
</FORM>
<BR><BR><BR>

</BODY>
</HTML>
```

This parent window has a button, which, when clicked, opens a child window. It also has two text fields, one for sending text to the child and one for receiving text from the child. The user will first click the button to create a new window. This is the child window. When the user enters text into the first text box and clicks the Send Text button, the input is sent to the child and appears in its appropriate text box. Take a look now at what the child window looks like in Listing 5.6.

*Listing 5.6    Child Window Code for Window Example*

```
<HTML>
<HEAD>
<TITLE> Window Example - Child</TITLE>
<SCRIPT LANGUAGE="Javascript">
<!-- Hide

// Function sends a value from the child window to the parent window.
// Function sends a text value from a child window
// to the parent window.
function sendToParent(){
  window.opener.document.parentForm.received.value =
document.childForm.sendText.value;
}

// End Hide -->
</SCRIPT>
</HEAD>

<BODY>
<P>
<CENTER>
<B>Window Example - Child window</B>
<BR><BR><BR>
</CENTER>
<FORM NAME="childForm">
<TABLE>
<TR><TD ALIGN=left>
<INPUT TYPE="text" NAME="sendText" size=45></TD>
<TD ALIGN=left>
<INPUT TYPE="button" NAME="submit" VALUE="Send Text" onclick="sendToParent()">
</TD>
</TR>
<BR>
<TR><TD ALIGN=left>
<INPUT TYPE="text" NAME="childText" size=45>
</TD>
<TD ALIGN=left>
Text Received from Parent:
</TD>
</TR>
</TABLE>
</FORM>
<BR><BR><BR>

</BODY>
</HTML>
```

The child window is similar to the parent except that there is no option to open another window. The child window has one text field for sending text to the parent window and one text field for receiving text from the parent. In the JavaScript code, you can see the use of the opener property to reference its parent. Remember, you cannot reference windows directly upward. The parent can call a child by name, but a child cannot call the parent by its name.

Manipulating windows provides you with the ability to greatly expand your site's functionality. There are many window properties that can be specified or modified to your individual needs.

# Dynamic HTML Element Positioning

Dynamically positioning HTML elements within a Web page using JavaScript allows developers to take Web page design to a new level. No longer is an HTML element forced to stay in the same place for the duration a Web page is viewed in a browser. Now elements can be moved all around the browser window after the page has completed loading. Elements can even exhibit three-dimensional movement where one element can appear in front of, or behind another element. Before you get too excited thinking about how you can change your existing Web pages to having flying buttons and disappearing text, there is one problem—browser compatibility.

Netscape initially tackled three-dimensional positioning with the <layer> tag in Netscape Navigator 4. Internet Explorer implemented three-dimensional positioning by extending the functionality of the existing HTML <div> tag, which had previously been of little use to most Web developers. So, you are probably thinking that the <div> is supported by Netscape. While it is true that both Netscape and Internet Explorer use the <div> tag to define static "layers" in their browsers, only Internet Explorer supports using it for dynamic positioning.

Now you have two ways of creating layers of elements within Web pages, but they are browser-specific. Cascading Style Sheets, which exist in both Netscape and Internet Explorer, are providing the base from which dynamic positioning will be handled on both platforms in the future. This area is still in a state of change, with standards being hammered out at this time.

What is known at this point is that using the <div> tag will be the way layers should be created in the future, and JavaScript will modify Cascading Style Sheet properties to make these layers dynamic in the future. Until both browsers support the standard that is currently being developed, you must understand the existing ways of creating layers and dynamically positioning them in three-dimensional space.

## Introduction to the <div> Block

Internet Explorer implemented the same functionality as the Netscape <layer> tag by using the <div> tag. The <div> tag has been around in HTML for quite a long time but was not used extensively. Originally, the <div> tag was used to divide a portion of a Web page so its alignment could be set to the left, right, or center of the browser window. Internet Explorer extends the functionality of this tag to allow the portion of HTML code defined by this tag to be placed and manipulated in three-dimensional space.

The `<div>` tag is nice because it provides a way to group numerous HTML tags together as one, but this does not mean you have to use the `<div>` tag all the time. In fact, you can dynamically position any HTML tag, such as `<b>` or `<spans>` using JavaScript, just like you would the `<div>` tag. So the concepts associated with the `<div>` tag that are about to be covered can be applied to any other HTML tag.

## Manipulating the <div> Block

To designate a portion of a Web page in Internet Explorer as a block that can later be positioned using JavaScript, simply place a `<div>` tag at the beginning of the HTML code and a `</div>` tag at the end. Any HTML tags can be placed within the `<div>` tags, which means you can have moving buttons, tables, check boxes, and so on. It is also possible to initialize various style sheet within the `<div>` tag by using the STYLE property. Listing 5.7 shows how the `<div>` tag is implemented.

*Listing 5.7    Internet Explorer `<div>` Tag Implementation*
```
<div id="mydiv" style="position:absolute; top:10; left:10; width:100;
height:50">
This is the Internet Explorer block implementation
</div>
```

The positioning of blocks can be either absolute or relative. With absolute positioning, you can specify the position within its containing block. Relative positioning is when the object appears in its natural location within the flow of the document.

After a portion of HTML code has been designated with the `<div>` tags, it is then possible to dynamically change the style sheet properties using the JavaScript. Thus, you can position, hide, show, and move designated elements in three-dimensional space by changing the values stored in the style sheet properties.

## <div> Block Example

In Listing 5.8, two `<div>` blocks are created (one yellow and another red) using the `<div>` and `</div>` tags. The red box contains buttons that will move the red box around the browser window. The red box also has a button that will make the yellow box disappear and reappear. The actual moving of elements is accomplished by changing the value of the style sheet properties associated with box. Keep in mind that even though Netscape Navigator will display the buttons and text only, Internet Explorer is capable of dynamically moving the elements when the buttons are pressed.

*Listing 5.8    Manipulating a <div> Block*

```
<HTML>
<BODY>

<DIV ID="redBox"
     STYLE="position:absolute;
            left:150px;
            top:150px;
            background-color:red;">
This is a block of moving buttons
<FORM>
<INPUT TYPE="button"
       VALUE="UP"
       onClick="moveUp()">
<INPUT TYPE="button"
       VALUE="DOWN"
       onCLick="moveDown()">
<INPUT TYPE="button"
       VALUE="LEFT"
       onClick="moveLeft()">
<INPUT TYPE="button"
       VALUE="RIGHT"
       onClick="moveRight()"><BR>
<INPUT TYPE="button"
       VALUE="SHOW/HIDE Yellow Box"
       onClick="showHide()">
</FORM>
</DIV>

<DIV ID="yellowBox" STYLE="background-color:yellow;">
Here is some text defined as a block
</DIV>

<SCRIPT LANGUAGE="JavaScript">
<!--

//Move the red box up 20 pixels
function moveUp()
{
  document.all.redBox.style.pixelTop+=(-20);
}

//Move the red box down 20 pixels
function moveDown()
{
  document.all.redBox.style.pixelTop+=20;
}

//Move the red box to the left 20 pixels
```

```
function moveLeft()
{
  document.all.redBox.style.pixelLeft+=(-20);
}

//Move the red box to the right 20 pixels.
function moveRight()
{
  document.all.redBox.style.pixelLeft+=20;
}

//Hide or show the yellow box
function showHide()
{
  if(document.all.yellowBox.style.visibility == "hidden")
    document.all.yellowBox.style.visibility="visible";
  else
    document.all.yellowBox.style.visibility="hidden";
}

//-->
</SCRIPT>
</BODY>
</HTML>
```

# Netscape's <layer> and <ilayer> Additions

As mentioned earlier, even though Internet Explorer's implementation of the <div> tag is the direction of how dynamic positioning will be handled in the future, it is important that you understand how Netscape handles positioning today. It uses the <layer> tag as well as the <div> tag.

# Quick Layer Background

Layers was a new object introduced within JavaScript version 1.2. Navigator 4.0 and later supports the layers property; however, the layers object is only supported in Navigator. Layers provide the ability to control multiple documents within a single window.

With the layer object, a new HTML tag called <layer> was created. The <layer> tag lets you use your JavaScript layer objects within an HTML page. Since layers are only supported in Navigator, the same applies to the <layer> tag. Listing 5.9 shows an example of Navigator's <layer> tag.

*Listing 5.9   Navigator* <LAYER> *Tag Implementation*
```
<LAYER ID="name" WIDTH=220 HEIGHT=100 BGCOLOR="red" TOP=150
LEFT=100 VISIBILITY="show"> This is the Navigator Layer Tag
</LAYER>
```

The positioning of layers can be either absolute or relative. With absolute positioning, you can specify the position within its containing layer. Relative positioning is when the object appears in its natural location within the flow of the document. The <layer> tag uses absolute positioning. It contains properties that let a developer specify a layer's position in a document.

For relative positioning, the <ilayer> tag is used. A layer created with the <ilayer> tag is considered an inflow or inline layer. The layer is sometimes called inflow because it appears in the document flow. It is also referred to as inline because it will share line space with the other HTML elements.

The type of layer and browser implementation to use depends on how the layer will be used and the audience. For most applications, the layer object with absolute positioning is used because it is more flexible. However, if you don't want to bother with specifying the coordinates of where your layer is positioned, relative positioning may work better. It depends on the situation.

So far, you have only considered creating layers using either the <layer> or <ilayer> tag, but there is one other way to create a layer. Because a layer is an object in Netscape, it can be created directly in JavaScript by using the Layer() constructor. This constructor takes two arguments—the width of the new layer in pixels and the parent of the new layer. Listing 5.10 demonstrates how to create a layer object using the Layer() constructor.

*Listing 5.10    Creating a Layer with the* Layer() *Constructor*
```
<script language="JavaScript">
<!--

myLayer = new Layer(150,document);

//-->
</script>
```

## Manipulating Layers

As with every object, the layer object is a child of the document object. It does have its own individual properties. Using these properties, you are able to control the layer settings.

Before you can manipulate a layer, you must be able to access the layer's properties. Similar to forms, there also exists a layers array. This array contains a list of all the layers in a specified document. For instance, if you wanted to set the visibility property of the second layer in a document to hide, you can do so with the following statement:

```
layers[1].visibility = hide;
```

The layers array also allows you to reference a layer object by the layer name. Suppose you have four layers within a document named Minnie, Mickey, Donald, and Goofy, respectively. If you wanted to reference the bgcolor property for the Goofy layer, but didn't want to count to determine what layer number Goofy was, you could just reference it by name. The following statements will each point to Goofy's `bgcolor` property:

```
layers["Goofy"].bgcolor
layers.Goofy.bgcolor
```

In an HTML document, any code inserted between the `<layer>` and `</layer>` tags is turned into a layer. This layer contains its own document and properties. There are two ways to manipulate this layer, depending on whether an ID was associated with this layer. If no ID is specified with the `ID` property in the layer tag, you would have to reference it first by using the `layers` array. From the `layers` array, you can either manipulate properties directly or with built-in methods. The following statement uses the layers array to assign the background color of the first layer to green:

```
document.layers[0].bgcolor = "green";
```

If an ID is specified, it can be used to reference the properties and methods associated with the layer. The following statement uses a layer ID to assign `"green"` to the background color of the layer called `"myLayer"`:

```
document.layer.myLayer.bgcolor = "green";
```

## Layer Example

In Listing 5.11, two blocks are created (one yellow and another red) using the `<layer>` and `</layer>` tags. The red box contains buttons that will move the red box around the browser window. The red box also has a button that will make the yellow box disappear and reappear. The actual moving of elements is accomplished by changing the value of the layer's properties. You will notice that when the buttons move, the text associated with buttons will sometimes get jumbled. This is because Netscape does not refresh the entire screen when a layer property is changed. Keep in mind that because Internet Explorer does not recognize the `<layer>` tag, this example will only work in Netscape Navigator.

*Listing 5.11   Manipulating Layers*
```
<html>
<body>

<layer id="redBox"
       style="position:absolute;
              left:150px;
              top:150px;
              background-color:red;">
This is a block of moving buttons
<form>
<input type="button"
       value="UP"
```

*continues*

*Listing 5.11    continued*

```
        onClick="moveUp()">
<input type="button"
        value="DOWN"
        onClick="moveDown()">
<input type="button"
        value="LEFT"
        onClick="moveLeft()">
<input type="button"
        value="RIGHT"
        onClick="moveRight()"><BR>
<input type="button"
        value="SHOW/HIDE Yellow Box"
        onClick="showHide()">
</form>
</layer>

<layer if="yellowBox" style="background-color:yellow;">
Here is some text defined as a block
</layer>

<script language="JavaScript">
<!--

//Move the red box up 20 pixels
function moveUp()
{
  document.layers.redBox.pageY+=(-20);
}

//Move the red box down 20 pixels
function moveDown()
{
  document.layers.redBox.pageY+=20;
}

//Move the red box to the left 20 pixels
function moveLeft()
{
  document.layers.redBox.pageX+=(-20);
}

//Move the red box to the right 20 pixels.
function moveRight()
{
  document.layers.redBox.pageX+=20;
}

//Hide or show the yellow box
```

```
function showHide()
{
  if(document.layers.yellowBox.visibility == "hide")
    document.layers.yellowBox.visibility="inherit";
  else
    document.layers.yellowBox.visibility="hide";
}


//-->
</script>
</body>
```

# Dynamic Positioning In Navigator and Internet Explorer

So far, the two ways of creating layers and dynamically positioning them after a page has loaded have been covered respective to the supporting browser. So how do you create HTML pages that use layering that will work on both Netscape Navigator as well as Internet Explorer? Until both browsers support the standard that is currently being developed, both methods must be used along with some extra code to determine browser type.

Listing 5.12 merges the code from the `<div>` example and the code from the `<layer>` example. Using JavaScript to determine the type of browser, two layers (one red and another plain text) are created using either the `<div>` tags or the `<layer>` tags. The red box contains buttons that will move the red box around the browser window. The red box also has a button that will make the text box disappear and reappear. The actual moving of elements is accomplished by changing the value of the layer's properties in the case of Netscape Layers or Cascading Style Sheet properties in the case of a `<div>` block. When using Netscape Navigator, you will notice that when the buttons move, the text associated with buttons will sometimes get jumbled. This is because Netscape does not refresh the entire screen when a layer property is changed. Internet Explorer does a much better job of refreshing the screen when the style sheet properties are changed.

*Listing 5.12   Manipulating Layers in Both Navigator and Internet Explorer*
```
<html>
<body>

<script language="JavaScript">
<!--

//Create a layer tag if Netscape
if(navigator.appName.indexOf("Netscape") != -1)
  document.write('<layer id="redBox" ');

//Create a div tag if Microsoft
```

*continues*

*Listing 5.12    continued*

```
if(navigator.appName.indexOf("Microsoft") != -1)
  document.write("<div id='redBox' ");

//Set the style used for the red box
document.write('style="position:absolute; ');
document.write('left:150px; ');
document.write('top:150px; ');
document.write('background-color:red;">');

//-->
</script>


This is a block of moving buttons
<form>
<input type="button"
       value="UP"
       onClick="moveUp()">
<input type="button"
       value="DOWN"
       onClick="moveDown()">
<input type="button"
       value="LEFT"
       onClick="moveLeft()">
<input type="button"
       value="RIGHT"
       onClick="moveRight()"><BR>
<input type="button"
       value="SHOW/HIDE Text Box"
       onClick="showHide()">
</form>

<script language="JavaScript">
<!--
//If Netscape close the layer tag
if(navigator.appName.indexOf("Netscape") != -1)
  document.write("</layer>");

//If Microsoft close div tag
if(navigator.appName.indexOf("Microsoft") != -1)
  document.write("</div>");
//-->
</script>

<script language="JavaScript">
<!--
//If Netscape create a text layer using layer tag
if(navigator.appName.indexOf("Netscape") != -1)
```

```
{
  document.write('<layer id="textBox" >');
  document.write("Here is some text defined as a block");
  document.write("</layer>");
}

//If Microsoft create a text block using div tag
if(navigator.appName.indexOf("Microsoft") != -1)
{
  document.write("</div>");
  document.write("<div id='textBox'>");
  document.write("Here is some text defined as a block");
  document.write("</div>");
}
//-->
</script>


<script language="JavaScript">
<!--

//Move the red box up 20 pixels
function moveUp()
{
  if(navigator.appName.indexOf("Netscape") != -1)
    document.layers.redBox.pageY+=(-20);
  if(navigator.appName.indexOf("Microsoft") != -1)
    document.all.redBox.style.pixelTop+=(-20);
}

//Move the red box down 20 pixels
function moveDown()
{
  if(navigator.appName.indexOf("Netscape") != -1)
    document.layers.redBox.pageY+=20;
  if(navigator.appName.indexOf("Microsoft") != -1)
    document.all.redBox.style.pixelTop+=20;
}

//Move the red box to the left 20 pixels
function moveLeft()
{
  if(navigator.appName.indexOf("Netscape") != -1)
    document.layers.redBox.pageX+=(-20);
  if(navigator.appName.indexOf("Microsoft") != -1)
    document.all.redBox.style.pixelLeft+=(-20);
```

*continues*

*Listing 5.12    continued*

```
}

//Move the red box to the right 20 pixels.
function moveRight()
{
  if(navigator.appName.indexOf("Netscape") != -1)
    document.layers.redBox.pageX+=20;
  if(navigator.appName.indexOf("Microsoft") != -1)
    document.all.redBox.style.pixelLeft+=20;
}

//Hide or show the text box
function showHide()
{
  if(navigator.appName.indexOf("Netscape") != -1)
  {
    //If text box is currently hidden, make it visible
    if(document.layers.textBox.visibility == "hide")
      document.layers.textBox.visibility="inherit";
    else
      document.layers.textBox.visibility="hide";
  }
  if(navigator.appName.indexOf("Microsoft") != -1)
  {
    //If text box is currently hidden, make it visible
    if(document.all.textBox.style.visibility == "hidden")
      document.all.textBox.style.visibility="visible";
    else
      document.all.textBox.style.visibility="hidden";
  }
}

//-->
</script>

</body>
</html>
```

# PART III

## JAVASCRIPT REFERENCE BY OBJECT

# CHAPTER 6

# Core Syntax

This chapter is a detailed reference of all the items and elements that make up the core JavaScript language. Every nuance of the language is covered, giving you a one-stop place to get answers to all your questions. Each entry includes version, environment support, syntax, a description, and an example, as well as many other details.

The chapter is in alphabetical order, by JavaScript objects, to provide you with quick, easy access to the major parts of the language. The methods, properties, functions, and event handlers of every object appear alphabetically after the respective parent object, using the simple dot notation that makes the language so easy to learn. For example, the sin() function is found after the Math object as Math.sin().

## Operators

### - (Subtraction)

*JavaScript 1.0+, ECMAScript 1.0+, JScript 1.0+*

*Nav2+, NES2+, IE 3+, Opera3+*

#### Syntax

```
num1 - num2
```

#### Description

The number to the right of the operator is subtracted from the number to the left of the operator. If either operand is a string, an attempt is made to convert the string to a number before performing the operation.

## Example

The code in Listing 6.1 creates a string out of the number "45". The string is converted to a number before being subtracted from the number 25.

*Listing 6.1    Using the Subtraction Operator*

```
<html>
<script language="JavaScript">
<!-- Hide

//Declare the number 45 as a string
aString = new String("45");

//Subtract 25 from 45
answer = aString - 25;
document.write("answer = (45-25)<br>");

//Answer is equal to 20
document.write("answer = ",answer);

// End Hide -->
</script>
</html>
```

# - (Unary Negation)

## *JavaScript 1.0+, ECMAScript 1.0+, JScript 1.0+*

## *Nav2+, NES2+, IE 3+, Opera3+*

## Syntax

*-num*

## Description

The unary negation operator changes the sign of *num*. When negating a variable, the contents of the variable do not change; only the value returned is negated. If the operand is a string, it is converted to a number before performing the unary negation operation.

## Example

The code in Listing 6.2 creates a string "45". The string is converted to a number before being negated.

*Listing 6.2    Using the Negation Operator*

```
<html>
<script language="JavaScript">
<!-- Hide
```

```
//Declare the number 36 as a string
aString = new String("36");

//negate the the number
answer = -aString;
document.write("answer = -aString<br>");

//Answer is equal to -36
document.write("answer = ",answer);

// End Hide -->
</script>
</html>
```

# -- (Decrement)

## *JavaScript 1.0+, ECMAScript 1.0+, JScript 1.0+*

## *Nav2+, NES2+, IE 3+, Opera3+*

### Syntax
```
--variable
variable--
```

### Description

The pre-decrement operator, defined in the first syntactical definition, decrements *variable* by 1. The new decremented value is returned by the operation.

The second syntactical definition contains the post-decrement operator. This operator is like the pre-decrement operator in that it decrements *variable* by 1. However, the original value is returned by the operation before being decremented.

In both cases, if the operand is a string, it is converted to a number before performing the operation.

### Example

Listing 6.3 demonstrates how the pre-decrement and post-decrement operators work. Notice that the variable num holds a string that is converted before performing the decrement operations. The result from executing this code is shown in Figure 6.1.

*Listing 6.3   Using the Decrement Operator*
```
<html>

<script language="JavaScript">
<!-- Hide

// Store value in variable before pre-decrement
```

*continues*

*Listing 6.3 continued*

```
document.write("<h3>Before Pre-decrement</h3>");
num = new String("807");   //num holds the string 807
document.write("num=",num,"<br>");   //807 is displayed

// Pre-decrement the value stored in num
returnValue = --num;
document.write("<h3>After Pre-decrement</h3>");
document.write("num=",num,"<br>");   //806 is displayed

//806 is displayed by returnValue
document.write("Value returned from operation is ",returnValue,"<br>");

// Post-decrement the value stored in num
returnValue = num--;
document.write("<h3>After Post-decrement</h3>");
document.write("num=",num,"<br>");     //805 is displayed

//806 is displayed by returnValue
document.write("Value returned from operation is ",returnValue,"<br>");

// End hide -->
</script>

</html>
```

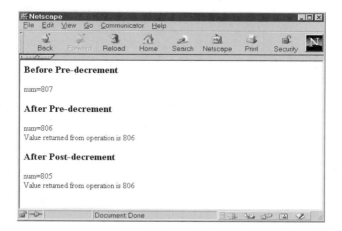

**Figure 6.1**

*The difference between pre-decrement and post-decrement.*

# ! (Logical NOT)

## *JavaScript 1.0+, ECMAScript 1.0+, JScript 1.0+*

## *Nav2+, NES2+, IE 3+, Opera3+*

## Syntax

!operand

## Description

If *operand* evaluates to true, the result of the operation is false. If the *operand* evaluates to false, the result is true. When the *operand* evaluates to a non-Boolean value, it is converted to true or false before performing the inversion.

## Example

In Listing 6.4 the character "1" is a Boolean true before inverting the value with the NOT operand. The variable theReverseTruth is assigned the Boolean false.

*Listing 6.4    Using the Logical* NOT *Operator*

```
<script language="JavaScript">
<!-- Hide

//Create a variable that contains 1
theTruth = new String("1");

//Invert the value stored in the previous variable
theReverseTruth = !theTruth;

//Output the values stored in the two variables
document.write("theTruth = ",theTruth,"<br>");
document.write("theReverseTruth = ",theReverseTruth);

// End Hide -->
</script>
```

# != (Not Equal)

## *JavaScript 1.0+, ECMAScript 1.0+, JScript 1.0+*

## *Nav2+, NES2+, IE 3+, Opera3+*

## Syntax

expression1 != expression2

## Description

The not equal operator compares the first expression to the second expression. If the expressions are not equal, true is returned from operation. If they are equal, false is returned.

JavaScript and Microsoft JScript attempt to convert the expressions to the same data type before evaluating the not equal operation using the following rules:

- `True` is converted to the number 1, and `false` is converted to zero before being compared.
- If either of the operands is `NaN`, the equality operator returns `false`.
- Null and undefined are equal.
- Null and undefined are not equal to `0` (zero), `""` , or `false`.
- If a string and a number are compared, attempt to convert the string to a number and then check for equality.
- If an object and a string are compared, attempt to convert the object to a string and then check for equality.
- If an object and a number are compared, attempt to convert the object to a number and then check for equality.
- If both operands of an equality operation are objects, the address of the two objects are checked for equality.

## CAUTION

In JavaScript 1.2, the decision was made to NOT do type-conversion on the operands of the not equal operator. JavaScript reverted back to using type-conversion with this operator in 1.3 and later.

## *Example*

In the following example, the string `"523"` is converted to a number (except in JavaScript 1.2, in which type-conversion is not performed), so that two numbers are compared. Since the left operand is equal to the right operand, the phrase `"The string 523 is EQUAL to 347"` is written to the browser window.

*Listing 6.5    Using the Not Equal Operator*

```
<script language="JavaScript">
<!-- Hide

//Before comparing this string to the number the
//string will be converted to a number.
if("523" != 523) {

  //If the two numbers are not equal then display this sentence.
  document.write("The string 523 is NOT equal to the number 523");

} else {

  //If the two numbers are equal then display this sentence.
  document.write("The string 523 is EQUAL to the number 523");
}

// End Hide -->
</script>
```

# !== (Non-Identity)

## JavaScript 1.3+, JScript 1.0+

## Nav4.06+, IE 3+

## Syntax

`expression1 !== expression2`

## Description

The non-identity operator compares the first expression to the second expression. If the value on the left is not equal to the value on the right side of the operator, `true` is returned from operation. If the values are equal, `false` is returned.

> **NOTE**
>
> No type-conversion is performed on the expressions before the comparison is made.

## Example

In Listing 6.6, the string `"8765"` is NOT converted to a number, so the two expressions are not the same type. Since the two operands are not the same type, they are not equal, so the phrase `"The string 8765 is NOT equal to 8765"` is written to the browser window.

*Listing 6.6  Using the Not-Identity Operator*

```
<script language="JavaScript">
<!-- Hide

//Compare the string to the number but do not
//convert the string to a number
if("8765" !== 8765)
{
  //If the string and number are not equal then display this sentence.
  document.write("The string 8765 is NOT equal to the number 8765");
}
else
{
  //If the string and number are equal then display this sentence.
  document.write("The string 8765 is EQUAL to the number 8765");
}

// End Hide -->
</script>
```

# % (Modulus)

## *JavaScript 1.0+, ECMAScript 1.0+, JScript 1.0+*

## *Nav2+, NES2+, IE 3+, Opera3+*

## Syntax

*num1 % num2*

## Description

The modulus operator begins like the division operator, by dividing the left value by the right; but instead of returning the normal result of division, only the remainder is returned by the operation. If either operand is a string, an attempt is made to convert the string to a number before performing the operation.

## Example

In Listing 6.7, the variable answer is assigned the value 1 because 7 is divided by the number 2 three times plus a reminder of 1. This reminder is stored in the variable answer.

*Listing 6.7    Using the Modulus Operator*

```
<script language="JavaScript">
<!-- Hide

//1 is stored in the variable answer.
answer = 7 % 2;

//Display the value in the variable answer
document.write("answer = ",answer);

// End Hide -->
</script>
```

# %= (Modulus Assignment)

## *JavaScript 1.0+, ECMAScript 1.0+, JScript 1.0+*

## *Nav2+, NES2+, IE 3+, Opera3+*

## Syntax

*variable %= value*

## Description

The modulus assignment operator divides the value stored in the left variable by the right value. The remainder is returned by the operation and stored in the variable to the left of the operator. If value is a string, an attempt is made to convert the string to a number before performing the modulus and assignment.

## Example

In Listing 6.8, the variable answer is initially assigned the value 3. The number 17 is divided by the number 3, which is stored in the variable answer—five times plus a reminder of 2. This reminder is stored in the variable answer overwriting the number 3.

*Listing 6.8    Using the Modulus Assignment Operator*

```
<script language="JavaScript">
<!-- Hide

//Initialize the variable answer with 3
answer = 3;

//The number 2 is stored in the variable answer.
answer %= 17;

//Display the value stored in the variable answer.
document.write("answer = ",answer);

// End Hide -->
</script>
```

# & (Bitwise AND)

## *JavaScript 1.0+, ECMAScript 1.0+, JScript 1.0+*

## *Nav2+, NES2+, IE 3+, Opera3+*

## Syntax

*num1* & *num2*

## Description

The bitwise AND operator looks at the integer numbers on both sides of the operator as 32-bit binary numbers. The logical AND (&&) operator individually evaluates each of the 32 bits representing the number to the left of the operator to the corresponding bit of the number to the right of the operator using the truth table shown in Table 6.1. The 32-bit binary result of the logical AND operation is converted to an integer value and returned from the bitwise AND operation.

*Table 6.1    Bitwise AND Truth Table*

| First Value | Second Value | Result |
|-------------|--------------|--------|
| true | true | true |
| true | false | false |
| false | true | false |
| false | false | false |

## Example

The code in Listing 6.9 uses the bitwise AND operator on the number 11 and 6. You see that the result of the operation is 2 in Figure 6.2.

*Listing 6.9    Using the Bitwise* AND *Operator*

```
<script language="JavaScript">
<!-- Hide

// integer = 32-bit binary representation
// 11 = 00000000000000000000000000001011
//  6 = 00000000000000000000000000000110
//  2 = 00000000000000000000000000000010

// answer is equal to 2
answer = 11 & 6;

//Display the value stored in the variable answer
document.write("11 & 6 = ",answer);

// End hide -->
</script>
```

**Figure 6.2**

*The result of using the bitwise* AND *operator on two numbers.*

# && (Logical AND)

## *JavaScript 1.0+, ECMAScript 1.0+, JScript 1.0+*

## *Nav2+, NES2+, IE 3+, Opera3+*

## *Syntax*

*expression1 && expression2*

## Description

The logical AND operator returns true if the expression to the left and the expression to the right of the operator evaluate to true. If either the left, right, or both evaluates to false, the result of the operation is false.

Be sure to note that the implementation of the logical AND operator in JavaScript is more complex than what was just mentioned. The AND operation begins by evaluating the left expression. If the left expression evaluates to false, the basic logic of the AND operator is complete, so the right expression is never evaluated. But if the left expression evaluates to true, the right expression must be evaluated to determine the final result of the AND operation. In either case, the final result returned by the AND operation is actually determined by the result of the last expression to be evaluated.

## Example

Listing 6.10 demonstrates the complications associated with the logical AND operator. In Figure 6.3, you see that the first expression evaluates to false, causing the logical AND operation to evaluate to false. Since the first expression evaluates to false, the second expression, which assigns the number 5 to the variable x, is not evaluated.

*Listing 6.10   The Complicated Logical* AND *Operator*

```
<html>

<script language="JavaScript">
<!-- Hide

//Initialize the variable x with the number 3
x = 3;

//The assignment of 5 to the variable x never occurs
//since the expression (2==x) evaluates to false in the if statement.
if((2==x) && (x=5))
{
  document.write("The && evaluated TRUE!<br>");
}
else
{
  document.write("The && evaluated FALSE!<br>");
}

// x is still equal to 3
document.write("x=",x,"<br>");

// End hide -->
</script>

</html>
```

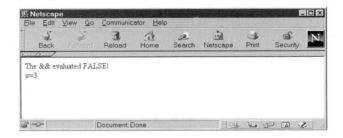

**Figure 6.3**

*Using the logical AND operator.*

# &= (Bitwise AND Assignment)

## JavaScript 1.0+, ECMAScript 1.0+, JScript 1.0+

## Nav2+, NES2+, IE 3+, Opera3+

## Syntax

```
variable &= value
```

## Description

The bitwise AND plus assignment operator looks at the integer numbers on both sides of the operator as 32-bit binary numbers. The logical AND (&&) operator individually evaluates each of the 32 bits representing the number to the left of the operator to the corresponding bit of the number to the right of the operator using the truth table shown in Table 6.2. The 32-bit binary result of the logical AND operation is converted to an integer value and stored in the variable to the left of the operator.

*Table 6.2    Bitwise AND Truth Table*

| First Value | Second Value | Result |
|-------------|--------------|--------|
| true | true | true |
| true | false | false |
| false | true | false |
| false | false | false |

## Example

In Listing 6.11, the bitwise AND plus assignment operator is used on the numbers 12 and 6 to generate a result of 4.

*Listing 6.11    Using the Bitwise AND Plus Assignment Operator*

```
<script language="JavaScript">
<!-- Hide
```

```
// integer = 32-bit binary representation
// 12 = 00000000000000000000000000001100
//  6 = 00000000000000000000000000000110
//  4 = 00000000000000000000000000000100

//Initialize the variable x with the number 6.
x = 6;

//x is now equal to 4
x &= 12;

//Display the value stored in the variable x
document.write("x = ",x);

// End Hide -->
</script>
```

# * (Multiplication)

## *JavaScript 1.0+, ECMAScript 1.0+, JScript 1.0+*

## *Nav2+, NES2+, IE 3+, Opera3+*

## Syntax

*num1 * num2*

## Description

The multiplication operator (*) multiplies the left operand by the right operand. If either of the operands is a string, an attempt is made to convert the string to a number.

## Example

In Listing 6.12 the string "5" is converted to a number before being multiplied by the number 6. The result of 30 is displayed in the browser window.

*Listing 6.12 Using the Multiplication Operator*

```
<script language="JavaScript">
<!-- Hide

//Initialize the variable aString.
aString = new String("5");

//x is now equal to 30
x = aString * 6;
document.write("x = ",x);

// End Hide -->
</script>
```

# *= (Multiplication Assignment)

## *JavaScript 1.0+, ECMAScript 1.0+, JScript 1.0+*

## *Nav2+, NES2+, IE 3+, Opera3+*

### Syntax

```
variable *= value
```

### Description

The number stored in the variable to the left of the operator is multiplied by the number to the right of the operator. The result of the multiplication is written into the variable to the left of the operand. If either of the operands is a string, it is converted to a number.

### Example

In Listing 6.13, the string "5" is converted to a number before being multiplied by the number 7. The result of the multiplication, which is 35, is stored in the variable x.

*Listing 6.13    Using the Multiplication Plus Assignment Operator*

```
<script language="JavaScript">
<!-- Hide

//Initialize the variable x with the number 7
//and the variable aString with "5"
x = 7;
aString = new String("5");

//The variable x is now equal to 35.
x *= aString;

//Display the value stored in the variable x.
document.write("x = ",x);

// End Hide -->
</script>
```

# , (Comma)

## *JavaScript 1.0+, ECMAScript 1.0+, JScript 1.0+*

## *Nav2+, IE 3+, Opera3+*

### Syntax

```
statement1, statement2, statement3
```

## Description

The comma allows multiple statements to be executed as one statement. The only value returned from this operation is the return value of the right-most statement.

## Example

In Listing 6.14, the comma is used to execute multiple assignment statements on one line. The number 3 is stored in y, and then 9 is stored in z. Since z=9 is the last statement in the group of comma-separated statements, its value is returned and stored in the variable x.

*Listing 6.14   Using the Comma to Separate Multiple Statements.*
```
<script language="JavaScript">
<!-- Hide

//Assign values to all three variables
x = (y = 3, z = 9);

//Display the values stored in all three variables.
document.write("x = ",x,"<br>y = ",y,"<br>z = ",z);

// End Hide -->
</script>
```

# / (Division)

## *JavaScript 1.0+, ECMAScript 1.0+, JScript 1.0+*

## *Nav2+, NES2+, IE 3+, Opera3+*

## Syntax

*num1 / num2*

## Description

The left number is divided by the right number. If either of the operands is a string, it is converted to a number.

## Example

In Listing 6.15, the string "168" is converted to a number before being divided by the number 14. The result of the multiplication is stored in the variable x.

*Listing 6.15   Using the Division Operator*
```
<script language="JavaScript">
<!-- Hide

//Initialize the variable aString with "168"
```

*continues*

*Listing 6.15   continued*
```
aString = new String("168");

//Create the variable x and set it equal to the number 12.
x = aString / 14;

//Display the value stored in the variable x.
document.write("x = ",x);

// End Hide -->
</script>
```

# /* */ (Multi-line Comment)

## JavaScript 1.0+, ECMAScript 1.0+, JScript 1.0+

## Nav2+, IE 3+, Opera3+

## Syntax
```
/* comments */
```

## Description

Every character that appears within the two comment tags is ignored by the JavaScript interpreter. Placing the tags on different lines allows comments to span multiple lines. Be careful not to nest comment tags within comment tags, as this will lead to errors.

## Example

Listing 6.16 demonstrates the use of multiple-line comments in JavaScript code.

*Listing 6.16   Using the Multi-Line Comments*
```
<script language="JavaScript">
<!-- Hide

document.write("<h2>Multi-line Comments</h2>");

/* Even though this sentences spans multiple lines it is treated
as a comment because it begins and ends with comment tags.
document.write("Not displayed!");
Notice that even the JavaScript statement above is treated as a comment*/

// End Hide -->
</script>
```

# // (Comment)

## *JavaScript 1.0+, ECMAScript 1.0+, JScript 1.0+*

## *Nav2+, IE 3+, Opera3+*

## Syntax

```
// comment
```

## Description

Every character that appears after this tag and on the same line as the tag is ignored by the JavaScript interpreter.

## Example

Listing 6.17 demonstrates the use of the single line comment in JavaScript code.

*Listing 6.17    Using Single Line Comments*

```
<script language="JavaScript">
<!-- Hide

document.write("<h2>Single Line Comments</h2>");

//Everything on this line is considered a comment.
//document.write("Not Displayed!");

// End Hide -->
</script>
```

# /= (Division Assignment)

## *JavaScript 1.0+, ECMAScript 1.0+, JScript 1.0+*

## *Nav2+, NES2+, IE 3+, Opera3+*

## Syntax

```
variable /= value
```

## Description

The number stored in the variable to the left of the operator is divided by the number on the right. The result of the division overwrites the value in the variable to the left of the operator. If either of the operands is a string, it is converted to a number.

## Example

In Listing 6.18, the string "8" is converted to a number before being divided into the number 7. The result of the division, which is 4, is stored in the variable x.

*Listing 6.18    Using the Division and Assignment Operator*

```
<script language="JavaScript">
<!-- Hide

//Initialize the the variables x and aString
x = 32;
aString = new String("8");

//The variable x is now equal to the number 4.
x /= aString;

//Display the value stored in the variable x.
document.write("x = ",x);

// End Hide -->
</script>
```

# ?: (Conditional)

## JavaScript 1.0+, ECMAScript 1.0+, JScript 1.0+

## Nav2+, NES2+, IE 3+, Opera3+

### Syntax

*expression ? value1 : value2*

### Description

An expression that evaluates to a Boolean is always placed to the left of the question mark (?). If the expression evaluates to true, *value1* is returned from the operation. If the expression evaluates to false, *value2* is returned.

The same functionality of the conditional operator can be achieved with an if...else statement.

### Example

In Listing 6.19, the conditional operator is shown along with a similar standard if statement. Both the conditional operator and the if statement have the same result, except that the conditional operator takes up less space. Figure 6.4 shows the result of using the conditional operator and the if statement.

*Listing 6.19    The Conditional Operator and* if *Statement Are Compared*

```
<html>

<script language="JavaScript">
<!-- Hide

// Set the cooking status flag to "YES"
doneCooking = "YES"
```

```
//Create 2 empty variables
var message1;
var message2;

//Standard if statement
if (doneCooking == "YES")
  message1 = "The hamburgers are done!";
else
  message1 = "The hamburgers are still cooking.";

//Same statement using conditional operator
message2 = (doneCooking == "YES") ?
  "The hotdogs are done!" :
  "The hotdogs are still cooking.";

// Print the message to the screen.  Notice both messages are the same!
document.write("The if statement returns: ",message1,"<br>");
document.write("The conditional operator returns: ",message2);

// End hide -->
</script>

</html>
```

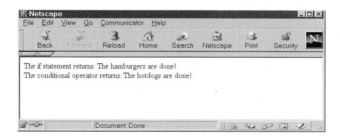

**Figure 6.4**

*The same result of using the conditional operator can be accomplished with the* if *statement.*

## ^ (Bitwise Exclusive OR)

### *JavaScript 1.0+, ECMAScript 1.0+, JScript 1.0+*

### *Nav2+, NES2+, IE 3+, Opera3+*

### *Syntax*

*num1 ^ num2*

## Description

The bitwise exclusive OR (XOR) operator looks at the integer numbers on both sides of the operator as 32-bit binary numbers. The bitwise exclusive OR uses a special version of the logical OR operator, called exclusive OR, to evaluate each individual bit of a binary number.

Each of the 32 bits representing the number to the left of the operator is evaluated to the corresponding bit of the number to the right of the operator using the exclusive OR truth table shown in Table 6.3. The 32-bit binary result of the operation is converted to an integer value and returned.

**Table 6.3   Bitwise Exclusive OR Truth Table**

| First Value | Second Value | Result |
|---|---|---|
| true | true | false |
| true | false | true |
| false | true | true |
| false | false | false |

## Example

The code in Listing 6.20 uses the bitwise exclusive OR operator on the numbers 6 and 3. The result of executing the code is the number 5, which is written to the browser window.

*Listing 6.20   Using the Bitwise Exclusive OR Operator*

```
<html>

<script language="JavaScript">
<!-- Hide

// integer = 32-bit binary representation
// 6 = 00000000000000000000000000000110
// 3 = 00000000000000000000000000000011
// 5 = 00000000000000000000000000000101

//Display the number 5 in the browser.
document.write("6 ^ 3 = ", (6 ^ 3) );

// End hide -->
</script>

</html>
```

# ^= (Bitwise Exclusive OR Assignment)

## *JavaScript 1.0+, ECMAScript 1.0+, JScript 1.0+*

## *Nav2+, NES2+, IE 3+, Opera3+*

## Syntax

```
variable ^= value
```

## Description

The bitwise exclusive OR operator looks at the integer numbers on both sides of the operator as 32-bit binary numbers. The bitwise exclusive OR uses a special version of the logical OR operator, called exclusive OR, to evaluate each individual bit of a binary number.

Each of the 32 bits representing the number to the left of the operator is evaluated to the corresponding bit of the number to the right of the operator using the exclusive OR truth table shown in Table 6.4. The 32-bit binary result of the operation is converted to an integer value and stored in the variable to the left of the operator.

**Table 6.4    Bitwise Exclusive OR Truth Table**

| First Value | Second Value | Result |
|-------------|--------------|--------|
| true        | true         | false  |
| true        | false        | true   |
| false       | true         | true   |
| false       | false        | false  |

## Example

Listing 6.21 uses the bitwise exclusive OR plus assignment operator on the numbers 12 and 6 to generate the result 4.

*Listing 6.21    Using Bitwise Exclusive OR Plus Assignment Operator*

```
<script language="JavaScript">
<!-- Hide

// integer = 32-bit binary representation
// 10 = 00000000000000000000000000001010
//  6 = 00000000000000000000000000000110
// 12 = 00000000000000000000000000001100

//Initialize the variable x with the number 10
x = 10;

//The variable x is now equal to 12.
```

*continues*

*Listing 6.21    continued*
```
x ^= 6;

//Display the value stored in the variable x
document.write("x = ",x);

// End Hide -->
</script>
```

# | (Bitwise OR)

## *JavaScript 1.0+, ECMAScript 1.0+, JScript 1.0+*

## *Nav2+, NES2+, IE 3+, Opera3+*

## *Syntax*

*num1 ¦ num2*

## Description

The bitwise OR operator looks at the integer numbers on both sides of the operator as 32-bit binary numbers. The truth table of the logical OR (¦¦) operator, shown in Table 6.5, is used to individually evaluate each of the 32 bits representing the number to the left of the operator to the corresponding bit of the number to the right of the operator. The 32-bit binary result of bitwise OR operation is converted to an integer value and returned from the operation.

**Table 6.5    Bitwise Exclusive OR Truth Table**

| First Value | Second Value | Result |
|---|---|---|
| true | true | true |
| true | false | true |
| false | true | true |
| false | false | false |

## Example

The code in Listing 6.22 uses the bitwise OR operator on the numbers 9 and 5. Executing the code displays the number 13 in the browser window.

*Listing 6.22    Using the Bitwise Exclusive OR Operator*
```
<html>

<script language="JavaScript">
<!-- Hide

// integer = 32-bit binary representation
//   9 = 00000000000000000000000000001001
//   5 = 00000000000000000000000000000101
```

```
// 13 = 00000000000000000000000000001101
```

Display the number 13 in the browser window.
```
document.write("9 ¦ 5 = ", (9 ¦ 5) );
```

```
// End hide -->
</script>
```

```
</html>
```

# || (Logical OR)

## *JavaScript 1.0+, ECMAScript 1.0+, JScript 1.0+*

## *Nav2+, NES2+, IE 3+, Opera3+*

### *Syntax*

*expression1* ¦¦ *expression2*

### *Description*

The logical OR operator returns true if the left operand, right operand, or both operands evaluates to true. If both the operands evaluate to false, the result of the operation is false.

The implementation of the logical OR operator in JavaScript and JScript is more complex than what was just mentioned. The OR operation begins by evaluating the left operand. If the left operand evaluates to true, the basic logic of the OR operator is complete, so the right operand is never evaluated. But if the left operand evaluates false, the right operand must be evaluated to determine the final result of the OR operation. In either case, the final result returned by the OR operation is actually the result of the last operand to be evaluated.

### *Example*

Listing 6.23 demonstrates the complications associated with the logical OR operator. In Figure 6.5, you see that the first expression evaluates to true, causing the logical OR operation to evaluate to true. Because the first expression evaluates to true, the second expression, which assigns the number 7 to the variable x, is not evaluated.

*Listing 6.23    The Complicated Logical* OR *Operator*
```
<html>

<script language="JavaScript">
<!-- Hide

//Initialize the variable x with the number 8.
```

*continues*

*Listing 6.23    continued*

```
x = 8;

//The assignment of 7 to the variable x never occurs
//since the first expression (8==x) evaluates to true.
if((8==x) || (x=7))
{
  document.write("The || evaluated TRUE!<br>");
}
else
{
  document.write("The || evaluated FALSE!<br>");
}

// x is equal to 8
document.write("x=",x,"<br>");

// End hide -->
</script>

</html>
```

**Figure 6.5**

*Using the logical OR operator.*

# |= (Bitwise OR Assignment)

## *JavaScript 1.0+, ECMAScript 1.0+, JScript 1.0+*

## *Nav2+, NES2+, IE 3+, Opera3+*

## *Syntax*

*variable |= value*

## *Description*

The bitwise OR operator looks at the integer numbers on both sides of the operator as 32-bit binary numbers. The logical OR (||) operator individually evaluates each of the

32 bits representing the number to the left of the operator to the corresponding bit of the number to the right of the operator. The 32-bit binary result of the logical OR operation is converted to an integer value and stored in the variable to the left of the operator.

## Example

Listing 6.24 uses the bitwise OR plus assignment operator on the numbers 2 and 5 to generate the number 7.

*Listing 6.24    Using the Bitwise OR and Assignment Operator*

```
<script language="JavaScript">
<!-- Hide

// integer = 32-bit binary representation
// 2 = 00000000000000000000000000000011
// 5 = 00000000000000000000000000000101
// 7 = 00000000000000000000000000000111

//Initialize the variable x with the number 2.
x = 2;

//The variable x now contains the number 7.
x |= 5;

//Display the value stored in the variable x.
document.write("x = ",x);

// End Hide -->
</script>
```

# ~ (Bitwise NOT)

## *JavaScript 1.0+, ECMAScript 1.0+, JScript 1.0+*

## *Nav2+, NES2+, IE 3+, Opera3+*

## Syntax

*~operand*

## Description

The bitwise NOT operator begins by looking at the number to the right of the operator as a 32-bit binary number. Each bit of the given number is reversed so that all ones become zeros and all zeros become ones. The 32-bit binary result is converted to an integer value and returned from the bitwise NOT operation.

The result of inverting a number can be very confusing due to the way signed numbers are represented. Just remember that applying the bitwise NOT operator to a positive number will return the original number with the sign changed, minus one.

## Example

The code in Listing 6.25 demonstrates the use of the bitwise NOT operator. Notice that the result of the operation, shown in Figure 6.6, is -3, which is the original number (2) with the sign reversed (−2) minus 1.

*Listing 6.25   The Complicated Bitwise NOT Operator*

```
<html>

<script language="JavaScript">
<!-- Hide

// integer = 32-bit binary representation
//   2 = 00000000000000000000000000000010
// -3 = 11111111111111111111111111111101
// -2 = 11111111111111111111111111111110
// -1 = 11111111111111111111111111111111

//Display the result of the Bitwise NOT Operator
document.write("~2 = ",(~2));   //Displays -3

// End hide -->
</script>

</html>
```

**Figure 6.6**

*Using the Bitwise NOT operator.*

# + (Addition)

## *JavaScript 1.0+, ECMAScript 1.0+, JScript 1.0+*

## *Nav2+, NES2+, IE 3+, Opera3+*

## Syntax

*operand1 + operand2*

## Description

The addition operator provides two types of functionality depending on the data type of the operands. The first type of functionality is simple addition, in which the value to the left of the addition operator is added to the value on the right. If either of the operands are not number strings, they will be converted to numbers.

The second type of functionality provided by the addition operator is string concatenation. If either of the operands is a string, string concatenation is performed by first converting any non-string operand to a string. String concatenation is then performed by appending the string to the right of the operator to the end of the string located to the left of the operator.

## Example

Listing 6.26 demonstrates the addition of numbers as well as string concatenation. Compare the Listing 6.26 to the result of executing the code as seen in Figure 6.7 to understand how addition is handled with various variable types.

*Listing 6.26    Addition of Numbers and String Concatenation*

```
<html>

<script language="JavaScript">
<!-- Hide

//Initialize the variable aString
aString = new String("67");

//answerNum contains the number 90
answerNum = 67 + 23;

//answerStr contains the string "6723"
answerStr = aString + 23;

//Print the result to the screen
document.write("answerNum =",answerNum,"<br>");   //Displays 90
document.write("answerStr =",answerStr);          //Displays 6723

// End hide -->
</script>

</html>
```

**Figure 6.7**

*Using the addition operator to add numbers and concatenate strings.*

## ++ *(Increment)*

## *JavaScript 1.0+, ECMAScript 1.0+, JScript 1.0+*

## *Nav2+, NES2+, IE 3+, Opera3+*

### Syntax

```
++variable       (Pre-Increment)
variable++       (Post-Increment)
```

### Description

The pre-increment operator increments `variable` by 1. The new incremented value is returned by the operation.

The post-increment operator is like the pre-increment operator in that it increments `variable` by 1. However, the original value is returned by the operation before being incremented.

In both cases, if the operand is a string, it is converted to a number before performing the operation.

### Example

Listing 6.27 demonstrates how the pre-increment and post-increment operators work. Notice that the variable num holds a string that is converted before performing the increment operations. The result from executing this code is shown in Figure 6.8.

*Listing 6.27    Using the   Increment Operator*

```html
<html>

<script language="JavaScript">
<!-- Hide

/* Store value in variable before pre-increment */
```

```
document.write("<h3>Before Pre-increment</h3>");
num = new String("807");    //num holds the string 807
document.write("num=",num,"<br>");    //807 is displayed

/* Pre-increment the value stored in num */
returnValue = ++num;
document.write("<h3>After Pre-increment</h3>");
document.write("num=",num,"<br>");    //808 is displayed

//808 is displayed by returnValue
document.write("Value returned from operation is ",returnValue,"<br>");

/* Post-increment the value stored in num */
returnValue = num++;
document.write("<h3>After Post-increment</h3>");
document.write("num=",num,"<br>");    //809 is displayed

//808 is displayed by returnValue
document.write("Value returned from operation is ",returnValue,"<br>");

// End hide -->
</script>

</html>
```

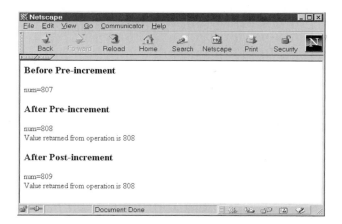

**Figure 6.8**

*The difference between pre-increment and post-increment.*

# += (Addition Assignment)

*JavaScript 1.0+, ECMAScript 1.0+, JScript 1.0+*

*Nav2+, NES2+, IE 3+, Opera3+*

## Syntax

```
variable += value
```

## Description

The addition assignment operator provides two types of functionality depending on the data type of the operands. The first type of functionality is simple addition in which the value stored in the variable to the right of the addition assignment operator is added to the value on the left. The result of the addition overwrites the value stored in the variable to the left of the operator. If either of the operands is not a number or string, it will be converted to a number.

The second type of functionality provided by the addition assignment operator is string concatenation. If either of the operands is a string, string concatenation is performed by first converting any non-string operand to a string. String concatenation is then performed by appending the string to the right of the operator to the end of the string located to the left of the operator. The new string is stored in the variable to the left of the operator.

## Example

In Listing 6.28, the addition assignment operator is used to add two numbers together as well as concatenate two strings.

*Listing 6.28    Using the Addition and Assignment Operator*

```
<script language="JavaScript">
<!-- Hide

//Initialize the variables num and str.
num = 42;
str = new String("42");

//Use the addition/assignment operator
num += 8;    //num contains the number 50
str += 8;    //str contains the string "428"

//Display the results of the addition/assignment operator
document.write("num = ",num,"<br>str = ",str);

// End Hide -->
</script>
```

# < (Less Than)

## *JavaScript 1.0+, ECMAScript 1.0+, JScript 1.0+*

## *Nav2+, NES2+, IE 3+, Opera3+*

## Syntax

num1 < num2

## Description

The less than operator compares the value to the left of the operator to the value on the right. If the value on the left is less than the value on the right, `true` is returned from the operation. If the value to the left of the operator is greater than or equal to the value on the right, `false` is returned. If either of the operands is not a number or string, it is converted to numbers before performing the comparison.

## Example

In Listing 6.29, the string `"45"` is converted to a number before performing the comparison. Because the number 45 is less than the number 68, the phrase `"45 is less than 68"` is returned.

*Listing 6.29    Using Less Than Operator*

```
<script language="JavaScript">
<!-- Hide

//Initialize the variable str with "45"
str = new String("45");

//Compare the variable to the number 68
if(str < 68)
  document.write("45 is less than 68");
else
  document.write("Returned FALSE!");

// End Hide -->
</script>
```

# << (Shift Left)

## *JavaScript 1.0+, ECMAScript 1.0+, JScript 1.0+*

## *Nav2+, NES2+, IE 3+, Opera3+*

## Syntax

num1 << num2

## Description

The shift left operator looks at the integer to the left of the operator as a 32-bit binary number. The number of positions specified by *num2* shifts all the bits of num1 to the left. As the bits are shifted to the left, zeros are filled in on the right. Because the number can only be 32-bits long, the extra bits on the left are lost. The 32-bit binary result of the shifting operation is converted to an integer value and returned from the shift left operation.

### NOTE

The result generated from the shift left operator can be quickly calculated by multiplying the number by 2 raised to the *x* power, where *x* is the number of positions shifted.

## Example

Listing 6.30 shifts the bits that make up the number 2 to the left two positions, which results in the number 8, as shown in Figure 6.9.

*Listing 6.30    Using the Shift Left Operator*

```
<html>

<script language="JavaScript">
<!-- Hide

// integer = 32-bit binary representation
// 2 = 00000000000000000000000000000010
// 8 = 00000000000000000000000000001000

//Assign the number 8 to the variable x
x = 2 << 2;

//Display the the value stored in the variable x.
document.write("2 << 2 = ",x);

// End hide -->
</script>

</html>
```

**Figure 6.9**

*Using the shift left operator.*

# <<= (Shift Left Assignment)

## *JavaScript 1.0+, ECMAScript 1.0+, JScript 1.0+*

## *Nav2+, NES2+, IE 3+, Opera3+*

### Syntax

```
variable <<= num
```

### Description

The shift left operator looks at the integer stored in the variable to the left of the operator as a 32-bit binary number. All the bits in this number are shifted to the left by the number of positions specified by the integer to the right of the operator. As the bits are shifted to the left, zeros are filled in on the right. Because the number can only be 32-bits long, the extra bits on the left are lost. The 32-bit binary result of shifting operation is converted to an integer value and stored in the variable to the left of the operator.

### Example

In Listing 6.31, the 32-bit binary version of the number 3, which is stored in the variable x, is shifted two positions to the left. The result of this operation, the number 12, is stored in the variable x.

*Listing 6.31    Using the Shift Left plus Assignment Operator*
```
<script language="JavaScript">
<!-- Hide

// integer = 32-bit binary representation
//   3 = 00000000000000000000000000000011
//  12 = 00000000000000000000000000001100

//Initialize the variable x with the number 3
```

*continues*

*Listing 6.31    continued*
```
x = 3;

//The variable x is now equal to the number 12
x <<= 2;

//Display the value stored in the variable x.
document.write("x = ",x);

// End Hide -->
</script>
```

# <= (Less Than or Equal)

## *JavaScript 1.0+, ECMAScript 1.0+, JScript 1.0+*

## *Nav2+, NES2+, IE 3+, Opera3+*

## Syntax

*num1 <= num2*

## Description

The less than or equal operator compares the number to the left of the operator to the number on the right. If the number on the left is less than or equal to the number on the right, true is returned from operation. If the number to the left of the operator is greater than the number on the right, false is returned.

## Example

In Listing 6.32, the string "34" would be converted to a number before performing the comparison. Because the number 34 is less than the number 77, the phrase "34 is less than or equal to 77" would be returned.

*Listing 6.32    Using the Less Than or Equal Operator*
```
<script language="JavaScript">
<!-- Hide

//Initialize the variable str to "34"
str = new String("34");

//Compare the value stored in the variable to the number 77.
if(str <= 77)
  document.write("34 is less than or equal to 77");
else
  document.write("Returned FALSE!");

// End Hide -->
</script>
```

# = (Assignment)

## *JavaScript 1.0+, ECMAScript 1.0+, JScript 1.0+*

## *Nav2+, NES2+, IE 3+, Opera3+*

## Syntax
```
variable = value
```

## Description
The value to the right of the operator is stored in the variable to the left of the operator.

## Example
In Listing 6.33, the assignment operator is used to assign various types of values to variables.

Listing 6.33    *Using the Assignment Operator*
```
<script language="JavaScript">
<!-- Hide

//Number
x = 456;                  //x contains a number
document.write("x is a ",typeof x,"<br>");

//String
y = new String("Hello")   //y contains a String
document.write("y is a ",typeof y,"<br>");

//Boolean
z = true;                 //z contains a Boolean
document.write("z is a ",typeof z);

// End Hide -->
</script>
```

# -= (Subtraction Assignment)

## *JavaScript 1.0+, ECMAScript 1.0+, JScript 1.0+*

## *Nav2+, NES2+, IE 3+, Opera3+*

## Syntax
```
variable -= value
```

## Description
The number to the right of the operator is subtracted from number stored in the variable to the left of the operator. The result of the operation overwrites the value stored

in the variable to the left of the operator. If either operand is a string, an attempt is made to convert the string to a number before performing the subtraction.

## Example

In Listing 6.34, the string `"878"` is converted to a number before the subtraction operation begins. The number 55 is subtracted from 878 and the result, 823, is stored in the variable `answer`.

*Listing 6.34    Using the Assignment Operator*

```
<script language="JavaScript">
<!-- Hide

//Initialize the variable aString with "878"
aString = new String("878");

//Assign the number 823 to the variable answer
answer -= 55;

//Display the values stored in the variable answer.
document.write("answer = ",answer);

// End Hide -->
</script>
```

# == (Equal)

## *JavaScript 1.0+, ECMAScript 1.0+, JScript 1.0+*

## *Nav2+, NES2+, IE 3+, Opera3+*

## Syntax

```
expression1 == expression2
```

## Description

The equal operator compares the value to the left of the operator to the value to the right of the operator. If the values are equal, `true` is returned from the operation. If the values are not equal, `false` is returned from the operation.

JavaScript attempts to convert the operands to the same data type before comparing the values for all versions of JavaScript except 1.2. JavaScript adheres to the following rules when performing type-conversion:

- `True` is converted to the number 1, and `false` is converted to zero before being compared.
- If either of the operands is `NaN`, the equality operator returns `false`.
- Null and undefined are equal.
- Null and undefined are not equal to `0` (zero), `""` , or `false`.

- If a string and a number are compared, attempt to convert the string to a number and then check for equality.
- If an object and a string are compared, attempt to convert the object to a string and then check for equality.
- If an object and a number are compared, attempt to convert the object to a number and then check for equality.
- If both operands of an equality operation are objects, the address of the two objects are check for equality.

## CAUTION

In JavaScript 1.2, the decision was made to NOT do type-conversion on the operands of the not equal operator. JavaScript reverted back to using type-conversion with this operator in 1.3 and later.

### Example

In Listing 6.35, the string `"749"` is converted to a number (except in JavaScript 1.2, in which type-conversion is not performed) so that two numbers are compared. Because the left operand is equal to the right operand, the phrase `"The string 749 is EQUAL to 749"` is written to the browser window.

*Listing 6.35   Using the Equal Operator*

```
<script language="JavaScript">
<!-- Hide

//The string is converted to a number before performing the comparison.
if("749" == 749)
{
  document.write("The string 749 is EQUAL to the number 749");
}
else
{
  document.write("The string 749 is NOT equal to the number 749");
}

// End Hide -->
</script>
```

# === (Identity)

## JavaScript 1.3+, JScript 1.0+

## Nav4.06+, IE 3+

## Syntax

*expression1 === expression2*

## Description

The identity operator compares the first operand to the second operand. If the value on the left is equal to the value on the right side of the operator, `true` is returned from operation. If the values are not equal, `false` is returned.

> **NOTE**
>
> No type-conversion is performed on the operands before the comparison is made.

## Example

In Listing 6.36, the string `"326"` is NOT converted to a number, so the two operands are not the same type. Because the two operands are not the same type, they are not equal, so the phrase `"The string 326 is NOT equal to 326"` is written to the browser window.

*Listing 6.36    Using the Identity Operator*

```
<script language="JavaScript">
<!-- Hide

//A string is compared to a number
if("326" === 326)
{
   document.write("The string 326 is NOT equal to the number 326");
}
else
{
   document.write("The string 326 is EQUAL to the number 326");
}
// End Hide -->
</script>
```

# > (Greater Than)

## *JavaScript 1.0+, ECMAScript 1.0+, JScript 1.0+*

## *Nav2+, NES2+, IE 3+, Opera3+*

## Syntax

*num1 > num2*

## Description

The greater than operator compares the value to the left of the operator to the value on the right. If the value on the left is greater than the value on the right, `true` is returned from the operation. If the value to the left of the operator is less than or equal to the value on the right, `false` is returned. If either of the operands is not a number, it is converted to a number before performing the comparison.

## Example

In Listing 6.37, the string "112" would be converted to a number before performing the comparison. Because the number 112 is greater than the number 23, the phrase "112 is greater than 23" would be returned.

*Listing 6.37    Using the Greater Than Operator*

```
<script language="JavaScript">
<!-- Hide

//Initialize the variable str with the string "112"
str = new String("112");

//Compare the value in the variable to a number
if(str > 68)
  document.write("112 is greater than 23");
else
  document.write("Returned FALSE!");

// End Hide -->
</script>
```

# >= (Greater Than or Equal)

## *JavaScript 1.0+, ECMAScript 1.0+, JScript 1.0+*

## *Nav2+, NES2+ IE 3+, Opera3+*

## Syntax

*variable >= value*

## Description

The greater than or equal operator compares the number to the left of the operator to the number on the right. If the number on the left is greater than or equal to the number on the right, true is returned from operation. If the number to the left of the operator is less than the number on the right, false is returned.

## Example

In Listing 6.38, the string "95" would be converted to a number before performing the comparison. Because the number 95 is greater than the number 44, the phrase "95 is greater than or equal to 44" would be returned.

*Listing 6.38    Using the Greater Than Or Equal Operator*

```
<script language="JavaScript">
<!-- Hide

//Initialize the variable str
```

*continues*

*Listing 6.38    continued*
```
str = new String("95");

//Compare the value stored in the variable to the number 44
if(str >= 44)
  document.write("95 is greater than or equal to 44");
else
  document.write("Returned FALSE!");

// End Hide -->
</script>
```

# >> (Shift Right with Sign)

## *JavaScript 1.0+, ECMAScript 1.0+, JScript 1.0+*

## *Nav2+, NES2+, IE 3+, Opera3+*

## Syntax

*num1 >> num2*

## Description

The shift right with sign operator looks at the integer to the left of the operator, *num1*, as a 32-bit binary number. All the bits in this number are shifted to the right by the number of positions specified by *num2*. As the bits are shifted to the right, either ones or zeros are filled in on the left. If the original number is positive, zeros are added to the left side of the binary number. On the other hand, if the original number is negative, ones are used. Because the result can only be 32-bits long, the extra bits on the right are lost. The 32-bit binary result of shifting operation is converted to an integer value and returned from the shift right with sign operation.

**NOTE**

The result generated from the shift right with sign operator can be quickly calculated by dividing the number by 2 raised to the $x$ power, where $x$ is the number of positions shifted. Discard the remainder.

## Example

Listing 6.39 shifts the bits that make up the number 14 to the right two positions, which results in the number 3. The number -2 results from shifting the bits that make up the number -4 one position to the right. The result of executing the code is shown in Figure 6.10.

*Listing 6.39    Using the Shift Right with Sign Operator*
```
<html>

<script language="JavaScript">
```

```
<!-- Hide

// integer = 32-bit binary representation
// 14 = 00000000000000000000000000001110
//  3 = 00000000000000000000000000000011

//The number 3 is assigned to the variable x
x = 14 >> 2;

//Display the value stored in the variable.
document.write("14 >> 2 = ",x);

//--------------------------------------
document.write("<br>");

// integer = 32-bit binary representation
// -4 = 11111111111111111111111111111100
// -2 = 11111111111111111111111111111110

//The number -2 is stored in the variable y
y = -4 >> 1;    //y is equal to -2

//Display the value stored in the variable y
document.write("-4 >> 2 = ",y);

// End hide -->
</script>

</html>
```

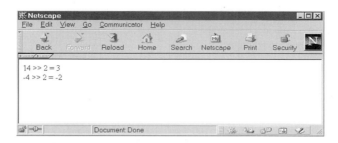

**Figure 6.10**

*Using the shift right with sign operator.*

# >>= (Shift Right with Sign Assignment)

## *JavaScript 1.0+, ECMAScript 1.0+, JScript 1.0+*

## *Nav2+, NES2+, IE 3+, Opera3+*

## Syntax

```
variable >>= value
```

## Description

The shift right with sign and assignment operator looks at the integer to the left of the operator as a 32-bit binary number. All the bits in this number are shifted to the right by the number of positions specified by the integer to the right of the operator. As the bits are shifted to the right, either ones or zeros are filled in on the left. If the original number is positive, zeros are added to the left side of the binary number. On the other hand, if the original number is negative, ones are used. Because the result can only be 32-bits long, the extra bits on the right are lost. The 32-bit binary result of shifting operation is converted to an integer value and stored in the variable to the left of the operator.

## Example

In Listing 6.40, the 32-bit binary version of the number 15, which is stored in the variable x, is shifted one position to the right. The result of this operation, the number 7, is stored in the variable x.

*Listing 6.40    Using the Shift Right with Sign and Assignment Operator*

```
<script language="JavaScript">
<!-- Hide

// integer = 32-bit binary representation
// 15 = 00000000000000000000000000001111
//  7 = 00000000000000000000000000000111

//Initialize the variable x with the number 15
x = 15;

//The variable x is now equal to 7.
x >>= 1;

//Display the values stored in the variable x.
document.write("x = ",x);

// End Hide -->
</script>
```

# >>> (Shift Right Zero Fill)

## JavaScript 1.0+, ECMAScript 1.0+, JScript 1.0+

## Nav2+, NES2+, IE 3+, Opera3+

## Syntax

num1 >>> num2

## Description

The shift right zero fill operator looks at the integer to the left of the operator as a 32-bit binary number. All the bits in this number are shifted to the right by the number of positions specified by the integer to the right of the operator. As the bits are shifted to the right, zeros are filled in on the left, regardless of the sign of the original integer. Because the result can only be 32-bits long, the extra bits on the right are lost. The 32-bit binary result of this shifting operation is converted to an integer value and returned from the shift right zero fill operation.

## Example

Listing 6.41 shifts the bits that make up the number 13 to the right one position, which results in the number 6. The number 1073741822 results from shifting the bits that make up the number –8 two positions to the right. Figure 6.11 displays the results of executing the code.

*Listing 6.41   Using the Shift Right Zero Fill Operator*

```
<html>

<script language="JavaScript">
<!-- Hide

// integer = 32-bit binary representation
// 13 = 00000000000000000000000000001101
//  6 = 00000000000000000000000000000110

//Asssign the number 6 to the variable x
x = 13 >>> 1;

//Display the value stored in the variable x
document.write("13 >>> 1 = ",x);

//-------------------------------------
document.write("<br>");

// integer = 32-bit binary representation
//      -8 = 11111111111111111111111111111000
```

*continues*

*Listing 6.41    continued*

```
// 1073741822 = 00111111111111111111111111111110

//Assign the number 1073741822 to the variable y
y = -8 >>> 2;

//Display the value stored in the variable y
document.write("-8 >>> 2 = ",y);

// End hide -->
</script>

</html>
```

**Figure 6.11**

*Using the shift right zero fill operator.*

# >>>= (Shift Right Zero Fill Assignment)

## *JavaScript 1.0+, ECMAScript 1.0+, JScript 1.0+*

## *Nav2+, NES2+, IE 3+*

## *Syntax*

```
variable >>>= value
```

## *Description*

The shift right zero fill with assignment operator looks at the integer to the left of the operator as a 32-bit binary number. All the bits in this number are shifted to the right by the number of positions specified by the integer to the right of the operator. As the bits are shifted to the right, zeros are filled in on the left, regardless of the sign of the original integer. Because the result can only be 32-bits long, the extra bits on the right are lost. The 32-bit binary result of this shifting operation is converted to an integer value and stored in the variable to the left of the operator.

## Example

In Listing 6.42, the 32-bit binary version of the number –6, which is stored in the variable x, is shifted one position to the right. The result of this operation, the number 1073741822, is stored in the variable x.

*Listing 6.42    Using the Shift Right Zero Fill with Assignment Operator*

```
<script language="JavaScript">
<!-- Hide

// integer = 32-bit binary representation
//          -6 = 11111111111111111111111111111010
// 1073741822 = 00111111111111111111111111111110

//Initialize the variable x with the number -6.
x = -6;

//The variable x now contains the number 1073741822
x >>>= 2;

//Display the value stored in the variable x.
document.write("x = ",x);

// End Hide -->
</script>
```

# abstract

## JavaScript 1.2+

## NES3+, Nav4+

## Syntax

```
Reserved Keyword
```

## Description

The abstract keyword has not been implemented in JavaScript to date, but has been reserved for future use.

## Example

This keyword has not been implemented, therefore no example is provided.

# arguments

## *JavaScript 1.1+, ECMAScript 1.0+*

## *Nav3+*

## *Syntax*

```
arguments
arguments[index]
```

## *Description*

The `Arguments` object is an array that contains all the arguments passed into the currently executing function as well as a few other useful properties. This object is automatically created and initialized when a function is invoked and goes out of scope as soon as the code function finishes executing. To access arguments passed into a function, simply use array brackets to specify an *index*. Table 6.6 lists the properties associated with `Argument` object.

## NOTE

To use the `Argument` object, you do not specify the function using dot notation as you might expect. This is because this object is different from the `Function.arguments[]` array associated with a `Function` object. Using this `Argument` object gives you the ability to access the arguments of functions that have no name.

**Table 6.6   *Properties Associated with the Arguments Object***

| Property | Description |
| --- | --- |
| callee | Contains the function that is currently executing |
| caller | Contains the `Arguments` object of the calling function |
| length | The length of the arguments array |

## *Example*

In Listing 6.43, a function is created to display a individual's favorite food in an alert box. The function is called when the buttons are pressed. The arguments passed to this function are accessed within the function with the `Arguments` object array brackets.

*Listing 6.43   Using the* Arguments *Object to Display People's Favorite Foods*

```
<html>
Select a person's name to discover their favorite food!

<form>
<input type="button"
    value="Meredith"
    OnClick=displayFood(this,"pizza")>
<input type="button"
```

```
        value="Allison"
        OnClick=displayFood(this,"beans")>
<input type="button"
        value="BayLeigh"
        OnClick=displayFood(this,"carrots")>
<input type="button"
        value="Michael"
        OnClick=displayFood(this,"corn")>
<input type="button"
        value="Rob"
        OnClick=displayFood(this,"hotdogs")>
</form>

<script language="JavaScript">
<!-- Hide

//Create a function that displays a person's favorite food
function displayFood()
{
  //Create a string that contains the name of the person
  var aString = arguments[0].value;
  aString += "'s favorite food is ";

  //Add the favorite food to the end of the string
  aString += arguments[1];

  //Display the string in an alert box
  alert(aString);
}

//Hide End -->
</script>
</html>
```

# arguments.callee

## *JavaScript 1.2+, ECMAScript 1.0+*

## *Nav4+*

## *Syntax*

```
arguments.callee
```

## *Description*

The callee property of the Arguments object contains the function that is currently
executing. This is useful if the function has no name.

## Example

In Listing 6.44, a function is created to display a individual's favorite food in an alert box. The function is called when the buttons are clicked. The code that makes up the executing function is displayed using the `callee` property.

*Listing 6.44    Using the* `callee` *Property of the* `Arguments` *Object*

```
<html>
Learn what functions are used when you press the buttons
below that represent a person's favorite food!

<form>
<input type="button"
       value="Meredith"
       OnClick=displayFood(this,"pizza")>
<input type="button"
       value="Allison"
       OnClick=displayFood(this,"beans")>
<input type="button"
       value="BayLeigh"
       OnClick=displayFood(this,"carrots")>
<input type="button"
       value="Michael"
       OnClick=displayFood(this,"corn")>
<input type="button"
       value="Rob"
       OnClick=displayFood(this,"hotdogs")>
</form>

<script language="JavaScript">
<!-- Hide

//Create a function that displays a person's favorite food
function displayFood()
{
  //Create a string that contains the name of the person
  var aString = arguments[0].value;
  aString += "'s favorite food is ";

  //Add the favorite food to the end of the string
  aString += arguments[1];

  //Display the string in an alert box
  alert(aString);

  //Display the this function using the callee property
  alert(arguments.callee.toString());
}
```

```
//Hide End -->
</script>
</html>
```

# arguments.caller

## JavaScript 1.2+

## Nav4+

## Syntax

```
arguments.caller
```

## Description

The `caller` property of the `Arguments` object contains the `Arguments` object of the calling function. If the given function was not executed from within another function, null is stored in this property.

## Example

Listing 6.45 creates two functions. One displays an individual's favorite food in an alert box, while the other displays the number of arguments associated with the calling function. Anytime a button is clicked, an alert box displays the favorite food. This function then calls the second function to display an alert box saying there were two arguments passed into the first function.

*Listing 6.45   Using the* `caller` *Property of the* `Arguments` *Object*

```
<html>
Select a person's name to discover their favorite food!

<form>
<input type="button"
       value="Meredith"
       OnClick=displayFood(this,"pizza")>
<input type="button"
       value="Allison"
       OnClick=displayFood(this,"beans")>
<input type="button"
       value="BayLeigh"
       OnClick=displayFood(this,"carrots")>
<input type="button"
       value="Michael"
       OnClick=displayFood(this,"corn")>
<input type="button"
       value="Rob"
       OnClick=displayFood(this,"hotdogs")>
```

*continues*

*Listing 6.45    continued*

```
</form>

<script language="JavaScript">
<!-- Hide

//Display the number of arguments in the function that calls this function.
function displayArgLength()
{
  var argLengthStr = "The calling function contained ";
  argLengthStr += arguments.caller.length;
  argLengthStr += " arguments.";
  alert(argLengthStr);
}

//Create a function that displays a person's favorite food
function displayFood()
{
  //Create a string that contains the name of the person
  var aString = arguments[0].value;
  aString += "'s favorite food is ";

  //Add the favorite food to the end of the string
  aString += arguments[1];

  //Display the string in an alert box
  alert(aString);

  displayArgLength();
}

//Hide End -->
</script>
</html>
```

# arguments.length

## *JavaScript 1.1+, ECMAScript 1.0+*

## *Nav3+*

## *Syntax*

```
arguments.length
```

## *Description*

The `length` property of the `Arguments` object contains the number of arguments that were passed into the function to which the `Argument` object is associated. If less arguments are passed in than are specified in the definition of the function, the `length` property will only contain the number of arguments passed into the function. This number matches the number of elements in the arguments array associated with the Argument object.

## Example

In Listing 6.46, the length property of the Argument object is used to process any number of arguments passed into the displayFood() function.

*Listing 6.46    Using the* length *Property to Access Elements of the* Arguments *Object*

```
<html>
Select a person's name to discover their favorite food!

<form>
<input type="button"
       value="Meredith"
       OnClick=displayFood(this,"pizza","salad","icecream")>
<input type="button"
       value="Allison"
       OnClick=displayFood(this,"beans","potatoes")>
<input type="button"
       value="BayLeigh"
       OnClick=displayFood(this,"carrots")>
<input type="button"
       value="Michael"
       OnClick=displayFood(this,"corn","beans")>
<input type="button"
       value="Rob"
       OnClick=displayFood(this,"hotdogs")>
</form>

<script language="JavaScript">
<!-- Hide

//Create a function that displays a person's favorite foods
function displayFood()
{
  //Create a string that contains the name of the person
  var aString = arguments[0].value;
  aString += "'s favorite foods are: ";

  //Add all the favorite foods to the end of the string
  for(var i=1; i<arguments.length; i++)
  {
    aString += arguments[i];
    aString += ", ";
```

*continues*

*Listing 6.46    continued*
```
  }

  //Display the string in an alert box
  alert(aString);
}

//Hide End -->
</script>
</html>
```

# Array

## JavaScript 1.1+, ECMAScript 1.0+, JScript 3.0+

## Nav3+, NES3+, IE 4+, Opera3+

### Syntax
```
var variable = new Array()
var variable = new Array(int)
var variable = new Array(arg1, ..., argN)
```

### Description

Although arrays can be created with the basic JavaScript object, the Array object provides a much easier way to create and manage arrays.

Table 6.7 lists the argument and return values associated with this object's constructors. These constructors create a new array and, in two cases, initialize the Array object based on the arguments passed in the parameter list. The constructor that has no arguments sets the length property to 0.

*Table 6.7    Arguments and Return Values Associated with the Array Object*

| Type | Item | Description |
|------|------|-------------|
| Arguments | int | When the array constructor contains one argument, an array is created, and its length property is set to the value int. |
| | arg1,...argN | When the parameter list of the array constructor contains more than one argument, an array is created and the array is populated with the arguments. The array length property is set to the number of arguments in the parameter list. |
| Returns | | The newly created array is returned from the constructor. |

Table 6.8 lists the properties and methods used by the Array object.

*Table 6.8    Properties and Methods Used by the Array Object*

| Type | Item | Description |
|------|------|-------------|
| Property | `length` | The number elements in the array |
| Methods | `concat()` | Concatenates an array on to an array |
| | `join()` | Concatenates all elements of an array into one string |
| | `pop()` | Deletes the last element from an array |
| | `push()` | Adds elements to the end of an array |
| | `reverse()` | Reverses the order of the elements in the array |
| | `shift()` | Deletes elements from the front of an array |
| | `slice()` | Returns a subsection of the array |
| | `sort()` | Sorts elements in array |
| | `splice()` | Inserts and removes elements from an array |
| | `toSource()` | Converts elements to a string with square brackets |
| | `toString()` | Converts elements to a string |
| | `unshift()` | Adds elements to the front of an array |

## Example

Listing 6.47 creates an array of numbers using the `Array` constructor. Once created, the elements are displayed on the screen using bracket notation (`[ ]`).

*Listing 6.47    Creating an Array and Accessing Its Elements*

```
<html>

<h2>Creating and Accessing Arrays</h2>

<script language="JavaScript">
<!-- Hide

//Create a new array that contains 3 numbers
numArray = new Array(45,67,34);
document.write("Created an array of numbers that contains 45, 67, and 34<br>");

//Display the contents of the array
document.write("[0]=",numArray[0],"<br>"); // will display 45
document.write("[1]=",numArray[1],"<br>"); // will display 67
document.write("[2]=",numArray[2]);        // will display 34

//End Hide-->
</script>

</html>
```

# Array.concat()

## *JavaScript 1.2+, JScript 3.0+*

## *Nav4+, NES3+, IE 4+*

## Syntax

`array.concat(arg1,...argN)`

## Description

The `concat()` method adds the elements listed in the parameter list to the end of the existing array and returns the result. The original is not changed by this method. Should any of the arguments be `Array`, the elements of that array are concatenated to the array that called the method.

Table 6.9 lists the argument and return values associated with this method.

### Table 6.9    Arguments and Return Values Associated with concat()

| Type | Item | Description |
|------|------|-------------|
| Arguments | arg1,...argN | The parameter list of the `concat()` method contains one or more elements to be concatenated to the end of the array. |
| Returns | | The original array with the new concatenated elements is returned from the method. |

## Example

Listing 6.48 uses the `concat()` method to display the total inventory of two grocery store shelves. Notice how the multidimensional arrays were concatenated together in Figure 6.12.

*Listing 6.48    Using* `concat()` *to Display Inventory*

```
<html>

<script language="JavaScript">

//Display the elements in the array
function displayElements(theArray)
{
  //Access each element in the array
  for(i=0; i<theArray.length; i++)
  {
    //Display the element
    document.write("  -  ",theArray[i][1]," ");
    document.write(theArray[i][0],"<br>");
  }
```

```
}

//Create a grocery shelf using an array to represent
//the items on each shelf.
shelf1 = new Array(["apples",10],["oranges",25]);
document.write("Shelf 1 contains:<br>");
//Display the items on shelf 1
displayElements(shelf1);

//Create a second grocery shelf using an array to represent
//the items on each shelf.
shelf2 = new Array(["grapes",50],["bananas",3],["lemons",8]);
document.write("Shelf 2 contains:<br>");
//Display the items on shelf 2
displayElements(shelf2);

//Create a master inventory list by concatenating
//the two shelf arrays into one array.
inventory = shelf1.concat(shelf2);

//Display the all the items on all the shelves.
document.write("<br>The total inventory contains:<br>");
displayElements(inventory);

</script>

</html>
```

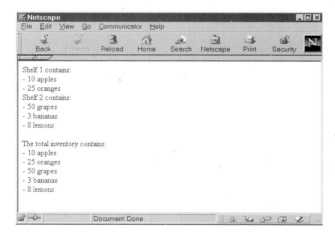

**Figure 6.12**

*Concatenate the items on two grocery store shelves.*

# Array.join()

## *JavaScript 1.1+, ECMAScript 1.0+, JScript 3.0+*

## *Nav3+, NES3+, IE 4+, Opera3+*

## *Syntax*

```
array.join()
array.join(string)
```

## *Description*

The join() method converts all the elements of the array to strings and then concatenates all the strings into one string. If an argument is provided in the parameter list, it is used to separate the elements in the string returned by the method.

Table 6.10 lists the argument and return values associated with this method. If an argument is passed into the method, it is used as a separator between the elements of the array.

**Table 6.10    Arguments and Return Values Associated with join()**

| Type | Item | Description |
|---|---|---|
| Arguments | string | A string that is used to separate the elements of the array in the string returned from the method. |
| Returns | | All the elements of the array are concatenated into one string and returned from the method. |

## *Example*

Listing 6.49 creates an array of fruits. The contents of this array are displayed on the screen using the join() method. A dash is specified as the delimiter used to separate the array elements when they are written to the screen as a string.

*Listing 6.49    Using the* join() *Method to Display the Elements of an Array*

```
<script language="JavaScript">
<!-- Hide

//Create an array that contains 3 fruits.
fruit = new Array("Apple","Orange","Grape");

//List the contents of the fruit array as a string
//with a dash seperating each item.
aString = fruit.join("-");  //aString = "Apple-Orange-Grape"

//Display the string generated from using the join() method.
document.write("The fruit array contains: ",aString);

// End hide -->
</script>
```

# Array.length

## *JavaScript 1.1+, ECMAScript 1.0+, JScript 3.0+*

## *Nav3+, NES3+, IE 4+, Opera3+*

## *Syntax*

```
array.length
```

## *Description*

The `length` property holds the number of elements in the array. This property is a read/write variable. If the `length` property is overwritten with a number that is larger than the original number, new elements are added to the end of the array and assigned undefined values. If the `length` property is overwritten with a number that is smaller than the original number, elements at the end of the array are lost.

## *Example*

Listing 6.50 creates an array of coins. The number of coins in the array is then reduced from 4 to 3 by modifying the `length` property so the array contains only three elements. Because the quarter was the last element in the array, it was removed when the `length` property was changed.

*Listing 6.50    Using the `length` Property to Reduce the Number of Elements in an Array*

```
<script language="JavaScript">
<!-- Hide

//Create an array of coins
coins = new Array("Penny","Nickle","Dime","Quarter");

x = coins.length;   //x contains 4
coins.length = 3    //"Quarter" was removed from array

//Display the contents of the array
document.write("The coins array contains: ", coins.join(','));

// End hide -->
</script>
```

# Array.pop()

## *JavaScript 1.2+*

## *Nav4+, NES3+*

## *Syntax*

```
array.pop()
```

## Description

The pop() method "pops" elements off the end of the array by deleting the last element of the array and setting the array's length property to one less than its current value. This last element is returned from the method. Table 6.11 shows the return value associated with this method.

*Table 6.11 Arguments and Return Values Associated with pop()*

| Type | Item | Description |
|---|---|---|
| Returns | | The last element in the array is returned from the method. |

## Example

In Listing 6.51, an array of pages is created to represent a stack of papers. The pop() method removes and returns the top-most paper. After the pop() method is executed, the variable currentPaper contains "Page3", and the array's length property is 2.

*Listing 6.51 Using the pop() Method to Remove Elements from the End of an Array*

```
<script language="JavaScript">
<!-- Hide

//Create an array of papers and remove the top page
pileOfPapers = new Array("Page1","Page2","Page3");
currentPaper = pileOfPapers.pop();   //Removed Page3
document.write(currentPaper," was removed from the pile.");

// End hide -->
</script>
```

# Array.prototype

## JavaScript 1.1+, ECMAScript 1.0+, JScript 3.0+

## Nav3+, NES3+, IE 4+

## Syntax

Array.prototype.*property*

Array.prototype.*method*

## Description

The prototype property allows you to add new properties and methods (designated as property/method in Syntax section) to the Array object that can be used throughout your code.

## *Example*

In Listing 6.52, the `prototype` property is used to provide a `pop()` method for work-ing with arrays. Even though the `pop()` method is already available to Netscape browsers, the method is not supported by Internet Explorer. To make this method avail-able to both browsers, a new `pop()` method is created. This method overrides the func-tionality of the Netscape `Array.pop()` method. The new `pop()` method is used at the end of the code to remove an element from an array.

*Listing 6.52   Assigning a New Method to the* `Array` *Object with the Prototype Property*

```
<html>

<script language="JavaScript">
<!-- Hide

//This function removes the last element in the array.  This last
//element is returned from the function.
function pop()
{
  if(this.length != 0)
  {
    var lastElement = this[this.length-1];  //Get last element
    this.length = this.length-1;            //Remove last element from array
    return(lastElement);                    //Return the last element
  }
}

//Make the pop() function available to all Array objects
//This will override the pop() method provided by the Array object in Netscape
Array.prototype.pop = pop;

//Create an Array of juice flavors.
var flavorArray = new Array("Strawberry","Blueberry","Peach");

//Display the contents of the flavor array
document.write("The flavor array initially contains: ");
document.write(flavorArray.join(', '),"<br>");

//Remove Peach from the array.
var removedElement = flavorArray.pop();
document.write(removedElement," was removed from the flavor array.<br>");

//Display the contents of the flavor array after the pop() method.
document.write("The flavor array now contains: ");
document.write(flavorArray.join(', '),"<br>");

//Hide End -->
</script>

</html>
```

# Array.push()

## *JavaScript 1.2+,*

## *Nav4+, NES3+*

## *Syntax*

```
array.push(arg1,...argN)
```

## *Description*

The push() method "pushes" the elements specified in the parameter list on to the end of the array in the order they were listed. Table 6.12 shows the arguments and return value associated with this method.

*Table 6.12    Arguments and Return Values Associated with push()*

| Type | Item | Description |
|------|------|-------------|
| Arguments | arg1,...argN | One or more elements to be added to the end of the array |
| Returns | | The last element added to the end of the array, which is also the last argument in the parameter list |

## *Example*

In Listing 6.53, an array of pages is created to represent a stack of papers. The push() method puts two more pages on the end of the array. After the push() method is executed, the variable currentPaper contains "Page4", and the array's length property is 4.

*Listing 6.53    Using the* push() *Method to Add Elements to the End of an Array*

```
<script language="JavaScript">
<!-- Hide

//Create an array of papers
pileOfPapers = new Array("Page1","Page2");

//Add 2 more pages to the end of the array.
currentPaper = pileOfPapers.push("Page3","Page4");

//Display the papers in the pile.
document.write(pileOfPapers.join(',')," are in the pile.");

// End hide -->
</script>
```

# Array.reverse()

## JavaScript 1.1+, ECMAScript 1.0+, JScript 3.0+

## Nav3+, NES3+, IE 4+

### Syntax
`array.reverse()`

### Description
The reverse() method reverses the order of the elements in the array according to the array index numbers.

### Example
Listing 6.54 creates an array representing a line of people. The reverse() method is called to reverse the order of the names so that Polly is the first element, Leslie is the second element, and Cheryl is the last element.

*Listing 6.54    Reversing Element Positions in an Array with the* reverse() *Method*

```
<script language="JavaScript">
<!-- Hide

//Create an array of names representing people in a grocery store line
lineOfPeople = new Array("Cheryl","Leslie","Polly");
lineOfPeople.reverse();    //Reverse the items in the array

//Display the names in the array. Notice the reversed ordering.
document.write("lineOfPeople[0]=",lineOfPeople[0],"<br>");
document.write("lineOfPeople[1]=",lineOfPeople[1],"<br>");
document.write("lineOfPeople[2]=",lineOfPeople[2],"<br>");

// End hide -->
</script>
```

# Array.shift()

## JavaScript 1.2+

## Nav4+, NES3+

### Syntax
`array.shift()`

### Description
The shift() method deletes and returns the first element of the array. Once deleted, all the remaining elements are shifted down one spot, so the first position is filled by

the element that was previously in the second position. Table 6.13 shows the return value associated with this method.

**Table 6.13    Arguments and Return Values Associated with shift()**

| Type | Item | Description |
|------|------|-------------|
| Returns | | The first element of the array, before the elements are shifted, is returned from the method. |

## Example

Listing 6.55 creates an array representing people waiting for a table at a restaurant. The `shift()` method pulls the first name off the list and shifts all the other names up one position. After the `shift()` method is executed, the variable `nextGroup` now contains Kent. Jon is shifted to `lineOfPeople[0]` and Jeremy to `lineOfPeople[1]`.

*Listing 6.55    Removing the First Element from an Array with the `shift()` Method*

```
<script language="JavaScript">
<!-- Hide

//Create an array representing a line of people at a resturant
lineOfPeople = new Array(""Kent","Jon","Jeremy");
personToSeat = lineOfPeople.shift();  //Kent pulled from array

//Display name of person removed from array
document.write("Please seat ",personToSeat,"<br>");

//Display people left in the array
document.write("People waiting for a seat: ",lineOfPeople.join(', '));
// End hide -->
</script>
```

# Array.slice()

## JavaScript 1.2+, JScript 3.0+

## Nav4+, NES3+, IE 4+

## Syntax

```
array.slice(start)
array.slice(start, stop)
```

## Description

The `slice()` method returns a new array that contains the elements of the original array starting at position `start` and ending at the element position *before* `stop`. If no `stop` position is specified, the new array will contain the elements of the original array, starting at the position stated in `start` through the end of the array. Table 6.14 lists the arguments and return values associated with this method.

*Table 6.14*  **Arguments and Return Values Associated with slice()**

| Type | Item | Description |
| --- | --- | --- |
| Arguments | start | The position in the array where the slice is to begin. Negative numbers can be used to count from the last element to the first. For example, −1 is the last element in the array, and −2 is the second to the last element in the array. |
| | stop | The position in the array where the slice is to stop. Like the start parameter, the stop parameter can be negative. |
| Returns | | A new array is returned from this method that contains the elements of the original array from index positions specified by start and stop. |

## Example

In Listing 6.56, an array of numbers is created. A new array of numbers is derived from the original array of numbers using the slice() method. After the slice() method is executed, the array newNumArray contains the elements 23 and 759.

*Listing 6.56  Selecting a Subsection from an Array with the slice() Method*

```
<script language="JavaScript">
<!-- Hide

//Create an array of 4 numbers and display the contents
numArray = new Array(345,23,759,5);
document.write("numArray contains the numbers: ",numArray.join(', '),"<br>");

//Create a new array from part of the original array
newNumArray = numArray.slice(1,3);    // new array contains [23,759]

//Display the contents of the new array
document.write("newNumArray contains the numbers: ",newNumArray.join(',
'),"<br>");

// End hide -->
</script>
```

# Array.sort()

## *JavaScript 1.1+, ECMAScript 1.0+, JScript 3.0+*

## *Nav3+, NES3+, IE 4+*

## Syntax

```
array.sort()
array.sort(function)
```

## Description

The sort() method rearranges the elements of the array based on a sorting order. Table 6.15 lists the argument associated with this method. If the method has no parameters, JavaScript attempts to convert all the elements of the array to strings and then sort them alphabetically. If the array should be sorted some other way, a function must be provided to handle the new sorting algorithm.

**Table 6.15   Argument Associated with sort()**

| Type | Item | Description |
|------|------|-------------|
| Argument | `function` | A function designated to handle the sorting of the array. |

As mentioned before, if the array should be sorted some other way than alphabetically, a function must be provided to handle the new sorting algorithm. The function specified must operate based on the following rules:

- The function must accept two arguments that are to be compared.
- The function must return a number indicating the order of the two arguments in relation to each other.
- If the first argument should appear before the second argument, a number less than zero should be returned from the function.
- If the first argument should appear after the second argument, a number greater than zero should be returned from the function.
- If both arguments are equivalent, zero should be returned from the function.

When the function specified by the sort() method returns zero, signifying that the arguments are equal, the arguments remain in the same order relative to each other after the function has been called.

## Example

To help solidify how the this method operates, Listing 6.57 demonstrates how to use the method to sort an array based on the number of characters in each argument. Notice how the sort() method changes the order of the elements of the array in Figure 6.13.

*Listing 6.57   Sorting Array Based on Argument Lengths*

```
<html>

<script language="JavaScript">

//Display the contents of an array
function contentsOfArray(theArray)
{
  document.write("the array contains:<br>");
  //Access each element in the array
  for(i=0; i<theArray.length; i++)
  {
```

```
      document.write("Position ",i," = ",theArray[i],"<br>");
   }
}

//Sort arguments based on their length
function sortOnArgLen(arg1,arg2)
{
  if(arg1.length < arg2.length)
    return -1;
  if(arg1.length > arg2.length)
    return 1;
  if(arg1.length == arg2.length)
    return 0;
}

//Create and display an array of shapes
shapes = new Array("triangle","rectangle","square");
document.write("Before the sort method ");
contentsOfArray(shapes);

//Sort the array
shapes.sort(sortOnArgLen);
document.write("<br>After the sort method ");
contentsOfArray(shapes);

</script>

</html>
```

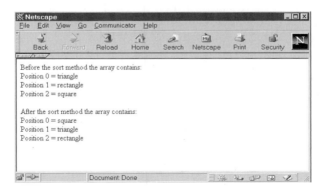

**Figure 6.13**

*Sort the array elements based on the character length of each element.*

# Array.splice()

## *JavaScript 1.2+*

## *Nav4+*

## *Syntax*

`array.splice(start,delete,arg3,...,argN)`

## *Description*

The `splice()` method provides a way for elements to be either added to or deleted from the array. When the `delete` parameter contains a number other than zero, the elements beginning at `start` and ending at index `start+ending` are deleted from the array. If `delete` is zero, no elements are deleted. All elements from `start` to the end of the array are deleted when `delete` is not specified. If arguments follow the `delete` parameter, they are added to the array as elements beginning at the position specified by `start`. Existing elements are shifted up to allow room for the new elements.

**NOTE**

There is a bug in Navigator 4 when just one element is deleted from an array. Rather than returning an array that contains the deleted element, the actual element is returned from the method. In addition, when no elements are deleted from the array, `null` is returned instead of an empty array.

Table 6.16 lists the arguments and return values associated with the `splice()` method.

*Table 6.16  Arguments and Return Values Associated with splice()*

| Type | Item | Description |
|------|------|-------------|
| Arguments | `start` | The position in the array where the slice is to begin. |
| | `delete` | The number of elements to be deleted from the array, beginning at the position specified by `start`. |
| | `arg3,...,argN` | New array elements to be inserted into the array, starting at the position specified by `start`. |
| Returns | | If any elements are deleted from the array, they are returned from the method as an array. |

## *Example*

To help understand how the `splice()` method works, Listing 6.58 uses the `delete` and `insert` abilities of the method to simulate a food order at a restaurant. In Figure 6.14, notice how the hamburger was replaced with a hotdog based on the customer's change in appetite.

*Listing 6.58    Using `splice()` to Simulate a Restaurant*

```
<html>

<script language="JavaScript">

//Display the current order
function printOrder(theArray)
{
  document.write("The current order is:<br>");
  //Access each element in the array
  for(i=0; i<theArray.length; i++)
  {
    document.write("- ",theArray[i],"<br>");
  }
}

//Create and display a food order
foodOrder = new Array("hamburger","fries","drink");
document.write("<h3>The initial order taken</h3>");
printOrder(foodOrder);

//Replace the hamburger with a hotdog
foodOrder.splice(0,1,"hotdog");
document.write("<h3>The customer wants a hotdog ");
document.write("instead of the hamburger.</h3>");

//Print the new order
printOrder(foodOrder);

</script>

</html>
```

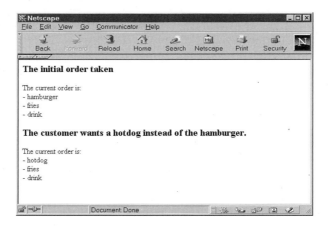

**Figure 6.14**

*Food order changed using the* `slice()` *method.*

# Array.toSource()

## *JavaScript1.3+, JScript3.0+, ECMAScript2.0+ (proposed)*

## *Nav4.06+, IE4+*

## *Syntax*

`array.toSource()`

## *Description*

The `toSource()` method returns one string representing the source of the `Array` object. The string that is returned contains all the elements in the array separated with commas. The entire string is enclosed with brackets (`[]`) to show it is an array. If another array is contained within an array, its contents are also part of the string with its own set of brackets.

## *Example*

Listing 6.59 creates an `Array` object of colors and an `Array` object of numbers. The array of numbers is included in the array of colors. The `toSource()` method is then applied to the `Array` object to return the source string.

`["Blue", "Green", "Red", [3, 6, 7]]`

*Listing 6.59   Accessing the source of an* `Array` *object with the* `toSource()`
*Method*
```
<script language="JavaScript">
<!-- Hide
```

```
//Create an array of numbers
numbers = new Array(3,6,7);

//Create an array of colors and a subarray of numbers
colors = new Array("Blue","Green","Red",numbers);

//Force JavaScript to display the array contents in a string
aString = colors.toSource();  //create a string from the array contents
document.write(aString); //display the string

// End hide -->
</script>
```

# Array.toString()

## *JavaScript 1.1+, ECMAScript 1.0+, JScript 3.0+*

## *Nav3+, IE 4+*

## *Syntax*

```
array.toString()
```

## *Description*

The toString() method returns one string that contains all the elements in the array separated with commas. You may be wondering why anyone would need this method when the join() method can do this and more. The reason is that the toString() method is what JavaScript uses to automatically convert an array to a string when the array is used in string context.

## CAUTION

JavaScript 1.2 does not use commas to separate the elements. Instead, each element is enclosed in square brackets.

Table 6.17 shows the return value associated with the toString() method.

### *Table 6.17   Return Value Associated with toString()*

| Type | Item | Description |
|------|------|-------------|
| Returns | | A string that contains all the elements of the array |

## *Example*

Listing 6.60 creates an array of colors and then forces JavaScript to use the toString() method by putting the array in a document.write() method, which normally accepts string arguments.

*Listing 6.60   Forcing JavaScript to Use an Array's* `toString()` *Method*

```
<script language="JavaScript">
<!-- Hide

//Create an array of colors
colors = new Array("Blue","Green","Red");

//Force JavaScript to display the array contents in a string
document.write(colors); //returns "Blue,Green,Red"


// End hide -->
</script>
```

# Array.unshift()

## *JavaScript 1.2+*

## *Nav4+, NES3+*

## *Syntax*

*array*.unshift(*arg1,...argN*)

## *Description*

The `unshift()` method adds the arguments listed in the parameter list to the front of the array as new elements. Existing elements are shifted up to allow room for the new elements. Table 6.18 lists the arguments and return values associated with this method.

**Table 6.18   Arguments and Return Values Associated with unshift()**

| Type | Item | Description |
|------|------|-------------|
| Arguments | arg1,...argN | Elements to be added to the array |
| Returns | | The length of the array after adding the new elements. |

## *Example*

Listing 6.61 creates an array of school grades. Two new grades, `100` and `93` are added to the front of the array using the `unshift()` method. After the `unshift()` method has executed, the grades array contains [`100,93,95,87`], and `newLength` contains the new length of the array, `4`.

*Listing 6.61   Adding Elements to the Front of an Array Using the* `unshift()` *Method*

```
<script language="JavaScript">
<!-- Hide

//Create an array of test grades
grades = new Array(95,87);
```

```
//Add two more grades to the array.
newLength = grades.unshift(100,93);

//Display the grades stored in the array.
for(i=0; i<newLength; i++)
{
  document.write("grades[",i,"]=",grades[i],"<br>");
}

// End hide -->
</script>
```

# Array.valueOf()

## *JavaScript1.1+, JScript3.0+, ECMAScript1.0+*

## *NES2+, Nav3+, IE4+, Opera3+*

### *Syntax*

```
array.valueOf()
```

### *Description*

The valueOf() method returns the primitive value of the object. In terms of an instance of an Array object, this method returns the array elements separated by commas. If an array contains another array, the contents are flattened when this method is used.

### *Example*

Listing 6.62 creates an Array object of colors and an Array object of numbers. The array of numbers is included in the array of colors. Because the valueOf() method returns the actual elements in the array, "Blue,Green,Red,3,6,7" is written to the browser.

*Listing 6.62   Using the* valueOf() *Method to Return the Value of the* Array *Object*

```
<script language="JavaScript">
<!-- Hide

//Create an array of numbers
numbers = new Array(3,6,7);

//Create an array of colors and a subarray of numbers
colors = new Array("Blue","Green","Red",numbers);

//Display the primitive value of the array
document.write(colors.valueOf()); //display the array elements

// End hide -->
</script>
```

# boolean

# JavaScript1.2

### NES3+, Nav4+

### Syntax

```
Reserved Keyword
```

### Description

The `boolean` keyword has not been implemented in JavaScript to date, but has been reserved for future use. Note that this keyword is not the same as the `Boolean` object.

### Example

This keyword has not been implemented; therefore, no example is provided.

# Boolean

### JavaScript 1.1+, ECMAScript 1.0+, JScript 3.0+

### Nav3+, NES3+, IE 4+

### Syntax

```
var variable = new Boolean(value)
var variable = Boolean(value)
```

### Description

The `Boolean` object is a wrapper object that holds a primitive Boolean value, as well as provides a method for converting the value to a string. A primitive `boolean` can have only one of two states: `true` or `false`. Internally, JavaScript uses the number 1 to represent `true` and 0 to represent `false` but provides the `toString()` method to return the strings `"true"` and `"false"`.

A `Boolean` object is created with the `Boolean()` constructor and the new operator or by the `Boolean()` function. The argument, return value, and method associated with this object are listed in Table 6.19.

**Table 6.19   Argument, Return Value, and Method Associated with the Boolean object**

| Type | Item | Description |
|------|------|-------------|
| Argument | value | The value to be converted to a Boolean value and stored in the object. The values null, NaN, "" (empty string), and 0 (zero) are converted to false. All other values (including the string "false") are converted to true. |
| Returns | | If the new operator is used, the new Boolean object is returned. If the Boolean() function is used, the primitive Boolean value is returned. |
| Properties | prototype | Represents the prototype of this class. |
| Method | toString() | This method returns a string representation of the primitive Boolean value stored in the object. If the object contains true, the string "true" is returned. Similarly, if the object contains false, the string "false" is returned. |

## Example

In Listing 6.63, a Boolean object and a primitive Boolean value are created. There are a couple key points to notice when examining the results generated by the code, shown in Figure 6.15. First, the Boolean() constructor converts the string "false" to the Boolean value true. Secondly, boolObj is a Boolean object, while boolVal is just a variable holding a primitive Boolean value.

*Listing 6.63*   **Boolean** *Object Verses Primitive Boolean Value*

```
<script language="JavaScript">
<!-- Hide

//Create a Boolean object
boolObj = new Boolean("false");
document.write("boolObj = ",boolObj);         //Display true
document.write(" [",typeof boolObj,"]<br>");  //Display object

//Create a primitive boolean value
boolVal = Boolean(false);
document.write("boolVal = ",boolVal);         //Display false
document.write(" [",typeof boolVal,"]");      //Display boolean

//Hide End -->
</script>
```

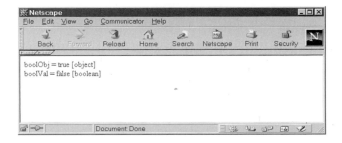

**Figure 6.15**

`Boolean` *object verses primitive Boolean value.*

# Boolean.prototype

## *JavaScript 1.1+, ECMAScript 1.0+, JScript 3.0+*

## *Nav3+, IE 4+*

## *Syntax*

`Boolean.prototype.`*property*

`Boolean.prototype.`*method*

## *Description*

The `prototype` property allows you to add new properties and methods to the `Boolean` object that can be used throughout your code.

## *Example*

In Listing 6.64, the `prototype` property is used to create a new method, called `letter()`, which can be used by all `Boolean` objects. The `letter()` method uses the `letterBoolean()` function to return `T` or `F` based on the status of the object.

*Listing 6.64   Assigning a New Method to the* `Boolean` *Object with the* `prototype` *Property*

```
<html>

<script language="JavaScript">
<!-- Hide

//This function returns the string "T" or "F" based on the value stored in the
//Boolean object that uses this function.
function letterBoolean()
{
  if(this == true)
    return("T");
  else
```

```
    return("F");
}

//Make the letterBoolean function available to all Boolean objects
Boolean.prototype.letter = letterBoolean;

//Create a Boolean object with an initial setting if true
var myBooleanObj = new Boolean(true);    //myBooleanObj equal to true

//Display the state of the Boolean object using the letter method.
document.write("myBooleanObj is set to ",myBooleanObj.letter());  //Return "T"

//Hide End -->
</script>

</html>
```

# Boolean.toSource()

## JavaScript1.3+, JScript3.0+, ECMAScript2.0+ (proposed)
## Nav4.06+, IE4+

### Syntax
*boolean*.toSource()

### Description

The toSource() method returns one string representing the source of the Boolean object. The string that is returned is enclosed in with parentheses.

### Example

Listing 6.65 creates a Boolean object to represent true. The toSource() method is then applied to the Boolean object to return the source string "(new Boolean(true))".

*Listing 6.65   Accessing the Source of a* Boolean *Object with the* toSource() *Method*

```
<script language="JavaScript">
<!-- Hide

//Create a Boolean object representing true
bool = new Boolean(1);

//Display the source of the Boolean object
document.write(bool.toSource());

// End hide -->
</script>
```

# Boolean.toString()

## *JavaScript 1.1+, ECMAScript 1.0+, JScript 3.0+*

## *Nav3+, IE 4+*

## *Syntax*

`boolean.toString()`

## *Description*

The `toString()` method returns the string representation (`"true"` or `"false"`) of the primitive Boolean value stored in the `Boolean` object. The return value associated with this object is listed in Table 6.20.

*Table 6.20   Return Value Associated with toString()*

| Type | Description |
| --- | --- |
| Returns | If `true`, the string `"true"` is returned. If `false`, the string `"false"` is returned. |

## *Example*

In Listing 6.66, the `toString()` method is used to force a comparison of strings rather than Boolean values. Without the `toString()` method, the `if` comparison would find the Boolean value not equal to the string value.

*Listing 6.66   Force the Correct Comparison Using Boolean's `toString()` Method*

```
<script language="JavaScript">
<!-- Hide

//Create a Boolean object that contains the boolean value "false"
boolObj = new Boolean(false);

//Force JavaScript to convert the boolObj object to the string "false"
//before comparing to the string "false"
if(boolObj.toString() == "false")     //Evalutes to true
  alert("EQUAL");                      //so display "EQUAL" on screen
else
  alert("NOT Equal");

//Hide End -->
</script>
```

# Boolean.valueOf()

*JavaScript1.1+, JScript3.0+, ECMAScript1.0+*

*NES2+, Nav3+, IE4+, Opera3+*

## Syntax

```
boolean.valueOf()
```

## Description

The `valueOf()` method returns the primitive value of the object. In terms of an instance of a `Boolean` object, this method returns a Boolean value contained in the object.

## Example

Listing 6.67 creates a `Boolean` object representing `true`. Because the `valueOf()` method returns the Boolean value in the object, `"true"` is written to the browser.

*Listing 6.67   Using the* `valueOf()` *Method to Return the Value of the* `Boolean` *Object*

```
<script language="JavaScript">
<!-- Hide

//Create a Boolean object representing true
bool = new Boolean(1);

//Display the source of the Boolean object
document.write(bool.valueOf());

// End hide -->
</script>
```

# break

*JavaScript 1.1+, ECMAScript 1.0+, JScript 1.0+*

*Nav3+, IE 3+, Opera3+*

## Syntax

```
break label;
```

## Description

The keyword `break` provides a way to exit out of loop structures and `switch` conditionals prematurely. Most of the time, the word `break` appears on a line by itself, but there are times when a label will follow the keyword (see Table 6.21). When a label is used, code execution completely breaks out of the area designated by `label` and proceeds to the code that follows the area. To label a statement, simply place the label name followed by a colon (:) in front of the code that needs to be broken out of during code execution.

**Table 6.21   Argument Associated with the break Keyword**

| Type | Item | Description |
| --- | --- | --- |
| Argument | label | A label that designates code from which to break. |

## Example

Listing 6.68 demonstrates the effect of using labels and break statements when working with nested loops. Figure 6.16 shows the result of executing this code.

*Listing 6.68   Using breaks and Labels*

```
<script language='JavaScript'>
<!--

//Loop through the outer loop (forLoop1) 4 times
forLoop1:
for (var counter1 = 1; counter1 <= 5; counter1++)
{
  //Go through this inner loop 4 times for each time through the outer loop.
  for (var counter2 = 1; counter2 <= 5; counter2++)
  {
    //Display the values in each for loop's counter
    document.write("Counter1=",counter1);
    document.write(" Counter2=",counter2,"<br>");

    //Break out of inner loop the 3rd time through the inner loop
    if (counter2 == 3)
      break;

    //Break out of the outer loop the 3rd time through the outer loop
    if (counter1 == 3)
      break forLoop1;
  }
}

document.write("All done!");

//-->
</script>
```

Notice how the break statement with no label, in Figure 6.16, breaks out of just the inner loop. When the break statement is used with a label, JavaScript knows at what level to break.

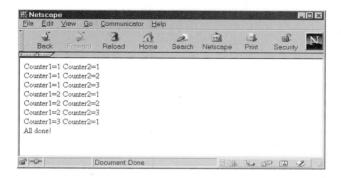

**Figure 6.16**

*Using labels and the* break *statement in nested loops.*

# byte

## *JavaScript1.2+*

## *NES3+, Nav4+*

## *Syntax*

Reserved Keyword

## *Description*

The byte keyword has not been implemented in JavaScript to date, but has been reserved for future use.

## *Example*

This keyword has not been implemented, therefore no example is provided.

# case

## *JavaScript1.2+, Jscript3.0+*

## *NES3+, Nav4+, IE4+*

## *Syntax*

Reserved Keyword

## *Description*

The case keyword has not been implemented in JavaScript to date, but has been reserved for future use.

## Example

This keyword has not been implemented, therefore no example is provided.

# char

## JavaScript1.2+

## NES3+, Nav4+

## Syntax

Reserved Keyword

## Description

The char keyword has not been implemented in JavaScript to date, but has been reserved for future use.

## Example

This keyword has not been implemented, therefore no example is provided.

# class

## JavaScript, ECMAScript 1.0+, JScript

## Syntax

Reserved Keyword

## Description

The word class is a reserved for future use, so there is no definition at this time.

## Example

No example can be provided because class is reserved for future use.

# const

## JavaScript, ECMAScript 1.0+, JScript

## Syntax

Reserved Keyword

## Description

The word const is a reserved for future use, so there is no definition at this time.

## Example

No example can be provided because const is reserved for future use.

# continue

*JavaScript 1.1+, ECMAScript 1.0+, JScript 3.0+*

*Nav3+, IE 4+, Opera3+*

## Syntax

```
continue label;
```

## Description

The `continue` statement forces the execution of the code within a loop to continue at the beginning of the loop. Normally, the `continue` keyword appears on a line by itself, but there are times when a label will follow the keyword (see Table 6.22). When a label is used, code execution immediately jumps to the beginning of the loop designated by the label and begins executing code.

**Table 6.22   Argument Associated with the continue Keyword**

| Type | Item | Description |
|------|------|-------------|
| Argument | label | A label that designates code to execute. |

The beginning of a loop varies depending on the type of loop structure. Table 6.23 shows where each looping structure jumps to when a `continue` structure is encountered.

**Table 6.23   Where the continue Statement Jumps**

| Looping Structure | Continue **Jumps to:** |
|-------------------|------------------------|
| for | Expression in parentheses following `for` keyword |
| while | Expression in parentheses following `while` keyword |
| do...while | Expression in parentheses following `while` keyword |
| for...in | Next property name in object |

### CAUTION

There is a bug in Navigator 4 that causes the expression in parentheses following the `while` keyword in a `do...while` loop to not get executed when jumped to using a `continue` statement. Instead, execution of code starts at the top of loop, after the `continue` statement. This problem can be avoided by using a `while` loop.

To label a statement, simply place the label name followed by a colon (`:`) in front of the code that code execution needs to continue.

## Example

Listing 6.69 demonstrates the use of labels and `continue`. This example is a bit complicated, so take time to compare Listing 6.61 to the output in Figure 6.17. Notice how the phrase "`Bottom of innerLoop`" was not printed after the "`Continue at top of innerLoop.`" because code execution jumped back to beginning of the inner-most loop. When a label was attached to the `continue` keyword, code execution jumped back to the beginning of the loop labeled `outerLoop`.

*Listing 6.69    Using the* `continue` *Statement*

```
<script language='JavaScript'>
<!--

//Loop through the outerLoop twice.
outerLoop:
  for (var counter1 = 1; counter1 <= 2; counter1++)
  {
    document.write("Top of outerLoop.<br>");

    //Loop through the innerLoop twice.
    innerLoop:
      for (var counter2 = 1; counter2 <= 2; counter2++)
      {
        //Display the values in each for loop's counter
        document.write("Top of innerLoop.<br>");
        document.write("Counter1=",counter1,"<br>");
        document.write("Counter2=",counter2,"<br>");

        //If this is the second time through the innerLoop then
        //don't go any further and jump back to the top of the innerLoop.
        if (counter2 == 2)
        {
          document.write("Continue at top of innerLoop.<br>");
          continue;
        }

        //If this is the second time through the outerLoop then
        //don't go any further and jump back to the top of the outerLoop.
        if (counter1 == 2)
        {
          document.write("Continue at top of outerLoop.<br>");
          continue outerLoop;
        }
        document.write("Bottom of innerLoop.<br>");
      }
    document.write("Bottom of outerLoop.<br>");
  }

document.write("All done!");

//-->
</script>
```

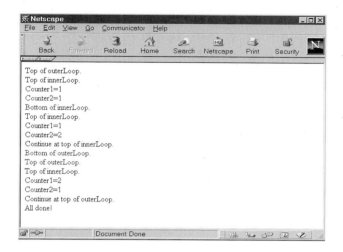

**Figure 6.17**

*The result of using the* continue *statement.*

# Date

## *JavaScript 1.0+, ECMAScript 1.0+, JScript 1.0+*

## *Nav2+, NES2+, IE 3+, Opera3+*

### *Syntax*

```
var variable = new Date();
var variable = new Date(milliseconds1);
var variable = new Date(string)
var variable = new Date(year, month, day, hours, minutes, seconds,
milliseconds2)
```

### *Description*

The Date object represents all aspects of a date and time from year to milliseconds. If arguments are provided when creating the Date object, the new object will contain the date specified, otherwise the object will be set to the current date. A Date object can also be created by calling Date as a function by excluding the new operator. The arguments and methods are listed in Table 6.24.

**CAUTION**

Navigator 3 and 4 return a string representation of the date rather than a Date object when the Date constructor is used as a function. To avoid this problem, simply don't use the Date constructor as a function.

*Table 6.24* **Arguments and Methods Associated with the Date Object**

| Type | Item | Description |
|---|---|---|
| Argument | `milliseconds1` | The desired date is calculated from the number of milliseconds between midnight January 1, 1970 GMT and the desired date. |
| | `string` | The desired date is calculated from the string representation. The format of the string should match the `parse()` method of the `Date` object. |
| | `year` | A four digit representation of the year. |
| | `month` | The month represented as an integer, where `0` represents January and `11` represents December. |
| | `day` | The day of the month represented as an integer from 1 to 31. Optional argument. |
| | `hours` | The hour represented as an integer where `0` represents 12 am (midnight) and `23` represents 11 pm. Optional argument. |
| | `minutes` | The minutes in the hour represented as an integer from `0` to `59`. Optional argument. |
| | `seconds` | The seconds in the minute represented as an integer from `0` to `59`. Optional argument. |
| | `milliseconds2` | The milliseconds in the second represented as an integer from `0` to `999`. Optional argument. |
| Methods | `getDate()` | Returns the day of the month. |
| | `getDay()` | Returns the day of the week. |
| | `getFullYear()` | Returns the year in local time with four digits. |
| | `getHours()` | Returns the hour. |
| | `getMilliseconds()` | Returns the milliseconds. |
| | `getMinutes()` | Returns the minutes. |
| | `getMonth()` | Returns the month. |
| | `getSeconds()` | Returns the seconds. |
| | `getTime()` | Returns the date and time in milliseconds. |
| | `getTimezoneOffset()` | Returns the time zone offset from GMT in minutes. |
| | `getUTCDate()` | Returns the day of the month converted to universal time. |
| | `getUTCDay()` | Returns the day of the week converted to universal time. |
| | `getUTCFullYear()` | Returns four-digit representation of the year converted to universal time. |

| Type | Item | Description |
|------|------|-------------|
| | getUTCHours() | Return the hour converted to universal time. |
| | getUTCMilliseconds() | Returns the milliseconds converted to universal time. |
| | getUTCMinutes() | Returns the minutes converted to universal time. |
| | getUTCMonth() | Returns the month converted to universal time. |
| | getUTCSeconds() | Returns the seconds converted to universal time. |
| | getYear() | Returns the year as either four-digits or two-digits. |
| | parse() | Converts a string, representing a date and time, into milliseconds. |
| | setDate() | Sets the day of the month. |
| | setFullYear() | Sets year as a four-digit number. |
| | setHours() | Sets the hour. |
| | setMilliseconds() | Sets the milliseconds. |
| | setMinutes() | Sets the minutes. |
| | setMonth() | Sets the month. |
| | setSeconds() | Sets the seconds. |
| | setTime() | Sets the date and time from a millisecond representation of a date and time. |
| | setUTCdate() | Sets the day of the month in universal time. |
| | setUTCFullYear() | Sets the year as a four-digit number in universal time. |
| | setUTCHours() | Sets the hour in universal time. |
| | setUTCMilliseconds() | Sets the milliseconds in universal time. |
| | setUTCMinutes() | Sets the minutes in universal time. |
| | setUTCMonth() | Sets the month in universal time. |
| | setUTCSeconds() | Sets the seconds in universal time. |
| | setYear() | Sets the year as either a four-digit number or a two-digit number. |
| | toGMTString() | Return the data and time as a string in universal time (GMT). |
| | toLocalString() | Return the date and time as a string in local time format. |
| | toSource() | Return the source of the Date object. |
| | toString() | Return the date and time as a string in local time. |
| | toUTCString() | Return the data and time as a string in universal time (GMT). |
| | UTC() | Convert a universal date and time (GMT) to milliseconds. |

## Example

Listing 6.70 demonstrates how to create Date objects using various arguments in the Date() constructor.

*Listing 6.70    Creating Date Objects*

```
<html>

<script language="JavaScript">
<!-- Hide

//Create a new Date object using all arguments.
theDate1 = new Date(2002,9,29,20,5,8,10);

//Create a new Date object using just milliseconds.
theDate2 = new Date(theDate1.getTime());

//Create a new Date object using a string.
theDate3 = new Date(theDate1.toString());

//Display all the date objects.
document.write("theDate1-> ",theDate1.toString());
document.write("<br>theDate2-> ",theDate2.toString());
document.write("<br>theDate3-> ",theDate3.toString());

//Hide End -->
</script>

</html>
```

# Date.getDate()

## *JavaScript 1.0+, ECMAScript 1.0+, JScript 1.0+*

## *Nav2+, NES2+, IE 3+, Opera3+*

## Syntax

*date.getDate()*

## Description

The getDate() method returns the day of the month expressed as an integer from 1 to 31.

## Example

The code in Listing 6.71 displays the current day of the month expressed as an integer from 1 to 31 using the getDate() method.

*Listing 6.71    Using the* `getDate()` *Method to Return the Day of the Month*

```
<html>

<script language="JavaScript">
<!-- Hide

//Create a Date object that contains the current date and time.
theDate = new Date();

//Display the date
document.write("The date is ",theDate.getDate());

//Hide End -->
</script>

</html>
```

# Date.getDay()

## *JavaScript 1.0+, ECMAScript 1.0+, JScript 1.0+*

## *Nav2+, NES2+, IE 3+, Opera3+*

## *Syntax*

*date.*getDay()

## *Description*

The `getDay()` method returns the day of the week expressed as an integer from 0 (Sunday) to 6 (Saturday).

## *Example*

The code in Listing 6.72 uses the `getDay()` method to return the day of the week expressed as an integer. This number is then converted to a string representation of the day of the week.

*Listing 6.72    Using the* `getDate()` *Method to Return the Day of the Week*

```
<html>

<script language="JavaScript">
<!-- Hide

//This function converts the day from a number to
//a string and returns the string.
function getDayString(num)
{
  var day;    //Create a local variable to hold the string
```

*continues*

*Listing 6.72    continued*

```
  switch(num)
  {
    case 0:
      day="Sunday";
      break;
    case 1:
      day="Monday";
      break;
    case 2:
      day="Tuesday";
      break;
    case 3:
      day="Wednesday";
      break;
    case 4:
      day="Thursday";
      break;
    case 5:
      day="Friday";
      break;
    case 6:
      day="Saturday";
      break;
    default:
      day="Invalid day";
  }
  return day;
}

//Create a Date object that contains the current date and time.
theDate = new Date();

//Display the day
document.write("Today is ",getDayString(theDate.getDay()));
//Hide End -->
</script>

</html>
```

# Date.getFullYear()

*JavaScript 1.2+, ECMAScript 1.0+, JScript 3.0+*

*Nav4+, IE 4+*

## Syntax

```
date.getFullYear()
```

## Description

The getFullYear() method returns the year in local time as a full four-digit number.

## Example

The code in Listing 6.73 displays the year using the getFullYear() method.

*Listing 6.73   Using the* getFullYear() *Method to Return the Year*

```
<html>

<script language="JavaScript">
<!-- Hide

//Create a Date object that contains the current date and time.
theDate = new Date();

//Display the full year
document.write("The year is ",theDate.getFullYear());

//Hide End -->
</script>

</html>
```

# Date.getHours()

## *JavaScript 1.0+, ECMAScript 1.0+, JScript 1.0+*

## *Nav2+, NES2+, IE 3+, Opera3+*

## Syntax

*date*.getHours()

## Description

The getHours() method returns the hour portion of the date expressed as an integer from 0 (12:00 a.m. midnight) to 23 (11:00 p.m.).

## Example

The code in Listing 6.74 displays the current hour as an integer from 0 to 23 using the getHours() method.

*Listing 6.74   Using the* getHours() *Method to Return the Current Hour*

```
<html>

<script language="JavaScript">
<!-- Hide

//Create a Date object that contains the current date and time.
```

*continues*

*Listing 6.74    continued*

```
theDate = new Date();

//Display the hour
document.write("The hour is ",theDate.getHours());

//Hide End -->
</script>

</html>
```

# Date.getMilliseconds()

## JavaScript 1.2+, ECMAScript 1.0+, JScript 3.0+

## Nav4+, IE 4+

## Syntax

```
date.getMilliseconds()
```

## Description

The getMilliseconds() method returns the millisecond portion of the date expressed as an integer from 0 to 999.

## Example

The code in Listing 6.75 displays the milliseconds in the Date object using the getMilliseconds() method.

*Listing 6.75    Using the* getMilliseconds() *Method to Return the Current Millisecond*

```
<html>

<script language="JavaScript">
<!-- Hide

//Create a Date object that contains the current date and time.
theDate = new Date();

//Display the milliseconds
document.write("The millisecond is ",theDate.getMilliseconds());

//Hide End -->
</script>

</html>
```

# Date.getMinutes()

## *JavaScript 1.0+, ECMAScript 1.0+, JScript 1.0+*

## *Nav2+, NES2+, IE 3+, Opera3+*

## Syntax
`date.getMinutes()`

## Description

The `getMinutes()` method returns the minutes portion of the `Date` object expressed as an integer from 0 to 59.

## Example

The code in Listing 6.76 displays the current minute using the `getMinutes()` method.

*Listing 6.76    Using the* `getMinutes()` *Method to Return the Current Minute*

```
<html>

<script language="JavaScript">
<!-- Hide

//Create a Date object that contains the current date and time.
theDate = new Date();

//Display the minutes
document.write("The minute is ",theDate.getMinutes());

//Hide End -->
</script>

</html>
```

# Date.getMonth()

## *JavaScript 1.0+, ECMAScript 1.0+, JScript 1.0+*

## *Nav2+, NES2+, IE 3+, Opera3+*

## Syntax
`date.getMonth()`

## Description

The `getMonth()` method returns the month portion of the `Date` object expressed as an integer from 0 (January) to 11 (December).

## Example

The code in Listing 6.77 displays the current month using the `getMonth()` method.

*Listing 6.77   Using the* `getMonth()` *Method to Return the Current Month*

```
<html>

<script language="JavaScript">
<!-- Hide

//This function converts the month from a number to
//a string and returns the string.
function getMonthString(num)
{
  var month;    //Create a local variable to hold the string
  switch(num)
  {
    case 0:
      month="January";
      break;
    case 1:
      month="February";
      break;
    case 2:
      month="March";
      break;
    case 3:
      month="April";
      break;
    case 4:
      month="May";
      break;
    case 5:
      month="June";
      break;
    case 6:
      month="July";
      break;
    case 7:
      month="August";
      break;
    case 8:
      month="September";
      break;
    case 9:
      month="October";
      break;
    case 10:
      month="November";
      break;
    case 11:
      month="December";
      break;
    default:
```

```
        month="Invalid month";
    }
    return month;
}

//Create a Date object that contains the current date and time.
theDate = new Date();

//Display the month
document.write("The month is ",getMonthString(theDate.getMonth()));

//Hide End -->
</script>

</html>
```

# Date.getSeconds()

## *JavaScript 1.0+, ECMAScript 1.0+, JScript 1.0+*

## *Nav2+, NES2+, IE 3+, Opera3+*

## *Syntax*

```
date.getSeconds()
```

## *Description*

The getSeconds() method returns the seconds portion of the Date object expressed as an integer from 0 to 59.

## *Example*

The code in Listing 6.78 displays the current seconds using the getSeconds() method.

*Listing 6.78    Using the* getSeconds() *Method to Return the Current Second*

```
<html>

<script language="JavaScript">
<!-- Hide

//Create a Date object that contains the current date and time.
theDate = new Date();

//Display the seconds
document.write("The second is ",theDate.getSeconds());

//Hide End -->
</script>

</html>
```

# Date.getTime()

## *JavaScript 1.0+, ECMAScript 1.0+, JScript 1.0+*

## *Nav2+, NES2+, IE 3+, Opera3+*

## Syntax

```
date.getTime()
```

## Description

The getTime() method returns the equivalence of the Date object in milliseconds. The milliseconds are expressed as an integer representing the number of milliseconds between midnight January 1, 1970 (GMT) to the date and time specified in the Date object.

> **TIP**
>
> It is much easier to compare two different dates as milliseconds by using the getTime() method, rather than having to examine the individual parts of the date.

## Example

The code in Listing 6.79 displays the number of milliseconds that passed between midnight January 1, 1970 to midnight January 1, 2000 using the getTime() method.

*Listing 6.79 Using the getTime() Method to Return the Milliseconds Between 1970 and 2000*

```
<html>

<script language="JavaScript">
<!-- Hide

//Create a Date object that contains midnight January 1,1970.
theDate = new Date(2000,1,1,0,0,0,0);

//Display the elapsed milliseconds
document.write(theDate.getTime());
document.write(" milliseconds passed between 1-1-1970 and 1-1-2000");

//Hide End -->
</script>

</html>
```

# Date.getTimezoneOffset()

## JavaScript 1.0+, ECMAScript 1.0+, JScript 1.0+

## Nav2+, NES2+, IE 3+, Opera3+

## Syntax

```
date.getTimezoneOffset()
```

## Description

The getTimezoneOffset() method returns the difference between the time zones of local time and Greenwich Mean Time (GMT). This difference is returned as an integer representing the number of minutes between the time zone of the local time and GMT. Although this is a method of a Date object, the actual date and time associated with the date is irrelevant because the time zone difference is based on the environment settings in which the JavaScript code is run.

## Example

The code in Listing 6.80 displays the time zone offset by using the getTimezoneOffset() method. Notice that when the date and time are changed, the time zone offset remains the same because the contents of the Date object are not used in the calculation.

*Listing 6.80   Using the* getTimezoneOffset() *Method to Return the Timezone Offset*

```
<html>

<script language="JavaScript">
<!-- Hide

//Create 2 very different date objects
aDate1 = new Date(1990,1,1,0,0,0,0);
aDate2 = new Date(1994,2,13,8,24,45,300);

//Display the timezone offsets
document.write("The timezone offset of aDate1 is ");
document.write(aDate1.getTimezoneOffset()," minutes.<br>");
document.write("The timezone offset of aDate2 is "
document.write(aDate2.getTimezoneOffset()," minutes.");

//Hide End -->
</script>

</html>
```

# Date.getUTCDate()

*JavaScript 1.2+, ECMAScript 1.0+, JScript 3.0+*

*Nav4+, IE 4+*

## Syntax

`date.getUTCDate()`

## Description

The `getUTCDate()` method returns the day of the month converted to universal time and expressed as an integer from 1 to 31.

## Example

The code in Listing 6.81 displays the day of the month in universal time using the `getUTCDate()` method.

*Listing 6.81    Using the* `getUTCDate()` *Method to Return the Day of the Month*

```
<html>

<script language="JavaScript">
<!-- Hide

//Create a Date object that contains the current date and time.
theDate = new Date();

//Display the UTC date
document.write("The UTC date is ",theDate.getUTCDate());

//Hide End -->
</script>

</html>
```

# Date.getUTCDay()

*JavaScript 1.2+, ECMAScript 1.0+, JScript 3.0+*

*Nav4+, IE 4+, Opera3+*

## Syntax

`date.getUTCDay()`

## Description

The `getUTCDay()` method returns the day of the week converted to universal time and expressed as an integer from 0 (Sunday) to 6 (Saturday).

## Example

The code in Listing 6.82 uses the getUTCDay() method to return the day of the week expressed as an integer in universal time. The number is then converted to a string equivalent to the day of the week.

*Listing 6.82    Using the* getUTCDay() *Method to Return the Day of the Week*

```
<html>

<script language="JavaScript">
<!-- Hide

//This function converts the day from a number to
//a string and returns the string.
function getDayString(num)
{
  var day;      //Create a local variable to hold the string
  switch(num)
  {
    case 0:
      day="Sunday";
      break;
    case 1:
      day="Monday";
      break;
    case 2:
      day="Tuesday";
      break;
    case 3:
      day="Wednesday";
      break;
    case 4:
      day="Thursday";
      break;
    case 5:
      day="Friday";
      break;
    case 6:
      day="Saturday";
      break;
    default:
      day="Invalid day";
  }
  return day;
}

//Create a Date object that contains the current date and time.
```

*continues*

*Listing 6.82    continued*
```
theDate = new Date();

//Display the UTC day
document.write("The UTC day is ",getDayString(theDate.getUTCDay()));

//Hide End -->
</script>

</html>
```

# Date.getUTCFullYear()

## *JavaScript 1.2+, ECMAScript 1.0+, JScript 3.0+*

## *Nav4+, IE 4+*

## Syntax

*date*.getUTCFullYear()

## Description

The getUTCFullYear() method returns the year as a full four-digit number converted to universal time.

## Example

The code in Listing 6.83 displays the year in universal time using the getUTCFullYear() method.

*Listing 6.83    Using the* getUTCFullYear() *Method to Return the Year*
```
<html>

<script language="JavaScript">
<!-- Hide

//Create a Date object that contains the current date and time.
theDate = new Date();

//Display the full UTC year
document.write("The UTC year is ",theDate.getUTCFullYear());

//Hide End -->
</script>

</html>
```

# Date.getUTCHours()

## *JavaScript 1.2+, ECMAScript 1.0+, JScript 3.0+*

## *Nav4+, IE 4+*

## Syntax

`date.getUTCHours()`

## Description

The `getUTCHours()` method returns the hour portion of the date expressed, converted to universal time and expressed as an integer from 0 (12:00 a.m. midnight) to 23 (11:00 p.m.).

## Example

The code in Listing 6.84 displays the current hour in universal time using the `getUTCHours()` method.

*Listing 6.84    Using the* `getUTCHours()` *Method to Return the Current Hour*

```
<html>

<script language="JavaScript">
<!-- Hide

//Create a Date object that contains the current date and time.
theDate = new Date();

//Display the hour
document.write("The UTC hour is ",theDate.getUTCHours());

//Hide End -->
</script>

</html>
```

# Date.getUTCMilliseconds()

## *JavaScript 1.2+, ECMAScript 1.0+, JScript 3.0+*

## *Nav4+, IE 4+*

## Syntax

`date.getUTCMilliseconds()`

## Description

The `getUTCMilliseconds()` method returns the millisecond portion of the date converted to universal time and expressed as an integer from 0 to 999.

## Example

The code in Listing 6.85 displays the current millisecond in universal time using the getUTCMilliseconds() method.

*Listing 6.85    Using the* `getUTCMilliseconds()` *Method to Return the Current Milliseconds*

```
<html>

<script language="JavaScript">
<!-- Hide

//Create a Date object that contains the current date and time.
theDate = new Date();

//Display the UTC milliseconds
document.write("The UTC millisecond is ",theDate.getUTCMilliseconds());

//Hide End -->
</script>

</html>
```

# Date.getUTCMinutes()

## JavaScript 1.2+, ECMAScript 1.0+, JScript 3.0+

## Nav4+, IE 4+

## Syntax

`date.getUTCMinutes()`

## Description

The getUTCMinutes() method returns the minutes portion of the Date object converted to universal time and expressed as an integer from 0 to 59.

## Example

The code in Listing 6.86 displays the current minute in universal time using the getUTCMinutes() method.

*Listing 6.86    Using the* `getUTCMinutes()` *Method to Return the Current Minutes*

```
<html>

<script language="JavaScript">
<!-- Hide

//Create a Date object that contains the current date and time.
```

```
theDate = new Date();

//Display the UTC minutes
document.write("The UTC minute is ",theDate.getUTCMinutes());

//Hide End -->
</script>

</html>
```

# Date.getUTCMonth()

## JavaScript 1.2+, ECMAScript 1.0+, JScript 3.0+

## Nav4+, IE 4+

### Syntax

`date.getUTCMonth()`

### Description

The getUTCMonth() method returns the month portion of the Date object converted to universal time and expressed as an integer from 0 (January) to 11 (December).

### Example

The code in Listing 6.87 uses the getUTCMonth() method to return the current month, expressed as an integer, in universal time. The integer is converted to string representation of the month.

*Listing 6.87    Using the* getUTCMonth() *Method to Return the Current Month*

```
<html>

<script language="JavaScript">
<!-- Hide

//This function converts the month from a number to
//a string and returns the string.
function getMonthString(num)
{
  var month;      //Create a local variable to hold the string
  switch(num)
  {
    case 0:
      month="January";
      break;
    case 1:
      month="February";
      break;
```

*continues*

*Listing 6.87  continued*

```
    case 2:
      month="March";
      break;
    case 3:
      month="April";
      break;
    case 4:
      month="May";
      break;
    case 5:
      month="June";
      break;
    case 6:
      month="July";
      break;
    case 7:
      month="August";
      break;
    case 8:
      month="September";
      break;
    case 9:
      month="October";
      break;
    case 10:
      month="November";
      break;
    case 11:
      month="December";
      break;
    default:
      month="Invalid month";
  }
  return month;
}

//Create a Date object that contains the current date and time.
theDate = new Date();

//Display the UTC month
document.write("The UTC month is ",theMonthString(theDate.getUTCMonth()));

//Hide End -->
</script>

</html>
```

# Date.getUTCSeconds()

*JavaScript 1.2+, ECMAScript 1.0+, JScript 3.0+*

*Nav4+, IE 4+*

## Syntax

`date.getUTCSeconds()`

## Description

The `getUTCSeconds()` method returns the seconds portion of the `Date` object, converted to universal time and expressed as an integer from 0 to 59.

## Example

The code in Listing 6.88 displays the current second in universal time using the `getUTCSeconds()` method.

*Listing 6.88    Using the `getUTCSeconds()` Method to Return the Current Second*

```
<html>

<script language="JavaScript">
<!-- Hide

//Create a Date object that contains the current date and time.
theDate = new Date();

//Display the UTC seconds
document.write("The UTC seconds is ",theDate.getUTCSeconds());

//Hide End -->
</script>

</html>
```

# Date.getYear()

*JavaScript 1.0+, ECMAScript 1.0+, JScript 1.0+*

*Nav2+, NES2+, IE 3+, Opera3+*

## Syntax

`date.getYear()`

## Description

The `getYear()` method returns the year portion of the `Date` object. Unfortunately, the year is represented as either a two-digit number or a four-digit number, depending on the browser version. For example, the year 1983 may be returned from the methods as 1983 or just 83. The getYear() method was depreciated in JavaScript 1.2 in favor of the getFullYear() method.

## CAUTION

Netscape version 2 and 3 display the years from 1900 to 1999 by subtracting 1900 from the year to effectively create a two-digit representation of the year. Years less than 1900 and greater than 1999 are displayed as four-digit numbers.

Netscape version 4.5 always subtracts 1900 from the year for all years.

## CAUTION

Internet Explorer 3 always subtracts 1900 from the year for all years since 1970. Dates prior to 1970 are not handled by Internet Explorer 3. This means the year 2001 would be returned as 101.

### Example

The code in Listing 6.89 displays the year using the getYear() method associated with your specific browser.

*Listing 6.89    Using the* getYear() *Method to Return the Current Year*

```
<html>

<script language="JavaScript">
<!-- Hide

//Create a Date object that contains the current date and time.
theDate = new Date();

//Display the year
document.write("The year is ",theDate.getYear());

//Hide End -->
</script>

</html>
```

# Date.parse()

## JavaScript 1.0+, ECMAScript 1.0+, JScript 1.0+

## Nav2+, NES2+, IE 3+

## Syntax

```
Date.parse(date)
```

## Description

The parse() method returns the time, represented in milliseconds between date argument string and midnight, January 1, 1970, GMT. Notice that this method is associated with the "Date" object rather than a date that was declared. The string date should use the format written by the Date toGMTString() method, which looks like the following:

Mon, 24 Oct 1982 12:03:27 -0200

The method will also accept strings that lack all or portions of the time and time zone.

## Example

The code in Listing 6.90 displays the milliseconds from 1970 to the string representation of the date and time.

*Listing 6.90    Using the* parse() *Method*

```
<html>
<script language="JavaScript">
<!-- Hide


//Display a date in milliseconds
document.write("<br>The milliseconds of the string: ");
document.write(Date.parse("Sun, 24 Oct 1982 12:03:27"));

//Hide End -->
</script>

</html>
```

# Date.prototype

## *JavaScript 1.1+, ECMAScript 1.0+, JScript 3.0+*

## *Nav3+, NES3+, IE 4+*

## Syntax

Date.prototype.*property*

Date.prototype.*method*

## Description

The prototype property allows you to add new properties and methods to the Date object that can be used throughout your code.

## Example

In Listing 6.91, the prototype property is used to create a new method, called getDayString, which can be used by all Date objects. The getDayString() method uses the getDayString() function to return a string representation of the day of the week (for example, Sunday, Monday, Tuesday,...). This new functionality is used to display the name of the current day.

*Listing 6.91    Creating a New Method to Get the String Representation of the Day*

```html
<html>

<script>
<!-- Hide

//This function returns a string representation of the day
function getDayString()
{
  var day
  switch(this.getDay())
  {
    case 0:
      day="Sunday";
      break;
    case 1:
      day="Monday";
      break;
    case 2:
      day="Tuesday";
      break;
    case 3:
      day="Wednesday";
      break;
    case 4:
      day="Thursday";
      break;
    case 5:
      day="Friday";
      break;
    case 6:
      day="Saturday";
      break;
    default:
      day="Invalid day";
  }
  return(day);
}

//Make the getDayString function available to all Date objects
Date.prototype.getDayString = getDayString;

//Create a Date object with current date and time
var currentDate = new Date();
```

```
//Display the day as a string
document.write("<h2>Today is ",currentDate.getDayString(),"</h2>");


//Hide End -->
</script>

</html>
```

# Date.setDate()

## *JavaScript 1.0+, ECMAScript 1.0+, JScript 1.0+*

## *Nav2+, NES2+, IE 3+, Opera3+*

### Syntax
`date.setDate(day)`

### Description

The setDate() method sets the day of the month in the Date object to the argument day, an integer from 1 to 31. The method returns an integer representing the number of milliseconds between midnight January 1, 1970 (GMT) to the date and time specified in the Date object after the day of the month has been adjusted.

**CAUTION**

Prior to JavaScript 1.2, this method returned nothing.

### Example

The code in Listing 6.92 displays the current date in milliseconds before setting the day to 4. Notice that the milliseconds specified after the setDate() method are the same as the result returned from the method.

*Listing 6.92   Setting the Day of the Month with the* setDate() *Method*
```
<html>

<script language="JavaScript">
<!-- Hide


//Create a Date object.
theDate = new Date();

//Set the day of the month and display the milliseconds
document.write("Initial milliseconds=",theDate.getTime());
document.write("<br>setDate returned ");
document.write(theDate.setDate(4)," milliseconds.")
```

*continues*

*Listing 6.92  continued*
```
document.write("<br>Final milliseconds=",theDate.getTime());

//Hide End -->
</script>

</html>
```

# Date.setFullYear()

## *JavaScript 1.2+, ECMAScript 1.0+, JScript 3.0+*

## *Nav4+, IE 4+*

## *Syntax*

```
date.setFullYear(year)
```

## *Description*

The setFullYear() method sets the year in the Date object to the argument year, a four-digit integer. The method returns an integer representing the number of milliseconds between midnight January 1, 1970 (GMT) to the date and time specified in the Date object after the year has been adjusted.

## *Example*

The code in Listing 6.93 displays the current date in milliseconds before setting the year to 2003. Notice that the milliseconds specified after the setFullYear() method are the same as the result returned from the method.

*Listing 6.93  Setting the Day of the Week with the setDay() Method*
```
<html>

<script language="JavaScript">
<!-- Hide

//Create a Date object.
theDate = new Date();

//Set the year and display the milliseconds
document.write("Initial milliseconds=",theDate.getTime());
document.write("<br>setFullYear returned ");
document.write(theDate.setFullYear(2003)," milliseconds.")
document.write("<br>Final milliseconds=",theDate.getTime());

//Hide End -->
</script>

</html>
```

# Date.setHours()

## JavaScript 1.0+, ECMAScript 1.0+, JScript 1.0+

## Nav2+, NES2+, IE 3+, Opera3+

## Syntax

`date.setHours(hours)`

## Description

The setHours() method sets the hour in the Date object to the argument hours, an integer from 0 (12:00 a.m. midnight) to 23 (11:00 p.m.). The method returns an integer representing the number of milliseconds between midnight January 1, 1970 (GMT) to the date and time specified in the Date object after the hour has been adjusted.

## Example

The code in Listing 6.94 displays the current date in milliseconds before setting the hour to 7 (8:00 a.m.). Notice that the milliseconds specified after the setHours() method are the same as the result returned from the method.

*Listing 6.94    Setting the Hour with the* `setHours()` *Method*

```
<html>

<script language="JavaScript">
<!-- Hide

//Create a Date object.
theDate = new Date();

//Set the hour and display the milliseconds
document.write("Initial milliseconds=",theDate.getTime());
document.write("<br>setHours returned ");
document.write(theDate.setHours(7)," milliseconds.")
document.write("<br>Final milliseconds=",theDate.getTime());

//Hide End -->
</script>

</html>
```

# Date.setMilliseconds()

## JavaScript 1.2+, ECMAScript 1.0+, JScript 3.0+

## Nav4+, IE 4+

## Syntax

`date.setMilliseconds(milliseconds)`

## Description

The `setMilliseconds()` method sets the milliseconds in the `Date` object to the argument `milliseconds`, an integer from 0 999. The method returns an integer representing the number of milliseconds between midnight January 1, 1970 (GMT) to the date and time specified in the `Date` object after the milliseconds have been adjusted.

## Example

Listing 6.95 displays the current date in milliseconds before setting the milliseconds to 792. Notice that the milliseconds specified after the `setMilliseconds()` method are the same as the result returned from the method.

*Listing 6.95   Setting the Milliseconds with the* `setMilliseconds()` *Method*

```
<html>

<script language="JavaScript">
<!-- Hide

//Create a Date object.
theDate = new Date();

//Set the milliseconds
document.write("Initial milliseconds=",theDate.getTime());
document.write("<br>setMilliseconds returned ");
document.write(theDate.setMilliseconds(792)," milliseconds.")
document.write("<br>Final milliseconds=",theDate.getTime());

//Hide End -->
</script>

</html>
```

# Date.setMinutes()

## *JavaScript 1.0+, ECMAScript 1.0+, JScript 1.0+*

## *Nav2+, NES2+, IE 3+, Opera3+*

## Syntax

`date.setMinutes(minutes)`

## Description

The `setMinutes()` method sets the minutes in the `Date` object to the argument `minutes`, an integer from 0 to 59. The method returns an integer representing the number of milliseconds between midnight January 1, 1970 (GMT) to the date and time specified in the `Date` object after the minutes have been adjusted.

## Example

The code in Listing 6.96 displays the current date in milliseconds before setting the minutes to 43. Notice that the milliseconds specified after the setMinutes() method are the same as the result returned from the method.

*Listing 6.96  Setting the Minutes with the* setMinutes() *Method*

```
<html>

<script language="JavaScript">
<!-- Hide

//Create a Date object.
theDate = new Date();

//Set the minutes and display the milliseconds
document.write("Initial milliseconds=",theDate.getTime());
document.write("<br>setMinutes returned ");
document.write(theDate.setMinutes(43)," milliseconds.")
document.write("<br>Final milliseconds=",theDate.getTime());

//Hide End -->
</script>

</html>
```

# Date.setMonth()

## *JavaScript 1.0+, ECMAScript 1.0+, JScript 1.0+*

## *Nav2+, NES2+, IE 3+, Opera3+*

## Syntax

*date.*setMonth(*month*)

## Description

The setMonth() method sets the month in the Date object to the argument month, an integer from 0 (January) to 11 (December). The method returns an integer representing the number of milliseconds between midnight January 1, 1970 (GMT) to the date and time specified in the Date object after the month has been adjusted.

**CAUTION**

Prior to JavaScript 1.2, this method returned nothing.

## Example

The code in Listing 6.97 displays the current date in milliseconds before setting the month to 2 (March). Notice that the milliseconds specified after the setMonth() method are the same as the result returned from the method.

*Listing 6.97    Setting the Month with the* `setMonth()` *Method*

```
<html>

<script language="JavaScript">
<!-- Hide

//Create a Date object.
theDate = new Date();

//Set the month and display the milliseconds
document.write("Initial milliseconds=",theDate.getTime());
document.write("<br>setMonth returned ");
document.write(theDate.setMonth(2)," milliseconds.")
document.write("<br>Final milliseconds=",theDate.getTime());

//Hide End -->
</script>

</html>
```

# Date.setSeconds()

## *JavaScript 1.0+, ECMAScript 1.0+, JScript 1.0+*

## *Nav2+, NES2+, IE 3+, Opera3+*

### Syntax

*date.*setSeconds(*seconds*)

### Description

The `setSeconds()` method sets the seconds in the `Date` object to the argument `seconds`, an integer from 0 to 59. The method returns an integer representing the number of milliseconds between midnight January 1, 1970 (GMT) to the date and time specified in the `Date` object after the seconds have been adjusted.

### CAUTION

Prior to JavaScript 1.2, this method returned nothing.

### Example

The code in Listing 6.98 displays the current date in milliseconds before setting the seconds to 16. Notice that the milliseconds specified after the `setSeconds()` method are the same as the result returned from the method.

*Listing 6.98    Setting the Seconds with the* `setSeconds()` *Method*

```
<html>

<script language="JavaScript">
```

```
<!-- Hide

//Create a Date object.
theDate = new Date();

//Set the seconds and display the milliseconds
document.write("Initial milliseconds=",theDate.getTime());
document.write("<br>setSeconds returned ");
document.write(theDate.setSeconds(16)," milliseconds.")
document.write("<br>Final milliseconds=",theDate.getTime());

//Hide End -->
</script>

</html>
```

# Date.setTime()

## *JavaScript 1.0+, ECMAScript 1.0+, JScript 1.0+*

## *Nav2+, NES2+, IE 3+, Opera3+*

### Syntax

```
date.setTime(milliseconds)
```

### Description

The setTime() method sets the time in the Date object to the argument milliseconds, an integer representing the number of milliseconds between midnight January 1, 1970 (GMT) to the desired date and time.

### Example

The code in Listing 6.99 uses the setTime() method to set the date to November, 17, 2005 using milliseconds.

*Listing 6.99   Setting the Date with the* setTime() *Method*

```
<html>

<script language="JavaScript">
<!-- Hide

//Create a Date object.
theDate = new Date();

//Set the date to Nov. 17, 2005
theDate.setTime(1132203600000);

//display the date
```

*continues*

*Listing 6.99    continued*
```
document.write(theDate.toString());

//Hide End -->
</script>

</html>
```

# Date.setUTCDate()

## JavaScript 1.2+, ECMAScript 1.0+, JScript 3.0+

## Nav4+, IE 4+

### Syntax

`date.setUTCDate(day)`

## Description

The `setUTCDate()` method sets the day of the month in the `Date` object to the argument `day`, an integer from 1 to 31 universal time. The method returns an integer representing the number of milliseconds between midnight January 1, 1970 (GMT) to the date and time specified in the `Date` object after the day of the month has been adjusted.

## Example

The code in Listing 6.100 displays the current date in milliseconds (universal time) before setting the day to 6. Notice that the milliseconds specified after the `setUTCDate()` method are the same as the result returned from the method.

*Listing 6.100    Setting the Date with the* `setUTCDate()` *Method*
```
<html>

<script language="JavaScript">
<!-- Hide

//Create a Date object.
theDate = new Date();

//Set the day of the month and display the milliseconds
document.write("Initial milliseconds=",theDate.getTime());
document.write("<br>setUTCDate returned ");
document.write(theDate.setUTCDate(6)," milliseconds.");
document.write("<br>Final milliseconds=",theDate.getTime());

//Hide End -->
</script>
```

# Date.setUTCFullYear()

## *JavaScript 1.2+, ECMAScript 1.0+, JScript 3.0+*

## *Nav4+, IE 4+*

## *Syntax*

`date.setUTCFullYear(year)`

## *Description*

The `setUTCFullYear()` method sets the year in the `Date` object to the argument `year`, a four-digit integer universal time. The method returns an integer representing the number of milliseconds between midnight January 1, 1970 (GMT) to the date and time specified in the `Date` object after the year has been adjusted.

## *Example*

The code in Listing 6.101 displays the current date in milliseconds (universal time) before setting the year to `2004`. Notice that the milliseconds specified after the `setUTCFullYear()` method are the same as the result returned from the method.

*Listing 6.101    Setting the Year with the* `setUTCFullYear()` *Method*

```
<html>

<script language="JavaScript">
<!-- Hide

//Create a Date object.
theDate = new Date();

//Set the year and display the milliseconds
document.write("Initial milliseconds=",theDate.getTime());
document.write("<br>setUTCFullYear returned ");
document.write(theDate.setUTCFullYear(2004)," milliseconds.")
document.write("<br>Final milliseconds=",theDate.getTime());

//Hide End -->
</script>

</html>
```

# Date.setUTCHours()

## *JavaScript 1.2+, ECMAScript 1.0+, JScript 3.0+*

## *Nav4+, IE 4+*

## *Syntax*

`date.setUTCHours(hours)`

## Description

The setUTCHours() method sets the hour in the Date object to the argument hours, an integer from 0 (12:00 a.m. midnight) to 23 (11:00 p.m.) universal time. The method returns an integer representing the number of milliseconds between midnight January 1, 1970 (GMT) to the date and time specified in the Date object after the hour has been adjusted.

## Example

The code in Listing 6.102 displays the current date in milliseconds (universal time) before setting the hour to 5 (6:00am). Notice that the milliseconds specified after the setUTCHours() method are the same as the result returned from the method.

*Listing 6.102   Setting the Hour with the* setUTCHours() *Method*

```
<html>

<script language="JavaScript">
<!-- Hide

//Create a Date object.
theDate = new Date();

//Set the hour and display the milliseconds
document.write("Initial milliseconds=",theDate.getTime());
document.write("<br>setUTCHours returned ");
document.write(theDate.setUTCHours(5)," milliseconds.")
document.write("<br>Final milliseconds=",theDate.getTime());

//Hide End -->
</script>

</html>
```

# Date.setUTCMilliseconds()

## *JavaScript 1.2+, ECMAScript 1.0+, JScript 3.0+*

## *Nav4+, IE 4+*

## Syntax

*date*.setUTCMilliseconds(*milliseconds*)

## Description

The setUTCMilliseconds() method sets the milliseconds in the Date object to the argument milliseconds, an integer from 0 999 universal time. The method returns an integer representing the number of milliseconds between midnight January 1, 1970 (GMT) to the date and time specified in the Date object after the milliseconds have been adjusted.

## Example

The code in Listing 6.103 displays the current date in milliseconds (universal time) before setting the milliseconds to 258. Notice that the milliseconds specified after the setUTCMilliseconds() method are the same as the result returned from the method.

*Listing 6.103   Setting the Milliseconds with the* setUTCMilliseconds() *Method*

```
<html>

<script language="JavaScript">
<!-- Hide

//Create a Date object.
theDate = new Date();

//Set the milliseconds
document.write("Initial milliseconds=",theDate.getTime());
document.write("<br>setUTCMilliseconds returned ");
document.write(theDate.setUTCMilliseconds(258)," milliseconds.")
document.write("<br>Final milliseconds=",theDate.getTime());

//Hide End -->
</script>

</html>
```

# Date.setUTCMinutes()

## *JavaScript 1.2+, ECMAScript 1.0+, JScript 3.0+*

## *Nav4+, IE 4+*

## Syntax

*date.*setUTCMinutes(*minutes*)

## Description

The setUTCMinutes() method sets the minutes in the Date object to the argument minutes, an integer from 0 to 59 universal time. The method returns an integer representing the number of milliseconds between midnight January 1, 1970 (GMT) to the date and time specified in the Date object after the minutes have been adjusted.

## Example

The code in Listing 6.104 displays the current date in milliseconds (universal time) before setting the minutes to 19. Notice that the milliseconds specified after the setUTCMinutes() method are the same as the result returned from the method.

*Listing 6.104    Setting the Minutes with the* `setUTCMinutes()` *Method*

```
<html>

<script language="JavaScript">
<!-- Hide

//Create a Date object.
theDate = new Date();

//Set the minutes and display the milliseconds
document.write("Initial milliseconds=",theDate.getTime());
document.write("<br>setUTCMinutes returned ");
document.write(theDate.setUTCMinutes(19)," milliseconds.")
document.write("<br>Final milliseconds=",theDate.getTime());

//Hide End -->
</script>

</html>
```

# Date.setUTCMonth()

## JavaScript 1.2+, ECMAScript 1.0+, JScript 3.0+

## Nav4+, IE 4+

## Syntax

`date.setUTCMonth(month)`

## Description

The `setUTCMonth()` method sets the month in the `Date` object to the argument `month`, an integer from 0 (January) to 11 (December) universal time. The method returns an integer representing the number of milliseconds between midnight January 1, 1970 (GMT) to the date and time specified in the `Date` object after the month has been adjusted.

## Example

The code in Listing 6.105 displays the current date in milliseconds (universal time) before setting the month to 4 (May). Notice that the milliseconds specified after the `setUTCMonth()` method are the same as the result returned from the method.

*Listing 6.105    Setting the Month with the* `setUTCMonth()` *Method*

```
<html>

<script language="JavaScript">
<!-- Hide

//Create a Date object.
```

```
theDate = new Date();

//Set the month and display the milliseconds
document.write("Initial milliseconds=",theDate.getTime());
document.write("<br>setUTCMonth returned ");
document.write(theDate.setUTCMonth(4)," milliseconds.")
document.write("<br>Final milliseconds=",theDate.getTime());

//Hide End -->
</script>

</html>
```

# Date.setUTCSeconds()

## *JavaScript 1.2+, ECMAScript 1.0+, JScript 3.0+*

## *Nav4+, IE 4+*

## Syntax

*date.* setUTCSeconds *(seconds)*

## Description

The setUTCSeconds() method sets the seconds in the Date object to the argument seconds, an integer from 0 to 59 universal time. The method returns an integer representing the number of milliseconds between midnight January 1, 1970 (GMT) to the date
and time specified in the Date object after the seconds have been adjusted.

## Example

The code in Listing 6.106 displays the current date in milliseconds (universal time)
before setting the seconds to 46. Notice that the milliseconds specified after the
setUTCSeconds() method are the same as the result returned from the method.

*Listing 6.106    Setting the Seconds with the* setUTCSeconds() *Method*

```
<html>

<script language="JavaScript">
<!-- Hide

//Create a Date object.
theDate = new Date();

//Set the seconds and display the milliseconds
document.write("Initial milliseconds=",theDate.getTime());
document.write("<br>setUTCSeconds returned ");
document.write(theDate.setUTCSeconds(46)," milliseconds.")
```

*continues*

*Listing 6.106    continued*
```
document.write("<br>Final milliseconds=",theDate.getTime());

//Hide End -->
</script>

</html>
```

# Date.setYear()

## *JavaScript 1.0+, ECMAScript 1.0+, JScript 1.0+*

## *Nav2+, NES2+, IE 3+, Opera3+*

## Syntax

`date.setYear(year)`

## Description

The setYear() method sets the year in the Date object to the argument year. The argument can be either a four-digit or two-digit integer. To create a two-digit representation, subtract 1900 from the desired date. The method returns an integer representing the number of milliseconds between midnight January 1, 1970 (GMT) to the date and time specified in the Date object after the year has been adjusted.

## CAUTION

Prior to JavaScript 1.2, this method returned nothing.

## Example

The code in Listing 6.107 displays the current date in milliseconds before setting the year to 1983. Notice that the milliseconds specified after the setYear() method are the same as the result returned from the method.

*Listing 6.107    Setting the Year with the setYear() Method*
```
<html>

<script language="JavaScript">
<!-- Hide

//Create a Date object.
theDate = new Date();

//Set the year and display the milliseconds
document.write("Initial milliseconds=",theDate.getTime());
document.write("<br>setYear returned ");
document.write(theDate.setYear(83)," milliseconds.")
```

```
document.write("<br>Final milliseconds=",theDate.getTime());

//Hide End -->
</script>

</html>
```

# Date.toGMTString()

## *JavaScript 1.0+, ECMAScript 1.0+, JScript 1.0+*

## *Nav2+, NES2+, IE 3+, Opera3+*

## *Syntax*

*date.*toGMTString()

## *Description*

The toGMTString() method returns a string representing the universal time of the Date object. The date is converted to the GMT time zone before being converted to a string. The format of the string will look similar to the following:

```
Mon, 24 Oct 1982 12:03:27 GMT
```

## *Example*

The code in listing 6.108 creates a Date object that contains the current date and time. The toGMTString() method returns the date as a string in GMT.

*Listing 6.108 Converting Date and Time to GMT with the* toGMTString() *Method*

```
<html>

<script language="JavaScript">
<!-- Hide

//Create a Date object.
theDate = new Date();

//Display date and time string in GMT
document.write(theDate.toGMTString());

//Hide End -->
</script>

</html>
```

# Date.toLocaleString()

*JavaScript 1.0+, ECMAScript 1.0+, JScript 1.0+*

*Nav2+, IE 3+*

## Syntax

```
date.toLocaleString()
```

## Description

The `toLocaleString()` method returns a string representation of the `Date` object in the local time zone. The format of the string can vary greatly, depending on the user's date and time format settings.

## Example

The code in Listing 6.109 creates a `Date` object that contains the current date and time. The `toLocaleString()` method returns the date and time as a string using the local time zone.

*Listing 6.109   Converting Date and Time to the Local Time Zone with the* `toLocaleString()` *Method*

```
<html>

<script language="JavaScript">
<!-- Hide

//Create a Date object.
theDate = new Date();

//Display date and time string
document.write(theDate.toLocaleString());

//Hide End -->
</script>

</html>
```

# Date.toSource()

*JavaScript1.3+, JScript3.0+, ECMAScript2.0+ (proposed)*

*Nav4.06+, IE4+*

## Syntax

```
date.toSource()
```

## Description

The toSource() method converts the Date object to a string that represents the source of the Date instance that was created.

## Example

Listing 6.110 creates a date object March 16, 2002. The toSource() method is then applied to the date object to return the source string "(new Date(1018986503234))" with the date expressed in milliseconds.

*Listing 6.110   Accessing the Source of a Date Object with the* toSource() *Method*

```
<script language="JavaScript1.3">
<!-- Hide

//Create a Date object for March 16, 2002.
theDate = new Date(2002,3,16,15,48,23,234);


//Display "Tue Apr 16 15:48:23 GMT-0400 (Eastern Daylight Time) 2002"
document.write(theDate.toString());

//Display source of date object
document.write(theDate.toSource());  //Display "(new Date(1018986503234))"

// End hide -->
</script>
```

# Date.toString()

## *JavaScript 1.0+, ECMAScript 1.0+, JScript 1.0+*

## *Nav2+, NES2+, IE 3+*

## Syntax

date.toString()

## Description

The toString() method returns a string representation of the Date object in the local time zone.

### NOTE

How does the toString() method differ from toGMTString() and toLocaleString()? Unlike the toGMTString() method, the toString() method displays the date in the local time zone. The toString() does not always display the date in the local format of the toLocaleString() method.

## Example

The code in Listing 6.111 creates a Date object from the current date and time. The toString() method is then used to display the date as a string in the local time zone.

*Listing 6.111   Accessing Date as a String with the* toString() *Method*

```
<html>

<script language="JavaScript">
<!-- Hide

//Create a Date object.
theDate = new Date();

//Display date and time string
document.write(theDate.toString());

//Hide End -->
</script>

</html>
```

# Date.toUTCString()

## *JavaScript 1.2+, ECMAScript 1.0+, JScript 3.0+*

## *Nav4+, IE 4+, Opera3+*

## Syntax

`date.toUTCString()`

## Description

The toUTCString() method returns a string representing the universal time of the Date object. The date is converted to the GMT time zone before being converted to a string. This method is exactly the same as the toGMTString().

## Example

The code in Listing 6.112 creates a Date object and initializes it to the current date and time. The toUTCString() method is then used to display the current date and time as a string in universal time.

*Listing 6.112   Accessing Date in Universal Time with the* toUTCString() *Method*

```
<html>

<script language="JavaScript">
<!-- Hide

//Create a Date object.
```

```
theDate = new Date();

//Display date and time string in universal time
document.write(theDate.toUTCString());

//Hide End -->
</script>

</html>
```

# Date.UTC()

## JavaScript 1.0+, ECMAScript 1.0+, JScript 1.0+

## Nav2+, NES2+, IE 3+, Opera3+

## Syntax

Date.UTC(*year*, *month*, *day*, *hours*, *minutes*, *seconds*, *milliseconds*)

## Description

Since the Date constructor creates new dates in local time, the UTC() method is provided to create dates in universal time (GMT). The method accepts arguments to allow you to set all aspects of a date and time, from the year to milliseconds. An integer, representing the number of milliseconds between midnight January 1, 1970 (GMT) to the date and time specified, is returned from the method. The integer can then be used to create a new Date object. The arguments and return value are in Table 6.25.

**CAUTION**

The milliseconds returned from the method are incorrect in Navigator 2.

**Table 6.25 Arguments and Return Value Associated with UTC()**

| Type | Item | Description |
|---|---|---|
| Argument | year | A four digit representation of the year. |
| | month | The month represented as an integer where 0 represents January and 11 represents December. |
| | day | The day of the month represented as an integer from 1 to 31. Optional argument. |
| | hours | The hour represented as an integer where 0 represents 12 am (midnight) and 23 represents 11 pm. Optional argument. |
| | minutes | The minutes in the hour represented as an integer from 0 to 59. Optional argument. |

*continues*

*Table 6.25 continued*

| Type | Item | Description |
|------|------|-------------|
| | seconds | The seconds in the minute represented as an integer from 0 to 59. Optional argument. |
| | milliseconds | The milliseconds in the second represented as an integer from 0 to 999. Optional argument. |
| Returns | | An integer, representing the number of milliseconds between midnight January 1, 1970 (GMT) to the date and time specified, is returned from the method. |

## Example

The code in Listing 6.113 creates a new Date object initialized to September 29, 2002 universal time. The newly created date and time are then displayed in the browser.

*Listing 6.113   Creating a Date in Universal Time with the* UTC() *Method*

```
<html>

<script language="JavaScript">
<!-- Hide

//Create a Date object in universal time.
theDate = new Date(Date.UTC(2002,9,29,20,5,8,10));

//Display date and time string.
document.write(theDate.toUTCString());

//Hide End -->
</script>

</html>
```

# Date.valueOf()

## JavaScript1.1+, JScript3.0+, ECMAScript1.0+

## NES2+, Nav3+, IE4+, Opera3+

## Syntax

*date*.valueOf()

## Description

The valueOf() method returns the primitive value of the object. In terms of an instance of a Date object, this method returns the equivalence of the Date object in milliseconds. The milliseconds are expressed as an integer representing the number of milliseconds between midnight January 1, 1970 (GMT) to the date and time specified in the Date object.

## Example

Listing 6.114 creates a Date object representing the current date and time. The result of the valueOf() method on this date object is displayed in the browser.

*Listing 6.114    Using the* valueOf() *Method to Return the Value of the* Date *Object*

```
<script language="JavaScript">
<!-- Hide

//Create a Date object.
theDate = new Date();

//Display the source of the Dateobject
document.write(theDate.valueOf());

// End hide -->
</script>
```

# debugger

## *JavaScript 1.2+, JScript 3.0+*

## *NES3+, Nav4+, IE4+*

## Syntax

Reserved Keyword

## Description

The keyword debugger is reserved for future use.

## Example

This keyword has not been implemented, therefore no example is provided.

# default

## *JavaScript1.2+, Jscript3.0+*

## *NES3+, Nav4+, IE4+*

## Syntax

Reserved Keyword

## Description

The default keyword has not been implemented in JavaScript to date, but has been reserved for future use.

## Example

This keyword has not been implemented, therefore no example is provided.

# delete

## *JavaScript 1.0+, ECMAScript 1.0+, JScript 3.0+*

## *Nav2+, NES3+, IE 4+, Opera*

## Syntax

delete *property*

## Description

The delete operator deletes properties from objects and array elements from arrays by making them undefined. Actual memory deallocation is done by JavaScript garbage collection. Some objects, such as variables created by the var statement, are not affected by the delete operator.

### CAUTION

Prior to JavaScript 1.2, the delete operator set the object property to null rather than undefined.

## Example

The code in Listing 6.115 demonstrates how to use the delete operator to delete a Date object. Notice that the last document.write() statement does not write anything to the browser because theDate is undefined after using the delete operator.

*Listing 6.115    Using the* delete *Operator*

```
<html>

<script language="JavaScript">
<!-- Hide

//Create a Date object in universal time.
theDate = new Date();

//Display the date object.
document.write("theDate=",theDate,"<br>Deleting theDate!<br>");

//Delete theDate
delete theDate;

//Attempt to display theDate
document.write("theDate=",theDate);    //theDate is undefined
```

```
//Hide End -->
</script>

</html>
```

# double

## *JavaScript1.2+*

## *NES3+, Nav4+*

## *Syntax*

Reserved Keyword

## *Description*

The double keyword has not been implemented in JavaScript to date, but has been reserved for future use.

## *Example*

This keyword has not been implemented, therefore no example is provided.

# do...while

## *JavaScript 1.0+ , ECMAScript 1.0, JScript 3.0+*

## *Nav2+, NES3+, IE 4+, Opera 3+*

## *Syntax*

```
do{
   statement;
}while(expression);
```

## *Description*

The do...while loop always executes the loop once before evaluating the expression for the first time. Once the loop has executed for the first time, the expression, in parenthesis, is evaluated. If true, the loop is executed again. When the expression evaluates to false, the next line of code following the while structure is executed. A statement must be included in the loop that modifies a variable in the expression to prevent an infinite loop. Also, notice that a semicolon (;) must be placed after the right parenthesis.

## *Example*

Listing 6.116 uses the do...while loop to control access through a gate. Only three individuals are allowed through the gate at once.

*Listing 6.116    The* do...while *Loop*

```
<html>
<script language="JavaScript">
<!-- Hide

names = new Array("Mendy","Michael","Jeff","Bill","Mike");
x = 0; //array counter

document.write("Allow these 3 individuals through gate:<br>");

//print names of the first 3 individuals who can pass through gate.
do
{
  document.write((x+1),". ",names[x],"<br>");
  x++;   //increment counter
}
while(x<3);

//Hide End -->
</script>

</html>
```

# enum

## *JavaScript 1.3+, ECMAScript 1.0+, Jscript 3.0+*

## *Nav4.06+, IE 4+*

## *Syntax*
```
Reserved Keyword
```

## *Description*
The enum keyword is newly introduced in JavaScript1.3 and is reserved for future use.

## *Example*
This entry has not yet been implemented in the JavaScript language, and no example is provided.

# escape()

## *JavaScript 1.0+, ECMAScript 1.0+, JScript 3.0+*

## *NES2+, Nav2+, IE 4+, Opera3+*

## *Syntax*
```
escape(string)
escape(expression)
```

## Description

The escape() method takes any string object or expression and returns a string object in which all non-alphanumeric characters are converted to their numeric equivalent in the form %*XX*. The *XX* is a hexadecimal number representing the non-alphanumeric character.

## Example

Listing 6.117 shows how to use the escape() method. It takes a string of text and returns the escaped value.

*Listing 6.117   Example of How to Use* escape()

```
<script lanuguage="JavaScript">
var newString = escape("Tom & Jerry Show");
</script>
```

This returns: "Tom%20%26%20Jerry%20show". Notice that the spaces were replaced with "%20" and the & sign was replaced with %26.

Listing 6.118 shows how to return the escape() method's interpretation of user input.

*Listing 6.118   Example of Returning a Value from the* escape() *Method*

```
<html>
<body>
<script lanuguage="JavaScript">
<!-- Hide
// writes the value of input after excape has been performed
function showEscapeVal(){
    alert("The escape value is: " + escape(document.form1.input1.value));
}
// End Hide -->
</script>

<form name="form1">
Enter input:
<input type="text" name="input1" size=30>
<input type="button" value="Show Escape Value" onClick='showEscapeVal()'>
</form>

</body>
</html>
```

# eval()

## *JavaScript 1.0+, JScript 1.0+*

## *NES2+, Nav2+, IE 3+, Opera3+*

## Syntax

```
eval(command)
eval(string)
```

## Description

The `eval()` function accepts a string of JavaScript statements and evaluates it as JavaScript source code. `eval()` returns the value of the executed JavaScript statement.

---

**NOTE**

`eval()` has evolved with JavaScript. In the early releases of JavaScript, version 1.0, `eval()` was only a built-in function. When version 1.1 was released, though, it was made a method as well. But when JavaScript version 1.2 was initially released, it was changed back to being just a built-in function. However, `eval()` was once again changed to a built-in function and method with the release of Navigator 4.02 and later.

---

## Example

Listing 6.119 shows how to use `eval()` to execute a JavaScript command input by a user. Simply enter a valid JavaScript command into the text box and click the Execute button. When the button is clicked, the `run()` function is called, which performs a `eval` on the user input.

*Listing 6.119   Simple Use of `eval()` Function*

```
<html>
<body>
<script lanuguage="JavaScript">
<!-- Hide
// executes the JavaScript command entered in the text box
function run(){
     eval (document.form1.input1.value);
}
// End Hide -->
</script>

<form name="form1">
Enter a JavaScript command in the text field and click
the "execute" button to execute the command.
<br><br>
Command:<input type="text" name="input1" size=30>
<br>
<input type="button" value="execute" onClick='run()'>
</form>

</body>
</html>
```

# export

## *JavaScript 1.2+, ECMAScript 1.0+*

## *Nav4+*

## *Syntax*

```
export
```

## *Description*

Export is a keyword used by scripts implementing security features that makes objects, properties, and methods accessible to other unsigned scripts.

## *Example*

Listing 6.120 shows how to use the export keyword. In the JavaScript code, the export keyword is used to make the variables, name, city, and function, showName() available to other unsigned scripts. Other scripts would access the information using the import keyword.

*Listing 6.120    Example of Using* export

```
<html>
<body>
<script language = "JavaScript">
<!-- Hide
// declare variables
var name = "John Smith";
var city = "Atlanta";

function showName(){
     alert("Your name is: " + name);
}

// makes two variables and function available to other scripts
export name, city, showName

// End Hide -->
</script>

</body>
</html>
```

# extends

*JavaScript 1.3+, ECMAScript 1.0+*

*Nav4.06+*

## Syntax

Reserved Keyword

## Description

The extends keyword is newly introduced in JavaScript 1.3 and is reserved for future use.

## Example

This entry has not yet been implemented in the JavaScript language.

# false

*JavaScript1.2+*

*NES3+, Nav4+*

## Syntax

Reserved Keyword

## Description

The false keyword has not been implemented in JavaScript to date. It has been reserved for future use.

## Example

This keyword has not been implemented, therefore no example is provided.

# final

*JavaScript1.2+*

*NES3+, Nav4+*

## Syntax

Reserved Keyword

## Description

The final keyword has not been implemented in JavaScript to date. It has been reserved for future use.

## Example

This keyword has not been implemented, therefore no example is provided.

# finally

*JavaScript 1.3+*

*Nav4.06+*

## Syntax

Reserved Keyword

## Description

The `finally` keyword is newly introduced in JavaScript 1.3 and is reserved for future use.

## Example

This entry has not yet been implemented in the JavaScript language. No example is provided.

# float

*JavaScript1.2+*

*NES3+, Nav4+*

## Syntax

Reserved Keyword

## Description

The `float` keyword has not been implemented in JavaScript to date. It has been reserved for future use.

## Example

This keyword has not been implemented, therefore no example is provided.

# for

*JavaScript 1.0+, ECMAScript 1.0+, JScript 1.0+*

*Nav2+, NES2+, IE 3+*

## Syntax

```
for( [initial statement;] [condition;] [num;]){

  code;

}
```

## Description

The for keyword is used to create a loop that consists of three optional expressions, enclosed in parentheses and separated by semicolons, followed by a block of statements executed in the loop.

The *initial statement* is a JavaScript statement or variable declaration. The *condition* is an optional statement which is evaluated through each iteration of the loop. If *condition* is satisfied, all statements contained in the loop are executed. *num* designates if the loop increments or decrements every loop iteration. And finally, the *code* contains JavaScript statements that are executed each time the condition is satisfied.

## Example

Listing 6.121 shows an example of a loop that performs a document.write eight times. An initial variable i is declared and set equal to zero. The variable is then evaluated against the condition that it is less than nine. If this evaluates to true, the variable is incremented and the document.write expression is performed.

*Listing 6.121    Example of* for *Loop*

```
<html>
<body>
<script language="JavaScript">
<!-- Hide

    for (i=0; i<9; i++){
        document.write("Loop iteration " + i + "<br>");
    }

// End Hide -->
</script>

</body>
</html>
```

# for...in

## *JavaScript 1.0+, ECMAScript 1.0+, JScript 1.0+*

## *Nav2+, NES2+, IE 3+, Opera3+*

## Syntax

```
for(variable in object){

  code;

}
```

## Description

The for...in object iterates a specified variable over all the properties of an object. The statements, contained in the body, are executed once for each property. The *variable* is a variable interated over each property in the *object*. *code* contains JavaScript statements to be executed.

## Example

Listing 6.122 shows how to use the for...in object. The showProperties function takes an object type and object name as arguments. A for...in loop is then executed on the object displaying each of the object's properties and their values.

*Listing 6.122    Using the* for...in *Object*

```
<html>
<body>
<script language = "JavaScript>
<!-- Hide
// function displays the properties for the specified object.
function showProperties(obj, objName) {
   var result;
   for (var i in obj) {
      result += i + " = " + obj[i] + "<br>";
   }
   document.write("The properties for the " + objName + " object:" +
               "<br><br>");
   document.write(result);
}
// End Hide -->
</script>
<form name="form1">
<input type="button" value="Get Button Properties" name="button1"
onClick='showProperties(this, this.name)'>
</form>
</body>
</html>
```

# function

## *JavaScript 1.0+, ECMAScript 1.0+, JScript 1.0+*

## *Nav2+, NES2+, IE 3+, Opera3+*

## Syntax

```
function name(parm1, parm2, …, paramN)

function name()
```

## Description

The function keyword is used for specifying JavaScript functions. Javascript functions typically contain a series of JavaScript statements that are grouped together to perform a specific task. The *name* is the name of the function and *parm1* through *paramN* are any optional parameters.

## Example

Listing 6.123 shows how the `function` keyword is used. The function keyword defines the `sendMessage` function.

*Listing 6.123   Example of* `function` *Keyword*

```
<html>
<script lanuguage="JavaScript">
<!-- Hide
function sendMessage(){
     alert("The function key word is used to declare the sendMessage
function");
}
// End Hide -->
</script>
</html>
```

# Function()

## JavaScript 1.0+, ECMAScript 1.0+, JScript 1.0+

## Nav2+, NES2+, IE 3+, Opera3+

## Syntax

```
var variable = new Function()
var variable = new Function(int)
var variable = new Function(arg1, ..., argN)
```

## Description

`Function()` is a constructor that creates a `Function` object. Table 6.26 lists the different methods and properties of the `Function` object.

*Table 6.26   Properties and Methods of the Function Object*

| Property/Method | Description |
| --- | --- |
| apply() | Applies method to multiple objects |
| arguments | Array reflecting function arguments |
| arity | Number of arguments expected by function |
| call() | Allows calling of methods belonging to other functions |
| caller | Reference to function caller |
| prototype | Prototype for a class of objects |
| toSource() | Created copy of function object |
| toString() | Converts function back to string which defines it |

## Example

Listing 6.124 shows how a new `Function` object can be created with a single line. In this example, the function, when called, will change the background color of the page to blue.

*Listing 6.124   Setting the Background Color with a New* Function *Object*

```
<script language="JavaScript">
<!-- Hide

// Create a function to change background color
var setBGColor = new Function(document.bgColor='blue');

// End hide -->
</script>
```

# Function.apply()

## JavaScript 1.3+, ECMAScript 1.0+, JScript 1.0+

## Nav4.06+, IE 3+, Opera3+

### Syntax

`function.apply()`

### Description

The apply() method of the Function object is used to apply a method of one object to another object. Using the apply() method keeps developers from rewriting methods for different objects.

### Example

Listing 6.125 shows how the apply() method can be used between two objects. The bigHome function adds a new property, numRooms, to the home object.

*Listing 6.125   Using the* apply() *Method*

```
<html>
<body>
<script lanuguage="JavaScript">
<!-- Hide

// function defines a home with two properties
function home(number, street){
    var num = number;
    var str = street;
    document.write("house number is: " + num + "<br>");
    document.write("Street name is: " + str + "<br>");
}

// function adds an additional property to the basic home.
// Applies the home function.
function bigHome(number, street, rooms){
    var numRooms = rooms;
```

*continues*

*Listing 6.125    continued*

```
    home.apply(home,arguments);
    document.write("The number of rooms is: " + numRooms + "<br>");
}

myHome = new bigHome(101, Main, 5);
// End Hide -->
</script>
</body>
</html>
```

# Function.arguments

## *JavaScript 1.1+, JScript 1.0+*

## *Nav3+, NES2+, IE 3+, Opera3+*

## *Syntax*

*function.*arguments

## Description

The arguments property of the Function object is an array that holds the arguments that are passed to a function. The number of arguments passed to a defined function can be more than the number of parameters if the arguments array is used. The arguments array can only be accessed while inside the function. Any attempt to access the arguments array outside the function will result in an error.

## Example

Listing 6.126 shows how the arguments array is used. A document.write is performed, which calls the foo function. The foo function is passed two arguments and calls the foobar function with the parameter 123. The foobar function outputs the number of arguments is has and the second argument to the function that called it, in this case the foo function.

*Listing 6.126    Using the* arguments *Property*

```
<html>
<body>
<script lanuguage="JavaScript">
<!-- Hide
// function foo, calls function foobar with the parameter 123.
function foo(a,b) {
    foobar(123);
    document.write("Done with function foo" + "<br>");
}

// function foobar writes output to the document
// using the arguments property of function.
function foobar(x) {
```

```
    document.write(foobar.arguments.length + "<br>");
    document.write(foobar.arguments.caller.b + "<br>");
}

document.write(foo(21,44) + "\n");
// End Hide -->
</script>
</body>
</html>
```

# Function.arity

## JavaScript 1.2

## Nav4+, NES3+

## Syntax

`function.arity`

## Description

The `arity` property of the `Function` object represents the number of declared arguments a function expects to receive. This is valid when the language attribute of the script tag is set to `JavaScript1.2`.

## Example

Listing 6.127 shows how `arity` can be used. The first line written to the user's page contains the number of arguments passed to the function. The second line is the result of running the script.

*Listing 6.127   Example of Using* `arity`

```
<html>
<body>
<script lanuguage="JavaScript1.2">
<!-- Hide
// function subtracts the second number from the first
function subtract(first, second){
  var result = first - second;
  return result;
}

// Write the results to the screen
document.write("arity = " + subtract.arity + "<br>")
document.write("The result of the subtract function is: " + subtract(4,3));

// End Hide -->
</script>
</body>
</html>
```

# Function.call()

## *JavaScript 1.3+, JScript 1.0+*

## *Nav4.06+, IE 3+, Opera3+*

## *Syntax*

```
function.call(this)

function.call(this, arg1, arg2, ..., argN)
```

## *Description*

The call() method of the Function object allows you to call another object's method. Optional arguments can be passed to the method as shown in the second syntactical definition.

## *Example*

Listing 6.128 shows an example of the call() method. The script creates a person and author object. The author object uses the call() method to perform some of its creation.

*Listing 6.128 Using the* call() *Method of the* Function *Object*

```
<script language="JavaScript1.3">
<!-- Hide

// Create a person object to handle the creation
// of people
function person (author, name){
  this.name = name;
  this.author = true;
}

// Create an author object
function authors(name, books){
  this.books = books;
  person.call(this, name);
}

authors.prototype = new person();

// Create a new author
var myAuthor = new authors("Allen", 5);

// End hide -->
</script>
```

# Function.caller

*JavaScript 1.1+, JScript 1.0+*

*Nav3+, NES2+, IE 3+, Opera3+*

## Syntax

```
function.caller
```

## Description:

The `caller` property of the `Function` object is used to reference the function that called the currently executing function.

## Example

Listing 6.129 shows how the `caller` property is used to get the name of the function calling `John()`.

*Listing 6.129    Accessing the* `caller` *Property*

```
<html>
<body>
<script lanuguage="JavaScript1.1">
<!-- Hide

// Define a simple function Alice(), which calls the John() function.
function Alice(){
     var Boss = true;
     John();
}

// function outputs its caller
function John(){
    myBoss = John.caller.name;
    document.write("The boss is: " + myBoss + "<br>");
}
// End Hide -->
</script>
</body>
</html>
```

# Function.prototype

*JavaScript 1.1+, ECMAScript 1.0+, JScript 1.0+*

*Nav3+, NES2+, IE 3+, Opera3+*

## Syntax

```
function.prototype.property
```

```
function.prototype.method
```

## Description

The prototype property of the Function object refers to the object that serves as the prototype from which classes are created. prototype allows you to add new properties of methods to an existing class by adding them to the prototype associated with the constructor of that class.

## Example

Listing 6.130 shows how the prototype property is used. The function setTask, which simply sets the "task" variable, is defined. Then a new prototype called duty is created for the String object. The duty prototype is set to call the setTask function. Now all String objects in the example have the setTask method.

*Listing 6.130    Example for* prototype *Property*

```
<html>
<body>
<script lanuguage="JavaScript">
<!-- Hide

var mytask = new String();

// sample function that sets the task string
function setTask(str){
    var task="Girls go shopping";

    if(str != null){
     task = str;
    }
    return task;
}

String.prototype.duty = setTask;

document.write("The first task is: " + mytask.duty("Nothing") + "<br>");
document.write("The next task is: " + mytask.duty());
// End Hide -->
</script>
</body>
</html>
```

# Function.toSource()

## JavaScript 1.3+, JScript 1.0+

## Nav4.06+, IE 3+, Opera3+

## Syntax

```
function.toSource()
```

## Description

The toSource() method of the Function object allows you to create a copy of an object.

## Example

Listing 6.131 uses the toSource() method on a newly created string. Running this script in a browser returns the following:

```
(new String("This is the source"))
```

*Listing 6.131   Using the* toSource() *Method*
```
<html>
<body>
<script lanuguage="JavaScript">
<!-- Hide

// Create a new String instance
var aString = new String("This is the source");

// Call the toSource() method
bString = aString.toSource();

// Write the returned value of calling the toSource()
// method to the page.
document.write(bString);

// End Hide -->
</script>

</body>
</html>
```

# Function.toString()

## JavaScript 1.1+, ECMAScript 1.0+, JScript 3.0+

## Nav3+, NES2+, IE 4+, Opera3+

## Syntax

```
function.toString()
```

## Description

The toString() method of the Function object is used to convert a function to string. The method converts the function back to the JavaScript source that defines the function. The converted string includes all aspects of the defined function.

## Example:

Listing 6.132 shows how the toString() method is used to convert a function to a text string.

*Listing 6.132   Use of* `toString()` *Method*

```
<html>
<body>
<script lanuguage="JavaScript">
<!-- Hide

// function just writes some text output
function writeText(){
    document.write("Some dummy text");
}

// Call the toString() method
var func = writeText.toString();

// Write the results to the page
document.write("The string representation of the writeText");
document.write(" function looks like: " + "<br><br><b>");
document.write(func + "</b>");
// End Hide -->
</script>

</body>
</html>
```

# Global

## *JavaScript 1.0+, JScript 1.0+*

## *Nav2+, NES2+, IE 3+, Opera3+*

## *Syntax*

Core JavaScript Object

## *Description*

The `Global` object is a core object in the JavaScript language. Properties and functions that are not associated with any other object belong to this object. Table 6.27 shows the properties and methods of this object

*Table 6.27   Properties and Functions of the Global Object*

| Property/Functions | Description |
|---|---|
| `escape()` | Returns a string object in which all non-alphanumeric characters are converted to their numeric equivalent |
| `eval()` | Accepts a string of JavaScript statements and evaluates it as JavaScript source code |
| `Infinity` | Keyword that represents positive infinity |

| Property/Functions | Description |
|---|---|
| isFinite() | Method used to determine if a variable has finite bounds |
| isNaN() | Method used to determine whether a variable is a valid number or not |
| NaN | Represents an object not equal to any number |
| parseFloat() | Method used to convert a string to a number of type float |
| parseInt() | Method used to convert a string to an integer |
| unescape () | Method that takes a hexadecimal value and returns the ISO-Latin-1 ASCII equivalent |

## Example

See the separate entries for each of these properties and functions for examples. Note that the properties and functions are not referred to with a preceeding Global reference.

# Global.escape()

## JavaScript 1.0+, ECMAScript 1.0+, JScript 1.0+

## Nav2+, NES2+, IE 3+, Opera3+

## Syntax

```
escape(string)
escape(expression)
```

## Description

The escape() method takes any string object or expression and returns a string object in which all non-alphanumeric characters are converted to their numeric equivalent in the form %XX. The XX is a hexadecimal number representing the non-alphanumeric character.

## Example

Listing 6.133 shows how to use the escape() method and what it returns. It takes a string of text and returns the escaped value.

*Listing 6.133   Example of How to Use* escape()
```
<script lanuguage="JavaScript">
var newString = escape("Tom & Jerry Show");
</script>
```

This returns: "Tom%20%26%20Jerry%20show". Notice that the spaces were replaced with "%20" and the & sign was replaced with %26.

Listing 6.134 shows how to return the escape() method's interpretation of user input.

*Listing 6.134   Example of Taking User Input and Passing Data to the Escape Method*

```
<html>
<body>
<script lanuguage="JavaScript">
<!-- Hide
// writes the value of input after escape has been performed
function showEscapeVal(){
    document.write(escape(document.form1.input1.value);
}
// End Hide -->
</script>

<form name="form1">
<input type="text" name="input1" size=30>
</form>

</body>
</html>
```

# Global.eval()

## *JavaScript 1.0+, JScript 1.0+*

## *Nav2+, NES2+, IE 3+, Opera3+*

## *Syntax*

```
eval(command)
eval(string)
```

## *Description*

The `eval()` function accepts a string of JavaScript statements and evaluates it as JavaScript source code. `eval()` returns the value of the executed JavaScript statement.

## NOTE

eval() has evolved with JavaScript. In the early releases of JavaScript, version 1.0, eval() was only a built-in function. When version 1.1 was released though, it was made a method as well. But when JavaScript version 1.2 was initially released, it was changed back to being just a built-in function. However, eval() was once again changed to a built-on function and method, with the release of Navigator 4.02 and later.

## *Example*

Listing 6.135 shows how to use `eval()` to execute a JavaScript command input by a user. Simply enter a valid JavaScript command into the text box and click the Execute button. When the button is clicked, the run() function is called, which performs a eval on the user input.

*Listing 6.135    Simple Use of* eval() *Function*
```
<html>
<body>
<script lanuguage="JavaScript">
<!-- Hide
// executes the javascript command entered in the text box
function run(){
     eval (document.form1.input1.value);
}
// End Hide -->
</script>

<form name="form1">
Enter a Javascript command in the text field and click
the "execute" button to execute the command.
<br><br>
Command:<input type="text" name="input1" size=30>
<br>
<input type="button" value="execute" onClick='run()'>
</form>

</body>
</html>
```

# Global.Infinity

## JavaScript 1.3+, JScript 1.0+

## Nav4.06+, IE 3+, Opera3+

## Syntax
```
Infinity
```

## Description
Infinity is a JavaScript keyword that represents positive infinity.

## Example
Listing 6.136 shows how the Infinity keyword is used. An input text box is provided to enter a value to be compared to Infinity. If any number is entered, it will result in being less than Infinity. However, if the word Infinity is entered, it will result in being equal to Infinity.

*Listing 6.136   Example of Using the* `Infinity` *Property*

```
<html>
<body>
<script language = "JavaScript">
<!-- Hide

// function checks to see if the input is greater, less than, or equal
// to the value input by the user.
function checkNum(){

 input=document.form1.num.value;

   if(input < Infinity){
       alert("Your number is less than Infinity");
   }
   else if(input > Infinity){
      alert("Your number is greater than Infinity");
   }
   else if(input == Infinity){
     alert("Your number if equal to Infinity");
   }

}
// End Hide -->
</script>

<form name="form1">
Enter a number to compare against Infinity.
<br><br>
<input type="text" size="35" name="num">
<br><br>
<input type="button" value="Check Number" onClick='checkNum()'>
</form>
// End Hide -->
</script>

</body>
</html>
```

# Global.isFinite()

*JavaScript 1.3+, ECMAScript 1.0+, JScript 3.0+*

*Nav4.06+, IE 4+, Opera3+*

## Syntax

```
isFinite()
```

## Description

The isFinite() method is used to determine if a variable has finite bounds.

## Example

In Listing 6.137, you see how the isFinite() method is used to verify if the user input value has finite bounds.

*Listing 6.137   Example of* isFinite() *Method*

```
<html>
<body>

<script lanuguage="JavaScript">
<!-- Hide

function checkNum(){
    var n = document.form1.text1.value;
    if(isFinite(n) == true){
       alert("Your entry had finite bounds");
     }
}
// End Hide -- >
</script>

<form name="form1">
Enter a number or character into the text box and then click the check value
button to verify if the input is a number.
<br><br>
<input type="text" name="text1" size=3>
<br><br>
<input type="button" value="Check value" onClick='checkNum()'>
<br>
</form>

</body>
</html>
```

# Global.isNaN()

## JavaScript 1.1+, JScript 1.0+

## Nav3+, NES2+, IE 3+, Opera3+

## Syntax

isNaN(*variable*)

## Description

The isNaN() function is used to determine whether *variable* is a valid number.

## Example

In Listing 6.138, you see how the isNaN() function can be used to check user input.

*Listing 6.138    Example of* isNaN() *Function*

```
<html>
<body>
<script lanuguage="JavaScript">
<!-- Hide

function checkNum(){
    var n = document.form1.text1.value;
    if(isNaN(n) == true){
        alert("Your entry is not a number");
    }
}
// End Hide -- >
</script>

<form name="form1">
Enter a number or character into the text box and then click the check value
button to verify if the input is a number.
<br><br>
<input type="text" name="text1" size=3>
<br><br>
<input type="button" value="Check value" onClick='checkNum()'>
<br>
</form>

</body>
</html>
```

# Global.NaN

## *JavaScript 1.3+, JScript 1.0+*

## *Nav4.06+, IE 3+*

## Syntax

NaN

## Description

The NaN object represents an object that is not equal to any number, including itself. NaN stands for *Not a Number*.

## Example

Listing 6.139 shows how the NaN object is used in a comparison.

*Listing 6.139    Example Using the* NaN *Object*

```
<html>
<body>
<script lanuguage="JavaScript">
<!-- Hide
if ("a" != NaN){
    document.write("This is not a number");
}
// End Hide -->
</script>

</body>
</html>
```

# Global.parseFloat()

## *JavaScript 1.0+, ECMAScript 1.0+, JScript 1.0+*

## *Nav2+, NES2+, IE 3+, Opera3+*

### *Syntax*

```
paraseFloat(string)
```

### *Description*

The parseFloat() method is used to convert a string to a number.

### *Example*

Listing 6.140 shows how the parseFloat() is used. In the example, parseFloat is called with two different strings. The first string, which contains numerical characters, is converted to a number without any problems. The second string, which contains alphabetic characters, is unable to be converted into a number.

*Listing 6.140    Example of the* parseFloat() *Method*

```
<html>
<body>
<script language="JavaScript">
<!-- Hide
// convert the "1245.31" string to a number
document.write("The string 1245.31 converted is" + parseFloat("1245.31") +
"<br>");

// try to convert the string "test" to a number.
// if not possible, then print error.
if( isNaN(parseFloat("test")) ){
    document.write("Cannot convert test string to a number.");
}
// End Hide -->
```

*continues*

*Listing 6.140    continued*
```
</script>

</body>
</html>
```

# Global.parseInt()

## *JavaScript 1.0+, ECMAScript 1.0+, JScript 1.0+*

## *Nav2+, NES2+, IE 3+, Opera3+*

## Syntax

```
parseInt(string, radix)

parseInt(string)
```

## Description

The parseInt() method is used to convert a string to an integer. It can take *string* input with an optional *radix* input. The *radix* input represents the base of the number in the string.

## Example

Listing 6.141 shows how parseInt() is used to parse a string. A few different examples are shown for different string types.

*Listing 6.141    Example of the parseInt() Method*
```
<html>
<body>
<script language="JavaScript">
<!-- Hide
// convert the "859" string to an integer
document.write("The string 859 converted to an integer is: ");
document.write(parseInt("859") + "<br>");

// converts a binary string into a integer
document.write("The binary string 101101 converted to an integer is: ");
document.write(parseInt("101101", 2) + "<br>");

// converts a hexidecimal string into an integer
document.write("The hexidecimal string FA832B converted to an integer is: ");
document.write(parseInt("FA832B", 16) + "<br>");

// End Hide -->
</script>

</body>
</html>
```

# Global.unescape()

## *JavaScript 1.0+, JScript 1.0+, ECMAScript 1.0+*

## *Nav2+, NES2+, IE3+, Opera3+*

## Syntax

```
unescape(string)
```

## Description

The unescape() method takes a hexadecimal value and returns the ISO-Latin-1 ASCII equivalent. This method performs the opposite operation of the escape() method and is commonly used to escape user-entered data before form submission.

## Example

Listing 6.142 declares a local variable, escapedVal and passes it to the unescaped() method. The result, "@", is then written to the page.

*Listing 6.142   Using the* unescape() *Method to Convert a Hexadecimal Value to Its ASCII Equivalent*

```
<script language="JavaScript">
<!-- Hide

// create a variable
var escapedVal = "%40";

// evaluate the variable and place the value in a variable
var unescapedVal = unescape(escapedVal);

document.write('The <I>escapedVal</I> value (' + escapedVal + ") ");
document.write("evaluates to " + unescapedVal);

// End hide -->
</script>
```

# if

## *JavaScript 1.0+, ECMAScript 1.0+, JScript 1.0+*

## *Nav2+, NES2+, IE 3+, Opera3+*

## Syntax

```
if(statement){
  code;
}
```

## Description

The if statement is used to perform logic statements on specific cases. If *statement* evaluates to true, *code* is executed.

## Example

In Listing 6.143, you see how the if statement is being used to determine if the temp Boolean value is true.

Listing 6.143    Example of if Statement

```
<html>
<body>
<script lanuguage="JavaScript">
<!-- Hide

var temp = 1;

if(temp == true){
     document.write("Statement is true");
}

// End Hide -- >
</script>

</body>
</html>
```

# if...else

## JavaScript 1.0+, ECMAScript 1.0+, JScript 1.0+

## Nav2+, NES2+, IE 3+, Opera3+

## Syntax

```
if(statement){
  code;
}else(statement){
  code;
}
```

## Description

The if...else statement is used to perform logic statements on specific cases. If *statement* is satisfied, its statements are executed. Otherwise, the else *statement* is evaluated. When *statement* evaluates to true, *code* is executed.

## Example

In Listing 6.144, you see how the if...else statement is being used to determine if the temp Boolean value is true.

*Listing 6.144    Example of* `if...else` *Statement*

```
<html>
<body>
<script lanuguage="JavaScript">
<!-- Hide

var temp = 1;

if(temp == true){
     document.write("Statement is true");
}
else{
     document.write("Statement is false");
}
// End Hide -- >
</script>

</body>
</html>
```

# implements

## *JavaScript1.2+*

## *NES3+, Nav4+*

## *Syntax*

Reserved Keyword

## *Description*

The `implements` keyword has not been implemented in JavaScript to date. It has been reserved for future use.

## *Example*

This keyword has not been implemented, therefore no example is provided.

# import

## *JavaScript 1.0+, ECMAScript 1.0+, JScript 1.0+*

## *Nav2+, IE 3+, Opera3+*

## *Syntax*

import

## *Description*

The `import` keyword allows a script to import properties, functions, and objects from a signed script that has exported the information.

## Example

Listing 6.145 shows how the `import` keyword is used to import multiple properties from another script.

*Listing 6.145   Example of* `import` *Keyword*

```
<html>
<body>
<script language = "JavaScript">
<!-- Hide

// imports the variables name, city and state from another script.
// This makes those properties accessible to myObj.
import myObj.name;
import myObj.city;
import myObj.state;

// End Hide -->
</script> ·

</body>
</html>
```

# in

## *JavaScript1.2+, Jscript3.0+*

## *NES3+, Nav4+, IE4+*

## *Syntax*

```
Reserved Keyword
```

## *Description*

The `in` keyword has not been implemented in JavaScript to date. It has been reserved for future use.

## *Example*

This keyword has not been implemented, therefore no example is provided.

# Infinity

## *JavaScript 1.3+, JScript 1.0+*

## *Nav4.06+, IE 3+, Opera3+*

## *Syntax*

```
Infinity
```

## Description

Infinity is a JavaScript keyword that represents positive infinity.

## Example

Listing 6.146 shows how the Infinity keyword is used. An input text box is provided to enter a value to be compared to Infinity. If any number is entered, it will result in being less than Infinity. However, if the word "Infinity" is entered, it will result in being equal to Infinity.

*Listing 6.146    Example of* infinity *Keyword*

```
<html>
<body>
<script language = "JavaScript">
<!-- Hide

// function checks to see if the input is greater, less than, or equal
// to the value input by the user.
function checkNum(){

 input=document.form1.num.value;

    if(input < Infinity){
        alert("Your number is less than Infinity");
    }
    else if(input > Infinity){
       alert("Your number if greater than Infinity");
    }
    else if(input == Infinity){
       alert("Your number if equal to Infinity");
    }

}
// End Hide -->
</script>

<form name="form1">
Enter a number to compare against Infinity.
<br><br>
<input type="text" size="35" name="num">
<br><br>
<input type="button" value="Check Number" onClick='checkNum()'>
</form>
// End Hide -->
</script>

</body>
</html>
```

# instanceof

## *JavaScript1.2+*

## *NES3+, Nav4+*

## *Syntax*

Reserved Keyword

## *Description*

The instanceof keyword has not been implemented in JavaScript to date. It has been reserved for future use.

## *Example*

This keyword has not been implemented, therefore no example is provided.

# int

## *JavaScript1.2+*

## *NES3+, Nav4+*

## *Syntax*

Reserved Keyword

## *Description*

The int keyword has not been implemented in JavaScript to date. It has been reserved for future use.

## *Example:*

This keyword has not been implemented, therefore no example is provided.

# interface

## *JavaScript1.2+*

## *NES3+, Nav4+*

## *Syntax*

Reserved Keyword

## *Description*

The interface keyword has not been implemented in JavaScript to date. It has been reserved for future use.

## Example

This keyword has not been implemented, therefore no example is provided.

# isFinite()

## *JavaScript 1.3+, ECMAScript 1.0+, JScript 3.0+*

## *Nav4.06+, IE 4+, Opera3+*

## Syntax

```
isFinite()
```

## Description

The isFinite() method is used to determine if a variable has finite bounds.

## Example

In Listing 6.147, isFinite() method is used to verify if the user input value has finite bounds.

*Listing 6.147    Example of* isFinite() *Method*

```
<html>
<body>
<script lanuguage="JavaScript">
<!-- Hide

function checkNum(){
    var n = document.form1.text1.value;
    if(isFinite(n) == true){
       alert("Your entry had finite bounds");
     }
}
// End Hide -- >
</script>

<form name="form1">
Enter a number or character into the text box and the click the check value
button to verify if the input is a number.
<br><br>
<input type="text" name="text1" size=3>
<br><br>
<input type="button" value="Check value" onClick='checkNum()'>
<br>
</form>

</body>
</html>
```

# isNaN()

## *JavaScript 1.1+, JScript 1.0+*

## *Nav3+, NES2+, IE 3+, Opera3+*

## Syntax

isNaN(*variable*)

## Description

The isNaN() function is used to determine whether or not *variable* is a valid number.

## Example

Listing 6.148, shows how the isNaN() function can be used to check user input.

*Listing 6.148   Example of* isNaN() *Function*

```
<html>
<body>
<script lanuguage="JavaScript">
<!-- Hide

function checkNum(){
    var n = document.form1.text1.value;
    if(isNaN(n) == true){
        alert("Your entry is not a number");
     }
}
// End Hide -- >
</script>

<form name="form1">
Enter a number or character into the text box and then click the check value
button to verify if the input is a number.
<br><br>
<input type="text" name="text1" size=3>
<br><br>
<input type="button" value="Check value" onClick='checkNum()'>
<br>
</form>

</body>
</html>
```

# label

*JavaScript 1.2+, JScript 1.0+*

*Nav4+, NES3+, IE 3+*

## Syntax

```
label:

  code;
```

## Description

The `label` keyword provides an identifier that can be used with `break` or `continue` to indicate where a program should continue execution. You can associate a block of JavaScript statements with each other using a label. When a label is called using `break` or `continue`, `code` is executed.

## Example

Listing 6.149 shows an example of the `label` statement in conjunction with `break`.

*Listing 6.149   Example of* `label`

```
<html>
<body>
<script language="JavaScript">
<!-- Hide
// define a label called doSomething
doSomething:
   var x = 2+2;
   var y = 5*5;
   document.write("The value of 2+2 is: " + x + "<br>");


   // define another label called doSomeMore
   doSomeMore:
      for(i=0; i<5; i++){
          document.write("Ths value of i is: " + i + "<br>");
          if(i==2){
             break doSomeMore;
          }
      }
      document.write("I did some more." + "<br>");

   document.write("The value of 5 x 5 is: " + y + "<br>");
// End Hide -->
</script>

</body>
</html>
```

# long

## *JavaScript1.2+*

## *NES3+, Nav4+*

## *Syntax*

Reserved Keyword

## *Description*

The long keyword has not been implemented in JavaScript to date. It has been reserved for future use.

## *Example*

This keyword has not been implemented, therefore no example is provided.

# Math()

## *JavaScript 1.0+, ECMAScript 1.0+, JScript 1.0+*

## *Nav2+, NES2+, IE 3+, Opera3+*

## *Syntax*

Core JavaScript Object

## *Description*

The Math object is a built-in object containing properties and methods used for mathematical computation. It is a predefined JavaScript object and can be accessed without the use of a constructor or calling method. All Math properties and methods are static. Table 6.28 shows the different methods and properties of the Math object.

### *Table 6.28  Properties and Methods of the Math Object*

| Property/Method | Description |
| --- | --- |
| abs() | Returns absolute value of a number |
| acos() | Returns the arccosine of a number |
| asin() | Returns the arcsine of a number |
| atan() | Returns the arctangent of a number |
| atan2() | Returns the arctangent of the quotient of its parameters |
| ceil | Returns the smallest integer greater than or equal to a number |
| cos() | Returns the cosine of a number |
| E | Returns the value for Euler's constant |
| exp() | Returns $E^x$, where $x$ is a number |
| floor() | Returns the largest integer less than or equal to a number |
| LN10 | Returns the natural logarithm of 10 |

| Property/Method | Description |
|---|---|
| LN2 | Returns the natural logarithm of 2 |
| log() | Returns the natural logarithm (base E) of a number |
| LOG10E | Returns the base 10 logarithm of E |
| LOG2E | Returns the base 2 logarithm of E |
| max() | Returns the larger of two arguments |
| min() | Returns the smaller of two arguments |
| PI | Returns the value of PI |
| pow() | Returns base to the exponent power, base$^{exp}$ |
| random() | Returns a random number between 0 and 1 |
| round() | Rounds a number to its nearest integer |
| sin() | Returns the sine of a number |
| sqrt() | Returns the square root of a number |
| SQRT1_2 | Returns the square root of fi |
| SQRT2 | Returns the square root of 2 |
| tan() | Returns the tangent of a number |
| toSource() | Creates a copy of an object |
| toString() | Returns a string representation of an object |

## Example

Listing 6.150 shows how to create a new Math object.

*Listing 6.150   Example of Creating a* Math *Object*

```
<html>
<body>
<title>Example of creating a Math object</title>
<script language="JavaScript">
<!-- Hide
var newMathObject = Math.E;
// End Hide -->
</script>

</body>
</html>
```

# Math.abs()

## *JavaScript 1.0+, ECMAScript 1.0+, Jscript 1.0+*

## *Nav2+, NES2+, IE 3+, Opera3+*

## Syntax

math.abs(*num*)

## Description

The abs() method of the Math object is used to calculate the absolute value of *num* compared to the Math object on which it is invoked.

## Example

Listing 6.151 shows how to use the abs() method and what it returns.

*Listing 6.151    Example of* abs() *Method*

```html
<html>
<body>
<script language="JavaScript">
<!-- Hide
// function calculates the absolute value of the input number
function doMath(){
    var inputNum=document.form1.input.value;
    var result = Math.abs(inputNum);
    document.form1.answer.value = result;
}
// End Hide -->
</script>

<form name=form1>
This example calculates the absolute value of the number entered.
<br><br>
Enter Number:
<input type="text" name="input" size=10>
<input type="button" value="Calculate" onClick='doMath()'>
<br>
Answer:
<input type="text" name="answer" size=10>
</form>

</body>
</html>
```

# Math.acos()

## *JavaScript 1.0+, ECMAScript 1.0+, JScript 1.0+*

## *Nav2+, NES2+, IE 3+, Opera3+*

## Syntax

```
math.acos(num)
```

## Description

The acos() method of the Math object is used to calculate the arccosine of a number. The return value is between 0 and PI and is measured in radians. If the return value is outside this range, 0 is returned.

## Example

Listing 6.152 shows how the acos() method is used and what values can be returned.

*Listing 6.152   Example of How to Use* `acos()`

```
<html>
<body>
<script language="JavaScript">
<!-- Hide
// function calculates the arccosine of the input number
function doMath(){
    var inputNum=document.form1.input.value;
    var result = Math.acos(inputNum);
    document.form1.answer.value = result;
}
// End Hide -->
</script>

<form name=form1>
This example calculates the arccosine of the number entered.
<br><br>
Enter Number:
<input type="text" name="input" size=10>
<input type="button" value="Calculate" onClick='doMath()'>
<br>
The arccosine is:
<input type="text" name="answer" size=10>
</form>

</body>
</html>
```

# Math.asin()

## *JavaScript 1.0+, ECMAScript 1.0+, JScript 1.0+*

## *Nav2+, NES2+, IE 3+, Opera3+*

## *Syntax*

*math.*asin*(num)*

## *Description*

The asin() method of the Math object calculates and returns the arcsine of a number. The return value is –PI/2 and PI/2 in radians. If the return value is not within this range, 0 is returned.

## *Example*

Listing 6.153 shows how the asin() method is used.

*Listing 6.153    Example of* `asin()`

```
<html>
<body>
<script language="JavaScript">
<!-- Hide
// function calculates the arcsine of the input number
function doMath(){
    var inputNum=document.form1.input.value;
    var result = Math.asin(inputNum);
    document.form1.answer.value = result;
}
// End Hide -->
</script>

<form name=form1>
This example calculates the arcsine of the entered number.
<br><br>
Enter Number:
<input type="text" name="input" size=10>
<input type="button" value="Calculate" onClick='doMath()'>
<br>
The arcsin is:
<input type="text" name="answer" size=10>
</form>

</body>
</html>
```

# Math.atan()

## *JavaScript 1.0+, ECMAScript 1.0+, JScript 1.0+*

## *Nav2+, NES2+, IE 3+, Opera3+*

## Syntax

*math.*atan*(num)*

## Description

The `atan()` method of the `Math` object is used to calculate the arctangent of a number. The return value is a numeric value between –PI/2 and PI/2 radians.

## Example

Listing 6.154 shows how the `atan()` method is used to calculate the arctangent of a number.

*Listing 6.154    Example of the* `atan()` *Method*

```
<html>
<body>
<script language="JavaScript">
<!-- Hide
// function calculates the arctangent of the input number
function doMath(){
    var inputNum=document.form1.input.value;
    var result = Math.atan(inputNum);
    document.form1.answer.value = result;
}
// End Hide -->
</script>

<form name=form1>
This example calculates the arctangent of the input number.
<br><br>
Enter Number:
<input type="text" name="input" size=10>
<input type="button" value="Calculate" onClick='doMath()'>
<br>
The arctan is:
<input type="text" name="answer" size=10>
</form>

</body>
</html>
```

# Math.atan2()

## *JavaScript 1.0+, ECMAScript 1.0+, Jscript 3.0+*

## *Nav2+, NES2+, IE4+*

## *Syntax*

`math.atan2(num1, num2)`

## *Description*

The `atan2()` method of the `Math` object is used to calculate the arctangent of the quotient of its parameters. It returns a numeric value between –PI and PI representing the angle theta of an (x,y) point.

## *Example*

Listing 6.155 shows an example how the `atan2()` method is used. The two inputs are taken and stored in variables, `inputNum1` and `inputNum2`. The `atan2()` method is then called using the user input, and the result is stored in the variable result.

*Listing 6.155   Example of the* `atan2()` *Method*

```
<html>
<body>
<script language="JavaScript">
<!-- Hide
// function calculates the arctangent of the
// quotient of the two arguments.
function doMath(){
    var inputNum1=document.form1.input1.value;
    var inputNum2=document.form1.input2.value;
    var result = Math.atan2(inputNum1, inputNum2);
    document.form1.answer.value = result;
}
// End Hide -->
</script>

<form name=form1>
Enter First Number:
<input type="text" name="input1" size=10>
<br>
Enter Second Number:
<input type="Text" name="input2" size=10>
<br><br>
<input type="button" value="Calculate" onClick='doMath()'>
<br>
Answer:
<input type="text" name="answer" size=10>
</form>

</body>
</html>
```

# Math.ceil()

## *JavaScript 1.0+, ECMAScript 1.0+, JScript 1.0+*

## *Nav2+, NES2+, IE3+, Opera3+*

## Syntax

`math.ceil(num)`

## Description

The `ceil()` method of the `Math` object is used to calculate the smallest integer that is greater than or equal to the number passed in as a parameter. This is similar to getting the ceiling of a number.

## Example

Listing 6.156 shows how the `ceil()` method is used to get the largest integer for the number input by the user.

*Listing 6.156   Example of the* `ceil()` *Method*

```
<html>
<body>
<title>Example of the ceil() method</title>
<script language="JavaScript">
<!-- Hide
// function calculates the ceiling integer.
// takes input and passes it to the ceil method.
function doMath(){
    var inputNum=document.form1.input.value;
    var result = Math.ceil(inputNum);
    document.form1.answer.value = result;
}
// End Hide -->
</script>

<form name=form1>
This example calculates ceiling of the entered number.
<br><br>
Enter First Number:
<input type="text" name="input" size=10>
<input type="button" value="Calculate" onClick='doMath()'>
<br>
The Ceil output is:
<input type="text" name="answer" size=10>
</form>

</body>
</html>
```

# Math.cos()

## *JavaScript 1.0+, ECMAScript 1.0+, JScript 1.0+*

## *Nav2+, NES2+, IE3+, Opera3+*

## *Syntax*

`math.cos(num)`

## *Description*

The `cos()` method of the `Math` object is used to calculate the cosine of a number. It returns a numeric value between –1 and 1, representing the cosine of an angle.

## *Example*

Listing 6.157 shows how the `cos()` method is used to get the cosine of the number input by the user.

*Listing 6.157   Example of the* `cos()` *Method*

```
<html>
<body>

<script language="JavaScript">
<!-- Hide
// function calculates the cosine of the input number
// takes the input from the user and passes the value to
// the cos() method which calculates the cosine value.
function doMath(){
    var inputNum=document.form1.input.value;
    var result = Math.cos(inputNum);
    document.form1.answer.value = result;
}
// End Hide -->
</script>

<form name=form1>
This exanple calculates the cosine of the entered number.
<br><br>
Enter First Number:
<input type="text" name="input" size=10>
<input type="button" value="Calculate" onClick='doMath()'>
<br>
The cosine is:
<input type="text" name="answer" size=10>
</form>

</body>
</html>
```

# Math.E

## *JavaScript 1.0+, ECMAScript 1.0+, JScript 1.0+*

## *Nav2+, NES2+, IE3+, Opera3+*

## Syntax

*math.E*

## Description

The E property of the Math object is used to get the value of Euler's constant. This is approximately 2.718.

## Example

Listing 6.158 shows how the E property is used.

*Listing 6.158    Example of the* E *Property*

```
<html>
<body>

<script language="JavaScript">
<!-- Hide
// function to return Euler's constant
function doMath(){
    var result = Math.E;
    document.form1.answer.value = result;
}
// End Hide -->
</script>

<form name=form1>
Click on the button to get Euler's constant.
<br><br>
Euler's constant is:
<input type="text" name="answer" size=20>
<input type="button" value="Calculate" onClick='doMath()'>
<br>
</form>

</body>
</html>
```

# Math.exp()

## *JavaScript 1.0+, ECMAScript 1.0+, JScript 1.0+*

## *Nav2+, NES2+, IE3+, Opera3+*

## *Syntax*

`math.exp(num)`

## *Description*

The exp() method of the Math object is used to calculate an exponent where the base is Euler's constant (the base of the natural logarithms).

## *Example*

Listing 6.159 shows how the exp() method is used to calculate an exponential value using the number input by the user.

*Listing 6.159   Example of the* `exp()` *Method*

```
<html>
<body>

<script language="JavaScript">
<!-- Hide
// function doMath calculates exponential value
function doMath(){
    var inputNum=document.form1.input.value;
    var result = Math.exp(inputNum);
    document.form1.answer.value = result;
}
// End Hide -->
</script>

<form name=form1>
Enter First Number:
<input type="text" name="input" size=10>
<input type="button" value="Calculate" onClick='doMath()'>
<br>
The exponent is:
<input type="text" name="answer" size=10>
</form>

</body>
</html>
```

# Math.floor()

## *JavaScript 1.0+, ECMAScript 1.0+, JScript 1.0+*

## *Nav2+, NES2+, IE3+, Opera3+*

## Syntax

`math.floor(num)`

## Description

The `floor()` method of the `Math` object is used to get the largest integer number, which is equivalent to or less than the number passed as the parameter.

## Example

Listing 6.160 shows how the `floor()` method is used.

*Listing 6.160   Example of the* `floor()` *Method*

```
<html>
<body>

<script language="JavaScript">
```

```
<!-- Hide
// function calculates the floor of to input number
function doMath(){
    var inputNum=document.form1.input.value;
    var result = Math.floor(inputNum);
    document.form1.answer.value = result;
}
// End Hide -->
</script>

<form name=form1>
This example calculates the floor of the number entered.
<br><br>
Enter First Number:
<input type="text" name="input" size=10>
<input type="button" value="Calculate" onClick='doMath()'>
<br>
The floor is:
<input type="text" name="answer" size=10>
</form>

</body>
</html>
```

# Math.LN10

## *JavaScript 1.0+, ECMAScript 1.0+, JScript 1.0+*

## *Nav2+, NES2+, IE3+, Opera3+*

## *Syntax*

*math*.LN10

## *Description*

The LN10 property of the Math object is used to get the natural logarithm of 10. This is approximately equal to 2.302.

## *Example*

Listing 6.161 shows how the LN10 property is used. When the user clicks the button, the doMath function is called, which calculates the natural logarithm of 10 and displays the result in the input box.

*Listing 6.161    Example of the* LN10 *Property*

```
<html>
<body>

<script language="JavaScript">
```

*continues*

*Listing 6.161  continued*

```
<!-- Hide
// function gets the natural log of 10
function doMath(){
    var result = Math.LN10;
    document.form1.answer.value = result;
}
// End Hide -->
</script>

<form name=form1>
The Natural Logarithm of 10 is:
<input type="text" name="answer" size=20>
<input type="button" value="Calculate" onClick='doMath()'>
<br>
</form>

</body>
</html>
```

# Math.LN2

## *JavaScript 1.0+, ECMAScript 1.0+, JScript 1.0+*

## *Nav2+, NES2+, IE3+, Opera3+*

## *Syntax*

```
math.LN2
```

## *Description*

The LN2 property of the Math object is used to get the natural logarithm of 2. This is approximately equal to 0.693.

## *Example*

Listing 6.162 shows how the LN2 property is used to get the natural logarithm of 2.

*Listing 6.162  Example of the LN2 Property*

```
<html>
<body>

<script language="JavaScript">
<!-- Hide
// function gets the natural log of 2
function doMath(){
    var result = Math.LN2;
    document.form1.answer.value = result;
}
// End Hide -->
```

```
</script>

<form name=form1>
The Natural Logarithm of 2 is:
<input type="text" name="answer" size=20>
<input type="button" value="Calculate" onClick='doMath()'>
<br>
</form>

</body>
</html>
```

# Math.log()

## *JavaScript 1.0+, ECMAScript 1.0+, JScript 1.0+*

## *Nav2+, NES2+, IE3+, Opera3+*

### Syntax

`math.log(num)`

### Description

The `log()` method of the `Math` object is used to calculate the natural logarithm (base E) of a number.

### Example

Listing 6.163 shows how the `log()` method is used.

*Listing 6.163   Example of the `log()` Method*

```
<html>
<body>

<script language="JavaScript">
<!-- Hide
function doMath(){
    var inputNum=document.form1.input.value;
    var result = Math.log(inputNum);
    document.form1.answer.value = result;
}
// End Hide -->
</script>

<form name=form1>
This example calculates the natural log of the number entered.
<br><br>
Enter First Number:
```

*Listing 6.163    continued*
```
<input type="text" name="input" size=15>
<input type="button" value="Calculate" onClick='doMath()'>
<br>
The log is:
<input type="text" name="answer" size=10>
</form>

</body>
</html>
```

# Math.LOG10E

## *JavaScript 1.0+, ECMAScript 1.0+, JScript 1.0+*

## *Nav2+, NES2+, IE3+, Opera3+*

## *Syntax*

`math.LOG10E`

## *Description*

The `LOG10E` property of the `Math` object calculates the base 10 logarithm of Euler's constant. The return value is approximately 0.434.

## *Example*

Listing 6.164 shows how the `LOG10E` property is used. When the user chooses the Calculate button, the `doMath` function is executed, which calculates the base 10 logarithm of Euler's constant and outputs the result in the text box.

*Listing 6.164    Example of the* `LOG10E` *Property*
```
<html>
<body>

<script language="JavaScript">
<!-- Hide
function doMath(){
    var result = Math.LN10E;
    document.form1.answer.value = result;
}
// End Hide -->
</script>

<form name=form1>
The Base 10 logarithm of Euler's constant is:
<input type="text" name="answer" size=20>
<input type="button" value="Calculate" onClick='doMath()'>
```

```
<br>
</form>

</body>
</html>
```

# Math.LOG2E

## *JavaScript 1.0+, ECMAScript 1.0+, JScript 1.0+*

## *Nav2+, NES2+, IE3+, Opera3+*

## *Syntax*

`math.LOG2E`

## *Description*

The LOG2E property of the Math object calculates the base 2 logarithm of Euler's constant. The return value is approximately 1.442.

## *Example*

Listing 6.165 shows how the LOG2E property is used.

*Listing 6.165    Example of the* `log2E` *Property*

```
<html>
<body>

<script language="JavaScript">
<!-- Hide
function doMath(){
    var result = Math.LN2E;
    document.form1.answer.value = result;
}
// End Hide -->
</script>

<form name=form1>
The Base 2 logarithm of Euler's constant is:
<input type="text" name="answer" size=20>
<input type="button" value="Calculate" onClick='doMath()'>
<br>
</form>

</body>
</html>
```

# Math.max()

## *JavaScript 1.0+, ECMAScript 1.0+, JScript 1.0+*

## *Nav2+, NES2+, IE3+, Opera3+*

## Syntax

```
math.max(num1, num2)
```

## Description

The max() method of the Math object gets the maximum number of the two parameters passed to it. The larger value is returned as the result.

## Example

Listing 6.166 shows how the max() method is used to get the larger of two values.

*Listing 6.166   Example of the* max() *Method*

```
<html>
<body>

<script language="JavaScript">
<!-- Hide
// function returns the maximum of two arguments
function doMath(){
    var inputNum1=document.form1.input1.value;
    var inputNum2=document.form1.input2.value;
    var result = Math.max(inputNum1, inputNum2);
    document.form1.answer.value = result;
}
// End Hide -->
</script>

<form name=form1>
This example takes the two numbers entered and determines which is
the larger number.
<br><br>
Enter First Number:
<input type="text" name="input1" size=10>
<br>
Enter Second Number:
<input type="text" name="input2" size=10>
<input type="button" value="Show Max number" onClick='doMath()'>
<br>
The Maximum number is:
<input type="text" name="answer" size=10>
</form>

</body>
</html>
```

# Math.min()

## *JavaScript 1.0+, ECMAScript 1.0+, JScript 1.0+*

## *Nav2+, NES2+, IE3+, Opera3+*

## *Syntax*

```
math.min(num1, num2)
```

## *Description*

The min() method of the Math object gets the minimum number of the two number parameters passed to it. The smaller value is returned as the result.

## *Example*

Listing 6.167 shows how to use the Math.min() method.

*Listing 6.167    Example of the* min() *Method*

```
<html>
<body>

<script language="JavaScript">
<!-- Hide
// function returns the minimum of two arguments
function doMath(){
    var inputNum1=document.form1.input1.value;
    var inputNum2=document.form1.input2.value;
    var result = Math.min(inputNum1, inputNum2);
    document.form1.answer.value = result;
}
// End Hide -->
</script>

<form name=form1>
This example takes the two numbers entered and determines which is
the smaller number.
<br><br>
Enter First Number:
<input type="text" name="input1" size=10>
<br>
Enter Second Number:
<input type="text" name="input2" size=10>
<input type="button" value="Show Min number" onClick='doMath()'>
<br>
The Minimum number is:
<input type="text" name="answer" size=10>
</form>

</body>
</html>
```

# Math.PI

## *JavaScript 1.0+, ECMAScript 1.0+, JScript 1.0+*

## *Nav2+, NES2+, IE 3+, Opera3+*

## *Syntax*

`math.PI`

## *Description*

The `PI` property of the `Math` object is used to get the constant PI. This is approximately 3.14159.

## *Example*

Listing 6.168 shows how the `PI` property is used. When the user clicks the Calculate button, the `doMath` function is called, which calculates the value of PI and returns the result to the text box.

*Listing 6.168   Example of the `PI` Property*

```
<html>
<body>

<script language="JavaScript">
<!-- Hide
// function returns the value of PI
function doMath(){
    var result = Math.PI;
    document.form1.answer.value = result;
}
// End Hide -->
</script>

<form name=form1>
The Approximate value of PI is:
<input type="text" name="answer" size=20>
<input type="button" value="Calculate" onClick='doMath()'>
<br>
</form>

</body>
</html>
```

# Math.pow()

*JavaScript 1.0+, ECMAScript 1.0+, JScript 1.0+*

*Nav2+, NES2+, IE 3+, Opera3+*

## Syntax

```
math.pow(num1, num2)
```

## Description

The pow() method of the Math object is used to calculate an exponent power.

## Example

Listing 6.169 shows how the pow() method is used.

*Listing 6.169    Example of the* pow() *Method*

```
<html>
<body>

<script language="JavaScript">
<!-- Hide
// function takes two numbers and calculates the
// exponential power.
function doMath(){
    var inputNum1=document.form1.input1.value;
    var inputNum2=document.form1.input2.value;
    var result = Math.pow(inputNum1, inputNum2);
    document.form1.answer.value = result;
}
// End Hide -->
</script>

<form name=form1>
Enter Base number:
<input type="text" name="input1" size=10>
<br>
Enter exponent to be raised to:
<input type="text" name="input2" size=10>
<input type="button" value="Calculate" onClick='doMath()'>
<br>
The result is:
<input type="text" name="answer" size=10>
</form>

</body>
</html>
```

# Math.random()

## *JavaScript 1.1+, ECMAScript 1.0+, JScript 1.0+*

## *Nav3+, NES2+, IE 3+, Opera3+*

## *Syntax*

`math.random(num)`

## *Description*

The `random()` method of the `Math` object is used to obtain a random number between values 0 and 1.

## *Example*

Listing 6.170 shows how the `random()` method is used to calculate random numbers.

*Listing 6.170  Example of the `random()` Method*

```
<html>
<body>

<script language="JavaScript">
<!-- Hide    .
// function generates a random number between 0 & 1
function doMath(){
    var result = Math.random();
    document.form1.answer.value = result;
}
// End Hide -->
</script>

<form name=form1>
The random number is:
<input type="text" name="answer" size=20>
<input type="button" value="Calculate" onClick='doMath()'>
<br>
</form>

</body>
</html>
```

# Math.round()

## *JavaScript 1.0+, ECMAScript 1.0+, JScript 1.0+*

## *Nav2+, NES2+, IE3+, Opera3+*

## *Syntax*

`math.round(num)`

## Description

The round() method of the Math object is used to round a number to its nearest integer value. If the fractional portion of the number is .5 or greater, the result is rounded to the next highest integer. If the fractional portion of number is less than .5, the result is rounded to the next lowest integer.

## Example

Listing 6.171 shows how the round() method is used.

*Listing 6.171    Example of the* round() *Method*

```html
<html>
<body>

<script language="JavaScript">
<!-- Hide
// function rounds input number to nearest integer
function doMath(){
    var inputNum1=document.form1.input1.value;
    var result = Math.round(inputNum1);
    document.form1.answer.value = result;
}
// End Hide -->
</script>

<form name=form1>
Enter Number:
<input type="text" name="input1" size=10>
<input type="button" value="Round" onClick='doMath()'>
<br>
The rounded value is:
<input type="text" name="answer" size=10>
</form>

</body>
</html>
```

# Math.sin()

## *JavaScript 1.0+, ECMAScript 1.0+, JScript 1.0+*

## *Nav2+, NES2+, IE3+, Opera3+*

## Syntax

*math.*sin*(num)*

## Description

The sin() method of the Math object is used to calculate the sine of a number. It returns a numeric value between −1 and 1.

## Example

Listing 6.172 shows how the `sin()` method is used.

*Listing 6.172    Example of the `sine()` Method*

```
<html>
<body>

<script language="JavaScript">
<!-- Hide
// function calculates the sine of input number
function doMath(){
    var inputNum1=document.form1.input1.value;
    var result = Math.sin(inputNum1);
    document.form1.answer.value = result;
}
// End Hide -->
</script>

<form name=form1>
Enter Number:
<input type="text" name="input1" size=10>
<input type="button" value="Calculate" onClick='doMath()'>
<br>
The sine is:
<input type="text" name="answer" size=20>
</form>

</body>
</html>
```

# Math.sqrt()

## *JavaScript 1.0+, ECMAScript 1.0+, JScript 1.0+*

## *Nav2+, NES2+, IE3+, Opera3+*

## Syntax

`math.sqrt(num)`

## Description

The `sqrt()` method of the `Math` object is used to calculate the square root of a number. If the return value is outside the required range, `sqrt()` returns 0.

## Example

Listing 6.173 shows how the `sqrt()` method is used.

*Listing 6.173   Example of the* `sqrt()` *Method*

```
<html>
<body>

<script language="JavaScript">
<!-- Hide
// function calculates the square root of input number
function doMath(){
    var inputNum1=document.form1.input1.value;
    var result = Math.sqrt(inputNum1);
    document.form1.answer.value = result;
}
// End Hide -->
</script>

<form name=form1>
Enter Number:
<input type="text" name="input1" size=10>
<input type="button" value="Calculate" onClick='doMath()'>
<br>
The square root is:
<input type="text" name="answer" size=20>
</form>

</body>
</html>
```

# Math.SQRT1_2

## *JavaScript 1.0+, ECMAScript 1.0+, JScript 1.0+*

## *Nav2+, NES2+, IE 3+, Opera3+*

## *Syntax*

*math.*SQRT1_2

## *Description*

The SQRT1_2 property of the Math object returns the square root of one half, which is approximately 0.707.

## *Example*

Listing 6.174 shows how SQRT1_2 can be used. The function, doMath, returns the square root of 1/2 to the text box on the page.

*Listing 6.174    Example of the* SQRT1_2 *Property*

```
<html>
<body>

<script language="JavaScript">
<!-- Hide
// function returns the square root of 1/2
function doMath(){
    var result = Math.SQRT1_2;
    document.form1.answer.value = result;
}
// End Hide -->
</script>

<form name=form1>
The square root of 1/2 is:
<input type="text" name="answer" size=20>
<input type="button" value="Calculate" onClick='doMath()'>
<br>
</form>

</body>
</html>
```

# Math.SQRT2

## *JavaScript 1.0+, ECMAScript 1.0+, JScript 1.0+*

## *Nav2+, NES2+, IE 3+, Opera3+*

## *Syntax*

*math*.SQRT2

## *Description*

The SQRT2 property of the Math object returns the value of the square root of 2. This is approximately equal to 1.414.

## *Example*

Listing 6.175 shows how the SQRT2 property is used. The function, doMath, returns the square root of 2 to the text box on the page.

*Listing 6.175    Example of the* SQRT2 *Property*

```
<html>
<body>

<script language="JavaScript">
<!-- Hide
// function returns the square root of 2
```

```
function doMath(){
    var result = Math.SQRT2;
    document.form1.answer.value = result;
}
// End Hide -->
</script>

<form name=form1>
The square root of 2 is:
<input type="text" name="answer" size=20>
<input type="button" value="Calculate" onClick='doMath()'>
<br>
</form>

</body>
</html>
```

# Math.tan()

*JavaScript 1.0+, ECMAScript 1.0+, JScript 1.0+*

*Nav2+, NES2+, IE3+, Opera3+*

## Syntax

`math.tan(num)`

## Description

The tan() method of the Math object is to calculate the tangent of a number. It returns a value representing the tangent of an angle.

## Example

Listing 6.176 shows how the tan() method is used.

*Listing 6.176    Example of the tan() Method*

```
<html>
<body>

<script language="JavaScript">
<!-- Hide
// function returns the tangent of input number
function doMath(){
    var inputNum1=document.form1.input1.value;
    var result = Math.tan(inputNum1);
    document.form1.answer.value = result;
}
// End Hide -->
```

*continues*

*Listing 6.176    continued*
```
</script>

<form name=form1>
This example calculates the tanget of the entered number.
<br><br>
Enter Number:
<input type="text" name="input1" size=10>
<input type="button" value="Calculate" onClick='doMath()'>
<br>
The tangent is:
<input type="text" name="answer" size=20>
</form>

</body>
</html>
```

# Math.toSource()

## *JavaScript 1.3+*

## *Nav4.06+*

## *Syntax*
```
math.toSource()
```

## *Description*

The toSource() method of the Math object is used to create a copy of the object. It returns a string representation of an object, which can be passed to the eval method to create a copy of the object.

## *Example*

Listing 6.177 shows how the toSource() method is used to make a copy of the Math object.

*Listing 6.177    Example of the* toSource() *Method*
```
<html>
<body>

<script language="JavaScript">
<!-- Hide
// function makes copy of math object
function copy(){
    var result = Math.toSource(Math.E);
    document.form1.answer.value = result;
}
// End Hide -->
```

```
</script>

<form name=form1>
Click on the button to create a copy of a Math object.
<br><br>
<input type="button" value="Copy" onClick='copy()'>
<br>
The result of toSource is:
<input type="text" name="answer" size=20>
</form>

</body>
</html>
```

# Math.toString()

## JavaScript 1.0+, JScript 3.0+

## Nav2+, NES2+, IE4+

### Syntax

*math*.toString()

### Description

The toString() method of the Math object returns a string value representing the object.

### Example

Listing 6.178 shows how the toString() method is used to get a string value representing the Math object.

*Listing 6.178   Example of the* toString() *Method*

```
<html>
<body>

<script language="JavaScript">
<!-- Hide
// function returns string representation of math object
function copy(){
    var result = Math.toString(Math.sqrt(45));
    document.form1.answer.value = result;
}
// End Hide -->
</script>

<form name=form1>
```

*continues*

*Listing 6.178    continued*

```
<input type="button" value="Get String" onClick='copy()'>
<br>
The result of toString is:
<input type="text" name="answer" size=20>
</form>

</body>
</html>
```

# NaN

## JavaScript 1.3+, JScript 1.0+

## Nav4.06+, IE 3+

## Syntax

```
NaN
```

## Description

The NaN object represents an object that is not equal to any number, including itself. NaN stands for *Not a Number*.

## Example

Listing 6.179 shows how the NaN object is used within a comparison.

*Listing 6.179    Example Using the NaN Object*

```
<html>
<body>

<script lanuguage="JavaScript">
<!-- Hide
if ("a" != NaN){
    document.write("This is not a number");
}
// End Hide -->
</script>

</body>
</html>
```

# native

## JavaScript1.2+

## NES3+, Nav4+

## Syntax

```
Reserved Keyword
```

## Description

The `native` keyword has not been implemented in JavaScript to date. It has been reserved for future use.

## Example

This keyword has not been implemented, therefore no example is provided.

# new

## JavaScript 1.0+, JScript 1.0+

## Nav2+, NES2+, IE 3+, Opera3+

## Syntax

```
new
```

## Description

The `new` operator is used to create a new object.

## Example

Listing 6.180 shows how `new` is used to create a new `Array` object.

*Listing 6.180   Example of* new

```
<html>
<body>

<script language="JavaScript">
<!-- Hide

//Creates a new array object with the name myArray
var myArray = new Array();

// End Hide -->
</script>

</body>
</html>
```

# null

## JavaScript1.2+, Jscript3.0+, ECMAScript1.0+

## NES3+, Nav4+, IE4+

## Syntax

```
Reserved Keyword
```

## Description

The null keyword has not been implemented in JavaScript to date. It has been reserved for future use.

## Example

This keyword has not been implemented, therefore no example is provided.

# Number()

## JavaScript 1.1+, JScript 1.0+

## Nav3+, NES2+, IE 3+, Opera3+

## Syntax

```
var variable = new Number(value)
```

## Description

The Number object represents numeric value types. You can create a Number object by specifying a value in the parameter for the number constructor. Table 6.29 shows the different methods and properties of the Number object.

**Table 6.29    Properties and Methods of the Number Object**

| Property/Method | Description |
| --- | --- |
| MAX_VALUE | Specifies the largest value a number can have. |
| MIN_VALUE | Specifies the smallest value a number can have without being equal to 0. |
| NaN | Stands for **Not a Number**. Represents a value that is not equal to any numeric value. |
| NEGATIVE_INFINITY | A special value that represents a negative infinity value. |
| POSITIVE_INFINITY | A special value that represents a positive infinity value. |
| prototype | Represents the prototype for the number class. |
| toSource() | Returns a string representation of the number object. |
| toString() | Returns a string representing the specified number object. |
| valueOf() | Returns the primitive value of a number object as a number data type. |

## Example

Listing 6.181 shows how a new Number object is created.

*Listing 6.181    Example of* Number *Constructor*
```
<html>
<body>
```

```
<script language="JavaScript">
<!-- Hide
// Creates a new number object

var aNum = new Number(3);
// End Hide -->
</script>

</body>
</html>
```

# Number.MAX_VALUE

## *JavaScript 1.1+, ECMAScript 1.0+, JScript 1.0+*

## *Nav3+, NES2+, IE 3+, Opera3+*

### Syntax

```
Number.MAX_VALUE
```

### Description

The MAX_VALUE property of the Number object is used to get the maximum representable value for a number. This is approximately: 1.79E¶308.

### Example

Listing 6.182 shows how the MAX_VALUE property is used.

*Listing 6.182   Example of the* MAX_VALUE
```
<html>
<body>

<script language="JavaScript">
<!-- Hide
// checks to see if the number is a MAX_VALUE

if((9999*9999) <= Number.MAX_VALUE){
    document.write("The number is not greater than the maximum value");
}
// End Hide -->
</script>

</body>
</html>
```

# Number.MIN_VALUE

## *JavaScript 1.1+, ECMAScript 1.0+, JScript 1.0+*

## *Nav3+, NES2+, IE 3+, Opera3+*

## *Syntax*

```
Number.MIN_VALUE
```

## *Description*

The MIN_VALUE property of the Number object is used to get the minimum possible numeric value known to JavaScript. This is approximately: 2.22E–308.

## *Example*

Listing 6.183 shows how the MIN_VALUE property is used.

*Listing 6.183   Example of MIN_VALUE*

```
<html>
<body>

<script language="JavaScript">
<!-- Hide
// Checks to see if the number is equal to the MIN_VALUE

if((0.00000002) >= Number.MIN_VALUE){
    document.write("The number is not the minimum value");
}
// End Hide -->
</script>

</body>
</html>
```

# Number.NaN

## *JavaScript 1.1+, ECMAScript 1.0+, JScript 1.0+*

## *Nav3+, NES2+, IE 3+, Opera3+*

## *Syntax*

```
Number.NaN
```

## *Description*

The NaN property of the Number object represents a value that is not equal to any numeric value.

## Example

Listing 6.184 shows how to use the NaN property. An integer constant, 123, is compared to the NaN constant to see if it is a numeric value or not.

*Listing 6.184 Example of NaN Property*

```
<html>
<body>

<script language="JavaScript">
<!-- Hide
// checks to see if 123 is a number or not

if(123 == Number.NaN){
    document.write("This is not a number");
}
// End Hide -->
</script>

</body>
</html>
```

# Number.NEGATIVE_INFINITY

## *JavaScript 1.1+, ECMAScript 1.0+, JScript 1.0+*

## *Nav3+, NES2+, IE 3+, Opera3+*

## Syntax

```
Number.NEGATIVE_INFINITY
```

## Description

The NEGATIVE_INFINITY property of the number object represents a negative infinity number. It is returned when a calculation returns a negative number greater than the largest negative number in JavaScript.

## Example

Listing 6.185 shows how the NEGATIVE_INFINITY property is used. The sqrt() method is used on a number and the result is compared to NEGATIVE_INFINITY.

*Listing 6.185 Example of NEGATIVE_INFINITY*

```
<html>
<body>

<script language="JavaScript">
<!-- Hide
// Performs a square root calculation to obtain a negative result
```

*continues*

*Listing 6.185    continued*
```
// and then checks against the NEGATIVE_INFINITY value.

if((Math.sqrt(-2)) != Number.NEGATIVE_INFINITY_){
    document.write("This is not equal to NEGATIVE_INFINITY");
}
else{
    document.write("This is equal to NEGATIVE_INFINITY");
}

// End Hide -->
</script>

</body>
</html>
```

# Number.POSITIVE_INFINITY

## *JavaScript 1.1+, ECMAScript 1.0+, JScript 1.0+*

## *Nav3+, NES2+, IE 3+, Opera3+*

### *Syntax*
```
Number.POSITIVE_INFINITY
```

### *Description*

The POSITIVE_INFINITY property of the Number object represents a positive infinity number. It is returned when a calculation returns a positive number greater than the largest number in JavaScript.

### *Example*

Listing 6.186 shows how the POSITIVE_INFINITY property is used.

*Listing 6.186    Example of POSITIVE_INFINITY*
```
<html>
<body>

<script language="JavaScript">
<!-- Hide
// Performs some math computation and then checks the
// result against the POSITIVE_INFINITY value
if((Math.exp(999)) <= Number.POSITIVE_INFINITY_){
    document.write("This is less than positive infinity");
}
else{
    document.write('This is greater than POSITIVE_INFINITY");
}

// End Hide -->
```

```
</script>

</body>
</html>
```

# Number.prototype

## *JavaScript 1.1+, JScript 1.0+*

## *Nav3+, NES2+, IE 3+, Opera3+*

### *Syntax*

```
Number.prototype.property
```

```
Number.prototype.method
```

### *Description*

The prototype property of the Number object allows you to add properties or methods to all instances of this class.

### *Example*

Listing 6.187 shows how the prototype property is used.

*Listing 6.187    Example of* prototype

```
<html>
<body>

<script language="JavaScript">
<!-- Hide

// Creates a new Number property myProp
var myProp = new Number();

// sample function multiplies number by 3
function triple(num){
    var result;
    result = (num * 3);
    return result;
}

// Add the prototype peoperty to the number object
Number.prototype.calc3 = triple;

document.write("Example demonstrates the prototype property for the number
object."
+ "<br><br>");
document.write("150 tripled is: " + myProp.calc3(150) + "<br>");
```

*continues*

*Listing 6.187    continued*
```
// End Hide -->
</script>

</body>
</html>
```

# Number.toSource()

## *JavaScript 1.3+, ECMAScript 1.0+*

## *Nav4.06+*

## *Syntax*

```
number.toSource()
```

## *Description*

The `toSource()` method of the `Number` object is used to get a string representation of the `Number` object.

## *Example*

Listing 6.188 shows how the `toSource()` method is used.

*Listing 6.188    Example of* `toSource()` *Method*
```
<html>
<body>

<script language="JavaScript">
<!-- Hide
// creates a new number object and then gets the string
// representation of that object.
var aNum = Number(21);
document.write(aNum.toSource());
// End Hide -->
</script>

</body>
</html>
```

# Number.toString()

## *JavaScript 1.1+, ECMAScript 1.0+, JScript 1.0+*

## *Nav3+, NES2+, IE 3+, Opera3+*

## *Syntax*

```
number.toString()
```

## Description

The toString() method of the Number object is used to get a string representation of the Number object.

## Example

Listing 6.189 shows how the toString() method is used.

*Listing 6.189   Example of* toString() *Method*

```
<html>
<body>

<script language="JavaScript">
<!-- Hide
var aNum = Number(21);
document.write("The string value for 21 is: " + "<b>" + aNum.toString() +
"</b>");
// End Hide -->
</script>

</body>
</html>
```

# Number.valueOf()

## JavaScript 1.1+, Jscript 3.0+

## Nav3+, NES2+, IE4+

## Syntax

*number.*valueOf()

## Description

The valueOf method of the Number object is used to get the primitive value of a Number object as a number data type.

## Example

Listing 6.190 shows an example for the valueOf method. A Number object is created and set to myNum. The document then outputs the result of performing a valueOf function on the number.

*Listing 6.190   Example of* Number.valueOf() *Method*

```
<html>
<body>

<script language="JavaScript1.1">
```

*continues*

*Listing 6.190    continued*

```
<!-- Hide

// create a new number object
myNum = new Number(24)

// output the valueOf result.
document.write("The value of myNum is: " + myNum.valueOf());

// End Hide -->
</script>

</body>
</html>
```

# Object()

## JavaScript 1.1+, JScript1.0+

## Nav3+, NES2+, IE3+, Opera3+

## Syntax

```
var variable = new Object(string)
```

## Description

The Object() object is a primitive data type from which all JavaScript objects are derived. Table 6.30 shows the different properties of the Object() object.

**Table 6.30    Properties of the Object() Object**

| Property | Description |
|---|---|
| constructor | Function that creates an object |
| eval() | Evaluates a string of JavaScript code for the specified object |
| prototype | Prototypes new properties for the specific object |
| toSource() | Returns a string representation for the object |
| toString() | Converts the object to its string representation |
| unwatch | Removes a watchpoint for the object |
| valueOf | Returns the value of the specific object |
| watch | Adds a watchpoint to the object property |

## Example

Listing 6.191 shows how the Object object is used.

*Listing 6.191    Example of* `Object` *Object*

```
<html>
<body>

<script language="JavaScript">
<!---Hide
var myObj = new Object(foo);
document.write(Object foo created);
// End Hide -->
</script>

</body>
</html>
```

# Object.constructor

## JavaScript 1.1+, Jscript 3.0+

## Nav3+, NES2+, IE4+

## Syntax

`object.constructor`

## Description

The `constructor` property of the `Object` object specifies the function that creates the object.

## Example

Listing 6.192 shows an example of the `constructor` property.

*Listing 6.192    Example Packages* `constructor` *Property*

```
<html>
<body>

<script language="JavaScript">
<!---Hide

// create a new number object using the constructor property
num = new Number(3)
if(num.constructor == Number){
    document.write("Object is created");
}
// End Hide -->
</script>

</body>
</html>
```

# Object.eval()

## *JavaScript 1.1+, Jscript 3.0+*

## *Nav3+, NES2+, IE4+*

## *Syntax*

```
object.eval(string)
```

## *Description*

The eval() method of the Object object evaluates a *string* of JavaScript code in reference to this object.

## *Example*

Listing 6.193 shows how the eval() method is used. Two variables are declared and set. A statement multiplying the two variables together is passed to the eval() method to be evaluated.

*Listing 6.193  Example of* eval() *Method*

```
<html>
<body>

<script language="JavaScript">
<!--Hide

var x = 9;
var y = 8;

document.write("The result of x * y is: " + eval(x * y));
// End Hide -->
</script>

</body>
</html>
```

# Object.prototype

## *JavaScript 1.1+, Jscript 3.0+*

## *Nav3+, NES2+, IE4+*

## *Syntax*

```
object.prototype.property
```

```
object.prototype.method
```

## *Description*

The prototype property of the Object object allows the addition of properties or method to the Object class.

## Example

Listing 6.194 shows how the prototype property is used.

*Listing 6.194    Example of the* prototype *Property*

```
<html>
<body>

<script language="JavaScript">
<!--Hide
Object.prototype.newProperty = 2;
document.write(document.object.newProperty.value);
// End Hide -->
</script>

</body>
</html>
```

# Object.toSource()

## *JavaScript 1.3+*

## *Nav4.06+*

## Syntax

```
object.toSource()
```

## Description

The toSource() method is used to get a string representation of the object.

## Example

Listing 6.195 shows how the toSource() is used.

*Listing 6.195    Example of* toSource() *Method*

```
<html>
<body>

<script language="JavaScript">
<!-- Hide
// creates a new number object and then gets the string
// representation of that object.
var aNum = Number(21);
document.write(aNum.toSource());
// End Hide -->
</script>

</body>
</html>
```

# Object.toString()

## *JavaScript 1.1+, ECMAScript 1.0+, JScript 3.0+*

## *Nav3+, NES2+, IE4+, Opera3+*

## *Syntax*

```
object.toString()
```

## *Description*

The toString() method is used to get a string representation of the Number object.

## *Example*

Listing 6.196 shows how the toString() method is used.

*Listing 6.196   Example of the* toString() *Method*
```
<html>
<body>

<script language="JavaScript">
<!--Hide
// creates a number object.
var aNum = Number(21);

// converts the number object to a string and outputs to document.
document.write(aNum.toString());
// End Hide -->
</script>

</body>
</html>
```

# Object.unwatch()

## *JavaScript 1.2+*

## *Nav4+, NES3+*

## *Syntax*

```
object.unwatch(prop)
```

## *Description*

The unwatch() method of the Object object allows you to remove a watchpoint set on a property with the watch() method. This method takes a the property, *prop*, as a parameter.

## Example

Listing 6.197 shows how the unwatch() object is used. A temporary variable, tmp, is created and initialized. It is then set to be watched by invoking the watch method. If any changes occur to the tmp variable, the inform function is called. After a change is made to the variable, unwatch is called to turn off watch operations on the variable. Once watch operations are disabled, the variable can be changed without notification.

*Listing 6.197  Example of* unwatch() *Method*

```
<html>
<body>

<script language="JavaScript">
<!--Hide
// function informs the user when the tmp variable is changed.
function inform(){
     document.write("Tmp variable changed from 1 to 3");
}

// declare a tmp variable
var tmp = 1;

// watch the tmp variable for any changes
watch("tmp",inform);
tmp=3;

// turn off watch on the tmp variable
unwatch("tmp");
tmp=7;
// End Hide -->
</script>

</body>
</html>
```

# Object.valueOf()

## *JavaScript 1.1+, JScript 3.0+*

## *Nav3+, NES2+, IE 4+, Opera3+*

## Syntax

```
object.valueOf()
```

## Description

The valueOf() method for the Object object is used to obtain the value of the specified object.

## Example

Listing 6.198 shows how the valueOf() method is used.

*Listing 6.198   Example of the valueOf() Method*
```
<html>
<body>

<script language="JavaScript">
<!--Hide

// declare an age variable which contains a Number object.
var age = Number(30);

// calculate the valueOf the variable and output to the document.
document.write(age.valueOf());
// End Hide -->
</script>

</body>
</html>
```

# Object.watch()

## JavaScript 1.2+

## Nav4+, NES3+

## Syntax

*object*.watch(*prop, function*)

## Description

The watch() method of the Object object is used to watch for the event in which a property gets assigned a value. When the assignment is made, a user defined function is executed. The method itself takes the property to watch, *prop*, and the function to call, *func*, when the event occurs.

## Example

Listing 6.199 shows how the watch() method is used.

*Listing 6.199   Example of the watch() Method*
```
<html>
<body>
<title>Example of the watch method</title>
<script language="JavaScript">
<!--Hide

// function informs the user when the tmp variable is changed.
function inform(){
```

```
        document.write("Tmp variable changed from 1 to 3");
}

// declare a tmp variable and initialize.
var tmp = 1;

// turn on watch operations on the variable. If the tmp
// variable is changed, then the inform function is run.
watch("tmp",inform);

// change the tmp variable.
tmp=3;
// End Hide -->
</script>

</body>
</html>
```

# package

## JavaScript1.2+

## NES3+, Nav4+

## Syntax

Reserved Keyword

## Description

The package keyword has not been implemented in JavaScript to date. It has been reserved for future use.

## Example

This keyword has not been implemented, therefore no example is provided.

# Packages

## JavaScript 1.1+

## Nav3+, NES2+

## Syntax

Packages.*packagename*

## Description

The Packages object is a built-in object that provides access to various Java packages within the browser. Each property of the Packages object refers to a JavaPackage object containing references to specific classes. Table 6.31 shows the default packages included in the Packages object.

*Table 6.31    Properties of the Packages Object*

| Package | Description |
|---------|-------------|
| java | Refers to the core Java classes |
| netscape | Refers to a set of Netscape classes |
| sun | Refers to the core Sun classes |

## Example

Listing 6.200 shows how the `Packages` object is used. The user is provided with an input text box. When something is entered in the input box and the button clicked, the input is sent to the Java Console using the Java `classes` package.

*Listing 6.200    Example of* `Packages` *Object*

```
<html>
<body>
<script language="JavaScript">
<!-- Hide

// function takes the users input and writes it out to
// the Java Console
function writeOut(input){
    Packages.java.lang.System.out.println(input);
}
// End Hide -->
</script>

<form name="form1">
This script takes the text input and write it out to the Java Console
using the Java package.
<br><br>
Input:
<input type="text" size="40" name="txt">
<br><br>
<input type="button" value="Write Out Text" name="button1"
onClick='writeOut(document.form1.txt.value)'>
<br>
</form>

</body>
</html>
```

# Packages.java

## JavaScript 1.1+

## Nav3+, NES2+

## Syntax

```
Packages.java.className.methodName
```

## Description

The java sub-package of the Packages object refers to the JavaPackage containing the core Java class library. This sub-package is used for several things, but most notably for adding security to LiveConnect and accessing the Java Console.

## Example

Listing 6.201 shows an example for the java package. It is used to write text to the Java Console.

*Listing 6.201    Example* Packages.java *Sub-package*

```
<html>
<body>
<script language="JavaScript1.1">
<!-- Hide

// Use the Java package to write text to the Java Console
Packages.java.lang.System.out.println("Hello World!");

// End Hide -->
</script>

</body>
</html>
```

# Packages.netscape

## JavaScript 1.1+

## Nav3+, NES2+

## Syntax

Packages.netscape.*className*.*methodName*

## Description

The netscape sub-package of the Packages object refers to the JavaPackage containing the netscape package. This sub-package is used by Java applets to access JavaScript code via LiveConnect. The package itself has two classes: plugin and javascript.

## Example

Use of this package occurs within the code of a Java applet, and not JavaScript code. However, Listing 6.202 shows an example of calling the netscape package directly to verify it is implemented in the operating browser.

*Listing 6.202   Example of Accessing the* `netscape` *Package*

```
<html>
<body>
<script language="JavaScript1.1">
<!--Hide

// Call the package to see if it exists
if(Packages.netscape){
  document.write("This browser has LiveConnect!");
}else{
  document.write("This browser does not have LiveConnect!");
}
// End Hide -->
</script>

</body>
</html>
```

# Packages.sun

## *JavaScript 1.1+*

## *Nav3+, NES2+*

## *Syntax*

`Packages.sun.className.methodName`

## *Description*

The sun sub-package of the `Packages` object refers to the `JavaPackage` for the sun property. This sub-package is used for several things, but most notably for adding security to LiveConnect.

## *Example*

Use of this package occurs within the code of a Java applet, and not JavaScript code. However, Listing 6.203 shows an example of calling the sun package directly to verify it is implemented in the operating browser.

*Listing 6.203   Example of Accessing the* sun *Package*

```
<html>
<body>
<script language="JavaScript1.1">
<!---Hide

// Call the package to see if it exists
if(Packages.sun){
  document.write("This browser has LiveConnect!");
}else{
  document.write("This browser does not have LiveConnect!");
```

```
}
// End Hide -->
</script>

</body>
</html>
```

# parseFloat()

## *JavaScript 1.0+, ECMAScript 1.0+, JScript 1.0+*

## *Nav2+, NES2+, IE 3+, Opera3+*

## *Syntax*

```
parseFloat(string)
```

## *Description*

The parseFloat() method is used to convert a string to a number.

## *Example*

Listing 6.204 shows how the parseFloat() is used. In the example, parseFloat is called with two different strings. The first string, which contains numeric characters, is converted into a number without any problem. The second string, which contains alphabetic characters, is unable to be converted into a number.

*Listing 6.204   Example of the* parseFloat() *Method*

```
<html>
<body>

<script language="JavaScript">
<!-- Hide
// convert the "1245.31" string to a number
document.write("The string 1245.31 converted is" + parseFloat("1245.31") +
"<br>");

// try to convert the string "test" to a number.
// if not possible, then print error.
if( isNaN(parseFloat("test")) ){
   document.write("Cannot convert test string to a number.");
}
// End Hide -->
</script>

</body>
</html>
```

# parseInt()

## *JavaScript 1.0+, ECMAScript 1.0+, JScript 1.0+*

## *Nav2+, NES2+, IE 3+, Opera3+*

## *Syntax*

```
parseInt(string, radix)

parseInt(string)
```

## *Description*

The parseInt() method is used to convert a string to an integer. It can take *string* input with an optional *radix* input. The *radix* input represents the base of the number in the string.

## *Example*

Listing 6.205 shows how parseInt() is used to parse a string. A few different examples are shown for different types of strings.

*Listing 6.205   Example of the* parseInt() *Method*

```
<html>
<body>
<script language="JavaScript">
<!-- Hide

// convert the "859" string to an integer
document.write("The string 859 converted to an integer is: ");
document.write(parseInt("859") + "<br>");

// converts a binary string into an integer
document.write("The binary string 101101 converted to an integer is: ");
document.write(parseInt("101101", 2) + "<br>");

// converts a hexidecimal string into an integer
document.write("The hexidecimal string FA832B converted to an integer is: ");
document.write(parseInt("FA832B", 16) + "<br>");

// End Hide -->
</script>

</body>
</html>
```

# private

## *JavaScript1.2+*

## *NES3+, Nav4+*

## *Syntax*
Reserved Keyword

## *Description*
The `private` keyword has not been implemented in JavaScript to date. It has been reserved for future use.

## *Example*
This keyword has not been implemented, therefore no example is provided.

# protected

## *JavaScript1.2*

## *NES3+, Nav4+*

## *Syntax*
Reserved Keyword

## *Description*
The `protected` keyword has not been implemented in JavaScript to date. It has been reserved for future use.

## *Example*
This keyword has not been implemented, therefore no example is provided.

# public

## *JavaScript1.2+*

## *NES3+, Nav4+*

## *Syntax*
Reserved Keyword

## *Description*
The `public` keyword has not been implemented in JavaScript to date. It has been reserved for future use.

## Example

This keyword has not been implemented, therefore no example is provided.

# RegExp()

## JavaScript 1.2+, Jscript 3.0+

## Nav4+, NES3+, IE4+

## Syntax

```
var variable = new RegExp(pattern, flags)
```

## Description

The RegExp() object represents a regular expression that is used for pattern matching. The creation of the object takes *pattern* and *flags* parameters. The *pattern* is a valid regular expression. The *flags* are either or both g (global) and i (ignore case). Table 6.32 displays the properties and methods of the RegExp() object.

**Table 6.32    Properties and Methods of the RegExp() Object**

| Property/Method | Description |
| --- | --- |
| RegExp.$* | Represents multiline |
| RegExp.$& | Represents lastmatch |
| RegExp.$_ | Represents input |
| RegExp.$` | Represents leftContext |
| RegExp.$' | Represents rightContext |
| RegExp.$+ | Represents lastParen |
| RegExp.$1,$2,...$9 | Represents substring of matches |
| compile() | Compiles a regular expression |
| exec() | Executes the search for a match in a specified string |
| global | Specifies whether to check the expressions against all possible matches |
| ignoreCase | Whether case is ignored or not during a string search |
| input | String that is matched |
| lastIndex | Specifies the index at which to start matching the next string. |
| lastMatch | Last matched characters |
| lastParen | The last parenthesized substring match |
| leftContext | The substring preceding the most recent match |
| multiline | Specifies whether to search on multiple lines |
| rightContext | The substring following the most recent match |
| source | The string pattern |
| test() | Tests for a string match |

## Example

Listing 6.206 shows how to use the RegExp object. The user is given an input field, which is used to input a Social Security Number (SSN). Once entered, the Validate button is clicked, which checks whether the input is valid. This is performed by using a RegExp object for the SSN.

*Listing 6.206    Example of* RegExp *Object*

```
<html>
<body>

<script language="JavaScript">
<!-- Hide
// function checks to see if the ssn is valid.
function isSSN(str){

    // define a RegExp object which checks for either
    // a 9 digit input or an input in the form:
    // xxx-xx-xxxx
    var regexp = /^(\d{9}|\d{3}-\d{2}-\d{4})$/;
    return regexp.test(str);
}

// checks the SSN input.
function checkInput(){
  var valid = true;
  var ssn = document.form1.ssn.value;
  if (!isSSN (ssn)){
      window.alert("Invalid SSN: " + ssn);
      valid = false;
  }
  else{
    alert(ssn + " is a valid SSN");
  }
}

// End Hide -->
</script>

<form name="form1">
Enter your SSN:
<input type="text" size="15" name="ssn">
<br><br>
<input type="button" value="Validate SSN" onClick='checkInput()'>
<br>
</form>
</body>
</html>
```

# RegExp,$*

## *JavaScript 1.2+, Jscript 3.0+*

## *Nav4+, NES3+, IE4+*

## *Syntax*

RegExp,$*

## *Description*

The RegExp,$* property reflects a multiline string search. This is a Boolean, read-only value that reflects whether or not strings should be searched across multiple lines. This is the same as using the multiline property.

## *Example*

Listing 6.207 shows how to use RegExp,$* for pattern matching.

*Listing 6.207    Example of RegExp,$\**

```
<html>
<body>

<script language="JavaScript">
<!-- Hide
// function checks for the "the" expression.  However, if
// multiple lines are read, an alert box is displayed
// indicating so.
function getinfo(){

var myPat = new RegExp("the", "i");
var str = document.form1.mytext.value;
myArray = myPat.exec(str);

    alert("RegExp.$* is: " + RegExp.multiline);
}
// End Hide -->
</script>

<form name="form1">
When the text in the text box is changed, and the document is clicked,
an alert box will be displayed showing the value of RegExp.$*.
<br><br>
<textarea name="mytext" cols="60" rows="8" onChange='getinfo()'>
This is a sample textarea containing some dummy text for
testing purposes. The text in this box will be used to
demonstrate how the multiline property is used. If multiple lines are
```

```
read, then RegExp.$* will be true.
</textarea>
<br>
</form>

</body>
</html>
```

# RegExp.$&

## JavaScript 1.2+, Jscript 3.0+

## Nav4+, NES3+, IE4+

## Syntax

```
RegExp.$&
```

## Description

The `RegExp.$&` property represents the last matched characters. This is the same as using the `lastMatch` property.

## Example

Listing 6.208 shows how `RegExp.$&` is used.

*Listing 6.208    Example of* RegExp.$&

```
<html>
<body>

<script language="JavaScript">
<!-- Hide
// define a pattern to search for
var pat = new RegExp("test", "gi");
str = "Testing Testing 123";
myArray = pat.exec(str);

// Once pattern is found, display message.
document.write("Pattern found: " + myArray[0] +
              ". the last match expression is: " + RegExp.lastMatch);
// End Hide -->
</script>

</body>
</html>
```

# RegExp,$_

## *JavaScript 1.2+, Jscript 3.0+*

## *Nav4+, NES3+, IE4+*

## Syntax

```
RegExp,$_
```

## Description

The `RegExp,$_` property represents the input to which a string is matched. This is the same as using the `input` property.

## Example

Listing 6.209 shows how to use the `RegExp,$_` property.

*Listing 6.209    Example of* `RegExp,$_`

```
<html>
<body>

<script language="JavaScript">
<!-- Hide
// function creates a new regular expression and
// then executes it against the text in the textbox.
// Outputs an alert message indicating the value
// of the RegExp.input property.
function getinput(){

var myPat = new RegExp("the", "i");
var str = document.form1.mytext.value;
myArray = myPat.exec(str);

    alert("The RegExp.input is: " + RegExp.input);
}
// End Hide -->
</script>

<form name="form1">
When the text in the text box below is changed, an alert message
will appear showing the value of the input.
<br><br>
Enter some Text:
<input type="text" name="mytext" size="40" onChange='getinput()'>
<br>
```

```
</form>

</body>
</html>
```

# RegExp.$`

## JavaScript 1.2+, Jscript 3.0+

## Nav4+, NES3+, IE4+

## Syntax

```
RegExp.$`
```

## Description

The `RegExp.$`` property represents the substring preceding the most recent pattern match. This is the same as using the `leftContext` property.

## Example

Listing 6.210 shows how to use `RegExp.$``

*Listing 6.210   Example of* RegExp.$`

```
<html>
<body>

<script language="JavaScript">
<!-- Hide
// define a regular expression pattern and match globally
pat = /is*/g;

// create a string object
var str = "I know where the fish is tonight.";

// create an array to hold the results
myArray = pat.exec(str);

document.write("In the string: " + "<b>");
document.write("I know where the fish is tonight" + "</b><br><br>");
document.write("The RegExp.leftContext is: " + RegExp.leftContext);

// End Hide -->
</script>

</body>
</html>
```

# RegExp.$'

## *JavaScript 1.2+, Jscript 3.0+*

## *Nav4+, NES3+, IE4+*

## Syntax

```
RegExp.$'
```

## Description

The `RegExp.$'` property represents the substring following the most pattern match. This is the same as using the `rightContext` property.

## Example

Listing 6.211 shows how to use `RegExp.$'`.

*Listing 6.211   Example of `RegExp.$'`*

```
<html>
<body>

<script language="JavaScript">
<!-- Hide
// define a regular expression pattern and match globally
pat = /be*/gi;

// create a string object
var str = "Eat Drink and be Merry.";

// create an array to hold the results
myArray = pat.exec(str);

document.write("In the string: " + "<b>" +
               "Eat Drink and be Merry" + "</b><br><br>");
document.write("The RegExp.rightContext is: " + RegExp.rightContext);

// End Hide -->
</script>

</body>
</html>
```

# RegExp.$+

## *JavaScript 1.2+, Jscript 3.0+*

## *Nav4+, NES3+, IE4+*

## Syntax

```
RegExp.$+
```

## Description

The RegExp.$+ property represents the last parenthesized substring pattern match. This is the same as using the lastParen property.

## Example

Listing 6.212 shows how RegExp.$+ is used.

*Listing 6.212    Example of* RegExp.$+

```
<html>
<body>

<script language="JavaScript">
<!-- Hide
// define a regular expression
exp = new RegExp("(please)", "g");

// create a string object
str = "Will you (please) stop yelling!";
myArray = exp.exec(str);

// inform user what the lastParen property is
document.write("The RegExp.lastParen is: " + "<b>"
                + RegExp.lastParen + "</b>");

// End Hide -->
</script>

</body>
</html>
```

# RegExp.$1,$2,..$9

## *JavaScript 1.2+, JScript 3.0+*

## *Nav4+, NES3+, IE4+*

## Syntax

RegExp.$1,$2,..$9

## Description

The RegExp.$1,$2,..$9 property represents parenthesized substring matches.

## Example

Listing 6.213 shows how RegExp.$1,$2,..$9 is used. The user will enter his or her phone number in the input text box and, when the button is clicked, the swap function swaps the last 4 digits in the phone number with the first three.

*Listing 6.213    Example of* `RegExp.$1,$2,..$9`

```
<html>
<body>

<script language="JavaScript1.2">
<!-- Hide
// function takes the input and swaps the last 4 digits with the
// first three digits
function swap(){
re = /(\w+)\D(\w+)/;
str = document.form1.text1.value;
newstr=str.replace(re, "$2, $1");
document.form1.text2.value = newstr;
}
// End Hide -->
</script>

<form name="form1">
Enter your 7 digit phone number in the form xxx-xxxx
<br><br><br>
Phone Number (7 digits):<input type="text" name="text1" size=10>
<br><br>
<input type="button" value="Swap" onClick='swap()'>
<br><br><br>
Output: <input type="text" name="text2" size=10
</form>

</body>
</html>
```

# RegExp.compile()

## *JavaScript 1.2+, JScript 3.0+*

## *Nav4+, NES3+, IE4+*

## *Syntax*

`regexp.compile(pattern, flag)`

## *Description*

The `compile()` method of the `RegExp` object compiles a regular expression object. The creation of the object takes *pattern* and *flags* parameters. The *pattern* is a valid regular expression. The *flags* are either or both g (global) and i (ignore case).

## *Example*

Listing 6.214 shows how to use the `compile()` method. A pattern is created using the `RegExp` constructor. It is then compiled using the `compile` method, and the result is displayed in the text area.

*Listing 6.214    Example of* `compile()` *Method*

```
<html>
<body>

<script language="JavaScript">
<!-- Hide
var myPat = new RegExp("jane", "i");
var newPat = myPat.compile(myPat);

// function displays the result of the compiled pattern
function getinfo(){
    document.form1.text1.value = newPat;
}
// End Hide -->
</script>

<form name="form1">
Click the button below to get the pattern for the following
command: new RegExp("jane", "i");
<br><br><br>
Compiled Pattern: <input type="text" name="text1" size=30>
<br><br>
<input type="button" value="Get Pattern" onClick='getinfo()'>
</form>

</body>
</html>
```

# RegExp.exec()

## *JavaScript 1.2+, JScript 3.0+*

## *Nav4+, NES3+, IE4+*

## *Syntax*

`regexp.exec(string)`

## *Description*

The `exec()` method of the `RegExp` object executes the search for a match in a specified string. The results are returned in an array. The `string` passed contains the string the regular expression is trying to match in.

## *Example*

In Listing 6.215, you see how the `exec()` method is used. A regular expression is defined and executed on the string using the `exec` method.

*Listing 6.215   Example of* `exec()` *Method*

```
<html>
<body>

<script language="JavaScript">
<!-- Hide
// checks for the pattern "xyz" in str. If found, then
// output written to document indicating that it was found and
// displays the index it was found in the string.

myRe=/xyz*/g;
str = "abcxyzdefhij"
myArray = myRe.exec(str);

document.writeln("Found " + myArray[0] + " in the pattern: " + "<b>" +
                "abcxyzdefhij " + "</b>" + " at index " +
                (myRe.lastIndex - 3));

// End Hide -->
</script>
</body>
</html>
```

# RegExp.global

## *JavaScript 1.2+, JScript 3.0+*

## *Nav4+, NES3+, IE4+*

## *Syntax*

*regexp*.global

## *Description*

The `global` property of the `RegExp` object specifies whether or not the g flag is used with the regular expression. If so, a global pattern match will be performed.

## *Example*

Listing 6.216 shows how the `global` property is used.

*Listing 6.216   Example of* `global` *Property*

```
<html>
<body>

<script language="JavaScript">
<!-- Hide
// defines a regular expression on the pattern "if"
// with the global flag set.
```

```
var myPat = new RegExp("if", "g");

// define a string
var str = "What if Angela is wondering about gifs?";

// store results of exec into myArray
myArray = myPat.exec(str);

document.write("The value of RegExp.global is: " + "<b>"
              + myPat.global + "</b>");
// End Hide -->
</script>

</body>
</html>
```

# RegExp.ignoreCase

## JavaScript 1.2+, JScript 3.0+

## Nav4+, NES3+, IE4+

## Syntax

*regexp*.ignoreCase

## Description

The ignoreCase property of the RegExp object is a flag that informs the user if case is to be ignored during pattern matching or not.

## Example

Listing 6.217 shows how ignoreCase is used.

*Listing 6.217    Example of* ignoreCase

```
<html>
<body>

<script language="JavaScript">
<!-- Hide
// defines a regular expression on the pattern "and"
// with the ignore case flag set.
var myPat = new RegExp("and", "i");

// define a string
var str = "Would Missy and Livvy like some Candy?";

// store results of exec into myArray
```

*continues*

*Listing 6.217    continued*

```
myArray = myPat.exec(str);

document.write("The value of RegExp.ignoreCase is: " + "<b>"
                + myPat.ignoreCase + "</b>");

// End Hide -->
</script>

</body>
</html>
```

# RegExp.input

## *JavaScript 1.2+, JScript 3.0+*

## *Nav4+, NES3+, IE4+*

## *Syntax*

*regexp*.input

## *Description*

The input property of the RegExp object represents the string on which the pattern matching is performed.

## *Example*

Listing 6.218 shows how to use the input property.

*Listing 6.218    Example of* input *Property*

```
<html>
<body>

<script language="JavaScript1.2">
<!-- Hide
// function creates a new regular expression and
// then executes it against the text in the textbox.
// Outputs an alert message indicating the value
// of the RegExp.input property.
function getinput(){

var myPat = new RegExp("the", "i");
var str = document.form1.mytext.value;
myArray = myPat.exec(str);

    alert("The RegExp.input is: " + RegExp.input);
}

// End Hide -->
</script>
```

```
<form name="form1">
When the text in the text box below is changed, an alert message
will appear showing the value of the input.
<br><br>
Enter some Text:
<input type="text" name="mytext" size="40" onChange='getinput()'>
<br>
<br><br><br><br><br><br><inputtype=name=size=<br><br><inputtype=value=</form>

</body>
</html>
```

# RegExp.lastIndex

## JavaScript 1.2+, JScript 3.0+

## Nav4+, NES3+, IE4+

## Syntax

*regexp*.lastIndex

## Description

The lastIndex property of the RegExp object is used to get the index of where the next match begins.

## Example

Listing 6.219 shows how the lastIndex property is used. A regular expression for "is" is created and checked against the string. When found, results are written to the document.

*Listing 6.219   Example of* lastIndex

```
<html>
<body>

<script language="JavaScript">
<!-- Hide
</script>

// creates a regular expression for "is".
exp=/is*/g;
str = "This is just a sample sentence.";
myArray = exp.exec(str);

document.write("Found: " + myArray[0] +
               ". Next match starts at index: " + exp.lastIndex);
// End Hide -->
</script>
</body>
</html>
```

# RegExp.lastMatch

## JavaScript 1.2+, JScript 3.0+

## Nav4+, NES3+, IE4+

## Syntax

`regexp.lastMatch`

## Description

The `lastMatch` property of the `RegExp` object represents the last matched characters.

## Example

Listing 6.220 shows how the `lastMatch` property is used.

*Listing 6.220    Example of* `lastMatch` *Property*

```
<html>
<body>

<script language="JavaScript">
<!-- Hide
// define a pattern to search for
var pat = new RegExp("test", "gi");
str = "Testing Testing 123";
myArray = pat.exec(str);

// Once pattern is found, display message.
document.write("Pattern found: " + myArray[0] +
            ". the last match expression is: " + RegExp.lastMatch);
// End Hide -->
</script>

</body>
</html>
```

# RegExp.lastParen

## JavaScript 1.2+, JScript 3.0+

## Nav4+, NES3+, IE4+

## Syntax

`regexp.lastParen`

## Description

The `lastParen` property of the `RegExp` object represents the last parenthesized substring match. It returns a string value for the last parenthesized substring.

## Example

Listing 6.221 shows how the lastParen property is used.

*Listing 6.221   Example of* lastParen *Property*

```
<html>
<body>

<script language="JavaScript">
<!-- Hide
// define a regular expression
exp = new RegExp("(please)", "g");

// create a string object
str = "Will you (please) stop yelling!";
myArray = exp.exec(str);

// inform user what the lastParen property is
document.write("The RegExp.lastParen is: " + "<b>"
              + RegExp.lastParen + "</b>");

// End Hide -->
</script>

</body>
</html>
```

# RegExp.leftContext

## JavaScript 1.2+, JScript 3.0+

## Nav4+, NES3+, IE4+

## Syntax

*regexp*.leftContext

## Description

The leftContext property of the RegExp object represents the substring preceding the most recent pattern match.

## Example

Listing 6.222 shows how the leftContext property is used.

*Listing 6.222    Example of the* `leftContext` *Property*

```
<html>
<body>

<script language="JavaScript">
<!-- Hide
// define a regular expression pattern and match globally
pat = /is*/g;

// create a string object
var str = "I know where the fish is tonight.";

// create an array to hold the results
myArray = pat.exec(str);

document.write("In the string: " + "<b>" +
              "I know where the fish is tonight" + "</b><br><br>");
document.write("The RegExp.leftContext is: " + RegExp.leftContext);
// End Hide -->
</script>

</body>
</html>
```

# RegExp.multiline

## JavaScript 1.2+, Jscript 3.0+

## Nav4+, NES3+, IE4+

## Syntax

*regexp*.multiline

## Description

The `multiline` property of the `RegExp` object is used to determine whether pattern matching should be performed across multiple lines.

## Example

Listing 6.223 shows how `multiline` is used.

*Listing 6.223    Example of* `multiline`

```
<html>
<body>

<script language="JavaScript">
<!-- Hide
// function creates a new regular expression and
// then executes it against the text in the textarea.
```

```
// Outputs an alert message indicating the boolean value
// of the RegExp.multiline property.
function getinfo(){

var myPat = new RegExp("the", "i");
var str = document.form1.mytext.value;
myArray = myPat.exec(str);

    alert("RegExp.$* is: " + RegExp.multiline);
}

// End Hide -->
</script>

<form name="form1">
When the text in the text box is changed, and the document is clicked,
an alert box will be displayed showing the value of RegExp.$*.
<br><br>
<textarea name="mytext" cols="60" rows="8" onChange='getinfo()'>
This is a sample textarea containing some dummy text for
testing purposes. The text in this box will be used to
demonstrate how the multiline property is used. If multiple lines are
read, then RegExp.$* will be true.
</textarea>
<br>
</form>

</body>
</html>
```

# RegExp.rightContext

## *JavaScript 1.2+, JScript 3.0+*

## *Nav4+, NES3+, IE4+*

## *Syntax*

*regexp*.rightContext

## *Description*

The rightContext property of the RegExp object represents the substring following the
most recent pattern match.

## *Example*

Listing 6.224 shows how the rightContext property is used.

*Listing 6.224    Example of* `rightContext`

```
<html>
<body>

<script language="JavaScript">
<!-- Hide
// define a regular expression pattern and match globally
pat = /be*/gi;

// create a string object
var str = "Eat Drink and be Merry.";

// create an array to hold the results
myArray = pat.exec(str);

document.write("In the string: " + "<b>" +
               "Eat Drink and be Merry" + "</b><br><br>");
document.write("The RegExp.rightContext is: " + RegExp.rightContext);

// End Hide -->
</script>

</body>
</html>
```

# RegExp.source

## JavaScript 1.2+, Jscript 3.0+

## Nav4+, NES3+, IE4+

## Syntax

*regexp.*source

## Description

The `source` property of the `RegExp` object represents the text being used for pattern matching.

## Example:

Listing 6.225 shows how the `source` property is used.

*Listing 6.225    Example of* `source` *Property*

```
<html>
<body>

<script language="JavaScript">
<!-- Hide

exp = new RegExp("am", "g");
```

```
str = "This is just a sample sentence.";
myArray = exp.exec(str);

document.write("The source is: " + "<b>" + exp.source + "</b>");
// End Hide -->
</script>

</body>
</html>
```

# RegExp.test()

## JavaScript 1.2+, JScript 3.0+

## Nav4+, NES3+, IE4+

### Syntax
`regexp.test()`

### Description
The `test()` method of the `RegExp` object is used to test for a pattern match in a string. Returns Boolean value `true` or `false`.

### Example
Listing 6.226 shows how the `test()` method is used.

*Listing 6.226    Example of `test()` Method*
```
<html>
<body>

<script language="JavaScript">
<!-- Hide
// create a new regular expression
myExp = new RegExp("hope", "g");

// define a string object
str = "I hope everything is going well.";

// test to see if the regular expression exists in the string
if(myExp.test(str)){
  document.write("The test found \"hope\" in the string: "
                 + "<b>" + " I hope everything is going well" + "</b>");
}

// End Hide -->
</script>

</body>
</html>
```

# return

## JavaScript 1.0+, JScript 1.0+

## Nav2+, NES2+, IE 3+, Opera3+

## Syntax

```
return
```

## Description

The return keyword will exit the existing function and return a value.

## Example

Listing 6.227 shows an example of using the return statement to return the value of the processing from the function.

*Listing 6.227   Example of* return

```
<html>
<body>

<script language="JavaScript">
<!-- Hide

function getValue(){
     var myValue = 4*3;
     return myValue;
}

function fill(){
     var x = getValue();
     document.form1.tmp.value = x;
}
// End Hide -->
</script>

<form name="form1">
Value: <input type="text" Name="tmp" Size=5>
<br>
<br>
<input type="button" name="get" value="Get Returned Value" onClick='fill()'>
<br>
<br>
</form>

</body>
</html>
```

# short

*JavaScript1.2+*

*NES3+, Nav4+*

*Syntax*

Reserved Keyword

## Description

The short keyword has not been implemented in JavaScript to date. It has been reserved for future use.

## Example

This keyword has not been implemented, therefore no example is provided.

# static

*JavaScript1.2+*

*NES3+, Nav4+*

*Syntax*

Reserved Keyword

## Description

The static keyword has not been implemented in JavaScript to date. It has been reserved for future use.

## Example

This keyword has not been implemented, therefore no example is provided.

# String()

*JavaScript1.0+, JScript1.0+, ECMAScript1.0+*

*NES2+, Nav2+, IE3+, Opera3+*

*Syntax*

```
var variable = new String(string);

"string"
```

## Description

The String() object is one of the core JavaScript objects. Instances are created when a program constructs an instance using the new keyword and passing it the String() object. In JavaScript 1.0, instances were also created when programmers quoted characters in their script. Table 6.33 lists the properties and methods used by this object.

**Table 6.33   Properties and Methods Used by the String Object**

| Type | Item | Description |
|------|------|-------------|
| Method | anchor() | Creates an instance of the <A> tag with the NAME attribute set to the string passed to the method. |
| | big() | Converts the string into an instance of the <BIG> tag. |
| | blink() | Converts the string into an instance of the <BLINK> tag. |
| | bold() | Converts the string into an instance of the <BOLD> tag. |
| | charAt() | Returns the character at the index passed to the method. |
| | charCodeAt() | Returns the ISO-Latin-1 number of the character at the index passed to the method. |
| | concat() | Concatenates the two strings passed to return a new string. This method was added in JavaScript 1.2. |
| | fixed() | Converts the string into an instance of the <TT>, fixed pitch font tag. |
| | fontcolor() | Sets the COLOR attribute of an instance of the <FONT> tag. |
| | fontsize() | Sets the SIZE attribute of an instance of the <FONT> tag. |
| | fromCharCode() | Returns the string value of the ISO-Latin-1 number passed to the method. |
| | indexOf() | Returns the index of the first occurrence of the string passed to the method within an instance of a String object. |
| | italics() | Converts the string into an instance of the <I> tag. |
| | lastIndexOf() | Returns the index of the last occurrence of the string passed to the method within an instance of a String object. |
| | link() | Converts the string into an instance of the <A> tag and sets the HREF attribute with the URL that is passed to the method. |
| | match() | Returns an array containing the matches found based on the regular expression passed to the method. This method was added in JavaScript 1.2. |

| Type | Item | Description |
|------|------|-------------|
| | `replace()` | Performs a search and replace, using the regular expression and replace string passed to the method, on the instance of a `string` that calls it. This method was added in JavaScript 1.2. |
| | `search()` | Returns the index location of the match found in the string passed to the method. A −1 is returned if the string is not found. This method was added in JavaScript 1.2. |
| | `slice()` | Returns the string between the beginning and ending index passed to the method. If a negative number is passed, the index is referenced from the end of the string passed. This method was added in JavaScript 1.2. |
| | `small()` | Converts the string into an instance of the `<SMALL>` tag. |
| | `split()` | Returns the string split into segments defined by the string and instance limit passed to the method. This method was added in JavaScript 1.1. |
| | `strike()` | Converts the string into an instance of the `<STRIKE>` tag. |
| | `sub()` | Converts the string into an instance of the `<SUB>` tag. |
| | `substr()` | Returns the string beginning with the indexed location and number of characters to return. If a negative number is passed, the index is referenced from the end of the string passed. This method was added in JavaScript 1.2. |
| | `substring()` | Returns the string between the beginning and ending index passed to the method. |
| | `sup()` | Converts the string into an instance of the `<SUP>` tag. |
| | `toLowerCase()` | Converts all the characters in the string to lowercase. |
| | `toSource()` | Returns the string representation of the `string` passed. This method was added in JavaScript 1.3. |
| | `toString()` | Returns the characters passed as type string. This method was added in JavaScript 1.3. |
| | `toUpperCase()` | Converts all the characters in the string to uppercase. |
| Property | `length` | Returns the length of the string. |
| | `prototype` | Provides the ability for a programmer to add properties to instances of the `string` object. This property was added in JavaScript 1.1. |

## Example

Listing 6.228 displays the use of some of the String properties and methods. It contains a single button. After the user clicks the button, a second window (see Figure 6.18) is opened. Various methods are called by a string instance created in the script. The results of such are displayed in the pop-up window.

*Listing 6.228   Examples of an Instance of the* String *Object*

```
<html>
<head>
  <title>Examples of the String Object</title>
<script language="JavaScript1.1">
<!-- Hide

// Define the openWin function called by pressing the button
function openWin(){

  // Open a window to store the results and create a new String object
  var myWin = open("", "","width=450,height=200");
  var myString = new String("Hello, World!");

  // Call various methods on this instance and write their results to the
  // window
  myWin.document.write("Original String, " + myString);
  myWin.document.write(" has " + myString.length + " characters.<br>");
  myWin.document.write("Big: " + myString.big() + "<br>");
  myWin.document.write("Small: " + myString.small() + "<br>");
  myWin.document.write("Blinking: " + myString.blink() + "<br>");
  myWin.document.write("Italics: " + myString.italics() + "<br>");
  myWin.document.write("Convert to Lower: " + myString.toLowerCase());
  myWin.document.write("<br>");
  myWin.document.write("Convert to Upper: " + myString.toUpperCase());
  myWin.document.write("<br>");

  // Close the stream to the window
  myWin.document.close();
}
// End hide -->
</script>
</head>
<body>
<form name="myForm">
  <input type=BUTTON value="Click to Process" name="myButton"
         onClick="openWin()">
</form>
</body>
</html>
```

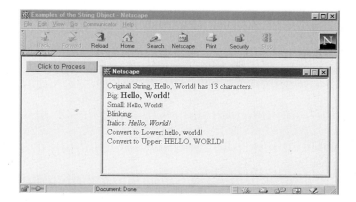

**Figure 6.18**

*Results of running Listing 6.228 in a browser and clicking the Click to Process button.*

# String.anchor()

## JavaScript1.0+, JScript1.0+

## NES2+, Nav2+, IE3+, Opera3+

## Syntax

```
string.anchor(name)
```

## Description

The anchor() method will convert the string it is called on to an instance of the <a> tag, setting the NAME attribute to the *name* that is passed.

## Example

Listing 6.229 creates an instance of the String object and uses the document.write() method to write the tag to the page. The results of running this script will be the following:

```
<a name="HELLO">Hello, World!</a>
```

*Listing 6.229   Using the anchor() Method of the* String *Object*
```
<script language="JavaScript">
<!-- Hide

// Create an instance of the String object
var myString = new String("Hello, World!");

// Write the string to the page after invoking the anchor() method on it
```

*continues*

*Listing 6.229   continued*

```
document.write(myString.anchor("HELLO"));

// Close the stream to the window
document.close();

// End hide -->
</script>
```

# String.big()

## *JavaScript1.0+, JScript1.0+*

## *NES2+, Nav2+, IE3+, Opera3+*

## *Syntax*

`string.big()`

## **Description**

The `big()` method will convert the string it is called on to an instance of the <big> tag.

## *Example*

Listing 6.230 creates an instance of the `String` object and uses the `document.write()` method to write the tag to the page. The results of running this script will be the following:

```
<big>Hello, World!</big>
```

*Listing 6.230   Using the `big()` Method of the `String` Object*

```
<script language="JavaScript">
<!-- Hide

// Create an instance of the String object
var myString = new String("Hello, World!");

// Write the string to the page after invoking the big() method on it
document.write(myString.big());

// Close the stream to the window
document.close();

// End hide -->
</script>
```

# String.blink()

*JavaScript1.0+*

*NES2+, Nav2+*

## Syntax

```
string.blink()
```

## Description

The `blink()` method will convert the string it is called on to an instance of the `<blink>` tag. This method is only supported in Netscape Navigator, because it is the only browser that has an implementation of the `<blink>` tag.

## Example

Listing 6.231 creates an instance of the `String` object and uses the `document.write()` method to write the tag to the page. The results of running this script will be the following:

```
<blink>Hello, World!</blink>
```

*Listing 6.231    Using the `blink()` Method of the `String` Object*
```
<script language="JavaScript">
<!-- Hide

// Create an instance of the String object
var myString = new String("Hello, World!");

// Write the string to the page after invoking the blink() method on it
document.write(myString.blink());

// Close the stream to the window
document.close();

// End hide -->
</script>
```

# String.bold()

*JavaScript1.0+, JScript1.0+*

*NES2+, Nav2+, IE3+, Opera3+*

## Syntax

```
string.bold()
```

## Description

The `bold()` method will convert the string it is called on to an instance of the `<bold>` tag.

## Example

Listing 6.232 creates an instance of the `String` object and uses the `document.write()` method to write the tag to the page. The results of running this script will be the following:

```
<bold>Hello, World!</bold>
```

*Listing 6.232    Using the `bold()` Method of the `String` Object*
```
<script language="JavaScript">
<!-- Hide

// Create an instance of the String object
var myString = new String("Hello, World!");

// Write the string to the page after invoking the bold() method on it
document.write(myString.bold());

// Close the stream to the window
document.close();

// End hide -->
</script>
```

# String.charAt()

## *JavaScript1.0+, JScript1.0+, ECMAScript1.0+*

## *NES2+, Nav2+, IE3+, Opera3+*

## Syntax

`string.charAt(num)`

## Description

The `charAt()` method of an instance of the `String` object returns the character located at the indexed, `num`, position passed. This indexing is done from left to right starting with the 0 (zero) position. If the `num` passed is not a valid index in the string, −1 is returned.

## Example

Listing 6.233 creates an instance of a `String` object. When the page is loaded, the user is prompted for an index number. After entering the index number and clicking OK, the character at that indexed location is written to the document. Notice that there is also a check to see if the character at that location is a space.

*Listing 6.233    Using the* `charAt()` *Method to Retrieve a Character at a User-specified Location in a String*

```
<html>
<head>
  <title>Using the String.charAt() method</title>
</head>
<body>
<script language="JavaScript">
<!-- Hide

// Create an instance of the String object
var myString = new String("Here is a short sentence.");

// Prompt the user for a number
var myIndex = prompt("Please enter a number", "");

// Store the character at that location in a variable
var myChar = myString.charAt(myIndex);

// Write the character to the page, but check to see if it
// is a space first.
document.write('<b>The string you searched through was: </b>' + myString);
document.write('<br>The ' + myIndex + ' character in this string is ');

if (myChar == " "){
  document.write('&lt;space&gt;');
}else{
  document.write(myChar);
}

// Close the stream to the window
myWin.document.close();

// End hide -->
</script>
</body>
</html>
```

# String.charCodeAt()

## *JavaScript1.0+, JScript1.0+, ECMAScript1.0+*

## *NES2+, Nav2+, IE3+, Opera3+*

## *Syntax*

*string*.charCodeAt(*num*)

## Description

The charCodeAt() method of an instance of the String object returns the ISO-Latin-1 number of the character located at the indexed, num, position passed. This indexing is done from left to right starting with the 0 (zero) position. If the num passed is not a valid index in the string, −1 is returned.

## Example

Listing 6.234 creates an instance of a String object. When the page is loaded, the user is then prompted for an index number. After entering the index number and OK, the ISO-Latin-1 number of the character at that indexed location is written to the document. Notice that there is also a check to see if the character at that location is a space.

*Listing 6.234   Using the* charCodeAt() *Method to Retrieve a Character at a User-specified Location in a String*

```
<html>
<head>
  <title>Using the String.charCodeAt() method</title>
</head>
<body>
<script language="JavaScript">
<!-- Hide

// Create an instance of the String object
var myString = new String("Here is a short sentence.");

// Prompt the user for a number
var myIndex = prompt("Please enter a number", "");

// Store the character code at that location in a variable
var myCharCode = myString.charCodeAt(myIndex);
var myChar = myString.charAt(myIndex);

// Write the character code to the page
document.write('<b>The string you searched through was: </b>' + myString);
document.write('<br>The ' + myIndex + ' character in this string is ');

// Check to see if it is a space
if (myChar == " "){
  document.write('&lt;space&gt;');
}else{
  document.write(myChar);
}

// Write the character code
document.write(' and its ISO-Latin-1 code is ' + myCharCode);

// Close the stream to the window
```

```
myWin.document.close();

// End hide -->
</script>
</body>
</html>
```

# String.concat()

## JavaScript1.2+, JScript3.0+

## NES3+, Nav4+, IE4+

## Syntax

`string.concat(string2)`

## Description

The concat() method of an instance of the String object concatenates the string in string2 to the end of string to return a new string.

## Example

Listing 6.235 creates two instances of the String object and uses the concat() method to concatenate them to create a new string. The string is then displayed in an alert box.

*Listing 6.235  Using the concat() Method to Concatenate Two Strings*

```
<script language="JavaScript1.2">
<!-- Hide

// Create 2 instances of the String object and concatenate
// them together.
var myString1 = new String("Hello, ");
var myString2 = new String("World!");
var myConcatString = myString1.concat(myString2);

// Popup an alert box showing the concatenation
alert(myConcatString);

// End hide -->
</script>
```

# String.fixed()

## JavaScript1.0+, JScript1.0+

## NES2+, Nav2+, IE3+, Opera3+

## Syntax

`string.fixed()`

## Description

The `fixed()` method will convert the string it is called on to an instance of the <tt> tag.

## Example

Listing 6.236 creates an instance of the `String` object and uses the `document.write()` method to write the tag to the page. The results of running this script will be the following:

```
<tt>Hello, World!</tt>
```

*Listing 6.236   Using the* `fixed()` *Method of the* `String` *Object*
```
<script language="JavaScript">
<!-- Hide

// Create an instance of the String object
var myString = new String("Hello, World!");

// Write the string to the page after invoking the fixed() method on it
document.write(myString.fixed());

// Close the stream to the window
document.close();

// End hide -->
</script>
```

# String.fontcolor()

## JavaScript1.0+, JScript1.0+

## NES2+, Nav2+, IE3+, Opera3+

## Syntax

```
string.fontcolor(hexnum)

string.fontcolor(color)
```

## Description

The `fontcolor()` method sets the `COLOR` attribute of an instance of the <font> tag, which it creates. This attribute can either be passed as the hexadecimal equivalent of the color or the actual string that represents that color.

## Example

Listing 6.237 creates an instance of the `String` object and uses the `document.write()` method to write two instances of the tag to the page. The results of running this script will be the following:

```
Hex usage: <font color="#FF0000">Hello, World!</font>
<br>Color usage: <font color="blue">Hello, World!</font>
```

*Listing 6.237   Using the* fontcolor() *Method of the* String *Object*
```
<script language="JavaScript">
<!-- Hide

// Create an instance of the String object
var myString = new String("Hello, World!");

// Write the string twice to the page after invoking the
// fontcolor() method on them
document.write("Hex usage: " + myString.fontcolor('FF0000'));
document.write("<br>Color usage: " + myString.fontcolor('blue'));

// Close the stream to the window
document.close();

// End hide -->
</script>
```

# String.fontsize()

## *JavaScript1.0+, JScript1.0+*

## *NES2+, Nav2+, IE3+, Opera3+*

## *Syntax*

*string*.fontsize(*num*)

*string*.fontsize(*string2*)

## *Description*

The fontsize() method sets the SIZE attribute of an instance of the <font> tag, which it creates. This attribute can be a number between 1 and 7. If you pass the method the number in the form of a string, the size displayed is relative to the <basefont> tag.

## *Example*

Listing 6.238 creates an instance of the String object and uses the document.write() method to write two instances of the tag to the page. The results of running this script will be the following:

```
Hex usage: <font size="6">Hello, World!</font>
<br>Color usage: <font size="-2">Hello, World!</font>
```

*Listing 6.238   Using the* `fontsize()` *Method of the* `String` *Object*
```
<script language="JavaScript">
<!-- Hide

// Create an instance of the String object
var myString = new String("Hello, World!");

// Write the string twice to the page after invoking the
// fontsize() method on them
document.write("Size=6: " + myString.fontsize(6));
document.write("<br>Size=-2: " + myString.fontsize('-2'));

// Close the stream to the window
document.close();

// End hide -->
</script>
```

# String.fromCharCode()

## JavaScript1.2+, JScript3.0+, ECMAScript1.0+

## NES3+, Nav4+, IE4+

### Syntax

`String.fromCharCode(num1, num2,..,numN)`

`String.fromCharCode(keyevent.which)`

### Description

The `fromCharCode()` method of the `String` object returns the characters that corre-spond to the ISO-Latin-1 numbers (num1, num2, ..., numN) position passed. You can also pass the method a key event and use the `which` property to determine which key has been pressed. The possible key events are `KeyDown`, `KeyPress`, and `KeyUp`.

As you can see in the syntax definition, this is a method of the actual `String` object and not an instance of this object. Because of this, you may want to store the results gen-erated by this method into a variable for future processing.

### Example

Listing 6.239 invokes the `fromCharCode()` method on the numbers 88, 89, and 90. The results of this processing are then written to the user's page.

*Listing 6.239   Using the* `fromCharCode()` *Method to Determine the Characters of the ISO-Latin-1 Numbers Passed*
```
<script language="JavaScript1.2">
<!-- Hide
```

```
// Invoke the fromCharCode() method and store the results in
// a variable.
var myString = String.fromCharCode(88,89,90);

// Write the results to the page
document.write("These numbers evaluate to: " + myString);

// Close the stream to the page
document.close();

// End hide -->
</script>
```

# String.indexOf()

## *JavaScript1.0+, JScript1.0+, ECMAScript1.0+*

## *NES2+, Nav2+, IE3+, Opera3+*

### Syntax

*string*.indexOf(*string*, *num*)

*string*.indexOf(*string*)

### Description

The indexOf() method of an instance of the String object returns the indexed start position of the string passed. Additionally, you can specify an index, defined by num in the syntax definition, to start your search for the string specified. This method is the same as the String.lastIndexOf() method, but it starts at the beginning of the string.

### Example

Listing 6.240 creates a simple instance of the String object. This instance is then passed to the indexOf() method on two occasions with the result written to the user's page. The first occasion looks for a space in the string, which returns 6. The second occasion starts the search at the fourth position, so it returns the location of the letter "l" in the word "world".

*Listing 6.240   Using the indexOf() Method to Find the Location of a Character in a String*

```
<script language="JavaScript">
<!-- Hide

// Create an instance of the String object
var myString = new String("Hello, World!");

// Look for the first instance of a space
```

*continues*

*Listing 6.240    continued*
```
document.write(myString.indexOf(" ") + '<br>');

// By specifying an indexed location to start looking you
// can return the indexed location of the third instance of
// the letter 'l'.
document.write(myString.indexOf("l", 4));

// Close the stream to the page
document.close();

// End hide -->
</script>
```

# String.italics()

## *JavaScript1.0+, JScript1.0+*

## *NES2+, Nav2+, IE3+, Opera3+*

## *Syntax*

```
string.italics()
```

## *Description*

The italics() method will convert the string it is called on to an instance of the <i> tag.

## *Example*

Listing 6.241 creates an instance of the String object and uses the document.write() method to write the tag to the page. The results of running this script will be the following:

```
<i>Hello, World!</i>
```

*Listing 6.241    Using the italics() Method of the String Object*
```
<script language="JavaScript">
<!-- Hide

// Create an instance of the String object
var myString = new String("Hello, World!");

// Write the string to the page after invoking the italics() method on it
document.write(myString.italics());

// Close the stream to the window
document.close();

// End hide -->
</script>
```

# String.lastIndexOf()

## *JavaScript1.0+, JScript1.0+, ECMAScript1.0+*

## *NES2+, Nav2+, IE3+, Opera3+*

## *Syntax*

*string*.lastIndexOf(*string, num*)

*string*.lastIndexOf(*string*)

## *Description*

The lastIndexOf() method of an instance of the String object returns the indexed start position of the string passed, starting from the right and going left. Additionally, you can specify an index, defined by num in the syntax definition, to start your search for the string specified. This method is the same as the String.indexOf() method, but it starts at the end of the string.

## *Example*

Listing 6.242 creates a simple instance of the String object. This instance is then passed to the lastIndexOf() method on two occasions with the result written to the user's page. The first occasion looks for the last occurrence of the letter e in the string, which returns 16. The second occasion starts the search at the third position, so it returns the location of the first l in the word "Hello".

*Listing 6.242    Using the* lastIndexOf() *Method to Find the Location of a Character in a String*

```
<script language="JavaScript">
<!-- Hide

// Create an instance of the String object
var myString = new String("Hello World, here I am!");

// Look for the last instance of the letter 'l'
document.write(myString.lastIndexOf("e") + '<br>');

// By specifying an indexed location to start looking, you
// can return the indexed location of the second instance of
// the letter 'l'.
document.write(myString.lastIndexOf("l", 3));

// Close the stream to the page
document.close();

// End hide -->
</script>
```

# String.length

## *JavaScript1.0+, JScript1.0+, ECMAScript1.0+*

## *NES2+, Nav2+, IE3+, Opera3+*

### *Syntax*

`string.length`

### *Description*

The `length` property of an instance of the `String` object returns the total length of the string.

### *Example*

Listing 6.243 creates three instances of the `String` object. The `length` property of each of these instances are accessed and written to the user's page.

*Listing 6.243   Accessing the `length` Property of an Instance of the `String` Object*

```
<script language="JavaScript">
<!-- Hide

// Create an instance of the String object
var myString1 = new String("Hello, World");
var myString2 = new String("Here is a longer string");
var myString3 = new String("Here is an even longer string");

// Write the lengths of these strings to the user's page.
document.write(myString1 + ": is " + myString1.length);
document.write(" characters long.<br>");
document.write(myString2 + ": is " + myString2.length);
document.write(" characters long.<br>");
document.write(myString3 + ": is " + myString3.length);
document.write(" characters long.<br>");

// Close the stream to the page
document.close();

// End hide -->
</script>
```

# String.link()

## *JavaScript1.0+, JScript1.0+*

## *NES2+, Nav2+, IE3+, Opera3+*

### *Syntax*

`string.link(URL)`

## Description

The `link()` method will convert the string it is called on to an instance of the <a> tag, setting the HREF attribute to the URL that is passed.

## Example

Listing 6.244 creates an instance of the `String` object and uses the `document.write()` method to write the tag to the page. The results of running this script will be the following:

```
<a href="http://www.purejavascript.com">The online book!</a>
```

Listing 6.244    Using the `link()` Method of the `String` Object
```
<script language="JavaScript">
<!-- Hide

// Create an instance of the String object
var myString = new String("The online book!");

// Write the string to the page after invoking the link() method on it
document.write(myString.link('http://www.purejavascript.com'));

// Close the stream to the window
document.close();

// End hide -->
</script>
```

# String.match()

## JavaScript1.2+, JScript3.0+

## NES3+, Nav4+, IE4+

## Syntax

`string.match(regexpression)`

## Description

The `match()` method of an instance of the `String` object searches the string in which it is invoked for the regular expression passed to the method. The regular expression is made up of a *pattern* and *flags* that dictate what is to be matched. The method returns an array containing the matches found in the string.

**TIP**

See the reference entry for `RegExp` for a list of the patterns and flags that can be used to create a regular expression.

## Example

Listing 6.245 creates an instance of the `String` object and tries to match instances that contain a space followed by some characters. If any matches were returned into the array, they are written to the user's page one at a time.

*Listing 6.245   Using the `match()` Method to Match Regular Expressions in a String*

```
<script language="JavaScript1.2">
<!-- Hide

// Create an instance of the String object and load it with a name.
var myString = new String("Mr. R. Allen Wyke");

// Match occurrences of a space followed by characters
var myRegExp = /\s\w*/g;
var answerArray = myString.match(myRegExp);

// Check to see if there were any matches found
if(answerArray == null){
  document.write('No matches were found');
}else{
  document.write('The following matches were found: <br>');

  // Write the contents of the array to the page. This will put
  // R, Allen, and Wyke each on a separate line.
  for(var i = 0; i < answerArray.length; i++){
    document.write(answerArray[i] + '<br>');
  }
}

// Close the stream to the window
document.close();

// End hide -->
</script>
```

# String.prototype

## JavaScript 1.1+, ECMAScript 1.0+, JScript 3.0+

## NES2+, Nav3+, IE 4+, Opera3+

## Syntax

```
String.prototype.property
```

```
String.prototype.method
```

## Description

The prototype property of the String object allows a programmer to add properties or methods to a core JavaScript object.

## Example

Listing 6.246 creates two instances of the String object. Then it prototypes a new property, type, and a new method, verify(). In the script, the type property is assigned to the string instances and then they are checked using the verify() method. The results of the validation are then written to the user's page.

*Listing 6.246  Using the* prototype *Property to Create New Properties and Methods of the* String *Object*

```
<script language="JavaScript1.1">
<!-- Hide

// Define the method that we prototyped
function myVerify(){

  // Check to see if the type property we added is set to "Name"
  // If it is, then return true. If not, then return false.
  if(this.type != "Name"){
    return false;
  }else{
    return true;
  }
}

// Create a new property and method of the String object.
String.prototype.type = null;
String.prototype.verify = myVerify;

// Create two instances of the String object and load it with a name.
var myString1 = new String("Mr. R. Allen Wyke");
var myString2 = new String("Mr. Robert J. Wyke");

// Using the prototype we defined, assign the type property to Name
// for the first string and to "Title" for the second.
myString1.type = "Name";
myString2.type = "Title";

// Check each of the types of the strings to see if they are valid
if(myString1.verify()){
  document.write(myString1 + " has a valid type of " + myString1.type);
}else{
  document.write(myString1 + " has an invalid type of " + myString1.type);
```

*continues*

*Listing 6.246    contnued*
```
}

document.write('<br>');

if(myString2.verify()){
  document.write(myString2 + " has a valid type of " + myString2.type);
}else{
  document.write(myString2 + " has an invalid type of " + myString2.type);
}

// Close the stream to the window
//document.close();

// End hide -->
</script>
```

# String.replace()

## JavaScript1.2+, JScript3.0+

## NES3+, Nav4+, IE4+

## Syntax

`string.replace(regexpression, replacestring)`

## Description

The `replace()` method of an instance of the `String` object searches the string in which it is invoked for the regular expression passed to the method. The regular expression is made up of a *pattern* and *flags* that dictate what is to be matched. If and when a match is found, the method returns a new string with that match replaced with the replacement string passed to the method.

**TIP**

See the reference entry for `RegExp` for a list of the patterns and flags that can be used to create a regular expression.

## Example

Listing 6.247 creates an instance of the `String` object. This instance is then searched through to see if any occurrences of the word `"Wyke"` is found. If so, it is replaced with `"White"`.

*Listing 6.247    Using the* `replace()` *Method to Replace Regular Expression Matches in a String*

```
<script language="JavaScript1.2">
<!-- Hide

// Create an instance of the String object and load it with a name.
var myString = new String("Mr. R. Allen Wyke");

// Search for "Wyke" and replace it with "White"
var myRegExp = /Wyke/g;
var newString = myString.replace(myRegExp, "White");

// Write the results to the page
document.write('Notice the last name in the original string, ' + myString);
document.write(', was replaced and is now '+ newString);

// Close the stream to the window
document.close();

// End hide -->
</script>
```

# String.search()

## *JavaScript1.2+, JScript3.0+*

## *NES3+, Nav4+, IE4+*

## *Syntax*

`string.search(regexpression)`

## *Description*

The `search()` method of an instance of the `String` object searches the string in which it is invoked for the regular expression passed to the method. The regular expression is made up of a *pattern* and *flags* that dictate what is to be matched. The method returns the indexed start location of the string if it is found and –1 if the string does not contain a regular expression match.

**TIP**

> See the reference entry for `RegExp` for a list of the patterns and flags that can be used to create a regular expression.

## *Example*

Listing 6.248 creates an instance of the `String` object, which is searched for the first instance of a space. If a match is found, the indexed start position is returned. The results of running this script are written to the user's page.

*Listing 6.248 Using the* `search()` *Method to Search Regular Expressions in a String*

```
<script language="JavaScript1.2">
<!-- Hide

// Create an instance of the String object and load it with a name.
var myString = new String("Mr. R. Allen Wyke");

// Find the first occurrences of any whitespace
var myRegExp = /\s/;
var answerIdx = myString.search(myRegExp);

// Check to see if there were any matches found
if(answerIdx == -1){
  document.write('No matches were found');
}else{
  document.write('Your search string was found starting at: ' + answerIdx);
}

// Close the stream to the window
document.close();

// End hide -->
</script>
```

# String.slice()

## *JavaScript1.0+, JScript1.0+*

## *NES2+, Nav2+, IE3+, Opera3+*

## *Syntax*

*string*.slice(*num1, num2*)

*string*.slice(*num*)

## Description

The slice() method of an instance of the String object returns the characters in the string between the indexed positions num1 and num2 in which the method is invoked. The string itself is zero based, so the first character is in position 0. It is also possible to pass num2 as a negative number. In this scenario, the string counts from the end of the string to end the slice.

As the syntax definition states, it is also possible to pass a single index location to the method. In this implementation, the method will not stop at a position and will return all characters until the end of the string.

## Example

Listing 6.249 creates an instance of the String object. The slice() method is invoked on this string and asked to return the first seven characters of the string. The results of running this script are written to the user's page.

Listing 6.249  *Using the* slice() *Method to Return Seven Characters in a String*

```
<script language="JavaScript">
<!-- Hide

// Create an instance of the String object and load it with a name.
var myString = new String("Mr. R. Allen Wyke");

// Grab the first 7 characters of the string
var mySlice = myString.slice(0,6);

// Write the results to the page
document.write('The first 7 characters of our string, ' + myString);
document.write(', are: ' + mySlice);

// Close the stream to the window
document.close();

// End hide -->
</script>
```

# String.small()

## *JavaScript1.0+, JScript1.0+*

## *NES2+, Nav2+, IE3+, Opera3+*

## Syntax

*string*.small()

## Description:

The small() method will convert the string it is called on to an instance of the <small> tag.

## Example

Listing 6.250 creates an instance of the String object and uses the document.write() method to write the tag to the page. The results of running this script will be the following:

```
<small>Hello, World!</small>
```

*Listing 6.250    Using the* `small()` *Method of the* `String` *Object*

```
<script language="JavaScript1.1">
<!-- Hide

// Create an instance of the String object
var myString = new String("Hello, World!");

// Write the string to the page after invoking the small() method on it
document.write(myString.small());

// Close the stream to the window
document.close();

// End hide -->
</script>
```

# String.split()

## *JavaScript1.1+, JScript1.0+, ECMAScript1.0+*

## *NES2+, Nav3+, IE3+, Opera3+*

## *Syntax*

`string.split(`*separator, num*`)`

`string.split(`*separator*`)`

`string.split(`*regexpression, num*`)`

`string.split(`*regexpression*`)`

## *Description*

The `split()` method of an instance of the `String` object splits the string in which it is invoked into separate strings based on the regular expression or separator passed to the method. If a regular expression is passed, it is made up of a *pattern* and *flags* that dictate what is to be matched. The `separator` is a string or character that is matched to perform the separation.

## NOTE

If the LANGUAGE attribute of the `<script>` tag is set to `"JavaScript1.2"` when using the second syntactical definition and the separator is a space, consecutive spaces are treated differently. In JavaScript 1.1, each space would be split and returned as part of the results. So if there were an instance of three consecutive spaces, two of the spaces would be returned in the array. Specifying JavaScript 1.2 tells the interpreter to treat the three spaces as a single space, so you are able to perform proper splits.

The method returns an array containing each of the segments found in the string.

## *Example*

Listing 6.251 creates an instance of the String object. This instance is then split, looking for a space as the separator, using each of the syntactical definitions. The results are then written to the user's page.

*Listing 6.251   Using the* split() *Method to Split the String Passed into Separate Strings*

```
<script language="JavaScript1.2">
<!-- Hide

// Define a function to handle writing the results
function genResults(arrayName, testName){
  document.write('<b>Currently Evaluating: ' + testName + '</b><hr>');

  // Check to see if there were any spaces found
  if(arrayName == null){
    document.write('No matches were found');
  }else{

    // Write the contents of the array to the page. This will put
    // R, Allen, and Wyke each on a separate line.
    for(var i = 0; i < arrayName.length; i++){
      document.write('[' + i + ']: ' + arrayName[i] + '<br>');
    }
  }
  document.write('<p>');
}

// Create an instance of the String object and load it with a name.
var myString = new String("Mr. R. Allen Wyke");

// Define a regular expression and a separator. Both are set to
// split on a single whitespace.
var myRegExp = /\s/g;
var mySeparator = " ";

genResults(myString.split(mySeparator), "Separator Only");
genResults(myString.split(mySeparator, 2), "Separator With Limit of 2");
genResults(myString.split(myRegExp), "Regular Expression Only");
```

*continues*

*Listing 6.251    continued*
```
genResults(myString.split(myRegExp, 3), "Regular Expression With Limit of 3");

// Close the stream to the window
document.close();

// End hide -->
</script>
```

# String.strike()

## *JavaScript1.0+, JScript1.0+*

## *NES2+, Nav2+, IE3+, Opera3+*

## *Syntax*
```
string.strike()
```

## *Description*

The `strike()` method will convert the string it is called on to an instance of the `<strike>` tag.

## *Example*

Listing 6.252 creates an instance of the `String` object and uses the `document.write()` method to write the tag to the page. The results of running this script will be the following:

```
<strike>Hello, World!</strike>
```

*Listing 6.252    Using the `strike()` Method of the `String` Object*
```
<script language="JavaScript">
<!-- Hide

// Create an instance of the String object
var myString = new String("Hello, World!");

// Write the string to the page after invoking the strike() method on it
document.write(myString.strike());

// Close the stream to the window
document.close();

// End hide -->
</script>
```

# String.sub()

## *JavaScript1.0+, JScript1.0+*

## *NES2+, Nav2+, IE3+, Opera3+*

## *Syntax*

`string.sub()`

## *Description*

The sub() method will convert the string it is called on to an instance of the <sub> tag.

## *Example*

Listing 6.253 creates an instance of the String object and uses the document.write() method to write the tag to the page. The results of running this script will be the following:

`<sub>Hello, World!</sub>`

*Listing 6.253   Using the* sub() *Method of the* String *Object*

```
<script language="JavaScript1.1">
<!-- Hide

// Create an instance of the String object
var myString = new String("Hello, World!");

// Write the string to the page after invoking the sub() method on it
document.write(myString.sub());

// Close the stream to the window
document.close();

// End hide -->
</script>
```

# String.substr()

## *JavaScript1.0+, JScript1.0+*

## *NES2+, Nav2+, IE3+, Opera3+*

## *Syntax*

`string.substr(num1, num2)`

`string.substr(num)`

## Description

The substr() method of an instance of the String object returns the characters in the string, starting with the indexed position num1 and counting to num2 characters. The string itself is zero based, so the first character is in position 0. It is also possible to pass num1 as a negative number. In this scenario, the string starts from the end of the string to begin the substring extraction.

As the syntax definition states, it is also possible to pass a single index location to the method. In this implementation, the method will not stop at a position and will return all characters until the end of the string.

## Example

Listing 6.254 creates an instance of the String object. The substr() method is invoked on this string and asked to return the first six characters of the string. The results of running this script are written to the user's page.

*Listing 6.254    Using the* substr() *Method to Return Six Characters in a String*

```
<script language="JavaScript1.1">
<!-- Hide

// Create an instance of the String object and load it with a name.
var myString = new String("Mr. R. Allen Wyke");

// Grab the first 6 characters of the string
var mySubString = myString.substr(0,6);

// Write the results to the page
document.write('The first 6 characters of our string, ' + myString);
document.write(', are: ' + mySubString);

// Close the stream to the window
document.close();

// End hide -->
</script>
```

# String.substring()

## JavaScript1.0+, JScript1.0+

## NES2+, Nav2+, IE3+, Opera3+

## Syntax

*string*.substring(*num1, num2*)

*string*.substring(*num*)

## Description

The substring() method of an instance of the String object returns the characters in the string starting with the indexed position num1 and ending with the character before num2. The string itself is zero based, so the first character is in position 0.

If you pass num1 as a negative number, it will be treated as 0. Likewise if you pass num2 as a value greater than the string.length property, it will be treated as string.length. And finally, if num1 equals num2, an empty string is returned.

As the syntax definition states, it is also possible to pass a single index location to the method. In this implementation, the method will not stop at a position and will return all characters until the end of the string.

### NOTE

If the LANGUAGE attribute of the <script> tag is set to "JavaScript1.2" and a Navigator browser is interpreting the script, a runtime out of memory error will be produced if num1 is greater than num2. Without this attribute set, the method returns a substring beginning with num2 and ending with num1 ·1.

## Example:

Listing 6.255 creates an instance of the String object. The substring() method is invoked on this string and asked to return the first ten characters of the string. The results of running this script are written to the user's page.

*Listing 6.255* *Using the* substring() *Method to Return Ten Characters in a String*

```
<script language="JavaScript">
<!-- Hide

// Create an instance of the String object and load it with a name.
var myString = new String("Mr. R. Allen Wyke");

// Grab the first 10 characters of the string
var mySubString = myString.substring(0,10);

// Write the results to the page
document.write('The first 10 characters of our string, ' + myString);
document.write(', are: ' + mySubString);

// Close the stream to the window
document.close();

// End hide -->
</script>
```

# String.sup()

## *JavaScript1.0+, JScript1.0+*

## *NES2+, Nav2+, IE3+, Opera3+*

## *Syntax*

```
string.sup()
```

## *Description*

The sup() method will convert the string it is called on to an instance of the <sup> tag.

## *Example*

Listing 6.256 creates an instance of the String object and uses the document.write() method to write the tag to the page. The results of running this script will be the following:

```
<sup>Hello, World!</sup>
```

*Listing 6.256   Using the* sup() *Method of the* String *Object*
```
<script language="JavaScript">
<!-- Hide

// Create an instance of the String object
var myString = new String("Hello, World!");

// Write the string to the page after invoking the sup() method on it
document.write(myString.sup());

// Close the stream to the window
document.close();

// End hide -->
</script>
```

# String.toLowerCase()

## *JavaScript1.0+, JScript1.0+, ECMAScript1.0+*

## *NES2+, Nav2+, IE3+, Opera3+*

## *Syntax*

```
string.toLowerCase()
```

## *Description*

The toLowerCase() method of an instance of a String object converts the characters in that string to all lowercase values. This is often used when a programmer is trying to evaluate a string a user has entered and does not care about case.

## Example

Listing 6.257 pops up a prompt box and asks the user to enter various case text. After the user clicks OK, the lowercase version of the string is written to the page.

*Listing 6.257   Using the `toLowerCase()` Method of the `String` Object to Convert a String Entered by a User to Lowercase*

```
<script language="JavaScript">
<!-- Hide

// Create an instance of the String object
var myString = new String(prompt("Please enter some various case text", ""));

// Convert the text to lowercase and write it to the page.
document.write(myString.toLowerCase());

// Close the stream to the window
document.close();

// End hide -->
</script>
```

# String.toSource()

## *JavaScript1.3+, JScript3.0+, ECMAScript2.0+ (proposed)*

## *Nav4.06+, IE4+*

## Syntax

```
string.toSource()

String.toSource()
```

## Description

The `toSource()` method of the `String` object is not defined in the first version of the ECMAScript standard, but is proposed for version 2. If this method is invoked on the core `String` object, it will return something like the following:

```
function String() { [native code] }
```

If it is invoked on an instance of the `String` object, it will contain the source of the instance you created. In Listing 6.258, the result of this application of the method should be something like the following:

```
(new String("Hello, World!"))
```

## Example

Listing 6.258 creates an instance of the `String` object. The `toSource()` method is then applied to the instance and the results are written to the page. A second `document.write()` method writes the results of applying the method to the core object.

*Listing 6.258    Using the* `toSource()` *Method of the* `String` *Object to Obtain the Source of the Object or an Instance of It*

```
<script language="JavaScript1.3">
<!-- Hide

// Create an instance of the String object
var myString = new String("Hello, World!");

// Apply the toSource() method to the instance and the core String
// object.
document.write(myString.toSource() + '<br>');
document.write(String.toSource());

// Close the stream to the window
document.close();

// End hide -->
</script>
```

# String.toString()

## JavaScript1.1+, JScript1.0+, ECMAScript1.0+

## NES2+, Nav3+, IE3+

## Syntax

*string*.toString()

String.toString()

## Description

The `toString()` method of the `String` object, if invoked on the core `String` object, will return the object type or the name of the constructor that created the object. This will be something like the following:

```
function String() { [native code] }
```

If it is invoked on an instance of the `String` object, it will contain the source string of the instance you created. In Listing 6.259, the result of this application of the method should be something like the following:

```
Hello, World!
```

## Example

Listing 6.259 creates an instance of the `String` object. The `toString()` method is then applied to the instance and the results are written to the page. A second `document.write()` method writes the results of applying the method to the core object.

*Listing 6.259   Using the* `toString()` *Method of the* `String` *Object to Obtain the Source of the Object or an Instance of It*

```
<script language="JavaScript1.3">
<!-- Hide

// Create an instance of the String object
var myString = new String("Hello, World!");

// Apply the toString() method to the instance and the core String
// object.
document.write(myString.toString() + '<br>');
document.write(String.toString());

// Close the stream to the window
document.close();

// End hide -->
</script>
```

# String.toUpperCase()

## *JavaScript1.0+, JScript1.0+, ECMAScript1.0+*

## *NES2+, Nav2+, IE3+, Opera3+*

## Syntax

*string*.toUpperCase()

## Description

The `toUpperCase()` method of an instance of a `String` object converts the characters in that string to all uppercase values. This is often used when a programmer is trying to evaluate a string a user has entered, and case is not an issue.

## Example

Listing 6.260 pops up a prompt box and asks the user to enter various case text. After the user clicks OK, the uppercase version of the string is written to the page.

*Listing 6.260   Using the* `toUpperCase()` *Method of the* `String` *Object to Convert a String Entered by a User to Uppercase*

```
<script language="JavaScript">
<!-- Hide

// Create an instance of the String object
var myString = new String(prompt("Please enter some various case text", ""));

// Convert the text to uppercase and write it to the page.
```

*continues*

*Listing 6.260    continued*
```
document.write(myString.toUpperCase());

// Close the stream to the window
document.close();

// End hide -->
</script>
```

# String.valueOf()

## *JavaScript1.1+, JScript3.0+, ECMAScript1.0+*

## *NES2+, Nav3+, IE4+, Opera3+*

## *Syntax*
```
string.valueOf()
```

## *Description*

The valueOf() method returns the primitive value of the object. In terms of an instance of a String object, this method returns the string itself.

### *Example*

In Listing 6.261, an instance of the String object is created. Since the valueOf() method returns the actual value of the string, "Here is some random text" is written to the user's page.

*Listing 6.261    Using the* valueOf() *Method to Return the Value of the* String *Instance*
```
<script language="JavaScript1.1">
<!-- Hide

// Create an instance of the String object
var myString = new String("Here is some random text.");

// Write the value of the string to the page.
document.write('The value of my string instance is: ' + myString.valueOf());

// Close the stream to the window
document.close();

// End hide -->
</script>
```

# super

*JavaScript1.3+*

*NES3+, Nav4.06+*

## Syntax

Reserved Keyword

## Description

The super keyword was reserved in JavaScript 1.3 for future use but has not currently been implemented.

## Example

No example can be provided because super has not been implemented.

# switch

*JavaScript1.2+, JScript 3.0+*

*NES3+, Nav4+, IE4+*

## Syntax

```
switch(expression){
  case label1:
    code;
    break;
  case label2:
    code;
    break;
  case labelN:
    code;
    break;
  default:
    code;
}
```

## Description

The switch statement allows you to process the expression passed by matching it with a label—from label1 to labelN. If there is a match, the code following that label is executed. If the expression passed does not match a label, the default section is executed. Note that you can have as many labels as you deem necessary in your script.

## *Example*

Listing 6.262 has a text field and a button. Users are asked to enter a day of the week into the field. When they press the button, a function is called that contains a `switch`, which verifies they entered a correct day. If so, an alert box pops up and tells users what part of the week they entered.

*Listing 6.262    Using a `switch` Statement to Process Data*

```
<html>
<head>
  <title>Using the switch statement</title>
<script language="JavaScript">
<!-- Hide

// Display an alert box that contains the value of the
// submit button.
function verifyDay(form){

  // Read the text entered in a variable and convert it to uppercase
  var myEntry = form.day.value.toUpperCase();

  // Define what you return
  var firstPart = "You have entered a day at the first of the week";
  var endPart = "You have entered a day at the end of the week";
  var weekEnd = "You have entered a weekend day";

  // Use a switch statement to perform your processing
  switch(myEntry){
    case "MONDAY" :
      alert(firstPart);
      break;
    case "TUESDAY" :
      alert(firstPart);
      break;
    case "WEDNESDAY" :
      alert('You have entered a "hump" day');
      break;
    case "THURSDAY" :
      alert(endPart);
      break;
    case "FRIDAY" :
      alert(endPart);
      break;
    case "SATURDAY" :
      alert(weekEnd);
      break;
    case "SUNDAY" :
      alert(weekEnd);
      break;
```

```
      default :
        alert('You have entered an invalid day');
    }
  }
  // End hide -->
  </script>
  </head>
  <body>
  <form name="myForm">
  <b>Please enter a day of the week:</b><br>
    <input type=TEXT value="" name="day">
    <input type=BUTTON value="Verify" name="myButton"
         onClick='verifyDay(this.form)'>
  </form>
  </body>
  </html>
```

# synchronized

## *JavaScript1.2+, JScript3.0+*

## *NES3+, Nav4+, IE4+*

## *Syntax*

Reserved Keyword

## *Description*

The synchronized keyword has not been implemented in JavaScript to date. It has been reserved for future use.

## *Example*

This keyword has not been implemented, therefore no example is provided.

# this

## *JavaScript1.0+, JScript1.0+*

## *NES2+, Nav2+, IE2+, Opera3+*

## *Syntax*

this
this.*property*

## *Description*

The this keyword is used to refer to the current object and is often used to pass entire objects, such as those contained in Form instances, to functions and methods specified in scripts.

## *Example*

Listing 6.263 contains a text box, a text area, and a button. When the user clicks the button, an onClick event handler passes the form's information, using the this keyword, to a function defined in the <head> of the document. The function opens a second, smaller window and writes several properties of the form to the page.

*Listing 6.263    Using this to Pass all Form Data to a Function*

```html
<html>
<head>
  <title> Using this in passing form information</title>
<script language="JavaScript">
<!-- Hide

function displayInfo(form){

  // Open a window to store the results
  var myWin = open("", "","width=450,height=200");

  // Write the text boxes properties to the window
  myWin.document.write("The defaultValue of the text box is: ");
  myWin.document.write(form.myText.defaultValue);
  myWin.document.write("<br>The name of the text area is: ");
  myWin.document.write(form.myTextArea.name);
  myWin.document.write("<br>The value of the button is: ");
  myWin.document.write(form.myButton.value);

  // Close the stream to the window
  myWin.document.close();
}
// End hide -->
</script>
</head>
<body>
<form name="myForm">
  <textarea name="myTextArea" rows=2 cols=50>
  Here is some text in my text area.
  </textarea>
  <br>
  <input type=TEXT value="Change Me?" name="myText">
  <br>
  <input type=BUTTON value="Display Information" name="myButton"
         onClick='displayInfo(this.form)'>
</form>
</body>
</html>
```

Listing 6.264 creates a vehicle object that has three properties: number of doors, color, and the type of vehicle. The this keyword is used to associate these properties with the object when it is referenced in other scripts. Further down in the example, an instance of the vehicle object is created and its properties are written to the page. The results of running this example are shown in Figure 6.19.

*Listing 6.264    Using* this *to Internally Reference Properties of a User-defined Object*

```
<html>
<head>
  <title>Using this in object creation</title>
<script language="JavaScript">
<!-- Hide

// Create vehicle object
function vehicle(nDoors, sColor, sType){

  // Define the characteristics of the vehicle and associate
  // them with a new instance using the "this" keyword.
  this.doors = nDoors;
  this.color = sColor;
  this.type = sType;
}

// End hide -->
</script>
</head>
<body>
<script language="JavaScript">
<!-- Hide

// Create an instance of the vehicle
var myVehicle = new vehicle(4, "red", "Toyota");

// Call the properties of your object using the dot convention
// found throughout JavaScript.
document.writeln("I have created a " + myVehicle.type);
document.writeln(" that is " + myVehicle.color);
document.writeln(" and has " + myVehicle.doors + " doors.");
// End hide -->
</script>
</body>
</html>
```

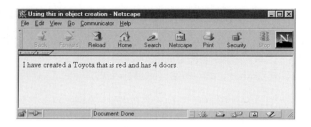

**Figure 6.19**

*Results of running Listing 6.264 in a browser.*

# throw

## *JavaScript1.4+, JScript5.0+*

## *NES3+, Nav5+, IE5+*

### Syntax

```
throw exception
```

### Description

The `throw` element of the JavaScript language was a reserved keyword in the JavaScript 1.3 and JScript 3.0 languages and in the Netscape Enterprise server 3 environment. Navigator 5 and Internet Explorer 5 were the first browsers to implement the keyword. It is used to generate an error condition handled by a `try..catch` statement or to pass errors found in these statements to higher level handlers.

### Example

Listing 6.265 contains a text box and button. The user is asked to insert a numeric value into the text box and press the button. When this is done, the `onClick` event handler of the button calls a function to check to see if the entered text was numeric. If it is not, the `myErrorHandler` function is called to handle the error. The `myErrorHandler` function contains a `try..catch` statement that allows the programmer to define what happens on an incorrect entry. In this example, an `alert` box is displayed containing an error code and message.

*Listing 6.265    This Example Uses* `throw` *in a* `try..catch` *Statement*

```
<html>
<head>
  <title>Listing 6.165: Using throw in a try..catch statement</title>
<script language="JScript1.3">
<!-- Hide

// Declare a function to handle errors
```

```
function myErrorHandler(data){
  try{
    // Check to see if the value passed is "string" or "NaN"
    // then "throw" the appropriate error
    if(data == "string"){
      throw "E0";
    }else{
      throw "E1";
    }
  }catch{

    // If the error thrown was "E0" then return the following
    if(e == "E0"){
      return("Error (" + e + "): Entry must be numeric.");
    }else{

      // Pass off to a higher level handler
      return("Error (" + e + "): Entry must be numeric.");
    }
  }
}

// This function reads in the form data and calls the appropriate error.
function processData(form){

  // Check to see if a number was passed
  if(isNaN(parseInt(form.myText.value))){
    alert(myErrorHandler("string"));
  }else{
    alert("You have correctly entered a number");
  }
}
// End hide -->
</script>
</head>
<body>
<form name="myForm">
  Please enter a number:
  <input type=TEXT size=10 value="" name="myText">
  <input type=BUTTON value="Process" name="myButton"
         onClick='processData(this.form)'>
</form>
</body>
</html>
```

# throws

## JavaScript1.2+

## NES3+, Nav4

## Syntax

Reserved Keyword

## Description

The throws keyword has not been implemented in JavaScript to date. It has been reserved for future use.

## Example

This keyword has not been implemented, therefore no example is provided.

# transient

## JavaScript1.2+

## NES3+, Nav4+

## Syntax

Reserved Keyword

## Description

The transient keyword has not been implemented in JavaScript to date. It has been reserved for future use.

## Example

This keyword has not been implemented, therefore no example is provided.

# true

## JavaScript1.2+

## NES3+, Nav4+

## Syntax

Reserved Keyword

## Description

The true keyword has not been implemented in JavaScript to date. It has been reserved for future use.

## Example

This keyword has not been implemented, therefore no example is provided.

# try...catch

## *JScript5.0+, JavaScript1.4*

## *NES3+, IE5+, Nav5+*

## *Syntax*

```
try{
    statement1
}catch(exception){
    statement2
}
```

## *Description*

The try...catch statement of the JavaScript language contained the try and catch reserve keywords in the JavaScript 1.3 and JScript 3.0 languages and in the Netscape Enterprise server 3 environments. Internet Explorer 5 and Navigator 5 were the first browsers to implement this feature. It can be used to handle all or some of the errors that can occur in a script. If an error is not handled by a try...catch statement, it is passed on so other statements can handle the error. If there are no other statements to handle the error, it is passed to the browser to handle. This usually means a pop-up dialog box to the user or writing the information to the "JavaScript Typein Console" for Navigator 4.06 and higher browsers.

*statement1* is where an error can occur, while *statement2* is used to handle the error. As soon as an error occurs, the value *thrown* is passed to the *catch* portion of the statement and stored in *exception*. If the error can not be handled, another throw statement is used to pass the error to a higher level handler if one is defined.

> **NOTE**
>
> It is possible to have nested try...catch statements within try...catch statements.

## *Example*

Listing 6.266 contains a text box and button. The user is asked to insert a numeric value into the text box and press the button. When this is done, the onClick event handler of the button calls a function to check to see if the entered text was numeric. If it is not, the myErrorHandler function is called to handle the error. The myErrorHandler function contains a try...catch statement that allows the programmer to define what happens on an incorrect entry. In this example, an alert box is displayed containing an error code and message.

Note that there are two levels of error handling contained in this example to demonstrate nested usage.

*Listing 6.266   This Example uses a* `try...catch` *Statement to Handle an Incorrect Entry*

```
<html>
<head>
  <title>Listing 6.166: Using a try..catch statement</title>
<script language="JScript1.3">
<!-- Hide

// Declare a function to handle errors
function myErrorHandler(data){
  try{
    try{
      // Check to see if the value passed is "string" or "NaN"
      // then "throw" the appropriate error
      if(data == "string"){
        throw "E0";
      }else{
        throw "E1";
      }
    }catch{

      // If the error thrown was "E0" then return the following
      if(e == "E0"){
        return("Error (" + e + "): Entry must be numeric.");
      }else{

        // Pass off to a higher level handler
        throw e;
      }
    }

  // This it the higher level handler for demonstration purposes
  }catch{
    return("Error (" + e + "): Entry was invalid.");
  }
}

// This function reads in the form data and calls the appropriate error.
function processData(form){

  // Check to see if a number was passed
  if(isNaN(parseInt(form.myText.value))){
    alert(myErrorHandler("string"));
  }else{
```

```
      alert("You have correctly entered a number");
   }
}
// End hide -->
</script>
</head>
<body>
<form name="myForm">
  Please enter a number:
  <input type=TEXT size=10 value="" name="myText">
  <input type=BUTTON value="Process" name="myButton"
       onClick='processData(this.form)'>
</form>
</body>
</html>
```

# typeof

## *JavaScript1.1+, JScript1.0+*

## *NES2+, Nav3+, IE3+, Opera3+*

## *Syntax*

typeof(*variable*)

## *Description*

The typeof unary operator is used to determine the type of the variable passed to it. The return values of this operator are boolean, number, object, string, or undefined.

## NOTE

Because undefined was not fully implemented until JavaScript 1.3 and JScript 3.0, many supporting browsers return null when passing a variable that has not been defined.

## *Example*

Listing 6.267 creates boolean, number, object, string, and undefined variable instances, and then uses the typeof operator to write their type to the page.

*Listing 6.267    This Example Uses the* typeof *Unary Operator to Return the Types for Four Different Variables*

```
<html>
<head>
  <title>Listing 6.167: Using typeof to determine the type of variables
  </title>
<script language="JavaScript1.1">
```

*continues*

*Listing 6.267 continued*

```
<!-- Hide

// Declare 4 variables of different types
var bMyVar = true;
var nMyVar = 35;
var sMyVar = "This is a string";
var uMyVar;

// End hide -->
</script>
</head>
<body>
<script language="JavaScript1.1">
<!-- Hide

// Declare 4 variables of different types
document.writeln("bMyVar = " + typeof(bMyVar));
document.writeln("<br>nMyVar = " + typeof(nMyVar));
document.writeln("<br>sMyVar = " + typeof(sMyVar));
document.writeln("<br>uMyVar = " + typeof(uMyVar));

// End hide -->
</script>
</body>
</html>
```

# undefined

## *JavaScript 1.3+, ECMAScript 1.0+, JScript 5.0+*

## *Nav4.06+, IE5+*

## *Syntax*

```
undefined
```

## *Description*

The undefined property is a primitive value of the global object. It is returned by variables that have not had values assigned to them. It is also returned by methods if the variable being evaluated is not assigned a value. Browsers not supporting this property return null on the undefined variables.

**NOTE**

> ECMAScript 1.0 only defines undefined as a primitive value, and does not define it as a property of the global object.

## Example

Listing 6.268 creates the variable myVariable, and then checks to see if it is undefined in an if clause. Note that Opera 3 and later browsers, even though they do not officially support this property, return null but evaluate the if clause in this example as true.

**NOTE**

At the time of this writing, Internet Explorer 5 was still in beta and incorrectly evaluated the if clause in this example.

*Listing 6.268   Testing a Variable to See if It is Undefined*

```
<script language="JavaScript1.3">
<!-- Hide

// create a variable
var myVariable;

// evaluate the variable in an if statement and write its
// value to the page.
if(myVariable == undefined){
  document.write("This variable is undefined at the moment");
}else{
  document.write("This variables value is: " + myVariable);
}
// End hide -->
</script>
```

# unescape()

## *JavaScript 1.0+, JScript 1.0+, ECMAScript 1.0+*

## *NES2+, Nav2+, IE3+, Opera3+*

## Syntax

unescape(*string*)

## Description

The unescape() method takes a hexadecimal value and returns the ISO-Latin-1 ASCII equivalent. This method performs the opposite operation of the escape() method and is commonly used to escape user-entered data before form submission.

## Example

Listing 6.269 declares a local variable, escapedVal, and passes it to the unescape() method. The result, "@", is then written to the page.

*Listing 6.269    Using the* `unescape()` *Method to Convert a Hexadecimal Value to its ASCII Equivalent*

```
<script language="JavaScript">
<!-- Hide

// create a variable
var escapedVal = "%40";

// evaluate the variable and place the value in a variable
var unescapedVal = unescape(escapedVal);

document.write('The <I>escapedVal</I> value (' + escapedVal + ") ");
document.write("evaluates to " + unescapedVal);

// End hide -->
</script>
```

# var

## *JavaScript 1.0, JScript 1.0, ECMAScript 1.0*

## *NES2+, Nav2+, IE3+, Opera3+*

## Syntax

```
var variable
var variable = value
```

## Description

The `var` keyword is used to declare variables within a script. If it is used in a function, the scope of the variable is confined to that function. If used outside of a function, it is not limited and can be accessed anywhere on the page.

## Example

Listing 6.270 declares the variable, `myVar`, in three different locations. It is declared once at a global level, once within a function where it is the returned value, and once in a function where it is written to the page. The result of running this script is shown in Figure 6.20.

*Listing 6.270    This Example Shows Using the* `var` *Keyword in Three Different Instances*

```
<html>
<head>
  <title>Listing 6.170: Examples of the var Keyword</title>
<script language="JavaScript">
<!-- Hide

// Declare a global variable
```

```
var myVar = "Global";

// Declare a variable of the same name in this function
// and return it
function myFunc(){
  var myVar = "Function";
  return myVar;
}

// Declare a variable of the same name in a second function
// and write it to the page
function mySecFunc(){
  var myVar = "Second Function";
  document.write("<br>The value of myVar when called by mySecFunc() is: ");
  document.write(myVar);
}
// End hide -->
</script>
</head>
<body>
<script language="JavaScript">
<!-- Hide

// Write the value of the global variable
document.write("The value of myVar when called is: " + myVar)

// Write the value returned by the function
document.write("<br>The value of myVar when called by myFunc() is: ");
document.write(myFunc());

// Call the second function to write its results.
mySecFunc();

// End hide -->
</script>
</body>
</html>
```

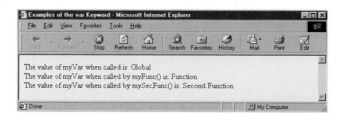

**Figure 6.20**

*Results of running Listing 6.270 in a browser.*

# void

## *JavaScript 1.1, JScript 1.0, ECMAScript 1.0*

## *NES2+, Nav3+, IE3+*

## *Syntax*

```
void(expression)
void expression
```

## *Description*

The `void` operator is used to evaluate an expression without returning a value. This operator returns `undefined` and is commonly used in place of the `onClick` event handler because of various bugs in early UNIX Navigator browsers. Note that Opera browsers do not support this operator.

## *Example*

In Listing 6.271, the `void` operator is used to keep an `<A>` link on a page from clicking through anywhere while still invoking the function specified.

*Listing 6.271    Using the* void *Operator to Call a Function*

```
<html>
<head>
  <title>Listing 6.171: Examples of the void Operator</title>
<script language="JavaScript">
<!-- Hide

// Define a function to be called by clicking the link
function myFunc(){
  alert("You clicked the link!");
}

// End hide -->
</script>
</head>
<body>
<A HREF="javascript:void(myFunc())">Click here to call the function</A>
</body>
</html>
```

# volatile

## *JavaScript1.2+*

## *NES3+, Nav4*

## *Syntax*

```
Reserved Keyword
```

## Description

The volatile keyword has not been implemented in JavaScript to date. It has been reserved for future use.

## Example

This keyword has not been implemented, therefore no example is provided.

# while

## JavaScript1.0+, JScript1.0+, ECMAScript1.0+

## NES2+, Nav2+, IE3+, Opera3+

## Syntax

```
while(condition){
  code;
}
```

## Description

The while conditional statement evaluates the condition passed and executes the code within the block until the condition is no longer met. This is often used to evaluate the value of variables, and then perform tasks as well as to iterate through lines in a file when implemented on the server-side.

## Example

Listing 6.272 defines a number and then asks the user for a second number. The user is continually asked for the second number until a number lower than the defined number is entered.

*Listing 6.272   Using the* while *Statement to Check the Value Passed in*

```
<html>
<head>
  <title>Using while</title>
</head>
<body>
<script language="JavaScript">
<!-- Hide

// Define the number to compare against and ask the user for a guess
var indexNum = 30;
var guess = parseInt(prompt("Please enter a number.", ""));

// As long as the user puts in a higher number, keep prompting.
```

*continues*

*Listing 6.272   continued*

```
while(guess >= indexNum){
  guess = parseInt(prompt("Try again. Guess lower!", ""));
}

// Once the user guesses a number lower than the indexed number
// write the following to the screen.
document.write('You have guessed a number lower than the index number. ');
document.write('You guessed ' + guess + ' and the index was ');
document.write(indexNum + '.');

// Close the stream to the browser.
document.close();

// End hide -->
</script>
</body>
</html>
```

# with

## *JavaScript1.0+, JScript1.0+, ECMAScript1.0+*

## *NES2+, Nav2+, IE3+, Opera3+*

## *Syntax*

```
with(object){
  code;
}
```

## *Description*

The with statement takes an object and refers to all of the properties, methods, and events of that object within the code without directly referencing the object itself. This allows you to use these characteristics of an object, such as the Math object, without specifically referencing the object.

## *Example*

Listing 6.273 creates a variable, and then assigns it and the methods called on it, as a Math object. Because the with statement is used, you do not have to reference the methods via the instance of this object.

*Listing 6.273    Using the* with *Statement*

```
<script language="JavaScript">
<!-- Hide

// Define the variables we are going to use
var myNum = 25;
var myE, mySin, mySqrt;

// Use a with statement to use the methods of the Math object
with (Math) {
   myE = E;
   mySqrt = sqrt(myNum)
   mySin = sin(PI/myNum)
}

// End hide -->
</script>
```

# CHAPTER 7

## Client-Side Browser Syntax

This chapter contains all the items and elements making up the JavaScript language in browsers. As with the other chapters in this section of the book, each entry includes the version, browser support, syntax, a description, an example, as well as many other details.

### NOTE

As discussed in earlier chapters, there are some differences in support for language elements among browsers. This is predominately seen in Internet Explorer 3.02 and Navigator 2.02 for OS/2, where features are present that are not in other 3.0 and 2.0 versions. In these instances, the displayed browser support will consist of the most accepted support. If there is an exception, it will be pointed out in the description of the entry.

JavaScript objects are in alphabetical order to provide you with quick, easy access. The methods, properties, functions, and event handlers of every object appear alphabetically after the respective parent object using the simple dot notation used in Chapter 6, "Core Syntax," Chapter 8, "Netscape's Server-Side Additions," and Chapter 9, "Microsoft's Scripting Engine Extensions."

**TIP**

A more general method of accessing client-side JavaScript items is cross-referenced in the Appendixes. It provides an alphabetical list of every client-side JavaScript item with its supporting browser.

# Anchor

## JavaScript 1.2+, JScript 3.0+

## Nav4+, IE 4+

## Syntax

Core client-side JavaScript object.

## Description

An instance of the Anchor object is created with each instance of the <a> tag with the NAME attribute set. An *anchor* itself is a point in an HTML document that can be reached by using a hypertext link. The hypertext link that references an anchor can appear within the same document as the anchor or in a completely different Web page. In either case, anchors allow access to specific parts of Web pages rather than always displaying the top of a document when a Web page is loaded in a browser. For an anchor to act like an anchor, the NAME property must be set for hyperlinks to reference the anchor's position in the document.

In HTML, the <a> tag is usually accompanied by an HREF property that contains a hypertext link. This is the complete opposite of the definition of an anchor, because when the HREF is used in conjunction with the <a> tag, it is a link rather than an anchor. In fact, JavaScript uses the Link object to access the anchor tag when the tag is used as a link.

Table 7.1 lists the properties used by the Anchor object.

**Table 7.1    Properties Used by the Anchor Object**

| Properties | Description |
|---|---|
| name | A name that provides access to the anchor from a link |
| text | The text that appears between the <a> and </a> tags |
| x | The x-coordinate of the anchor |
| y | The y-coordinate of the anchor |

## Example

Listing 7.1 demonstrates how anchors are created and used in HTML document by creating a dictionary of fruit. The heading for each letter of the dictionary is designated as an anchor. At the bottom of the document, some properties of the anchors are accessed using JavaScript.

*Listing 7.1    Creating Anchors in a Document*

```
<html>

<center>
<h1><u>Fruit Dictionary</u></h1>

Pick a letter:
<a href="#A">A</a>¦<a href="#B">B</a>¦<a href="#C">C</a>
</center>

<hr><a name="A"><h4>The Letter A</h4></a>
Apple = A round, juicy fruit that comes in red, yellow, and green.<br>
Apricot = A round yellow-orange fruit.<br>

<hr><a name="B"><h4>The Letter B</h4></a>
Banana = A long, yellow, curved fruit with a soft core.<br>
Blackberry = A black, tart fruit from a prickly bush.<br>
Blueberry = A small, round, blue berry that grows on a bush.<br>

<hr><a name="C"><h4>The Letter C</h4></a>
Cantaloupe = A large orange melon with hard outer surface.<br>
Coconut = A large round fruit with a hard, fuzzy outer surface.<br>

<script language="JavaScript">
<!-- Hide
document.write("<hr>The Anchor Properties:<br>");

//Display the values of the properties associated with each anchor.
for(var counter=0; counter<=document.anchors.length; counter++)
{
  document.write("anchors[",counter,"].name=");
  document.write(document.anchors[counter].name,"<br>");
  document.write("anchors[",counter,"].text=");
  document.write(document.anchors[counter].text,"<br>");
  document.write("anchors[",counter,"].x=");
  document.write(document.anchors[counter].x,"<br>");
  document.write("anchors[",counter,"].y=");
  document.write(document.anchors[counter].y,"<br>");
}

// End hide --->
</script>

</html>
```

# Anchor.name

*JavaScript 1.2+, JScript 3.0+*

*Nav4+, IE 4+*

## *Syntax*

```
document.anchors[num].name
```

## *Description*

The name property holds the name of the anchor and is the way hyperlinks reference the anchor's position. This property is originally set by the NAME attribute in the <a> tag.

## *Example*

Listing 7.2 creates a dictionary of fruit where the heading for each letter of the dictionary is designated as an anchor. At the bottom of the document, the name property of each anchor is used to create the hyperlink text and reference each anchor.

*Listing 7.2   Accessing the* name *Property of the* Anchor *Object*

```
<html>

<center>
<h1><u>Fruit Dictionary</u></h1>

Pick a letter:
<a href="#A">A</a>¦<a href="#B">B</a>¦<a href="#C">C</a>
</center>

<hr><a name="A"><h4>The Letter A</h4></a>
Apple = A round, juicy fruit that comes in red, yellow, and green.<br>
Apricot = A round yellow-orange fruit.<br>

<hr><a name="B"><h4>The Letter B</h4></a>
Banana = A long, yellow, curved fruit with a soft core.<br>
Blackberry = A black, tart fruit from a prickly bush.<br>
Blueberry = A small, round, blue berry that grows on a bush.<br>

<hr><a name="C"><h4>The Letter C</h4></a>
Cantaloupe = A large orange melon with hard outer surface.<br>
Coconut = A large round fruit with a hard, fuzzy outer surface.<br>

<script language="JavaScript">
<!-- Hide
document.write("<hr>Pick a letter:");

//Create a link for each anchor using the Anchor object
for(var counter=0; counter<=document.anchors.length; counter++)
{
  document.write("<a href='#",document.anchors[counter].name,"'>");
  document.write(document.anchors[counter].name,"</a>¦");
}

// End hide --->
</script>

</html>
```

# Anchor.text

## *JavaScript 1.2+*

## *Nav4+*

## *Syntax*

```
document.anchors[num].text
```

## *Description*

The `text` property contains the text that appears between the `<a>` and `</a>` tags. If other HTML tags appear within these two anchor tags, the `text` property might not contain all of the text between the anchor tags.

## *Example*

Listing 7.3 creates a dictionary of fruit where the heading for each letter of the dictionary is designated as an anchor. At the bottom of the document, the `text` property of the anchors is used to create hyperlink text that points to each anchor.

*Listing 7.3    Accessing the `text` Property of the `Anchor` Object*

```
<html>

<center>
<h1><u>Fruit Dictionary</u></h1>

Pick a letter:
<a href="#A">A</a>¦<a href="#B">B</a>¦<a href="#C">C</a>
</center>

<hr><a name="A"><h4>The Letter A</h4></a>
Apple = A round, juicy fruit that comes in red, yellow, and green.<br>
Apricot = A round yellow-orange fruit.<br>

<hr><a name="B"><h4>The Letter B</h4></a>
Banana = A long, yellow, curved fruit with a soft core.<br>
Blackberry = A black, tart fruit from a prickly bush.<br>
Blueberry = A small, round, blue berry that grows on a bush.<br>

<hr><a name="C"><h4>The Letter C</h4></a>
Cantaloupe = A large orange melon with hard outer surface.<br>
Coconut = A large round fruit with a hard, fuzzy outer surface.<br>

<script language="JavaScript">
<!-- Hide
document.write("<hr>Pick a letter:<br>");

//Create a link for each anchor using the Anchor object
for(var counter=0; counter<=document.anchors.length; counter++)
```

*continues*

*Listing 7.3    continued*

```
{
  document.write("<a href='#',document.anchors[counter].name,"'>");
  document.write(document.anchors[counter].text,"</a><br>");
}

// End hide --->
</script>

</html>
```

# Anchor.x

## *JavaScript 1.2+*

## *Nav4+*

## *Syntax*

```
document.anchors[num].x
```

## Description

The x property contains the x-coordinate of the anchor, in pixels, from the left edge of the document to the anchor.

## Example

Listing 7.4 creates a single anchor out of a header at the top of the document. The x property is used to display the horizontal position of the Anchor object on the bottom of the page.

*Listing 7.4    Accessing the x Property of the Anchor Object*

```
<html>

<center><a name="A"><h4>Apple</h4></a></center>
A round, juicy fruit that comes in red, yellow, and green.<hr>

<script language="JavaScript">
<!-- Hide

//Display the x property of the anchor
document.write("The x property is equal to ",document.anchors[0].x);

// ---End Hide>
</script>

</html>
```

# Anchor.y

## *JavaScript 1.2+*

## Nav4+

### Syntax

```
document.anchors[num].y
```

### Description

The y property contains the y-coordinate of the anchor, in pixels, from the top edge of the document to the anchor.

### Example

Listing 7.5 creates a single anchor out of a header at the top of the document. The y property is used to display the vertical position of the Anchor object on the bottom of the page.

*Listing 7.5   Accessing the* y *Property of the* Anchor *Object*

```
<html>

<center><a name="B"><h4>Banana</h4></a></center>
A long, yellow, curved fruit with a soft core.<hr>

<script language="JavaScript">
<!-- Hide

//Display the y property of the anchor
document.write("The y property is equal to ",document.anchors[0].y);

// ---End Hide>
</script>

</html>
```

# Applet

## JavaScript 1.1+, JScript 3.0+

## Nav3+, IE 4+

### Syntax

Core client-side JavaScript object.

### Description

In JavaScript, applets embedded in HTML Web pages are represented by the Applet object. This object, which is created with each instance of the <applet> tag in a document, allows access to the public fields and methods of the applet through JavaScript properties and methods. Table 7.2 lists the properties and methods used by the Applet object.

**Table 7.2    Properties and Methods used by the Applet Object**

| Type | Description |
| --- | --- |
| Property | All the public fields in a Java applet are accessed as properties of the Applet object in JavaScript. |
| Method | All the public methods in a Java applet are accessed as methods of the Applet object in JavaScript. |

## Example

Assume, for the sake of the example code in Listing 7.6, that you have a calculator applet that you want to embed in an HTML document. Also assume that this applet has a method called add(), which adds two numbers and returns the result. If you wanted to access this method from within JavaScript, you would begin by defining the applet using <applet> tags. Then the JavaScript code would pass the numbers 2 and 5 into the add() method, using dot notation, and the result of 7 would be returned and displayed in the browser.

*Listing 7.6    Accessing the Method of an Applet Object*

```
<html>

<applet name="calculator" code="calculator.class" width=50 height=50></applet>

<script language="JavaScript">
<!-- Hide

//Use the calculator applet to add two numbers
document.write("2+5=",calculator.add(2,5));        //7 is returned

// End hide --->
</script>
</html>
```

# Area

## JavaScript 1.1+, JScript 1.0+

## Nav3+, IE 3+, Opera3+

## Syntax

Core client-side JavaScript object.

## Description

An instance of the Area object is created with each occurrence of the <area> tag within an HTML document. In HTML documents, the <area> tag is used in conjunction with the <map> tag to define an area within a picture that will act as a hyperlink. Because the Area object is a hyperlink, it is equivalent to the Link object in JavaScript. In fact, the Area object is stored in the same array where Link objects are stored. Table 7.3 lists the properties, methods, and event handlers used by the Area object.

*Table 7.3    Properties, Methods, and Event Handlers Used by the Area Object*

| Type | Item | Description |
|---|---|---|
| Properties | `hash` | The portion of the URL that is the anchor, including the # symbol |
| | `host` | The hostname (IP address) and port specified in the URL |
| | `hostname` | The hostname specified within the URL |
| | `href` | The entire URL |
| | `pathname` | The path of the file specified in the URL beginning with the / symbol |
| | `port` | The port specified in the URL |
| | `protocol` | The protocol specified in the URL, including the ending colon (`:`) |
| | `search` | The search part of the URL, including the beginning question mark (`?`) |
| | `target` | The name of the target window in which the URL should be displayed |
| Methods | `handleEvent()` | Calls the event handler associated with this event |
| Event Handlers | `onDblClick` | Invoked when the mouse is double-clicked while in the region defined by the `Area` object |
| | `onMouseOut` | Invoked when the mouse moves outside the region defined by the `Area` object |
| | `onMouseOver` | Invoked when the mouse moves into the region defined by the `Area` object |

## Example

Listing 7.7 creates a paint store Web page complete with a box of colors that contains hyperlinks to bogus color sites. The hyperlinks are created over the graphic using the <map>, <img>, and <area> tags. When the mouse is moved over an area, the properties associated with that area are displayed in the text fields at the bottom of the screen. Figure 7.1 shows what happens when the mouse pointer is placed in the green box.

*Listing 7.7    Creating Areas and Accessing Their Properties*

```
<html>
<body>

<h2>The Paint Store</h2>

Select one of the 4 colors to find out more about the colors we carry.<br>

<map name="colorMap">
  <area name="redArea"
        coords="1,1,48,48"
        href="http://www.red.com:1234/red.html
```

*continues*

*Listing 7.7    continued*

```
                ?query=red#RED"
        target="_top"
        onMouseOver="overBox(0)"
        onMouseOut="clearBox()">
  <area name="greenArea"
        coords="51,1,99,49"
        href="http://www.green.com:5678/green.html
                ?query=green#GREEN"
        target="_top"
        onMouseOver="overBox(1)"
        onMouseOut="clearBox()">
  <area name="yellowArea"
        coords="1,51,51,99"
        href="http://www.yellow.com:9876/yellow.html
                ?query=yellow#YELLOW"
        target="_top"
        onMouseOver="overBox(2)"
        onMouseOut="clearBox()">
  <area name="blueArea"
        coords="51,51,99,99"
        href="http://www.blue.com:5432/blue.html
                ?query=blue#BLUE"
        target="_top"
        onMouseOver="overBox(3)"
        onMouseOut="clearBox()">
</map>
<img src="box4.gif" align="top"
     height="100"   width="100" usemap="#colorMap">

<br><br><b><u>AREA Properties</u></b>

<form name="myForm">
  hash=<input name="tHash" type="textarea"><br>
  host=<input name="tHost" type="textarea"><br>
  hostname=<input name="tHostName" type="textarea"><br>
  href=<input name="tHref" type="textarea"><br>
  pathname<input name="tPathName" type="textarea"><br>
  port=<input name="tPort" type="textarea"><br>
  protocol=<input name="tProtocol" type="textarea"><br>
  search=<input name="tSearch" type="textarea"><br>
  target=<input name="tTarget" type="textarea"><br>
</form>


<script language="JavaScript">
<!-- Hide

//Fill in the text area fields
function overBox(num)
```

```
{
  document.myForm.tHash.value = document.links[num].hash;
  document.myForm.tHost.value = document.links[num].host;
  document.myForm.tHostName.value = document.links[num].hostname;
  document.myForm.tHref.value = document.links[num].href;
  document.myForm.tPathName.value = document.links[num].pathname;
  document.myForm.tPort.value = document.links[num].port;
  document.myForm.tProtocol.value = document.links[num].protocol;
  document.myForm.tSearch.value = document.links[num].search;
  document.myForm.tTarget.value = document.links[num].target;
}

//Clear text in the text area fields
function clearBox()
{
  document.myForm.tHash.value = "";
  document.myForm.tHost.value = "";
  document.myForm.tHostName.value = "";
  document.myForm.tHref.value = "";
  document.myForm.tPathName.value = "";
  document.myForm.tPort.value = "";
  document.myForm.tProtocol.value = "";
  document.myForm.tSearch.value = "";
  document.myForm.tTarget.value = "";
}
// End Hide--->
</script>

</body>
</html>
```

**Figure 7.1**

*Accessing an area's properties.*

# Area.handleEvent()

## *JavaScript 1.2+, JScript 1.0+*

## *Nav4+, IE 3+, Opera3+*

## *Syntax*

```
document.links[num].handleEvent(event)
```

## *Description*

The `handleEvent()` method invokes the event handler associated with the `event` argument. Table 7.4 lists the argument and return value associated with this method.

*Table 7.4    Arguments and Return Values Associated with the handleEvent() Method*

| Type | Item | Description |
| --- | --- | --- |
| Argument | event | An Event object. |
| Returns | | The value returned from the event handler associated with event is returned from this method. |

## *Example*

Listing 7.8 creates a Web page for learning more about the toppings used on a pizza. When an area is clicked, the user is taken to a place within the document to learn more about the pizza topping. The `handleEvent()` method is used to pass all the mouse events from the first area (represented by peppers) to the event handlers of the second area (represented by onion). Normally, you would want to display a special notice when the mouse moves over the pepper area, but use the `handleEvent()` method to make the pepper area do the same thing as the onion area. Notice that "onion" is placed in the text box when the mouse is moved over either of the two defined areas, thanks to the `handleEvent()` method.

*Listing 7.8    Passing Events to Other Area Objects to be Handled*

```
<html>
<body>

<center><h1><u>Learn more about the toppings we use on our
pizza</u></h1></center>

<h3>Choose A Pizza Topping from Pictures to learn more.</h3>

<map name="toppingsMap">
  <area name="peppers"
        coords="1,1,48,48"
        href="#PEPPERS"
        target="_top"
        onMouseOver="document.pizzaForm.textbox.value='peppers'"
        onMouseOut="document.pizzaForm.textbox.value=''"><br>
```

```
      <area name="onion"
            coords="51,1,99,49"
            href="#ONION"
            target="_top"
            onMouseOver="document.pizzaForm.textbox.value='onion'"
            onMouseOut="document.pizzaForm.textbox.value=''">
</map>
<img src="toppingsBox.gif"
     align="top"
     height="50"
     width="100"
     usemap="#toppingsMap">
<hr>
<form name="pizzaForm">
  <input type="text"
         name="textbox">
</form>

<script "JavaScript">
<!-- Hide

//This function passes event to another Area object to handle
function fillTextField(event)
{
  //Pass event to 2nd area link
  document.links[1].handleEvent(event);
}

// End hide --->
</script>

<a name="PEPPERS"><h3>The peppers we use:</h3></a>
<ul>
  <li>Yellow</li>
  <li>Red</li>
  <li>Green</li>
</ul>

<a name="ONION"><h3>The onions we use:</h3></a>
<ul>
  <li>Mild</li>
  <li>Hot</li>
</ul>

</body>
</html>
```

# Area.hash

## *JavaScript 1.1+, JScript 1.0+*

## Nav3+, IE 3+, Opera3+

## Syntax

```
document.links[num].hash
```

## Description

The hash property associated with an Area object contains the anchor specified in the URL including the leading hash symbol (#). This property is a read/write string.

## Example

Listing 7.9 creates an auto parts page that allows users to find model numbers of parts by clicking a picture of the part (see Figure 7.2). Selecting either Car or Truck at the top of the page changes the links associated with the pictures. Selecting Car or Truck causes the hash property to be modified so that the user is taken to a different location within the page.

Listing 7.9    *Modifying the* hash *Property of the* Area *Object*

```
<html>
<body>

<center><h1><u>Wild Bill's Auto Parts</u></h1></center>

<h3>Step 1: Choose Auto Type.</h3>

<form name="step1">
<input name="autoType"
       type="radio"
       checked
       onClick="updateLinks('TRUCK')">Truck<br>
<input name="autoType"
       type="radio"
       onClick="updateLinks('CAR')">Car
</form>

<h3>Step 2: Choose Part from Pictures.</h3>

<map name="partsMap">
   <area name="sparkPlug"
         coords="1,1,48,48"
         href="#"
         target="_top">
   <area name="tires"
         coords="51,1,99,49"
         href="#"
         target="_top">
   <area name="headlights"
         coords="1,51,51,99"
         href="#"
         target="_top">
```

```
  <area name="fuses"
        coords="51,51,99,99"
        href="#"
        target="_top">
</map>
<img src="partsBox.gif" align="top"
     height="100"   width="100" usemap="#partsMap">

<hr>

<script language="JavaScript">
<!-- Hide

//update the picture hash links based on the radio box settings
function updateLinks(autoType)
{
  //Set truck links
  if(autoType=="TRUCK")
  {
    document.links[0].hash="TRUCK_SPARKPLUGS";
    document.links[1].hash="TRUCK_TIRES";
    document.links[2].hash="TRUCK_HEADLIGHTS";
    document.links[3].hash="TRUCK_FUSES";
  }

  //Set car links
  if(autoType=="CAR")
  {
    document.links[0].hash="CAR_SPARKPLUGS";
    document.links[1].hash="CAR_TIRES";
    document.links[2].hash="CAR_HEADLIGHTS";
    document.links[3].hash="CAR_FUSES";
  }
}

updateLinks("TRUCK");

// End hide --->
</script>

<a name="TRUCK_SPARKPLUGS"><h3>Truck Spark Plugs</h3></a>
<ul>
  <li>SP93654</li>
  <li>SP34710</li>
  <li>SP19374</li>
</ul>

<a name="TRUCK_TIRES"><h3>Truck Tires</h3></a>
<ul>
```

*continues*

*Listing 7.9    continued*

```
  <li>Mud Stompers</li>
  <li>Low Riders</li>
  <li>Standard</li>
</ul>

<a name="TRUCK_HEADLIGHTS"><h3>Truck Headlights</h3></a>
<ul>
  <li>Night Vision bulbs</li>>
  <li>Standard</li>
</ul>

<a name="TRUCK_FUSES"><h3>Truck Fuses</h3></a>
<ul>
  <li>Red</li>
  <li>Yellow</li>
  <li>Green</li>
  <li>Blue</li>
</ul>

<a name="CAR_SPARKPLUGS"><h3>Car Spark Plugs</h3></a>
<ul>
  <li>SP003856</li>
  <li>SP993874</li>
  <li>SP118305</li>
</ul>

<a name="CAR_TIRES"><h3>Car Tires</h3></a>
<ul>
  <li>Racers</li>
  <li>Low Profilers</li>
  <li>Standard</li>
</ul>

<a name="CAR_HEADLIGHTS"><h3>Car Headlights</h3></a>
<ul>
  <li>Sport lights</li>
  <li>Standard</li>
</ul>

<a name="CAR_FUSES"><h3>Car Fuses</h3></a>
<ul>
  <li>Red</li>
  <li>Yellow</li>
  <li>Green</li>
  <li>Blue</li>
</ul>

</body>
</html>
```

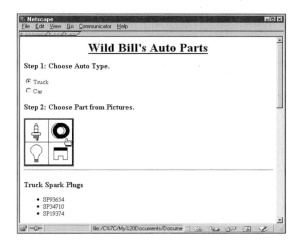

**Figure 7.2**

*Selecting a part causes the* hash *property to change.*

# Area.host

## *JavaScript 1.1+, JScript 1.0+*

## *Nav3+, IE 3+, Opera3+*

## *Syntax*

```
document.links[num].host
```

## *Description*

The host property associated with an Area object contains the hostname and port that is specified in the URL and separated with a colon (:). This property is a read/write string.

## *Example*

In Listing 7.10, a sports car picture site is created. Selecting your location determines from which site a large picture of the sports car is retrieved. This is accomplished by modifying the host property based on what site from which the user wants to receive the sport car pictures.

*Listing 7.10    Modifying the* host *Property of the* Area *Object*

```
<html>
<body>

<center><h1><u>Sports Car Pictures</u></h1></center>

<h3>Step 1: Choose a site close to you.</h3>
```

*continues*

*Listing 7.10    continued*

```
<form name="question">
<input name="site"
       type="radio"
       checked
       onClick="updateLinks('US')">US<br>
<input name="site"
       type="radio"
       onClick="updateLinks('EUROPE')">Europe
</form>

<h3>Step 2: Choose one of the small pictures.</h3>

<MAP name="carsMap">
  <area name="car1"
        coords="1,1,48,48"
        href="http://www.uscars.com:3498/car1.html"
        target="_top">
  <area name="car2"
        coords="51,1,99,49"
        href="http://www.uscars.com:3498/car2.html""
        target="_top">
</map>
<img src="cars.gif" align="top"
     height="50"   width="100" usemap="#carsMap">

<hr>

<script language="JavaScript">
<!-- Hide

//update the picture host links based on the radio box settings
function updateLinks(site)
{
  //Set to a US site
  if(site=="US")
  {
    document.links[0].host="www.uscars.com:3498";
    document.links[1].host=document.links[0].host;
  }

  //Set to a European site
  if(site=="EUROPE")
  {
    document.links[0].host="www.europecars.com:7412";
    document.links[1].host=document.links[0].host;
  }
}
```

```
// End hide --->
</script>

</body>
</html>
```

# Area.hostname

## JavaScript 1.1+, JScript 1.0+

## Nav3+, IE 3+, Opera3+

## Syntax

```
document.links[num].hostname
```

## Description

The hostname property associated with the Area object contains just the hostname that is specified in the URL. This property is a read/write string.

## Example

In Listing 7.11, a sports car picture site is created. Selecting your location determines from which site a large picture of the sports car is retrieved. This is accomplished by modifying the hostname property based on the site from which the user wants to receive the sport car pictures. Notice that, unlike the host property, the port number stays the same when modifying the hostname property.

*Listing 7.11   Modifying the hostname Property of the Area Object*

```
<html>
<body>

<center><h1><u>Sports Car Pictures</u></h1></center>

<h3>Step 1: Choose a site close to you.</h3>

<form name="question">
<input name="site"
       type="radio"
       checked
       onClick="updateLinks('US')">US<br>
<input name="site"
       type="radio"
       onClick="updateLinks('EUROPE')">Europe
</form>

<h3>Step 2: Choose one of the small pictures.</h3>

<MAP name="carsMap">
```

*continues*

*Listing 7.11    continued*

```
  <area name="car1"
        coords="1,1,48,48"
        href="http://www.uscars.com:3498/car1.html"
        target="_top">
  <area name="car2"
        coords="51,1,99,49"
        href="http://www.uscars.com:3498/car2.html"
        target="_top">
</map>
<img src="cars.gif" align="top"
     height="50"   width="100" usemap="#carsMap">

<hr>

<script language="JavaScript">
<!-- Hide

//update the picture host links based on the radio box settings
function updateLinks(site)
{
  //Set to a US site
  if(site=="US")
  {
    document.links[0].hostname="www.uscars.com";
    document.links[1].hostname=document.links[0].hostname;
  }

  //Set to a European site
  if(site=="EUROPE")
  {
    document.links[0].hostname="www.europecars.com";
    document.links[1].hostname=document.links[0].hostname;
  }
}

// End hide --->
</script>

</body>
</html>
```

# Area.href

## *JavaScript 1.1+, JScript 1.0+*

## *Nav3+, IE 3+, Opera3+*

## *Syntax*

```
document.links[num].href
```

## Description

The href property associated with the Area property contains the entire URL specified by the HREF attribute of the <area> tag. This property is a read/write string.

## Example

In Listing 7.12, a sports car picture site is created. Selecting your location determines from which site a large picture of the sports car is retrieved. This is accomplished by modifying the href property to link to a completely different site based on the user's choice of cars.

Listing 7.12    Modifying the href Property of the Area Object

```
<html>
<body>

<center><h1><u>Sports Car Pictures</u></h1></center>

<h3>Step 1: Choose a car.</h3>

<form name="question">
<input name="carType"
       type="radio"
       checked
       onClick="updateLinks('LAMBORGINI')">Lamborgini<br>
<input name="carType"
       type="radio"
       onClick="updateLinks('FERRARI')">Ferrari
</form>

<h3>Step 2: Click on the picture to see the car.</h3>

<map name="carMap">
  <area name="car"
       coords="1,1,48,48"
       href="http://www.cars.com:5678/cars.html?query=fast#LAMBORGINI"
       target="_top">
</map>
<img src="cars.gif" align="top"
     height="50"   width="50" usemap="#carMap">

<hr>

<script language="JavaScript">
<!-- Hide

//update the picture host links based on the radio box settings
function updateLinks(car)
{
  //Set to Lamborgini site
  if(car=="LAMBORGINI")
```

*continues*

*Listing 7.12    continued*

```
document.links[0].href="http://www.cars.com:5678/cars.html?query=fast#LAMBORGIN
I";

  //Set to Ferrari site
  if(car=="FERRARI")
document.links[0].href="http://www.sportscars.com:2020/fastcars.html?query=fast
#FERRARI";
}

// End hide --->
</script>

</body>
</html>
```

# Area.onDblClick

## *JavaScript 1.1*

## *Nav3, IE 4*

## *Syntax*

```
onDblClick="command"
```

## *Description*

The onDblClick event handler associated with the Area object is invoked when the user double-clicks the mouse pointer while in the region defined by the <area> tag.

## *Example*

Listing 7.13 creates a clothing site with a picture of a shirt. Double-clicking the shirt displays a message about red shirts, thanks to the onDblClick event handler.

*Listing 7.13    Using the onDblClick Property of the Area Object*

```
<html>
<body>

<h2>The Clothes Site</h2>

<map name="clothesMap">
  <area name="redShirt"
        coords="1,1,48,48"
        target="_top"
        onDblClick="alert('You must like red shirts.')">
</map>
<img src="clothes.gif" align="top"
     height="100"   width="100" usemap="#clothesMap">

</body>
</html>
```

# Area.onMouseOut

## JavaScript 1.1+, JScript 1.0+

## Nav3+, IE 3+, Opera3+

## Syntax

```
onMouseOut="command"
```

## Description

The `onMouseOut` event handler associated with the `Area` object is invoked when the user moves the mouse pointer into the region defined by the `<area>` tag.

## Example

Listing 7.14 creates a clothing site with a picture of a shirt. Clicking the shirt graphic takes you to a site about red shirts. If the mouse is moved out of the region, an alert box posts a message to the screen, thanks to the `onMouseOut` event handler.

*Listing 7.14    Using the `onMouseOut` Property of the `Area` Object*

```
<html>
<body>

<h2>The Clothes Site</h2>

<map name="clothesMap">
  <area name="redShirt"
        coords="1,1,48,48"
        href="http://www.clothes.com/redShirts.html"
        target="_top"
        onMouseOut="alert('You did not want to go the red shirt site?')">
</map>
<img src="clothes.gif" align="top"
     height="100"   width="100" usemap="#clothesMap">

</body>
</html>
```

# Area.onMouseOver

## JavaScript 1.1+, JScript 1.0+

## Nav3+, IE 3+, Opera3+

## Syntax

```
onMouseOver="command"
```

## Description

The `onMouseOver` event handler is invoked when the user moves the mouse pointer out of the region defined by the `<area>` tag.

## Example

Listing 7.15 creates a clothing site with a picture of a shirt. Clicking the shirt graphic takes you to a site about red shirts. By simply moving the mouse over the region causes an alert box to be posted alerting the user that a mouseover event occurred.

Listing 7.15   Using the onMouseOver Property of the Area Object

```
<html>
<body>

<h2>The Clothes Page</h2>

Click on the sales tag to see the clothes that are on sale:<br>

<map name="clothesMap">
  <area name="sale"
        coords="1,1,48,48"
        href="http://www.clothes.comspecials.html"
        target="_top"
        onMouseOver="alert('An onMouseOver event occured.')">
</map>
<img src="sale.gif" align="top"
     height="100"   width="100" usemap="#colorMap">

</body>
</html>
```

# Area.pathname

## *JavaScript 1.1+, JScript 1.0+*

## *Nav3+, IE 3+, Opera3+*

## Syntax

```
document.links[num].pathname
```

## Description

The pathname property contains the path of the file specified in the URL, including the leading slash (/). This property is a read/write string.

## Example

In Listing 7.16, a sports car picture site is created. The user is instructed to click the type of sports car he or she would like to see. Based on the car selected, the pathname property is modified to direct the link to a different HTML file.

Listing 7.16   Modifying the pathname Property of an Area Object

```
<html>
<body>

<center><h1><u>Sports Car Pictures</u></h1></center>
```

```
<h3>Step 1: Choose a car.</h3>

<form name="question">
<input name="carType"
       type="radio"
       checked
       onClick="updateLinks('LAMBORGINI')">Lamborgini<br>
<input name="carType"
       type="radio"
       onClick="updateLinks('FERRARI')">Ferrari
</form>

<h3>Step 2: Click on the picture to see the car.</h3>

<map name="carMap">
  <area name="car"
        coords="1,1,48,48"
        href="http://www.cars.com/hotrod.html"
        target="_top">
</map>
<img src="cars.gif" align="top"
     height="50"   width="50" usemap="#carMap">

<hr>

<script language="JavaScript">
<!-- Hide

//update the picture host links based on the radio box settings
function updateLinks(car)
{
  //Set to Lamborgini page
  if(car=="LAMBORGINI")
    document.links[0].pathname="/lamborgini.html";

  //Set to Ferrari page
  if(car=="FERRARI")
    document.links[0].pathname="/ferrari.html";
}

// End hide --->
</script>

</body>
</html>
```

# Area.port

## *JavaScript 1.1+, JScript 1.0+*

## Nav3+, IE 3+

## Syntax

```
document.links[num].port
```

## Description

The port property contains just the port specified in the URL. This property is a read/write string.

## Example

In Listing 7.17, a Plant Supply Company page is created. The user is instructed to select the port number he or she wants to use when he or she clicks the company logo. The port number used by the area is modified based on the user's port selection.

*Listing 7.17   Modifying the port Property of an Area Object*

```
<html>
<body>

<center><h1><u>Plant Supply Company< u></h1></center>

<h3>Step 1: Choose a port number.</h3>

<form name="port">
<input name="portType"
       type="radio"
       checked
       onClick="updateLinks('8080')">Port 8080<br>
<input name="portType"
       type="radio"
       onClick="updateLinks('4545')">Port 4545
</form>

<h3>Step 2: Click on the Plant Supply Company logo.</h3>

<map name="plantMap">
  <area name="plant"
       coords="1,1,48,48"
       href="http://www.plantsuppl.com/index.html"
       target="_top">
</map>
<img src="logo.gif" align="top"
     height="50"   width="50" usemap="#plantMap">

<hr>

<script language="JavaScript">
<!-- Hide

//update the picture port settings based on the radio box settings
function updateLinks(portSetting)
```

```
{
  //Use the port setting that is passed in the set property
  document.links[0].port=portSetting;
}

// End hide --->
</script>

</body>
</html>
```

# Area.protocol

## *JavaScript 1.1+, JScript 1.0+*

## *Nav3+, IE 3+, Opera3+*

### *Syntax*

```
document.links[num].protocol
```

### *Description*

The protocol property contains the protocol (http:, file:, ftp:, and so on) specified in the URL, including the ending colon (:). This property is a read/write string.

### *Example*

In Listing 7.18, the protocol property containing http: is displayed below the area link.

*Listing 7.18   Accessing the protocol Property of an Area Object*

```
<html>

<h2>The Color Page</h2>

<map name="colorMap">
  <area name="greenArea"
        coords="1,1,48,48"
        href="http://www.green.com:5678/green.html?query=green#GREEN"
        target="_top">
</map>
<img src="box4.gif" align="top"
     height="100"   width="100" usemap="#colorMap">

<script>
<!-- Hide

//Display the protocol associated with the area
document.write("protocol = ",document.links[0].protocol);

// End hide --->
</script>
</html>
```

# Area.search

## *JavaScript 1.1+, JScript 1.0+*

## *Nav3+, IE 3+, Opera3+*

## Syntax

```
document.links[num].search
```

## Description

The search property contains the search string specified in the URL, including the leading question mark (?). This property is a read/write string.

## Example

In Listing 7.19, a sports car picture site is created. The user is instructed to click the type of sports car he or she would like to see. Based on the car selected, the search property is modified to search for the car on another page.

*Listing 7.19    Modifying the search Property of an Area Object*

```
<html>
<body>

<center><h1><u>Sports Car Pictures</u></h1></center>

<h3>Step 1: Choose a car.</h3>

<form name="question">
<input name="carType"
       type="radio"
       checked
       onClick="updateLinks('LAMBORGINI')">Lamborgini<br>
<input name="carType"
       type="radio"
       onClick="updateLinks('FERRARI )">Ferrari
</form>

<h3>Step 2: Click on the picture to see the car.</h3>

<map name="carMap">
  <area name="car"
        coords="1,1,48,48"
        href="http://www.cars.com:5678/cars.html"
        target="_top">
</map>
<img src="cars.gif" align="top"
     height="50"   width="50" usemap="#carMap">

<hr>
```

```
<script language="JavaScript">
<!-- Hide

//update the picture search query based on the radio box settings
function updateLinks(car)
{
  //Set to Lamborgini site
  if(car=="LAMBORGINI")
    document.links[0].search="?query=Lamborgini";

  //Set to Ferrari site
  if(car=="FERRARI")
    document.links[0].search="?query=Ferrari";
}

// End hide --->
</script>

</body>
</html>
```

# Area.target

## *JavaScript 1.1+, JScript 1.0+*

## *Nav3+, IE 3+, Opera3+*

## *Syntax*

```
document.links[num].target
```

## *Description*

The `target` property contains the name of target window or frame in which the URL should be displayed. This property is a read/write string.

## *Example*

In Listing 7.20, a truck parts site is created that allows the user to find out what parts the store carries. The target of the spark plugs and tires link is modified to make the information appear in a new browser window.

*Listing 7.20    Modifying the `target` Property of an `Area` Object*

```
<html>
<body>

<center><h1><u>Wild Bill's Truck Parts</u></h1></center>

<h3>Choose Part from Pictures.</h3>

<map name="partsMap">
```

*continues*

*Listing 7.20    continued*

```
  <area name="sparkPlug"
        coords="1,1,48,48"
        href="#SPARKPLUGS"
        target="_top">
  <area name="tires"
        coords="51,1,99,49"
        href="#TIRES"
        target="_top">
  <area name="headlights"
        coords="1,51,51,99"
        href="#HEADLIGHTS"
        target="_top">
  <area name="fuses"
        coords="51,51,99,99"
        href="#FUSES"
        target="_top">
</map>
<img src="partsBox.gif" align="top"
     height="100"   width="100" usemap="#partsMap">

<hr>

<script language="JavaScript">
<!-- Hide

//Make the result of the sparkplugs and tires appear in a new window.
document.links[0].target="_blank";     //sparkplugs
document.links[1].target="_blank";     //tires

// End hide --->
</script>

<a name="SPARKPLUGS"><h3>Truck Spark Plugs</h3></a>
<ul>
  <li>SP93654</li>
  <li>SP34710</li>
  <li>SP19374</li>
</ul>

<a name="TIRES"><h3>Truck Tires</h3></a>
<ul>
  <li>Mud Stompers</li>
  <li>Low Riders</li>
  <li>Standard</li>
</ul>

<a name="HEADLIGHTS"><h3>Truck Headlights</h3></a>
<ul>
  <li>Night Vision bulbs</li>>
```

```
  <li>Standard</li>
</ul>

<a name="FUSES"><h3>Truck Fuses</h3></a>
<ul>
  <li>Red</li>
  <li>Yellow</li>
  <li>Green</li>
  <li>Blue</li>
</ul>

</body>
</html>
```

# Button

## *JavaScript 1.0+, JScript 1.0+*

## *Nav2+, IE 3+, Opera3+*

## *Syntax*

Core client-side JavaScript object.

## *Description*

The Button object represents a graphical button that the user can click to initiate an action. Buttons are created as part of a form by using the `<input>` tag with the TYPE attribute set to button in an HTML document. Once created, buttons can be accessed in JavaScript as an element of a form using dot notation. The arguments, properties, methods, and event handlers for the Button object are listed in Table 7.5.

**Table 7.5   Arguments, Properties, Methods, and Event Handlers Associated with the Button Object**

| Type | Item | Description |
| --- | --- | --- |
| Arguments | string | The string to appear in the graphical representation of a button. |
| | num | An index number that allows access to buttons through a forms elements list. |
| Properties | form | Returns the form object of a button. |
| | name | The string that is specified in the NAME attribute of the HTML `<input>` tag. |
| | type | The string that is specified in the TYPE attribute of the HTML `<input>` tag. This string is always button for the Button object. |
| | value | The string that appears in the graphical representation of a button. |

*continues*

**Table 7.5 continued**

| Type | Item | Description |
|------|------|-------------|
| Methods | `blur()` | Removes focus from a button. |
| | `click()` | Calls the button's `onClick` event handler. |
| | `focus()` | Applies focus to a button. |
| | `handleEvent()` | Passes an event to the appropriate event handler associated with a button. |
| Event Handlers | `onBlur` | The handler invoked when focus is removed from a button. |
| | `onClick` | The handler invoked when a button is clicked. |
| | `onFocus` | The handler invoked when focus is applied to a button. |
| | `onMouseDown` | The handler invoked when the mouse is clicked to select a button. |
| | `onMouseUp` | The handler invoked when the mouse is clicked to unselect a button. |

## Example

In Listing 7.21, a button is created by using the `<input>` tag. When the button is clicked, the button's name is displayed in the adjacent text box.

*Listing 7.21    Creating a Button and Displaying Its Name*

```
<html>

<h2>The Button NAME Property</h2>

<form name="myForm">
  <input type="button"
         value="Press here to see the name of this button"
         name="myBigButton"
         onClick="displayButtonName()">
  <input type="text"
         name="textBox">
</form>

<script language="JavaScript">
<!-- Hide

//This function displays the button's name in the textbox.
function displayButtonName()
{
  //Display button name in textbox.
  document.myForm.textBox.value=document.myForm.myBigButton.name;
}

//Hide End --->
```

```
</script>

</html>
```

# Button.blur()

## *JavaScript 1.1+, JScript 1.0+*

## *Nav3+, IE 3+*

## *Syntax*

document.*form*.*button*.blur()

## *Description*

The blur() method removes the focus from a button.

## WARNING

In the UNIX versions of Navigator 2 and Navigator 3, the blur() method does not work for buttons.

## *Example*

In Listing 7.22, two buttons are created by using the <input> tag to demonstrate focus. The first button retains focus after being clicked, but the second button loses focus as soon as it is clicked due to the use of the blur() method. There are not a lot of uses for this method, but it is provided for your use all the same.

*Listing 7.22    Removing Focus from a Button with the blur() Method*

```
<html>

<h2>The Button Focus Game</h2>

Click both buttons. Notice that the second button does not
hold its focus after being clicked.

<form name="myForm">
  <input type="button"
         value="I hold my focus after a click"
         name="button1"><br>
  <input type="button"
         value="I can not hold my focus after a click"
         name="button2"
         onClick="removeFocus()">
</form>

<script language="JavaScript">
<!-- Hide
```

*continues*

*Listing 7.22    continued*
```
//This function takes the focus off of button2.
function removeFocus()
{
  //Remove the focus from button2
  document.myForm.button2.blur();
}

//Hide End --->
</script>

</html>
```

# Button.click()

## *JavaScript 1.0+, JScript 1.0+*

## *Nav2+, IE 3+*

### Syntax

```
document.form.button.click()
```

### Description

The click() method simulates the click event.

### Example

In Listing 7.23, two buttons are created by using the <input> tag. The first button displays an alert box when it is clicked. When the second button is clicked, it causes the first button's onClick event handler to be activated, displaying the alert box associated with the first button.

*Listing 7.23    Simulating a click Event with the click() Method*
```
<html>

<form name="myForm">
  <input type="button"
         value="Display alert box"
         name="button1"
         onClick="alert('You clicked the first button.')"><br>
  <input type="button"
         value="Call on button 1"
         name="button2"
         onClick="clickFirstButton()">
</form>

<script language="JavaScript">
<!-- Hide

//This function activates the first button's onClick handler.
```

```
function clickFirstButton()
{
  //Click first button
  document.myForm.button1.click();
}

//Hide End --->
</script>

</html>
```

# Button.focus()

## *JavaScript 1.1+, JScript 1.0+*

## *Nav3+, IE 3+*

## *Syntax*

```
document.form.button.focus()
```

## *Description*

The focus() method applies focus to the button without invoking the button's onFocus event handler.

## WARNING

In the UNIX versions of Navigator 2 and Navigator 3, the focus() method does not work for buttons.

## *Example*

In Listing 7.24, two buttons are created to demonstrate focus. Choosing the second button causes the focus to shift to the first button instead of the focus staying on the second button, thanks to the focus() method.

*Listing 7.24    Shifting the Focus to a Button Using the focus() Method*

```
<html>

<h2>The Button Focus Game</h2>

Click both buttons. Notice that when the second button is clicked
focus is shifted to the first button.

<form name="myForm">
  <input type="button"
         value="I hold my focus after a click"
         name="button1"><br>
  <input type="button"
         value="I shift my focus when click"
```

*continues*

*Listing 7.24    continued*
```
        name="button2"
        onClick="moveFocus()">
</form>

<script language="JavaScript">
<!-- Hide

//This function puts button1 in focus
function moveFocus()
{
  //Give button1 the focus.
  document.myForm.button1.focus();
}

//Hide End --->
</script>

</html>
```

# Button.form

## *JavaScript 1.0+, JScript 1.0+*

## *Nav2+, IE 3+, Opera3+*

## *Syntax*

document.*form*.*button*.form

## *Description*

The form property provides access to the button's parent Form object.

## *Example*

Listing 7.25 proves that the button's form property contains the parent form object by
evaluating the if statement to true.

*Listing 7.25    Accessing a Button's Parent with the form Property*
```
<html>
<form name="myForm">
  <input type="button"
        value="Big Button"
        name="myButton">
</form>

<script language="JavaScript">
<!-- Hide

//Does the parent of the myButton equal myForm?
if(document.myForm.myButton.form == document.myForm)
  alert("myButton's form property is equal to myForm object");    //Equal
```

```
else
   alert("myButton's form property is NOT equal to myForm object"); //Not equal

//Hide End --->
</script>

</html>
```

# Button.handleEvent()

## *JavaScript 1.2+*

## *Nav4+*

## *Syntax*

document.*form*.*button*.handleEvent(*event*)

## *Description*

The handleEvent() method provides a way to invoke a button's event handler, even though the event was not triggered by the user. The argument associated with this method is listed in Table 7.6.

*Table 7.6    Argument Associated with the handleEvent() Method*

| Argument | Description |
| --- | --- |
| event | An event object to be handled |

## *Example*

The code in Listing 7.26 provides information about a car that is for sale. By choosing one of the buttons labeled Doors, Engine, or Transmission, the related information is entered into the text boxes. The text boxes can be cleared by clicking the Clear All Info button. Unlike the other buttons, the Show All Info button passes the click event along to each of the other buttons using the handleEvent() method. This way, each button takes care of filling in its respective text box. Figure 7.3 shows the result of pressing the Show All Info button.

*Listing 7.26    Handling the click Event with the handleEvent() Method*

```
<html>

<center><h2>Car For Sale!</h2></center>

Click on a button for more information:

<form name="myForm">
   <input type="button"
          value="Doors"
          name="doorsButton"
```

*continues*

*Listing 7.26    continued*

```
        onClick="document.myForm.doorsBox.value='4 doors'">
  <input type="text"
         name="doorsBox"><br>
  <input type="button"
         value="Engine"
         name="engineButton"
         onClick="document.myForm.engineBox.value='4 cylinder'">
  <input type="text"
         name="engineBox"><br>
  <input type="button"
         value="Transmission"
         name="transmissionButton"
         onClick="document.myForm.transmissionBox.value='manual transmission'">
  <input type="text"
         name="transmissionBox"><hr>
  <input type="button"
         value="Clear All Info"
         name="clearAllButton"
         onClick="clearAll()">
  <input type="button"
         value="Show All Info"
         name="showAllButton"
         onClick="showAll()">
</form>

<script language="JavaScript">
<!-- Hide

//This function clears all the text boxes.
function clearAll()
{
   document.myForm.doorsBox.value="";
   document.myForm.engineBox.value="";
   document.myForm.transmissionBox.value="";
}

//This function passes the click event to all of the buttons.
//Each button then fills its respective information into the text boxes.
function showAll(event)
{
   document.myForm.doorsButton.handleEvent(event);
   document.myForm.engineButton.handleEvent(event);
   document.myForm.transmissionButton.handleEvent(event);
}

//Hide End --->
</script>

</html>
```

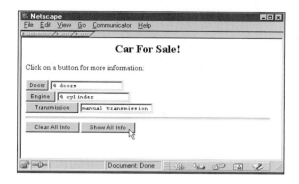

**Figure 7.3**

*Passing events to buttons using the* `handleEvent()` *method.*

# Button.name

## *JavaScript 1.0+, JScript 1.0+*

## *Nav2+, IE 3+, Opera 3+*

## *Syntax*

```
document.form.button.name
```

## *Description*

The `name` property provides access to the NAME attribute of the button as specified by the `<input>` tag. This property is a read-only string.

## *Example*

In Listing 7.27, a button is created. When the button is clicked, the button's `name` property is displayed.

*Listing 7.27   Accessing a Button's Name with the `name` Property*

```
<html>

<form name="myForm">
  <input type="button"
         value="Big Button"
         name="myButton"
         onClick="displayMessage()">
</form>

<script language="JavaScript">
```

*continues*

*Listing 7.27    continued*

```
<!-- Hide

//This function displays an alert box the contains the name of the button.
function displayMessage()
{
  //Create a string with name of button
  var alertString = String("You pressed the button named ");
  alertString += document.myForm.myButton.name;

  //Create alert box
  alert(alertString);
}

//Hide End --->
</script>

</html>
```

# Button.onBlur

## JavaScript 1.1+, JScript 1.0+

## Nav3+, IE 3+

## Syntax

```
onBlur="command"
```

## Description

The onBlur event handler is defined in an <input> tag and specifies what to do when the button loses focus.

## Example

The code in Listing 7.28 uses the onBlur event handler to display an alert box any time the button loses focus.

*Listing 7.28    Use onBlur Event Handler to Display an Alert Box When the Button Loses Focus*

```
<html>

<form name="myForm">
  <input type="button"
         value="Big Button"
         name="myButton"
         onBlur="alert('Blur event occurred')">
</form>

</html>
```

# Button.onClick

## *JavaScript 1.0+, JScript 1.0+*

## *Nav2+, IE 3+*

## Syntax

`onClick="command"`

## Description

The `onClick` event handler is defined in an `<input>` tag and specifies what to do when the button is clicked.

## Example

The code in Listing 7.29 uses the `onClick` event handler to display an alert box any time the button is clicked.

*Listing 7.29   Use `onClick` Event Handler to Display an Alert Box When the Button Is Clicked*

```
<html>

<form name="myForm">
  <input type="button"
         value="Big Button"
         name="myButton"
         onClick="alert('Click event occurred')">
</form>

</html>
```

# Button.onFocus

## *JavaScript 1.1+, JScript 1.0+*

## *Nav3+, IE 3+*

## Syntax

`onFocus="command"`

## Description

The `onFocus` event handler is defined in an `<input>` tag and specifies what to do when the button gains focus.

## Example

The code in Listing 7.30 uses the `onFocus` event handler to display an alert box any time the button gains focus.

*Listing 7.30    Use onFocus Event Handler to Display an Alert Box When the Button Gains Focus*

```
<html>

<form name="myForm">
  <input type="button"
         value="Big Button"
         name="myButton"
         onFocus="alert('Focus event occured')">
</form>

</html>
```

# Button.onMouseDown

## *JavaScript 1.0+, JScript 1.0+*

## *Nav2+, IE 3+*

## Syntax

```
onMouseDown="command"
```

## Description

The onMouseDown event handler is defined in an <input> tag and specifies what to do when the button is chosen.

## Example

The code in Listing 7.31 uses the onMouseDown event handler to display an alert box any time the button is chosen.

*Listing 7.31    Use onMouseDown Event Handler to Display an Alert Box When the Button Is Chosen*

```
<html>

<form name="myForm">
  <input type="button"
         value="Big Button"
         name="myButton"
         onMouseDown="alert('MouseDown event occured')">
</form>

</html>
```

# Button.onMouseUp

## *JavaScript 1.0+, JScript 1.0+*

## *Nav2+, IE 3+*

## Syntax

```
onMouseUp="command"
```

## Description

The `onMouseUp` event handler is defined in an `<input>` tag and specifies what to do when the mouse button is released while over the button.

## Example

The code in Listing 7.32 uses the `onMouseUp` event handler to display an alert box any time the mouse button is released while over the button.

*Listing 7.32    Use onMouseUp Event Handler to Display an Alert Box When the Mouse Button Is Released over the Button*

```
<html>

<form name="myForm">
  <input type="button"
         value="Big Button"
         name="myButton"
         onMouseUp="alert('MouseUp event occured')">
</form>

</html>
```

# Button.type

## JavaScript 1.1+, JScript 1.0+

## Nav3+, IE 3+, Opera3+

## Syntax

```
document.form.button.type
```

## Description

The `type` property provides access to the TYPE attribute of the button. This property is a read-only string that always contains `button`.

## Example

Listing 7.33 creates buttons that relate to various math problems. The `type` property is used to determine the number of buttons on the page. This number is then used in the instructions displayed on the bottom of the page.

*Listing 7.33    Accessing a Button's type Property*

```
<html>

<h2>The Math Page</h2>

<form name="mathForm">
```

*continues*

*Listing 7.33    continued*

```
  <input type="button"
         name="4plus2"
         value="(4 + 2)"
         onClick="document.mathForm.answer.value='(4 + 2) = 6'">
  <input type="button"
         name="4minus2"
         value="(4 - 2)"
         onClick="document.mathForm.answer.value='(4 - 2) = 2'"><HR>
  Answer:
  <input type="text"
         name="answer">
</form>

<script language="JavaScript">
<!-- Hide

//Create a counter to count the number of buttons in mathForm
var buttonCount = 0;

//Loop through all the elements of mathForm
for(var x=0; x<document.mathForm.length; x++)
{
  //Is element a button?
  if(document.mathForm.elements[x].type=="button")
    buttonCount++;        //Increment buttonCount
}

//Display the number of buttons in the mathForm
document.write("Please select one of the ",buttonCount);    //2 buttons
document.write(" buttons above to find out the answer to the math problem.");

//Hide End --->
</script>

</html>
```

# Button.value

## *JavaScript 1.0+, JScript 1.0+*

## *Nav2+, IE 3+, Opera3+*

## *Syntax*

document.*form.button.*value

## *Description*

The value property provides access to the VALUE attribute of the button. This property is a read-only string that is displayed in the graphical button.

## Example

Listing 7.34 uses the `value` property to customize the text in a button. To modify the button value, enter your name into the text field and then click the Customize the Button button. The button at the bottom of the document will no longer contain just the word "Press".

*Listing 7.34    Modifying Text in a Button Using the `value` Property*

```
<html>

<h2>Customize the Button</h2>

<form name="myForm">
  Please enter your name:
  <input type="text"
         name="nameBox">
  <input type="button"
         name="customizeTheButton"
         value="Customize the button"
         onClick="customizeButton()"><HR>
  <input type="button"
         name="theButton"
         value="Press                 "
         onClick="displayAlert()">
</form>

<SCRIPT LANGUAGE="JavaScript">
<!-- Hide

//This function customizes the button
function customizeButton()
{
  //Create a string using the name entered in text box
  var aString = document.myForm.nameBox.value;
  aString += " press this button!";

  //Change the value displayed in the button
  document.myForm.theButton.value=aString;
}

//This function creates an alert box
function displayAlert()
{
  //Create an alert box
  alert("You pressed the button.");
}

//Hide End --->
</script>

</html>
```

# Checkbox

## *JavaScript 1.0+, JScript 1.0+*

## *Nav2+, IE 3+, Opera3+*

## *Syntax*

Core client-side JavaScript object.

## *Description*

The Checkbox object represents a graphical check box that the user can click to toggle the check on or off. Check boxes are created as part of a form by using the <input> tag with the TYPE attribute set to checkbox in an HTML document. Once created, check boxes can be accessed in JavaScript as an element of a form using dot notation. Check boxes can also be grouped together under the same name and accessed as an array by using brackets. The arguments, properties, methods, and event handlers of the Checkbox object are listed in Table 7.7.

*Table 7.7    Arguments, Properties, Methods, and Event Handlers Associated with the Checkbox Object*

| Type | Item | Description |
| --- | --- | --- |
| Arguments | num1 | An index number that allows access to check boxes through a form's element list. |
| | num2 | An index number that allows access to individual check boxes that are grouped together under the same name. |
| Properties | checked | A Boolean value that determines if the check box is checked. |
| | defaultChecked | A Boolean value that holds the initial state of the check box. This value is set with the CHECKED attribute. |
| | form | Returns the Form object of the check box. |
| | name | The string that is specified in the NAME attribute of the HTML <input> tag. |
| | type | The string that is specified in the TYPE attribute of the HTML <input> tag. This string is always checkbox for the Checkbox object. |
| | value | The value returned when the form is submitted. |
| Methods | blur() | Removes focus from the check box. |
| | click() | Calls the check box's onClick event handler. |
| | focus() | Applies focus to this check box. |
| | handleEvent() | Passes an event to the appropriate event handler associated with the check box. |

| Type | Item | Description |
|---|---|---|
| Event Handlers | onBlur | The handler invoked when focus is removed from the check box. |
| | onClick | The handler invoked when the check box is selected. |
| | onFocus | The handler invoked when focus is applied to the check box. |

## CAUTION

In Navigator 2, there is a bug when working with check boxes that are grouped together and share the same NAME attribute. If the onClick event handler is not set, the check boxes will be placed into the array in reverse order. The bug was fixed in Navigator 3. To prevent this problem, simply set the onClick event handler equal to zero.

## Example

Listing 7.35 creates a hamburger order page. Check boxes are used to select toppings for the hamburger. When the Submit Order button is clicked, an alert box is displayed with the selected toppings.

*Listing 7.35    Creating Check Boxes and Accessing Some of Their Properties*

```
<html>

<h2>Hamburger Order</h2>

Step 1: Please select the toppings you would like on your hamburger:<BR>

<form name="orderForm">
  Lettuce
  <input type="checkbox"
         value="lettuce"
         name="lettuceCB"><br>
  Cheese
  <input type="checkbox"
         value="cheese"
         name="cheeseCB"><br>
  Tomatoe
  <input type="checkbox"
         value="tomato"
         name="tomatoCB"><hr>
  Step 2:
  <input type="button"
         value="Submit Order"
         name="orderButton"
         onClick="submitOrder()">
```

*continues*

*Listing 7.35   continued*

```
</form>

<script language="JavaScript">
<!-- Hide

//This function creates a box alerting what toppings were selected.
function submitOrder()
{
  //Create a string to display in alert box
  var alertString = String("Order: Hamburger ");
  if(document.orderForm.lettuceCB.checked == true)
    alertString += " with lettuce ";        //Add lettuce to string
  if(document.orderForm.cheeseCB.checked == true)
    alertString += "with cheese ";          //Add cheese to string
  if(document.orderForm.tomatoCB.checked == true)
    alertString += "with tomato ";          //Add tomato to string

  //Create alert box
  alert(alertString);
}

//Hide End --->
</script>

</html>
```

# Checkbox.blur()

## *JavaScript 1.1+, JScript 3.0+*

## *Nav3+, IE 4+*

## *Syntax*

```
document.form.checkbox.blur()
```

## *Description*

The `blur()` method removes the focus from a check box.

## WARNING

In the UNIX versions of Navigator 2 and Navigator 3, the `blur()` method does not work for check boxes.

## *Example*

In Listing 7.36, two check boxes are created by using the <input> tag. The first check box retains focus after being clicked, but the second check box loses focus as soon as it is clicked due to the use of the `blur()` method. Do not be surprised if you do not see a difference between the check boxes in this example. In most browsers, you will not be able to detect the difference between a check box that is focused versus one that is not focused. For this reason, you will probably find very little use for this method.

*Listing 7.36   Removing Focus from a Check Box with the `blur()` Method*

```
<html>

<h2>The Checkbox Focus Test</h2>

Click both check boxes. Notice that the second check box does not
hold its focus after being clicked.

<form name="myForm">
  I hold my focus after a click
  <input type="checkbox"
       name="checkBox1"><br>
  I cannot hold my focus after a click
  <input type="checkbox"
       name="checkBox2"
       onClick="removeFocus()">
</form>

<script language="JavaScript">
<!-- Hide

//This function takes the focus off of checkBox2.
function removeFocus()
{
  //Remove the focus from checkBox2
  document.myForm.checkBox2.blur();
}

//Hide End --->
</script>

</html>
```

# Checkbox.checked

## *JavaScript 1.0+, JScript 3.0+*

## *Nav2+, IE 4+, Opera3+*

## *Syntax*

document.*form*.*checkbox*.checked

## *Description*

The checked property holds the current state of a check box. Because this property is a read/write Boolean, the state of the check box can be altered by changing this property.

## *Example*

In Listing 7.37, the user is asked to select the door style wanted on his or her new car. When the order is submitted, the `checked` property of each check box is analyzed to determine if two different door styles were selected or none at all. If two styles were selected, the check boxes are reset by altering the `checked` property.

*Listing 7.37    Modifying the `checked` Property of a Check Box*

```
<html>

<h2>Car Purchase Sheet</h2>

Step1: Please select the door style you want on your new car:<BR>

<form name="orderForm">
  <input type="checkbox"
         name="door4">4 doors<br>
  <input type="checkbox"
         name="door2">2 doors<hr>
  Step 2:
  <input type="button"
         value="Submit Order"
         name="orderButton"
         onClick="submitOrder()">
</form>

<script language="JavaScript">
<!-- Hide

//This function creates a box alerting what door styles were selected.
function submitOrder()
{
  //Check for duplicate door selections
  if((document.orderForm.door4.checked == true) &&
(document.orderForm.door2.checked == true))
  {
    //Create alert box
    alert("You selected two different door styles. Reselect door style.");

    //Uncheck check boxes for door styles
    document.orderForm.door4.checked = false;
    document.orderForm.door2.checked = false;
  }
  //Check for no door selection
  else if((document.orderForm.door4.checked == false) &&
(document.orderForm.door2.checked == false))
  {
    //Create alert box
    alert("You did not select a door style! Please select a door style.");
  }
  //Display the car order
```

```
  else
  {
    //Create a string to display in alert box
    var alertString = String("Order: Car with ");
    if(document.orderForm.door4.checked == true)
      alertString += "4 doors.";        //Add 4 doors to string
    if(document.orderForm.door2.checked == true)
      alertString += "2 doors.";        //Add 2 door to string

    //Create alert box
    alert(alertString);
  }
}

//Hide End --->
</script>

</html>
```

# Checkbox.click()

## *JavaScript 1.1+, JScript 3.0+*

## *Nav3+, IE 4+*

## *Syntax*

```
document.form.checkbox.click()
```

## *Description*

The click() method simulates the click event. The clicked property is adjusted accordingly when this method is used.

## *Example*

In Listing 7.38, the user is asked to select the door style wanted on his or her new car. If the user selects the 4-door option, the user is alerted that the 4-door has lots of leg room. If the 2-door option is selected, a message is posted to encourage the user to consider the 4-door model. In addition to this message, the message about extra leg room is displayed, thanks to the click() method.

*Listing 7.38    Using the Check Box's click() Method*
```
<html>

<h2>Car Purchase Sheet</h2>

Step1: Please select the door style you want on your new car:<BR>

<form name="orderForm">
  <input type="checkbox"
```

*continues*

*Listing 7.38 continued*

```
        name="door4"
        onClick="alert('The 4-door version has lots of leg room.')">4
doors<br>
  <input type="checkbox"
        name="door2"
        onClick="displayNote()">2 doors<hr>
  Step 2:
  <input type="button"
        value="Submit Order"
        name="orderButton"
        onClick="alert('Your order has been submitted')">
</form>

<script language="JavaScript">
<!-- Hide

//This function calls on another click handler
function displayNote()
{
  //Alert user to consider the 4-door version
  alert("Have you considered the 4-door version?");

  //Display the 4 door note using click() method.
  document.orderForm.door4.click();
}

//Hide End --->
</script>

</html>
```

# Checkbox.defaultChecked

## *JavaScript 1.0+, JScript 3.0+*

## *Nav2+, IE 4+*

## *Syntax*

document.*form.checkbox*.defaultChecked

## *Description*

The defaultChecked property holds the initial state of a check box as defined by the checked attribute of the <input> tag. Because this property only holds the initial state of the check box, it is a read-only Boolean value.

## *Example*

In Listing 7.39, the defaultChecked property is used to reset the car door check boxes to their initial state.

*Listing 7.39    Resetting Check Boxes with the `defaultChecked` Property*

```html
<html>

<h2>Car Purchase Sheet</h2>

Step1: Please select the door style you want on your new car:<BR>

<form name="orderForm">
  <input type="checkbox"
         name="door4">4 doors<br>
  <input type="checkbox"
         name="door2"
         checked>2 doors<hr>
  Step 2:
  <input type="button"
         value="Submit Order"
         name="orderButton"
         onClick="alert('Your order has been submitted')">
  <input type="button"
         value="Reset Checkboxes"
         name="resetButton"
         onClick="resetCheckboxes()">
</form>

<script language="JavaScript">
<!-- Hide

//This function resets the check boxes back to their initial state
function resetCheckboxes()
{
  //Access initial state with the defaultChecked property
  document.orderForm.door4.checked = document.orderForm.door4.defaultChecked;
  document.orderForm.door2.checked = document.orderForm.door2.defaultChecked;
}

//Hide End --->
</script>

</html>
```

# Checkbox.focus()

## *JavaScript 1.0+, JScript 3.0+*

## *Nav2+, IE 4+*

## *Syntax*

document.*form.checkbox*.focus()

## Description

The `focus()` method applies focus to a check box without invoking the checkbox's onFocus event handler.

**WARNING**

In the UNIX versions of Navigator 2 and Navigator 3, the `focus()` method does not work for check boxes.

## Example

In Listing 7.40, two check boxes are created by using the `<input>` tag. Click the first check box and then the second check box. Finally, click the Move Focus button to move the focus back to the first check box. Do not be surprised if you do not see a difference in the check boxes in this example. In most browsers, you will not be able to detect the difference between a check box that is focused versus one that is not focused. For this reason, you will probably find very little use for this method.

*Listing 7.40    Applying Focus to a Check Box Using the `focus()` Method*

```
<html>

<h2>The Checkbox Focus Test</h2>

Click both checkboxes and then click the button to return focus to
the first checkbox.

<form name="myForm">
  <input type="checkbox"
         name="checkBox1">Option 1<br>
  <input type="checkbox"
         name="checkBox2">Option 2<hr>
  <input type="button"
         name="focusButton"
         value="Move Focus"
         onClick="moveFocus()">
</form>

<script language="JavaScript">
<!-- Hide

//This function moves the focus to checkBox1.
function moveFocus()
{
  //Move the focus to from checkBox1
  document.myForm.checkBox1.focus();
}

//Hide End --->
</script>

</html>
```

# Checkbox.form

## JavaScript 1.0+, JScript 3.0+

## Nav2+, IE 4+, Opera3+

## Syntax

```
document.form.checkbox.form
```

## Description

The form property provides access to a check box's parent Form object.

## Example

The code in Listing 7.41 proves that the check box's form property contains the parent Form object by evaluating the if statement to true.

Listing 7.41    Accessing a Check Box's Parent with the form Property

```
<html>

<form name="myForm">
  <input type="checkbox"
         value="YES"
         name="myCheckBox"
         checked>
</form>

<script language="JavaScript">
<!-- Hide

//Does the parent of the myCheckBox equal myForm?

if(document.myForm.myCheckBox.form == document.myForm)
  alert("myCheckBox's form property is equal to myForm object");      //Equal
else
  alert("myCheckBox's form property is NOT equal to myForm object");  //Not
equal

//Hide End --->
</script>

</html>
```

# Checkbox.handleEvent()

## JavaScript 1.2+

## Nav4+

## Syntax

```
document.form.checkbox.handleEvent(event)
```

## Description

The handleEvent() method provides a way to invoke a check box's event handler, even though the event never happened. The argument associated with this method is listed in Table 7.8.

**Table 7.8    Argument Associated with the handleEvent() Method**

| Argument | Description |
| --- | --- |
| event | An Event object to be handled |

## Example

In Listing 7.42, the user is asked to select the engine wanted in his or her new car. If the user selects the V6 engine, the user is alerted that the V6 has lots of power. If the 4 cylinder is selected, a message is posted to encourage the user to consider the V6. The click event is passed to the first check box via the handleEvent() method. This causes the message about more power to be displayed. Figure 7.4 shows the result of selecting the 4-cylinder engine check box.

*Listing 7.42    Passing Events to a Check Box with the handleEvent() Method*

```
<html>

<h2>Car Purchase Sheet</h2>

Step1: Please select the engine style you want on your new car:<BR>

<form name="orderForm">
  <input type="checkbox"
         name="v6"
         onClick="alert('The V6 has lots of power!')">V6<br>
  <input type="checkbox"
         name="cylinder4"
         onClick="displayNote()">4 Cylinder<hr>
  Step 2:
  <input type="button"
         value="Submit Order"
         name="orderButton"
         onClick="alert('Your order has been submitted')">
</form>

<script language="JavaScript">
<!-- Hide

//This function passes the click event along to another check box
//using the check box's handleEvent method.
function displayNote(event)
{
```

```
  //Display not about V6 engine
  alert("Have you considered the V6 engine?");

  //Pass event along to first V6 check box.
  document.orderForm.v6.handleEvent(event);
}

//Hide End --->
</script>

</html>
```

**Figure 7.4**

*Alert box prompted by checking the 4-cylinder engine check box.*

# Checkbox.name

## *JavaScript 1.0+, JScript 3.0+*

## *Nav2+, IE 4+, Opera3+*

## *Syntax*

```
document.form.checkbox.name
```

## *Description*

The name property provides access to the name attribute of the check box. This property is a read-only string.

## *Example*

Listing 7.43 uses the name property of the check boxes to display what engine type was selected.

*Listing 7.43    Display the Name of the Check Box with the* name *Property*

```
<html>

<h2>Truck Purchase Sheet</h2>

Step1: Please select the engine style you want on your new truck:<BR>

<form name="orderForm">
  <input type="checkbox"
         name="V6">V6<br>
  <input type="checkbox"
         name="V8">V8<hr>
  Step 2:
  <input type="button"
         value="Submit Order"
         name="orderButton"
         onClick="submitOrder()">
</form>

<script language="JavaScript">
<!-- Hide

//This function uses the name property to let the user
//know what options were selected.
function submitOrder()
{
  //Create a string to be displayed in the alert box
  var alertString = String("You have selected a ");

  //Determine what type of engine was selected.
  if(document.orderForm.V6.checked == true)
    alertString += document.orderForm.V6.name;  //Display V6
  else
    alertString += document.orderForm.V8.name;  //Display V8
  alertString += " truck.";

  //Create alert box
  alert(alertString);
}

//Hide End --->
</script>

</html>
```

# Checkbox.onBlur

## *JavaScript 1.1+, JScript 3.0+*

## *Nav3+, IE 4+*

## Syntax

```
onBlur="command"
```

## Description

The onBlur event handler is defined in an <input> tag and specifies what to do when a check box loses focus.

## Example

The code in Listing 7.44 uses the onBlur event handler to display a message alerting the customer that the peppers he or she is ordering are hot.

*Listing 7.44    Use onBlur Event Handler to Display Alert Box When Check Box Loses Focus*

```
<html>

<h2>Pizza Machine</h2>

Step 1: Please select your pizza toppings:<BR>

<form name="orderForm">
  <input type="checkbox"
         name="peppers"
         onBlur="pepperAlert()">Peppers<br>
  <input type="checkbox"
         name="sausage">Sausage<hr>
  Step 2:
  <input type="button"
         value="Order Pizza"
         name="orderButton"
         onClick="alert('Your pizza has been ordered.')">
</form>

<script language="JavaScript">
<!-- Hide

//This function alerts the customer that peppers are hot!
function pepperAlert()
{
  //If peppers are selected then display alert
  if(document.orderForm.peppers.checked == true)
  {
    //Create alert box
    alert("These are extremely hot peppers.");
  }
}

//Hide End --->
</script>

</html>
```

# Checkbox.onClick
## *JavaScript 1.1+, JScript 3.0+*
## *Nav3+, IE 4+*

## *Syntax*

onClick="*command*"

## *Description*

The onClick event handler is defined in an <input> tag and specifies what to do when
a check box is clicked.

## *Example*

The code in Listing 7.45 uses the onClick event handler to display a message alerting
the customer that sausage goes well with peppers.

*Listing 7.45   Use onClick Event Handler to Display Message*

```
<html>

<h2>Pizza Machine</h2>

Step 1: Please select your pizza toppings:<BR>

<form name="orderForm">
  <input type="checkbox"
         name="peppers"
         onClick="recommendSausage()">Peppers<br>
  <input type="checkbox"
         name="sausage">Sausage<hr>
  Step 2:
  <input type="button"
         value="Order Pizza"
         name="orderButton"
         onClick="alert('Your pizza has been ordered.')">
</form>

<script language="JavaScript">
<!-- Hide

//This function recommends the customer consider sausage.
function recommendSausage()
{
  //If peppers are selected, display alert
  if(document.orderForm.peppers.checked == true)
  {
    //Create alert box
    alert("Sausage goes well with peppers.");
  }
}
```

```
//Display the event handler associated with onClick
document.write("The pepper checkbox onClick event handler: ");
document.write(document.orderForm.peppers.onclick);


//Hide End --->
</script>

</html>
```

# Checkbox.onFocus

## JavaScript 1.1+, JScript 3.0+

## Nav3+, IE 4+

## Syntax

```
onFocus="command"
```

## Description

The onFocus event handler is defined in an `<input>` tag and specifies what to do when a check box gains focus.

## Example

The code in Listing 7.46 uses the onFocus event handler to automatically select extra cheese when the customer selects sausage.

*Listing 7.46   Using the onFocus Event Handler to Select Extra Cheese*
```
<html>

<h2>Pizza Machine</h2>

Step1: Please select your pizza toppings:<BR>

<form name="orderForm">
  <input type="checkbox"
         name="peppers">Peppers<br>
  <input type="checkbox"
         name="sausage"
         onFocus="chooseExtraCheese()">Sausage<br>
  <input type="checkbox"
         name="cheese">Extra Cheese<hr>
  Step 2:
  <input type="button"
         value="Order Pizza"
         name="orderButton"
         onClick="alert('Your pizza has been ordered.')">
```

*continues*

*Listing 7.46    continued*

```
</form>

<script language="JavaScript">
<!-- Hide

//This function chooses the extra cheese checkbox.
function chooseExtraCheese()
{
  //If sausage is selected, select extra cheese
  if(document.orderForm.sausage.checked == false)
  {
    //select extra cheese
    document.orderForm.cheese.checked = true;
  }
}

//Display the event handler associated with onFocus
document.write("The sausage checkbox onFocus event handler: ");
document.write(document.orderForm.sausage.onFocus);


//Hide End --->
</script>

</html>
```

# Checkbox.type

## *JavaScript 1.1+, JScript 3.0+*

## *Nav3+, IE 4+, Opera3+*

## *Syntax*

document.*form*.*checkbox*.type

## *Description*

The type property provides access to type attribute of the check box. This property is a read-only string that always contains checkbox.

## *Example*

Listing 7.47 instructs the customer to select only two toppings (check boxes) of all those offered. To determine the number of toppings, the type property of the check box is used to determine how many check boxes are in orderForm. The program finds there are four check boxes representing the possible pizza toppings.

*Listing 7.47    Accessing a Check Box's type Property*

```
<html>

<h2>Pizza Machine</h2>
```

```
Step 1: Please select your pizza toppings:<br>

<form name="orderForm">
  <input type="checkbox"
         name="peppers">Peppers<br>
  <input type="checkbox"
         name="sausage">Sausage<br>
  <input type="checkbox"
         name="onion">Onion<br>
  <input type="checkbox"
         name="bacon">Bacon<hr>
  Step 2:
  <input type="button"
         value="Order Pizza"
         name="orderButton"
         onClick="alert('Your pizza has been ordered.')">
</form>

<script language="JavaScript">
<!-- Hide

//Initialize a counter to zero
var counter = 0;

//Count the number of check boxes in orderForm
for(var x=0; x<document.orderForm.length; x++)
{
  //Is element a check box?
  if(document.orderForm.elements[x].type == "checkbox")
  {
    //Increment the counter
    counter++;
  }
}

//display the topping instructions.
document.write("Please select no more than 2 of the ");
document.write(counter," possible toppings.");    //Insert 4

//Hide End --->
</script>

</html>
```

# Checkbox.value

## *JavaScript 1.0+, JScript 3.0+*

## *Nav2+, IE 4+, Opera3+*

## Syntax

document.*form.checkbox*.value

## Description

The value property provides access to value attribute of the check box. This property is a read/write value that is sent to the server when the form is submitted.

## Example

Listing 7.48 uses the value property of each check box to create instructions for the customer on how to order his or her custom pizza.

*Listing 7.48   Accessing a Check Box's* value *Property*

```
<html>

<h2>Pizza Machine</h2>

Step1: Please select your pizza toppings:<BR>

<form name="orderForm">
  <input type="checkbox"
         name="onion"
         value="hot onion">Onion<br>
  <input type="checkbox"
         name="bacon"
         value="spicy bacon">Bacon<hr>
  Step 2:
  <input type="button"
         value="Order Pizza"
         name="orderButton"
         onClick="alert('Your pizza has been ordered.')">
</form>

<script language="JavaScript">
<!-- Hide

//Display instructions using the check box value property
document.write("Please select either ");
document.write(document.orderForm.onion.value);   //Insert hot onion
document.write(" or ",document.orderForm.bacon.value);  //Insert spicy bacon
document.write(" on your custom pizza!");

//Hide End --->
</script>

</html>
```

# Document

## *JavaScript 1.0+, ECMAScript 1.0+, JScript 1.0+*

# Nav2+, IE 3+, Opera3+

## Syntax

Core client-side JavaScript object.

## Description

The Document object represents a Web page that is displayed in a browser window, frame, or layer. An instance is created with each document that is loaded by the browser. This object has many properties and methods that vary greatly between JavaScript and JScript. Table 7.9 lists all the properties, methods, and event handlers associated with Document object.

**Table 7.9   Properties, Methods, and Event Handlers Associated with the Document Object**

| Type | Item | Description |
| --- | --- | --- |
| Properties | alinkColor | Color of activated link |
| | all | Array of all HTML tags in the document |
| | anchors | Array of Anchor objects |
| | applets | Array of Applet objects |
| | bgcolor | Background color of document |
| | classes | Style sheet classes array |
| | cookie | Cookie associated with document |
| | domain | Domain of document |
| | embeds | Array of embedded objects |
| | fgcolor | Color of text in document |
| | forms | Array of Form objects |
| | ids | Style sheet IDs array |
| | images | Array of Image objects |
| | lastModified | Date when document was last modified |
| | layers | Array of Layer objects |
| | linkColor | Color of links |
| | links | Array of Link objects |
| | plugins | Array of embedded objects |
| | referrer | URL of document to which the current document was linked |
| | tags | Style sheet tag array |
| | title | Title of document |
| | URL | URL of current document |
| | vlinkColor | Color of visited links |
| Methods | captureEvents() | Captures events to be handled by document |
| | close() | Closes output stream to document |
| | getSelection() | Returns the selected text |
| | open() | Opens output stream to document |
| | releaseEvents() | Releases events captured by document |

*continues*

*Table 7.9 continued*

| Type | Item | Description |
|------|------|-------------|
| | `routeEvent()` | Routes captured events to other objects |
| | `write()` | Appends text to document |
| | `writeln()` | Appends text and a newline character to document |
| Event Handlers | `onClick` | Handler for click events |
| | `onDblClick` | Handler for double-click events |
| | `onKeyDown` | Handler for `KeyDown` events |
| | `onKeyPress` | Handler for `KeyPress` events |
| | `onKeyUp` | Handler for `KeyUp` events |
| | `onLoad` | Handler that is used when `Document` has finished loading |
| | `onMouseDown` | Handler for `MouseDown` events |
| | `onMouseUp` | Handler for `MouseUp` events |
| | `onUnLoad` | Handler that is used when `Document` unloaded from window |

# document.alinkColor

## *JavaScript 1.0+, JScript 1.0+*

## *Nav2+, IE 3+*

## Syntax

```
document.alinkColor
```

## Description

The `alinkColor` property specifies the color of activated links. A link is considered activated between the time the mouse button is pressed and released over a link. The color is expressed as a string in hexadecimal digits or as one of the JavaScript standard color names. The hexadecimal form is made up of six digits that follow the pattern "RRGGBB."

## Example

The sample code in Listing 7.49 sets the activated links color to green for all links on the page, even if they are placed before the `<script>` tags.

*Listing 7.49   Setting Document Properties*

```
<html>

<a href="myGreenPage.html">The Green Site</a><br>

<script language="JavaScript">
<!-- Hide
```

```
//Set the activated links color to green.
document.alinkColor="00ff00";

//Hide End --->
</script>

<a href="myGreenGrassPage.html">The Green Grass Page</a>

</html>
```

# document.all

## *JScript 3.0+*

## *IE 4+*

## *Syntax*

```
document.all[index]
```

## *Description*

The `document.all` property is an array of all the HTML elements that are in the document. The elements appear in the array in the order in which they were created. Table 7.10 lists the methods associated with `document.all` array.

*Table 7.10   Methods Associated with the document.all Array*

| Method | Description |
| --- | --- |
| item() | Returns an HTML element based on element's name |
| tags() | Returns an array of elements that have the specified tag |

## *Example*

Listing 7.50 uses the `document.all` property array and array notation (brackets) to access the `Paint` anchor. Using dot notation, the name of the anchor is used to create a link to the top of the page.

*Listing 7.50   Using document.all*

```
<html>

<a name="Paint"><h2><u>Paint Colors</u></h2></a>
Red<br>
Green<br>
Blue<br>
Orange<br>
<hr>

<script language="JavaScript">
<!-- Hide
```

*continues*

*Listing 7.50    continued*

```
//Create a link using the name associated with HTML element 4.
document.write("<a href='#',document.all[4].name,"'>");   //Insert "Paint"
document.write(document.all[4].name,"</a>");              //Insert "Paint"

//Hide End --->
</script>

</html>
```

# document.all.item()

## *JScript 3.0+*

## *IE 4+*

## Syntax

```
document.all.item(name)
```

## Description

The item() method provides a way to retrieve an HTML element out of the document.all array without having to know its position in the array. Instead of using an index position, the item() method allows you to just pass in the name of the element as specified by the name or id attribute of HTML tags. Normally, the method returns the element, but, if more than one element is found with the same name, an array of elements is returned.

## Example

Listing 7.51 uses the item() method to access the Paint anchor. Using dot notation, the name of the anchor is used to create a link to the top of the page.

*Listing 7.51    Using the item() Method to Find a Particular HTML Element*

```
<HTML name="top">

<a name="Paint"><h2><u>Paint Colors</u></h2></a>
Red<br>
Green<br>
Blue<br>
Orange<br>
<hr>

<script language="JavaScript">
<!-- Hide

//Create a link using the name associated with HTML element 4.
document.write("<a href='#")                //Create first part of link tag
document.write(document.all.item("Paint").name,"'>");   //Insert "Paint"
document.write(document.all.item("Paint").name,"</a>"); //Insert "Paint"
```

```
//Hide End --->
</script>

</html>
```

# document.all.tags()

## *JScript 3.0+*

## *IE 4+*

## *Syntax*

```
document.all.tags(tag)
```

## *Description*

The tags() method provides a way to retrieve all HTML elements of a particular tag type from the document.all array. The method returns an array of elements.

## *Example*

Listing 7.52 uses the tags() method to create an array of all the anchor tags in the document. Using dot notation, the name of the first anchor in the temporary array is used to create a link to the top of the page.

*Listing 7.52    Using the tags() Method to Find HTML Elements with a Particular Tag*

```
<html>

<a name="Paint"><h2><u>Paint Colors</u></h2></a>
Red<br>
Green<br>
Blue<br>
Orange<br>
<hr>

<script language="JavaScript">
<!-- Hide

//Get all the anchor tags
var arrayOfAnchors = document.all.tags("A");

//Create a link using name of the first element in the arrayOfAnchors
document.write("<a href='#",arrayOfAnchors[0].name,"'>");   //Insert "Paint"
document.write(arrayOfAnchors[0].name,"</a>");              //Insert "Paint"

//Hide End --->
</script>

</html>
```

# document.anchors

## *JavaScript 1.2+, JScript 3.0+*

## *Nav4+, IE 4+*

## *Syntax*

```
document.anchors
document.anchors[index]
```

## *Description*

The anchors property is an array that contains all the Anchor objects that appear within the HTML document from using the <a name="*string*"> tag. The anchors property has one property of its own, called length, which contains the number of Anchor objects in the array. The *index* number ranges from zero to the length of the array minus 1. See "Anchor," earlier in the chapter, for a detailed explanation of all the properties associated with anchors.

## WARNING

Although hyperlinks are created using the <a> tag, they are not accessible through the anchors array. Hyperlinks are stored in the document's links array.

## *Example*

Listing 7.53 demonstrates how to access anchor names using the document's anchors array.

*Listing 7.53   Accessing Anchor Names Using the anchors Array*

```
<html>

<a name="A"><h4>The Letter A</h4></a>
apple<br>
aligator<hr>

<a name="B"><h4>The Letter B</h4></a>
baby.<br>
basketball<br>
banana<hr>

<script language="JavaScript">
<!-- Hide

document.write("Anchor Names:<br>");        //Title

//Set up a loop to display the name of each anchor in document
for(var x=0; x<=document.anchors.length; x++)
{
   //Display the name of each anchor
```

```
    document.write(document.anchors[x].name,"<br>");
}

//Hide End --->
</script>

</html>
```

# document.anchors.length

## *JavaScript 1.2+, JScript 3.0+*

## *Nav4+, IE 4+*

## *Syntax*

```
document.anchors.length
```

## *Description*

The length property contains the number of Anchor objects that are in the document.

## *Example*

Listing 7.54 uses the anchor length property to loop through all the anchors in the document. During each pass through the loop, a link to each anchor in the document is created.

*Listing 7.54    Using the Anchor* length *Property to Create Hyperlinks*

```
<html>

<center><h1><u>The Music Intrument Page</u></h1></center>

<hr><a name="Trumpet"><h4>Trumpet</h4></a>
The trumpet is a brass instrument that can create bright, loud tones.  The
horn has 3 valves for changing the tone being played.<br>

<hr><a name="Guitar"><h4>Guitar</h4></a>
The guitar is a stringed instrument that has a hollow wooden body with a long
wooden neck.  Most guitars have 6 strings each tuned to a different tone.
By pressing different combinations of strings chords can be created.<br>

<hr><a name="Piano"><h4>Piano</h4></a>
The piano has one of the largest tonal ranges of any instrument.  Tones
are created by pressing keys which are attached to small wood hammers that
hit strings tuned to specific tones.<br>

<script language="JavaScript">
<!-- Hide
document.write("<hr>Pick an instrument:<br>");
```

*continues*

*Listing 7.54    continued*

```
//Create a link for each anchor using the Anchor object and the length property
for(var counter=0; counter<document.anchors.length; counter++)
{
  document.write("<a href='#",document.anchors[counter].name,"'>");
  document.write(document.anchors[counter].text,"</a><br>");
}

// End hide --->
</script>

</html>
```

# document.applets

## JavaScript 1.1+, JScript 1.0+

## Nav3+, IE 3+

## Syntax

```
document.applets
document.applets[index]
```

## Description

The `applets` property is an array that contains all the `Applet` objects that appear within the HTML document from using the `<applet>` tag. The `applet` property has one property of its own, called `length`, which contains the number of `Applet` objects in the array. The `index` number ranges from zero to the length of the array minus 1. See "Applet," earlier in this chapter, for a detailed explanation of all the properties associated with applets.

## Example

Listing 7.55 includes two fictitious calculator applets that are embedded in the HTML document. Using the `applets` array, the names of the calculators are displayed on the screen.

*Listing 7.55    Accessing Applets with the `applets` Array*

```
<html>

<applet name="Home Calculator" code="homeCalculator.class" width=50 height=50
mayscript></applet>
<applet name="Office Calculator" code="officeCalculator.class" width=50
height=50 mayscript></applet>

Special thanks goes to the individuals who provided us with the following
calculators:<br>

<script language="JavaScript">
```

```
<!-- Hide

//Display the names of the calculator applets
document.write(document.applets[0].name,"<br>");
document.write(document.applets[1].name);

</script>
</html>
```

# document.applets.length

## *JavaScript 1.1+, JScript 3.0+*

## *Nav3+, IE 4+*

## *Syntax*

```
document.applets.length
```

## *Description*

The length property contains the number of Applet objects that are in a document.

## *Example*

Listing 7.56 uses the length property to display the number of applets in a HTML document.

*Listing 7.56  Accessing the Number of Applets in a Document with the length Property*

```
<html>

<h2>The Applets Page</h2>

<applet name="myAddApplet" code="add.class" width=50 height=50
mayscript></applet>
<applet name="mySubtractApplet" code="subtract.class" width=50 height=50
mayscript></applet>

<script language="JavaScript">
<!-- Hide

//Tell the user how many applets are currently available.
document.write("There are currently ",document.applets.length);
document.write("applets available on this page.  Check back as");
document.write("new applets are added daily.");
//Hide End -->
</script>

</html>
```

# document.bgColor

## *JavaScript 1.0+, JScript 1.0+*

## *Nav2+, IE 3+, Opera3+*

## Syntax

```
document.bgColor
```

## Description

The bgColor property specifies the background color of HTML document. The color is expressed as a string in hexadecimal digits or as one of the JavaScript standard color names. The hexadecimal form is made up of six digits that follow the pattern "RRGGBB." The color of the background can also be set with bgcolor attribute of the <body> tag.

## Example

Listing 7.57 changes the document's background color based on which button is chosen.

*Listing 7.57    Modifying the Document bgColor Property*

```
<html>

<form>
<input  type="button"
        value="Yellow"
        name="Yellow"
        onClick="changeBG('yellow')">
<input  type="button"
        value="Green"
        name="Green"
        onClick="changeBG('green')">
<input  type="text"
        name="color">
</form>

<script language="JavaScript">
<!-- Hide

//This function changes the background color and fills in the text box
function changeBG(color)
{
  document.bgColor=color;                //Change background color
  document.myForm.color.value=color;     //Display the  color
}

//Hide End --->
</script>

</html>
```

# document.captureEvents()

## *JavaScript 1.2+*

## *Nav4+*

## *Syntax*

```
document.captureEvents(eventMask)
```

## *Description*

The captureEvents() method specifies the type of events that should be passed to the document rather than to the object for which they were intended. The *eventMask* argument(s) specifies what events to capture. The following list shows all the possible event masks. Multiple events can be captured by using the bitwise OR (¦) operator.

- Event.ABORT
- Event.BLUR
- Event.CHANGE
- Event.CLICK
- Event.DBCLICK
- Event.DRAGDROP
- Event.ERROR
- Event.FOCUS
- Event.KEYDOWN
- Event.KEYPRESS
- Event.KEYUP
- Event.LOAD
- Event.MOUSEDOWN
- Event.MOUSEMOVE
- Event.MOUSEOUT
- Event.MOUSEOVER
- Event.MOUSEUP
- Event.MOVE
- Event.RESET
- Event.RESIZE
- Event.SELECT
- Event.SUBMIT
- Event.UNLOAD

## *Example*

Listing 7.58 attempts to change the background color from yellow to purple when the mouse button is pressed and released. Before the Event.MOUSEDOWN and Event.MOUSEUP events can be handled by the button, they are intercepted by Document's captureEvent() method and routed to special functions that change the background colors to red and blue.

*Listing 7.58    Capture Events with the* `captureEvent()` *Method*

```
<html>

Normally the button below would toggle the background color between
yellow and purple but since the mouseup and mousedown events are captured
and handled by the document the events are never allowed to reach the button
level.

<form>
<input type="button"
       value="Yellow/Purple"
       onMouseDown="document.bgColor='yellow'"
       onMouseUp="document.bgColor='purple'">
</form>

<script>
<!-- Hide

//Intercept all mouseup and mousedown events and handle them
//by document event handlers.  This will cause the button event handlers
//to be intercepted.
document.captureEvents(Event.MOUSEDOWN ¦ Event.MOUSEUP);

//Define event handlers within document to handle the mousedown
//and mouseup events.
document.onmousedown = function(event){document.bgColor='red'};
document.onmouseup = function(event){document.bgColor='blue'};

//Hide End --->
</script>

</html>
```

# document.classes

## JavaScript 1.2+

## Nav4+

## Syntax

`document.classes.className.tagName`

## Description

The `classes` property is an associative array that contains classes associated with Netscape style sheets. Using dot notation, `className` specifies the `class` attribute and associated HTML tag (`tagName`) for which the style is applied. When `tagName` is set to all, the style is applied to all tags with a class attribute of *className*. The style sheet classes are created within <style> or <script> using JavaScript or HTML.

> **NOTE**
>
> When creating a class, make sure the declaration appears before the new class is used, because many HTML objects cannot be changed once they have been created in the document.

> **NOTE**
>
> If JavaScript dot notation is used when creating a new class within <style> tags, document does not have to be specified.

## *Example*

Listing 7.59 demonstrates three different ways to create style sheet classes using JavaScript and HTML within <style> and <script> tags. Notice how the order in which the classes are declared and used ultimately affects the style result in Figure 7.5.

*Listing 7.59    Creating New Style Sheet Classes*

```
<html>

<style type="text/css">
  all.TEXTFORMAT {font-style: italic;}
</style>

<p CLASS=TEXTFORMAT>After first STYLE tag.<p>

<style type="text/javascript">
  classes.TEXTFORMAT.all.fontWeight = "bold";
</style>

<p class=TEXTFORMAT>After second STYLE tag.<p>

<script>
<!-- Hide
document.classes.TEXTFORMAT.all.textDecoration = "underline";
//Hide End --->
</script>

<p class=TEXTFORMAT>After SCRIPT tag.<p>

</html>
```

**Figure 7.5**

*Three lines of text with different style sheet settings.*

# document.classes.align

## JavaScript 1.2+

## Nav4+

## Syntax

```
document.classes.className.tagName.align
```

## Description

The `align` property specifies the alignment of an element within its parent as associated with the `class` called *className*. The definition can be further defined by specifying a tag (*tagName*) or the word `all` for *tagName*.

The `align` property can be assigned one of the following values: `left`, `right`, `none`.

## NOTE

The `align` property is referred to as `float` when using CSS syntax. JavaScript could not use the word "float" because it was a reserved word.

## Example

Listing 7.60 uses the `align` property to align a paragraph to the right of its parent, the document. Figure 7.6 shows what happens to the text that is directly after the paragraph that uses the `RIGHT` class.

*Listing 7.60    Aligning Right with the `align` Property*

```
<html>

<script>
<!-- Hide

//Create a style sheet class that aligns right
document.classes.RIGHT.all.align = "right";

//Hide End --->
</script>
```

```
<p class=RIGHT>Send me to the right!</p>

<p>Where am I?</p>

</html>
```

**Figure 7.6**

*Paragraph aligned to the right of its parent.*

# document.classes.backgroundColor

## *JavaScript 1.2+*

## *Nav4+*

## *Syntax*

```
document.classes.className.tagName.backgroundColor
```

## *Description*

The `backgroundColor` property specifies the background color associated with the class called `className`. The definition can also specify a tag (`tagName`) or the word all for `tagName`.

## *Example*

Listing 7.61 uses the `backgroundColor` property to make the background color around an anchor red.

*Listing 7.61    Setting the Background Color with the `backgroundColor` Property*

```
<html>

<script>
<!-- Hide

//Create a style sheet class that contains the background color
```

*continues*

*Listing 7.61    continued*

```
document.classes.BG.all.backgroundColor = "red";

//Hide End --->
</script>

<b class=BG>This</b> is an anchor that uses
styles from the BG class.

</html>
```

# document.classes.backgroundImage

## JavaScript 1.2+

## Nav4+

## Syntax

```
document.classes.className.tagName.backgroundImage
```

## Description

The `backgroundImage` property specifies the background image of an element as associated with the `class` called *className*. The definition can also specify a tag or the word `all` for *tagName*.

## Example

Listing 7.62 makes the image `logo.gif` the background for the header text.

*Listing 7.62    Setting the Background Image with the `backgroundImage` Property*

```
<html>

<script>
<!-- Hide

//Create a style sheet class that uses an image as a background
document.classes.BGI.all.backgroundImage = "logo.gif";

//Hide End --->
</script>

<h2 class=BGI>Look at my background image!</h2>

</html>
```

# document.classes.borderBottomWidth

## JavaScript 1.2+

## Nav4+

## Syntax

```
document.classes.className.tagName.borderBottomWidth
```

## Description

The `borderBottomWidth` property specifies the width of the bottom border of an element as associated with the `class` called *className*. The definition can also specify a tag or the word `all` for *tagName*.

## Example

Listing 7.63 uses the `borderBottomWidth` property to set the size of the bottom border that surrounds a text header. Notice that only the bottom portion of the border is shown.

*Listing 7.63    Setting the Bottom Border Width with the* `borderBottomWidth` *Property*

```
<html>

<script>
<!-- Hide

//Create a style sheet class that creates a bottom border
document.classes.BBW.all.borderBottomWidth = "10";

//Hide End --->
</script>

<h2 class=BBW>This text has a bottom border</h2>

</html>
```

# document.classes.borderColor

## JavaScript 1.2+

## Nav4+

## Syntax

```
document.classes.className.tagName.borderColor
```

## Description

The `borderColor` property specifies the color of the border of an element as associated with the `class` called *className*. The definition can be further defined by specifying a tag or the word `all` for *tagName*.

## Example

Listing 7.64 uses the `borderColor` property to set the color of the border that surrounds a text header to blue.

*Listing 7.64    Setting the Border Color with the `borderColor` Property*

```html
<html>

<script>
<!-- Hide

//Create a style sheet class that creates a left border
document.classes.ABORDER.all.borderWidths(10);
document.classes.ABORDER.all.borderColor = "blue";

//Hide End --->
</script>

<h2 class=Aborder=1>This text has a blue border</h2>

</html>
```

# document.classes.borderLeftWidth

## JavaScript 1.2+

## Nav4+

## Syntax

```
document.classes.className.tagName.borderLeftWidth
```

## Description

The `borderLeftWidth` property specifies the width of the left border of an element as associated with the `class` called *className*. The definition can also specify a tag or the word `all` for *tagName*.

## Example

Listing 7.65 uses the `borderLeftWidth` property to set the size of the left border that surrounds a text header. Notice that only the left portion of the border is shown.

*Listing 7.65    Setting the Left Border Width with the `borderLeftWidth` Property*

```html
<html>

<script>
<!-- Hide

//Create a style sheet class that creates a left border
document.classes.BLW.all.borderLeftWidth = "10";

//Hide End --->
</script>

<h2 class=BLW>This text has a left border</h2>

</html>
```

# document.classes.borderRightWidth

## JavaScript 1.2+

## Nav4+

## Syntax

```
document.classes.className.tagName.borderRightWidth
```

## Description

The `borderRightWidth` property specifies the width of the right border of an element as associated with the `class` called `className`. The definition can also specify a tag or the word `all` for `tagName`.

## Example

Listing 7.66 uses the `borderRightWidth` property to set the size of the right border that surrounds a text header. Notice that only the right portion of the border is shown.

*Listing 7.66    Setting the Right Border Width with the* `borderRightWidth` *Property*

```
<html>

<script>
<!-- Hide

//Create a style sheet class that creates a right border
document.classes.BRW.all.borderRightWidth = "10";

//Hide End --->
</script>

<h2 class=BRW>This text has a right border</h2>

</html>
```

# document.classes.borderStyle

## JavaScript 1.2+

## Nav4+

## Syntax

```
document.classes.className.tagName.borderStyle
```

## Description

The `borderStyle` property specifies the style of the border that surrounds an element as associated with the `class` called `className`. The definition can also specify a tag or the word `all` for `tagName`.

The borderStyle property can be assigned one of the following values: none, solid, double, inset, outset, groove, or ridge.

## Example

Listing 7.67 uses the borderStyle property to set the border around a text header to a double line.

*Listing 7.67  Setting the Border Style with the borderStyle Property*

```
<html>

<script>
<!-- Hide

//Create a style sheet class that creates a double border
document.classes.ABORDER.all.borderWidths(10);
document.classes.ABORDER.all.borderColor = "red";
document.classes.ABORDER.all.borderStyle = "double";

//Hide End --->
</script>

<h2 class=ABORDER1>This text has a double border</h2>

</html>
```

# document.classes.borderTopWidth

## JavaScript 1.2+

## Nav4+

## Syntax

```
document.classes.className.tagName.borderTopWidth
```

## Description

The borderTopWidth property specifies the width of the top border of an element as associated with the class called *className*. The definition can also specify a tag or the word all for *tagName*.

## Example

Listing 7.68 uses the borderTopWidth property to set the size of the top border that surrounds a text header. Notice that only the top portion of the border is shown.

*Listing 7.68  Setting the Top Border Width with the borderTopWidth Property*

```
<html>

<script>
<!-- Hide
```

```
//Create a style sheet class that creates a top border
document.classes.BTW.all.borderTopWidth = "10";

//Hide End --->
</script>

<h2 class=BTW>This text has a top border</h2>

</html>
```

# document.classes.borderWidths()

## JavaScript 1.2+

## Nav4+

## Syntax

```
document.classes.className.tagName.borderWidths(top,right,bottom,left)
document.classes.className.tagName.borderWidths(top-bootom,right-left)
document.classes.className.tagName.borderWidths(all)
```

## Description

The borderWidths() method specifies the width of the border that surrounds an element as associated with the class called *className*. The definition can also specify a tag or the word all for *tagName*. Setting border widths is equivalent to setting the borderBottomWidth, borderLeftWidth, borderRightWidth, and borderTopWidth properties. Table 7.11 lists all the arguments associated with the borderWidths() method.

**Table 7.11  Arguments Associated with the borderWidths() Method**

| Item | Description |
| --- | --- |
| top | Width of the top border |
| right | Width of the right border |
| left | Width of the left border |
| bottom | Width of the bottom border |
| top-bottom | Width of the both the top and bottom border |
| left-right | Width of the both the left and right border |
| all | Width of all four sides of the border |

## Example

Listing 7.69 uses the borderWidths() method to set the width of the border that surrounds a text header.

*Listing 7.69    Setting All the Border Widths with the* `borderWidths()` *Method*

```
<html>

<script>
<!-- Hide

//Create a style sheet class that creates a border
document.classes.ABORDER.all.borderWidths(5,10,15,20);

//Hide End --->
</script>

<h2 class=Aborder=1>This text has a border</h2>

</html>
```

# document.classes.clear

## *JavaScript 1.2+*

## *Nav4+*

## *Syntax*

```
document.classes.className.tagName.clear
```

## *Description*

The `clear` property specifies the sides of an element where floating elements (elements that define the `align` property) are not allowed. Using dot notation, this property is associated with the `class` called *className*. The definition can also specify a tag or the word `all` for *tagName*.

The `clear` property can be assigned one of the following values: `left`, `right`, `both`, or `none`.

## *Example*

Listing 7.70 uses the `clear` property to prevent floating elements from being on either side of an element.

*Listing 7.70    Using the* `clear` *Property*

```
<html>

<script>
<!-- Hide

//Create a style sheet classes that sets alignments
document.classes.LEFT.all.align = "left";
document.classes.LEFT.all.backgroundColor = "yellow";
document.classes.RIGHT.all.align = "right";
document.classes.RIGHT.all.backgroundColor = "red";
document.classes.KEEPAWAY.all.clear = "both";
```

```
//Hide End --->
</script>

<p class=LEFT>Send me to the left!</p>
<p class=RIGHT>Send me to the right!</p>
<p>I like other elements next to me!</p>

<p class=LEFT>Send me to the left!</p>
<p class=RIGHT>Send me to the right!</p>
<p class=KEEPAWAY>I don't like other elements next to me!</p>

</html>
```

# document.classes.color

## JavaScript 1.2+

## Nav4+

## Syntax

document.classes.*className*.*tagName*.color

## Description

The color property specifies foreground color of an element as associated with the class called *className*. The definition can also specify a tag or the word all for *tagName*.

## Example

Listing 7.71 uses the color property to set the color of various text.

*Listing 7.71    Set the Color of Text Using the color Property*

```
<html>

<script>
<!-- Hide

//Create a style sheet classes that defines colors
document.classes.BLUE.all.color = "blue";
document.classes.RED.all.color = "red";

//Hide End --->
</script>

<p class=BLUE>The blue boat floated on the blue ocean.</p>
<p class=RED>The red car stopped at a red stop sign.</p>

</html>
```

# document.classes.display

## JavaScript 1.2+

## Nav4+

## Syntax

```
document.classes.className.tagName.display
```

## Description

The `display` property specifies an element is displayed when associated with the class called *className*. The definition can also specify a tag or the word `all` for *tagName*.

The `display` property can be assigned one of the following values: `inline`, `block`, `list-item`, or `none`.

Specifying an `inline` value is equivalent to using the `<em>` tag. The `block` value is the same as creating header text with the `<h>` tag. Using `list-item` is equivalent to using the `<li>` tag. If `none` is specified, the element is not displayed.

## Example

Listing 7.72 sets the `display` property equal to "block" to create header text. Block consists of a line break and resetting margins to their default values. Notice that in this example, a carriage return is automatically entered before the bold tag.

*Listing 7.72    Set the `display` Property*

```
<html>

<script>
<!-- Hide

//Create a style sheet class that defines a block display
//A block consists of a line break and default margins
document.classes.H.all.display = "block";

//Hide End --->
</script>

Some text before the header
<b class=H>Big Header</b><br>
Just some regular text following the Big Header.

</html>
```

# document.classes.fontFamily

## JavaScript 1.2+

## Nav4+

### Syntax

document.classes.*className*.*tagName*.fontFamily

### Description

The fontFamily property specifies the font an element should use when associated with the class called *className*. The definition can also specify a tag or the word all for *tagName*. More than one font can be specified, in case a particular font has not been loaded.

### Example

Listing 7.73 uses the fontFamily property to create text with an Arial font. If that font is not available, Helvetica is used.

*Listing 7.73   Set the* fontFamily *Property*

```
<html>

<script>
<!-- Hide

//Create a style sheet class that defines a font
document.classes.F.all.fontFamily = "Arial,Helvetica";

//Hide End --->
</script>

<p class=F>Do you like this font?</p>

</html>
```

# document.classes.fontSize

## JavaScript 1.2+

## Nav4+

### Syntax

document.classes.*className*.*tagName*.fontSize

### Description

The fontSize property specifies the size of fonts used by an element when associated with the class called *className*. The definition can also specify a tag or the word all for *tagName*. The values that can be used to set font size can divided into four categories, as shown in Table 7.12.

*Table 7.12    Font Sizes*

| Category | Value |
|---|---|
| Absolute | `xx-small` |
| | `x-small` |
| | `small` |
| | `medium` |
| | `large` |
| | `x-large` |
| | `xx-large` |
| Relative | `smaller` (relative font size of parent) |
| | `larger` (relative font size of parent) |
| Length | A number followed by a unit of measurement |
| Percentage | The size relative to font size of parent |

## Example

Listing 7.74 uses absolute font sizing to define the `fontSize` property and associate it with text.

*Listing 7.74    Set the `fontSize` Property*

```
<html>

<script>
<!-- Hide

//Create a style sheet class that defines a font size
document.classes.XXS.all.fontSize = "xx-small";
document.classes.XXL.all.fontSize = "xx-large";

//Hide End --->
</script>

<p class=XXS>Extra, extra small text</p>
<p class=XXL>Extra, extra large text</p>

</html>
```

# document.classes.fontStyle

## JavaScript 1.2+

## Nav4+

## Syntax

`document.classes.`*className*`.`*tagName*`.fontStyle`

## Description

The fontStyle property specifies the font style used by an element when associated with the class called *className*. The definition can also specify a tag or the word all for *tagName*.

The fontStyle property can be assigned one of the following values: normal or italic.

## Example

Listing 7.75 uses the fontStyle property to italicize the header text.

*Listing 7.75  Set the fontStyle Property*

```
<html>

<script>
<!-- Hide

//Create a style sheet class that defines a font style
document.classes.I.all.fontStyle = "italic";

//Hide End --->
</script>

<h2 class=I>Italicized Heading</h2>

</html>
```

# document.classes.fontWeight

## JavaScript 1.2+

## Nav4+

## Syntax

document.classes.*className*.*tagName*.fontWeight

## Description

The fontWeight property specifies the font weight used by an element when associated with the class called *className*. The definition can also specify a tag or the word all for *tagName*.

The fontWeight property can be assigned one of the following values: normal, bold, bolder, lighter, or a number from 100 to 900.

## Example

Listing 7.76 uses the fontWeight property to set different levels of weight on various text. Even though the fontWeight can be set from 100 to 900, this does not mean that there are 800 different font weights. In Listing 7.76, you will find that fontWeight 400 looks the same as fontWeight 100.

*Listing 7.76   Set the `fontWeight` Property*

```
<html>

<script>
<!-- Hide

//Create a style sheet class that defines a font style
document.classes.W1.all.fontWeight = 100;
document.classes.W4.all.fontWeight = 400;
document.classes.W9.all.fontWeight = 900;

//Hide End --->
</script>

<p class=W1>Font weight of 100</p>
<p class=W4>Font weight of 400</p>
<p class=W9>Font weight of 900</p>

</html>
```

# document.classes.lineHeight

## JavaScript 1.2+

## Nav4+

## Syntax

```
document.classes.className.tagName.lineHeight
```

## Description

The `lineHeight` property specifies the distance between two lines that are next to each other. Using dot notation, the property is associated with the class called `className`. The definition can also specify a tag or the word `all` for `tagName`.

There are four types of values that are valid for the `lineHeight` property: `number`, `length`, `percentage`, and the value `normal`.

When a number is given without a unit of measure, it is multiplied by the font size of the element to give the line height. Length is specified by including a unit of measure after the number. A percentage is designated by including a percent sign (%) after the number to represent the line height as it relates to its parent.

## Example

Listing 7.77 uses the `lineHeight` property to set the distance between lines.

*Listing 7.77   Set the `lineHeight` Property*

```
<html>

<script>
<!-- Hide
```

```
//Create a style sheet class that defines a line height
document.classes.D1.all.lineHeight = "1in";
document.classes.D2.all.lineHeight = "30pt";

//Hide End --->
</script>

<p>This is the first line of text</p>
<p class=D1>This is a second line of text.</p>
<p>This is a third line of text.</p>
<p class=D2>This is a fourth line of text.</p>
<p>This is a fith line of text.</p>

</html>
```

# document.classes.listStyleType

## JavaScript 1.2+

## Nav4+

## Syntax

`document.classes.`*className.tagName.*`listStyleType`

## Description

The `listStyleType` property specifies the format of list items elements that are associated with the `class` called *className*. The definition can also specify a tag or the word `all` for *tagName*.

There are nine types of values that are valid for the `listStyleType` property: `disc`, `circle`, `square`, `decimal`, `lower-roman`, `upper-roman`, `lower-alpha`, `upper-alpha`, and `none`.

**NOTE**

The `listStyleType` property is only valid if the element also has the `display` property set to `list-item`.

## Example

Listing 7.78 uses the `listStyleType` property to format a list of items.

*Listing 7.78    Set the `listStyleType` Property*
```
<html>

<script>
<!-- Hide
```

*continues*

*Listing 7.78    continued*

```
//Create a style sheet class that defines a list format
document.classes.LIST.all.display = "list-item";
document.classes.LIST.all.listStyleType = "circle";

//Hide End --->
</script>

<h2>The days in a week</h2>

<ul class=LIST>
  <li>Monday
  <li>Tuesday
  <li>Wednesday
  <li>Thursday
  <li>Friday
  <li>Saturday
  <li>Sunday
</ul>

</html>
```

# document.classes.marginBottom

## *JavaScript 1.2+*

## *Nav4+*

## *Syntax*

```
document.classes.className.tagName.marginBottom
```

## *Description*

The `marginBottom` property specifies the distance between the bottom border of an element and the top border of another element. Dot notation is used to associate this property with the `class` called *className*. The definition can also specify a tag or the word `all` for *tagName*.

## *Example*

Listing 7.79 uses `marginBottom` property to set the distance between adjacent elements.

*Listing 7.79    Set the Bottom Margin with the* `marginBottom` *Property*

```
<html>

<script>
<!-- Hide

//Create a style sheet class that defines bottom margin
document.classes.FORMAT.all.borderWidths(10);
```

```
document.classes.FORMAT.all.marginBottom = 40;

//Hide End --->
</script>

<b>My margins are set automatically</b>
<b class=FORMAT>I have a large bottom margin!</b>
<b>My margins are set automatically</b>

</html>
```

# document.classes.marginLeft

## JavaScript 1.2+

## Nav4+

## Syntax
```
document.classes.className.tagName.marginLeft
```

## Description

The `marginLeft` property specifies the distance between the left border of an element and the right border of another element. Dot notation is used to associate this property with the `class` called `className`. The definition can also specify a tag or the word `all` for `tagName`.

## Example

Listing 7.80 uses `marginLeft` property to set the distance between adjacent elements. Notice the distance between the border and the right edge of the browser window.

*Listing 7.80    Set the Left Margin with the `marginLeft` Property*
```
<html>

<script>
<!-- Hide

//Create a style sheet class that defines left margin
document.classes.FORMAT1.all.borderWidths(10);
document.classes.FORMAT1.all.marginLeft = 40;
document.classes.FORMAT2.all.borderWidths(10);

//Hide End --->
</script>

<p class=FORMAT1>I have a large left margin!</p>
<p class=FORMAT2>I have an automatic left margin</p>

</html>
```

# document.classes.marginRight

## JavaScript 1.2+

## Nav4+

## Syntax

```
document.classes.className.tagName.marginRight
```

## Description

The `marginRight` property specifies the distance between the right border of an element and the left border of another element. Dot notation is used to associate this property with the `class` called `className`. The definition can also specify a tag or the word `all` for `tagName`.

## Example

Listing 7.81 uses `marginRight` property to set the distance between adjacent elements. Notice the distance between the border and the right edge of the browser window.

Listing 7.81   Set the Right Margin with the `marginRight` Property

```
<html>

<script>
<!-- Hide

//Create a style sheet class that defines right margin
document.classes.FORMAT1.all.borderWidths(10);
document.classes.FORMAT1.all.marginRight = 40;
document.classes.FORMAT2.all.borderWidths(10);

//Hide End --->
</script>

<p class=FORMAT1>I have a large right margin!</p>
<p class=FORMAT2>I have an automatic right margin</p>

</html>
```

# document.classes.margins()

## JavaScript 1.2+

## Nav4+

## Syntax

```
document.classes.className.tagName.margins(top,right,bottom,left)
document.classes.className.tagName.margins(top-bottom,right-left)
document.classes.className.tagName.margins(all)
```

## Description

The margins() method specifies the margin distance between border of an element and the border of adjacent elements. Dot notation is used to associate the property with the class called *className*. The definition can also specify a tag or the word all for *tagName*. Setting margin widths is equivalent to setting the marginBottom, marginLeft, marginRight, and marginTop properties. Table 7.13 lists all the arguments associated with the margins() method.

**Table 7.13 Arguments Associated with the margins() Method**

| Item | Description |
|------|-------------|
| top | Width of the top margin |
| right | Width of the right margin |
| left | Width of the left margin |
| bottom | Width of the bottom margin |
| top-bottom | Width of both the top and bottom margins |
| left-right | Width of both the left and right margins |
| all | Width of all four margins |

## Example

Listing 7.82 uses the margins() method to set the margin widths around a text element.

*Listing 7.82   All Margins Set with the margins() Method*

```
<html>

<script>
<!-- Hide

//Create a style sheet class that defines margins
document.classes.margin.all.borderWidths(10);
document.classes.margin.all.margins(50);

//Hide End --->
</script>

<h2 class=margin>This text has margins set to 50</h2>

</html>
```

# document.classes.marginTop

## JavaScript 1.2+

## Nav4+

## Syntax

document.classes.*className*.*tagName*.marginTop

## Description

The marginTop property specifies the distance between the top border of an element and the bottom border of another element. Dot notation is used to associate this property with the class called *className*. The definition can also specify a tag or the word all for *tagName*.

## Example

Listing 7.83 uses marginTop property to set the distance between adjacent elements.

*Listing 7.83    Set the Top Margin with the marginTop Property*

```
<html>

<script>
<!-- Hide

//Create a style sheet class that defines top margin
document.classes.FORMAT.all.borderWidths(10);
document.classes.FORMAT.all.marginTop = 40;

//Hide End --->
</script>

<b>My margins are set automatically</b>
<b class=FORMAT>I have a large top margin!</b>
<b>My margins are set automatically</b>

</html>
```

# document.classes.paddingBottom

## JavaScript 1.2+

## Nav4+

## Syntax

document.classes.*className*.*tagName*.paddingBottom

## Description

The paddingBottom property specifies the distance between the bottom border of an element and its content. Using dot notation, the property is associated with the class called *className*. The definition can also specify a tag or the word all for *tagName*.

## Example

Listing 7.84 uses paddingBottom property to set the distance between a line of text and its border.

*Listing 7.84    Set the Bottom Padding with the `paddingBottom` Property*

```
<html>

<script>
<!-- Hide

//Create a style sheet class that defines the bottom padding
document.classes.PAD.all.borderWidths(10)
document.classes.PAD.all.paddingBottom = "40";

//Hide End --->
</script>

<p class=PAD>This text has extra padding on the bottom.</p>

</html>
```

# document.classes.paddingLeft

## JavaScript 1.2+

## Nav4+

## Syntax

```
document.classes.className.tagName.paddingLeft
```

## Description

The `paddingLeft` property specifies the distance between the left border of an element and its content. Using dot notation, the property is associated with the `class` called *className*. The definition can also specify a tag or the word `all` for *tagName*.

## Example

Listing 7.85 uses `paddingLeft` property to set the distance between a line of text and its border.

*Listing 7.85    Set the Left Padding with the `paddingLeft` Property*

```
<html>

<script>
<!-- Hide

//Create a style sheet class that defines the left padding
document.classes.PAD.all.borderWidths(10)
document.classes.PAD.all.paddingLeft = "40";

//Hide End --->
</script>

<p class=PAD>This text has extra padding on the left.</p>

</html>
```

# document.classes.paddingRight

*JavaScript 1.2+*

*Nav4+*

## Syntax

```
document.classes.className.tagName.paddingRight
```

## Description

The `paddingRight` property specifies the distance between the right border of an element and its content. Using dot notation, the property is associated with the class called `className`. The definition can also specify a tag or the word `all` for `tagName`.

## Example

Listing 7.86 uses `paddingRight` property to set the distance between a line of text and its border.

*Listing 7.86    Set the Right Padding with the `paddingRight` Property*

```
<html>

<script>
<!-- Hide

//Create a style sheet class that defines the right padding
document.classes.PAD.all.borderWidths(10)
document.classes.PAD.all.paddingRight = "40";

//Hide End --->
</script>

<p class=PAD>This text has extra padding on the right.</p>

</html>
```

# document.classes.paddings()

*JavaScript 1.2+*

*Nav4+*

## Syntax

```
document.classes.className.tagName.paddings(top,right,bottom,left)
document.classes.className.tagName.paddings(top-bottom,right-left)
document.classes.className.tagName.paddings(all)
```

## Description

The paddings() method specifies the distance between the borders of an element and its content. Using dot notation, the property is associated with the class called *className*. The definition can also specify a tag or the word all for *tagName*. Setting the sizes is equivalent to setting the paddingBottom, paddingLeft, paddingRight, and paddingTop properties. Table 7.14 lists all the arguments associated with the paddings() method.

**Table 7.14    Arguments Associated with the paddings() Method**

| Item | Description |
| --- | --- |
| top | Padding between top border and content |
| right | Padding between right border and content |
| left | Padding between left border and content |
| bottom | Padding between bottom border and content |
| top-bottom | Padding between the content and both the top and bottom border |
| left-right | Padding between the content and both the left and right border |
| all | Padding between content and all four sides of the border |

## Example

Listing 7.87 uses paddings() method to set the distance between text and all sides of its border.

*Listing 7.87    Set all Paddings with the paddings() Method*

```
<html>

<script>
<!-- Hide

//Create a style sheet class that defines all paddings
document.classes.PAD.all.borderWidths(5);
document.classes.PAD.all.paddings(0,20,40,60);

//Hide End --->
</script>

<p class=PAD>This text has padding on all sides of its border.</p>

</html>
```

# document.classes.paddingTop

## JavaScript 1.2+

## Nav4+

## Syntax

document.classes.*className*.*tagName*.paddingTop

## Description

The paddingTop property specifies the distance between the left border of an element and its content. Using dot notation, the property is associated with the class called *className*. The definition can also specify a tag or the word all for *tagName*.

## Example

Listing 7.88 uses paddingTop property to set the distance between a line of text and its border.

Listing 7.88    *Set Top Padding with the* paddingTop *Property*

```
<html>

<script>
<!-- Hide

//Create a style sheet class that defines the top padding
document.classes.PAD.all.borderWidths(10)
document.classes.PAD.all.paddingTop = "40";

//Hide End --->
</script>

<p class=PAD>This text has extra padding on the top.</p>

</html>
```

# document.classes.textAlign

## JavaScript 1.2+

## Nav4+

## Syntax

document.classes.*className.tagName*.textAlign

## Description

The textAlign property specifies the alignment of text within an element as associated with the class called *className*. The definition can also specify a tag or the word all for *tagName*.

There are four types of values that are valid for the textAlign property: left, right, center, and justify.

## Example

Listing 7.89 uses textAlign property to align the text to the right.

Listing 7.89    *Set the* textAlign *Property*

```
<html>
```

```
<script>
<!-- Hide

//Create a style sheet class that defines right alignment
document.classes.RIGHT.all.borderWidths(10)
document.classes.RIGHT.all.textAlign = "right";

//Hide End --->
</script>

<p class=RIGHT>This text is aligned right.</p>

</html>
```

# document.classes.textDecoration

## *JavaScript 1.2+*

## *Nav4+*

## *Syntax*

document.classes.*className*.*tagName*.textDecoration

## *Description*

The textDecoration property specifies the type of decoration that is added to text as associated with the class called *className*. The definition can also specify a tag or the word all for *tagName*.

There are four types of values that are valid for the textDecoration property: underline, line-through, blink, and none.

## *Example*

Listing 7.90 uses the textDecoration property to put a line through a line of text.

*Listing 7.90    Set the textDecoration Property*

```
<html>

<script>
<!-- Hide

//Create a style sheet class that defines text decoration
document.classes.CROSSOUT.all.textDecoration = "line-through";

//Hide End --->
</script>

<p class=CROSSOUT>This text is crossed out.</p>

</html>
```

# document.classes.textIndent

## *JavaScript 1.2+*

## *Nav4+*

## *Syntax*

```
document.classes.className.tagName.textIndent
```

## *Description*

The `textIndent` property specifies the indention should appear before text as associated with the `class` called *className*. The definition can also specify a tag or the word `all` for *tagName*. The property is assigned a number that represents either length or a percentage.

## *Example*

Listing 7.91 uses the `textIndent` property to set the text indention to 1 inch.

*Listing 7.91    Set the `textIndent` Property*

```
<html>

<script>
<!-- Hide

//Create a style sheet class that defines text indention
document.classes.INDENT.all.textIndent = "1in";

//Hide End --->
</script>

<p>This text has no indention.</p>
<p class=INDENT>This text is indented 1 inch.</p>

</html>
```

# document.classes.textTransform

## *JavaScript 1.2+*

## *Nav4+*

## *Syntax*

```
document.classes.className.tagName.textTransform
```

## *Description*

The `textTransform` property specifies the transformation that should be applied to text as associated with the `class` called *className*. The definition can also specify a tag or the word `all` for *tagName*.

There are four types of values that are valid for the `textTransform` property: `capitalize`, `uppercase`, `lowercase`, and `none`.

## Example

Listing 7.92 uses the `textTransform` property to capitalize the first letter of every word in the sentence.

*Listing 7.92    Set the `textTransform` Property*

```
<html>

<script>
<!-- Hide

//Create a style sheet class that defines capitalization
document.classes.CAP.all.textTransform = "capitalize";

//Hide End --->
</script>

<p class=CAP>This line demonstrates the ability to capitalize words.</p>

</html>
```

# document.classes.whiteSpace

## JavaScript 1.2+

## Nav4+

## Syntax

`document.classes.className.tagName.whiteSpace`

## Description

The `whiteSpace` property specifies how whitespace should be handled within an element. Using dot notation, the property can be associated with the `class` called `className`. The definition can also specify a tag or the word `all` for `tagName`.

There are two types of values that are valid for the `whiteSpace` property: `normal` and `pre`.

## Example

Listing 7.93 uses the `whiteSpace` property to make whitespace collapsed within the text element.

*Listing 7.93    Set the `whiteSpace` Property*

```
<html>

<script>
```

*continues*

*Listing 7.93    continued*

```
<!-- Hide

//Create a style sheet class that defines white space
document.classes.NOPRE.all.whiteSpace = "normal";

//Hide End --->
</script>

<p><pre>This line used to PRE tag to format white space.</pre></p>
<p class=NOPRE>This line should have collapsed white space.</p>

</html>
```

# document.close()

## *JavaScript 1.0+, JScript 1.0+*

## *Nav2+, IE 3+, Opera3+*

## Syntax

```
document.close()
```

## Description

The `close()` method closes the output stream to the document. Any output that has not been written prior to calling the method will be displayed.

## Example

Listing 7.94 uses the `close()` method to close the output stream to a document. Notice that a portion of the last paragraph is not displayed until after the `close()` method is called and the alert box has been displayed.

*Listing 7.94    Close Document Output Stream with `close()` Method*

```
<html>

<script>
<!-- Hide

//Write some text to the screen and then close the document.
document.write("This line is a long line that should wrap around the ");
document.write("browser.  If it does not wrap around the screen then ");
document.write("resize your browser window so that it does wrap and ");
document.write("reexecute this code.<br>");


//Close document and write all lines that are currently in the buffer
document.close();

//Write another paragraph
```

```
document.write("If the paragraph above wrapped around the browser then ");
document.write("you will notice that this paragraph was only written after ");
document.write("the close method was called.");

//Create an alert box so you can see where the close operation takes place.
alert("Press to continue");

//Hide End --->
</script>

</html>
```

# document.cookie

## JavaScript 1.0+, JScript 1.0+

## Nav2+, IE 3+

## Syntax

```
document.cookie
```

## Description

The `cookie` property provides the ability to read and write cookies. A cookie represents a small amount of data that a Web browser stores to allow information to be shared among Web pages

## Example

Listing 7.95 creates a cookie and then reads back the result.

*Listing 7.95    Create a Cookie and Read It back Using the `cookie` Property*

```
<html>

<script>
<!-- Hide

//Create a cookie
document.cookie = "temperature=75";

//Display the contents of the cookie
document.write("The cookie contains: ",document.cookie);

//Hide End --->
</script>

</html>
```

# document.domain

## JavaScript 1.1+, JScript 1.0+

## Nav3+, IE 3+, Opera3+

### Syntax

```
document.domain
```

### Description

The `domain` property initially contains the hostname of the server from which the document was loaded. The document is allowed to change the value to the domain minus the prefix. For example, if a Web page originated from *www.example.com*, the document could change this to *example.com*. The reason this is allowed is so different pages that come from different servers within the same Web site can share properties. The restrictive quality of this property keeps unrelated documents from wrongfully seeing the data each document might have collected.

### Example

No example is provided, because the document would have to originate from a server that has a domain name for this property not to be empty.

# document.embeds

## JavaScript 1.1+, JScript 1.0+

## Nav3+, IE 3+, Opera3+

### Syntax

```
document.embeds
document.embeds[index]
```

### Description

The `embeds` property is an array that contains all the embedded objects and plug-ins that appear within the HTML document from using the `<embed>` tag. The `embeds` property has one property of its own, called `length`, which contains the number of items in the array. The *index* number ranges from zero to the `length` minus one.

> **NOTE**
>
> The `embeds` array property accesses the same data as the `document.plugins` array property.

### Example

Listing 7.96 uses the `length` property to display the number of embedded objects in a HTML document.

*Listing 7.96    List the Number of Embedded Objects*

```
<html>

<h2>Learn your shapes</h2>
```

```
<h2>A Circle</h2>
<embed src="circle.gif">

<h2>A Square</h2>
<embed src="square.gif">

<script language="JavaScript">
<!-- Hide

//Display the length of the embeds array.
document.write(document.embeds.length," embedded objects.");

//Hide End --->
</script>

</html>
```

# document.embeds.length

## *JavaScript 1.1+, JScript 1.0+*

## *Nav3+, IE 3+, Opera3+*

## *Syntax*

```
document.embeds.length
```

## *Description*

The length property contains the number of objects that are in the embeds[] array.

## *Example*

Listing 7.97 uses the length property to display the number of embedded objects in an HTML document.

*Listing 7.97    List the Number of Embedded Objects*
```
<html>

<h2>A Circle</h2>
<embed src="circle.gif">

<h2>A Square</h2>
<embed src="square.gif">

<script language="JavaScript">
<!-- Hide

//Display the length of the embeds array.
document.write(document.embeds.length," embedded objects.");
```

*continues*

*Listing 7.97   continued*

```
//Hide End --->
</script>

</html>
```

# document.fgColor

## *JavaScript 1.0+, JScript 1.0+*

## *Nav2+, IE 3+, Opera3+*

## *Syntax*

```
document.fgColor
```

## *Description*

The `fgColor` property specifies the default text color of all the text that appears in a Web document. This is equivalent to assigning the color to the `text` attribute in the `<body>` tag. The color is expressed as a string in hexadecimal digits or as one of the JavaScript standard color names. The hexadecimal form is made up of 6 digits that follow the pattern "RRGGBB."

## *Example*

Listing 7.98 sets the default color of all the text on the page to blue.

*Listing 7.98   Set the Text Color with the `fgColor` Property*

```
<html>

<script language="JavaScript">
<!-- Hide

//Set the text color to blue.
document.fgColor="0000ff";

//Hide End --->
</script>

<body>
The color of all text on this page is blue.
</body>

</html>
```

# document.forms

## *JavaScript 1.0+, JScript 1.0+*

## *Nav2+, IE 3+, Opera3+*

## Syntax

```
document.forms
document.forms[index]
```

## Description

The forms property is an array that contains all the forms that exist within the HTML document from using the <form> tag. The forms property has one property of its own, called length, which contains the number of items in the array. The *index* number ranges from zero to the length minus one.

## Example

Listing 7.99 accesses the names of each form using the forms[] array.

*Listing 7.99    Accesses Form Names Using the forms Array*

```
<html>

<form name="Form1">
  <input type="button"
         value="Green"
         onClick = "document.bgColor='green'">
</form>
<form name="Form2">
  <input type="button"
         value="Blue"
         onClick = "document.bgColor='blue'">
</form>

<script language="JavaScript">
<!-- Hide

//Display the name of the form objects.
for(i=0;i<document.forms.length;i++)
{
  document.write("The name of form object ",(i+1));
  document.write(" is <i><b>",document.forms[i].name,"</b></i><br>");
}

//Hide End --->
</script>

</html>
```

# document.forms.length

## *JavaScript 1.0+, JScript 1.0+*

## *Nav2+, IE 3+, Opera3+*

## Syntax

```
document.forms.length
```

## Description

The `length` property contains the number of `Form` objects that are in the `forms[]` array.

## Example

Listing 7.100 uses the `length` property to display the number of `Form` objects in the document.

*Listing 7.100   Access the Number of Forms in the Document with the `length` Property*

```html
<html>

<form name="Form1">
  <input type="button"
         value="Green"
         onClick = "document.bgColor='green'">
</form>
<form name="Form2">
  <input type="button"
         value="Blue"
         onClick = "document.bgColor='blue'">
</form>

<script language="JavaScript">
<!-- Hide

//How many items in forms[] array?
document.write(document.forms.length," Form objects in document.");

//Hide End --->
</script>

</html>
```

# document.getSelection()

## JavaScript 1.2+

## Nav4+

## Syntax

```
document.getSelection()
```

## Description

The `getSelection()` method returns the text that is selected within the HTML document.

## Example

Listing 7.101 uses the `getSelection()` method to display all captured text in a text box. The result of selecting JavaScript is Great! from the text is shown in Figure 7.7.

*Listing 7.101   Displaying the Selected Text*

```html
<html>

The following text area will display any text that you
select within the Web page.  Try selecting the phrase
"JavaScript is Great!" with the mouse.

<form name="Form1">
  <input type="text"
         name="TextArea">
</form>

<script language="JavaScript">
<!-- Hide

//Fill in textarea when mouse button is released
document.captureEvents(Event.MOUSEUP);
document.onmouseup = function(event){document.Form1.TextArea.value =
document.getSelection()};

//Hide End --->
</script>

</html>
```

**Figure 7.7**

*Selecting a portion of text and displaying it in a text box.*

# document.handleEvent()

## *JavaScript 1.2+*

## *Nav4+*

## Syntax

```
document.handleEvent(event)
```

## Description

The handleEvent() method provides a way to invoke a document's event handler, even though the event never happened. The argument associated with this method is listed in Table 7.15.

*Table 7.15    Argument associated with the handleEvent() method.*

| Type | Item | Description |
|------|------|-------------|
| Argument | event | An event object to be handled |

## Example

In Listing 7.102, an event handler is designated to handle all document Click events. When the user selects the button labeled 9, the eventHandler() method is used to route the event to the document's event handler.

*Listing 7.102    Pass Events to Document with the handleEvent() Method*

```
<html>

<h2>Math Quiz</h2>

What is 6+3?

<form name="answerForm">
  <input type="button"
         value="   8   "
         name="answer8"
         onClick="alert('Incorrect. Try again.')">
  <input type="button"
         value="   9   "
         name="answer9"
         onClick="document.handleEvent(event)">
</form>

<script language="JavaScript">
<!-- Hide

//Function designated to handle click events
function clickHandler(event)
{
  //Display an alert box
  alert("A click event occured within the document.");
}

//Register the Click event with the document event handler
document.onClick = clickHandler;
```

```
//Hide End --->
</script>

</html>
```

# document.ids

## *JavaScript 1.2+,*

## *Nav4+*

## *Syntax*

```
document.ids.idName
```

## *Description*

The ids property is an associative array that contains IDs associated with Netscape style sheets. Using dot notation, *idName* specifies an ID associated with a style. The style sheet IDs are created within the <style> or <script> tags using JavaScript or HTML.

**NOTE**

> When creating an ID, make sure the declaration appears before the new ID is used, because many HTML objects cannot be changed after they have been created in the document.

**NOTE**

> If JavaScript dot notation is used when creating a new ID within <style> tags, document does not have to be specified.

## *Example*

Listing 7.103 demonstrates three different ways to create style sheet IDs using JavaScript and HTML within <style> and <script> tags. Notice how the order in which the IDs are declared and used ultimately affects the style result.

*Listing 7.103    Creating Style Sheet IDs*

```
<html>

<style type="text/css">
  #TEXTFORMAT {font-style: italic;}
</style>

<p id=TEXTFORMAT>After first STYLE tag.<p>

<style type="text/javascript">
```

*continues*

*Listing 7.103    continued*

```
  ids.TEXTFORMAT.fontWeight = "bold";
</style>

<p id=TEXTFORMAT>After second STYLE tag.<p>

<script>
<!-- Hide
document.ids.TEXTFORMAT.textDecoration = "underline";
//Hide End --->
</script>

<p id=TEXTFORMAT>After SCRIPT tag.<p>

</html>
```

# document.ids.align

## JavaScript 1.2+

## Nav4+

## Syntax

```
document.ids.idName.align
```

## Description

The `align` property specifies the alignment of an element within its parent as associated with the ID called *idName*.

The `align` property can be assigned one of the following values: `left`, `right`, or `none`.

### NOTE

The `align` property is referred to as `float` when using CSS syntax. JavaScript could not use the word "float" because it was a reserved word.

## Example

Listing 7.104 uses the `align` property to align a paragraph to the right of its parent, the document.

*Listing 7.104    Aligning Right with the `align` Property*

```
<html>

<script>
<!-- Hide

//Create a style sheet id that aligns right
document.ids.RIGHT.align = "right";
```

```
//Hide End --->
</script>

<p id=RIGHT>Send me to the right!</p>

<p>Where am I?</p>

</html>
```

# document.ids.backgroundColor

## *JavaScript 1.2+*

## *Nav4+*

## *Syntax*

`document.ids.`*idName*`.backgroundColor`

## Description

The `backgroundColor` property specifies the background color associated with the ID called *idName*.

## Example

Listing 7.105 uses the `backgroundColor` property to make the background color around an anchor red.

*Listing 7.105    Setting the Background Color with the `backgroundColor` Property*

```
<html>

<script>
<!-- Hide

//Create a style sheet id that contains the background color
document.ids.BG.backgroundColor = "red";

//Hide End --->
</script>

<a id=BG name="THIS">This</a> is an anchor that uses
styles from the BG id.

</html>
```

# document.ids.backgroundImage

## *JavaScript 1.2+*

## *Nav4+*

## Syntax

```
document.ids.idName.backgroundImage
```

## Description

The `backgroundImage` property specifies the background image of an element as associated with the ID called *idName*.

## Example

The code in Listing 7.106 makes the image `logo.gif` the background for the header text.

*Listing 7.106    Setting the Background Image with the `backgroundImage` Property*

```
<html>

<script>
<!-- Hide

//Create a style sheet id that uses an image as a background
document.ids.BGI.backgroundImage = "logo.gif";

//Hide End --->
</script>

<h2 id=BGI>Look at my background image!</h2>

</html>
```

# document.ids.borderBottomWidth

## JavaScript 1.2+

## Nav4+

## Syntax

```
document.ids.idName.borderBottomWidth
```

## Description

The `borderBottomWidth` property specifies the width of the bottom border of an element as associated with the ID called *idName*.

## Example

Listing 7.107 uses the `borderBottomWidth` property to set the size of bottom border that surrounds a text header. Notice that only the bottom portion of the border is shown.

*Listing 7.107    Setting the Bottom Border Width with the `borderBottomWidth` Property*

```
<html>

<script>
```

```
<!-- Hide

//Create a style sheet id that creates a bottom border
document.ids.BBW.borderBottomWidth = "10";

//Hide End --->
</script>

<h2 id=BBW>This text has a bottom border</h2>

</html>
```

# document.ids.borderColor

## JavaScript 1.2+

## Nav4+

## Syntax

```
document.ids.idName.borderColor
```

## Description

The borderColor property specifies the color of the border of an element as associated with the ID called idName.

## Example

Listing 7.108 uses the borderColor property to set the color of the border that surrounds a text header to blue.

Listing 7.108    *Setting the Border Color with the borderColor Property*

```
<html>

<script>
<!-- Hide

//Create a style sheet id that creates a left border
document.ids.ABORDER.borderWidths(10);
document.ids.ABORDER.borderColor = "blue";

//Hide End --->
</script>

<h2 id=ABORDER>This text has a blue border</h2>

</html>
```

# document.ids.borderLeftWidth

## JavaScript 1.2+

## *Nav4+*

### *Syntax*

```
document.ids.idName.borderLeftWidth
```

### *Description*

The `borderLeftWidth` property specifies the width of the left border of an element as associated with the ID called *idName*.

### *Example*

Listing 7.109 uses the `borderLeftWidth` property to set the size of left border that surrounds a text header. Notice that only the left portion of the border is shown.

*Listing 7.109   Setting the Left Border Width with the `borderLeftWidth` Property*

```
<html>

<script>
<!-- Hide

//Create a style sheet id that creates a left border
document.ids.BLW.borderLeftWidth = "10";

//Hide End --->
</script>

<h2 id=BLW>This text has a left border</h2>

</html>
```

# document.ids.borderRightWidth

## *JavaScript 1.2+*

## *Nav4+*

### *Syntax*

```
document.ids.idName.borderRightWidth
```

### *Description*

The `borderRightWidth` property specifies the width of the right border of an element as associated with the ID called *idName*.

### *Example*

Listing 7.110 uses the `borderRightWidth` property to set the size of right border that surrounds a text header. Notice that only the right portion of the border is shown.

*Listing 7.110   Setting the Right Border Width with the `borderRightWidth` Property*

```
<html>
```

```
<script>
<!-- Hide

//Create a style sheet id that creates a right border
document.ids.BRW.borderRightWidth = "10";

//Hide End --->
</script>

<h2 id=BRW>This text has a right border</h2>

</html>
```

# document.ids.borderStyle
## *JavaScript 1.2+*
## *Nav4+*

## *Syntax*

```
document.ids.idName.borderStyle
```

## *Description*

The borderStyle property specifies the style of the border that surrounds an element as associated with the ID called *idName*.

The borderStyle property can be assigned one of the following values: none, solid, double, inset, outset, groove, and ridge.

## *Example*

Listing 7.111 uses borderStyle property to set the border around a text header to a double line.

*Listing 7.111    Setting the Border Style with the borderStyle Property*

```
<html>

<script>
<!-- Hide

//Create a style sheet id that creates a double border
document.ids.ABORDER.borderWidths(10);
document.ids.ABORDER.borderColor = "red";
document.ids.ABORDER.borderStyle = "double";

//Hide End --->
</script>

<h2 id=ABORDER>This text has a double border</h2>

</html>
```

# document.ids.borderTopWidth

## JavaScript 1.2+

## Nav4+

## Syntax

```
document.ids.idName.borderTopWidth
```

## Description

The `borderTopWidth` property specifies the width of the top border of an element as associated with the ID called *idName*.

## Example

Listing 7.112 uses the `borderTopWidth` property to set the size of top border that surrounds a text header. Notice that only the top portion of the border is shown.

*Listing 7.112    Setting the Top Border Width with the `borderTopWidth` Property*

```
<html>

<script>
<!-- Hide

//Create a style sheet id that creates a top border
document.ids.BTW.borderTopWidth = "10";

//Hide End --->
</script>

<h2 id=BTW>This text has a top border</h2>

</html>
```

# document.ids.borderWidths()

## JavaScript 1.2+

## Nav4+

## Syntax

```
document.ids.idName.borderWidths(top,right,bottom,left)
document.ids.idName.borderWidths(top-bottom,right-left)
document.ids.idName.borderWidths(all)
```

## Description

The `borderWidths()` method specifies the width of the border that surrounds an element as associated with the ID called *idName*. Setting border widths is equivalent to setting the `borderBottomWidth`, `borderLeftWidth`, `borderRightWidth`, and `borderTopWidth` properties. Table 7.16 lists all the arguments associated with the `borderWidths()` method.

**Table 7.16   Arguments Associated with the borderWidths() Method**

| Item | Description |
| --- | --- |
| `top` | Width of the top border |
| `right` | Width of the right border |
| `left` | Width of the left border |
| `bottom` | Width of the bottom border |
| `top-bottom` | Width of both the top and bottom border |
| `left-right` | Width of both the left and right border |
| all | Width of all four sides of the border |

## Example

Listing 7.113 uses the `borderWidths()` method to set the width of the border that surrounds a text header.

*Listing 7.113   Setting All the Border Widths with the `borderWidths()` Method*

```
<html>

<script>
<!-- Hide

//Create a style sheet id that creates a border
document.ids.ABORDER.borderWidths(5,10,15,20);

//Hide End --->
</script>

<h2 id=ABORDER>This text has a border</h2>

</html>
```

# document.ids.clear

## JavaScript 1.2+

## Nav4+

## Syntax

`document.ids.idName.clear`

## Description

The `clear` property specifies the sides of an element where floating elements (elements that define the align property) are not allowed. Using dot notation, this property is associated with the ID called *idName*.

The clear property can be assigned one of the following values: left, right, both, and none.

## Example

Listing 7.114 uses the clear property to prevent floating elements from being on either side.

*Listing 7.114    Using the clear Property*

```
<html>

<script>
<!-- Hide

//Create a style sheet classes and id that set alignments
document.classes.LEFT.all.align = "left";
document.classes.LEFT.all.backgroundColor = "yellow";
document.classes.RIGHT.all.align = "right";
document.classes.RIGHT.all.backgroundColor = "red";
document.ids.KEEPAWAY.clear = "both";

//Hide End --->
</script>

<p class=LEFT>Send me to the left!</p>
<p class=RIGHT>Send me to the right!</p>
<p>I like other elements next to me!</p>

<p class=LEFT>Send me to the left!</p>
<p class=RIGHT>Send me to the right!</p>
<p id=KEEPAWAY>I don't like other elements next to me!</p>

</html>
```

# document.ids.color

## *JavaScript 1.2+*

## *Nav4+*

## *Syntax*

```
document.ids.idName.color
```

## Description

The color property specifies foreground color of an element as associated with the ID called *idName*.

## Example

Listing 7.115 uses the color property to set the color of various text.

*Listing 7.115   Set the Color of Text Using the* `color` *Property*

```
<html>

<script>
<!-- Hide

//Create a style sheet classes that defines colors
document.ids.BLUE.color = "blue";
document.ids.RED.color = "red";

//Hide End --->
</script>

<p id=BLUE>The blue boat floated on the blue ocean.</p>
<p id=RED>The red car stopped at a red stop sign.</p>

</html>
```

# document.ids.display

## JavaScript 1.2+

## Nav4+

## Syntax

```
document.ids.idName.display
```

## Description

The `display` property specifies an element to be displayed when associated with the ID called *idName*.

The `display` property can be assigned one of the following values: `inline`, `block`, `list-item`, and `none`.

Specifying an `inline` value is equivalent to using the <em> tag. The `block` value is the same as creating header text with the <h> tag. Using `list-item` is equivalent to using the <li> tag. If `none` is specified, the element is not displayed.

## Example

Listing 7.116 uses the `display` property to create header text. `block` consists of a line break and resetting margins to their default values. Notice that in this example a carriage return is automatically entered before the bold tag.

*Listing 7.116   Set the* `display` *Property*

```
<html>

<script>
<!-- Hide
```

*continues*

*Listing 7.116   continued*

```
//Create a style sheet id that defines a block display
document.ids.H.display = "block";

//Hide End --->
</script>

<u id=H>A BIG HEADER</u>

Just some regular text following the Big Header.

</html>
```

# document.ids.fontFamily

## *JavaScript 1.2+*

## *Nav4+*

## *Syntax*

```
document.ids.idName.fontFamily
```

## *Description*

The `fontFamily` property specifies the font an element should use when associated with the ID called *idName*. More than one font can be specified, in case a particular font has not been loaded.

## *Example*

Listing 7.117 uses the `fontFamily` property to create text with an Arial font. If that font is not available, Helvetica is used.

*Listing 7.117   Set the `fontFamily` Property*

```
<html>

<script>
<!-- Hide

//Create a style sheet id that defines a font
document.ids.F.fontFamily = "Arial, Helvetica";

//Hide End --->
</script>

<p id=F>Do you like this font?</p>

</html>
```

# document.ids.fontSize

## *JavaScript 1.2+*

## *Nav4+*

## *Syntax*

document.ids.*idName*.fontSize

## *Description*

The fontSize property specifies the size of fonts used by an element when associated with the ID called *idName*. The values that can be used to set font size can be divided into four categories, as shown in Table 7.17.

### *Table 7.17    Font Sizes*

| Category | Value |
|---|---|
| Absolute | xx-small |
| | x-small |
| | small |
| | medium |
| | large |
| | x-large |
| | xx-large |
| Relative | smaller (relative font size of parent) |
| | larger (relative font size of parent) |
| Length | A number followed by a unit of measurement |
| Percentage | The size relative to font size of parent |

## *Example*

Listing 7.118 uses absolute font sizing to define the fontSize property and associate with text.

*Listing 7.118    Set the fontSize Property*

```
<html>

<script>
<!-- Hide

//Create a style sheet id that defines a font size
document.ids.XXS.fontSize = "xx-small";
document.ids.XXL.fontSize = "xx-large";

//Hide End --->
</script>
```

*continues*

*Listing 7.118 continued*

```
<p id=XXS>Extra, extra small text</p>
<p id=XXL>Extra, extra large text</p>

</html>
```

# document.ids.fontStyle

## *JavaScript 1.2+*

## *Nav4+*

## *Syntax*

```
document.ids.idName.fontStyle
```

## **Description**

The fontStyle property specifies the font style used by an element when associated with the ID called *idName*.

The fontStyle property can be assigned one of the following values: normal or italic.

## *Example*

Listing 7.119 uses fontStyle property to italicize the header text.

*Listing 7.119   Set the fontStyle Property*

```
<html>

<script>
<!-- Hide

//Create a style sheet id that defines a font style
document.ids.I.fontStyle = "italic";

//Hide End --->
</script>

<h2 id=I>Italicized Heading</h2>

</html>
```

# document.ids.fontWeight

## *JavaScript 1.2+*

## *Nav4+*

## *Syntax*

```
document.ids.idName.fontWeight
```

## Description

The `fontWeight` property specifies the font weight used by an element when associated with the ID called *idName*.

The `fontStyle` property can be assigned one of the following values: `normal`, `bold`, `bolder`, `lighter`, or a number from 100 to 900.

## Example

Listing 7.120 uses the `fontWeight` property to set different levels of weight on various text.

*Listing 7.120    Set the `fontWeight` Property*

```
<html>

<script>
<!-- Hide

//Create a style sheet id that defines a font style
document.ids.W1.fontWeight = 100;
document.ids.W4.fontWeight = 400;
document.ids.W9.fontWeight = 900;

//Hide End --->
</script>

<p id=W1>Font weight of 100</p>
<p id=W4>Font weight of 400</p>
<p id=W9>Font weight of 900</p>

</html>
```

# document.ids.lineHeight

## JavaScript 1.2+

## Nav4+

## Syntax

`document.ids.`*idName*`.lineHeight`

## Description

The `lineHeight` property specifies the distance between two lines that are next to each other. Using dot notation, the property is associated with the ID called *idName*.

There are four types of values that are valid for the `lineHeight` property: `number`, `length`, `percentage`, and the value `normal`.

When a number is given without a unit of measure, it is multiplied by the font size of the element to give the line height. Length is specified by including a unit of measure after the number. A percentage is designated by including a percent sign (%) after the number to represent the line height as it relates to its parent.

## Example

Listing 7.121 uses the lineHeight property to set the distance between lines.

*Listing 7.121    Set the lineHeight Property*

```html
<html>

<script>
<!-- Hide

//Create a style sheet id that defines a line height
document.ids.D1.lineHeight = "1in";
document.ids.D2.lineHeight = "50pt";

//Hide End --->
</script>

<p>This is the first line of text</p>
<p id=D1>This is a second line of text.</p>
<p>This is a third line of text.</p>
<p id=D2>This is a fourth line of text.</p>
<p>This is a fifth line of text.</p>

</html>
```

# document.ids.listStyleType

## JavaScript 1.2+

## Nav4+

## Syntax

document.ids.*idName*.listStyleType

## Description

The listStyleType property specifies the format of list items elements that are associated with the ID called *idName*.

There are nine types of values that are valid for the listStyleType property: disc, circle, square, decimal, lower-roman, upper-roman, lower-alpha, upper-alpha, and none.

### NOTE

The listStyleType property is only valid if the element also has the display property set to list-item.

## Example

Listing 7.122 uses the `listStyleType` property to format a list of items.

*Listing 7.122   Set the `listStyleType` Property*

```
<html>

<script>
<!-- Hide

//Create a style sheet class and id that define a list format
document.classes.LIST.all.display = "list-item";
document.ids.FORMAT.listStyleType = "upper-roman";

//Hide End --->
</script>

<h2>Presentation Outline</h2>

<ol class=LIST id=FORMAT>
  <li>Introduction
  <li>Overview of new product
  <li>Cost of product
  <li>Conclusion
</ol>

</html>
```

# document.ids.marginBottom

## JavaScript 1.2+

## Nav4+

## Syntax

document.ids.*idName*.marginBottom

## Description

The `marginBottom` property specifies the distance between the bottom border of an element and the top border of another element. Dot notation is used to associate this property with the ID called *idName*.

## Example

Listing 7.123 uses the `marginBottom` property to set the distance between adjacent elements.

*Listing 7.123    Set the Bottom Margin with the `marginBottom` Property*

```
<html>

<script>
<!-- Hide

//Create a style sheet class and id that define the bottom margin
document.classes.FORMAT.all.borderWidths(10);
document.ids.margin.marginBottom = 40;

//Hide End --->
</script>

<b>My margins are set automatically</b>
<b class=FORMAT ID=margin>I have a large bottom margin!</b>
<b>My margins are set automatically</b>

</html>
```

# document.ids.marginLeft

## *JavaScript 1.2+*

## *Nav4+*

## *Syntax*

```
document.ids.idName.marginLeft
```

## Description

The `marginLeft` property specifies the distance between the left border of an element and the right border of another element. Dot notation is used to associate this property with the ID called *idName*.

## Example

Listing 7.124 uses the `marginLeft` property to set the distance between adjacent elements. Notice the distance between the border and the right edge of the browser window.

*Listing 7.124    Set the Left Margin with the `marginLeft` Property*

```
<html>

<script>
<!-- Hide

//Create a style sheet id that defines the left margin
document.classes.FORMAT1.all.borderWidths(10);
document.ids.margin.marginLeft = 40;
document.classes.FORMAT2.all.borderWidths(10);
```

```
//Hide End --->
</script>

<p class=FORMAT1 id=margin>I have a large left margin!</p>
<p class=FORMAT2>I have an automatic left margin</p>

</html>
```

# document.ids.marginRight

## JavaScript 1.2+

## Nav4+

## Syntax

```
document.ids.idName.marginRight
```

## Description

The `marginRight` property specifies the distance between the right border of an element and the left border of another element. Dot notation is used to associate this property with the ID called `idName`.

## Example

Listing 7.125 uses the `marginRight` property to set the distance between adjacent elements. Notice the distance between the border and the right edge of the browser window.

*Listing 7.125   Set the Right Margin with the `marginRight` Property*

```
<html>

<script>
<!-- Hide

//Create a style sheet id that defines the right margin
document.classes.FORMAT.all.borderWidths(10);
document.ids.margin1.marginRight = 40;
document.ids.margin2.marginRight = 0;

//Hide End --->
</script>

<p class=FORMAT id=margin1>I have a large right margin!</p>
<p class=FORMAT id=margin2>I have no right margin</p>

</html>
```

# document.ids.margins()

## JavaScript 1.2+

## *Nav4+*

## *Syntax*

```
document.ids.idName.margins(top,right,bottom,left)
document.ids.idName.margins(top-bottom,right-left)
document.ids.idName.margins(all)
```

## *Description*

The margins() method specifies the margin distance between border of an element and the border of adjacent elements. Dot notation is used to associate the property with the ID called *idName*. Setting margin widths is equivalent to setting the marginBottom, marginLeft, marginRight, and marginTop properties. Table 7.18 lists all the arguments associated with the margins() method.

*Table 7.18   Arguments Associated with the margins() Method*

| Item | Description |
|---|---|
| top | Width of the top margin |
| right | Width of the right margin |
| left | Width of the left margin |
| bottom | Width of the bottom margin |
| top-bottom | Width of both the top and bottom margins |
| left-right | Width of both the left and right margins |
| all | Width of all four margins |

## *Example*

Listing 7.126 uses the margins() method to set the margin widths around a text element.

*Listing 7.126   All Margins Set with the margins() Method*

```
<html>

<script>
<!-- Hide

//Create a style sheet id that defines the margins
document.classes.FORMAT.all.borderWidths(10);
document.ids.margin.margins(50);

//Hide End --->
</script>

<h2 CLASS=FORMAT ID=margin>This text has margins set to 50</h2>

</html>
```

# document.ids.marginTop

## JavaScript 1.2+

## Nav4+

## Syntax

document.ids.*idName*.marginTop

## Description

The marginTop property specifies the distance between the top border of an element and the bottom border of another element. Dot notation is used to associate this property with the ID called *idName*.

## Example

Listing 7.127 uses the marginTop property to set the distance between adjacent elements.

Listing 7.127    *Set the Top Margin with the marginTop Property*

```
<html>

<script>
<!-- Hide

//Create a style sheet id that defines the top margin
document.classes.FORMAT.all.borderWidths(10);
document.ids.margin.marginTop = 40;

//Hide End --->
</script>

<b>My margins are set automatically</b>
<b class=FORMAT id=margin>I have a large top margin!</b>
<b>My margins are set automatically</b>

</html>
```

# document.ids.paddingBottom

## JavaScript 1.2+

## Nav4+

## Syntax

document.ids.*idName*.paddingBottom

## Description

The `paddingBottom` property specifies the distance between the bottom border of an element and its content. Using dot notation, the property is associated with the ID called *idName*.

## Example

Listing 7.128 uses the `paddingBottom` property to set the distance between a line of text and its border.

*Listing 7.128    Set the Bottom Padding with the `paddingBottom` Property*

```
<html>

<script>
<!-- Hide

//Create a style sheet id that defines the bottom padding
document.classes.FORMAT.all.borderWidths(10)
document.ids.PAD.paddingBottom = "40";

//Hide End --->
</script>

<p class=FORMAT id=PAD>This text has extra padding on the bottom.</p>

</html>
```

# document.ids.paddingLeft

## JavaScript 1.2+

## Nav4+

## Syntax

```
document.ids.idName.paddingLeft
```

## Description

The `paddingLeft` property specifies the distance between the left border of an element and its content. Using dot notation, the property is associated with the ID called *idName*.

## Example

Listing 7.129 uses the `paddingLeft` property to set the distance between a line of text and its border.

*Listing 7.129    Set the Left Padding with the `paddingLeft` Property*

```
<html>

<script>
<!-- Hide
```

```
//Create a style sheet id that defines the left padding
document.classes.FORMAT.all.borderWidths(10)
document.ids.PAD.paddingLeft = "40";

//Hide End --->
</script>

<p CLASS=FORMAT ID=PAD>This text has extra padding on the left.</p>

</html>
```

# document.ids.paddingRight

## *JavaScript 1.2+*

## *Nav4+*

## *Syntax*

```
document.ids.idName.paddingRight
```

## *Description*

The paddingRight property specifies the distance between the right border of an element and its content. Using dot notation, the property is associated with the ID called *idName*.

## *Example*

Listing 7.130 uses the paddingRight property to set the distance between a line of text and its border.

*Listing 7.130   Set the Right Padding with the paddingRight Property*

```
<html>

<script>
<!-- Hide

//Create a style sheet id that defines the right padding
document.classes.FORMAT.all.borderWidths(10)
document.ids.PAD.paddingRight = "40";

//Hide End --->
</script>

<p class=FORMAT id=PAD>This text has extra padding on the right.</p>

</html>
```

# document.ids.paddings()

## *JavaScript 1.2+*

## *Nav4+*

## *Syntax*

```
document.ids.idName.paddings(top,right,bottom,left)
document.ids.idName.paddings(top-bottom,right-left)
document.ids.idName.paddings(all)
```

## *Description*

The paddings() method specifies the distance between the borders of an element and its content. Using dot notation, the property is associated with the ID called *idName*. Setting the sizes is equivalent to setting the paddingBottom, paddingLeft, paddingRight, and paddingTop properties. Table 7.19 lists all the arguments associated with this method.

**Table 7.19    Arguments Associated with the paddings() Method**

| Item | Description |
| --- | --- |
| top | Padding between top border and content |
| right | Padding between right border and content |
| left | Padding between left border and content |
| bottom | Padding between bottom border and content |
| top-bottom | Padding between the content and both the top and bottom borders |
| left-right | Padding between the content and both the left and right borders |
| all | Padding between content and all four sides of the border |

## *Example*

Listing 7.131 uses the paddings() method to set the distance between text and all sides of its border.

*Listing 7.131    Set All Paddings with the paddings() Method*

```
<html>

<script>
<!-- Hide

//Create a style sheet id that defines all paddings
document.classes.FORMAT.all.borderWidths(5);
document.ids.PAD.paddings(0,20,40,60);

//Hide End --->
</script>

<p class=FORMAT id=PAD>This text has padding on all sides of its border.</p>

</html>
```

# document.ids.paddingTop

## JavaScript 1.2+

## Nav4+

## Syntax

```
document.ids.idName.paddingTop
```

## Description

The paddingTop property specifies the distance between the left border of an element and its content. Using dot notation, the property is associated with the ID called idName.

## Example

Listing 7.132 uses the paddingTop property to set the distance between a line of text and its border.

Listing 7.132    Set Top Padding with the paddingTop Property

```
<html>

<script>
<!-- Hide

//Create a style sheet id that defines the top padding
document.classes.FORMAT.all.borderWidths(10)
document.ids.PAD.paddingTop = "40";

//Hide End --->
</script>

<p class=FORMAT id=PAD>This text has extra padding on the top.</p>

</html>
```

# document.ids.textAlign

## JavaScript 1.2+

## Nav4+

## Syntax

```
document.ids.idName.textAlign
```

## Description

The textAlign property specifies the alignment of text within an element as associated with the ID called idName.

There are four types of values that are valid for the textAlign property: left, right, center, and justify.

## Example

Listing 7.133 uses the `textAlign` property to align the text to the right.

*Listing 7.133   Set the `textAlign` Property*

```
<html>

<script>
<!-- Hide

//Create a style sheet id that defines the right alignment
document.classes.FORMAT.all.borderWidths(10)
document.ids.RIGHT.textAlign = "right";

//Hide End --->
</script>

<p class=FORMAT id=RIGHT>This text is aligned right.</p>

</html>
```

# document.ids.textDecoration

## JavaScript 1.2+

## Nav4+

## Syntax

```
document.ids.idName.textDecoration
```

## Description

The `textDecoration` property specifies the type of decoration that is added to text as associated with the ID called *idName*.

There are four types of values that are valid for the `textDecoration` property: under-line, line-through, blink, and none.

## Example

Listing 7.134 uses the `textDecoration` property to put a line through a line of text.

*Listing 7.134   Set the `textDecoration` Property*

```
<html>

<script>
<!-- Hide

//Create a style sheet id that defines the text decoration
document.ids.CROSSOUT.textDecoration = "line-through";

//Hide End --->
</script>
```

```
<p id=CROSSOUT>This text is crossed out.</p>

</html>
```

# document.ids.textIndent

## JavaScript 1.2+

## Nav4+

## Syntax

```
document.ids.idName.textIndent
```

## Description

The textIndent property specifies that the indention should appear before text as associated with the ID called *idName*. The property is assigned a number that represents either length or a percentage.

## Example

Listing 7.135 uses the textIndent property to set the text indention to 1 inch.

Listing 7.135   Set the *textIndent* Property

```
<html>

<script>
<!-- Hide

//Create a style sheet id that defines the text indention
document.ids.INDENT.textIndent = "1in";

//Hide End --->
</script>

<p>This text has no indention.</p>
<p id=INDENT>This text is indented 1 inch.</p>

</html>
```

# document.ids.textTransform

## JavaScript 1.2+

## Nav4+

## Syntax

```
document.ids.idName.textTransform
```

## Description

The textTransform property specifies the transformation that should be applied to text as associated with the ID called *idName*.

There are four types of values that are valid for the textTransform property: capitalize, uppercase, lowercase, and none.

## Example

Listing 7.136 uses the textTransform property to capitalize the first letter of every word in the sentence.

*Listing 7.136    Set the textTransform Property*

```
<html>

<script>
<!-- Hide

//Create a style sheet id that defines capitalization
document.ids.CAP.textTransform = "capitalize";

//Hide End --->
</script>

<p id=CAP>This line demonstrates the ability to capitalize words.</p>

</html>
```

# document.ids.whiteSpace

## JavaScript 1.2+

## Nav4+

## Syntax

```
document.ids.idName.whiteSpace
```

## Description

The whiteSpace property specifies how whitespace should be handled within an element. Using dot notation, the property can be associated with the ID called *idName*.

There are two types of values that are valid for the whiteSpace property: normal and pre.

## Example

Listing 7.137 uses the whiteSpace property to make whitespace collapsed within the text element.

*Listing 7.137    Set the whiteSpace Property*

```
<html>
```

```
<script>
<!-- Hide

//Create a style sheet id that defines whitespace
document.ids.NOPRE.whiteSpace = "normal";

//Hide End --->
</script>

<p><pre>This line used to PRE tag to format whitespace.</pre></p>
<p id=NOPRE>This line should have collapsed whitespace.</p>

</html>
```

# document.images

## *JavaScript 1.1+, JScript 1.0+*

## *Nav3+, IE 3+, Opera3+*

## *Syntax*

```
document.images
document.images[index]
```

## *Description*

The `images` property is an array that contains all the objects that appear within the HTML document from using the `<img>` tag. The `images` property has one property of its own, called `length`, which contains the number of items in the array. The *index* number ranges from zero to the length of the array minus 1.

## *Example*

The code in Listing 7.138 accesses the source of each image using the `images[]` array.

*Listing 7.138   Accessing Images with `images` Array*

```
<html>

<h2>A Circle</h2>
<img src="circle.gif">

<h2>A Square</h2>
<img src="square.gif"><br>

<script language="JavaScript">
<!-- Hide

//Display the source of the image objects.
for(i=0;i<document.images.length;i++)
{
```

*continues*

*Listing 7.138   continued*

```
  document.write("The source of image object ",(i+1));
  document.write(" is <i><b>",document.images[i].src,"</b></i><br>");
}

//Hide End --->
</script>

</html>
```

# document.images.length

## JavaScript 1.1+, JScript 1.0+

## Nav3+, IE 3+

## Syntax

```
document.images.length
```

## Description

The length property contains the number of objects that are in the images[] array.

## Example

The code in Listing 7.139 uses the length property to display the number of images in the HTML document.

*Listing 7.139   Display the Number of Images in Document Using the length Property*

```
<html>

<h2>A Circle</h2>
<img src="circle.gif">

<h2>A Square</h2>
<img src="square.gif"><br>

<script language="JavaScript">
<!-- Hide

//Display the length of the images array.
document.write(document.images.length," image objects.");

//Hide End --->
</script>

</html>
```

# document.lastModified

## *JavaScript 1.0+, JScript 3.0+*
## *Nav2+, IE 3+, Opera3+*

## *Syntax*

```
document.lastModified
```

## *Description*

The lastModified property contains the date and time the document was last modified on the server. This property can be very useful when dealing with documents that contain information that is very date-specific. Be careful when using this date because Web servers are not required to provide this timestamp. If the timestamp is not provided, JavaScript will set the lastModified property to midnight, January 1, 1970 (GMT).

## *Example*

The code in Listing 7.140 lists limited discount prices on clothing, starting when the document was last modified.

*Listing 7.140   Display Prices based on lastModified Property*

```
<html>
<center>
<h2>LIMITED TIME SALE ON CLOTHING</h2>

<script language="JavaScript">
<!-- Hide
document.write("Starting ",document.lastModified," the following ");
document.write("clothing items will be on sale for one week ");
document.write("so order now!<br>");
//Hide End --->
</script>

<table border=ON>
  <tr>
    <th>Item</th>
    <th>Retail Price</th>
    <th>Sale Price</th>
  </tr>
  <tr>
    <td>T-shirt</td>
    <td>$20.00</td>
    <td><font color="RED">$10.99</font></td>
  </tr>
  <tr>
    <td>Jeans</td>
    <td>$60.00</td>
```

*continues*

*Listing 7.140 continued*

```
    <td><font color="RED">$30.99</font></td>
  </tr>
  <tr>
    <td>Hats</td>
    <td>$25.00</td>
    <td><font color="RED">$15.00</font></td>
  </tr>
</table>
</center>

</html>
```

# document.layers

## *JavaScript 1.2+*

## *Nav4+*

## *Syntax*

```
document.layers
document.layers[index]
```

## *Description*

The `layers` property is an array that contains all the objects that appear within the HTML document from using the `<layer>` tag. The `layers` property has one property of its own, called `length`, which contains the number of items in the array. The `index` number ranges from zero to the length.

## *Example*

The code in Listing 7.141 creates two layers and then displays their names at the bottom of the page using the `layers[]` array.

*Listing 7.141 Accessing `Layer` Objects Using the `layers[]` Array*

```
<html>

<layer name="Layer1"
       PAGEX=50
       PAGEY=50
       width=100
       height=100
 bgcolor="blue">Layer 1</layer>
<layer name="Layer2"
       PAGEX=150
       PAGEY=150
       width=100
       height=100
 bgcolor="red">Layer 2</layer>
```

```
<script language="JavaScript">
<!-- Hide

//Display the name of the layer objects.
for(i=0;i<document.layers.length;i++)
{
  document.write("The name of layer object ",(i+1));
  document.write(" is <i><b>",document.layers[i].name,"</b></i><br>");
}

//Hide End --->
</script>

</html>
```

# document.layers.length

## JavaScript 1.2+

## Nav4+

## Syntax

```
document.layers.length
```

## Description

The length property contains the number of objects that are in the layers[] array.

## Example

Listing 7.142 creates two layers and then displays the number of layers on the bottom of the page using the length property.

*Listing 7.142   Display the Number of Layers in the Document*

```
<html>

<layer name="Layer1"
       pagex=50
       pagey=50
       width=100
       height=100
 bgcolor="blue">Layer 1</layer>
<layer name="Layer2"
       pagex=150
       pagey=150
       width=100
       height=100
 bgcolor="red">Layer 2</layer>

<script language="JavaScript">
```

*continues*

*Listing 7.142    continued*

```
<!-- Hide

//Display the length of the layers array.
document.write(document.layers.length," layer objects.");

//Hide End --->
</script>

</html>
```

# document.linkColor

## *JavaScript 1.0+, ECMAScript 1.0+, JScript 1.0+*

## *Nav2+, IE 3+*

### *Syntax*

```
document.linkColor
```

### *Description*

The `linkColor` property specifies the color of unvisited links. The color is expressed as a string in hexadecimal digits or as one of the JavaScript standard color names. The hexadecimal form is made up of 6 digits that follow the pattern "RRGGBB."

### *Example*

Listing 7.143 sets the unvisited links color to green for all links on the page only if they are placed before the `<script>` tags.

*Listing 7.143    Setting Link Colors with the `linkColor` Property*

```
<html>

<a href="myGreenPage.html">The Green Site</a><br>

<script language="JavaScript">
<!-- Hide

//Set the unvisited links color to green.
document.linkColor="00ff00";

//Hide End --->
</script>

<a href="myGreenGrassPage.html">The Green Grass Page</a>

</html>
```

# document.links

## *JavaScript 1.0+, JScript 1.0+*

## *Nav2+, IE 3+, Opera3+*

### Syntax

```
document.links
document.links[index]
```

### Description

The links property is an array that contains all the Link objects that appear within the HTML document from using the <a href="*source*"> tag. The links property has one property of its own, called length, which contains the number of Link objects in the array. The *index* number ranges from zero to the length minus one. See Link, earlier in this chapter, for a detailed explanation of all the properties associated with links.

## WARNING

Although anchors are created using the <a> tag, they are not accessible through the links array. Anchors are stored in the document's anchors array.

### Example

Listing 7.144 displays the URL of each link using the links[] array.

*Listing 7.144   Display the URL of each Link in the Document*

```
<html>

<a href="EmployeeList.html">The Employee List Page</a><br>
<a href="EmployeeBenefits.html">The Employee Benefits Page</a><br>

<script language="JavaScript">
<!-- Hide

//Display the URL of the link objects.
for(i=0;i<document.links.length;i++)
{
  document.write("The URL of link object ",(i+1));
  document.write(" is <i><b>",document.links[i].href,"</b></i><br>");
}

//Hide End --->
</script>

</html>
```

# document.links.length

## *JavaScript 1.0+, JScript 1.0+*

### Nav2+, IE 3+, Opera3+

### Syntax

```
document.links.length
```

### Description

The length property contains the number of Link objects that are in the document.links array.

### Example

Listing 7.145 uses the length property to display the number of links in the HTML document.

*Listing 7.145    Display the Number of Links in the Document*

```html
<html>

<a href="EmployeeList.html">The Employee List Page</a><br>
<a href="EmployeeBenefits.html">The Employee Benefits Page</a><br>

<script language="JavaScript">
<!-- Hide

//Display the length of the links array.
document.write(document.links.length," links.");

//Hide End --->
</script>

</html>
```

# document.onClick

### JavaScript1.0+, JScript1.0+

### Nav2+, IE3+

### Syntax

```
document.onClick
```

### Description

The onClick event handler specifies what should happen when the mouse is clicked within the Document object.

### Example

In Listing 7.146, the script in the <head> of the document specifies a function to handle all Click events in the document. To be able to do this, the document's captureEvents() method is used to capture all events of type Event.CLICK. When the page itself is clicked, Document's event handler generates an alert box notifying the user of the event.

*Listing 7.146    Handle the* Click *Event with the* onClick *Event Handler*

```
<head>

<script language="JavaScript1.2">
<!-- Hide

// Tell the browser you want to intercept ALL click events
// on the page and then define a function to handle them.
document.captureEvents(Event.CLICK);
document.onClick = myClickHandler;

// Define the myClickHandler function to handle click events
function myClickHandler{
  alert("The document was clicked!");
}

// End hide --->
</script>
</head>
<body>
Any time you click anywhere within this document you will
get a message alerting you that a Click event has taken place.
</body>
</html>
```

# document.onDblClick

## *JavaScript1.0+, JScript1.0+*

## *Nav2+, IE3+*

## *Syntax*

```
document.onDblClick
```

## *Description*

The onDblClick event handler specifies what should happen when the mouse is dou-ble-clicked within the Document object.

## *Example*

In Listing 7.147, the script in the <head> of the document specifies a function to han-dle all DblClick events in the document. To be able to do this, the document's captureEvents() method is used to capture all events of type Event.DBLCLICK. When the page itself is double-clicked, Document's event handler generates an alert box noti-fying the user of the event.

*Listing 7.147    Handle the* DblClick *Event with the* onDblClick *Event Handler*

```
<html>
<head>
```

*continues*

*Listing 7.147    continued*

```
<script language="JavaScript1.2">
<!-- Hide

// Tell the browser you want to intercept ALL DblClick events
// on the page and then define a function to handle them.
document.captureEvents(Event.DBLCLICK);
document.onDblClick = myDblClickHandler;

// Define the myDblClickHandler function to handle DblClick events
function myDblClickHandler{
  alert("The document was double clicked!");
}

// End hide --->
</script>
</head>
<body>
Any time you double-click anywhere within this document, you will
get a message alerting you that a DblClick event has taken place.
</body>
</html>
```

# document.onKeyDown

## *JavaScript1.0+, JScript1.0+*

## *Nav2+, IE3+*

## *Syntax*

```
document.onKeyDown
```

## *Description*

The onKeyDown event handler specifies what should happen when any key is pressed when the Document object is in focus.

## *Example*

In Listing 7.148, the script in the <head> of the document specifies a function to handle all KeyDown events in the document. To be able to do this, the document's captureEvents() method is used to capture all events of type Event.KEYDOWN. When any key is pressed within the page, the document's event handler generates an alert box notifying the user of the event.

*Listing 7.148    Handle the KeyDown Event with the onKeyDown Event Handler*
```
<html>
<head>

<script language="JavaScript1.2">
```

```
<!-- Hide

// Tell the browser you want to intercept ALL key down events
// on the page and then define a function to handle them.
document.captureEvents(Event.KEYDOWN);
document.onKeyDown = myKeyDownHandler;

// Define the myKeyDownHandler function to handle
// key down events
function myKeyDownHandler{
  alert("A key down event took place within the document!");
}

// End hide --->
</script>
</head>
<body>
Anytime you press a key within this document, you will
get a message alerting you that a KeyDown event has taken place.
</body>
</html>
```

# document.onKeyPress

## JavaScript1.0+, JScript1.0+

## Nav2+, IE3+

## Syntax

```
document.onKeyPress
```

## Description

The onKeyPress event handler specifies what should happen when any key is pressed when the Document object is in focus.

## Example

In Listing 7.149, the script in the <head> of the document specifies a function to handle all KeyPress events in the document. To be able to do this, the document's captureEvents() method is used to capture all events of type Event.KEYPRESS. When any key is pressed within the page, the document's event handler generates an alert box notifying the user of the event.

*Listing 7.149   Handle the KeyPress Event with the onKeyPress Event Handler*
```
<html>
<head>

<script language="JavaScript1.2">
<!-- Hide
```

*continues*

*Listing 7.149    continued*

```
// Tell the browser you want to intercept ALL key press events
// on the page and then define a function to handle them.
document.captureEvents(Event.KEYPRESS);
document.onKeyPress = myKeyPressHandler;

// Define the myKeyPressHandler function to handle
// key press events
function myKeyPressHandler{
  alert("A key press event took place within the document!");
}

// End hide --->
</script>
</head>
<body>
Anytime you press a key within this document, you will
get a message alerting you that a KeyPress event has taken place.
</body>
</html>
```

# document.onKeyUp

## *JavaScript1.0+, JScript1.0+*

## *Nav2+, IE3+*

## *Syntax*

```
document.onKeyUp
```

## *Description*

The onKeyUp event handler specifies what should happen when any key is pressed and then released when the Document object is in focus.

## *Example*

In Listing 7.150, the script in the <head> of the document specifies a function to handle all KeyUp events in the document. To be able to do this, the document's captureEvents() method is used to capture all events of type Event.KEYUP. When any key is pressed and then released within the page, the document's event handler generates an alert box notifying the user of the event.

*Listing 7.150    Handle the KeyUp Event with the onKeyUp Event Handler*
```
<html>
<head>

<script language="JavaScript1.2">
<!-- Hide
```

```
// Tell the browser you want to intercept ALL key up events
// on the page and then define a function to handle them.
document.captureEvents(Event.KEYUP);
document.onKeyUp = myKeyUpHandler;

// Define the myKeyUpHandler function to handle
// key up events
function myKeyUpHandler{
  alert("A key up event took place within the document!");
}

// End hide --->
</script>
</head>
<body>
Anytime you press a key and release it within this document, you will
get a message alerting you that a KeyUp event has taken place.
</body>
</html>
```

# document.onLoad

## *JavaScript1.0+, JScript1.0+*

## *Nav2+, IE3+*

## *Syntax*

onLoad="*command*"

## *Description*

The onLoad event handler of the Document object is fired when the page has finished loading in that particular window instance. This event handler actually belongs to the Window object but is accessible through the Document object.

## NOTE

The onLoad event in the <body> of a document that is loaded in a frame will fire before an event loaded in the <frameset> tag that loaded the document.

## *Example*

The sample of code in Listing 7.151 pops up an alert box when the page has finished loading using the onLoad event handler.

*Listing 7.151    Handle the Load Event with the onLoad Event Handler*
```
<body onLoad='alert("The document has completely loaded.")'>
```

# document.onMouseDown

## *JavaScript1.0+, JScript1.0+*

## Nav2+, IE3+

## Syntax

```
document.onMouseDown
```

## Description

The onMouseDown event handler specifies what should happen when the mouse button is pressed within the Document object.

## Example

In Listing 7.152, the script in the <head> of the document specifies a function to handle all MouseDown events in the document. To be able to do this, the document's captureEvents() method is used to capture all events of type Event.MOUSEDOWN. When the mouse button is pressed within the page, the document's event handler generates an alert box notifying the user of the event.

Listing 7.152    Handle the MouseDown Event with the onMouseDown Event Handler

```
<html>
<head>

<script language="JavaScript1.2">
<!-- Hide

// Tell the browser you want to intercept ALL mouse
// down events on the page and then define a function
// to handle them.
document.captureEvents(Event.MOUSEDOWN);
document.onMouseDown = myMouseDownHandler;

// Define the myMouseDownHandler function to handle
// mouse down events
function myMouseDownHandler{
  alert("A mouse down event took place within the document!");
}

// End hide --->
</script>
</head>
<body>
Anytime you press the mouse button down within this document, you will
get a message alerting you that a MouseDown event has taken place.
</body>
</html>
```

# document.onMouseUp

## JavaScript1.0+, JScript1.0+

## Nav2+, IE3+

## Syntax

```
document.onMouseUp
```

## Description

The onMouseUp event handler specifies what should happen when the mouse button is pressed and then released within the Document object.

## Example

In Listing 7.153, the script in the <head> of the document specifies a function to handle all MouseUp events in the document. To be able to do this, the document's captureEvents() method is used to capture all events of type Event.MOUSEUP. When the mouse button is pressed and then released within the page, the document's event handler generates an alert box notifying the user of the event.

*Listing 7.153   Handle the MouseUp Event with the onMouseUp Event Handler*

```
<html>
<head>

<script language="JavaScript1.2">
<!-- Hide

// Tell the browser you want to intercept ALL mouse
// up events on the page and then define a function
// to handle them.
document.captureEvents(Event.MOUSEUP);
document.onMouseUp = myMouseUpHandler;

// Define the myMouseUpHandler function to handle
// mouse up events
function myMouseUpHandler{
  alert("A mouse up event took place within the document!");
}

// End hide --->
</script>
</head>
<body>
Anytime you press the mouse button and then release it within this
Document, you will get a message alerting you that a MouseUp
event has taken place.
</body>
</html>
```

# document.onUnLoad

## *Nav2+, IE3+, Opera3+*

## Syntax

```
onUnLoad="command"
```

## Description

The onUnLoad event handler of a Document object is fired when the page is unloaded in that particular window instance. This occurs when the user leaves the page for another page. This event handler actually belongs to the Window object but is accessible through the Document object. See Window.onUnLoad, later in this chapter, for more information.

> **NOTE**
>
> The onUnLoad event handler in the `<body>` of a document that is loaded in a frame will fire before an event loaded in the `<frameset>` tag that loaded the document.

## Example

The code in Listing 7.154 pops up an alert box when the user leaves the page, thanks to the onUnLoad event handler.

Listing 7.154  *Handle the UnLoad Event with the onUnLoad Event Handler*
```
<body onUnLoad='alert("Please do not leave!")'>
```

# document.open()

## JavaScript1.0+, JScript1.0+

## Nav2+, IE3+, Opera3+

## Syntax

```
document.open()
document.open(mimetype)
```

## Description

The open() method of the Document object clears the current document and opens a stream for new data to be placed in the document. This method accepts one argument, *mimetype*, that specifies what type of data will be written to the document. The argument can be one of the following standard mimetypes: text/html, text/plain, image/gif, image/jpeg, or image/x-bitmap.

## Example

Listing 7.155 opens a document with the open() method and then writes text to the document.

Listing 7.155  *Open a Document with the open() Method*
```
<script language="JavaScript">
<!-- Hide

document.open()
document.write("Stream text to document");
document.close()
```

```
//Hide End --->
</script>
```

# document.plugins

## *JavaScript 1.1+, JScript 1.0+*

## *Nav3+, IE 3+, Opera3+*

### *Syntax*

```
document.plugins
document.plugins[index]
```

### *Description*

The `plugins` property is an array that contains all the embedded objects and plug-ins that appear within the HTML document from using the <embed> tag. The `plugins` property has one property of its own, called `length`, which contains the number of items in the array. The *index* number ranges from zero to the `length` minus one.

> **NOTE**
>
> The `plugins[]` array property accesses the same data as the `document.embeds[]` array property.

### *Example*

Listing 7.156 uses the `length` property to display the number of embedded objects in the HTML document.

*Listing 7.156    Access the Plug-ins Using the embeds Array*

```
<html>

<h2>Learn Shapes</h2>

<h2>A Circle</h2>
<embed src="circle.gif">

<h2>A Square</h2>
<embed src="square.gif">

<script language="JavaScript">
<!-- Hide

//Display the length of the plugins array.
document.write(document.plugins.length," embedded objects.");

//Hide End --->
</script>

</html>
```

# document.plugins.length

## *JavaScript 1.1+, JScript 1.0+*

## *Nav3+, IE 3+, Opera3+*

## *Syntax*

```
document.plugins.length
```

## *Description*

The `length` property contains the number of objects that are in the `plugins[]` array.

## *Example*

Listing 7.157 uses the `length` property to display the number of embedded objects in the HTML document.

*Listing 7.157   Display the Number of Plug-ins in the Document*

```
<html>

<h2>A Circle</h2>
<embed src="circle.gif">

<h2>A Square</h2>
<embed src="square.gif">

<script language="JavaScript">
<!-- Hide

//Display the length of the plugins array.
document.write(document.plugins.length," embedded objects.");

//Hide End --->
</script>

</html>
```

# document.referrer

## *JavaScript 1.0+, JScript 3.0+*

## *Nav2+, IE 4+*

## *Syntax*

```
document.referrer
```

## *Description*

The `referrer` property contains the URL of the document that was used to reach the current document. If the URL was typed directly into the browser's location field, this property will be empty.

## Example

In Listing 7.158, the `referrer` property is used to create a link back to the previous document from within the current document in the example.

*Listing 7.158   Create a Link Back to the Calling Document Using the `referrer` Property*

```
<script language="JavaScript">
<!-- Hide

//Create a link back to the referring document.
document.write("<a href='",document.referrer,"'>Go back</a>");

//Hide End --->
</script>
```

# document.releaseEvents()

## JavaScript1.2+

## Nav4+

## Syntax

```
document.releaseEvents(event)
document.releaseEvents(event1 | event2 | eventN)
```

## Description

The `releaseEvents()` method of the `Document` object releases all previously captured events of the event type passed. These events can be captured with the `Document.captureEvents()` method. The following events can be released:

- `Event.ABORT`
- `Event.BLUR`
- `Event.CHANGE`
- `Event.CLICK`
- `Event.DBLCLICK`
- `Event.DRAGDROP`
- `Event.ERROR`
- `Event.FOCUS`
- `Event.KEYDOWN`
- `Event.KEYPRESS`
- `Event.KEYUP`
- `Event.LOAD`
- `Event.MOUSEDOWN`
- `Event.MOUSEMOVE`
- `Event.MOUSEOUT`
- `Event.MOUSEOVER`
- `Event.MOUSEUP`
- `Event.MOVE`

- Event.RESET
- Event.RESIZE
- Event.SELECT
- Event.SUBMIT
- Event.UNLOAD

After one of these events has been captured, you can define a function to replace the built-in method for handling the event. Use the `releaseEvents()` method to free the event after a capture.

## Example

Listing 7.159 has a single text box and a button. The script in the <head> of the document specifies a function to handle all `Click` events in the document. To be able to do this, the `captureEvents()` method had to be used to capture all events of type `Event.CLICK`. When the page itself is clicked, a counter, which is displayed in the text box, is incremented.

When the mouse button is pressed down, the `MouseDown` event is fired and the `Event.CLICK` is released and no longer increments the page when the page is clicked.

Listing 7.159    *Using the `releaseEvents()` Method to Stop Capturing Specific Events*

```
<html>
<head>

<script language="JavaScript1.2">
<!-- Hide

// Define a click counter variable
var counter = 0;

// Tell the browser you want to intercept ALL click events
// on the page. Then define a function to handle them.
document.captureEvents(Event.CLICK);
document.onClick = myClickHandler;

// Define the myClickHandler function to handle click events
function myClickHandler{

  // Pass all click events to the onClick event of the text box
  document.myForm.myText.handleEvent;
}

// Function is called by onClick of text box. Displays the number
// of clicks that have occurred.
function changeText(){
  document.myForm.myText.value = counter++;
}

// Releases the click event capturing
```

```
function releaseClick(){
  document.releaseEvents(Event.CLICK);
  document.onClick="";
}

// End hide --->
</script>
</head>
<body>
<form name="myForm">
  <input type=TEXT size=2 value="" name="myText" onClick='changeText()'>
  <input type=BUTTON value="Release Event" onMouseDown='releaseClick()'>
</form>
</body>
</html>
```

# document.routeEvent()

## JavaScript1.2+

## Nav4+

## Syntax

```
document.routeEvent(event)
```

## Description

The routeEvent() method of the Document object passes all previously captured events of the event type passed through their normal event processes. The events that can be passed are as follows:

- Event.ABORT
- Event.BLUR
- Event.CHANGE
- Event.CLICK
- Event.DBLCLICK
- Event.DRAGDROP
- Event.ERROR
- Event.FOCUS
- Event.KEYDOWN
- Event.KEYPRESS
- Event.KEYUP
- Event.LOAD
- Event.MOUSEDOWN
- Event.MOUSEMOVE
- Event.MOUSEOUT
- Event.MOUSEOVER
- Event.MOUSEUP
- Event.MOVE

- Event.RESET
- Event.RESIZE
- Event.SELECT
- Event.SUBMIT
- Event.UNLOAD

After one of these events has been captured using the `Document.captureEvents()` method, you can define a function to replace the built-in method for handling the event. Use the `releaseEvents()` method to free the event after a capture, and use `routeEvent()` to allow normal processing to take place.

## Example

Listing 7.160 has a single text box and a link. The script in the `<head>` of the document specifies a function to handle all `Click` events in the window. To be able to do this, the `captureEvents()` method had to be used to capture all events of type `Event.CLICK`. When the page itself is clicked, a counter, which is displayed in the text box, is incremented.

When the link is clicked, the `MouseDown` event is fired and the `Event.CLICK` is routed through its normal means and no longer increments the page when the page is clicked.

*Listing 7.160    Using the `routeEvent()` Method to Continue Routing a Captured Event*

```
<html>
<head>

<script language="JavaScript1.2">
<!-- Hide

// Define a click counter variable
var counter = 0;

// Tell the browser you want to intercept ALL click events
// on the page. Then define a function to handle them.
document.captureEvents(Event.CLICK);
document.onClick = myClickHandler;

// Define the myClickHandler function to handle click events
function myClickHandler{

  // Pass all click events to the onClick event of the text box
  document.myForm.myText.handleEvent;
}

// Function is called by onClick of text box. Displays the number
// of clicks that have occurred.
function changeText(){
  document.myForm.myText.value = counter++;
}
```

```
// Releases the click event capturing
function releaseClick(){
  document.routeEvent(Event.CLICK);
}

// End hide --->
</script>
</head>
<body>
<form name="myForm">
  <input type=TEXT size=2 value="" name="myText" onClick='changeText()'>
  <a href="http://www.purejavascript.com"
onMouseDown='window.routeEvent(Event.CLICK)'>Click Here!</a>
</form>
</body>
</html>
```

# document.tags

## JavaScript 1.2+

## Nav4+

## Syntax

document.tags.*tagName*

## Description

The `tags` property is an associative array that contains tags associated with Netscape style sheets. Using dot notation, *tagName* specifies a tag associated with a style. The style sheet tags are created within the `<style>` or `<script>` tags using JavaScript or HTML.

> **NOTE**
>
> When creating a tag, make sure the declaration appears before the new tag is used, because many HTML objects cannot be changed after they have been created in the document.

> **NOTE**
>
> If JavaScript dot notation is used when creating a new tag within `<style>` tags, `document` does not have to be specified.

## Example

Listing 7.161 demonstrates three different ways to create style sheet tags using JavaScript and HTML within `<style>` and `<script>` tags. Notice that the order in which the tags are declared and used ultimately affects the style result.

*Listing 7.161    Creating New Style Sheet Tags*

```
<html>

<style type="text/css">
  P {font-style: italic;}
</style>

<p>After first STYLE tag.<p>

<style type="text/javascript">
  tags.P.fontWeight = "bold";
</style>

<p>After second STYLE tag.<p>

<script>
<!-- Hide
document.tags.P.textDecoration = "underline";
//Hide End --->
</script>

<p>After SCRIPT tag.<p>

</html>
```

# document.tags.align

## *JavaScript 1.2+*

## *Nav4+*

## *Syntax*

```
document.tags.tagName.align
```

## *Description*

The `align` property specifies the alignment of an element within its parent as associated with the tag called *tagName*.

The `align` property can be assigned one of the following values: `left`, `right`, or `none`.

> **NOTE**
>
> The `align` property is referred to as `float` when using CSS syntax. JavaScript could not use the word "float" because it was a reserved word.

## *Example*

Listing 7.162 uses the `align` property to align a paragraph to the right of its parent, the document.

*Listing 7.162    Aligning Right with the `align` Property*

```
<html>

<script>
<!-- Hide

//Create a style sheet tag that aligns right
document.tags.P.align = "right";

//Hide End --->
</script>

<p>Send me to the right!</p>

I appear to the left of the document.

</html>
```

# document.tags.backgroundColor

## JavaScript 1.2+

## Nav4+

## Syntax

```
document.tags.tagName.backgroundColor
```

## Description

The `backgroundColor` property specifies the background color associated with the tag called *tagName*.

## Example

Listing 7.163 uses the `backgroundColor` property to make the background color around an anchor red.

*Listing 7.163    Setting the Background Color with the `backgroundColor` Property*

```
<html>

<script>
<!-- Hide

//Create a style sheet id that contains the background color
document.tags.A.backgroundColor = "red";

//Hide End --->
</script>

<a name="THIS">This</a> is an anchor that uses
```

*continues*

*Listing 7.163 continued*
```
styles from the A tag.

</html>
```

# document.tags.backgroundImage

## *JavaScript 1.2+*

## *Nav4+*

## *Syntax*

```
document.tags.tagName.backgroundImage
```

## *Description*

The backgroundImage property specifies the background image of an element as associated with the tag called *tagName*.

## *Example*

Listing 7.164 makes the image logo.gif the background for the header text.

*Listing 7.164 Setting the Background Image with the backgroundImage Property*
```
<html>

<script>
<!-- Hide

//Create a style sheet tag that uses an image as a background
document.tags.H2.backgroundImage = "logo.gif";

//Hide End --->
</script>

<h2>Look at my background image!</h2>

</html>
```

# document.tags.borderBottomWidth

## *JavaScript 1.2+*

## *Nav4+*

## *Syntax*

```
document.tags.tagName.borderBottomWidth
```

## *Description*

The borderBottomWidth property specifies the width of the bottom border of an element as associated with the tag called *tagName*.

## Example

Listing 7.165 uses the `borderBottomWidth` property to set the size of the bottom border that surrounds a text header. Notice that only the bottom portion of the border is shown.

*Listing 7.165   Setting the Bottom Border Width with the `borderBottomWidth` Property*

```
<html>

<script>
<!-- Hide

//Create a style sheet id that creates a bottom border
document.tags.H2.borderBottomWidth = "10";

//Hide End --->
</script>

<h2>This text has a bottom border</h2>

</html>
```

# document.tags.borderColor

## JavaScript 1.2+

## Nav4+

## Syntax

```
document.tags.tagName.borderColor
```

## Description

The `borderColor` property specifies the color of the border of an element as associated with the tag called *tagName*.

## Example

Listing 7.166 uses the `borderColor` property to set the color of the border that surrounds a text header to blue.

*Listing 7.166   Setting the Border Color with the `borderColor` Property*

```
<html>

<script>
<!-- Hide

//Create a style sheet tag that creates a left border
document.tags.H2.borderWidths(10);
```

*continues*

*Listing 7.166   continued*

```
document.tags.H2.borderColor = "blue";

//Hide End --->
</script>

<h2>This text has a blue border</h2>

</html>
```

# document.tags.borderLeftWidth

## JavaScript 1.2+

## Nav4+

## Syntax

```
document.tags.tagName.borderLeftWidth
```

## Description

The `borderLeftWidth` property specifies the width of the left border of an element as associated with the tag called *tagName*.

## Example

Listing 7.167 uses the `borderLeftWidth` property to set the size of left border that surrounds a text header. Notice that only the left portion of the border is shown.

*Listing 7.167   Setting the Left Border Width with the `borderLeftWidth` Property*

```
<html>

<script>
<!-- Hide

//Create a style sheet tag that creates a left border
document.tags.H2.borderLeftWidth = "10";

//Hide End --->
</script>

<h2>This text has a left border</h2>

</html>
```

# document.tags.borderRightWidth

## JavaScript 1.2+

## Nav4+

## Syntax

```
document.tags.tagName.borderRightWidth
```

## Description

The `borderRightWidth` property specifies the width of the right border of an element as associated with the tag called *tagName*.

## Example

Listing 7.168 uses the `borderRightWidth` property to set the size of right border that surrounds a text header. Notice that only the right portion of the border is shown.

*Listing 7.168 Setting the Right Border Width with the `borderRightWidth` Property*

```
<html>

<script>
<!-- Hide

//Create a style sheet tag that creates a right border
document.tags.H2.borderRightWidth = "10";

//Hide End --->
</script>

<h2>This text has a right border</h2>

</html>
```

# document.tags.borderStyle

## JavaScript 1.2+

## Nav4+

## Syntax

```
document.tags.tagName.borderStyle
```

## Description

The `borderStyle` property specifies the style of the border that surrounds an element as associated with the tag called *tagName*.

The `borderStyle` property can be assigned one of the following values: `none`, `solid`, `double`, `inset`, `outset`, `groove`, or `ridge`.

## Example

Listing 7.169 uses the `borderStyle` property to set the border around a text header to a double line.

*Listing 7.169    Setting the Border Style with the borderStyle Property*

```
<html>

<script>
<!-- Hide

//Create a style sheet tag that creates a double border
document.tags.H2.borderWidths(10);
document.tags.H2.borderColor = "red";
document.tags.H2.borderStyle = "double";

//Hide End --->
</script>

<h2>This text has a double border</h2>

</html>
```

# document.tags.borderTopWidth

## JavaScript 1.2+

## Nav4+

## Syntax

document.tags.*tagName*.borderTopWidth

## Description

The borderTopWidth property specifies the width of the top border of an element as associated with the tag called *tagName*.

## Example

Listing 7.170 uses the borderTopWidth property to set the size of top border that surrounds a text header. Notice that only the top portion of the border is shown.

*Listing 7.170    Setting the Top Border Width with the borderTopWidth Property*

```
<html>

<script>
<!-- Hide

//Create a style sheet tag that creates a top border
document.tags.H2.borderTopWidth = "10";

//Hide End --->
</script>

<h2>This text has a top border</h2>

</html>
```

# document.tags.borderWidths()

## *JavaScript 1.2+*

## *Nav4+*

## *Syntax*

```
document.tags.tagName.borderWidths(top,right,bottom,left)
document.tags.tagName.borderWidths(top-bottom,right-left)
document.tags.tagName.borderWidths(all)
```

## *Description*

The `borderWidths()` method specifies the width of the border that surrounds an element as associated with the tag called *tagName*. Setting border widths is equivalent to setting the `borderBottomWidth`, `borderLeftWidth`, `borderRightWidth`, and `borderTopWidth` properties. Table 7.20 lists all the arguments associated with the `borderWidths()` method.

**Table 7.20    Arguments Associated with the borderWidths() Method**

| Item | Description |
|------|-------------|
| `top` | Width of the top border |
| `right` | Width of the right border |
| `left` | Width of the left border |
| `bottom` | Width of the bottom border |
| `top-bottom` | Width of both the top and bottom borders |
| `left-right` | Width of both the left and right borders |
| `all` | Width of all four sides of the border |

## *Example*

Listing 7.171 uses the `borderWidths()` method to set the width of the border that surrounds a text header.

*Listing 7.171    Setting All Border Widths with the borderWidths() Method*

```
<html>

<script>
<!-- Hide

//Create a style sheet tag that creates a border
document.tags.H2.borderWidths(5,10,15,20);

//Hide End --->
</script>

<h2>This text has a border</h2>

</html>
```

# document.tags.clear

## JavaScript 1.2+

## Nav4+

## Syntax

```
document.tags.tagName.clear
```

## Description

The clear property specifies the sides of an element where floating elements (elements that define the align property) are not allowed. Using dot notation, this property is associated with the tag called *tagName*.

The clear property can be assigned one of the following values: left, right, both, or none.

## Example

Listing 7.172 uses the clear property to prevent floating elements from being on either side of the text I don't like other elements next to me!.

*Listing 7.172    Using the clear Property*

```
<html>

<script>
<!-- Hide

//Create style sheet tags that set alignments
document.tags.P.align = "left";
document.tags.P.backgroundColor = "yellow";
document.tags.I.align = "right";
document.tags.I.backgroundColor = "red";
document.tags.B.clear = "both";

//Hide End --->
</script>

<p>Send me to the left!</p>
<i>Send me to the right!</i>
I like other elements next to me!

<p>Send me to the left!</p>
<i>Send me to the right!</i>
<b>I don't like other elements next to me!</b>

</html>
```

# document.tags.color

## JavaScript 1.2+

## Nav4+

## Syntax

```
document.tags.tagName.color
```

## Description

The `color` property specifies the foreground color of an element as associated with the tag called *tagName*.

## Example

Listing 7.173 uses the `color` property to set the color of various text.

*Listing 7.173   Set the Color of Text Using the `color` Property*

```
<html>

<script>
<!-- Hide

//Create a style sheet tags that defines colors
document.tags.I.color = "blue";
document.tags.B.color = "red";

//Hide End --->
</script>

<i>The blue boat floated on the blue ocean.</i>
<b>The red car stopped at a red stop sign.</b>

</html>
```

# document.tags.display

## JavaScript 1.2+

## Nav4+

## Syntax

```
document.tags.tagName.display
```

## Description

The `display` property specifies an element that is displayed when associated with the tag called *tagName*.

The `display` property can be assigned one of the following values: `inline`, `block`, `list-item`, or `none`.

Specifying an inline value is equivalent to using the <em> tag. The block value is the same as creating header text with the <h> tag. Using list-item is equivalent to using the <li> tag. If none is specified, the element is not displayed.

## Example

Listing 7.174 uses the display property to create header text. block consists of a line break and resetting margins to their default values. Notice that a carriage return is automatically entered before the bold tag.

*Listing 7.174    Set the display Property*

```
<html>

<script>
<!-- Hide

//Create a style sheet tag that defines a block display
document.tags.H2.display = "block";

//Hide End --->
</script>

<h2>A BIG HEADER</h2>

Just some regular text following the Big Header.

</html>
```

# document.tags.fontFamily

## JavaScript 1.2+

## Nav4+

## Syntax

```
document.tags.tagName.fontFamily
```

## Description

The fontFamily property specifies the font an element should use when associated with the tag called *tagName*. More than one font can be specified, in case a particular font has not been loaded.

## Example

Listing 7.175 uses the fontFamily property to create text with an Arial font. If that font is not available, Helvetica is used.

*Listing 7.175    Set the fontFamily Property*

```
<html>

<script>
```

```
<!-- Hide

//Create a style sheet tag that defines a font
document.tags.P.fontFamily = "Arial, Helvetica";

//Hide End --->
</script>

<p>Do you like this font?</p>

</html>
```

# document.tags.fontSize

## JavaScript 1.2+

## Nav4+

## Syntax

document.tags.*tagName*.fontSize

## Description

The fontSize property specifies the size of fonts used by an element when associated with the tag called *tagName*. The values that can be used to set font size can be divided into four categories as shown in Table 7.21.

*Table 7.21    Font Sizes*

| Category | Value |
|---|---|
| Absolute | xx-small |
| | x-small |
| | small |
| | medium |
| | large |
| | x-large |
| | xx-large |
| Relative | smaller (relative font size of parent) |
| | larger (relative font size of parent) |
| Length | A number followed by a unit of measurement. |
| Percentage | The size relative to font size of parent. |

## Example

Listing 7.176 uses absolute font sizing to define the fontSize property and associate it with text.

*Listing 7.176    Set the `fontSize` Property*

```
<html>

<script>
<!-- Hide

//Create a style sheet tag that defines a font size
document.tags.P.fontSize = "xx-small";
document.tags.I.fontSize = "xx-large";

//Hide End --->
</script>

<p>Extra, extra small text</p>
<i>Extra, extra large text</i>

</html>
```

# document.tags.fontStyle

## JavaScript 1.2+

## Nav4+

## Syntax

```
document.tags.tagName.fontStyle
```

## Description

The `fontStyle` property specifies the font style used by an element when associated with the tag called `tagName`.

The `fontStyle` property can be assigned one of the following values: `normal` or `italic`.

## Example

Listing 7.177 uses the `fontStyle` property to italicize the header text.

*Listing 7.177    Set the `fontStyle` Property*

```
<html>

<script>
<!-- Hide

//Create a style sheet tag that defines a font style
document.tags.H2.fontStyle = "italic";

//Hide End --->
</script>
```

```
<h2>Italicized Heading</h2>

</html>
```

# document.tags.fontWeight

## *JavaScript 1.2+*

## *Nav4+*

## *Syntax*

document.tags.*tagName*.fontWeight

## Description

The fontWeight property specifies the font weight used by an element when associated with the tag called *tagName*.

The fontStyle property can be assigned one of the following values: normal, bold, bolder, lighter, or a number from 100 to 900.

## Example

Listing 7.178 uses the fontWeight property to set different levels of weight on various text.

*Listing 7.178    Set the fontWeight Property*

```
<html>

<script>
<!-- Hide

//Create a style sheet tags that defines a font style
document.tags.P.fontWeight = 100;
document.tags.I.fontWeight = 900;

//Hide End --->
</script>

<p>Font weight of 100</p>
<i>Font weight of 900</i>

</html>
```

# document.tags.lineHeight

## *JavaScript 1.2+*

## *Nav4+*

## *Syntax*

document.tags.*tagName*.lineHeight

## Description

The lineHeight property specifies the distance between two lines that are next to each other. Using dot notation, the property is associated with the tag called *tagName*.

There are four types of values that are valid for the lineHeight property: number, length, percentage, and the value normal.

When a number is given without a unit of measure, it is multiplied by the font size of the element to give the line height. Length is specified by including a unit of measure after the number. A percentage is designated by including a percent sign (%) after the number to represent the line height as it relates to its parent.

## Example

Listing 7.179 uses the lineHeight property to set the distance between lines.

*Listing 7.179    Set the lineHeight Property*

```
<html>

<script>
<!-- Hide

//Create a style sheet tags that defines a line height
document.tags.I.lineHeight = "1in";
document.tags.U.lineHeight = "50pt";

//Hide End --->
</script>

This is the first line of text<br>
<i>This is a second line of text.</i><br>
This is a third line of text.<br>
<u>This is a fourth line of text.</u><br>
This is a fifth line of text.<br>

</html>
```

# document.tags.listStyleType

## JavaScript 1.2+

## Nav4+

## Syntax

```
document.tags.tagName.listStyleType
```

## Description

The listStyleType property specifies the format of list items elements associated with the tag called *tagName*.

There are nine types of values that are valid for the `listStyleType` property: `disc`, `circle`, `square`, `decimal`, `lower-roman`, `upper-roman`, `lower-alpha`, `upper-alpha`, and `none`.

**NOTE**

> The `listStyleType` property is only valid if the element also has the `display` property set to `list-item`.

## Example

Listing 7.180 uses the `listStyleType` property to format a list of items.

*Listing 7.180 Set the `listStyleType` Property*

```
<html>

<script>
<!-- Hide

//Create a style sheet tag that defines a list format
document.tags.OL.display = "list-item";
document.tags.OL.listStyleType = "upper-roman";

//Hide End --->
</script>

<h2>Presentation Outline</h2>

<ol>
  <li>Introduction
  <li>Overview of new product
  <li>Cost of product
  <li>Conclusion
</ol>

</html>
```

# document.tags.marginBottom

## JavaScript 1.2+

## Nav4+

## Syntax

`document.tags.`*tagName*`.marginBottom`

## Description

The `marginBottom` property specifies the distance between the bottom border of an element and the top border of another element. Dot notation is used to associate this property with the tag called *tagName*.

## Example

Listing 7.181 uses the `marginBottom` property to set the distance between adjacent elements.

*Listing 7.181   Set the Bottom Margin with the `marginBottom` Property*

```
<html>

<script>
<!-- Hide

//Create a style sheet class and id that define bottom margin
document.tags.B.borderWidths(10);
document.tags.B.marginBottom = 40;

//Hide End --->
</script>

My margins are set automatically<br>
<b>I have a large bottom margin!</b>
My margins are set automatically

</html>
```

# document.tags.marginLeft

## JavaScript 1.2+

## Nav4+

## Syntax

```
document.tags.tagName.marginLeft
```

## Description

The `marginLeft` property specifies the distance between the left border of an element and the right border of another element. Dot notation is used to associate this property with the tag called *tagName*.

## Example

Listing 7.182 uses the `marginLeft` property to set the distance between adjacent elements. Notice the distance between the border and the right edge of the browser window.

*Listing 7.182   Set the Left Margin with the `marginLeft` Property*

```
<html>

<script>
<!-- Hide

//Create a style sheet id and tags that defines left margin
```

```
document.ids.FORMAT.borderWidths(10);
document.tags.B.marginLeft = 40;
document.tags.I.marginLeft = 0;

//Hide End --->
</script>

<b id=FORMAT>I have a large left margin!</b>
<i id=FORMAT>I have no left margin</i>

</html>
```

# document.tags.marginRight

## *JavaScript 1.2+*

## *Nav4+*

## *Syntax*

```
document.tags.tagName.marginRight
```

## Description

The marginRight property specifies the distance between the right border of an element and the left border of another element. Dot notation is used to associate this property with the tag called *tagName*.

## Example

Listing 7.183 uses the marginRight property to set the distance between adjacent elements. Notice the distance between the border and the right edge of the browser window.

*Listing 7.183    Set the Right Margin with the marginRight Property*

```
<html>

<script>
<!-- Hide

//Create a style sheet id and tags that defines right margin
document.ids.FORMAT.borderWidths(10);
document.tags.B.marginRight = 40;
document.tags.I.marginRight = 0;

//Hide End --->
</script>

<b id=FORMAT>I have a large right margin!</b>
<i id=FORMAT>I have no right margin</i>

</html>
```

# document.tags.margins()

## *JavaScript 1.2+*

## *Nav4+*

## *Syntax*

```
document.tags.tagName.margins(top,right,bottom,left)
document.tags.tagName.margins(top-bottom,right-left)
document.tags.tagName.margins(all)
```

## *Description*

The margins() method specifies the margin distance between the border of an element and the border of adjacent elements. Dot notation is used to associate the property with the tag called *tagName*. Setting margin widths is equivalent to setting the marginBottom, marginLeft, marginRight, and marginTop properties. Table 7.22 lists all the arguments associated with the margins() method.

**Table 7.22    Arguments Associated with the margins() Method**

| Item | Description |
| --- | --- |
| top | Width of the top margin |
| right | Width of the right margin |
| left | Width of the left margin |
| bottom | Width of the bottom margin |
| top-bottom | Width of both the top and bottom margins |
| left-right | Width of both the left and right margins |
| all | Width of all four margins |

## *Example*

Listing 7.184 uses the margins() method to set the margin widths around a text element.

*Listing 7.184    All Margins Set with the margins() Method*

```
<html>

<script>
<!-- Hide

//Create a style sheet tag that defines margins
document.tags.H2.borderWidths(10);
document.tags.H2.margins(50);

//Hide End --->
</script>

<h2>This text has margins set to 50</h2>

</html>
```

# document.tags.marginTop

## JavaScript 1.2+

## Nav4+

## Syntax

```
document.tags.tagName.marginTop
```

## Description

The `marginTop` property specifies the distance between the top border of an element and the bottom border of another element. Dot notation is used to associate this property with the tag called *tagName*.

## Example

Listing 7.185 uses the `marginTop` property to set the distance between adjacent elements.

*Listing 7.185    Set the Top Margin with the `marginTop` Property*

```
<html>

<script>
<!-- Hide

//Create a style sheet id and tag that defines top margin
document.ids.BORDER.borderWidths(10);
document.tags.B.marginTop = 40;

//Hide End --->
</script>

<i id=BORDER>My margins are set automatically</i><br>
<b id=BORDER>I have a large top margin!</b>
<i id=BORDER>My margins are set automatically</i>

</html>
```

# document.tags.paddingBottom

## JavaScript 1.2+

## Nav4+

## Syntax

```
document.tags.tagName.paddingBottom
```

## Description

The `paddingBottom` property specifies the distance between the bottom border of an element and its content. Using dot notation, the property is associated with the tag called *tagName*.

## Example

Listing 7.186 uses the `paddingBottom` property to set the distance between a line of text and its border.

*Listing 7.186   Set the Bottom Padding with the `paddingBottom` Property*

```
<html>

<script>
<!-- Hide

//Create a style sheet tag that defines the bottom padding
document.tags.P.borderWidths(10)
document.tags.P.paddingBottom = "40";

//Hide End --->
</script>

<p>This text has extra padding on the bottom.</p>

</html>
```

# document.tags.paddingLeft

## JavaScript 1.2+

## Nav4+

## Syntax

document.tags.*tagName*.paddingLeft

## Description

The `paddingLeft` property specifies the distance between the left border of an element and its content. Using dot notation, the property is associated with the tag called *tagName*.

## Example

Listing 7.187 uses the `paddingLeft` property to set the distance between a line of text and its border.

*Listing 7.187   Set the Left Padding with the `paddingLeft` Property*

```
<html>

<script>
<!-- Hide

//Create a style sheet tag that defines the left padding
document.tags.P.borderWidths(10)
document.tags.P.paddingLeft = "40";
```

```
//Hide End --->
</script>

<p>This text has extra padding on the left.</p>

</html>
```

# document.tags.paddingRight

## JavaScript 1.2+

## Nav4+

## Syntax

```
document.tags.tagName.paddingRight
```

## Description

The paddingRight property specifies the distance between the right border of an element and its content. Using dot notation, the property is associated with the tag called tagName.

## Example

Listing 7.188 uses the paddingRight property to set the distance between a line of text and its border.

Listing 7.188    *Set the Right Padding with the paddingRight Property*

```
<html>

<script>
<!-- Hide

//Create a style sheet tag that defines the right padding
document.tags.P.borderWidths(10)
document.tags.P.paddingRight = "40";

//Hide End --->
</script>

<p>This text has extra padding on the right.</p>

</html>
```

# document.tags.paddings()

## JavaScript 1.2+

## Nav4+

## Syntax

```
document.tags.tagName.paddings(top,right,bottom,left)
document.tags.tagName.paddings(top-bottom,right-left)
document.tags.tagName.paddings(all)
```

## Description

The `paddings()` method specifies the distance between the borders of an element and its content. Using dot notation, the property is associated with the tag called *tagName*. Setting the sizes is equivalent to setting the `paddingBottom`, `paddingLeft`, `paddingRight`, and `paddingTop` properties. Table 7.23 lists all the arguments associated with the `paddings()` method.

**Table 7.23    Arguments Associated with the paddings() Method**

| Item | Description |
| --- | --- |
| top | Padding between top border and content |
| right | Padding between right border and content |
| left | Padding between left border and content |
| bottom | Padding between bottom border and content |
| top-bottom | Padding between the content and both the top and bottom border |
| left-right | Padding between the content and both the left and right border |
| all | Padding between content and all four sides of the border |

## Example

Listing 7.189 uses the `paddings()` method to set the distance between text and all sides of its border.

*Listing 7.189    Set All Paddings with the `paddings()` Method*

```html
<html>

<script>
<!-- Hide

//Create a style sheet tag that defines all paddings
document.tags.P.borderWidths(5);
document.tags.P.paddings(0,20,40,60);

//Hide End --->
</script>

<p>This text has padding on all sides of its border.</p>

</html>
```

# document.tags.paddingTop

## JavaScript 1.2+

## Nav4+

## Syntax

```
document.tags.tagName.paddingTop
```

## Description

The `paddingTop` property specifies the distance between the left border of an element and its content. Using dot notation, the property is associated with the tag called `tagName`.

## Example

Listing 7.190 uses the `paddingTop` property to set the distance between a line of text and its border.

*Listing 7.190    Set Top Padding with the `paddingTop` Property*

```html
<html>

<script>
<!-- Hide

//Create a style sheet tag that defines the top padding
document.tags.P.borderWidths(10)
document.tags.P.paddingTop = "40";

//Hide End --->
</script>

<p>This text has extra padding on the top.</p>

</html>
```

# document.tags.textAlign

## JavaScript 1.2+

## Nav4+

## Syntax

```
document.tags.tagName.textAlign
```

## Description

The `textAlign` property specifies the alignment of text within an element as associated with the tag called `tagName`.

There are four types of values that are valid for the `textAlign` property: `left`, `right`, `center`, and `justify`.

## Example

Listing 7.191 uses the `textAlign` property to align the text to the right side of the browser window.

*Listing 7.191    Set the `textAlign` Property*

```
<html>

<script>
<!-- Hide

//Create a style sheet tag that defines right alignment
document.tags.P.borderWidths(10)
document.tags.P.textAlign = "right";

//Hide End --->
</script>

<p>This text is aligned right.</p>

</html>
```

# document.tags.textDecoration

## JavaScript 1.2+

## Nav4+

## Syntax

```
document.tags.tagName.textDecoration
```

## Description

The `textDecoration` property specifies the type of decoration that is added to text as associated with the tag called *tagName*.

There are four types of values that are valid for the `textDecoration` property: `under-line`, `line-through`, `blink`, and `none`.

## Example

Listing 7.192 uses the `textDecoration` property to put a line through a line of text.

*Listing 7.192    Set the `textDecoration` Property*

```
<html>

<script>
<!-- Hide

//Create a style sheet tag that defines text decoration
document.tags.P.textDecoration = "line-through";

//Hide End --->
```

```
</script>

<p>This text is crossed out.</p>

</html>
```

# document.tags.textIndent

## *JavaScript 1.2+*

## *Nav4+*

## *Syntax*

```
document.tags.tagName.textIndent
```

## *Description*

The textIndent property specifies the indention should appear before text as associated with the tag called *tagName*. The property is assigned a number that represents either length or a percentage.

## *Example*

Listing 7.193 uses the textIndent property to set the text indention to 1 inch.

*Listing 7.193   Set the textIndent Property*
```
<html>

<script>
<!-- Hide

//Create a style sheet tag that defines text indention
document.tags.I.textIndent = "1in";

//Hide End --->
</script>

This text has no indention.<br>
<i>This text is indented 1 inch.</i>

</html>
```

# document.tags.textTransform

## *JavaScript 1.2+*

## *Nav4+*

## *Syntax*

```
document.tags.tagName.textTransform
```

## Description

The textTransform property specifies the transformation that should be applied to text as associated with the tag called *tagName*.

There are four types of values that are valid for the textTransform property: capitalize, uppercase, lowercase, and none.

## Example

Listing 7.194 uses the textTransform property to capitalize the first letter of every word in the sentence.

*Listing 7.194    Set the textTransform Property*

```
<html>

<script>
<!-- Hide

//Create a style sheet tag that defines capitalization
document.tags.P.textTransform = "capitalize";

//Hide End --->
</script>

<p>This line demonstrates the ability to capitalize words.</p>

</html>
```

# document.tags.whiteSpace

## JavaScript 1.2+

## Nav4+

## Syntax

document.tags.*tagName*.whiteSpace

## Description

The whiteSpace property specifies how whitespace should be handled within an element. Using dot notation, the property can be associated with the tag called *tagName*.

There are two types of values that are valid for the whiteSpace property: normal and pre.

## Example

Listing 7.195 uses the whiteSpace property to make whitespace collapsed within the text element.

*Listing 7.195   Set the whiteSpace Property*

```
<html>

<script>
<!-- Hide

//Create a style sheet tag that defines whitespace
document.tags.B.whiteSpace = "normal";

//Hide End --->
</script>

<p><pre>This line used to PRE tag to format whitespace.</pre></p>
<p><b>This line should have collapsed whitespace.</b></p>

</html>
```

# document.title

## JavaScript 1.0+, JScript1.0+

## Nav2+, IE3+, Opera3+

## Syntax

```
document.title
```

## Description

The `title` property is a read-only string that specifies the title of the document. This property is commonly set with the `<title>` tag.

## Example

In Listing 7.196, the title of the Web page is written to the screen using the `title` property.

*Listing 7.196   Accessing the title Property of a Document*

```
<html>
<head><title>My Web Page</title></head>

<script>
<!-- Hide

//Output the title of the document
document.write("The title of this page is <i>");
document.write(document.title,"</i>");

//Hide End --->
</script>

</html>
```

# document.URL

## *JavaScript 1.1+, JScript1.0+*

## *Nav3+, IE3+, Opera3+*

## *Syntax*

```
document.URL
```

## *Description*

The URL property specifies the URL of the document. This property is read-only.

## *Example*

Listing 7.197 uses the URL property to write the document's URL to the screen.

*Listing 7.197    Accessing a Document's URL Property*

```
<html>

<script>
<!-- Hide

//Output the URL of the document
document.write("The URL of this page is -->",document.URL);

//Hide End --->
</script>

</html>
```

# document.vlinkColor

## *JavaScript 1.0+, JScript 1.0+*

## *Nav2+, IE 3+*

## *Syntax*

```
document.vlinkColor
```

## *Description*

The vlinkColor property specifies the color of visited links. The color is expressed as a string in hexadecimal digits or as one of the JavaScript standard color names. The hexadecimal form is made up of 6 digits that follow the pattern "RRGGBB".

## *Example*

Listing 7.198 sets the visited links color to green for all links on the page only if they are placed before the <script> tags.

*Listing 7.198    Setting the Visited Links Color with the `vLinkColor` Property*

```
<html>

<a href="myGreenPage.html">The Green Site</a><br>

<script language="JavaScript">
<!-- Hide

//Set the visited links color to green.
document.vlinkColor="00ff00";

//Hide End --->
</script>

<a href="myGreenGrassPage.html">The Green Grass Page</a>

</html>
```

# document.write()

## JavaScript 1.0+, JScript 1.0+

## Nav2+, IE 3+, Opera3+

## Syntax

```
document.write(value,....)
```

## Description

The `write()` method appends the comma-separated argument(s) (*value*) to the document as a string. If any of the arguments are not strings, they are converted to strings before being appended to the document.

## Example

Listing 7.199 writes some text, as well as the value of a property, to the current document using the `write()` method.

*Listing 7.199    Displaying Text in a Document Using the `write()` Method*

```
<html>
<head><title>Movies</title></head>

<script language="JavaScript">
<!-- Hide

//write data to the current document.
document.write("The title of this web page is called <u>");
document.write(document.title,"</u>");

//Hide End --->
</script>

</html>
```

# document.writeln()

## *JavaScript 1.0+, JScript 1.0+*

## *Nav2+, IE 3+, Opera3+*

## Syntax

```
document.writeln(value,....)
```

## Description

The `writeln()` method appends the comma-separated argument(s) (`value`) to the document as a string. Unlike the `write()` method, the `writeln()` method appends a newline character to the document after the last argument has been written. If any of the arguments are not strings, they are converted to strings before being appended to the document.

## Example

Listing 7.200 writes some text, as well as the value of a property, to the current document using the `writeln()` method. The `<pre>` tag is used to make the newline character, which was created by the `writeln()` method, appear in the Web page.

*Listing 7.200   Displaying Text on a Line in a Document Using the `writeln()` Method*

```
<html>
<head><title>Movies</title></head>

<script language="JavaScript">
<!-- Hide

//write data to the current document.
document.writeln("<pre>The title of this web page is called <u>");
document.writeln(document.title,"</u></pre>");

//Hide End --->
</script>

</html>
```

# Embed

## *JavaScript 1.0+, JScript 3.0+*

## *Nav2+, IE 4+, Opera3+*

## *Syntax*

Core client-side JavaScript object.

## *Description*

The Embed object references any object that is embedded within a Web page using the HTML <embed> tag. It is inherited from the document object. Embed is typically used for audio and video files, but can be used for any type of embedded file. Embedded objects are referenced by either the embeds array or by name.

## *Example*

Listing 7.201 shows an example of how an embedded midi file can be referenced using the embeds array.

When this HTML code is loaded in a browser, the AUTOSTART option for the <embed> tag will start playing the midi file automatically. The stopsong() function calls the stop method, which is part of browser audio plug-in, to stop playing the midi file.

*Listing 7.201   Accessing an Embedded Object by Array*

```
<html>
<head>
<title>Accessing an embedded object by array</title>
</head>
<body>
<script language="JavaScript">
<!--Hide
// function stops the playing of the midi song
function stopsong(){
     document.embeds[0].stop();
}
// End Hide --->
</script>

<embed src="phantom.mid" name="phantom" width="100" height="50"
AUTOSTART="true">
<br>
<form>
Click on the stop button to stop playing the midi file.
<input type="button" value="stop" onCLick='stopsong()'>
</form>

</body>
</html>
```

# Event

## JavaScript 1.2+, JScript 1.0+

## Nav4+, IE 3+

## Syntax

Core client-side JavaScript object.

## Description

The Event object is a built-in object that handles the passing of properties to an event handler. The available properties are shown in Table 7.24.

**Table 7.24    Properties of the Event Object**

| Property | Description |
| --- | --- |
| data | Array of URL's for dragged and dropped objects |
| height | Height of window |
| layerX | Horizontal cursor position within layer |
| layerY | Vertical cursor position within layer |
| modifiers | Bit mask representing modifier keys |
| pageX | Horizontal cursor position within Web page |
| pageY | Vertical cursor position within Web page |
| screenX | Horizontal cursor position within computer screen |
| screenY | Vertical cursor position within computer screen |
| target | Object for captured events |
| type | Type of event |
| which | The mouse button that is pressed |
| width | Width of window |

In addition to the Event properties, events exist that get handled. The available events are shown in Table 7.25.

**Table 7.25    Handled Events**

| Events | Description |
| --- | --- |
| ABORT | Loading of Web page interrupted by user. |
| BLUR | Focus is removed from the object. |
| CHANGE | Contents or setting for document object changed. |
| CLICK | Mouse button is clicked once. |
| DBLCLICK | Mouse button is clicked twice. |
| DRAGDROP | Object is dragged and dropped. |
| ERROR | Error occurred during loading. |
| FOCUS | Focus is applied to an object. |
| KEYDOWN | A key is pressed down. |
| KEYPRESS | A key is pressed. |
| KEYUP | A key is let up after being pressed down. |

| Events | Description |
|---|---|
| LOAD | Load document within a browser. |
| MOUSEDOWN | The mouse button is pressed down. |
| MOUSEMOVE | The mouse cursor is moved. |
| MOUSEOUT | The mouse cursor is moved away from a specific object. |
| MOUSEOVER | The mouse cursor is moved over a specific object. |
| MOUSEUP | The pressed mouse button is let up. |
| MOVE | Object is moved on the screen. |
| RESET | Reset button is pressed. |
| RESIZE | Window or frame has been resized. |
| SELECT | Document object is selected. |
| SUBMIT | Submit button is pressed. |
| UNLOAD | Document is unloaded from browser. |

## Example

Without using the Event properties, Event is used only as an argument to functions for event capturing. An example of this is shown in Listing 7.202. The example captures all KEYPRESS and DBLCLICK events for the Window object and captures SUBMIT events for the document. After the events are captured, they are passed to event handlers that perform specific functions on them. In two of the event handlers, event properties are returned.

*Listing 7.202    Use of* event *Keyword*

```
<html>
<head>
<title>Using the event object</title>
</head>
<body>

<script language = "JavaScript">
<!--Hide

// sets up the document to capture multiple events
window.captureEvents(Event.KEYPRESS | Event.DBLCLICK);
document.captureEvents(Event.SUBMIT);

// function handles the KEYPRESS event.
function handlePress(evnt){
   alert("You pressed a key down. The event it triggered was: " + evnt.type);
   return true;
}

// function handles the DBLCLICK event
function handleDblClick(evnt){
   alert("You double clicked at location: " + evnt.pageX + "," + evnt.pageY);
   return(true);
```

*continues*

*Listing 7.202    continued*

```
}

// function handles the SUBMIT event
function handleSubmit(){
   alert("You clicked on the submit button");
}

// This registers the :
//       handlePress function as the event handler for the KEYPRESS event
//       handleDblClick as the event handler for the DBLCLICK event
//       handleSubmit as the event handler for the SUBMIT event
window.onKeyPress = handlePress;
window.onDblClick = handleDblClick;
document.onSubmit = handleSubmit;

// End Hide --->
</script>


This example shows a number of different things.
<br><br>
<ul>
<li>How to capture multiple events</li>
<li>How to process those events using the event handlers</li>
<li>How to access properties of the <b>event</b> object</li>
</ul>
<br><br><br>
When you click on the submit button, it triggers the <b>SUBMIT</b>
event which displays an alert box.
<br><br>
If you double click somewhere in the page, it triggers the
<b>DBLCLICK</b> event which displays an alert box showing the
coordinates of where you double clicked.
<br><br>
When a key is pressed down in the browser, the <b>KEYPRESS</b>
event is triggered and an alert box is displayed indicating the type of event.
<br><br><br>
<form>
<input type="submit" value="Submit">
</form>

</body>
</html>
```

# event.data

*JavaScript 1.2+*

*Nav4+*

## Syntax

*event*.data

## Description

The data property of the Event object references an array of strings for events of objects that have been dragged and dropped. Each string in the array contains a URL representing the dropped object. The data property can be read only if the script has the UniversalBrowserRead privilege.

## Example

Listing 7.203 shows an example of how the data property can be used to determine the URL of objects that have been dragged and dropped. The example captures all DRAG-DROP events and passes them to a function called handleDrapDrop(). The function extracts the data property from the event and outputs it.

*Listing 7.203   Accessing the* event.data *Property*

```
<html>
<head>
<title>Example of the event.data property</title>
</head>
<body>


<script language="JavaScript">
<!--Hide
// sets up the window to capture DRAGDROP events
window.captureEvents(Event.DRAGDROP);

// function that handles the specific event. The evnt parameter refers to
// the event object.
function handleDragDrop(evnt){

   // request the Universal Browser Read privilege
  netscape.security.PrivilegeManager.enablePrivilege("UniversalBrowserRead");

   // declare a temporary array to hold the URL data from the event.data
   // property.
   tmp = new Array();
   tmp = evnt.data;

   // informs the user of the URL for the dragged and dropped object.
   alert("The URL for the dragdrop object is: " + tmp);
   return true;
}

// This registers the handleDragDrop function as the event handler for the
// DRAGDROP event.
```

*continues*

*Listing 7.203    continued*
```
window.onDragDrop = handleDragDrop;

// End Hide --->
</script>

This example requires the use of <b>UniversalBrowserRead</b> privilege.
<br><br>
Simply drag and drop an object, gif image, folder, file, etc. to the browser
and an alert box will appear indicating the URL path for the object.
</body>
</html>
```

# event.height

## JavaScript 1.2+

## Nav4+

## Syntax

*event*.height

## Description

The height property of the Event object controls the height of a window or frame during the RESIZE event.

## Example

Listing 7.204 shows how the height property can be accessed when an event such as RESIZE occurs. The RESIZE event means that the corresponding window or frame has changed size, thereby changing the height property.

*Listing 7.204    Accessing* event.height *Property*
```
<html>
<head>
<title>Example of the event.height property</title>
</head>
<body>

<script language = "JavaScript">
<!--Hide
// sets up the window to capture RESIZE events
window.captureEvents(Event.RESIZE);

// function that changes the size of the window.
function changeSize(){
    window.resizeTo(300,400);
}

// function that handles the specific event. The evnt parameter refers to
```

```
// the event object.
function handle(evnt){
    alert("A RESIZE event has occurred. The new height of the window is: " +
evnt.height);
    return true;
}

// This registers the handle function as the event handler for the
// RESIZE event.
window.onResize = handle;

// End Hide --->
</script>

<form name="form1">
Click button to change the window size:
<input type="button" value="Resize window" onClick = 'changeSize()'>
</form>
</body>
</html>
```

# event.layerX

## *JavaScript 1.2+*

## *Nav4+*

## *Syntax*

*event*.layerX

## *Description*

The layerX property of the Event object controls the horizontal (x-coordinate) positioning within the layer in which the event occurred.

## *Example*

Listing 7.205 shows an example of a function that is listening for a RESIZE event. When one occurs, a variable stores the new x-coordinate position of the window in the layerX property. In the example, when the user resizes the window, an alert box appears informing him or her of the new X value.

*Listing 7.205   Accessing* layerX *Property of the* event *Object*

```
<html>
<head>
<title>Using the layerX property for the event object</title>
</head>
<body>
<script language="JavaScript">
<!--Hide
```

*continues*

*Listing 7.205   Accessing* `layerX` *Property of the* `event` *Object*

```
// sets up the window to capture RESIZE events
window.captureEvents(Event.RESIZE);

// function that changes the size of the window.
function changeSize(){
    window.resizeTo(300,400);
}

// function that handles the specific event. The evnt parameter refers to
// the event object.
function handle(evnt){
    alert("The new width (X value) after the resize is: " + evnt.layerX);
    return true;
}

// This registers the handle function as the event handler for the
// RESIZE event.
window.onResize = handle;
// End Hide --->
</script>

<form name="form1">
Click button to resize:
<input type="Button" value="Resize Window" onClick='changeSize()'>
</form>
</body>
</html>
```

# event.layerY

## JavaScript 1.2+

## Nav4+

## Syntax

`event.layerY`

## Description

The `layerY` property of the `Event` object controls the vertical (y-coordinate) positioning within the layer in which the event occurred. When a window or frame is resized, the new value for the vertical coordinate is stored in the `layerY` property.

## Example

Listing 7.206 shows an example of how the `layerY` property is used. When a RESIZE event occurs, it invokes the event handler that displays an alert box indicating the new y value. The y value is obtained from the `layerY` property of the `event` object.

*Listing 7.206    Example of How to Change the* `layerY` *Property*

```
<html>
<head>
<title>Using the layerY property for the event object</title>
</head>
<body>
<script language="JavaScript">
<!--Hide

// sets up the window to capture RESIZE events
window.captureEvents(Event.RESIZE);

// function that changes the size of the window.
function changeSize(){
    window.resizeTo(200,350);
}

// function that handles the specific event. The evnt parameter refers to
// the event object.
function handle(evnt){
    alert("The new height (Y value) of the window object after the resize is: "
+ evnt.layerY);
    return true;
}

// This registers the handle function as the event handler for the
// RESIZE event.
window.onResize = handle;
// End Hide --->
</script>

<form name="form1">
Click button to resize:

<input type="Button" value="Resize Window" onClick='changeSize()'>
</form>
</body>
</html>
```

# event.modifiers

## *JavaScript 1.2+*

## *Nav4+*

## *Syntax*

*event*.modifiers

## Description

The `modifiers` property of the `Event` object refers to any keyboard modifier that occurs during an event. Modifiers are in the form of a bitmask object and may consist of the following values: `ALT_MASK`, `CONTROL_MASK`, `META_MASK`, and `SHIFT_MASK`.

## Example

Listing 7.207 shows how the `modifiers` property can be accessed when some sort of modifier, such as a mouse or keyboard event, has occurred. The `KEYPRESS` event is captured and the `modifiers` property checked to see which type of key was pressed. If a match is found, a message is sent to the user so indicating.

*Listing 7.207   Accessing the* `modifiers` *Property*

```
<html>
<head>
<title>Using the modifiers property for the event object</title>
</head>
<body>
<script language = "Javascript">
<!--Hide
// sets up the window to capture KEYPRESS events
document.captureEvents(Event.KEYPRESS);

// function that handles the KEYPRESS event.
// It checks the event.modifiers property to see
// what button was pressed.
//
// The available values are:
//          META_MASK = 0
//          CONTROL_MASK = 2
//          ALT_MASK = 3
//          SHIFT_MASK = 4
function handlePress(evnt){

    if(evnt.modifiers == "0"){
        alert("The Meta key was pressed");
    }

    if(evnt.modifiers == '2'){
        alert("The Ctrl key was pressed");
    }

    if(evnt.modifiers == "4"){
        alert("The Shift key was pressed");
     }
     return true;
}
// This registers the handlePress function as the event handler for the
// KEYPRESS event.
document.onKeyPress = handlePress;
```

```
// End Hide --->
</script>

This example demonstrates the modifiers property of the event object.
<br><br>
The modifier checks for pressing of the <b>Meta</b> key.
<br><br>
If you press the "<b>Ctrl</b>" key the modifiers property indicates so.
<br><br>
By pressing the "<b>Shift</b>" key, you trigger an event which checks for the
SHIFT_MASK modifier.
<br><br>
</body>
</html>
```

To access a specific modifier value, simply reference it using the Event object. Listing 7.208 shows how to access the ALT_MASK modifier.

*Listing 7.208   Accessing a Specific Modifier Value*
```
Event.ALT_MASK
```

# event.pageX

## *JavaScript 1.2+*

## *Nav4+*

## *Syntax*

```
event.pageX
```

## *Description*

The pageX property of the Event object controls the horizontal (x-coordinate) positioning within a Web page in which the event occurred.

## *Example*

Listing 7.209 shows an example of how you can find the x-coordinate positioning of where the click event occurred within the browser. Simply click in the browser window and an alert box will appear indicating the value of the x-coordinate of where the mouse was clicked.

*Listing 7.209   Example of Using the pageX Property*
```
<html>
<head>
<title>Example of the event.pageX property</title>
</head>
<body>

<script language = "JavaScript">
```

*continues*

*Listing 7.209    continued*

```
<!--Hide

// sets up the window to capture CLICK events
window.captureEvents(Event.CLICK);

// function that handles the specific event. The evnt parameter refers to
// the event object.
function handle(evnt){
  alert("The X coordinate of where the click event occurred is: " +
evnt.pageX);
    return true;
}

// This registers the handle function as the event handler for the
// CLICK event.
window.onClick = handle;

// End Hide --->
</script>

<form>
This example shows you how to access the <b>pageX</b>
property of the <i>event</i> object.  As you click in the
web browser, an alert box will pop up indicating the value of
the X-coordinate of where you clicked.
</form>

</body>
</html>
```

# event.pageY

## *JavaScript 1.2+*

## *Nav4+*

## *Syntax*

`event.pageY`

## *Description*

The pageY property of the Event object controls the vertical (y-coordinate) positioning within the Web page in which the event occurred.

## *Example*

Listing 7.210 shows an example of how to determine the y-coordinate cursor positioning by using the pageY event property. The JavaScript code listens for a CLICK event to occur. When this happens, it calls the handle() function, which is defined to handle any captured click events. The `handle()` function simply pops up an alert box indicating the y-coordinate value of where the click occurred.

*Listing 7.210   Example of Using the* `pageY` *Event Property*

```
<html>
<head>
<title>Example of the event.pageY property</title>
</head>
<body>

<script language = "JavaScript">
<!--Hide

// sets up the window to capture CLICK events
window.captureEvents(Event.CLICK);

// function that handles the specific event. The evnt parameter refers to
// the event object.
function handle(evnt){
  alert("The Y coordinate of where the click event occurred is: " +
evnt.pageY);
    return true;
}

// This registers the handle function as the event handler for the
// CLICK event.
window.onClick = handle;

// End Hide --->
</script>

This example shows you how to access the <b>pageY</b> property of the
<i>event</i> object.  As you click in the web browser, an alert box will
pop up indicating the value of the Y-coordinate of where you clicked.

</body>
</html>
```

# event.screenX

## *JavaScript 1.2+, JScript 3.0+*

## *Nav4+, IE 4+*

## *Syntax*

`event.screenX`

## *Description*

The `screenX` property of the event object controls the horizontal (x-coordinate) positioning within the computer screen in which the event occurred.

## Example

Listing 7.211 shows an example of how to determine the x-coordinate of the cursor relative to the screen of where the click event occurred. The code captures the CLICK event. When captured, control is passed to the handle() function, which determines the x-coordinate position using the screenX property.

*Listing 7.211    Using the screenX Property*

```
<html>
<head>
<title>Example of the event.screenX property</title>
</head>
<body>

<script language = "JavaScript">
<!--Hide

// sets up the window to capture CLICK events
window.captureEvents(Event.CLICK);

// function that handles the specific event. The evnt parameter refers to
// the event object.
function handle(evnt){
   alert("The X coordinate relative to the computer screen of where the click
occurred is: " + evnt.screenX);
      return true;
}

// This registers the handle function as the event handler for the
// CLICK event.
window.onClick = handle;

// End Hide --->
</script>

This example shows you how to access the <b>screenX</b>
property of the <i>event</i> object.  As you click in
the web browser, an alert box will pop up indicating
the value of the X-coordinate (relative to the computer screen)
of where you clicked.

</body>
</html>
```

# event.screenY

## *JavaScript 1.2+, JScript 3.0+*

## *Nav4+, IE 4+*

## Syntax

*event*.screenY

## Description

The screenY property of the Event object controls the vertical (y-coordinate) positioning within the computer screen in which the event occurred.

## Example

Listing 7.212 shows an example of how to determine the y-coordinate of the cursor positioning relative to the computer screen when the click event occurs. The code captures the CLICK event. When captured, control is passed to the handle() function, which determines the y-coordinate position using the screenY property.

*Listing 7.212   Accessing the* screenY *Property of the* Event *Object*

```
<html>
<head>
<title>Example of the event.screenY property</title>
</head>
<body>

<script language = "JavaScript">
<!--Hide

// sets up the window to capture CLICK events
window.captureEvents(Event.CLICK);

// function that handles the specific event. The evnt parameter refers to
// the event object.
function handle(evnt){
  alert("The Y coordinate relative to the computer screen of where the click
occurred is: " + evnt.screenY);
    return true;
}

// This registers the handle function as the event handler for the
// CLICK event.
window.onClick = handle;

// End Hide --->
</script>

This example shows you how to access the <b>screenY</b>
property of the <i>event</i> object.  As you click in
the web browser, an alert box will pop up indicating
the value of the Y-coordinate (relative to the computer screen)
of where you clicked.


</body>
</html>
```

# event.target

*JavaScript 1.2+*

*Nav4+*

## Syntax

*event*.target

## Description

The target property of the Event object refers to the object on which the event takes place.

## Example

Listing 7.213 shows an example of how the target property can be used to determine to which object an event occurred. In the HTML document, there are three buttons. When the button is clicked, a JavaScript function catches the click event and, using the target property, tells the user which button was clicked.

*Listing 7.213   Accessing the* target *Property*

```
<html>
<head>
<title>Using the target property of the event object</title>
</head>
<body>
<script language = "JavaScript">
<!--Hide
// informs the user which mouse button was pressed
function whichButton(evnt){
    window.captureEvents(evnt.CLICK);
    alert("The button you pressed was:" + evnt.target.value);
}
// End Hide --->
</script>

<form name="form1">
Choose a button and click on it.
<br><br>
<input type="button" value="Button1" name="Button1" onClick =
whichButton(event)>
<input type="button" value="Button2" name="Button2" onClick =
whichButton(event)>
<input type="button" value="Button3" name="Button3" onClick =
whichButton(event)>
</form>

</body>
</html>
```

# event.type

## *JavaScript 1.2+, JScript 3.0+*

## *Nav4+, IE 4+*

## *Syntax*

`event.type`

## *Description*

The type property of the Event object refers to the type of event that occurred. The value assigned to type is a string representing the name of the event. See Table 7.25 for the valid event types supported by each browser.

## *Example*

Listing 7.214 shows how the type property can be used to figure out what type of event is being set. This example checks for a few different events. When an event is detected, a message is displayed in the message box indicating to the user which type of event occurred. This example can be expanded to include many different events.

*Listing 7.214    Accessing the* type *Property*

```
<html>
<head>
<title>Using the type property for the event object</title>
</head>
<body>

<script language = "Javascript">
<!--Hide

// sets up the window to capture multiple events
document.captureEvents(Event.CLICK¦Event.KEYPRESS¦Event.MOUSEDOWN);

// function that handles the specific event. The evnt parameter refers to
// the event object.
function handle(evnt){

//alert(evnt.type)
    if(evnt.type == "click"){
        document.form1.msg.value += "The click event occurred.\n"
    }

    if(evnt.type == "mousedown"){
        document.form1.msg.value += "The mousedown event occurred.\n"
    }

    if(evnt.type == "keypress"){
        document.form1.msg.value += "The keypress event occurred.\n"
```

```
    }

    return true;
}

// This registers the handle function as the event handler for the
// multiple events.
document.onKeyPress = handle;
document.onClick = handle;
document.onMouseDown = handle;

// End Hide --->
</script>

<form name="form1">
This page demonstrates a few different events. Upon events occurring, a message
will be displayed in the textarea indicating which event occurred.
<br><br><br>
<ul>
<li><input type="Button" value="Click Me"></li>
<br><br>
<li>
Dummy text area.
<input type="text" size="20">
<br>
Click mouse in text field.
<br><br>
</li>

<br><br>
<b>Message output:</b>
<textarea name="msg" rows="10" cols="60"></textarea>
<br><br>
<input type="reset" value="Clear">
</form>

</body>
</html>
```

# event.which

## *JavaScript 1.2+*

## *Nav4+*

## *Syntax*

*event*.which

## Description

The which property of the Event object refers to which key or mouse button was pressed or clicked. The value returned for mouse events is a numeric value 1, 2, or 3, representing the left, middle, and right mouse buttons, respectively. The value returned for keyboard events is a character representation for the key that was pressed.

## Example

Listing 7.215 shows how the which property can be used to determine which mouse button was pressed. When the user clicks the radio button, an alert box is shown informing you of the corresponding number for the mouse button clicked.

*Listing 7.215    Accessing the which Property of Event Object*

```
<html>
<head>
<title>Using the which property of the event object</title>
</head>
<body>

<form>
This example uses the which property of the event object to determine
which mouse button is pressed.
<br><br>
<input type="radio" onClick = 'alert("Mouse button Number " + event.which +
"was pressed.")'>
</form>

</body>
</html>
```

# event.width

## JavaScript 1.2+

## Nav4+

## Syntax

```
event.width
```

## Description

The width property of the Event object refers to the width of a window or frame. It is set during the RESIZE event to the new width of window or frame being resized.

## Example

Listing 7.216 shows an example using the width property. The RESIZE event is captured and passed to the handle() function. This function informs the user that a RESIZE event has occurred and outputs the new width of the window.

*Listing 7.216   Accessing the* width *Property*

```
<html>
<head>
<title>Example of the event.width property</title>
</head>
<body>

<script language = "JavaScript">
<!--Hide

// sets up the window to capture RESIZE events
window.captureEvents(Event.RESIZE);

// function that changes the size of the window.
function changeSize(){
    window.resizeTo(300,400);
}

// function that handles the specific event. The evnt parameter refers to
// the event object.
function handle(evnt){
    alert("An RESIZE event has occurred. The new width of the window is: " +
evnt.height);
    return true;
}

// This registers the handle function as the event handler for the
// RESIZE event.
window.onResize = handle;

// End Hide --->
</script>

<form name="form1">
<inputtype=value=
Click the button to resize the window:
<input type="Button" value="Resize">
</form>

</body>
</html>
```

# Event.ABORT

## *JavaScript 1.0+, JScript 1.0+*

## *Nav2+, IE 3+, Opera3+*

## *Syntax*

```
Event.ABORT
```

## Description

The ABORT property of the Event object is used by images and refers to the event in which a transfer is interrupted or aborted by a user.

## Example

Listing 7.217 shows an example in which an HTML document may have a large .gif file embedded within it, but, during the document loading process, the loading of the .gif file is aborted (by clicking the Stop button in the browser). The captureEvents() method catches the ABORT event and passes it to the handleAbort(), method which handles it accordingly.

*Listing 7.217   Using the ABORT Event Property*

```
<html>
<head>
<title>Example of Event.ABORT</title>
</head>
<body>
<script language = "JavaScript">
<!--Hide

// sets up the window to capture ABORT events
document.captureEvents(Event.ABORT);

// function that handles the specific event. The evnt parameter refers to
// the event object. In this case the function is handling any type of ABORT
events.
function handleAbort(evnt){
    alert("An ABORT event has occurred.");
    return true;
}

// This registers the handle function as the event handler for the
// ABORT event.
document.onAbort = handleAbort;
// End Hide --->
</script>

This page loads the sample.gif image. Assuming this is a large image and takes
some time to load, if the user clicks the stop button on the browser, an
<b>abort</b> event will be captured.
<br><br><br>
<img src="sample.gif" width="350" height="500" onAbort=''>

</body>
</html>
```

# Event.BLUR

## *JavaScript 1.0+, JScript 1.0+*

## Nav2+, IE 3+, Opera3+

## Syntax

```
Event.BLUR
```

## Description

The BLUR property of the Event object is used by all windows, frames, and form elements when focus is removed from a particular object.

## Example

Listing 7.218 shows an example in which the user wants to be alerted when the focus had been removed from the text area. A function is created to capture the BLUR event that occurs when focus is removed from an object. When the event is captured, the handlerBlur() function alerts the user of the event.

*Listing 7.218    Using the BLUR Event Property*

```
<html>
<head>
<title>Example of Event.BLUR</title>
</head>
<body>

<script language = "JavaScript">
<!--Hide

// sets up the window to capture BLUR events
document.captureEvents(Event.BLUR);

// function that handles the specific event. The evnt parameter refers to
// the event object.
function handleBlur(evnt){
    document.form1.msg.value += "A BLUR event has occurred.\n";
    return true;
}

// This registers the handle function as the event handler for the
// BLUR event.
document.onBlur = handleBlur;

// End Hide --->
</script>

<form>
Set focus to the first text box. Then click in the second
text box to remove focus from text 1.
<br><br>
Text 1:<input type="text" size="20">
<br><br>
```

```
Text 2:<input type="text" size="20">
<br><br>
<b>Message box:</b>
<textarea name="msg" rows="5" cols="50"></textarea>
</form>

</body>
</html>
```

# Event.CHANGE

## JavaScript 1.0+, JScript 1.0+

## Nav2+, IE 3+, Opera3+

### Syntax

```
Event.CHANGE
```

### Description

The CHANGE property of the Event object is used by any text-related and select-box form elements to indicate a change in the element settings.

### Example

Listing 7.219 shows an example of a function checking for any occurrences of the CHANGE event. When a CHANGE event occurs, it is captured by the Document object and then passed to the handleChange() function, which alerts the user.

Listing 7.219  Accessing the CHANGE Property

```
<html>
<head>
<title>Example of Event.CHANGE</title>
</head>
<body>

<script language = "JavaScript">
<!--Hide

// sets up the window to capture CHANGE event
document.captureEvents(Event.CHANGE);

// function that handles the specific event. The evnt parameter
// refers to the event object.
function handleChange(evnt){
    alert("The text in TextBox1 has been changed");
    return true;
}

// This registers the handle function as the event handler for the
```

*continues*

*Listing 7.219 continued*

```
// CHANGE event.
document.onChange = handleChange;

// End Hide --->
</script>
```

This example demonstrates the change event. Initially TextBox1
is empty, however when you enter information into the textbox,
the CHANGE event occurs. This triggers an alert box to open
up informing you that the text in box 1 has been changed.

```
<br><br>
<form name="form1">
TextBox1:
<input type="text" size="20" name="text1">
<br><br>
TextBox2:
<input type="text" size="20" name="text2">
</form>
</body>
</html>
```

# Event.CLICK

## *JavaScript 1.0+*

## *Nav2+, Opera3+*

## *Syntax*

```
Event.CLICK
```

## *Description*

The CLICK property of the Event object is used by all button objects, documents, and
links to indicate a single mouse button click.

## *Example*

Listing 7.220 shows how the CLICK property is used to determine whether the mouse
was clicked or not. When you click the browser window, the captureEvents() method
captures the CLICK event. The event handler then alerts you that a click has been performed.

*Listing 7.220   Accessing the CLICK Property*

```
<html>
<head>
<title>Example of Event.CLICK</title>
</head>
<body>
<script language = "JavaScript">
<!--Hide
```

```
// sets up the window to capture CLICK events
window.captureEvents(Event.CLICK);

// function that handles the specific event. The evnt parameter refers to
// the event object.
function handleClick(evnt){
    alert("A CLICK event has occurred in this window.");
    return true;
}

// This registers the handle function as the event handler for the
// CLICK event.
window.onClick = handleClick;

// End Hide --->
</script>

<form>
<input type="button" value="Click Here" onClick = 'findClick(event)'>
</form>

</body>
</html>
```

# Event.DBLCLICK

## *JavaScript 1.2+, JScript 3.0+*

## *Nav4+, IE 4+*

## *Syntax*

```
Event.DBLCLICK
```

## *Description*

The DBLCLICK property of the Event object is used by documents and links to indicate a double mouse click.

## *Example*

Listing 7.221 shows an example of the onDblClick event handler being used to handle the DBLCLICK event. When the user double-clicks the button or anywhere in the window, an alert box appears informing the user that he or she double-clicked.

*Listing 7.221    Accessing the* DBLCLICK *Object*
```
<html>
<head>
<title>Example of Event.DBLCLICK</title>
```

*continues*

*Listing 7.221    continued*

```
</head>
<body>


<script language = "JavaScript">
<!--Hide                    *

// sets up the window to capture DBLCLICK events
window.captureEvents(Event.DBLCLICK);

// function that handles the specific event. The evnt parameter refers to
// the event object.
function handle(evnt){
    alert("A DBLCLICK event has occurred in this window.");
    return true;
}

// This registers the handle function as the event handler for the
// DBLCLICK event.
window.onDblClick = handle;

// End Hide --->
</script>

This example demonstrates the double-click event. Double-click
anywhere in the browser window and an alert box will appear
indicating that a <b>DBLCLICK</b> event has been captured.
<br><br>

<form>
<input type="button" value="Double-click me">
</form>
</body>
</html>
```

# Event.DRAGDROP

## *JavaScript 1.2+*

## *Nav4+*

## *Syntax*

Event.DRAPDROP

## *Description*

The DRAGDROP property of the Event object is used by the window to indicate the event
that an object has been dragged and dropped.

## Example

Listing 7.222 shows the how the DRAGDROP event is used to check for any object that has been dragged and dropped into the browser window. If this occurs, an alert box is shown indicating that the DRAGDROP event has occurred.

*Listing 7.222   Using the* DragDrop *Event Handler*

```
<html>
<head>
<title>Example of Event.DRAGDROP</title>
</head>
<body>


<script language = "JavaScript">
<!--Hide

// sets up the window to capture DRAGDROP events
window.captureEvents(Event.DRAGDROP);

// function that handles the specific event. The evnt parameter refers to
// the event object.
function handleDragDrop(evnt){
    alert("An object has been dragged and dropped.");
    return true;
}

// This registers the handle function as the event handler for the
// DRAGDROP event.
window.onDragDrop = handleDragDrop;

// End Hide --->
</script>

This example demonstrates the dragdrop event. Drag and drop an
object in the browser window and an alert box will appear
indicating that a <b>DRAGDROP</b> event has occurred.
<br><br>

</body>
</html>
```

# Event.ERROR

## *JavaScript 1.1+, JScript 3.0+*

## *Nav3+, IE 4+, Opera3+*

## *Syntax*

```
Event.ERROR
```

## Description

The ERROR property of the Event object is used by windows and images to indicate any errors that occurred during the loading of the Web page.

## Example

Listing 7.223 shows an example of how ERROR events can be handled. When an ERROR event is captured, it is passed to the handle() function, which informs the user of the error.

*Listing 7.223    Accessing the* ERROR *Property*

```
<html>
<head>
<title>Using the Event.ERROR</title>
</head>
<body>

<script language = "JavaScript">
<!--Hide

// sets up the window to capture ERROR event
window.captureEvents(Event.ERROR);

// function that handles the specific event. The evnt parameter refers to
// the event object.
function handle(evnt){
    alert("ERROR: The image was unable to be loaded.");
    return true;
}

// This registers the handle function as the event handler for the
// ERROR event.
window.onError = handle;
// End Hide --->
</script>

This page only contains a gif image. However since this gif doesn't
exist there will be an error loading the page. This error event will
be captured and alerted to the user.
<br><br>
<img src="nothing.gif">

</body>
</html>
```

# Event.FOCUS

## *JavaScript 1.0+, JScript 1.0+*

## *Nav2+, IE 3+, Opera3+*

## Syntax

.Event.FOCUS

## Description

The FOCUS property of the Event object is used by windows, frames, and form elements to indicate when focus is applied to an object.

## Example

Listing 7.224 shows an example of how the FOCUS property is used to determine when focus is set on a certain object. As you click each object, a message is displayed in the message box indicating which object has focus. The onFocus event handler handles all Event.FOCUS events by default.

*Listing 7.224   Accessing the FOCUS Property*

```
<html>
<head>
<title>Example of Event.FOCUS</title>
</head>
<body>
<script language="JavaScript">
<!--Hide

function showMsg1(){
    document.form1.msg.value += "Focus set on Text 1.\n";
}

function showMsg2(){
    document.form1.msg.value += "Focus set on Text 2.\n";
}

function showMsg3(){
    document.form1.msg.value += "Focus set on Button 1.\n";
}

function showMsg4(){
    document.form1.msg.value += "Focus set on the Message Box.\n";
}
// End Hide --->
</script>

<form name="form1">
Set focus to an object.
<br><br>
Text 1:<input type="text" size="20" onFocus='showMsg1()'>
<br><br>
Text 2:<input type="text" size="20" onFocus='showMsg2()'>
<br><br>
```

*continues*

*Listing 7.224    continued*

```
Button 1:<input type="button" value="Click Me" onfocus='showMsg3()'>
<br><br>
<b>Message box:</b>
<textarea name="msg" rows="5" cols="50" onfocus='showMsg4()'></textarea>
</form>

</body>
</html>
```

# Event.KEYDOWN

## *JavaScript 1.2+*

## *Nav4+*

## Syntax

Event.KEYDOWN

## Description

The KEYDOWN property of the Event object is used by documents, images, links, and text area for elements to indicate when a key is pressed by the user.

## Example

Listing 7.225 shows an example of how a JavaScript function can use the KEYDOWN event to determine if a key was pressed down. When the KEYDOWN event is captured, the handle() function processes the event and informs the user that a key has been pressed down.

*Listing 7.225    Accessing the KEYDOWN Property*

```
<html>
<head>
<title>Example of Event.KEYDOWN</title>
</head>
<body>
<script language="JavaScript">
<!--Hide

// sets up the window to capture KEYDOWN events
window.captureEvents(Event.KEYDOWN);

// function that handles the specific event. The evnt parameter refers to
// the event object.
function handle(evnt){
    document.form1.msg.value += " A key was pressed down.\n";
    return true;
}
```

```
// This registers the handle function as the event handler for the
// KEYPRESS event.
window.onKeyDown = handle;
// End Hide --->
</script>
<form name="form1">
<inputtype=
Press a key down. When a key is pressed down, a message is displayed in the
message box indicating that the <b>KEYDOWN</b> event has occurred.
<br><br>
<b>Message box:</b>
<textarea name="msg" rows="5" cols="50"></textarea>
<br><br>
<input type="reset" value="Clear Message Box">
</form>

</body>
</html>
```

# Event.KEYPRESS

## *JavaScript 1.2+*

## *Nav4+*

## *Syntax*

```
Event.KEYPRESS
```

## *Description*

The KEYPRESS property of the Event object is used by documents, images, links, and text area form elements to indicate when a key is pressed and held by the user.

## *Example*

Listing 7.226 shows how the KEYPRESS property is used to determine when a key has been pressed. When the KEYPRESS event is captured, it is sent to the handle() function, which informs the user that a key has been pressed.

*Listing 7.226  Accessing the KEYPRESS Object*

```
<html>
<head>
<title>Example of Event.KEYPRESS</title>
</head>
<body>
<script language="JavaScript">
<!--Hide

// sets up the window to capture KEYPRESS events
```

*continues*

*Listing 7.226   continued*
```
window.captureEvents(Event.KEYPRESS);

// function that handles the specific event. The evnt parameter refers to
// the event object.
function handle(evnt){
    document.form1.msg.value += " A key was pressed.\n";
    return true;
}

// This registers the handle function as the event handler for the
// KEYPRESS event.
window.onKeyPress = handle;
// End Hide --->
</script>

<form name="form1">
Press a key. When a key is pressed, a message is displayed in the message box
indicating that a key has been pressed.
<br><br>
<b>Message box:</b>
<textarea name="msg" rows="5" cols="50"></textarea>
</form>

</body>
</html>
```

# Event.KEYUP

## *JavaScript 1.2+*

## *Nav4+*

## *Syntax*

```
Event.KEYUP
```

## *Description*

The KEYUP property of the Event object is used by documents, images, links, and text area form elements to indicate when a pressed key is released by the user.

## *Example*

Listing 7.227 shows how to determine when a key has been released. The KEYUP event is captured. When this occurs, the handle() function is invoked, which informs the user that a key that had been pressed down has been released.

*Listing 7.227   Accessing the KEYUP Property*
```
<html>
<head>
<title>Example of Event.KEYUP</title>
```

```
</head>
<body>
<script language="JavaScript">
<!--Hide

// sets up the window to capture KEYUP events
window.captureEvents(Event.KEYUP);

// function that handles the specific event. The evnt parameter refers to
// the event object.
function handle(evnt){
    document.form1.msg.value += " A key was pressed down and let up.\n";
    return true;
}

// This registers the handle function as the event handler for the
// KEYPRESS event.
window.onKeyUp = handle;
// End Hide --->
</script>

<form name="form1">

Press a key down. When a key is pressed down and let back up, a message is
displayed in the message box indicating that the <b>KEYUP</b> event has
occurred.
If you press a key down and hold it down, no message displayed. Only when the
key
is let backup is a message displayed.
<br><br>
<b>Message box:</b>
<textarea name="msg" rows="5" cols="50"></textarea>
<br><br>
<input type="reset" value="Clear Message Box">
</form>

</body>
</html>
```

# Event.LOAD

## *JavaScript 1.0+, JScript 1.0+*

## *Nav2+, IE 3+*

## *Syntax*

```
Event.LOAD
```

## Description

The LOAD property of the Event object is used by the Document object to indicate when a page is loaded by the browser.

## Example

Listing 7.228 shows an example of how to inform the user when a Web page has loaded. The LOAD event is captured. When this occurs, the handle() function is invoked, which informs the user that the page has finished being loaded.

*Listing 7.228    Example of Using the LOAD Event Property*

```
<html>
<head>
<title>Using the Event.LOAD</title>
</head>
<body>
<script language = "JavaScript">
// sets up the window to capture LOAD events
window.captureEvents(Event.LOAD);

// function that handles the specific event. The evnt parameter refers to
// the event object.
function handle(evnt){
    alert("The page is finish being loaded.");
    return true;
}

// This registers the handle function as the event handler for the
// LOAD event.
window.onload = handle;

// End Hide --->
</script>

This page only contains a gif image. When the page is finished loading,
a message is displayed indicating so.
<br><br>
<img src="mypic.gif" onload='handle()'>
</body>
</html>
```

# Event.MOUSEDOWN

## *JavaScript 1.2+, JScript 3.0+*

## *Nav4+, IE 4+*

## Syntax

```
Event.MOUSEDOWN
```

## Description

The MOUSEDOWN property of the Event object is used by button objects, documents, and links to indicate when the mouse button is pressed by the user.

## Example

Listing 7.229 shows how to use the MOUSEDOWN property to determine when the mouse has been pressed down. The onMouseDown event handler is used to catch the MOUSEDOWN event. When it is caught, an alert box is used to inform the user that the event has just occurred.

*Listing 7.229   Accessing* MOUSEDOWN *Property*

```
<html>
<head>
<title>Using Event.MOUSEDOWN</title>
</head>
<body>

<script language = "JavaScript">
<!--Hide

// sets up the window to capture MOUSEDOWN events
window.captureEvents(Event.MOUSEDOWN);

// function that handles the specific event. The evnt parameter refers to
// the event object.
function handle(evnt){
    alert("The mouse has been pressed down.");
    return true;
}

// This registers the handle function as the event handler for the
// MOUSEDOWN event.
window.onMouseDown = handle;

// End Hide --->
</script>

This example uses the <b>MOUSEDOWN</b> event. When the mouse button
is pressed down, an alert box is shown.

</body>
</html>
```

# Event.MOUSEMOVE

## *JavaScript 1.2+, JScript 3.0+*

## *Nav4+, IE 4+*

## Syntax

Event.MOUSEMOVE

## Description

The MOUSEMOVE property of the Event object indicates when the mouse cursor is moved by the user.

## Example

Listing 7.230 shows how the MOUSEMOVE event is used to determine when the user is moving the mouse. As the mouse cursor is moved, the coordinates are displayed in the text boxes.

*Listing 7.230   Accessing the MOUSEMOVE Property*

```
<html>
<head>
<title>Using Event.MOUSEMOVE</title>
</head>
<body>
<script language = "JavaScript">
<!--Hide

// sets up the window to capture MOUSEMOVE events
window.captureEvents(Event.MOUSEMOVE);

// function that handles the specific event. The evnt parameter refers to
// the event object. The function sets the x and y coordinates into the text
// areas.
function handle(evnt){
    document.form1.x.value=evnt.pageX;
    document.form1.y.value=evnt.pageY;
    return true;
}

// This registers the handle function as the event handler for the
// MOUSEMOVE event.
window.onMouseMove = handle;
// End Hide --->
</script>

<form name="form1">
This example uses the <b>MOUSEMOVE</b> event. When the mouse is moved,
then the coordinates are changed.
<br><br>
Mouse x-Coordinate value:<input type="text" name="x" size="3"><br><br>
Mouse y-Coordinate value:<input type="text" name="y" size="3">
</form>
</body>
</html>
```

# Event.MOUSEOUT

## *JavaScript 1.1+, JScript 3.0+*

## *Nav3+, IE 4+, Opera3+*

### Syntax

Event.MOUSEOUT

### Description

The MOUSEOUT property of the Event object is used by links and document layers to indicate when the focus of the mouse cursor is moved away from an object.

### Example

Listing 7.231 shows how the onMouseOut event handler is used to catch the MOUSEOUT event that occurs when the mouse cursor is removed from a HTML link.

*Listing 7.231   Using the* MOUSEOUT *Property*
```
<html>
<head>
<title>Example of Event.MOUSEOUT</title>
</head>
<body>

<a href="http://www.microsoft.com" onMouseout = 'alert("The mouse has moved out
of the area of this link")'>
Microsoft Website</a>

</body>
</html>
```

# Event.MOUSEOVER

## *JavaScript 1.0+, Jscript 1.0+*

## *Nav2+, IE3+, Opera3+*

### Syntax

Event.MOUSEOVER

### Description

The MOUSEOVER property of the Event object is used by links and document layers to indicate when the mouse cursor is moved over an object.

### Example

Listing 7.232 shows an example of how the MOUSEOVER event property can be used to modify form element values. As the user moves the mouse cursor over the link, the MOUSEOVER event is captured and the user is alerted.

*Listing 7.232    Accessing the* MOUSEOVER *Property*

```
<html>
<head>
<title>Example of Event.MOUSEOVER</title>
</head>
<body>

<script language="JavaScript">
<!--Hide

// sets up the window to capture MOUSEOVER events
window.captureEvents(Event.MOUSEOVER);

// function that handles the specific event. The evnt parameter refers to
// the event object.
function handle(evnt){
    alert("Your mouse cursor is over the Netscape link.");
    return true;
}

// This registers the handle function as the event handler for the
// MOUSEOVER event.
window.onMouseOver = handle;

// End Hide --->
</script>

<form name="form1">
Move the mouse cursor over the link to Netscape. When you do,
it will trigger a <b>MOUSEOVER</b> event which is captured.
An alert box will then appear indicating that the mouse cursor
is over the link.
<br><br><br>
<a href="http://www.netscape.com">
Link to Netscape Website</a>
<br>
</form>

</body>
</html>
```

# Event.MOUSEUP

## *JavaScript 1.2+, JScript 3.0+*

## *Nav4+, IE 4+*

## *Syntax*

```
Event.MOUSEUP
```

## Description

The MOUSEUP property of the Event object is used by button objects, documents, and links to indicate when a mouse button is released.

## Example

Listing 7.233 shows how the onMouseUp event handler is used to determine when the mouse button is released after being pressed. The user clicks the button and, when the mouse button is released, a message is displayed indicating the action.

*Listing 7.233    Accessing the* MOUSEUP *Property*

```
<html>
<head>
<title>Example of Event.MOUSEUP</title>
</head>
<body>

<form>
This example demonstrates the MOUSEUP event. When you click the
➥button and let the
mouse up, an alert message is
➥displayed indicating that the event occurred.
<input type="button" value="Click Me"
➥onMouseup = 'alert("The Mouse button was let up")'>
</form>

</body>
</html>
```

# Event.MOVE

## *JavaScript 1.2+*

## *Nav4+*

## Syntax

```
Event.MOVE
```

## Description

The MOVE property of the Event object is used by windows and frames to indicate when movement by the window or frame occurs.

## Example

Listing 7.234 shows the syntax for accessing the MOVE property. When you begin to move the browser window, the MOVE event will be captured, and the coordinates for the upper-left of the window will be displayed.

*Listing 7.234    Accessing the* MOVE *Property*

```
<html>
<head>
<title>Using Event.MOVE</title>
</head>
<body>

<script language = "JavaScript">
<!--Hide

// sets up the window to capture MOVE events
window.captureEvents(Event.MOVE);

// function that handles the specific event. The evnt parameter refers to
// the event object. The function sets the x and y coordinates into the text
// areas.
function handleMove(evnt){
    document.form1.msg.value="The window has been moved to coordinates: " +
evnt.screenX + "," + screenY;
    document.form1.x.value=evnt.screenX;
    document.form1.y.value=evnt.screenY;
    return true;
}

// This registers the handleMove function as the event handler for the
// MOVE event.
window.onMove = handleMove;

// End Hide --->
</script>

<form name="form1">
This example uses the <b>MOVE</b> event. When the browser window is moved,
then the coordinates are displayed and updated in the field.
<br><br>
Upper-Left Corner X-Coordinate value:
<input type="text" name="x" size="3"><br><br>
Upper-Left Corner Y-Coordinate value:
<input type="text" name="y" size="3">
<br><br><br>
Message Box:
<br>
<textarea name="msg" rows="3" cols="60"></textarea>
<br>
<input type="reset" value="Clear">
</form>

</body>
</html>
```

# Event.RESET

## *JavaScript 1.1+, JScript 1.0+*

## *Nav3+, IE 3+, Opera3+*

## Syntax

```
Event.RESET
```

## Description

The RESET property of the Event object is used solely by forms to indicate when the Reset button is clicked.

## Example

Listing 7.235 shows an example of how to determine if a Reset button has been pressed. When the RESET event is captured, the function handle() alerts the user that the button has been clicked.

*Listing 7.235   Accessing the RESET Property*

```
<html>
<head>
<title>Example of Event.RESET</title>
</head>
<body>
<script language="JavaScript">
<!--Hide

// sets up the window to capture RESET events
window.captureEvents(Event.RESET);

// function that handles the specific event. The evnt parameter refers to
// the event object.
function handle(evnt){
    alert("You have clicked the Reset button");
    return true;
}

// This registers the handle function as the event handler for the
// RESET event.
window.onReset = handle;
// End Hide --->
</script>

This example demonstrates the <b>Reset</b> event. Click the different buttons
below. Only the Reset button will trigger the submit event.
<br><br>
<form>
```

*continues*

*Listing 7.235    continued*

```
<br><br>
Dummy Text:<input type="text" size="20">
<br><br>
<input type="button" value="Click Button 1">
<br><br>
<input type="button" value="Click Button 2">
<br><br>
<input type="reset" value="Reset">
</form>
</body>
</html>
```

# Event.RESIZE

## *JavaScript 1.2+, JScript 3.0+*

## *Nav4+, IE 4+*

### *Syntax*

```
Event.RESIZE
```

### *Description*

The RESIZE property of the Event object is used by windows and frames to indicate the event of resizing the window or frame.

### *Example*

Listing 7.236 shows how to determine when the window has been resized using the RESIZE event. When the RESIZE event is captured, the handle() function outputs the height and width properties of the window.

*Listing 7.236    Using the RESIZE Property*

```
<html>
<head>
<title>Example of Event.RESIZE</title>
</head>
<body>
<script language="JavaScript">
<!--Hide

// sets up the window to capture RESIZE events
window.captureEvents(Event.RESIZE);

// function that handles the specific event. The evnt parameter refers to
// the event object.
function handle(evnt){
    alert("You have resized the window to: " + evnt.height + "x" + evnt.width);
    return true;
}
```

```
// This registers the handle function as the event handler for the
// RESIZE event.
window.onResize = handle;
// End Hide --->
</script>

<form name="form1">
Click button to resize:
<input type="Button" value="Resize" onClick="window.resizeTo(250,400)">
</form>

</body>
</html>
```

# Event.SELECT

## *JavaScript 1.0+*

## *Nav2+, Opera3+*

## *Syntax*

Event.SELECT

## *Description*

The SELECT property of the Event object is used by text objects and select-box form elements to indicate when an element is selected by the user.

## *Example*

Listing 7.237 shows how the SELECT event can be used to determine which form object has been selected. When some text in the textarea is selected, the SELECT event is invoked. The document will then capture the event and call the handleSelect() function, which informs the user that the SELECT event occurred.

*Listing 7.237    Using the SELECT Property*

```
<html>
<head>
<title>Example of Event.SELECT</title>
</head>
<body>
<script language="JavaScript">
<!--Hide

// sets up the window to capture SELECT events
document.captureEvents(Event.SELECT);

// handles the SELECT event
function handleSelect(evnt){
```

*continues*

*Listing 7.237    continued*
```
        alert("You have selected some text in the textarea");
}


// This registers the handle function as the event handler for the
// SELECT event.
document.onSelect = handleSelect;


// End Hide --->
</script>

<form name="form1">
Message:
<input type="text" size="25" name="txtbox" value="">
<br><br><br>
Display text:<br>
<textarea name="msg" rows="5" cols="60">
In this example we check for the SELECT event to
occur. This occurs when some text in a textarea or
textbox is selected. To see this, select some text
in this paragraph and an alert box will pop up
indicating that the select event has occurred.
</textarea>
<br><br>
</form>

</body>
</html>
```

# Event.SUBMIT

## *JavaScript 1.0+, JScript 1.0+*

## *Nav2+, IE 3+, Opera3+*

## *Syntax*

```
Event.SUBMIT
```

## *Description*

The SUBMIT property of the Event object is used solely by forms to indicate the clicking of the Submit button.

## *Example*

Listing 7.238 shows an example of how JavaScript can be used to process a form when the Submit button is clicked. The Window listens for the SUBMIT event. When captured, it will call the handle() function. This function informs the user that the Submit button was clicked.

*Listing 7.238   Example of Using the* SUBMIT *Property*

```
<html>
<head>
<title>Example of Event.SUBMIT</title>
</head>
<body>
<script language="JavaScript">
<!--Hide

// sets up the window to capture SUBMIT events
window.captureEvents(Event.SUBMIT);

// function that handles the specific event. The evnt parameter refers to
// the event object.
function handle(evnt){
    alert("You have clicked the Submit button");
    return true;
}

// This registers the handle function as the event handler for the
// SUBMIT event.
window.onSubmit = handle;
// End Hide --->
</script>
```

This example demonstrates the submit event. Click the different buttons below. Only the Submit button will trigger the submit event.

```
<br><br>
<form>
<input type="button" value="Click Me">
<br><br>
<input type="Submit" value="Submit">
<br><br>
<input type="button" value="Click on Me too">
</form>
</body>
</html>
```

# Event.UNLOAD

## *JavaScript 1.0+, JScript 1.0+*

## *Nav2+, IE 3+, Opera3+*

## *Syntax*

```
Event.UNLOAD
```

## *Description*

The UNLOAD property of the Event object is used by documents to indicate when a new document is loaded in a browser or when the browser window is closed.

## Example

Listing 7.239 shows how the UNLOAD property can be used to find out when a browser has finished unloading a Web page. When the UNLOAD event has been captured, the han- dle() function is called, which informs the user that the page has been unloaded.

*Listing 7.239   Accessing the* UNLOAD *Property*

```
<html>
<head>
<title>Using the Event.UNLOAD</title>
</head>
<body>
<script language = "JavaScript">
<!--Hide

// sets up the window to capture UNLOAD events
window.captureEvents(Event.UNLOAD);

// function that handles the specific event. The evnt parameter refers to
// the event object.
function handle(evnt){
    alert("The page has been unloaded.");
    return true;
}

// This registers the handle function as the event handler for the
// LOAD event.
window.onUnload = handle;

// End Hide --->
</script>

This page only contains a gif image. When is unloaded, an alert
message is displayed indicating so.<i> (To unload the page, simply l
oad another page or click on the browser back button.)</i>
<br><br>
<img src="star.gif" onUnload=''>

</body>
</html>
```

# FileUpload

## *JavaScript 1.0+, Jscript 3.0+*

## *Nav2+, IE 4+, Opera3+*

## *Syntax*

Core client-side JavaScript object.

## Description

The `FileUpload` object represents a file upload box within an HTML form. An upload box is created by using the HTML `<input>` tag and specifying the `TYPE` attribute as `file`. The `FileUpload` object has specific properties and methods associated with it, which are shown in Table 7.26.

**Table 7.26    Properties and Methods of FileUpload object**

| Property/Method | Description |
| --- | --- |
| `blur()` | Removes focus from `FileUpload` box |
| `focus()` | Sets focus on `FileUpload` box |
| `form` | Reference form object containing `FileUpload` box |
| `handleEvent()` | Handles specific event |
| `name` | HTML `NAME` attribute for `FileUpload` box |
| `onBlur` | Event handler for `Blur` event |
| `onChange` | Event handler for `Change` event |
| `onFocus` | Event handler for `Focus` event |
| `select()` | Selects input area for `FileUpload` box |
| `type` | HTML `TYPE` attribute for `FileUpload` box |
| `value` | String specifying pathname of selected file |

## Example

Listing 7.240 shows how an upload box is created and then how the `name` property is accessed using the `FileUpload` object.

A `FileUpload` object in the HTML page contains a Browse button that allows you to browse the computer for a file to upload. Once this is chosen, normally it would be sent to a server to be uploaded. However, this example only demonstrates how to get the full pathname for the file to be uploaded.

*Listing 7.240    Example of How the* `FileUpload` *Object Is Used*

```
<html>
<head>
<title>Example using FileUpload object </title>
</head>
<body>
<script language="JavaScript">
<!-- Hide
// function demonstrates how to obtain property values of the FileUpload
object.
function showname(){
    // declare a variable to hold the name of the upload box.
    var  file = document.form1.uploadBox.value ;
     document.form1.filename.value = file ;
}
// End Hide --->
```

*continues*

*Listing 7.240    continued*
```
</script>

<form name="form1">
Click on browse to choose a file to send.
<br>
Click on the Send button to see the full path for the file sent.
<br><br>
File to send: <input type="file" name="uploadBox">
<br><br>
<input type="button" value="Send" name="get" onClick='showname()'>
<br><br>
<input type="text" name="filename" size="40">
</form>
</body>
</html>
```

# FileUpload.blur()

## JavaScript 1.1+

## Nav3+, Opera3+

## Syntax

*fileupload*.blur()

## Description

The blur() method of the FileUpload object is used to remove focus from the FileUpload box.

## Example

Listing 7.241 shows how the blur() method is used to remove focus from the upload box. When the OK button is clicked, the focus is removed from the upload box and a message is displayed.

*Listing 7.241    Example of* blur() *Method*
```
<html>
<head>
<title>Using the blur() method of the FileUpload object</title>
</head>
<body>
<script language="JavaScript">
<!-- Hide
function showMessage(){
// Removes focus from the upload box and writes text
    document.form1.uploadbox.blur();
    document.form1.textbox.value = "File Submitted";
}
// End Hide --->
```

```
</script>

<form name="form1">
Enter Filename:
<input type="file" name="uploadbox">
<input type="button" value="Okay" onClick=showMessage()>
<br><br>
Confirmation:
<input type="text" name="textbox">

</form>

</body>
</html>
```

# FileUpload.focus()

## *JavaScript 1.1+, Jscript 3.0+*

## *Nav3+, IE 4+, Opera3+*

## *Syntax*

`fileupload.focus()`

## *Description*

The `focus()` method is used to set focus to the `FileUpload` object.

## *Example*

Listing 7.242 shows how to set the focus on the `FileUpload` object. When the user clicks the OK button, the JavaScript function `checkFile()` is called to reset the focus to the upload box and display a message.

*Listing 7.242    Setting Focus to the Upload Box*

```
<html>
<head>
<title>Using the focus method to set focus to FileUpload box</title>
</head>
<body>
<script language="JavaScript">
<!-- Hide
function checkFile(){
// sets focus to the upload box
    document.form1.uploadbox.focus();
    document.form1.textbox.value = "Verify that filename is correct";
}
// End Hide --->
</script>
```

*continues*

*Listing 7.242    continued*

```
<form name="form1">
Enter Filename:
<input type="file" name="uploadbox">
<input type="button" value="Okay" onClick=checkFile()>
<br><br>
Confirmation Message:
<input type="text" name="textbox" size=35>

</form>

</body>
</html>
```

# FileUpload.form

## *JavaScript 1.0+, Jscript 3.0+*

## *Nav2+, IE4+, Opera3+*

## Syntax

`fileupload.form`

## Description

The `form` property of the `FileUpload` object is used to reference the form object that contains the `FileUpload` box.

## Example

Listing 7.243 shows an example of how the `form` property can be used to extract any attributes of the form containing the `FileUpload` box. The page contains two boxes in which a file can be specified to be uploaded. The `checkFiles()` function verifies whether a file has been chosen for each upload box. If a file hasn't been chosen, the script will alert the user.

*Listing 7.243    Using the `FileUpload` `form` Property*

```
<html>
<head>
<title>Using FileUpload form property</title>
</head>
<body>
<script language="JavaScript">
<!-- Hide

// function verifies whether a file has been chosen for each FileUpload box.
function checkFiles(){

    if (document.secret.file1.value == ""){
        alert("You did not enter anything for file 1");
    }
```

```
    if (document.secret.file2.value == ""){
        alert("You did not enter anything for file 2");
    }
    else {
        alert("The files are okay and will be uploaded");
    }
}
// End Hide --->
</script>

<form name="secret">

Please choose two files to upload.
<br><br>
File 1:<input type="file" name="file1">
<br><br>
File 2:<input type="file" name="file2">
<br><br>
<input type="button" value="Verify" onClick='checkFiles()'>
</form>

</body>
</html>
```

The first example shows one method of referencing the upload box. There is a second way, though. It can also be referenced by using the form elements array. An example of this in Listing 7.244.

*Listing 7.244    Second Method of Referencing* FileUpload *Object Using the* forms *Elements Array*

```
<html>
<head>
<title>Using form elements array to access FileUpload object</title>
</head>
<body>
<script language="JavaScript">
<!-- Hide
function showUploadName(){
    alert("The FileUpload box name is: " + document.secret.elements[0].name);
}
// End Hide --->
</script>

<form name="secret">
Please choose a file to be uploaded.
<br><br>
<input type="file" name="mybox" >
<br><br>
Click the button to get the name of the form containing the FileUpload box.
```

*continues*

*Listing 7.243    continued*

```
<br><br>
<input type="button" value="Get Form Name" onClick='showUploadName()'>
</form>

</body>
</html>
```

# FileUpload.handleEvent()

## *JavaScript 1.2+*

## *Nav4+*

## *Syntax*

*fileupload*.handleEvent(*event*)

## **Description**

The handleEvent() method of the FileUpload object invokes the event handler for the specific event.

## **Example**

Listing 7.245 shows how the handleEvent() method is used to handle all CHANGE events. When the user chooses or enters a filename in the FileUpload box and then changes the information, the CHANGE event occurs and is captured. The handleChange function processes the CHANGE event and passes it to the handleEvent() method of the upload box. So the event handler for the upload box will handle all CHANGE events.

*Listing 7.245    Using* handleEvent *Method*

```
<html>
<head>
<title>Using the handleEvent method</title>
</head>
<body>

<script language = "JavaScript">
<!--Hide

// sets up the window to capture CHANGE events
window.captureEvents(Event.CHANGE);

// function that handles the specific event. The evnt parameter refers to
// the event object.
function handleChange(evnt){
    window.document.uploadbox.handleEvent(evnt);
}

function displayText(){
    document.form1.msg.value += "Change made to object\n";
```

```
}

// This registers the handle function as the event handler for the
// CHANGE event.
window.onChange = handleChange;
// End Hide --->
</script>


Choose a file:
<br>
<form name="form1">
<input type="file" size="40" name="uploadbox" onChange='displayText()'>
<br><br>
<textarea name="msg" rows="10" cols="50"></textarea>

</form>

</body>
</html>
```

# FileUpload.name

## JavaScript 1.0+

## Nav2+, Opera3+

## Syntax

*fileupload*.name

## Description

The name property of the FileUpload object represents the NAME attribute of the HTML <input> tag that creates the FileUpload box. This allows you to reference a FileUpload object directly by name.

## Example

Listing 7.246 shows how the name of the upload box is used to access its properties. The function getname() uses the form object and the name of the upload box to access the name property.

*Listing 7.246   Accessing* FileUpload *Object by Name*
```
<html>
<head>
<title> Using the name property of the FileUpload object</title>
</head>
<body>
<script language="JavaScript">
<!--Hide
```

*continues*

*Listing 7.246    continued*

```
// Function alerts the user to what the name of the upload box is.
function getname(){
    var boxname = document.form1.myUploadbox.name;
    alert("The name of the FileUpload box is: " + boxname);
}
// End Hide --->
</script>

<formform name="form1">
Click on the button below to get the name of the upload box.
<br><br>
<inputinput type="file" name="myUploadbox">
<br><br>
<input type="button" value="Get Name" onClick='getname()'>
</form>

</form>
</html>
```

# FileUpload.onBlur

## JavaScript 1.1+

## Nav3+, Opera3+

## Syntax

onBlur="*command*"

## Description

The onBlur event handler is an event handler for the FileUpload object that notifies you when the focus is removed from an upload box.

## Example

Listing 7.247 shows how the onBlur event handler is used to detect when the focus is removed from the specified upload box. The user chooses a file from the FileUpload box and then clicks the text box that removes the focus from the FileUpload box, causing the Blur event to be thrown.

*Listing 7.247    Example of FileUpload onBlur Method*
```
<html>
<head>
<title>Using the onBlur event handler</title>
</head>
<body>
<script language="JavaScript">
<!--Hide
function inform(){
```

```
      document.form1.msg.value="File submitted and focus removed from FileUpload
object";
}

// End Hide
</script>

<formform name="form1">
Please choose a file to upload to the server.
<br><br>
<input type="file" onBlur= 'inform()'>
<br><br>
Click on the text box.
<br><br>
Message:
<input type="text" name="msg" size="50">
</form>

</body>
</html>
```

# FileUpload.onChange

## *JavaScript 1.1+*

## *Nav3+, Opera3+*

## *Syntax*

onChange="*command*"

## *Description*

The onChange event handler of the FileUpload object is an event handler that notifies you when the upload box information has been changed.

## *Example*

Listing 7.248 uses the onChange event handler to check for a user entering information into an upload box. When the filename entered has been changed, the onChange event handler is triggered and a message is displayed in the text box.

*Listing 7.248    Example of* onChange *Event Handler*

```
<html>
<head>
<title>Using the onChange event handler</title>
</head>
<body>
<script language="JavaScript">
<!-- Hide
// function that informs the user that the filename in the FileUpload box
```

*continues*

*Listing 7.248    continued*

```
// has been changed.
function inform(){
    document.form1.msg.value = "Filename has been changed";
}

// End Hide --->
</script>

<form name="form1">
<inputtype=name=
Please choose a file.
<input type="file" name="uploadbox" size="35" onChange='inform()'>
<br><br>
Message:
<input type="text" name="msg" size="40">
</form>

</body>
</html>
```

# FileUpload.onFocus

## JavaScript 1.1+

## Nav3+, Opera3+

## Syntax

```
onFocus="command"
```

## Description

The onFocus event handler of the FileUpload object notifies you when the focus is set on the upload box.

## Example

In Listing 7.249, the onFocus event handler is used to notify the user when the focus is moved to the upload box. If the user sets the focus to the FileUpload box, a message is displayed. If the user removes the focus from the FileUpload box, another message is displayed.

*Listing 7.249    Example of the onFocus Event Handler*

```
<html>
<head>
<title>Using the onFocus event handler</title>
</head>
<body>
<script language="JavaScript">
<!-- Hide
```

```
// function that displays a message whenever focus is set on the FileUpload //
box.
function showMsg1(){
    document.form1.msg.value += "Focus on the FileUpload box\n";
}

// function displays a message when focus is removed from the FileUpload box.
function showMsg2(){
    document.form1.msg.value += "Focus removed from FileUpload box\n";
}

// End Hide --->
</script>
<form name="form1">
<form name="form1">
Click in the FileUpload box to set focus to it.
<br><br>
<input type="file" name="uploadbox" onFocus = 'showMsg1()'>
<br><br>
Click on the button to remove focus from the FileUpload box.
<br>
<input type="button" value="Click here" onClick='showMsg2()'>
<br><br>
<textarea name="msg" rows="5" cols="50"></textarea>
</form>

</body>
</html>
```

# FileUpload.select()

## *JavaScript 1.0+*

## *Nav2+, Opera3+*

## Syntax

*fileupload*.select()

## Description

The select() method of the FileUpload box is used to select the input area of the upload field.

## Example

Listing 7.250 shows an example of how the select() method is used to select the input text box of the FileUpload box.

*Listing 7.250    Using* `select()` *Method of* `FileUpload` *Object*

```
<html>
<head>

<title>Using select() method of the FileUpload object</title>
</head>
<body>
<script language = "JavaScript">
<!-- Hide
function enterName(){
// selects the input area of upload box when button is clicked.
    document.form1.uploadbox.select();
}
// End Hide --->
</script>

<form name="form1">
<input type="file" name="uploadbox">
<br><br>
<input type="button"  value="Go to Filename Box" onClick=enterName()>

</body>
</html>
```

# FileUpload.type

## JavaScript 1.1+

## Nav3+, Opera3+

## Syntax

`fileupload.type`

## Description

The `type` property of the `FileUpload` object represents the TYPE attribute of the HTML `<input>` tag used to create the upload box.

## Example

Listing 7.251 shows how to access the `type` property. When the user clicks the Get Type button, an alert box appears indicating the type of input.

*Listing 7.251    Accessing the* `FileUpload` *Type Property*

```
<html>
<head>
<title>Using the type property of the FileUpload object</title>
</head>
<body>
<script language="JavaScript">
<!-- Hide
```

```
// function informs the user what type of input the first element is.
function getType(){
    var mytype = document.form1.uploadbox.type;

    alert("The input box type is: " + mytype);
}
// End Hide --->
</script>

<form name="form1">
<input type="file" name="webfile">
<br><br>
Interested in finding out what type in input box is above? Click on the button
below.
<br>
<input type="button" value="Get Type" onClick='getType()'>
</form>
</body>
</html>
```

# FileUpload.value

## *JavaScript 1.0+*

## *Nav2+, Opera3+*

## *Syntax*

*fileupload*.value

## *Description*

The value property of the FileUpload object specifies the filename of the file selected or input by the user.

## *Example*

Listing 7.252 shows how to access the value property. The form object is used in conjunction with the upload box name to get the value attribute of the FileUpload box.

*Listing 7.252   Accessing FileUpload Value Property*
```
<html>
<head>
<title>Using the value property of the FileUpload object</title>
</head>
<body>
<script language="JavaScript">
<!-- Hide
function showFile(){
    var input = document.form1.uploadbox.value;
    alert("The filename entered is: " + input);
```

*continues*

*Listing 7.252    continued*
```
}
// End Hide --->
</script>

<form name="form1">
Please select a file.
<input type="file" name="uploadbox">
<br><br>
Click on the button to see the value of the FileUpload object.
<br>
<input type="button" value="Submit" onClick=showFile()>
</form>

</body>
</html>
```

# Form

## *JavaScript 1.0+, JScript 1.0+*

## *Nav2+, IE 3+, Opera3+*

## *Syntax*

Core client-side JavaScript object.

## *Description*

The Form object represents an HTML property created by the <form> tag. The Form object can be used to access all the properties of the specified form. Forms can be referenced by either the forms array or directly by name. Table 7.27 shows the different Form methods and properties.

**Table 7.27    Properties and Methods of the Form Object**

| Property/Method | Description |
| --- | --- |
| action | HTML ACTION attribute of Form object |
| elements | Array reflecting elements within form |
| elements.length | Length of elements array |
| encoding | HTML ENCTYPE attribute of Form object |
| handleEvent() | Handles specific event |
| length | Number of elements within form |
| method | HTML METHOD attribute of Form object |
| name | HTML NAME attribute of Form object |
| onReset | Event handler for Reset button |
| onSubmit | Event handler for Submit button |
| reset() | Resets form elements |
| submit() | Submit for data |
| target | HTML TARGET attribute of Form object |

## *Example*

Listing 7.253 uses the method of accessing the Form object directly by name.

*Listing 7.253    Accessing* Form *Object by Name*

```
<html>
<head>
<title> Using the name property to access a form object</title>
</head>
<body>
<script language = "JavaScript">
<!-- Hide
// Function shows the name enterd to the user to verify that the information is
correct.
function checkName(){


    var firstName = document.formEx.first.value;
    var lastName = document.formEx.last.value;
    alert("The name you entered is: " + firstName + " " + lastName);
}
// End Hide --->
</script>

<form namename="formEx">
First Name:
<input typetype="text" namename="first" size="20">
Last Name:
<input type="text" name="last" size="25">
<br><br>
Click the button to check that the information is correct.
<br>
<input type="button" value="verify" name="check" onClick='checkName()'>
</form>
</body>
</html>
```

Listing 7.254 accesses the Form object by using the forms array. The form simply contains one text box. Clicking the button shows an alert box containing the name of the form. Because it is the first form in the document, it is index 0 in the forms array.

*Listing 7.254    Using the Forms Array*

```
<html>
<head>
<title> Using the forms array to access a form element</title>
</head>
<body>
<script language = "JavaScript">
<!-- Hide
```

*continues*

*Listing 7.254    continued*

```
function showFormName(){
    var name = document.forms[0].name;

    alert("The name of the form is: " + name);
}
// End Hide --->
</script>

<form name="form1">
This text box belongs to a form.
<input type="text" name="street">
<br><br>
Click on the button to get the name of the form.
<br>
<input type="button" value="Get Form name" onClick='showFormName()'>
</form>

<form name="form2">
This is the second form in the document. It contains a FileUpload object.
<input type="file" name="uploadbox" size="25">
</form>
</body>
</html>
```

# Form.action

## *JavaScript 1.0+, JScript 1.0+*

## *Nav2+, IE 3+, Opera3+*

## *Syntax*

*form.*action

## *Description*

The action property represents the ACTION attribute of the HTML <form> tag. It is typically the URL to which the form is being submitted.

## *Example*

Listing 7.255 shows one method of how to use the Form object to access the action property of the HTML form. The action property specifies the server and program to which the form is submitted.

*Listing 7.255    Accessing the Action Value of the Form Object*

```
<html>
<head>
<title> Using the action property of the Form object</title>
</head>
<body>
```

```
<script language="JavaScript">
<!-- Hide
function getAction(){
     var actionValue = document.form1.action;
document.form1.msg.value =
       "Your form was submitted to the following URL:\n " + actionValue;
}
// End Hide --->
</script>

<form name="form1" action="http://www.test.org/cgi-bin/process.pl">
Enter your street address:
<input type="text" name="address" size="40">
<br><br>
<input type="button" value="Submit"onClick=getAction()>
<br><br><br>
<textarea name="msg" rows="5" cols="62"></textarea>
</form>
</body>
</html>
```

# Form.elements

## JavaScript 1.0+, JScript 1.0+

## Nav2+, IE 3+, Opera3+

### Syntax

*form.*elements

### Description

The elements property of the Form object represents the elements array, which is used to access each element within a form. The order of the form elements in the elements array is the order in which they appear in the HTML source.

### Example

Listing 7.256 shows how to access form elements using the elements array. Because it is accessing the first element in the form, the index 0 is used. The second element in the form can be accessed with elements[1].

*Listing 7.256   Accessing Form Elements*
```
<html>
<head>
<title> Using the form elements property</title>
</head>
<body>
<script language="JavaScript">
<!-- Hide
```

*continues*

*Listing 7.256    continued*
```
function getName(){
    var textName = document.form1.elements[0].name;
    alert("The textbox name is: " + textName);
}
    // End Hide --->
</script>

<form name="form1">
This is a blank input textbox. Click on the button below to get the name of the
textbox.
<br>
<input type="text" name="textbox1" size=25>
<br><br>
<input type="button" value="Get Name" onClick = getName()>
</form>
</body>
</html>
```

# Form.elements.length

## *JavaScript 1.0+, JScript 1.0+*

## *Nav2+, IE 3+, Opera3+*

## *Syntax*

`form.elements.length`

## *Description*

The `elements.length` property of the `Form` object specifies the number of items in the `elements` array. Each item in the array refers to an object in the HTML form.

## *Example*

Listing 7.257 shows how to use the `elements.length` property. When the user clicks the Get Elements button, an alert box is displayed indicating the number of elements in the form.

*Listing 7.257    Using the `elements.length` Property*
```
<html>
<head>
<title> Using the elements.length property of the Form object</title>
</head>
<body>
<script language="JavaScript">
<!-- Hide
// function uses the elements.length property to get the number of elements in
the form.
function getNum(){
    var numOfElements = document.form1.elements.length;
```

```
alert("The number of elements in this document are:" + numOfElements);
}
// End Hide --->
</script>

<form name="form1">
Dummy text box:
<input type="text" name="textbox1" size="25">
<br>
<input type="button" value="Dummy Button">
<input type="text" size="20" namename="Sample">
<br><br>
Click on the button to get the number of elements in this form.
<input type="button" value="Get Elements" onClick='getNum()'>
</form>
</body>
</html>
```

# Form.encoding

## *JavaScript 1.0+, JScript 1.0+*

## *Nav2+, IE 3+, Opera3+*

## Syntax

*form.*encoding

## Description

The encoding property of the Form object represents the type of encoding used by the form. It can be specified in the HTML <form> tag as the ENCTYPE attribute.

**NOTE**

Setting the encoding property will override the HTML ENCTYPE attribute.

## Example

In Listing 7.258, the encoding property of the Form object is used to get the type of encoding being used by the form.

*Listing 7.258 Accessing Form Encoding Property*
```
<html>
<head>
<title> Using the encoding property for the Form object</title>
</head>
<body>
<script language="JavaScript">
<!-- Hide
```

*continues*

*Listing 7.258    continued*
```
// This function returns the encoding type for the specified form.
function getEncoding(){
     var encodingType = document.form1.encoding;
     return encodingType;
}
// End Hide --->
</script>

<form name="form1" action="post" enctype="application/x-www-form-urlencoded">
<input type="button" value="Get Encoding" onClick='getEncoding()'>
</fpr,>
</body>
</html>
```

# Form.handleEvent()

## *JavaScript 1.2+, JScript 1.0+*

## *Nav4+, IE 3+*

## *Syntax*

`form.handleEvent(event)`

## *Description*

The handleEvent() method of the Form property invokes the handler for the specified event. It takes one parameter, which is the event to be handled.

## *Example*

In Listing 7.259, the handleEvent() method is being used to handle the event being passed. The script captures the CLICK event. When this occurs, the handleMyClick() function calls the handleEvent() method to handle the CLICK event.

*Listing 7.259    Using the* handleEvent() *Method*
```
<html>
<head>
<title> Using the handleEvent method of the Form object</title>
</head>
<body>
<script language = "JavaScript">
<!--Hide

// sets up the document to capture CLICK events
document.captureEvents(Event.CLICK);

// function that handles the specific event. The evnt parameter refers to
// the event object.
```

```
function handleMyClick(evnt){
    window.document.button1.handleEvent(evnt);
}

function displayMsg(){
    document.form1.msg.value += "Click event occurred.\n";
}

// This registers the handle function as the event handler for the
// CLICK event.
document.onClick = handleMyClick;

// End Hide --->
</script>


<form name="form1">
<input type="button" value="Click on Me" name="button1" onClick='displayMsg()'>
<br><br>
<textarea name="msg" rows="10" cols="50" onClick='displayMsg()'></textarea>
</form>

</body>
</html>
```

# Form.length

## *JavaScript 1.0+, JScript 1.0+*

## *Nav2+, IE 3+, Opera3+*

## *Syntax*

*form*.length

## *Description*

The length property of the Form object represents the number of elements within a form.

### NOTE

This property works the same as the elements.length property.

## *Example*

Listing 7.260 shows an example of how the length property is used to determine the number of elements in the document. The showNumElements() function informs the user of the form length, which represents the number of form elements.

*Listing 7.260    Using the* `Form.length` *Property*

```
<html>
<head>
<title> Using the length property of the Form object</title>
</head>
<body>
<script language="JavaScript">
<!-- Hide
// function displays an alert box indicating the number of elements in the
form.
function showNumElements(){
     alert("There are " + document.form1.length + " elements in this
document");
}
// End Hide --->
</script>

<form name="form1">
Enter First Name:
<input type="text" size=15><br>
Enter Last Name:
<input type="text" size=20><br>
Enter address:
<input type="text" size=40><br><br>
<input type="button" value="Submit" onClick=showNumElements()>
</form>

</body>
</html>
```

# Form.method

## *JavaScript 1.0+, JScript 1.0+*

## *Nav2+, IE 3+, Opera3+*

## *Syntax*

`form.method`

## *Description*

The `method` property of the `Form` object represents the type of submission, GET or POST, being used by the form.

## *Example*

In Listing 7.261, the `method` property is used to get the type of method being used by the form. The `informMethod()` function alerts the user of the method, GET or POST, being used by the form.

*Listing 7.261    Accessing Method Object*

```html
<html>
<head>
<title> Using the method property of the Form object</title>
</head>
<body>
<script language="JavaScript">
<!--Hide

function informMethod(){
alert("The form method is:" + document.form1.method);
}
// End Hide --->
</script>

<form name="form1" method="get">
First Name:<input type=text" name="first" size=15>
Last Name:<input type=text" name="last" size=25>
<br>
City:<input type=text" name="city" size=20>
State:<input type=text" name="state" size=2 maxlength=2>
Zip:<input type=text" name="zip" size=5 maxlength=5>
<br><br>
Click the button to see what type of Method is used for submission.
<input type="button" value="Click Here" onClick='informMethod()'>
</form>
</body>
</html>
```

# Form.name

## JavaScript 1.0+, JScript 1.0+

## Nav2+, IE 3+, Opera3+

## Syntax

*form*.name

## Description

The name property of the Form object represents the name of the form as specified in the HTML <form> tag.

## Example

Listing 7.262 shows how the name property is used to get the HTML NAME attribute of the form. The showName function uses the Form object to access the name attribute of the form.

*Listing 7.262   Accessing* name *Property*

```
<html>
<head>
<title>Access the name property of the Form object</title>
</head>
<body>
<script language="JavaScript">
<!-- Hide
function showName(){
// Alert box tells what the name of the form is
alert("Form Name is: " + document.form1.name);
}
// End Hide --->
</script>

<form name ="form1" >
Dummy input text box.
<input type= "text" size="15">
<br><br>
Click on the button to get the name of the form
<input type="button" value="click me" onclick='showName()'>

</form>
</body>
</html>
```

# Form.onReset

## JavaScript 1.1+, JScript 1.0+

## Nav3+, IE 3+, Opera3+

## Syntax

```
onReset="command"
```

## Description

The onReset method of the Form object executes JavaScript code when a reset event occurs.

## Example

Listing 7.263 demonstrates the use of the onReset event handler. The JavaScript function checks to see if the Reset button has been clicked. If so, all the text values are reset to a specified value.

*Listing 7.263   Using the* onReset *Event Handler*

```
<html>
<head>
<title>Using the onReset event handler</title>
</head>
```

```
<body>
<script language="JavaScript">
<!-- Hide
// function displays a message when the onReset event handler determines that
// the reset button has been pressed.
function showMsg(){
    document.form2.msg.value = "You have cleared the Entry Fields.";
}
// End Hide --->
</script>

<form name="form1" onReset='showMsg()'>
Entry 1:<input type= "text" name="text1" size="20"><br>
Entry 2:<input type= "text" name="text2" size="20"><br>
Entry 3:<input type= "text" name="text3" size="20"><br>
<input type="reset" value= namename="Reset"
</form>

<form name="form2">
Message:<input type="text" name="msg" size="50">
<br><br>
</form>
</body>
</html>
```

# Form.onSubmit

## *JavaScript 1.0+, JScript 1.0+*

## *Nav2+, IE 3+, Opera3+*

## *Syntax*

onSubmit="*command*"

## *Description*

The onSubmit method of the Form property executes JavaScript code when a submit
event occurs.

## *Example*

Listing 7.264 shows how the onSubmit event handler is used for a Form object. A user
would enter his or her comments in the text area provided. Once done, he or she clicks
the Submit button to submit the form. Using the onSubmit event handler, you can display a thank you note when the user has submitted his or her comments.

*Listing 7.264   Using the* onSubmit() *Form Method*
```
<html>
<head>
<title> Using the onSubmit event handler for the Form object</title>
```

*continues*

*Listing 7.264    continued*
```
</head>
<body>

<script language="JavaScript">
<!-- Hide
//function displays a confirmation message when a for is submitted.
function confirm(){
    alert("Your comments have been submitted. Thank you.");
}
// End Hide --->
</script>

<form name="form1" onSubmit = 'confirm()'
<b>Enter Comments:</b>
<br>
<textarea name="comments" rows="5" cols="60"></textarea>
<br><br>
<input type = "submit" Value="Submit Comments">
</form>
</body>
</html>
```

# Form.reset()

## *JavaScript 1.1+, JScript 1.0+*

## *Nav3+, IE 3+, Opera3+*

## *Syntax*

```
form.reset()
```

## *Description*

The reset method of the Form object resets all the form elements to their default values. It operates the same as a mouse click on a Reset button for the calling form.

## *Example*

Listing 7.265 shows how the reset method is used to reset a form. When the Reset button is clicked, all values in the form object are reset (text boxes are cleared of their values).

*Listing 7.265   Accessing the reset() Method*
```
<html>
<head>
<title> Using the reset method of the Form object</title>
</head>
<body>
<script language="JavaScript">
<!-- Hide
```

```
function resetForm(form){
    document.form1.reset(form);
}
// End Hide --->
</script>

<form name="form1">
Field 1:<input type="text" size="20" name="text1"><br>
Field 2:<input type="text" size="20" name="text2"><br>
Field 3:<input type="text" size="20" name="text3"><br>
<input type="button" name=reset value="reset" onClick='resetForm(this.form)'>
</form>

</body>
</html>
```

# Form.submit()

## *JavaScript 1.0+, JScript 1.0+*

## *Nav2+, IE 3+, Opera3+*

## *Syntax*

*form*.submit()

## *Description*

The submit method of the Form object is used to submit a form. It operates the same as if a Submit button was clicked.

## *Example*

Listing 7.266 shows how you would submit a form using the submit() method. The form is submitted to the value specified in the ACTION attribute of the HTML <form> tag. In this specific example, a made up script processes the form.

*Listing 7.266    Accessing the submit() Method*

```
<html>
<head>
<title> Using the submit method for the Form object</title>
</head>
<body>
<script language="JavaScript">
<!-- Hide
// function submits a form to a server specified in the <form> tag
function submitForm(form){
    document.form1.submit(form);
}
// End Hide --->
```

*continues*

*Listing 7.266    continued*

```
</script>

<form name= "form1" method="post" action="http://www.myserver.com/cgi-
bin/test.pl">
This is a sample form
<br><br>
Name:<input type="text" size="40" name="name">
<br>
Age:<input type="text" size="3" name="age">
<br>
Phone Number:<input type="text" size="10" name="phone">
<br><br>
<input type= "button" value="Submit" onclick = submitForm(this.form)>
</form>
</body>
</html>
```

# Form.target

## *JavaScript 1.0+, JScript 1.0+*

## *Nav2+, IE 3+, Opera3+*

## *Syntax*

```
form.target
```

## *Description*

The target property of the Form object represents the target window or frame in which the form results will be displayed. This can also reflect the TARGET attribute of the HTML <form> tag. Valid target attributes are: _blank, _parent, _self, and _top.

## *Example*

The code in Listing 7.267 is for an HTML document that contains two frames, frameA and frameB, respectively. The target property is used from the frameA object to specify that the returned result is displayed in frameB.

*Listing 7.267    Displaying Results Using the target Property*

```
<html>
<head>
<title> Using the target property of the Form object</title>
</head>
<body>
<script language="JavaScript">
<!-- Hide
function show(){

var tar = document.form1.target;
```

```
      if(tar == "_self"){
        alert("The target for this form submission is this window");
      }
      else{
        alert("The target has not been specifically specified");
      }
    }
    // End Hide --->
    </script>

    <form name="form1" action="post" target="_self">
    First Name:<input type="text" size="15" name="first">
    Last Name:<input type="text" size="20" name="last">
    <br>
    Street:<input type="text" size="40" name="street">
    <br>
    City:<input type="text" size="15" name="city">
    State:<input type="text" size="2" name="st">
    Zip:<input type="text" size="5" name="zip">
    <br><br><br>
    <input type="button" value="submit" onClick='show()'>
    </form>

    </body>
    </html>
```

# Frame

## *JavaScript 1.0+, JScript 1.0+*

## *Nav2+, IE 3+, Opera3+*

## *Syntax*

Core client-side JavaScript object.

## *Description*

A window can display multiple, independently scrollable frames on a single screen, each with its own distinct URL. The Frame object, which has an instance created with each occurrence of the <frame> tag, is a convenience for thinking about the objects that make up these frames. However, JavaScript actually represents a frame using a Window object. Every Frame object is a Window object, and has all the methods and properties of a Window object. Table 7.28 shows Frames available methods and properties.

**NOTE**

The majority of examples for the Frame object assume that top.html and bottom.html files exist. Some examples also only display the JavaScript code that would be contained in a document.

*Table 7.28* **Properties and Methods of the Frame Object**

| Property/Method | Description |
| --- | --- |
| blur() | Removes focus from the frame |
| clearInterval() | Cancels a repeated execution |
| clearTimeout() | Cancels any delayed execution |
| document | Current document loaded within frame |
| focus() | Applies focus to frame |
| frames | Array containing references to child frames |
| length | Length of the frames array |
| name | HTML NAME attribute of Frame object. |
| onBlur | Event handler for blur event |
| onFocus | Event handler for focus event |
| onMove | Event handler for move event |
| onResize | Event handler for resize event |
| parent | Main window or frame from which child frames are created |
| print() | Invokes the print dialog box |
| self | Refers to the current frame |
| setInterval() | Sets function schedule for repeated execution |
| setTimeout() | Sets function schedule for delayed execution |
| top | Browser window that executes script |
| window | Refers to current window or frame. |

## Example

Listing 7.268 shows the code to create an HTML frame and access its properties. This example assumes that the files top.html and bottom.html already exist.

*Listing 7.268* Frame *Example*

```
<html>
<title> Example of Frame object</title>

<script language="JavaScript">
<!--Hide

//Function returns the name of the frame
function getName(){
    var frameName = document.window.frame.name;
    return frameName;
}
// End Hide --->
</script>

<frameset rows="100,*">
<frame src="top.html" name=upper>
<frame src="bottom.html" name=bottom scrolling=yes>
</frameset>

</html>
```

# Frame.blur()

## *JavaScript 1.1+, JScript 1.0+*

## *Nav3+, IE 3+, Opera3+*

## *Syntax*

```
frame.blur()
```

## *Description*

The `blur()` method of the `Frame` object removes focus from the frame.

## *Example*

Listing 7.269 uses the `blur()` method to remove focus from the frame.

*Listing 7.269   Example of* `blur()` *Method*

```
<html>
<title> Example of blur method of Frame object</title>

<script language="JavaScript">
<!-- Hide
function removeFocus(){
    document.upper.blur()
}
// End Hide --->
</script>

<frameset rows="100,*">
<frame src="top.html" name=upper onDblClick=removeFocus()>
<frame src="bottom.html" name=bottom scrolling=yes>
</frameset>

</html>
```

# Frame.clearInterval()

## *JavaScript 1.2+, JScript 1.0+*

## *Nav4+, IE 3+*

## *Syntax*

```
frame.clearInterval()
```

## *Description*

The `clearInterval()` method of the `Frame` object is used to cancel a repeated execution.

## Example

Listing 7.270 shows the syntax for accessing the `clearInterval()` method. For a more detailed example, see `window.clearInterval()`.

*Listing 7.270   Example of the `clearIntercal()` Method*
```
<script language="JavaScript">
<!-- Hide
function cancel(){
    framename.clearInterval();
}
// End Hide --->
</script>
```

# Frame.clearTimeout()

## *JavaScript 1.0+, JScript 1.0+*

## *Nav2+, IE 3+, Opera3+*

## Syntax

`frame.clearTimeout()`

## Description

The `clearTimeout()` method of the `Frame` object is used to cancel a delayed execution. For a more detailed example, see `window.clearTimeout()`. .

## Example

Listing 7.271 shows the syntax for accessing the `clearTimeout()` method.

*Listing 7.271   Accessing the `clearTimeout()` Method*
```
<script language="JavaScript">
<!-- Hide
function stop(){
    framename.clearTimeout();
}
// End Hide --->
</script>
```

# Frame.document

## *JavaScript 1.0+, JScript 1.0+*

## *Nav2+, IE 3+, Opera3+*

## Syntax

`frame.document`

## Description

The document property of the Frame object contains information about the current document. The document property is created by the HTML <body> tag and is available in every Frame or Window object. The document property is used to access other aspects of the HTML document.

## Example

Listing 7.272 shows how the document property can be used to access document elements within a specific frame. For a more detailed example, see window.document.

*Listing 7.272    Accessing the* document *Property*

```
<script language="JavaScript">
<!-- Hide
function getName(){
    var name = framename.document.elements[1].name;
}
// End Hide --->
</script>
```

# Frame.focus()

## JavaScript 1.1+, JScript 1.0+

## Nav3+, IE 3+, Opera3+

## Syntax

```
frame.focus()
```

## Description

The focus() method of the Frame object is used to set the focus to a specific frame.

## Example

Listing 7.273 shows the syntax for using the focus() method. When the document is loaded, the focus is automatically set to the bottom frame.

*Listing 7.273    Accessing the* focus() *Method*

```
<html>
<title> Example of focus method of Frame object</title>

<script>
<!-- Hide
//set initial focus to bottom frame
document.bottom.focus;
// End Hide --->
</script>

<frameset rows="80, *">
```

*continues*

*Listing 7.273    continued*
```
<frame name=top src=top.html>
<frame name=bottom src=bottom.html>
</frameset>

</html>
```

# Frame.frames

## *JavaScript 1.0+, JScript 1.0+*

## *Nav2+, IE 3+, Opera3+*

## Syntax
```
frame.frames[num]
```

## Description

The `frames` property of the `Frame` object represents an array that stores child frame objects. Array entries of the child frame can be referenced either by index number or by the name assigned from the `NAME` attribute.

## Example

In Listing 7.274, the `frames` array is used to access the length of the child frame.

*Listing 7.274    Example Using the* `frames` *Property*
```
<script language="JavaScript">
<!-- Hide
function getFrameLength(){
    var childLength = document.frames["firstChild"].length;
}
// End Hide --->
</script>
```

# Frame.length

## *JavaScript 1.0+, ECMAScript 1.0+, JScript 1.0+*

## *Nav2+, IE 3+, Opera3+*

## Syntax
```
frame.length
```

## Description

The `length` property of the `frames` object represents the length of the `frames` array, which is the number of child frames.

## Example

Listing 7.275 shows a simple function call that uses the `length` property to set a variable for the number of child frames.

*Listing 7.275   Example Using the* `length` *Property*

```
<script language = "JavaScript">
<!-- Hide
function getLength(){
    var numOfChildFrames = window.frameName.length;
}
// End Hide --->
</script>
```

# Frame.name

## *JavaScript 1.0+, JScript 1.0+*

## *Nav2+, IE 3+, Opera3+*

## Syntax

`frame.name`

## Description

The `name` property of the `Frame` object represents the name given to a frame as specified from the NAME attribute of the HTML <frame> tag.

## Example

In Listing 7.276, the `name` property is used to inform the user of the active frame.

*Listing 7.276   Example of the* `name` *Property*

```
<script language = "JavaScript">
<!-- Hide
function activeFrame(){
    var frameName = window.myframe.name;
    alert("The active frame is: " + frameName);
}
// End Hide --->
</script>
```

# Frame.onBlur

## *JavaScript 1.1+, JScript 1.0+*

## *Nav3+, IE 3+, Opera3+*

## Syntax

`onBlur="command"`

## Description

The `onBlur` event handler specifies when the focus has been removed from a frame.

## Example

In Listing 7.277, the `onBlur` event handler is used to change the color of the upper frame when the focus is set on it.

*Listing 7.277   Using the* onBlur *Event Handler*

```
<html>
<title> Example of onBlur event handler of the Frame object</title>

<script language = "JavaScript">
<!-- Hide
function change(){
    frames[0].onBlur=new Function("document.bgColor='green'")
}
// End Hide --->
</script>

<frameset rows="50%,*" onLoad=change()>
<frame name="topFrame" src="top.html">
<frame name="bottomFrame" src=bottom.html>
</frameset>

</html>
```

# Frame.onFocus

## *JavaScript 1.1+, JScript 1.0+*

## *Nav3+, IE 3+, Opera3+*

## Syntax

onFocus="*command*"

## Description

The onFocus event handler is used to specify when the focus is brought to a frame. The user can set the focus by either pressing the mouse button or by using the Tab key.

## Example

The syntax for accessing the onFocus event handler is shown in Listing 7.278. When the focus is set on the top frame, an alert box is displayed.

*Listing 7.278   Syntax for the* onFocus *Event Handler*

```
<html>
<title> Example of onFocus event handler of the Frame object</title>

<frameset rows="80, *">
<frame src=top.html name=top onFocus='alert("You are now in the top frame")'>
<frame src=bottom.html name=bottom>
</frameset>

</html>
```

# Frame.onMove

## *JavaScript 1.2+, ECMAScript 1.0+, JScript 1.0+*

## *Nav4+, IE 3+*

### *Syntax*

```
onMove="command"
```

### *Description*

The onMove frame event handler is used to specify when a move event occurs within a frame.

### *Example*

Listing 7.279 shows the onMove event handler being used to inform the user when the frame is being moved.

*Listing 7.279    Example of the onMove Event Handler*
```
<html>
<title> Example of onMove event handler of the Frame object</title>

<frameset rows="80, *" onMove='alert("You are now moving the frame")'>
<frame src=top.html name=top >
<frame src=bottom.html name=bottom>
</frameset>

</html>
```

# Frame.onResize

## *JavaScript 1.2+, ECMAScript 1.0+*

## *Nav4+*

### *Syntax*

```
onResize="command"
```

### *Description*

The onResize frame event handler is used to specify when a frame has been resized.

### *Example*

Listing 7.280 shows how you would use the onResize event handler to check for when a frame is being resized.

*Listing 7.280    Syntax of the onResize Event Handler*
```
<html>
<title> Example of onResize event handler of the Frame object</title>

<frameset rows="80, *">
<frame src=top.html name=top >
<frame src=bottom.html name=bottom onResize='alert("You are resizing the bottom
```

*continues*

*Listing 7.280   continued*
```
frame")'>
</frameset>

</html>
```

# Frame.parent

## *JavaScript 1.0+, JScript 1.0+*

## *Nav2+, IE 3+, Opera3+*

## Syntax

```
frame.parent
```

## Description

The `parent` property of the `Frame` object specifies the frame containing the current frame.

## Example

Listing 7.281 shows a small example of how the name of the `Frame` parent can be accessed.

*Listing 7.281   Example of the `Frame.parent` Property*
```
<script language="JavaScript">
<!-- Hide
function getParent(){
     var parentName = parent.frameName.name;
}
// End Hide --->
</script>
```

# Frame.print()

## *JavaScript 1.2+, JScript 1.0+*

## *Nav4+, IE 3+*

## Syntax

```
frame.print(options)
```

## Description

The `print` method of the `Frame` object is used to send the document output of a particular frame to a printer. This works the same as executing the Print command from a browser menu.

## Example

Listing 7.282 shows an example of the `print` method. Using the `onClick` event handler, when the bottom frame is clicked, the `print()` method is executed.

*Listing 7.282    Example of* `print()` *Method*

```
<html>
<title> Example of print method of the Frame object</title>

<frameset rows="80, *">
<frame src=top.html name=top >
<frame src=bottom.html name=bottom onClick='document.window.bottom.print()'>
</frameset>

</html>
```

# Frame.self

## *JavaScript 1.0+, JScript 1.0+*

## *Nav2+, IE 3+, Opera3+*

## *Syntax*

`frame.self`

## *Description*

The `self` property of the `Frame` object is used as a keyword to reference the current frame.

## *Example*

Listing 7.283 shows an example of the `self` property being used to get the name for the current frame.

*Listing 7.283    Syntax for the* `self` *Property*

```
<script language="JavaScript">
<!-- Hide
function getName(){
    var name=window.frame.self.name;
}
// End Hide --->
</script>
```

# Frame.setInterval()

## *JavaScript 1.2+, JScript 1.0+*

## *Nav4+, IE 3+*

## *Syntax*

`frame.setInterval()`

## *Description*

The `setInterval` method of the `Frame` object is used to schedule a function for repeated execution. It takes two parameters. The first parameter is the expression being executed. The second parameter is the time in milliseconds that elapses before the expression is executed again. The function being executed is stopped by calling the `clearInterval` method.

## Example

Listing 7.284 shows a simple example of a `setInterval` method call. For a more detailed example, see `window.setInterval`.

*Listing 7.284   Example of* `setInterval()` *Method Call*

```
<script language="JavaScript">
<!-- Hide
Frame.setInterval(document.write('Begin writing", 50);
 // End Hide --->
</script>
```

# Frame.setTimeout()

## JavaScript 1.0+, JScript 1.0+

## Nav2+, IE 3+, Opera3+

## Syntax

```
frame.setTimeout()
```

## Description

The `setTimeout` method of the `Frame` object is used to schedule a function for delayed execution. The method accepts two parameters. The first parameter is the function or expression being evaluated. The second parameter is a numeric value specifying the millisecond units that elapse before the function or expression is executed.

## Example

Listing 7.285 shows a example of the `setTimeout` method being used to delay the printing of text.

*Listing 7.285   Example of* `setTimeout()` *Method*

```
<html>
<title> Example of setTimeout method of the Frame object</title>

<script language="JavaScript">
<!-- Hide
document.bottom.setTimeout(document.bottom.print("Keep on running"), 500);
// End Hide --->
</script>

<frameset rows="100,*">
<frame src="top.html" name=upper>
<frame src="bottom.html" name=bottom scrolling=yes>
</frameset>

</html>
```

# Frame.top

## *JavaScript 1.0+, JScript 1.0+*

## *Nav2+, IE 3+, Opera3+*

## Syntax

```
frame.top
```

## Description

The top property of the Frame object specifies the top-most browser window containing frames.

## Example

Listing 7.286 shows an example of how the top property is used to get the name of the top frame.

*Listing 7.286  Example of* top *Property*
```
<script language="JavaScript">
<!-- Hide

var topBrowserName = myframe.document.top.name;
alert("The name of the top most browser is: " + topBrowser);
// End Hide --->
</script>
```

# Frame.window

## *JavaScript 1.0+, JScript 1.0+*

## *Nav2+, IE 3+, Opera3+*

## Syntax

```
frame.window
```

## Description

The window property of the Frame object is used to reference the current frame. This works the same as using the self property.

## Example

Listing 7.287 shows an example of the syntax of the window property.

*Listing 7.287  Syntax for the* window *Property*
```
<html>
<title> Example of the window property of the Frame object</title>

<script language="JavaScript">
```

*continues*

*Listing 7.287    continued*

```
<!--Hide
//sets focus to the upper frame
document.upper.window.focus();
// End Hide --->
</script>

<frameset rows="100,*">
<frame src="top.html" name=upper>
<frame src="bottom.html" name=bottom>
</frameset>

</html>
```

# Hidden

## *JavaScript 1.0+, JScript 1.0+*

## *Nav2+, IE 3+, Opera3+*

## *Syntax*

Core client-side JavaScript object.

## *Description*

The Hidden object is created with the HTML <input> tag. Specifying the TYPE parameter of the <input> tag as hidden creates the Hidden object. It is a text object that is
suppressed from form display in an HTML form. The Hidden object is primarily used
for passing name/value pairs from a form. Table 7.29 shows the properties of the
Hidden object.

*Table 7.29    Properties of the Hidden Object*

| Property | Description |
| --- | --- |
| form | Specifies the form containing the Hidden object. |
| name | Refers to the name of Hidden object. |
| type | Refers to HTML TYPE attribute of Hidden object. |
| value | Refers to HTML VALUE attribute of Hidden object. |

## *Example*

Listing 7.288 shows how a Hidden object is created and how some of its properties are
accessed.

*Listing 7.288    Creating a Hidden Object*

```
<html>
<head>
<title> Creating hidden objects</title>
</head>
```

```
<body>
<form name="form1">
<input type="hidden" name="hide1" value="Test">
<p>
<input type="button" value="Get Hidden Attributes"
   onClick='alert("The Hidden object Name is: " + form1.hide1.name +
" The Hidden Type is: " + form1.hide1.type + " The Hidden Value is: " +
form1.hide1.value)'>
</form>

</body>
</html>
```

# Hidden.form

## *JavaScript 1.0+, Jscript 1.0+*

## *Nav2+, IE 3+, Opera3+*

## Syntax

```
hidden.form
```

## Description

The form property of the Hidden object is used to reference the form containing the Hidden object.

## Example

Listing 7.289 shows how the form property is used to store the name of the form.

*Listing 7.289    Example of the* form *Property*

```
<html>
<head>
<title> Using the form property of the Hidden object</title>
</head>
<body>
<form namename="form1">
Form name:<input typetype="hidden" namename="hide1" valuevalue="Test">
<p>
<input typetype="button" valuevalue="Form Name"
   onClick="this.form.hide1.value=this.form.name">
</form>

</body>
</html>
```

# Hidden.name

## *JavaScript 1.0+, JScript 1.0+*

## Nav2+, IE 3+, Opera3+

### Syntax

`hidden.name`

### Description

The `name` property of the `Hidden` object is used get the name for the `Hidden` object. This is the HTML `NAME` attribute for the `Hidden` object.

### Example

Listing 7.290 shows an example of how the `name` property is used. The form object is used to access the `name` property.

*Listing 7.290    Example of* name *Property*

```
<html>
<head>
<title> Using the name property of the Hidden object</title>
</head>
<body>
< form name="form1">
Form name:<input type="hidden" name="hide1" value="Test">
<p>
<input type="button" value="Hidden Name"
   onClick='alert("The Hidden object name is: " + form1.hide1.name)'>
</form>

</body>
</html>
```

# Hidden.type

## JavaScript 1.1+, JScript 3.0+

## Nav3+, IE 4+, Opera3+

### Syntax

`hidden.type`

### Description

The `type` property of the `Hidden` object specifies the hidden type. For all `Hidden` objects, the type value is `Hidden`.

### Example

Listing 7.291 shows an example of how the `type` property is used to get the `hidden` type. The form object is used to access the `type` property.

*Listing 7.291    Example of the* type *Property*

```
<html>
<head>
<title> Using the type property of the Hidden object</title>
</head>
<body>
<form name="form1">
Form name:<input type="hidden" name="hide1" value="Test">
<p>
<input type="button" value="Hidden Type"
   onClick='alert("The Hidden object type is: " + form1.hide1.type)'>
</form>

</body>
</html>
```

# Hidden.value

## *JavaScript 1.0+, JScript 1.0+*

## *Nav2+, IE 3+, Opera3+*

## *Syntax*

*hidden*.value

## Description

The value property of the hidden object reflects the HTML VALUE attribute of the Hidden object.

## Example

Listing 7.292 shows how the value property of the Hidden object is used. The onClick event handler is used to display an alert box to the user indicating the value of the Hidden object.

*Listing 7.292    Using the* value *Property of* Hidden *Object*

```
<html>
<head>
<title> Using the value property of the Hidden Object</title>
</head>
<body>
<form name="form1">
Form name:<input type="hidden" name="hide1" value="Test">
<p>
<input type="button" value="Get Hidden Value"
   onClick='alert("The Hidden object value is: " + form1.hide1.value)'>
</form>

</body>
</html>
```

# History

## JavaScript 1.0+, ECMAScript 1.0+, JScript 1.0+

## Nav2+, IE 3+, Opera3+

### Syntax

Core client-side JavaScript object.

### Description

The History object is a predefined JavaScript object that allows you to navigate through the history of Websites that a browser has displayed. The browser stores a history of visited URLs in a list, which the History object references. Table 7.30 shows the methods and properties of the History object.

**Table 7.30    Properties and Methods of the History Object**

| Property | Description |
| --- | --- |
| back() | Loads the URL for the previous visited Web site |
| current | Refers to the current URL in the history list |
| forward() | Loads the next URL in the history list |
| go() | Loads a URL from the history list |
| length | Returns the number of entries in the history list |
| next | Refers to the next URL in the history list |
| previous | Refers to the previous URL in the history list |

### Example

Listing 7.293 shows an example of how the History object is used. A for loop is used to loop through the history list and outputs the Web site entries in the list.

*Listing 7.293    Example of the History Object*

```
<html>
<head>
<title> Using the history object to view a list of the browser history</title>
</head>
<body>
<script language="JavaScript">
<!-- Hide
// code loops though the history list and outputs a history list of web sites
visited.
for (i=0; i<history.length; i++){
document.writeln(window.history.previous);
}
//-->
</script>

</body>
</html>
```

# History.back()

## *JavaScript 1.0+, ECMAScript 1.0+, JScript 1.0+*

## *Nav2+, IE 3+, Opera3+*

### Syntax

```
history.back()
```

### Description

The back() method of the History object is used to load the URL for the previously visited Web site.

### Example

Listing 7.294 shows an example of how a JavaScript button can use the back() method to simulate the browser's back functionality.

*Listing 7.294    Example of the* back() *Method*
```
<html>
<head>
<title> Using the back method of the History object</title>
</head>
<body>

<form name=form1>
Click on the button to go back to the previous page.
<input type="button" value="Go Back" onClick='window.history.back()'>
</form>

</body>
</html>
```

# History.current

## *JavaScript 1.1+, ECMAScript 1.0+, JScript 3.0+*

## *Nav3+, IE 4+*

### Syntax

```
history.current
```

### Description

The current property of the History object contains a string that specifies the complete URL of the current history entry.

> **NOTE**
>
> In Navigator 4 and higher, getting the current value requires the
> `UniversalBrowserRead` privilege.

## Example

Listing 7.295 shows an example of how the `current` property is used. For this example, the `UniversalBrowserRead` privilege must be set. Once this is done, the `onClick` event handler alerts the user of the `History current` property.

*Listing 7.295    Example of the `current` Property*

```html
<html>
<head>
<title> Using the current property of the History object</title>
</head>
<body>

<script language="JavaScript">
<!--Hide

// request the Universal Browser Read privilege
netscape.security.PrivilegeManager.enablePrivilege("UniversalBrowserRead");

// End Hide --->
</script>

<form name=form1>
<input type="button" value="Get Current"
onClick='alert(window.history.current)'>
</form>

</body>
</html>
```

# History.forward()

## *JavaScript 1.0+, ECMAScript 1.0+, JScript 1.0+*

## *Nav2+, IE 3+, Opera3+*

### Syntax

```
history.forward()
```

### Description

The `forward()` method of the `History` object is used to load the URL for the next Web site in the history list.

## Example

Listing 7.296 shows an example of how the `forward()` method is used to simulate the forward functionality of the browser.

*Listing 7.296   Example of the `forward()` Method*
```
<html>
<head>
<title> Using the forward method of the History object</title>
</head>
<body>

<form name=form1>
Click on the button to go to the forward browser page.
<input type="button" value="Go Forward" onClick='window.history.forward()'>
</form>

</body>
</html>
```

# History.go()

## *JavaScript 1.0+, ECMAScript 1.0+, JScript 1.0+*

## *Nav2+, IE 3+, Opera3+*

## Syntax

```
history.go(num)
```

## Description

The `go()` method of the `History` object loads a URL from the history list.

## Example

Listing 7.297 shows how the `go()` method can be used to navigate to another Web site in the history list.

*Listing 7.297   Example of the `History go()` Method*
```
<html>
<head>
<title> Using the go method of the History object</title>
</head>
<body>

<form name=form1>
Click on the button to go back 2 pages.
<input type="button" value="Go" onClick='window.history.go(-2)'>
</form>

</body>
</html>
```

# History.length

## *JavaScript 1.0+, ECMAScript 1.0+, JScript 1.0+*

## *Nav2+, IE 3+, Opera3+*

### *Syntax*

```
history.length
```

### *Description*

The `length` property of the `History` object is used to get the number of URLs in the history list.

### *Example*

Listing 7.298 shows an example of how the `length` property is used to determine how many URLs are in the history list.

*Listing 7.298    Example of the `length` Property*

```
<html>
<head>
<title> Using the length property of the History object</title>
</head>
<body>

<script language="JavaScript">
<!-- Hide
//write the number of elements in the history list
var numOfURL = window.history.length;
document.write("The number of URL's in the history list is: " + numOfURL);
// End Hide
</script>

</body>
</html>
```

# History.next

## *JavaScript 1.1+, ECMAScript 1.0+, JScript 3.0+*

## *Nav3+, IE 4+*

### *Syntax*

```
history.next
```

### *Description*

The `next` property of the `History` object is used to get the URL for the next entry in the history list.

**NOTE**

> In Navigator 4 and later, getting the next value requires the `UniversalBrowserRead` privilege.

## Example

Listing 7.299 shows an example of how the `next` property is used to get the next URL in the history list. If nothing is displayed for the `nextURL`, you are at the end of the history list.

*Listing 7.299    Example of the next Property*

```
<html>
<head>
<title> Using the next property of the History object</title>
</head>
<body>

<script language="JavaScript">
<!-- Hide
// request the Universal Browser Read privilege
netscape.security.PrivilegeManager.enablePrivilege("UniversalBrowserRead");

//get the next URL in the history list
var nextURL = window.history.next;
document.write("The next URL in the history list is: " + nextURL);
// End Hide -- >
</script>

</body>
</html>
```

# History.previous

## *JavaScript 1.1+, ECMAScript 1.0+, JScript 3.0+*

## *Nav3+, IE 4+*

## Syntax

`history.previous`

## Description

The `previous` property of the `History` object is used to get the URL for the previous entry in the history list.

**NOTE**

> In Navigator 4 and later, getting the previous value requires the `UniversalBrowserRead` privilege.

## Example

Listing 7.300 shows an example of how the `previous` property is used to get the previous URL in the history list.

*Listing 7.300   Example of the* `previous` *Property*

```
<html>
<head>
<title> Using the previous property of the History object</title>
</head>
<body>
<script language="JavaScript">
<!-- Hide
// request the Universal Browser Read privilege
netscape.security.PrivilegeManager.enablePrivilege("UniversalBrowserRead");
// End Hide --->
</script>

<form name=form1>
<input type="button" value="Get Previous"
onClick='alert(window.history.previous)'>
</form>

</body>
</html>
```

# Image

## JavaScript 1.1+, JScript 1.0+

## Nav3+, IE 3+, Opera3+

## Syntax

Core client-side JavaScript object.

## Description

The `Image` object represents an image that was created with the `<img>` tag. Images can be downloaded and cached dynamically by using the `Image()` constructor, but they cannot be displayed using the constructor. The constructor takes two optional arguments, `width` and `height`. The argument *width* specifies the width of the image in pixels, while the argument *height* specifies the height of the image in pixels. If these arguments are larger or smaller than the actual image, the image will be stretched to these dimensions. You have probably noticed that there is no argument specifying the image to load. The image to load is specified using dot notation and the `src` property after the image constructor has been called. Table 7.31 lists all the properties, methods, and events associated with `Image` object.

*Table 7.31    Properties, Methods, and Events Associated with the Image Object*

| Type | Item | Description |
|---|---|---|
| Properties | border | Width of border around image |
| | complete | Has image finished loading? |
| | height | Height of image |
| | hspace | Padding on left and right of image. |
| | lowsrc | Alternate image for low-resolution displays |
| | name | Name of image |
| | src | URL of image |
| | vspace | Padding on top and bottom of image |
| | width | Width of image |
| Method | handleEvent() | Invokes an images event handler |
| Events | onAbort | Handler when image load is aborted |
| | onError | Handler when error occurs while loading image |
| | onKeyDown | Handler for KeyDown events within image |
| | onKeyPress | Handler for KeyPress events within image |
| | onKeyUp | Handler for KeyUp events within image |
| | onLoad | Handler when image is finished loading |

## Example

Listing 7.301 demonstrates how to use the <img> tag and the Image() constructor to alternate images in a document.

*Listing 7.301    Example of Image Object*

```
<html>
<head>
<title>Example of Image Object</title>
</head>
<script language="JavaScript">
<!-- Hide

//Alternate flag
alternate=0;

//Create an Image object and preload image
circle = new Image();
circle.src = "circle.gif";
square = new Image();
square.src = "square.gif";

function changeImage()
{
```

*continues*

*Listing 7.301    continued*

```
  if(alternate==0)
  {
    document.magic.src=circle.src;
    alternate=1;
  }
  else
  {
    document.magic.src=square.src;
    alternate=0;
  }
}

//End Hide --->
</script>

<center>
<h2>Magic Trick</h2>

<form>
<input type="button"
       value="Change Image"
       onClick="changeImage()">
</form>

<img name="magic" src="square.gif">
</center>

</html>
```

# Image.border

## JavaScript 1.1+, Jscript 1.0+

## Nav3+, IE 3+, Opera3+

### Syntax

*image*.border

### Description

The border property of the Image object specifies the width of the border around an image in pixels. This property can only be set by the BORDER attribute of the <img> tag.

### Example

Listing 7.302 shows how the border property is used.

*Listing 7.302    Example of* border *Property*

```
<html>
<head>
<title>Example of border Property</title>
```

```
</head>
<img name="circle"
     src="circle.gif"
     border=10>
<br>

<script language="JavaScript">
<!-- Hide

//Display width of border
document.write("The image has a border with of ");
document.write(document.circle.border," pixels.");

//Hide End --->
</script>

</html>
```

# Image.complete

## *JavaScript 1.1+, JScript 1.0+*

## *Nav3+, IE 3+, Opera3+*

## *Syntax*

*image*.complete

## *Description*

The complete property of the Image object is a Boolean value that specifies if an image has finished loading. After an image has completely loaded, the property is changed to false. If the load is aborted or an error occurs during the loading process, the property will be set to true.

## *Example*

Listing 7.303 displays a message based on the value of the complete property.

*Listing 7.303   Example of the* complete *Property*

```
<html>
<head>
<title>Example of complete Property</title>
</head>
<img name="circle" src="circle.gif">
<br>

<script language="JavaScript">
<!-- Hide

//Display message about loading progress of image
```

*continues*

*Listing 7.303  continued*
```
if(document.circle.complete == true)
  document.write("The image has finished loading.");
else
  document.write("The image has not finished loading.");

//Hide End --->
</script>

</html>
```

# Image.handleEvent()

## JavaScript 1.2+,

## Nav4+

### Syntax
```
image.handleEvent(event)
```

### Description

The handleEvent() method provides a way to invoke an image's event handler, even though the event never happened. The *event* argument associated with this method can be any of the events handled by the Image object.

### Example

Listing 7.304 shows how to force an image to handle a KEYDOWN event.

*Listing 7.304  The* handleEvent() *Method*
```
<img name="circle" src="circle.gif" onKeyDown="alert('Key pressed')">

<script language="JavaScript">
<!-- Hide
document.circle.handleEvent(Event.KEYDOWN);
//Hide End --->
</script>
```

# Image.height

## JavaScript 1.1+, JScript 1.0+

## Nav3+, IE 3+, Opera3+

### Syntax
```
image.height
```

### Description

The height property of the Image object specifies the height of the image in pixels. This property can only be set by the HEIGHT attribute of the <img> tag.

## Example

Listing 7.305 displays the value of the height property.

*Listing 7.305   Example of* height *Property*

```
<html>
<head>
<title>Example of height property</title>
</head>
<img name="circle"
     src="circle.gif"
     height=200>
<br>

<script LANGUAGE=language="JavaScript">
<!-- Hide

//Display height of image
document.write("The height of the image is ");
document.write(document.circle.height, " pixels.");

//Hide End --->
</script>

</html>
```

# Image.hspace

## *JavaScript 1.1+, JScript 1.0+*

## *Nav3+, IE 3+, Opera3+*

## Syntax

*image*.hspace

## Description

The hspace property of the Image object specifies the number of extra pixels that should appear on the left and right of the image. This property can only be set by the HSPACE attribute of the <img> tag.

## Example

Listing 7.306 demonstrates the hspace property.

*Listing 7.306   Example of* hspace *Property*

```
<html>
<head>
<title>Example of hspace property</title>
</head>
```

*continues*

*Listing 7.306   continued*
```
Text to left of image.
<img name="circle" src="circle.gif" HSPACE=100>
Text to right of image.<br>

<script language="JavaScript">
<!-- Hide

//Display value of hspace property
document.write("The hspace property of the image is ");
document.write(document.circle.hspace);

//Hide End --->
</script>

</html>
```

# Image.lowsrc

## *JavaScript 1.1+, JScript 1.0+*

## *Nav3+, IE 3+, Opera3+*

### Syntax

*image*.lowsrc

### Description

The lowsrc property of the Image object specifies the URL of an alternate image to use on low-resolution displays. This property can only be set by the LOWSRC attribute of the <img> tag.

### Example

Listing 7.307 displays the URL of the low-resolution image.

*Listing 7.307   Example of* lowsrc *Property*
```
<html>
<head>
<title>Example of lowsrc property</title>
</head>
<img name="circle"
     src="circle.gif"
     lowsrc="circle_low.gif">
<br>

<script language="JavaScript">
<!-- Hide

//Display the low resolution image
document.write("The URL of the low resolution image is ");
```

```
document.write("<i><b>",document.circle.lowsrc,"</b></i>");

//Hide End --->
</script>

</html>
```

# Image.name

## *JavaScript 1.1+, JScript 1.0+*

## *Nav3+, IE 3+, Opera3+*

## *Syntax*

*image*.name

## *Description*

The name property of the Image object specifies the name of the image. This property can only be set by the NAME attribute of the <img> tag.

## *Example*

Listing 7.308 displays the name of the image.

*Listing 7.308  Example the of* name *Property*

```
<html>
<head>
<title>Example of name property</title>
</head>
<img name="circle" src="circle.gif">
<br>

<script language="JavaScript">
<!-- Hide

//Display name of image
document.write("The name of the image is <i>");
document.write(document.circle.name,"</i>");

//Hide End --->
</script>

</html>
```

# Image.onAbort

## *JavaScript 1.1+, JScript 1.0+*

## *Nav3+, IE 3+*

## Syntax

```
onAbort="command"
```

## Description

The onAbort event defines a handler when the loading of the image is aborted.

## Example

Listing 7.309 creates an alert box when the loading of the image is aborted.

*Listing 7.309    Example of the onAbort Event*
```
<img name="circle"
    src="circle.gif"
    onAbort="alert('This image did not finish loading!')">
```

# Image.onError

## JavaScript 1.1+, JScript 3.0+

## Nav3+, IE 4+

## Syntax

```
onError="command"
```

## Description

The onError event handler is triggered when an error occurs while loading the image.

## Example

Listing 7.310 creates an alert box when an error occurs while loading the image.

*Listing 7.310    Example of the onError Event Handler*
```
<img name="circle"
    src="circle.gif"
    onError="alert('An error occurred while this image was loading!')">
```

# Image.onKeyDown

## JavaScript 1.2+, JScript 3.0+

## Nav4+, IE 4+

## Syntax

```
onKeyDown="command"
```

## Description

The onKeyDown event handler is triggered when a key is pressed down in the image.

## Example

Listing 7.311 defines an event handler for the onKeyDown event within an image.

*Listing 7.311   Example of the* onKeyDown *Event*
```
<img name="circle"
     src="circle.gif"
     onKeyDown="alert('An ONKEYDOWN event occurred!')">
```

# Image.onKeyPress

## *JavaScript 1.2+, JScript 3.0+*

## *Nav4+, IE 4+*

## *Syntax*
```
onKeyPress="command"
```

## *Description*

The onKeyPress event defines a handler when a key is pressed in the image.

## *Example*

Listing 7.312 defines an event handler for the onKeyPress event within an image.

*Listing 7.312   Example of the* onKeyPress *Event Handler*
```
<img name="circle"
     src="circle.gif"
     onKeyPress="alert('An ONKEYPRESS event occurred!')">
```

# Image.onKeyUp

## *JavaScript 1.2+, JScript 3.0+*

## *Nav4+, IE 4+*

## *Syntax*
```
onKeyUp="command"
```

## *Description*

The onKeyUp event defines a handler when a key is pressed and then released in the image.

## *Example*

Listing 7.313 defines an event handler for the onKeyUp event within an image.

*Listing 7.313   Example of the* onKeyUp *Event*
```
<img name="circle"
     src="circle.gif"
     onKeyUp="alert('An ONKEYUP event occurred!')">
```

# Image.onLoad

## *JavaScript 1.1+, JScript 1.0+*

## Nav3+, IE 3+

### Syntax

onLoad="*command*"

### Description

The onLoad event handler defines what should happen once the image has finished loading.

### Example

Listing 7.314 displays a message once the image has finished loading.

*Listing 7.314    Example of the onLoad Event Handler*

```
<img name="circle"
    src="circle.gif"
    onLoad="alert('This image has finished loading!')">
```

# Image.src

## JavaScript 1.1+, JScript 1.0+

## Nav3+, IE 3+, Opera3+

### Syntax

*image*.src

### Description

The src property of the Image object specifies the URL of the image. This property can only be set by the SRC attribute of the <img> tag.

### Example

Listing 7.315 displays the URL of the image.

*Listing 7.315    Example of the src Property*

```
<html>
<head>
<title>Example of src property</title>
</head>
<img name="circle" src="circle.gif"><br>

<script language="JavaScript">
<!-- Hide

//Display the URL of the image
document.write("The URL of the image is ");
document.write("<i><b>",document.circle.src,"</b></i>");

//Hide End --->
```

```
</script>

</html>
```

# Image.vspace

## *JavaScript 1.1+, JScript 1.0+*

## *Nav3+, IE 3+, Opera3+*

## Syntax

*image*.vspace

## Description

The vspace property of the Image object specifies the number of extra pixels that should appear on the top and bottom of the image. This property can only be set by the VSPACE attribute of the <img> tag.

## Example

Listing 7.316 demonstrates the vspace property.

*Listing 7.316    Example of the* vspace *Property*

```
<html>
<head>
<title>Example of vspace property</title>
</head>
Text at top of image.<br>
<img name="circle" src="circle.gif" VSPACE=100><br>
Text at bottom of image.<br>

<script language="JavaScript">
<!-- Hide

//Display value of vspace property
document.write("The vspace property of the image is ");
document.write(document.circle.vspace);

//Hide End --->
</script>

</html>
```

# Image.width

## *JavaScript 1.1+, JScript 1.0+*

## *Nav3+, IE 3+, Opera3+*

## Syntax

*image*.width

## Description

The width property of the Image object specifies the width of the image in pixels. This property can only be set by the WIDTH attribute of the <img> tag.

## Example

Listing 7.317 displays the value of the width property.

*Listing 7.317    Example of the* width *Property*

```
<html>
<head>
<title>Example of width property</title>
</head>
<img name="circle"
     src="circle.gif"
     width=150>
<br>

<script language="JavaScript">
<!-- Hide

//Display width of image
document.write("The width of the image is ");
document.write(document.circle.width, " pixels.");

//Hide End --->
</script>

</html>
```

# Layer

## JavaScript 1.2+

## Nav4+

## Syntax

Core client-side JavaScript object.

## Description

The Layer object represents an object that contains a single document. A document can contain multiple layers, and thereby contain multiple documents. Layers are useful for displaying graphics which overlay each other within a browser. The Layer object has specific properties and methods associated with it, as shown in Table 7.32.

*Table 7.32* **Properties and Methods of the Layer Object**

| Property/Method | Description |
| --- | --- |
| `above` | Specifies the layer above |
| `background` | Refers to the background image of the layer |
| `below` | Specifies the layer below |
| `bgColor` | Refers to the background color of the layer |
| `captureEvents()` | Specifies the event types to capture |
| `clip.bottom` | Refers to the bottom of the layer's clipping area |
| `clip.height` | Refers to the height of the layer's clipping area |
| `clip.left` | Refers to the left of the layer's clipping area |
| `clip.right` | Refers to the right of the layer's clipping area |
| `clip.top` | Refers to the top of the layer's clipping area |
| `clip.width` | Refers to the width of the layer's clipping area |
| `document` | The document object that contains the layer |
| `handleEvent()` | Invokes handler for specified event |
| `left` | The x-coordinate of the layer |
| `load()` | Loads a new URL |
| `moveAbove()` | Moves the layer above another layer |
| `moveBelow()` | Moves the layer below another layer |
| `moveBy()` | Moves the layer to a specified position |
| `moveTo()` | Moves the top-left corner of the window to the specified screen coordinates |
| `moveToAbsolute()` | Changes the layer position to the specified pixel coordinates within the page |
| `name` | Refers to the name of the layer |
| `onBlur` | Event handler when focus is removed from the layer |
| `onFocus` | Event handler when focus is set to a layer |
| `onLoad` | Event handler when a document is loaded in a layer |
| `onMouseOut` | Event handler when the mouse cursor is removed from a layer's area |
| `onMouseOver` | Event handler when the mouse cursor is moved over a layer's area |
| `pageX` | The x-coordinate relative to the document |
| `pageY` | The y-coordinate relative to the document |
| `parentLayer` | The containing layer |
| `releaseEvents()` | Sets the layer to release captured events of the specified type |
| `resizeBy()` | Resizes the layer by the specified height and width values |
| `resizeTo()` | Resizes the layer to have the specified height and width values |
| `routeEvent()` | Passes a captured event along the normal event hierarchy |
| `siblingAbove` | The layer above in the zIndex |

*continues*

**Table 7.32    continued**

| Property/Method | Description |
| --- | --- |
| siblingBelow | The layer below in the zIndex |
| src | The source URL for the layer |
| top | The y-coordinate of the layer |
| visibility | Specifies the visibility state of the layer |
| zIndex | The relative z-order of this layer with respect to its siblings |

## Example

Listing 7.318 creates a layer. When the mouse cursor is moved over the `layer` object, an alert message is displayed informing which layer the cursor was moved over.

*Listing 7.318    Example of the* Layer *Object*

```
<html>
<head>
<title> Creating a Layer object<title>
</head>
<body>
<layer id="layer1" width="150" height="200" bgcolor="yellow" TOP="170"
left=200 visibility="show" onMouseOut='alert("This is layer 1")'>
<center>Layer 1</center>
</layer>

<layer id="layer2" width="150" height="160" bgcolor="green" TOP="100"
left="70" visibility="show" onMouseOut='alert("This is layer 2")'>
<center>Layer 2</center>
</layer>

</body>
</html>
```

# Layer.above

## JavaScript 1.2+

## Nav4+

## Syntax

`layer.above`

## Description

The above property of the Layer object refers to the layer immediately above the layer in the zIndex. If this does not exist, the value is null.

## Example

Listing 7.319 shows how the above property is used. Two layers are created and when the Get Above button is clicked, an alert box is displayed with the value of the above attribute.

*Listing 7.319    Example of the* above *Property*

```
<html>
<head>
<title> Using the above property of the Layer object</title>
</head>
<body>

<layer id="layer1" width=200 height=200 color= bgcolor="yellow" TOP=170
LEFT=200 VISIBILITY="show">
<center>Layer 1</center>
</layer>

<layer ID="layer2" width=150 height=160 color= bgcolor="green" TOP=100
LEFT=70 VISIBILITY="show">
<center>Layer 2</center>
</layer>

<form name="form1">
<input type="button" value="Get above" onClick=alert(document.layers.above)>
</form>

</body>
</html>
```

# Layer.background

## JavaScript 1.2+

## Nav4+

## Syntax

`layer.background`

## Description

The background property of the Layer object refers to the BACKGROUND attribute of the <layer> tag. The background images for the layer object can be changed by setting the background.src property.

## Example

Listing 7.320 shows an example of how to change the layer background image. Two layers are created and when the Change Background button is clicked, the change() function is called. The change() function sets the background property of layer1 to water.gif.

*Listing 7.320    Example of the* background *Property*

```
<html>
<head>
<title> Using the background property of the Layer object</title>
</head>
<body>

<script language="JavaScript">
<!-- Hide
function change(){
    document.layer1.background.src = "water.gif";
}
// End Hide --->
</script>

<layer id="layer1" width=200 height=200 color= bgcolor="yellow" TOP=170
LEFT=200 VISIBILITY="show">
<center>Layer 1</center>
</layer>

<layer id="layer2" width=150 height=160 color= bgcolor="green" TOP=100
LEFT=70 VISIBILITY="show">
<center>Layer 2</center>
</layer>

<form name="form1">
<input type="button" value="Change Background" onClick=change()>
</form>


</body>
</html>
```

# Layer.below

## *JavaScript 1.2+*

## *Nav4+*

## *Syntax*

`layer.below`

## *Description*

The below property of the Layer object specifies the layer object immediately below the layer in the zIndex. If this does not exist, the below value is null.

## Example

Listing 7.321 shows an example of the below property. Two layers are created using the <layer> tag. When the Get Below button is clicked, an alert box is displayed showing the value of the below property.

*Listing 7.321    Example of the* below *Property*

```
<html>
<head>
<title> Using the below property of the Layer object</title>
</head>
<body>

<layer id="layer1" width=200 height=200 color= bgcolor="yellow" TOP=170
LEFT=200 VISIBILITY="show">
<center>Layer 1</center>
</layer>

<layer id="layer2" width=150 height=160 color= bgcolor="green" TOP=100
LEFT=70 VISIBILITY="show">
<center>Layer 2</center>
</layer>

<form name="form1">
<input type="button" value="Get below" onClick=alert(document.layers.below)>
</form>

</body>
</html>
```

# Layer.bgColor

## JavaScript 1.2+

## Nav4+

## Syntax

`layer.bgColor`

## Description

The bgColor property of the Layer object represents the BGCOLOR attribute of the <layer> tag. The background color for the Layer object can be changed by setting the bgColor.src property. The color can only be changed if the background property is not set.

## Example

Listing 7.322 shows how the bgColor property is used to change the background colors of the layer's objects.

*Listing 7.322    Example of the* bgColor *Property*

```
<html>
<head>
<title> Using the bgColor property of the Layer object</title>
</head>
<body>

<script language="JavaScript">
<!-- Hide

// function changes the color of layer1
function change1(){
    document.layer1.bgColor = "#FF00FA";
}

// function changes the color of Layer2
function change2(){
    document.layer2.bgColor="orange";
}
// End Hide --->
</script>

<layer id="layer1" width=200 height=200 color= bgcolor="yellow" TOP=170
LEFT=200 VISIBILITY="show">
<center>Layer 1</center>
</layer>

<layer id="layer2" width=150 height=160 color= bgcolor="green" TOP=100
LEFT=70 VISIBILITY="show">
<center>Layer 2</center>
</layer>

<form name="form1">
<input type="button" value="Change Layer 1 Background" onClick=change1()>
<br><br>
<input type="button" value="Change Layer 2 Background" onClick=change2()>
</form>

</body>
</html>
```

# Layer.captureEvents()

## JavaScript 1.2+

## Nav4+

## Syntax

*layer*.captureEvents(*event.type*)

## Description

The captureEvents() method of the Layer object is used to handle all events of a specific type.

## Example

Listing 7.323 shows how the captureEvents() method is used. The captureEvents() method is used for layer2 to listen for the RESIZE event. When this occurs, the resize2() function is called, which displays a message to the user.

*Listing 7.323    Example of the* captureEvents() *Method*

```
<html>
<head>
<title> Using the captureEvents of the Layer object</title>
</head>
<body>

<script language="JavaScript">
<!-- Hide
document.layer2.captureEvents(Event.RESIZE);

// function resizes layer2 and upon the resize event alerts the
// user that the layer was resized.
function resize2(){
    document.layer2.resizeTo(300,100);
    onResize=alert("Layer2 has been resized.");
}
// End Hide --->
</script>

<layer id="layer1" width=200 height=200 color= bgcolor="yellow" TOP=170
LEFT=200 VISIBILITY="show">
<center>Layer 1</center>
</layer>

<layer id="layer2" width=150 height=160 color= bgcolor=green" TOP=100
LEFT=70 VISIBILITY="show">
<center>Layer 2</center>
</layer>

<form>
Click the button to resize Layer 2
<br>
<input type="button" value="Resize Layer2" onClick='resize2()'>
</form>
</body>
</html>
```

# Layer.clip.bottom

## *JavaScript 1.2+*

## *Nav4+*

## *Syntax*

```
layer.clip.bottom
```

## *Description*

The `clip.bottom` property of the `Layer` object refers to the bottom of the layer's clipping area.

## *Example*

Listing 7.324 shows an example of how `clip.bottom` is used. Two layers are created using the `<layer>` tag. When the button is clicked, the `clip1` function is called, which clips the bottom of `layer1` by 100 pixels.

*Listing 7.324   Example of the* `clip.bottom` *Property*

```
<html>
<head>
<title> Using the clip.bottom property of the Layer object</title>
</head>
<body>

<script language="JavaScript">
<!-- Hide

// function clips the bottom of layer 1 by 100 pixels
function clip1(){
    document.layer1.clip.bottom = 100;
}
// End Hide --->
</script>

<layer id="layer1" width=200 height=200 color= bgcolor="yellow" TOP=170
LEFT=200 VISIBILITY="show">
<center>Layer 1</center>
</layer>

<layer id="layer2" width=150 height=160 color= bgcolor="green" TOP=100
LEFT=70 VISIBILITY="show">
<center>Layer 2</center>
</layer>

<form name="form1">
<input type="button" value="Clip bottom of Layer 1" onClick=clip1()>
</form>

</body>
</html>
```

# Layer.clip.height

## *JavaScript 1.2+*

## *Nav4+*

## *Syntax*

```
layer.clip.height
```

## *Description*

The `clip.height` property of the `Layer` object refers to the height of the layer's clipping area.

## *Example*

Listing 7.325 shows how the `clip.height` property is used. Two layers are created using the <layer> tag. When the button is clicked, the `clip1()` function is called, which clips the height of `layer1` by 75 pixels.

*Listing 7.325    Example of the `clip.height` Property*

```
<html>
<head>
<title> Using the clip.height property of the Layer object</title>
</head>
<body>

<script language="JavaScript">
<!-- Hide

// function clips the height of layer 1 by 75 pixels
function clip1(){
    document.layer1.clip.height = 75;
}
// End Hide --->
</script>

<layer id="layer1" width=200 height=200 color= bgcolor="yellow" TOP=170
LEFT=200 VISIBILITY="show">
<center>Layer 1</center>
</layer>

<layer id="layer2" width=150 height=160 color= bgcolor="green" TOP=100
LEFT=70 VISIBILITY="show">
<center>Layer 2</center>
</layer>

<form name="form1">
<input type="button" value="Clip Height of Layer 1" onClick=clip1()>
</form>

</body>
</html>
```

# Layer.clip.left
## *JavaScript 1.2+*
## *Nav4+*
## *Syntax*
```
layer.clip.left
```
## *Description*
The `clip.left` property of the `Layer` object represents the left of the layer's clipping area.

## *Example*
Listing 7.326 shows how the `clip.left` property is used. Two layers are created using the `<layer>` tag. When the button is clicked, the `clip1()` function is called, which clips the left side of `layer1` by 90 pixels.

*Listing 7.326    Example of the `clip.left` Property*
```html
<html>
<head>
<title> Using the clip.left property of the Layer object</title>
</head>
<body>

<script language="JavaScript">
<!-- Hide

// function clips the left side of layer1 by 90 pixels
function clip1(){
     document.layer1.clip.left = 90;
}
// End Hide --->
</script>

<layer id="layer1" width=200 height=200 color= bgcolor="yellow" TOP=170
LEFT=200 VISIBILITY="show">
<center>Layer 1</center>
</layer>

<layer id="layer2" width=150 height=160 color= bgcolor="green" TOP=100
LEFT=70 VISIBILITY="show">
<center>Layer 2</center>
</layer>

<form name="form1">
<input type="button" value="Clip Left of Layer 1" onClick=clip1()>
</form>

</body>
</html>
```

# Layer.clip.right

## JavaScript 1.2+

## Nav4+

## Syntax

```
layer.clip.right
```

## Description

The `clip.right` property of the `Layer` object represents the right of the layer's clipping area.

## Example

Listing 7.327 shows how the `clip.right` property is used to shorten the right side of the layer. Two layers are created using the `<layer>` tag. When the button is clicked, the `clip1()` function is called, which clips the right side of `layer1` by 110 pixels.

*Listing 7.327   Example of the* `clip.right` *Property*

```
<html>
<head>
<title> Using the clip.right property of the Layer object</title>
</head>
<body>

<script language="JavaScript">
<!-- Hide

// function clips the right side of layer1 by 110 pixels
function clip1(){
    document.layer1.clip.right = 110;
}
// End Hide --->
</script>

<layer id="layer1" width=200 height=200 color= bgcolor="yellow" TOP=170
LEFT=200 VISIBILITY="show">
<center>Layer 1</center>
</layer>

<layer id="layer2" width=150 height=160 color= bgcolor="green" TOP=100
LEFT=70 VISIBILITY="show">
<center>Layer 2</center>
</layer>

<form name="form1">
<input type="button" value="Clip Right of Layer 1" onClick=clip1()>
```

*continues*

*Listing 7.327    continued*

```
</form>

</body>
</html>
```

# Layer.clip.top

## JavaScript 1.2+

## Nav4+

## Syntax

```
layer.clip.top
```

## Description

The clip.top property of the Layer object represents the top part of the layer's clipping area.

## Example

Listing 7.328 uses the clip.top property to shorten the height of the layer. Two layers are created using the <layer> tag. When the button is clicked, the clip1() function is called, which clips the top of layer1 by 88 pixels.

*Listing 7.328    Example of the* clip.top *Property*

```
<html>
<head>
<title> Using the clip.top property of the Layer object</title>
</head>
<body>

<script language="JavaScript">
<!-- Hide

// function clips the top of layer 1 by 88 pixels.
function clip1(){
    document.layer1.clip.top = 88;
}
// End Hide --->
</script>

<layer id="layer1" width=200 height=200 color= bgcolor="yellow" TOP=170
LEFT=200 VISIBILITY="show">
<center>Layer 1</center>
</layer>

<layer id="layer2" width=150 height=160 color= bgcolor="green" TOP=100
LEFT=70 VISIBILITY="show">
<center>Layer 2</center>
```

```
</layer>

<form name="form1">
<input type="button" value="Clip Top of Layer 1" onClick=clip1()>
</form>

</body>
</html>
```

# Layer.clip.width

## JavaScript 1.2+

## Nav4+

## Syntax

```
layer.clip.width
```

## Description

The `clip.width` property of the `Layer` object represents the width of the layer's clipping area.

## Example

Listing 7.329 shows how the `clip.width` property is used to shorten the width of the layer. Two layers are created using the `<layer>` tag. When the button is clicked, the `clip1()` function is called, which clips the width of `layer1` by 60 pixels.

Listing 7.329    Example of the `clip.width` Property

```
<html>
<head>
<title> Using the clip.width property of the Layer object</title>
</head>
<body>

<script language="JavaScript">
<!-- Hide

// function changes the width of Layer 1
function clip1(){
     document.layer1.clip.width = 60;
}
// End Hide --->
</script>

<layer id="layer1" width=200 height=200 color= bgcolor="yellow" TOP=170
LEFT=200 VISIBILITY="show">
<center>Layer 1</center>
</layer>
```

*Listing 7.329    continued*

```
<layer id="layer2" width=150 height=160 color= bgcolor="green" TOP=100
LEFT=70 VISIBILITY="show">
<center>Layer 2</center>
</layer>

<form name="form1">
<input type="button" value="Clip Width of Layer 1" onClick=clip1()>
</form>

</body>
</html>
```

# Layer.document

## *JavaScript 1.2+*

## *Nav4+*

## *Syntax*

*layer*.document

## **Description**

The document property of the Layer object references the Document object contained
in the layer.

## **Example**

Listing 7.330 shows how the document property is used. When the button is clicked,
the getInfo() function is called. This displays the name of the document in layer1.

*Listing 7.330    Example of the* document *Property*
```
<html>
<head>
<title> Using the document property of the Layer object</title>
</head>
<body>

<script language="JavaScript">
<!-- Hide

// function displays an alert box indicating the name of Layer 1 document
function getInfo(){
     alert("The name of Layer 1's document is: " +
document.layer1.document.name);
}
// End Hide --->
</script>

<layer id="layer1" width=200 height=200 color= bgcolor="yellow" TOP=170
```

```
LEFT=200 VISIBILITY="show">
<center>Layer 1</center>
</layer>

<layer id="layer2" width=150 height=160 color= bgcolor="green" TOP=100
LEFT=70 VISIBILITY="show">
<center>Layer 2</center>
</layer>

<form name="form1">
<input type="button" value="Get Layer1 document info" onClick=getInfo()>
</form>

</body>
</html>
```

# Layer.handleEvent()

## *JavaScript 1.2+*

## *Nav4+*

## *Syntax*

`layer.handleEvent(event)`

## *Description*

The handleEvent method of the Layer object determines what type of event occurred and passes the event to the object's appropriate event handler.

## *Example*

Listing 7.331 shows how to use the handleEvent method. The document is set up to capture any FOCUS events. When one occurs, it is sent to the handle() function, which passes it to the default handler for layer2 object. This calls the displayMsg() function for any FOCUS events that occur.

*Listing 7.331   Example of the* handleEvent() *Method*

```
<html>
<head>
<title> Using the handleEvent property of the Layer object</title>
</head>
<body>

<script language="JavaScript">
<!-- Hide

// sets up the document to capture FOCUS events
document.captureEvents(Event.FOCUS);
```

*continues*

*Listing 7.331    continued*

```
// function that handles the specific event. The evnt parameter refers to
// the event object.
function handle(evnt){
    window.document.layer2.handleEvent(evnt);
}

function displayMsg(){
    alert("Focus event occurred.");
}

// This registers the handle function as the event handler for the
// FOCUS event.
document.onFocus = handle;
// End Hide --->
</script>

<layer id="layer1" width=200 height=200 color= bgcolor="yellow" top=170
left=200 visibility="show">
<center>Layer 1</center>
</layer>

<layer id="layer2" width=150 height=160 color= bgcolor="green" top=100
left="70" visibility="show" onFocus='displayMsg()'>
<center>Layer 2</center>
</layer>

<form name="form1">
<input type="button" value="Get Layer1 document info" onClick=getInfo()>
</form>

</body>
</html>
```

# Layer.left

## *JavaScript 1.2+*

## *Nav4+*

## *Syntax*

`layer.left`

## *Description*

The left property of the Layer object represents the x-coordinate position of the layer within the document. Changing this property can move the layer left or right.

## Example

Listing 7.332 shows how the `left` property is used to move the layer from left to right across the screen. When the button is clicked, the `move()` function is called, which moves the `layer1` to the left by 60 pixels.

*Listing 7.332    Example of the `left` Property*

```
<html>
<head>
<title> Using the left property of the Layer object</title>
</head>
<body>

<script language="JavaScript">
<!-- Hide

// function moves Layer 1 to the left
function move(){
    document.layer1.left = document.layer1.left + 10;
}
// End Hide --->
</script>

<layer id="layer1" width=200 height=200 color= bgcolor="yellow" TOP=170
LEFT=200 VISIBILITY="show">
<center>Layer 1</center>
</layer>

<layer id="layer2" width=150 height=160 color= bgcolor="green" TOP=100
LEFT=70 VISIBILITY="show">
<center>Layer 2</center>
</layer>

<form name="form1">
<input type="button" value="Move layer 1" onClick=move()>
</form>

</body>
</html>
```

# Layer.load()

## JavaScript 1.2+

## Nav4+

## Syntax

`layer.load(src, width)`

## Description

The load() method of the Layer object is used to load a new document in the layer. As described in the syntactical definition, this method takes the URL of the source of the layer and the width.

## Example

Listing 7.333 shows how to use the load() method. When the button is clicked, the onClick event handler loads the tmp.html file.

*Listing 7.333   Example of the load() Method*
```
<html>
<head>
<title> Using the load method of the Layer object</title>
</head>
<body>

<layer id="layer1" width=200 height=200 color= bgcolor="yellow" TOP=170
LEFT=200 VISIBILITY="show">
<center>Layer 1</center>
</layer>

<layer id="layer2" width=150 height=160 color= bgcolor="green" TOP=100
LEFT=70 VISIBILITY="show">
<center>Layer 2</center>
</layer>

<form name="form1">
<input type="button" value="Load Layer 2"
onClick='document.layer2.load("tmp.html", 400)'>
</form>

</body>
</html>
```

# Layer.moveAbove()

## *JavaScript 1.2+*

## *Nav4+*

## Syntax

`layer.moveAbove(layername)`

## Description

The moveAbove() method of the Layer object is used to move the current layer above another specified layer. The parameter, *layername*, is the layer object that gets moved to the back.

## Example

Listing 7.334 an example of how the moveAbove() method is used. When the button is clicked, the onClick event handler handles the CLICK event and moves Layer1 above Layer2.

*Listing 7.334   Example of the* moveAbove() *Method*

```
<html>
<head>
<title> Using the moveAbove method of the Layer object</title>
</head>
<body>

<layer id="layer1" width=200 height=200 color= bgcolor="yellow" TOP=170
LEFT=150 VISIBILITY="show">
<center>Layer 1</center>
</layer>

<layer id="layer2" width=150 height=160 color= bgcolor="green" TOP=100
LEFT=70 VISIBILITY="show">
<center>Layer 2</center>
</layer>

<form name="form1">
<input type="button" value="Move layer 1 above layer 2"
onClick='document.layer1.moveAbove(document.layer2)'>
</form>

</body>
</html>
```

# Layer.moveBelow()

## JavaScript 1.2+

## Nav4+

## Syntax

`layer.moveBelow(layername)`

## Description

The moveBelow() method of the Layer object is used to move a layer object below another specified layer. The function takes a single parameter, *layername*, representing the layer object that gets moved to the front.

## Example

Listing 7.335 shows how the moveBelow() method is used to move Layer2 below Layer1.

*Listing 7.335   Example of the* moveBelow() *Method*

```
<html>
<head>
<title> Using the moveBelow method of the Layer object</title>
</head>
<body>

<layer id="layer1" width=200 height=200 color= bgcolor="yellow" TOP=170
LEFT=150 VISIBILITY="show">
<center>Layer 1</center>
</layer>

<layer id="layer2" width=150 height=160 color= bgcolor="green" TOP=100
LEFT=70 VISIBILITY="show">
<center>Layer 2</center>
</layer>

<form name="form1">
<input type="button" value="Move layer 2 below layer 1"
onClick='document.layer2.moveBelow(document.layer1)'>
</form>

</body>
</html>
```

# Layer.moveBy()

## JavaScript 1.2+

## Nav4+

## Syntax

```
layer.moveBy(x,y)
```

## Description

The moveBy() method of the Layer object moves the layer object to the right and down from its current position. The method takes two parameters, *x* and *y*. The *x* parameter refers to the number of pixels the layer is moved to the right. The *y* parameter refers to the number of pixels the layer is moved down.

## Example

Listing 7.336 shows how the moveBy() method is used. When the button is clicked, the onClick event handler uses the moveBy method to move layer2 50 pixels to the right and 30 pixels down.

*Listing 7.336   Example of the* moveBy() *Method*

```
<html>
<head>
<title> Using the moveBy method of the Layer object</title>
```

```
</head>
<body>

<layer id="layer1" width=200 height=200 color= bgcolor="yellow" TOP=170
LEFT=150 VISIBILITY="show">
<center>Layer 1</center>
</layer>

<layer id="layer2" width=150 height=160 color= bgcolor="green" TOP=100
LEFT=70 VISIBILITY="show">
<center>Layer 2</center>
</layer>

<form name="form1">
<input type="button" value="Move layer 2"
onClick='document.layer2.moveBy(50,30)'>
</form>

</body>
</html>
```

# Layer.moveTo()

## *JavaScript1.2+*

## *Nav4+*

## *Syntax*

`Layer.moveTo(x,y)`

## *Description*

The `moveTo()` method of the `Layer` object moves the top-left corner of the layer object to the specified screen coordinates. The *x* parameter refers to an integer representing the top edge of the window in screen coordinates. The *y* parameter refers to an integer representing the left edge of the window in screen coordinates.

## *Example*

Listing 7.337 shows how the `moveTo()` method is used. Two layers are created using the `<layer>` tag. When the button is clicked, the `onClick` event handler for `layer2` invokes the `moveTo` method, which moves the layer to the screen coordinates 100,200.

*Listing 7.337 Example of the `moveTo()` Method*
```
<html>
<head>
<title> Using the moveTo method of the Layer object</title>
</head>
<body>
```

*continues*

*Listing 7.337    continued*

```
<layer id="layer1" WIDTH=200 HEIGHT=200 BGCOLOR="yellow" TOP=170
LEFT=150 VISIBILITY="show">
<center>Layer 1</center>
</layer>

<layer id="layer2" WIDTH=150 HEIGHT=160 BGCOLOR="green" TOP=100
LEFT=70 VISIBILITY="show">
<center>Layer 2</center>
</layer>

<FORM NAME="form1">
<INPUT TYPE="button" VALUE="Move layer 2"
onClick='document.layer2.moveTo(100,200)'>
</FORM>

</body>
</html>
```

# Layer.moveToAbsolute()

## JavaScript 1.2+

## Nav4+

## Syntax

`layer.moveToAbsolute(x,y)`

## Description

The `moveToAbsolute()` method of the `Layer` object moves the upper-left corner of the layer to the specified position. This position is relative to the top-level document. The method takes two parameters, *x* and *y*. The *x* parameter refers to the number of pixels the layer is moved to the right. The *y* parameter refers to the number of pixels the layer is moved down.

## Example

Listing 7.338 an example of how the `moveToAbsolute()` method is used.

*Listing 7.338    Example of the* `moveToAbsolute()` *Method*

```
<html>
<head>
<title> Using the moveToAbsolute method of the Layer object</title>
</head>
<body>

<layer id="layer1" width=200 height=200 color= bgcolor="yellow" TOP=170
LEFT=150 VISIBILITY="show">
<center>Layer 1</center>
</layer>
```

```
<layer id="layer2" width=150 height=160 color= bgcolor="green" TOP=100
LEFT=70 VISIBILITY="show">
<center>Layer 2</center>
</layer>

<form name="form1">
<input type="button" value="Move layer 2"
onClick='document.layer2.moveToAbsolute(350,400)'>
</form>

</body>
</html>
```

# Layer.name

## *JavaScript 1.2+*

## *Nav4+*

## *Syntax*

`layer.name`

## *Description*

The name property of the Layer object refers to the NAME or ID attribute of the <layer> tag.

## *Example*

Listing 7.339 shows how to access the layer's name.

*Listing 7.339    Example of the* name *Property*

```
<html>
<head>
<title> Using the name property of the Layer object</title>
</head>
<body>

<layer id="Tarzan" width=200 height=200 color= bgcolor="yellow" TOP=170
LEFT=250 VISIBILITY="show">
<center>Layer 1</center>
</layer>

<layer id="Jane" width=150 height=160 color= bgcolor="green" TOP=100
LEFT=70 VISIBILITY="show">
<center>Layer 2</center>
</layer>

<form name="form1">
```

*continues*

*Listing 7.339    continued*

```
<input type="button" value="Get Layer 1 Name"
onClick='alert("The name of this layer is: " + document.layer1.name)'>
<br><br><br>
<input type="button" value="Get Layer 2 Name"
onClick='alert("The name of this layer is: " + document.layer2.name)'>
</form>

</body>
</html>
```

# Layer.onBlur

## JavaScript 1.2+

## Nav4+

## Syntax

```
onBlur="command"
```

## Description

The onBlur event handler of the Layer object handles the event when the focus is removed from the layer object.

## Example

Listing 7.340 shows how the onBlur event handler is used. When focus is removed from layer1, the onBlur event handler calls the showMsg() function.

*Listing 7.340    Example of the* onBlur *Event Handler*

```
<html>
<head>
<title> Using the onBlur event handler of the Layer object</title>
</head>
<body>

<script language="JavaScript">
<!-- Hide
function showMsg(){
    document.form1.text1.value = "Focus was removed from Layer 1";
}
// End Hide --->
</script>

<layer id="layer1" width=200 height=200 color= bgcolor="yellow" TOP=170
LEFT=200 VISIBILITY="show"onBlur='showMsg()'>
<center>Layer 1</center>
</layer>

<layer id="layer2" width=150 height=160 color= bgcolor="green" TOP=100
LEFT=70 VISIBILITY="show">
```

```
<center>Layer 2</center>
</layer>

<form name="form1">
Click on Layer 1 and the click on Layer 2.
<br><br>
<input type="text" name="text1" size=40>
</form>

</body>
</html>
```

# Layer.onFocus

## *JavaScript 1.2+*

## *Nav4+*

## *Syntax*

onFocus="*command*"

## *Description*

The onFocus property is an event handler for the Layer object that notifies you when the focus is set on a layer object.

## *Example*

Listing 7.341 shows how the onFocus method is used to detect when focus is set on Layer 1.

*Listing 7.341    Example of* the onFocus *Event Handler*

```
<html>
<head>
<title> Using the onFocus event handler of the Layer object</title>
</head>
<body>

<script language="JavaScript">
<!-- Hide
function showMsg(){
    document.form1.text1.value = "Focus set on Layer 1";
}
// End Hide --->
</script>

<layer id="layer1" width=200 height=200 color= bgcolor="yellow" TOP=170
LEFT=200 VISIBILITY="show"onFocus='showMsg()'>
<center>Layer 1</center>
</layer>
```

*continues*

*Listing 7.341    continued*

```
<layer id="layer2" width=150 height=160 color= bgcolor="green" TOP=100
LEFT=70 VISIBILITY="show">
<center>Layer 2</center>
</layer>

<form name="form1">
Click on Layer 2 and then click on layer 1.
<br><br>
<input type="text" name="text1" size=40>
</form>

</body>
</html>
```

# Layer.onLoad

## JavaScript 1.2+

## Nav4+

## Syntax

onLoad="*command*"

## Description

The onLoad property of the Layer object is an event handler that notifies you when the layer's contents are being loaded.

## Example

Listing 7.342 shows how the onLoad event handler is used.

*Listing 7.342    Example of the* onLoad *Event Handler*

```
<html>
<head>
<title> Using the onLoad event handler of the Layer object</title>
</head>
<body>

<script language="JavaScript">
<!-- Hide
function showMsg(){
    document.form1.text1.value = "Layer contents being loaded";
}
// End Hide --->
</script>

<layer id="layer1" width=200 height=200 color= bgcolor="yellow" TOP=170
LEFT=200 VISIBILITY="show"onLoad='showMsg()'>
<center>Layer 1</center>
</layer>
```

```
<layer id="layer2" width=150 height=160 color= bgcolor="green" TOP=100
LEFT=70 VISIBILITY="show">
<center>Layer 2</center>
</layer>

<form name="form1">
<input type="text" name="text1" size=40>
<br><br>
<input type="button" value="Load Layer 1"
onClick='document.layer1.load("tmp.html",300)'>
</form>

</body>
</html>
```

# Layer.onMouseOut

## JavaScript 1.2+

## Nav4+

## Syntax

onMouseOut="*command*"

## Description

The onMouseOut property of the Layer object is an event handler that notifies you when the mouse cursor has moved out of the layer region.

## Example

Listing 7.343 shows how the onMouseOut event handler is used.

*Listing 7.343    Example of the* onMouseOut *Event Handler*
```
<html>
<head>
<title> Using the onMouseOut event handler of the Layer object</title>
</head>
<body>

<script language="JavaScript">
<!-- Hide
function showMsg1(){
    document.form1.text1.value = "Mouse Moved out of Layer 1 area.";
}
// End Hide --->
</script>

<layer id="layer1" width=200 height=200 color= bgcolor="yellow" TOP=170
```

*continues*

*Listing 7.343    continued*
```
LEFT=200 VISIBILITY="show"onMouseOut='showMsg1()'>
<center>Layer 1</center>
</layer>

<layer id="layer2" width=150 height=160 color= bgcolor="green" TOP=100
LEFT=70 VISIBILITY="show">
<center>Layer 2</center>
</layer>

<form name="form1">
<input type="text" name="text1" size=40>
<br><br>
</form>

</body>
</html>
```

# Layer.onMouseOver

## JavaScript 1.2+

## Nav4+

## Syntax

```
onMouseOver="command"
```

## Description

The onMouseOver event handler of the Layer object handles the events when the mouse cursor is moved over the layer area.

## Example

Listing 7.344 shows an example of the onMouseOver event handler.

*Listing 7.344    Example of the onMouseOver Event Handler*
```
<html>
<head>
<title> Using the onMouseOver event handler of the Layer object</title>
</head>
<body>

<script language="JavaScript">
<!-- Hide

// function displays a message everytime the mouse is moved over Layer 2
function showMsg1(){
    document.form1.text1.value = "Mouse Moved over Layer 2 area.";
}
// End Hide --->
</script>
```

```
<layer id="layer1" width=200 height=200 color= bgcolor="yellow" TOP=170
LEFT=200 VISIBILITY="show">
<center>Layer 1</center>
</layer>

<layer id="layer2" width=150 height=160 color= bgcolor="green" TOP=100
LEFT=70 VISIBILITY="show" onMouseOver='showMsg1()'>
<center>Layer 2</center>
</layer>

<form name="form1">
<input type="text" name="text1" size=40>
<br><br>
</form>

</body>
</html>
```

# Layer.pageX

## JavaScript 1.2+

## Nav4+

## Syntax

`layer.pageX`

## Description

The `pageX` property of the `Layer` object represents the x-coordinate position of the layer relative to the top-level document.

## Example

Listing 7.345 shows how to use the `pageX` property.

*Listing 7.345    Example of the `pageX` Property*

```
<html>
<head>
<title> Using the pageX property of the Layer object</title>
</head>
<body>

<script language="JavaScript">
<!-- Hide

// function increases the size of Layer 1 pageX property
function size(){
     document.layer1.pageX = document.layer1.pageX +20;
```

*continues*

*Listing 7.345    continued*

```
}
// End Hide --->
</script>

<layer id="layer1" width=200 height=200 color= bgcolor="yellow" TOP=170
LEFT=200 VISIBILITY="show">
<center>Layer 1</center>
</layer>

<layer id="layer2" width=150 height=160 color= bgcolor="green" TOP=100
LEFT=70 VISIBILITY="show">
<center>Layer 2</center>
</layer>

<form name="form1">
<input type="button" value="Change Layer 1 X-coordinate" onClick=size()>
</form>

</body>
</html>
```

# Layer.pageY

## *JavaScript 1.2+*

## *Nav4+*

## *Syntax*

```
layer.pageY
```

## *Description*

The pageY property of the Layer object represents the y-coordinate position of the layer relative to the top-level document.

## *Example*

Listing 7.346 shows how to manipulate the pageY property. When the button is clicked, the size function is called, which adds 20 pixels to pageY attribute of layer1.

*Listing 7.346    Example of the pageY Property*

```
<html>
<head>
<title> Using the pageY property of the Layer object</title>
</head>
<body>

<script language="JavaScript">
<!-- Hide
```

```
// function changes the value of the PageY attribute
function size(){
     document.layer1.pageY = document.layer1.pageY +20;
}
// End Hide --->
</script>

<layer id="layer1" width=200 height=200 color= bgcolor="yellow" TOP=170
LEFT=200 VISIBILITY="show">
<center>Layer 1</center>
</layer>

<layer id="layer2" width=150 height=160 color= bgcolor="green" TOP=100
LEFT=70 VISIBILITY="show">
<center>Layer 2</center>
</layer>

<form name="form1">
<input type="button" value="Change Layer 1 Y-coordinate" onClick=size()>
</form>

</body>
</html>
```

# Layer.parentLayer

## *JavaScript 1.2+*

## *Nav4+*

## *Syntax*

```
layer.parentLayer
```

## *Description*

The parentLayer property of the Layer object represents the window or layer object that contains the current layer object.

## *Example*

Listing 7.347 shows how to use the parentLayer. The function getname() gets and returns the name of the parent layer.

*Listing 7.347   Example of the* parentLayer *Property*

```
<html>
<head>
<title>Using the parentLayer property of the Layer object</title>
</head>
<body>
```

*continues*

*Listing 7.347    continued*

```
<script language="JavaScript">
<!-- Hide

// function gets the name of the parent layer
function getname(){
    document.form1.text1.value = document.layer1.parentLayer.name;
}
// End Hide --->
</script>

<layer id="layer1" width=200 height=200 color= bgcolor="yellow" TOP=170
LEFT=200 VISIBILITY="show">
<center>Layer 1</center>
</layer>

<layer id="layer2" width=150 height=160 color= bgcolor="green" TOP=100
LEFT=70 VISIBILITY="show"'>
<center>Layer 2</center>
</layer>

<form name="form1">
<input type="button" value="Get Layer 1 parent name" onClick='getname()'>
<br><br>
<input type="text" name="text1" size=40>
</form>

</body>
</html>
```

# Layer.releaseEvents()

## JavaScript 1.2+

## Nav4+

## Syntax

`layer.releaseEvents(event)`

## Description

The releaseEvents() method of the Layer object specifies that the layer object should no longer capture events of the specified type.

## Example

Listing 7.348 is an example of how the releaseEvents() method is used. When the FOCUS event is captured, it is handled by the handle() method. Once this is done, executing the event is released using the releaseEvents() method.

*Listing 7.348    Example of the* `releaseEvents()` *Method*

```
<html>
<head>
<title> Using the releaseEvents method of the Layer object</title>
</head>
<body>

<script language="JavaScript">
<!-- Hide
// sets up the document to capture FOCUS events
document.captureEvents(Event.FOCUS);

// function that handles the specific event. The evnt parameter refers to
// the event object.
function handle(evnt){
   alert("The layer got a FOCUS event and calls releaseEvents");
   return true;
}

function releaseFocus(){
    document.layer2.releaseEvents(Event.FOCUS);
}

// This registers the handle function as the event handler for the
// FOCUS event.
document.onFocus = handle;

// End Hide --->
</script>

<layer id="layer1" width=200 height=200 color= bgcolor="yellow" TOP=170
LEFT=200 VISIBILITY="show">
<center>Layer 1</center>
</layer>

<layer id="layer1" width=150 height=160 color= bgcolor=green" TOP=100
LEFT=70 VISIBILITY="show">
<center>Layer 2</center>
</layer>

</body>
</html>
```

# Layer.resizeBy()

## *JavaScript 1.2+*

## *Nav4+*

## Syntax

`layer.resizeBy(x,y)`

## Description

The `resizeBy()` method of the `Layer` object resizes the layer by a relative size. The *x* parameter refers to the number of pixels the layer width is increased. The *y* parameter refers to the number of pixels the layer height is increased.

## Example

Listing 7.349 shows how to resize a `Layer` object. When the button is clicked, the onClick event handler executes the `resizeBy()` method to resize `layer2`.

Listing 7.349   Example of the `resizeBy()` Method

```
<html>
<head>
<title> Using the resizeBy method of the Layer object</title>
</head>
<body>

<layer id="layer1" width=200 height=200 color= bgcolor="yellow" TOP=170
LEFT=200 VISIBILITY="show">
<center>Layer 1</center>
</layer>

<layer id="layer2" width=150 height=160 color= bgcolor="green" TOP=100
LEFT=70 VISIBILITY="show">
<center>Layer 2</center>
</layer>

<form name="form1">
<input type="button" value="Resize Layer 2"
onClick='document.layer2.resizeBy(30, 50)'>
<br>
</form>

</body>
</html>
```

# Layer.resizeTo()

## JavaScript 1.2+

## Nav4+

## Syntax

`layer.resizeTo(x,y)`

## Description

The resizeTo() method of the Layer object resizes the layer object to the specified value. The *x* parameter refers to the number of pixels the layer width is increased. The *y* parameter refers to the number of pixels the layer height is increased.

## Example

Listing 7.350 shows how to resize a layer. When the button is clicked, the onClick event handler uses the resizeTo() method to resize layer2.

*Listing 7.350   Example of the resizeTo() Method*

```
<html>
<head>
<title> Using the resizeTo method of the Layer object</title>
</head>
<body>

<layer id="layer1" width=200 height=200 color= bgcolor="yellow" TOP=170
LEFT=200 VISIBILITY="show">
<center>Layer 1</center>
</layer>

<layer id="layer2" width=150 height=160 color= bgcolor="green" TOP=100
LEFT=70 VISIBILITY="show">
<center>Layer 2</center>
</layer>

<form name="form1">
<input type="button" value="Resize Layer 2"
onClick='document.layer2.resizeTo(100, 300)'>
<br>
</form>

</body>
</html>
```

# Layer.routeEvent()

## JavaScript 1.2+

## Nav4+

## Syntax

*layer*.routeEvent(*event*)

## Description

The routeEvent() method of the Layer object reroutes a captured event to another event handler. The method takes a single parameter representing the event to be routed.

## *Example*

Listing 7.351 shows an example of the routeEvent() method.

*Listing 7.351   Example of the* routeEvent() *Method*

```html
<html>
<head>
<title> Using the routeEvent method of the Layer object</title>
</head>
<body>

<script language="JavaScript">
<!-- Hide

// sets up the document to capture FOCUS events
document.captureEvents(Event.FOCUS);

// function that handles the specific event. The evnt parameter refers to
// the event object.
function handle(evnt){
   alert("The layer got a FOCUS event and executes routeEvent");
   document.routeEvent(evnt);
   alert("Event has been routed");
   return true;
}

// This registers the handle function as the event handler for the
// FOCUS event.
document.onFocus = handle;

// End Hide --->
</script>

<layer id="layer1" width=200 height=200 color= bgcolor="yellow" TOP=170
LEFT=200 VISIBILITY="show">
<center>Layer 1</center>
</layer>

<layer id="layer2" width=150 height=160 color= bgcolor="green" TOP=100
LEFT=70 VISIBILITY="show">
<center>Layer 2</center>
</layer>

</body>
</html>
```

# Layer.siblingAbove

## *JavaScript 1.2+*

## *Nav4+*

## Syntax

`layer.siblingAbove`

## Description

The `siblingAbove` property of the `Layer` object refers to the sibling layer immediately above the current layer in the zIndex. If this doesn't exist, `null` is returned.

## NOTE

Any child of a parent layer is considered a sibling.

## Example

Listing 7.352 shows how to get the `siblingAbove` property value. When the button is clicked, the `siblingAbove` value is displayed.

*Listing 7.352   Example of the* `siblingAbove` *Property*

```
<html>
<head>
<title> Using siblingAbove property of the Layer object</title>
</head>
<body>


<layer id="layer1" width=200 height=200 color= bgcolor="yellow" TOP=170
LEFT=200 VISIBILITY="show">
<center>Layer 1</center>
</layer>

<layer id="layer2" width=150 height=160 color= bgcolor="green" TOP=100
LEFT=70 VISIBILITY="show">
<center>Layer 2</center>
</layer>

<form name="form1">
<input type="button" value="Get Sibling Above Layer 1"
onClick='alert(document.layer2.siblingAbove)'>
<br>
</form>

</body>
</html>
```

# Layer.siblingBelow

## *JavaScript 1.2+*

## *Nav4+*

## Syntax

```
layer.siblingBelow
```

## Description

The `siblingBelow` property of the `Layer` object refers to the sibling layer immediately below the current layer in the zIndex. If this doesn't exist, `null` is returned.

## Example

Listing 7.353 shows the `siblingBelow` property. When the button is clicked, the `siblingBelow` value is displayed.

**Listing 7.353**   *Example of the* `siblingBelow` *Property*

```
<html>
<head>
<title> Using the siblingBelow property of the Layer object</title>
</head>
<body>

<layer id="layer2" width=200 height=200 color= bgcolor="yellow" TOP=170
LEFT=200 VISIBILITY="show">
<center>Layer 1</center>
</layer>

<layer id="layer1" width=150 height=160 color= bgcolor="green" TOP=100
LEFT=70 VISIBILITY="show">
<center>Layer 2</center>
</layer>

<form name="form1">
<input type="button" value="Get Sibling Above Layer 1"
onClick='alert(document.layer1.siblingBelow)'>
<br>
</form>

</body>
</html>
```

# Layer.src

## JavaScript 1.2+

## Nav4+

## Syntax

```
layer.src
```

## Description

The `src` property of the `Layer` object represents the source URL of a particular layer.

## Example

Listing 7.354 shows how the src property is used. When the button is clicked, the src property is displayed.

*Listing 7.354   Example of the* src *Property*

```html
<html>
<head>
<title> Using the src property of the Layer object</title>
</head>
<body>

<layer id="layer1" width=200 height=200 color= bgcolor="yellow" TOP=170
LEFT=200 VISIBILITY="show">
<center>Layer 1</center>
</layer>

<layer id="layer2" width=150 height=160 color= bgcolor="green" TOP=100
LEFT=70 VISIBILITY="show">
<center>Layer 2</center>
</layer>

<form name="form1">
<input type="button" value="Get Layer 1 src"
onClick=alert(document.layer1.src)>
</form>

</body>
</html>
```

# Layer.top

## *JavaScript 1.2+*

## *Nav4+*

## *Syntax*

```
layer.top
```

## Description

The top property of the Layer object represents the y-coordinate position of the layer relative to the top-level document. Increasing or decreasing this value can move the layer object up or down.

## Example

Listing 7.355 uses the top property to move the layer up. When the button is clicked, the move() function is executed, which will move the layer up by 10 pixels.

*Listing 7.355    Example of the* top *Property*

```
<html>
<head>
<title> Using the top property of the Layer object</title>
</head>
<body>

<script language="JavaScript">
<!-- Hide
function move(){
     document.layer1.top = document.layer1.top - 10;
}
// End Hide --->
</script>

<layer id="layer1" width=200 height=200 color= bgcolor="yellow" TOP=170
LEFT=200 VISIBILITY="show">
<center>Layer 1</center>
</layer>

<layer id="layer2" width=150 height=160 color= bgcolor="green" TOP=100
LEFT=70 VISIBILITY="show">
<center>Layer 2</center>
</layer>

<form name="form1">
<input type="button" value="Move layer 1 Up" onClick=move()>
</form>

</body>
</html>
```

# Layer.visibility

## JavaScript 1.2+

## Nav4+

## Syntax

```
layer.visibility
```

## Description

The visibility property of the Layer object controls whether the layer is displayed or hidden. Valid values for this property are: hide, show, and inherit. This property also represents the HTML VISIBILITY attribute of the <layer> tag.

## Example

Listing 7.356 shows how the visibility property is used to hide a Layer object.

*Listing 7.356   Example of the* `visibility` *Property*

```
<html>
<head>
<title> Using the visibility property of the Layer object</title>
</head>
<body>

<script language="JavaScript">
<!-- Hide
function hide(){
    document.layer2.visibility ="hide";
}
// End Hide --->
</script>

<layer id="layer1" width=200 height=200 color= bgcolor="yellow" TOP=170
LEFT=200 VISIBILITY="show">
<center>Layer 1</center>
</layer>

<layer id="layer2" width=150 height=160 color= bgcolor="green" TOP=100
LEFT=70 VISIBILITY="show">
<center>Layer 2</center>
</layer>

<form name="form1">
<input type="button" value="Hide Layer 2" onClick=hide()>
</form>

</body>
</html>
```

# Layer.zIndex

## *JavaScript 1.2+*

## *Nav4+*

## *Syntax*

`layer.zIndex`

## *Description*

The `zIndex` property of the `Layer` object represents the stacking order of the layers.

## *Example*

Listing 7.357 shows an example of the `zIndex` property. When the button is clicked, an alert box is displayed showing the value of `zIndex`.

*Listing 7.357    Example of the* `zIndex` *Property*

```
<html>
<head>
<title> Using the zIndex property of the Layer object</title>
</head>
<body>

<layer id="layer1" width=200 height=200 color= bgcolor="yellow" TOP=170
LEFT=200 VISIBILITY="show">
<center>Layer 1</center>
</layer>

<layer id="layer2" width=150 height=160 color= bgcolor="green" TOP=100
LEFT=70 VISIBILITY="show">
<center>Layer 2</center>
</layer>

<form name="form1">
<input type="button" value="Get Layer 2 zIndex"
onClick=alert(document.layer2.zIndex)>
</form>

</body>
</html>
```

# Link

## JavaScript 1.0+, JScript 1.0+

## Nav2+, IE 3+, Opera3+

## Syntax

Core client-side JavaScript object.

## Description

The Link object represents an HTML hypertext link. This can be an image, text, or pre-defined area within the Web page. All HTML links are stored in a `links[]` array. The Link object has specific properties and methods associated with it, as shown in Table 7.33.

**Table 7.33    Properties and Methods of the Link Object**

| Property/Method | Description |
|---|---|
| handleEvent | Event Handler |
| hash | Represents an anchor name in the URL for the link, which begins with the # character |
| host | Represents the host portion of the URL associated with a link |

| Property/Method | Description |
|---|---|
| hostname | Represents the hostname portion of the URL associated with a link |
| href | Represents the complete URL associated with a link |
| onClick | Event handler for mouse click events |
| onDblClick | Event handler for double mouse click events |
| onKeyDown | Event handler for pressing a key down on a Link object |
| onKeyPress | Event handler for pressing a key on the Link object |
| onKeyUp | Event handler for releasing a key on the Link object |
| onMouseDown | Event handler for pressing the mouse button down on the link |
| onMouseOut | Event handler for moving the mouse cursor away from the link |
| onMouseOver | Event handler for moving the mouse cursor over the link |
| onMouseUp | Event handler for releasing the mouse button on the link |
| pathname | Represents the pathname portion of the link URL |
| port | Represents the port portion of the URL link |
| protocol | Specifies the protocol portion of the URL link |
| search | Represents the query portion of the URL link |
| target | Represents the name of the Window object in which the link is displayed |
| text | The text used to create the link |

## Example

Listing 7.358 shows how to use the Link object. When the link is clicked, the text of the link is displayed.

*Listing 7.358   Example of the* Link *Object*

```
<html>
<head>
<title> Creating a Link object</title>
</head>
<body>

Click on the link to go to the site.
<br><br>
<a href=http://www.mcp.com
onClick='alert("Go to:" + document.links[0].text)'> Macmillian Publishing</a>

</body>
</html>
```

# Link.handleEvent()

## *JavaScript 1.2+*

## *Nav4+*

## Syntax

*link*.handleEvent(*event*)

## Description

The handleEvent() method invokes the event handler for the Link object.

## Example

Listing 7.359 shows how to access the handleEvent() method. All click events are handled by the first link in the document.

*Listing 7.359   Example of the* handleEvent() *Method*

```
<html>
<head>
<title> Using the handleEvent method of the Link object</title>
</head>
<body>

<script language="JavaScript">
<!-- Hide
// sets up the document to capture CLICK events
document.captureEvents(Event.CLICK);

// function that handles the specific event. The evnt parameter refers to
// the event object.
function handle(evnt){
     document.form1.links[0].handleEvent(Event.CLICK);
}

function displayMsg(){
    alert("Click event occurred.");
}

// This registers the handle function as the event handler for the
// CLICK event.
document.onClick = handle;

// End Hide --->
</script>

<form name="form1">
<a href=http://www.mcp.com:80/foo?something#foobar onClick='displayMsg()'>
http://www.mcp.com:80/foo?something#foobar</a>
<br>
</form>

</body>
</html>
```

# Link.hash

## JavaScript 1.0+

## Nav2+, Opera3+

## Syntax

```
link.hash
```

## Description

The hash property represents a portion of the currently displayed URL.

## Example

Listing 7.360 shows an example of how the hash property is used. When the button is clicked, the showHash() function displays the value of the hash property for the link.

*Listing 7.360    Example of the hash Property*

```
<html>
<head>
<title> Using the hash property of the Link object</title>
</head>
<body>

<script language="JavaScript">
<!-- Hide
// function shows the hash value of the link
function showHash(){
    document.form1.text1.value = document.links[0].hash;
}
// End Hide --->
</script>

Click the button to see the hash for the URL
<form name="form1">
<a href=http://www.mcp.com:80/foo?something#foobar>
http://www.mcp.com:80/foo?something#foobar</a>
<br><br>
Hash value: <input type="text" name="text1" size=20>
<br>
<input type="button" name="hash" value="Get hash value" onClick='showHash()'>
<br><br>
</form>

</body>
</html>
```

# Link.host

*JavaScript 1.0+, JScript 1.0+*

*Nav2+, IE 3+, Opera3+*

## Syntax

`link.host`

## Description

The host property represents the host portion of the URL.

## Example

Listing 7.361 shows how to use the host property. When the button is clicked, the showHost() function is called to show the value of the host property.

*Listing 7.361    Example of the host Property*

```
<html>
<head>
<title> Using the host property of the Link object</title>
</head>
<body>

<script language="JavaScript">
<!-- Hide
// function shows the host value
function showHost(){
    document.form1.text1.value = document.links[0].host;
}
// End Hide --->
</script>

Click the button to see the host for the URL
<form name="form1">
<a href=http://www.mcp.com:80/foo?something#foobar>
http://www.mcp.com:80/foo?something#foobar</a>
<br><br>
Host value: <input type="text" name="text1" size=20>
<br><br>
<input type="button" name="host" value="Get Host Value" onClick='showHost()'>
<br>
</form>

</body>
</html>
```

# Link.hostname

*JavaScript 1.0+, JScript 1.0+*

## Nav2+, IE 3+, Opera3+

## Syntax

`link`.hostname

## Description

The `hostname` property of the `Link` object represents the hostname portion of the link's URL.

## Example

Listing 7.362 shows an example of how the `hostname` is used. When the button is clicked, the `showHostname()` function is called, which displays the value of the `hostname` for the link.

Listing 7.362   *Example of the* `hostname` *Property*

```
<html>
<head>
<title> Using the hostname property of the Link object</title>
</head>
<body>

<script language="JavaScript">
<!-- Hide

// displays the hostname for the URL
function showHostname(){
    document.form1.text1.value = document.links[0].hostname;
}
// End Hide --->
</script>

Click the button to see the hostname for the URL
<form name="form1">
<a href=http://www.mcp.com:80/foo?something#foobar>
http://www.mcp.com:80/foo?something#foobar</a>
<br><br>
Host value: <input type="text" name="text1" size=20>
<br><br>
<input type="button" name="host" value="Get Hostname Value"
onClick='showHostname()'>
<br>
</form>

</body>
</html>
```

# Link.href

## *JavaScript 1.0+, JScript 1.0+*

## *Nav2+, IE 3+, Opera3+*

## *Syntax*

`link.href`

## Description

The `href` property of the `Link` object represents the whole URL for the link.

## *Example*

Listing 7.363 shows how to use the `href` property. When the button is clicked, the `showhref()` function displays the value of the `href` property of the link.

*Listing 7.363    Example of the* `href` *Property*

```
<html>
<head>
<title> Using the href property of the Link object</title>
</head>
<body>

<script language="JavaScript">
<!-- Hide

// displays the value of the href property in the text box.
function showhref(){
    document.form1.text1.value = document.links[0].href;
}
// End Hide --->
</script>

Click the button to see the href property for the URL
<form name="form1">
<a href=http://www.mcp.com:80/foo?something#foobar>
http://www.mcp.com:80/foo?something#foobar</a>
<br><br>
Host value: <input type="text" name="text1" size=45>
<br><br>
<input type="button" name="href" value="Get href Value" onClick='showhref()'>
<br>
</form>

</body>
</html>
```

# Link.onClick

## *JavaScript 1.0+, JScript 1.0+*

## *Nav2+, IE 3+, Opera3+*

## Syntax

```
onClick="command"
```

## Description

The onClick event handler for the Link object is used to handle the event when the mouse cursor is clicked on the link.

## Example

Listing 7.364 shows how to determine a mouse click using the onClick event handler.

*Listing 7.364    Example of the* onClick *Event Handler*

```
<html>
<head>
<title> Using the onClick event handler of the Link object</title>
</head>
<body>

Click the link.
<form name="form1">
<a href=http://www.mcp.com:80/foo?something#foobar onClick='alert("You clicked
the link")'>
http://www.mcp.com:80/foo?something#foobar</a>
<br><br>
</form>

</body>
</html>
```

# Link.onDblClick

## *JavaScript 1.2+, JScript 1.0+*

## *Nav4+, IE 3+*

## Syntax

```
onDblClick="command"
```

## Description

The onDblClick event handler of the Link object is used to handle the event when the mouse cursor is double-clicked on the link.

## Example

Listing 7.365 shows how to use the onDblClick event handler.

*Listing 7.365   Example of the* `onDblClick` *Event Handler*

```
<html>
<head>
<title> Using the onDblClick event handler of the Link object</title>
</head>
<body>

Click the link.
<form name="form1">
<a href=http://www.mcp.com:80/foo?something#foobar
onDblClick='alert("You double-clicked the link")'>
http://www.mcp.com:80/foo?something#foobar</a>
<br><br>
</form>

</body>
</html>
```

# Link.onKeyDown

## *JavaScript 1.2+, JScript 1.0+*

## *Nav4+, IE 3+*

## *Syntax*

onKeyDown="*command*"

## *Description*

The onKeyDown event handler for the Link object is used to handle the event when a key is pressed down while the focus is on the link.

## *Example*

Listing 7.366 shows how the onKeyDown event handler operates.

*Listing 7.366   Example of the* `onKeyDown` *Event Handler*

```
<html>
<head>
<title> Using the onKeyDown event handler of the Link object</title>
</head>
<body>

Click the link.
<form name="form1">
<a href=http://www.mcp.com:80/foo?something#foobar
onKeyDown='alert("You pressed the key DOWN on the link")'>
http://www.mcp.com:80/foo?something#foobar</a>
<br><br>
</form>

</body>
</html>
```

# Link.onKeyPress

## *JavaScript 1.2+, JScript 1.0+*

## *Nav4+, IE 3+*

## *Syntax*

onKeyPress="*command*"

## *Description*

The onKeyPress event handler for the Link object is used to handle the event when a key is pressed when the focus is set on the link.

## *Example*

Listing 7.367 shows how the onKeyPress event handler is used. The onKeyPress event handler is invoked any time a key is pressed on the link.

*Listing 7.367    Example of the* onKeyPress *Event Handler*

```
<html>
<head>
<title> Using the onKeyPress event handler of the Link object</title>
</head>
<body>

Click the link.
<form name="form1">
<a href=http://www.mcp.com:80/foo?something#foobar
onKeyPress='alert("You pressed the key on the link")'>
http://www.mcp.com:80/foo?something#foobar</a>
<br><br>
</form>

</body>
</html>
```

# Link.onKeyUp

## *JavaScript 1.2+, JScript 1.0+*

## *Nav4+, IE 3+*

## *Syntax*

onKeyUp="*command*"

## *Description*

The onKeyUp event handler for the Link object is used to handle events in which a key is pressed and then released.

## Example

Listing 7.368 shows an example of how the onKeyUp event handler is used. The onKeyUp event handler is invoked any time a key is pressed and released on the link.

*Listing 7.368 Example of the* onKeyUp *Event Handler*

```
<html>
<head>
<title> Using the onKeyUp event handler of the Link object</title>
</head>
<body>

Highlight the link, press a key and let it up.
<form name="form1">
<a href=http://www.mcp.com:80/foo?something#foobar
onKeyUp='alert("You let the key up")'>
http://www.mcp.com:80/foo?something#foobar</a>
<br><br>
</form>

</body>
</html>
```

# Link.onMouseDown

## *JavaScript 1.2+, JScript 1.0+*

## *Nav4+, IE 3+*

## Syntax

onMouseDown="*command*"

## Description

The onMouseDown event handler of the Link object is used to handle the event when the mouse button is pressed down while the mouse pointer is over the link.

## Example

Listing 7.369 shows how the onMouseDown event handler is used. The onMouseDown event handler is invoked any time the mouse button is pressed down while the cursor is on the link.

*Listing 7.369   Example of the* onMouseDown *Event Handler*

```
<html>
<head>
<title> Using the onMouseDown event handler of the Link object</title>
</head>
<body>

Click the mouse button while the cursor is on the link.
<form name="form1">
```

```
<a href=http://www.mcp.com:80/foo?something#foobar
onMouseDown='alert("The mouse button was pressed DOWN.")'>
http://www.mcp.com:80/foo?something#foobar</a>
<br><br>
</form>

</body>
</html>
```

# Link.onMouseOut

## *JavaScript 1.1+, JScript 1.0+*

## *Nav3+, IE 3+, Opera3+*

## *Syntax*

onMouseOut="*command*"

## *Description*

The onMouseOut event handler of the Link object is used to handle the event when the mouse cursor is moved away from the link.

## *Example*

Listing 7.370 shows how the onMouseOut event handler is used.

*Listing 7.370   Example of the* onMouseOut *Event Handler*

```
<html>
<head>
<title> Using the onMouseOut event handler of the Link object</title>
</head>
<body>

<script language="JavaScript">
<!--Hide
// displays message when the MouseEvent occurs.
function showMsg(){
    document.form1.text1.value = "The Mouse cursor was removed from the link";
}
// End Hide --->
</script>


Click the mouse button while the cursor is on the link.
<form name="form1">
<a href=http://www.mcp.com:80/foo?something#foobar
onMouseOut='showMsg()'>
http://www.mcp.com:80/foo?something#foobar</a>
<br><br>
```

*continues*

*Listing 7.370    continued*
```
<input type="text" name="text1" size=50>
</form>

</body>
</html>
```

# Link.onMouseOver

## JavaScript 1.0+, JScript 1.0+

## Nav2+, IE 3+, Opera3+

## Syntax

```
onMouseOver="command"
```

## Description

The onMouseOver event handler of the Link handles the event when the mouse cursor is moved over the HTML link.

## Example

Listing 7.371 shows how the onMouseOver event handler is used to display a message when the mouse cursor is moved over the link.

*Listing 7.371 Example of the onMouseOver Event Handler*
```
<html>
<head>
<title> Using the onMouseOver event handler of the Link object</title>
</head>
<body>

<script language="JavaScript">
<!--Hide
// sets the text in the textbox to display the message.
function showMsg(){
     document.form1.text1.value = "The Mouse cursor was moved over the link";
}

// End Hide --->
</script>

Move the mouse cursor over the link.
<form name="form1">
<a href=http://www.mcp.com:80/foo?something#foobar
onMouseOver='showMsg()'>
http://www.mcp.com:80/foo?something#foobar</a>
<br><br>
<input type="text" name="text1" size=50>
</form>
```

```
</body>
</html>
```

# Link.onMouseUp

## *JavaScript 1.2+, JScript 1.0+*

## *Nav4+, IE 3+*

## *Syntax*

onMouseUp="*command*"

## *Description*

The onMouseUp event handler for the Link object is used to handle the event when the mouse button is pressed on the link and then released.

### *Example*

Listing 7.372 shows how the onMouseUp event handler is used.

*Listing 7.372    Example of the* onMouseUp *Event Handler*
```
<html>
<head>
<title> Using the onMouseUp event handler of the Link object</title>
</head>
<body>

Click the mouse button while the cursor is on the link.
<form name="form1">
<a href=http://www.mcp.com:80/foo?something#foobar
onMouseUp='alert("The Mouse button was let up")'>
http://www.mcp.com:80/foo?something#foobar</a>
<br><br>
<input type="text" name="text1" size=50>
</form>

</body>
</html>
```

# Link.pathname

## *JavaScript 1.0+, JScript 1.0+*

## *Nav2+, IE 3+, Opera3+*

## *Syntax*

*link*.pathname

## *Description*

The pathname property of the Link object represents the pathname portion of the link URL.

## Example

Listing 7.373 shows how the pathname property is used. When the button is clicked, the showpathname function is executed. This displays the pathname for the link.

*Listing 7.373 Example of the* pathname *Property*

```
<html>
<head>
<title> Using the pathname property of the Link object</title>
</head>
<body>

<script language="JavaScript">
<!-- Hide

// displays the pathname for the specified URL
function showpathname(){
    document.form1.text1.value = document.links[0].pathname;
}
// End Hide --->
</script>

Click the button to see the pathname for the URL
<form name="form1">
<a href=http://www.mcp.com:80/tmp/foo.html?something#foobar>
http://www.mcp.com:80/tmp/foo.html?something#foobar</a>
<br><br>
Pathname value: <input type="text" name="text1" size=20>
<br><br>
<input type="button" name="path" value="Get Pathname Value"
onClick='showpathname()'>
<br>
</form>

</body>
</html>
```

# Link.port

## JavaScript 1.0+, JScript 1.0+

## Nav2+, IE 3+, Opera3+

## Syntax

`link.port`

## Description

The port property of the Link object represents the port number in the URL. This is not always present in all URLs.

## Example

Listing 7.374 shows how to obtain the `port` number if available. When the button is clicked, the port number for the link is displayed.

*Listing 7.374   Accessing the* `port` *Number*

```
<html>
<head>
<title> Using the port property of the Link object</title>
</head>
<body>

<script language="JavaScript">
<!-- Hide

// displays the port number of the URL
function showport(){
    document.form1.text1.value = document.links[0].port;
}
// End Hide --->
</script>

Click the button to see the port number for the URL
<form name="form1">
<a href=http://www.mcp.com:80/foo?something#foobar>
http://www.mcp.com:80/foo?something#foobar</a>
<br><br>
Port value: <input type="text" name="text1" size=20>
<br><br>
<input type="button" name="port" value="Get Port Number" onClick='showport()'>
<br>
</form>

</body>
</html>
```

# Link.protocol

## *JavaScript 1.0+, JScript 1.0+*

## *Nav2+, IE 3+, Opera3+*

### Syntax

`link.protocol`

### Description

The `protocol` property of the `Link` object represents the protocol being used in the current Web browser. This is the first piece of text in the URL.

## Example

Listing 7.375 shows how you can get the `protocol` type being used. When the button is clicked, the protocol for the link is displayed.

*Listing 7.375   Example of the `protocol` Property*

```
<html>
<head>
<title> Using the protocol property of the Link object</title>
</head>
<body>

<script language="JavaScript">
<!-- Hide

// displays the type of protocol being used for the URL
function showproto(){
    document.form1.text1.value = document.links[0].protocol;
}
// End Hide --->
</script>

Click the button to see the protocol used for the URL
<form name="form1">
<a href=http://www.mcp.com:80/foo?something#foobar>
http://www.mcp.com:80/foo?something#foobar</a>
<br><br>
Protocol value: <input type="text" name="text1" size=20>
<br><br>
<input type="button" name="proto" value="Get Protocol" onClick='showproto()'>
<br>
</form>

</body>
</html>
```

# Link.search

## JavaScript 1.0+, JScript 1.0+

## Nav2+, IE 3+, Opera3+

## Syntax

`link.search`

## Description

The `search` property of the `Link` object represents the query portion of the URL (if available). This includes the leading question mark (?).

## Example

Listing 7.376 shows how the search property can be determined. When the button is clicked, the showsearch() function displays the search value of the link.

*Listing 7.376   Example of the* search *Property*

```
<html>
<head>
<title> Using the search property of the Link object</title>
</head>
<body>

<script language="JavaScript">
<!-- Hide

// display the information being queried
function showsearch(){
    document.form1.text1.value = document.links[0].search;
}
// End Hide --->
</script>

Click the button to see the search portion of the URL
<form name="form1">
<a href=http://www.mcp.com:80/foo?something#foobar>
http://www.mcp.com:80/foo?something#foobar</a>
<br><br>
Search value: <input type="text" name="text1" size=20>
<br><br>
<input type="button" name="search" value="Get Search portion"
onClick='showsearch()'>
<br>
</form>

</body>
</html>
```

# Link.target

## *JavaScript 1.0+, JScript 1.0+*

## *Nav2+, IE 3+, Opera3+*

## *Syntax*

*link*.target

## Description

The target property of the Link object represents the name of the window in which the URL is to be displayed.

## Example

Listing 7.377 shows how the `target` property is used. When the button is clicked, the `showtarget()` function displays the target value of the link.

*Listing 7.377   Example of the `target` Property*

```
<html>
<head>
<title> Using the target property of the Link object</title>
</head>
<body>

<script language="JavaScript">
<!-- Hide

// displays the name of the window in which the link will be displayed.
function showtarget(){
    document.form1.text1.value = document.links[0].target;
}
// End Hide --->
</script>

Click the button to see the target of the URL
<form name="form1">
<a href=http://www.mcp.com:80/foo?something#foobar>
http://www.mcp.com:80/foo?something#foobar</a>
<br><br>
Target value: <input type="text" name="text1" size=20>
<br><br>
<input type="button" name="tar" value="Get Target" onClick='showtarget()'>
<br>
</form>

</body>
</html>
```

# Link.text

## JavaScript 1.2+

## Nav4+

## Syntax

*link*.text

## Description

The `text` property of the `Link` object is used to get the text value of the link.

## Example

Listing 7.378 shows how to use the `text` property. When the button is clicked, the showtext function displays the text value of the link.

*Listing 7.378   Example of the `text` Property*

```
<html>
<head>
<title> Using the text property of the Link object</title>
</head>
<body>

<script language="JavaScript">
<!-- Hide
// function to display the value of the text property
function showtext(){
    document.form1.text1.value = document.links[0].text;
}
// End Hide --->
</script>

Click the button to see the text value of the link.
<form name="form1">
<a href=http://www.mcp.com:80/foo?something#foobar>
Link to Something</a>
<br><br>
Text value: <input type="text" name="text1" size=50>
<br><br>
<input type="button" name="txt" value="Get Text Value" onClick='showtext()'>
<br>
</form>

</body>
</html>
```

# Location

## *JavaScript 1.0+, JScript 1.0+*

## *Nav2+, IE 3+, Opera3+*

## Syntax

Core client-side JavaScript object.

## Description

The `Location` object represents the current Web address displayed in the browser. The `Location` object has specific properties and methods associated with it, as shown in Table 7.34.

*Table 7.34* **Properties and Methods of the Location Object**

| Property/Method | Description |
|---|---|
| hash | Represents an anchor name in the URL that begins with the # character |
| host | Represents the hostname and port number of the URL |
| hostname | Represents the hostname part of the URL |
| href | Represents the complete URL |
| pathname | Represents the pathname part of the URL |
| port | Represents the port part of the URL |
| protocol | Represents the protocol part of the URL |
| reload() | Reloads the current URL |
| replace() | Loads a new Web page in the current browser |
| search | The search part of the URL, including the ? |

## Example

Listing 7.379 shows how to access the Location object.

*Listing 7.379    Example of the* Location *Object*

```
<html>
<head>
<title> Creating a Location object</title>
</head>
<body>

<form name="form1">
Click the button to get the current location value.
<br><br><br>
<input type="button" name="getLoc" value="Get Location"
onClick='alert("The current location is: " + document.location)'>
<br>
</form>

</body>
</html>
```

# Location.hash

## JavaScript 1.0+, JScript 1.0+

## Nav2+, IE 3+, Opera3+

## Syntax

```
location.hash
```

## Description

The hash property of the Location object refers to the anchor portion of the URL, including the hash symbol (#).

In the following fictitious Web address:

```
http://www.mcp.com:80/foo?something#foobar
```

the hash value would be the #foobar portion.

## Example

Listing 7.380 shows an example of how to get the hash value.

*Listing 7.380   Example of the hash Property*

```html
<html>
<head>
<title> Using the hash property of the Location object</title>
</head>
<body>

<script language="JavaScript">
<!-- Hide

// displays the anchor portion of the URL
function show(){
      document.form1.text1.value=document.location.hash;
}
// End Hide --->
</script>

<form name="form1">
Click the button to get the current location.hash
➥value of the following address:
<br>
http://www.mcp.com:80/foo?something#foobar
<br><br>
Location.hash value: <input type="text" name="text1" size=20>
<br>
<input type="button" name="getLoc"➥ value="Get hash value" onClick='show()'>
<br>
</form>

</body>
</html>
```

# Location.host

## *JavaScript 1.0+, JScript 1.0+*

## *Nav2+, IE 3+, Opera3+*

## *Syntax*

```
location.host
```

## Description

The host property of the Location object represents the host portion of the URL. This is composed of the hostname and the port number (if available).

In the following fictitious Web address:

```
http://www.mcp.com:80/foo?something#foobar
```

the host value would be the www.mcp.com:80 portion.

## Example

Listing 7.381 shows the how the host property is used.

*Listing 7.381    Example of the host Property*

```
<html>
<head>
<title> Using the hash property of the Location object</title>
</head>
<body>

<script language="JavaScript">
<!-- Hide

// shows the host part of the URL
function show(){
    document.form1.text1.value=document.location.host
}
// End Hide --->
</script>

<form name="form1">
Click the button to get the current location.host value of the following
address:
<br>
http://www.mcp.com:80/foo?something#foobar
<br><br>
Location.host value: <input type="text" name="text1" size=20>
<br>
<input type="button" name="getLoc" value="Get host" onClick='show()'>
<br>
</form>

</body>
</html>
```

# Location.hostname

## *JavaScript 1.0+, JScript 1.0+*

## *Nav2+, IE 3+, Opera3+*

## Syntax

```
location.hostname
```

## Description

The `hostname` property of the `Location` object represents the hostname portion of the URL.

In the following fictitious Web address:

```
http://www.mcp.com:80/foo?something#foobar
```

the `hostname` value would be the `www.mcp.com` portion.

## Example

Listing 7.382 shows an example of how the `hostname` property is used. When the button is clicked, the `show()` function is called, which displays the value of `hostname` in the text box.

*Listing 7.382   Example of the* `hostname` *Property*

```html
<html>
<head>
<title> Using the hostname property of the Location object</title>
</head>
<body>

<script language="JavaScript">
<!-- Hide

// displays the hostname of the URL
function show(){
    document.form1.text1.value=document.location.hostname;
}
// End Hide --->
</script>

<form name="form1">
Click the button to get the current location.hostname
➥value of the following address:
<br>
http://www.mcp.com:80/foo?something#foobar
<br><br>
Location.hostname value: <input type="text" name="text1" size=20>
<br>
<input type="button" name="gethost"
➥value="Get hostname" onClick='show()'>
<br>
</form>

</body>
</html>
```

# Location.href

## *JavaScript 1.0+, JScript 1.0+*

## *Nav2+, IE 3+, Opera3+*

## Syntax

```
location.href
```

## Description

The `href` property of the `Location` object represents the entire URL string for the current page displayed in the browser.

In the following fictitious Web address:

```
http://www.mcp.com:80/foo?something#foobar
```

the `href` value would be the entire URL address.

## Example

An example of how to get the `href` value is shown in Listing 7.383.

*Listing 7.383    Example of the* `href` *Property*

```
<html>
<head>
<title> Using the href property of the Location object</title>
</head>
<body>

<script language="JavaScript">
<!-- Hide
function show(){
    document.location.href ="http://www.mcp.com:80/foo?something#foobar";
}
// End Hide --->
</script>

<form name="form1">
Click the button to set the current location.href
➥value of the following address:
<br>
http://www.mcp.com:80/foo?something#foobar
<br><br>
Location.href value: <input type="text" name="text1" size=20>
<br>
<input type="button" name="sethref" value="Set href" onClick='show()'>
<br>
</form>

</body>
</html>
```

# Location.pathname

## *JavaScript 1.0+, JScript 1.0+*

## *Nav2+, IE 3+, Opera3+*

### Syntax

```
location.pathname
```

### Description

The `pathname` property of the `Location` object represents the pathname portion of the URL.

In the following fictitious Web address:

```
http://www.mcp.com:80/foo?something#foobar
```

the `pathname` value would be the `/foo` portion.

### Example

Listing 7.384 shows an example of how to get the `pathname`.

*Listing 7.384    Example of the* pathname *Property*

```
<html>
<head>
<title> Using the pathname property of the Location object</title>
</head>
<body>

<script language="JavaScript">
<!-- Hide
// function to display the pathname value
function show(){
     document.form1.text1.value=document.location.pathname;
}
// End Hide --->
</script>

<form name="form1">
Click the button to get the current location.pathname
➥value of the following address:
<br>
http://www.mcp.com:80/foo?something#foobar
<br><br>
Location.pathname value: <input type="text" name="text1" size=20>
<br>
<input type="button" name="getLoc" value="Get pathname" onClick='show()'>
<br>
</form>

</body>
</html>
```

# Location.port

## *JavaScript 1.0+, JScript 1.0+*

## *Nav2+, IE 3+, Opera3+*

## *Syntax*

```
location.port
```

## *Description*

The `port` property of the `Location` object represents the port portion of the URL. This normally follows the hostname, but is not always available.

In the following fictitious Web address:

```
http://www.mcp.com:80/foo?something#foobar
```

the port value would be the `80` portion.

## *Example*

Listing 7.385 shows how to get the `port` number.

*Listing 7.385   Example of the* `port` *Property*

```
<html>
<head>
<title> Using the port property of the Location object</title>
</head>
<body>

<script language="JavaScript">
<!-- Hide
// Function to display the port value
function show(){
    document.form1.text1.value=document.location.port;
}
// End Hide --->
</script>

<form name="form1">
Click the button to get the current location.port
➥value of the following address:
<br>
http://www.mcp.com:80/foo?something#foobar
<br><br>
Location.port value: <input type="text" name="text1" size=20>
<br>
<input type="button" name="getport" value="Get port"
➥onClick='show()'>
<br>
</form>
```

```
</body>
</html>
```

# Location.protocol

## *JavaScript 1.0+, JScript 1.0+*

## *Nav2+, IE 3+, Opera3+*

## *Syntax*

```
location.protocol
```

## *Description*

The protocol property of the Location object represents the protocol portion of the URL. This is located in the beginning of the URL address (the text before ://).

In the following fictitious Web address:

```
http://www.mcp.com:80/foo?something#foobar
```

the protocol value would be the http portion.

## *Example*

The protocol property is used in Listing 7.386.

*Listing 7.386    Example of the* protocol *Property*

```
<html>
<head>
<title> Using the protocol property of the Location object</title>
</head>
<body>

<script language="JavaScript">
<!-- Hide
// Function to display the protocol value
function show(){
     document.form1.text1.value=document.location.protocol;
}
// End Hide --->
</script>

<form name="form1">
Click the button to get the current location.protocol
➥value of the following address:
<br>
http://www.mcp.com:80/foo?something#foobar
<br><br>
Location.protocol value: <input type="text" name="text1" size=20>
```

*continues*

*Listing 7.386    continued*

```
<br>
<input type="button" name="getproto" value="Get protocol" onClick='show()'>
<br>
</form>

</body>
</html>
```

# Location.reload()

## *JavaScript 1.1+, JScript 3.0+*

## *Nav3+, IE 4+, Opera3+*

## *Syntax*

```
location.reload()
```

## *Description*

The reload() method is used to reload the current page displayed in the browser.

## *Example*

Listing 7.387 shows an example of how the reload() method is used.

*Listing 7.387    Example of the reload() Method*

```
<html>
<head>
<title> Using the reload method of the Location object</title>
</head>
<body>

<form name="form1">
Click the button to reload the current page.
<br><br>
Location.hash value: <input type="text" name="text1" size=20>
<br>
<input type="button" name="load" value="Reload page"
onClick='document.location.reload()'>
<br>
</form>

</body>
</html>
```

# Location.replace()

## *JavaScript 1.1+, JScript 3.0+*

## *Nav3+, IE 4+, Opera3+*

## Syntax

```
location.replace(URL)
```

## Description

The `replace()` method is used to load a new page, specified by *URL*, in the current browser window. The new page replaces the previous page's position in the history list.

## Example

Listing 7.388 shows the `replace()` method being used to load the new Web site.

*Listing 7.388    Example of the* `replace()` *Method*

```
<html>
<head>
<title> Using the replace method of the Location object</title>
</head>
<body>

<form name="form1">
Click the button to load the new page: http://www.mcp.com
<br>
<br>
<input type="button" name="load" value="Load new page"
onClick='document.location.replace("http://www.mcp.com")'>
<br>
</form>

</body>
</html>
```

# Location.search

## JavaScript 1.0+, JScript 1.0+

## Nav2+, IE 3+, Opera3+

## Syntax

```
location.search
```

## Description

The `search` property of the `Location` object represents the query portion of the URL, including the preceding question mark.

In the following fictitious Web address:

```
http://www.mcp.com:80/foo?something#foobar
```

the `search` value would be the `?something` portion.

## Example

Listing 7.389 shows how to use the search property. When the button is clicked, the show function displays the value of the search property in the text box.

*Listing 7.389   Example of the* search *Property*

```html
<html>
<head>
<title> Using the search property of the Location object</title>
</head>
<body>

<script language="JavaScript">
<!-- Hide
// function displays the search property value
function show(){
    document.form1.text1.value=document.location.search;
}
// End Hide --->
</script>

<form name="form1">
Click the button to get the current location.search
➥value of the following address:
<br>
http://www.mcp.com:80/foo?something#foobar
<br><br>
Location.search value: <input type="text" name="text1" size=20>
<br>
<input type="button" name="getsearch" value="Get search"
➥onClick='show()'>
<br>
</form>

</body>
</html>
```

# MimeType

## *JavaScript 1.1+*

## *Nav3+*

## *Syntax*

Core client-side JavaScript object.

## *Description*

The MimeType object is a predefined JavaScript object that you access through the mimeTypes array of the Navigator or Plugin object. MIME stands for Multipart Internet Mail Extension. Table 7.35 shows the different methods and properties of the MimeType object.

**Table 7.35   Properties and Methods of the MimeType Object**

| Property/Method | Description |
|---|---|
| description | Returns description of MimeType |
| enabledPlugin | Returns plug-in for specific MimeType |
| suffixes | Returns file extension for MimeType |
| type | Returns string representation of MimeType |

## Example

Listing 7.390 shows an example of accessing a MimeType though the mimeTypes array. It prints out a few mimeTypes to the browser window.

*Listing 7.390   Example of* MimeType

```
<html>
<head>
<title> Example of how to determine the available MimeTypes</title>
</head>
<body>
<script language="JavaScript">
<!-- Hide

// function prints the first three MimeTypes
 for (i=0; i < 3; i++) {
    document.writeln(navigator.mimeTypes[i].type);
    document.writeln(navigator.mimeTypes[i].description);
    document.writeln(navigator.mimeTypes[i].suffixes);
    //
}
// End Hide --->
</script>

</body>
</html>
```

# MimeType.description

## *JavaScript 1.1+*

## *Nav3+*

## *Syntax*

*mimetype*.description

## Description

The description property of the MimeType object is used to obtain a description of the data type described by the MimeType object.

## Example

Listing 7.391 shows an example of how the description property is used. A for loop is used to output the suffixes of the first three MimeTypes.

*Listing 7.391   Accessing the* description *Property*

```
<html>
<head>
<title> Using the description property of the MimeType object</title>
</head>
<body>

<script language="javascript">
<!---Hide
// function prints the suffixes for the first three MimeTypes
 for (i=0; i < 3; i++) {
    document.write("MimeType description " + i + " : ");
    document.writeln(navigator.mimeTypes[i].description);
    document.write("<br>");
}
// End Hide --->
</script>

</body>
</html>
```

# MimeType.enabledPlugin

## JavaScript 1.1+

## Nav3+

## Syntax

*mimetype*.enabledPlugin

## Description

The enabledPlugin property of the MimeType object is used to determine which plug-in is configured for a specific MIME type.

## Example

Listing 7.392 shows how the enabledPlugin property is used. A for loop is used to output the first three enabledPlugin values.

*Listing 7.392   Accessing the* enabledPlugin *Property*

```
<html>
<head>
<title> Using the enabledPlugin property of the MimeType object</title>
</head>
<body>
```

```
<script language="javascript">
<!---Hide

// loop through and output enabledPlugin values
 for (i=0; i < 3; i++) {
    document.write("MimeType enabledPlugin " + i + " : ");
    document.writeln(navigator.mimeTypes[i].enabledPlugin);
    document.write("<br>");
}
// End Hide --->
</script>

</body>
</html>
```

# MimeType.suffixes

## JavaScript 1.1+

## Nav3+

## Syntax

*mimetype*.suffixes

## Description

The suffixes property of the MimeType object is used to obtain a string listing the possible file suffixes or filename extensions for the MIME type.

## Example

Listing 7.393 shows an example of how the suffixes property is used. A for loop is used to output the first three suffix values.

*Listing 7.393    Accessing the* suffixes *Property*

```
<html>
<head>
<title> Using the suffixes property of the MimeType object</title>
</head>
<body>

<script language="javascript">
<!---Hide
// function prints the suffixes for the first three MimeTypes
 for (i=0; i < 3; i++) {
    document.write("MimeType suffix " + i + " : ");
    document.writeln(navigator.mimeTypes[i].suffixes);
    document.write("<br>");
}
// End Hide --->
```

*continues*

*Listing 7.393    continued*
```
</script>

</body>
</html>
```

# MimeType.type

## *JavaScript 1.1+*

## *Nav3+*

## *Syntax*

```
mimetype.type
```

## *Description*

The type property of the MimeType object is used to obtain a string specifying the name of the MIME type.

## *Example*

Listing 7.394 shows how the type property is used. A for loop is used to output the first three MIME types.

*Listing 7.394    Example of the* type *Property*
```
<html>
<head>
<title> Using the type property of the MimeType object</title>
</head>
<body>

<script language="javascript">
<!---Hide
// function prints the types for the first 3 MimeTypes
 for (i=0; i < 3; i++) {
    document.write("MimeType type " + i + " :");
    document.writeln(navigator.mimeTypes[i].type);
    document.write("<br>");
}
// End Hide --->
</script>

</body>
</html>
```

# navigator

## *JavaScript 1.0+, Jscript 1.0+*

## *Nav2+, IE 3+, Opera3+*

## Syntax

Core client-side JavaScript object.

## Description

The `navigator` object is a built-in object that is used to obtain information related to the Navigator browser. Table 7.36 shows the different methods and properties of the `navigator` object.

**Table 7.36   Properties and Methods of the navigator object**

| Property/Method | Description |
|---|---|
| appCodeName | Represents the code name of the browser |
| appName | Refers to the official browser name |
| appVersion | Refers to the version information of the browser |
| javaEnabled() | Function that tests to see that Java is supported in the browser |
| language | Refers to the language of the browser |
| mimeTypes | Refers to an array of MimeType objects that contains all the MIME types that the browser supports |
| platform | A string representing the platform on which the browser is running |
| plugins | Refers to an array of Plugin objects that contains all the plug-ins installed in the browser |
| plugins.refresh() | Checks for any newly installed plug-ins |
| preference() | Allows reading and setting of various user preferences in the browser |
| taintEnabled() | Tests to see whether data-tainting is enabled |
| userAgent | String that represents the user-agent header |

## Example

Listing 7.395 shows an example for the `navigator` object.

*Listing 7.395   Example of the* `navigator` *Object*

```
<html>
<head>
<title> Example of the navigator object</title>
</head>
<body>

<script language="JavaScript">
<!--Hide
// Output the navigate appName property
document.write(navigator.appName);
// End Hide --->
</script>

</body>
</html>
```

# navigator.appCodeName

## JavaScript 1.0+, JScript 1.0+

## Nav2+, IE 3+, Opera3+

## Syntax

```
navigator.appCodeName
```

## Description

The appCodeName property of the navigator object refers to the internal code name of the browser.

## Example

Listing 7.396 shows an example of how the appCodeName property is used.

Listing 7.396   Example of the appCodeName Property
```
<html>
<head>
<title> Example of the appCodeName property of the navigator object</title>
</head>
<body>

<script language="JavaScript">
<!--Hide
// Output the navigate appCodeName property
document.write(navigator.appCodeName);
// End Hide --->
</script>

</body>
</html>
```

# navigator.appName

## JavaScript 1.0+, JScript 1.0+

## Nav2+, IE 3+, Opera3+

## Syntax

```
navigator.appName
```

## Description

The appName property of the navigator object refers to the browser name.

## Example

Listing 7.397 shows an example of how the appName property is used.

*Listing 7.397    Example of the* `appName` *Property*

```
<html>
<head>
<title> Example of the appName property of the navigator object</title>
</head>
<body>

<script language="JavaScript">
<!--Hide
// output the appName property
document.write(navigator.appName);
// End Hide --->
</script>

</body>
</html>
```

# navigator.appVersion

## JavaScript 1.0+, JScript 1.0+

## Nav2+, IE 3+, Opera3+

## Syntax

```
navigator.appVersion
```

## Description

The `appVersion` property of the `navigator` object is used to get the browser version. The returned property contains the browser version, platform on which the browser is running, and the country (either international or domestic).

## Example

Listing 7.398 shows an example of how the `appVersion` property is used.

*Listing 7.398    Example of the* `appVersion` *Property*

```
<html>
<head>
<title> Example of the appVersion property of the navigator object</title>
</head>
<body>

<script language="JavaScript">
<!--Hide
// output the appVersion property
document.write(navigator.appVersion);
// End Hide --->
</script>

</body>
</html>
```

# navigator.javaEnabled()

*JavaScript 1.1+, JScript 1.0+*

*Nav3+, IE 3+, Opera3+*

## Syntax

```
navigator.javaEnabled()
```

## Description

The javaEnabled() method is used to test whether the browser supports Java.

## Example

Listing 7.399 shows an example of how the javaEnabled() method is used. A check is made to determine whether Java is enabled on the browser. If so, a message is output indicating that to be the case.

*Listing 7.399   Example of the javaEnabled() Method*

```html
<html>
<head>
<title> Example of the javaEnabled method of the navigator object</title>
</head>
<body>

<script language="JavaScript">
<!--Hide

// check to determine if Java is enabled on the browser.
// If so then output a message.
if (navigator.javaEnabled()){
    document.write("This browser supports Java");
}
// End Hide --->
</script>

</body>
</html>
```

# navigator.language

*JavaScript 1.2+*

*Nav4+*

## Syntax

```
navigator.language
```

## Description

The language property of the navigator object is used to determine what language the browser supports. The return value is a string.

## Example

Listing 7.400 shows an example of how the language property is used.

*Listing 7.400   Example of the* language *Property*

```
<html>
<head>
<title> Example of the language property of the navigator object</title>
</head>
<body>

<script language="JavaScript">
<!--Hide
// output the navigator language property
     document.write(navigator.language);
// End Hide --->
</script>

</body>
</html>
```

# navigator.mimeTypes

## JavaScript 1.1+

## Nav3+, Opera3+

## Syntax

```
navigator.mimeTypes
```

## Description

The mimeTypes property of the navigator object is used to obtain a list of all the MIME types supported by the browser. The returned object is an array containing all supported MIME types. The mimetypes array contains all the properties of the Array object.

## Example

Listing 7.401 shows an example of how the mimeTypes property is used.

*Listing 7.401   Example of the* mimeTypes *Property*

```
<html>
<head>
<title> Example of the mimetypes property of the navigator object</title>
```

*continues*

*Listing 7.401    continued*

```
</head>
<body>

<script language="JavaScript">
<!--Hide
// output the navigator mimeTypes length property
     document.write(navigator.mimeTypes.length);
// End Hide --->
</script>

</body>
</html>
```

# navigator.platform

## *JavaScript 1.2+, JScript 1.0+*

## *Nav4+, IE 4+*

## *Syntax*

```
navigator.platform
```

## *Description*

The `platform` property of the `navigator` object returns a string representing the platform on which the browser is running. Valid platform values are: `Win32`, `Win16`, `Mac68k`, and `MacPPC`. There are also various values for UNIX platforms.

## *Example*

Listing 7.402 shows an example of how the `platform` property is used.

*Listing 7.402    Example of the* `platform` *Property*

```
<html>
<head>
<title> Example of the platform property of the navigator object</title>
</head>
<body>

<script language="JavaScript">
<!--Hide
// output the navigator platform property
     document.write(navigator.platform);
// End Hide -->
</script>

</body>
</html>
```

# navigator.plugins

## JavaScript 1.1+, JScript 1.0+

## Nav3+, IE 3+

## Syntax

```
navigator.plugins[num]
```

## Description

The `plugins` property of the `navigator` object returns an array of the `Plugins` object representing all the plug-ins installed on a particular browser. These can be accessed by the indexed *num* passed.

## Example

Listing 7.403 shows an example of how the `plugins` property is used. A loop is used to output a list of all the plug-ins for the browser.

*Listing 7.403   Example of the* `plugins` *Property*

```
<html>
<head>
<title> Example of the plugins property of the navigator object</title>
</head>
<body>

<script language="JavaScript">
<!--Hide
var plugLength = navigator.plugins.length

// loop through and output all the plugins
// present in the browser
for(i=0; i<plugLength; i++){
    document.write(navigator.plugins[i].name);
}
// End Hide --->
</script>

</body>
</html>
```

# navigator.plugins.refresh()

## JavaScript 1.1+, JScript 1.0+

## Nav3+, IE 3+

## Syntax

```
navigator.plugins.refresh()
```

## Description

The `plugins.refresh()` method of the `navigator` object is used to check for any new plug-ins installed on the browser.

## Example

Listing 7.404 shows an example of how the `plugins.refresh()` method is used.

*Listing 7.404   Example of the* `plugins.refresh()` *Method*

```
<html>
<head>
<title> Example of the plugins.refresh method of the navigator object</title>
</head>
<body>

<script language="JavaScript">
<!--Hide
    document.write(navigator.plugins.refresh());
// End Hide -->
</script>

</body>
</html>
```

# navigator.preference()

## *JavaScript 1.2+, JScript 1.0+*

## *Nav4+, IE 4+, Opera3+*

## Syntax

```
navigator.preference(name)

navigator.preference(name, value)
```

## Description

The `preference()` method of the `navigator` object is used to read or set any user preferences in the browser. For security reasons, reading a preference with the `preference()` method requires the `UniversalPreferencesRead` privilege. Setting a preference with this method requires the `UniversalPreferencesWrite` privilege.

## Example

Listing 7.405 shows an example of how the `preference()` method can be used to set a preference.

*Listing 7.405   Example of the* `preference()` *Method*

```
<html>
<head>
<title> Example of the preference method of the navigator object</title>
</head>
```

```
<body>

<script language="JavaScript">
<!--Hide
// This disables Java support in the browser
navigator.preference(security.enable_java, false);
// End Hide --->
</script>

</body>
</html>
```

# navigator.taintEnabled()

## JavaScript 1.1+

## Nav3+

## Syntax

```
navigator.taintEnabled()
```

## Description

The taintEnabled() method of the navigator specifies whether data tainting is enabled.

**NOTE**

This method is removed in Navigator 4 and later releases.

## Example

Listing 7.406 shows an example of how the taintEnabled() method is used.

*Listing 7.406    Example of the* taintEnabled() *Method*

```
<html>
<head>
<title> Example of the taintEnabled method of the navigator object</title>
</head>
<body>

<script language="JavaScript">
<!--Hide

// determine if tainting is enabled in the browser
if(navigator.taintEnabled()){
    document.write("Data tainting is enabled");
}
else{
```

*continues*

*Listing 7.406    continued*
```
    document.write("There is no data tainting");
}
// End Hide --->
</script>

</body>
</html>
```

# navigator.userAgent

## JavaScript 1.0+, JScript 1.0+

## Nav2+, IE 3+, Opera3+

## Syntax

```
navigator.userAgent
```

## Description

The userAgent property of the navigator object returns a string identifying the browser. This value is often sent to servers during HTTP data requests.

## Example

Listing 7.407 shows an example of how the userAgent property is used.

*Listing 7.407    Example of the userAgent Property*
```
<html>
<head>
<title> Example of the userAgent property of the navigator object</title>
</head>
<body>

<script language="JavaScript">
<!--Hide
//Returns the userAgent property of the browser

document.write(navigator.userAgent);
// End Hide --->
</script>

</body>
</html>
```

# Option

## JavaScript 1.0+, JScript 1.0+

## Nav2+, IE 3+

## Syntax

Core client-side JavaScript object.

## Description

The Option object is used to reference a property of an HTML select list. An Option object can be created by using the option constructor and specifying the appropriate values. Table 7.37 shows the different properties of the Option object.

**Table 7.37   Properties and Methods of the Option Object**

| Property | Description |
| --- | --- |
| defaultSelected | Refers to the option that is selected by default from the select box |
| selected | Refers to the selected value of the select box |
| text | Refers to the text for the option |
| value | Refers to the value that is returned to when the option is selected |

## Example

Listing 7.408 shows an example of how a select list is populated.

*Listing 7.408   Example of the* Option *Object*

```
<html>
<head>
<title> Example of the option object</title>
</head>
<body>

<script>
<script language="JavaScript">
<!--Hide
// function adds the options to the select list.
function add(myForm) {

   var option0 = new Option("Joe", "person1");
   var option1 = new Option("Jane", "person2");
   var option2 = new Option("Mark", "person3");
   var option3 = new Option("Melissa", "person4");

   for (var i=0; i < 4; i++) {
      eval("myForm.people.options[i]=option" + i)
}

   history.go(0)
}
// End Hide --->
```

*continues*

*Listing 7.408    continued*
```
</script>

<form>
<select name="people" multiple></select><p>
<input type="button" value="Add People" onClick="add(this.form)">
</form>
</body>
</html>
```

# Option.defaultSelected

## JavaScript 1.1+, JScript 1.0+

## Nav3+, IE 3+

## Syntax

`option.defaultSelected`

## Description

The `defaultSelected` property of the `Option` object specifies the initial option selection of the select list.

## Example

Listing 7.409 shows an example of how the `defaultSelected` property is used. The `check` function checks for the default selected option.

*Listing 7.409    Example of the* `defaultSelected` *Property*
```
<html>
<head>
<title> Example of the defaultSelected property of the option object</title>
</head>
<body>


<script language="JavaScript">
<!--Hide
// function checks the form to see what is the default selected.
function check(myForm){
    for (var i = 0; i < document.form1.myList.length; i++) {
        if (document.form1.myList.options[i].defaultSelected == true) {
            alert("The default value is: 2");
        }
    }
}
// End Hide --->
</script>

<form name=form1>
```

```
<select name="myList" multiple>
<option value=1>One
<option value=2 SELECTED>Two
<option value=3>Three
<option value=4>Four
</select><p>
<input type="button" value="Get Default Value" onClick='check(this.form)'>
</form>

</body>
</html>
```

# Option.selected

## *JavaScript 1.2+*

## *Nav4+*

## *Syntax*

*option*.selected

## *Description*

The selected property of the Option object specifies the current selected option of the select list.

## *Example*

Listing 7.410 shows an example of how the selected property is used. The check function checks to see what the selected property is.

*Listing 7.410   Example of the* selected *Property*

```
<html>
<head>
<title> Example of the selected property of the option object</title>
</head>
<body>


<script language="JavaScript">
<!--Hide
// function checks the forms to see what the selected property is
function check(myForm){
    for (var i = 0; i < document.form1.myList.length; i++) {
        if (document.form1.myList.options[i].selected == true) {
            alert("The selected value is: " +
document.form1.myList.options[i].value);
        }
    }
}
```

*continues*

*Listing 7.410    continued*
```
// End Hide --->
</script>

<form name=form1>
<select name="myList" multiple>
<option value=1>One
<option value=2>Two
<option value=3>Three
<option value=4>Four
</select><p>
<input type="button" value="Get Value" onClick='check(this.form)'>
</form>

</body>
</html>
```

# Option.text

## *JavaScript 1.0+, JScript 1.0+*

## *Nav2+, IE 3+*

## *Syntax*

`option.text`

## *Description*

The `text` property of the `Option` object specifies the text for the selected option of the select list.

## *Example*

Listing 7.411 shows an example of how the `text` property is used. The `check` function determines what the text is for the selected value.

*Listing 7.411    Example of the* `text` *Property*
```
<html>
<head>
<title> Example of the text property of the option object</title>
</head>
<body>

<script>
<script language="JavaScript">
<!--Hide
// function check the form to see what the selected value's text is
function check(myForm){
    for (var i = 0; i < document.form1.myList.length; i++) {
        if (document.form1.myList.options[i].selected == true) {
            alert("The selected text value is: " +
```

```
document.form1.myList.options[i].text);
      }
   }
}
// End Hide --->
</script>

<form name=form1>
<select name="myList" multiple>
<option value=1>One
<option value=2>Two
<option value=3>Three
<option value=4>Four
</select><p>
<input type="button" value="Get Text Value" onClick='check(this.form)'>
</form>

</body>
</html>
```

# Option.value

## *JavaScript 1.0+, JScript 1.0+*

## *Nav2+, IE 3+*

## *Syntax*

*option*.value

## *Description*

The value property of the Option object specifies the value that is returned to the server when the option is selected and the form is submitted.

## *Example*

Listing 7.412 shows an example of how the value property is used. The function getValue gets the value of the selected option.

*Listing 7.412   Example of the* value *Property*

```
<html>
<head>
<title> Example of the text value of the option object</title>
</head>
<body>

<script language="JavaScript">
<!--Hide
```

*continues*

*Listing 7.412    continued*

```
// Function gets the value of the selected option
function getValue(myForm){
    for (var i = 0; i < document.form1.myList.length; i++) {
        if (document.form1.myList.options[i].selected == true) {
            alert("The selected value is: " +
document.form1.myList.options[i].value);
        }
    }
}
// End Hide --->
</script>

<form name=form1>
<select name="myList" multiple>
<option value=1>One
<option value=2>Two
<option value=3>Three
<option value=4>Four
</select><p>
<input type="button" value="Get Value" onClick='getValue(this.form)'>
</form>

</body>
</html>
```

# Password

## *JavaScript 1.0+, JScript 1.0+*

## *Nav2+, IE 3+, Opera3+*

## *Syntax*

Core client-side JavaScript object.

## *Description*

The Password object refers to the HTML element created with the <input> tag setting the type to specify password. It operates similarly to a standard HTML text input box as input is entered into the box. Instead of displaying the input in cleartext, input is displayed using the * symbol. Table 7.38 shows the different methods and properties of the Password object.

**Table 7.38   Properties and Methods of the Password Object**

| Property/Method | Description |
| --- | --- |
| blur() | Removes focus from the password box |
| defaultValue | Refers to the VALUE attribute of the HTML password box |
| focus() | Sets focus to the password box |
| form | Refers to the form that contains the password box |

| Property/Method | Description |
| --- | --- |
| handleEvent() | Invokes the event handler |
| name | Refers to the NAME attribute of the HTML password box |
| onBlur | Event handler used when the focus is removed from the password box |
| onFocus | Event handler used when the focus is put on the password box |
| select() | Selects the text entered in the password box |
| type | Refers to the TYPE attribute of the HTML password box |
| value | Refers to the current contents of the password box |

## Example

Listing 7.413 shows an example of how the Password object is used to read the value entered in a password box.

*Listing 7.413   Example of the* Password *Object*

```
<html>
<head>
<title> Creating a password object</title>
</head>
<body>

<form name="form1">
<input type="PASSWORD" Name="pass" size=10>
<br>
<input type="BUTTON" value="Show Password"
onClick=alert(document.form1.pass.value)>
</form>

</body>
</html>
```

# Password.blur()

## *JavaScript 1.0+, JScript 1.0+*

## *Nav2+, IE 3+, Opera3+*

## Syntax

password.blur()

## Description

The blur method for the Password object is used to remove the focus from the password box.

## Example

Listing 7.414 shows an example of how the focus is removed from the password box.

*Listing 7.414   Example of the* `blur()` *Method*

```
<html>
<head>
<title> Example of the blur method of the password object</title>
</head>
<body>

<script language="JavaScript">
<!--Hide
// function that shifts focus when the button is clicked
function shift(){
    document.form1.pass.blur();
    document.form1.txt.value="Get Focus";
}
// End Hide --->
</script>

<form name="form1">
<input type="PASSWORD" Name="pass" size=10>
<br>
<input type="Text" name="txt" size=10>
<br>
<input type="BUTTON" value="Show Password" onClick=shift()>
</form>

</body>
</html>
```

# Password.defaultValue

## JavaScript 1.0+, JScript 1.0+

## Nav2+, IE 3+

## Syntax

*password.*defaultValue

## Description

The defaultValue property of the Password object is used to get the HTML VALUE attribute of the password box.

## Example

Listing 7.415 shows an example of how the defaultValue is used to get the password value.

*Listing 7.415   Example of the* defaultValue *Property*

```
<html>
<head>
<title> Example of the password defaultValue property</title>
</head>
```

```
<body>

<form name="form1">
<input type="PASSWORD" Name="pass" size=10 value="pass123">
<br>
<input type="BUTTON" value="Show Password"
onClick=alert(document.form1.pass.defaultValue)>
</form>

</body>
</html>
```

# Password.focus()

## JavaScript 1.0+, JScript 1.0+

## Nav2+, IE 3+, Opera3+

## Syntax
`password.focus()`

## Description
The focus() method of the Password object sets the focus to the password box.

## Example
Listing 7.416 shows an example of how the focus() method is used to move the focus back to the password box.

Listing 7.416   Example of the focus() Method
```
<html>
<head>
<title> Example of the password focus method</title>
</head>
<body>

<form name="form1">
<input type="PASSWORD" Name="pass" size=10>
<br>
<input type="BUTTON" value="Show Password" onClick=document.form1.pass.focus()>
</form>

</body>
</html>
```

# Password.form

## JavaScript 1.0+, JScript 1.0+

## Nav2+, IE 3+, Opera3+

## Syntax

`password.form`

## Description

The `form` property of the `Password` object is used to access the `Form` object in which the password box resides.

## Example

Listing 7.417 shows an example of how the `form` property is used to get the form name.

*Listing 7.417   Example of the* `form` *Property*

```
<html>
<head>
<title> Example of the password form property</title>
</head>
<body>

<form name="form1">
<input type="PASSWORD" Name="pass" size=10>
<br>
<input type="BUTTON" value="Show Formname"
onClick=alert(document.form1.pass.form.name)>
</form>

</body>
</html>
```

# Password.handleEvent()

## JavaScript 1.2+, JScript 1.0+

## Nav4+, IE 3+, Opera3+

## Syntax

`password.handleEvent(event)`

## Description

The `handleEvent()` method of the `Password` object is used to handle events of the type *event* passed.

## Example

Listing 7.418 shows an example of how the `handleEvent()` method is used to handle the `Click` event when the button is clicked.

*Listing 7.418   Example of the* `handleEvent()` *Method*

```
<html>
<head>
<title> Example of the password handleEvent property</title>
</head>
```

```
<body>

<script language="JavaScript">
<!--Hide

// sets up the document to capture CHANGE events
document.captureEvents(Event.CHANGE);

// function that handles the specific event. The evnt parameter refers to
// the event object.
function handleChange(evnt){
    window.document.pass.handleEvent(evnt);
}

function showMsg(){
    alert("Password Changed.");
}

// This registers the handle function as the event handler for the
// CHANGE event.
document.onChange = handleChange;
// End Hide --->
</script>

<form name="form1">

Enter password:
<input type="PASSWORD" name="pass" size=15 onChange='showMsg()'>
</form>

</body>
</html>
```

# Password.name

## *JavaScript 1.0+, JScript 1.0+*

## *Nav2+, IE 3+, Opera3+*

## *Syntax*

*password.*name

## *Description*

The name property of the Password object is used to get the HTML NAME attribute of the password box.

## *Example*

Listing 7.419 shows an example of how the name property is used. When the button is clicked, an alert box is displayed showing the password object name.

*Listing 7.419   Example of the* name *Property*
```
<html>
<head>
<title> Example of the password name property</title>
</head>
<body>

<form name="form1">
<input type="PASSWORD" Name="pass" size=10>
<br>
<input type="BUTTON" value="Show Formname"
onClick=alert(document.form1.pass.name)>
</form>

</body>
</html>
```

# Password.onBlur

## *JavaScript 1.0+, JScript 1.0+*

## *Nav2+, IE 3+, Opera3+*

## *Syntax*

```
onBlur="command"
```

## *Description*

The onBlur event handler of the Password object is used to handle the event that occurs when the focus is removed from the password box.

## *Example*

Listing 7.420 shows an example of how the onBlur event handler is used. When the focus is removed from the Password object, the setTxt() function is called to display a message in the text box.

*Listing 7.420   Example of the* onBlur *Event Handler*
```
<html>
<head>
<title> Example of the password onBlur event handler</title>
</head>
<body>

<script language="JavaScript">
<!--Hide
// function that sets the text value
function setTxt(){
    document.form1.txt.value="setup";
}
// End Hide --->
```

```
</script>


<form name="form1">
<input type="PASSWORD" Name="pass" size=10 onBlur=setTxt()>
<br>
<input type="Text" name="txt" size=10 >
</form>

</body>
</html>
```

# Password.onFocus

## *JavaScript 1.0+, JScript 1.0+*

## *Nav2+, IE 3+, Opera3+*

## *Syntax*

onFocus="*command*"

## *Description*

The onFocus event handler of the Password object is used to handle the Focus event for the password box.

## *Example*

Listing 7.421 shows an example of the onFocus event handler.

*Listing 7.421    Example of the* onFocus *Event Handler*

```
<html>
<head>
<title> Example of the password onFocus event handler</title>
</head>
<body>

<script language="JavaScript">
<!--Hide
// sets a message in the text box
function set(){
     document.form1.pass.value="aha123";
}
// End Hide --->
</script>

<form name="form1">
<input type="PASSWORD" Name="pass" size=10 onFocus=set()>
<br>
```

*continues*

*Listing 7.421    continued*
```
<input type="BUTTON" value="Show Formname" >
</form>

</body>
</html>
```

# Password.select()

## *JavaScript 1.0+, JScript 1.0+*

## *Nav2+, IE 3+, Opera3+*

## *Syntax*

`password.select()`

## *Description*

The `select()` method of the `Password` object is used to select the value entered into the password box. The selected value is highlighted.

## *Example*

Listing 7.422 shows an example of how the password value can be selected.

*Listing 7.422    Example of the* `select()` *Method*
```
<html>
<head>
<title> Example of the password select method</title>
</head>
<body>

<form name="form1">
<input type="PASSWORD" Name="pass" size=10>
<br>
<input type="BUTTON" value="Select Password"
➥onClick=document.form1.pass.select()>
</form>

</body>
</html>
```

# Password.type

## *JavaScript 1.1+, JScript 1.0+*

## *Nav3+, IE 3+, Opera3+*

## *Syntax*

`password.type`

## Description

The type property of the Password object is used to get the HTML TYPE attribute associated with the password box. For the Password object, this value is always password.

## Example

Listing 7.423 shows an example of how the type property is used. When the button is clicked, an alert box is displayed showing the value of the type property.

*Listing 7.423   Example of the type Property*

```
<html>
<head>
<title> Example of the password type property</title>
</head>
<body>

<form name="form1">
<input type="PASSWORD" Name="pass" size=10>
<br>
<input type="BUTTON" value="Get Type" onClick=alert(document.form1.pass.type)>
</form>

</body>
</html>
```

# Password.value

## JavaScript 1.0+, JScript 1.0+

## Nav2+, IE 3+, Opera3+

## Syntax

*password.*value

## Description

The value property of the Password object is used to get the value entered in the password box.

## Example

Listing 7.424 shows an example of how the value property is used.

*Listing 7.424   Example of the value Property*

```
<html>
<head>
<title> Example of the password value property</title>
</head>
<body>
```

*continues*

*Listing 7.424    continued*

```
<form name="form1">
<input type="PASSWORD" Name="pass" size=10>
<br>
<input type="BUTTON" value="Get Value"
onClick=alert(document.form1.pass.value)>
</form>

</body>
</html>
```

# Plugin

## JavaScript 1.1+, JScript 1.0+

## Nav3+, IE 3+, Opera3+

## Syntax

Core client-side JavaScript object.

## Description

The Plugin object is used to obtain plug-in information from the browser. The Plugin object contains an array of elements containing the MIME types handled by each plug-in. Table 7.39 shows the different properties of the Plugin object.

**Table 7.39    Properties of the Plugin Object**

| Property | Description |
| --- | --- |
| description | Refers to a description of the plug-in |
| filename | Refers to the filename of a plug-in program |
| length | Refers to the number of MIME types supported |
| name | Refers to the plug-in name |

## Example

Listing 7.425 shows an example where all the browser's plug-ins are printed to the document.

*Listing 7.425    Example Using the Plugin Object*

```
<html>
<head>
<title> Example of the Plugin object</title>
</head>
<body>

<script language="JavaScript">
<!--Hide
// function that prints all the browser plug-ins
for(i=0; i<navigator.plugins.length; i++){
    document.write(navigator.plugins[i].description);
```

```
}
// End Hide --->
</script>

</body>
</html>
```

# Plugin.description

## JavaScript 1.1+, JScript 1.0+

## Nav3+, IE 3+, Opera3+

## Syntax

`plugin`.description

## Description

The description property of the Plugin object is used to obtain a description of the browser plug-ins.

## Example

Listing 7.426 shows an example of how the description property is used.

*Listing 7.426   Example of the* description *Property*

```
<html>
<head>
<title> Example of the plugin description property</title>
</head>
<body>

<script language="JavaScript">
<!--Hide
// print the description for the first plug-in
    document.write(navigator.plugins[0].description);

// End Hide --->
</script>

</body>
</html>
```

# Plugin.filename

## JavaScript 1.1+, JScript 1.0+

## Nav3+, IE 3+, Opera3+

## Syntax

`plugin`.filename

## Description

The `filename` property of the `Plugin` object is used to get the path and filename for a plug-in.

## Example

Listing 7.427 shows an example of how the `filename` property is used.

*Listing 7.427   Example of the* `filename` *Property*

```
<html>
<head>
<title> Example of the plugin filename property</title>
</head>
<body>

<script language="JavaScript">
<!--Hide
// print the filename for the first browser plug-in
    document.write(navigator.plugins[0].filename);

// End Hide --->
</script>

</body>
</html>
```

# Plugin.length

## JavaScript 1.1+, JScript 1.0+

## Nav3+, IE 3+, Opera3+

## Syntax

`plugin.length`

## Description

The `length` property of the `Plugin` object determines the number of MIME data types the plug-in can support.

## Example

Listing 7.428 shows an example of how the `length` property is used.

*Listing 7.428   Example of the* `length` *Property*

```
<html>
<head>
<title> Example of the plugin length property</title>
</head>
<body>

<script language="JavaScript">
```

```
<!--Hide
// print the number of browser plug-ins
    document.write(navigator.plugins.length);

// End Hide --->
</script>

</body>
</html>
```

# Plugin.name

## *JavaScript 1.1+, JScript 1.0+*

## *Nav3+, IE 3+, Opera3+*

### Syntax

*plugin*.name

### Description

The name property of the Plugin object is used to get the plug-in's name.

### Example

Listing 7.429 shows an example of how the name property is used.

*Listing 7.429   Example of the* name *Property*
```
<html>
<head>
<title> Example of the plugin name property</title>
</head>
<body>

<script language="JavaScript">
<!--Hide
// print the name of the first browser plug-in
    document.write(navigator.plugins[0].name);

// End Hide --->
</script>

</body>
</html>
```

# Radio

## *JavaScript 1.0+, JScript 1.0+*

## *Nav2+, IE 3+, Opera3+*

## Syntax

Core client-side JavaScript object.

## Description

The Radio object represents a check box within an HTML form. A check box is created using the HTML `<input>` tag and specifying the TYPE attribute as radio. The Radio object has specific properties and methods associated with it, as shown in Table 7.40.

### Table 7.40   Properties and Methods of the Radio Object

| Property/Method | Description |
| --- | --- |
| blur() | Removes focus from Radio object |
| checked | Specifies whether a button is checked or unchecked |
| click() | Simulates a mouse click on the button |
| defaultChecked | Refers to the CHECKED attribute of the HTML `<input>` tag |
| focus() | Sets the focus to a button |
| form | Refers to the Form object that contains the Radio object |
| handleEvent() | Invokes the default handler for the specified event |
| name | Refers to the NAME attribute of the HTML `<input>` tag |
| onBlur | Event handler for Blur event |
| onClick | Event handler for Click event |
| onFocus | Event handler for Focus event |
| type | Refers to the TYPE attribute of the HTML `<input>` tag |
| value | Refers to the VALUE attribute of the HTML `<input>` tag |

## Example

Listing 7.430 shows how a check box is created and then how the name property is accessed using the Radio object.

*Listing 7.430   Example of the Radio Object*

```
<html>
<head>
<title> Example of the Radio object title>
</head>
<body>

<form name="form1">
<input type="radio" name=button1
➥onClick='alert(document.form1.button1.name)'>Box 1
<br>
<input type="radio" name=button2>Box 2
<br>
</form>

</body>
</html>
```

# Radio.blur()

## *JavaScript 1.0+, JScript 1.0+*

## *Nav2+, IE 3+, Opera3+*

## *Syntax*

```
radio.blur()
```

## *Description*

The `blur()` method of the `Radio` object is used to remove the focus from the check box.

## *Example*

Listing 7.431 shows how the `blur()` method is used to remove focus from the radio button. When the Remove Focus button is clicked, the focus is removed from the radio button and a text message is displayed.

*Listing 7.431    Example of the* `blur()` *Method*

```
<html>
<head>
<title> Example of the radio blur method</title>
</head>
<body>

<script language="JavaScript">
<!--Hide

// function removes focus from the button
function change(){
document.form1.button1.blur();
document.form1.text1.value="Focus removed from button";
}
// End Hide --->
</script>

<form name="form1">
<input type="radio" name=button1 CHECKED>Box 1
<br>
<input type="radio" name=button2>Box 2
<br>
<input type="button" value="Remove Focus" onClick='change()'>
<br>
<input type="text" name="text1" size=15>
</form>

</body>
</html>
```

# Radio.checked

## *JavaScript 1.0+, JScript 1.0+*

## *Nav2+, IE 3+, Opera3+*

## Syntax

`radio.checked`

## Description

The `checked` property of the `Radio` object is a Boolean value used to determine whether a radio button is in a checked or unchecked state.

## Example

Listing 7.432 shows an example of how to determine whether the radio button is checked by using the `checked` property.

*Listing 7.432   Example of the `checked` Property*

```
<html>
<head>
<title> Example of the radio checked property</title>
</head>
<body>

<script language="JavaScript">
<!-- Hide

// function looks to see if button 1 is checked and displays
// an appropriate alert message.
function checkButton(){
if(document.form1.button1.checked == true){
    alert("Box1 is checked");
}
else if(document.form1.button2.checked == true){
    alert("Box 2 is checked");
}
}
// End Hide --->
</script>

<form name="form1">
<input type="radio" name=button1>Box 1
<br>
<input type="radio" name=button2 CHECKED>Box 2
<br>
< INPUT type="button" value="Get Checked" onClick='checkButton()'>
</form>

</body>
</html>
```

# Radio.click()

*JavaScript 1.0+, JScript 1.0+*

*Nav2+, IE 3+, Opera3+*

## Syntax

`radio.click()`

## Description

The `click()` property of the `Radio` object is used to simulate a mouse click on the radio button.

## Example

Listing 7.433 shows an example of how the `click()` property is used.

*Listing 7.433   Example of the `click()` Property*

```
<html>
<head>
<title> Example of the radio click property</title>
</head>
<body>

By pressing the "Simulate Click" button below,  box 2 becomes checked
because a simulated mouse click is performed.
<form name="form1">
<input type="radio" name=button1 CHECKED>Box 1
<br>
<input type="radio" name=button2>Box 2
<br>
<input type="button" value="Simulate Click"
onClick='document.form1.button2.click()'>
</form>

</body>
</html>
```

# Radio.defaultChecked

*JavaScript 1.0+, Jscript 1.0+*

*Nav2+, IE 3+, Opera3+*

## Syntax

`radio.defaultChecked`

## Description

The `defaultChecked` property of the `Radio` object is a Boolean value that reports which radio buttons contain the HTML CHECKED attribute. If the CHECKED attribute is contained in the `Radio` object, `true` is returned. Otherwise, `false` is returned.

## Example

Listing 7.434 shows how the `defaultChecked` property is used to find out which box is checked by default.

*Listing 7.434   Example of the* `defaultChecked` *Property*

```
<html>
<head>
<title> Example of the radio defaultChecked property</title>
</head>
<body>

<script language="JavaScript">
<!-- Hide
function checkBox(){
if(document.form1.button1.defaultChecked == true){
    alert("Box1 is checked by default");
}
else if(document.form1.button2.defaultChecked == true){
    alert("Box 2 is checked by default");
}
}
// End Hide --->
</script>

<form name="form1">
<input type="radio" name=button1>Box 1
<br>
<input type="radio" name=button2 CHECKED>Box 2
<br><br>
<input type="button" value="Get Default" onClick='checkBox()'>
</form>

</body>
</html>
```

# Radio.focus()

## JavaScript 1.0+, JScript 1.0+

## Nav2+, IE 3+, Opera3+

## Syntax

`radio.focus()`

## Description

The `focus()` method of the `Radio` object sets the focus to the radio button.

## Example

Listing 7.435 shows how the `focus()` method is used.

*Listing 7.435    Example of the* `focus()` *Method*

```
<html>
<head>
<title> Example of the radio focus method</title>
</head>
<body>

<form name="form1">
<input type="radio" name=button1>Box 1
<br>
<input type="radio" name=button2>Box 2
<br><br>
<input type="button" value="Set Focus to Box 1"
onClick='document.form1.button1.focus()'>
</form>

</body>
</html>
```

# Radio.form

## JavaScript 1.0+, JScript 1.0+

## Nav2+, IE 3+, Opera3+

## Syntax

`radio.form`

## Description

The `form` property of the `Radio` object is used to reference the `Form` object that contains the `Radio` box.

## Example

Listing 7.436 shows an example of how the `form` property can be used to get the name of the form that contains the `Radio` object.

*Listing 7.436    Example of the* `form` *Property*

```
<html>
<head>
<title> Example of the radio form property</title>
</head>
<body>

<form name="form1">
<input type="radio" name=button1>Box 1
<br>
<input type="radio" name=button2>Box 2
```

*continues*

*Listing 7.436   continued*

```
<br><br>
<input type="button" value="Get Form Name"
  onClick='alert("The form name is: " + document.form1.button1.form.name)'>
</form>

</body>
</html>
```

# Radio.handleEvent()

## JavaScript 1.0+, JScript 1.0+

## Nav2+, IE 3+, Opera3+

## Syntax

`radio.handleEvent(event)`

## Description

The handleEvent() method of the Radio object invokes the event handler for the specific event.

## Example

Listing 7.437 shows how the handleEvent() method is used to capture all CLICK events and pass them to the but1 object event handler.

*Listing 7.437   Using the handleEvent() Method*

```
<html>
<head>
<title> Example of the radio handleEvent method</title>
</head>
<body>

<script language="JavaScript">
<!-- Hide
// sets up the document to capture CLICK events
document.captureEvents(Event.CLICK);

// function that handles the specific event. The evnt parameter refers to
// the event object.
function handleClick(evnt){
    window.document.but1.handleEvent(evnt);
}

function showMsg(){
    alert("Button clicked.");
}

// This registers the handle function as the event handler for the
// CLICK event.
```

```
document.onClick = handleClick;
// End Hide --->
</script>

<form name="form1">
<input type="radio" name="but1" onClick='showMsg()'>Choice 1
<br>
<input type="radio" name="but1" onClick='showMsg()'>Choice 2
<br>
</form>

</body>
</html>
```

# Radio.name

## *JavaScript 1.0+, JScript 1.0+*

## *Nav2+, IE 3+, Opera3+*

### Syntax

*radio*.name

### Description

The name property of the Radio object represents the NAME attribute of the HTML <input> tag that creates the Radio button. This allows you to reference a Radio object directly by name.

### Example

Listing 7.438 shows how the name of the radio button is used to access its properties.

*Listing 7.438    Accessing Radio Button by Name*
```
<html>
<head>
<title> Example of the radio name property</title>
</head>
<body>

<form name="form1">
<input type="radio" name=myButton>Box 1
<br><br>
<input type="button" value="Get Name"
➥onClick='alert("The name of the button is: " +
document.form1.myButton.name)'>

</form>

</body>
</html>
```

# Radio.onBlur

## JavaScript 1.0+, JScript 1.0+

## Nav2+, IE 3+, Opera3+

## Syntax

onBlur="*command*"

## Description

The onBlur property is an event handler for the Radio object that notifies you when the focus is removed from a radio button.

## Example

Listing 7.439 shows how the onBlur event handler is used to detect when the focus is removed from the specified radio button.

*Listing 7.439    Example of the* onBlur *Event Handler*

```
<html>
<head>
<title> Example of the Radio onBlur event handler</title>
</head>
<body>

<script language="JavaScript">
<!--Hide
function showChange(){
    document.form1.text1.value = "Focus removed from Radio Button";
}
// End Hide --->
</script>


<form name="form1">
Click the radio button first, then click in the text area.
<br><br>
<input type="radio" name=button1 onBlur='showChange()'>Box 1
<br>
Click the text box
<input type="text" name="text1" size=40>
<br>
</form>

</body>
</html>
```

# Radio.onClick

## *JavaScript 1.0+, JScript 1.0+*

## *Nav2+, IE 3+, Opera3+*

## Syntax

```
onClick="command"
```

## Description

The onClick property of the Radio object is an event handler that notifies you when the mouse has been clicked on the button.

## Example

Listing 7.440 uses the onClick event handler to check for a mouse click event.

*Listing 7.440   Example of the* onClick *Event Handler*
```
<html>
<head>
<title> Example of the radio onClick event handler</title>
</head>
<body>

<form name="form1">
<input type="radio" name=button1
➥onClick='alert("mouse was clicked on this object")'>Box 1
<br>
</form>

</body>
</html>
```

# Radio.onFocus()

## *JavaScript 1.0+, JScript 1.0+*

## *Nav2+, IE 3+, Opera3+*

## Syntax

```
onFocus="command"
```

## Description

The onFocus event handler of the Radio object is an event handler that notifies you when the focus is set on the radio button.

## Example

In Listing 7.441, the onFocus event handler notifies the user with a text message when the focus is set on the radio button.

*Listing 7.441   Example of the* onFocus *Event Handler*

```
<html>
<head>
<title> Example of the radio onFocus event handler</title>
</head>
<body>

<script language="JavaScript">
<!--Hide

// function sets the focus to box 1
function showFocus(){
    document.form1.text1.value = "Focus set on Box 1";
}
// End Hide --->
</script>

<form name="form1">
Click on the radio button
<br><br>
<input type="radio" name=button1 onFocus='showFocus()'>Box 1
<br><br>
<input type="text" name="text1" size=40>
</form>

</body>
</html>
```

# Radio.type

## *JavaScript 1.0+, JScript 1.0+*

## *Nav2+, IE 3+, Opera3+*

## Syntax

*radio*.type

## Description

The type property of the Radio button represents the button's TYPE HTML attribute. For this object, it is always radio.

## Example

Listing 7.442 shows an example of the type property.

*Listing 7.442   Example of the* type *Property*

```
<html>
<head>
<title> Example of the radio type property</title>
</head>
<body>
```

```
<form name="form1">
<input type="radio" name=button1>Box 1
<br><br>
<input type="button" value="Get Button Type"
onClick='alert("The button type is: " + document.form1.button1.type)'>
</form>

</body>
</html>
```

# Radio.value

## *JavaScript 1.0+, JScript 1.0+*

## *Nav2+, IE 3+, Opera3+*

## *Syntax*

```
radio.value
```

## *Description*

The value property of the Radio object represents the VALUE attribute of the HTML
<input> tag used to create the radio button.

## *Example*

Listing 7.443 shows how to access the value property.

*Listing 7.443    Example of the* value *Property*
```
<html>
<head>
<title> Example of the radio value property</title>
</head>
<body>

<form name="form1">
<input type="radio" name=button1 value=1>Box 1
<br><br>
<input type="button" value="Get Button Value"
onClick='alert("The button value is: " + document.form1.button1.value)'>
</form>

</body>
</html>
```

# Reset

## *JavaScript 1.2+, JScript 1.0+*

## *Nav4+, IE 3+*

## Syntax

Core client-side JavaScript object.

## Description

The Reset object represents a Reset button within an HTML form. The button is created using the HTML <input> tag and specifying the TYPE attribute as reset. Reset buttons are used for form submissions. The Reset object has specific properties and methods associated with it, as shown in Table 7.41.

**Table 7.41    Properties and Methods of the Reset Object**

| Property/Method | Description |
| --- | --- |
| blur() | Removes focus from Reset button |
| click() | Simulates a mouse click on a Reset button |
| focus() | Sets the focus to the Reset button |
| form | Specifies the form name that contains the Reset button |
| handleEvent() | Invokes the event handler |
| name | HTML NAME attribute for the Reset button |
| onBlur | Event handler for Blur event |
| onClick | Event handler for Click event |
| onFocus | Event handler for Focus event |
| type | HTML TYPE attribute for the Reset button |
| value | HTML VALUE attribute for the Reset button |

## Example

Listing 7.444 shows the syntax for using the Reset object.

*Listing 7.444    Example of the Reset Object*

```
<html>
<head>
<title> Example of the reset object</title>
</head>
<body>

<form name="form1">
Click the Reset button to reset the form.
<br><br><br>
Enter Name: <input type="text" Name="name" Size=15>
<br>
Enter Phone: <input type="text" Name="phone" Size=10>
<br><br>
<input type="reset" name=resetbutton value=Reset>
<br>
<br>
</form>

</body>
</html>
```

# Reset.blur()

## *JavaScript 1.0+, JScript 1.0+*

## *Nav2+, IE 3+, Opera3+*

## *Syntax*

```
reset.blur()
```

## *Description*

The blur() method of the Reset object is used to remove the focus from the Reset button.

## *Example*

Listing 7.445 shows an example of how the blur() method is used.

*Listing 7.445   Example of the* blur() *Method*

```
<html>
<head>
<title> Example of the reset blur method</title>
</head>
<body>

<script language="JavaScript">
<!-- Hide

// displays a message when focus is removed from the reset button
function showMsg(){
     document.form1.msg.value="Focus removed from the Reset button.";
}
// End Hide --->
</script>

<form name="form1">
Enter Name: <input type="text" Name="name" Size=15>
<br>
Enter Phone: <input type="text" Name="phone" Size=10>
<br>
Message: <input type="text" Name="msg" Size=40>
<br>
<input type="reset" name=resetbutton value=Reset onBlur='showMsg()'>
<br>
<br>
</form>

</body>
</html>
```

# Reset.click()

## *JavaScript 1.0+, JScript 1.0+*

## *Nav2+, IE 3+, Opera3+*

## *Syntax*

```
reset.click()
```

## *Description*

The click method of the Reset object is used to simulate a mouse click on the Reset button.

## *Example*

Listing 7.446 shows how the click() method is used.

*Listing 7.446    Example of the* click() *Method*

```
<html>
<head>
<title> Example of the reset click method</title>
</head>
<body>

<script language="JavaScript">
<!-- Hide
function clickReset(){
    document.form1.resetbutton.click();
}

function inform(){
    alert("The reset button was clicked");
 }
// End Hide --->
</script>

<form name="form1">
Enter Name: <input type="text" Name="name" Size=15>
<br>
Enter Phone: <input type="text" Name="phone" Size=10>
<br><br>
<input type="reset" name=resetbutton value=Reset onClick='inform()'>
<br>
<br>
<input type="button" value="Simulate Click" onClick='clickReset()'>
</form>

</body>
</html>
```

# Reset.focus()

## *JavaScript 1.1+, JScript 1.0+*

## *Nav3+, IE 3+, Opera3+*

## Syntax

`reset.focus()`

## Description

The focus() method of the Reset object is used to set the focus to the Reset button.

## Example

Listing 7.447 shows an example of how the focus() method is used.

*Listing 7.447   Accessing the focus() Method*

```
<html>
<head>
<title> Example of the reset focus method</title>
</head>
<body>

<script language="JavaScript">
<!-- Hide
function focusReset(){
     document.form1.resetbutton.focus();
}
// End Hide --->
</script>

<form name="form1">
Enter Name: <input type="text" Name="name" Size=15>
<br>
Enter Phone: <input type="text" Name="phone" Size=10>
<br><br>
<input type="reset" name=resetbutton value=Reset>
<br>
<br>
<input type="button" value="Set Focus to Reset" onClick='focusReset()'>
<br>
</form>

</body>
</html>
```

# Reset.form

## *JavaScript 1.0+, JScript 1.0+*

## Nav2+, IE 3+, Opera3+

### Syntax

`reset.form`

### Description

The `form` property of the `Reset` object is used to obtain the name of the form that contains the Reset button.

### Example

Listing 7.448 shows an example of how to get the form name.

*Listing 7.448    Example of Using the `form` Property*

```
<html>
<head>
<title> Example of the reset form property</title>
</head>
<body>

<form name="form1">
Enter Name: <input type="text" Name="name" Size=15>
<br>
Enter Phone: <input type="text" Name="phone" Size=10>
<br><br>
<input type="reset" name=resetbutton value=Reset
onClick='alert("The form name is: " + document.form1.resetbutton.form.name)'>
<br>
<br>
</form>

</body>
</html>
```

# Reset.handleEvent()

## JavaScript 1.0+, JScript 1.0+

## Nav2+, IE 3+, Opera3+

### Syntax

`reset.handleEvent(event)`

### Description

The `handleEvent()` method of the `Reset` object invokes the event handler for the object.

### Example

Listing 7.449 shows an example of how the `handleEvent()` method is used.

*Listing 7.449    Example of the* `handleEvent()` *Method*

```
<html>
<head>
<title> Example of the reset handleEvent method</title>
</head>
<body>

<script language="JavaScript">
<!-- Hide
// sets up the document to capture CLICK events
document.captureEvents(Event.CLICK);

// function that handles the specific event. The evnt parameter refers to
// the event object.
function handleMyClick(evnt){
    window.document.resetbutton.handleEvent(evnt);
}

function showMsg(){
    alert("Form has been reset");
}

// This registers the handle function as the event handler for the
// CLICK event.
document.onClick = handleMyClick;
// End Hide --->
</script>

<form name="form1">
Enter Name: <input type="text" Name="name" Size=15>
<br>
Enter Phone: <input type="text" Name="phone" Size=10>
<br><br>
<input type="reset" name=resetbutton value="Reset" onClick='showMsg()'>
<br>
<br>
</form>

</body>
</html>
```

# Reset.name

## *JavaScript 1.0+, JScript 1.0+*

## *Nav2+, IE 3+, Opera3+*

## *Syntax*

*reset.name*

## Description

The name property of the Reset object represents the name given to a Reset button as specified from the NAME attribute of the HTML <input type="reset"> tag.

## Example

In Listing 7.450, the name property is used to inform the user of the active frame.

*Listing 7.450    Example of the* name *Property*

```
<html>
<head>
<title> Example of the reset name property</title>
</head>
<body>

<form name="form1">
Enter Name: <input type="text" Name="name" Size=15>
<br>
Enter Phone: <input type="text" Name="phone" Size=10>
<br><br>
<input type="reset" name=resetbutton value=Reset
onClick='alert("The reset button name is: " +
➥document.form1.resetbutton.name)'>
<br>
<br>
</form>

</body>
</html>
```

# Reset.onBlur

## *JavaScript 1.1+, JScript 1.0+*

## *Nav3+, IE 3+, Opera3+*

## Syntax

onBlur="*command*"

## Description

The onBlur event handler for the Reset object is an event handler that specifies when the focus has been removed from the Reset button.

## Example

In Listing 7.451, the onBlur event handler is used.

*Listing 7.451    Using the* onBlur *Event Handler*

```
<html>
<head>
<title> Example of the reset onBlur event handler</title>
```

```
</head>
<body>

<script language="JavaScript">
<!-- Hide
function setMsg(){
     document.form1.text1.value = "Focus was removed from the reset object";
}
// End Hide --->
</script>

<form name="form1">
Click the reset button and then click in a text area.
<br><br>
Enter Name: <input type="text" Name="name" Size=15>
<br>
Enter Phone: <input type="text" Name="phone" Size=10>
<br><br>
Message: <input type="text" name="text1" size=45>
<br><br>
<input type="reset" name=resetbutton value=Reset onBlur='setMsg()'>
<br>
<br>
</form>

</body>
</html>
```

# Reset.onClick

## *JavaScript 1.1+, JScript 1.0+*

## *Nav3+, IE 3+, Opera3+*

## Syntax

```
onClick="command"
```

## Description

The onClick property is an event handler used to handle the event of a mouse click on the Reset button.

## Example

Listing 7.452 shows an example of how the onClick event handler is used.

*Listing 7.452    Example of the* onClick *Event Handler*

```
<html>
<head>
<title> Example of the reset onClick event handler</title>
```

*continues*

*Listing 7.452    continued*

```
</head>
<body>

<form name="form1">
Enter Name: <input type="text" Name="name" Size=15>
<br>
Enter Phone: <input type="text" Name="phone" Size=10>
<br><br>
<input type="reset" name=resetbutton value=Reset
➥onClick='alert("The reset button was clicked")'>
<br>
<br>
</form>

</body>
</html>
```

# Reset.onFocus

## JavaScript 1.2+, ECMAScript 1.0+, JScript 1.0+

## Nav4+, IE 3+

### Syntax

onFocus="*command*"

### Description

The onFocus event handler is used to specify when the focus is set on the Reset button.

### Example

Listing 7.453 shows the onFocus event handler being used to inform the user when the focus is set.

*Listing 7.453    Example of the* onFocus *Event Handler*

```
<html>
<head>
<title> Example of the reset onFocus event handler</title>
</head>
<body>

<script language="JavaScript">
<!-- Hide
function setMsg(){
     document.form2.text1.value = "Focus is set on the reset button.";
}
// End Hide --->
</script>

<form name="form1">
```

```
Click the reset button.
<br><br>
Enter Name: <input type="text" Name="name" Size=15>
<br>
Enter Phone: <input type="text" Name="phone" Size=10>
<br><br>
<input type="reset" name=resetbutton value=Reset onFocus='setMsg()'>
<br>
</form>

<form name="form2">
<br><br>
Message: <input type="text" name="text1" size=45>
</form>

</body>
</html>
```

# Reset.type

## *JavaScript 1.2+, ECMAScript 1.0+*

## *Nav4+*

## *Syntax*

`reset.type`

## Description

The `type` property of the `Reset` object represents the HTML `TYPE` attribute of the Reset button. In the case of a Reset button, this will always be `reset`.

## Example

Listing 7.454 shows how to get the Reset button type.

*Listing 7.454    Example of the* type *Property*

```
<html>
<head>
<title> Example of the reset type property</title>
</head>
<body>

<form name="form1">
Enter Name: <input type="text" Name="name" Size=15>
<br>
Enter Phone: <input type="text" Name="phone" Size=10>
<br><br>
<input type="reset" name=resetbutton value=Reset
```

*continues*

*Listing 7.454    continued*
```
onClick='alert("The button type is: " + document.form1.resetbutton.type)'>
<br>
<br>
</form>

</body>
</html>
```

# Reset.value

## *JavaScript 1.0+, JScript 1.0+*

## *Nav2+, IE 3+, Opera3+*

## *Syntax*

```
reset.value
```

## *Description*

The value property of the Reset object represents the HTML VALUE attribute of the Reset button.

## *Example*

Listing 7.455 shows how the Reset button value can be accessed.

*Listing 7.455    Example of the* value *Property*
```
<html>
<head>
<title> Example of the reset value property</title>
</head>
<body>

<form name="form1">
Enter Name: <input type="text" Name="name" Size=15>
<br>
Enter Phone: <input type="text" Name="phone" Size=10>
<br><br>
<input type="reset" name=resetbutton value=Reset
onClick='alert("The button value is: " + document.form1.resetbutton.value)'>
<br>
<br>
</form>

</body>
</html>
```

# screen

## *JavaScript 1.2+, JScript 3+*

## *Nav4+, IE4+*

## *Syntax*

Core client-side JavaScript object.

## *Description*

The screen object provides a programmer with access to various properties of the user's screen. These properties are often accessed and used sizing windows that various scripts open. Table 7.42 shows the properties of the screen object.

*Table 7.42    Properties of the screen Object*

| Item | Description |
| --- | --- |
| availHeight | Accesses the pixel height of the user's screen, minus the toolbar or any other "permanent" objects. |
| availWidth | Accesses the pixel width of the user's screen, minus the toolbar or any other "permanent" objects. |
| colorDepth | Accesses the maximum number of colors the user's screen can display. This is in bit format. |
| height | Accesses the pixel height of the user's screen. |
| pixelDepth | Accesses the number of bits per pixel of the user's screen. Internet Explorer did not support this property at the time of this writing and returns undefined. |
| width | Accesses the pixel width of the user's screen. |

## *Example*

Listing 7.456 has a button that, when clicked, opens a secondary window that displays all the properties of the screen object. Figure 7.8 shows the results of running this script.

*Listing 7.456    Displaying the Properties of the screen Object*

```
<html>
<head>
<script language="JavaScript1.2">
<!-- Hide

// Define the openWin function called by pressing the button
function openWin(){

  // Open a window to store the results
  var myWin = open("", "","width=450,height=200");
```

*continues*

*Listing 7.456    continued*

```
// Write the screen properties to the window
myWin.document.write("The availHeight is: " + screen.availHeight + "<br>");
myWin.document.write("The availWidth is: " + screen.availWidth + "<br>");
myWin.document.write("The colorDepth is: " + screen.colorDepth + "<br>");
myWin.document.write("The height is: " + screen.height + "<br>");
myWin.document.write("The pixelDepth is: " + screen.pixelDepth + "<br>");
myWin.document.write("The width is: " + screen.width + "<br>");

// Close the stream to the window
myWin.document.close();
}
// End hide --->
</script>
</head>
<body>
<form name="myForm">
  <input type=BUTTON value="Click to See Screen Properties" name="myButton"
onClick="openWin()">
</form>
</body>
</html>
```

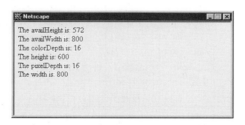

**Figure 7.8**

*Results of running Listing 7.456 in a browser and clicking the Click to See Screen Properties button.*

# screen.availHeight

## *JavaScript 1.2+, JScript 3+*

## *Nav4+, IE4+*

## Syntax

```
screen.availHeight
```

## Description

The availHeight property of the screen object accesses the available pixel height of the user's screen. This height is minus any toolbar or any other "permanent" objects that may be on the user's screen.

## Example

Listing 7.457 displays the available height of the user's screen to the page.

*Listing 7.457    Accessing the* `availHeight` *Property of the* `screen` *Object*

```
<script language="JavaScript1.2">
<!-- Hide

document.write("The available height of this user's screen is <b>");
document.write(screen.availHeight + '</b> pixels');

// End hide --->
</script>
```

# screen.availWidth

## *JavaScript 1.2+, JScript 3+*

## *Nav4+, IE4+*

## Syntax

```
screen.availWidth
```

## Description

The `availWidth` property of the `screen` object accesses the available pixel width of the user's screen. This width is minus any toolbar or any other "permanent" objects that may be on the user's screen.

## Example

Listing 7.458 displays the available width of the user's screen to the page.

*Listing 7.458    Accessing the* `availWidth` *Property of the* `screen` *Object*

```
<script language="JavaScript1.2">
<!-- Hide

document.write("The available width of this user's screen is <b>");
document.write(screen.availWidth + '</b> pixels');

// End hide --->
</script>
```

# screen.colorDepth

## *JavaScript 1.2+, JScript 3+*

## *Nav4+, IE4+*

## Syntax

```
screen.colorDepth
```

## Description

The `colorDepth` property of the `screen` object accesses the maximum number of colors the user's screen can display. The returned value is in terms of bits.

## Example

Listing 7.459 displays the color depth of the user's screen to the page.

*Listing 7.459   Accessing the `colorDepth` Property of the `screen` Object*

```
<script language="JavaScript1.2">
<!-- Hide

document.write("The color depth of this user's screen is <b>");
document.write(screen.colorDepth + '</b> bit');

// End hide --->
</script>
```

# screen.height

## JavaScript 1.2+, JScript 3+

## Nav4+, IE4+

## Syntax

```
screen.height
```

## Description

The `height` property of the `screen` object accesses the height of the user's screen in pixels.

## Example

Listing 7.460 displays the height of the user's screen to the page.

*Listing 7.460   Accessing the `height` Property of the `screen` Object*

```
<script language="JavaScript1.2">
<!-- Hide

document.write("The height of this user's screen is <b>");
document.write(screen.height + '</b> pixels');

// End hide --->
</script>
```

# screen.pixelDepth

## JavaScript 1.2+

## Nav4+

## Syntax

```
screen.pixelDepth
```

## Description

The `pixelDepth` property of the `screen` object accesses the number of bits per pixel of the user's screen.

## Example

Listing 7.461 displays the pixel depth of the user's screen to the page.

*Listing 7.461   Accessing the `pixelDepth` Property of the `screen` Object*
```
<script language="JavaScript1.2">
<!-- Hide

document.write("The pixel depth of this user's screen is <b>");
document.write(screen.pixelDepth + '</b> bit');

// End hide --->
</script>
```

# screen.width

## JavaScript 1.2+, JScript 3+

## Nav4+, IE4+

## Syntax

```
screen.width
```

## Description

The `width` property of the `screen` object accesses the width of the user's screen in pixels.

## Example

Listing 7.462 displays the width of the user's screen to the page.

*Listing 7.462   Accessing the `width` Property of the `screen` Object*
```
<script language="JavaScript1.2">
<!-- Hide

document.write("The width of this user's screen is <b>");
document.write(screen.width  + '</b> pixels');

// End hide --->
</script>
```

# Select

## JavaScript1.0+, JScript1.0+

## Nav2+, IE3+, Opera3+

## Syntax

Core client-side JavaScript object.

## Description

The Select object is one of the core JavaScript objects. Instances are created by the browser when it encounters an HTML <select> tag. In the JavaScript object hierarchy, the Select object is located at window.document.Form.Select. Table 7.43 lists the properties, methods, and event handlers used by the Select object.

**Table 7.43  Event Handlers, Methods, and Properties Used by the Select Object**

| Type | Item | Description |
| --- | --- | --- |
| Event Handlers | onBlur | Executes code when the select box loses the focus. |
| | onChange | Executes code when the select box loses the focus and has had its value modified. |
| | onFocus | Executes code when the select box receives the focus. |
| Methods | blur() | Removes the focus from the select box. |
| | focus() | Gives the focus to the select box. |
| | handleEvent() | Invokes the handler for the event specified and was added in JavaScript 1.2. |
| Properties | form | Returns the entire form the select box is in. |
| | length | Returns the number of options in the select box. |
| | name | Returns the name of this select box specified by the NAME attribute. |
| | options | Returns an array containing each of the items in the select box. These items are created using the <option> HTML tag. There is also a length and selectedIndex subproperty of this property. |
| | selectedIndex | Returns an integer specifying the indexed location of the selected option in the select box. |
| | type | Returns the type of this select box specified by the TYPE attribute. For <select> instances that contain the multiple attribute, this property returns select-multiple. Instances without this attribute return select-one. Note that this property was added in JavaScript 1.1. |

## Example

Listing 7.463 displays the use of the Select properties. It contains a select box and a button. When the button is clicked, a second window, as shown in Figure 7.9, is opened. The values of the properties of this Select object are displayed in this window.

*Listing 7.463    Displaying the Properties of an Instance of a* Select *Object*

```
<html>
<head>
<script language="JavaScript">
<!-- Hide

// Define the openWin function called by pressing the button
function openWin(){

  // Place the reference to the select box in a variable for easier access
  var myInstance = document.myForm.mySelect;

  // Open a window to store the results
  var myWin = open("", "","width=450,height=200");

  // Write the select box's properties to the window
  myWin.document.write("The length is: " + myInstance.length + "<br>");
  myWin.document.write("The name is: " + myInstance.name + "<br>");
  myWin.document.write("The selected option is located at position: ");
  myWin.document.write(myInstance.selectedIndex + "<br>");
  myWin.document.write("The type is: " + myInstance.type + "<br>");

  // Note that the entire form object is passed with this property.
  // This allows you to then drill down and get the value of other
  // components in the form.
  myWin.document.write("The form can be used to grab ");
  myWin.document.write("the value of the button: ");
  myWin.document.write(myInstance.form.myButton.value);

  // Close the stream to the window
  myWin.document.close();
}
// End hide --->
</script>
</head>
<body>
<form name="myForm">My Favorite Sport is:
  <select name="mySelect">
    <option value=BASE>Baseball</option>
    <option value=FOOT>Football</option>
    <option value=BASKET>Basketball</option>
    <option value=SOCCER>Soccer</option>
  </select>
```

*continues*

*Listing 7.463    continued*
```
<input type=BUTTON value="Click to Process" name="myButton"
       onClick="openWin()">
</form>
</body>
</html>
```

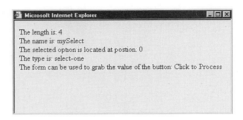

**Figure 7.9**

*Results of running Listing 7.463 in a browser and clicking the Click to Process button.*

# Select.blur()

## *JavaScript1.0+, JScript1.0+*

## *Nav2+, IE3+, Opera3+*

## *Syntax*
```
select.blur()
```

## *Description*

The `blur()` method of the `Select` object removes focus from the select box. Note that this does not mean that the selected option is unselected, but rather, the focus on this option and the select box as a whole are removed. Be careful when using this method in conjunction with the `Select.focus()` method. It can lead to a focus/blur loop, where the browser blurs a focus as soon as it is done, and vice versa.

## *Example*

Listing 7.464 has a multiple select box and a button. If the user selects any of the options in the box and then clicks the Click Here to Remove Focus button, the option and entire select box will no longer have focus.

*Listing 7.464    Using the `blur()` Method to Remove Focus from the Select Box*
```
<html>
<head>
<script language="JavaScript">
<!-- Hide

// Define the removeFocus function called by pressing the button
function removeFocus(){
```

```
  // Remove focus from the select box.
  document.myForm.mySelect.blur();
}
// End hide --->
</script>
</head>
<body>
<p>
<form name="myForm">
  <select name="mySelect" multiple>
    <option value=BASE>Baseball</option>
    <option value=FOOT>Football</option>
    <option value=BASKET>Basketball</option>
    <option value=SOCCER>Soccer</option>
  </select>
  <input type=BUTTON value="Click to Remove Focus" name="myButton"
       onClick="removeFocus()">
</form>
</body>
</html>
```

# Select.focus()

## *JavaScript1.0+, JScript1.0+*

## *Nav2+, IE3+, Opera3+*

## *Syntax*

```
select.focus()
```

## *Description*

The focus() method of the Select object gives the focus to the select box. Be careful when using this method in conjunction with the Select.blur() method. It can lead to a focus/blur loop, where the browser blurs a focus as soon as it is done, and vice versa.

## *Example*

Listing 7.465 has two text boxes and two buttons. If the user clicks the first button, the cursor is set inside the first text box. If the user clicks the second text box, the cursor is set inside the second text box.

*Listing 7.465   Using the* focus() *Method to Place the Cursor in the Desired Select Box*

```
<html>
<head>
<script language="JavaScript">
<!-- Hide
```

*continues*

*Listing 7.465    continued*

```
// Define the setFocus function called by pressing the button
function setFocus(num){

  // Determine which button was clicked and set the cursor
  // in the appropriate select box.
  if(num == 1){
    document.myForm.mySelect1.focus();
  }else if(num == 2){
    document.myForm.mySelect2.focus();
  }
}
// End hide --->
</script>
</head>
<body>
<p>
<form name="myForm">
  <select name="mySelect1" multiple>
    <option value=BASE>Baseball</option>
    <option value=FOOT>Football</option>
    <option value=BASKET>Basketball</option>
    <option value=SOCCER>Soccer</option>
  </select>
  <input type=BUTTON value="Click to Set Cursor" name="myButton1"
         onClick="setFocus(1)">
  <br>
  <select name="mySelect2" multiple>
    <option value=HOCK>Hockey</option>
    <option value=RUG>Rugby</option>
    <option value=GOLF>Golf</option>
    <option value=TENNIS>Tennis</option>
  </select>
  <input type=BUTTON value="Click to Set Cursor" name="myButton2"
         onClick="setFocus(2)">
</form>
</body>
</html>
```

# Select.form

## *JavaScript1.0+, JScript1.0+*

## *Nav2+, IE3+, Opera3+*

## Syntax

`select.form`

## Description

The form property of an instance of a Select object holds all the data of the form in which the select box is contained. This allows a developer to obtain specific information about the form in which the select box is located.

## Example

Listing 7.466 has a select box and a button. When the button is clicked, three properties of the form as a whole are displayed. These properties were referenced through the form property of the select box.

*Listing 7.466   Accessing a Form Via the* form *Property of an Instance of a* Select *Object*

```
<html>
<head>
<script language="JavaScript">
<!-- Hide

// Define the openWin function called by pressing the button
function openWin(){

  // Place the reference to the form property of select box
  // in a variable for easier access
  var formData = document.myForm.mySelect.form;

  // Open a window to display the results
  var myWin = open("", "","width=450,height=200");

  // Write the form properties accessed through the form
  // property to the window
  myWin.document.write("The name of the form is: " + formData.name + "<br>");
  myWin.document.write("The selectedIndex of the option is: ");
  myWin.document.write(formData.mySelect.selectedIndex + "<br>");
  myWin.document.write("The name of the button is: ");
  myWin.document.write(formData.elements[1].name + "<br>");

  // Close the stream to the window
  myWin.document.close();
}
// End hide --->
</script>
</head>
<body>
<form name="myForm">
  <select name="mySelect" multiple>
    <option value=BASE>Baseball</option>
    <option value=FOOT>Football</option>
    <option value=BASKET>Basketball</option>
```

*continues*

*Listing 7.466    continued*
```
    <option value=SOCCER>Soccer</option>
  </select>
<input type=BUTTON value="Click to Process" name="myButton"
       onClick="openWin()">
</form>
</body>
</html>
```

# Select.handleEvent()

## *JavaScript1.2+, JScript3.0+*

## *Nav4+, IE4+*

## *Syntax*
```
select.handleEvent(event)
```

## *Description*
The handleEvent() method of the Select object invokes the handler for the event specified. This method was added in JavaScript 1.2.

## *Example*
Listing 7.467 has a single select box. The script tells the browser that it wants to intercept all Click events and that it wants the myClickHandler function to handle them. Within this function, the handleEvent() method of the select box has been specified to handle the click.

When the user clicks anywhere on the page, the onClick event handler in the <select> tag calls a function to change the selection in a select box. The change increments through the four options in the box.

*Listing 7.467    Using the handleEvent() Method of a Select Object to Handle all Clicks on a Page*
```
<html>
<head>
<script language="JavaScript1.2">
<!-- Hide

// Define a click counter variable
var counter = 0;

// Tell the browser you want to intercept ALL click events
// on the page. Then define a function to handle them.
window.captureEvents(Event.CLICK)
window.onClick = myClickHandler;

// Define the myClickHandler function to handle click events
function myClickHandler{
```

```
  // Pass all click events to the onClick event of the select box
  window.document.myForm.mySelect.handleEvent;

}

// Function is called by onClick of select box.
function changeSelect(){
  if(counter > 3){
    counter = 0;
    document.myForm.mySelect.selectedIndex = counter;
  }else{
    document.myForm.mySelect.selectedIndex = counter++;
  }
}
// End hide --->
</script>
</head>
<body>
<form name="myForm">
  <select name="mySelect" onClick='changeSelect()'>
    <option value=BASE>Baseball</option>
    <option value=FOOT>Football</option>
    <option value=BASKET>Basketball</option>
    <option value=SOCCER>Soccer</option>
  </select>
</form>
</body>
</html>
```

# Select.length

## *JavaScript1.0+, JScript1.0+*

## *Nav2+, IE3+, Opera3+*

### Syntax

*select*.length

### Description

The length property of an instance of a Select object returns the number of items in the select box.

### Example

Listing 7.468 has a single select box and button. The length property of a Select object is displayed in an alert box when the button is clicked.

*Listing 7.468    Using the* `length` *Property to Retrieve the Name of a Select Box*

```html
<html>
<head>
<script language="JavaScript">
<!-- Hide

// Display an alert box that contains the length of the
// select box.
function getName(){
  alert("The length of this select box is " +
        document.myForm.mySelect.length);
}
// End hide --->
</script>
</head>
<body>
<form name="myForm">
  <select name="mySelect">
    <option value=BASE>Baseball</option>
    <option value=FOOT>Football</option>
    <option value=BASKET>Basketball</option>
    <option value=SOCCER>Soccer</option>
  </select>
  <input type=BUTTON value="Get Name" name="myButton" onClick='getName()'>
</form>
</body>
</html>
```

# Select.name

## *JavaScript1.0+, JScript1.0+*

## *Nav2+, IE3+, Opera3+*

## *Syntax*

`select.name`

## *Description*

The name property of an instance of a `Select` object returns the name of the select box. This property is often accessed via the `elements` array of a `Form` object and used to return the name of the select area. It is most useful when there are many forms on a given page, and determining the name helps you determine what function you want to perform.

## *Example*

Listing 7.469 has a single select box and button. The `elements` array of a `Form` object is used to retrieve the name and display it in an alert box.

*Listing 7.469    Using the* name *Property to Retrieve the Name of a Select Box*

```
<html>
<head>
<script language="JavaScript">
<!-- Hide

// Display an alert box that contains the name of the
// select box.
function getName(){
  alert("The name of this select box is " +
        document.myForm.elements[0].name);
}
// End hide --->
</script>
</head>
<body>
<form name="myForm">
  <select name="mySelect" multiple>
    <option value=BASE>Baseball</option>
    <option value=FOOT>Football</option>
    <option value=BASKET>Basketball</option>
    <option value=SOCCER>Soccer</option>
  </select>
  <input type=BUTTON value="Get Name" name="myButton" onClick='getName()'>
</form>
</body>
</html>
```

# Select.onBlur

## *JavaScript1.0+, JScript1.0+*

## *Nav2+, IE3+, Opera3+*

## *Syntax*

onBlur="*command*"

## *Description*

The onBlur event handler of an instance of a Select object is fired when the focus is moved away from that particular select box. Care should be taken when using this event handler, because it is possible to get into an infinite loop when using onFocus event handler or focus() method.

## *Example*

Listing 7.470 contains two select boxes, one of which has the Blur event intercepted within its tag and a text box. The text box is used for a counter for the number of times the Blur event is fired.

In the script, the event is fired and the event handler calls a function that reassigns the first select box focus. The result of this is that when a user tries to click or tab away from the first select box, the counter is incremented and the focus returns. Note that this does not mean the selected item in the select box becomes unselected, but rather the first select box gains the focus.

As you will see if you run Listing 7.470, even clicking in other windows or the URL bar increments the counter.

*Listing 7.470    Example of Using the* onBlur *Event Handler*

```
<html>
<head>
<script language="JavaScript">
<!-- Hide

// Initialize a counter to show clicks
var counter = 0;

// Set the focus on the first select box, and increment
// counter in the text box.
function comeBack(){
  document.myForm.mySelect1.focus();
  document.myForm.counter.value = counter++;
}
// End hide --->
</script>
</head>
<body onLoad='comeBack()'>
<form name="myForm">
  <select name="mySelect1" multiple onBlur='comeBack()'>
    <option value=BASE>Baseball</option>
    <option value=FOOT>Football</option>
    <option value=BASKET>Basketball</option>
    <option value=SOCCER>Soccer</option>
  </select>
  <br>
  <select name="mySelect2" multiple>
    <option value=HOCK>Hockey</option>
    <option value=RUG>Rugby</option>
    <option value=GOLF>Golf</option>
    <option value=TENNIS>Tennis</option>
  </select>
  <input type=TEXT size=2 value="" name="counter">
</form>
</body>
</html>
```

# Select.onChange

*JavaScript1.0+, JScript1.0+*

## Nav2+, IE3+, Opera3+

## Syntax

```
onChange="command"
```

## Description

The onChange event handler of an instance of a Select object is fired when the option selected in the select box is changed. Care should be taken when using this event handler, because it is possible to get into an infinite loop when using other event handlers or methods that are fired when focus is placed on or away from the select box.

## Example

Listing 7.471 has a single select box. If the user changes the selected option, an alert box is displayed showing the option that has been selected.

*Listing 7.471    Using the* onChange *Event Handler to Display an Alert Box When an Option Is Selected in the Select Box*

```
<html>
<head>
<script language="JavaScript">
<!-- Hide

// Pop up an alert box displaying the option selected
function changeBack(form){
  for (var i = 0; i < form.mySelect.options.length; i++) {
    if (form.mySelect.options[i].selected){
      alert("You have selected " + form.mySelect.options[i].text);
    }
  }
}
// End hide --->
</script>
</head>
<body>
<form name="myForm">
  <select name="mySelect" onChange='changeBack(this.form)'>
    <option value=HOCK>Hockey</option>
    <option value=RUG>Rugby</option>
    <option value=GOLF>Golf</option>
    <option value=TENNIS>Tennis</option>
  </select>
</form>
</body>
</html>
```

# Select.onFocus

## JavaScript1.0+, JScript1.0+

## *Nav2+, IE3+, Opera3+*

## *Syntax*

onFocus="*command*"

## *Description*

The onFocus event handler of an instance of a Select object is fired when the focus is set on that particular select box. Care should be taken when using this event handler, because it is possible to get into an infinite loop when using onBlur event handler or blur() method.

## *Example*

Listing 7.472 contains a multiple select box and a text box. The select box has an onFocus event handler within its tag that is fired every time you select an option in the box. In the script, the onFocus event handler within the <select> tag calls a function that assigns the text box focus. Each time a user clicks or tabs to the select box, the counter is incremented and the focus is returned to the text box.

*Listing 7.472   Example of Using the* onFocus *Event Handler*

```
<html>
<head>
<script language="JavaScript">
<!-- Hide

// Initialize a counter to show clicks
var counter = 0;

// Set the focus on the counter text box, and increment
// counter.
function sendAway(){
  document.myForm.counter.focus();
  document.myForm.counter.value = counter++;
}
// End hide --->
</script>
</head>
<body onLoad='sendAway()'>
<form name="myForm">
  <select name="mySelect" multiple onFocus='sendAway()'>
    <option value=HOCK>Hockey</option>
    <option value=RUG>Rugby</option>
    <option value=GOLF>Golf</option>
    <option value=TENNIS>Tennis</option>
  </select>
  <input type=TEXT size=2 value="" name="counter">
</form>
</body>
</html>
```

# Select.options

## JavaScript1.0+, JScript1.0+

## Nav2+, IE3+, Opera3+

## Syntax

`select.options`

## Description

The `options` property of the `Select` object is an array that contains the elements of each of the options in the select box. This property is often used to retrieve properties of the options in a select box, such as the value or text.

## Example

Listing 7.473 has a select box with four options in it. When an option is selected, a second window pops up. In this window, the `document.write()` method is used to write the properties of the selected option to the page.

*Listing 7.473   Example of Using the* `option` *Array to Retrieve the Properties of a Selected Option in a Select Box*

```
<html>
<head>
<script language="JavaScript">
<!-- Hide

// Pop up an alert box displaying the option selected
function infoBox(form){

  // Store the passed info into a variable for easier coding.
  var myIn = form.mySelect;

  // Open a window to store the results
  var myWin = open("", "","width=400,height=150");

  // Write the header info
  myWin.document.write("The following is information about the ");
  myWin.document.write("option you selected");
  myWin.document.write('<hr height=1>');

  // Determine which option was selected
  for (var i = 0; i < form.mySelect.options.length; i++) {
    if (form.mySelect.options[i].selected){

      // Write the option's properties to the window
      myWin.document.write('<br><b>Value:</b> ' + myIn.options[i].value);
      myWin.document.write('<br><b>Text:</b> ' + myIn.options[i].text);
```

*continues*

*Listing 7.473   continued*

```
    myWin.document.close();
  }
 }
}
// End hide --->
</script>
</head>
<body>
<form name="myForm">
  <select name="mySelect" onChange='infoBox(this.form)'>
    <option value=HOCK>Hockey</option>
    <option value=RUG>Rugby</option>
    <option value=GOLF>Golf</option>
    <option value=TENNIS>Tennis</option>
  </select>
</form>
</body>
</html>
```

# Select.options.length

## *JavaScript1.0+, JScript1.0+*

## *Nav2+, IE3+, Opera3+*

## Syntax

`select.options.length`

## Description

The `length` property of the `options` array of the `Select` object returns the number of options in that instance of a select box.

## Example

Listing 7.474 has a single select box. When the user makes a selection, the `onChange` event handler is used to pop up an alert box that displays the number of options in this select box.

*Listing 7.474   Accessing the `length` Property of the `options` Array of a*
`Select` *Object*

```
<form name="myForm">
  <select name="mySelect" onChange='alert(mySelect.options.length)'>
    <option value=HOCK>Hockey</option>
    <option value=RUG>Rugby</option>
    <option value=GOLF>Golf</option>
    <option value=TENNIS>Tennis</option>
  </select>
</form>
```

# Select.options.selectedIndex

## *JavaScript1.0+, JScript1.0+*

## *Nav2+, IE3+, Opera3+*

## *Syntax*

`select`.options.selectedIndex

## *Description*

The `selectedIndex` property of the `options` array of the `Select` object returns the index number of the selected option in that instance of a select box.

## *Example*

Listing 7.475 has a single select box. When the user makes a selection, the `onChange` event handler is used to pop up an alert box that displays the index number of the selected option in this select box.

*Listing 7.475    Accessing the* `selectedIndex` *Property of the* `options` *Array of a* `Select` *Object*

```
<form name="myForm">
  <select name="mySelect" onChange='alert(mySelect.options.selectedIndex)'>
    <option value=HOCK>Hockey</option>
    <option value=RUG>Rugby</option>
    <option value=GOLF>Golf</option>
    <option value=TENNIS>Tennis</option>
  </select>
</form>
```

# Select.options.value

## *JavaScript1.0+, JScript1.0+*

## *Nav2+, IE3+, Opera3+*

## *Syntax*

`select`.options.value

## *Description*

The `value` property of the `options` array of the `Select` object returns the value of the option that is selected in that instance of a select box.

## *Example*

Listing 7.476 has a single select box. When the user makes a selection, the `onChange` event handler is used to pop up an alert box that displays the value of the selected option in this select box.

*Listing 7.476   Accessing the* value *Property of the* options *Array of a* Select *Object*

```
<form name="myForm">
<select name="mySelect"
          onChange='alert(mySelect.options[selectedIndex].value)'>
   <option value=HOCK>Hockey</option>
   <option value=RUG name=TEST>Rugby</option>
   <option value=GOLF>Golf</option>
   <option value=TENNIS>Tennis</option>
  </select>
</form>
```

# Select.selectedIndex

## *JavaScript1.0+, JScript1.0+*

## *Nav2+, IE3+, Opera3+*

## *Syntax*

```
select.selectedIndex
```

## *Description*

The selectedIndex property of the Select object returns the index number of the selected option in that instance of a select box. If this property is used to access a multiple select box, it will return the index number of the first selected item.

## *Example*

Listing 7.477 has a single select box. When the user makes a selection, the onChange event handler is used to pop up an alert box that displays the index number of the selected option in this select box.

*Listing 7.477   Accessing the* selectedIndex *Property of the* Select *Object*

```
<form name="myForm">
  <select name="mySelect" onChange='alert(mySelect.selectedIndex)'>
   <option value=HOCK>Hockey</option>
   <option value=RUG>Rugby</option>
   <option value=GOLF>Golf</option>
   <option value=TENNIS>Tennis</option>
  </select>
</form>
```

# Select.type

## *JavaScript1.1+, JScript1.0+*

## *Nav3+, IE3+, Opera3+*

## *Syntax*

```
select.type
```

## Description

The `type` property of an instance of a `Select` object returns the type of the select box. This is either `select-multiple`, if the multiple attribute is set in the `<select>` tag, or `select-one` if it is not.

## Example

Listing 7.478 has a select box and a button. When the button is clicked, an `alert` box is popped up that displays the `type` property of the select box.

*Listing 7.478    Displaying the* type *Property in an Alert Box*

```
<html>
<head>
<script language="JavaScript1.1">
<!-- Hide

// Display an alert box that contains the type of the
// select box.
function getType(){
  alert("The name of this text box is " +
        document.myForm.elements[0].type);
}
// End hide --->
</script>
</head>
<body>
<form name="myForm">
  <select name="mySelect">
    <option value=HOCK>Hockey</option>
    <option value=RUG>Rugby</option>
    <option value=GOLF>Golf</option>
    <option value=TENNIS>Tennis</option>
  </select>
  <input type=BUTTON value="Get Type" name="myButton" onClick='getType()'>
</form>
</body>
</html>
```

# Submit

## JavaScript1.0+, JScript1.0+

## Nav2+, IE3+, Opera3+

## Syntax

Core client-side JavaScript object.

## Description

The `Submit` object is one of the core JavaScript objects. Instances are created by the browser when it encounters an HTML `<input>` tag with the `TYPE` attribute set to

SUBMIT. In the JavaScript object hierarchy, the Submit object is located at window.document.Form.Submit. Table 7.44 lists the properties, methods, and events used by the Submit object.

## NOTE

Starting with Navigator 4, if you submit a form to a mailto: or news: protocol, the UniversalSendMail security privilege must be set.

**Table 7.44   Event Handlers, Methods, and Methods Used by the Submit Object**

| Type | Item | Description |
| --- | --- | --- |
| Event Handlers | onBlur | Executes code when the submit button loses focus. This event handler was added in JavaScript 1.1. |
| | onClick | Executes code when the submit button is clicked. |
| | onFocus | Executes code when the submit button receives the focus. This event handler was added in JavaScript 1.1. |
| Methods | blur() | Removes focus from the submit button. This method was added in JavaScript 1.1. |
| | click() | Simulates a mouse click on the submit button. |
| | focus() | Gives the focus to the submit button. This method was added in JavaScript 1.1. |
| | handleEvent() | Invokes the handler for the event specified and was added in JavaScript 1.2. |
| Properties | form | Returns the entire form the submit button is in. |
| | name | Returns the name of the submit button specified by the NAME attribute. |
| | type | Returns the type of this submit button specified by the TYPE attribute. This property always returns submit. This property was added in JavaScript 1.1. |
| | value | Returns the value of this submit button specified by the VALUE attribute. |

## *Example*

Listing 7.479 displays the use of the Submit properties. It contains a select box and a submit button. When the button is clicked, a second window is opened (see Figure 7.10). The values of the properties of this Submit object are displayed in this window.

*Listing 7.479   Displaying the Properties of an Instance of a* Submit *Object*

```
<html>
<head>
<script language="JavaScript">
<!-- Hide

// Define the openWin function called by clicking the button
function openWin(){

  // Place the reference to the Submit button in a variable for easier access
  var myInstance = document.myForm.mySubmit;

  // Open a window to store the results
  var myWin = open("", "","width=450,height=200");

  // Write the Submit button's properties to the window
  myWin.document.write("The name is: " + myInstance.name + "<br>");
  myWin.document.write("The type is: " + myInstance.type + "<br>");

  // Note that the entire form object is passed with this property.
  // This allows you to then drill down and get the value of other
  // components in the form.
  myWin.document.write("The form can be used to grab the ");
  myWin.document.write("value of the button: ");
  myWin.document.write(myInstance.form.mySubmit.value);

  // Close the stream to the window
  myWin.document.close();
}
// End hide --->
</script>
</head>
<body>
<form name="myForm">
  <input type=TEXT value="Hello, World!" name="myText">
<input type=SUBMIT value="Click to Submit" name="mySubmit"
        onClick="openWin()">
</form>
</body>
</html>
```

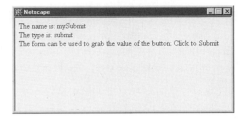

**Figure 7.10**
*Results of running Listing 7.479 in a browser and clicking the Click to Submit button.*

# Submit.blur()

## *JavaScript1.0+, JScript1.0+*

## *Nav2+, IE3+, Opera3+*

## *Syntax*
`submit.blur()`

## *Description*

The `blur()` method of the `Submit` object removes the focus from the submit button. Be careful when using this method in conjunction with the `Submit.focus()` method. It can lead to a focus/blur loop, where the browser blurs a focus as soon as it is done, and vice versa.

## *Example*

Listing 7.480 has a text box and a submit button. If the user clicks the Click Here to Remove Focus button, the button will no longer be focused. The best way to see this is to tab to the button and then click it. When tabbing to the button, you should see that it becomes selected.

*Listing 7.480   Using the* `blur()` *Method to Remove the Focus from the Submit Button*

```
<html>
<head>
<script language="JavaScript">
<!-- Hide

// Define the removeFocus function called by pressing the button
function removeFocus(){

  // Remove focus from the submit button.
  document.myForm.mySubmit.blur();
}
// End hide --->
</script>
```

```
</head>
<body>
<form name="myForm">
  <input type=TEXT value="Hello, World!" name="myText">
  <input type=SUBMIT value="Click to Remove Focus" name="mySubmit"
       onClick="removeFocus()">
</form>
</body>
</html>
```

# Submit.click()

## JavaScript1.0+, JScript1.0+

## Nav2+, IE3+, Opera3+

### Syntax

*submit*.click()

### Description

The click() method of an instance of the Submit object simulates a click on the submit button. Note that if you have an onClick event handler assigned to this button, it will not be executed.

### Example

Listing 7.481 has a text field, a submit button, and a link. If the user clicks the link, a function will be called to check if the user entered any text. If the user did not, an alert box is displayed. If the user did enter text, the function submits the form by calling the click() method of the submit button.

*Listing 7.481   Using the* click() *Method to Submit a Form*

```
<html>
<head>
<script language="JavaScript">
<!-- Hide

// Define the submitForm function to submit the form
function submitForm(){

  // Check to see if some text has been entered
  if(document.myForm.myText.value == ""){
    alert("Please enter some text first");
  }else{

    // Use the click() method to submit the form.
    document.myForm.mySubmit.click();
  }
```

*continues*

*Listing 7.481    continued*
```
}
// End hide --->
</script>
</head>
<body>
<form name="myForm">
Please Enter some text and click the link.<br>
  <input type=TEXT value="" name="myText">
  <input type=SUBMIT value="Submit" name="mySubmit">
</form>
<br>
<a href="javascript:submitForm()">Click here to submit the form</a>
</body>
</html>
```

# Submit.focus()

## JavaScript1.0+, JScript1.0+

## Nav2+, IE3+, Opera3+

## Syntax

```
submit.focus()
```

## Description

The focus() method of the Submit object places focus on the Submit button. Be careful when using this method in conjunction with the Submit.blur() method. It can lead to a focus/blur loop, where the browser blurs a focus as soon as it is done, and vice versa.

## Example

Listing 7.482 has a text box and a submit button. If the user clicks in the text box, focus is placed on the submit button.

*Listing 7.482    Using the* `focus()` *Method to Set the Focus on the Submit Button*
```
<html>
<head>
<script language="JavaScript">
<!-- Hide

// Define the setFocus function called by clicking in the text box
function setFocus(){

  // Place focus from the submit button.
  document.myForm.mySubmit.focus();
}
// End hide --->
</script>
```

```
</head>
<body>
<form name="myForm">
  <input type=TEXT value="Hello, World!" name="myText" onFocus="setFocus()">
  <input type=SUBMIT value="Submit" name="mySubmit">
</form>
</body>
</html>
```

# Submit.form

## JavaScript1.0+, JScript1.0+

## Nav2+, IE3+, Opera3+

## Syntax

`submit.form`

## Description

The form property of an instance of the Submit object provides access to all the data of the form in which the submit button is located.

## Example

Listing 7.483 has a text box and a submit button. When the button is clicked, three properties of the form as a whole are displayed. These properties were referenced through the form property of the submit button.

Listing 7.483   *Accessing a Form Via the* form *Property of an Instance of a* Submit *Object*

```
<html>
<head>
<script language="JavaScript">
<!-- Hide

// Define the openWin function called by pressing the button
function openWin(){

  // Place the reference to the form property of submit button
  // in a variable for easier access
  var formData = document.myForm.mySubmit.form;

  // Open a window to display the results
  var myWin = open("", "","width=450,height=200");

  // Write the form properties accessed through the form
  // property to the window
  myWin.document.write("The name of the form is: " + formData.name + "<br>");
```

*continues*

*Listing 7.483    continued*

```
myWin.document.write("The value of the text box is: ");
myWin.document.write(formData.myText.value + "<br>");
myWin.document.write("The name of the button is: ");
myWin.document.write(formData.elements[1].name + "<br>");

// Close the stream to the window
myWin.document.close();
}
// End hide --->
</script>
</head>
<body>
<form name="myForm">
  <input type=TEXT value="Hello, World!" name="myText">
<input type=BUTTON value="Click to Process" name="mySubmit"
        onClick="openWin()">
</form>
</body>
</html>
```

# Submit.handleEvent()

## *JavaScript1.2+, JScript3.0+*

## *Nav4+, IE4+*

## Syntax

*submit*.handleEvent(*event*)

## Description

The handleEvent() method of the Submit object invokes the handler for the event specified. This method was added in JavaScript 1.2.

## Example

Listing 7.484 has a single text box. The script tells the browser that it wants to intercept all Click events and that it wants the myClickHandler function to handle them. Within this function, the handleEvent() method of the submit button has been specified to handle the click.

When the user clicks anywhere on the page, the onClick event handler in the <input type=SUBMIT> tag calls a function to change the text in the text box. The change is nothing more than a simple number that is incremented counting the number of times the page has been clicked.

*Listing 7.484    Using the* handleEvent() *Method of a* Submit *Object to Handle all Clicks on a Page*

```
<html>
<head>
```

```
<script language="JavaScript1.2">
<!-- Hide

// Define a click counter variable
var counter = 0;

// Tell the browser you want to intercept ALL click events
// on the page. Then define a function to handle them.
window.captureEvents(Event.CLICK)
window.onClick = myClickHandler;

// Define the myClickHandler function to handle click events
function myClickHandler{

  // Pass all click events to the onClick event of the submit button
  window.document.myForm.mySubmit.handleEvent;

}

// Function is called by onClick of submit button. Displays the number
// of clicks that have occurred in the text box. Note that you have to
// return false so the form is not submitted.
function changeText(){
  counter++;
  document.myForm.myText.value = counter;
  return false;
}
// End hide --->
</script>
</head>
<body>
<form name="myForm">
  <input type=TEXT size=2 value="" name="myText">
  <input type=SUBMIT value="Submit" name="mySubmit" onClick='changeText()'>
</form>
</body>
</html>
```

# Submit.name

## *JavaScript1.0+, JScript1.0+*

## *Nav2+, IE3+, Opera3+*

## *Syntax*

*submit*.name

## *Description*

The name property of an instance of a Submit object returns the name of the submit button. This property is often accessed via the elements array of a Form object and used

to return the name of the button. It is most useful when there are many forms on a given page, and determining the name helps you determine what function you want to perform.

## Example

Listing 7.485 has a single text box and submit button. The `elements` array of a `Form` object is used to retrieve the name and display it in an alert box.

*Listing 7.485   Using the `name` Property to Retrieve the Name of a Submit Button*

```
<html>
<head>
<script language="JavaScript">
<!-- Hide

// Display an alert box that contains the name of the
// submit button.
function getName(){
  alert("The name of this submit button is " +
        document.myForm.elements[1].name);
}
// End hide --->
</script>
</head>
<body>
<form name="myForm">
  <input type=TEXT value="First Box" name="myText">
  <input type=SUBMIT value="Submit" name="mySubmit" onClick='getName()'>
</form>
</body>
</html>
```

# Submit.onBlur

## *JavaScript1.0+, JScript1.0+*

## *Nav2+, IE3+, Opera3+*

## Syntax

```
onBlur="command"
```

## Description

The `onBlur` event handler is fired when the focus is moved away from that particular submit button. Care should be taken when using this event handler, because it is possible to get into an infinite loop when using `onFocus` event handler or `focus()` method.

## Example

Listing 7.486 contains two text boxes and a submit button. The button has the `Blur` event intercepted within its tag. The second text box is used for a counter for the number of times the `onBlur` event handler is fired.

In the script, the event calls a function that reassigns the submit button focus. The result of this is that when a user tries to click or tab away from the submit button box, the counter is incremented and the focus returns. As you will see if you run Listing 7.486, even clicking in other windows or the URL bar increments the counter.

*Listing 7.486    Example of Using the* onBlur *Event Handler*

```
<html>
<head>
<script language="JavaScript">
<!-- Hide

// Initialize a counter to show clicks
var counter = 0;

// Set the focus on the submit button, and increment
// counter in the text box.
function comeBack(){
  document.myForm.mySubmit.focus();
  document.myForm.counter.value = counter++;
}
// End hide --->
</script>
</head>
<body onLoad='comeBack()'>
<form name="myForm">
  <input type=TEXT value="Text Box" name="myText">
  <input type=SUBMIT value="Submit" name="mySubmit" onBlur='comeBack()'><br>
  <input type=TEXT size=2 value="" name="counter">
</form>
</body>
</html>
```

# Submit.onClick

## *JavaScript1.0+, JScript1.0+*

## *Nav2+, IE3+, Opera3+*

## *Syntax*

onClick="*command*"

## *Description*

The onClick event handler is fired when a submit button is clicked. Note that this is not fired in the instances where a single form object is in the form, such as a text box, and the user presses the Enter or Return key to submit the form.

## Example

Listing 7.487 has a single text box and a button. If the user presses the submit button, the Click event is fired, calling a function that changes the text in the text box to all uppercase.

*Listing 7.487   Using the* onClick *Event Handler to Verify a Form Before It Is Submitted*

```
<html>
<head>
<script language="JavaScript1.2">
<!-- Hide

// Define the setText function to change the text to uppercase
function setText(){

  // Change the text to uppercase
  document.myForm.myText.value = document.myForm.myText.value.toUpperCase();

}
// End hide --->
</script>
</head>
<body>
<form name="myForm">
Please Enter some text and click the Submit Button.<br>
  <input type=TEXT value="Enter Text Here" name="myText">
  <input type=BUTTON value="Submit" name="mySubmit" onClick="setText()">
</form>
</body>
</html>
```

# Submit.onFocus

## *JavaScript1.0+, JScript1.0+*

## *Nav2+, IE3+, Opera3+*

## Syntax

onFocus="*command*"

## Description

The onFocus event handler of an instance of a Submit object is fired when focus is set to that particular submit button. Care should be taken when using this event handler, because it is possible to get into an infinite loop when using the onBlur event handler or blur() method.

## Example

Listing 7.488 contains two text boxes and a submit button. The submit button has the Focus event intercepted within its tag. The second text box is used for a counter for the number of times the onFocus event handler is fired.

In the script, the event calls a function that assigns the first text box focus. The result of this is that when a user tries to click or tab to the submit button, the counter is incremented and the focus is returned to the text box.

*Listing 7.488    Example of Using the* onFocus *Event Handler*

```
<html>
<head>
<script language="JavaScript">
<!-- Hide

// Initialize a counter to show clicks
var counter = 0;

// Set the focus on the text box, and increment
// counter in text box.
function sendAway(){
  document.myForm.myText.focus();
  document.myForm.counter.value = counter++;
}
// End hide --->
</script>
</head>
<body onLoad='sendAway()'>
<form name="myForm">
  <input type=TEXT value="First Box" name="myText">
  <input type=SUBMIT value="Submit" name="mySubmit" onFocus='sendAway()'><br>
  <input type=TEXT size=2 value="" name="counter">
</form>
</body>
</html>
```

# Submit.type

## JavaScript1.1+, JScript1.0+

## Nav3+, IE3+, Opera3+

## Syntax

*submit*.type

## Description

The type property of an instance of a Submit object returns the type of the text box. This always returns submit.

## Example

Listing 7.489 has a text box and a submit button. When the button is clicked, an `alert` box is popped up that displays the `type` property of the submit button.

*Listing 7.489   Displaying the `type` Property in an Alert Box*

```
<html>
<head>
<script language="JavaScript1.1">
<!-- Hide

// Display an alert box that contains the type of the
// submit button.
function getType(){
  alert("The name of this submit button is " +
        document.myForm.elements[1].type);
}
// End hide --->
</script>
</head>
<body>
<form name="myForm">
  <input type=TEXT value="First Box" name="myText">
  <input type=SUBMIT value="Submit" name="mySubmit" onClick='getType()'>
</form>
</body>
</html>
```

# Submit.value

## *JavaScript1.0+, JScript1.0+*

## *Nav2+, IE3+, Opera3+*

## Syntax

`submit.value`

## Description

The `value` property of an instance of a `Submit` object returns the current value of the submit button. This value is what is displayed on the button itself.

## Example

Listing 7.490 contains a text box and button. When a user clicks the submit button, an alert box pops up displaying the `value` of this instance.

*Listing 7.490   Accessing the Value of a `Submit` Object*

```
<html>
<head>
<script language="JavaScript1.1">
<!-- Hide
```

```
// Display an alert box that contains the value of the
// submit button.
function getValue(){
  alert("The value of this submit button is " +
        document.myForm.elements[1].value);
}
// End hide --->
</script>
</head>
<body>
<form name="myForm">
  <input type=TEXT value="First Box" name="myText">
  <input type=SUBMIT value="Submit" name="mySubmit" onClick='getValue()'>
</form>
</body>
</html>
```

# taint()

## JavaScript1.1

## Nav3

## Syntax

taint(*object*)

## Description

The taint() method was a security measure that was only implemented in JavaScript 1.1 and that allowed a developer to keep return values from being used by and propagated to other scripts. This method does not change the data element passed to it, but rather returns a marked reference to the element.

Because taint() and the functionality of data tainting was removed in JavaScript 1.2, you should avoid using this method. You should use it only if you have a specific security reason for compatibility with Navigator 3 browsers. See Chapter 1, "What Is JavaScript to a Programmer?" for more information on the security model that is now used in Navigator browsers.

## Example

Listing 7.491 simply taints a variable that is defined in a separate window.

Listing 7.491   Use of the taint() Method, Which Is No Longer Supported
```
<script language="JavaScript1.1">
<!-- Hide

// store the tainted variable from the second window
```

*continues*

*Listing 7.491    continued*
```
// in the variable taintMyVar.
var taintMyvar = taint(myWin.myVar);

// End hide --->
</script>
```

# Text

## JavaScript1.0+, JScript1.0+

## Nav2+, IE3+, Opera3+

## Syntax

Core client-side JavaScript object.

## Description

The Text object is one of the core JavaScript objects. Instances are created by the browser when it encounters an HTML <input> tag with the TYPE attribute set to text. In the JavaScript object hierarchy, the Text object is located at window.document. Form.Text. Table 7.45 lists the properties, methods, and events used by the Text object.

**Table 7.45    Event Handlers, Methods, and Properties Used by the Text Object**

| Type | Item | Description |
|---|---|---|
| Event Handlers | onBlur | Executes code when the text box loses the focus. |
| | onChange | Executes code when the text box loses the focus and has had its value modified. |
| | onFocus | Executes code when the text box receives the focus. |
| | onSelect | Executes code when a user selects some of the text within the text box. |
| Methods | blur() | Removes the focus from the text box. |
| | focus() | Gives the focus to the text box. |
| | handleEvent() | Invokes the handler for the event specified and was added in JavaScript 1.2. |
| | select() | Selects the text in the text box. |
| Properties | defaultValue | Returns the value of this text box specified by the VALUE attribute. Note that this property is not supported by the Opera browsers. |
| | form | Returns the entire form the text box is in. |
| | name | Returns the name of this text box specified by the NAME attribute. |

| Type | Item | Description |
|------|------|-------------|
| | type | Returns the type of this text box specified by the TYPE attribute. Note that this is always text and was added in JavaScript 1.1. |
| | value | Returns the value that is actually displayed in the text box. |

## Example

Listing 7.492 displays the use of the Text properties. It contains a text box and a button. When the button is clicked, a second window is opened (see Figure 7.11). The values of the properties of this Text object are displayed in this window.

*Listing 7.492   Displaying the Properties of an Instance of a* Text *Object*

```
<html>
<head>
<script language="JavaScript">
<!-- Hide

// Define the openWin function called by pressing the button
function openWin(){

  // Place the reference to the text box in a variable for easier access
  var myInstance = document.myForm.myText;

  // Open a window to store the results
  var myWin = open("", "","width=450,height=200");

  // Write the text boxes' properties to the window
  myWin.document.write("The defaultValue is: " + myInstance.defaultValue);
  myWin.document.write("<br>");
  myWin.document.write("The name is: " + myInstance.name + "<br>");
  myWin.document.write("The type is: " + myInstance.type + "<br>");
  myWin.document.write("The value is: " + myInstance.value + "<br>");

  // Note that the entire form object is passed with this property.
  // This allows you to then drill down and get the value of other
  // components in the form.
  myWin.document.write("The form can be used to grab the value ");
  myWin.document.write("of the button: ");
  myWin.document.write(myInstance.form.myButton.value);

  // Close the stream to the window
  myWin.document.close();
}
// End hide --->
</script>
```

*continues*

*Listing 7.492    continued*
```
</head>
<body>
<form name="myForm">
  <input type=TEXT value="hello world" name="myText">
  <input type=BUTTON value="Click to Process" name="myButton"
onClick="openWin()">
</form>
</body>
</html>
```

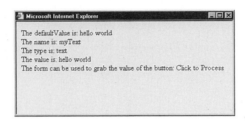

**Figure 7.11**

*Results of running Listing 7.492 in a browser and clicking the Click to Process button.*

# Text.blur()

## *JavaScript1.0+, JScript1.0+*

## *Nav2+, IE3+, Opera3+*

## *Syntax*

```
text.blur()
```

## *Description*

The blur() method of the Text object removes focus from the text box. Be careful when using this method in conjunction with the Text.focus() method. It can lead to a focus/blur loop, where the browser blurs a focus as soon as it is done, and vice versa.

## *Example*

Listing 7.493 has a text box and a button. If the user highlights some of the text in the box and then clicks the Click Here to Remove Focus button, the text will no longer be highlighted.

*Listing 7.493    Using the* blur() *Method to Remove the Focus from the Text Box*
```
<html>
<head>
<script language="JavaScript">
<!-- Hide
```

```
// Define the removeFocus function called by pressing the button
function removeFocus(){

  // Remove focus from the text box.
  document.myForm.myText.blur();
}
// End hide --->
</script>
</head>
<body>
<b>Highlight some of the text in the following text box:</b>
<p>
<form name="myForm">
  <input type=TEXT value="hello world" name="myText">
  <input type=BUTTON value="Click to Remove Focus" name="myButton"
        onClick="removeFocus()">
</form>
</body>
</html>
```

# Text.defaultValue

## JavaScript1.0+, JScript1.0+

## Nav2+, IE3+

### Syntax

*text*.defaultValue

### Description

The defaultValue property of a Text object instance contains the default value specified by the VALUE attribute of the <input> tag. This property is often used to reset forms to their default values after a user has entered some data.

### Example

Listing 7.494 has a text box and a button. If the user edits some of the text in the box and then clicks the Click to Reset button, the text will change back to the default value.

*Listing 7.494   Using the* defaultValue *Property to Set the Value of the Text Box back to Its Original Value*

```
<html>
<head>
<script language="JavaScript">
<!-- Hide

// Define the resetForm function called by pressing the button
function resetForm(){
```

*continues*

*Listing 7.494    continued*

```
  // Set the text in the text box back to "hello world"
  document.myForm.myText.value = document.myForm.myText.defaultValue;
}
// End hide --->
</script>
</head>
<body>
<b>Edit the text in the following text box:</b>
<p>
<form name="myForm">
  <input type=TEXT value="hello world" name="myText">
  <input type=BUTTON value="Click to Reset" name="myButton"
         onClick="resetForm()">
</form>
</body>
</html>
```

# Text.focus()

## JavaScript1.0+, JScript1.0+

## Nav2+, IE3+, Opera3+

## Syntax

`text.focus()`

## Description

The focus() method of the Text object gives focus to the text box. Be careful when using this method in conjunction with the Text.blur() method. It can lead to a focus/blur loop, where the browser blurs a focus as soon as it is done, and vice versa.

## Example

Listing 7.495 has two text boxes and two buttons. If the user clicks the first button, the cursor is set inside the first text box. If the user clicks the second text box, the cursor is set inside the second text box.

*Listing 7.495    Using the* focus() *Method to Place the Cursor in the Desired Text Box*

```
<html>
<head>
<script language="JavaScript">
<!-- Hide

// Define the setFocus function called by pressing the button
function setFocus(num){

  // Determine which button was clicked and set the cursor
```

```
// in the appropriate text box.
if(num == 1){
  document.myForm.myText1.focus();
}else if(num == 2){
  document.myForm.myText2.focus();
}
}
// End hide --->
</script>
</head>
<body>
<p>
<form name="myForm">
  <input type=TEXT value="Textbox 1" name="myText1">
  <input type=BUTTON value="Click to Set Cursor" name="myButton1"
        onClick="setFocus(1)">
  <br>
  <input type=TEXT value="Textbox 2" name="myText2">
  <input type=BUTTON value="Click to Set Cursor" name="myButton2"
        onClick="setFocus(2)">
</form>
</body>
</html>
```

# Text.form

## *JavaScript1.0+, JScript1.0+*

## *Nav2+, IE3+, Opera3+*

## *Syntax*

`text.form`

## *Description*

The `form` property of an instance of a `Text` object holds all the data of the form in which the text box is contained. This allows a developer to obtain specific information about the form in which the text box is located.

## *Example*

Listing 7.496 has a text box and a button. When the button is clicked, three properties of the form as a whole are displayed. These properties were referenced though the `form` property of the text box.

*Listing 7.496    Accessing a Form via the `form` Property of an Instance of a `Text` Object*

```
<html>
<head>
<script language="JavaScript">
```

*continues*

*Listing 7.496    continued*

```
<!-- Hide

// Define the openWin function called by pressing the button
function openWin(){

  // Place the reference to the form property of text box
  // in a variable for easier access
  var formData = document.myForm.myText.form;

  // Open a window to display the results
  var myWin = open("", "","width=450,height=200");

  // Write the form properties accessed through the form
  // property to the window
  myWin.document.write("The name of the form is: " + formData.name + "<br>");
  myWin.document.write("The value of the text box is: ");
  myWin.document.write(formData.myText.value + "<br>");
  myWin.document.write("The name of the button is: ");
  myWin.document.write(formData.elements[1].name + "<br>");

  // Close the stream to the window
  myWin.document.close();
}
// End hide --->
</script>
</head>
<body>
<form name="myForm">
  <input type=TEXT value="hello world" name="myText">
<input type=BUTTON value="Click to Process" name="myButton"
        onClick="openWin()">
</form>
</body>
</html>
```

# Text.handleEvent()

## *JavaScript1.2+, JScript3.0+*

## *Nav4+, IE4+*

## *Syntax*

`text.handleEvent(event)`

## *Description*

The handleEvent() method of the Text object invokes the handler for the event specified. This method was added in JavaScript 1.2.

## *Example*

Listing 7.497 has a single text box. The script tells the browser that it wants to inter-cept all `Click` events and that it wants the `myClickHandler` function to handle them. With in this function, the `handleEvent()` method of the text box has been specified to handle the click.

When the user clicks anywhere on the page, the `onClick` event handler in the `<input type=TEXT>` tag calls a function to change the text in the text box. The change is noth-ing more than a simple number that is incremented counting the number of times the page has been clicked.

*Listing 7.497   Using the* `handleEvent()` *Method of a* `Text` *Object to Handle all Clicks on a Page*

```
<html>
<head>
<script language="JavaScript1.2">
<!-- Hide

// Define a click counter variable
var counter = 0;

// Tell the browser you want to intercept ALL click events
// on the page. Then define a function to handle them.
window.captureEvents(Event.CLICK)
window.onClick = myClickHandler;

// Define the myClickHandler function to handle click events
function myClickHandler{

   // Pass all click events to the onClick event of the text box
   window.document.myForm.myText.handleEvent;
}

// Function is called by onClick of text box. Displays the number
// of clicks that have occurred.
function changeText(){
   document.myForm.myText.value = counter++;
}
// End hide --->
</script>
</head>
<body>
<form name="myForm">
   <input type=TEXT size=2 value="" name="myText" onClick='changeText()'>
</form>
</body>
</html>
```

# Text.name

## *JavaScript1.0+, JScript1.0+*

## *Nav2+, IE3+, Opera3+*

## *Syntax*

```
text.name
```

## *Description*

The name property of an instance of a Text object returns the name of the text box. This property is often accessed via the elements array of a Form object and used to return the name of the text area. It is most useful when there are many forms on a given page, and determining the name helps you determine what function you want to perform.

## *Example*

This simple example has a single text box and button. The elements array of a Form object is used to retrieve the name and display it in an alert box. The result of running Listing 7.498 and clicking the button is shown in Figure 7.12.

*Listing 7.498    Using the name Property to Retrieve the Name of a Text Box*

```
<html>
<head>
<script language="JavaScript">
<!-- Hide

// Display an alert box that contains the name of the
// text box.
function getName(){
  alert("The name of this text box is " +
        document.myForm.elements[0].name);
}
// End hide --->
</script>
</head>
<body>
<form name="myForm">
  <input type=TEXT value="First Box" name="myText">
  <input type=BUTTON value="Get Name" name="myButton" onClick='getName()'>
</form>
</body>
</html>
```

**Figure 7.12**

*Results of running Listing 7.498 in a browser and clicking the Get Name button.*

# Text.onBlur

## *JavaScript1.0+, JScript1.0+*

## *Nav2+, IE3+, Opera3+*

## *Syntax*

```
onBlur="command"
```

## *Description*

The onBlur event handler of an instance of a Text object is fired when the focus is moved away from that particular text box. Care should be taken when using this event handler, because it is possible to get into an infinite loop when using the onFocus event handler or focus() method.

## *Example*

Listing 7.499 contains three text boxes, one of which has the onBlur event handler intercepted within its tag. The third text box is used for a counter for the number of times the onBlur event handler is fired.

In the script, the event calls a function that reassigns the first text box focus. The result of this is that when a user tries to click or tab away from the first text box, the counter is incremented and the focus returns. As you will see if you run Listing 7.499, even clicking in other windows or the URL bar increments the counter.

*Listing 7.499    Example of Using the* onBlur *Event Handler*

```
<html>
<head>
<script language="JavaScript">
<!-- Hide

// Initialize a counter to show clicks
var counter = 0;

// Set the focus on the first text box, and increment
// counter in last text box.
function comeBack(){
  document.myForm.myText1.focus();
  document.myForm.counter.value = counter++;
```

*continues*

*Listing 7.499    continued*

```
}
// End hide --->
</script>
</head>
<body onLoad='comeBack()'>
<form name="myForm">
  <input type=TEXT value="First Box" name="myText1" onBlur='comeBack()'>
  <input type=TEXT value="Second Box" name="myText2"><br>
  <input type=TEXT size=2 value="" name="counter">
</form>
</body>
</html>
```

# Text.onChange

## *JavaScript1.0+, JScript1.0+*

## *Nav2+, IE3+, Opera3+*

## *Syntax*

onChange="*command*"

## *Description*

The onChange event handler of an instance of a Text object is fired when the text in the box is modified. Care should be taken when using this event handler, because it is possible to get into an infinite loop when using other events or methods that are fired when focus is placed on or away from the text box.

## *Example*

Listing 7.500 has a single text box. If the user changes the text and then shifts the focus away from the text box by clicking elsewhere or pressing Return, the default text is placed back in the text box.

*Listing 7.500    Using the* onChange *Event Handler to Change the Text Back to the Default*

```
<html>
<head>
<script language="JavaScript">
<!-- Hide

// Change the text back to the default if user tries to change it.
// Note that the user has to click away or hit return for this
// to change back.
function changeBack(){
  document.myForm.myText.value = document.myForm.myText.defaultValue;
}
// End hide --->
</script>
```

```
</head>
<body>
<form name="myForm">
  <input type=TEXT value="Change Me?" name="myText" onChange='changeBack()'>
</form>
</body>
</html>
```

# Text.onFocus

## *JavaScript1.0+, JScript1.0+*

## *Nav2+, IE3+, Opera3+*

## *Syntax*

```
onFocus="command"
```

## *Description*

The onFocus event handler of an instance of a Text object is fired when focus is made on that particular text box. Care should be taken when using this event handler, because it is possible to get into an infinite loop when using onBlur event handler or blur() method.

## *Example*

Listing 7.501 contains three text boxes, one of which has the onFocus event handler intercepted within its tag. The third text box is used for a counter for the number of times the Focus event is fired.

In the script, the event handler calls a function that assigns the second text box focus. The result of this is that when a user tries to click or tab to the first text box, the counter is incremented and the focus is returned to the second text box.

*Listing 7.501    Example of Using the onFocus Event Handler*
```
<html>
<head>
<script language="JavaScript">
<!-- Hide

// Initialize a counter to show clicks
var counter = 0;

// Set the focus on the second text box, and increment
// counter in last text box.
function sendAway(){
  document.myForm.myText2.focus();
  document.myForm.counter.value = counter++;
}
// End hide --->
```

*continues*

*Listing 7.501    continued*
```
</script>
</head>
<body onLoad='sendAway()'>
<form name="myForm">
  <input type=TEXT value="First Box" name="myText1" onFocus='sendAway()'>
  <input type=TEXT value="Second Box" name="myText2"><br>
  <input type=TEXT size=2 value="" name="counter">
</form>
</body>
</html>
```

# Text.onSelect

## *JavaScript1.0+, JScript1.0+*

## *IE3+*

## *Syntax*

```
onSelect="command"
```

## *Description*

The onSelect event handler of an instance of a Text object is fired when the text in the
box is highlighted. Care should be taken when using this event handler, because it is
possible to get into an infinite loop when using other events or methods that are fired
when focus is placed on the text box.

**NOTE**

> Note that Netscape defined this function in JavaScript 1.0, however is not fully
> implemented in any version released to date. Opera browsers do not support this
> function either.

## *Example*

Listing 7.502 has two text boxes. If the user highlights the text in the first text box, the
default text of the first text box is written to the second text box.

*Listing 7.502    Using the onSelect Event Handler to Set the Text in the Second
Text Box*
```
<html>
<head>
<script language="JavaScript">
<!-- Hide

// Change the text of the second text box to the default
// of the first if user highlights text in the first.
function setText(){
  document.myForm.myText2.value = document.myForm.myText1.defaultValue;
}
```

```
// End hide --->
</script>
</head>
<body>
<form name="myForm">
  <input type=TEXT value="Change Me?" name="myText1" onSelect='setText()'>
  <br>
  <input type=TEXT value="" name="myText2">
</form>
</body>
</html>
```

# Text.select()

## JavaScript1.0+, JScript1.0+

## Nav2+, IE3+, Opera3+

## Syntax

`text.select()`

## Description

The `select()` method of the Text object selects the text in the text box. Be careful when using this method in conjunction with the `blur()` and `focus()` methods. It can lead to a focus/blur loop where the browser blurs or focuses as soon as it is has been selected, and vice versa.

## Example

Listing 7.503 has a text box and a button. If the user clicks the button, the text inside the text box will be highlighted. Notice the `focus()` method had to be used to tell the browser to actually highlight the text.

*Listing 7.503    Using the* `select()` *Method to Select the Text in a Text Box*

```
<html>
<head>
<script language="JavaScript">
<!-- Hide

// Define the selectText function called by pressing the button
function selectText(){

  // Select the text in the box, then place focus on it.
  document.myForm.myText.select();
  document.myForm.myText.focus();
}
// End hide --->
</script>
```

*continues*

*Listing 7.503    continued*
```
</head>
<body>
<form name="myForm">
  <input type=TEXT value="hello world" name="myText">
  <input type=BUTTON value="Click to Select Text" name="myButton"
      onClick="selectText()">
</form>
</body>
</html>
```

# Text.type

## *JavaScript1.1+, JScript1.0+*

## *Nav3+, IE3+, Opera3+*

## *Syntax*

```
text.type
```

## *Description*

The `type` property of an instance of a `Text` object returns the type of the text box. This always returns `text`.

## *Example*

Listing 7.504 has a text box and a button. When the button is clicked, an `alert` box is popped up that displays the `type` property of the text box.

*Listing 7.504    Displaying the `type` Property in an Alert Box*
```
<html>
<head>
<script language="JavaScript1.1">
<!-- Hide

// Display an alert box that contains the type of the
// text box.
function getType(){
  alert("The name of this text box is " +
      document.myForm.elements[0].type);
}
// End hide --->
</script>
</head>
<body>
<form name="myForm">
  <input type=TEXT value="First Box" name="myText">
  <input type=BUTTON value="Get Type" name="myButton" onClick='getType()'>
</form>
</body>
</html>
```

# Text.value

*JavaScript1.0+, JScript1.0+*

*Nav2+, IE3+, Opera3+*

## Syntax

`text.value`

## Description

The `value` property of an instance of a `Text` object returns the current value of the text box. Note that this is not the default value that can be accessed via the `Text.defaultValue` property and is often used to set the value of a text box.

## Example

Listing 7.505 contains a text box and button. You can edit the text in the text box and then click the Reset button to reset the text back to the default value.

*Listing 7.505   Resetting the Value of a Text Box to the Default Value*

```
<html>
<head>
<script language="JavaScript">
<!-- Hide

// Reset the text in the text box to its default value.
function resetText(){
   document.myForm.myText.value = document.myForm.myText.defaultValue;
}
// End hide --->
</script>
</head>
<body>
<form name="myForm">
   <input type=TEXT value="First Box" name="myText">
   <input type=BUTTON value="Reset" name="myButton" onClick='resetText()'>
</form>
</body>
</html>
```

# Textarea

*JavaScript1.0+, JScript1.0+*

*Nav2+, IE3+, Opera3+*

## Syntax

Core client-side JavaScript object.

## Description

The Textarea object is one of the core JavaScript objects. Instances are created by the browser when it encounters an HTML <textarea> tag. In the JavaScript object hierarchy, the Textarea object is located at window.document.Form.Textarea. Table 7.46 lists the event handlers, methods, and properties used by the Textarea object.

**Table 7.46   Event Handlers, Methods, and Properties Used by the Textarea Object**

| Type | Item | Description |
| --- | --- | --- |
| Event Handlers | onBlur | Executes code when the text area loses the focus. |
| | onChange | Executes code when the text area loses the focus and has had its value modified. |
| | onFocus | Executes code when the text area receives the focus. |
| | onKeyDown | Executes code when a key is pressed down. This occurs before an onKeyPress event handler is triggered and was added in JavaScript 1.2. |
| | onKeyPress | Executes code when a key is pressed down immediately after an onKeyDown event handler is triggered. This event handler was added in JavaScript 1.2. |
| | onKeyUp | Executes code when a key is released. This was added in JavaScript 1.2. |
| | onSelect | Executes code when a user selects some of the text within the text area. |
| Methods | blur() | Removes the focus from the text area. |
| | focus() | Gives the focus to the text area. |
| | handleEvent() | Invokes the handler for the event specified and was added in JavaScript 1.2. |
| | select() | Selects the text in the text area. |
| Properties | defaultValue | Returns the value of this text area defined between the beginning and ending <textarea> tags. Note that this property is not supported by the Opera browsers. |
| | form | Returns the entire form the text area is in. |
| | name | Returns the name of this text area specified by the NAME attribute. |
| | type | Returns the type of this text area. Note that this is always textarea and was added in JavaScript 1.1. |
| | value | Returns the value that is actually displayed in the text area. |

## *Example*

Listing 7.506 displays the use of the Textarea properties. It contains a text area and a button. When the button is clicked, a second window is opened (see Figure 7.13). The values of the properties of this Textarea object are displayed in this window.

*Listing 7.506   Displaying the Properties of an Instance of a* Textarea *Object*

```
<html>
<head>
<script language="JavaScript">
<!-- Hide

// Define the openWin function called by pressing the button
function openWin(){

  // Place the reference to the text area in a variable for easier access
  var myInstance = document.myForm.myTextArea;

  // Open a window to store the results
  var myWin = open("", "","width=450,height=200");

  // Write the text areas properties to the window
  myWin.document.write("The defaultValue is: " + myInstance.defaultValue +
"<br>");
  myWin.document.write("The name is: " + myInstance.name + "<br>");
  myWin.document.write("The type is: " + myInstance.type + "<br>");
  myWin.document.write("The value is: " + myInstance.value + "<br>");

  // Note that the entire form object is passed with this property.
  // This allows you to then drill down and get the value of other
  // components in the form.
  myWin.document.write("The form can be used to grab the value of the button:
");
  myWin.document.write(myInstance.form.myButton.value);

  // Close the stream to the window
  myWin.document.close();
}
// End hide --->
</script>
</head>
<body>
<form name="myForm">
  <textarea name="myTextArea" rows=6 cols=50>
  Here is some text in my text area.
  </textarea>
  <input type=BUTTON value="Click to Process" name="myButton"
         onClick="openWin()">
</form>
</body>
</html>
```

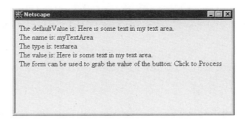

**Figure 7.13**

*Results of running Listing 7.506 in a browser and clicking the Click to Process button.*

# Textarea.blur()

## *JavaScript1.0+, JScript1.0+*

## *Nav2+, IE3+, Opera3+*

## *Syntax*

`textarea.blur()`

## *Description*

The `blur()` method of the `Textarea` object removes the focus from the text area. Be careful when using this method in conjunction with the `Textarea.focus()` method. It can lead to a focus/blur loop, where the browser blurs a focus as soon as it is done, and vice versa.

## *Example*

Listing 7.507 has a text area and a button. If the user highlights some of the text in the box and then clicks the Click Here to Remove Focus button, the text will no longer be highlighted.

*Listing 7.507   Using the* `blur()` *Method to Remove the Focus from the Text Area*

```
<html>
<head>
<script language="JavaScript">
<!-- Hide

// Define the removeFocus function called by pressing the button
function removeFocus(){

  // Remove focus from the text area.
  document.myForm.myTextArea.blur();
}
// End hide --->
</script>
</head>
```

```
<body>
<b>Highlight some of the text in the following text area:</b>
<p>
<form name="myForm">
  <textarea name="myTextArea" rows=6 cols=50>
  Here is some text in my text area.
  </textarea>
  <input type=BUTTON value="Click to Remove Focus" name="myButton"
       onClick="removeFocus()">
</form>
</body>
</html>
```

# Textarea.defaultValue

## *JavaScript1.0+, JScript1.0+*

## *Nav2+, IE3+*

### Syntax

`textarea.defaultValue`

### Description

The `defaultValue` property of a `Textarea` object instance contains the text between the beginning and ending `<textarea>` tags. This property is often used to reset areas to their default values after a user has modified them.

### Example

Listing 7.508 has a text area and a button. If the user edits some of the text in the box and then clicks the Click to Reset button, the text will change back to the default value.

*Listing 7.508    Using the* `defaultValue` *Property to Set the Value of the Text Area Back to Its Original Value*

```
<html>
<head>
<script language="JavaScript">
<!-- Hide

// Define the resetForm function called by pressing the button
function resetForm(){

  // Set the text in the text area back to "hello world"
  document.myForm.myTextArea.value = document.myForm.myTextArea.defaultValue;
}
// End hide --->
</script>
</head>
<body>
```

*continues*

*Listing 7.508   continued*

```
<b>Edit the text in the following text box:</b>
<p>
<form name="myForm">
    <textarea name="myTextArea" rows=6 cols=50>
    Here is some text in my text area.
  </textarea>
<input type=BUTTON value="Click to Reset" name="myButton"
        onClick="resetForm()">
</form>
</body>
</html>
```

# Textarea.focus()

## JavaScript1.0+, JScript1.0+

## Nav2+, IE3+, Opera3+

## Syntax

`textarea.focus()`

## Description

The `focus()` method of the `Textarea` object gives the focus to the text area. Be careful when using this method in conjunction with the `Textarea.blur()` method. It can lead to a focus/blur loop, where the browser blurs a focus as soon as it is done, and vice versa.

## Example

Listing 7.509 has two text areas and two buttons. If the user clicks the first button, the cursor is set inside the first text area. If the user clicks the second text box, the cursor is set inside the second text area.

*Listing 7.509   Using the* `focus()` *Method to Place the Cursor in the Desired Text Area*

```
<html>
<head>
<script language="JavaScript">
<!-- Hide

// Define the setFocus function called by pressing the button
function setFocus(num){

  // Determine which button was clicked and set the cursor
  // in the appropriate text area.
  if(num == 1){
    document.myForm.myTextArea1.focus();
  }else if(num == 2){
    document.myForm.myTextArea2.focus();
```

```
   }
}
// End hide --->
</script>
</head>
<body>
<p>
<form name="myForm">
  <textarea name="myTextArea1" rows=2 cols=50>
  Here is the first text area.
  </textarea>
<input type=BUTTON value="Click to Set Cursor" name="myButton1"
       onClick="setFocus(1)">
  <br>
  <textarea name="myTextArea2" rows=2 cols=50>
  Here is the second text area.
  </textarea>
  <input type=BUTTON value="Click to Set Cursor" name="myButton2"
       onClick="setFocus(2)">
</form>
</body>
</html>
```

# Textarea.form

## *JavaScript1.0+, JScript1.0+*

## *Nav2+, IE3+, Opera3+*

## *Syntax*

```
textarea.form
```

## *Description*

The `form` property of an instance of a `Textarea` object holds all the data of the form in which the text box is contained. This allows a developer to obtain specific information about the form in which the text area is located.

## *Example*

Listing 7.510 has a text area and a button. When the button is clicked, three properties of the form as a whole are displayed. These properties were referenced through the `form` property of the text area.

*Listing 7.510   Accessing a Form via the `form` Property of an Instance of a*
Textarea *Object*

```
<html>
<head>
<script language="JavaScript">
```

*continues*

*Listing 7.510    continued*

```
<!-- Hide

// Define the openWin function called by pressing the button
function openWin(){

  // Place the reference to the form property of text area
  // in a variable for easier access
  var formData = document.myForm.myTextArea.form;

  // Open a window to display the results
  var myWin = open("", "","width=450,height=200");

  // Write the form properties accessed through the form
  // property to the window
  myWin.document.write("The name of the form is: " + formData.name + "<br>");
  myWin.document.write("The value of the text box is: ");
  myWin.document.write(formData.myTextArea.value + "<br>");
  myWin.document.write("The name of the button is: ");
  myWin.document.write(formData.elements[1].name + "<br>");

  // Close the stream to the window
  myWin.document.close();
}
// End hide --->
</script>
</head>
<body>
<form name="myForm">
  <textarea name="myTextArea" rows=6 cols=50>
  Here is some text in my text area.
  </textarea>
<input type=BUTTON value="Click to Process" name="myButton"
        onClick="openWin()">
</form>
</body>
</html>
```

# Textarea.handleEvent()

## *JavaScript1.2+, JScript3.0+*

## *Nav4+, IE4+*

## *Syntax*

`textarea.handleEvent(event)`

## *Description*

The handleEvent() method of the Textarea object invokes the handler for the event specified. This method was added in JavaScript 1.2.

## Example

Listing 7.511 has a single text area. The script tells the browser that it wants to intercept all Click events and that it wants the myClickHandler function to handle them. Within this function, the handleEvent() method of the text area has been specified to handle the click.

When the user clicks anywhere on the page, the onClick event handler in the <textarea> tag calls a function to change the text in the text area. The change is nothing more than a simple number that is incremented counting the number of times the page has been clicked on.

*Listing 7.511    Using the* handleEvent() *Method of a* Textarea *Object to Handle All Clicks on a Page*

```
<html>
<head>
<script language="JavaScript1.2">
<!-- Hide

// Define a click counter variable
var counter = 0;

// Tell the browser you want to intercept ALL click events
// on the page. Then define a function to handle them.
window.captureEvents(Event.CLICK)
window.onClick = myClickHandler;

// Define the myClickHandler function to handle click events
function myClickHandler{

    // Pass all click events to the onClick event of the text area
    window.document.myForm.myTextArea.handleEvent;

}

// Function is called by onClick of text box. Displays the number
// of clicks that have occurred.
function changeText(){
    document.myForm.myTextArea.value = counter++;
}
// End hide --->
</script>
</head>
<body>
<form name="myForm">
    <textarea name="myTextArea" rows=6 cols=50 onClick='changeText()'>
    Here is some text in my text area.
    </textarea>
</form>
</body>
</html>
```

# Textarea.name

## *JavaScript1.0+, JScript1.0+*

## *Nav2+, IE3+, Opera3+*

## *Syntax*

```
textarea.name
```

## *Description*

The name property of an instance of a Textarea object returns the name of the text area. This property is often accessed via the elements array of a Form object and used to return the name of the text area. It is most useful when there are many forms on a given page, and determining the name helps you determine what function you want to perform.

## *Example*

Listing 7.512 has a text area and button. The elements array of a Form object is used to retrieve the name and display it in an alert box. The result of running Listing 7.557 and clicking the button is shown in Figure 7.14.

*Listing 7.512   Using the name Property to Retrieve the Name of a Text Area*

```
<html>
<head>
<script language="JavaScript">
<!-- Hide

// Display an alert box that contains the name of the
// text area.
function getName(){
  alert("The name of this text area is " +
        document.myForm.elements[0].name);
}
// End hide --->
</script>
</head>
<body>
<form name="myForm">
  <textarea name="myTextArea" rows=6 cols=50>
  Here is some text in my text area.
  </textarea>
  <input type=BUTTON value="Get Name" name="myButton" onClick='getName()'>
</form>
</body>
</html>
```

**Figure 7.14**

*Results of running Listing 7.512 in a browser and clicking the Get Name button.*

# Textarea.onBlur

## *JavaScript1.0+, JScript1.0+*

## *Nav2+, IE3+, Opera3+*

## *Syntax*

onBlur="*command*"

## *Description*

The onBlur event handler of an instance of a Textarea object is fired when the focus is moved away from that particular text area. Care should be taken when using this event handler, because it is possible to get into an infinite loop when using onFocus event handler or focus() method.

## *Example*

Listing 7.513 contains three text areas, one of which has the onBlur event handler used within its tag. The third text box is used for a counter for the number of times the onBlur event handler is used.

In the script, the event calls a function that reassigns the first text area focus. The result of this is that when a user tries to click or tab away from the first text area, the counter is incremented and the focus returns. As you will see if you run Listing 7.513, even clicking in other windows or the URL bar increments the counter.

*Listing 7.513   Example of Using the* onBlur *Event Handler*

```
<html>
<head>
<script language="JavaScript">
<!-- Hide

// Initialize a counter to show clicks
var counter = 0;

// Set the focus on the first text area, and increment
// counter in last text area.
function comeBack(){
  document.myForm.myTextArea1.focus();
```

*continues*

*Listing 7.513    continued*
```
  document.myForm.counter.value = counter++;
}
// End hide --->
</script> .
</head>
<body onLoad='comeBack()'>
<form name="myForm">
  <textarea name="myTextArea1" rows=2 cols=50 onBlur='comeBack()'>
    Here is some text in my text area.
  </textarea>
  <textarea name="myTextArea2" rows=2 cols=50>
  Here is some text in my text area.
  </textarea><br>
  <input type=TEXT size=2 value="" name="counter">
</form>
</body>
</html>
```

# Textarea.onChange

## *JavaScript1.0+, JScript1.0+*

## *Nav2+, IE3+, Opera3+*

## *Syntax*

onChange="*command*"

## *Description*

The onChange event handler of an instance of a Textarea object is fired when the text in the area is modified. Care should be taken when using this event handler, because it is possible to get into an infinite loop when using other events or methods that are fired when focus is placed on or away from the text area.

## *Example*

Listing 7.514 has a single text area. If the user changes the text and then shifts the focus away from the text area by clicking elsewhere, the default text is placed back in the text area.

*Listing 7.514    Using the onChange Event Handler to Change the Text Back to the Default*
```
<html>
<head>
<script language="JavaScript">
<!-- Hide

// Change the text back to the default if user tries to change it.
// Note that the user has to click away or hit return for this
// to change back.
```

```
function changeBack(){
   document.myForm.myTextArea.value = document.myForm.myTextArea.defaultValue;
}
// End hide --->
</script>
</head>
<body>
<form name="myForm">
   <textarea name="myTextArea" rows=2 cols=50 onChange='changeBack()'>
   Here is some text in my text area.
   </textarea>
</form>
</body>
</html>
```

# Textarea.onFocus

## *JavaScript1.0+, JScript1.0+*

## *Nav2+, IE3+, Opera3+*

## *Syntax*

onFocus="*command*"

## *Description*

The onFocus event handler of an instance of a Textarea object is fired when focus is made on that particular text area. Care should be taken when using this event handler since it is possible to get into an infinite loop when using onBlur event handler or blur() method.

## *Example*

Listing 7.515 contains three text boxes, one of which has the Focus event intercepted within its tag. The third text box is used for a counter for the number of times the Focus event is fired.

In the script, the event calls a function that assigns the second text box focus. The result of this is that when a user tries to click or tab to the first text box, the counter is incremented and the focus is returned to the second text box.

*Listing 7.515    Example of Using the* onFocus *Event Handler*
```
<html>
<head>
<script language="JavaScript">
<!-- Hide

// Initialize a counter to show clicks
var counter = 0;
```

*continues*

*Listing 7.515    continued*

```
// Set the focus on the second text area, and increment
// counter in last text area.
function sendAway(){
  document.myForm.myTextArea2.focus();
  document.myForm.counter.value = counter++;
}
// End hide --->
</script>
</head>
<body onLoad='sendAway()'>
<form name="myForm">
  <textarea name="myTextArea1" rows=2 cols=50 onFocus='sendAway()'>
  Here is some text in my text area.
  </textarea>
  <textarea name="myTextArea2" rows=2 cols=50>
  Here is some text in my text area.
  </textarea>
  <br>
  <input type=TEXT size=2 value="" name="counter">
</form>
</body>
</html>
```

# Textarea.onKeyDown

## *JavaScript1.2+, JScript3.0+*

## *Nav4+, IE4+*

## Syntax

onKeyDown="*command*"

## Description

The onKeyDown event handler of an instance of a Textarea object is fired when a key is pressed down within the text area. Care should be taken when using this event handler, because it is possible to get into an infinite loop when using other events or methods that are fired when the focus is placed on or away from the text area or other key-related events are used. The onKeyDown event handler is called followed by a onKeyPress event handler.

## Example

Listing 7.516 has a single text area. If the user presses a key while the focus is on the text area, an alert box is displayed as soon as the key is pressed.

*Listing 7.516    The onKeyDown Event Handler Causes an Alert Box to be Displayed*

```
<html>
<head>
```

```
<script language="JavaScript1.2">
<!-- Hide

// Pop up an alert box when the user presses a key.
function showDialog(){
  alert("A key was pressed down");
}
// End hide --->
</script>
</head>
<body>
<form name="myForm">
  <textarea name="myTextArea" rows=2 cols=50 onKeyDown='showDialog()'>
  Here is some text in my text area.
  </textarea>
</form>
</body>
</html>
```

# Textarea.onKeyPress

## *JavaScript1.2+, JScript3.0+*

## *Nav4+, IE4+*

## *Syntax*

onKeyPress="*command*"

## Description

The onKeyPress event handler of an instance of a Textarea object is fired when a key
is pressed within the text area. Care should be taken when using this event handler,
because it is possible to get into an infinite loop when using other events or methods
that are fired when the focus is placed on or away from the text area or other key-
related events are used. This event is called after an onKeyDown event handler.

## Example

Listing 7.517 has a single text area. If the user presses a key while the focus is on the
text area, an alert box is displayed as soon as the key is pressed showing the type of
event that was fired. The first event handler is onKeyDown, which is followed by an
onKeyPress event handler.

*Listing 7.517   The* onKeyDown *and* onKeyPress *Event Handlers Cause an Alert
Box to be Displayed*

```
<html>
<head>
<script language="JavaScript1.2">
<!-- Hide
```

*continues*

*Listing 7.517    continued*

```
// Pop up an alert box when the user presses a key.
function showDialog(type){
  alert("An onKey" + type + " event just occurred");
}
// End hide --->
</script>
</head>
<body>
<form name="myForm">
  <textarea name="myTextArea" rows=2 cols=50
            onKeyDown='showDialog("Down")'
            onKeyPress='showDialog("Press")'>
  Here is some text in my text area.
  </textarea>
</form>
</body>
</html>
```

# Textarea.onKeyUp

## *JavaScript1.2+, JScript3.0+*

## *Nav4+, IE4+*

## *Syntax*

onKeyUp="*command*"

## *Description*

The onKeyUp event handler of an instance of a Textarea object is fired when a key is released within the text area. Care should be taken when using this event handler, because it is possible to get into an infinite loop when using other events or methods that are fired when the focus is placed on or away from the text area or other key-related events are used. The onKeyUp event handler is called after an onKeyPress event handler.

## *Example*

Listing 7.518 has a single text area. If the user releases a key while the focus is on the text area, an alert box is displayed as soon as the key is released.

*Listing 7.518    The* onKeyUp *Event Handler Causes an Alert Box to be Displayed*

```
<html>
<head>
<script language="JavaScript1.2">
<!-- Hide

// Pop up an alert box when the user presses a key.
```

```
function showDialog(){
  alert("A key was released");
}
// End hide --->
</script>
</head>
<body>
<form name="myForm">
  <textarea name="myTextArea" rows=2 cols=50 onKeyUp='showDialog()'>
  Here is some text in my text area.
  </textarea>
</form>
</body>
</html>
```

# Textarea.onSelect

## JavaScript1.0+, JScript1.0+

## IE3+

## Syntax

onSelect="*command*"

## Description

The onSelect event handler of an instance of a Textarea object is fired when the text in the area is highlighted. Care should be taken when using this event handler, because it is possible to get into an infinite loop when using other events or methods that are fired when the focus is placed on the text area.

### NOTE

Note that Netscape defined this function in JavaScript 1.0, however, it is not fully implemented in any version released to date. Opera browsers do not support this function either.

## Example

Listing 7.519 has two text areas. If the user highlights the text in the first text area, the default text of the first text area is written to the second text area.

*Listing 7.519    Using the* onSelect *Event Handler to Set the Text in the Second Text Box*

```
<html>
<head>
<script language="JavaScript">
<!-- Hide
```

*continues*

*Listing 7.519    continued*
```
// Change the text of the second text area to the default
// of the first if user highlights text in the first.
function setText(){
  document.myForm.myTextArea2.value = document.myForm.myTextArea1.defaultValue;
}
// End hide --->
</script>
</head>
<body>
<form name="myForm">
  <textarea name="myTextArea1" rows=2 cols=50 onSelect='setText()'>
  Here is some text in my text area.
  </textarea>
  <br>
  <textarea name="myTextArea2" rows=2 cols=50>
  </textarea>
</form>
</body>
</html>
```

# Textarea.select()

## *JavaScript1.0+, JScript1.0+*

## *Nav2+, IE3+, Opera3+*

## *Syntax*

```
textarea.select()
```

## *Description*

The select() method of the Textarea object selects the text in the text area. Be careful when using this method in conjunction with the blur() and focus() methods. It can lead to a focus/blur loop where the browser blurs or focuses as soon as it is has been selected, and vice versa.

## *Example*

Listing 7.520 has a text area and a button. If the user clicks the button, the text inside the text area will be highlighted. Notice the focus() method had to be used to tell the browser to actually highlight the text.

*Listing 7.520    Using the* select() *Method to Select the Text in a Text Area*
```
<html>
<head>
<script language="JavaScript">
<!-- Hide

// Define the selectText function called by pressing the button
function selectText(){
```

```
    // Select the text in the area, then place focus on it.
    document.myForm.myTextArea.select();
    document.myForm.myTextArea.focus();
}
// End hide --->
</script>
</head>
<body>
<form name="myForm">
  <textarea name="myTextArea" rows=6 cols=50>
  Here is some text in my text area.
  </textarea>
<input type=BUTTON value="Click to Select Text" name="myButton"
       onClick="selectText()">
</form>
</body>
</html>
```

# Textarea.type

## *JavaScript1.1+, JScript1.0+*

## *Nav3+, IE3+, Opera3+*

## *Syntax*

`textarea.type`

## Description

The `type` property of an instance of a `Textarea` object returns the type of the text area. This always returns `textarea`.

## Example

Listing 7.521 has a text area and a button. When the button is clicked, an alert box is popped up that displays the `type` property of the text area.

*Listing 7.521    Displaying the* `type` *Property in an Alert Box*

```
<html>
<head>
<script language="JavaScript1.1">
<!-- Hide

// Display an alert box that contains the type of the
// text area.
function getType(){
  alert("The name of this text area is " +
        document.myForm.elements[0].type);
```

*continues*

*Listing 7.521    continued*

```
}
// End hide --->
</script>
</head>
<body>
<form name="myForm">
  <textarea name="myTextArea" rows=6 cols=50>
  Here is some text in my text area.
  </textarea>
  <input type=BUTTON value="Get Type" name="myButton" onClick='getType()'>
</form>
</body>
</html>
```

# Textarea.value

## JavaScript1.0+, JScript1.0+

## Nav2+, IE3+, Opera3+

## Syntax

`textarea.value`

## Description

The `value` property of an instance of a `Textarea` object returns the current value of the text area. Note that this is not the default value that can be accessed via the `Textarea.defaultValue` property and is often used to set the value of a text area.

## Example

Listing 7.522 contains a text area and button. You can edit the text in the text area, and then click the Reset button to reset the text back to the default value.

*Listing 7.522    Resetting the Value of a Text Area to the Default Value*

```
<html>
<head>
<script language="JavaScript">
<!-- Hide

// Reset the text in the text area to its default value.
function resetText(){
  document.myForm.myTextArea.value = document.myForm.myTextArea.defaultValue;
}
// End hide --->
</script>
</head>
<body>
<form name="myForm">
  <textarea name="myTextArea" rows=6 cols=50>
```

```
 Here is some text in my text area.
 </textarea>
 <input type=BUTTON value="Reset" name="myButton" onClick='resetText()'>
</form>
</body>
</html>
```

# untaint()

## *JavaScript 1.1*

## *Nav3*

## *Syntax*

```
untaint(property)
untaint(variable)
untaint(function)
untaint(object)
```

## *Description*

The untaint() method, a security measure that was only implemented in JavaScript 1.1, allowed a developer to allow return values to be used by and propagated to other scripts. This method does not change the data element passed to it, but rather returns an unmarked reference to the element.

Because untaint() and the functionality of data tainting was removed in JavaScript 1.2, you should avoid using this method. You should use it only if you have a specific security reason for compatibility with Navigator 3 browsers. See Chapter 1 for more information on the security model that is now used in Navigator browsers.

## *Example*

Listing 7.523 simply untaints a variable that is defined in a separate window.

*Listing 7.523   Use of the* untaint() *Method, Which Is No Longer Supported*

```
<script language="JavaScript1.1">
<!-- Hide

// store the untainted variable from the second window
// in the variable utMyVar.
var utMyvar = untaint(myWin.myVar);

// End hide --->
</script>
```

# Window

## *JavaScript1.0+, JScript1.0+*

## *Nav2+, IE3+, Opera3+*

## Syntax

Core client-side JavaScript object.

## Description

The `Window` object is one of the top-level JavaScript objects that are created when a `<body>`, `<frameset>`, or `<frame>` tag is encountered. Instances of this object can also be created by using the `Window.open()` method. Table 7.47 lists the properties and methods associated with the `Window` object.

**Table 7.47    Methods and Properties of the Window Object**

| Type | Item | Description |
| --- | --- | --- |
| Methods | alert | Displays an alert dialog box with the text string passed. |
| | back | Loads the previous page in place of the window instance. |
| | blur | Removes the focus from a window. |
| | captureEvents | Sets the window to capture all events of a specified type. |
| | clearInterval | Clears the interval set with the setInterval method. |
| | clearTimeout | Clears the timeout set with the setTimeout method. |
| | close | Closes the instance of the window. |
| | confirm | Displays a confirmation dialog box. |
| | disableExternalCapture | Disables external event capturing. |
| | enableExternalCapture | Enables external event capturing for the pages loaded from other servers. |
| | find | Displays a Find dialog box where the user can enter text to search the current page. |
| | focus | Assigns the focus to the specified window instance. |
| | forward | Loads the next page in place of the window instance. |
| | handleEvent | Invokes the handler for the event passed. |
| | home | Loads the user's specified home page in place of the window instance. |
| | moveBy | Moves the window by the amounts specified. |
| | moveTo | Moves the window to the specified location. |
| | open | Opens a new instance of a window. |
| | print | Invokes the Print dialog box so the user can print the current window. |

| Type | Item | Description |
|---|---|---|
| | `prompt` | Displays a prompt dialog box. |
| | `releaseEvents` | Releases the captured events of a specified type. |
| | `resizeBy` | Resizes the window by the specified amount. |
| | `resizeTo` | Resizes the window to the specified size. |
| | `routeEvent` | Passes the events of a specified type to be handled natively. |
| | `scroll` | Scrolls the document in the window to a specified location. |
| | `scrollBy` | Scrolls the document in the window by a specified amount. |
| | `scrollTo` | Scrolls the document, both width and height, in the window to a specified location. |
| | `setInterval` | Invokes a function or evaluates an expression every time the number of milliseconds has passed. |
| | `setTimeout` | Invokes a function or evaluates an expression when the number of milliseconds has passed. |
| | `stop` | Stops the current window from loading other items within it. |
| Properties | `closed` | Specifies if the window instance has been closed. |
| | `defaultStatus` | Is the default message in the window's status bar. |
| | `document` | References all the information about the document within this window. See the `Document` object for more information. |
| | `frames` | References all the information about the frames within this window. See the `Frame` object for more information. |
| | `history` | References the URLs the user has visited. |
| | `innerHeight` | Contains the height of the display area of the current window in pixels. |
| | `innerWidth` | Contains the width of the display area of the current window in pixels. |
| | `length` | Represents the number of frames in the current window. |

*continues*

*Table 7.47 continued*

| Type | Item | Description |
|------|------|-------------|
| | location | Contains the current URL loaded into the window. |
| | locationbar | Reference to the browser's location bar. |
| | menubar | Reference to the browser's menu bar. |
| | name | Name of the window. |
| | opener | Contains the name of the window from which a second window was opened. |
| | outerHeight | Contains the height of the outer area of the current window in pixels. |
| | outerWidth | Contains the width of the outer area of the current window in pixels. |
| | pageXOffset | Contains the x-coordinate of the current window. |
| | pageYOffset | Contains the y-coordinate of the current window. |
| | parent | Reference to the upper most window that is displaying the current frame. |
| | personalbar | Reference to the browser's personal bar. |
| | scrollbars | Reference to the browser's scroll bars. |
| | self | Reference for the current window. |
| | status | Reference to the message in the window's status bar. |
| | statusbar | Reference to the browser's status bar. |
| | toolbar | Reference to the browser's tool bar. |
| | top | Reference to the upper most window that is displaying the current frame. |
| | window | Reference for the current window. |

Any of the methods or properties of this object can have the instance name left off if it refers to the window in which they are invoked. Setting the `status` property, for instance, would set the status in the current window, while setting `myWin.status` sets the status in the window named `myWin`. The only exception to this rule is in using the `location` property and the `close()` and `open()` methods, which must take the instance's name when called within an event handler.

**NOTE**

Each of the entries for the `Window` object's methods and properties in this chapter will be preceded by the `Window` object name in its syntax definition.

## *Example*

Listing 7.524 contains a button. When the button is clicked, a new window instance is created using the open() method. Information is then written to the window before the stream is closed. There is also a button in the new window to close it. The result of running this script and clicking the button to open the window can be seen in Figure 7.15.

*Listing 7.524    Creating a New Instance of the* Window *Object*

```
<html>
<head>

<script language="JavaScript">
<!-- Hide

// Define the openWin() function
function openWin(){

  // Create variables to hold the various options that can be set
  // when a new Window instance is created.
  var myBars = 'directories=no,location=no,menubar=no,status=no';
  myBars += ',titlebar=no,toolbar=no';
  var myOptions = 'scrollbars=no,width=400,height=200,resizeable=no';
  var myFeatures = myBars + ',' + myOptions;
  var myReadme = "Welcome to Pure JavaScript!\n" +
        "----------------------------------------\n" +
        'You can enter some text here.'

  // Open the window. Give the window instance the name newDoc and
  // name the document in the window myWin.
  var newWin = open('', 'myWin', myFeatures);

  newWin.document.writeln('<form>');
  newWin.document.writeln('<table cellspacing=0 cellpadding=0 border=1>');
  newWin.document.writeln('<tr valign=TOPcolor= bgcolor="#000099"><td>');
  newWin.document.writeln('<font size=-1 color="#FFFFFF"><b>');
  newWin.document.writeln('  Readme</b></font>');
  newWin.document.writeln('</td></tr>');
  newWin.document.writeln('<tr valign=TOP><td>');
  newWin.document.writeln('<textarea cols=45 rows=7 wrap=SOFT>');
  newWin.document.writeln(myReadme + '</textarea>');
  newWin.document.writeln('</td></tr>');
  newWin.document.writeln('<tr valign=BOTTOM align=RIGHT');
  newWin.document.writeln(' bgcolor="#C0C0C0"><td>');
  newWin.document.writeln('<input type=BUTTON value="Close"');
  newWin.document.writeln(' onClick="window.close()">');
  newWin.document.writeln('</td></tr>');
  newWin.document.writeln('</table></form>');

  // Close the stream to the document and bring the window to the front.
```

*continues*

*Listing 7.524    continued*
```
  newWin.document.close();
  newWin.focus();
}

// End hide --->
</script>
</head>
<body>
<form>
  <b>Click the following button to open a new window: </b>
  <input type=BUTTON value="Open" onClick='openWin()'>
</form>
</body>
</html>
```

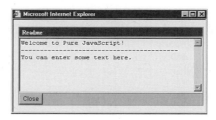

**Figure 7.15**
*Result of running Listing 7.524 in a browser and clicking the Open button.*

# window.alert()

## *JavaScript1.0+, JScript1.0*

## *Nav2+, IE3+, Opera3+*

## *Syntax*
window.alert(*string*)

## *Description*
The alert() method of the Window object displays an alert dialog box when invoked.
The value of the string passed to the method is displayed in the box.

## *Example*
Listing 7.525 pops up an alert box when the script is loaded. The result of running this
script can be seen in Figure 7.16.

*Listing 7.525    An Alert Box*
```
<script language="JavaScript">
<!-- Hide
```

```
alert('Here is an alert dialog box.');

// End hide --->
</script>
```

**Figure 7.16**

*An alert box created with the* Window.alert() *method.*

# window.back()

## *JavaScript1.2+, Jscript3.0*

## *Nav4+, IE4+*

## *Syntax*

*window*.back()

## *Description*

The back() method of the Window object simulates the user clicking the Back button on the browser. It returns the browser's page or frame to the previous page or frame.

## *Example*

Listing 7.526 has two buttons. One of the buttons takes the browser back one page and the other button takes it forward. Note that there has to be a back and previous page during your session for the button to have somewhere to go.

*Listing 7.526    Using the* back() *Method*

```
<html>
<body>
<form>
  <input type=BUTTON value="Back" onClick="window.back()">
  <input type=BUTTON value="Forward" onClick="window.forward()">
</form>
</body>
</html>
```

# window.blur()

## *JavaScript1.0+, JScript1.0+*

## *Nav2+, IE3+, Opera3+*

## Syntax

```
window.blur()
```

## Description

The `blur()` method of the `Window` object removes the focus from the window. Be careful when using this method in conjunction with the `focus()` method of objects. It can lead to a focus/blur loop, where the browser blurs a focus as soon as it is done, and vice versa.

## Example

Listing 7.527 has two buttons. When the user clicks the Open button, a second, smaller window is opened. If the Blur button is clicked, the focus is removed from the parent window and placed on the child window.

*Listing 7.527    Using the `blur()` Method to Remove the Focus from a Window*

```html
<html>
<head>
  <title>Using the blur() Method</title>
<script language="JavaScript">
<!-- Hide

// Define the openWin() function
function openWin(){

  // Create variables to hold the various options that can be set
  // when a new Window instance is created.
  var myBars = 'directories=no,location=no,menubar=no,status=no';
  myBars += ',titlebar=no,toolbar=no';
  var myOptions = 'scrollbars=no,width=400,height=200,resizeable=no';
  var myFeatures = myBars + ',' + myOptions;

  // Open a child window
  newWin = open('', 'myDoc', myFeatures);

  newWin.document.writeln('Here is the child window');

  // Close the stream to the document.
  newWin.document.close();

  // Return focus to the parent window
  self.focus();
}

// Define the blurWin() function
function blurWin(){

  // Blur the parent window and focus on the child
```

```
  self.blur();
  newWin.focus();
}

// End hide --->
</script>
</head>
<body>
<form>
  <input type=BUTTON value="Open" onClick='openWin()'>
  <input type=BUTTON value="Blur" onClick='blurWin()'>
</form>
</body>
</html>
```

# window.captureEvents()

## *JavaScript1.2+, JScript3.0+*

## *Nav4+, IE4+*

## *Syntax*

```
window.captureEvents(event)
window.captureEvents(event1 ¦ event2 ¦ eventN)
```

## *Description*

The captureEvents() method of the Window object captures all the events of the event type passed. Because you can capture the events that are natively handled by the language itself, programmers can now define a function to handle events in a manner they want. If you have multiple events that you want to capture, separate them with the pipe, ¦, character. The types of events that can be captured are as follows:

- Event.ABORT
- Event.BLUR
- Event.CHANGE
- Event.CLICK
- Event.DBLCLICK
- Event.DRAGDROP
- Event.ERROR
- Event.FOCUS
- Event.KEYDOWN
- Event.KEYPRESS
- Event.KEYUP
- Event.LOAD
- Event.MOUSEDOWN
- Event.MOUSEMOVE
- Event.MOUSEOUT
- Event.MOUSEOVER

- Event.MOUSEUP
- Event.MOVE
- Event.RESET
- Event.RESIZE
- Event.SELECT
- Event.SUBMIT
- Event.UNLOAD

After an event has been captured, you can define a function to replace the built-in method for handling the event.

## Example

Listing 7.528 has a single text box. The script in the <head> of the document specifies a function to handle all onClick events in the window. To be able to do this, the captureEvents() method had to be used to capture all events of type Event.CLICK. When the page itself is clicked, a counter, which is displayed in the text box, is incremented.

*Listing 7.528    Capturing Events with the* Window.captureEvents() *Method*

```
<html>
<head>
  <title>Using window.captureEvents</title>
<script language="JavaScript1.2">
<!-- Hide

// Define a click counter variable
var counter = 0;

// Tell the browser you want to intercept ALL click events
// on the page. Then define a function to handle them.
window.captureEvents(Event.CLICK)
window.onClick = myClickHandler;

// Define the myClickHandler function to handle click events
function myClickHandler{

  // Pass all click events to the onClick event of the text box
  window.document.myForm.myText.handleEvent;

}

// Function is called by onClick of text box. Displays the number
// of clicks that have occurred.
function changeText(){
  document.myForm.myText.value = counter++;
}
// End hide --->
</script>
</head>
<body>
```

```
<form name="myForm">
  <input type=TEXT size=2 value="" name="myText" onClick='changeText()'>
</form>
</body>
</html>
```

# window.clearInterval()

## JavaScript1.2+, JScript3.0+

## Nav4+, IE4+

### Syntax

```
window.clearInterval(interval)
```

### Description

The clearInterval() method of the Window object clears the interval that is passed to the method. The interval that is passed has to be previously defined using the setInterval() method.

### Example

Listing 7.529 sets an interval in the <head> of the document that displays a counter in a text box on the page. An interval is set to update the counter in the text box every five seconds. There is also a button on the page that can be clicked to clear the interval and stop the counting.

Listing 7.529    Clearing an Interval with the clearInterval() Method

```
<html>
<head>
  <title>Using window.clearInterval()</title>
<script language="JavaScript1.2">
<!-- Hide

// Create a variable to hold a counter
var counter = 1;

// Define a function to display the counter
function startCounter(){
  document.myForm.myText.value = counter++;
}

// Define a function to stop the counter
function stopCounter(){
  window.clearInterval(myInterval);
}

// Set the interval to call the function every 5 seconds
var myInterval = window.setInterval("startCounter()", 5000)
```

*continues*

*Listing 7.529    continued*

```
// End hide --->
</script>
</head>
<body onLoad="startCounter()">
<form name="myForm">
  <input type=TEXT size=20 value="" name="myText">
  <input type=BUTTON value="Clear Interval" onClick="stopCounter()">
</form>
</body>
</html>
```

# window.clearTimeout()

## JavaScript1.0+, JScript1.0+

## Nav2+, IE3+, Opera3+

## Syntax

```
window.clearTimeout(timeout)
```

## Description

The `clearTimeout()` method of the `Window` object clears the timeout passed to the method. The timeout that is passed has to be previously defined using the `setTimeout()` method.

## Example

Listing 7.530 has a button and text box. By the default, the time will be displayed in the text box after five seconds. This is done using the `setTimeout()` method. If the button is clicked, a function is called that invokes the `clearTimeout()` method preventing the time from being displayed in the text box.

*Listing 7.530    Using the `clearTimeout()` Method*

```
<html>
<head>
<script language="JavaScript">
<!-- Hide

// Define a function to show the time
function showTime(){
  myTime = new Date();
  myTime = myTime.getHours() + ":" + myTime.getMinutes() + ":";
  myTime += myTime.getSeconds();
  document.myForm.myText.value = myTime;
}

// Define a function to stop the display of the time
function stopTime(){
  window.clearTimeout(myTimeout);
```

```
}

// Set the interval to call the function after 5 seconds
var myTimeout = window.setTimeout("showTime()", 5000)

// End hide --->
</script>
</head>
<body>
<form name="myForm">
  <input type=TEXT size=20 value="" name="myText">
  <input type=BUTTON value="Clear Timeout" onClick="stopTime()">
</form>
</body>
</html>
```

# window.close()

## JavaScript1.0+, JScript1.0+

## Nav2+, IE3+, Opera3+

## Syntax

`window.close()`

## Description

The `close()` method of the `Window` object is used to close browser windows. Even though this method was first introduced in JavaScript 1.0, there have been some changes. In the first version, this method could be used to close any window. In JavaScript 1.1, it was restricted to close only windows opened using JavaScript. In JavaScript 1.2, you must have the `UniversalBrowserWrite` privilege to unconditionally close a window.

## Example

Listing 7.531 has a button that opens a window. Within the opened window there is a Close button. Clicking this button invokes the `close()` method and closes the browser window.

*Listing 7.531    Using the* `close()` *Method to Close a Window*
```
<html>
<head>

<script language="JavaScript">
<!-- Hide

// Define the openWin() function
function openWin(){
```

*continues*

*Listing 7.531    continued*

```
// Create variables to hold the various options that can be set
// when a new Window instance is created.
var myBars = 'directories=no,location=no,menubar=no,status=no';
myBars += ',titlebar=no,toolbar=no';
var myOptions = 'scrollbars=no,width=400,height=200,resizeable=no';
var myFeatures = myBars + ',' + myOptions;
var myReadme = "Welcome to Pure JavaScript!\n" +
     "----------------------------------------\n" +
     "Click the Close button to invoke the close() " +
     "method and close the window."

// Open the window. Give the window instance the name newDoc and
// name the document in the window myDoc.
var newWin = open('', 'myDoc', myFeatures);

newWin.document.writeln('<form>');
newWin.document.writeln('<table cellspacing=0 cellpadding=0 border=1>');
newWin.document.writeln('<tr valign=TOPcolor= bgcolor="#000099"><td>');
newWin.document.writeln('<font size=-1 color="#FFFFFF"><b>');
newWin.document.writeln('  Readme</b></font>');
newWin.document.writeln('</td></tr>');
newWin.document.writeln('<tr valign=TOP><td>');
newWin.document.writeln('<textarea cols=45 rows=7 wrap=SOFT>');
newWin.dpcument.writeln(myReadme + '</textarea>');
newWin.document.writeln('</td></tr>');
newWin.document.writeln('<tr valign=BOTTOM align=RIGHT);
newWin.document.writeln(' bgcolor="#C0C0C0"><td>');

// Write the close() method on the new window. Invoke it with an onClick
// event.
newWin.document.writeln('<input type=BUTTON value="Close");
newWin.document.writeln(' onClick="window.close()">');

newWin.document.writeln('</td></tr>');
newWin.document.writeln('</table></form>');

// Close the stream to the document and bring the window to the front.
newWin.document.close();
newWin.focus();
}


// End hide --->
</script>
</head>
<body>
<form>
  <b>Click the following button to open a new window: </b>
  <input type=BUTTON value="Open" onClick='openWin()'>
</form>
```

```
</body>
</html>
```

# window.closed

## *JavaScript1.1+, JScript1.0+*

## *Nav3+, IE3+, Opera3+*

## *Syntax*

*window.closed*

## *Description*

The closed property of the Window object returns a Boolean value specifying if the window instance it is referencing is closed or not. If the window is still open, the property returns false. If it is closed, the property returns true.

## *Example*

Listing 7.532 has two buttons. When the Open button is clicked, a second window is opened and focused. When the Check button is clicked, the script checks to see if the window is still open or not. If it is, the text in the text area of the second window is changed. If it is not, an alert dialog box is displayed.

*Listing 7.532   Using the* closed *Property to See If a Window Is Still Open*

```
<html>
<head>

<script language="JavaScript1.1">
<!-- Hide

// Define the openWin() function
function openWin(){

  // Create variables to hold the various options that can be set
  // when a new Window instance is created.
  var myBars = 'directories=no,location=no,menubar=no,status=no';
  myBars += ',titlebar=no,toolbar=no';
  var myOptions = 'scrollbars=no,width=400,height=200,resizeable=no';
  var myFeatures = myBars + ',' + myOptions;
  var myReadme = "Welcome to Pure JavaScript!\n" +
      "----------------------------------------\n" +
      "Click the Close button to invoke the close() " +
      "method and close the window."

  // Open the window. Give the window instance the name newDoc and
  // name the document in the window myDoc.
  newWin = open('', 'myDoc', myFeatures);
```

*continues*

*Listing 7.532    continued*

```
  newWin.document.writeln('<form name="secondForm">');
  newWin.document.writeln('<table cellspacing=0 cellpadding=0 border=1>');
  newWin.document.writeln('<tr valign=TOPcolor= bgcolor="#000099"><td>');
  newWin.document.writeln('<font size=-1 color="#FFFFFF"><b>');
  newWin.document.writeln('  Readme</b></font>');
  newWin.document.writeln('</td></tr>');
  newWin.document.writeln('<tr valign=TOP><td>');
  newWin.document.writeln('<textarea name="myTextArea"cols=45 rows=7');
  newWin.document.writeln(' wrap=SOFT>' + myReadme + '</textarea>');
  newWin.document.writeln('</td></tr>');
  newWin.document.writeln('<tr valign=BOTTOM align=RIGHT');
  newWin.document.writeln(' bgcolor="#C0C0C0"><td>');
  newWin.document.writeln('<input type=BUTTON value="Close" ');
  newWin.document.writeln('onClick="window.close()">');
  newWin.document.writeln('</td></tr>');
  newWin.document.writeln('</table></form>');

  // Close the stream to the document and bring the window to the front.
  newWin.document.close();
  newWin.focus();
}


function checkWin(){

  // Use the closed property to see if the window has been closed.
  if(newWin.closed){
      alert("Sorry, the window has been closed.");
  }else{
    var myText = "This window is still opened";
    newWin.document.secondForm.myTextArea.value = myText;
    newWin.focus();
  }
}
// End hide --->
</script>
</head>
<body>
<form>
  <input type=BUTTON value="Open" onClick='openWin()'>
  <input type=BUTTON value="Check" onClick='checkWin()'>
</form>
</body>
</html>
```

# window.confirm()

## *JavaScript1.0+, JScript1.0*

## Nav2+, IE3+, Opera3+

## Syntax

`window.confirm(string)`

## Description

The `confirm()` method of the `Window` object displays a confirmation dialog box when invoked. The value of the string passed to the method is displayed in the box. This box will contain both an OK and Cancel button. The method returns a Boolean value of `true` if the user clicks OK and `false` if the user clicks Cancel.

## Example

Listing 7.533 pops up a confirmation box when the script is loaded to see if the user wishes to proceed. Once the user makes a decision, the script writes his choice to the page. The result of running this script can be seen in Figure 7.17.

*Listing 7.533   A Confirm Box*

```
<script language="JavaScript">
<!-- Hide

// Ask the user if they want to proceed
if(confirm("Are you sure you want to do this?")){
  document.write("You clicked the OK button");
}else{
  document.write("You clicked the Cancel button");
}

// Close the stream to the document
document.close();

// End hide --->
</script>
```

**Figure 7.17**

*A confirmation box created with the* `Window.confirm()` *method.*

# window.defaultStatus

## JavaScript1.0+, JScript1.0+

## Nav2+, IE3+, Opera3+

## Syntax

```
window.defaultStatus = string
```

## Description

The `defaultStatus` property of the `Window` object reflects the message that is displayed in the status bar of the browser. Note that in JavaScript 1.1, this property was tainted. See Chapter 1 for more information on JavaScript security and data tainting.

## Example

Listing 7.534 shows how you can set the default status to be displayed after a document has finished loading. This is done in conjunction with the `onLoad` event handler within the <body> tag.

*Listing 7.534    Setting the Default Status of a Page*

```
<body onLoad="window.defaultStatus='Please make a selection'">
```

# window.disableExternalCapture()

## JavaScript1.2+

## Nav4+

## Syntax

```
window.disableExternalCapture()
```

## Description

The `disableExternalCapture()` method of the `Window` object disables any external event capturing set up using the `enableExternalCapture()` method. The functionality of this method provides the capturing of events in frames loaded from a different server. Before you can enable the capturing of these external events, you must first obtain `UniversalBrowserWrite` privileges. Once obtained and the method has been invoked, you use the `Window.captureEvents()` method to specify the events you wish to capture.

> **NOTE**
>
> For more information on privileges, JavaScript security, and signed scripts, see Chapter 1.

## Example

Listing 7.535 enables external event capturing when the document loads. The document itself has a button that, when clicked, calls a function to disable the external event captures.

*Listing 7.535    Disabling External Event Capturing*

```
<html>
<head>
<script language="JavaScript1.2">
<!-- Hide

// Ask the user for permission to enable the UniversalBrowserWrite
// privilege
netscape.security.PrivilegeManager.enablePrivilege("UniversalBrowserWrite");

// Enable the external capturing of events.
window.enableExternalCapture();

// Specifically capture submit events.
window.captureEvents(Event.SUBMIT);

// Define a function to turn off these external event captures
function turnOffEvents(){
  window.disableExternalCapture();
  alert("You have sucessfully turned off external event captures");
}
// End hide --->
</script>
</head>
<body>
<form>
  <input type=BUTTON value="Disenable External Capturing"
         onClick="turnOffEvents()">
</form>
</body>
</html>
```

# window.document

## *JavaScript1.0+, JScript1.0+*

## *Nav2+, IE3+, Opera3+*

## Syntax

```
Creates Instance of Document Object
window.document.event
window.document.method()
window.document.property
```

## Description

The document property, which is a child object of the Window object, is a core JavaScript object that is created when instances of the <body> tag are encountered. The properties, methods, and events associated with this object are in Table 7.48.

**Table 7.48** *Event Handlers, Methods, and Properties Used by the Window.document Property*

| Type | Item | Description |
|------|------|-------------|
| Event Handlers | onClick | Executes code when the document is clicked. |
| | onDblClick | Executes code when the document is double-clicked. |
| | onKeyDown | Executes code when a key is pressed down. This occurs before an onKeyPress event handler and was added in JavaScript 1.2. |
| | onKeyPress | Executes code when a key is pressed down immediately after an onKeyDown event handler. This event handler was added in JavaScript 1.2. |
| | onKeyUp | Executes code when a key is released. This was added in JavaScript 1.2. |
| | onMouseDown | Executes code when the mouse button is pressed down. |
| | onMouseUp | Executes code when the mouse button is released. |
| Methods | captureEvents() | Allows you to capture all events of the type passed in the document. Note that this method was added in JavaScript 1.2. |
| | close() | Closes the stream to the document. |
| | getSelection() | Returns the currently selected text. Note that this method was added in JavaScript 1.2. |
| | handleEvent() | Invokes the handler for the event specified and was added in JavaScript 1.2. |
| | open() | Opens a stream to the document. |
| | releaseEvents() | Releases the events that you have captured of the type passed in the document. Note that this method was added in JavaScript 1.2. |
| | routeEvent() | Passes the specified event along the normal route of execution. Note that this method was added in JavaScript 1.2. |
| | write() | Writes the string passed to the document. |
| | writeln() | Writes the string, followed by a newline character, to the document. |
| Properties | alinkColor | Specifies the ALINK attribute of the <body> tag. |

| Type | Item | Description |
|------|------|-------------|
| | anchors | Array containing each `<a>` tag in a document. |
| | applets | Array containing each `<applet>` tag in a document. Note that this property was added in JavaScript 1.1. |
| | bgColor | Specifies the BGCOLOR attribute of the `<body>` tag. |
| | cookie | Specifies a cookie. |
| | domain | Specifies the domain that served the document. Note that this property was added in JavaScript 1.1. |
| | embeds | Array containing each `<embed>` tag in a document. Note that this property was added in JavaScript 1.1. |
| | fgColor | Specifies the TEXT attribute of the `<body>` tag. |
| | *formName* | The actual name of each `<form>` in a document. Note that this property was added in JavaScript 1.1. |
| | forms | Array containing each `<form>` tag in a document. Note that this property was added in JavaScript 1.1. |
| | images | Array containing each `<img>` tag in a document. Note that this property was added in JavaScript 1.1. |
| | lastModified | Specifies the date the document was last changed. |
| | layers | Array containing each `<layer>` tag in a document. Note that this property was added in JavaScript 1.2. |
| | linkColor | Specifies the LINK attribute of the `<body>` tag. |
| | links | Array containing each `<a>` and `<area>` tag in a document. |
| | plugins | Array containing each plug-in in a document. Note that this property was added in JavaScript 1.1. |
| | referrer | Specifies the referral URL. |
| | title | Contains the text between the beginning `<title>` and ending `</title>` tags. |
| | URL | Specifies the URL of the document. |
| | vlinkColor | Specifies the VLINK attribute of the `<body>` tag. |

Please see the entries in this chapter for the Document object for more information on each of these events, methods, and properties.

## Example

Listing 7.536 uses the write() method of the document property to write text to the user's page.

*Listing 7.536   Accessing Methods of the document Property*

```
<script language="JavaScript">
<!-- Hide

window.document.write("Hello, World!");

// End hide --->
</script>
```

# window.enableExternalCapture()

## JavaScript1.2+

## Nav4+

## Syntax

window.enableExternalCapture(*event*)

## Description

The enableExternalCapture() method of the Window object enables external event capturing of the event that is passed to the method. This method provides the capturing of events in frames loaded from a different server. Before you can enable the capturing of these external events, you must first obtain UniversalBrowserWrite privileges. Obtaining this privilege will send a security dialog box to the user to decide whether or not to accept the request. This dialog box is like the one in Figure 7.18.

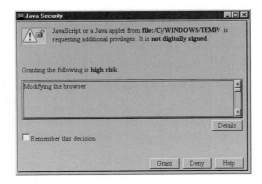

**Figure 7.18**

*The security dialog box that is displayed when a script asks for UniversalBrowserWrite privileges.*

Once obtained and the method has been invoked, you use the `Window.captureEvents()` method to specify the events you want to capture. To remove the ability to capture these events, you can invoke the `Window.disableExternalCapture()` method. The types of events that can be captured are as follows:

- `Event.ABORT`
- `Event.BLUR`
- `Event.CHANGE`
- `Event.CLICK`
- `Event.DBLCLICK`
- `Event.DRAGDROP`
- `Event.ERROR`
- `Event.FOCUS`
- `Event.KEYDOWN`
- `Event.KEYPRESS`
- `Event.KEYUP`
- `Event.LOAD`
- `Event.MOUSEDOWN`
- `Event.MOUSEMOVE`
- `Event.MOUSEOUT`
- `Event.MOUSEOVER`
- `Event.MOUSEUP`
- `Event.MOVE`
- `Event.RESET`
- `Event.RESIZE`
- `Event.SELECT`
- `Event.SUBMIT`
- `Event.UNLOAD`

**NOTE**

For more information on privileges, JavaScript security, and signed scripts, see Chapter 1.

## *Example*

Listing 7.537 enables external event capturing when the document loads.

*Listing 7.537    Enabling External Event Capturing*

```
<script language="JavaScript1.2">
<!-- Hide

// Ask the user for permission to enable the UniversalBrowserWrite
// privilege
netscape.security.PrivilegeManager.enablePrivilege("UniversalBrowserWrite");
```

*continues*

*Listing 7.537    continued*
```
// Enable the external capturing of events.
window.enableExternalCapture();

// Specifically capture submit events.
window.captureEvents(Event.SUBMIT);

// End hide --->
</script>
```

# window.find()

## JavaScript1.2+, JScript3.0

## Nav4+, IE4+

## Syntax

```
window.find()
```

## Description

The find() method of the Window object displays a find dialog box when invoked. This allows a user to search for a string in the page from which it was invoked.

## Example

Listing 7.538 has a function that pops up a Find box when it is called. The result of running this script can be seen in Figure 7.19.

*Listing 7.538    A Find Box That Can Be Used to Search for Text in the Document*
```
<script language="JavaScript1.2">
<!-- Hide

function mySearch(){
  window.find();
}

// End hide --->
</script>
```

## Figure 7.19

*A find box created with the Window.find() method.*

# window.focus()

## *JavaScript1.1+, JScript1.0+*

## *Nav3+, IE3+, Opera3+*

## *Syntax*

```
window.focus()
```

## *Description*

The `focus()` method of the `Window` object places focus on the window. Be careful when using this method in conjunction with the `blur()` method of objects. It can lead to a focus/blur loop, where the browser blurs a focus as soon as it is done, and vice versa.

## *Example*

Listing 7.539 has a button. When the user clicks the Open button, a second, smaller window is opened and the focus is placed back on the parent window.

*Listing 7.539   Using the `focus()` Method to Remove the Focus from a Window*

```
<html>
<head>
</head>

<script language="JavaScript1.1">
<!-- Hide

// Define the openWin() function
function openWin(){

  // Create variables to hold the various options that can be set
  // when a new Window instance is created.
  var myBars = 'directories=no,location=no,menubar=no,status=no';
  myBars += ',titlebar=no,toolbar=no';
  var myOptions = 'scrollbars=no,width=400,height=200,resizeable=no';
  var myFeatures = myBars + ',' + myOptions;

  // Open a child window
  newWin = open('', 'myDoc', myFeatures);

  newWin.document.writeln('Here is the child window');

  // Close the stream to the document.
  newWin.document.close();

  // Return focus to the parent window
  self.focus();
```

*continues*

*Listing 7.539    continued*
```
}

// End hide --->
</script>
<body>
<form>
  <input type=BUTTON value="Open" onClick='openWin()'>
</form>
</body>
</html>
```

# window.forward()

## *JavaScript1.2+, Jscript3.0*

## *Nav4+, IE4+*

## Syntax

```
window.forward()
```

## Description

The `forward()` method of the `Window` object simulates the user clicking the Forward button on the browser. It returns the browser's page or frame to the next page or frame in its history.

## Example

Listing 7.540 has two buttons. One of the buttons takes the browser back one page and the other button takes it forward. Note that there has to be a back and previous page during your session for the button to have somewhere to go.

*Listing 7.540    Using the* `forward()` *Method to Take the User to the Next Page in Their History*
```
<html>
<body>
<form>
  <input type=BUTTON value="Back" onClick="window.back()">
  <input type=BUTTON value="Forward" onClick="window.forward()">
</form>
</body>
</html>
```

# window.frames

## *JavaScript1.0+, JScript1.0+*

## *Nav2+, IE3+, Opera3+*

## Syntax

```
window.frames["frameName"]
window.frames[num]
```

## Description

The `frames` property of the `Window` object contains an array that stores each frame instance created with the `<frame>` tag, in a document. Array entries of the child frame can be referenced either by index number or by the name assigned by the NAME attribute of the `<frame>` tag.

## Example

Listing 7.541 uses the `length` property of `frames` array and a `for` loop to access the name of each frame in the window. This information is then written to the document window.

*Listing 7.541    Example of Using the* `frames` *Property*

```
<script language="JavaScript">
<!-- Hide

// Use a for loop to write out the name of each frame.
for(var i = 0; i <window.frames.length; i++){
  newWin.document.write("The name of frame #" + i);
  newWin.document.write(" is " + window.frames[i].name + "<br>");
}
// End Hide --->
</script>
```

# window.frames.length

```
window.frames["frameName"].length
window.frames[num].length
```

## Description

The `length` sub property of the `frames` property of the `Window` object contains the number of frame instances in a document created with the `<frame>` tag.

## Example

Listing 7.542 uses the `length` property of `frames` array and a `for` loop to access the name of each frame in the window. This information is then written to the document window.

*Listing 7.542    Using the* `length` *Property*

```
<script language="JavaScript">
<!-- Hide

// Use a for loop to write out the name of each frame.
for(var i = 0; i <window.frames.length; i++){
```

*continues*

*Listing 7.542    continued*
```
  newWin.document.write("The name of frame #" + i);
  newWin.document.write(" is " + window.frames[i].name + "<br>");
}
// End Hide --->
</script>
```

# window.handleEvent()

## *JavaScript1.2+, JScript3.0+*

## *Nav4+, IE4+*

## *Syntax*

*window.object*.handleEvent(*event*)

## Description

The handleEvent() method of the Window object invokes the handler for the event specified of the specified object. This method was added in JavaScript 1.2.

## Example

Listing 7.543 has a single text box. The script tells the browser that it wants to intercept all Click events and that it wants the myClickHandler function to handle them. Within this function, the handleEvent() method of the text box has been specified to handle the click.

When the user clicks anywhere on the page, the onClick event handler in the <input type=TEXT> tag calls a function to change the text in the text box. The change is nothing more than a simple number that is incremented counting the number of times the page has been clicked.

*Listing 7.543    Using the* handleEvent() *Method of a* Window *Object to Handle all Clicks on a Page*
```
<html>
<head>
<script language="JavaScript1.2">
<!-- Hide

// Define a click counter variable
var counter = 0;

// Tell the browser you want to intercept ALL click events
// on the page. Then define a function to handle them.
window.captureEvents(Event.CLICK)
window.onClick = myClickHandler;

// Define the myClickHandler function to handle click events
function myClickHandler{
```

```
  // Pass all click events to the onClick event of the text box
  window.document.myForm.myText.handleEvent;
}

// Function is called by onClick of text box. Displays the number
// of clicks that have occurred.
function changeText(){
  document.myForm.myText.value = counter++;
}
// End hide --->
</script>
</head>
<body>
<form name="myForm">
  <input type=TEXT size=2 value="" name="myText" onClick='changeText()'>
</form>
</body>
</html>
```

# window.history

## JavaScript1.1+, JScript1.0+

## Nav3+, IE3+, Opera3+

## Syntax

*window*.history[*num*]
*window*.history.*method()*
*window*.history.*property*

## Description

The history property of the Window object is actually one of the core JavaScript objects. This object contains an array of the names and URLs of the pages the window has visited. A specific URL in the history array can be accessed by specifying the indexed location, *num*, that represents the URL about which you want to retrieve information.

Also, as defined in the syntax definition, the methods and properties of this object are also accessible for programming use. Table 7.49 has a list of each of these, followed by a description.

**Table 7.49    Methods and Properties Used by the Window.history Property**

| Type | Item | Description |
| --- | --- | --- |
| Methods | back | References the URL that is located one page back from the current page. |

*continues*

*Table 7.49 continued*

| Type | Item | Description |
|------|------|-------------|
| | `forward` | References the URL that is located one page forward of the current page. |
| | `go` | Loads the URL passed to the method. This can be in relation to the current URL or a string representing part or the whole URL you wish to access. |
| Properties | `current` | Reflects the current URL of the window. This property was added in JavaScript 1.1. |
| | `length` | Reflects the number of URLs in the history of the window. |
| | `next` | Reflects the next URL in the history in relation to the current URL. This property was added in JavaScript 1.1. |
| | `previous` | Reflects the last URL in the history in relation to the current URL. This property was added in JavaScript 1.1. |

For more information on the `History` object and its properties and methods, please see its entry in this chapter.

## Example

Listing 7.544 has two buttons that allow a user to move forward and back in his or her history.

*Listing 7.544   Using the `history` Array to Access Pages Visited*

```
<html>
<body>
<form>
  <input type=BUTTON value="Back" onClick="window.history.back()">
  <input type=BUTTON value="Forward" onClick="window.history.forward()">
</form>
</body>
</html>
```

# window.home()

## *JavaScript1.2+, Jscript3.0*

## *Nav4+, IE4+*

## Syntax

`window.home()`

## Description

The home() method of the Window object simulates the user clicking the Home button on the browser. It takes the browser to the user's specified home page.

## Example

Listing 7.545 has a single button that, when clicked, takes the browser to the user's home page.

*Listing 7.545    Using the* home() *Method to Go to the User's Home Page*

```
<html>
<body>
<form>
<h3>Home James!</h3>
  <input type=BUTTON value="Home" onClick="window.home()">
</form>
</body>
</html>
```

# window.innerHeight

## JavaScript1.2+

## Nav4+

## Syntax

window.innerHeight

## Description

The innerHeight property of the Window object references the pixel height of the document within the browser's frame. This does not include any of the toolbars or other "chrome" that makes up the frame itself.

## Example

Listing 7.546 has a button that, when clicked, opens up a second, smaller window. The innerHeight property is written to this new window.

*Listing 7.546    Using the* innerHeight *Property*

```
<html>
<head>
<script language="JavaScript1.2">
<!-- Hide

// Define a function to open a small window
function openWin(){

  // Create variables to hold the various options that can be set
  // when a new Window instance is created.
```

*continues*

*Listing 7.546    continued*

```
var myBars = 'directories=no,location=no,menubar=no,status=no';
myBars += ',titlebar=no,toolbar=no';
var myOptions = 'scrollbars=no,width=400,height=200,resizeable=no';
var myFeatures = myBars + ',' + myOptions;

// Open the window. Give the window instance the name newDoc and
// name the document in the window myDoc.
var newWin = open('', 'myDoc', myFeatures);

// Write the window height and width properties to the new window.
newWin.document.writeln('<h4>Properties for this Window</h4>');
newWin.document.writeln('innerHeight: ' + newWin.innerHeight + '<br>');
newWin.document.writeln('innerWidth: ' + newWin.innerWidth + '<br>');
newWin.document.writeln('outerHeight: ' + newWin.outerHeight + '<br>');
newWin.document.writeln('outerWidth: ' + newWin.outerWidth + '<br>');
newWin.document.writeln('<form>');
newWin.document.writeln('<input type=BUTTON value="Close"');
newWin.document.writeln(' onClick="window.close()">');
newWin.document.writeln('</form>');

// Close the stream to the document.
newWin.document.close();

}
// End hide --->
</script>
</head>
<body>
<form>
  <input type=BUTTON value="Open" onClick="openWin()">
</form>
</body>
</html>
```

# window.innerWidth

## *JavaScript1.2+*

## *Nav4+*

## *Syntax*

*window*.innerWidth

## *Description*

The innerWidth property of the Window object references the pixel width of the document within the browser's frame. This does not include any of the toolbars or other "chrome" that makes up the frame itself.

## *Example*

Listing 7.547 has a button that, when clicked, opens up a second, smaller window. The innerWidth property is written to this new window.

*Listing 7.547    Using the* innerWidth *Property*

```
<html>
<head>
<script language="JavaScript1.2">
<!-- Hide

// Define a function to open a small window
function openWin(){

  // Create variables to hold the various options that can be set
  // when a new Window instance is created.
  var myBars = 'directories=no,location=no,menubar=no,status=no';
  myBars += ',titlebar=no,toolbar=no';
  var myOptions = 'scrollbars=no,width=400,height=200,resizeable=no';
  var myFeatures = myBars + ',' + myOptions;

  // Open the window. Give the window instance the name newDoc and
  // name the document in the window myDoc.
  var newWin = open('', 'myDoc', myFeatures);

  // Write the window height and width properties to the new window.
  newWin.document.writeln('<h4>Properties for this Window</h4>');
  newWin.document.writeln('innerHeight: ' + newWin.innerHeight + '<br>');
  newWin.document.writeln('innerWidth: ' + newWin.innerWidth + '<br>');
  newWin.document.writeln('outerHeight: ' + newWin.outerHeight + '<br>');
  newWin.document.writeln('outerWidth: ' + newWin.outerWidth + '<br>');
  newWin.document.writeln('<form>');
  newWin.document.writeln('<input type=BUTTON value="Close"');
  newWin.document.writeln(' onClick="window.close()">');
  newWin.document.writeln('</form>');

  // Close the stream to the document.
  newWin.document.close();

}
// End hide --->
</script>
</head>
<body>
<form>
  <input type=BUTTON value="Open" onClick="openWin()">
</form>
</body>
</html>
```

# window.length

## JavaScript1.0+, JScript1.0+, ECMAScript1.0+

## Nav2+, IE3+, Opera3+

### Syntax

```
window.length
```

### Description

The `length` property of the `Window` object represents the number of frames within a window. This returns the same results as `Window.frames.length`.

### Example

Listing 7.548 shows a function that can be used to return the number of frames in a window.

*Listing 7.548    Using the `length` Property of the `Window` Object*

```
<script language="JavaScript">
<!-- Hide

// Define a function to return the number of frames in the
// window passed.
function numFrames(win){
  return win.length;
}

// End hide --->
</script>
```

# window.location

## JavaScript1.0+, JScript1.0+

## Nav2+, IE3+, Opera3+

### Syntax

```
window.location
```

### Description

The `location` property of the `Window` object returns the current URL of the document in the window.

### Example

Listing 7.549 pops up an alert box that contains the URL of the current window.

*Listing 7.549    Using the `location` Property of the `Window` Object*

```
<script language="JavaScript">
<!-- Hide
```

```
// Display the current URL in an alert box
alert(window.location);

// End hide --->
</script>
```

# window.locationbar

## JavaScript1.2+

## Nav4+

## Syntax

*window*.locationbar.*property*

## Description

The locationbar property of the Window object is, to some degree, an object itself. The real use of this property is to access its visible property to determine if the location bar is visible to the user or not.

**NOTE**

As of this writing, the locationbar property only has one subproperty: visible.

## Example

Please see the example of Window.locationbar.visible for an example of using the locationbar property.

# window.locationbar.visible

## JavaScript1.2+

## Nav4+

## Syntax

*window*.locationbar.visible

## Description

The visible subproperty of the locationbar property of the Window is used to determine if the location bar is visible to the user or not. If it is visible, the property returns true. It returns false if the bar is not visible.

## Example

Listing 7.550 determines if several of the browser bars are displayed or not. In the example, you will see if the location bar is visible by using the visible property.

*Listing 7.550    Using the* `visible` *Property of* `locationbar`

```
<script language="JavaScript">
<!-- Hide

// Write the browser's bar status to the page. If the value
// is true, then it is displayed.
document.writeln('<h3>Browser Chrome Status</h3>')
document.writeln('Menu Bar: ' + window.menubar.visible + '<br>');
document.writeln('Tool Bar: ' + window.toolbar.visible + '<br>');
document.writeln('Location Bar: ' + window.locationbar.visible + '<br>');
document.writeln('Personal Bar: ' + window.personalbar.visible + '<br>');
document.writeln('Scroll Bars: ' + window.scrollbars.visible + '<br>');
document.writeln('Status Bar: ' + window.statusbar.visible + '<br>');

// Close the stream to the document.
document.close();

// End hide --->
</script>
```

# window.menubar

## JavaScript1.2+

## Nav4+

## Syntax

*window.menubar.property*

## Description

The `menubar` property of the `Window` object is, to some degree, an object itself. The real use of this property is to access its `visible` property to determine if the menu bar is visible to the user or not.

### NOTE

As of this writing, the `menubar` property only has one subproperty: `visible`.

## Example

Please see the example of `Window.menubar.visible` for an example of using the `menubar` property.

# window.menubar.visible

## JavaScript1.2+

## Nav4+

## Syntax

```
window.menubar.visible
```

## Description

The `visible` subproperty of the `menubar` property of the `Window` is used to determine if the menu bar is visible to the user or not. If it is visible, the property returns `true`. It returns `false` if the bar is not visible.

## Example

Listing 7.551 determines if several of the browser bars are displayed or not. In the example, you will see if the menu bar is visible by using the `visible` property.

*Listing 7.551    Using the* `visible` *Property of* `menubar`

```
<script language="JavaScript">
<!-- Hide

// Write the browser's bar status to the page. If the value
// is true, then it is displayed.
document.writeln('<h3>Browser Chrome Status</h3>')
document.writeln('Menu Bar: ' + window.menubar.visible + '<br>');
document.writeln('Tool Bar: ' + window.toolbar.visible + '<br>');
document.writeln('Location Bar: ' + window.locationbar.visible + '<br>');
document.writeln('Personal Bar: ' + window.personalbar.visible + '<br>');
document.writeln('Scroll Bars: ' + window.scrollbars.visible + '<br>');
document.writeln('Status Bar: ' + window.statusbar.visible + '<br>');

// Close the stream to the document.
document.close();

// End hide --->
</script>
```

# window.moveBy()

## JavaScript1.2+, JScript3.0+

## Nav4+, IE4+

## Syntax

```
window.moveBy(numHort, numVert)
```

## Description

The `moveBy()` method of the `Window` object moves the specified window by the number of pixels passed to the method. As shown in the syntax definition, the first numeric value passed to the method represents the number of vertical pixels you wish to move the window, while the second numeric value represents the horizontal number of pixels.

If the numbers passed are positive, the window is moved to the right horizontally, and up vertically. Negative numbers move the window in the opposite direction.

## Example

Listing 7.552 has four buttons: Up, Down, Right, and Left. If you click these buttons, the window the document is loaded in will move one pixel at a time in that direction.

*Listing 7.552 Using the* moveBy() *Method to Move the Location of a Window*

```
<html>
<head>
</head>
<script language="JavaScript1.2">
<!-- Hide

// Define a function to handle the window movement
function moveWin(dir, dist){

  // Define varaibles to hold the movement values
  var myVert;
  var myHorz;

  // Determine the type of movement
  if(dir == "vert"){
    myHorz = 0;
    myVert = dist;
  }else{
    myHorz = dist;
    myVert = 0;
  }

  // Move the window
  window.moveBy(myHorz, myVert);
}
// End hide --->
</script>
<body>
<form>
<table border=0>
  <tr>
    <td></td>
    <td><input type=BUTTON value="  Up  " onClick="moveWin('vert',-1)"></td>
    <td></td>
  </tr>
  <tr>
    <td><input type=BUTTON value=" Left " onClick="moveWin('horz',-1)"></td>
    <td></td>
    <td><input type=BUTTON value="Right" onClick="moveWin('horz',1)"></td>
  </tr>
  <tr>
    <td></td>
```

```
      <td><input type=BUTTON value="Down" onClick="moveWin('vert',1)"></td>
      <td></td>
    </tr>
  </table>
  </form>
  </body>
  </html>
```

# window.moveTo()

## JavaScript1.2+, JScript3.0+

## Nav4+, IE4+

## Syntax

window.moveTo(*numX, numY*)

## Description

The moveTo() method of the Window object, moves the specified window to the specified location passed to the method. As shown in the syntax definition, the first numeric value passed to the method represents the x-coordinate to which you want to move the window, while the second numeric value represents the y-coordinate.

## Example

Listing 7.553 has two text fields and a button. If the user enters an integer value in each of the text fields and clicks the button, the window will move to that location.

*Listing 7.553    Using the* moveTo() *Method to Move the Location of a Window*

```
<html>
<head>
</head>
<script language="JavaScript1.2">
<!-- Hide

// Define a function to handle the window movement
function moveWin(form){

  // Define varaibles to hold the movement values
  var myX = form.X.value;
  var myY = form.Y.value;

  // Move the window
  window.moveTo(myX, myY);
}
// End hide --->
</script>
<body>
```

*continues*

*Listing 7.553    continued*

```
<form>
  <b>X-Coordinate:</b>
  <input type=TEXT name="X"><br>
  <b>Y-Coordinate:</b>
  <input type=TEXT name="Y"><br>
  <input type=BUTTON value="Move Window" onClick="moveWin(this.form)"></td>
</form>
</body>
</html>
```

# window.name

## *JavaScript1.0+, JScript1.0+*

## *Nav2+, IE3+, Opera3+*

## Syntax

`window.name`

## Description

The `name` property of an instance of a `Window` object returns the name of the window. This property contains the name specified when new windows are created using the `Window.open()` method. In JavaScript 1.0, this property was read only, but this was changed in JavaScript 1.1 so you can assign a name to a window not created with the `Window.open()` method. This property was tainted in JavaScript 1.1 as well.

## Example

Listing 7.554 has a button that launches a second window. The name of the window is written to it using the `name` property of the `Window` object.

*Listing 7.554    Using the* `name` *Property to Retrieve the Name of a Window*

```
<html>
<head>
<script language="JavaScript">
<!-- Hide

// Define a function to open a small window
function openWin(){

  // Create variables to hold the various options that can be set
  // when a new Window instance is created.
  var myBars = 'directories=no,location=no,menubar=no,status=no';
  myBars += ',titlebar=no,toolbar=no';
  var myOptions = 'scrollbars=no,width=400,height=200,resizeable=no';
  var myFeatures = myBars + ',' + myOptions;

  // Open the window. Give the window instance the name newWin and
  // name the document in the window myDoc.
```

```
  var newWin = open('', 'myDoc', myFeatures);

  // Write the window's name to the new window.
  newWin.document.writeln('This window\'s name is: ' + newWin.name + '<br>');
  newWin.document.writeln('<form>');
  newWin.document.writeln('<input type=BUTTON value="Close"');
  newWin.document.writeln(' onClick="window.close()">');
  newWin.document.writeln('</form>');

  // Close the stream to the document.
  newWin.document.close();

}
// End hide --->
</script>
</head>
<body>
<form>
  <input type=BUTTON value="Open" onClick="openWin()">
</form>
</body>
</html>
```

# window.onBlur

## *JavaScript1.0+, JScript1.0+*

## *Nav2+, IE3+, Opera3+*

## *Syntax*

onBlur="*command*"

## *Description*

The onBlur event handler is a property of a Window object and is fired when the focus is moved away from that particular window instance. Care should be taken when using this event handler, because it is possible to get into an infinite loop when using onFocus event handler or focus() method. Note that when this event handler is called within the <body> tag, it is overridden if a <frame> tag that also uses this event handler loaded the document.

**NOTE**

Some Navigator 3 browsers do not fully support this event handler when called in a <frameset> tag.

## Example

Listing 7.555 has a frame set with two frames. The first frame, `toc`, has the `onBlur` event handler specified in its tag. When focus leaves this frame, the event is fired and the `myBlurFunc()` function will be called.

*Listing 7.555   Example of Using the* onBlur *Event*

```
<frameset cols="150,*">
  <frame name="toc"
         src="/toc.htm"
         onBlur='myBlurFunc()'
         marginwidth=1 marginheight=1 scrolling=AUTO>
  <frame name="body"
         src="/body.htm"
         marginwidth=10 marginheight=5 scrolling=AUTO>
</frameset>
```

# window.onDragDrop

## JavaScript1.2+

## Nav4+

## Syntax

`onDragDrop="command"`

## Description

The `onDragDrop` event handler of a property of a `Window` object is fired when the user drops an object, such as a file, on that particular window instance. Care should be taken when using this event handler, because it is possible to get into an infinite loop when using other event handlers such as `onFocus` and `onBlur`.

## Example

In Listing 7.556, if you try to drop a new file on to the browser when this page is loaded, you will be asked to confirm this operation. If you accept, the page will load. If you cancel, the page will not be loaded.

*Listing 7.556   Example of Using the* onDragDrop *Event*

```
<html>
<body onDragDrop='return(confirm("Are you sure you want to continue?"))'>
</body>
Try to drop an element on this page.
</html>
```

# window.onError

## JavaScript1.1+, JScript1.0+

## Nav3+, IE3+, Opera3+

## Syntax

```
onError="command"
```

## Description

The onError event handler of the Window object is fired when an error occurs loading the page. You may find this useful to try and reload the page, using the reload() method of the Location object.

## Example

Listing 7.557 is an example of placing the onError event handler in the <body> tag. If there is an error when loading this page, an alert box will be displayed to the user.

*Listing 7.557  Example of Using the onError Event Handler*

```
<body onError='alert("Error: There has been an error loading this page.")'>
```

# window.onFocus

## JavaScript1.0+, JScript1.0+

## Nav2+, IE3+, Opera3+

## Syntax

```
onFocus="command"
```

## Description

The onFocus event handler of a property of a Window object is fired when the focus is placed on that particular window instance. Care should be taken when using this event handler, because it is possible to get into an infinite loop when using onBlur event handler or blur() method. Note that when this event handler is called within the <body> tag, it is overridden if a <frame> tag that also uses this event handler loaded the document.

NOTE

Some Navigator 3 browsers do not fully support this event handler when called in a <frameset> tag.

## Example

Listing 7.558 has a frame set with two frames. The first frame, toc, has the onFocus event handler specified in its tag. When the focus leaves this frame, the event is fired and the myFocusFunc() function will be called.

*Listing 7.558  Example of Using the onFocus Event*

```
<frameset cols="150,*">
  <frame name="toc"
         src="/toc.htm"
```

*continues*

*Listing 7.558 continued*
```
        onFocus='myFocusFunc()'
        marginwidth=1 marginheight=1 scrolling=AUTO>
  <frame name="body"
        src="/body.htm"
        marginwidth=10 marginheight=5 scrolling=AUTO>
</frameset>
```

# window.onLoad

## *JavaScript1.0+, JScript1.0+*

## *Nav2+, IE3+, Opera3+*

## Syntax

onLoad="*command*"

## Description

The onLoad event handler of a property of a Window object is fired when the page has finished loading in that particular window instance.

> **NOTE**
>
> The onLoad event handler in the <body> of a document that is loaded in a frame will fire before an event handler loaded in the <frameset> tag that loaded the document.

## Example

Listing 7.559 pops up an alert box when the page has finished loading.

*Listing 7.559 Example of Using the onLoad Event*
```
<body onLoad='alert("The document has completely loaded.")'>
```

# window.onMove

## *JavaScript1.2+*

## *Nav4+*

## Syntax

onMove="*command*"

## Description

The onMove event handler of a property of a Window object is fired when the window it is referenced in is moved. The user physically moving the window or a script moving it can fire this event.

## Example

Listing 7.560 pops up an alert box if the user tries to move the window.

*Listing 7.560    Using the* onMove *Event to Display an Alert Box*

```
<body onMove='alert("Do NOT move this window!")'>
```

# window.onResize

## JavaScript1.2+

## Nav4+

## Syntax

```
onResize="command"
```

## Description

The onResize event handler of a property of a Window object is fired when the window it is referenced in is resized. The user physically resizing the window or a script resizing it can fire this event.

## Example

Listing 7.561 pops up an alert box if the user tries to resize the window.

*Listing 7.561    Using the* onResize *Event to Display an Alert Box*

```
<body onResize='alert("Do NOT resize this window!")'>
```

# window.onUnLoad

## Nav2+, IE3+, Opera3+

## Syntax

```
onUnLoad="command"
```

## Description

The onUnLoad event handler of a property of a Window object is fired when the page is unloaded in that particular window instance. This occurs when the user leaves the page for another page.

**NOTE**

The onUnLoad event handler in the <body> of a document that is loaded in a frame will fire before an event handler loaded in the <frameset> tag that loaded the document.

## Example

Listing 7.562 pops up an alert box when the user leaves the page.

*Listing 7.562    Example of Using the* onUnLoad *Event*

```
<body onUnLoad='alert("Please do not leave!")'>
```

# window.open()

## JavaScript1.0+, JScript1.0+

## Nav2+, IE3+, Opera3+

## Syntax

```
window.open(pageURL, name, parameters)
```

## Description

The open() method of the Window object creates a new instance of a window. It loads the *pageURL* passed to the method in a window based on the *parameters* specified. The ACTION attribute of the <form> tag and the TARGET attribute of the <a> tag can reference the window by the *name* passed.

Most of the *parameters* passed, which are listed without spaces and commas, are toggled on and off by setting them to yes or no. It is also possible to use 1 or 0 to turn these features on or off. Either way, you should be consistent across each of the options. Table 7.50 has the different *parameters* that can be passed and how to turn them on and off.

## NOTE

If you place spaces in the parameter string, the options will not work. Be sure to comma separate each of these options and do not insert any spaces.

**Table 7.50    Parameters That Can Be Passed When Creating a New Instance of the Window Object Using the open() Method**

| Parameter | Initialize With | Description |
| --- | --- | --- |
| alwaysLowered | yes/no | This parameter tells the window to stay behind all other windows. This must be done in signed scripts because it is a secure feature and was implemented in JavaScript 1.2. |
| alwaysRaised | yes/no | This parameter tells the window to stay on top of all other windows. This must be done in signed scripts because it is a secure feature and was implemented in JavaScript 1.2. |

| Parameter | Initialize With | Description |
|---|---|---|
| dependent | yes/no | This parameter opens the window as a true child window of the parent window. When the parent window is closed, so is the child window. This feature was implemented in JavaScript 1.2. |
| directories | yes/no | Specifies if the Directory Bar on Navigator 2 and 3 is visible on the new window. |
| height | pixel value | Sets the height in pixels of the window. This feature, though still existent for backward compatibility, was removed in JavaScript 1.2 and replaced with `innerHeight`. |
| hotkeys | yes/no | Disables all but the Security and Quit hotkeys in a new window with no Menu Bar. This feature was implemented in JavaScript 1.2. |
| innerHeight | pixel value | Sets the height in pixels of the document in the window. This feature was implemented in JavaScript 1.2. |
| innerWidth | pixel value | Sets the width in pixels of the document in the window. This feature was implemented in JavaScript 1.2. |
| location | yes/no | Specifies if the Location Bar is visible on the new window. |
| menubar | yes/no | Specifies if the Menu Bar is visible on the new window. |
| outerHeight | pixel value | Sets the height in pixels of the window, including the chrome. This feature was implemented in JavaScript 1.2. |
| outerWidth | pixel value | Sets the width in pixels of the window, including the chrome. This feature was implemented in JavaScript 1.2. |
| resizable | yes/no | Specifies if the window can be resized. |
| screenX | pixel value | Sets the distance in pixels of the window from the left side of the screen. This feature was implemented in JavaScript 1.2. |
| screenY | pixel value | Sets the distance in pixels of the window from the top of the screen. This feature was implemented in JavaScript 1.2. |

*continues*

*Table 7.50 continued*

| Parameter | Initialize With | Description |
|-----------|-----------------|-------------|
| scrollbars | yes/no | Specifies if the Scroll Bars are visible on the new window. |
| titlebar | yes/no | Specifies if the Title Bar is visible on the new window. |
| toolbar | yes/no | Specifies if the toolbar is visible on the new window. |
| width | pixel value | Sets the width in pixels of the window. This feature, though still existent for backward compatibility, was removed in JavaScript 1.2 and replaced with innerWidth. |
| z-lock | yes/no | Specifies that the window is not supposed to be located above other windows when it is made active. This feature was implemented in JavaScript 1.2. |

## NOTE

It is possible to open windows that are not on the physical screen. However, this is a secure feature and must be in a signed script to implement.

## Example

Listing 7.563 has a single button that opens a new window when clicked. As you can see in the creation of the window, there are various parameters passed that define how the window should look when opened.

*Listing 7.563    Using the* open() *Method to Open a New Window*

```
<html>

<script language="JavaScript">
<!-- Hide

// Define the openWin() function
function openWin(){

  // Create variables to hold the various options that can be set
  // when a new Window instance is created.
  var myBars = 'directories=no,location=no,menubar=no,status=no';
  myBars += ',titlebar=no,toolbar=no';
  var myOptions = 'scrollbars=no,width=400,height=200,resizeable=no';
  var myFeatures = myBars + ',' + myOptions;
  var myReadme = "Welcome to Pure JavaScript!\n" +
      "------------------------------------------------\n" +
      'You can enter some text here.'
```

```
        // Open the window. Give the window instance the name newWin and
        // name the document in the window myDoc.
        var newWin = open('', 'myDoc', myFeatures);

        newWin.document.writeln('<form>');
        newWin.document.writeln('<table cellspacing=0 cellpadding=0 border=1>');
        newWin.document.writeln('<tr valign=TOP color= bgcolor="#000099"><td>');
        newWin.document.writeln('<font size=-1 color="#FFFFFF"><b>');
        newWin.document.writeln('  Readme</b></font>');
        newWin.document.writeln('</td></tr>');
        newWin.document.writeln('<tr valign=TOP><td>');
        newWin.document.writeln('<textarea cols=45 rows=7 wrap=SOFT>');
        newWin.document.writeln(myReadme + '</textarea>');
        newWin.document.writeln('</td></tr>');
        newWin.document.writeln('<tr valign=BOTTOM align=RIGHT');
        newWin.document.writeln(' bgcolor="#C0C0C0"><td>');
        newWin.document.writeln('<input type=BUTTON value="Close"');
        newWin.document.writeln(' onClick="window.close()">');
        newWin.document.writeln('</td></tr>');
        newWin.document.writeln('</table></form>');

        // Close the stream to the document and bring the window to the front.
        newWin.document.close();
        newWin.focus();
    }

// End hide --->
</script>
<body>
<form>
    <b>Click the following button to open a new window: </b>
    <input type=BUTTON value="Open" onClick='openWin()'>
</form>
</body>
</html>
```

# window.opener

## *JavaScript1.1+, JScript1.0+*

## *Nav3+, IE3+, Opera3+*

## *Syntax*

*window*.opener
*window*.opener.*method*
*window*.opener.*property*

## *Description*

The opener property of the Window object corresponds to the window that opens the window from which the property was accessed. When accessed by a child window, it returns the parent window. With this property, you can then invoke methods and access properties of the Window object on the "opener" window. This property can also be set in scripts that allow the browser to clean up the reference to the parent window if it is closed before the child window. Most browsers have limits on the number of open windows they can have, and, by cleaning up these closed windows, you are able to regain the ability to open more windows if your limit has been reached. This is done by setting the opener property to null.

## Example

Listing 7.564 has a button that opens a second window when clicked. In the second window, there is a button that closes the parent window by referencing it via the opener property. Once the close() method has been called on this window, the opener property is set to null to clean up the parent window.

*Listing 7.564    Using the opener Property to Return the Parent Window*

```
<html>
<head>

<script language="JavaScript">
<!-- Hide

// Define the openWin() function
function openWin(){

  // Create variables to hold the various options that can be set
  // when a new Window instance is created.
  var myBars = 'directories=no,location=no,menubar=no,status=no';
  myBars += ',titlebar=no,toolbar=no';
  var myOptions = 'scrollbars=no,width=400,height=200,resizeable=no';
  var myFeatures = myBars + ',' + myOptions;
  var myReadme = "Welcome to Pure JavaScript!\n" +
      "---------------------------------------\n" +
      'You can enter some text here.'

  // Open the window. Give the window instance the name newWin and
  // name the document in the window myDoc.
  var newWin = open('', 'myDoc', myFeatures);

  newWin.document.writeln('<form>');
  newWin.document.writeln('<table cellspacing=0 cellpadding=0 border=1>');
  newWin.document.writeln('<tr valign=TOP color= bgcolor="#000099"><td>');
  newWin.document.writeln('<font size=-1 color="#FFFFFF"><b>');
  newWin.document.writeln('  Readme</b></font>');
  newWin.document.writeln('</td></tr>');
  newWin.document.writeln('<tr valign=TOP><td>');
  newWin.document.writeln('<textarea cols=45 rows=7 wrap=SOFT>');
  newWin.document.writeln(myReadme + '</textarea>');
  newWin.document.writeln('</td></tr>');
  newWin.document.writeln('<tr valign=BOTTOM align=RIGHT color=
```

```
bgcolor="#C0C0C0"><td>');

    // Close the opener window and clean it up
    newWin.document.writeln('<input type=BUTTON value="Close"');
    var myJS = "window.opener.close();window.opener=null"
    newWin.document.writeln('onClick="' + myJS + '">');

    newWin.document.writeln('</td></tr>');
    newWin.document.writeln('</table></form>');

    // Close the stream to the document and bring the window to the front.
    newWin.document.close();
    newWin.focus();
}

// End hide --->
</script>
</head>
<body>
<form>
  <b>Click the following button to open a new window: </b>
  <input type=BUTTON value="Open" onClick='openWin()'>
</form>
</body>
</html>
```

# window.outerHeight

## *JavaScript1.2+*

## *Nav4+*

## *Syntax*

*window*.outerHeight

## *Description*

The outerHeight property of the Window object references the pixel height of the browser's frame. This includes any of the toolbars or other "chrome" that makes up the frame itself.

## *Example*

Listing 7.565 has a button that, when clicked, opens up a second, smaller window. The outerHeight property is written to this new window.

*Listing 7.565   Using the* outerHeight *Property*
```
<html>
<head>
<script language="JavaScript1.2">
```

*continues*

*Listing 7.565    continued*

```
<!-- Hide

// Define a function to open a small window
function openWin(){

  // Create variables to hold the various options that can be set
  // when a new Window instance is created.
  var myBars = 'directories=no,location=no,menubar=no,status=no';
  myBars += ',titlebar=no,toolbar=no';
  var myOptions = 'scrollbars=no,width=400,height=200,resizeable=no';
  var myFeatures = myBars + ',' + myOptions;

  // Open the window. Give the window instance the name newWin and
  // name the document in the window myDoc.
  var newWin = open('', 'myDoc', myFeatures);

  // Write the window height and width properties to the new window.
  newWin.document.writeln('<h4>Properties for this Window</h4>');
  newWin.document.writeln('innerHeight: ' + newWin.innerHeight + '<br>');
  newWin.document.writeln('innerWidth: ' + newWin.innerWidth + '<br>');
  newWin.document.writeln('outerHeight: ' + newWin.outerHeight + '<br>');
  newWin.document.writeln('outerWidth: ' + newWin.outerWidth + '<br>');
  newWin.document.writeln('<form>');
  newWin.document.writeln('<input type=BUTTON value="Close"');
  newWin.document.writeln(' onClick="window.close()">');
  newWin.document.writeln('</form>');

  // Close the stream to the document.
  newWin.document.close();

}
// End hide --->
</script>
</head>
<body>
<form>
  <input type=BUTTON value="Open" onClick="openWin()">
</form>
</body>
</html>
```

# window.outerWidth

## *JavaScript1.2+*

## *Nav4+*

## *Syntax*

*window*.outerWidth

## Description

The outerWidth property of the Window object references the pixel width of the browser's frame. This includes any of the toolbars or other "chrome" that make up the frame itself.

## Example

Listing 7.566 has a button that, when clicked, opens up a second, smaller window. The outerWidth property is written to this new window.

*Listing 7.566   Using the* outerWidth *Property*

```
<html>
<head>
<script language="JavaScript1.2">
<!-- Hide

// Define a function to open a small window
function openWin(){

  // Create variables to hold the various options that can be set
  // when a new Window instance is created.
  var myBars = 'directories=no,location=no,menubar=no,status=no';
  myBars += ',titlebar=no,toolbar=no';
  var myOptions = 'scrollbars=no,width=400,height=200,resizeable=no';
  var myFeatures = myBars + ',' + myOptions;

  // Open the window. Give the window instance the name newWin and
  // name the document in the window myDoc.
  var newWin = open('', 'myDoc', myFeatures);

  // Write the window height and width properties to the new window.
  newWin.document.writeln('<h4>Properties for this Window</h4>');
  newWin.document.writeln('innerHeight: ' + newWin.innerHeight + '<br>');
  newWin.document.writeln('innerWidth: ' + newWin.innerWidth + '<br>');
  newWin.document.writeln('outerHeight: ' + newWin.outerHeight + '<br>');
  newWin.document.writeln('outerWidth: ' + newWin.outerWidth + '<br>');
  newWin.document.writeln('<form>');
  newWin.document.writeln('<input type=BUTTON value="Close"');
  newWin.document.writeln(' onClick="window.close()">');
  newWin.document.writeln('</form>');

  // Close the stream to the document.
  newWin.document.close();

}
// End hide --->
</script>
</head>
```

*continues*

*Listing 7.566    continued*

```
<body>
<form>
  <input type=BUTTON value="Open" onClick="openWin()">
</form>
</body>
</html>
```

# window.pageXOffset

## *JavaScript1.2+, JScript3+*

## *Nav4+, IE4+*

## *Syntax*

```
window.pageXOffSet
```

## Description

The pageXOffSet property of the Window object reflects the current horizontal pixel location of the top-left corner of the document in the window. In chromeless windows, this property can be referenced if you are moving a window with the moveTo() method before the actual move is made to see if the window needs to be moved. It is also useful when using the scrollTo() method because it returns the current location of the viewable document in relation to the whole page.

## Example

Listing 7.567 has a button that, when clicked, displays the current x- and y-coordinates of the window.

*Listing 7.567    Using the pageXoffSet Property to See the Current Location of the Window*

```
<html>
<head>
<script language="JavaScript1.2">
<!-- Hide

// Define a function to display an alert box with the current
// window location
function showLocation(){

  // Store the offset in variables
  var x = self.pageXOffset;
  var y = self.pageYOffset

  // Build a string to display
  var currX = "X-coordinate: " + x + "\n";
  var currY = "Y-coordinate: " + y;

  // Display the coordinates
```

```
  window.alert(currX + currY);
}

// End hide --->
</script>
</head>
<body>
<form>
  <input type=BUTTON value="Show Location" onClick="showLocation()">
</form>
</body>
</html>
```

# window.pageYOffset

## *JavaScript1.2+, JScript3+*

## *Nav4+, IE4+*

## *Syntax*

*window*.pageYOffSet

## *Description*

The pageYOffSet property of the Window object reflects the current vertical pixel location of the top-left corner of the document in the window. In chromeless windows, this
property can be referenced if you are moving a window with the moveTo() method
before the actual move is made to see if the window needs to be moved. It is also useful when using the scrollTo() method because it returns the current location of the
viewable document in relation to the whole page.

## *Example*

Listing 7.568 has a button that, when clicked, displays the current x- and y-coordinates
of the window.

*Listing 7.568    Using the* pageYoffSet *Property to See the Current Location of
the Window*

```
<html>
<head>
<script language="JavaScript1.2">
<!-- Hide

// Define a function to display an alert box with the current
// window location
function showLocation(){

  // Store the offset in variables
  var x = self.pageXOffset;
```

*continues*

*Listing 7.568    continued*

```
  var y = self.pageYOffset

  // Build a string to display
  var currX = "X-coordinate: " + x + "\n";
  var currY = "Y-coordinate: " + y;

  // Display the coordinates
  window.alert(currX + currY);
}

// End hide --->
</script>
</head>
<body>
<form>
  <input type=BUTTON value="Show Location" onClick="showLocation()">
</form>
</body>
</html>
```

# window.parent

## JavaScript1.0+, JScript1.0

## Nav2+, IE3+, Opera3+

## Syntax

```
window.parent.frames[num]
window.parent.frameName
```

## Description

The parent property of the Window object contains a reference to the parent window of any frames that are loaded. In the instance where Frame A loads a page with a <frame-set> with Frame A.1 and A.2, the parent of the documents in A.1 and A.2 is Frame A. Frame A's parent is the top level window.

The referencing of these sibling frames can either be done using the frames array and passing an index number, or you can directly reference a frame using the name that is assigned by the NAME attribute of the <frame> tag.

## Example

Listing 7.569 shows how to reference the parent of the third frame on a page.

*Listing 7.569    Using the* parent *Property to Reference a Frame*
```
var myFrameReference = myWin.parent.frames[2];
```

# window.personalbar

## JavaScript1.2+

## Nav4+

## Syntax

`window.personalbar.property`

## Description

The `personalbar` property of the `Window` object is, to some degree, an object itself. The real use of this property is to access its `visible` property to determine if the personal bar is visible to the user or not.

> **NOTE**
>
> As of this writing, the `personalbar` property only has one subproperty: `visible`.

## Example

Listing 7.570 determines if several of the browser bars are displayed or not. In the example, you will see if the personal bar is visible by using the `visible` property.

Listing 7.570 *Using the* visible *Property of* personalbar

```
<script language="JavaScript">
<!-- Hide

// Write the browser's bar status to the page. If the value
// is true, then it is displayed.
document.writeln('<h3>Browser Chrome Status</h3>')
document.writeln('Menu Bar: ' + window.menubar.visible + '<br>');
document.writeln('Tool Bar: ' + window.toolbar.visible + '<br>');
document.writeln('Location Bar: ' + window.locationbar.visible + '<br>');
document.writeln('Personal Bar: ' + window.personalbar.visible + '<br>');
document.writeln('Scroll Bars: ' + window.scrollbars.visible + '<br>');
document.writeln('Status Bar: ' + window.statusbar.visible + '<br>');

// Close the stream to the document.
document.close();

// End hide --->
</script>
```

# window.personalbar.visible

## JavaScript1.2+

## Nav4+

## Syntax

*window*.personalbar.visible

## Description

The visible subproperty of the personalbar property of the Window is used to determine if the Personal Bar is visible to the user or not. If it is visible, the property returns true. It returns false if the bar is not visible.

## Example

Listing 7.571 determines if several of the browser bars are displayed or not. In the example, you will see if the Personal Bar is visible by using the visible property.

*Listing 7.571    Using the* visible *Property of* personalbar

```
<script language="JavaScript">
<!-- Hide

// Write the browser's bar status to the page. If the value
// is true, then it is displayed.
document.writeln('<h3>Browser Chrome Status</h3>')
document.writeln('Menu Bar: ' + window.menubar.visible + '<br>');
document.writeln('Tool Bar: ' + window.toolbar.visible + '<br>');
document.writeln('Location Bar: ' + window.locationbar.visible + '<br>');
document.writeln('Personal Bar: ' + window.personalbar.visible + '<br>');
document.writeln('Scroll Bars: ' + window.scrollbars.visible + '<br>');
document.writeln('Status Bar: ' + window.statusbar.visible + '<br>');

// Close the stream to the document.
document.close();

// End hide --->
</script>
```

# window.print()

## Nav4+, IE4+

## Syntax

*window*.print()

## Description

The print() method of the Window object simulates the user clicking the Print button on the browser. It tells the browser to open the print dialog box to print the current page.

## Example

Listing 7.572 has a button. Clicking the button will tell the browser to open the Print dialog box to allow the user to print the current page.

*Listing 7.572 Using the* `print()` *Method to Print the Current Page*

```
<html>
<body>
<form>
  <input type=BUTTON value="Print" onClick="window.print()">
</form>
</body>
</html>
```

# window.prompt()

## JavaScript1.0+, JScript1.0

## Nav2+, IE3+, Opera3+

### Syntax

`window.prompt(string1, string2)`

### Description

The `prompt()` method of the `Window` object displays a prompt dialog box when invoked. The value of *string1* passed to the method is displayed in the box, and the value of *string2* is contained in the text field of the prompt dialog box. The returned value of this method is the text in the text field.

### Example

Listing 7.573 pops up a prompt box when the script is loaded asking the user for a password. If the correct password is entered, the page finishes loading. The result of running this script can be seen in Figure 7.20.

*Listing 7.573 A Prompt Box*

```
<script language="JavaScript">
<!-- Hide

// Keep asking the user for a password until they get it right
while(prompt('Please enter your password', 'HERE') != 'admin'){
  alert('That was an incorrect response, please try again');
}

// This is only executed if 'admin' is entered.
document.write('You have entered the correct password!');

// End hide --->
</script>
```

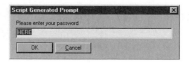

**Figure 7.20**

*An alert box created with the* Window.prompt() *method.*

# window.releaseEvents()

## *JavaScript1.2+, JScript3.0+*

## *Nav4+, IE4+*

## *Syntax*

```
window.releaseEvents(event)
window.releaseEvents(event1 ¦ event2 ¦ eventN)
```

## *Description*

The releaseEvents() method of the Window object releases all previously captured events of the event type passed. These events can be captured with the Window.captureEvents() method. The events that can be released are as follows:

- Event.ABORT
- Event.BLUR
- Event.CHANGE
- Event.CLICK
- Event.DBLCLICK
- Event.DRAGDROP
- Event.ERROR
- Event.FOCUS
- Event.KEYDOWN
- Event.KEYPRESS
- Event.KEYUP
- Event.LOAD
- Event.MOUSEDOWN
- Event.MOUSEMOVE
- Event.MOUSEOUT
- Event.MOUSEOVER
- Event.MOUSEUP
- Event.MOVE
- Event.RESET
- Event.RESIZE
- Event.SELECT
- Event.SUBMIT
- Event.UNLOAD

After one of these events has been captured, you can define a function to replace the built-in method for handling the event. Use the `releaseEvents()` method to free the event after a capture.

## Example

Listing 7.574 has a single text box and a button. The script in the `<head>` of the document specifies a function to handle all `onClick` events in the window. To be able to do this, the `captureEvents()` method has to be used to capture all events of type `Event.CLICK`. When the page itself is clicked, a counter, which is displayed in the text box, is incremented.

When the button is pressed down, the `onMouseDown` event handler is fired and the `Event.CLICK` is released and no longer increments the page when the page is clicked.

*Listing 7.574   Capturing Events with the* `Window.releaseEvents()` *Method*

```
<html>
<head>
<script language="JavaScript1.2">
<!-- Hide

// Define a click counter variable
var counter = 0;

// Tell the browser you want to intercept ALL click events
// on the page. Then define a function to handle them.
window.captureEvents(Event.CLICK);
window.onClick = myClickHandler;

// Define the myClickHandler function to handle click events
function myClickHandler{

  // Pass all click events to the onClick event of the text box
  window.document.myForm.myText.handleEvent;
}

// Function is called by onClick of text box. Displays the number
// of clicks that have occurred.
function changeText(){
  document.myForm.myText.value = counter++;
}

// Releases the click event capturing
function releaseClick(){
  window.releaseEvents(Event.CLICK);
}

// End hide --->
</script>
```

*continues*

*Listing 7.574    continued*

```
</head>
<body>
<form name="myForm">
  <input type=TEXT size=2 value="" name="myText" onClick='changeText()'>
  <input type=BUTTON value="Release Event" onMouseDown='releaseClick()'>
</form>
</body>
</html>
```

# window.resizeBy()

## *JavaScript1.2+, JScript3.0+*

## *Nav4+, IE4+*

## Syntax

```
window.resizeBy(numHort, numVert)
```

## Description

The resizeBy() method of the Window object resizes the specified window by the number of pixels passed to the method. As shown in the syntax definition, the first numeric value passed to the method represents the number of vertical pixels you want to size the window by, while the second numeric value represents the horizontal number of pixels.

If the numbers passed are positive, the window size is increased. Negative numbers reduce the size of the window.

## Example

Listing 7.575 has four buttons. Two buttons are for increasing height, and the other two are for increasing width. If you click these buttons, the window will resize 10 pixels at a time.

*Listing 7.575    Using the resizeBy() Method to Resize a Window*

```
<html>
<head>
<script language="JavaScript1.2">
<!-- Hide

// Define a function to handle the window resizing
function resizeWin(dir, dist){

  // Define varaibles to hold the sizing values
  var myVert;
  var myHorz;

  // Determine the type of movement
  if(dir == "vert"){
    myHorz = 0;
```

```
    myVert = dist;
  }else{
    myHorz = dist;
    myVert = 0;
  }

  // Resize the window
  window.resizeBy(myHorz, myVert);
}
// End hide --->
</script>
</head>
<body>
<form>
<table border=0>
  <tr>
    <td></td>
<td><input type=BUTTON value="Expand Down"
            onClick="resizeWin('vert',10)"></td>
    <td></td>
  </tr>
  <tr>
<td><input type=BUTTON value="Retract From Right"
            onClick="resizeWin('horz',-10)"></td>
    <td></td>
    <td><input type=BUTTON value="Grow Right"
            onClick="resizeWin('horz',10)"></td>
  </tr>
  <tr>
    <td></td>
<td><input type=BUTTON value="Retrack Up"
            onClick="resizeWin('vert',-10)"></td>
    <td></td>
  </tr>
</table>
</form>
</body>
</html>
```

# window.resizeTo()

## JavaScript1.2+, JScript3.0+

## Nav4+, IE4+

## Syntax

window.resizeTo(*numWidth*, *numHeight*)

## Description

The resizeTo() method of the Window object resizes the specified window to the specified size passed to the method. As shown in the syntax definition, the first numeric value passed to the method represents the width you want to size the window to, while the second numeric value represents the height.

## Example

Listing 7.576 has two text fields and a button. If the user enters an integer value in each of the text fields and clicks the button, the window will resize to those settings.

*Listing 7.576    Using the* resizeTo() *Method to Resize the Window*

```
<html>
<head>
<script language="JavaScript1.2">
<!-- Hide

// Define a function to handle the window resizing
function resizeWin(form){

  // Define variables to hold the resize values
  var myWidth = form.width.value;
  var myHeight = form.height.value;

  // Resize the window
  window.resizeTo(myWidth, myHeight);
}
// End hide --->
</script>
</head>
<body>
<form>
  <b>New Width:</b>
  <input type=TEXT name="width"><br>
  <b>New Height:</b>
  <input type=TEXT name="height"><br>
  <input type=BUTTON value="Resize Window"
         onClick="resizeWin(this.form)"></td>
</form>
</body>
</html>
```

# window.routeEvent()

## JavaScript1.2+, JScript3.0+

## Nav4+, IE4+

## Syntax

```
window.routeEvent(event)
```

## Description

The routeEvent() method of the Window object passes all previously captured events of the event type passed through their normal event process. The events that can be passed are as follows:

- Event.ABORT
- Event.BLUR
- Event.CHANGE
- Event.CLICK
- Event.DBLCLICK
- Event.DRAGDROP
- Event.ERROR
- Event.FOCUS
- Event.KEYDOWN
- Event.KEYPRESS
- Event.KEYUP
- Event.LOAD
- Event.MOUSEDOWN
- Event.MOUSEMOVE
- Event.MOUSEOUT
- Event.MOUSEOVER
- Event.MOUSEUP
- Event.MOVE
- Event.RESET
- Event.RESIZE
- Event.SELECT
- Event.SUBMIT
- Event.UNLOAD

After one of these events has been captured using the Window.captureEvents() method, you can define a function to replace the built-in method for handling the event. Use the releaseEvents() method to free the event after a capture, and use routeEvent() to allow the normal processing to take place.

## Example

Listing 7.577 has a single text box and a link. The script in the <head> of the document specifies a function to handle all onClick events in the window. To be able to do this, the captureEvents() method has to be used to capture all events of type Event.CLICK. When the page itself is clicked, a counter, which is displayed in the text box, is incremented.

When the link is clicked, the onMouseDown event handler is fired and the Event.CLICK is routed through its normal means and no longer increments the page when the page is clicked.

*Listing 7.577  Capturing Events with the* `Window.routeEvent()` *Method*

```
<html>
<head>
<script language="JavaScript1.2">
<!-- Hide

// Define a click counter variable
var counter = 0;

// Tell the browser you want to intercept ALL click events
// on the page. Then define a function to handle them.
window.captureEvents(Event.CLICK);
window.onClick = myClickHandler;

// Define the myClickHandler function to handle click events
function myClickHandler{

  // Pass all click events to the onClick event of the text box
  window.document.myForm.myText.handleEvent;
}

// Function is called by onClick of text box. Displays the number
// of clicks that have occurred.
function changeText(){
  document.myForm.myText.value = counter++;
}

// Releases the click event capturing
function releaseClick(){
  window.routeEvent(Event.CLICK);
}

// End hide --->
</script>
</head>
<body>
<form name="myForm">
  <input type=TEXT size=2 value="" name="myText" onClick='changeText()'>
  <a href="http://www.purejavascript.com"
     onMouseDown='window.routeEvent(Event.CLICK)'>Click Here!</a>
</form>
</body>
</html>
```

# window.scroll()

## *JavaScript1.1, JScript3.0*

## *Nav3, IE3, Opera3*

## Syntax

window.scroll(*numX, numY*)

## Description

The scroll() method of the Window object scrolls the specified window to the specified location passed to the method. As shown in the syntax definition, the first numeric value passed to the method represents the x-coordinate to which you want to scroll the window, while the second numeric value represents the y-coordinate. Note that this method has been deprecated in JavaScript 1.2 and replaced with the scrollBy() and scrollTo() methods.

## Example

Listing 7.578 has two text fields and a button. If the user enters an integer value in each of the text fields and clicks the button, the window will be scrolled to those settings.

*Listing 7.578   Using the* scroll() *Method to Scroll the Window*

```
<html>
<head>
<script language="JavaScript1.2">
<!-- Hide

// Define a function to handle the window scrolling
function scrollWin(dir, dist){

  // Define variables to hold the scrolling values
  var myVert;
  var myHorz;

  // Determine the type of scrolling
  if(dir == "vert"){
    myHorz = 0;
    myVert = dist;
  }else{
    myHorz = dist;
    myVert = 0;
  }

  // Scroll the window
  window.scroll(myHorz, myVert);
}
// End hide --->
</script>
</head>
<body>
<form>
<table border=0>
  <tr>
```

*continues*

*Listing 7.578 continued*

```
  <td></td>
  <td><input type=BUTTON value="Down" onClick="scrollWin('vert',10)"></td>
  <td></td>
</tr>
<tr>
  <td><input type=BUTTON value=" Left " onClick="scrollWin('horz',-10)"></td>
  <td></td>
  <td><input type=BUTTON value="Right" onClick="scrollWin('horz',10)"></td>
</tr>
<tr>
  <td></td>
  <td><input type=BUTTON value=" Up " onClick="scrollWin('vert',-10)"></td>
  <td></td>
</tr>
</table>
</form>
</body>
</html>
```

# window.scrollbars

## JavaScript1.2+

## Nav4+

## Syntax

window.scrollbars.*property*

## Description

The scrollbars property of the Window object is, to some degree, an object itself. The real use of this property is to access its visible property to determine if the scrollbars are visible to the user or not.

## NOTE

As of this writing, the scrollbars property only has one subproperty: visible.

## Example

Please see the example of Window.scrollbars.visible for an example of using the scrollbars property.

# window.scrollbars.visible

## JavaScript1.2+

## Nav4+

## Syntax

*window*.scrollbars.visible

## Description

The `visible` subproperty of the `scrollbars` property of the `Window` is used to determine if the scrollbars are visible to the user or not. If they are visible, the property
returns `true`. It returns `false` if the bars are not visible.

## Example

Listing 7.579 determines if several of the browser scrollbars are displayed or not. In the
example, you will see if the scrollbars are visible by using the `visible` property.

*Listing 7.579   Using the* `visible` *Property of* `scrollbars`

```
<script language="JavaScript">
<!-- Hide

// Write the browser's bar status to the page. If the value
// is true, then it is displayed.
document.writeln('<h3>Browser Chrome Status</h3>')
document.writeln('Menu Bar: ' + window.menubar.visible + '<br>');
document.writeln('Tool Bar: ' + window.toolbar.visible + '<br>');
document.writeln('Location Bar: .' + window.locationbar.visible + '<br>');
document.writeln('Personal Bar: ' + window.personalbar.visible + '<br>');
document.writeln('Scroll Bars: ' + window.scrollbars.visible + '<br>');
document.writeln('Status Bar: ' + window.statusbar.visible + '<br>');

// Close the stream to the document.
document.close();

// End hide --->
</script>
```

# window.scrollBy()

## JavaScript1.2+, JScript3.0+

## Nav4+, IE4+

## Syntax

*window*.scrollBy(*numHort, numVert*)

## Description

The `scrollBy()` method of the `Window` object scrolls the specified window by the number of pixels passed to the method. As shown in the syntax definition, the first numeric
value passed to the method represents the number of vertical pixels by which you want
to scroll the window, while the second numeric value represents the horizontal number
of pixels.

If the numbers passed are positive, the window is scrolled in the positive direction. Negative numbers are scrolled in the negative direction.

## Example

Listing 7.580 has four buttons. Each of these buttons scroll the windows contents in different directions when clicked.

*Listing 7.580    Using the* `scrollBy()` *Method to Resize a Window*

```
<html>
<head>
<script language="JavaScript1.2">
<!-- Hide

// Define a function to handle the window scrolling
function scrollWin(dir, dist){

  // Define variables to hold the scrolling values
  var myVert;
  var myHorz;

  // Determine the type of scrolling
  if(dir == "vert"){
    myHorz = 0;
    myVert = dist;
  }else{
    myHorz = dist;
    myVert = 0;
  }

  // Scroll the window
  window.scrollBy(myHorz, myVert);
}
// End hide --->
</script>
</head>
<body>
<form>
<table border=0>
  <tr>
    <td></td>
    <td><input type=BUTTON value="Down"
            onClick="scrollWin('vert',10)"></td>
    <td></td>
  </tr>
  <tr>
    <td><input type=BUTTON value=" Left "
            onClick="scrollWin('horz',-10)"></td>
    <td></td>
    <td><input type=BUTTON value="Right"
            onClick="scrollWin('horz',10)"></td>
```

```
  </tr>
  <tr>
    <td></td>
    <td><input type=BUTTON value="  Up  "
             onClick="scrollWin('vert',-10)"></td>
    <td></td>
  </tr>
</table>
</form>
</body>
</html>
```

# window.scrollTo()

## *JavaScript1.2+, JScript3.0+*

## *Nav4+, IE4+*

## *Syntax*

*window*.scrollTo(*numX, numY*)

## *Description*

The scrollTo() method of the Window object scrolls the specified window to the specified location passed to the method. As shown in the syntax definition, the first numeric value passed to the method represents the x-coordinate to which you want to scroll the window, while the second numeric value represents the y-coordinate.

## *Example*

Listing 7.581 has two text fields and a button. If the user enters an integer value in each of the text fields and clicks the button, the window will be scrolled to those settings.

*Listing 7.581   Using the* scrollTo() *Method to Scroll the Window*

```
<html>
<head>
<script language="JavaScript1.2">
<!-- Hide

// Define a function to handle the window scrolling
function scrollWin(form){

  // Define variables to hold the scroll values
  var myX = form.X.value;
  var myY = form.Y.value;

  // Scroll the window
  window.scrollTo(myX, myY);
}
// End hide --->
```

*continues*

*Listing 7.581    continued*

```
</script>
</head>
<body>
<form>
  <b>X-Coordinate:</b>
  <input type=TEXT name="X"><br>
  <b>Y-Coordinate:</b>
  <input type=TEXT name="Y"><br>
  <input type=BUTTON value="Scroll Window"
         onClick="scrollWin(this.form)"></td>
</form>
</body>
</html>
```

# window.self

## *JavaScript1.0+, JScript1.0*

## *Nav2+, IE3+, Opera3+*

## *Syntax*

```
window.self.method
window.self.property
```

## *Description*

The `self` property of the `Window` object contains a reference to the current window. This allows you to invoke functions or call properties on the current window without any confusion when multiple windows are displayed.

## *Example*

Listing 7.582 shows how to close the current window through the `self` reference.

*Listing 7.582    Using the `self` Property to Reference the Current Window*

```
<script language="JavaScript">
<!-- Hide

// Define a function to close the current window
function closeWin(){

  self.close()

// End hide --->
</script>
```

# window.setInterval()

## *JavaScript1.2+, JScript3.0+*

## Nav4+, IE4+

## Syntax

```
window.setInterval(expression, milliseconds)
window.setInterval(function, milliseconds)
window.setInterval(function, milliseconds, arg1, ..., argN)
```

## Description

The setInterval() method of the Window object sets an interval to invoke the expression or function that is passed to the method. The expression or function is invoked after every elapse of the *milliseconds* passed. As shown in the syntax definition, it is possible to pass arguments to the function you want to invoke. This interval can be cleared by using the clearInterval() method.

## Example

Listing 7.583 sets an interval in the <head> of the document that displays the current time in a text box on the page. The interval is set so it only updates the time in the text box every five seconds. There is also a button on this page that allows you to clear the interval if you click it.

*Listing 7.583    Clearing an Interval with the* setInterval() *Method*

```
<html>
<head>
<script language="JavaScript1.2">
<!-- Hide

// Create a variable to hold a counter
var counter = 1;

// Define a function to display the counter
function startCounter(){
  document.myForm.myText.value = counter++;
}

// Define a function to stop the counter
function stopCounter(){
  window.clearInterval(myInterval);
}

// Set the interval to call the function every 5 seconds
var myInterval = window.setInterval("startCounter()", 5000)

// End hide --->
</script>
</head>
<body onLoad="startCounter()">
<form name="myForm">
```

*continues*

*Listing 7.583    continued*
```
  <input type=TEXT size=20 value="" name="myText">
  <input type=BUTTON value="Clear Interval" onClick="stopCounter()">
</form>
</body>
</html>
```

# window.setTimeout()

## JavaScript1.0+, JScript1.0+

## Nav2+, IE3+, Opera3+

## Syntax

```
window.setTimeout(expression, milliseconds)
window.setTimeout(function, milliseconds)
window.setTimeout(function, milliseconds, arg1, ..., argN)
```

## Description

The setTimeout() method of the Window object sets a timeout to invoke the expression or function that is passed to the method. The expression or function is invoked after the elapse of the *milliseconds* passed. As shown in the syntax definition, it is possible to pass arguments to the function you want to invoke. This timeout can be cleared by using the clearTimeout() method.

## Example

Listing 7.584 has a button and text box. By the default, the time will be displayed in the text box after five seconds. This is done using the setTimeout() method. If the button is clicked, a function is called that invokes the clearTimeout() method, preventing the time from being displayed in the text box.

*Listing 7.584    Using the* setTimeout() *Method*
```
<html>
<head>
<script language="JavaScript">
<!-- Hide

// Define a function to show the time
function showTime(){
  myTime = new Date();
  myTime = myTime.getHours() + ":" + myTime.getMinutes() + ":";
  myTime += myTime.getSeconds();
  document.myForm.myText.value = myTime;
}

// Define a function to stop the display of the time
function stopTime(){
  window.clearTimeout(myTimeout);
}
```

```
// Set the interval to call the function after 5 seconds
var myTimeout = window.setTimeout("showTime()", 5000)

// End hide --->
</script>
</head>
<body>
<form name="myForm">
  <input type=TEXT size=20 value="" name="myText">
  <input type=BUTTON value="Clear Timeout" onClick="stopTime()">
</form>
</body>
</html>
```

# window.status

## JavaScript1.0+, JScript1.0+

## Nav2+, IE3+, Opera3+

## Syntax

```
window.status = string
```

## Description

The status property of the Window object allows you to specify the message that is displayed in the status bar of the browser. Note that in JavaScript 1.1, this property was tainted. See Chapter 1 for more information on JavaScript security and data tainting.

**NOTE**

When setting the Window.status property, be sure that your function returns true. This also applies when setting the property within the body of an HTML tag.

## Example

Listing 7.585 shows how you can set the status in the Status Bar by rolling over a link.

*Listing 7.585   Setting the Status of a Page*

```
<a href="http://www.purejavascript.com/book"
   onMouseOver="window.status='Please Visit Our Online Book!'; return true"
   onMouseOut="window.status='Document: Done'"
   >Click Here!</a>
```

# window.statusbar

## JavaScript1.2+

## Nav4+

## Syntax

*window*.statusbar.*property*

## Description

The statusbar property of the Window object is, to some degree, an object itself. The real use of this property is to access its visible property to determine if the status bar is visible to the user or not.

> **NOTE**
>
> As of this writing, the statusbar property only has one subproperty: visible.

## Example

Please see the example of Window.statusbar.visible for an example of using the statusbar property.

# window.statusbar.visible

## JavaScript1.2+

## Nav4+

## Syntax

*window*.statusbar.visible

## Description

The visible subproperty of the statusbar property of the Window is used to determine if the status bar is visible to the user or not. If it is visible, the property returns true. It returns false if the bar is not visible.

## Example

Listing 7.586 determines if several of the browser bars are displayed or not. In the example, you will see if the status bar is visible by using the visible property.

*Listing 7.586   Using the* visible *Property of* statusbar

```
<script language="JavaScript">
<!-- Hide

// Write the browser's bar status to the page. If the value
// is true, then it is displayed.
document.writeln('<h3>Browser Chrome Status</h3>')
document.writeln('Menu Bar: ' + window.menubar.visible + '<br>');
document.writeln('Tool Bar: ' + window.toolbar.visible + '<br>');
document.writeln('Location Bar: ' + window.locationbar.visible + '<br>');
document.writeln('Personal Bar: ' + window.personalbar.visible + '<br>');
document.writeln('Scroll Bars: ' + window.scrollbars.visible + '<br>');
document.writeln('Status Bar: ' + window.statusbar.visible + '<br>');
```

```
// Close the stream to the document.
document.close();

// End hide --->
</script>
```

# window.stop()

## JavaScript1.2+, JScript3.0

## Nav4+, IE4+

## Syntax

```
window.stop()
```

## Description

The stop() method of the Window object simulates the user clicking the Stop button on the browser. It stops the browser from downloading and rendering the current page.

## Example

Listing 7.587 has a button and an image reference to a nonexistent image. The browser will continue to try and download the image until it times out or the download is stopped. Clicking the button will stop the download.

*Listing 7.587   Using the* stop() *Method to Stop a Page from Loading*

```
<html>
<body>
<form>
  <input type=BUTTON value="Stop" onClick="window.stop()">
</form>
<p>
  <table border=1color= bgcolor="#FF0000"><tr><td>
    <img src="http://www.purejavascript.com/images/fake.gif"
        width=468 height=60>
  </td></tr></table>
</p>
</body>
</html>
```

# window.toolbar

## JavaScript1.2+

## Nav4+

## Syntax

```
window.toolbar.property
```

## Description

The `toolbar` property of the `Window` object is, to some degree, an object itself. The real use of this property is to access its `visible` property to determine if the toolbar is visible to the user or not.

> **NOTE**
>
> As of this writing, the `toolbar` property only has one subproperty: `visible`.

## Example

Please see the example of `Window.toolbar.visible` for an example of using the `toolbar` property.

# window.toolbar.visible

## JavaScript1.2+

## Nav4+

## Syntax

`window.toolbar.visible`

## Description

The `visible` subproperty of the `toolbar` property of the `Window` is used to determine if the toolbar is visible to the user or not. If it is visible, the property returns `true`. It returns `false` if the bar is not visible.

## Example

Listing 7.588 determines if several of the browser bars are displayed or not. In the example, you will see if the toolbar is visible by using the `visible` property.

*Listing 7.588   Using the* `visible` *Property of* `toolbar`

```
<script language="JavaScript">
<!-- Hide

// Write the browser's bar status to the page. If the value
// is true, then it is displayed.
document.writeln('<h3>Browser Chrome Status</h3>')
document.writeln('Menu Bar: ' + window.menubar.visible + '<br>');
document.writeln('Tool Bar: ' + window.toolbar.visible + '<br>');
document.writeln('Location Bar: ' + window.locationbar.visible + '<br>');
document.writeln('Personal Bar: ' + window.personalbar.visible + '<br>');
document.writeln('Scroll Bars: ' + window.scrollbars.visible + '<br>');
document.writeln('Status Bar: ' + window.statusbar.visible + '<br>');

// Close the stream to the document.
```

```
document.close();

// End hide --->
</script>
```

# window.top

## *JavaScript1.0+, JScript1.0*

## *Nav2+, IE3+, Opera3+*

## *Syntax*

```
window.top.frames[num]
window.top.frameName
window.top.method
window.top.property
```

## *Description*

The top property of the Window object contains a reference to the topmost browser window of any frames or pages that are loaded. In the instance where a Frame A loads a page with a <frameset> with Frame A.1 and A.2, the top of the documents in A.1 and A.2 is the window that actually has Frame A loaded. Frame A's top is also this window.

As shown in the syntax definition, the referencing of sibling frames can either be done using the frames array and passing an index number, or you can directly reference a frame using the name that is assigned by the NAME attribute of the <frame> tag. From within the current page or any of the frames, you can reference the top window and execute any methods or reference any properties that might reside there.

## *Example*

Assuming that the page with this script lies within a <frameset>, Listing 7.589 shows how you can call a function that is defined in the topmost page.

*Listing 7.589   Using the* top *Property to Call a Function in the Top Frame*

```
<script language="JavaScript">
<!-- Hide

// Call a function in the top
top.myFunc(myVar1, myVar2);

// End hide --->
</script>
```

# CHAPTER 8

## Netscape's Server-Side Additions

This chapter is a detailed reference of all the items and elements making up the server-side JavaScript language. Like Chapters 6, 7, and 9, the details of the language are covered in this chapter. Each entry includes the language version, syntax, description, and an example of each server-side–specific language element.

The chapter is in alphabetical order, by JavaScript objects, to provide you with quick, easy access to the methods, properties, functions, and event handlers of every server-side object. These appear alphabetically after the respective parent object using simple dot notation.

## addClient()

### NES2+

### Syntax

```
addClient(URL)
```

### Description

The `addClient()` function is a top-level function that is not associated with any core object. This function is used to preserve the property values of a `client` object when you generate dynamic links or use the `redirect` method. The `addClient()` function takes a URL as its only parameter.

### Example

This example demonstrates how you can use the `addClient()` function when dynamically building links. In Listing 8.1, a link is built by using a property of the `project` object.

*Listing 8.1    Using the* `addClient()` *Function to Dynamically Build a Link*

```
<A HREF='<SERVER>addClient("/myApp/page" + project.pagenum +
".html")</SERVER>'>
Please proceed to the next page</A>
```

In Listing 8.2, the `addClient()` function is used in conjunction with the `redirect()` function. This will send the user to the URL specified in the `addClient()` function.

*Listing 8.2    Using the* `addClient()` *Function with the* `redirect()` *Function*

```
<SERVER>

// Check to see if the browser is Internet Explorer
if(request.agent.indexOf('MSIE') != -1){
  redirect(addClient("/iepages/index.html"));

// Redirect to another page if it is not IE
}else{
  redirect(addClient("/defaultpages/index.html"));
}
</SERVER>
```

# addResponseHeader

## NES3+

## Syntax

`addResponseHeader(key, value)`

## Description

The `addResponseHeader` function is a top-level function that is not associated with any core object. This function is used to add fields and values to the HTTP header sent back to the client. Because of when the actual header is sent in relation to the body of the data, you should be sure to set these fields and values before you call the `flush` or `redirect` functions.

## NOTE

Because the JavaScript runtime engine flushes the output buffer after 64KB of content has been generated, you should be sure to call the `addResponseHeader` function before this time.

## Example

Listing 8.3 shows how you can send back a dynamically built external JavaScript source file to a browser with the proper content-type header field and value.

*Listing 8.3    Using the* `addResponseHeader` *Function to Set the* `content.type` *of a File Being Sent to a Browser*

```
<SERVER>

// Add a field to the header
addResponseHeader("content-type", "application/x-javascript");

</SERVER>
```

# blob

## NES2+

## Syntax

Core object is created with the `blob.blobImage()` and `blob.blobLink()` methods.

`blob(path)`

## Description

`BLOb` data represents Binary Large Objects that can be stored in a database. This allows you to store various types of information, such as images, movie files, and sounds in the database. The `blob` implementation in server-side JavaScript has two different purposes, as shown in the syntax definition.

> **NOTE**
>
> Be sure to consult the documentation on your specific database to see if there are any limitations to `BLOb` data types.

The first instance is a core object that is created when you use the methods of this object. Table 8.1 has the methods of the `blob` object and a description of what they do when invoked.

**Table 8.1    Methods of the blob Object**

| Method | Description |
| --- | --- |
| `blobImage()` | Retrieves and displays a BLOb data instance stored in a database |
| `blobLink()` | Retrieves and displays a link that references a BLOb data instance stored in a database |

The second instance is the `blob()` function that is used to store `BLOb` data in your database. This function takes the path to a `BLOb` file as its only parameter. Note that this path must be an absolute pathname and not a relative one.

## Example

In Listing 8.4, a `cursor` instance has been created to perform a query on the database to find a specific row. Focus is then placed on that row and the `blob()` function is used to assign the data to a column. The final step in the process is to use the `updateRow()` method to commit the change.

*Listing 8.4    Using the `blob()` Function to Insert BLOb Data into a Database*

```
<SERVER>

// SQL statement and instance of a cursor to execute it
var myStatement = 'SELECT * FROM family WHERE pic = null';
var myCursor = database.cursor(myStatement);

// Iterate through the returned rows
while(myCursor.next()){

  // Assign 'blank.gif' in the PIC column of the returned rows
  myCursor.pic = blob("/pictures/blank.gif");
  myCursor.updateRow("family");
}

// Close the cursor and write it to the page if there was an error
var dbError = myCursor.close();

if(dbError) write(myCursor.close());
</SERVER>
```

# blob.blobImage()

## NES2+

## Syntax

`cursor.column.blobImage(fileType, altText, align, width, height, border, ismap)`

## Description

The `blobImage()` method retrieves and displays a BLOb image stored in a database. The method actually returns the HTML for the `<IMG>` tag used to display the image. The `HREF` attribute of the `<IMG>` tag references the instance of this image in memory and does not have to contain a "normal" URL of the image itself.

This method can take up to seven parameters that set the various attributes of the `<IMG>` tag. These attributes are contained in Table 8.2. At a minimum, you must pass the `fileType` of the image.

*Table 8.2   Properties That Can Be Set with the blobImage() Method*

| Parameter | Attribute It Sets | Description |
|-----------|-------------------|-------------|
| fileType | none | This parameter does not set an attribute. It specifies the type of file that is being displayed, such as gif or jpeg. |
| altText | ALT | A string that is displayed when the browser has been set to not display images or when a mouse is over an image for a specified period of time. |
| align | ALIGN | This can be set to LEFT, RIGHT, or any other value your target browser supports. |
| width | WIDTH | The width in pixels of your image. |
| height | HEIGHT | The height in pixels of your image. |
| border | BORDER | An integer value that specifies the size of any border that may appear around the image if the image is surrounded by the <A> tag. |
| ismap | ISMAP | Specifies if the image has a map file associated with it to handle any clicks that may occur within it. This parameter is set by specifying true if the image has a map file associated with it or false if not. |

## Example

Listing 8.5 queries a database for a specific image. The image is then written to the page using the write() and blobImage() methods. The actual tag written will be as follows:

```
<IMG ALT="Click Here!" ALIGN="" WIDTH=468 HEIGHT=60 BORDER=0 ISMAP=false>
```

*Listing 8.5   Using the* blobImage() *Method to Dormat a* <IMG> *Tag*
```
<SERVER>

// Find the image you want to display
myCursor = myConn.cursor("SELECT path FROM images WHERE img = 1");

// Write the <IMG> tag to the page with the following attributes set
write(myCursor.path.blobImage("gif", "Click Here!", "", 468, 60, 0, false));

// Close the cursor
myCursor.close();
</SERVER>
```

# blob.blobLink()

## NES2+

## Syntax

```
cursor.column.blobLink(mimeType, text)
```

## Description

The blobLink() method retrieves BLOb data stored in a database, stores it in memory, and creates a temporary link to it. The method actually returns the HTML for the <A> tag used to display the link. The HREF attribute of the <A> tag references the BLOb data type, which has been stored in a temporary memory location, and does not contain a "normal" URL of this attribute. The data is stored in memory until the user clicks the link or until 60 seconds have elapsed.

The parameters this method takes are the MIME type of the file referenced, and the *text* that is displayed to the user as a link.

## Example

Listing 8.6 queries a database for a specific image. A link referencing the image is then written to the page using the write() and blobLink() methods. The actual tag written will be as follows:

```
<A HREF="LIVEWIRE_TEMP1">Click Here!</A>
```

*Listing 8.6    Using the blobLink() Method to Format a <A> Tag*
```
<SERVER>

// Find the image you want to display
myCursor = myConn.cursor("SELECT path FROM images WHERE img = 1");

// Write the <A> tag to the page with the attributes set
write(myCursor.path.blobLink("image/gif", "Click Here!"));

// Close the cursor
myCursor.close();
</SERVER>
```

# callC

## NES2+

## Syntax

```
callC(JSFuncName, arg1, arg2, ..., argN)
```

## Description

The callC function is a top-level function that is not associated with any core object. callC is used to call a JavaScript function that references a C function in a shared library. These libraries are the pre-built .dll files on Windows machines and .so files on UNIX machines. callC takes the JavaScript name you have assigned the C function and any arguments the function needs as arguments.

Before you can call this function, you must register the C library using the server-side JavaScript registerCFunction. registerCFunction takes the JavaScript name with which you want to reference the function, the path to the library, and the C function name as parameters.

## Example

Listing 8.7 registers an external C library, extlib.dll, that contains a function named getMyDate. The registration of this function assigns the name JSExtLib to be used within the script. If the function successfully registers, the callC function is used to call the C function and passes it two parameters. The results are written to the user's page. If the function does not register properly, an error is written to the user's page.

*Listing 8.7    Using a C Function with* callC *That Has Been Registered*

```
<SERVER>

// Register the library and function, assigning it a JavaScript
// function name
var myExternalLib = registerCFunction("JSExtLib", "c:/winnt/extlib.dll",
➥"getMyDate")

// If the library registered without error, then call it using the
// callC function. If it failed, then write an error to the page.
if (myExternalLib) {
  write(callC("getMyDate", 1999, 2000));
}else{
  write("There was an error processing this external library function");
}

</SERVER>
```

# client

## NES2+

## Syntax

Core object is created with each connection of a client to your application.

## Description

An instance of the client object is created with each connection of a user to your application. This object is used to maintain session variables for that user as he or she moves through your application's pages. Because the object is not created until a user connects to your application, you cannot use the object on the first page of your application.

> ## NOTE
>
> The `client` object is created for each user's connection to each application, so a single user connected to two applications will have two `client` objects created.

The object itself is held until the user is inactive a set period of time or the object is destroyed. At that time, the JavaScript runtime engine cleans up the object. The default timeout is ten minutes, but this can be changed by using the `expiration()` method or can be destroyed manually by using the `destroy()` method.

`client` objects do not have any default properties, but properties can be created for them. Do note that because of the method used to maintain user sessions, these properties are all converted to strings. If you have a property you have created that must be evaluated as a numeric value, use the `parseInt()` and `parseFloat()` methods for processing.

If you must store an object as a property, you will have to create an array of objects in the `project` or `server` objects. Then you can create a property to hold the index of your object in the `client` object.

## Example

Listing 8.8 contains a form the user fills out with his or her name, email address, and phone number. When the Submit button is clicked, the form is sent back to itself and the script sees information being passed in. This information is then assigned to three created properties of the `client` object and is then written to the user's page.

*Listing 8.8    Assigning Properties to the `client` Object*

```
<HTML>
<HEAD>
  <TITLE>Listing 8-8: Using the client object</TITLE>
</HEAD>
<BODY>
<SERVER>

// See if they have submitted or just need the form
if(request.method == "POST"){

  // Assign the client properties their values
  client.name = request.name;
  client.email = request.email;
  client.phone = request.phone;

  // Write the user's information to the page
  write('Hello ' + client.name + '!<BR>');
  write('Please confirm your email, ' + client.email + ', and ');
  write('phone number, ' + client.phone);
}else{

  // If this page was called and a form was not submitted
```

```
   write('<FORM NAME="myForm" METHOD=POST>');
   write('<TABLE BORDER=1><TR><TD>');
   write('<TABLE BORDER=0>');
   write('<TR ALIGN=LEFT VALIGN=TOP>');
   write('<TD><B>Name:</B></TD>');
   write('<TD><INPUT TYPE=TEXT NAME="name" SIZE=30></TD>');
   write('</TR>');
   write('<TR ALIGN=LEFT VALIGN=TOP>');
   write('<TD><B>E-mail:</B></TD>');
   write('<TD><INPUT TYPE=TEXT NAME="email" SIZE=30></TD>');
   write('</TR>');
   write('<TR ALIGN=LEFT VALIGN=TOP>');
   write('<TD><B>Phone:</B></TD>');
   write('<TD><INPUT TYPE=TEXT NAME="phone" SIZE=30></TD>');
   write('</TR>');
   write('<TR ALIGN=LEFT VALIGN=TOP>');
   write('<TD COLSPAN=2 ALIGN=RIGHT><INPUT TYPE=SUBMIT VALUE="Submit"></TD>');
   write('</TR>');
   write('</TABLE>');
   write('</TD></TR></TABLE>');
   write('</FORM>');
}
</SERVER>
</BODY>
</HTML>
```

# client.destroy()

## NES2+

## Syntax

```
client.destroy()
```

## Description

The destroy() method of the client object explicitly destroys that instance of the object and all its associated properties. If this method is not called, the JavaScript runtime will destroy the object after 10 minutes or after the time specified with the client.expiration() method.

If you are using cookies to maintain your client object, calling the destroy() method acts in the same manner but does not remove information stored in the browser's cookie file. To remove the cookie information, set the expiration to 0 seconds by using the client.expiration() method.

When using URL encoding to maintain the client object, the destroy() method will destroy all information with the exception that the links created before the method call will retain their properties. Because of this, good programming practice warrants calling the method at the top or bottom of a page.

## Example

Listing 8.9 shows how to destroy the properties of your user's `client` object.

*Listing 8.9    Using the `destroy()` Method to Destroy the `client` Object Properties*

```
<SERVER>

// Destroy the client properties
client.destroy()

</SERVER>
```

# client.expiration()

## NES2+

## Syntax

```
client.expiration(seconds)
```

## Description

The `expiration()` method of the `client` objects sets the number of seconds of user inactivity before the JavaScript runtime destroys all properties associated with that session. The default timeout is ten minutes if you do not explicitly set this property. Also, this method has no effect when using URL encoding to maintain your `client` objects.

**NOTE**

> Setting this to **0** will remove any cookies associated with the `client` object when using client cookies to maintain sessions.

## Example

Listing 8.10 sets the destruction of the `client` object to occur after five minutes of inactivity.

*Listing 8.10    Using the `expiration()` Method of the `client` Property*

```
<SERVER>

// Set the expiration to 5 minutes
client.expiration(300)

</SERVER>
```

# Connection

## NES3+

## Syntax

Core object is created when the DbPool.connection() method is called.

## Description

The Connection object represents a given connection, pulled from a "pool", to a database. This object has only one property, the prototype property, which you can use to add properties to the object. Table 8.3 shows the methods associated with this object.

**NOTE**

If you only need a single connection to the database and do not need to create a pool, use the database object for your connection.

**Table 8.3 Methods of the Connection Object**

| Method | Description |
| --- | --- |
| beginTransaction() | Begins a new SQL transaction |
| commitTransaction () | Commits the current SQL transaction |
| connected() | Tests to see if the pool connection is connected to the database |
| cursor() | Creates a Cursor object for the specified SQL SELECT statement |
| execute() | Performs the non-SELECT SQL statement passed |
| majorErrorCode() | Returns the major error code numeric value returned by the database or ODBC |
| majorErrorMessage() | Returns the major error message string value returned by the database or ODBC |
| minorErrorCode() | Returns the secondary error code numeric value returned by the database or ODBC |
| minorErrorMessage() | Returns the secondary error message string value returned by the database or ODBC |
| release() | Releases the specified connection back to the pool |
| rollbackTransaction() | Rolls back the specified transaction |
| SQLTable() | Formats the query results from a SELECT in HTML <TABLE> format for easy writing to a client |
| storedProc() | Creates a Stproc object and runs the specified stored procedure |
| toString() | Returns a string representing the specified object |

## Example

Listing 8.11 creates a pool of connections to an Oracle database and initializes a connection from that pool. It takes a user's UID and name that was passed in, runs a query (based on the UID) against the database to find that user's information, and updates the user's name. If a connection is not made, the error code and message is returned to the screen.

*Listing 8.11    Creating and Using a* Connection *Object*

```
<SERVER>

// Assign the user submitted ID and name to the client object as properties
client.uid = request.uid;
client.name = request.name;

// Create a pool of connections
var myPool = new DbPool("ORACLE", "mySID", "myApp", "appsPWD", "myTNS");

// Open a connection from the pool.  Give error if connection could
// not be made.
var myConn = myPool.connection('Employees', 15);
if(myConn.connected()){

  // Start a new SQL transaction to perform a SELECT
  myConn.beginTransaction();
var currRow = myConn.cursor('SELECT * FROM employees WHERE uid = '
➥ + client.uid);

  // Focus on that line, change the name column for that user,
  // and update the row.
  currRow.next();
  currRow.name = client.name;
  currRow.updateRow("employees");

  // Close the cursor
  currRow.close();

// If the connection fails, write an error message
}else{
write('Error ('+myConn.majorErrorCode()+'): '+myConn.majorErrorMessage);
  }

</SERVER>
```

# Connection.beginTransaction()

## NES3+

## Syntax

connection.beginTransaction()

## Description

The beginTransaction() method of the Connection object begins a new SQL transaction. This groups all the actions against the database together until the user exits the
page or either the commitTransaction() or rollbackTransaction() methods are

called. In the instance of the user exiting the page, the transaction is either committed or rolled back, depending on the setting of the commit flag when the DbPool object instance is created.

> **NOTE**
>
> You cannot have nested transactions.

## *Example*

Listing 8.12 creates a pool of connections to an Oracle database and pulls one of the connections from the pool. After the connection has been verified, the beginTransaction() method is called and a SQL query is performed. The results are formatted in a table with the SQLTable() method and written to the user's page.

*Listing 8.12    Starting a New Transaction with the* beginTransaction() *Method*

```
<SERVER>

// Assign the user submitted ID to the client object as properties
client.uid = request.uid;

// Create a pool of connections
var myPool = new DbPool("ORACLE", "mySID", "myApp", "appsPWD", "myTNS");

// Open a connection from the pool.  Give error if connection could
// not be made.
var myConn = myPool.connection('Employees', 15);
if(myConn.connected()){

  // Start a new transaction and write the results to a page, formatting
  // them with the SQLTable method.
  myConn.beginTransaction();
write(myConn.SQLTable('SELECT * FROM employees WHERE uid >= '+client.uid));

  // Commit the transaction
  myConn.commitTransaction();

// If the connection fails, write an error message
}else{
write('Error ('+myConn.majorErrorCode()+'): '+myConn.majorErrorMessage);
  }

</SERVER>
```

# Connection.commitTransaction()

## NES3+

## Syntax

```
connection.commitTransaction()
```

## Description

The commitTransaction() method of the Connection object commits a new SQL transaction. This commits all the actions against the database since the last commit. If the commit is successful, 0 is returned. If a non-zero number is returned, an error is encountered. In this case, various methods of the Connection object can be used to retrieve the code and message of the error.

## Example

Listing 8.13 creates a pool of connections to an Oracle database and pulls one of the connections from the pool. After the connection has been verified, the beginTransaction() method is called and a SQL query is performed. The results are formatted in a table with the SQLTable() method and written to the user's page.

*Listing 8.13    Starting a New Transaction with the* commitTransaction() *Method*

```
<SERVER>

// Assign the user submitted ID to the client object as properties
client.uid = request.uid;

// Create a pool of connections
var myPool = new DbPool("ORACLE", "mySID", "myApp", "appsPWD", "myTNS");

// Open a connection from the pool.  Give error if connection could
// not be made.
var myConn = myPool.connection('Employees', 15);
if(myConn.connected()){

  // Start a new transaction and write the results to a page, formatting
  // them with the SQLTable method.
  myConn.beginTransaction();
write(myConn.SQLTable('SELECT * FROM employees WHERE uid >= '+client.uid));

  // Commit the transaction
  myConn.commitTransaction();

// If the connection fails, write an error message
}else{
write('Error (' + myConn.majorErrorCode()+'): '+myConn.majorErrorMessage);
  }

</SERVER>
```

# Connection.connected()

## NES3+

## Syntax

`connection.connected()`

## Description

The `connected()` method of the `Connection` object tells if the pool of connections to the database is still connected.

## Example

Listing 8.14 creates a pool of connections and pulls a connection from the pool for processing. If the connection is made, any code within that section is executed. If the connection fails, the error is written to the page.

*Listing 8.14   Testing a Connection with the* `connected()` *Method*

```
<SERVER>

// Create a pool of connections
var myPool = new DbPool("ORACLE", "mySID", "myApp", "appsPWD", "myTNS");

// Open a connection from the pool.  Give error if connection could
// not be made.
var myConn = myPool.connection('Employees', 15);

if (myConn.connected()) {

  // You are connected, so perform any tasks here

}else{

  // There was an error connecting to the database
write('Error ('+myConn.majorErrorCode()+'): '+myConn.majorErrorMessage);
}

</SERVER>
```

# Connection.cursor()

## NES3+

## Syntax

`connection.cursor(sql)`
`connection.cursor(sql, boolean)`

## Description

The cursor() method of the Connection object creates a Cursor object that can be used to run SQL queries against the database. The method takes the SQL statement as a parameter, as well as an optional Boolean value that specifies if the cursor is update-able.

## Example

Listing 8.15 shows how you would run a query against the database using the cursor() method. The while loop is used to write the results to the user's page.

*Listing 8.15   Using the* cursor() *Method to Run Query Against the Database*

```
<SERVER>

// Set the query to run
var mySQL = myConn.cursor('SELECT name,title FROM employees');

// Iterate through the results and write them to the page.
while(mySQL.next()){
  write(mySQL.name + ': ' + mySQL.title + '<BR>');
}

</SERVER>
```

# Connection.execute()

## NES3+

## Syntax

```
connection.execute(statement)
```

## Description

The execute() method of the Connection object enables your application to execute a DDL (Data Definition Language) or DML (Data Manipulation Language) query, which does not return a Cursor, supported by your database. This includes statements such as CREATE, ALTER, and DROP.

> **NOTE**
>
> Be sure to use SQL that conforms to your database.

## Example

Listing 8.16 deletes all rows with a UID less than the number passed to the script.

*Listing 8.16    Using the* `execute()` *Method to Run DML Queries*
```
<SERVER>

// Assign the UID passed to the client object
client.uid = request.uid;

// Execute a DELETE based on the UID passed
myConn.execute('DELETE FROM employees WHERE uid < ' + client.uid);

</SERVER>
```

# Connection.majorErrorCode()

## NES3+

## Syntax

`connection.majorErrorCode()`

## Description

The `majorErrorMessage()` method of the `Connection` object contains the ODBC or database numeric error code that is returned if an error occurs.

## Example

Listing 8.17 shows how you would create a pool of connections, pull a connection from it, and test for the connection. If the test fails, the `majorErrorCode()` is used when writing the error to the page.

*Listing 8.17    Using* `majorErrorCode()` *to Retrieve a Database Connection Error*
```
<SERVER>

// Create a pool of connections
var myPool = new DbPool("ORACLE", "mySID", "myApp", "appsPWD", "myTNS");

// Open a connection from the pool.  Give error if connection could
// not be made.
var myConn = myPool.connection('Employees', 15);

if (myConn.connected()) {

  // You are connected, so perform any tasks here

}else{

  // There was an error connecting to the database
write('Error ('+myConn.majorErrorCode()+'): '+myConn.majorErrorMessage);
}

</SERVER>
```

# Connection.majorErrorMessage()

## NES3+

## Syntax

`connection.majorErrorMessage()`

## Description

The `majorErrorMessage()` method of the `Connection` object contains the ODBC or database string error message that is returned if an error occurs.

## Example

Listing 8.18 shows how you would create a pool of connections, pull a connection from it, and test for the connection. If the test fails, the `majorErrorMessage()` is used when writing the error to the page.

*Listing 8.18    Using `majorErrorMessage()` to Retrieve a Database Connection Error*

```
<SERVER>

// Create a pool of connections
var myPool = new DbPool("ORACLE", "mySID", "myApp", "appsPWD", "myTNS");

// Open a connection from the pool.  Give error if connection could
// not be made.
var myConn = myPool.connection('Employees', 15);

if (myConn.connected()) {

  // You are connected, so perform any tasks here

}else{

  // There was an error connecting to the database
write('Error ('+myConn.majorErrorCode()+'): '+myConn.majorErrorMessage);
}

</SERVER>
```

# Connection.minorErrorCode()

## NES3+

## Syntax

`connection.minorErrorCode()`

## Description

The `minorErrorMessage()` method of the `Connection` object contains the secondary ODBC or database numeric error code that is returned if an error occurs.

## Example

Listing 8.19 shows how you would create a pool of connections, pull a connection from it, and test for the connection. If the test fails, the `minorErrorCode()` is used when writing the secondary error to the page.

*Listing 8.19    Using `minorErrorCode()` to Retrieve a Secondary Database Connection Error*

```
<SERVER>

// Create a pool of connections
var myPool = new DbPool("ORACLE", "mySID", "myApp", "appsPWD", "myTNS");

// Open a connection from the pool.  Give error if connection could
// not be made.
var myConn = myPool.connection('Employees', 15);

if (myConn.connected()) {

   // You are connected, so perform any tasks here

}else{

   // There was an error connecting to the database
write('Error ('+myConn.minorErrorCode()+'): '+myConn.minorErrorMessage);
}

</SERVER>
```

# Connection.minorErrorMessage()

## NES3+

## Syntax

`connection.minorErrorMessage()`

## Description

The `minorErrorMessage()` method of the `Connection` object contains the secondary ODBC or database string error message that is returned if an error occurs.

## Example

Listing 8.20 shows how you would create a pool of connections, pull a connection from it, and test for the connection. If the test fails, the `minorErrorMessage()` is used when writing the secondary error to the page.

*Listing 8.20   Using* `minorErrorMessage()` *to Retrieve a Secondary Database Connection Error*

```
<SERVER>

// Create a pool of connections
var myPool = new DbPool("ORACLE", "mySID", "myApp", "appsPWD", "myTNS");

// Open a connection from the pool.  Give error if connection could
// not be made.
var myConn = myPool.connection('Employees', 15);

if (myConn.connected()) {

  // You are connected, so perform any tasks here

}else{

  // There was an error connecting to the database
write('Error ('+myConn.minorErrorCode()+'): '+myConn.minorErrorMessage);
}

</SERVER>
```

# Connection.prototype

## NES3+, ECMAScript 1.0+

## Syntax

```
connection.prototype.method = methodName
connection.prototype.property
```

## Description

The `prototype` property of the `Connection` object allows you to add methods and properties to the `Connection` object. If you are adding a method, you set the instance equal to the *methodName* of the method you have defined.

## Example

Listing 8.21 creates a new property and method of the `Connection` object. An instance is created and the new property is set. The new method is then called to verify the property and, if it is incorrect (which it is), an error is written to the page.

*Listing 8.21   Using the* `prototype` *Property to Create a New Property and Method*

```
<SERVER>

// Define the method that we prototyped
function verifyODBC(){
```

```
// Check to see if the type property we added is set to a valid value
if(this.type == "ODBC"){
  return true;
}else{
  return false;
}
}

// Create a new property and method of the Connection object.
Connection.prototype.type = null;
Connection.prototype.isODBC = verifyODBC;

// Create a pool of connections
var myPool = new DbPool("ORACLE", "mySID", "myApp", "appsPWD", "myTNS");

// Open a connection from the pool.
var myConn = myPool.connection('Employees', 15);

// Using the prototype we defined, assign the type property
myConn.type = "Oracle";

// Check the type of the connection to see if it is valid
if(myConn.isODBC()){
  write(myConn + " has a valid type of " + myConn.type);
}else{
  write(myConn + " has an invalid type of " + myConn.type);
}

</SERVER>
```

# Connection.release()

## *NES3+*

## *Syntax*

`connection.release()`

## *Description*

The release() method of the Connection object returns the connection to the DbPool instance after all cursors have been closed. If you do not close the cursor, the connection will remain until it times out or the variable holding your connection, assuming you assigned it to one, goes out of scope. Depending on how you have written your application, this can happen when the application is stopped, the Web server is stopped, or when control leaves the HTML page.

## Example

Listing 8.22 shows a pool being created, a connection being pulled from the pool, and a query run against the database. Once the cursor is closed, the connection is released.

*Listing 8.22   Releasing a Connection Back to the Pool Using the* release() *Method*

```
<SERVER>

// Assign the user submitted ID and name to the client object as properties
client.uid = request.uid;
client.name = request.name;

// Create a pool of connections
var myPool = new DbPool("ORACLE", "mySID", "myApp", "appsPWD", "myTNS");

// Open a connection from the pool.  Give error if connection could
// not be made.
var myConn = myPool.connection('Employees', 15);
if(myConn.connected()){

  // Start a new SQL transaction to perform a SELECT
  myConn.beginTransaction();
var currRow = myConn.cursor('SELECT * FROM employees WHERE uid = '
➥ + client.uid);

  // Focus on that line, change the name column for that user,
  // and update the row.
  currRow.next();
  currRow.name = client.name;
  currRow.updateRow("employees");

  // Close the cursor
  currRow.close();

// If the connection fails, write an error message
}else{
write('Error ('+myConn.majorErrorCode()+'): '+myConn.majorErrorMessage);
}

// Release the connection
myConn.release();

</SERVER>
```

# Connection.rollbackTransaction()

## NES3+

## Syntax

*connection*.rollbackTransaction()

## Description

The `rollbackTransaction()` method of the `Connection` object will undo all actions performed since the last `beginTransaction()` method call.

**NOTE**

You cannot have nested transactions.

## Example

Listing 8.23 takes a *commit* field sent to the application from the user. If this evaluates to TRUE, the transaction is committed. If not, it is rolled back.

*Listing 8.23   Rolling Back a Transaction with the* `rollbackTransaction()` *Method*

```
<SERVER>

// See if the user wants to commit the last transaction
client.commit = request.commit;

if(client.commit = "YES"){

  // Commit the transaction
  myConn.commitTransaction();

}else{

  // Rollback the transaction
  myConn.rollbackTransaction();
}

</SERVER>
```

# Connection.SQLTable()

## *NES3+*

## Syntax

```
connection.SQLTable(SQL)
```

## Description

The `SQLTable()` method of the `Connection` object takes a SQL `SELECT` statement as a parameter and executes a query through the connection from which it was called. It returns the result formatted in an HTML table for easy writing to a client's page. This is a simple table in the following format:

```
<TABLE BORDER>
<TR>
<TH>column 1</TH>
<TH>column 2</TH>
```

```
...
<TH>column N</TH>
</TR>
<TR>
<TD>value 1 of column 1</TD>
<TD>value 1 of column 2</TD>
...
<TD>value 1 of column N</TD>
</TR>
<TR>
<TD>value 2 of column 1</TD>
<TD>value 2 of column 2</TD>
...
<TD>value 2 of column N</TD>
</TR>
...
</TABLE>
```

## Example

Listing 8.24 runs a user passed query and formats the result using the `SQLTable()` method. This information is then written to the user's page.

*Listing 8.24    Using the `SQLTable()` Method to Format the Results of a SELECT Query*

```
<SERVER>

// Assign the user submitted query to the client object
client.sql = request.sql;

// Create a pool of connections
var myPool = new DbPool("ORACLE", "mySID", "myApp", "appsPWD", "myTNS");

// Open a connection from the pool.  Give error if connection could
// not be made.
var myConn = myPool.connection('Employees', 15);
if(myConn.connected()){

  // Start a new transaction and write the results to a page, formatting
  // them with the SQLTable method.
  myConn.beginTransaction();
  write(myConn.SQLTable(client.sql));

  // Commit the transaction
  myConn.commitTransaction();

// If the connection fails, write an error message
}else{
```

```
write('Error ('+myConn.majorErrorCode()+'): '+myConn.majorErrorMessage);
}

// Release the connection
myConn.release();

</SERVER>
```

# Connection.storedProc()

## NES3+

## Syntax

```
connection.storedProc(procName)
connection.storedProc(procName, arg1, arg2, ... , argN)
```

## Description

The storedProc() method of the Connection object creates a Stproc object that allows you to execute a database-specific stored procedure using the connection from which it was invoked.

As shown in the syntactical definition, you can also pass any arguments needed to the method for processing. If you are using a stored procedure that requires arguments, or if you want to have the procedure run using default arguments, you must pass /Default/ as the argument. The following shows an example of passing a default value:

```
var myStproc = myConn.storedProc("sp_employees", "/Default/");
```

The scope of this procedure is restricted to the current page. Any methods of the Stproc object must be invoked on the current page. If this is not possible, a new object will have to be created on subsequent pages to access the properties needed.

## Example

Listing 8.25 creates a pool of connections and pulls one of the connections. Once the connection has been verified, the storedProc() method is used to invoke the fictitious *sp_employees* stored procedure.

Listing 8.25    *Using the* storedProc() *Method to Invoke a Stored Procedure on a Database*

```
<SERVER>

// Create a pool of connections
var myPool = new DbPool("ORACLE", "mySID", "myApp", "appsPWD", "myTNS");

// Open a connection from the pool.  Give error if connection could
// not be made.
```

*continues*

*Listing 8.25    continued*

```
var myConn = myPool.connection('Employees', 15);
if(myConn.connected()){

  myConn.beginTransaction();

  // Run the stored procedure
  var myStproc = myConn.storedProc("sp_employees");

  // Commit the transaction
  myConn.commitTransaction();

// If the connection fails, write an error message
}else{
write('Error ('+myConn.majorErrorCode()+'): '+myConn.majorErrorMessage);
}

// Release the connection
myConn.release();

</SERVER>
```

# Connection.toString()

## *NES3+, ECMAScript1.0+*

## *Syntax*

`connection.toString()`

## *Description*

The `toString()` method of the `Connection` object returns a text value of the object. When invoked on an instance of a `Connection` object, the string is returned in the following format:

`"dbName" "uid" "dbType" "dbInstance"`

If parameter is unknown, an empty string is returned. Table 8.4 contains the value of these returned values.

**Table 8.4    Return Values of the toString() Method**

| Method | Description |
| --- | --- |
| dbName | The name of the database you want to log into. For Oracle, DB2, and ODBC connections this is a blank (`""`), string. In Oracle, the name of the database for these connections is set up in the `tnsnames.ora` file and is defined by the DSN for ODBC connections. DB2 does not have a database name and is referenced only by the `dbInstance`. |

| Method | Description |
|--------|-------------|
| uid | The username or ID you want the connections to connect as. |
| dbType | The type of database it is. Possible values are: ORACLE, SYBASE, INFORMIX, DB2, or ODBC. |
| dbInstance | This is the instance name of the database. For ODBC, it is the DSN entry name. |

## Example

Listing 8.26 creates an instance of the Connection object. Once created, the write() method is used to write its string value to the page.

*Listing 8.26    Write the Results of Calling the* toString() *Method to a Page*

```
<SERVER>

// Create a pool of connections
var myPool = new DbPool("ORACLE", "mySID", "myApp", "appsPWD", "myTNS");

// Open a connection from the pool.  Give error if connection could
// not be made.
var myConn = myPool.connection('Employees', 15);
if(myConn.connected()){

  // Write the string value of the object to the page
  write(myConn.toString());

// If the connection fails, write an error message
}else{
write('Error ('+myConn.majorErrorCode()+'): '+myConn.majorErrorMessage);
}

// Release the connection
myConn.release();

</SERVER>
```

# Cursor

## NES2+

### Syntax

```
connection.cursor()
database.cursor()
```

### Description

The Cursor object is a core object created when the cursor() method of the Connection or database object is called. A database query is said to return a cursor, so this object contains references to the rows returned from a query.

When working with cursor objects, you should explicitly close them using the `close()` method when you are finished. Not doing so will call the JavaScript runtime to hold the cursor in memory until the connection or pool to which the cursor was tied goes out of scope.

The `Cursor` object has several methods and properties associated with it. These are listed in Table 8.5.

**Table 8.5   Properties and Methods of the Cursor Object**

| Type | Item | Description |
| --- | --- | --- |
| property | `columnName` | This property represents the column names that are returned from the SQL statement you passed to the `cursor()` method. |
| | `prototype` | This property allows you to add methods and properties to the `Cursor` object to be used when new instances are created. |
| method | `close()` | This method closes the cursor and frees any memory used by it. |
| | `columnName()` | This method takes an indexed numbered location and returns the column name of the column in that location. |
| | `columns()` | This method returns the number of columns in the cursor. |
| | `deleteRow()` | This method deletes the current row of the table passed to the method. |
| | `insertRow()` | This method inserts a new row in the table passed to the method. |
| | `next()` | This method moves from the current row in the `Cursor` object to the next row. |
| | `updateRow()` | This method updates the current row in the table passed to the method.> |

## Example

Listing 8.27 takes a UID, passed as an area code, that is assigned to the `client` object. A pool of connections is then opened to the database, and one of the connections is pulled to run query. The results of the query are stored in a `Cursor` object and are iterated through use of the `next()` method. Once all rows have been updated with the new area code, the cursor is closed and the connection is released.

*Listing 8.27   Using the* `Cursor` *Object*

```
<SERVER>

// Assign the user submitted ID and area code to the client object
// as properties
client.uid = request.uid;
```

```
client.areacode = request.areacode;

// Create a pool of connections
var myPool = new DbPool("ORACLE", "mySID", "myApp", "appsPWD", "myTNS");

// Open a connection from the pool.  Give error if connection could
// not be made.
var myConn = myPool.connection('Employees', 15);
if(myConn.connected()){

  // Start a new SQL transaction to perform a SELECT
  myConn.beginTransaction();
  var currRow = myConn.cursor('SELECT areacode FROM employees WHERE uid >= '
➥ + client.uid);

  // For all the lines that matched, update the area code
  while(currRow.next()){
    currRow.areacode = client.areacode;
    currRow.updateRow("employees");
  }

  // Close the cursor
  currRow.close();

// If the connection fails, write an error message
}else{
write('Error ('+myConn.majorErrorCode()+'): '+myConn.majorErrorMessage);
}

// Release the connection
myConn.release();

</SERVER>
```

# Cursor.close()

## *NES2+*

## *Syntax*

`cursor.close()`

## *Description*

The `close()` method of the `Cursor` object closes the cursor and frees all memory that had been used to store its information. If successful, the method returns `0`, otherwise it returns an error code that can be obtained by using the `majorErrorCode()` and `majorErrorMessage()` methods of the `Connection` or database objects.

## Example

Listing 8.28 creates a cursor and then closes it.

*Listing 8.28    Closing a Cursor with the* `close()` *Method*

```
<SERVER>

// Create cursor
var currRow = myConn.cursor('SELECT areacode FROM employees WHERE uid >= '
➡ + client.uid);

// Close the cursor
currRow.close();

</SERVER>
```

# Cursor.columnName

## NES2+

## Syntax

`cursor.columnName`

## Description

The `columnName` property of the `Cursor` object is an array of objects that corresponds to the name of the columns in the cursor.

## Example

Listing 8.29 shows a cursor object being created. The various values are then written to the page using the `columnName` property as their reference.

*Listing 8.29    Using the* `columnName` *Property*

```
<SERVER>

var currRow = myConn.cursor('SELECT areacode,phone,name FROM employees);

// Write each person's name and phone number to the page in the form:
// "<name>'s phone number is (<areacode>) <phone>"
while(currRow.next()){
  write(currRow.name + "'s phone number is (" + currRow.areacode + ") ");
  write(currRow.phone + "<BR>");
}

// Close the cursor
currRow.close();

</SERVER>
```

# Cursor.columnName()

## NES2+

## Syntax

```
cursor.columnName(num)
```

## Description

The columnName() method of the Cursor object takes the zero-based indexed number location, *num*, passed to the method and returns the name of the column in that location. Note that these names are not returned in any specific order unless you order them as such. Successive calls to the method, however, will return all the columns. See the example for more information on this.

## Example

Listing 8.30 has two cursors. One of the cursors returns specific column names and the other returns all columns. See the comments in the code for the output.

*Listing 8.30    Using the* columnName() *Method to Return the Names of the Columns in a Table*

```
<SERVER>

// Create a pool of connections
var myPool = new DbPool("ORACLE", "mySID", "myApp", "appsPWD", "myTNS");

// Open a connection from the pool.  Give error if connection could
// not be made.
var myConn = myPool.connection('Employees', 15);
if(myConn.connected()){

  // Start a new SQL transaction to perform a SELECT
  myConn.beginTransaction();
  var currRow1 = myConn.cursor('SELECT areacode,phone FROM employees
►WHERE uid >= 100');
  var currRow2 = myConn.cursor('SELECT * FROM employees WHERE uid >= 100');

  // Writes 'areacode', from the first cursor, to the page
  write(currRow1.columnName(0));

  // Writes 'phone', from the first cursor, to the page
  write(currRow1.columnName(1));

  // Writes all column names stored in the second cursor to the page.
  // This will include 'areacode' and 'phone' as well as any other
  // columns.
  for(var i = 0; i <= currRow2.columns(); i++){
```

*continues*

*Listing 8.30    continued*
```
    write(currRow2.columnName(i));
  }

  // Close the cursors
  currRow1.close();
  currRow2.close();

// If the connection fails, write an error message
}else{
write('Error ('+myConn.majorErrorCode()+'): '+myConn.majorErrorMessage);
}

// Release the connection
myConn.release();

</SERVER>
```

# Cursor.columns()

## NES2+

## Syntax

`cursor.columns()`

## Description

The `columns()` method of the `Cursor` object returns the number of columns in the cursor on which it is invoked. If the SQL string that was passed to create the cursor specified a set number of columns to return, this is the number returned by the method.

## Example

Listing 8.31 shows how you can return all the column names of the columns in your cursor.

*Listing 8.31    Using the `columns()` Method to Determine How Many Columns Are in the Cursor Before Writing Them to the Page*
```
<SERVER>

var currRow = myConn.cursor('SELECT * FROM employees');

// Writes all column names stored in the cursor to the page.
for(var i = 0; i <= currRow.columns(); i++){
  write(currRow.columnName(i));
}

// Close the cursors
currRow.close();

</SERVER>
```

# Cursor.deleteRow()

## NES2+

## Syntax

`cursor.deleteRow(table)`

## Description

The `deleteRow()` method of the `Cursor` object uses an updateable cursor and deletes the current row in the specified *table* of the cursor object. If the delete was successful, `0` is returned, otherwise it returns an error code that can be obtained by using the `majorErrorCode()` and `majorErrorMessage()` methods of the `Connection` or database objects.

## Example

Listing 8.32 creates a cursor object and selects all instances of a given *id*. The `deleteRow()` method is then used to delete each of these instances.

*Listing 8.32    Deleting a Row from the Cursor Using the `deleteRow()` Method*

```
<SERVER>

// Assign the user submitted ID to the client object as properties
client.uid = request.uid;

// Create a pool of connections
var myPool = new DbPool("ORACLE", "mySID", "myApp", "appsPWD", "myTNS");

// Open a connection from the pool.  Give error if connection could
// not be made.
var myConn = myPool.connection('Employees', 15);
if(myConn.connected()){

  // Start a new SQL transaction to perform a SELECT
  myConn.beginTransaction();
  var currRow = myConn.cursor('SELECT * FROM employees WHERE uid = '
➥ + client.uid, true);

  // Delete each row in the cursor.
  while(currRow.next()){
    currRow.delete("employees");
  }

  // Close the cursor
  currRow.close();

// If the connection fails, write an error message
```

*continues*

*Listing 8.32    continued*
```
}else{
write('Error ('+myConn.majorErrorCode()+'): '+myConn.majorErrorMessage);
}

</SERVER>
```

# Cursor.insertRow()

## NES2+

## Syntax

```
cursor.insertRow(table)
```

## Description

The insertRow() method of the Cursor object uses an updateable cursor and inserts a new row in the specified *table* of the cursor object. If the insert was successful, 0 is returned; otherwise, it returns an error code that can be obtained by using the majorErrorCode() and majorErrorMessage() methods of the Connection or database objects.

**NOTE**

> Depending on your database, you may have to close the current cursor and reopen it if you want to access a newly inserted row. Also, if the next() method has been called on the cursor, any columns you do not specify values for will get the same values as the current row.

## Example

Listing 8.33 creates a Cursor object and selects all rows. The insertRow() method is then used to insert a new row with three specified columns.

*Listing 8.33    Inserting a Row from the Cursor Using the* insertRow() *Method*
```
<SERVER>

// Assign the user submitted ID to the client object as properties
client.uid = request.uid;
client.name = request.name;
client.pwd = request.pwd;

// Create a pool of connections
var myPool = new DbPool("ORACLE", "mySID", "myApp", "appsPWD", "myTNS");

// Open a connection from the pool.  Give error if connection could
```

```
// not be made.
var myConn = myPool.connection('Employees', 15);
if(myConn.connected()){

    // Start a new SQL transaction to perform a SELECT. Notice the
    // cursor is updateable
    myConn.beginTransaction();
    var currRow = myConn.cursor('SELECT uid,name,pwd FROM employees', true);

    // Assign values to the columns and insert a new row
    currRow.uid = client.uid;
    currRow.name = client.name;
    currRow.pwd = client.pwd;
    currRow.insertRow("employees");
    myConn.commitTransaction();

    // Close the cursor and release the connection
    currRow.close();
    myConn.release();

// If the connection fails, write an error message
}else{
write('Error ('+myConn.majorErrorCode()+'): '+myConn.majorErrorMessage);
}

</SERVER>
```

# Cursor.next()

## *NES2+*

## *Syntax*

```
cursor.next()
```

## *Description*

The next() method of the Cursor object moves the point in the current row to the next row in the cursor. This method is used to iterate through each of the rows returned by the cursor. This method returns true, unless it is the last row of the cursor, at which time it returns false.

## *Example*

Listing 8.34 creates an instance of the Cursor object and iterates through its results, deleting each row. This is performed by using the next() method.

*Listing 8.34   Using the* next() *Method to Iterate Through the Rows in a Cursor*

```
<SERVER>

var currRow = myConn.cursor('SELECT * FROM employees WHERE uid <= 200');

// Delete each row in the cursor.
while(currRow.next(){
  currRow.delete("employees");
}

// Close the cursor
currRow.close();

</SERVER>
```

# Cursor.prototype

## NES2+, ECMAScript1.0+

### Syntax

```
cursor.prototype.method = methodName
cursor.prototype.property
```

### Description

The prototype property of the Cursor object allows you to create new properties and methods of the object. If you are adding a method, you set the instance equal to the *methodName* of the method you have defined.

### Example

Listing 8.35 creates a new property and method of the Cursor object. An instance is created and the new property is set. The new method is then called to verify the property, and, if it is incorrect, an error is written to the page.

*Listing 8.35   Using the* prototype *Property to Create a New Property and Method*

```
<SERVER>

// Define the method that we prototyped
function verifySELECT(){

  // Check to see if the type property we added is set to a valid value
  if(this.type == "SELECT"){
    return true;
  }else{
    return false;
  }
}
```

```
// Create a new property and method of the Cursor object.
Cursor.prototype.type = null;
Cursor.prototype.isSELECT = verifySELECT;

// Create a pool of connections, a connection, and a cursor
var myPool = new DbPool("ORACLE", "mySID", "myApp", "appsPWD", "myTNS");
var myConn = myPool.connection('Employees', 15);
var currRow = myConn.cursor('SELECT * FROM employees');

// Using the prototype we defined, assign the type property
currRow.type = "SELECT";

// Check the type of the connection to see if it is valid
if(currRow.verifySELECT()){
  write(currRow + " has a valid type of " + currRow.type);
}else{
  write(currRow + " has an invalid type of " + currRow.type);
}

</SERVER>
```

# Cursor.updateRow()

## NES2+

## Syntax

`cursor.updateRow(table)`

## Description

The `updateRow()` method of the `Cursor` object uses an updateable cursor and updates the current row in the specified *table* of the cursor object. If the insert was successful, 0 is returned; otherwise, it returns an error code that can be obtained by using the `majorErrorCode()` and `majorErrorMessage()` methods of the `Connection` or database objects.

## Example

Listing 8.36 creates a `Cursor` object and selects all rows. The `updateRow()` method is then used to update the current row with three specified values.

*Listing 8.36    Updating a Row from the Cursor Using the* `updateRow()` *Method*
```
<SERVER>

// Assign the user submitted ID to the client object as properties
client.uid = request.uid;
client.name = request.name;
```

*continues*

*Listing 8.36    continued*

```
client.pwd = request.pwd;

// Create a pool of connections
var myPool = new DbPool("ORACLE", "mySID", "myApp", "appsPWD", "myTNS");

// Open a connection from the pool.  Give error if connection could
// not be made.
var myConn = myPool.connection('Employees', 15);
if(myConn.connected()){

  // Start a new SQL transaction to perform a SELECT. Notice the
  // cursor is updateable
  myConn.beginTransaction();
  var currRow = myConn.cursor('SELECT uid,name,pwd FROM employees WHERE uid = '
➥ + client.uid, true);

  // Select the row and assign values to the columns
  currRow.next();
  currRow.uid = client.uid;
  currRow.name = client.name;
  currRow.pwd = client.pwd;
  currRow.updateRow("employees");
  myConn.commitTransaction();

  // Close the cursor and release the connection
  currRow.close();
  myConn.release();

// If the connection fails, write an error message
}else{
write('Error ('+myConn.majorErrorCode()+'): '+myConn.majorErrorMessage);
}

</SERVER>
```

# database

## NES2+

## Syntax

Core object is created when the `database.connect()` method is called.

## Description

The `database` object represents a given connection to a database. This object has only one property, the `prototype` property, which you can use to add properties to the object. Table 8.6 lists the methods associated with this object.

**NOTE**

If you only need a pool of connections to the database, use the DbPool object for your connection to initialize a pool, and then use the Connection.connection() method to assign a connection.

**Table 8.6    Methods of the database Object**

| Method | Description |
| --- | --- |
| beginTransaction() | Begins a new SQL transaction. |
| commitTransaction () | Commits the current SQL transaction. |
| connect() | Connects to a particular database as a particular user. |
| connected() | Tests to see if the connection is connected to the database. |
| cursor() | Creates a Cursor object for the specified SQL SELECT statement. |
| disconnect() | Disconnects a particular connection from the database. |
| execute() | Performs the non-SELECT SQL statement passed. |
| majorErrorCode() | Returns the major error code numeric value returned by the database or ODBC. |
| majorErrorMessage() | Returns the major error message string value returned by the database or ODBC. |
| minorErrorCode() | Returns the secondary error code numeric value returned by the database or ODBC. |
| minorErrorMessage() | Returns the secondary error message string value returned by the database or ODBC. |
| rollbackTransaction() | Rolls back the specified transaction. |
| SQLTable() | Formats the query results from a SELECT in HTML <TABLE> format for easy writing to a client. |
| storedProc() | Creates a Stproc object and runs the specified stored procedure. This method was added in NES 3.0. |
| storedProcArgs() | Creates a prototype for DB2, ODBC, or Sybase stored procedures. This method was added in NES 3.0. |
| toString() | Returns a string representing the specified object. |

## Example

Listing 8.37 creates a connection to an Oracle database. It takes a user's UID and name that was passed in, runs a query (based on the UID) against the database to find that user's information and updates his or her name. If a connection is not made, the error code and message are returned to the screen.

*Listing 8.37    Creating and Using a* database *Object*

```
<SERVER>

// Assign the user submitted ID and name to the client object as properties
client.uid = request.uid;
client.name = request.name;

// Open a connection
var myConn = database.connect("ORACLE", "mySID", "myApp", "appsPWD", "myTNS");

if(myConn.connected()){

  // Start a new SQL transaction to perform a SELECT
  myConn.beginTransaction();
  var currRow = myConn.cursor('SELECT * FROM employees WHERE uid = '
➥ + client.uid);

  // Focus on that line, change the name column for that user,
  // and update the row.
  currRow.next();
  currRow.name = client.name;
  currRow.updateRow("employees");
  myConn.commitTransaction();

  // Close the cursor and drop the connection.
  currRow.close();
  myConn.disconnect();

// If the connection fails, write an error message
}else{
write('Error ('+myConn.majorErrorCode()+'): '+myConn.majorErrorMessage);
}

</SERVER>
```

# database.beginTransaction()

## *NES2+*

## *Syntax*

*database*.beginTransaction()

## *Description*

The beginTransaction() method of the database object begins a new SQL transaction. This groups all the actions against the database together until the user exits the page or either the commitTransaction() or rollbackTransaction() methods are called. In the instance of the user exiting the page, the transaction is either committed or rolled back, depending on setting of the commit flag when the database object instance is created.

**NOTE**

You cannot have nested transactions.

## Example

Listing 8.38 creates a connection to an Oracle database. After the connection has been verified, the beginTransaction() method is called and a SQL query is performed. The results are formatted in a table with the SQLTable() method and written to the user's page.

*Listing 8.38   Starting a New Transaction with the* beginTransaction() *Method*

```
<SERVER>

// Assign the user submitted ID to the client object as properties
client.uid = request.uid;

// Open a connection
var myConn = database.connect("ORACLE", "mySID", "myApp", "appsPWD", "myTNS");

if(myConn.connected()){

  // Start a new transaction and write the results to a page, formatting
  // them with the SQLTable method.
  myConn.beginTransaction();
  write(myConn.SQLTable('SELECT * FROM employees WHERE uid >= ' + client.uid));

  // Commit the transaction
  myConn.commitTransaction();

// If the connection fails, write an error message
}else{
write('Error ('+myConn.majorErrorCode()+'): '+myConn.majorErrorMessage);
}

</SERVER>
```

# database.commitTransaction()

## NES2+

## Syntax

*database*.commitTransaction()

## Description

The commitTransaction() method of the database object commits a new SQL transaction. This commits all the actions against the database since the last commit. If the commit is successful, 0 is returned. If a non-zero number is returned, an error was encountered. In this case, you can use the various methods of the database object to retrieve the code and message of the error.

## Example

Listing 8.39 creates a connection to an Oracle database. After the connection has been verified, the beginTransaction() method is called and a SQL query is performed. The results are formatted in a table with the SQLTable() method and written to the user's page.

*Listing 8.39 Starting a New Transaction with the commitTransaction() Method*

```
<SERVER>

// Assign the user submitted ID to the client object as properties
client.uid = request.uid;

// Open a connection
var myConn = database.connect("ORACLE", "mySID", "myApp", "appsPWD", "myTNS");

if(myConn.connected()){

  // Start a new transaction and write the results to a page, formatting
  // them with the SQLTable method.
  myConn.beginTransaction();
  write(myConn.SQLTable('SELECT * FROM employees WHERE uid >= ' + client.uid));

  // Commit the transaction
  myConn.commitTransaction();

// If the connection fails, write an error message
}else{
write('Error ('+myConn.majorErrorCode()+'): '+myConn.majorErrorMessage);
  }

</SERVER>
```

# database.connect()

## NES2+

## Syntax

database.connect(*dbType, dbInstance, uid, pwd, dbName*)

database.connect(*dbType, dbInstance, uid, pwd, dbName, maxConn*)

database.connect(*dbType, dbInstance, uid, pwd, dbName, maxConn, commitFlag*)

## Description

The connect method of the database object is the actual method that connects to a database given the parameters passed. Before you open a connection to a database and have the ability to run queries against it, you should create an instance of this object. Each parameter is defined in Table 8.7.

**Table 8.7 Parameters of the connect Method**

| Parameter | Description |
|---|---|
| dbType | The type of database it is. Possible values are: ORACLE, SYBASE, INFORMIX, DB2, or ODBC. |
| dbInstance | This is the instance name of the database. For ODBC it is the DSN entry name. |
| uid | The username or ID you want the connections to connect as. |
| pwd | The password for the user you are connecting as. |
| dbName | The name of the database you want to log in to. For Oracle, DB2, and ODBC connections this should be a blank, "", string. In Oracle, the name of the database for these connections is set up in the tnsnames.ora file and is defined by the DSN for ODBC connections. DB2 does not have a database name and is referenced only by the dbInstance. |
| maxConn | The maximum number of connections to the pool. This is effectively the number of connections the pool will open to the database. |
| commitFlag | This flag determines if a pending transaction is committed when connection is released. If it is set to false, the transaction is rolled back. If it is set to true, it is committed. |

Depending on your database, it is possible to create an instance of this object by passing a limited set of these parameters. Please see your database documentation for this information.

## Example

Listing 8.40 creates a connection to an Oracle database. It takes a user's UID and name that was passed in, runs a query (based on the UID) against the database to find that user's information, and updates his or her name. If a connection is not made, the error code and message are returned to the screen.

*Listing 8.40 Connecting to a Database Using the* connect() *Method*

```
<SERVER>

// Assign the user submitted ID and name to the client object as properties
client.uid = request.uid;
client.name = request.name;

// Open a connection
var myConn = database.connect("ORACLE","mySID","myApp","appsPWD","myTNS",true);

if(myConn.connected()){
```

*continues*

*Listing 8.40    continued*

```
// Start a new SQL transaction to perform a SELECT
myConn.beginTransaction();
var currRow = myConn.cursor('SELECT * FROM employees WHERE uid = '
➡ + client.uid);

// Focus on that line, change the name column for that user,
// and update the row.
currRow.next();
currRow.name = client.name;
currRow.updateRow("employees");
myConn.commitTransaction();

// Close the cursor and the connection
currRow.close();
myConn.disconnect();

// If the connection fails, write an error message
}else{
write('Error ('+myConn.majorErrorCode()+'): '+myConn.majorErrorMessage);
}

</SERVER>
```

# database.connected()

## *NES2+*

## *Syntax*

```
database.connected()
```

## *Description*

The connected() method of the database object tells if the connection to the database is still active.

## *Example*

Listing 8.41 creates a connection to a database. If the connection is made, any code within that section is executed. If the connection fails, the error is written to the page.

*Listing 8.41    Testing a Connection with the connected() Method*

```
<SERVER>

// Open a connection
var myConn = database.connect("ORACLE", "mySID", "myApp", "appsPWD", "myTNS");

if (myConn.connected()) {
```

```
  // You are connected, so perform any tasks here

}else{

  // There was an error connecting to the database
write('Error ('+myConn.majorErrorCode()+'): '+myConn.majorErrorMessage);
}

</SERVER>
```

# database.cursor()

## NES2+

## Syntax

```
database.cursor(sql)
database.cursor(sql, boolean)
```

## Description

The cursor() method of the database object creates a Cursor object that can be used to run SQL queries against the database. The method takes the SQL statement as a parameter, as well as an optional Boolean value that specifies if the cursor is update-able.

## Example

Listing 8.42 shows how you would run a query against the database using the cursor() method. The while loop is used to write the results to the user's page.

*Listing 8.42    Using the* cursor() *Method to Run Query Against the Database*

```
<SERVER>

// Set the query to run
var mySQL = myConn.cursor('SELECT name,title FROM employees');

// Iterate through the results and write them to the page.
while(mySQL.next()){
  write(mySQL.name + ': ' + mySQL.title + '<BR>');
}

</SERVER>
```

# database.disconnect()

## NES2+

## Syntax

```
database.disconnect()
```

## Description

The `disconnect` method of the `database` object disconnects a connection to a database.

## Example

Listing 8.43 creates a connection to an Oracle database. It takes a user's UID and name that was passed in, runs a query (based on the UID) against the database to find that user's information, and updates his or her name. If a connection is not made, the error code and message are returned to the screen. Once the processing has been completed, the connection is dropped using the `disconnect()` method.

*Listing 8.43 Disconnecting from a Database Using the* `disconnect()` *Method*

```
<SERVER>

// Assign the user submitted ID and name to the client object as properties
client.uid = request.uid;
client.name = request.name;

// Open a connection
var myConn = database.connect("ORACLE","mySID","myApp","appsPWD","myTNS",true);

if(myConn.connected()){

  // Start a new SQL transaction to perform a SELECT
  myConn.beginTransaction();
  var currRow = myConn.cursor('SELECT * FROM employees WHERE uid = '
➥ + client.uid);

  // Focus on that line, change the name column for that user,
  // and update the row.
  currRow.next();
  currRow.name = client.name;
  currRow.updateRow("employees");
  myConn.commitTransaction();

  // Close the cursor and the connection
  currRow.close();
  myConn.disconnect();

// If the connection fails, write an error message
}else{
write('Error ('+myConn.majorErrorCode()+'): '+myConn.majorErrorMessage);
}

</SERVER>
```

# database.execute()

## *NES2+*

## *Syntax*

`database.execute(`*statement*`)`

## *Description*

The `execute()` method of the `database` object enables your application to execute a DDL (Data Definition Language) or DML (Data Manipulation Language) query, which does not return a `Cursor`, supported by your database. This includes statements such as `CREATE`, `ALTER`, and `DROP`.

> **NOTE**
>
> Be sure to use Syntax that conforms to your database.

## *Example*

Listing 8.44 deletes all rows with a UID less than the number passed to the script.

*Listing 8.44   Using the* `execute()` *Method to Run DML Queries*

```
<SERVER>

// Assign the UID passed to the client object
client.uid = request.uid;

// Execute a DELETE based on the UID passed
myConn.execute('DELETE FROM employees WHERE uid < ' + client.uid);

</SERVER>
```

# database.majorErrorCode()

## *NES2+*

## *Syntax*

`database.majorErrorCode()`

## *Description*

The `majorErrorMessage()` method of the `database` object contains the ODBC or database numeric error code that is returned if an error occurs.

## *Example*

Listing 8.45 shows how you would create a connection and test for a successful connection. If the test fails, the `majorErrorCode()` is used when writing the error to the page.

*Listing 8.45   Using* `majorErrorCode()` *to Retrieve a Database Connection Error*
```
<SERVER>

// Open a connection
var myConn = database.connect("ORACLE", "mySID", "myApp", "appsPWD", "myTNS");

if (myConn.connected()) {

  // You are connected, so perform any tasks here

}else{

  // There was an error connecting to the database
write('Error ('+myConn.majorErrorCode()+'): '+myConn.majorErrorMessage);
}

</SERVER>
```

# database.majorErrorMessage()

## *NES2+*

## *Syntax*

*database*`.majorErrorMessage()`

## *Description*

The `majorErrorMessage()` method of the `database` object contains the ODBC or database string error message that is returned if an error occurs.

## *Example*

Listing 8.46 shows how you would create a connection and test for a successful connection. If the test fails, the `majorErrorMessage()` is used when writing the error to the page.

*Listing 8.46   Using* `majorErrorMessage()` *to Retrieve a Database Connection Error*
```
<SERVER>

// Open a connection
var myConn = database.connect("ORACLE", "mySID", "myApp", "appsPWD", "myTNS");

if (myConn.connected()) {

  // You are connected, so perform any tasks here

}else{
```

```
  // There was an error connecting to the database
write('Error ('+myConn.majorErrorCode()+'): '+myConn.majorErrorMessage);
}

</SERVER>
```

# database.minorErrorCode()

## NES2+

## Syntax

*database.minorErrorCode()*

## Description

The `minorErrorMessage()` method of the `database` object contains the secondary ODBC or database numeric error code that is returned if an error occurs.

## Example

Listing 8.47 shows how you would create a connection and test for a successful connection. If the test fails, the `minorErrorCode()` is used when writing the secondary error to the page.

*Listing 8.47    Using `minorErrorCode()` to Retrieve a Secondary Database Connection Error*

```
<SERVER>

// Open a connection
var myConn = database.connect("ORACLE", "mySID", "myApp", "appsPWD", "myTNS");

if (myConn.connected()) {

  // You are connected, so perform any tasks here

}else{

  // There was an error connecting to the database
write('Error ('+myConn.minorErrorCode()+'): '+myConn.minorErrorMessage);
}

</SERVER>
```

# database.minorErrorMessage()

## NES2+

## Syntax

*database.minorErrorMessage()*

## Description

The `minorErrorMessage()` method of the `database` object contains the secondary ODBC or database string error message that is returned if an error occurs.

## Example

Listing 8.48 shows how you would create a connection and test for a successful connection. If the test fails, the `minorErrorMessage()` is used when writing the secondary error to the page.

*Listing 8.48    Using `minorErrorMessage()` to Retrieve a Secondary Database Connection Error*

```
<SERVER>

// Open a connection
var myConn = database.connect("ORACLE", "mySID", "myApp", "appsPWD", "myTNS");

if (myConn.connected()) {

  // You are connected, so perform any tasks here
}else{

  // There was an error connecting to the database
  write('Error ('+myConn.minorErrorCode()+'): '+myConn.minorErrorMessage);
}

</SERVER>
```

# database.prototype

## NES2+, ECMAScript 1.0+

## Syntax

```
database.prototype.method = methodName
database.prototype.property
```

## Description

The `prototype` property of the `database` object allows you to add methods and properties to the `database` object. If you are adding a method, you set the instance equal to the `methodName` of the method you have defined.

## Example

Listing 8.49 creates a new property and method of the `database` object. An instance is created and the new property is set. The new method is then called to verify the property, and, if it is incorrect (which it is), an error is written to the page.

*Listing 8.49    Using the* prototype *Property to Create a New Property and Method*

```
<SERVER>

// Define the method that we prototyped
function verifyODBC(){

  // Check to see if the type property we added is set to a valid value
  if(this.type == "ODBC"){
    return true;
  }else{
    return false;
  }
}

// Create a new property and method of the database object.
database.prototype.type = null;
database.prototype.isODBC = verifyODBC;

// Open a connection
var myConn = database.connect("ORACLE", "mySID", "myApp", "appsPWD", "myTNS");

// Using the prototype we defined, assign the type property
myConn.type = "Oracle";

// Check the type of the connection to see if it is valid
if(myConn.isODBC()){
  write(myConn + " has a valid type of " + myConn.type);
}else{
  write(myConn + " has an invalid type of " + myConn.type);
}

</SERVER>
```

# database.rollbackTransaction()

## *NES2+*

## *Syntax*

database.rollbackTransaction()

## *Description*

The rollbackTransaction() method of the database object will undo all actions performed since the last beginTransaction() method call.

**NOTE**

You cannot have nested transactions.

## Example

Listing 8.50 takes a *commit* field sent to the application from the user. If this evaluates to TRUE, the transaction is committed. If not, it is rolled back.

*Listing 8.50   Rolling Back a Transaction with the* rollbackTransaction() *Method*

```
<SERVER>

// See if the user wants to commit the last transaction
client.commit = request.commit;

if(client.commit = "YES"){

  // Commit the transaction
  myConn.commitTransaction();

}else{

  // Rollback the transaction
  myConn.rollbackTransaction();
}

</SERVER>
```

# database.SQLTable()

## NES2+

## Syntax

*database*.SQLTable(*SQL*)

## Description

The SQLTable() method of the database object takes a SQL SELECT statement as a parameter and executes this query through the connection from which it was called. It returns the results formatted in an HTML table for easy writing to a client's page. This is a simple table in the following format:

```
<TABLE BORDER>
<TR>
<TH>column 1</TH>
<TH>column 2</TH>
...
<TH>column N</TH>
</TR>
<TR>
<TD>value 1 of column 1</TD>
```

```
<TD>value 1 of column 2</TD>
...
<TD>value 1 of column N</TD>
</TR>
<TR>
<TD>value 2 of column 1</TD>
<TD>value 2 of column 2</TD>
...
<TD>value 2 of column N</TD>
</TR>
...
</TABLE>
```

## Example

Listing 8.51 runs a user passed query and formats the result using the SQLTable() method. This information is then written to the user's page.

*Listing 8.51    Using the* SQLTable() *Method to Format the Result of a* SELECT *Query*

```
<SERVER>

// Assign the user submitted query to the client object
client.sql = request.sql;

// Open a connection
var myConn = database.connect("ORACLE", "mySID", "myApp", "appsPWD", "myTNS");

if(myConn.connected()){

    // Start a new transaction and write the results to a page, formatting
    // them with the SQLTable method.
    myConn.beginTransaction();
    write(myConn.SQLTable(client.sql));

    // Commit the transaction
    myConn.commitTransaction();

// If the connection fails, write an error message
}else{
write('Error ('+myConn.majorErrorCode()+'): '+myConn.majorErrorMessage);
}

// Release the connection
myConn.release();

</SERVER>
```

# database.storedProc()

## NES3+

## Syntax

```
database.storedProc(procName)
database.storedProc(procName, arg1, arg2, ... , argN)
```

## Description

The storedProc() method of the database object creates a Stproc object that allows you to execute a database-specific stored procedure using the connection from which it was invoked.

As shown in the syntactical definition, you can also pass any arguments needed to the method for processing. If you are using a stored procedure that requires arguments, or if you want to have the procedure run using default arguments, you must pass /Default/ as the argument. The following shows an example of passing a default value:

```
var myStproc = myConn.storedProc("sp_employees", "/Default/");
```

The scope of this procedure is restricted to the current page. Any methods of the Stproc object must be invoked on the current page. If this is not possible, a new object will have to be created on subsequent pages to access the properties needed.

## Example

Listing 8.52 creates a connection to a database. Once the connection has been verified, the storedProc() method is used to invoke the fictitious *sp_employees* stored procedure.

Listing 8.52   Using the storedProc() *Method to Invoke a Stored Procedure on a Database*

```
<SERVER>

// Open a connection
var myConn = database.connect("ORACLE", "mySID", "myApp", "appsPWD", "myTNS");

if(myConn.connected()){

  myConn.beginTransaction();

  // Run the stored procedure
  var myStproc = myConn.storedProc("sp_employees");

  // Commit the transaction
  myConn.commitTransaction();

// If the connection fails, write an error message
```

```
}else{
write('Error ('+myConn.majorErrorCode()+'): '+myConn.majorErrorMessage);
}

// Release the connection
myConn.release();

</SERVER>
```

# database.storedProcArgs()

## *NES3+*

## *Syntax*

```
database.storedProcArgs(procName)
database.storedProcArgs(procName, type1, type2, ... , typeN)
```

## *Description*

The storedProcArgs() method of the database object creates a Stproc object that allows you to execute a database-specific stored procedure using the connection from which it was invoked on DB2, ODBC, and Sybase databases. If this method is invoked on Informix or Oracle databases, it has no effect. The difference between this method and the storedProc() method is that this method takes a type as a parameter for the arguments passed. These types can be IN, OUT, or INOUT. The following shows an example of passing these types:

```
var myStproc = myConn.storedProc("sp_employees", "INOUT", "OUT");
```

The scope of this procedure is restricted to the current page. Any methods of the Stproc object must be invoked on the current page. If this is not possible, a new object will have to be created on subsequent pages to access the properties needed.

## *Example*

Listing 8.53 creates a connection to a database. Once the connection has been verified, the storedProc() method is used to invoke the fictitious *sp_employees* stored procedure, and the storedProcArgs() method is used to specify the argument types.

*Listing 8.53   Using the* storedProcArgs() *Method to Set the Argument Types of a Stored Procedure*

```
<SERVER>

// Open a connection
var myConn = database.connect("ORACLE", "mySID", "myApp", "appsPWD", "myTNS");

if(myConn.connected()){
```

*continues*

*Listing 8.53    continued*

```
myConn.beginTransaction();

// Run the stored procedure
var myStprocArgs = myConn.storedProcArgs("sp_employees", "IN", "INOUT");
var myStproc = myConn.storedProc("sp_employees", 3, "%John%");

// Commit the transaction
myConn.commitTransaction();

// If the connection fails, write an error message
}else{
write('Error ('+myConn.majorErrorCode()+'): '+myConn.majorErrorMessage);
}

// Release the connection
myConn.release();

</SERVER>
```

# database.toString()

## NES2+, ECMAScript1.0+

## Syntax

`database.toString()`

## Description

The `toString()` method of the `database` object returns a text value of the object. When invoked on an instance of a `database` object, the string is returned in the following format:

`"dbName" "uid" "dbType" "dbInstance"`

If parameter is unknown, an empty string is returned. Table 8.8 contains the value of these returned values.

**Table 8.8    Return Values of the toString() Method**

| Method | Description |
|---|---|
| dbName | The name of the database you want to log in to. For Oracle, DB2, and ODBC connections this is a blank, `""`, string. In Oracle, the name of the database for these connections are set up in the `tnsnames.ora` file and are defined by the DSN for ODBC connections. DB2 does not have a database name and is referenced only by the `dbInstance`. |

| Method | Description |
|---|---|
| uid | The username or ID you want the connections to connect as. |
| dbType | The type of database it is. Possible values are: ORACLE, SYBASE, INFORMIX, DB2, or ODBC. |
| dbInstance | This is the instance name of the database. For ODBC, it is the DSN entry name. |

## Example

Listing 8.54 creates an instance of the database object. Once created, the write() method is used to write its string value to the page.

*Listing 8.54   Write the Results of Calling the* toString() *Method to a Page*

```
<SERVER>

// Open a connection
var myConn = database.connect("ORACLE", "mySID", "myApp", "appsPWD", "myTNS");

if(myConn.connected()){

  // Write the string value of the object to the page
  write(myConn.toString());

// If the connection fails, write an error message
}else{
write('Error ('+myConn.majorErrorCode()+'): '+myConn.majorErrorMessage);
}

// Release the connection
myConn.release();

</SERVER>
```

# DbPool()

## NES3+

## Syntax

```
new DbPool()

new DbPool(dbType, dbInstance, uid, pwd, dbName)

new DbPool(dbType, dbInstance, uid, pwd, dbName, maxConn)

new DbPool(dbType, dbInstance, uid, pwd, dbName, maxConn, commitFlag)
```

## Description

The DbPool object is an object that holds a "pool" of connections to a database. Before you open a connection to a database and have the ability to run queries against it, you should create an instance of this object. Once the instance is created, connections can be obtained from the pool as needed. The pool object itself takes all the parameters necessary to make the connection. It is possible to create a pool without specifying any parameters; however, you must pass the parameters when the first connection is attempted.

The creation of a DbPool object is done using the format defined in the syntax definition. Each parameter is defined in Table 8.9.

**Table 8.9    Parameters of the DbPool Object**

| Parameter | Description |
|---|---|
| dbType | The type of database it is. Possible values are: ORACLE, SYBASE, INFORMIX, DB2, or ODBC. |
| dbInstance | This is the instance name of the database. For ODBC, it is the DSN entry name. |
| uid | The username or ID you want the connections to connect as. |
| pwd | The password for the user you are connecting as. |
| dbName | The name of the database you want to log in to. For Oracle, DB2, and ODBC connections this should be a blank, " ", string. In Oracle, the name of the database for these connections is set up in the tnsnames.ora file and is defined by the DSN for ODBC connections. DB2 does not have a database name and is referenced only by the dbInstance. |
| maxConn | The maximum number of connections to the pool. This is effectively the number of connections the pool will open to the database. |
| commitFlag | This flag determines if a pending transaction is committed when connection is released. If it is set to false, the transaction is rolled back. If it is set to true, it is committed. |

Depending on your database, it is possible to create an instance of this object by passing a limited set of these parameters, as well as passing none. The object itself has the methods listed in Table 8.10.

**Table 8.10    Methods of the DbPool Object**

| Method | Description |
|---|---|
| connect() | Connects to a particular pool of database connections |
| connected() | Tests to see if the pool is still connected to the database |
| connection() | Obtains an available connection from the pool |
| DbPool() | Creates the pool of connections to a database |

| Method | Description |
|---|---|
| disconnect() | Disconnects all connections in the pool from the database |
| majorErrorCode() | Returns the major error code numeric value returned by the database or ODBC |
| majorErrorMessage() | Returns the major error message string value returned by the database or ODBC |
| minorErrorCode() | Returns the secondary error code numeric value returned by the database or ODBC |
| minorErrorMessage() | Returns the secondary error message string value returned by the database or ODBC |
| storedProcArgs() | Creates a prototype for DB2, ODBC, or Sybase stored procedures |
| toString() | Returns a string representing the specified object |

## Example

Listing 8.55 creates a pool of connections to an Oracle database and initializes a connection from that pool. It takes a user's UID and name that was passed in, runs a query (based on the UID) against the database to find that user's information, and updates his or her name. If a connection is not made, the error code and message are returned to the screen.

*Listing 8.55  Creating and Using a* DbPool *Object*

```
<SERVER>

// Assign the user submitted ID and name to the client object as properties
client.uid = request.uid;
client.name = request.name;

// Create a pool of connections
var myPool = new DbPool("ORACLE", "mySID", "myApp", "appsPWD", "myTNS");

// Open a connection from the pool.  Give error if connection could
// not be made.
var myConn = myPool.connection('Employees', 15);
if(myConn){

  // Start a new SQL transaction to perform a SELECT
  myConn.beginTransaction();
  var currRow = myConn.cursor('SELECT * FROM employees WHERE uid = '
➡ + client.uid);

  // Focus on that line, change the name column for that user,
  // and update the row.
  currRow.next();
  currRow.name = client.name;
```

*continues*

*Listing 8.55 continued*
```
  currRow.updateRow("employees");

  // Close the cursor
  currRow.close();

// If the connection fails, write an error message
}else{
write('Error ('+myConn.majorErrorCode()+'): '+myConn.majorErrorMessage);
}

</SERVER>
```

# DbPool.connect()

## *NES3+*

## *Syntax*

*DbPool.connect(dbType, dbInstance, uid, pwd, dbName)*

*DbPool.connect(dbType, dbInstance, uid, pwd, dbName, maxConn)*

*DbPool.connect(dbType, dbInstance, uid, pwd, dbName, maxConn, commitFlag)*

## *Description*

The connect method of the DbPool object is used to connect to a database when the connection was not made with the initialization of the original DbPool object. The method takes all the parameters necessary to connect to the database. Each parameter is defined in Table 8.11.

### *Table 8.11 Parameters of the connect() Method*

| Parameter | Description |
| --- | --- |
| dbType | The type of database it is. Possible values are: ORACLE, SYBASE, INFORMIX, DB2, or ODBC. |
| dbInstance | This is the instance name of the database. For ODBC it is the DSN entry name. |
| uid | The username or ID you want the connections to connect as. |
| pwd | The password for the user you are connecting as. |
| dbName | The name of the database you want to log into. For Oracle, DB2, and ODBC connections this should be a blank, "", string. In Oracle, the name of the database for these connections is set up in the tnsnames.ora file and is defined by the DSN for ODBC connections. DB2 does not have a database name and is referenced only by the dbInstance. |

| Parameter | Description |
|-----------|-------------|
| maxConn | The maximum number of connections to the pool. This is effectively the number of connections the pool will open to the database. |
| commitFlag | This flag determines if a pending transaction is committed when connection is released. If it is set to false, the transaction is rolled back. If it is set to true, it is committed. |

Depending on your database, it is possible to create an instance of this object by passing a limited set of these parameters. Please see your database documentation for this information.

## Example

Listing 8.56 creates a connection pool. The connect() method is then called to open the pool to an Oracle database. If a connection is not made, the error code and message are returned to the screen.

*Listing 8.56    Connecting to a Database Using the* connect() *Method*

```
<SERVER>

// Assign the user submitted ID and name to the client object as properties
client.uid = request.uid;
client.name = request.name;

// Create a pool of connections
var myPool = new DbPool();

// Create a connection for the pool
myPool.connect("ORACLE", "mySID", "myApp", "appsPWD", "myTNS");

// Open a connection from the pool.  Give error if connection could
// not be made.
var myConn = myPool.connection('Employees', 15);

if(myConn.connected()){

  // Do any database stuff here

// If the connection fails, write an error message
}else{
write('Error ('+myConn.majorErrorCode()+'): '+myConn.majorErrorMessage);
}

</SERVER>
```

# DbPool.connected()

## NES3+

## Syntax

```
DbPool.connected()
```

## Description

The connected() method of the DbPool object tells if the pool of connections to the database is still connected.

## Example

Listing 8.57 creates a pool of connections and pulls a connection from the pool for processing. If the connection is made, any code within that section is executed. If the connection fails, the error is written to the page.

*Listing 8.57    Testing a Connection with the* connected() *Method*

```
<SERVER>

// Create a pool of connections
var myPool = new DbPool("ORACLE", "mySID", "myApp", "appsPWD", "myTNS");

// Open a connection from the pool.  Give error if connection could
// not be made.
var myConn = myPool.connection('Employees', 15);

if (myConn.connected()) {

  // You are connected, so perform any tasks here

}else{

  // There was an error connecting to the database
write('Error ('+myConn.majorErrorCode()+'): '+myConn.majorErrorMessage);
}

</SERVER>
```

# DbPool.connection()

## NES2+

## Syntax

```
DbPool.connection(name, seconds);
```

## Description

The connection() method of the DbPool object pulls a connection from the pool. The connection is returned from the method and can be stored in a variable to be used for processing.

The method takes two parameters. The first parameter is a *name*, which is a name you can give your connection. Because you actually store the connection in a variable, this name's primary function becomes one for debugging purposes. The second parameter is a *seconds* value for the number of seconds you give the instance to connect.

## Example

Listing 8.58 creates a pool of connections to an Oracle database and initializes a connection from that pool. It takes a user's UID and name that was passed in, runs a query (based on the UID) against the database to find that user's information, and updates his or her name. If a connection is not made, the error code and message are returned to the screen.

*Listing 8.58    Creating and Using a* connection *Method*

```
<SERVER>

// Create a pool of connections
var myPool = new DbPool("ORACLE", "mySID", "myApp", "appsPWD", "myTNS");

// Open a connection from the pool.  Give error if connection could
// not be made.
var myConn = myPool.connection('Employees', 15);

if (myConn.connected()) {

  // You are connected, so perform any tasks here

}else{

  // There was an error connecting to the database
write('Error ('+myConn.majorErrorCode()+'): '+myConn.majorErrorMessage);
}

</SERVER>
```

# DbPool.DbPool()

## NES3+

## Syntax

```
new DbPool()

new DbPool(dbType, dbInstance, uid, pwd, dbName)
```

```
new DbPool(dbType, dbInstance, uid, pwd, dbName, maxConn)

new DbPool(dbType, dbInstance, uid, pwd, dbName, maxConn, commitFlag)
```

## Description

The DbPool method of the DbPool object is the underlying method that creates a "pool" of connections to a database. The creation of a DbPool object is done using the format defined in the syntax definition. Each parameter is defined in Table 8.12.

*Table 8.12    Parameters of the DbPool Method*

| Parameter | Description |
| --- | --- |
| dbType | The type of database it is. Possible values are: ORACLE, SYBASE, INFORMIX, DB2, or ODBC. |
| dbInstance | This is the instance name of the database. For ODBC it is the DSN entry name. |
| uid | The username or ID you want the connections to connect as. |
| pwd | The password for the user you are connecting as. |
| dbName | The name of the database you want to log in to. For Oracle, DB2, and ODBC connections this should be a blank, "", string. In Oracle, the name of the database for these connections is set up in the tnsnames.ora file and is defined by the DSN for ODBC connections. DB2 does not have a database name and is referenced only by the dbInstance. |
| maxConn | The maximum number of connections to the pool. This is effectively the number of connections the pool will open to the database. |
| commitFlag | This flag determines if a pending transaction is committed when connection is released. If it is set to false, the transaction is rolled back. If it is set to true, it is committed. |

Depending on your database, it is possible to create an instance of this object by passing a limited set of these parameters.

## Example

Listing 8.59 creates a pool of connections and pulls a connection from the pool for processing. If the connection is made, any code within that section is executed. If the connection fails, the error is written to the page.

*Listing 8.59    The DbPool Method is the Underlying Method Used When a DbPool Object Instance Is Created*

```
<SERVER>

// Create a pool of connections
var myPool = new DbPool("ORACLE", "mySID", "myApp", "appsPWD", "myTNS");

// Open a connection from the pool.  Give error if connection could
```

```
// not be made.
var myConn = myPool.connection('Employees', 15);

if (myConn.connected()) {

  // You are connected, so perform any tasks here

}else{

  // There was an error connecting to the database
write('Error ('+myConn.majorErrorCode()+'): '+myConn.majorErrorMessage);
}

</SERVER>
```

# DbPool.disconnect()

## NES3+

## Syntax

`DbPool.disconnect()`

## Description

The `disconnect` method of the `DbPool` object disconnects all connections to a database within that pool.

## Example

Listing 8.60 creates a connection to an Oracle database. The next line drops the connection by using the `disconnect()` method.

*Listing 8.60   Disconnecting from a Database Using the* `disconnect()` *Method*

```
<SERVER>

// Create a pool of connections
var myPool = new DbPool("ORACLE", "mySID", "myApp", "appsPWD", "myTNS");

// Drop the connections
myPool.disconnect();

</SERVER>
```

# DbPool.majorErrorCode()

## NES3+

## Syntax

`DbPool.majorErrorCode()`

## Description

The `majorErrorMessage()` method of the `DbPool` object contains the ODBC or database numeric error code that is returned if an error occurs.

## Example

Listing 8.61 shows how you would create a pool of connections and test for the connection. If the test fails, then the `majorErrorCode()` is used when writing the error to the page.

*Listing 8.61  Using* `majorErrorCode()` *to Retrieve a Database Connection Error*

```
<SERVER>

// Create a pool of connections
var myPool = new DbPool("ORACLE", "mySID", "myApp", "appsPWD", "myTNS");

if (myPool.connected()) {

  // You are connected, so perform any tasks here

}else{

  // There was an error connecting to the database
write('Error ('+myPool.majorErrorCode()+'): '+myPool.majorErrorMessage);
}

</SERVER>
```

# DbPool.majorErrorMessage()

## NES3+

## Syntax

`DbPool.majorErrorMessage()`

## Description

The `majorErrorMessage()` method of the `DbPool` object contains the ODBC or database string error message that is returned if an error occurs.

## Example

Listing 8.62 shows how you would create a pool of connections and test for the connection. If the test fails, the `majorErrorMessage()` method is used to write the error to the page.

*Listing 8.62  Using* `majorErrorMessage()` *to Retrieve a Database Connection Error*

```
<SERVER>

// Create a pool of connections
```

```
var myPool = new DbPool("ORACLE", "mySID", "myApp", "appsPWD", "myTNS");

if (myPool.connected()) {

   // You are connected, so perform any tasks here

}else{

   // There was an error connecting to the database
write('Error ('+myPool.majorErrorCode()+'): '+myPool.majorErrorMessage);
}

</SERVER>
```

# DbPool.minorErrorCode()

## NES3+

## Syntax

*DbPool*.minorErrorCode()

## Description

The minorErrorMessage() method of the DbPool object contains the secondary ODBC or database numeric error code that is returned if an error occurs.

## Example

Listing 8.63 shows how to create a pool of connections and test for the connection. If the test fails, the minorErrorCode() method is used to write the secondary error to the page.

*Listing 8.63   Using* minorErrorCode() *to Retrieve a Secondary Database Connection Error*

```
<SERVER>

// Create a pool of connections
var myPool = new DbPool("ORACLE", "mySID", "myApp", "appsPWD", "myTNS");

if (myPool.connected()) {

   // You are connected, so perform any tasks here

}else{

   // There was an error connecting to the database
write('Error ('+myPool.minorErrorCode()+'): '+myPool.minorErrorMessage);
}

</SERVER>
```

# DbPool.minorErrorMessage()

## NES3+

## Syntax

`DbPool.minorErrorMessage()`

## Description

The `minorErrorMessage()` method of the `DbPool` object contains the secondary ODBC or database string error message that is returned if an error occurs.

## Example

Listing 8.64 shows how to create a pool of connections and test for the connection. If the test fails, the `minorErrorMessage()` method is used to write the secondary error to the page.

Listing 8.64    Using `minorErrorMessage()` to Retrieve a Secondary Database Connection Error

```
<SERVER>

// Create a pool of connections
var myPool = new DbPool("ORACLE", "mySID", "myApp", "appsPWD", "myTNS");

if (myPool.connected()) {

  // You are connected, so perform any tasks here

}else{

  // There was an error connecting to the database
write('Error ('+myPool.minorErrorCode()+'): '+myPool.minorErrorMessage);
}

</SERVER>
```

# DbPool.prototype

## NES3+, ECMAScript 1.0+

## Syntax

`DbPool.prototype.method = methodName`
`DbPool.prototype.property`

## Description

The `prototype` property of the `DbPool` object allows you to add methods and properties to the `DbPool` object. If you are adding a method, you set the instance equal to the `methodName` of the method you have defined.

## *Example*

Listing 8.65 creates a new property and method of the DbPool object. An instance is created and the new property is set. The new method is then called to verify the property, and, if it is incorrect, an error is written to the page.

*Listing 8.65    Using the* prototype *Property to Create a New Property and Method*

```
<SERVER>

// Define the method that we prototyped
function verifyOracle(){

  // Check to see if the type property we added is set to a valid value
  if(this.type == "Oracle"){
    return true;
  }else{
    return false;
  }
}

// Create a new property and method of the DbPool object.
DbPool.prototype.type = null;
DbPool.prototype.isOracle = verifyOracle;

// Create a pool of connections
var myPool = new DbPool("ORACLE", "mySID", "myApp", "appsPWD", "myTNS");

// Using the prototype we defined, assign the type property
myPool.type = "Oracle";

// Check the type of the connection to see if it is valid
if(myPool.isOracle()){
  write(myPool + " has a valid type of " + myPool.type);
}else{
  write(myPool + " has an invalid type of " + myPool.type);
}

</SERVER>
```

# DbPool.storedProcArgs()

## *NES3+*

## *Syntax*

```
database.storedProcArgs(procName)
database.storedProcArgs(procName, type1, type2, ... , typeN)
```

## Description

The `storedProcArgs()` method of the `database` object creates a `Stproc` object that allows you to execute a database-specific stored procedure using the connection from which it was invoked on DB2, ODBC, and Sybase databases. If this method is invoked on Informix or Oracle databases, it has no effect. The difference between this method and the `storedProc()` method is that this method takes a type as a parameter for the arguments passed. These types can be IN, OUT, or INOUT. The following shows an example of passing these types:

```
var myStproc = myConn.storedProc("sp_employees", "INOUT", "OUT");
```

The scope of this procedure is restricted to the current page. Any methods of the `Stproc` object must be invoked on the current page. If this is not possible, a new object will have to be created on subsequent pages to access the properties needed.

## Example

Listing 8.66 creates a pool of connections to a database. The `storedProc()` method is used to invoke the fictitious *sp_employees* stored procedure and the `storedProcArgs()` method is used to specify the argument types.

*Listing 8.66    Using the `storedProcArgs()` Method to Set the Argument Types of a Stored Procedure*

```
<SERVER>

// Create a pool of connections
var myPool = new DbPool("ORACLE", "mySID", "myApp", "appsPWD", "myTNS");

// Set the stored procedure arguments
var myStprocArgs = myPool.storedProcArgs("sp_employees", "IN", "INOUT");
var myStproc = myPool.storedProc("sp_employees", 3, "%John%");

</SERVER>
```

# DbPool.toString()

## NES3+, ECMAScript1.0+

## Syntax

```
DbPool.toString()
```

## Description

The `toString()` method of the `DbPool` object returns a text value of the object. When invoked on an instance of a `DbPool` object, the string is returned in the following format:

```
"dbName" "uid" "dbType" "dbInstance"
```

If parameter is unknown, an empty string is returned. Table 8.13 contains the value of these returned values.

**Table 8.13   Return Values of the toString() Method**

| Method | Description |
| --- | --- |
| dbName | The name of the database you want to log in to. For Oracle, DB2, and ODBC connections this is a blank, `""`, string. In Oracle, the name of the database for these connections is set up in the `tnsnames.ora` file and is defined by the DSN for ODBC connections. DB2 does not have a database name and is referenced only by the `dbInstance`. |
| uid | The username or ID you want the connections to connect as. |
| dbType | The type of database it is. Possible values are: `ORACLE`, `SYBASE`, `INFORMIX`, `DB2`, or `ODBC`. |
| dbInstance | This is the instance name of the database. For ODBC, it is the DSN entry name. |

## *Example*

Listing 8.67 creates an instance of the `DbPool` object. Once created, the `write()` method is used to write its string value to the page.

*Listing 8.67   Write the Results of Calling the `toString()` Method to a Page*

```
<SERVER>

// Create a pool of connections
var myPool = new DbPool("ORACLE", "mySID", "myApp", "appsPWD", "myTNS");

// Open a connection from the pool.  Give error if connection could
// not be made.
var myConn = myPool.connection('Employees', 15);
if(myConn.connected()){

  // Write the string value of the object to the page
  write(myPool.toString());

// If the connection fails, write an error message
}else{
write('Error ('+myConn.majorErrorCode()+'): '+myConn.majorErrorMessage);
}

// Release the connection
myConn.release();

</SERVER>
```

# debug()

## NES2+

## Syntax

```
debug(expression)
debug(variable)
```

## Description

The debug function is a top-level function that is not associated with any core object. This function is used to display the value of an expression or variable in the Trace Information window when running the application in the JavaScript Application Manager's debug window.

## Example

Listing 8.68, when run in the JavaScript Application Manager's debugger, will display the value of the *request.name* when encountered.

*Listing 8.68    Using the* debug() *Function to Write Information to the Trace Information Window*

```
<SERVER>

// Display the value of the name passed in the request
// to the application
debug(request.name);

</SERVER>
```

# deleteResponseHeader()

## NES3+

## Syntax

```
deleteResponseHeader(key)
```

## Description

The deleteResponseHeader function is a top-level function and is not associated with any core object. This function is used to delete fields in the HTTP header before it is sent back to the client. Because of when the actual header is sent in relation to the body of the data, you should be sure to delete these fields before you call the flush or redirect functions.

> **NOTE**
>
> The JavaScript runtime engine flushes the output buffer after 64KB of content has been generated. You should be sure to call the deleteResponseHeader function before this time.

## Example

Listing 8.69 shows how you can delete the content-type header field before it is sent back to the browser.

*Listing 8.69   Using the* `deleteResponseHeader` *Function to Delete the* `content.type` *of a File Being Sent to a Browser*

```
<SERVER>

// Delete a field to the header
deleteResponseHeader("content-type");

</SERVER>
```

# File()

## NES2+

## Syntax

```
new File(path)
```

## Description

The `File` object allows you to perform various tasks such as reading and writing to a file on your disk. The object itself has many methods to use and a `prototype` property that allows a programmer to create new properties and methods of the object. Table 8.14 lists the methods accessible and a brief description of each. An instance of this object is created by simply passing the *path* of the file you want to create or read.

*Table 8.14   Methods of the File Object*

| Method | Description |
| --- | --- |
| `byteToString()` | Converts the byte number passed into its string equivalent |
| `clearError()` | Clears the `File.eof()` and `File.error()` error status |
| `close()` | Closes the file you opened |
| `eof()` | Returns `true` if you are at the end of the file you have opened |
| `error()` | Returns the current error |
| `exists()` | Checks to see if the file you want to process exists |
| `flush()` | Writes the contents of the current buffer to the file |
| `getLength()` | Returns the length of the file |
| `getPosition()` | Returns your current position within a file |
| `open()` | Opens the file |
| `read()` | Reads the number of specified characters into a string |
| `readByte()` | Reads the next byte, or character, in the file |

*continues*

*Table 8.14 continued*

| Method | Description |
|--------|-------------|
| readln() | Reads the current line, starting at your current position, into a string |
| setPosition() | Sets your position in a file |
| stringToByte() | Converts the string passed into its byte number equivalent |
| write() | Writes a string to the file you opened |
| writeByte() | Writes a byte of data to a binary file you opened |
| writeln() | Writes a string and a carriage return to the file you opened |

The usage of the File object is very straightforward. The methods provided allow you to perform the various tasks needed on the files on your file system. Part of this functionality of working with these files is to allow programmers to specify how they want to open the files. A file can be opened to read, write, append, or open in binary mode. These options are specified in the open() method in the following form:

```
myFile.open("option");
```

Table 8.15 gives a list and description of these options.

*Table 8.15 Options of the open() Method*

| Option | Description |
|--------|-------------|
| a | This option opens a file for appending. If the file does not exist, it is created. This method always returns true. |
| a+ | This option opens a file for reading and appending. If the file does not exist, it is created. This method always returns true. |
| r | This option opens a file for reading. If the file exists, the method returns true; otherwise, it returns false. |
| r+ | This option opens a file for reading and writing. If the file exists, the method returns true; otherwise, it returns false. Reading and writing start at the beginning of the file. |
| w | This option opens a file for writing. If the file does not exist, it is created. If it does exist, it is overwritten. This method always returns true. |
| w+ | This option opens a file for reading and writing. If the file does not exist, it is created. If it does exist, it is overwritten. This method always returns true. |
| optionb | Appending b to the end of any of these options specifies that you wish to perform the operation in binary mode. |

## Example

Listing 8.70 displays an option menu that allows a user to select a file to read. When the form is submitted, the script reads the file and displays its contents on a page.

*Listing 8.70 Using the* File *Object*

```
<HTML>
<HEAD>
  <TITLE>Listing 8-70: Using the File object</TITLE>
</HEAD>
<BODY>
<SERVER>

// See if they have submitted or just need the form
if(request.method == "POST"){

  // Create an instance of the File object and pass it the file
  // the user specified they wanted to view.
  var myLog = new File(request.file);

  // Try to open the file.
  if(!myLog.open("r")){

    // If there was an error, tell the user.
    write("There was an error opening the file: " + request.file);
  }else{

    // If there was not an error, then open the file and display it.
    write('<H3>The contents of ' + request.file + ' are as follows:</H3>');
    while(!myLog.eof()){
      write(myLog.readln());
    }
  }
}else{

  // If this page was called then write the select box to the page for
  // the user to use select which log they want to see.

  write('<FORM NAME="myForm" METHOD=POST>');
  write('<SELECT NAME=file>');
  write('<OPTION VALUE="/logs/admin.log">Admin Log</OPTION>');
  write('<OPTION VALUE="/logs/user.log">User Log</OPTION>');
  write('<OPTION VALUE="/logs/error.log">Error Log</OPTION>');
  write('</SELECT>');
  write('<INPUT TYPE=SUBMIT VALUE="View Log">');
  write('</FORM>');
}

</SERVER>
</BODY>
</HTML>
```

# File.byteToString()

## NES2+

## Syntax

```
File.byteToString(num)
```

## Description

The byteToString() method of the File object is used to convert the numeric value passed to its ASCII equivalent. If the method is not passed a number, an empty string is returned.

## Example

Listing 8.71 opens two files, one for reading and the other for appending. Bytes are then read using the readByte() method from the first file, converted back to string characters using the byteToString() method, and written to the second file. Both files are closed when the process has completed.

*Listing 8.71    Using the byteToString() Method to Convert the Bytes Read into Strings*

```
<SERVER>

// Open a log file and a summary file
var myLog = new File("/data/logs/today.log");
var mySummary = new File("/data/logs/summary.log");

// Open the log file for reading and the summary file for
// appending.
myLog.open("r");
mySummary.open("a");

// Append the contents of the log file to the summary file
while (!myLog.eof()){
  myBytes = myLog.byteToString(myLog.readByte());
  mySummary.write(myBytes);
}

// Close the files
myLog.close();
mySummary.close();

</SERVER>
```

# File.clearError()

## NES2+

## Syntax

```
file.clearError()
```

## Description

The `clearError()` method of the `File` object clears the file error status and the value returned by the `eof()` method.

## Example

Listing 8.72 opens a file for reading. If the operation returned an error, the error is written to the page. If there was an error, it is cleared after writing it.

*Listing 8.72  Using the `clearError()` Method to Clear File Errors*

```
<SERVER>

// Open a log file
var myLog = new File("/data/logs/today.log");

// Open the log file for reading
myLog.open("r");

if (myLog.error() == 0) {

  // Perform actions on file

}else{

  // Write out the error
  write('Error: ' + myLog.error());

  // Clear the error
  myLog.clearError()
}

// Close the file
myLog.close();

</SERVER>
```

# File.close()

## NES2+

## Syntax

`file.close()`

## Description

The `close()` method of the `File` object closes the file on which it has been invoked. This method returns `true` if it was successful and `false` if it was unsuccessful.

## Example

Listing 8.73 shows how to open a file and then close it.

*Listing 8.73    Closing a File with the* `close()` *Method*

```
<SERVER>

// Open a log file
var myLog = new File("/data/logs/today.log");

// Open the log file for reading
myLog.open("r");

// Close the file
myLog.close();

</SERVER>
```

# File.eof()

## NES2+

## Syntax

```
file.eof()
```

## Description

The `eof()` method of the `File` object returns `true` if the position of the pointer within the file is past the end of the file. It returns `false` otherwise.

## Example

Listing 8.74 reads a file and writes its contents to the page until the end of the file is found with the `eof()` method.

*Listing 8.74    Reading a File Until You Come to the End of It*

```
<SERVER>

// Open a log file for reading
var myLog = new File("/data/logs/today.log");
myLog.open("r");

// Write the contents of the log file to the page
while (!myLog.eof()){
  myBytes = File.byteToString(myLog.readByte());
  write(myBytes);
}

// Close the file
myLog.close();

</SERVER>
```

# File.error()

## *NES2+*

## *Syntax*

`file.error()`

## *Description*

The `error()` method of the `File` object returns the operating system error code when an error occurs opening a file. This method returns 0 if there is no error, and -1 if the file you invoke the method on is not open.

## *Example*

Listing 8.75 opens a file for reading. If there was a problem during this operation, the error is written to the user's page.

*Listing 8.75    Using the `error()` Method to Access an Error to Write to the User's Page*

```
<SERVER>

// Open a log file
var myLog = new File("/data/logs/today.log");

// Open the log file for reading
myLog.open("r");

if (myLog.error() == 0) {

  // Perform actions on file

}else{

  // Write out the error
  write('Error: ' + myLog.error());

  // Clear the error
  myLog.clearError()
}

// Close the file
myLog.close();

</SERVER>
```

# File.exists()

*NES2+*

## Syntax

`file.exists()`

## Description

The `exists()` method of the `File` object returns a `boolean` value based on the existence of the file in which it was invoked. If the file exists, the method returns `true`. It returns `false` if the file does not exist.

## Example

Listing 8.76 opens a file and then checks to see if it exists.

*Listing 8.76   Using the `exists()` Method to See If a File Exists*

```
<SERVER>

// Open a log file
var myLog = new File("/data/logs/today.log");

// See if the file exists
if(myLog.exists()){
  write('The file exists');
}else{
  write('The file does not exist');
}

</SERVER>
```

# File.flush()

*NES2+*

## Syntax

`file.flush()`

## Description

The `flush()` method of the `File` object is used to write buffered information to a file. This information is placed in a buffer when the `write()`, `writeln()`, and `writeByte()` methods are used. Note that this is not the same as the top-level `flush` function.

## Example

Listing 8.77 opens a file for reading and another file for writing. If the file for reading exists, a string is written to the other file. The `flush()` method is used to write the actual buffer of information to the file.

*Listing 8.77    Using the* flush() *Method*
```
<SERVER>

// Open a log file
var myLog = new File("/data/logs/today.log");
var mySummary = new File("/data/logs/summary.log");

myLog.open("r");
mySummary.open("w");

// See if the file exists
if(myLog.exists()){
  mySummary.write('The file exists');
}else{
  mySummary.write('The file does not exist');
}

// Write the data in the buffer to the file
mySummary.flush();

// Close the file
myLog.close();
mySummary.close();

</SERVER>
```

# File.getLength()

## *NES2+*

## *Syntax*
```
file.getLength()
```

## *Description*

The getLength() of the File object returns the number of characters in a text file or the number of bytes in a binary file. If the method is unsuccessful, –1 is returned.

## *Example*

Listing 8.78 opens a file for reading and another file for writing. The getLength() method is used in a for loop to determine when to stop reading from the file.

*Listing 8.78    Using the* getLength() *Method*
```
<SERVER>

// Open the files
var myLog = new File("/data/logs/today.log");
```

*continues*

*Listing 8.78 continued*

```
var mySummary = new File("/data/logs/summary.log");
myLog.open("r");
mySummary.open("w");

// Write the contents of the log file to the page
for(var i = 0; i <= myLog.getLength(); i++){
  myBytes = File.byteToString(myLog.readByte());
  mySummary.write(myBytes);
}

mySummary.flush();

// Close the files
myLog.close();
mySummary.close();

</SERVER>
```

# File.getPosition()

## *NES2+*

## *Syntax*

```
file.getPosition()
```

## *Description*

The getPosition() method of the File object returns the zero-based index position of the current pointer in the file. If the pointer is on the first character, 0 is returned. If there is an error, -1 is returned.

## *Example*

Listing 8.79 loops through each character, printing it on a new line next to its indexed location.

*Listing 8.79 Using the getPosition() Method*

```
<SERVER>

// Open the files
var myLog = new File("/data/logs/today.log");
var mySummary = new File("/data/logs/summary.log");
myLog.open("r");
mySummary.open("w");

// Write the contents of the log file to the page
for(var i = 0; i <= myLog.getLength(); i++){
  myBytes = File.byteToString(myLog.readByte());
```

```
mySummary.write('Character '+mySummary.getPosition()+' is '+myBytes+'<BR>');
}

mySummary.flush();

// Close the files
myLog.close();
mySummary.close();

</SERVER>
```

# File.open()

## NES2+

## Syntax

`file.open(option)`

## Description

The `open()` method of the `File` object is used to open a file to read, write, and/or append to. The method returns `true` if it is successful and `false` otherwise. The options passed determine the mode in which the file is opened. The options are specified in Table 8.16.

### Table 8.16   Options of the open() Method

| Option | Description |
|--------|-------------|
| a | This option opens a file for appending. If the file does not exist, it is created. This method always returns `true`. |
| a+ | This option opens a file for reading and appending. If the file does not exist, it is created. This method always returns `true`. |
| r | This option opens a file for reading. If the file exists, the method returns `true`; otherwise, it returns `false`. |
| r+ | This option opens a file for reading and writing. If the file exists, the method returns `true`; otherwise, it returns `false`. Reading and writing start at the beginning of the file. |
| w | This option opens a file for writing. If the file does not exist, it is created. If it does exist, it is overwritten. This method always returns `true`. |
| w+ | This option opens a file for reading and writing. If the file does not exist, it is created. If it does exist, it is overwritten. This method always returns `true`. |
| optionb | Appending b to the end of any of these options specifies that you want to perform the operation in binary mode. |

## Example

Listing 8.80 shows how to open a file in read mode.

*Listing 8.80    Using the* open() *Method to Open a File*

```
<SERVER>

// Initialize a file
var myLog = new File("/data/logs/today.log");

// Open the file in read mode
myLog.open("r");

// Close the file
myLog.close();

</SERVER>
```

# File.prototype

## NES3+, ECMAScript 1.0+

## Syntax

```
file.prototype.method = methodName
file.prototype.property
```

## Description

The prototype property of the File object allows you to add methods and properties to the File object. If you are adding a method, you set the instance equal to the methodName of the method you have defined.

## Example

Listing 8.81 creates a new property and method of the File object. An instance is created and the new property is set. The new method is then called to verify the property, and, if it is incorrect (which it is), an error is written to the page.

*Listing 8.81    Using the* prototype *Property to Create a New Property and Method*

```
<SERVER>

// Define the method that we prototyped
function verifyTEXT(){

  // Check to see if the type property we added is set to a valid value
  if(this.type == "text"){
    return true;
  }else{
```

```
      return false;
   }
}

// Create a new property and method of the connection object.
File.prototype.type = null;
File.prototype.isText = verifyTEXT;

// Initialize a file
var myLog = new File("/data/logs/today.log");

// Open the file in read mode
myLog.open("r");

// Using the prototype we defined, assign the type property
myLog.type = "text";

// Check the type of the connection to see if it is valid
if(myLog.isText()){
   write(myLog + " has a valid type of " + myLog.type);
}else{
   write(myLog + " has an invalid type of " + myLog.type);
}

</SERVER>
```

# File.read()

## *NES2+*

## *Syntax*

`file.read(num)`

## *Description*

The read() method of the File object starts at the current pointer in the file and reads *num* characters in the file. If you try to read characters past the end of the file, the method will read all of the characters and stop. Use the readByte() method if you are trying to read the byte data.

## *Example*

Listing 8.82 reads information from a text file and writes every other character to the user's page. The setPosition() method is used to move the pointer correctly, and the read() method is used to read the data.

*Listing 8.82    Using the* `read()` *Method*

```
<SERVER>

// Open the files
var myLog = new File("/data/logs/today.log");
myLog.open("r");

// Write some characters to the page
for(var i = 1; i <= myLog.getLength(); i + 2){

  // Set the position of the pointer
  myLog.setPosition(i);

  // Write every other character to the page
  write(myLog.read(1));
}

// Close the file
myLog.close();

</SERVER>
```

# File.readByte()

## NES2+

## Syntax

`file.readByte(num)`

## Description

The `readByte()` method of the `File` object starts at the current pointer in the file and reads *num* bytes in the file. If you try to read bytes past the end of the file, the method will read all of the bytes and stop. Use the `read()` method if you are trying to read the characters in text data.

## Example

Listing 8.83 reads information from a text file and writes every other byte to the user's page. The `setPosition()` method is used to move the pointer correctly, and the `readByte()` method is used to read the data.

*Listing 8.83    Using the* `readByte()` *Method*

```
<SERVER>

// Open the files
var myLog = new File("/data/logs/today.dat");
myLog.open("rb");

// Write some characters to the page
```

```
for(var i = 1; i <= myLog.getLength(); i + 2){

  // Set the position of the pointer
  myLog.setPosition(i);

  // Write every other byte to the page
  write(myLog.readByte(1));
}

// Close the file
myLog.close();
```

```
</SERVER>
```

# File.readIn()

## NES2+

## Syntax

`file.readln()`

## Description

The `readln()` method of the `File` object starts at the current pointer position and reads the rest of the line. Once the method is complete, it will return the pointer to the first character on the next line.

> **NOTE**
>
> The return (\r) and newline (\n) characters are not contained in the string this method returns. However, the newline character determines when the end of the line is reached.

## Example

Listing 8.84 reads in the first line of a file and writes it to the user's page.

*Listing 8.84   Using the* `readln()` *Method*

```
<SERVER>

// Open the files
var myLog = new File("/data/logs/today.log");
myLog.open("r");

// Write the first line
write(myLog.readln());

// Close the file
myLog.close();

</SERVER>
```

# File.setPosition()

## NES2+

## Syntax

```
file.setPosition(num)
file.setPosition(num, refPoint)
```

## Description

The setPosition() method of the File object sets the pointer's position to a relative *num* location in the file. By default, this is relative to the beginning of the file, but you can pass a reference point to determine where this relative location is located. The possible values of this reference point are listed in Table 8.17.

**Table 8.17    Possible Values of the Reference Point**

| Value | Description |
| --- | --- |
| 0 | Sets the pointer relative to the beginning of the file |
| 1 | Sets the pointer relative to the current pointer position |
| 2 | Sets the pointer relative to the end of the file |

## Example

Listing 8.85 uses the setPosition() method to access every other character in the file.

*Listing 8.85    Using the* setPosition() *Method*

```
<SERVER>

// Open the files
var myLog = new File("/data/logs/today.log");
myLog.open("r");

// Write some characters to the page
for(var i = 1; i < myLog.getLength(); i + 2){

  // Set the position of the pointer
  myLog.setPosition(i);

  // Write every other character to the page
  write(myLog.read(1));
}

// Close the file
myLog.close();

</SERVER>
```

# File.stringToByte()

## NES2+

## Syntax

```
File.stringToByte(string)
```

## Description

The `stringToByte()` method of the `File` object is used to convert the first character of the string passed to its binary equivalent.

## Example

Listing 8.86 opens two files, one for reading and the other for appending. Strings are then read using the `read()` method from the first file, converted back to byte characters using the `stringToByte()` method, and then written to the second file. Both files are closed when the process has completed.

*Listing 8.86    Using the `stringToByte()` Method to Convert the Strings Read into Bytes*

```
<SERVER>

// Open a log file and a summary file
var myLog = new File("/data/logs/today.dat");
var mySummary = new File("/data/logs/summary.dat");

// Open the log file for reading and the summary file for
// appending.
myLog.open("rb");
mySummary.open("ab");

// Append the contents of the log file to the summary file
for(var i = 0; i < myLog.getLength(); i++){
  myLog.setPosition(i);
  myByte = File.stringToBytes(myLog.read(1));
  mySummary.writeByte(myByte);
}

// Flush the buffer to the file
mySummary.flush();

// Close the files
myLog.close();
mySummary.close();

</SERVER>
```

# File.write()

## NES2+

## Syntax

```
file.write(string)
```

## Description

The `write()` method of the `File` object writes the string passed to the method to the file on which it was invoked. The method returns `true` if it was successful and `false` otherwise. You should use the `read()` or `readln()` methods to read any string information from other files that you want to write. If you need to write binary information, use the `writeByte()` method.

## Example

Listing 8.87 writes "Hello, World!" to the summary file opened.

*Listing 8.87   Using* `write()` *to Write a String to a File*

```
<SERVER>

// Set an instance of a File
var mySummary = new File("/data/logs/summary.log");

// Open the log file for writing
mySummary.open("w");

// Write a string to the file
mySummary.write('Hello, World!');

// Flush the buffer to the file
mySummary.flush();

// Close the file
mySummary.close();

</SERVER>
```

# File.writeByte()

## NES2+

## Syntax

```
file.writeByte(byte)
```

## Description

The `writeByte()` method of the `File` object writes the byte passed to the method to the file on which it was invoked. The method returns `true` if it was successful and false otherwise. You should use the readByte() method to read any byte information from other files that you want to write. If you need to write text information, use the write() method.

## Example

Listing 8.88 reads data out of a binary file and writes it to another file.

*Listing 8.88    Using* writeByte() *to Write Binary Data to a File*

```
<SERVER>

// Open a log file and a summary file
var myLog = new File("/data/logs/today.dat");
var mySummary = new File("/data/logs/summary.dat");

// Open the log file for reading and the summary file for
// appending.
myLog.open("br");
mySummary.open("ba");

// Append the contents of the log file to the summary file
for(var i = 0; i < myLog.getLength(); i++){
  myLog.setPosition(i);
  myByte = myLog.readByte(1);
  mySummary.writeByte(myByte);
}

// Flush the buffer to the file
mySummary.flush();

// Close the files
myLog.close();
mySummary.close();

</SERVER>
```

# File.writeln()

## NES2+

## Syntax

*file*.writeln(*string*)

## Description

The writeln() method of the File object writes the string passed to the method, followed by a carriage return to the file on which it was invoked. The method returns true if it was successful and false otherwise. You should use the read() or readln() methods to read any string information from other files you want to write. If you need to write binary information, use the writeByte() method.

## Example

Listing 8.89 writes the line "Hello, World!" to the summary file opened.

*Listing 8.89    Using* `writeln()` *to Write a String and Carriage Return to a File*

```
<SERVER>

// Set an instance of a File
var mySummary = new File("/data/logs/summary.log");

// Open the log file for writing
mySummary.open("w");

// Write a string to the file
mySummary.writeln('Hello, World!');

// Flush the buffer to the file
mySummary.flush();

// Close the file
mySummary.close();

</SERVER>
```

# flush()

## NES2+

## Syntax

`flush()`

## Description

The `flush` function is a top-level function that is not associated with any object. The JavaScript runtime buffers the HTML page it is constructing in memory, and then sends it to the client after 64KB has been obtained. The `flush()` method can be used to send this data on demand, which is useful when done before large database queries. Note this is not the same flush as the `File.flush()` method.

> **NOTE**
>
> The `flush` function updates the cookie file as part of the HTTP header. If you are using a client cookie to maintain the `client` object, you should make any changes to this object before calling the `flush` function.

## Example

Listing 8.90 uses the `flush` function to flush the buffer to the page after the initial write.

*Listing 8.90    Using the* `flush()` *Function to Flush the Buffer to the Page*

```
<SERVER>

// Write a string to the page
write('Hello, World!');

// Flush the buffer to the client
flush();

</SERVER>
```

# getOptionValue()

## Nes2+

## Syntax

```
getOptionValue(key, num)
```

## Description

The `getOptionValue` function is a top-level function that is not associated with any object. This function returns the same value as the client-side `Option.text` property. The *key* passed in as an argument represents the NAME attribute of the <SELECT> tag, while the *num* parameter is the indexed position of the selected option. Specifying *num* to 0 can reference the first selected option, which may not be the first option.

## Example

Listing 8.91 displays a multi-select option box that allows a user to select different sports. When the Submit button is clicked, the form is sent back to itself and the script then uses a `for` loop and the `getOptionValue` function to write the submitted selections to the user's page.

*Listing 8.91    Using the* `getOptionValue` *Function*

```
<HTML>
<HEAD>
  <TITLE>Listing 8-91: Using the getOptionValue Function</TITLE>
</HEAD>
<BODY>
<SERVER>

// See if they have submitted or just need the form
if(request.method == "POST"){

  // Store the number of selected options in a variable
  var counter = getOptionValueCount("sports");

  // Write the title
```

*continues*

*Listing 8.91   continued*

```
  write('<B>You selected the following options</B><HR SIZE=1>');

  // Iterate through the options and write which ones were selected
  for(var i = 0; i < counter; i++){

    // Get the Option.text values of the selected options
    var optionValue = getOptionValue("sports", i)
    write('Option ' + i + ': ' + optionValue + '<BR>')
  }
}else{
  // If this page was called and a form was not submitted, then write the
  // form to the page for the user to use.

  write('<FORM NAME="myForm" METHOD=POST>');
  write('<SELECT NAME="sports" MULTIPLE SIZE=4>');
  write('<OPTION>Baseball</OPTION>');
  write('<OPTION>Football</OPTION>');
  write('<OPTION>Basketball</OPTION>');
  write('<OPTION SELECTED>Soccer</OPTION>');
  write('<OPTION>Rugby</OPTION>');
  write('</SELECT>');
  write('<INPUT TYPE=SUBMIT VALUE="Submit">');
  write('</FORM>');
}

</SERVER>
</BODY>
</HTML>
```

# getOptionValueCount()

## *NES2+*

## *Syntax*

```
getOptionValueCount(key)
```

## *Description*

The `getOptionValueCount` function is a top-level function that is not associated with any object. This function returns the number of selected options passed to the function. The *key* parameter represents the NAME attribute of the `<SELECT>` tag on which you want to invoke the function.

## *Example*

Listing 8.92 shows how to use the `getOptionValueCount` function to determine how many options were selected in a "sports" select box.

*Listing 8.92    Using the* getOptionValueCount *Function*

```
<SERVER>

// Store the number of selected options in a variable
var counter = getOptionValueCount("sports");

</SERVER>
```

# Lock()

## *NES3+*

## *Syntax*

```
new Lock()
```

## *Description*

A Lock object is used when you enter a section of code that can only be accessed from a single user at a time. Not implementing an instance of this object when needed can cause you to run out of system resources and will generate a runtime error. This object has only one property, which is the prototype property.

This property can be used to create new methods and properties for the Lock object. Table 8.18 contains the methods accessible from this object.

*Table 8.18    Methods of the Lock Object*

| Method | Description |
| --- | --- |
| isValid() | Verifies the construction of the Lock object instance |
| lock() | Locks the code |
| unlock() | Unlocks the code |

## *Example*

Listing 8.93 shows how you would create a new Lock object instance. See the examples for Lock.lock() and Lock.unlock() for examples on locking and unlocking your code segments.

*Listing 8.93    Creating a New* Lock *Object*

```
<SERVER>

// Create a new Lock object
var myLock = new Lock();

</SERVER>
```

# Lock.isValid()

*NES3+*

## Syntax

```
lock.isValid()
```

## Description

The isValid() method of the Lock object verifies if the lock was properly constructed. The method returns true if the lock was constructed successfully and false otherwise.

## Example

Listing 8.94 shows how you can check if a lock was properly constructed with an if statement.

*Listing 8.94    Verifying a Lock with the* isValid() *Method*
```
<SERVER>

// Create a new Lock object
var myLock = new Lock();

// Verify the lock
if(!myLock.isValid()){
  write('There has been an error constructing your lock');
}else{

  // Success: perform operations here

}

</SERVER>
```

# Lock.lock()

*NES3+*

## Syntax
```
lock.lock()
```

## Description

The lock() method of the Lock object locks the code in which you are working until you perform an unlock. If the code is already locked, this method will wait until it can get the lock, a timeout occurs, or an error occurs.

## Example

Listing 8.95 assumes there is a `project` object with a counter property, *num*. Because you only want to increment the counter with each new user request, it must be locked.

*Listing 8.95    Using the* `lock()` *Method to Lock Your Code*

```
<SERVER>

// Create a new Lock object under the project object
var project.myLock = new Lock();

// Verify the lock
if(!project.myLock.isValid()){
  write('There has been an error constructing your lock');
}else{

  // Lock the code and increment a project counter
  project.myLock.lock();
  project.hitCount.num += 1;

  // Unlock the code
  project.myLock.unlock();

}

</SERVER>
```

# Lock.prototype

## *NES3+, ECMAScript1.0+*

## Syntax

```
lock.prototype.method = methodName
lock.prototype.property
```

## Description

The `prototype` property of the `Lock` object allows you to add methods and properties to the `Lock` object. If you are adding a method, you set the instance equal to the *methodName* of the method you have defined.

## Example

Listing 8.96 creates a new property and method of the `Lock` object. An instance is created and the new property is set. The new method is then called to verify the property, and, if it is incorrect, an error is written to the page.

*Listing 8.96    Using the* `prototype` *Property to Create a New Property and Method*

```
<SERVER>

// Define the method that we prototyped
function verifyProject(){

  // Check to see if the type property we added is set to a valid value
  if(this.type == "project"){
    return true;
  }else{
    return false;
  }
}

// Create a new property and method of the Lock object.
Lock.prototype.type = null;
Lock.prototype.isProject = verifyProject;

// Create a new Lock object under the project object
var project.myLock = new Lock();

// Using the prototype we defined, assign the type property
project.myLock.type = "project";

// Check the type of the lock to see if it is valid
if(project.myLock.isProject()){
  write(project.myLock + " has a valid type of " + project.myLock.type);
}else{
  write(project.myLock + " has an invalid type of " + project.myLock.type);
}

</SERVER>
```

# Lock.unlock()

## NES3+

## Syntax

`lock`.unlock()

## Description

The `unlock()` method of the `Lock` object unlocks the code you have locked. This method returns `true` if the unlocking was successful and `false` if otherwise.

## Example

Listing 8.97 assumes there is a `project` object with a counter property, *num*. Because you only want to increment the counter with each new user request, it must be locked. Once the counter has been incremented, the project is unlocked.

*Listing 8.97   Using the* `unlock()` *Method to Unlock Your Code*

```
<SERVER>

// Create a new Lock object under the project object
var project.myLock = new Lock();

// Verify the lock
if(!project.myLock.isValid()){
  write('There has been an error constructing your lock');
}else{

  // Lock the code and increment a project counter
  project.myLock.lock();
  project.hitCount.num += 1;

  // Unlock the code
  project.myLock.unlock();

}

</SERVER>
```

# project

## NES2+

### Syntax

```
Created by the server-side JavaScript runtime when the application starts
```

### Description

The `project` object is an object shared by all users accessing the application. This object is created when the application is started, and destroyed when it is stopped. The `project` object is often used to store global properties that need to be accessed or modified by all user sessions. A common use of this object might be a counter holding the number of users that have accessed your application.

The object itself has no default properties, but properties can be created simply by specifying a name and value for the property. The following is an example of how to create a property and assign it a value, which is the IP address of the client requesting the application.

```
var project.lastIP = request.ip;
```

Table 8.19 contains a list and a description of the methods of the `project` object.

*Table 8.19    Methods of the property Object*

| Method | Description |
|---|---|
| lock() | Locks the code |
| unlock() | Unlocks the code |

## Example

Listing 8.98 shows how you can create and increment a counter property of the project object. Before this counter is incremented, the project is locked and then is unlocked afterwards.

*Listing 8.98    Using the project Object*

```
<SERVER>

// Lock the code and increment a project counter
project.lock();
project.hitCount += 1;

// Unlock the code
project.unlock();

</SERVER>
```

# project.lock()

## NES2+

## Syntax

```
project.lock()
```

## Description

The lock() method of the project object locks the code in which you are working until you perform an unlock. If the code is already locked, this method will wait until it can get the lock, a timeout occurs, or an error occurs.

## Example

Listing 8.99 sets a project object with a counter property, *hitCount*. Because you only want to increment the counter with each new user request, it must be locked.

*Listing 8.99    Using the lock() Method to Lock Your Code*

```
<SERVER>

// Lock the code and increment a project counter
project.lock();
project.hitCount += 1;
```

```
// Unlock the code
project.unlock();
```

```
</SERVER>
```

# project.unlock()

## *NES2+*

## *Syntax*

```
project.unlock()
```

## *Description*

The `unlock()` method of the `project` object unlocks the code that you have locked. This method returns `true` if the unlocking was successful and `false` if otherwise.

## *Example*

Listing 8.100 sets a `project` object with a counter property, *hitCount*. Because you only want to increment the counter with each new user request, it must be locked. Once the counter has been incremented, the project is unlocked.

*Listing 8.100    Using the* unlock() *Method to Unlock Your Code*
```
<SERVER>
```

```
// Lock the code and increment a project counter
project.lock();
project.hitCount += 1;
```

```
// Unlock the code
project.unlock();
```

```
</SERVER>
```

# redirect()

## *NES2+*

## *Syntax*

```
redirect(URL)
```

## *Description*

The `redirect` function is a top-level function that is not associated with any core object. This function is used to redirect the requesting browser to the URL it was passed as a parameter.

> **NOTE**
>
> Use the addClient function to preserve client object properties and their values.

## Example

Listing 8.101 checks to see if the browser asking for the page is Internet Explorer. The redirect function is then used to redirect the browser accordingly.

*Listing 8.101   Using the* redirect *Function to Redirect a User's Browser*

```
<SERVER>

// Check to see if the browser is Internet Explorer
if(request.agent.indexOf('MSIE') != -1){
  redirect(addClient("/iepages/index.html"));

// Redirect to another page if it is not IE
}else{
  redirect(addClient("/defaultpages/index.html"));
}

</SERVER>
```

# registerCFunction

## NES2+

## Syntax

```
registerCFunction(JSFuncName, libPath, CFunc)
```

## Description

registerCFunction is a top-level function that is not associated with any core object. registerCFunction is used to register a C function in a shared library as a JavaScript function so it can be used in your scripts. These libraries are the pre-built .dll files on Windows machines and .so files on UNIX machines. registerCFunction takes the JavaScript name you want to assign the C function, the path to the library, and the actual name of the C function you want to register in the library. The function returns a boolean value based on the success of the registration.

After you call this function, you can use the C library with the server-side JavaScript callC function. callC takes the JavaScript name you assigned and any parameters that need to be passed to the function.

## Example

Listing 8.102 registers an external C library, extlib.dll that contains a function named getMyDate. The registration of this function assigns the name JSExtLib to be used within the script. If the function successfully registers, the callC function is used to call the C function and pass it two parameters. The results are written to the user's page. If the function does not register properly, an error is written to the user's page.

*Listing 8.102    Registering a C Function in a Shared Library with*
```
registerCFunction
<SERVER>

// Register the library and function, assigning it a JavaScript
// function name
var myExternalLib = registerCFunction("JSExtLib", "c:/winnt/extlib.dll",
➥"getMyDate")

// If the library registered without error, then call it using the
// callC function. If it failed, then write an error to the page.
if (myExternalLib) {
  write(callC("getMyDate", 1999, 2000));
}else{
  write("There was an error processing this external library function");
}

</SERVER>
```

# request

## NES2+

## Syntax

Core object created by JavaScript runtime for each client request.

## Description

The request object contains specific information about the client's request. The object itself has several properties, as well as any properties that you may be passing from a form. This object also inherits Object.watch() and Object.unwatch(), which are defined in Chapter 6, "Core Syntax." The properties of this object are listed in Table 8.20.

*Table 8.20    Properties of the request Object*

| Property | Description |
|----------|-------------|
| agent | Contains the user-agent string sent in the HTTP request. |
| imageX | The x-coordinate of an imagemap request. |
| imageY | The y-coordinate of an imagemap request. |
| *formKey* | This could be any key, of a *key=value* pair, passed from within a <FORM> tag on a page. |
| ip | The IP address of the user request. |
| method | The HTTP method used in the request. |
| protocol | The protocol level the requesting agent supports. |

## Example

Listing 8.103 writes the various properties of a request to the page.

*Listing 8.103    Using the* request *Object to See Properties of the Requesting Agent*

```
<SERVER>

// Write each of the properties of the request to the page
write('User Agent: ' + request.agent + '<BR>');
write('Y-coordinate of ISMAP: ' + request.imageY + '<BR>');
write('X-coordinate of ISMAP: ' + request.imageX + '<BR>');
write('IP Address: ' + request.ip + '<BR>');
write('HTTP Method: ' + request.method + '<BR>');
write('Protocol Version: ' + request.protocol);

</SERVER>
```

# request.agent

## NES2+

## Syntax

```
request.agent
```

## Description

The agent property of the request object contains the user agent string of the requesting application. The following is an example of a user agent string for Navigator 4.5 on Windows 98.

```
Mozilla/4.5 [en] (Win98; U)
```

You can use several methods of the String object in conjunction with this property to determine the type and version of the browser requesting the page.

## Example

Listing 8.104 examines the requesting browser's agent string and redirects Internet Explorer browsers to an alternative page.

*Listing 8.104    Accessing the* agent *Property of the* request *Object*

```
<SERVER>

// Check to see if the browser is Internet Explorer
if(request.agent.indexOf('MSIE') != -1){
  redirect(addClient("/iepages/index.html"));
}

</SERVER>
```

# request.*formKey*

## *NES2+*

## *Syntax*

request.*formKey*

## *Description*

The *formKey* property of the request object represents any form key that is sent. A key is specified by the NAME attribute in any element of an HTML <FORM>.

## *Example*

Listing 8.105 shows how you can have a form with a "sports" key and use the request.*formKey* property to read the value.

*Listing 8.105    Reading a* formKey *Property*

```
<HTML>
<HEAD>
  <TITLE>Listing 8-105: Using the formKey Property</TITLE>
</HEAD>
<BODY>
<SERVER>

// See if they have submitted or just need the form
if(request.method == "POST"){

  // Print the selected option to the user's page
  write('You selected ' + request.sports);

}else{
  // If this page was called and a form was not submitted, then write the
  // form to the page for the user to use.

  write('<FORM NAME="myForm" METHOD=POST>');
  write('<SELECT NAME="sports">');
  write('<OPTION>Baseball</OPTION>');
  write('<OPTION>Football</OPTION>');
  write('<OPTION>Basketball</OPTION>');
  write('<OPTION>Soccer</OPTION>');
  write('<OPTION>Rugby</OPTION>');
  write('</SELECT>');
  write('<INPUT TYPE=SUBMIT VALUE="Submit">');
  write('</FORM>');
}

</SERVER>
</BODY>
</HTML>
```

# request.imageX

## NES2+

## Syntax

```
request.imageX
```

## Description

The `imageX` property of the `request` object contains the x-coordinate of the imagemap request sent from the browser. These requests come in the following form, where *x* is the numeric x-coordinate and *y* is the numeric y-coordinate:

```
http://www.purejavascript.com/clickthru.html?x,y
```

## Example

Listing 8.106 pulls out the x and y coordinates passed in the request and writes them to the user's page.

*Listing 8.106 Accessing the `imageX` Property*
```
<SERVER>

// Write the imageX and imageY properties to the page.
write('Y-coordinate of ISMAP: ' + request.imageY + '<BR>');
write('X-coordinate of ISMAP: ' + request.imageX);

</SERVER>
```

# request.imageY

## NES2+

## Syntax

```
request.imageY
```

## Description

The `imageY` property of the `request` object contains the y-coordinate of the imagemap request sent from the browser. These requests come in the following form, where *x* is the numeric x-coordinate and *y* is the numeric y-coordinate:

```
http://www.purejavascript.com/clickthru.html?x,y
```

## Example

Listing 8.107 pulls out the x and y coordinates passed in the request and writes them to the user's page.

*Listing 8.107    Accessing the* imageY *Property*
```
<SERVER>

// Write the imageX and imageY properties to the page.
write('Y-coordinate of ISMAP: ' + request.imageY + '<BR>');
write('X-coordinate of ISMAP: ' + request.imageX);

</SERVER>
```

# request.ip

## NES2+

## Syntax

```
request.ip
```

## Description

The ip property of the request object specifies the IP address of the requesting client.

## Example

Listing 8.108 checks the IP address of the requesting client. If the IP address is not within the correct domain, the browser is redirected to an "unauthorized IP" page.

*Listing 8.108    Using the* ip *Property to Verify Authorization*
```
<SERVER>

// See if the IP address is ok
if(request.ip.indexOf("207.200.75.") != -1){

   // Send them to an authorized page
   redirect(addClient("/authorized.html"));

}else{

   // Send them to an error page
   redirect(addClient("/unauthorized.html"));
}

</SERVER>
```

# request.method

## NES2+

## Syntax

```
request.method
```

## Description

The method property of the request object specifies the HTTP method used in the request. This can either be PUT or GET, depending on the submission type.

## Example

Listing 8.109 shows how you can use the same page to display a form and interpret it. If the method is POST, you know it was a form submission. If it was GET, you display the form.

*Listing 8.109   Evaluating the* method *Property*

```
<SERVER>

// See if they have submitted or just need the form
if(request.method == "POST"){

  // Perform your processing of the form here

}else{

  //  Write the actual HTML form here

}

</SERVER>
```

# request.protocol

## NES2+

## Syntax

```
request.protocol
```

## Description

The protocol property of the request object specifies the version of the HTTP protocol used in the request. This version is conveyed in the following format:

```
HTTP/1.0
```

## Example

Listing 8.110 takes a look at the protocol property to see if the request is HTTP 1.1. You can then insert any processing code needed, based on the protocol version supported by the client.

*Listing 8.110    Accessing the* protocol *Property*
```
<SERVER>

// Check the protocol version
if(request.protocol.indexOf("1.1") != -1){

  // Perform your HTTP 1.1 processing of the form here

}else{

  // Perform non-HTTP 1.1 processing here

}

</SERVER>
```

# Resultset

## *NES3+*

## *Syntax*

Core object created by the Stproc.resultSet().

## *Description*

The Resultset object is one of the core server-side JavaScript objects. This object is created by the resultSet() method of the Stproc object. For stored procedures run against DB2, Oracle, Sybase, and ODBC databases, the stored procedure object has one Resultset object for each SQL SELECT statement executed by the procedure. An Informix stored procedure, on the other hand, has one Resultset object.

Each instance of this object has a property for each column in the result set. For Oracle, Sybase, and ODBC stored procedures, these properties can be referred to by the column name. Informix and DB2 stored procedures do not have named columns, so you must use a zero-based numeric index to refer to the column.

You should always call the close() method of the Resultset object after you have finished. The JavaScript runtime will attempt to close the object when the associate DbPool or database object goes out of scope.

> **NOTE**
>
> After creating a result set, you must perform all operations on the set before calling the commitTransaction(), returnValue(), outParameters(), Connection.cursor(), or Connection.SQLTable() method.

This object has only one property—prototype. This property can be used to create new methods and properties for the Resultset object. Table 8.21 contains the methods accessible from this object.

*Table 8.21*  **Methods of the Resultset Object**

| Method | Description |
|---|---|
| close() | Closes the result set object and frees any memory used |
| columnName() | Takes an indexed numbered location and returns the column name of the column in that location |
| columns() | Returns the number of columns in the Resultset |
| next() | Moves from the current row in the Resultset object to the next row |

## Example

Listing 8.111 creates a connection to a database. Once the connection has been verified, the storedProc() method is used to invoke the fictitious *sp_employees* stored procedure. The result sets for this stored procedure are then held in an instance of the Resultset object.

*Listing 8.111*   *The* Resultset *Object*

```
<SERVER>

// Open a connection
var myConn = database.connect("ORACLE", "mySID", "myApp", "appsPWD", "myTNS");

if(myConn.connected()){

  myConn.beginTransaction();

  // Run the stored procedure
  var myStproc = myConn.storedProc("sp_employees");

  var myResultSet = myStproc.resultSet();

  // Commit the transaction
  myConn.commitTransaction();

  // Close the result set
  myResultSet.close();

  // Release the connection
  myConn.release();

// If the connection fails, write an error message
}else{
write('Error ('+myConn.majorErrorCode()+'): '+myConn.majorErrorMessage);
}

</SERVER>
```

# Resultset.close()

## NES3+

## Syntax

`resultset.close()`

## Description

The `close()` method of the `Resultset` object closes the result set and frees all memory used to store its information. If successful, the method returns 0; otherwise, it returns an error code that can be obtained by using the `majorErrorCode()` and `majorErrorMessage()` methods of the `Connection` or `database` objects.

## Example

Listing 8.112 creates a result set and then closes it.

*Listing 8.112   Closing a Cursor with the `close()` Method*

```
<SERVER>

// Open a connection
var myConn = database.connect("ORACLE", "mySID", "myApp", "appsPWD", "myTNS");

myConn.beginTransaction();

// Run the stored procedure
var myStproc = myConn.storedProc("sp_employees");

// Store the result set
myResultSet = myStproc.resultSet();

// Commit the transaction
myConn.commitTransaction();

// Close the result set
myResultSet.close();

</SERVER>
```

# Resultset.columnName()

## NES3+

## Syntax

`resultset.columnName(num)`

## Description

The columnName() method of the Resultset object takes the zero-based indexed number location, *num*, passed to the method and returns the name of the column in that location. Note that these names are not returned in any specific order unless you order them as such. Successive calls to the method, however, will return all the columns. See the example for more information.

## Example

Listing 8.113 has two result sets. One of the sets returns specific column names and the other returns all columns. See the comments in the code for the output.

*Listing 8.113 Using the* columnName() *Method to Return the Names of the Columns in a Table*

```
<SERVER>

// Create a pool of connections
var myPool = new DbPool("ORACLE", "mySID", "myApp", "appsPWD", "myTNS");

// Open a connection from the pool.  Give error if connection could
// not be made.
var myConn = myPool.connection('Employees', 15);

if(myConn.connected()){

  // Start a new SQL transaction
  myConn.beginTransaction();

  // Run the stored procedure
  var myStproc = myConn.storedProc("sp_employees");

  // Store the result sets
  var myResultSet1 = myStproc.resultSet();
  var myResultSet2 = myStproc.resultSet();

  // Writes column #1, from the first result set, to the page
  write(myResultSet1.columnName(0));

  // Writes column #1, from the first result set, to the page
  write(myResultSet1.columnName(1));

  // Writes all column names stored in the second result set to the page.
  for(var i = 0; i < myResultSet2.columns(); i++){
    write(myResultSet2.columnName(i));
  }

  // Close the result sets
  myResultSet1.close();
  myResultSet2.close();
```

```
// End SQL transaction
myConn.commitTransaction();

// If the connection fails, write an error message
}else{
write('Error ('+myConn.majorErrorCode()+'): '+myConn.majorErrorMessage);
}

// Release the connection
myConn.release();

</SERVER>
```

# Resultset.columns()

## NES3+

## Syntax

```
resultset.columns()
```

## Description

The columns() method of the Resultset object returns the number of columns in the result set on which it is invoked. If the SQL used to create the result set specifies a set number of columns to return, that is the number returned by this method.

## Example

Listing 8.114 shows how you can return all the column names of the columns in your result set.

*Listing 8.114    Using the columns() Method to Determine How Many Columns Are in the Result Set Before Writing Them to the Page*

```
<SERVER>

// Run the stored procedure
var myStproc = myConn.storedProc("sp_employees");

// Store the result set
var myResultSet = myStproc.resultSet();

// Writes all column names stored in the result set to the page.
for(var i = 0; i < myResultSet.columns(); i++){
  write(myResultSet.columnName(i));
}

// Close the result set
myResultSet.close();

</SERVER>
```

# Resultset.next()

*NES3+*

## Syntax

```
resultset.next()
```

## Description

The next() method of the Resultset object moves the point in the current row to the next row in the result set. This method is used to iterate through each of the rows returned by the result set. This method returns true, unless it is the last row of the result set, at which time it returns false.

## Example

Listing 8.115 creates an instance of the Resultset object and iterates through its results. This is performed by using the next() method.

*Listing 8.115 Using the next() Method to Iterate Through the Rows in a Result Set*

```
<SERVER>

// Run the stored procedure
var myStproc = myConn.storedProc("sp_employees");

// Store the result set
var myResultSet = myStproc.resultSet();

// Iterate through each return of the result set
while(myResultSet.next()){

  // Perform processing here

}

// Close the result set
myResultSet.close();

</SERVER>
```

# Resultset.prototype

*NES3+, ECMAScript1.0+*

## Syntax

```
resultset.prototype.method = methodName
resultset.prototype.property
```

## Description

The `prototype` property of the `Resultset` object allows you to create new properties and methods of the object. If you are adding a method, set the instance equal to the *methodName* of the method you have defined.

## Example

Listing 8.116 creates a new property and method of the `Resultset` object. An instance is created and the new property is set. The new method is then called to verify the property, and, if it is incorrect, an error is written to the page.

*Listing 8.116    Using the* prototype *Property to Create a New Property and Method*

```
<SERVER>

// Define the method that we prototyped
function verifyWork(){

  // Check to see if the type property we added is set to a valid value
  if(this.type == "work"){
    return true;
  }else{
    return false;
  }
}

// Create a new property and method of the Resultset object.
Resultset.prototype.type = null;
Resultset.prototype.isWORK = verifyWork;

// Create a pool of connections, a connection, a stored procedure,
// and a result set
var myPool = new DbPool("ORACLE", "mySID", "myApp", "appsPWD", "myTNS");
var myConn = myPool.connection('Employees', 15);
var myStproc = myConn.storedProc("sp_employees");
var myResultSet = myStproc.resultSet();

// Using the prototype we defined, assign the type property
myResultSet.type = "work";

// Check the type of the result set to see if it is valid
if(myResultSet.isWORK()){
  write(myResultSet + " has a valid type of " + myResultSet.type);
}else{
  write(myResultSet + " has an invalid type of " + myResultSet.type);
}

</SERVER>
```

# SendMail()

## *NES3+*

## *Syntax*

```
new SendMail()
```

## *Description*

The SendMail object is a core server-side object that is created using the new keyword. This object provides the properties and methods necessary to send email with your JavaScript applications. Table 8.22 lists the properties and methods of this object.

*Table 8.22   SendMail Methods and Properties*

| Function or Property | Description |
| --- | --- |
| Bcc | Property that contains the email addresses of those users you want to blind carbon copy |
| Body | Property that contains the actual body of the message |
| Cc | Property that contains the email addresses of those users you want to carbon copy |
| errorCode() | Returns an integer error code that may be incurred when sending email |
| errorMessage() | Returns a string related to any error messages that may be incurred when sending email |
| Errorsto | Property that contains the email address to which to send error messages |
| From | Property that contains the sender's email address |
| Organization | Property that contains the sender's organization |
| Replyto | Property that contains the sender's reply to email address |
| send() | Method that sends the email |
| Smtpserver | Property that specifics the IP address or hostname of the mail server to send the message |
| Subject | Property that contains the subject of the email |
| To | Property that contains the email address of the recipient |

Using the SendMail object is very straightforward. Simply set the same properties contained in the everyday email you send and invoke the send() method. If an error is encountered, it can be analyzed by using the error methods supplied.

## *Example*

Listing 8.117 shows the use of the SendMail object to create a page for users to send email. Figure 8.1 shows what is displayed to users when they encounter this page, and Figure 8.2 shows the results of submitting a successful email.

*Listing 8.117    Example of Using the* SendMail *Object*

```
<HTML>
<HEAD>
  <TITLE>Listing 8-117: Using the SendMail object</TITLE>
</HEAD>
<BODY>
<SERVER>

// See if they have submitted or just need the form
if(request.method == "POST"){

  // Create an instance of the SendMail object
  var myMail = new SendMail();

  // Assign the properties their values
  myMail.To = request.toAddress;
  myMail.From = request.fromAddress;
  myMail.Subject = request.subject;
  myMail.Body = request.body;
  myMail.Smtpserver = "mail.purejavascript.com";
  myMail.Errorsto = "errors@purejavascript.com";

  // Try to send the mail.
  if(!myMail.send()){

    // If there was an error, give the user the email address of who they
    // should contact about the error, as well as the error code and message.
    write("There was an error sending your message. Please send email to ");
    write(myMail.Errorsto + " with the following error message");
    write("Error " + myMail.errorCode() + ": " + myMail.errorMessage());
  }else{

    // If there was not an error, tell the user they were successful.
    write("Your message was sent successfully!");
  }
}else{

  // If this page was called and a form was not submitted, then write the
  // email form to the page for the user to use.

  write('<FORM NAME="myForm" METHOD=POST>');
  write('<TABLE BORDER=1><TR><TD>');
  write('<TABLE BORDER=0>');
  write('<TR ALIGN=LEFT VALIGN=TOP>');
  write('<TD><B>To:</B></TD>');
  write('<TD><INPUT TYPE=TEXT NAME="toAddress" SIZE=30></TD>');
  write('</TR>');
```

*continues*

*Listing 8.117    continued*

```
  write('<TR ALIGN=LEFT VALIGN=TOP>');
  write('<TD><B>From:</B></TD>');
  write('<TD><INPUT TYPE=TEXT NAME="fromAddress" SIZE=30></TD>');
  write('</TR>');
  write('<TR ALIGN=LEFT VALIGN=TOP>');
  write('<TD><B>Subject:</B></TD>');
  write('<TD><INPUT TYPE=TEXT NAME="subject" SIZE=30></TD>');
  write('</TR>');
  write('<TR ALIGN=LEFT VALIGN=TOP>');
  write('<TD><B>Body:</B></TD>');
  write('<TD><TEXTAREA NAME="body" COLS=60 ROWS=10 WRAP=SOFT>');
  write('</TEXTAREA></TD>');
  write('</TR>');
  write('<TR ALIGN=LEFT VALIGN=TOP>');
  write('<TD COLSPAN=2 ALIGN=RIGHT>');
  write('<INPUT TYPE=SUBMIT VALUE="Send Mail"></TD>');
  write('</TR>');
  write('</TABLE>');
  write('</TD></TR></TABLE>');
  write('</FORM>');
}
</SERVER>
</BODY>
</HTML>
```

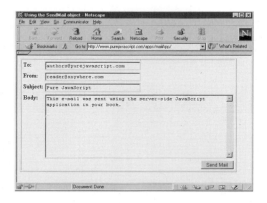

**Figure 8.1**

*Building an email page for your applications.*

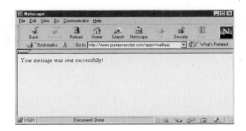

**Figure 8.2**

*The results of submitting an email successfully using the code in Listing 8.117.*

# SendMail.Bcc

## NES3+

## Syntax

`sendmail.Bcc`

## Description

The `Bcc` property of the `SendMail` objects specifies the email addresses of those recipients you want to blind carbon copy. If you want to specify more than one recipient, separate their email addresses with commas.

## Example

Listing 8.118 shows you how to set the `Bcc` property of an instance of the `SendMail` object.

*Listing 8.118    Setting the `Bcc` Property*

```
<SERVER>

// Set the Bcc property
myMail.Bcc = "publisher@purejavascript.com";

</SERVER>
```

# SendMail.Body

## NES3+

## Syntax

`sendmail.Body`

## Description

The `Body` property of the `SendMail` objects specifies the body of the email you want to send.

## Example

Listing 8.119 shows you how to set the `Body` property of an instance of the `SendMail` object.

*Listing 8.119    Setting the `Body` Property*

```
<SERVER>

// Set the Body property
myMail.Body = "Here is the text of the message";

</SERVER>
```

# SendMail.Cc

## NES3+

## Syntax

`sendmail.Cc`

## Description

The `Cc` property of the `SendMail` objects specifies the email addresses of those recipients you want to carbon copy. If you want to specify more than one recipient, separate their email addresses with commas.

## Example

Listing 8.120 shows you how to set the `Cc` property of an instance of the `SendMail` object.

*Listing 8.120    Setting the `Cc` Property*

```
<SERVER>

// Set the Cc property
myMail.Cc = "techedit@purejavascript.com";

</SERVER>
```

# SendMail.errorCode()

## NES3+

## Syntax

```
sendmail.errorCode()
```

## Description

The errorCode() method of the SendMail object returns one of six error codes after attempting to send an email. These codes are defined in Table 8.23.

*Table 8.23   Error Codes Generated from Sending Email with the SendMail.send() Method*

| Code | Description |
| --- | --- |
| 0 | The email was sent successfully. |
| 1 | The SMTP sending mail server was not specified. |
| 2 | The SMTP sending mail server was down or does not exist. |
| 3 | No recipient email address was specified. |
| 4 | No sender's email address was specified. |
| 5 | Connection problems and data not sent. |

## Example

Listing 8.121 tries to send an instance of the SendMail object. If the send() method fails, the errors it encountered are written to the page.

*Listing 8.121   Displaying the Error Code on a Failed Email Delivery*

```
<SERVER>

// Try to send an instance of the mail
if(!myMail.send()){

    // If there was an error, give the user the email address of who they
    // should contact about the error, as well as the error code and message.
    write("There was an error sending your message. Please send email to ");
    write(myMail.Errorsto + " with the following error message");
    write("Error " + myMail.errorCode() + ": " + myMail.errorMessage());

}else{

  // If there was not an error, tell the user they were successful.
  write("Your message was sent successfully!");
}

</SERVER>
```

# SendMail.errorMessage()

## *NES3+*

## *Syntax*

`sendmail.errorMessage()`

## *Description*

The `errorMessage()` method of the `SendMail` object returns the string error message generated after attempting to send an email.

## *Example*

Listing 8.122 tries to send an instance of the `SendMail` object. If the `send()` method fails, the errors it encountered are written to the page.

*Listing 8.122    Displaying the Error Message on a Failed Email Delivery*

```
<SERVER>

// Try to send an instance of the mail
if(!myMail.send()){

    // If there was an error, give the user the email address of who they
    // should contact about the error, as well as the error code and message.
    write("There was an error sending your message. Please send email to ");
    write(myMail.Errorsto + " with the following error message");
    write("Error " + myMail.errorCode() + ": " + myMail.errorMessage());

}else{

    // If there was not an error, tell the user they were successful.
    write("Your message was sent successfully!");
}

</SERVER>
```

# SendMail.Errorsto

## *NES3+*

## *Syntax*

`sendmail.Errorsto`

## *Description*

The `Errorsto` property of the `SendMail` objects specifies the email address of a recipient that should receive the error message. The default value of this error is the sender's address. If you want to specify more than one recipient, separate their email addresses with commas.

## Example

Listing 8.123 shows you how to set the Errorsto property of an instance of the SendMail object.

*Listing 8.123  Setting the Errorsto Property*

```
<SERVER>

// Set the Errorsto property
myMail.Errorsto = "authors@purejavascript.com";

</SERVER>
```

# SendMail.From

## NES3+

## Syntax

```
sendmail.From
```

## Description

The From property of the SendMail objects specifies the email address of the sender of the message.

## Example

Listing 8.124 shows you how to set the From property of an instance of the SendMail object.

*Listing 8.124  Setting the From Property*

```
<SERVER>

// Set the From property using the email key in a form sent by the client
myMail.From = request.email;

</SERVER>
```

# SendMail.Organization

## NES3+

## Syntax

```
sendmail.Organization
```

## Description

The Organization property of the SendMail objects specifies the organization of the sender.

## Example

Listing 8.125 shows you how to set the Organization property of an instance of the SendMail object.

*Listing 8.125  Setting the Organization Property*
```
<SERVER>

// Set the Organization property
myMail.Organization = "TIPs Technical Publishing";

</SERVER>
```

# SendMail.prototype

## NES3+, ECMAScript1.0+

## Syntax

```
sendmail.prototype.method = methodName
sendmail.prototype.property
```

## Description

The prototype property of the SendMail object allows you to create new properties and methods of the object. If you are adding a method, set the instance equal to the *methodName* of the method you have defined.

## Example

Listing 8.126 creates a new property and method of the SendMail object. An instance is created and the new property is set. The new method is then called to verify the property, and, if it is incorrect, an error is written to the page.

*Listing 8.126  Using the prototype Property to Create a New Property and Method*
```
<SERVER>

// Define the method that we prototyped
function verifyAttach(){

  // Check to see if the type property we added is set to a valid value
  if(this.type){
    return true;
  }else{
    return false;
  }
}

// Create a new property and method of the SendMail object.
SendMail.prototype.attachment = null;
```

```
SendMail.prototype.hasAttach = verifyAttach;

// Create a SendMail object
var myMail = new SendMail();

// Using the prototype we defined, assign the type property
myMail.type = false;

// Check to see if there is an attachment
if(myMail.hasAttach()){
  write(myMail + " has a valid type of " + myMail.type);
}else{
  write(myMail + " has an invalid type of " + myMail.type);
}

</SERVER>
```

# SendMail.Replyto

## *NES3+*

## *Syntax*

*sendmail*.ReplyTo

## *Description*

The ReplyTo property of the SendMail objects specifies the email addresses to which the sender wants any replies to be routed.

## *Example*

Listing 8.127 shows you how to set the ReplyTo property of an instance of the SendMail object.

*Listing 8.127    Setting the* ReplyTo *Property*
```
<SERVER>

// Set the ReplyTo property using the email key in a form sent by the client
myMail.ReplyTo = request.replyto;

</SERVER>
```

# SendMail.send()

## *NES3+*

## *Syntax*

*sendmail*.send()

## Description

The send() method of the SendMail objects attempts to send the email from the value specified in the From property to those specified in the To, Cc, and Bcc properties through the email server specified in the Smtpserver property. This method returns true if successful and false otherwise.

## Example

Listing 8.128 tries to send a message. If an error occurs when trying to send the message, an error message is written to the user's page.

*Listing 8.128   Sending a Message with the* send() *Method*

```
<SERVER>

// Try to send an instance of the mail
if(!myMail.send()){

    // If there was an error, give the user the email address of whom they
    // should contact about the error, as well as the error code and message.
    write("There was an error sending your message. Please send email to ");
    write(myMail.Errorsto + " with the following error message");
    write("Error " + myMail.errorCode() + ": " + myMail.errorMessage());

}else{

    // If there was not an error, tell the user they were successful.
    write("Your message was sent successfully!");
}

</SERVER>
```

# SendMail.Smtpserver

## NES3+

## Syntax

*sendmail*.Smtpserver

## Description

The Smtpserver property of the SendMail objects specifies the SMTP sending email IP address or server name. This value defaults to the value set in the Netscape Administration Server settings for the instance of Enterprise Server under which your application is running.

## Example

Listing 8.129 shows you how to set the Smtpserver property of an instance of the SendMail object.

*Listing 8.129    Setting the* Smtpserver *Property*
```
<SERVER>

// Set the Smtpserver property using the email key in a form
// sent by the client
myMail.Smtpserver = request.smtp;

</SERVER>
```

# SendMail.Subject

## NES3+

## Syntax

```
sendmail.Subject
```

## Description

The Subject property of the SendMail objects specifies the subject of the email you want to send.

## Example

Listing 8.130 shows you how to set the Subject property of an instance of the SendMail object.

*Listing 8.130    Setting the* Subject *Property*
```
<SERVER>

// Set the Subject property
myMail.Subject = "I really liked your book!";

</SERVER>
```

# SendMail.To

## NES3+

## Syntax

```
sendmail.To
```

## Description

The To property of the SendMail objects specifies the email addresses of the recipients of the message. If you want to specify more than one recipient, separate their email addresses with commas.

## Example

Listing 8.131 shows you how to set the To property of an instance of the SendMail object.

*Listing 8.131    Setting the* To *Property*

```
<SERVER>

// Set the To property
myMail.To = "authors@purejavascript.com";

</SERVER>
```

## server

### *NES2+*

### *Syntax*

Core object created when the instance of Netscape Enterprise Server is started.

### *Description*

The `server` object is one of the core server-side objects. An instance of this object is created for each instance of the Enterprise server you have running. This object is destroyed when the server process is stopped.

This object should be used to store global data you want to share and manage across your applications. Because of this, you will need to lock and unlock your code if you are changing any properties you have defined in your applications. The `server` object has the properties and methods listed in Table 8.24. Note that the properties are all read-only.

*Table 8.24    Properties and Methods of the server Object*

| Type | Item | Description |
|------|------|-------------|
| method | lock() | Locks your code while you perform data manipulation that should only have a single thread connected to it. |
| | unlock() | Unlocks previously locked code. |
| property | host | String specifying the server name, sub-domain, and domain name of the Web server. |
| | hostname | Contains the same information as concatenating the host property with the port property and separating them with a colon. |
| | port | The port number on which the server is running. |
| | protocol | Contains the protocol portion of the URL. This includes the information up to the first colon, as in http:. |

### *Example*

Listing 8.132 uses the `lock()` and `unlock()` methods of the `server` object to lock the working code while the property, `totalHits`, is modified.

*Listing 8.132   Accessing Properties of the* server *Object*

```
<SERVER>

// Lock the code and increment a server counter
server.lock();
server.totalHits += 1;

// Unlock the code
server.unlock();

</SERVER>
```

# server.host

## NES2+

## Syntax

```
server.host
```

## Description

The host property of the server object contains the server name, any sub-domain, and domain name of the Web server.

## Example

Listing 8.133 writes the host of the server to the user's page.

*Listing 8.133   Accessing the* host *Property*

```
<SERVER>

// Write the host property to the user's page
write(server.host);

</SERVER>
```

# server.hostname

## NES2+

## Syntax

```
server.hostname
```

## Description

The hostname property of the server object contains the server name, any sub-domain, domain name, and port of the Web server. This property is the same as concatenating the host property with the port property and separating them with a colon.

## Example

Listing 8.134 writes the hostname of the server to the user's page.

*Listing 8.134   Accessing the hostname Property*
```
<SERVER>

// Write the hostname property to the user's page
write(server.hostname);

</SERVER>
```

# server.lock()

## NES2+

## Syntax

```
server.lock()
```

## Description

The lock() method of the server object locks the code in which you are working until you perform an unlock. If the code is already locked, this method will wait until it can get the lock, a timeout occurs, or an error occurs.

## Example

Listing 8.135 sets a server object with a counter property, *totalHits*. Because you only want to increment the counter with each new user request on each application, it must be locked.

*Listing 8.135   Using the lock() Method to Lock Your Code*
```
<SERVER>

// Lock the code and increment a server counter
server.lock();
server.totalHits += 1;

// Unlock the code
server.unlock();

</SERVER>
```

# server.port

## NES2+

## Syntax

```
server.port
```

## Description

The port property of the server object contains the port number to which the Web server is responding.

## Example

Listing 8.136 writes the port of the server to the user's page.

*Listing 8.136   Accessing the* port *Property*
```
<SERVER>

// Write the port property to the user's page
write(server.port);

</SERVER>
```

# server.protocol

## NES2+

## Syntax
```
server.protocol
```

## Description

The protocol property of the server object contains the protocol to which the server is responding. This includes the information up to the first colon, as in http:.

## Example

Listing 8.137 writes the port of the server to the user's page.

*Listing 8.137   Accessing the* port *Property*
```
<SERVER>

// Write the port property to the user's page
write(server.port);

</SERVER>
```

# server.unlock()

## NES2+

## Syntax
```
server.unlock()
```

## Description

The unlock() method of the server object unlocks the code that you have locked. This method returns true if the unlocking was successful and false if otherwise.

## Example

Listing 8.138 sets a server object with a counter property, *totalHits*. Because you only want to increment the counter with each new user request, it must be locked. Once the counter has been incremented, the project is unlocked.

*Listing 8.138   Using the* unlock() *Method to Unlock Your Code*

```
<SERVER>

// Lock the code and increment a server counter
server.lock();
server.hitCount += 1;

// Unlock the code
server.unlock();

</SERVER>
```

# ssjs_generateClientID()

## NES3+

## Syntax

```
ssjs_generateClientID()
```

## Description

The ssjs_generateClientID function is a top-level function that is not associated with any core server-side object. This function returns a unique identifier from the run-time engine. This allows you to track a user's session across several pages when using client-side maintenance. You may want to store the identifier as a property of the client object, but be careful to keep it from being accessed from other clients.

## Example

Listing 8.139 shows how you can assign a property of the client object an identifier to track a user.

*Listing 8.139   Using the* ssjs_generateClientID *Function*

```
<SERVER>

// Store the identifier in a client property
client.sessionID = ssjs_generateClientID();

</SERVER>
```

# ssjs_getCGIVariable()

## NES3+

## Syntax

```
ssjs_getCGIVariable(envVariable)
```

## Description

The ssjs_getCGIVariable function is a top-level function that is not associated with any core server-side object. This function allows you to retrieve environment variables that are available to your CGI processes. When a variable cannot be found, the function returns null. Table 8.25 contains the default list of variables you can access.

**Table 8.25    Environment Variables Accessible by the ssjs_getCGIVariable Function**

| Variable | Description |
| --- | --- |
| AUTH_TYPE | The authorization type if the request is protected by a type of authorization. This returns values such as basic. |
| HTTPS | If security is active on the server. This returns values of ON or OFF. |
| HTTPS_KEYSIZE | The number of bits in the key used to encrypt the session. |
| HTTPS_SECRETKEYSIZE | The number of bits used to generate the server's private key. |
| PATH_INFO | Path information to the file you want to retrieve. This would be something like /sports/baseball.html. |
| PATH_TRANSLATED | The actual path to the file you want to retrieve. This would be something like /netscape/suitespot/docs/sports/baseball.html. |
| QUERY_STRING | Any information after a ? character in the URL. |
| REMOTE_ADDR | The IP address of the host submitting the request. |
| REMOTE_HOST | The hostname address of the host submitting the request. DNS must be turned on for this feature. |
| REMOTE_USER | The name of the local HTTP user of the Web browser, if access authorization is turned on for this URL. |
| REQUEST_METHOD | The type of request that is being made, such as GET or POST. |
| SCRIPT_NAME | The filename you are trying to retrieve, such as index.html. |
| SERVER_NAME | The hostname or IP under which the server is running. |
| SERVER_PORT | The port number to which the server is responding. |
| SERVER_PROTOCOL | The protocol version supported by the requesting client, such as HTTP/1.0. |
| SERVER_URL | The URL a user would have to enter to access the server, such as http://www.purejavascript.com:6969. |

## Example

Listing 8.140 returns the SERVER_URL variable to a property of the server object.

*Listing 8.140    Retrieving an Environment Variable*

```
<SERVER>

// Store the identifier in a server property
server.serverURL = ssjs_getCGIVariable(SERVER_URL);

</SERVER>
```

# ssjs_getClientID()

## *NES3+*

## *Syntax*

```
ssjs_getClientID()
```

## *Description*

The `ssjs_getClientID` function is a top-level function that is not associated with any core server-side object. This function returns a unique identifier from the runtime engine. This allows you to track a user's session across several pages when using server-side maintenance. When using this function, there is no need to store the identifier as a property of the `client` object.

## *Example*

Listing 8.141 writes the identifier generated by the `ssjs_getClientID` function to the page.

*Listing 8.141    Seeing the* `ssjs_getClientID` *Function*

```
<SERVER>

// Store the identifier in a variable
var myIdentifier = ssjs_getClientID();

// Write the ID to the page
write(myIdentifier);

</SERVER>
```

# Stproc

## *NES3+*

## *Syntax*

Core object created by the `storedProc()` method of the `database` or `Connection` objects.

## *Description*

The `Stproc` object is a core server-side object that is created by the `storedProc()` method of the `database` or `Connection` objects. Because of the nature of connections to a database, you should call the `close()` method of this object when you have completed your processing. This will free any and all memory used by the stored procedure. Otherwise, the object will be destroyed when the `database` or `Connection` objects go out of scope.

The object itself has only one property—`prototype`. This property can be used to add methods and properties to the object as needed. Table 8.26 lists the methods of the `Stproc` object.

*Table 8.26*    *Methods of the Stproc Object*

| Method | Description |
|---|---|
| close() | Closes a stored procedure instance |
| outParamCount() | Returns the number of output parameters from the stored procedure |
| outParameters() | Returns the value of the output parameter passed to the method |
| resultSet() | Creates a new Resultset object |
| returnValue() | Returns the return value for the stored procedure |

## Example

Listing 8.142 creates an instance of the Stproc object, via a Connection.storedProc() method call, and then closes it.

*Listing 8.142    Creating an Instance of the* stproc *Object*

```
<SERVER>

// Open a connection
var myConn = database.connect("ORACLE", "mySID", "myApp", "appsPWD", "myTNS");

myConn.beginTransaction();

// Run the stored procedure
var myStproc = myConn.storedProc("sp_employees");

// Commit the transaction
myConn.commitTransaction();

// Close the result set
myResultSet.close();

</SERVER>
```

# Stproc.close()

## NES3+

## Syntax

stproc.close()

## Description

The close() method of the Stproc object closes the stored procedure and frees all memory used to store its information. If successful, the method returns 0; otherwise, it returns an error code that can be obtained by using the majorErrorCode() and majorErrorMessage() methods of the Connection or database objects.

## Example

Listing 8.143 creates a stored procedure and then closes it.

*Listing 8.143    Closing a Cursor with the* `close()` *Method*

```
<SERVER>

// Open a connection
var myConn = database.connect("ORACLE", "mySID", "myApp", "appsPWD", "myTNS");

myConn.beginTransaction();

// Run the stored procedure
var myStproc = myConn.storedProc("sp_employees");

// Store the result set
var myResultSet = myStproc.resultSet();

// Commit the transaction
myConn.commitTransaction();

// Close the result set
myResultSet.close();

</SERVER>
```

# Stproc.outParamCount()

## NES3+

## Syntax

`stproc.outParamCount()`

## Description

The `outParamCount()` method of the `Stproc` object returns the number of output parameters from the stored procedure. Be sure to call this method before calling the `outParameters()` method to make sure parameters have been returned.

**NOTE**

Informix stored procedures do not have output parameters, so this method always returns 0 when run against an Informix database.

## Example

Listing 8.144 opens a connection to the database and runs a stored procedure. Based on the number of output parameters, the script writes the parameters to the user's screen.

*Listing 8.144    Using the* `outParamCount()` *Method*
```
<SERVER>

// Open a connection
var myConn = database.connect("ORACLE", "mySID", "myApp", "appsPWD", "myTNS");

myConn.beginTransaction();

// Run the stored procedure
var myStproc = myConn.storedProc("sp_employees");

// Write the output parameters of this stored procedure to the
// user's page.
for(var i = 0; i <= myStproc.outParamCount(); i++){
  write(myStproc.outParameters(i) + '<BR>');
}

// Close the result set
myStproc.close();

// Commit the transaction
myConn.commitTransaction();

</SERVER>
```

# Stproc.outParameters()

## NES3+

## Syntax

`stproc.outParameters(num)`

## Description

The `outParameters()` method of the `Stproc` object returns the output parameter from the stored procedure that is indexed at the *num* location. The return value of this method can be a `string`, `number`, `double`, or `object`. Be sure to call the `outParamCount()` method before calling this method to make sure parameters have been returned.

> **NOTE**
>
> Informix stored procedures do not have output parameters, so there is no need to run this method.

## Example

Listing 8.145 opens a connection to the database and runs a stored procedure. Based on the number of output parameters, the script writes the parameters to the user's screen.

*Listing 8.145    Using the* outParameters() *Method*

```
<SERVER>

// Open a connection
var myConn = database.connect("ORACLE", "mySID", "myApp", "appsPWD", "myTNS");

myConn.beginTransaction();

// Run the stored procedure
var myStproc = myConn.storedProc("sp_employees");

// Write the output parameters of this stored procedure to the
// user's page.
for(var i = 0; i <= myStproc.outParamCount(); i++){
  write(myStproc.outParameters(i) + '<BR>');
}

// Close the result set
myStproc.close();

// Commit the transaction
myConn.commitTransaction();

</SERVER>
```

# Stproc.prototype

## NES2+, ECMAScript1.0+

## Syntax

```
stproc.prototype.method = methodName
stproc.prototype.property
```

## Description

The prototype property of the Stproc object allows you to create new properties and methods of the object. If you are adding a method, set the instance equal to the methodName of the method you have defined.

## Example

Listing 8.146 creates a new property and method of the Stproc object. An instance is created and the new property is set. The new method is then called to verify the property, and, if it is incorrect, an error is written to the page.

*Listing 8.146    Using the* `prototype` *Property to Create a New Property and Method*

```
<SERVER>

// Define the method that we prototyped
function verifyWork(){

  // Check to see if the type property we added is set to a valid value
  if(this.type == "work"){
    return true;
  }else{
    return false;
  }
}

// Create a new property and method of the Stproc object.
Stproc.prototype.type = null;
Stproc.prototype.isWORK = verifyWork;

// Create a pool of connections, a connection, a stored procedure,
// and a result set
var myPool = new DbPool("ORACLE", "mySID", "myApp", "appsPWD", "myTNS");
var myConn = myPool.connection('Employees', 15);
var myStproc = myConn.storedProc("sp_employees");

// Using the prototype we defined, assign the type property
myStproc.type = "work";

// Check the type of the stored procedure to see if it is valid
if(myStproc.isWORK()){
  write(myStproc + " has a valid type of " + myStproc.type);
}else{
  write(myStproc + " has an invalid type of " + myStproc.type);
}

</SERVER>
```

# Stproc.resultSet()

## *NES3+*

## *Syntax*

`stproc.resultSet()`

## *Description*

The `resultSet()` object of the `Stproc` object creates a `Resultset` object for storing the results of running a stored procedure. For stored procedures run against DB2, Oracle, Sybase, and ODBC databases, the stored procedure object has one `Resultset` object for each SQL `SELECT` statement executed by the procedure. An Informix stored procedure, on the other hand, has one `Resultset` object.

Each instance of this object has a property for each column in the result set. For Oracle, Sybase, and ODBC stored procedures, these properties can be referred to by the column name. Informix and DB2 stored procedures do not have named columns, so you must use a zero-based numeric index to refer to the column.

You should always call the close() method of the Stproc object after you have finished. The JavaScript runtime will attempt to close the object when the associated DbPool or database object goes out of scope.

## NOTE

After creating a result set, you must perform all operations on the set before calling the commitTransaction(), returnValue(), outParameters(), Connection. cursor(), or Connection.SQLTable() method.

## *Example*

Listing 8.147 creates a connection to a database. Once the connection has been verified, the storedProc() method is used to invoke the fictitious *sp_employees* stored procedure. The result sets for this stored procedure are then held in an instance of the Resultset object that was created with the resultSet() method.

*Listing 8.147  Calling the* resultset() *Method*

```
<SERVER>

// Open a connection
var myConn = database.connect("ORACLE", "mySID", "myApp", "appsPWD", "myTNS");

if(myConn.connected()){

  myConn.beginTransaction();

  // Run the stored procedure
  var myStproc = myConn.storedProc("sp_employees");

  myResultSet = myStproc.resultSet();

  // Commit the transaction
  myConn.commitTransaction();

  // Close the result set
  myResultSet.close();

  // Release the connection
  myConn.release();

// If the connection fails, write an error message
}else{
```

```
write('Error ('+myConn.majorErrorCode()+'): '+myConn.majorErrorMessage);
}

</SERVER>
```

# Stproc.returnValue()

## NES3+

## Syntax

*stproc*.returnValue()

## Description

The returnValue() method of the Stproc object returns the return value of the stored procedure. For DB2, Informix, and ODBC, this method always returns null. Oracle only returns null if the stored procedure did not return a value. Sybase always returns a value.

**NOTE**

Before you call this method, you must retrieve any Resultset objects. Once this method is called, no more data can be obtained from the current result set and no more result sets can be created.

## Example

Listing 8.148 calls a stored procedure, creates a result set, and obtains the result value. This value is then written to the user's page.

*Listing 8.148    Accessing a Stored Procedure's Return Value*

```
<SERVER>

// Call the stored procedure
var myStproc = database.storedProc("sp_employees");

// Generate a result set
var myResultset = myStproc.resultSet();

// Get the return value. Note that you can no longer
// reference the myResultset variable
var myReturnValue = myStproc.returnValue();

// Write the result set to the page
write(myReturnValue);

</SERVER>
```

# write()

*NES2+*

## Syntax

```
write(string)

write(num)

write(expression)
```

## Description

The write function is a top-level function that is not associated with any object. This function writes information to the HTML page the script is generating to send back to the client. This function can take and write a string, numeric value, or an expression that returns an alphanumeric result. To write data to a file, see the entry for File.write() and File.writeln().

> **TIP**
>
> The JavaScript runtime buffers all write data until 64KB have been collected. Then the buffer is flushed to the file. You can manually call the top-level flush function to improve performance of your pages, if they are waiting on database query results, by calling the function before you run the query.

## Example

Listing 8.149 writes a string "Hello, World!" to the user's page.

*Listing 8.149    Using the* write *Function*

```
<SERVER>

// Write a string to the page
write('Hello, World!');

</SERVER>
```

# CHAPTER 9

## Microsoft's Scripting Engine Extensions

This chapter contains all the items and elements making up Microsoft's Scripting Engine additions. This contains JScript elements that are partial to Microsoft's interpreters. These elements can be used with IIS ASP pages, Windows Scripting Host, and within the Internet Explorer browser. Table 9.1 shows the JScript support in the various applications that are shipped with Microsoft's Scripting Engine.

> **NOTE**
>
> Microsoft products provide the ability to upgrade the scripting engines, which are separate from the application, in its products. This means that it is possible for Internet Explorer 3 to have JScript 5.0 with full backward compatibility. The following table only lists the engine version that was shipped with the product.

*Table 9.1 JScript Support in Various Microsoft Applications*

| Application | JScript Version |
|---|---|
| Internet Explorer 3.x | 1.0 |
| IIS 1.0 | 2.0 |
| Internet Explorer 4.x | 3.0 |
| IIS 4.0 | 3.0 |
| Windows Scripting Host 1.0 | 3.0 |
| Visual Studio | 4.0 |
| Internet Explorer 5.x | 5.0 |
| IIS 5.0 | 5.0 |

> **NOTE**
>
> Microsoft did release JScript 2.0 for Internet Explorer 3.02 as a standalone download from `http://msdn.microsoft.com/scripting`. Additionally, it released a 3.1 version for Internet Explorer 4.

Most of the extensions discussed in this chapter are objects supplied in Microsoft's Scripting Runtime Library, which is named `scrrun.dll`. They are not intrinsic members of the JScript language itself, which is found in the `jscript.dll` library. However, there are some exceptions. These are the conditional compilation flags, `GetObject` and `ActiveXObject`, and the various `ScriptEngine` functions.

This fact alone is probably the most notable difference between JScript and JavaScript. JScript is an automation-compatible language—it can create and manipulate COM (Component Object Model) objects. Both the `Dictionary` and `FileSystemObject` objects are examples of this, as are Excel, Word, and other Microsoft Office applications. The binaries for these applications, in the world of COM, are called COM servers.

It is worth noting the Microsoft Scripting Runtime Library did not come with Internet Explorer until version 5. It was available with IIS and the Windows Scripting Host. As mentioned in the previous note, you can download versions 2.0 and 3.1 from Microsoft's Scripting Technologies page at http://msdn.microsoft.com/scripting.

Now that you have taken a quick look at Microsoft's JScript and COM, you can get on to the reference. As with the other chapters in this section of the book, each entry includes a version, syntax, description, example, as well as many other details.

# @_alpha

## JScript3.0+

## Syntax

`@_alpha`

## Description

The `@_alpha` variable is used in conditional compilation to determine if a DEC Alpha processor is being used. When the variable is not `true`, it is defined as NaN.

## Example

Listing 9.1 alerts the user when a DEC Alpha processor is used.

*Listing 9.1   Detect a DEC Alpha Processor*

```
<script language="JScript">
<!-- Hide

@if (@_alpha)
  alert("You are using a DEC Alpha processor.");
```

```
@else
  alert("You are NOT using a DEC Alpha processor.");
@end

//Hide End -->
</script>
```

# @_jscript

## JScript3.0+

## Syntax

```
@_jscript
```

## Description

The `@_jscript` variable is used in conditional compilation to determine if JScript is being used. This variable is always `true`.

## Example

Listing 9.2 displays an alert box based on the value of the `@_jscript` variable.

*Listing 9.2    Detect a JScript*
```
<script language="JScript">
<!-- Hide

@if (@_jscript)
  alert("The @_jscript variable is true.");
@else
  alert("The @_jscript variable is NOT true.");
@end

//Hide End -->
</script>
```

# @_jscript_build

## JScript3.0+

## Syntax

```
@_jscript_build
```

## Description

The `@_jscript_build` variable is used in conditional compilation to hold the build number of the JScript scripting engine.

## WARNING

Before accessing the `@_jscript_build` variable, use the `@cc_on` statement to define the variable.

## Example

Listing 9.3 uses the `@_jscript_build` variable to display the build number of the JScript engine that is being used.

*Listing 9.3   Retrieve JScript Build Number*

```
<script language="JScript">
<!-- Hide

//Set conditional compilation so @_jscript_build variable will be defined.
@cc_on

//Display the JScript build number using the @_jscript_build variable
document.write("The JScript engine build number is ",@_jscript_build);

//Hide End -->
</script>
```

# @_jscript_version

## JScript3.0+

## Syntax

```
@_jscript_version
```

## Description

The `@_jscript_version` variable is used in conditional compilation to hold the JScript version number in *major.minor* format.

## WARNING

Before accessing the `@_jscript_version` variable, use the `@cc_on` statement to define the variable.

## Example

Listing 9.4 uses the `@jscript_version` variable to display the JScript version that is being used.

*Listing 9.4   Determine JScript Version*

```
<script language="JScript">
<!-- Hide

//Set conditional compilation so @_jscript_version variable will be defined.
```

```
@cc_on

//Display the JScript verision number using the @_jscript_version variable
document.write("The JScript version is ",@_jscript_version);

//Hide End -->
</script>
```

# @_mac

## *JScript3.0+*

### Syntax

```
@_mac
```

### Description

The @_mac variable is used in conditional compilation to determine if an Apple
Macintosh system is being used. When the variable is not true, it is defined as NaN.

### Example

Listing 9.5 alerts the user when an Apple Macintosh system is used.

*Listing 9.5    Detect an Apple Macintosh System*
```
<script language="JScript">
<!-- Hide

@if (@_mac)
   alert("You are using an Apple Macintosh system.");
@else
   alert("You are NOT using an Apple Macintosh system.");
@end

//Hide End -->
</script>
```

# @_mc680x0

## *JScript3.0+*

### Syntax

```
@_mc680x0
```

### Description

The @_mc680x0 variable is used in conditional compilation to determine if a Motorola
680×0 processor is being used. When the variable is not true, it is defined as NaN.

## Example

Listing 9.6 alerts the user when a Motorola 680×0 processor is used.

*Listing 9.6    Detect a Motorola 680×0 Processor*

```
<script language="JScript">
<!-- Hide

@if (@_mc680x0)
  alert("You are using a Motorola 680x0 processor.");
@else
  alert("You are NOT using a Motorola 680x0 processor.");
@end

//Hide End -->
</script>
```

# @_PowerPC

## JScript3.0+

## Syntax

```
@_PowerPC
```

## Description

The @_PowerPC variable is used in conditional compilation to determine if a Motorola PowerPC processor is being used. When the variable is not true, it is defined as NaN.

## Example

Listing 9.7 alerts the user when a Motorola PowerPC processor is used.

*Listing 9.7    Detect a Motorola PowerPC Processor*

```
<script language="JScript">
<!-- Hide

@if (@_PowerPC)
  alert("You are using a Motorola PowerPC processor.");
@else
  alert("You are NOT using a Motorola PowerPC processor.");
@end

//Hide End -->
</script>
```

# @_win16

## JScript3.0+

## Syntax

```
@_win16
```

## Description

The @_win16 variable is used in conditional compilation to determine if a win16 system is being used. When the variable is not true, it is defined as NaN.

## Example

Listing 9.8 alerts the user when a win16 system is used.

*Listing 9.8  Detect a win16 System*

```
<script language="JScript">
<!-- Hide

@if (@_win16)
  alert("You are using a win16 system.");
@else
  alert("You are NOT using a win16 system.");
@end

//Hide End -->
</script>
```

# @_win32

## JScript3.0+

## Syntax

```
@_win32
```

## Description

The @_win32 variable is used in conditional compilation to determine if a win32 system is being used. When the variable is not true, it is defined as NaN.

## Example

Listing 9.9 alerts the user when a win32 system is used.

*Listing 9.9  Detect a win32 System*

```
<script language="JScript">
<!-- Hide

@if (@_win32)
  alert("You are using a win32 system.");
@else
  alert("You are NOT using a win32 system.");
@end

//Hide End -->
</script>
```

# @_x86

## JScript3.0+

## Syntax

```
@_x86
```

## Description

The @_x86 variable is used in conditional compilation to determine if a Intel processor is being used. When the variable is not true, it is defined as NaN.

## Example

Listing 9.10 alerts the user when an Intel processor is used.

*Listing 9.10   Detect an Intel Processor*
```
<script language="JScript">
<!-- Hide

@if (@_x86)
  alert("You are using an Intel processor.");
@else
  alert("You are NOT using an Intel processor.");
@end

//Hide End -->
</script>
```

# @cc_on

## JScript3.0+

## Syntax

```
@cc_on
```

## Description

The @cc_on statement is used to activate conditional compilation in the scripting engine.

## Example

Listing 9.11 shows where the @cc_on statement would be used within JScript code to get the JScript revision.

*Listing 9.11   Activate Conditional Compilation*
```
<script language="JScript">
<!-- Hide

//Set conditional compilation so @_jscript_version variable will be defined.
```

```
@cc_on

//Display the JScript verision number using the @_jscript_version variable
document.write("The JScript version is ",@_jscript_version);

//Hide End -->
</script>
```

# @if

## JScript3.0+

## Syntax

```
@if (condition1)
   statement1
@elif (condition2)
   statement2
@else
   statement3
@end
```

## Description

The @if statement operates much like a typical if conditional statement but evaluates compiled variables and has a slightly different syntax. If the expression in *condition1* evaluates to *true*, *statement1* is executed. Otherwise, the *condition2* is evaluated to determine if *statement2* should be evaluated. The @elif statement operates the same as the JavaScript else... if statement, even though it looks different. You can use as many @elif statements as needed or none at all. Only one @else statement should be used to catch conditions that don't meet any of the previous conditionals. Like the @elif statement, the @else statement is optional. The @end statement is required at the end of all if conditionals.

## Example

Listing 9.12 displays a message based on the type of processor being used.

*Listing 9.12    Using @if to Display Processor Type*
```
<script language="JScript">
<!-- Hide

//Alert the user as to which type of processor they are using.
@if(@_alpha)
   alert("You are using a DEC Alpha processor.");
@elif(@_mc680x0)
   alert("You are using a Motorola 680x0 processor.");
@elif(@_PowerPC)
   alert("You are using a Motorola PowerPC processor.");
```

*continues*

*Listing 9.12 continued*

```
@elif(@_x86)
  alert("You are using an Intel processor.");
@else
  alert("I don't know what type of processor you have!");
@end

//Hide End -->
</script>
```

# @set

## *JScript3.0+*

## *Syntax*

```
@set @varName = value
```

## *Description*

The @set property allows the creation of custom compiled variables. The name of a custom variable must start with an ampersand character. If the variable is used before being defined, its value will be NaN.

## *Example*

Listing 9.13 uses the @set property to create a custom compiled variable called @number and assigns the number 25 to the variable. The variable is then used to display a sentence in the browser.

*Listing 9.13 Create Custom Compiled Variable*

```
<script language="JScript">
<!-- Hide

//Create a custom compiled variable called @number and set it to 25
@set @number = 25;

//Display a sentence in the browser based on the value stored in the
//custom compiled variable @number.
@if(@number == 25)
  document.write("Number is equal to ",@number);
@else
  document.write("Number is not equal to 25.");
@end

//Hide End -->
</script>
```

# ActiveXObject

## *JScript3.0+*

## *Syntax*

```
var variable = new ActiveXObject("serverName.typeName",location)
```

## *Description*

The `ActiveXObject` creates a reference to an object that is connected to another application or programming tool through automation interfaces. The arguments used by this object are listed in Table 9.2.

### Table 9.2 Argument Associated with ActiveXObject

| Argument | Description |
| --- | --- |
| `serverName` | The name of the application that provides the object. |
| `typeName` | The type or class of the object to create. |
| `location` | The name of the network server where the object is to be created. This field is optional. |

## *Example*

Listing 9.14 uses the `ActiveXObject` to create a multiplication table in a Microsoft Excel document. Excel will be started automatically.

> **NOTE**
>
> If you are not using Excel 97, you will need to change the portion of the code in Listing 9.14 that reads `Excelsheet.Activesheet.Cell` to `Excelsheet.Cells` for the code to execute properly.

*Listing 9.14    Create a Multiplication Table in an Excel Document*

```
<html>

See the Excel Application for the result of loading this web page.

<script language="JScript">
<!-- Hide

var ExcelSheet = new ActiveXObject("Excel.Sheet");

// Make Excel visible through the Application object.
ExcelSheet.Application.Visible = true;

//Create multiplication table in Excel
for(i=1;i<11;i++)
```

*continues*

*Listing 9.14    continued*

```
{
  // numbers to be multiplied in first two rows.
  ExcelSheet.ActiveSheet.Cells(i,1).Value = i;
  ExcelSheet.ActiveSheet.Cells(i,2).Value = 9;

  // Create Excel string to handle multiplication
  var aString = new String("=A");
  aString += i;
  aString += "*B";
  aString += i;
  ExcelSheet.ActiveSheet.Cells(i,3).Value = aString;
}

//Hide End -->
</script>
</html>
```

# Automation

## JScript3.0+

### Syntax

```
Core JScript Object
```

### Description

Automation objects are objects that are connected to other applications or programming tools through automation interfaces. These objects give JScript developers access to properties and methods applications from within the JScript code. See `ActiveXObject()` and `GetObject()` for details on using automation objects.

### Example

See `ActiveXObject()` and `GetObject()` for examples of using automation objects.

# Dictionary

## JScript3.0+

### Syntax

Core JScript object created by calling the `ActiveXObject()` method passing `Scripting.Dictionary`.

### Description

The `Dictionary` object is an associative array of items that can be of any type. Each item is associated with a unique key that provides access to each item in the array. The key is usually an integer or a string, but can be anything except an array. A `Dictionary` object is created and returned when the `ActiveXObject()` method has the server and type name set to `"Scripting.Dictionary"`.

A number of properties and methods are provided by the `Dictionary` object to provide access to the items in the dictionary. These properties and methods are listed in Table 9.3.

**Table 9.3 Arguments Associated with Document Object**

| Type | Item | Description |
| --- | --- | --- |
| Properties | Count | Returns the number of items in a collection or dictionary |
| | Item | Sets or returns an item for a specified key |
| | Key | Sets a key in a dictionary |
| Methods | Add() | Adds a key and item pair to dictionary |
| | Exists() | Determines if specified key exists in dictionary |
| | Items() | Returns array of all items in dictionary |
| | Keys() | Returns array of all existing keys in dictionary |
| | Remove() | Removes a *key*, *item* pair from dictionary |
| | RemoveAll() | Removes all *key*, *item* pairs from a dictionary |

## Example

Listing 9.15 creates a dictionary object using the `ActiveXObject()` constructor and assigns the new dictionary object to the variable "fruits".

*Listing 9.15   Create a Dictionary Object*
```
var fruits = new ActiveXObject("Scripting.Dictionary");
```

# Dictionary.Add()

## JScript3.0+

## Syntax

```
dictionaryobj.Add(key, item)
```

## Description

The Add() method of the Dictionary object adds new items to the dictionary using `key`, `item` pairs. The `item` can be of any type, but the `key` cannot be an array. Nothing is returned from this method.

## Example

Listing 9.16 creates a fruit dictionary and then uses the `Add()` method to add fruit items to the dictionary.

*Listing 9.16    Create and Add Items to a Fruit Dictionary*

```
<html>

<script language="JScript">
<!-- Hide

//Create dictionary
var fruits = new ActiveXObject("Scripting.Dictionary");

//define elements of dictionary
fruits.Add("A","apple");
fruits.Add("B","berry");
fruits.Add("O","orange");
</html>
```

# Dictionary.Count

## JScript3.0+

## Syntax

`dictionaryobj.Count`

## Description

The Count property of the Dictionary object contains the number of items in the dictionary. This property is read only, so it cannot be used to change the size of the dictionary.

## Example

Listing 9.17 creates a dictionary and displays the number of items that it contains.

*Listing 9.17    Number of Items in Dictionary*

```
<html>
<script language="JScript">
<!-- Hide

//Create dictionary
var fruits = new ActiveXObject("Scripting.Dictionary");

//define elements of dictionary
fruits.Add("A","apple");
fruits.Add("B","berry");
fruits.Add("G","grape");
fruits.Add("O","orange");

document.write("There are ",fruits.Count," items in this dictionary.");

//Hide End -->
</script>
</html>
```

# Dictionary.Exists()

## *JScript3.0+*

## *Syntax*

```
dictionaryobj.Exists(key)
```

## *Description*

The Exists() method of the Dictionary object determines if an item exists in the dictionary based on the *key* that is passed in to the method. If *key* exists, true is returned, otherwise false is returned from the method.

## *Example*

Listing 9.18 creates a dictionary and determines if any fruits that begin with "s" are in the dictionary.

*Listing 9.18   Do "s" Fruits Exist in Dictionary*
```
<html>
<script language="JScript">
<!-- Hide

//Create dictionary
var fruits = new ActiveXObject("Scripting.Dictionary");

//define elements of dictionary
fruits.Add("A","apple");
fruits.Add("B","berry");
fruits.Add("G","grape");
fruits.Add("O","orange");

if(fruits.Exists("S"))
   document.write("The fruit ",fruits.Item('S')," exists in dictionary.");
else
   document.write("No fruits that begin with <b>s</b> exist in dictionary.");

//Hide End -->
</script>
</html>
```

# Dictionary.Item()

## *JScript3.0+*

## *Syntax*

```
dictionaryobj.Item(key)
dictionaryobj.Item(key) = newItem
```

## Description

The Item() property of the Dictionary object provides the capability to retrieve, create, and modify items in the dictionary.

To retrieve an item from the dictionary, simply specify the *key* of the item to be returned in the argument list. The item associated with the *key* will be returned. If the *key* does not exist in the dictionary, a new *key, item* pair will be created in the dictionary and the item will be left empty. Nothing is returned from the method when this scenario occurs.

To create a new *key, item* pair in the dictionary specify a new unique *key* as the method's argument. Directly after the Item() method, place an equal sign followed by the *newItem* to be associated with the *key*. The newly created item will be returned from the method.

Finally, an item can be changed by specifying the *key* associated with the item in the argument list. Directly after the Item() method, place an equal sign followed by the *newItem* that will replace the existing item. The new item will be returned from the method.

## Example

Listing 9.19 uses Item() to create, modify, and retrieve an item from the dictionary.

*Listing 9.19    Retrieving, Creating, and Modifying Items Using* Item()

```
<html>
<html>
<script language="JScript">
<!-- Hide

//Create dictionary
var fruits = new ActiveXObject("Scripting.Dictionary");

//define elements of dictionary
fruits.Add("A","apple");
fruits.Add("B","berry");
fruits.Add("O","orange");

//Use Item() method to create a new item in dictionary.
fruits.Item("G") = "grape";

//Use Item() method to change item associated with G.
fruits.Item("G") = "grapefruit"

//Return item associated with G and display it on screen
document.write("The item ",fruits.Item('G')," is associated with G.");

//Hide End -->
</script>
</html>
```

# Dictionary.Items()

## *JScript3.0+*

## *Syntax*

```
dictionaryobj.Items()
```

## *Description*

The Items() method of the Dictionary object returns all the items in the dictionary in an array.

## *Example*

Listing 9.20 uses Items() method to retrieve all the items that are in the dictionary.

*Listing 9.20    Retrieve Array of Items Using Items() Method*

```
<html>
<script language="JScript">
<!-- Hide

//Create dictionary
var fruits = new ActiveXObject("Scripting.Dictionary");

//define elements of dictionary
fruits.Add("A","apple");
fruits.Add("B","berry");
fruits.Add("G","grape");
fruits.Add("O","orange");

//Create an array
theArray = (new VBArray(fruits.Items())).toArray();

document.write("The array contains:<br>");

//Display items in array
for (i in theArray)
{
   document.write("theArray[",i,"]=",theArray[i],"<br>");
}

//Hide End -->
</script>
</html>
```

# Dictionary.Key()

## *JScript3.0+*

## Syntax

```
dictionaryobj.Key(key) = newKey
```

## Description

The Key() property of the Dictionary object provides the ability to change an existing key in the dictionary. To change a key simply specify the *key* of the item you want changed followed by an equal sign and the *newKey*. If the *key* does not exist in the dictionary, a new *key, item* pair will be created in the dictionary using *newKey* and leaving the item empty. In either case, the new *key* is returned by the method.

## Example

Listing 9.21 uses Key() to change an existing key in the dictionary.

*Listing 9.21    Changing Existing Key Using* Key()

```
<script language="JScript">
<!-- Hide

//Create dictionary
var fruits = new ActiveXObject("Scripting.Dictionary");

//define elements of dictionary
fruits.Add("A","apple");
fruits.Add("B","berry");
fruits.Add("G","grape");
fruits.Add("O","orange");

//Change key "O" to "R"
fruits.Key("O") = "R";

//Hide End -->
</script>
```

# Dictionary.Keys()

## *JScript3.0+*

## Syntax

```
dictionaryobj.Keys()
```

## Description

The Keys() method of the Dictionary object returns all the items in the dictionary in an array.

## Example

Listing 9.22 uses the Keys() method to retrieve all the keys that are in the dictionary.

*Listing 9.22    Retrieve Array of Keys Using* Keys() *Method*

```
<html>
<script language="JScript">
<!-- Hide

//Create dictionary
var fruits = new ActiveXObject("Scripting.Dictionary");

//define elements of dictionary
fruits.Add("A","apple");
fruits.Add("B","berry");
fruits.Add("G","grape");
fruits.Add("O","orange");

//Create an array
theArray = (new VBArray(fruits.Keys())).toArray();

document.write("The array contains:<br>");

//Display keys in array
for (i in theArray)
{
   document.write("theArray[",i,"]=",theArray[i],"<br>");
}

//Hide End -->
</script>
</html>
```

# Dictionary.Remove()

## JScript3.0+

## Syntax

*dictionaryobj*.Remove(key)

## Description

The Remove() method of the Dictionary object removes the *key, item* pair from the dictionary that matches the *key* passed into the method. If no match is found, an error is returned. Nothing is returned from this method.

## Example

Listing 9.23 uses the Remove() method to remove berry from the dictionary.

*Listing 9.23   Remove* `berry` *Item and Associated Key from the Dictionary*

```
<script language="JScript">
<!-- Hide

//Create dictionary
var fruits = new ActiveXObject("Scripting.Dictionary");

//define elements of dictionary
fruits.Add("A","apple");
fruits.Add("B","berry");
fruits.Add("G","grape");
fruits.Add("O","orange");

//Delete berry from dictionary
fruits.Remove("B");

//Hide End -->
</script>
```

# Dictionary.RemoveAll()

## *JScript3.0+*

## *Syntax*

`dictionaryobj.RemoveAll()`

## *Description*

The `RemoveAll()` method of the `Dictionary` object removes all *key, item* pairs from the dictionary. Nothing is returned from this method.

## *Example*

Listing 9.24 uses `RemoveAll()` to remove items from the dictionary.

*Listing 9.24   Remove All Items from the Dictionary*

```
<script language="JScript">
<!-- Hide

//Create dictionary
var fruits = new ActiveXObject("Scripting.Dictionary");

//define elements of dictionary
fruits.Add("A","apple");
fruits.Add("B","berry");
fruits.Add("G","grape");
fruits.Add("O","orange");

//Delete all items from the dictionary
```

```
fruits.RemoveAll();

//Hide End -->
</script>
```

# Drive

## *JScript3.0+*

## *Syntax*

Core JScript object created by calling the `GetDrive()` method of the `FileSystemObject` object.

## *Description*

File System Objects (FSO) provide access to properties, methods, and events, using simple dot notation, to allow you to work with folders and files. A `Drive` is a file system object that provides access to the properties of disk drives and shared networks. A `Drive` object is created using the `GetDrive()` method of the `file system` object. The properties associated with the `Drive` object are listed in Table 9.4. For more information on file system objects, see the `FileSystemObject` section in this chapter.

### *Table 9.4 Properties Associated with Drive Object*

| Item | Description |
| --- | --- |
| AvailableSpace | Returns amount of space available to user on the specified drive or shared network |
| DriveLetter | Returns drive letter of a physical local drive or a shared network |
| DriveType | Returns value indicating the type of the specified drive |
| FileSystem | Returns type of file system in use for the specified drive |
| FreeSpace | Returns amount of free space available to user on the specified drive or shared network |
| IsReady | Returns status the specified drive |
| Path | Returns path for a specified file, folder, or drive |
| RootFolder | Returns a `Folder` object representing the root folder of a specified drive |
| SerialNumber | Returns decimal serial number used to uniquely identify a disk volume |
| ShareName | Returns shared network's name for a specified drive |
| TotalSize | Returns total space of a drive or shared network |
| VolumeName | Sets or returns the volume name of the specified drive |

## *Example*

Listing 9.25 creates a `Drive` object using the `GetDrive()` method associated with the file system object.

*Listing 9.25    Create a* Drive *Object*

```
//Create a string to hold the drive path
var drivePath = "C:";

//Create a file system object
var fileSysObj = new ActiveXObject("Scripting.FileSystemObject");

//Create a Drive object for drive C
var drive = fileSysObj.GetDrive(fileSysObj.GetDriveName(drivePath));
```

# Drive.AvaliableSpace

## JScript3.0+

## Syntax

*driveobject*.AvaliableSpace

## Description

The AvaliableSpace property of the Drive object contains the amount of space available to the user on the specified drive or shared network.

## Example

Listing 9.26 displays the available space on drive C.

*Listing 9.26    Find Available Space on Drive C*

```
<script language="JScript">
<!-- Hide

// Create a string to hold the drive path
var drivePath = "C:";

//Create a file system object
var fileSysObj = new ActiveXObject("Scripting.FileSystemObject");

//Create a Drive object for drive C
var drive = fileSysObj.GetDrive(fileSysObj.GetDriveName(drivePath));

//Display the available space
document.write("Available space for drive ",drivePath," is ");
document.write(drive.AvailableSpace);

//Hide End -->
</script>
```

# Drive.DriveLetter

## *JScript3.0+*

## *Syntax*

`driveobject.DriveLetter`

## *Description*

The `DriveLetter` property of the `Drive` object contains the drive letter of the local drive or a shared network.

## *Example*

Listing 9.27 retrieves the drive letter for the specified drive.

*Listing 9.27   Display the Drive Letter*

```
<script language="JScript">
<!-- Hide

//Create a string to hold the drive path
var drivePath = "C:";

//Create a file system object
var fileSysObj = new ActiveXObject("Scripting.FileSystemObject");

//Create a Drive object for drive C
var drive = fileSysObj.GetDrive(fileSysObj.GetDriveName(drivePath));

//Display the drive letter
document.write("The driver letter for ",drivePath," is ",drive.DriveLetter);

//Hide End -->
</script>
```

# Drive.DriveType

## *JScript3.0+*

## *Syntax*

`driveobject.DriveType`

## *Description*

The `DriveType` property of the `Drive` object contains a numeric value indicating type of the specified drive. The values associated with the `DriveType` are listed in Table 9.5.

### Table 9.5 Drive Type Value Definitions

| Value | Description |
|-------|-------------|
| 0 | Unknown |
| 1 | Removable |
| 2 | Fixed |
| 3 | Network |
| 4 | CD-ROM |
| 5 | RAM Disk |

## Example

Listing 9.28 retrieves the drive type for the specified drive.

*Listing 9.28    Display the Drive Type*

```
<script language="JScript">
<!-- Hide

//Create a string to hold the drive path
var drivePath = "C:";

//Create a file system object
var fileSysObj = new ActiveXObject("Scripting.FileSystemObject");

//Create a Drive object for drive C
var drive = fileSysObj.GetDrive(fileSysObj.GetDriveName(drivePath));

//Display the drive type
document.write("The drive type for ",drivePath," is ",drive.DriveType);

//Hide End -->
</script>
```

# Drive.FileSystem

## JScript3.0+

## Syntax

`driveobject.FileSystem`

## Description

The `FileSystem` property of the `Drive` object contains the type of file system used by the specified drive.

## Example

Listing 9.29 retrieves the file system of the specified drive.

*Listing 9.29   Display the File System*

```
<script language="JScript">
<!-- Hide

//Create a string to hold the drive path
var drivePath = "C:";

//Create a file system object
var fileSysObj = new ActiveXObject("Scripting.FileSystemObject");

//Create a Drive object for drive C
var drive = fileSysObj.GetDrive(fileSysObj.GetDriveName(drivePath));

//Display the file system used by the drive
document.write("Drive ",drivePath," uses the ");
document.write(drive.FileSystem," file system.");

//Hide End -->
</script>
```

# Drive.FreeSpace

## JScript3.0+

## Syntax

*driveobject*.FreeSpace

## Description

The FreeSpace property of the Drive object contains the amount of free space available to the user on the specified drive or shared network.

## Example

Listing 9.30 retrieves the free space associated with the specified drive.

*Listing 9.30   Display the Free Space*

```
<script language="JScript">
<!-- Hide

//Create a string to hold the drive path
var drivePath = "C:";

//Create a file system object
var fileSysObj = new ActiveXObject("Scripting.FileSystemObject");

//Create a Drive object for drive C
```

*continues*

*Listing 9.30    contnued*
```
var drive = fileSysObj.GetDrive(fileSysObj.GetDriveName(drivePath));

//Display free space on the drive
document.write("Drive ",drivePath," has ",drive.FreeSpace," free space.");

//Hide End -->
</script>
```

# Drive.IsReady

## JScript3.0+

## Syntax

```
driveobject.IsReady
```

## Description

The IsReady property of the Drive object contains the status of the specified drive. If the drive is ready, true is returned, otherwise false is returned.

## Example

Listing 9.31 determines if drive A is ready.

*Listing 9.31    Is Drive A Ready*
```
<script language="JScript">
<!-- Hide

//Create a string to hold the drive path
var drivePath = "A:";

//Create a file system objectvar fileSysObj = new
ActiveXObject("Scripting.FileSystemObject");

//Create a Drive object for drive A
var drive = fileSysObj.GetDrive(fileSysObj.GetDriveName(drivePath));

//Determine if drive is ready
if(drive.IsReady)
  document.write("Drive ",drivePath," is ready.");
else
  document.write("Drive ",drivePath," is NOT ready.");

//Hide End -->
</script>
```

# Drive.Path

## *JScript3.0+*

## Syntax

`driveobject.Path`

## Description

The `Path` property of the `Drive` object contains the path of the specified file, folder, or drive.

## Example

Listing 9.32 displays drive C's path.

*Listing 9.32   Display the Path of Drive C*
```jscript
<script language="JScript">
<!-- Hide

//Create a string to hold the drive path
var drivePath = "C:";

//Create a file system objectvar fileSysObj = new
ActiveXObject("Scripting.FileSystemObject");

//Create a Drive object for drive C
var drive = fileSysObj.GetDrive(fileSysObj.GetDriveName(drivePath));

//Display the path of drive C
document.write("The path of drive C is ",drive.Path);

//Hide End -->
</script>
```

# Drive.RootFolder

## *JScript3.0+*

## Syntax

`driveobject.RootFolder`

## Description

The `RootFolder` property of the `Drive` object contains a `Folder` object that represents the root folder of the specified drive.

## Example

Listing 9.33 provides a function that returns the root folder of drive C.

*Listing 9.33   Return the Root Folder*

```
function getCRootFolder()
{
  //Create a string to hold the drive path
  var drivePath = "C:";

  //Create a file system object
  var fileSysObj = new ActiveXObject("Scripting.FileSystemObject");

  //Create a Drive object for drive C
  var drive = fileSysObj.GetDrive(fileSysObj.GetDriveName(drivePath));

  //Return root folder object for drive C
  return(drive.RootFolder);
}
```

# Drive.SerialNumber

## *JScript3.0+*

## *Syntax*

*driveobject*.SerialNumber

## *Description*

The SerialNumber property of the Drive object contains the decimal serial number that uniquely identifies the specified disk volume.

## *Example*

Listing 9.34 displays the unique serial number of drive C.

*Listing 9.34   Unique Serial Number of Drive C*

```
<script language="JScript">
<!-- Hide

//Create a string to hold the drive pathvar drivePath = "C:";

//Create a file system object
var fileSysObj = new ActiveXObject("Scripting.FileSystemObject");

//Create a Drive object for drive C
var drive = fileSysObj.GetDrive(fileSysObj.GetDriveName(drivePath));

//Display the serial number associated with the drive
document.write("Drive serial number is ",drive.SerialNumber);

//Hide End -->
</script>
```

# Drive.ShareName

## *JScript3.0+*

## Syntax

*driveobject*.ShareName

## Description

The ShareName property of the Drive object contains the network share name for the specified drive.

## Example

Listing 9.35 provides a function that returns the share name of a drive.

*Listing 9.35   Return the Share Name*
```
function getShareName(drivePath)
{

  //Create a file system object
  var fileSysObj = new ActiveXObject("Scripting.FileSystemObject");

  //Create a Drive object for the drivePath
  var drive = fileSysObj.GetDrive(fileSysObj.GetDriveName(drivePath));

  //Return share name of the drive
  return(drive.ShareName);
}
```

# Drive.TotalSize

## *JScript3.0+*

## Syntax

*driveobject*.TotalSize

## Description

The TotalSize property of the Drive object returns the total size of the specified drive in bytes.

## Example

Listing 9.36 shows the total size of the drive.

*Listing 9.36   Return the Total Size of Drive*

```
<script language="JScript">
<!-- Hide

//Create a string to hold the drive path
var drivePath = "C:";

//Create a file system object
var fileSysObj = new ActiveXObject("Scripting.FileSystemObject");

//Create a Drive object for drive C
var drive = fileSysObj.GetDrive(fileSysObj.GetDriveName(drivePath));

//Display total space on the drive
document.write("Drive ",drivePath," is ",drive.TotalSize," bytes.");

//Hide End -->
</script>
```

# Drive.VolumeName

## JScript3.0+

## Syntax

```
driveobject.VolumeName
driveobject.VolumeName = newVolumeName
```

## Description

The VolumeName property of the Drive object contains the volume name of the speci-fied drive. If an equal sign follows this property, the volume name is set to *newVolumeName*.

## Example

Listing 9.37 provides a function that returns the volume name of a drive.

*Listing 9.37   Return the Volume Name*

```
function getVolumeName(drivePath)
{

  //Create a file system object
  var fileSysObj = new ActiveXObject("Scripting.FileSystemObject");

  //Create a Drive object for the drivePath
  var drive = fileSysObj.GetDrive(fileSysObj.GetDriveName(drivePath));

  //Return volume name of the drive
  return(drive.VolumeName);
}
```

# Drives

## *JScript3.0+*

## *Syntax*

Core JScript Collection of `Drive` objects.

## *Description*

The `Drives` collection holds a read-only collection of all the available drives. A collection is similar to an array except that an item pointer is used to navigate through the items in the collection rather than an array index. As you would with arrays, you can only move the current item pointer to the first or next element of a collection. Because the Drive object is a collection the drives can only be accessed by using and `Enumerator` object. The properties associated with the `Drives` object are listed in Table 9.6. For more information on accessing collections see the `Enumerator` section in this chapter.

**Table 9.6 Properties Associated with Drives Collection**

| Item | Description |
| --- | --- |
| Count | Returns the number of items in the collection |
| Item | Set or return an item for a specified key in a `Drives` dictionary object |

## *Example*

Listing 9.38 accesses the `Drives` collection using the `FileSystemObject`.

*Listing 9.38   Access a* `Drives` *Object*
```
var fileSysObj = new ActiveXObject("Scripting.FileSystemObject ");
document.write(fileSysObj.Drives.count);
```

# Drives.Count

## *JScript3.0+*

## *Syntax:*

```
Drives.Count
```

## *Description*

The `Count` property of the Drives collection contains the number of items in the collection.

## *Example*

Listing 9.39 displays the number of items contained in the `Drives` collection.

*Listing 9.39   Number of Items in Drives Collection.*

```
<html>
<script language="JScript">
<!-- Hide

//Create a file system object
var fileSysObj = new ActiveXObject("Scripting.FileSystemObject");

//Display number of drives
document.write("There are ",fileSysObj.Drives.count," drives.");

//Hide End -->
</script>
</html>
```

# Drives.Item()

## JScript3.0+

## Syntax

```
new enumeratorobj = Enumerator(Drives)
enumeratorobj.Item()
```

## Description

Because the `Drives` object is a collection, the `Item()` property relates to an enumerated `Drives` collection.

## Example

Listing 9.40 begins by creating an `Enumerator` object to access the `Drives` collection. The `Item()` property is used by the `enumerator` object to access the letter and type of each drive.

*Listing 9.40   Retrieving Drives Using* `Item()`

```
<html>

<H1>Drive Letters and drive types:</H1>

<script language="JScript">
<!-- Hide

//Create enumerator object
var fileSysObj = new ActiveXObject("Scripting.FileSystemObject");
var en = new Enumerator(fileSysObj.Drives);

//Display drive letter and type for each drive.
for (;!en.atEnd();en.moveNext())
{
  document.write("Drive ",en.item().DriveLetter);
```

```
    document.write(" is of type ",en.item().DriveType,"<br>");
}

//Hide End -->
</script>
</html>
```

# Enumerator

## *JScript3.0+*

## *Syntax*

```
var variable = new Enumerator(collection)
```

## *Description*

The `Enumerator` object provides access to items in a collection by allowing iteration through a collection. Accessing items in a collection requires moving the `Enumerator` object to the first element or the next element using special methods. Unlike arrays, enumerators can not access a specific position. To create and `Enumerator` object use the `Enumerator()` constructor. This constructor requires that a collection be passed in as an argument. The methods associated with the `Enumerator` object are listed in Table 9.7.

### *Table 9.7 Methods Associated with Enumerator Object*

| Method | Description |
|---|---|
| atEnd() | Determines if Enumerator is at the end of the collection |
| item() | Returns the current item in the collection |
| moveFirst() | Resets the Enumerator to the first item in the collection |
| moveNext() | Moves Enumerator to the next item in the collection |

## *Example*

Listing 9.41 creates an `Enumerator` object for accessing items in the `Drives` collection.

*Listing 9.41    Creating* Enumerator *Object*
```
var fileSysObj = new ActiveXObject("Scripting.FileSystemObject");
var en = new Enumerator(fileSysObj.Drives);
```

# Enumerator.atEnd()

## *JScript3.0+*

## *Syntax*

```
enumeratorobj.atEnd()
```

## Description

The atEnd() method of the Enumerator object returns true if the enumerator is pointing to the last element in the collection; otherwise, it returns false. True is also returned if the collection is empty or undefined.

## Example

The atEnd() method is used in Listing 9.42 to determine when to stop looping through the for loop.

Listing 9.42    *Stop Looping with the* atEnd() *Method*

```
<html>

<H1>Drive Letters and drive types:</H1>

<script language="JScript">
<!-- Hide

//Create enumerator object
var fileSysObj = new ActiveXObject("Scripting.FileSystemObject");
var en = new Enumerator(fileSysObj.Drives);

//Display drive letter and type for each drive.
for (;!en.atEnd();en.moveNext())
{
  document.write("Drive ",en.item().DriveLetter);
  document.write(" is of type ",en.item().DriveType,"<br>");
}

//Hide End -->
</script>
</html>
```

# Enumerator.item()

## JScript3.0+

## Syntax

```
enumeratorobj.item()
```

## Description

The item() method of the Enumerator object returns the element that the enumerator is pointing to in the collection. If the collection is empty or undefined, undefined is returned.

## Example

The item() method is used in Listing 9.43 to access the drive letter and drive type of the current drive.

*Listing 9.43    Accessing Drives with the* `item()` *Method*

```
<html>

<h1>Drive Letters and drive types:</h1>

<script language="JScript">
<!-- Hide

//Create enumerator object
var fileSysObj = new ActiveXObject("Scripting.FileSystemObject");
var en = new Enumerator(fileSysObj.Drives);

//Display drive letter and type for each drive.
for (;!en.atEnd();en.moveNext())
{
  document.write("Drive ",en.item().DriveLetter);
  document.write(" is of type ",en.item().DriveType,"<br>");
}

//Hide End -->
</script>
</html>
```

# Enumerator.moveFirst()

## *JScript3.0+*

## *Syntax*

*enumeratorobj*.moveFirst()

## *Description*

The `moveFirst()` method of the `Enumerator` object moves the enumerator to the beginning of the collection. If the collection is empty or undefined, `undefined` is returned.

## *Example*

In Listing 9.44, the enumerator is used to access the drive letters and types. The `moveFirst()` method moves the enumerator back to the beginning of the collection so the drive status can be determined for each drive.

*Listing 9.44    Moving the Enumerator to the Beginning of the Collection*

```
<html>

<H1>Drive Letters and drive types:</H1>

<script language="JScript">
```

*continues*

*Listing 9.44    continued*

```
<!-- Hide

//Create enumerator object
var fileSysObj = new ActiveXObject("Scripting.FileSystemObject");
var en = new Enumerator(fileSysObj.Drives);

//Display drive letter and type for each drive.
for (;!en.atEnd();en.moveNext())
{
  document.write("Drive ",en.item().DriveLetter);
  document.write(" is of type ",en.item().DriveType,"<br>");
}

document.write("<h1>Drive Status:</h1>");

//Move enumerator to the beginning of the collection
en.moveFirst();

//Determine if drive is ready.
for (;!en.atEnd();en.moveNext())
{
  if(en.item().IsReady)
  {
    document.write("Drive ",en.item().DriveLetter);
    document.write(" is ready!<br>");
  }
  else
  {
    document.write("Drive ",en.item().DriveLetter);
    document.write(" is not ready!<br>");
  }
}

//Hide End -->
</script>
</html>
```

# Enumerator.moveNext()

## *JScript3.0+*

## *Syntax*

*enumeratorobj*.moveNext()

## Description

The moveNext() method of the Enumerator object moves the enumerator to the next element in the collection. If the collection is empty, undefined is returned.

## Example

The moveNext() method is used in Listing 9.45 to move the enumerator to the next drive in the collection.

*Listing 9.45    Move to the Next Drive Using* moveNext()

```
<html>

<H1>Drive Letters and drive types:</H1>

<script language="JScript">
<!-- Hide

//Create enumerator object
var fileSysObj = new ActiveXObject("Scripting.FileSystemObject");
var en = new Enumerator(fileSysObj.Drives);

//Display drive letter and type for each drive.
for (;!en.atEnd();en.moveNext())
{
  document.write("Drive ",en.item().DriveLetter);
  document.write(" is of type ",en.item().DriveType,"<br>");
}

//Hide End -->
</script>
</html>
```

# Error

## JScript5.0+

## Syntax

```
var variable = new Error();
var variable = new Error(num);
var variable = new Error(num, description);
```

## Description

The Error object contains information about errors. The Error() constructors can be used to create custom errors. The arguments and properties associated with the Error object are listed in Table 9.8.

**Table 9.8 Arguments and Properties Associated with the Error Object**

| Type | Item | Description |
|---|---|---|
| Arguments | number | A number assigned to an error—Zero, if no number is provided in constructor. |
| | description | A string that describes the error—empty string, if no string is provided in constructor. |
| Properties | description | Sets or returns the description string associated with a specific error. |
| | number | Sets or returns the number associated with a specific error. |

**NOTE**

An error number is a 32-bit value where the upper 16-bit word is the facility code and the lower word is the actual error code.

## Example

Listing 9.46 creates an Error object.

*Listing 9.46   Creating Error Object*
```
var myError = Error(35,"My Error");
```

# Error.description

## JScript5.0+

## Syntax

```
errorobj.description
errorobj.description = string
```

## Description

The description property associated with the Error object contains the description of the error. This method is read/write so you can assign descriptions using this property.

## Example

Listing 9.47 creates an Error object and then displays the description.

*Listing 9.47   Description of an Error*
```
<html>

<script language="JScript">
<!-- Hide

//Create an Error object
var myError = new Error(45,"A really big error!");
```

```
//Display description associated with the custom error
document.write("The custom error description is '");
document.write(myError.description,"'");

//Hide End -->
</script>
</html>
```

# Error.number

## *JScript5.0+*

## *Syntax*

```
errorobj.number
errorobj.number = number;
```

## *Description*

The number property associated with the Error object contains the error number of the error. This method is read/write, so you can assign an error number using this property.

## *Example*

Listing 9.48 creates an Error object and then displays the error number.

*Listing 9.48   Error Number Associated with Custom Error*

```
<html>

<script language="JScript">
<!-- Hide

//Create an Error object
var myError = new Error(45,"A really big error!");

//Display error number associated with the custom error
document.write("The custom error number is ");
document.write(myError.number);

//Hide End -->
</script>
</html>
```

# File

## *JScript3.0+*

## *Syntax*

Core JScript object created by calling the ActiveXObject() method and passing Scripting.FileSystemObject.

## Description

The File object provides access to all the properties of a file. The File object has specific properties and methods associated with it, shown in Table 9.9.

**Table 9.9 Properties and Methods of the File Object**

| Property/Method | Description |
| --- | --- |
| Attributes | Refers to the attributes of the file |
| Copy() | Copies a file from one location to another |
| DateCreated | Returns the date a file was created |
| DateLastAccessed | Returns the date a file was last accessed |
| DateLastModified | Returns the date a file was last modified |
| Delete() | Removes a file |
| Drive | Returns the drive on which a file exists |
| Move() | Moves a file from one location to another |
| Name | Returns the name for a file |
| OpenAsTextStream() | Opens a text stream for a file |
| ParentFolder | Returns the parent folder name for a file |
| Path | Returns the path to a file |
| ShortName | Returns the shortname of the file |
| ShortPath | Returns the shortpath of the file |
| Size | Returns the size of a file |
| Type | Returns the file type |

## Example

Listing 9.49 shows how to create a new File object.

*Listing 9.49    Example of the File Object*

```
<html>
<body>

<script language="JavaScript">
<!-- Hide

var myObject, f;

// Create instance of new FileSystemObject
myObject = new ActiveXObject("Scripting.FileSystemObject");
f = myObject.GetFile("f:\\test.txt");
document.write("The name of the file is: " + f.Name);
```

```
// End Hide -->
</script>

</body>
</html>
```

# File.Attributes

## JScript3.0+

## Syntax

`file.Attributes[newattributes]`

## Description

The `Attributes` property is used to determine and/or set the attributes of a file. This property is an array that takes the optional parameter *newattributes*, to set any new attributes. Attributes can be read/write or read-only. The list of valid attributes is shown in Table 9.10.

### Table 9.10 Attribute properties

| Property | Description |
| --- | --- |
| 0 | Specifies a Normal file. No attributes set. |
| 1 | Specifies that a file is a Read-only file. Attribute is read/write. |
| 2 | Specifies that a file is Hidden. Attribute is read/write. |
| 4 | Refers to a system file. Attribute is read/write. |
| 8 | Refers to the disk drive volume label. Attribute is read-only. |
|  | Refers to a folder in a directory. Attribute is read-only. |
| 32 | Specifies that a file has changed since the last backup. Attribute is read/write. |
| 64 | Refers to a link or shortcut. Attribute is read-only. |
| 128 | Refers to the disk drive volume label. Attribute is read-only. |

## Example

Listing 9.50 shows how the `Attributes` property is used.

*Listing 9.50  Example of `Attributes`*

```
<html>
<body>

<script language="JScript">
<!--Hide
function get()
{
// declare variables.
```

*continues*

*Listing 9.50    continued*

```
var myObject, f;

// create a new File object
myObject = new ActiveXObject("Scripting.FileSystemObject");
f = myObject.GetFile("c:\\test.txt");

// check for all the attributes for the file.
if(!f.attributes) alert("no attributes set");
var strAttributes = "";
if (f.attributes & 1) strAttributes += "Read only\n";
if (f.attributes & 2) strAttributes +="Hidden\n";
if (f.attributes & 4) strAttributes +="System\n";
if (f.attributes & 8) strAttributes +="Volume label\n";
if (f.attributes & 16) strAttributes +="Folder\n";
if (f.attributes & 32) strAttributes +="Archive bit set\n";
if (f.attributes & 64) strAttributes +="Shortcut or link\n";
if (f.attributes & 128) strAttributes +="File is compressed\n";
alert(strAttributes);

}
// End Hide -->
</script>

Gets a files attributes.

<form name="myForm">
<input type="Button" value="Get Attributes" onClick='get()'>
</form>

</body>
</html>
```

# File.Copy()

## JScript3.0+

## Syntax

`file.Copy(destination, overwrite)`

## Description

The Copy() method is used to copy a specified file from one location to another. This method takes two parameters. *destination* is the location to which to copy the file. *overwrite* is a Boolean value indicating whether to overwrite an existing file of the same name.

## Example

Listing 9.51 shows how to use the Copy() method to copy the test.txt file to mytest.txt.

*Listing 9.51   Example of* Copy()

```
<html>
<BODY>

<script language="JScript">
<!-- Hide

// function creates a new file object and then copies it to
// another file.
function copy()
{
  var myObject, f;
  //Create an instance of the FileSystemObject
  myObject = new ActiveXObject("Scripting.FileSystemObject");
  f = myObject.file.copy("c:\\test.txt", "c:\\mytest.txt");
// End Hide -->
}
</script>

Copy test.txt to mytest.txt

<form name="myForm">
<INPUT type="Button" value="Copy File" onClick='copy()'>
</form>

</BODY>
</html>
```

# File.DateCreated

## JScript3.0+

## Syntax

`file`.DateCreated

## Description

The DateCreated property is used to get the date in which the file was created.

## Example

Listing 9.52 shows how to use to DateCreated property.

*Listing 9.52    Example of* `DateCreated`

```
<html>
<BODY>

<script language="JScript">
<!-- Hide

// function gets the date of when the file "mytest.txt" was
// created.
function get()
{
  var myObject, f, date;
  // Create an instance of the FileSystemObject
  myObject = new ActiveXObject("Scripting.FileSystemObject");
  f = myObject.GetFile("c:\\mytest.txt");

  // determine the date when the file was created.
  date = f.DateCreated;
  alert ("The date this file was created is: " + date);
}

//-->
</script>

Get the date that mytest.txt was created.

<form name="myForm">
<INPUT type="Button" value="Get Date" onClick='get()'>
</form>

</BODY>
</html>
```

# File.DateLastAccessed

## JScript3.0+

## Syntax

`file.DateLastAccessed`

## Description

The `DateLastAccessed` property is used to find out the last date that the file was accessed.

## Example

Listing 9.53 shows how the `DateLastAccessed` property is used.

*Listing 9.53    Example of* `DateLastAccessed`

```
<html>
<BODY>

<script language="JScript">
<!-- Hide

// function determines the date of when the file was
// last accessed.
function get()
{
  var myObject, f, date;
  // Create an instance of the FileSystemObject
  myObject = new ActiveXObject("Scripting.FileSystemObject");
  f = myObject.GetFile("c:\\mytest.txt");
  date = f.DateLastAccessed;

  // inform the user of the date when the file was last accessed.
  alert ("The date this file was last accessed is: " + date);
}

//-->
</script>

Get the date that mytest.txt was last accessed.

<form name="myForm">
<INPUT type="Button" value="Get Date" onClick='get()'>
</form>

</BODY>
</html>
```

# File.DateLastModified

## JScript3.0+

## Syntax

`file.DateLastModified`

## Description

The `DateLastModified` property returns the date when the file was last modified.

## Example

Listing 9.54 shows how the `DateLastModified` property is used.

*Listing 9.54   Example of* `DateLastModified`

```
<html>
<BODY>

<script language="JScript">
<!-- Hide

// function creates a new file object and the determines when
// it was last modified.
function get()
{
  var myObject, f, date;
  // Create an instance of the FileSystemObject
  myObject = new ActiveXObject("Scripting.FileSystemObject");
  f = myObject.GetFile("c:\\mytest.txt");
  date = f.DateLastModified;

  // inform the user of the date when the file was last modified.
  alert ("The date this file was last modified is: " + date);
}

//-->
</script>

Get the date that mytest.txt was last modified.

<form name="myForm">
<INPUT type="Button" value="Get Date" onClick='get()'>
</form>

</BODY>
</html>
```

# File.Delete()

## *JScript3.0+*

## *Syntax*

`file.Delete()`

## *Description*

The `Delete()` method is used to delete a specified file.

## *Example*

Listing 9.55 shows how to delete a file.

*Listing 9.55    Example of the* `Delete()` *Method*

```
<html>
<body>

<script language="JScript">
<!-- Hide

// function creates a new file and then delete it using the
// delete method
function remove()
{
  var myObject;
  // Create an instance of the FileSystemObject
  myObject = new ActiveXObject("Scripting.FileSystemObject");

  var f = myObject.GetFile("c:\\mytest.txt");
  f.Delete();

}

//-->
</script>

Delete file "mytest.txt".

<form name="myForm">
<input type="Button" vvalue="Delete File" onClick='remove()'>
</form>

</body>
</html>
```

# File.Drive

## JScript3.0+

## Syntax

`file.Drive`

## Description

The `Drive` property returns the drive letter of the drive on which the specified file or folder resides.

## Example

Listing 9.56 shows how the `Drive` property is used to get the letter of the drive that contains the specified file.

*Listing 9.56    Example of the* `Drive` *Property*

```
<html>
<BODY>

<script language="JScript">
<!-- Hide

// function gets the drive letter on which the file resides and
// then informs the user of the drive.
function get()
{
  var myObject, f, d;
  // Create an instance of the FileSystemObject
  myObject = new ActiveXObject("Scripting.FileSystemObject");
  f = myObject.GetFile("c:\\test.txt");
  d = f.drive;
  alert("The drive that test.txt resides is: " + d);
}

//-->
</script>

Get Drive for test.txt

<form name="myForm">
<INPUT type="Button" value="Get Drive" onClick='get()'>
</form>

</BODY>
</html>
```

# File.Move()

## JScript3.0+

## Syntax

`file.Move(destination)`

## Description

The Move method is used to move a file from one location to another. This method takes a single parameter, *destination*, which represents the location to which the file is to be moved.

## Example

Listing 9.57 shows how the to move a file from one location to another.

*Listing 9.57    Example of* Move *Method*

```
<html>
<body>

<script language="JScript">
<!-- Hide

// function creates a new file and then moves it from the
// C drive to the E drive.
function move()
{
  var myObject, f;
  // Create an instance of the FileSystemObject
  myObject = new ActiveXObject("Scripting.FileSystemObject");
  f =   myObject.GetFile("c:\\test.txt");
  f.Move("e:\\");
}

//-->
</script>

Move the file test.txt

<form name="myForm">
<input type="Button" vvalue="Move File" onClick='move()'>
</form>

</body>
</html>
```

# File.Name

## *JScript3.0+*

## *Syntax*

`file`.Name

## *Description*

The Name property is used to either set or get the name of a file object.

## *Example*

Listing 9.58 shows how the Name property is used to get the filename.

*Listing 9.58    Example of* Name *Property*

```
<html>
<BODY>

<script language="JScript">
```

*continues*

*Listing 9.58   continued*

```
<!-- Hide

// function creates a new file and uses the name property
// to display the name of the newly created file.
function get()
{
  var myObject, f;
  // Create an instance of the FileSystemObject
  myObject = new ActiveXObject("Scripting.FileSystemObject");
  f =   myObject.GetFile("c:\\test.txt");
  alert("The name of the file is: " + f.Name);
}

//-->
</script>

<form name="myForm">
<INPUT type="Button" value="Get Name" onClick='get()'>
</form>

</BODY>
</html>
```

# File.OpenAsTextStream()

## JScript3.0+

## Syntax

```
file.OpenAsTextStream(iomode, format)
```

## Description

The OpenAsTextStream method is used to open a specified text stream that can be used to read or write to a file. This method takes two parameters. The first parameter, *iomode*, specifies the mode for the file. Valid modes are ForReading, ForWriting, and ForAppending. The second parameter, *format*, specifies the format of the file. The default value is ASCII, however you can have one of the three settings shown in Table 9.11.

### Table 9.11 Settings for the format Parameter

| Constant | Value | Description |
|---|---|---|
| TristateUseDefault | -2 | Opens the file using the systemdefault |
| TristateTrue | -1 | Opens the file as Unicode |
| TristateFalse | 0 | Opens the file as ASCII mode |

## *Example*

Listing 9.59 uses the `OpenAsTextStream` method to open a stream to the file `dummy.txt`.

*Listing 9.59    Example of* `OpenAsTextStream`

```
<html>
<body>

<script language="JScript">
<!-- Hide

function open()
{
  var myObject, f, text;

  // define the variables locally
  var TristateFalse = 0;
  var ForWriting = 2;

  // Create an instance of the FileSystemObject
  myObject = new ActiveXObject("Scripting.FileSystemObject");
  myObject.CreateTextFile( "c:\\tmp\\dummy.txt" );
  f = myObject.GetFile("c:\\tmp\\dummy.txt");
  text = f.OpenAsTextStream(ForWriting, TristateFalse);
  text.Write( "Just some nonsense" );
  text.Close( );
}

//-->
</script>

<form name="myForm">
<input type="Button" value="open a filestream" onClick='open()'>
</form>

</body>
</html>
```

# File.ParentFolder

## *JScript3.0+*

## *Syntax*

`file.ParentFolder`

## *Description*

The `ParentFolder` property is used to determine the parent folder from which the file was obtained.

## Example

Listing 9.60 shows how the `ParentFolder` property is used.

*Listing 9.60    Example of* `ParentFolder`

```
<html>
<body>

<script language="JScript">
<!-- Hide

// function displays the path to the name of the parent folder.
function get()
{
  var myObject, f;
  // Create an instance of the FileSystemObject
  myObject = new ActiveXObject("Scripting.FileSystemObject");
  f = myObject.GetFile("c:\\tmp\\myTest.txt");
  alert("The name of the parent folder is: " + f.ParentFolder.Path);
}

//-->
</script>

Click to get the name of the parent folder
<form name="myForm">
<input type="Button" value="Get Parent Folder" onClick='get()'>
</form>

</body>
</html>
```

# File.Path

## JScript3.0+

## Syntax

`file`.Path

## Description

The `Path` property is used to get the path for a specified file.

## Example

Listing 9.61 shows an example of the `Path` property.

*Listing 9.61    Example of the* `Path` *Property*

```
<html>
<body>
```

```
<script language="JScript">
<!-- Hide
function getPath()
{
  var myObject, f;
  // Create an instance of the FileSystemObject
  myObject = new ActiveXObject("Scripting.FileSystemObject");
  f = myObject.GetFile("c:\\tmp\\myTest.txt");
  alert("The name of the path is: " + f.Path);
}

//-->
</script>

<form name="myForm">
<input type="Button" value="Get Path" onClick='getPath()'>
</form>
</body>
</html>
```

# File.ShortName

## JScript3.0+

## Syntax

*file*.ShortName

## Description

The ShortName property returns the short name used by programs that require the earlier 8.3 naming convention.

## Example

Listing 9.62 shows how to access the short name of the file.

*Listing 9.62    Example of the* ShortName *Property*

```
<html>
<body>

<script language="JScript">
<!-- Hide

// function gets the shortname for the file.
function get()
{
  var myObject, f;
// Create an instance of the FileSystemObject
```

*continues*

Listing 9.62    *continued*
```
  myObject = new ActiveXObject("Scripting.FileSystemObject");
  f = myObject.GetFile("c:\\tmp\\myTest.txt");
  alert("The file ShortName is: " + f.ShortName);
}


//-->
</script>

<form name="myForm">
<input type="Button" value="Get Shortname" onClick='get()'>
</form>

</body>
</html>
```

# File.ShortPath

## JScript3.0+

## Syntax

`file`.ShortPath

## Description

The ShortPath property returns the short path used by programs that require the earlier 8.3 naming convention.

## Example

Listing 9.63 shows how to get the short path for the specified file.

Listing 9.63    *Example of* ShortPath
```
<html>
<BODY>

<script language="JScript">
<!-- Hide

// function gets the shortpath of the file object.
function get()
{
  var myObject, f;
  // Create an instance of the FileSystemObject
  myObject = new ActiveXObject("Scripting.FileSystemObject");
  f = myObject.GetFile("c:\\tmp\\myTest.txt");
  alert("The file ShortPath name is: " + f.ShortPath);
}

//-->
```

```
</script>

<form name="myForm">
<INPUT type="Button" value="Get Shortpath" onClick='get()'>
</form>

</BODY>
</html>
```

# File.Size

## JScript3.0+

## Syntax

`file.Size`

## Description

The Size property returns the size of the specified file.

## Example

In Listing 9.64, the Size property is used to get the filesize.

*Listing 9.64    Example of Size*

```
<html>
<BODY>

<script language="JScript">
<!-- Hide
function get()
{
  var myObject, f;
  // Create an instance of the FileSystemObject
  myObject = new ActiveXObject("Scripting.FileSystemObject");
  f = myObject.GetFile("c:\\tmp\\myTest.txt");
  alert("The file size is: " + f.Size);
}

//-->
</script>

<form name="myForm">
type=value=<input type="Button" value="Get File Size" onClick='get()'>
</form>

</body>
</html>
```

# File.Type

## JScript3.0+

## Syntax

`file.Type`

## Description

The Type property is used to get information pertaining to the type of file.

## Example

Listing 9.65 shows an example of how the Type property is used to get the type return the type of file that myTest.txt is.

*Listing 9.65   Example of the* Type *Property*

```
<html>
<body>

<script language="JScript">
<!-- Hide
function get()
{
  var myObject, f;
  // Create an instance of the FileSystemObject
  myObject = new ActiveXObject("Scripting.FileSystemObject");

  // Gets the file myTest.txt
  f = myObject.GetFile("c:\\tmp\\myTest.txt");
  alert("The name type is: " + f.Type);
}

//-->
</script>

<form name="myForm">
<input type="Button" value="Get File Type" onClick='get()'>
</form>

</body>
</html>
```

# Files

## JScript3.0+

## Syntax

Core JScript Collection of File objects.

## Description

The Files object represents a collection of files in a folder. The Files object has specific properties and methods associated with it, which are shown in Table 9.12.

### Table 9.12 Properties and Methods of the Files Object

| Property/Method | Description |
|---|---|
| Count | Returns the number of items in a collection |
| Item | Sets or returns an item based on a specific key |

## Example

Listing 9.66 shows how to create a new Files object.

*Listing 9.66   Example of Files Object*

```
<html>
<body>

<script language="JScript">
<!-- Hide

// function displays a list of the files
// in the specified folder.
function ShowList(foldername)
{
  var myObject, f, MyFiles, names;
  // Create an instance of the FileSystemObject
  myObject = new ActiveXObject("Scripting.FileSystemObject");
  f = myObject.GetFolder(foldername);

  // stores the files in an enumerator
  myFiles = new Enumerator(f.files);
  names="";
  for (i=0; !myFiles.atEnd(); myFiles.moveNext()){
      names += myFiles.item();
      names += "<br>";
  }
  document.write(names);
}

// End Hide -->
</script>

<form name="form1">
Enter the name of an existing folder
including the drive letter if it is not on the C drive.
<input type="text" size="35" name="file">
```

*continues*

*Listing 9.66    continued*

```
<br><br>
<input type="Button" value="Get File List"
onClick='ShowList(document.form1.file.value)'>
</form>

</body>
</html>
```

# Files.Count

## JScript2.0+

## Syntax

```
files.Count
```

## Description

The Count property returns the number of items in the Files collection.

## Example

Listing 9.67 shows how to use the Count property to get the number of items in the Files collection.

*Listing 9.67    Example of the Count Property*

```
<html>
<body>

<script language="JScript">
<!-- Hide

// function gets the count of the file collection
// in a specified folder.
function getCount(foldername)
{
  var myObject, f, filesCount;
  // Create an instance of the FileSystemObject
  myObject = new ActiveXObject("Scripting.FileSystemObject");
  f = myObject.GetFolder(foldername);

  // gets the number of files in a folder
  filesCount = f.files.Count;

  document.write("The number of files in this folder is: " + filesCount);
}

// End Hide -->
</script>
```

```
<form name="myForm">

Enter the name of a folder which contains files.
<input type="text" size="35" name="file">
<br><br>
<input type="Button" value="Get File Count"
onClick='getCount(document.form1.file.value)'>
</form>

</body>
</html>
```

# Files.Item

## JScript2.0+

## Syntax

`files.Item`

## Description

The `Item` property sets or returns an `item` based on a specified `key` in a `collection` of files.

## Example

Listing 9.68 shows how to use the `Item` property.

*Listing 9.68   Example of the `Item` Property*

```
<html>
<body>

<script language="JScript">
<!-- Hide

// function gets the Item of the file collection
// in a specified folder.
function getItem(foldername)
{
  var myObject, f, filesItem;

  // create instance of the FileSystemObject
  myObject = new ActiveXObject("Scripting.FileSystemObject");

  f = myObject.GetFolder(foldername);

  // gets the setup.exe file
```

*continues*

*Listing 9.68    continued*

```
  filesItem = f.files.Item("Setup.exe");

  document.write("The file that you got is: " + filesItem);
}// End Hide -->
</script>

<form name="myForm">
Enter the name of a folder which contains files.
<input type="text" size="35" name="file">
<br><br>
<input type="Button" value="Get File Item"
onClick='getItem(document.form1.file.value)'>
</form>

</body>
</html>
```

# FileSystemObject

## JScript3.0+

## Syntax

Core JScript object created by calling the `ActiveXObject()` method passing `Scripting.FileSystemObject`.

## Description

The `FileSystemObject` object provides access to the computer's file system. The `FileSystemObject` object has specific properties and methods associated with it, which are shown in Table 9.13.

### Table 9.13 Properties and Methods of the FileSystemObject Object

| Property/Method | Description |
| --- | --- |
| `BuildPath()` | Appends information to a file path |
| `CopyFile()` | Copies a file from one location to another |
| `CopyFolder()` | Copies a folder from one location to another |
| `CreateFolder()` | Creates a new folder object |
| `CreateTextfile()` | Creates a new text file object |
| `DeleteFile()` | Removes a file |
| `DeleteFolder()` | Removes a folder object |
| `DriveExists()` | Determines whether a drive exists |
| `Drives` | Returns a `Drives` collection, containing all the available drive objects |
| `FileExists()` | Determines whether a file exists |
| `FolderExists()` | Determines whether a folder exists |

| Property/Method | Description |
|---|---|
| GetAbsolutePathName() | Returns the absolute pathname for a file |
| GetBaseName() | Gets the base name of the last component |
| GetDrive() | Gets the drive letter for a file |
| GetDriveName() | Gets the drive name on which a file resides |
| ExtensionName() | Returns the extension for a file |
| GetFile() | Gets the file object |
| GetFileName() | Gets the name of a file |
| GetFolder() | Gets the folder name that contains a file |
| GetParentFolderName() | Gets the parent folder's name |
| GetSpecialFolder() | Gets the folder names for special folders |
| GetTempName() | Creates a randomly generated temporary file |
| MoveFile() | Moves a file from one location to another |
| MoveFolder() | Moves a folder and its contents from one location to another |
| OpentextFile() | Opens a text file stream to a file |

## Example

Listing 9.69 shows how to create a new FileSystemObject object.

*Listing 9.69   Example of* FileSystemObject *Object*

```
<html>
<body>

<script language="JScript">
<!-- Hide

// create a new FileSystemObject
var myObject;
myObject = new ActiveXObject("Scripting.FileSystemObject");

// End Hide -->
</script>

</body>
</html>
```

# FileSystemObject.BuildPath()

## JScript3.0+

## Syntax

`filesystemobject.BuildPath(path, name)`

*path*   String representing existing path

*name*   Name being appended to existing path

## Description

The BuildPath() method is used to append a name to an existing path. A separator is inserted between the existing path and the appended name if necessary.

## Example

Listing 9.70 shows how to use the BuildPath() method.

*Listing 9.70    Example of BuildPath()*

```
<html>
<body>

<script language="JScript">
<!--Hide

function GetNewPath(path)
{
  var myObject, newpath;
  // Create an instance of the FileSystemObject
  myObject = new ActiveXObject("Scripting.FileSystemObject");
  newpath = myObject.BuildPath(path, "/newstuff");
  alert("The result is: " + newpath);
}
// End Hide -->
</script>

Append "/newstuff" to the existing path: "c:/tmp"

<form name="myForm">
<input type="Button" value="Build Path" onClick='GetNewPath("c:/tmp")'>
</form>

</body>
</html>
```

# FileSystemObject.CopyFile()

## JScript3.0+

## Syntax

`filesystemobject.CopyFile(source, destination, overwrite)`

## Description

The CopyFile() method is used to copy one or more files to a specified directory. This method takes three parameters. The first parameter, *source*, is a string specifying source path and filename from which to copy. The second parameter, *destination*, is a string specifying destination path a filename to which to copy. The final parameter, *overwrite*, is a Boolean value indicating whether to overwrite an existing file or not.

## Example

Listing 9.71 shows how to copy a file from one location to another.

*Listing 9.71  Example of* `CopyFile()`

```
<html>
<body>

<script language="JScript">
<!-- Hide

function copy()
{
  var myObject, newpath;
  // Create an instance of the FileSystemObject
  myObject = new ActiveXObject("Scripting.FileSystemObject");

  // Copies file test.txt from the root C drive to the tmp folder.
  myObject.CopyFile ("c:\\test.txt", "c:\\tmp\\myTest.txt");
}

// End Hide -->
</script>

Copy "c:\test.txt" to the existing path: "c:\tmp\myTest.txt"

<form name="myForm">
<input type="Button" value="Copy File" onClick='copy()'>
</form>

</body>
</html>
```

# FileSystemObject.CopyFolder()

## JScript3.0+

## Syntax

`filesystemobject.CopyFolder(source, destination, overwrite)`

## Description

The `CopyFolder()` method copies a folder from a source to a destination. This method takes three parameters. The first parameter, *source*, is a string specifying source path and filename from which to copy. The second parameter, *destination*, is a string specifying destination path a filename to which to copy. The final parameter, *overwrite*, is a Boolean value indicating whether to overwrite an existing file or not.

## Example

Listing 9.72 shows how to use the CopyFolder() method. A new FileSystemObject is created, providing access to the computer's file system. It is then used to copy all the contents of the folder tmp to newtmp. The * specifies that all the contents of tmp are to be copied.

*Listing 9.72    Example of* CopyFolder()

```
<html>
<body>

<script language="JScript">
<!-- Hide

// function creates a new FileSystemObject and copies
// the file from one folder to another
function copy()
{
  var myObject;
  // Create an instance of the FileSystemObject
  myObject = new ActiveXObject("Scripting.FileSystemObject");

  // Copies all files and folders from "tmp" to "newtmp"
  myObject.CopyFolder ("c:\\tmp\\*", "c:\\newtmp\\");
}

// End Hide -->
</script>

Copy Folder "c:\tmp" to the folder "c:\newtmp"

<form name="myForm">
<input type="Button" value="Copy Folder" onClick='copy()'>
</form>

</body>
</html>
```

# FileSystemObject.CreateFolder()

## JScript3.0+

## Syntax

*filesystemobject*.CreateFolder(*name*)

## Description

The CreateFolder() method is used to create a new folder. This method takes the *name* parameter, which is a string specifying folder name to create.

## Example

Listing 9.73 shows how to use the CreateFolder() method.

*Listing 9.73   Example of* CreateFolder()

```
<html>
<body>

<script language="JScript">
<!-- Hide

// Function creates a new folder called "newtmp"
function create()
{
  var myObject, newfolder;
  // Create an instance of the FileSystemObject
  myObject = new ActiveXObject("Scripting.FileSystemObject");

  // Creates the folder newtmp
  newfolder = myObject.CreateFolder ("c:\\newtmp\\");
}

// End Hide -->
</script>

Create Folder: "c:\newtmp"

<form name="myForm">
<input type="Button" value="Click to Create New Folder" onClick='create()'>
</form>

</body>
</html>
```

# FileSystemObject.CreateTextFile()

## JScript2.0+

## Syntax

*filesystemobject*.CreateTextFile(*filename*, *overwrite*)

## Description

The CreateTextFile() method is used to create a new text file. This method takes two parameters. The first parameter, *filename*, is a string specifying the name of the file to create, while the second parameter, *overwrite*, is a Boolean value indicating whether to overwrite an existing file.

## Example

Listing 9.74 shows how to use the `CreateTextFile()` method. An instance of the `FileSystemObject` is created, which in turn uses the `CreateTextFile()` method to create the file `testing.txt`.

*Listing 9.74 Example of* `CreateTextFile()`

```
<html>
<body>

<script language="JScript">
<!-- Hide

// function creates a new text file called "testing.txt"
function createFile()
{
  var myObject, newfile;
  // Create an instance of the FileSystemObject
  myObject = new ActiveXObject("Scripting.FileSystemObject");

  // Creates a text file called "testing.txt"
  newfile = myObject.CreateTextFile("c:\\testing.txt", false);
}

// End Hide -->
</script>

Create Text file "testing.txt"

<form name="myForm">
<input type="Button" value="Click to Create New File" onClick='createFile()'>
</form>

</body>
</html>
```

# FileSystemObject.DeleteFile()

## JScript3.0+

## Syntax

`filesystemobject.DeleteFile(filename, force)`

## Description

The DeleteFile() method is used to delete an existing file. An instance of the `FileSystemObject` is created, which uses the `DeleteFile()` method to remove the file `testing.txt`. This method takes two parameters. The first parameter, *filename*, is a string specifying the name of the file to delete, while *force* is a Boolean value indicating whether a file that has read only permissions can be deleted.

## *Example*

Listing 9.75 shows how to delete a file.

*Listing 9.75   Example of* `DeleteFile()`

```
<html>
<body>

<script language="JScript">
<!-- Hide

// function deletes the file "texting.txt"
function deleteFile()
{
  var myObject;
  // Create an instance of the FileSystemObject
  myObject = new ActiveXObject("Scripting.FileSystemObject");

  // Delete the file texting.txt
  myObject.DeleteFile("c:\\testing.txt");
}

// End Hide -->
</script>

Delete Text file "testing.txt"

<form name="myForm">
<input type="Button" value="Click to Delete File" onClick='deleteFile()'>
</form>

</body>
</html>
```

# FileSystemObject.DeleteFolder()

## *JScript3.0+*

## *Syntax*

`filesystemobject.DeleteFolder(foldername, force)`

## *Description*

The `DeleteFolder()` method is used to remove an existing folder and all its contents. This method takes two parameters. The first parameter, `foldername`, is a string specifying the name of the folder to delete, while `force` is a Boolean value indicating whether a file that has read only permissions can be deleted.

## Example

Listing 9.76 shows how the DeleteFolder() method is used. An instance of the FileSystemObject is created, which uses the DeleteFolder() method to remove the folder newtmp.

*Listing 9.76  Example of* DeleteFolder()

```
<html>
<body>

<script language="JScript">
<!-- Hide

// function deletes the folder "newtmp"
function deleteFolder()
{
  var myObject;
  // Create an instance of the FileSystemObject
  myObject = new ActiveXObject("Scripting.FileSystemObject");

  // Delete the folder "newtmp"
  myObject.DeleteFolder("c:\\newtmp");
}

// End Hide -->
</script>

Delete Folder: "newtmp"

<form name="myForm">
<input type="Button" value="Click to Delete Folder" onClick='deleteFolder()'>
</form>

</body>
</html>
```

# FileSystemObject.DriveExists()

## JScript3.0+

## Syntax

*filesystemobject*.DriveExists(*letter*)

## Description

The DriveExists() method is used to determine whether a drive exists or not. This method takes *letter* as a parameter, which specifies a drive letter to look for.

## Example

Listing 9.77 shows how to check for the existence of a D drive.

*Listing 9.77   Example of* `DriveExists()`

```
<html>
<body>

<script language="JScript">
<!-- Hide

// function checks for the existance of drive D.
function checkDrive()
{
  var myObject;
  // Create an instance of the FileSystemObject
  myObject = new ActiveXObject("Scripting.FileSystemObject");

  // Check for the existance of a D drive
    if(myObject.DriveExists("d")){
    alert("Drive D exists");
    }
    else {
    alert("Drive D doesn't exist");
    }
}

// End Hide -->
</script>

Check for drive "D"

<form name="myForm">
<input type="Button" value="Check drive" onClick='checkDrive()'>
</form>

</body>
</html>
```

# FileSystemObject.Drives

## JScript3.0+

## Syntax

`filesystemobject.Drives`

## Description

The `Drives` collection is a collection that holds all the `Drive` objects. It is used to get an object consisting of all the drives.

## Example

Listing 9.78 shows how to check for drives.

*Listing 9.78    Example of* Drives

```
<html>
<body>

<script language="JScript">
<!-- Hide

function getdrive()
{
  var myObject, drive, e;
  // Create an instance of the FileSystemObject
  myObject = new ActiveXObject("Scripting.FileSystemObject");
  drive = myObject.Drives;

  // Store drives in a enumerator e
  e = new Enumerator(drive);
  alert("The first drive is: " + e.item());
}

// End Hide -->
</script>

<form name="myForm">
<input type="Button" value="Get Drive Name" onClick='getdrive()'>
</form>

</body>
</html>
```

# FileSystemObject.FileExists()

## JScript3.0+

## Syntax

`filesystemobject.FileExists(filename)`

## Description

The FileExists() method is used to determine whether or not a file exists on the current system. This method takes *filename* as its only parameter, which represents the name of file to check.

## Example

Listing 9.79 shows how to use the FileExists() method to check to see if the file test.txt exists.

*Listing 9.79   Example of* `FileExists()`

```
<html>
<body>

<script language="JScript">
<!-- Hide

function checkfile()
{
  var myObject;
  // Create an instance of the FileSystemObject
  myObject = new ActiveXObject("Scripting.FileSystemObject");

  // check to see if the file exists and alert user of status
  if(myObject.FileExists("c:\\test.txt")){
  alert("File Exists");
  }
  else {
  alert("File doesn't exist");
   }
}

// End Hide -->
</script>

Check for file "test.txt"

<form name="myForm">
<input type="Button" value="Check file" onClick='checkfile()'>
</form>

</body>
</html>
```

# FileSystemObject.FolderExists()

## *JScript3.0+*

## *Syntax:*

*filesystemobject*.FolderExists(*foldername*)

## *Description*

The `FolderExists()` method is used to determine whether or not a specified folder exists on the current system. This method takes *foldername* as its only parameter, which represents the name of folder to check.

## Example

Listing 9.80 shows an example of how to determine if the tmp folder exists.

*Listing 9.80    Example of* FolderExists()

```
<html>
<body>

<script language="JScript">
<!-- Hide

function checkfolder()
{
  var myObject;
  // Create an instance of the FileSystemObject
  myObject = new ActiveXObject("Scripting.FileSystemObject");


  // Check for the tmp folder
  if(myObject.FolderExists("c:\\tmp")){
  alert("tmp Folder Exists");
    }
    else {
    alert("tmp Folder doesn't exist");
    }
}

// End Hide -->
</script>

Check for folder "tmp"

<form name="myForm">
<input type="Button" value="Check Folder" onClick='checkfolder()'>
</form>

</body>
</html>
```

# FileSystemObject.GetAbsolutePathName()

## JScript3.0+

## Syntax

`filesystemobject.GetAbsolutePathName(/Pathname/)`

## Description

The GetAbsolutePathName() method returns a complete and unambiguous path from a provided path specification.

## Example

Listing 9.81 shows how to use the GetAbsolutePathName() method.

*Listing 9.81   Example of* GetAbsolutePathName()

```
<html>
<body>

<script language="JScript">
<!-- Hide

// function gets the absolute path and informs the user
function getpath()
{
  var myObject, path;
  // Create an instance of the FileSystemObject
  myObject = new ActiveXObject("Scripting.FileSystemObject");
  path = myObject.GetAbsolutePathName("c:\\")
  alert("Absolute Path Name is: " + path);
}

// End Hide -->
</script>

Get the Absolute Path for C:\

<form name="myForm">
<input type="Button" value="Get Absolute Path" onClick='getpath()'>
</form>

</body>
</html>
```

# FileSystemObject.GetBaseName()

## JScript3.0+

## Syntax

```
filesystemobject.GetBaseName(path)
```

*path*   Required parameter specifying the component whose base name is to be returned.

## Description

The GetBaseName() method returns a string containing the base name of a file or folder, without any extension or path.

## Example

Listing 9.82 shows how the GetBaseName() method is used.

*Listing 9.82    Example of* GetBaseName()

```
<html>
<body>

<script language="JScript">
<!-- Hide

// function gets the Base name of the FileSystemObject
function get()
{
  var myObject, b;
  // Create an instance of the FileSystemObject
  myObject = new ActiveXObject("Scripting.FileSystemObject");

  // Gets the specified base name
  b = myObject.GetBaseName("c:\\tmp\\myTest.txt");
  alert("The base name is: " + b);
}

// End Hide -->
</script>

<form name="myForm">
<input type="Button" value="Get Base" onClick='get()'>
</form>

</body>
</html>
```

# FileSystemObject.GetDrive()

## JScript3.0+

## Syntax

`filesystemobject.GetDrive(drive)`

## Description

The GetDrive() method is used to determine the drive specified in the drive parameter. This method takes *drive* as its only parameter, which represents the letter of drive for which to get information.

## Example

Listing 9.83 shows how the GetDrive() method is used.

*Listing 9.83    Example of* GetDrive()

```
<html>
<body>
```

```
<script language="JScript">
<!-- Hide

function getdrive()
{
  var myObject, drive;
  // Create an instance of the FileSystemObject
  myObject = new ActiveXObject("Scripting.FileSystemObject");
  drive = myObject.GetDrive("c:\\")
  alert("Drive Name of drive C is: " + drive.VolumeName);
}

// End Hide -->
</script>
```

Get the name for Drive C.

```
<form name="myForm">
<input type="Button" value="Get Drive Name" onClick='getdrive()'>
</form>

</body>
</html>
```

# FileSystemObject.GetDriveName()

## JScript3.0+

## Syntax

```
filesystemobject.GetDriveName(letter)
```

## Description

The GetDriveName() method is used to get the name of a specified drive. This method takes *drive* as its only parameter, which represents the letter of drive for which to get the name.

## Example

Listing 9.84 shows how the GetDriveName() method is used. An instance of the FileSystemObject is created and then used to get the name of the C drive.

*Listing 9.84   Example of* GetDriveName()
```
<html>
<body>

<script language="JScript">
```

*continues*

*Listing 9.84    continued*

```
<!-- Hide

function getdrive()
{
  var myObject, drive;
  // Create an instance of the FileSystemObject
  myObject = new ActiveXObject("Scripting.FileSystemObject");

  // Gets the name of the specified drive
  drive = myObject.GetDriveName("c:\\");

  // Informs the user of the drive name
  alert("Name for drive C is: " + drive);
}

// End Hide -->
</script>

Get the name for Drive C.

<form name="myForm">
<input type="Button" value="Get Drive Name" onClick='getdrive()'>
</form>

</body>
</html>
```

# FileSystemObject.GetExtensionName()

## JScript3.0+

## Syntax

`filesystemobject.GetExtensionName(path)`

## Description

The `GetExtensionName()` method is used to get the file extension name for a specified file. This method takes *path* as its only parameter, which represents the full path to the file.

## Example

Listing 9.85 shows how the `GetExtensionName()` method is used. An instance of the `FileSystemObject` is created and then used to get the extension name of the specified file type.

*Listing 9.85   Example of* `GetExtensionName()`

```
<html>
<body>

<script language="JScript">
<!-- Hide
// gets the extension name for the file and informs the user
// of the results
function getExt()
{
  var myObject, ext;
  // Creates an instance of the FileSystemObject
  myObject = new ActiveXObject("Scripting.FileSystemObject");

  //Gets the extension of the specified file
  ext = myObject.GetExtensionName("c:\\testing.txt");

  //Informs the user of the file extension
  alert("The extension for the testing file is: " + ext);
}

// End Hide -->
</script>

Get the extension for the file "testing.txt".

<form name="myForm">
<input type="Button" value="Get Extension" onClick='getExt()'>
</form>

</body>
</html>
```

# FileSystemObject.GetFile()

## *JScript3.0+*

## Syntax

`filesystemobject.GetFile(/file name/)`

## Description

The `GetFile()` method is used to get a specified file object.

## Example

Listing 9.86 shows how you can use the `GetFile()` method to get the size of a file.

*Listing 9.86   Example of* GetFile()

```
<html>
<body>

<script language="JScript">
<!-- Hide

function getsize()
{
  var myObject, afile, size;
  // Creates an instance of the FileSystemObject
  myObject = new ActiveXObject("Scripting.FileSystemObject");
  afile = myObject.GetFile("c:\\test.txt")

  //Gets the size of the file
  size = afile.Size;

  // Informs user of the file size
  alert("The size of the test.txt file is:" + size);
}

// End Hide -->
</script>

Get the size for the file "test.txt"

<form name="myForm">
<input type="Button" value="Get Size" onClick='getsize()'>
</form>

</body>
</html>
```

# FileSystemObject.GetFileName()

## JScript3.0+

## Syntax

`filesystemobject.GetFileName(filename)`

## Description

The GetFileName() method is used to get a specified filename. This method takes *filename* as its only parameter, which represents the absolute or relative path to the file.

## Example

Listing 9.87 shows how the GetFileName() property is used.

*Listing 9.87    Example of* GetFileName()

```
<html>
<body>

<script language="JScript">
<!-- Hide

function getname()
{
  var myObject, name;
  // Creates an instance of the FileSystemObject
  myObject = new ActiveXObject("Scripting.FileSystemObject");

  // Gets the file name
  name = myObject.GetFileName("c:\\test.txt");

  // Informs the user of the name
  alert("The file name is:" + name);
}

// End Hide -->
</script>

Get the name value for the file "test.txt"

<form name="myForm">
<input type="Button" value="Get File Name" onClick='getname()'>
</form>

</body>
</html>
```

# FileSystemObject.GetFolder()

## *JScript3.0+*

## *Syntax*

`filesystemobject.GetFolder(/Path/)`

## *Description*

The GetFolder() method is used to get the specified folder object.

## *Example*

Listing 9.88 shows how to retrieve a folder object. An instance of the FileSystemObject is created and then used to get a folder name. Then the DateLastAccessed property is applied to the folder object to get the actual date that the folder was last accessed. The result is then returned to the user.

*Listing 9.88    Example of* `GetFolder()`

```
<html>
<body>

<script language="JScript">
<!-- Hide

// function gets the folder object and then checks the date
// property of when the folder was last accessed.
function getfolder()
{
  var myObject, afolder, date;
  // Creates an instance of the FileSystemObject
  myObject = new ActiveXObject("Scripting.FileSystemObject");

  // Gets the folder object
  afolder = myObject.GetFolder("c:\\tmp");

  // Gets the date the folder was last accessed
  date = afolder.DateLastAccessed;

  // Informs the user of the date result
  alert("The folder"+name+" is a temporary folder.");
}

// End Hide -->
</script>

Get the date that the folder "tmp" was last accessed.

<form name="myForm">
<input type="Button" value="Get Folder Date" onClick='getfolder()'>
</form>

</body>
</html>
```

# FileSystemObject.GetParentFolderName()

## JScript3.0+

## Syntax

`filesystemobject.GetParentFolderName(foldername)`

## Description

The `GetParentFolderName()` method is used to get the name of the parent folder for a specified file or folder. This method takes *foldername* as its only parameter, which represents the path for the name of the subfolder.

## Example

Listing 9.89 shows how to get the name for the parent folder.

*Listing 9.89  Example of* `GetParentFolderName()`

```
<html>
<body>

<script language="JScript">
<!-- Hide

function getparent()
{
  var myObject, name;
  // Creates an instance of the FileSystemObject
  myObject = new ActiveXObject("Scripting.FileSystemObject");
  name = myObject.GetParentFolderName("c:\\tmp\\subfolder");
  alert("The parent folder name is:" + name);
}

// End Hide -->
</script>

Get the parent folder name for "subtmp" folder.

<form name="myForm">
<input type="Button" value="Get Parent Folder" onClick='getparent()'>
</form>

</body>
</html>
```

# FileSystemObject.GetSpecialFolder()

## JScript3.0+

## Syntax

`filesystemobject.GetSpecialFolder(num)`

## Description

The `GetSpecialFolder()` method is used to get the special folder object specified. This method takes *num* as its only parameter, which represents one of the following values:

- 0   Windows folder
- 1   System folder
- 2   Temporary folder

## Example

Listing 9.90 shows how the `GetSpecialFolder()` method is used to get the Temporary folder.

*Listing 9.90   Example of* `GetSpecialFolder()`

```
<html>
<body>

<script language="JScript">
<!-- Hide

function get()
{
  var myObject, name;
  // Creates an instance of the FileSystemObject
  myObject = new ActiveXObject("Scripting.FileSystemObject");
  name = myObject.GetSpecialFolder(2);
  alert("The folder is a temporary folder" + name);
}

// End Hide -->
</script>

Check to see if the folder "Temp" is a temporary folder.

<form name="myForm">
<input type="Button" value="Get Special Folder" onClick='get()'>
</form>

</body>
</html>
```

# FileSystemObject.GetTempName()

## JScript3.0+

## Syntax

`filesystemobject.GetTempName()`

## Description

The `GetTempName()` method is used to get a randomly generated temporary file or folder.

## Example

Listing 9.91 shows how the `GetTempName()` method is used. An instance of the `FileSystemObject` is created and then used to get the name of a randomly generated temporary file.

*Listing 9.91    Example of* GetTempName()

```
<html>
<body>

<script language="JScript">
<!-- Hide

function get()
{
  var myObject, name;
  // Create an instance of the FileSystemObject
  myObject = new ActiveXObject("Scripting.FileSystemObject");

  // Get the name of a temporary file
  name = myObject.GetTempName();
  alert("The temp file name is: " + name);
}

// End Hide -->
</script>

Get a temp file.

<form name="myForm">
<input type="Button" value="Get Temp Name" onClick='get()'>
</form>

</body>
</html>
```

# FileSystemObject.MoveFile()

## JScript3.0+

## Syntax

*filesystemobject*.MoveFile(*source, destination*)

## Description

The MoveFile() method is used to move a file from a source to a destination. This method takes two parameters. The first parameter, *source*, is the location of the file to be moved, while the second parameter, *destination*, is the new location of the moved file.

## Example

Listing 9.92 shows how the MoveFile() method is used. An instance of the FileSystemObject is created and then used to move the test.txt from the root directory on the C drive to the tmp folder.

*Listing 9.92    Example of* MoveFile()

```
<html>
<body>

<script language="JScript">
<!-- Hide

function move()
{
  var myObject;
  // Create an instance of the FileSystemObject
  myObject = new ActiveXObject("Scripting.FileSystemObject");

  // File is moved from root to tmp folder
  myObject.MoveFile("c:\\test.txt", "c:\\tmp\\test.txt");
}

// End Hide -->
</script>

Move the file "test.txt" from c:\ to c:\tmp

<form name="myForm">
<input type="Button" value="Move file" onClick='move()'>
</form>

</body>
</html>
```

# FileSystemObject.MoveFolder()

## JScript3.0+

## Syntax

`filesystemobject.MoveFolder(/arguments/)`

## Description

The MoveFolder() method is used to move one or more folders from one location to another.

## Example

Listing 9.93 shows how the NewFolder() method is used. An instance of the FileSystemObject is created and then used to move the subtmp folder to the root directory on the C drive.

*Listing 9.93    Example of* MoveFolder()

```
<html>
<body>

<script language="JScript">
<!-- Hide

function move()
{
  var myObject;
  // Create an instance of the FileSystemObject
  myObject = new ActiveXObject("Scripting.FileSystemObject");

  // Folder is moved
  myObject.MoveFolder("c:\\tmp\\subtmp", "c:\\");
}

// End Hide -->
</script>

Move the folder "subtmp" from c:\tmp\subtmp to c:\

<form name="myForm">
<input type="Button" value="Move folder" onClick='move()'>
</form>

</body>
</html>
```

# FileSystemObject.OpentextFile()

## *JScript2.0+*

## *Syntax*

*filesystemobject*.OpentextFile(*filename, iomode, create, format*)

## *Description*

The OpentextFile() method is used to open a text stream object to a specified file, which can be used to read and write from that file. This method takes four parameters. The first parameter, *filename*, is the name of the file to be created. The second parameter, *iomode*, is the mode of the file. The third parameter, *create*, is a Boolean value indicating whether the file can be created if it doesn't exist. And the final parameter, *format*, is a value indicating the format of the opened file. The default is ASCII.

## *Example*

Listing 9.94 shows how the OpentextFile() method is used. An instance of the FileSystemObject is created and the used to open a text stream to the file dummy.txt. The file is opened in append mode.

*Listing 9.94    Example of* OpentextFile()

```
<html>
<body>

<script language="JScript">
<!-- Hide

function open()
{
  var myObject, afile;
  // Create an instance of the FileSystemObject
  myObject = new ActiveXObject("Scripting.FileSystemObject");

  // Create a File called "dummy.txt" and open for appending
  afile = myObject.OpenTextFile("c:\\dummy.txt", ForAppending, false);
  afile.close();
}

// End Hide -->
</script>

Open a text stream for the file dummy.txt

<form name="myForm">
<input type="Button" value="Open File" onClick='open()'>
</form>

</body>
</html>
```

# Folder

## JScript3.0+

## Syntax

Core JScript object created by calling the GetFolder() method of the FileSystemObject object.

## Description

The Folder object, when created, provides access to all the properties of a folder. This object is created by using the GetFolder() method of the FileSystemObject object. The *folder* passed is the name the folder for which you want to create a JScript object.

Table 9.14 contains a list of methods and properties of the Folder object.

## Table 9.14 Methods and Properties of the Folder Object

| Type | Item | Description |
| --- | --- | --- |
| Method | Copy() | Copies the folder from one location to another |
| | Delete() | Deletes the specified folder |
| | Move() | Moves the specified folder |
| Property | Attributes | Sets or returns the file system attributes of the folder |
| | DateCreated | Returns the date the folder was created |
| | DateLastAccessed | Returns the date the folder was last accessed |
| | DateLastModified | Returns the date the folder was last modified |
| | Drive | Returns the drive on which the folder is located |
| | Files | Returns a Files collection containing all the File objects in the folder |
| | IsRootFolder | Returns true if the folder is the root folder, false otherwise |
| | Name | Sets or returns the name of the folder |
| | ParentFolder | Returns a folder object for the parent folder of the folder |
| | Path | Returns the path to the folder |
| | ShortName | Returns the 8.3 version of the name of the folder |
| | ShortPath | Returns the 8.3 version of the path to the folder |
| | Size | Returns the byte size of all the contents of the folder |
| | SubFolders | Returns a Folders collection of all the folders contained in the folder |
| | Type | Returns the type of folder |

## Example

Listing 9.95 creates an instance of the FileSystemObject object, and then creates an instance of the Folder object. The drive letter of the folder instance is written to the user's page if this script is run in a browser window.

*Listing 9.95   Creating an Instance of the* Folder *Object*

```
<script language="JScript1.1">
<!-- Hide

// Create an instance of the FileSystemObject
```

*continues*

*Listing 9.95   continued*

```
var myFileSysObj = new ActiveXObject("Scripting.FileSystemObject");

// Create an instance of the Folder object for the "temp" folder
var myFolder = myFileSysObj.GetFolder("\\temp");

// Write the drive the folder appears to a web page
document.write(myFolder.Drive);

// End hide -->
</script>
```

# Folder.Attributes

## JScript3.0+

## Syntax

```
folder.Attributes
```

```
folder.Attributes = attrib
```

## Description

The `Attributes` property of an instance of the `Folder` object is used to set or retrieve the attributes of a folder. If the property is called, as in the first syntactical definition, you can retrieve the current attributes of the folder. If you set the property equal to `attrib`, you are able to set new attributes. Table 9.15 has the values of the attributes.

### Table 9.15 Attribute values

| Value | Stands For | Description |
|-------|-----------|-------------|
| 0 | Normal | Normal folder with no attributes set |
| 1 | Read Only | Read-only folder with read/write attribute |
| 2 | Hidden | Hidden folder with read/write attribute |
| 4 | System | System folder with read/write attribute |
| 8 | Volume | Disk drive volume label with read-only attribute |
| 16 | Directory | Folder or directory with read-only attribute |
| 32 | Archive | Folder has changed since last backup with read/write attribute |
| 64 | Alias | Link or shortcut to a folder with read-only attribute |
| 128 | Compressed | Compressed folder with read-only attribute |

## Example

This example, which is run in an Internet Explorer browser, has a button. When the button is pressed, an alert box pops up displaying the attribute setting of the folder specified in the script. See the entry for `File.Attributes` for a more detailed example.

*Listing 9.96   Using the* Attributes *Property*

```
<html>
<body>

<script language="JScript1.2">
<!--Hide
function get(){

  // Create an instance of the FileSystemObject
  var myObject = new ActiveXObject("Scripting.FileSystemObject");

  // Create an instance of a Folder object
  var myFolder = myObject.GetFolder("c:\\Temp");

  // Display an alert box with the folder attributes
  alert(myFolder.Attributes);
}

// End Hide -->
</script>

Gets a folders attributes.

<form name="myForm">
<input type="Button" value="Get Attributes" onClick='get()'>
</form>

</body>
</html>
```

# Folder.Copy()

## *JScript3.0+*

## *Syntax*

*folder.Copy(destination)*
*folder.Copy(destination, boolean)*

## *Description*

The Copy() method is used to copy a specified folder from one location to another. The *destination* specified is the location to which to copy the folder. If the *boolean* parameter is set to true, and if there is an existing folder in the *destination* location, the copy will overwrite the folder.

## *Example*

Listing 9.97 creates an instance of the Folder object, and then makes a copy using the Copy() method. If the new folder already exists, it will be overwritten.

*Listing 9.97   Using the* `Copy()` *Method*

```
// Create a FileSystemObject
var myObject = new ActiveXObject("Scripting.FileSystemObject");

// Create a Folder object
var myFolder = myObject.GetFolder("c:\Temp");

// Copy the folder to another location. Overwrite the folder
// if it already exists.
myFolder.Copy("c:\\Test", true);
```

# Folder.DateCreated

## *JScript3.0+*

## *Syntax*

`folder.DateCreated`

## *Description*

The `DateCreated` property of an instance of the `Folder` object is used to get the date when the folder was created.

## *Example*

Listing 9.98 is run in an Internet Explorer browser, and it contains a single button. When the button is clicked, an alert box pops up displaying the creation date of the folder specified.

*Listing 9.98    Using the* `DateCreated` *Property*

```
<html>
<body>

<script language="JScript">
<!-- Hide
function get(){

  // Create a FileSystemObject object
  var myObject = new ActiveXObject("Scripting.FileSystemObject");

  // Create a Folder object
  var myFolder = myObject.GetFolder("c:\\Temp");

  // Display the creation date of the folder
  alert (myFolder.DateCreated);
}

// End hide-->
</script>
```

Get the date the c:\temp folder was created.

```
<form name="myForm">
<input type="Button" value="Get Date" onClick='get()'>
</form>

</body>
</html>
```

# Folder.DateLastAccessed

## JScript3.0+

## Syntax

`folder.DateLastAccessed`

## Description

The `DateLastAccessed` property of an instance of the `Folder` object is used to get the date the folder was last accessed.

## Example

Listing 9.99 is run in an Internet Explorer browser, and it contains a single button. When the button is clicked, an alert box pops up displaying the date the folder was last accessed.

Listing 9.99    Using the `DateLastAccessed` Property

```
<html>
<body>

<script language="JScript">
<!-- Hide
function get(){

  // Create a FileSystemObject object
  var myObject = new ActiveXObject("Scripting.FileSystemObject");

  // Create a Folder object
  var myFolder = myObject.GetFolder("c:\\Temp");

  // Display the date the folder was last accessed
  alert (myFolder.DateLastAccessed);
}

// End hide-->
```

*continues*

*Listing 9.99    continued*
```
</script>
```

Get the date the c:\temp folder was last accessed.

```
<form name="myForm">
<input type="Button" value="Get Last Access" onClick='get()'>
</form>

</body>
</html>
```

# Folder.DateLastModified

## JScript3.0+

## Syntax
```
folder.DateLastModified
```

## Description

The DateLastModified property of an instance of the Folder object is used to get the date the folder was last modified.

## Example

Listing 9.100 is run in an Internet Explorer browser, and it contains a single button. When the button is clicked, an alert box pops up displaying the date the folder was last modified.

*Listing 9.100    Using the DateLastModified Property*
```
<html>
<body>

<script language="JScript">
<!-- Hide
function get(){

  // Create a FileSystemObject object
  var myObject = new ActiveXObject("Scripting.FileSystemObject");

  // Create a Folder object
  var myFolder = myObject.GetFolder("c:\\Temp");

  // Display the date the folder was last modified
  alert (myFolder.DateLastModified);
}

// End hide-->
```

```
</script>
```

Get the date the c:\temp folder was last modified.

```
<form name="myForm">
<input type="Button" value="Get Last Modified" onClick='get()'>
</form>

</body>
</html>
```

# Folder.Delete()

## JScript3.0+

## Syntax

*folder*.Delete(*boolean*)

*folder*.Delete()

## Description

The Delete() method of an instance of the Folder object is used to delete a specified folder. The optional *boolean* parameter the method takes will cause the method to delete all read-only files and folders in the folder if set to true.

## Example

Listing 9.101 deletes the specified folder.

*Listing 9.101    Using the* Delete() *Method*
```
// Create a FileSystemObject object
var myObject = new ActiveXObject("Scripting.FileSystemObject");

// Create a Folder object
var myFolder = myObject.GetFolder("c:\Test");

// Delete the folder
myFolder.Delete();
```

# Folder.Drive

## JScript3.0+

## Syntax

*folder*.Drive

## Description

The Drive property of an instance of the Folder object returns the drive letter of the folder.

## Example

Listing 9.102 is run in an Internet Explorer browser, and it contains a single button. When the button is clicked, an alert box pops up displaying the drive on which the folder is located.

*Listing 9.102    Using the* `Drive` *Property*

```
<html>
<body>

<script language="JScript">
<!-- Hide
function get(){

  // Create a FileSystemObject object
  var myObject = new ActiveXObject("Scripting.FileSystemObject");

  // Create a Folder object
  var myFolder = myObject.GetFolder("c:\\Temp");

  // Display the drive of the folder
  alert (myFolder.Drive);
}

// End hide-->
</script>

Get the drive the c:\temp folder is located on.

<form name="myForm">
<input type="Button" value="Get Drive" onClick='get()'>
</form>

</body>
</html>
```

# Folder.Files

## JScript3.0+

## Syntax

`folder`.Files

## Description

The `Files` property of an instance of the `Folder` object, returns a collection consisting of all the `File` objects contained in the `folder`. This includes hidden and system files.

## Example

Listing 9.103 creates and instance of the Folder object, and then creates an instance of the Enumerator object to access the collection of files contained in the Files property. If this example is loaded in a browser, each of the files contained in the folder will be written to the page.

*Listing 9.103    Using the* Files *Property*

```
<script language="JScript1.1">
<!-- Hide

// Create an instance of the FileSystemObject
var myFileSysObj = new ActiveXObject("Scripting.FileSystemObject");

// Create an instance of the Folder object for the "temp" folder
var myFolder = myFileSysObj.GetFolder("\\temp");

// Use an instance of the Enumerator object to access the files
// in this folder.
var myEnum = new Enumerator(myFolder.Files);

// Write file names of the files in this folder
while(!myEnum.atEnd()){
  document.write(myEnum.item() + '<br>');
  myEnum.moveNext();
}

// End hide -->
</script>
```

# Folder.IsRootFolder

## JScript3.0+

## Syntax

folder.IsRootFolder

## Description

The IsRootFolder property of an instance of the Folder object, evaluates to true if the folder is the root folder, and false otherwise.

## Example

Listing 9.104 creates an instance of the Folder object, and then checks to see if it is the root folder. If this example is loaded in a browser, a string will be written to the user's page stating whether or not the folder is the root folder.

*Listing 9.104    Using the* IsRootFolder *Property*

```
<script language="JScript1.1">
<!-- Hide

// Create an instance of the FileSystemObject
var myFileSysObj = new ActiveXObject("Scripting.FileSystemObject");

// Create an instance of the Folder object for the "temp" folder
var myFolder = myFileSysObj.GetFolder("\\temp");

// See if the folder is the root folder.
if(myFolder.IsRootFolder){
  document.write(myFolder.Name + " is the root folder.");
}else{
  document.write(myFolder.Name + " is not the root folder.");
}

// End hide -->
</script>
```

# Folder.Move()

## JScript3.0+

## Syntax

folder.Move(destination)

## Description

The Move() method is used to move a specified folder from one location to another. The *destination* specified is the location to which to move the folder.

## Example

Listing 9.105 creates an instance of the Folder object, and then moves it by using the Move() method.

*Listing 9.105    Using the* Move() *Method*

```
// Create a FileSystemObject
var myObject = new ActiveXObject("Scripting.FileSystemObject");

// Create a Folder object
var myFolder = myObject.GetFolder("c:\\Temp");

// Move the folder to another location.
myFolder.Move("c:\\Test");
```

# Folder.Name

## *JScript3.0+*

## Syntax

`folder.Name`

## Description

The `Name` property of an instance of the `Folder` object is used to either `set` or `get` the name of the folder.

## Example

Listing 9.106 is run in an Internet Explorer browser, and it contains a single button. When the button is clicked, an alert box pops up displaying the name of the folder.

*Listing 9.106   Example of the* Name *Property*

```
<html>
<body>

<script language="JScript">
<!-- Hide
function get(){

  // Create a FileSystemObject object
  var myObject = new ActiveXObject("Scripting.FileSystemObject");

  // Create a Folder object
  var myFolder = myObject.GetFolder("c:\\Temp");

  // Display the name of the folder
  alert (myFolder.Name);
}

// End hide-->
</script>

Get the name of the c:\temp folder.

<form name="myForm">
<input type="Button" value="Get Name" onClick='get()'>
</form>

</body>
</html>
```

# Folder.ParentFolder

## *JScript3.0+*

## *Syntax*

`folder`.ParentFolder

## *Description*

The `ParentFolder` property of an instance of the `Folder` object is used to return a new `Folder` object for the parent folder.

## *Example*

Listing 9.107 is run in an Internet Explorer browser, and it contains a single button. When the button is clicked, an alert box pops up displaying the name of the parent folder.

*Listing 9.107  Using the* `ParentFolder` *Property*

```
<html>
<body>

<script language="JScript">
<!-- Hide
function get(){

  // Create a FileSystemObject object
  var myObject = new ActiveXObject("Scripting.FileSystemObject");

  // Create a Folder object
  var myFolder = myObject.GetFolder("c:\\Temp");

  // Display the name of the parent folder
  alert (myFolder.ParentFolder.Path);
}

// End hide-->
</script>

Get the name of the c:\temp parent folder.

<form name="myForm">
<input type="Button" value="Get Parent Folder" onClick='get()'>
</form>

</body>
</html>
```

# Folder.Path

## *JScript3.0+*

## *Syntax*

`folder`.Path

## *Description*

The Path property of an instance of the Folder object returns the full path to the folder.

## *Example*

Listing 9.108 is run in an Internet Explorer browser, and it contains a single button. When the button is clicked, an alert box pops up displaying the path of the folder.

*Listing 9.108    Using the* Path *Property*

```
<html>
<body>

<script language="JavaScript1.2">
<!-- Hide
function get(){

  // Create a FileSystemObject object
  var myObject = new ActiveXObject("Scripting.FileSystemObject");

  // Create a Folder object
  var myFolder = myObject.GetFolder("c:\\Temp");

  // Display the path of the  folder
  alert (myFolder.Path);
}

// End hide-->
</script>

Get the path of the c:\temp folder.

<form name="myForm">
<input type="Button" value="Get Path" onClick='get()'>
</form>

</body>
</html>
```

# Folder.ShortName

## JScript3.0+

## Syntax

`folder`.ShortName

## Description

The ShortName property of an instance of the Folder object returns the 8.3 name of the folder.

## Example

Listing 9.109 is run in an Internet Explorer browser, and it contains a single button. When the button is clicked, an alert box pops up displaying the short name of the folder.

*Listing 9.109    Using the* ShortName *Property*

```
<html>
<body>

<script language="JScript">
<!-- Hide
function get(){

  // Create a FileSystemObject object
  var myObject = new ActiveXObject("Scripting.FileSystemObject");

  // Create a Folder object
  var myFolder = myObject.GetFolder("c:\\Program Files");

  // Display the short name of the folder
  alert (myFolder.ShortName);
}

// End hide-->
</script>

Get the short name of the "C:\Program Files" folder.

<form name="myForm">
<input type="Button" value="Get Short Name" onClick='get()'>
</form>

</body>
</html>
```

# Folder.ShortPath

## *JScript3.0+*

## *Syntax*

```
folder.ShortPath
```

## *Description*

The `ShortPath` property of an instance of the `Folder` object returns the 8.3 path to the folder.

## *Example*

Listing 9.110 is run in an Internet Explorer browser, and it contains a single button. When the button is clicked, an alert box pops up displaying the short path to the folder.

*Listing 9.110    Using the `ShortPath` Property*

```
<html>
<body>

<script language="JScript">
<!-- Hide
function get(){

    // Create a FileSystemObject object
    var myObject = new ActiveXObject("Scripting.FileSystemObject");

    // Create a Folder object
    var myFolder = myObject.GetFolder("c:\\Program Files");

    // Display the short path of the folder
    alert (myFolder.ShortPath);
}

// End hide-->
</script>

Get the short path of the "c:\\Program Files" folder.

<form name="myForm">
<input type="Button" value="Get Short Path" onClick='get()'>
</form>

</body>
</html>
```

# Folder.Size

## JScript3.0+

## Syntax

`folder`.Size

## Description

The Size property of an instance of the Folder object returns the byte size of the folder.

## Example

Listing 9.111 is run in an Internet Explorer browser, and it contains a single button. When the button is clicked, an alert box pops up displaying the byte size of the folder.

*Listing 9.111    Using the* Size *Property*

```
<html>
<body>

<script language="JScript">
<!-- Hide
function get(){

  // Create a FileSystemObject object
  var myObject = new ActiveXObject("Scripting.FileSystemObject");

  // Create a Folder object
  var myFolder = myObject.GetFolder("c:\\Program Files");

  // Display the size of the folder
  alert (myFolder.Size);
}

// End hide-->
</script>

Get the size of the "c:\\Program Files" folder.

<form name="myForm">
<input type="Button" value="Get Size" onClick='get()'>
</form>

</body>
</html>
```

# Folder.SubFolders

## JScript3.0+

## Syntax

`folder.SubFolders`

## Description

The `SubFolders` property of an instance of the `Folder` object returns a collection consisting of all the `Folder` objects contained in the *folder*. This includes hidden and system folders.

## Example

Listing 9.112 creates an instance of the `Folder` object, and then creates an instance of the `Enumerator` object to access the collection of folders contained in the `Folders` property. If this example is loaded in a browser, the names of each of the folders contained in the folder will be written to the page.

*Listing 9.112    Using the* `SubFolders` *Property*

```
<script language="JScript">
<!-- Hide

// Create an instance of the FileSystemObject
var myFileSysObj = new ActiveXObject("Scripting.FileSystemObject");

// Create an instance of the Folder object for the "temp" folder
var myFolder = myFileSysObj.GetFolder("\\temp");

// Use an instance of the Enumerator object to access the sub folders
// in this folder.
var myEnum = new Enumerator(myFolder.SubFolders);

// Write file names of the folders in this folder
while(!myEnum.atEnd()){
  document.write(myEnum.item() + '<br>');
  myEnum.moveNext();
}

// End hide -->
</script>
```

# Folder.Type

## JScript3.0+

## Syntax

`folder.Type`

## Description

The Type property of an instance of the Folder object returns the type of the folder. For a folder, the return value is File Folder.

## Example

Listing 9.113 is run in an Internet Explorer browser, and it contains a single button. When the button is clicked, an alert box pops up displaying the type of the folder.

*Listing 9.113    Using the* Type *Property*

```
<html>
<body>

<script language="JScript">
<!-- Hide
function get(){

  // Create a FileSystemObject object
  var myObject = new ActiveXObject("Scripting.FileSystemObject");

  // Create a Folder object
  var myFolder = myObject.GetFolder("c:\\Program Files");

  // Display the type of the folder
  alert (myFolder.Type);
}

// End hide-->
</script>

Get the type of the "c:\\Program Files" folder.

<form name="myForm">
<input type="Button" value="Get Type" onClick='get()'>
</form>

</body>
</html>
```

# Folders

## JScript3.0+

## Syntax

Core JScript Collection of Folder objects.

## Description

The Folders collection holds a read-only collection of all the available folders. A collection is similar to an array except that an item pointer is used to navigate through the items in the collection rather than an array index. As you would with arrays, you can only move the current item pointer to the first or next element of a collection. Because the `Folder` object is a collection, the folders can be accessed only by using an `Enumerator` object. The properties associated with the `Folders` collection are listed in Table 9.16. For more information on accessing collections see the `Enumerator` section in this chapter.

**Table 9.16 Properties Associated with Folders Collection**

| Item | Description |
|------|-------------|
| Add | Allows you to add a folder to the collection |
| Count | Returns the number of items in the collection |
| Item | Set or return an item for a specified key in a Drives dictionary object |

## Example

Listing 9.114 accesses the `Folders` collection by using `FileSystemObject`.

*Listing 9.114    Using the* **Add()** *Method of the* **Folders** *Collection*
```
var fileSysObj = new ActiveXObject("Scripting.FileSystemObject");
document.write(fileSysObj.Folders.count);
```

# Folders.Add()

## JScript3.0+

## Syntax

```
folderscollection.Add(foldername)
```

## Description

The `Add()` method of the `Folders` collection is used to add folders to the collection. This can be used to create new folders on the file system.

## Example

Listing 9.115 creates a `test` folder inside the `\temp` folder on the file system. This script can be executed by using the Windows Scripting Host (`wscript.exe` or `cscript.exe`). Be sure you are on a drive that contains a folder named `temp`, and make sure there is no folder named `test` already present. Not doing so will result in an error.

*Listing 9.115    Using the* **Add()** *Method of the* **Folders** *Collection*
```
// Create an instance of the FileSystemObject
var myFileSysObj = new ActiveXObject("Scripting.FileSystemObject");

// Create an instance of the Folder object for the "temp" folder
```

*continues*

*Listing 9.115   continued*
```
var myFolder = myFileSysObj.GetFolder("\\temp");

// Access the sub folders collection of our folder
var myFolderCollection = myFolder.SubFolders;

// Add a new folder called "test"
myFolderCollection.Add("test");
```

# Folders.Count

## JScript1.0+

## Syntax

`folderscollection.Count`

## Description

The Count property of the Folders collection returns the number of folders in the collection. Folders are added to this collection by using the Folders.Add() method.

## Example

Listing 9.116 is run in an Internet Explorer browser, and it contains a single button. When the button is clicked, an alert box pops up displaying the number of folders in the Folders collection.

*Listing 9.116   Accessing the Count Property*
```
<html>
<body>

<script language="JScript">
<!-- Hide
function get(){

  // Create an instance of the FileSystemObject
  var myFileSysObj = new ActiveXObject("Scripting.FileSystemObject");

  // Create two instances of the Folder object for the "temp" folder
  var myFolder = myFileSysObj.GetFolder("c:\\Temp");

  // Access the sub folders collection of our folder
  var myFolderCollection = myFolder.SubFolders;

  // Add two new folders
  myFolderCollection.Add("test1");
  myFolderCollection.Add("test2");

  // Display the number of folders in the collection
```

```
    alert(myFolderCollection.Count);

}

// End hide-->
</script>

Get the count of the c:\temp Folders collection.

<form name="myForm">
<input type="Button" value="Get Count" onClick='get()'>
</form>

</body>
</html>
```

# Folders.Item

## JScript1.0+

## Syntax

*folderscollection*.Item(*foldername*)

## Description

The Item property of an instance of the Folders collection returns *foldername* folder.

## Example

Listing 9.117 is run in an Internet Explorer browser, and it contains a single button. When the button is clicked, an alert box pops up displaying the second folder added to the Folders collection.

*Listing 9.117   Accessing the Item Property*

```
<html>
<body>

<script language="JScript">
<!-- Hide              .
function get(){

  // Create an instance of the FileSystemObject
  var myFileSysObj = new ActiveXObject("Scripting.FileSystemObject");

  // Create two instances of the Folder object for the "temp" folder
  var myFolder = myFileSysObj.GetFolder("c:\\Temp");

  // Access the sub folders collection of our folder
```

*continues*

*Listing 9.117    continued*

```
  var myFolderCollection = myFolder.SubFolders;

  // Add two new folders
  myFolderCollection.Add("test1");
  myFolderCollection.Add("test2");

  // Display the second folder added to the collection
  alert(myFolderCollection.Item(2).Name);

}

// End hide-->
</script>
```

Get the second item added to the c:\temp Folders collection.

```
<form name="myForm">
<input type="Button" value="Get Item" onClick='get()'>
</form>

</body>
</html>
```

# GetObject

## JScript3.0+

## Syntax

```
GetObject(path)

GetObject(path, app.type)
```

## Description

The GetObject function returns a reference to an Automation object from a file. The function can take up to two parameters. The *path* parameter represents the full path and name to the file containing the object you wish to retrieve.

> **NOTE**
>
> Some of the applications you can retrieve objects from allow you to activate only part of the file. This can be achieved by placing an exclamation point, !, at the end of the *path* followed by the string that specifies the part you want to activate.

The *app.type* attribute is the program ID or formal definition of the object. The *app* portion represents the name of the application providing the object, and the *type* designates the type of object to create. If this parameter is not passed, the Automation object will try to determine which application to start.

## Example

Listing 9.118 shows the syntax that can be used to return an Automation object from a file. The second entry shows how you can activate only part of the object.

*Listing 9.118    Using the GetObject Function*
```
// Returning an object for this Excel file
var myObj = GetObject("C:\\TEMP\\TESTOBJ.XLS");

// Activating the first sheet in the file
var myObjRef = GetObject("C:\\TEMP\\TESTOBJ.XLS!sheet1");
```

# ScriptEngine

## JScript2+

## Syntax
```
ScriptEngine()
```

## Description

The ScriptEngine function has three possible return values: JScript, VBScript, and VBA. When implemented in JavaScript scripts, this function returns JScript.

## Example

Listing 9.119 prints the complete version information for the Internet Explorer browser interpreting the script. In addition to the ScriptEngine function, it also uses other Internet Explorer specific functions. The results of loading this example can be seen in Figure 9.1.

*Listing 9.119    Using the ScriptEngine Function to Retrieve Information About the Version of the Scripting Engine in an Internet Explorer Browser*
```
<script language="JScript1.1">
<!-- Hide

// Write the scripting engine type
document.write(ScriptEngine());

// Write the "major" version value to the page
document.write(" " + ScriptEngineMajorVersion() + ".");

// Write the "minor" version value to the page
```

*continues*

*Listing 9.119    continued*
```
document.write(ScriptEngineMinorVersion());

// Write the build number to the page
document.write(" build " + ScriptEngineBuildVersion());

// End hide -->
</script>
```

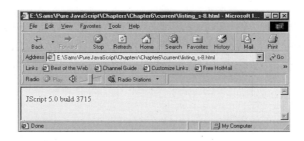

**Figure 9.1**
*Results of running Listing 9.119 in Internet Explorer 5.*

# ScriptEngineBuildVersion

## *JScript2+*

## *Syntax*
```
ScriptEngineBuildVersion
```

## *Description*
The `ScriptEngineBuildVersion` function returns the actual build number of the scripting engine contained on the user's machine.

## *Example*
Listing 9.120 prints the build number of the Internet Explorer browser interpreting the script.

*Listing 9.120    Using the* `ScriptEngineBuildVersion` *Function to Retrieve the Build Number of the Scripting Engine in an Internet Explorer Browser*

```
<script language="JScript">
<!-- Hide

// Write the build number to the page
document.write("Build " + ScriptEngineBuildVersion());

// End hide -->
</script>
```

# ScriptEngineMajorVersion

## *JScript2.0+*

## Syntax

```
ScriptEngineMajorVersion()
```

## Description

The `ScriptEngineMajorVersion` function returns the actual major version number of the scripting engine contained on the user's machine.

### Example

Listing 9.121 prints the major version number of the Internet Explorer browser interpreting the script.

*Listing 9.121    Using the* `ScriptEngineMajorVersion` *Function to Retrieve the Major Version Number of the Scripting Engine in an Internet Explorer Browser*

```
<script language="JScript">
<!-- Hide

// Write the build number to the page
document.write("Major Version: " + ScriptEngineMajorVersion());

// End hide -->
</script>
```

# ScriptEngineMinorVersion

## *JScript2.0+*

## Syntax

```
ScriptEngineMinorVersion()
```

## Description

The `ScriptEngineMinorVersion` function returns the actual minor version number of the scripting engine contained on the user's machine.

## Example

Listing 9.122 prints the minor version number of the Internet Explorer browser interpreting the script.

*Listing 9.122   Using the* `ScriptEngineMinorVersion` *Function to Retrieve the Minor Version Number of the Scripting Engine in an Internet Explorer Browser*

```
<script language="JScript">
<!-- Hide

// Write the build number to the page
document.write("Minor Version: " + ScriptEngineMinorVersion());

// End hide -->
</script>
```

# TextStream

## JScript2.0+

## Syntax

Core JScript object created by calling the `CreateTextFile()` method of the `FileSystemObject` object.

## Description

The `TextStream` object is created by calling the `CreateTextFile()` method of an instance of the `FileSystemObject`. An instance of the `TextStream` object is created by calling the `CreateTextFile()` method of the `FileSystemObject` object.

Table 9.17 contains a list of methods and properties of the `TextStream` object.

### Table 9.17 Methods and Properties of the TextStream Object

| Type | Item | Description |
|------|------|-------------|
| Method | `Close()` | Closes the file |
| | `Read()` | Reads in a specified number of characters |
| | `ReadAll()` | Reads the entire file |
| | `ReadLine()` | Reads a line of the file up to the newline character |
| | `Skip()` | Skips the specified number of characters |
| | `SkipLine()` | Skips the next line when reading the file |
| | `Write()` | Writes a string to the file |
| | `WriteBlankLines()` | Writes the specified number of blank lines to the file |
| | `WriteLine()` | Writes a string followed by a newline character to the file |

| Type | Item | Description |
|---|---|---|
| Property | AtEndOfLine | Returns true if the pointer is immediately before the end-of-line marker |
| | AtEndOfStream | Returns true if the pointer is at the end of the file |
| | Column | Returns the column number of the current pointer position |
| | Line | Returns the line number of the current pointer position |

## Example

Listing 9.123 creates an example of the TextStream object, and then writes a string to the file. After the string has been written, the stream is closed. This file can be executed with the Windows Scripting Host (wscript.exe or cscript.exe).

*Listing 9.123    Creating an Instance of the TextStream Object*

```
// Create a FileSystemObject object
var myFileSysObj = new ActiveXObject("Scripting.FileSystemObject")

// Create a TextStream object
var myTextStream = myFileSysObj.OpenTextFile("c:\\temp\\test.txt", 2, true)

// Write a string to the file
myTextStream.Write("Hello, World!");

// Close the stream to the file
myTextStream.Close();
```

# TextStream.AtEndOfLine

## JScript2.0+

## Syntax

*textstream*.AtEndOfLine

## Description

The AtEndOfLine property of the TextStream object returns true when the end of a line in a text line is found.

## Example

Listing 9.124 opens two files. The first file is for reading a string from, while the second file is written to—one character at a time—as the script iterates through. The result is that the first line of the file opened for reading is written to the second file. This file can be executed with the Windows Scripting Host (wscript.exe or cscript.exe).

*Listing 9.124    Using the* `AtEndOfLine` *Property to Find the End of the First Line in a File*

```
// Create a FileSystemObject object
var myFileSysObj = new ActiveXObject("Scripting.FileSystemObject");

// Create a TextStream object to read from and one to write to
var myInputTextStream = myFileSysObj.OpenTextFile("c:\\temp\\test.txt", 1,
true);
var myOutputTextStream = myFileSysObj.OpenTextFile("c:\\temp\\test2.txt", 2,
true);

// Iterate through the file one character at a time and write it
// to the second file.
while(!myInputTextStream.AtEndOfLine){
  myOutputTextStream.Write(myInputTextStream.Read(1));
}

// Close the stream to the files
myInputTextStream.Close();
myOutputTextStream.Close();
```

# TextStream.AtEndOfStream

## JScript2.0+

## Syntax

`textstream.AtEndOfStream`

## Description

The `AtEndOfStream` property of the `TextStream` object returns `true` when the end of a line in a text file is found.

## Example

Listing 9.125 opens two files. The first file is for reading a string from, while the second file is written to—one character at a time—as the script iterates through. The result is that the file opened for reading is written to the second file. This file can be executed with the Windows Scripting Host (`wscript.exe` or `cscript.exe`).

*Listing 9.125    Using the* `AtEndOfStream` *Property to Find the End of the File*

```
// Create a FileSystemObject object
var myFileSysObj = new ActiveXObject("Scripting.FileSystemObject");

// Create a TextStream object to read from and one to write to
var myInputTextStream = myFileSysObj.OpenTextFile("c:\\temp\\test.txt", 1,
true);
```

```
var myOutputTextStream = myFileSysObj.OpenTextFile("c:\\temp\\test2.txt", 2,
true);

// Iterate through the file one character at a time and write it
// to the second file.
while(!myInputTextStream.AtEndOfStream){
  myOutputTextStream.Write(myInputTextStream.Read(1));
}

// Close the stream to the files
myInputTextStream.Close();
myOutputTextStream.Close();
```

# TextStream.Close()

## *JScript2.0+*

## *Syntax*

`textstream.Close()`

## *Description*

The `Close()` method of the `TextStream` object closes the previously opened file.

## *Example*

Listing 9.126 shows you how to open and close a text file. This file can be executed with the Windows Scripting Host (`wscript.exe` or `cscript.exe`).

*Listing 9.126   Using the* `Close()` *Method to Close a Text File*
```
// Create a FileSystemObject object
var myFileSysObj = new ActiveXObject("Scripting.FileSystemObject");

// Create a TextStream object
var myTextStream = myFileSysObj.OpenTextFile("c:\\temp\\test.txt", 1, true);

// Close the stream to the file
myTextStream.Close();
```

# TextStream.Column

## *JScript2.0+*

## *Syntax*

`textstream.Column`

## *Description*

The `Column` property of the `TextSream` object returns the column number of the current pointer position.

## Example

Listing 9.127 opens a file for reading and a file for writing. The script iterates through each character of the first file, and then writes it and the column number to the second file. This file can be executed with the Windows Scripting Host (`wscript.exe` or `cscript.exe`).

*Listing 9.127    Using the* Column *Property*

```
// Create a FileSystemObject object
var myFileSysObj = new ActiveXObject("Scripting.FileSystemObject");

// Create a TextStream object to read from and one to write to
var myInputTextStream = myFileSysObj.OpenTextFile("c:\\temp\\test.txt", 1,
true);
var myOutputTextStream = myFileSysObj.OpenTextFile("c:\\temp\\test2.txt", 2,
true);

// Iterate through the file one character at a time and write it
// to the second file. Include the column number with each character.
while(!myInputTextStream.AtEndOfStream){
  myOutputTextStream.Write(myInputTextStream.Column + ": ");
  myOutputTextStream.WriteLine(myInputTextStream.Read(1));
}

// Close the stream to the files
myInputTextStream.Close();
myOutputTextStream.Close();
```

# TextStream.Line

## JScript2.0+

## Syntax

`textstream`.Line

## Description

The `Line` property of the `TextSream` object returns the line number of the current pointer position.

## Example

Listing 9.128 opens a file for reading and a file for writing. The script iterates through each character of the first file, and then writes it and the line number to the second file. This file can be executed with the Windows Scripting Host (`wscript.exe` or `cscript.exe`).

*Listing 9.128   Using the* Column *Property*
```
// Create a FileSystemObject object
var myFileSysObj = new ActiveXObject("Scripting.FileSystemObject");

// Create a TextStream object to read from and one to write to
var myInputTextStream = myFileSysObj.OpenTextFile("c:\\temp\\test.txt", 1,
true);
var myOutputTextStream = myFileSysObj.OpenTextFile("c:\\temp\\test2.txt", 2,
true);

// Iterate through the file one character at a time and write it
// to the second file. Include the column number with each character.
while(!myInputTextStream.AtEndOfStream){
  myOutputTextStream.Write(myInputTextStream.Line + ": ");
  myOutputTextStream.WriteLine(myInputTextStream.Read(1));
}

// Close the stream to the files
myInputTextStream.Close();
myOutputTextStream.Close();
```

# TextStream.Read()

## *JScript2.0+*

## *Syntax*

```
textstream.Read(num)
```

## *Description*

The Read() method of an instance of the TextStream object reads the *num* characters passed to the method starting at the current pointer position.

## *Example*

Listing 9.129 opens two files. The first file is for reading a string from, while the second file is written to—one character at a time—as the script iterates through. The result is that the file opened for reading is written to the second file. This file can be executed with the Windows Scripting Host (wscript.exe or cscript.exe).

*Listing 9.129   Using the* Read() *Method*
```
// Create a FileSystemObject object
var myFileSysObj = new ActiveXObject("Scripting.FileSystemObject");

// Create a TextStream object to read from and one to write to
var myInputTextStream = myFileSysObj.OpenTextFile("c:\\temp\\test.txt", 1,
true);
```

*continues*

*Listing 9.129    continued*
```
var myOutputTextStream = myFileSysObj.OpenTextFile("c:\\temp\\test2.txt", 2,
true);

// Iterate through the file one character at a time and write it
// to the second file.
while(!myInputTextStream.AtEndOfStream){
  myOutputTextStream.Write(myInputTextStream.Read(1));
}

// Close the stream to the files
myInputTextStream.Close();
myOutputTextStream.Close();
```

# TextStream.ReadAll()

## JScript2.0+

## Syntax

```
textstream.ReadAll()
```

## Description

The `ReadAll()` method of an instance of the `TextStream` object reads the entire text file. Be careful when using this method with large files because it will use up a good amount of system memory.

## Example

Listing 9.130 opens two files. The first file is for reading a string from, while the second file is written to. The result is that the file opened for reading is written to the second file. This file can be executed with the Windows Scripting Host (`wscript.exe` or `cscript.exe`).

*Listing 9.130    Using the* `ReadAll()` *Method*
```
// Create a FileSystemObject object
var myFileSysObj = new ActiveXObject("Scripting.FileSystemObject");

// Create a TextStream object to read from and one to write to
var myInputTextStream = myFileSysObj.OpenTextFile("c:\\temp\\test.txt", 1,
true);
var myOutputTextStream = myFileSysObj.OpenTextFile("c:\\temp\\test2.txt", 2,
true);

// Iterate through the file one character at a time and write it
// to the second file.
while(!myInputTextStream.AtEndOfStream){
```

```
  myOutputTextStream.Write(myInputTextStream.ReadAll());
}

// Close the stream to the files
myInputTextStream.Close();
myOutputTextStream.Close();
```

# TextStream.ReadLine()

## *JScript2.0+*

## *Syntax*

```
textstream.ReadLine()
```

## *Description*

The ReadLine() method of an instance of the TextStream object reads a line from a text file up to a newline character. Be careful when using this method with large files because it will use up a good amount of system memory.

## *Example*

Listing 9.131 opens two files. The first file is for reading a string from, while the second file is written to. Each line is read and written one at a time. The result is that the file opened for reading is written to the second file. This file can be executed with the Windows Scripting Host (wscript.exe or cscript.exe).

*Listing 9.131    Using the* ReadLine() *Method*

```
// Create a FileSystemObject object
var myFileSysObj = new ActiveXObject("Scripting.FileSystemObject");

// Create a TextStream object to read from and one to write to
var myInputTextStream = myFileSysObj.OpenTextFile("c:\\temp\\test.txt", 1,
true);
var myOutputTextStream = myFileSysObj.OpenTextFile("c:\\temp\\test2.txt", 2,
true);

// Iterate through the file one character at a time and write it
// to the second file.
while(!myInputTextStream.AtEndOfStream){
  myOutputTextStream.WriteLine(myInputTextStream.ReadLine());
}

// Close the stream to the files
myInputTextStream.Close();
myOutputTextStream.Close();
```

# TextStream.Skip()

## *JScript2.0+*

## *Syntax*

`textstream.Skip(num)`

## *Description*

The `Skip()` method of an instance of the `TextStream` object skips *num* characters.

## *Example*

Listing 9.132 opens two files. The first file is for reading a string from, while the second file is written to. The `Skip()` method is used to skip the first 5 characters before the file is read. This file can be executed with the Windows Scripting Host (`wscript.exe` or `cscript.exe`).

*Listing 9.132   Using the* `Skip()` *Method*

```
// Create a FileSystemObject object
var myFileSysObj = new ActiveXObject("Scripting.FileSystemObject");

// Create a TextStream object to read from and one to write to
var myInputTextStream = myFileSysObj.OpenTextFile("c:\\temp\\test.txt", 1,
true);
var myOutputTextStream = myFileSysObj.OpenTextFile("c:\\temp\\test2.txt", 2,
true);

// The Skip method is used to skip the first 5 characters.
myInputTextStream.Skip(5);

// Iterate through the file one character at a time and write it
// to the second file.
while(!myInputTextStream.AtEndOfStream){
  myOutputTextStream.Write(myInputTextStream.Read(1));
}

// Close the stream to the files
myInputTextStream.Close();
myOutputTextStream.Close();
```

# TextStream.SkipLine()

## *JScript2.0+*

## *Syntax*

`textstream.SkipLine()`

## *Description*

The `SkipLine()` method of an instance of the `TextStream` object skips the next line.

## Example

Listing 9.133 opens two files. The first file is for reading a string from, while the second file is written to. The `SkipLine()` method is used to skip the first line before the file is read. This file can be executed with the Windows Scripting Host (`wscript.exe` or `cscript.exe`).

*Listing 9.133    Using the* `SkipLine()` *Method*

```
// Create a FileSystemObject object
var myFileSysObj = new ActiveXObject("Scripting.FileSystemObject");

// Create a TextStream object to read from and one to write to
var myInputTextStream = myFileSysObj.OpenTextFile("c:\\temp\\test.txt", 1,
true);
var myOutputTextStream = myFileSysObj.OpenTextFile("c:\\temp\\test2.txt", 2,
true);

// The SkipLine method is used to skip the first line of the input file.
myInputTextStream.SkipLine();

// Iterate through the file one character at a time and write it
// to the second file.
while(!myInputTextStream.AtEndOfStream){
  myOutputTextStream.Write(myInputTextStream.Read(1));
}

// Close the stream to the files
myInputTextStream.Close();
myOutputTextStream.Close();
```

# TextStream.Write()

## JScript2.0+

## Syntax

*textstream*.Write(*string*)

## Description

The `Write()` method of an instance of the `TextStream` object is used to write a string to the text file.

## Example

Listing 9.134 opens a text file and writes a string to it. This file can be executed with the Windows Scripting Host (`wscript.exe` or `cscript.exe`).

*Listing 9.134   Using the* Write() *Method*

```
// Create a FileSystemObject object
var myFileSysObj = new ActiveXObject("Scripting.FileSystemObject")

// Create a TextStream object
var myTextStream = myFileSysObj.OpenTextFile("c:\\temp\\test.txt", 2, true)

// Write a string to the file
myTextStream.Write("Hello, World!");

// Close the stream to the file
myTextStream.Close();
```

# TextStream.WriteBlankLines()

## JScript2.0+

## Syntax

*textstream*.WriteBlankLines(*num*)

## Description

The WriteBlankLines() method of an instance of the TextStream object is used to write *num* newline characters to the text file.

## Example

Listing 9.135 opens a text file and writes a string to it. The WriteBlankLines() method is then used to place a newline before a second string is written. This file can be executed with the Windows Scripting Host (wscript.exe or cscript.exe).

*Listing 9.135   Using the* WriteBlankLines() *Method*

```
// Create a FileSystemObject object
var myFileSysObj = new ActiveXObject("Scripting.FileSystemObject")

// Create a TextStream object
var myTextStream = myFileSysObj.OpenTextFile("c:\\temp\\test.txt", 2, true)

// Write the first string to the file
myTextStream.Write("Hello, World!");

// Write a newline character to the file
myTextStream.WriteBlankLines(1);

// Write a second string to the file
myTextStream.Write("Hello, World Again!");

// Close the stream to the file
myTextStream.Close();
```

# TextStream.WriteLine()

## JScript2.0+

## Syntax

```
textstream.WriteLine()
```

## Description

The WriteLine() method of an instance of the TextStream object is used to write a string followed by a newline to the text file.

## Example

Listing 9.136 opens a text file and writes a string followed by a newline to it. This file can be executed with the Windows Scripting Host (wscript.exe or cscript.exe).

*Listing 9.136    Using the* WriteLine() *Method*

```
// Create a FileSystemObject object
var myFileSysObj = new ActiveXObject("Scripting.FileSystemObject")

// Create a TextStream object
var myTextStream = myFileSysObj.OpenTextFile("c:\\temp\\test.txt", 2, true)

// Write a string followed by a newline to the file
myTextStream.WriteLine("Hello, World!");

// Close the stream to the file
myTextStream.Close();
```

# VBArray

## JScript3.0+

## Syntax

```
var variable = new VBArray(vbarray)
```

## Description

The VBArray object provides access to Visual Basic safeArrays. These arrays are often written on the same HTML page and are written in VBScript. Table 9.18 lists the methods of the VBArray is object.

**Table 9.18 Methods of the VBArray Object**

| Method | Description |
| --- | --- |
| dimensions() | Returns the number of dimensions in the array |
| getItem() | Returns the item at a specified location |
| lbound() | Returns the lowest index value of the dimension in the array |
| toArray() | Returns a JScript array from the VBArray passed |
| ubound() | Returns the highest index value of the dimension in the array |

## Example

Listing 9.137 calls a VBScript function from a JavaScript new operator to create a Visual Basic safe array. The function itself writes the contents of this two-dimensional array to the user's page.

*Listing 9.137    Creating a* VBArray

```
<script LANGUAGE="VBScript">
<!-- Hide
' Define the VB Array
Function myVBArray()

   ' Define variables for 2-D array positioning
   Dim i
   Dim j

   ' Define variable to hold incremented values to put into
   ' array and assign it an initial value of 1
   Dim k
   k = 1

   ' Create a 2-D array
   Dim myArray(1, 1)

   ' Iterate through 2-D array and put incremented value in
   For i = 0 To 1
     For j = 0 To 1
       myArray(j, i) = k

       ' Write the value to the screen
       document.writeln(k)
       k = k + 1
     Next
     document.writeln("<br>")
   Next

   ' Return the array to the calling function
   myVBArray = myArray
End Function
' End Hide -->
</script>
<script language="JScript">
<!-- Hide

// Create a new instance of VBArray
var myArray = new VBArray(myVBArray());

// End hide -->
</script>
```

# VBArray.dimensions()

## *JScript3.0+*

## *Syntax*

```
vbarray.dimensions()
```

## *Description*

The `dimensions()` method of an instance of a `VBArray` returns the number of dimensions of the array.

## *Example*

Listing 9.138 calls a VBScript function from a JavaScript `new` operator to create a Visual Basic safe array. The array itself writes the contents of this two-dimensional array to the user's page. An alert box is also invoked that contains the number of dimensions the array contains.

*Listing 9.138    Viewing the Number of Dimensions of a* VBArray *Object*

```
<script LANGUAGE="VBScript">
<!-- Hide
' Define the VB Array
Function myVBArray()

  ' Define variables for 2-D array positioning
  Dim i
  Dim j

  ' Define variable to hold incremented values to put into
  ' array and assign it an initial value of 1
  Dim k
  k = 1

  ' Create a 2-D array
  Dim myArray(1, 1)

  ' Iterate through 2-D array and put incremented value in
  For i = 0 To 1
    For j = 0 To 1
      myArray(j, i) = k

      ' Write the value to the screen
      document.writeln(k)
      k = k + 1
    Next
    document.writeln("<br>")
```

*continues*

*Listing 9.138   continued*
```
  Next

  ' Return the array to the calling function
  myVBArray = myArray
End Function
' End Hide -->
</script>
<script language="JScript">
<!-- Hide

// Create a new instance of VBArray
var myArray = new VBArray(myVBArray());
alert(myArray.dimensions());

// End hide -->
</script>
```

# VBArray.getItem()

## JScript3.0+

## Syntax

```
vbarray.getItem(index)

vbarray.getItem(indexA, indexB, ..., indexN)
```

## Description

The getItem() method of an instance of a VBArray returns the value at the *index*
passed. If the array is multi-dimensional, you pass the necessary coordinates to access
the location you want.

## Example

Listing 9.139 calls a VBScript function from a JavaScript new operator to create a
Visual Basic safe array. The array itself writes the contents of this two-dimensional
array to the user's page. An alert box is also invoked that contains the value in the second column of the second row.

*Listing 9.139   Using the* getItem() *Method*
```
<script LANGUAGE="VBScript">
<!-- Hide
' Define the VB Array
Function myVBArray()

  ' Define variables for 2-D array positioning
  Dim i
```

```
Dim j

' Define variable to hold incremented values to put into
' array and assign it an initial value of 1
Dim k
k = 1

' Create a 2-D array
Dim myArray(1, 1)

' Iterate through 2-D array and put incremented value in
For i = 0 To 1
  For j = 0 To 1
    myArray(j, i) = k

    ' Write the value to the screen
    document.writeln(k)
    k = k + 1
  Next
  document.writeln("<br>")
Next

' Return the array to the calling function
  myVBArray = myArray
End Function
' End Hide -->
</script>
<script language="JScript">
<!-- Hide

// Create a new instance of VBArray
var myArray = new VBArray(myVBArray());
alert(myArray.getItem(1,1));

// End hide -->
</script>
```

# VBArray.lbound()

## *JScript3.0+*

## *Syntax*

*vbarray*.lbound(*dimension*)

*vbarray*.lbound()

## *Description*

The lbound() method of an instance of a VBArray returns the lowest index value in the *dimension* passed. If no *dimension* is passed, then the method defaults to using 1.

## Example

Listing 9.140 calls a VBScript function from a JavaScript new operator to create a Visual Basic safe array. The array itself writes the contents of this two-dimensional array to the user's page. An alert box is also invoked that contains the lowest index number used in the second dimension.

*Listing 9.140   Using the* `lbound()` *Method*

```
<script LANGUAGE="VBScript">
<!-- Hide
' Define the VB Array
Function myVBArray()

  ' Define variables for 2-D array positioning
  Dim i
  Dim j

  ' Define variable to hold incremented values to put into
  ' array and assign it an initial value of 1
  Dim k
  k = 1

  ' Create a 2-D array
  Dim myArray(1, 1)

  ' Iterate through 2-D array and put incremented value in
  For i = 0 To 1
    For j = 0 To 1
      myArray(j, i) = k

      ' Write the value to the screen
      document.writeln(k)
      k = k + 1
    Next
    document.writeln("<br>")
  Next

  ' Return the array to the calling function
  myVBArray = myArray
End Function
' End Hide -->
</script>
<script language="JScript">
<!-- Hide

// Create a new instance of VBArray
var myArray = new VBArray(myVBArray());
alert(myArray.lbound(2));

// End hide -->
</script>
```

# VBArray.toArray()

## *JScript3.0+*

## Syntax

```
vbarray.toArray()
```

## Description

The `toArray()` method of an instance of a `VBArray` returns a valid JScript array from a `VBArray`.

## Example

Listing 9.141 calls a VBScript function from a JavaScript new operator to create a Visual Basic safe array. The array itself writes the contents of this two-dimensional array to the user's page. The array is then converted into a valid JScript array and an alert box is invoked to display a value in this array.

*Listing 9.141   Using the* `toArray()` *Method*

```
<script LANGUAGE="VBScript">
<!-- Hide
' Define the VB Array
Function myVBArray()

  ' Define variables for 2-D array positioning
  Dim i
  Dim j

  ' Define variable to hold incremented values to put into
  ' array and assign it an initial value of 1
  Dim k
  k = 1

  ' Create a 2-D array
  Dim myArray(1, 1)

  ' Iterate through 2-D array and put incremented value in
  For i = 0 To 1
    For j = 0 To 1
      myArray(j, i) = k

      ' Write the value to the screen
      document.writeln(k)
      k = k + 1
    Next
    document.writeln("<br>")
```

*continues*

*Listing 9.141    continued*
```
  Next

   ' Return the array to the calling function
   myVBArray = myArray
End Function
' End Hide -->
</script>
<script language="JScript">
<!-- Hide

// Create a new instance of VBArray
var myArray = new VBArray(myVBArray());

// Convert the VBArray to a JScript Array
var myJSArray = myArray.toArray();

// Display the second column, first row value
alert(myJSArray[0,1]);

// End hide -->
</script>
```

# VBArray.ubound()

## *JScript3.0+*

## *Syntax*

*vbarray*.ubound(*dimension*)

## *Description*

The ubound() method of an instance of a VBArray returns the highest index value in the *dimension* passed.

## *Example*

Listing 9.142 calls a VBScript function from a JavaScript new operator to create a Visual Basic safe array. The array itself writes the contents of this two-dimensional array to the user's page. An alert box is also invoked that contains the highest index number used in the second dimension.

*Listing 9.142    Using the* ubound() *Method*
```
<script LANGUAGE="VBScript">
<!-- Hide
' Define the VB Array
Function myVBArray()

   ' Define variables for 2-D array positioning
   Dim i
```

```
Dim j

' Define variable to hold incremented values to put into
' array and assign it an initial value of 1
Dim k
k = 1

' Create a 2-D array
Dim myArray(1, 1)

' Iterate through 2-D array and put incremented value in
For i = 0 To 1
  For j = 0 To 1
    myArray(j, i) = k

    ' Write the value to the screen
    document.writeln(k)
    k = k + 1
  Next
  document.writeln("<br>")
Next

' Return the array to the calling function
  myVBArray = myArray
End Function
' End Hide -->
</script>
<script language="JScript">
<!-- Hide

// Create a new instance of VBArray
var myArray = new VBArray(myVBArray());
alert(myArray.ubound(2));

// End hide -->
</script>
```

# PART IV

## APPENDIXES

# APPENDIX A

## Navigator-Supported Syntax

The following table contains a list of JavaScript syntax that Netscape Navigator browsers support. Each supported object, method, property, or Event Handler is followed by the version of the browser that supports it.

# Netscape Navigator-Supported Syntax

| Syntax | Type | 2.0 | 3.0 | 4.0 -4.05 | 4.06 -4.5 | 5.0 |
|---|---|---|---|---|---|---|
| - | Operator | X | X | X | X | X |
| - - | Operator | X | X | X | X | X |
| ! | Operator | X | X | X | X | X |
| != | Operator | X | X | X | X | X |
| !== | Operator | | | | X | X |
| % | Operator | X | X | X | X | X |
| %= | Operator | X | X | X | X | X |
| & | Operator | X | X | X | X | X |
| && | Operator | X | X | X | X | X |
| &= | Operator | X | X | X | X | X |
| * | Operator | X | X | X | X | X |
| *= | Operator | X | X | X | X | X |
| , | Operator | X | X | X | X | X |
| / | Operator | X | X | X | X | X |
| /**/ | Operator | X | X | X | X | X |
| // | Operator | X | X | X | X | X |
| /= | Operator | X | X | X | X | X |
| ?: | Operator | X | X | X | X | X |
| ^ | Operator | X | X | X | X | X |
| ^= | Operator | X | X | X | X | X |
| ¦ | Operator | X | X | X | X | X |
| ¦¦ | Operator | X | X | X | X | X |
| ¦= | Operator | X | X | X | X | X |
| ~ | Operator | X | X | X | X | X |
| + | Operator | X | X | X | X | X |
| ++ | Operator | X | X | X | X | X |
| += | Operator | X | X | X | X | X |
| < | Operator | X | X | X | X | X |
| << | Operator | X | X | X | X | X |
| <<= | Operator | X | X | X | X | X |
| <= | Operator | X | X | X | X | X |
| = | Operator | X | X | X | X | X |
| -= | Operator | X | X | X | X | X |
| == | Operator | X | X | X | X | X |
| === | Operator | | | | X | X |
| > | Operator | X | X | X | X | X |
| >= | Operator | X | X | X | X | X |
| >> | Operator | X | X | X | X | X |
| >>= | Operator | X | X | X | X | X |
| >>> | Operator | X | X | X | X | X |
| >>>= | Operator | X | X | X | X | X |

| Syntax | Type | 2.0 | 3.0 | 4.0 -4.05 | 4.06 -4.5 | 5.0 |
|---|---|---|---|---|---|---|
| abstract | Reserved | | | | | |
| Anchor | Object | | | X | X | X |
| Anchor.name | Property | | | X | X | X |
| Anchor.text | Property | | | X | X | X |
| Anchor.x | Property | | | X | X | X |
| Anchor.y | Property | | | X | X | X |
| Applet | Object | | X | X | X | X |
| Area | Object | | X | X | X | X |
| Area.handleEvent | Method | | | X | X | X |
| Area.hash | Property | | X | X | X | X |
| Area.host | Property | | X | X | X | X |
| Area.hostname | Property | | X | X | X | X |
| Area.href | Property | | X | X | X | X |
| Area.onMouseOut | Event Handler | | X | X | X | X |
| Area.onMouseOver | Event Handler | | X | X | X | X |
| Area.pathname | Property | | X | X | X | X |
| Area.port | Property | | X | X | X | X |
| Area.protocol | Property | | X | X | X | X |
| Area.search | Property | | X | X | X | X |
| Area.target | Property | | X | X | X | X |
| Array() | Object | | X | X | X | X |
| Array.concat() | Method | | | X | X | X |
| Array.join() | Method | | X | X | X | X |
| Array.length | Property | | X | X | X | X |
| Array.pop() | Method | | | X | X | X |
| Array.push() | Method | | | X | X | X |
| Array.reverse() | Method | | X | X | X | X |
| Array.shift() | Method | | | X | X | X |
| Array.slice() | Method | | | X | X | X |
| Array.sort() | Method | | X | X | X | X |
| Array.splice() | Method | | | X | X | X |
| Array.toSource() | Method | | | | X | X |
| Array.toString() | Method | | X | X | X | X |
| Array.unshift() | Method | | | X | X | X |
| boolean | Reserved | | | | | |
| Boolean() | Object | | X | X | X | X |
| Boolean.prototype | Property | | X | X | X | X |
| Boolean.toSource() | Method | | X | X | X | X |
| Boolean.toString() | Method | | X | X | X | X |
| break | Keyword | | X | X | X | X |

*continues*

| Syntax | Type | 2.0 | 3.0 | 4.0 -4.05 | 4.06 -4.5 | 5.0 |
|---|---|---|---|---|---|---|
| byte | Reserved | | | | | |
| Button | Object | X | X | X | X | X |
| Button.blur() | Method | | X | X | X | X |
| Button.click() | Method | X | X | X | X | X |
| Button.focus() | Method | | X | X | X | X |
| Button.form | Property | X | X | X | X | X |
| Button.handleEvent() | Method | | | X | X | X |
| Button.name | Property | X | X | X | X | X |
| Button.onBlur | Event Handler | | X | X | X | X |
| Button.onClick | Event Handler | X | X | X | X | X |
| Button.onFocus | Event Handler | | X | X | X | X |
| Button.onMouseDown | Event Handler | X | X | X | X | X |
| Button.onMouseUp | Event Handler | X | X | X | X | X |
| Button.type | Property | | X | X | X | X |
| Button.value | Property | X | X | X | X | X |
| catch | Statement | | | | | X |
| case | Reserved | | | | | |
| char | Reserved | | | | | |
| Checkbox | Object | X | X | X | X | X |
| Checkbox.blur() | Method | | X | X | X | X |
| Checkbox.checked | Property | X | X | X | X | X |
| Checkbox.click() | Method | | X | X | X | X |
| Checkbox.defaultChecked | Property | X | X | X | X | X |
| Checkbox.focus() | Method | X | X | X | X | X |
| Checkbox.form | Property | X | X | X | X | X |
| Checkbox.handleEvent() | Method | | | X | X | X |
| Checkbox.name | Property | X | X | X | X | X |
| Checkbox.onBlur | Event Handler | | X | X | X | X |
| Checkbox.onClick | Event Handler | | X | X | X | X |
| Checkbox.onFocus | Event Handler | | X | X | X | X |
| Checkbox.type | Property | | X | X | X | X |
| Checkbox.value | Property | X | X | X | X | X |
| class | Reserved | | | | | |
| const | Reserved | | | | | |
| continue | Statement | | X | X | X | X |
| Date() | Object | X | X | X | X | X |
| Date.getDate() | Method | X | X | X | X | X |
| Date.getDay() | Method | X | X | X | X | X |
| Date.getFullYear() | Method | | | X | X | X |
| Date.getHours() | Method | X | X | X | X | X |
| Date.getMilliseconds() | Method | | | X | X | X |

| Syntax | Type | 2.0 | 3.0 | 4.0 -4.05 | 4.06 -4.5 | 5.0 |
|---|---|---|---|---|---|---|
| Date.getMinutes() | Method | X | X | X | X | X |
| Date.getMonth() | Method | X | X | X | X | X |
| Date.getSeconds() | Method | X | X | X | X | X |
| Date.getTime() | Method | X | X | X | X | X |
| Date. getTimezoneOffset() | Method | X | X | X | X | X |
| Date.getUTCDate() | Method | | | X | X | X |
| Date.getUTCDay() | Method | | | X | X | X |
| Date.getUTCFullYear() | Method | | | X | X | X |
| Date.getUTCHours() | Method | | | X | X | X |
| Date. getUTCMilliseconds() | Method | | | X | X | X |
| Date.getUTCMinutes() | Method | | | X | X | X |
| Date.getUTCMonth() | Method | | | X | X | X |
| Date.getUTCSeconds() | Method | | | X | X | X |
| Date.getYear() | Method | X | X | X | X | X |
| Date.parse() | Method | X | X | X | X | X |
| Date.prototype | Property | X | X | X | X | X |
| Date.setDate() | Method | X | X | X | X | X |
| Date.setFullYear() | Method | | | X | X | X |
| Date.setHours() | Method | X | X | X | X | X |
| Date.setMilliseconds() | Method | | | X | X | X |
| Date.setMinutes() | Method | X | X | X | X | X |
| Date.setMonth() | Method | X | X | X | X | X |
| Date.setSeconds() | Method | X | X | X | X | X |
| Date.setTime() | Method | X | X | X | X | X |
| Date.setUTCDate() | Method | | | X | X | X |
| Date.setUTCFullYear() | Method | | | X | X | X |
| Date.setUTCHours() | Method | | | X | X | X |
| Date. setUTCMilliseconds() | Method | | | X | X | X |
| Date.setUTCMinutes() | Method | | | X | X | X |
| Date.setUTCMonth() | Method | | | X | X | X |
| Date.setUTCSeconds() | Method | | | X | X | X |
| Date.setYear() | Method | X | X | X | X | X |
| Date.toGMTString() | Method | X | X | X | X | X |
| Date.toLocaleString() | Method | X | X | X | X | X |
| Date.toSource() | Method | | | | X | X |
| Date.toString() | Method | X | X | X | X | X |
| Date.toUTCString() | Method | | | X | X | X |
| Date.UTC() | Method | X | X | X | X | X |

*continues*

| Syntax | Type | 2.0 | 3.0 | 4.0 -4.05 | 4.06 -4.5 | 5.0 |
|---|---|---|---|---|---|---|
| debugger | Reserved | | | | | |
| default | Reserved | | | | | |
| delete | Statement | X | X | X | X | X |
| do...while | Statement | X | X | X | X | X |
| document | Object | X | X | X | X | X |
| document.alinkColor | Property | X | X | X | X | X |
| document.anchors | Property | | | X | X | X |
| document.anchors.length | Property | | | X | X | X |
| document.applets | Property | | X | X | X | X |
| document.applets.length | Property | | X | X | X | X |
| document.bgColor | Property | X | X | X | X | X |
| document. captureEvents() | Method | | | X | X | X |
| document.classes | Property | | | X | X | X |
| document.classes. backgroundColor | Property | | | X | X | X |
| document.classes. backgroundImage | Property | | | X | X | X |
| document.classes. borderBottomWidth | Property | | | X | X | X |
| document.classes. borderColor | Property | | | X | X | X |
| document.classes. borderLeftWidth | Property | | | X | X | X |
| document.classes. borderRightWidth | Property | | | X | X | X |
| document.classes. borderStyle | Property | | | X | X | X |
| document.classes. borderTopWidth | Property | | | X | X | X |
| document.classes. borderWidths() | Method | | | X | X | X |
| document.classes.clear | Property | | | X | X | X |
| document.classes.color | Property | | | X | X | X |
| document.classes. display | Property | | | X | X | X |
| document.classes. fontFamily | Property | | | X | X | X |
| document.classes. fontSize | Property | | | X | X | X |
| document.classes. | | | | | | |

| Syntax | Type | 2.0 | 3.0 | 4.0 -4.05 | 4.06 -4.5 | 5.0 |
|--------|------|-----|-----|-----------|-----------|-----|
| fontStyle document.classes. | Property | | | X | X | X |
| fontWeight document.classes. | Property | | | X | X | X |
| lineHeight document.classes. | Property | | | X | X | X |
| listStyleType document.classes. | Property | | | X | X | X |
| marginBottom document.classes. | Property | | | X | X | X |
| marginLeft document.classes. | Property | | | X | X | X |
| marginRight document.classes. | Property | | | X | X | X |
| margins() document.classes. | Method | | | X | X | X |
| marginTop document.classes. | Property | | | X | X | X |
| paddingBottom document.classes. | Property | | | X | X | X |
| paddingLeft document.classes. | Property | | | X | X | X |
| paddingRight document.classes. | Property | | | X | X | X |
| paddings() document.classes. | Method | | | X | X | X |
| paddingTop document.classes. | Property | | | X | X | X |
| textAlign document.classes. | Property | | | X | X | X |
| TextDecoration document.classes. | Property | | | X | X | X |
| textIndent document.classes. | Property | | | X | X | X |
| textTransform document.classes. | Property | | | X | X | X |
| whiteSpace | Property | | | X | X | X |
| document.close() | Method | X | X | X | X | X |
| document.cookie | Property | X | X | X | X | X |
| document.domain | Property | | X | X | X | X |
| document.embeds | Property | | X | X | X | X |

*continues*

| Syntax | Type | 2.0 | 3.0 | 4.0 -4.05 | 4.06 -4.5 | 5.0 |
|--------|------|-----|-----|-----------|-----------|-----|
| document.embeds.length | Property | | X | X | X | X |
| document.fgColor | Property | X | X | X | X | X |
| document.*formName* | Property | | X | X | X | X |
| document.forms | Property | | X | X | X | X |
| document.forms.length | Property | | X | X | X | X |
| document.getSelection() | Property | | | X | X | X |
| document.handleEvent() | Property | | | X | X | X |
| document.height | Property | | | X | X | X |
| document.ids | Property | | | X | X | X |
| document.ids. backgroundColor | Property | | | X | X | X |
| document.ids. backgroundImage | Property | | | X | X | X |
| document.ids. borderBottomWidth | Property | | | X | X | X |
| document.ids. borderColor | Property | | | X | X | X |
| document.ids. borderLeftWidth | Property | | | X | X | X |
| document.ids. borderRightWidth | Property | | | X | X | X |
| document.ids. borderStyle | Property | | | X | X | X |
| document.ids. borderTopWidth | Property | | | X | X | X |
| document.ids. borderWidths() | Method | | | X | X | X |
| document.ids.clear | Property | | | X | X | X |
| document.ids.color | Property | | | X | X | X |
| document.ids.display | Property | | | X | X | X |
| document.ids.fontFamily | Property | | | X | X | X |
| document.ids.fontSize | Property | | | X | X | X |
| document.ids.fontStyle | Property | | | X | X | X |
| document.ids. fontWeight | Property | | | X | X | X |
| document.ids. lineHeight | Property | | | X | X | X |
| document.ids. listStyleType | Property | | | X | X | X |
| document.ids. marginBottom | Property | | | X | X | X |

| Syntax | Type | 2.0 | 3.0 | 4.0 -4.05 | 4.06 -4.5 | 5.0 |
|---|---|---|---|---|---|---|
| marginLeft document.ids. | Property | | | X | X | X |
| marginRight document.ids. | Property | | | X | X | X |
| margins() document.ids. | Method | | | X | X | X |
| marginTop document.ids. | Property | | | X | X | X |
| paddingBottom document.ids. | Property | | | X | X | X |
| paddingLeft document.ids. | Property | | | X | X | X |
| paddingRight document.ids. | Property | | | X | X | X |
| paddings() document.ids. | Method | | | X | X | X |
| paddingTop document.ids. | Property | | | X | X | X |
| textAlign document.ids. | Property | | | X | X | X |
| textDecoration document.ids. | Property | | | X | X | X |
| textIndent document.ids. | Property | | | X | X | X |
| textTransform document.ids. | Property | | | X | X | X |
| verticalAlign | Property | | | X | X | X |
| document.ids.whiteSpace | Property | | | X | X | X |
| document.images | Property | | X | X | X | X |
| document.images.length | Property | | X | X | X | X |
| document.lastModified | Property | X | X | X | X | X |
| document.layers | Property | | | X | X | X |
| document.layers.length | Property | | | X | X | X |
| document.linkColor | Property | X | X | X | X | X |
| document.links | Property | X | X | X | X | X |
| document.links.length | Property | X | X | X | X | X |
| document.location | Property | X | X | X | X | X |
| document.onClick | Event Handler | X | X | X | X | X |
| document.onDblClick | Event Handler | X | X | X | X | X |
| document.onKeyDown | Event Handler | X | X | X | X | X |
| document.onKeyPress | Event Handler | X | X | X | X | X |

*continues*

| Syntax | Type | 2.0 | 3.0 | 4.0 -4.05 | 4.06 -4.5 | 5.0 |
|--------|------|-----|-----|-----------|-----------|-----|
| document.onKeyUp | Event Handler | X | X | X | X | X |
| document.onMouseDown | Event Handler | X | X | X | X | X |
| document.onMouseUp | Event Handler | X | X | X | X | X |
| document.open() | Method | X | X | X | X | X |
| document.plugins | Property | | X | X | X | X |
| document.referrer | Property | X | X | X | X | X |
| document. releaseEvents() | Method | | | X | X | X |
| document.routeEvent() | Method | | | X | X | X |
| document.tags | Property | | | X | X | X |
| document.tags. backgroundColor | Property | | | X | X | X |
| document.tags. backgroundImage | Property | | | X | X | X |
| document.tags. borderBottomWidth | Property | | | X | X | X |
| document.tags. borderColor | Property | | | X | X | X |
| document.tags. borderLeftWidth | Property | | | X | X | X |
| document.tags. borderRightWidth | Property | | | X | X | X |
| document.tags. borderStyle | Property | | | X | X | X |
| document.tags. borderTopWidth | Property | | | X | X | X |
| document.tags. borderWidths() | Method | | | X | X | X |
| document.tags.clear | Property | | | X | X | X |
| document.tags.color | Property | | | X | X | X |
| document.tags.display | Property | | | X | X | X |
| document.tags. fontFamily | Property | | | X | X | X |
| document.tags. fontSize | Property | | | X | X | X |
| document.tags. fontStyle | Property | | | X | X | X |
| document.tags. fontWeight | Property | | | X | X | X |
| document.tags. lineHeight | Property | | | X | X | X |
| document.tags. | | | | | | |

| Syntax | Type | 2.0 | 3.0 | 4.0 -4.05 | 4.06 -4.5 | 5.0 |
|---|---|---|---|---|---|---|
| listStyleType | Property | | | X | X | X |
| document.tags. marginBottom | Property | | | X | X | X |
| document.tags. marginLeft | Property | | | X | X | X |
| document.tags. marginRight | Property | | | X | X | X |
| document.tags. margins() | Method | | | X | X | X |
| document.tags. marginTop | Property | | | X | X | X |
| document.tags. paddingBottom | Property | | | X | X | X |
| document.tags. paddingLeft | Property | | | X | X | X |
| document.tags. paddingRight | Property | | | X | X | X |
| document.tags. paddings() | Method | | | X | X | X |
| document.tags. paddingTop | Property | | | X | X | X |
| document.tags. textAlign | Property | | | X | X | X |
| document.tags. textDecoration | Property | | | X | X | X |
| document.tags. textIndent | Property | | | X | X | X |
| document.tags. textTransform | Property | | | X | X | X |
| document.tags. whiteSpace | Property | | | X | X | X |
| document.title | Property | X | X | X | X | X |
| document.URL | Property | X | X | X | X | X |
| document.vlinkColor | Property | X | X | X | X | X |
| document.width | Property | | | X | X | X |
| document.write() | Method | X | X | X | X | X |
| document.writeln() | Method | X | X | X | X | X |
| Embed | Object | X | X | X | X | X |
| enum | Keyword | | | | X | X |
| escape() | Method | X | X | X | X | X |
| eval() | Method | X | X | X | X | X |

*continues*

| Syntax | Type | 2.0 | 3.0 | 4.0 -4.05 | 4.06 -4.5 | 5.0 |
|---|---|---|---|---|---|---|
| event | Object | | | X | X | X |
| event.data | Property | | | X | X | X |
| event.height | Property | | | X | X | X |
| event.layerX | Property | | | X | X | X |
| event.layerY | Property | | | X | X | X |
| event.modifiers | Property | | | X | X | X |
| event.pageX | Property | | | X | X | X |
| event.pageY | Property | | | X | X | X |
| event.screenX | Property | | | X | X | X |
| event.screenY | Property | | | X | X | X |
| event.target | Property | | | X | X | X |
| event.type | Property | | | X | X | X |
| event.which | Property | | | X | X | X |
| event.width | Property | | | X | X | X |
| Event.ABORT | Event | | X | X | X | X |
| Event.BLUR | Event | X | X | X | X | X |
| Event.CHANGE | Event | X | X | X | X | X |
| Event.CLICK | Event | X | X | X | X | X |
| Event.DBLCLICK | Event | | | X | X | X |
| Event.DRAGDROP | Event | | | X | X | X |
| Event.ERROR | Event | | X | X | X | X |
| Event.FOCUS | Event | X | X | X | X | X |
| Event.KEYDOWN | Event | | | X | X | X |
| Event.KEYPRESS | Event | | | X | X | X |
| Event.KEYUP | Event | | | X | X | X |
| Event.LOAD | Event | X | X | X | X | X |
| Event.MOUSEDOWN | Event | | | X | X | X |
| Event.MOUSEMOVE | Event | | | X | X | X |
| Event.MOUSEOUT | Event | | X | X | X | X |
| Event.MOUSEOVER | Event | X | X | X | X | X |
| Event.MOUSEUP | Event | | | X | X | X |
| Event.MOVE | Event | | | X | X | X |
| Event.RESET | Event | | X | X | X | X |
| Event.RESIZE | Event | | | X | X | X |
| Event.SELECT | Event | X | X | X | X | X |
| Event.SUBMIT | Event | X | X | X | X | X |
| Event.UNLOAD | Event | X | X | X | X | X |
| export | Statement | | | X | X | X |
| extends | Keyword | | | | X | X |
| false | Reserved | | | | | |
| FileUpload | Object | X | X | X | X | X |
| FileUpload.blur() | Method | | X | X | X | X |

| Syntax | Type | 2.0 | 3.0 | 4.0 -4.05 | 4.06 -4.5 | 5.0 |
|---|---|---|---|---|---|---|
| FileUpload.focus() | Method | | X | X | X | X |
| FileUpload.form | Property | X | X | X | X | X |
| FileUpload. handleEvent() | Method | | | X | X | X |
| FileUpload.name | Property | X | X | X | X | X |
| FileUpload.onBlur | Event Handler | | X | X | X | X |
| FileUpload.onChange | Event Handler | | X | X | X | X |
| FileUpload.onFocus | Event Handler | | X | X | X | X |
| FileUpload.select() | Method | X | X | X | X | X |
| FileUpload.type | Property | | X | X | X | X |
| FileUpload.value | Property | X | X | X | X | X |
| finally | Keyword | | | | X | X |
| for | Statement | X | X | X | X | X |
| for...in | Statement | X | X | X | X | X |
| Form | Object | X | X | X | X | X |
| Form.action | Property | X | X | X | X | X |
| Form.elements | Property | X | X | X | X | X |
| Form.elements.length | Property | X | X | X | X | X |
| Form.encoding | Property | X | X | X | X | X |
| Form.handleEvent() | Method | | | X | X | X |
| Form.length | Property | X | X | X | X | X |
| Form.method | Property | X | X | X | X | X |
| Form.name | Property | X | X | X | X | X |
| Form.onReset | Event Handler | | X | X | X | X |
| Form.onSubmit | Event Handler | X | X | X | X | X |
| Form.reset() | Method | | X | X | X | X |
| Form.submit() | Method | X | X | X | X | X |
| Form.target | Property | X | X | X | X | X |
| Frame | Object | X | X | X | X | X |
| Frame.blur() | Method | | X | X | X | X |
| Frame.clearInterval() | Method | | | X | X | X |
| Frame.clearTimeout() | Method | | | X | X | X |
| Frame.document | Property | X | X | X | X | X |
| Frame.focus() | Method | | X | X | X | X |
| Frame.frames | Property | X | X | X | X | X |
| Frame.length | Property | X | X | X | X | X |
| Frame.name | Property | X | X | X | X | X |
| Frame.onBlur | Event Handler | | X | X | X | X |
| Frame.onFocus | Event Handler | | X | X | X | X |
| Frame.onMove | Event Handler | | | X | X | X |
| Frame.onResize | Event Handler | | | X | X | X |

*continues*

| Syntax | Type | 2.0 | 3.0 | 4.0 -4.05 | 4.06 -4.5 | 5.0 |
|---|---|---|---|---|---|---|
| Frame.parent | Property | X | X | X | X | X |
| Frame.print() | Method | | | X | X | X |
| Frame.self | Property | X | X | X | X | X |
| Frame.setInterval() | Method | | | X | X | X |
| Frame.setTimeout() | Method | X | X | X | X | X |
| Frame.top | Property | X | X | X | X | X |
| Frame.window | Property | X | X | X | X | X |
| function | Statement | X | X | X | X | X |
| Function() | Object | X | X | X | X | X |
| Function.apply() | Method | | | | X | X |
| Function.arguments | Property | | X | X | X | X |
| Function.arity | Property | | | X | X | X |
| Function.call() | Method | | | | X | X |
| Function.caller | Property | | X | X | X | X |
| Function.prototype | Property | | X | X | X | X |
| Function.toSource() | Method | | | | X | X |
| Function.toString() | Method | | X | X | X | X |
| Hidden | Object | X | X | X | X | X |
| Hidden.form | Property | X | X | X | X | X |
| Hidden.name | Property | X | X | X | X | X |
| Hidden.type | Property | | X | X | X | X |
| Hidden.value | Property | X | X | X | X | X |
| History | Object | X | X | X | X | X |
| History.back() | Method | X | X | X | X | X |
| History.current | Property | | X | X | X | X |
| History.forward() | Method | X | X | X | X | X |
| History.go() | Method | X | X | X | X | X |
| History.length | Property | X | X | X | X | X |
| History.next | Property | | X | X | X | X |
| History.previous | Property | X | X | X | X | X |
| if...else | Statement | X | X | X | X | X |
| Image() | Object | | X | X | X | X |
| Image.border | Property | | X | X | X | X |
| Image.complete | Property | | X | X | X | X |
| Image.handleEvent() | Method | | | X | X | X |
| Image.height | Property | | X | X | X | X |
| Image.hspace | Property | | X | X | X | X |
| Image.lowsrc | Property | | X | X | X | X |
| Image.name | Property | | X | X | X | X |
| Image.onAbort | Event Handler | | X | X | X | X |
| Image.onError | Event Handler | | X | X | X | X |
| Image.onKeyDown | Event Handler | | | X | X | X |

| Syntax | Type | 2.0 | 3.0 | 4.0 -4.05 | 4.06 -4.5 | 5.0 |
|---|---|---|---|---|---|---|
| Image.onKeyPress | Event Handler | | | X | X | X |
| Image.onKeyUp | Event Handler | | | X | X | X |
| Image.onLoad | Event Handler | | X | X | X | X |
| Image.prototype | Property | | X | X | X | X |
| Image.src | Property | | X | X | X | X |
| Image.vspace | Property | | X | X | X | X |
| Image.width | Property | | X | X | X | X |
| implements | Reserved | | | | | |
| import | Statement | | | X | X | X |
| in | Operator | | | | | X |
| Infinity | Keyword | | | | X | X |
| instanceof | Operator | | | | | X |
| int | Reserved | | | | | |
| interface | Reserved | | | | | |
| isFinite() | Method | | | | X | X |
| isNaN() | Method | | | | X | X |
| labeled | Statement | | | X | X | X |
| Layer() | Object | | | X | X | X |
| Layer.above | Property | | | X | X | X |
| Layer.background | Property | | | X | X | X |
| Layer.below | Property | | | X | X | X |
| Layer.bgColor | Property | | | X | X | X |
| Layer.captureEvents() | Method | | | X | X | X |
| Layer.clip.bottom | Property | | | X | X | X |
| Layer.clip.height | Property | | | X | X | X |
| Layer.clip.left | Property | | | X | X | X |
| Layer.clip.right | Property | | | X | X | X |
| Layer.clip.top | Property | | | X | X | X |
| Layer.clip.width | Property | | | X | X | X |
| Layer.document | Property | | | X | X | X |
| Layer.handleEvent() | Method | | | X | X | X |
| Layer.left | Property | | | X | X | X |
| Layer.load() | Method | | | X | X | X |
| Layer.moveAbove() | Method | | | X | X | X |
| Layer.moveBelow() | Method | | | X | X | X |
| Layer.moveBy() | Method | | | X | X | X |
| Layer.moveTo() | Method | | | X | X | X |
| Layer.moveToAbsolute() | Method | | | X | X | X |
| Layer.name | Property | | | X | X | X |
| Layer.onBlur | Event Handler | | | X | X | X |
| Layer.onFocus | Event Handler | | | X | X | X |

*continues*

| Syntax | Type | 2.0 | 3.0 | 4.0 -4.05 | 4.06 -4.5 | 5.0 |
|---|---|---|---|---|---|---|
| Layer.onLoad | Event Handler | | | X | X | X |
| Layer.onMouseOut | Event Handler | | | X | X | X |
| Layer.onMouseOver | Event Handler | | | X | X | X |
| Layer.pageX | Property | | | X | X | X |
| Layer.pageY | Property | | | X | X | X |
| Layer.parentLayer | Property | | | X | X | X |
| Layer.releaseEvents() | Method | | | X | X | X |
| Layer.resizeBy() | Method | | | X | X | X |
| Layer.resizeTo() | Method | | | X | X | X |
| Layer.routeEvent() | Method | | | X | X | X |
| Layer.siblingAbove | Property | | | X | X | X |
| Layer.siblingBelow | Property | | | X | X | X |
| Layer.src | Property | | | X | X | X |
| Layer.top | Property | | | X | X | X |
| Layer.visibility | Property | | | X | X | X |
| Layer.zIndex | Property | | | X | X | X |
| Link | Object | X | X | X | X | X |
| Link.handleEvent() | Method | | | X | X | X |
| Link.hash | Property | X | X | X | X | X |
| Link.host | Property | X | X | X | X | X |
| Link.hostname | Property | X | X | X | X | X |
| Link.href | Property | X | X | X | X | X |
| Link.onClick | Event Handler | X | X | X | X | X |
| Link.onDblClick | Event Handler | | | X | X | X |
| Link.onKeyDown | Event Handler | | | X | X | X |
| Link.onKeyPress | Event Handler | | | X | X | X |
| Link.onKeyUp | Event Handler | | | X | X | X |
| Link.onMouseDown | Event Handler | | | X | X | X |
| Link.onMouseOut | Event Handler | | X | X | X | X |
| Link.onMouseOver | Event Handler | X | X | X | X | X |
| Link.onMouseUp | Event Handler | | | X | X | X |
| Link.pathname | Property | X | X | X | X | X |
| Link.port | Property | X | X | X | X | X |
| Link.protocol | Property | X | X | X | X | X |
| Link.search | Property | X | X | X | X | X |
| Link.target | Property | X | X | X | X | X |
| Link.text | Property | | | X | X | X |
| Location | Object | X | X | X | X | X |
| Location.hash | Property | X | X | X | X | X |
| Location.host | Property | X | X | X | X | X |
| Location.hostname | Property | X | X | X | X | X |
| Location.href | Property | X | X | X | X | X |

| Syntax | Type | 2.0 | 3.0 | 4.0 -4.05 | 4.06 -4.5 | 5.0 |
|---|---|---|---|---|---|---|
| Location.pathname | Property | X | X | X | X | X |
| Location.port | Property | X | X | X | X | X |
| Location.protocol | Property | X | X | X | X | X |
| Location.reload() | Method | | X | X | X | X |
| Location.replace() | Method | | X | X | X | X |
| Location.search | Property | X | X | X | X | X |
| long | Reserved | | | | | |
| Math() | Object | X | X | X | X | X |
| Math.abs() | Method | X | X | X | X | X |
| Math.acos() | Method | X | X | X | X | X |
| Math.asin() | Method | X | X | X | X | X |
| Math.atan() | Method | X | X | X | X | X |
| Math.atan2() | Method | X | X | X | X | X |
| Math.ceil() | Method | X | X | X | X | X |
| Math.cos() | Method | X | X | X | X | X |
| Math.E | Property | X | X | X | X | X |
| Math.exp() | Method | X | X | X | X | X |
| Math.floor() | Method | X | X | X | X | X |
| Math.LN10 | Property | X | X | X | X | X |
| Math.LN2 | Property | X | X | X | X | X |
| Math.log() | Method | X | X | X | X | X |
| Math.LOG10E | Property | X | X | X | X | X |
| Math.LOG2E | Property | X | X | X | X | X |
| Math.max() | Method | X | X | X | X | X |
| Math.min() | Method | X | X | X | X | X |
| Math.PI | Property | X | X | X | X | X |
| Math.pow() | Method | X | X | X | X | X |
| Math.random() | Method | X | X | X | X | X |
| Math.round() | Method | X | X | X | X | X |
| Math.sin() | Method | X | X | X | X | X |
| Math.sqrt() | Method | X | X | X | X | X |
| Math.SQRT1_2 | Property | X | X | X | X | X |
| Math.SQRT2 | Property | X | X | X | X | X |
| Math.tan() | Method | X | X | X | X | X |
| Math.toSource() | Method | X | X | X | X | X |
| Math.toString() | Method | X | X | X | X | X |
| MimeType | Object | | X | X | X | X |
| MimeType.description | Property | | X | X | X | X |
| MimeType.enabledPlugin | Property | | X | X | X | X |
| MimeType.suffixes | Property | | X | X | X | X |
| MimeType.type | Property | | X | X | X | X |

*continues*

| Syntax | Type | 2.0 | 3.0 | 4.0 -4.05 | 4.06 -4.5 | 5.0 |
|---|---|---|---|---|---|---|
| NaN | Keyword | | | | X | X |
| native | Reserved | | | | | |
| navigator | Object | X | X | X | X | X |
| navigator.appCodeName | Property | X | X | X | X | X |
| navigator.appName | Property | X | X | X | X | X |
| navigator.appVersion | Property | X | X | X | X | X |
| navigator.javaEnabled() | Method | | X | X | X | X |
| navigator.language | Property | | | X | X | X |
| navigator.mimeTypes | Property | | X | X | X | X |
| navigator.platform | Property | | | X | X | X |
| navigator.plugins | Property | | X | X | X | X |
| navigator.plugins. refresh() | Method | | X | X | X | X |
| navigator.preference() | Method | | | X | X | X |
| navigator. taintEnabled() | Method | | X | | | |
| navigator.userAgent | Property | X | X | X | X | X |
| new | Operator | X | X | X | X | X |
| Number() | Object | | X | X | X | X |
| Number.MAX_VALUE | Property | | X | X | X | X |
| Number.MIN_VALUE | Property | | X | X | X | X |
| Number.NaN | Property | | X | X | X | X |
| Number. NEGATIVE_INFINITY | Property | | X | X | X | X |
| Number. POSITIVE_INFINITY | Property | | X | X | X | X |
| Number.prototype | Property | | X | X | X | X |
| Number.toSource() | Method | | | | X | X |
| Number.toString() | Method | | X | X | X | X |
| Object() | Object | | X | X | X | X |
| Object.constructor | Property | | X | X | X | X |
| Object.eval() | Method | | X | X | X | X |
| Object.prototype | Property | | X | X | X | X |
| Object.toSource() | Method | | | | X | X |
| Object.toString() | Method | | X | X | X | X |
| Object.unwatch() | Method | | | X | X | X |
| Object.valueof() | Method | | X | X | X | X |
| Object.watch() | Method | | | X | X | X |
| Option | Object | X | X | X | X | X |
| Option.defaultSelected | Property | | X | X | X | X |
| Option.selected | Property | X | X | X | X | X |
| Option.text | Property | X | X | X | X | X |

| Syntax | Type | 2.0 | 3.0 | 4.0 -4.05 | 4.06 -4.5 | 5.0 |
|--------|------|-----|-----|-----------|-----------|-----|
| Option.value | Property | X | X | X | X | X |
| packages | Reserved | | | | | |
| Packages | Object | | X | X | X | X |
| Packages.java | Property | | X | X | X | X |
| Packages.netscape | Property | | X | X | X | X |
| Packages.sun | Property | | X | X | X | X |
| parseFloat() | Method | X | X | X | X | X |
| parseInt() | Method | X | X | X | X | X |
| Password | Object | X | X | X | X | X |
| Password.blur() | Method | X | X | X | X | X |
| Password.defaultValue | Property | X | X | X | X | X |
| Password.focus() | Method | X | X | X | X | X |
| Password.form | Property | X | X | X | X | X |
| Password.handleEvent() | Method | | | X | X | X |
| Password.name | Property | X | X | X | X | X |
| Password.onBlur | Event Handler | X | X | X | X | X |
| Password.onFocus | Event Handler | X | X | X | X | X |
| Password.select() | Method | X | X | X | X | X |
| Password.type | Property | | X | X | X | X |
| Password.value | Property | X | X | X | X | X |
| Plugin | Object | | X | X | X | X |
| Plugin.description | Property | | X | X | X | X |
| Plugin.filename | Property | | X | X | X | X |
| Plugin.length | Property | | X | X | X | X |
| Plugin.name | Property | | X | X | X | X |
| private | Reserved | | | | | |
| protected | Reserved | | | | | |
| public | Reserved | | | | | |
| Radio | Object | X | X | X | X | X |
| Radio.blur() | Method | X | X | X | X | X |
| Radio.checked | Property | X | X | X | X | X |
| Radio.click() | Method | X | X | X | X | X |
| Radio.defaultChecked | Property | X | X | X | X | X |
| Radio.focus() | Method | X | X | X | X | X |
| Radio.form | Property | X | X | X | X | X |
| Radio.handleEvent() | Method | | | X | X | X |
| Radio.name | Property | X | X | X | X | X |
| Radio.onBlur | Event Handler | X | X | X | X | X |
| Radio.onClick | Event Handler | X | X | X | X | X |
| Radio.onFocus | Event Handler | X | X | X | X | X |
| Radio.type | Property | | X | X | X | X |

*continues*

| Syntax | Type | 2.0 | 3.0 | 4.0 -4.05 | 4.06 -4.5 | 5.0 |
|--------|------|-----|-----|-----------|-----------|-----|
| Radio.value | Property | X | X | X | X | X |
| RegExp() | Object | | | X | X | X |
| RegExp,$* | Property | | | X | X | X |
| RegExp.$& | Property | | | X | X | X |
| RegExp.$_ | Property | | | X | X | X |
| RegExp.$` | Property | | | X | X | X |
| RegExp.$' | Property | | | X | X | X |
| RegExp.$+ | Property | | | X | X | X |
| RegExp.$1,$2,...$9 | Property | | | X | X | X |
| RegExp.compile() | Method | | | X | X | X |
| RegExp.exec() | Method | | | X | X | X |
| RegExp.global | Property | | | X | X | X |
| RegExp.ignoreCase | Property | | | X | X | X |
| RegExp.input | Property | | | X | X | X |
| RegExp.lastIndex | Property | | | X | X | X |
| RegExp.lastMatch | Property | | | X | X | X |
| RegExp.lastParen | Property | | | X | X | X |
| RegExp.leftContext | Property | | | X | X | X |
| RegExp.multiline | Property | | | X | X | X |
| RegExp.rightContext | Property | | | X | X | X |
| RegExp.source | Property | | | X | X | X |
| RegExp.test() | Method | | | X | X | X |
| Reset | Object | X | X | X | X | X |
| Reset.blur() | Method | X | X | X | X | X |
| Reset.click() | Method | X | X | X | X | X |
| Reset.focus() | Method | X | X | X | X | X |
| Reset.form | Property | X | X | X | X | X |
| Reset.handleEvent() | Method | | | X | X | X |
| Reset.name | Property | X | X | X | X | X |
| Reset.onBlur | Event Handler | X | X | X | X | X |
| Reset.onClick | Event Handler | X | X | X | X | X |
| Reset.onFocus | Event Handler | X | X | X | X | X |
| Reset.type | Property | | X | X | X | X |
| Reset.value | Property | X | X | X | X | X |
| return | Statement | X | X | X | X | X |
| screen | Object | | | X | X | X |
| screen.availHeight | Property | | | X | X | X |
| screen.availWidth | Property | | | X | X | X |
| screen.colorDepth | Property | | | X | X | X |
| screen.height | Property | | | X | X | X |
| screen.pixelDepth | Property | | | X | X | X |
| screen.width | Property | | | X | X | X |

| Syntax | Type | 2.0 | 3.0 | 4.0 -4.05 | 4.06 -4.5 | 5.0 |
|---|---|---|---|---|---|---|
| Select | Object | X | X | X | X | X |
| Select.blur() | Method | X | X | X | X | X |
| Select.focus() | Method | X | X | X | X | X |
| Select.form | Property | X | X | X | X | X |
| Select.handleEvent() | Method | | | X | X | X |
| Select.length | Property | X | X | X | X | X |
| Select.name | Property | X | X | X | X | X |
| Select.onBlur | Event Handler | X | X | X | X | X |
| Select.onChange | Event Handler | X | X | X | X | X |
| Select.onFocus | Event Handler | X | X | X | X | X |
| Select.options | Property | X | X | X | X | X |
| Select.options.length | Property | X | X | X | X | X |
| Select.options. selectedIndex | Property | X | X | X | X | X |
| Select.selectedIndex | Property | X | X | X | X | X |
| Select.type | Property | | X | X | X | X |
| short | Reserved | | | | | |
| static | Reserved | | | | | |
| String() | Object | | X | X | X | X |
| String.anchor() | Method | X | X | X | X | X |
| String.big() | Method | X | X | X | X | X |
| String.blink() | Method | X | X | X | X | X |
| String.bold() | Method | X | X | X | X | X |
| String.charAt() | Method | X | X | X | X | X |
| String.charCodeAt() | Method | X | X | X | X | X |
| String.concat() | Method | | | X | X | X |
| String.fixed() | Method | X | X | X | X | X |
| String.fontcolor() | Method | X | X | X | X | X |
| String.fontsize() | Method | X | X | X | X | X |
| String.fromCharCode() | Method | X | X | X | X | X |
| String.indexOf() | Method | X | X | X | X | X |
| String.italics() | Method | X | X | X | X | X |
| String.lastIndexOf() | Method | X | X | X | X | X |
| String.length | Property | X | X | X | X | X |
| String.link() | Method | X | X | X | X | X |
| String.match() | Method | | | X | X | X |
| String.prototype | Property | | X | X | X | X |
| String.replace() | Method | | | X | X | X |
| String.search() | Method | | | X | X | X |
| String.slice() | Method | | | X | X | X |
| String.small() | Method | X | X | X | X | X |

*continues*

| Syntax | Type | 2.0 | 3.0 | 4.0 -4.05 | 4.06 -4.5 | 5.0 |
|---|---|---|---|---|---|---|
| String.split() | Method | | X | X | X | X |
| String.strike() | Method | X | X | X | X | X |
| String.sub() | Method | X | X | X | X | X |
| String.substr() | Method | | | X | X | X |
| String.substring() | Method | X | X | X | X | X |
| String.sup() | Method | X | X | X | X | X |
| String.toLowerCase() | Method | X | X | X | X | X |
| String.toSource() | Method | | | | X | X |
| String.toString() | Method | | | | X | X |
| String.toUpperCase() | Method | X | X | X | X | X |
| Submit | Object | X | X | X | X | X |
| Submit.blur() | Method | | X | X | X | X |
| Submit.click() | Method | X | X | X | X | X |
| Submit.focus() | Method | | X | X | X | X |
| Submit.form | Property | X | X | X | X | X |
| Submit.handleEvent() | Method | | | X | X | X |
| Submit.name | Property | X | X | X | X | X |
| Submit.onBlur | Event Handler | | X | X | X | X |
| Submit.onClick | Event Handler | X | X | X | X | X |
| Submit.onFocus | Event Handler | | X | X | X | X |
| Submit.type | Property | | X | X | X | X |
| Submit.value | Property | X | X | X | X | X |
| super | Reserved | | | X | X | X |
| switch | Statement | | | X | X | X |
| synchronized | Reserved | | | | | |
| taint() | Method | | X | | | |
| Text | Object | X | X | X | X | X |
| Text.blur() | Method | X | X | X | X | X |
| Text.defaultValue | Property | X | X | X | X | X |
| Text.focus() | Method | X | X | X | X | X |
| Text.form | Property | X | X | X | X | X |
| Text.handleEvent() | Method | | | X | X | X |
| Text.name | Property | X | X | X | X | X |
| Text.onBlur | Event Handler | X | X | X | X | X |
| Text.onChange | Event Handler | X | X | X | X | X |
| Text.onFocus | Event Handler | X | X | X | X | X |
| Text.onSelect | Event Handler | X | X | X | X | X |
| Text.select() | Method | X | X | X | X | X |
| Text.type | Property | | X | X | X | X |
| Text.value | Property | X | X | X | X | X |
| Textarea | Object | X | X | X | X | X |
| Textarea.blur() | Method | X | X | X | X | X |

| Syntax | Type | 2.0 | 3.0 | 4.0 -4.05 | 4.06 -4.5 | 5.0 |
|---|---|---|---|---|---|---|
| Textarea.defaultValue | Property | X | X | X | X | X |
| Textarea.focus() | Method | X | X | X | X | X |
| Textarea.form | Property | X | X | X | X | X |
| Textarea.handleEvent() | Method | | | X | X | X |
| Textarea.name | Property | X | X | X | X | X |
| Textarea.onBlur | Event Handler | X | X | X | X | X |
| Textarea.onChange | Event Handler | X | X | X | X | X |
| Textarea.onFocus | Event Handler | X | X | X | X | X |
| Textarea.onKeyDown | Event Handler | | | X | X | X |
| Textarea.onKeyPress | Event Handler | | | X | X | X |
| Textarea.onKeyUp | Event Handler | | | X | X | X |
| Textarea.onSelect | Event Handler | X | X | X | X | X |
| Textarea.select() | Method | X | X | X | X | X |
| Textarea.type | Property | | X | X | X | X |
| Textarea.value | Property | X | X | X | X | X |
| this | Keyword | X | X | X | X | X |
| throw | Statement | | | | | X |
| throws | Reserved | | | | | |
| transient | Reserved | | | | | |
| true | Reserved | | | | | |
| try | Statement | | | | | X |
| typeof | Operator | | X | X | X | X |
| Reserved | Property | | | | X | X |
| unescape() | Method | X | X | X | X | X |
| untaint() | Method | | X | | | |
| var | Keyword | X | X | X | X | X |
| void | Operator | | X | X | X | X |
| volatile | Reserved | | | | | |
| while | Statement | X | X | X | X | X |
| Window | Object | X | X | X | X | X |
| window.alert() | Method | X | X | X | X | X |
| window.back() | Method | | | X | X | X |
| window.blur() | Method | | X | X | X | X |
| window.captureEvents() | Method | | | X | X | X |
| window.clearInterval() | Method | | | X | X | X |
| window.clearTimeout() | Method | X | X | X | X | X |
| window.close() | Method | X | X | X | X | X |
| window.closed | Property | | X | X | X | X |
| window.confirm() | Method | X | X | X | X | X |
| window.defaultStatus | Property | X | X | X | X | X |
| window.disable | | | | | | |

*continues*

| Syntax | Type | 2.0 | 3.0 | 4.0 -4.05 | 4.06 -4.5 | 5.0 |
|---|---|---|---|---|---|---|
| ExternalCapture() | Method | | | X | X | X |
| window.document | Property | X | X | X | X | X |
| window.enable ExternalCapture() | Method | | | X | X | X |
| window.find() | Method | | | X | X | X |
| window.focus() | Method | | X | X | X | X |
| window.forward() | Method | | | X | X | X |
| window.frames | Property | X | X | X | X | X |
| window.frames.length | Property | X | X | X | X | X |
| window.handleEvent() | Method | | | X | X | X |
| window.history | Property | | X | X | X | X |
| window.home() | Method | | | X | X | X |
| window.innerHeight | Property | | | X | X | X |
| window.innerWidth | Property | | | X | X | X |
| window.length | Property | X | X | X | X | X |
| window.location | Property | X | X | X | X | X |
| window.locationbar | Property | | | X | X | X |
| window.menubar | Property | | | X | X | X |
| window.menubar.visible | Property | | | X | X | X |
| window.moveBy() | Method | | | X | X | X |
| window.moveTo() | Method | | | X | X | X |
| window.name | Property | X | X | X | X | X |
| window.onBlur | Event Handler | | X | X | X | X |
| window.onDragDrop | Event Handler | | | X | X | X |
| window.onError | Event Handler | | X | X | X | X |
| window.onFocus | Event Handler | | X | X | X | X |
| window.onLoad | Event Handler | X | X | X | X | X |
| window.onMove | Event Handler | | | X | X | X |
| window.onResize | Event Handler | | | X | X | X |
| window.onUnLoad | Event Handler | X | X | X | X | X |
| window.open() | Method | X | X | X | X | X |
| window.opener | Property | | X | X | X | X |
| window.outerHeight | Property | | | X | X | X |
| window.outerWidth | Property | | | X | X | X |
| window.pageXOffset | Property | | | X | X | X |
| window.pageYOffset | Property | | | X | X | X |
| window.parent | Property | X | X | X | X | X |
| window.personalbar | Property | | | X | X | X |
| window.personalbar. visible | Property | | | X | X | X |
| window.print() | Method | | | X | X | X |
| window.prompt() | Method | X | X | X | X | X |

| Syntax | Type | 2.0 | 3.0 | 4.0 -4.05 | 4.06 -4.5 | 5.0 |
|---|---|---|---|---|---|---|
| window.releaseEvents() | Method | | | X | X | X |
| window.resizeBy() | Method | | | X | X | X |
| window.resizeTo() | Method | | | X | X | X |
| window.routeEvent() | Method | | | X | X | X |
| window.scroll() | Method | | X | | | |
| window.scrollbars | Property | | | X | X | X |
| window.scrollbars. visible | Property | | | X | X | X |
| window.scrollBy() | Method | | | X | X | X |
| window.scrollTo() | Method | | | X | X | X |
| window.self | Property | X | X | X | X | X |
| window.setInterval() | Method | | | X | X | X |
| window.setTimeout() | Method | X | X | X | X | X |
| window.status | Property | X | X | X | X | X |
| window.statusbar | Property | | | X | X | X |
| window.statusbar. visible | Property | | | X | X | X |
| window.stop() | Method | | | X | X | X |
| window.toolbar | Property | | | X | X | X |
| window.top | Property | X | X | X | X | X |
| with | Statement | X | X | X | X | X |

# APPENDIX B

## Internet Explorer-Supported Syntax

The following table contains a list of JScript syntax that Microsoft Internet Explorer browsers support. Each supported object, method, property, or event is listed, followed by the version of the browser that supports it.

# Internet Explorer-Supported Syntax

| Syntax | Type | 3.0 | 4.0 | 5.0 |
|---|---|:---:|:---:|:---:|
| - | Operator | X | X | X |
| - - | Operator | X | X | X |
| ! | Operator | X | X | X |
| != | Operator | X | X | X |
| !== | Operator | | | X |
| % | Operator | X | X | X |
| %= | Operator | X | X | X |
| & | Operator | X | X | X |
| && | Operator | X | X | X |
| &= | Operator | X | X | X |
| * | Operator | X | X | X |
| *= | Operator | X | X | X |
| , | Operator | X | X | X |
| / | Operator | X | X | X |
| /**/ | Operator | X | X | X |
| // | Operator | X | X | X |
| /= | Operator | X | X | X |
| ?: | Operator | X | X | X |
| ^ | Operator | X | X | X |
| ^= | Operator | X | X | X |
| ¦ | Operator | X | X | X |
| ¦¦ | Operator | X | X | X |
| ¦= | Operator | X | X | X |
| ~ | Operator | X | X | X |
| + | Operator | X | X | X |
| ++ | Operator | X | X | X |
| += | Operator | X | X | X |
| < | Operator | X | X | X |
| << | Operator | X | X | X |
| <<= | Operator | X | X | X |
| <= | Operator | X | X | X |
| = | Operator | X | X | X |
| -= | Operator | X | X | X |
| == | Operator | X | X | X |
| === | Operator | | | X |
| > | Operator | X | X | X |
| >= | Operator | X | X | X |
| >> | Operator | X | X | X |
| >>= | Operator | X | X | X |
| >>> | Operator | X | X | X |
| >>>= | Operator | X | X | X |

| Syntax | Type | 3.0 | 4.0 | 5.0 |
|--------|------|-----|-----|-----|
| Anchor | Object | | X | X |
| Anchor.name | Property | | X | X |
| Applet | Object | | X | X |
| Area | Object | X | X | X |
| Area.handleEvent | Method | | X | X |
| Area.hash | Property | X | X | X |
| Area.host | Property | X | X | X |
| Area.hostname | Property | X | X | X |
| Area.href | Property | X | X | X |
| Area.onMouseOut | Event Handler | X | X | X |
| Area.onMouseOver | Event Handler | X | X | X |
| Area.pathname | Property | X | X | X |
| Area.port | Property | X | X | X |
| Area.protocol | Property | X | X | X |
| Area.search | Property | X | X | X |
| Area.target | Property | X | X | X |
| Array() | Object | | X | X |
| Array.concat() | Method | | X | X |
| Array.join() | Method | | X | X |
| Array.length | Property | | X | X |
| Array.reverse() | Method | | X | X |
| Array.slice() | Method | | X | X |
| Array.sort() | Method | | X | X |
| Array.toSource() | Method | | X | X |
| Array.toString() | Method | | X | X |
| Boolean() | Object | | X | X |
| Boolean.prototype | Property | | X | X |
| Boolean.toSource() | Method | | X | X |
| Boolean.toString() | Method | | X | X |
| break | Keyword | X | X | X |
| Button | Object | X | X | X |
| Button.blur() | Method | X | X | X |
| Button.click() | Method | X | X | X |
| Button.focus() | Method | X | X | X |
| Button.form | Property | X | X | X |
| Button.handleEvent() | Method | | X | X |
| Button.name | Property | X | X | X |
| Button.onBlur | Event Handler | X | X | X |
| Button.onClick | Event Handler | X | X | X |
| Button.onFocus | Event Handler | X | X | X |
| Button.onMouseDown | Event Handler | X | X | X |
| Button.onMouseUp | Event Handler | X | X | X |

*continues*

| Syntax | Type | 3.0 | 4.0 | 5.0 |
|---|---|---|---|---|
| Button.type | Property | X | X | X |
| Button.value | Property | X | X | X |
| case | Reserved | | | |
| catch | Statement | | | X |
| Checkbox | Object | X | X | X |
| Checkbox.blur() | Method | X | X | X |
| Checkbox.checked | Property | | X | X |
| Checkbox.click() | Method | | X | X |
| Checkbox.defaultChecked | Property | | X | X |
| Checkbox.focus() | Method | | X | X |
| Checkbox.form | Property | | X | X |
| Checkbox.handleEvent() | Method | | X | X |
| Checkbox.name | Property | | X | X |
| Checkbox.onBlur | Event Handler | | X | X |
| Checkbox.onClick | Event Handler | | X | X |
| Checkbox.onFocus | Event Handler | | X | X |
| Checkbox.type | Property | | X | X |
| Checkbox.value | Property | | X | X |
| class | Reserved | | | |
| const | Reserved | | | |
| continue | Statement | | X | X |
| Date() | Object | X | X | X |
| Date.getDate() | Method | X | X | X |
| Date.getDay() | Method | X | X | X |
| Date.getFullYear() | Method | | X | X |
| Date.getHours() | Method | X | X | X |
| Date.getMilliseconds() | Method | | X | X |
| Date.getMinutes() | Method | X | X | X |
| Date.getMonth() | Method | X | X | X |
| Date.getSeconds() | Method | X | X | X |
| Date.getTime() | Method | X | X | X |
| Date.getTimezoneOffset() | Method | X | X | X |
| Date.getUTCDate() | Method | | X | X |
| Date.getUTCDay() | Method | | X | X |
| Date.getUTCFullYear() | Method | | X | X |
| Date.getUTCHours() | Method | | X | X |
| Date.getUTCMilliseconds() | Method | | X | X |
| Date.getUTCMinutes() | Method | | X | X |
| Date.getUTCMonth() | Method | | X | X |
| Date.getUTCSeconds() | Method | | X | X |
| Date.getYear() | Method | X | X | X |
| Date.parse() | Method | X | X | X |
| Date.prototype | Property | | X | X |

| Syntax | Type | 3.0 | 4.0 | 5.0 |
|---|---|:---:|:---:|:---:|
| Date.setDate() | Method | X | X | X |
| Date.setFullYear() | Method | | X | X |
| Date.setHours() | Method | X | X | X |
| Date.setMilliseconds() | Method | | X | X |
| Date.setMinutes() | Method | X | X | X |
| Date.setMonth() | Method | X | X | X |
| Date.setSeconds() | Method | X | X | X |
| Date.setTime() | Method | X | X | X |
| Date.setUTCDate() | Method | | X | X |
| Date.setUTCFullYear() | Method | | X | X |
| Date.setUTCHours() | Method | | X | X |
| Date.setUTCMilliseconds() | Method | | X | X |
| Date.setUTCMinutes() | Method | | X | X |
| Date.setUTCMonth() | Method | | X | X |
| Date.setUTCSeconds() | Method | | X | X |
| Date.setYear() | Method | X | X | X |
| Date.toGMTString() | Method | X | X | X |
| Date.toLocaleString() | Method | X | X | X |
| Date.toSource() | Method | | X | X |
| Date.toString() | Method | X | X | X |
| Date.toUTCString() | Method | | X | X |
| Date.UTC() | Method | X | X | X |
| debugger | Reserved | | | |
| default | Reserved | | | |
| delete | Statement | | X | X |
| do...while | Statement | | X | X |
| document | Object | X | X | X |
| document.all | Property | | X | X |
| document.all.item() | Method | | X | X |
| document.all.tags() | Method | | X | X |
| document.alinkColor | Property | X | X | X |
| document.anchors | Property | | X | X |
| document.anchors.length | Property | | X | X |
| document.applets | Property | X | X | X |
| document.applets.length | Property | X | X | X |
| document.bgColor | Property | X | X | X |
| document.close() | Method | X | X | X |
| document.cookie | Property | X | X | X |
| document.domain | Property | | X | X |
| document.embeds | Property | | X | X |
| document.embeds.length | Property | | X | X |
| document.fgColor | Property | X | X | X |

*continues*

| Syntax | Type | 3.0 | 4.0 | 5.0 |
|---|---|---|---|---|
| document.*formName* | Property | | X | X |
| document.forms | Property | | X | X |
| document.forms.length | Property | | X | X |
| document.handleEvent() | Property | | X | X |
| document.images | Property | | X | X |
| document.images.length | Property | | X | X |
| document.lastModified | Property | X | X | X |
| document.linkColor | Property | X | X | X |
| document.links | Property | X | X | X |
| document.links.length | Property | X | X | X |
| document.location | Property | X | X | X |
| document.onClick | Event Handler | X | X | X |
| document.onDblClick | Event Handler | X | X | X |
| document.onKeyDown | Event Handler | X | X | X |
| document.onKeyPress | Event Handler | X | X | X |
| document.onKeyUp | Event Handler | X | X | X |
| document.onMouseDown | Event Handler | X | X | X |
| document.onMouseUp | Event Handler | X | X | X |
| document.open() | Method | X | X | X |
| document.plugins | Property | | X | X |
| document.referrer | Property | X | X | X |
| document.title | Property | X | X | X |
| document.URL | Property | X | X | X |
| document.vlinkColor | Property | X | X | X |
| document.write() | Method | X | X | X |
| document.writeln() | Method | X | X | X |
| Embed | Object | X | X | X |
| enum | Keyword | | X | X |
| escape() | Method | X | X | X |
| eval() | Method | X | X | X |
| event | Object | | X | X |
| event.data | Property | | X | X |
| event.height | Property | | X | X |
| event.layerX | Property | | X | X |
| event.layerY | Property | | X | X |
| event.modifiers | Property | | X | X |
| event.pageX | Property | | X | X |
| event.pageY | Property | | X | X |
| event.screenX | Property | | X | X |
| event.screenY | Property | | X | X |
| event.target | Property | | X | X |
| event.type | Property | | X | X |
| event.which | Property | | X | X |

| Syntax | Type | 3.0 | 4.0 | 5.0 |
| --- | --- | --- | --- | --- |
| event.width | Property | | X | X |
| Event.ABORT | Event | | X | X |
| Event.BLUR | Event | X | X | X |
| Event.CHANGE | Event | X | X | X |
| Event.CLICK | Event | X | X | X |
| Event.DBLCLICK | Event | | X | X |
| Event.DRAGDROP | Event | | X | X |
| Event.ERROR | Event | | X | X |
| Event.FOCUS | Event | X | X | X |
| Event.KEYDOWN | Event | | X | X |
| Event.KEYPRESS | Event | | X | X |
| Event.KEYUP | Event | | X | X |
| Event.LOAD | Event | X | X | X |
| Event.MOUSEDOWN | Event | | X | X |
| Event.MOUSEMOVE | Event | | X | X |
| Event.MOUSEOUT | Event | | X | X |
| Event.MOUSEOVER | Event | X | X | X |
| Event.MOUSEUP | Event | | X | X |
| Event.MOVE | Event | | X | X |
| Event.RESET | Event | | X | X |
| Event.RESIZE | Event | | X | X |
| Event.SELECT | Event | X | X | X |
| Event.SUBMIT | Event | X | X | X |
| Event.UNLOAD | Event | X | X | X |
| export | Statement | | X | X |
| extends | Keyword | | X | X |
| FileUpload | Object | X | X | X |
| FileUpload.blur() | Method | | X | X |
| FileUpload.focus() | Method | | X | X |
| FileUpload.form | Property | X | X | X |
| FileUpload.handleEvent() | Method | | X | X |
| FileUpload.name | Property | X | X | X |
| FileUpload.onBlur | Event | | X | X |
| FileUpload.onChange | Event | | X | X |
| FileUpload.onFocus | Event | | X | X |
| FileUpload.select() | Method | X | X | X |
| FileUpload.type | Property | | X | X |
| FileUpload.value | Property | X | X | X |
| finally | Keyword | | X | X |
| for | Statement | X | X | X |
| for...in | Statement | X | X | X |
| Form | Object | X | X | X |

*continues*

| Syntax | Type | 3.0 | 4.0 | 5.0 |
|---|---|:---:|:---:|:---:|
| Form.action | Property | X | X | X |
| Form.elements | Property | X | X | X |
| Form.elements.length | Property | X | X | X |
| Form.encoding | Property | X | X | X |
| Form.handleEvent() | Method | | X | X |
| Form.length | Property | X | X | X |
| Form.method | Property | X | X | X |
| Form.name | Property | X | X | X |
| Form.onReset | Event | | X | X |
| Form.onSubmit | Event | X | X | X |
| Form.reset() | Method | | X | X |
| Form.submit() | Method | X | X | X |
| Form.target | Property | X | X | X |
| Frame | Object | X | X | X |
| Frame.blur() | Method | | X | X |
| Frame.clearInterval() | Method | | X | X |
| Frame.clearTimeout() | Method | | X | X |
| Frame.document | Property | X | X | X |
| Frame.focus() | Method | | X | X |
| Frame.frames | Property | X | X | X |
| Frame.length | Property | X | X | X |
| Frame.name | Property | X | X | X |
| Frame.onBlur | Event | | X | X |
| Frame.onFocus | Event | | X | X |
| Frame.onMove | Event | | X | X |
| Frame.onResize | Event | | X | X |
| Frame.parent | Property | X | X | X |
| Frame.print() | Method | | X | X |
| Frame.self | Property | X | X | X |
| Frame.setInterval() | Method | | X | X |
| Frame.setTimeout() | Method | X | X | X |
| Frame.top | Property | X | X | X |
| Frame.window | Property | X | X | X |
| function | Statement | X | X | X |
| Function() | Object | X | X | X |
| Function.apply() | Method | | | X |
| Function.arguments | Property | | X | X |
| Function.arity | Property | | X | X |
| Function.call() | Method | | | X |
| Function.caller | Property | | X | X |
| Function.prototype | Property | | X | X |
| Function.toSource() | Method | | X | X |
| Function.toString() | Method | | X | X |

| Syntax | Type | 3.0 | 4.0 | 5.0 |
|---|---|---|---|---|
| Hidden | Object | X | X | X |
| Hidden.form | Property | X | X | X |
| Hidden.name | Property | X | X | X |
| Hidden.type | Property | | X | X |
| Hidden.value | Property | X | X | X |
| History | Object | X | X | X |
| History.back() | Method | X | X | X |
| History.current | Property | | X | X |
| History.forward() | Method | X | X | X |
| History.go() | Method | X | X | X |
| History.length | Property | X | X | X |
| History.next | Property | | X | X |
| History.previous | Property | X | X | X |
| If...else | Statement | X | X | X |
| Image() | Object | | X | X |
| Image.border | Property | | X | X |
| Image.complete | Property | | X | X |
| Image.handleEvent() | Method | | X | X |
| Image.height | Property | | X | X |
| Image.hspace | Property | | X | X |
| Image.lowsrc | Property | | X | X |
| Image.name | Property | | X | X |
| Image.onAbort | Event | | X | X |
| Image.onError | Event | | X | X |
| Image.onKeyDown | Event | | X | X |
| Image.onKeyPress | Event | | X | X |
| Image.onKeyUp | Event | | X | X |
| Image.onLoad | Event | | X | X |
| Image.prototype | Property | | X | X |
| Image.src | Property | | X | X |
| Image.vspace | Property | | X | X |
| Image.width | Property | | X | X |
| import | Statement | | X | X |
| in | Operator | | | X |
| Infinity | Keyword | | | X |
| instanceof | Operator | | | X |
| isFinite() | Method | | | X |
| isNaN() | Method | | | X |
| labeled | Statement | | X | X |
| Link | Object | X | X | X |
| Link.handleEvent() | Method | | X | X |
| Link.hash | Property | X | X | X |

*continues*

| Syntax | Type | 3.0 | 4.0 | 5.0 |
|---|---|:---:|:---:|:---:|
| Link.host | Property | X | X | X |
| Link.hostname | Property | X | X | X |
| Link.href | Property | X | X | X |
| Link.onClick | Event | X | X | X |
| Link.onDblClick | Event | | X | X |
| Link.onKeyDown | Event | | X | X |
| Link.onKeyPress | Event | | X | X |
| Link.onKeyUp | Event | | X | X |
| Link.onMouseDown | Event | | X | X |
| Link.onMouseOut | Event | | X | X |
| Link.onMouseOver | Event | X | X | X |
| Link.onMouseUp | Event | | X | X |
| Link.pathname | Property | X | X | X |
| Link.port | Property | X | X | X |
| Link.protocol | Property | X | X | X |
| Link.search | Property | X | X | X |
| Link.target | Property | X | X | X |
| Link.text | Property | | X | X |
| Location | Object | X | X | X |
| Location.hash | Property | X | X | X |
| Location.host | Property | X | X | X |
| Location.hostname | Property | X | X | X |
| Location.href | Property | X | X | X |
| Location.pathname | Property | X | X | X |
| Location.port | Property | X | X | X |
| Location.protocol | Property | X | X | X |
| Location.reload() | Method | | X | X |
| Location.replace() | Method | | X | X |
| Location.search | Property | X | X | X |
| Math() | Object | X | X | X |
| Math.abs() | Method | X | X | X |
| Math.acos() | Method | X | X | X |
| Math.asin() | Method | X | X | X |
| Math.atan() | Method | X | X | X |
| Math.atan2() | Method | X | X | X |
| Math.ceil() | Method | X | X | X |
| Math.cos() | Method | X | X | X |
| Math.E | Property | X | X | X |
| Math.exp() | Method | X | X | X |
| Math.floor() | Method | X | X | X |
| Math.LN10 | Property | X | X | X |
| Math.LN2 | Property | X | X | X |
| Math.log() | Method | X | X | X |

| Syntax | Type | 3.0 | 4.0 | 5.0 |
|---|---|---|---|---|
| Math.LOG10E | Property | X | X | X |
| Math.LOG2E | Property | X | X | X |
| Math.max() | Method | X | X | X |
| Math.min() | Method | X | X | X |
| Math.PI | Property | X | X | X |
| Math.pow() | Method | X | X | X |
| Math.random() | Method | X | X | X |
| Math.round() | Method | X | X | X |
| Math.sin() | Method | X | X | X |
| Math.sqrt() | Method | X | X | X |
| Math.SQRT1_2 | Property | X | X | X |
| Math.SQRT2 | Property | X | X | X |
| Math.tan() | Method | X | X | X |
| Math.toSource() | Method | X | X | X |
| Math.toString() | Method | X | X | X |
| MimeType | Object | | X | X |
| MimeType.description | Property | | X | X |
| MimeType.enabledPlugin | Property | | X | X |
| MimeType.suffixes | Property | | X | X |
| MimeType.type | Property | | X | X |
| NaN | Keyword | | X | X |
| navigator | Object | X | X | X |
| navigator.appCodeName | Property | X | X | X |
| navigator.appName | Property | X | X | X |
| navigator.appVersion | Property | X | X | X |
| navigator.javaEnabled() | Method | | X | X |
| navigator.language | Property | | X | X |
| navigator.mimeTypes | Property | | X | X |
| navigator.platform | Property | | X | X |
| navigator.plugins | Property | | X | X |
| navigator.plugins.refresh() | Method | | X | X |
| navigator.preference() | Method | | X | X |
| navigator.userAgent | Property | X | X | X |
| new | Operator | X | X | X |
| Number() | Object | | X | X |
| Number.MAX_VALUE | Property | | X | X |
| Number.MIN_VALUE | Property | | X | X |
| Number.NaN | Property | | X | X |
| Number.NEGATIVE_INFINITY | Property | | X | X |
| Number.POSITIVE_INFINITY | Property | | X | X |
| Number.prototype | Property | | X | X |
| Number.toSource() | Method | | X | X |

*continues*

| Syntax | Type | 3.0 | 4.0 | 5.0 |
|---|---|:---:|:---:|:---:|
| Number.toString() | Method | | X | X |
| Object() | Object | | X | X |
| Object.constructor | Property | | X | X |
| Object.eval() | Method | | X | X |
| Object.prototype | Property | | X | X |
| Object.toSource() | Method | | X | X |
| Object.toString() | Method | | X | X |
| Object.unwatch() | Method | | X | X |
| Object.valueof() | Method | | X | X |
| Object.watch() | Method | | X | X |
| Option | Object | X | X | X |
| Option.defaultSelected | Property | | X | X |
| Option.selected | Property | X | X | X |
| Option.text | Property | X | X | X |
| Option.value | Property | X | X | X |
| parseFloat() | Method | X | X | X |
| parseInt() | Method | X | X | X |
| Password | Object | X | X | X |
| Password.blur() | Method | X | X | X |
| Password.defaultValue | Property | X | X | X |
| Password.focus() | Method | X | X | X |
| Password.form | Property | X | X | X |
| Password.handleEvent() | Method | | X | X |
| Password.name | Property | X | X | X |
| Password.onBlur | Event | X | X | X |
| Password.onFocus | Event | X | X | X |
| Password.select() | Method | X | X | X |
| Password.type | Property | | X | X |
| Password.value | Property | X | X | X |
| Plugin | Object | | X | X |
| Plugin.description | Property | | X | X |
| Plugin.filename | Property | | X | X |
| Plugin.length | Property | | X | X |
| Plugin.name | Property | | X | X |
| Radio | Object | X | X | X |
| Radio.blur() | Method | X | X | X |
| Radio.checked | Property | X | X | X |
| Radio.click() | Method | X | X | X |
| Radio.defaultChecked | Property | X | X | X |
| Radio.focus() | Method | X | X | X |
| Radio.form | Property | X | X | X |
| Radio.handleEvent() | Method | | X | X |
| Radio.name | Property | X | X | X |

| Syntax | Type | 3.0 | 4.0 | 5.0 |
|---|---|:---:|:---:|:---:|
| Radio.onBlur | Event | X | X | X |
| Radio.onClick | Event | X | X | X |
| Radio.onFocus | Event | X | X | X |
| Radio.type | Property | | X | X |
| Radio.value | Property | X | X | X |
| RegExp() | Object | | X | X |
| RegExp.$* | Property | | X | X |
| RegExp.$& | Property | | X | X |
| RegExp.$_ | Property | | X | X |
| RegExp.$` | Property | | X | X |
| RegExp.$' | Property | | X | X |
| RegExp.$+ | Property | | X | X |
| RegExp.$1,$2,...$9 | Property | | X | X |
| RegExp.compile() | Method | | X | X |
| RegExp.exec() | Method | | X | X |
| RegExp.global | Property | | X | X |
| RegExp.ignoreCase | Property | | X | X |
| RegExp.input | Property | | X | X |
| RegExp.lastIndex | Property | | X | X |
| RegExp.lastMatch | Property | | X | X |
| RegExp.lastParen | Property | | X | X |
| RegExp.leftContext | Property | | X | X |
| RegExp.multiline | Property | | X | X |
| RegExp.rightContext | Property | | X | X |
| RegExp.source | Property | | X | X |
| RegExp.test() | Method | | X | X |
| Reset | Object | X | X | X |
| Reset.blur() | Method | X | X | X |
| Reset.click() | Method | X | X | X |
| Reset.focus() | Method | X | X | X |
| Reset.form | Property | X | X | X |
| Reset.handleEvent() | Method | | X | X |
| Reset.name | Property | X | X | X |
| Reset.onBlur | Event | X | X | X |
| Reset.onClick | Event | X | X | X |
| Reset.onFocus | Event | X | X | X |
| Reset.type | Property | | X | X |
| Reset.value | Property | X | X | X |
| return | Statement | X | X | X |
| screen | Object | | X | X |
| screen.availHeight | Property | | X | X |
| screen.availWidth | Property | | X | X |

*continues*

| Syntax | Type | 3.0 | 4.0 | 5.0 |
|---|---|---|---|---|
| screen.colorDepth | Property | | X | X |
| screen.height | Property | | X | X |
| screen.width | Property | | X | X |
| Select | Object | X | X | X |
| Select.blur() | Method | X | X | X |
| Select.focus() | Method | X | X | X |
| Select.form | Property | X | X | X |
| Select.handleEvent() | Method | | X | X |
| Select.length | Property | X | X | X |
| Select.name | Property | X | X | X |
| Select.onBlur | Event Handler | X | X | X |
| Select.onChange | Event Handler | X | X | X |
| Select.onFocus | Event Handler | X | X | X |
| Select.options | Property | X | X | X |
| Select.options.length | Property | X | X | X |
| Select.options.selectedIndex | Property | X | X | X |
| Select.selectedIndex | Property | X | X | X |
| Select.type | Property | | X | X |
| String() | Object | X | X | X |
| String.anchor() | Method | X | X | X |
| String.big() | Method | X | X | X |
| String.blink() | Method | X | X | X |
| String.bold() | Method | X | X | X |
| String.charAt() | Method | X | X | X |
| String.charCodeAt() | Method | X | X | X |
| String.concat() | Method | | X | X |
| String.fixed() | Method | X | X | X |
| String.fontcolor() | Method | X | X | X |
| String.fontsize() | Method | X | X | X |
| String.fromCharCode() | Method | X | X | X |
| String.indexOf() | Method | X | X | X |
| String.italics() | Method | X | X | X |
| String.lastIndexOf() | Method | X | X | X |
| String.length | Property | X | X | X |
| String.link() | Method | X | X | X |
| String.match() | Method | | X | X |
| String.prototype | Property | | X | X |
| String.replace() | Method | | X | X |
| String.search() | Method | | X | X |
| String.slice() | Method | | X | X |
| String.small() | Method | | X | X |
| String.split() | Method | | X | X |
| String.strike() | Method | X | X | X |

| Syntax | Type | 3.0 | 4.0 | 5.0 |
|---|---|:---:|:---:|:---:|
| String.sub() | Method | X | X | X |
| String.substr() | Method | | X | X |
| String.substring() | Method | X | X | •X |
| String.sup() | Method | X | X | X |
| String.toLowerCase() | Method | X | X | X |
| String.toSource() | Method | | X | X |
| String.toString() | Method | | X | X |
| String.toUpperCase() | Method | X | X | X |
| Submit | Object | X | X | X |
| Submit.blur() | Method | | X | X |
| Submit.click() | Method | X | X | X |
| Submit.focus() | Method | | X | X |
| Submit.form | Property | X | X | X |
| Submit.handleEvent() | Method | | X | X |
| Submit.name | Property | X | X | X |
| Submit.onBlur | Event Handler | | X | X |
| Submit.onClick | Event Handler | X | X | X |
| Submit.onFocus | Event Handler | | X | X |
| Submit.type | Property | | X | X |
| Submit.value | Property | X | X | X |
| super | Reserved | | | |
| switch | Statement | | X | X |
| Text | Object | X | X | X |
| Text.blur() | Method | X | X | X |
| Text.defaultValue | Property | X | X | X |
| Text.focus() | Method | X | X | X |
| Text.form | Property | X | X | X |
| Text.handleEvent() | Method | | X | X |
| Text.name | Property | X | X | X |
| Text.onBlur | Event Handler | X | X | X |
| Text.onChange | Event Handler | X | X | X |
| Text.onFocus | Event Handler | X | X | X |
| Text.onSelect | Event Handler | X | X | X |
| Text.select() | Method | X | X | X |
| Text.type | Property | | X | X |
| Text.value | Property | X | X | X |
| Textarea | Object | X | X | X |
| Textarea.blur() | Method | X | X | X |
| Textarea.defaultValue | Property | X | X | X |
| Textarea.focus() | Method | X | X | X |
| Textarea.form | Property | X | X | X |
| Textarea.handleEvent() | Method | | X | X |

*continues*

| Syntax | Type | 3.0 | 4.0 | 5.0 |
|---|---|:-:|:-:|:-:|
| Textarea.name | Property | X | X | X |
| Textarea.onBlur | Event Handler | X | X | X |
| Textarea.onChange | Event Handler | X | X | X |
| Textarea.onFocus | Event Handler | X | X | X |
| Textarea.onKeyDown | Event Handler | | X | X |
| Textarea.onKeyPress | Event Handler | | X | X |
| Textarea.onKeyUp | Event Handler | | X | X |
| Textarea.onSelect | Event Handler | X | X | X |
| Textarea.select() | Method | X | X | X |
| Textarea.type | Property | | X | X |
| Textarea.value | Property | X | X | X |
| this | Keyword | X | X | X |
| throw | Statement | | | X |
| try | Statement | | | X |
| typeof | Operator | | X | X |
| undefined | Property | | X | X |
| unescape() | Method | X | X | X |
| var | Keyword | X | X | X |
| void | Operator | | X | X |
| while | Statement | X | X | X |
| Window | Object | X | X | X |
| window.alert() | Method | X | X | X |
| window.back() | Method | | X | X |
| window.blur() | Method | | X | X |
| window.captureEvents() | Method | | X | X |
| window.clearInterval() | Method | | X | X |
| window.clearTimeout() | Method | X | X | X |
| window.close() | Method | X | X | X |
| window.closed | Property | | X | X |
| window.confirm() | Method | X | X | X |
| window.defaultStatus | Property | X | X | X |
| window.disableExternal Capture() | Method | | X | X |
| window.document | Property | X | X | X |
| window.enableExternal Capture() | Method | | X | X |
| window.find() | Method | | X | X |
| window.focus() | Method | | X | X |
| window.forward() | Method | | X | X |
| window.frames | Property | X | X | X |
| window.frames.length | Property | X | X | X |
| window.handleEvent() | Method | | X | X |
| window.history | Property | | X | X |

| Syntax | Type | 3.0 | 4.0 | 5.0 |
|---|---|:---:|:---:|:---:|
| window.home() | Method | | X | X |
| window.innerHeight | Property | | X | X |
| window.innerWidth | Property | | X | X |
| window.length | Property | | X | X |
| window.location | Property | X | X | X |
| window.locationbar | Property | | X | X |
| window.menubar | Property | | X | X |
| window.menubar.visible | Property | | X | X |
| window.moveBy() | Method | | X | X |
| window.moveTo() | Method | | X | X |
| window.name | Property | X | X | X |
| window.onBlur | Event Handler | | X | X |
| window.onDragDrop | Event Handler | | X | X |
| window.onError | Event Handler | | X | X |
| window.onFocus | Event Handler | | X | X |
| window.onLoad | Event Handler | X | X | X |
| window.onMove | Event Handler | | X | X |
| window.onResize | Event Handler | | X | X |
| window.onUnLoad | Event Handler | X | X | X |
| window.open() | Method | X | X | X |
| window.opener | Property | | X | X |
| window.outerHeight | Property | | X | X |
| window.outerWidth | Property | | X | X |
| window.pageXOffset | Property | | X | X |
| window.pageYOffset | Property | | X | X |
| window.parent | Property | X | X | X |
| window.personalbar | Property | | X | X |
| window.personalbar.visible | Property | | X | X |
| window.print() | Method | | X | X |
| window.prompt() | Method | X | X | X |
| window.releaseEvents() | Method | | X | X |
| window.resizeBy() | Method | | X | X |
| window.resizeTo() | Method | | X | X |
| window.routeEvent() | Method | | X | X |
| window.scroll() | Method | | X | X |
| window.scrollbars | Property | | X | X |
| window.scrollbars.visible | Property | | X | X |
| window.scrollBy() | Method | | X | X |
| window.scrollTo() | Method | | X | X |
| window.self | Property | X | X | X |
| window.setInterval() | Method | | X | X |
| window.setTimeout() | Method | X | X | X |

*continues*

| Syntax | Type | 3.0 | 4.0 | 5.0 |
|---|---|---|---|---|
| window.status | Property | X | X | X |
| window.statusbar | Property | | X | X |
| window.statusbar.visible | Property | | X | X |
| window.stop() | Method | | X | X |
| window.toolbar | Property | | X | X |
| window.top | Property | X | X | X |
| with | Statement | X | X | X |

# APPENDIX C

## Opera-Supported Syntax

The following table contains a list of JavaScript syntax that Opera browsers support. Each supported object, method, property, or event is listed, followed by the version of the browser that supports it.

# Opera-Supported Syntax

| Syntax | Type | 3.0 | 3.5 |
|---|---|---|---|
| - | Operator | X | X |
| -- | Operator | X | X |
| ! | Operator | X | X |
| != | Operator | X | X |
| % | Operator | X | X |
| %= | Operator | X | X |
| & | Operator | X | X |
| & | Operator | X | X |
| &= | Operator | X | X |
| * | Operator | X | X |
| *= | Operator | X | X |
| , | Operator | X | X |
| / | Operator | X | X |
| /**/ | Operator | X | X |
| // | Operator | X | X |
| /= | Operator | X | X |
| ?: | Operator | X | X |
| ^ | Operator | X | X |
| ^= | Operator | X | X |
| ¦ | Operator | X | X |
| ¦¦ | Operator | X | X |
| ¦= | Operator | X | X |
| ~ | Operator | X | X |
| + | Operator | X | X |
| ++ | Operator | X | X |
| += | Operator | X | X |
| < | Operator | X | X |
| << | Operator | X | X |
| <<= | Operator | X | X |
| <= | Operator | X | X |
| = | Operator | X | X |
| -= | Operator | X | X |
| == | Operator | X | X |
| > | Operator | X | X |
| >= | Operator | X | X |
| >> | Operator | X | X |
| >>= | Operator | X | X |
| >>> | Operator | X | X |
| >>>= | Operator | X | X |
| Applet | Object | X | X |
| Area | Object | X | X |
| Area.hash | Property | X | X |

| Syntax | Type | 3.0 | 3.5 |
|---|---|:---:|:---:|
| Area.host | Property | X | X |
| Area.hostname | Property | X | X |
| Area.href | Property | X | X |
| Area.onMouseOut | Event Handler | X | X |
| Area.onMouseOver | Event Handler | X | X |
| Area.pathname | Property | X | X |
| Area.port | Property | X | X |
| Area.protocol | Property | X | X |
| Area.search | Property | X | X |
| Area.target | Property | X | X |
| Array() | Object | X | X |
| Array.join() | Method | X | X |
| Array.length | Property | X | X |
| Array.reverse() | Method | X | X |
| Array.sort() | Method | X | X |
| Array.toString() | Method | X | X |
| Boolean() | Object | X | X |
| Boolean.prototype | Property | X | X |
| Boolean.toSource() | Method | X | X |
| Boolean.toString() | Method | X | X |
| break | Keyword | X | X |
| Button | Object | X | X |
| Button.blur() | Method | X | X |
| Button.click() | Method | X | X |
| Button.focus() | Method | X | X |
| Button.form | Property | X | X |
| Button.name | Property | X | X |
| Button.onBlur | Event Handler | X | X |
| Button.onClick | Event Handler | X | X |
| Button.onFocus | Event Handler | X | X |
| Button.onMouseDown | Event Handler | X | X |
| Button.onMouseUp | Event Handler | X | X |
| Button.type | Property | X | X |
| Button.value | Property | X | X |
| Checkbox | Object | X | X |
| Checkbox.blur() | Method | X | X |
| Checkbox.checked | Property | X | X |
| Checkbox.click() | Method | X | X |
| Checkbox.defaultChecked | Property | X | X |
| Checkbox.focus() | Method | X | X |
| Checkbox.form | Property | X | X |
| Checkbox.name | Property | X | X |

*continues*

| Syntax | Type | 3.0 | 3.5 |
|---|---|---|---|
| Checkbox.onBlur | Event Handler | X | X |
| Checkbox.onClick | Event Handler | X | X |
| Checkbox.onFocus | Event Handler | X | X |
| Checkbox.type | Property | X | X |
| Checkbox.value | Property | X | X |
| continue | Statement | X | X |
| Date() | Object | X | X |
| Date.getDate() | Method | X | X |
| Date.getDay() | Method | X | X |
| Date.getHours() | Method | X | X |
| Date.getMinutes() | Method | X | X |
| Date.getMonth() | Method | X | X |
| Date.getSeconds() | Method | X | X |
| Date.getTime() | Method | X | X |
| Date.getTimezoneOffset() | Method | X | X |
| Date.getYear() | Method | X | X |
| Date.parse() | Method | X | X |
| Date.prototype | Property | X | X |
| Date.setDate() | Method | X | X |
| Date.setHours() | Method | X | X |
| Date.setMinutes() | Method | X | X |
| Date.setMonth() | Method | X | X |
| Date.setSeconds() | Method | X | X |
| Date.setTime() | Method | X | X |
| Date.setYear() | Method | X | X |
| Date.toGMTString() | Method | X | X |
| Date.toLocaleString() | Method | X | X |
| Date.toString() | Method | X | X |
| Date.UTC() | Method | X | X |
| delete | Statement | X | X |
| do...while | Statement | X | X |
| document | Object | X | X |
| document.alinkColor | Property | X | X |
| document.applets | Property | X | X |
| document.applets.length | Property | X | X |
| document.bgColor | Property | X | X |
| document.close() | Method | X | X |
| document.cookie | Property | X | X |
| document.domain | Property | X | X |
| document.embeds | Property | X | X |
| document.embeds.length | Property | X | X |
| document.fgColor | Property | X | X |
| document.formName | Property | X | X |

| Syntax | Type | 3.0 | 3.5 |
| --- | --- | --- | --- |
| document.forms | Property | X | X |
| document.forms.length | Property | X | X |
| document.images | Property | X | X |
| document.images.length | Property | X | X |
| document.lastModified | Property | X | X |
| document.linkColor | Property | X | X |
| document.links | Property | X | X |
| document.links.length | Property | X | X |
| document.location | Property | X | X |
| document.onClick | Event Handler | X | X |
| document.onDblClick | Event Handler | X | X |
| document.onKeyDown | Event Handler | X | X |
| document.onKeyPress | Event Handler | X | X |
| document.onKeyUp | Event Handler | X | X |
| document.onMouseDown | Event Handler | X | X |
| document.onMouseUp | Event Handler | X | X |
| document.open() | Method | X | X |
| document.plugins | Property | X | X |
| document.referrer | Property | X | X |
| document.title | Property | X | X |
| document.URL | Property | X | X |
| document.vlinkColor | Property | X | X |
| document.write() | Method | X | X |
| document.writeln() | Method | X | X |
| Embed | Object | X | X |
| escape() | Method | X | X |
| eval() | Method | X | X |
| Event.ABORT | Event | X | X |
| Event.BLUR | Event | X | X |
| Event.CHANGE | Event | X | X |
| Event.CLICK | Event | X | X |
| Event.ERROR | Event | X | X |
| Event.FOCUS | Event | X | X |
| Event.LOAD | Event | X | X |
| Event.MOUSEOUT | Event | X | X |
| Event.MOUSEOVER | Event | X | X |
| Event.RESET | Event | X | X |
| Event.SELECT | Event | X | X |
| Event.SUBMIT | Event | X | X |
| Event.UNLOAD | Event | X | X |
| FileUpload | Object | X | X |
| FileUpload.blur() | Method | X | X |

*continues*

| Syntax | Type | 3.0 | 3.5 |
|---|---|---|---|
| FileUpload.focus() | Method | X | X |
| FileUpload.form | Property | X | X |
| FileUpload.name | Property | X | X |
| FileUpload.onBlur | Event | X | X |
| FileUpload.onChange | Event | X | X |
| FileUpload.onFocus | Event | X | X |
| FileUpload.select() | Method | X | X |
| FileUpload.type | Property | X | X |
| FileUpload.value | Property | X | X |
| for | Statement | X | X |
| for...in | Statement | X | X |
| Form | Object | X | X |
| Form.action | Property | X | X |
| Form.elements | Property | X | X |
| Form.elements.length | Property | X | X |
| Form.encoding | Property | X | X |
| Form.length | Property | X | X |
| Form.method | Property | X | X |
| Form.name | Property | X | X |
| Form.onReset | Event | X | X |
| Form.onSubmit | Event | X | X |
| Form.reset() | Method | X | X |
| Form.submit() | Method | X | X |
| Form.target | Property | X | X |
| Frame | Object | X | X |
| Frame.blur() | Method | X | X |
| Frame.document | Property | X | X |
| Frame.focus() | Method | X | X |
| Frame.frames | Property | X | X |
| Frame.length | Property | X | X |
| Frame.name | Property | X | X |
| Frame.onBlur | Event | X | X |
| Frame.onFocus | Event | X | X |
| Frame.parent | Property | X | X |
| Frame.self | Property | X | X |
| Frame.setTimeout() | Method | X | X |
| Frame.top | Property | X | X |
| Frame.window | Property | X | X |
| function | Statement | X | X |
| Function() | Object | X | X |
| Function.arguments | Property | X | X |
| Function.caller | Property | X | X |
| Function.prototype | Property | X | X |

| Syntax | Type | 3.0 | 3.5 |
|---|---|---|---|
| Function.toString() | Method | X | X |
| Hidden | Object | X | X |
| Hidden.form | Property | X | X |
| Hidden.name | Property | X | X |
| Hidden.type | Property | X | X |
| Hidden.value | Property | X | X |
| History | Object | X | X |
| History.back() | Method | X | X |
| History.current | Property | X | X |
| History.forward() | Method | X | X |
| History.go() | Method | X | X |
| History.length | Property | X | X |
| History.next | Property | X | X |
| History.previous | Property | X | X |
| If...else | Statement | X | X |
| Image() | Object | X | X |
| Image.border | Property | X | X |
| Image.complete | Property | X | X |
| Image.height | Property | X | X |
| Image.hspace | Property | X | X |
| Image.lowsrc | Property | X | X |
| Image.name | Property | X | X |
| Image.onAbort | Event | X | X |
| Image.onError | Event | X | X |
| Image.onLoad | Event | X | X |
| Image.prototype | Property | X | X |
| Image.src | Property | X | X |
| Image.vspace | Property | X | X |
| Image.width | Property | X | X |
| Link | Object | X | X |
| Link.hash | Property | X | X |
| Link.host | Property | X | X |
| Link.hostname | Property | X | X |
| Link.href | Property | X | X |
| Link.onClick | Event | X | X |
| Link.onMouseOut | Event | X | X |
| Link.onMouseOver | Event | X | X |
| Link.pathname | Property | X | X |
| Link.port | Property | X | X |
| Link.protocol | Property | X | X |
| Link.search | Property | X | X |
| Link.target | Property | X | X |

*continues*

| Syntax | Type | 3.0 | 3.5 |
|---|---|---|---|
| Location | Object | X | X |
| Location.hash | Property | X | X |
| Location.host | Property | X | X |
| Location.hostname | Property | X | X |
| Location.href | Property | X | X |
| Location.pathname | Property | X | X |
| Location.port | Property | X | X |
| Location.protocol | Property | X | X |
| Location.reload() | Method | X | X |
| Location.replace() | Method | X | X |
| Location.search | Property | X | X |
| Math() | Object | X | X |
| Math.abs() | Method | X | X |
| Math.acos() | Method | X | X |
| Math.asin() | Method | X | X |
| Math.atan() | Method | X | X |
| Math.atan2() | Method | X | X |
| Math.ceil() | Method | X | X |
| Math.cos() | Method | X | X |
| Math.E | Property | X | X |
| Math.exp() | Method | X | X |
| Math.floor() | Method | X | X |
| Math.LN10 | Property | X | X |
| Math.LN2 | Property | X | X |
| Math.log() | Method | X | X |
| Math.LOG10E | Property | X | X |
| Math.LOG2E | Property | X | X |
| Math.max() | Method | X | X |
| Math.min() | Method | X | X |
| Math.PI | Property | X | X |
| Math.pow() | Method | X | X |
| Math.random() | Method | X | X |
| Math.round() | Method | X | X |
| Math.sin() | Method | X | X |
| Math.sqrt() | Method | X | X |
| Math.SQRT1_2 | Property | X | X |
| Math.SQRT2 | Property | X | X |
| Math.tan() | Method | X | X |
| Math.toSource() | Method | X | X |
| Math.toString() | Method | X | X |
| navigator | Object | X | X |
| navigator.appCodeName | Property | X | X |
| navigator.appName | Property | X | X |

| Syntax | Type | 3.0 | 3.5 |
|---|---|---|---|
| navigator.appVersion | Property | X | X |
| navigator.javaEnabled() | Method | X | X |
| navigator.mimeTypes | Property | X | X |
| navigator.plugins | Property | X | X |
| navigator.plugins.refresh() | Method | X | X |
| navigator.userAgent | Property | X | X |
| new | Operator | X | X |
| Number() | Object | X | X |
| Number.MAX_VALUE | Property | X | X |
| Number.MIN_VALUE | Property | X | X |
| Number.NaN | Property | X | X |
| Number.NEGATIVE_INFINITY | Property | X | X |
| Number.POSITIVE_INFINITY | Property | X | X |
| Number.prototype | Property | X | X |
| Number.toString() | Method | X | X |
| Object() | Object | X | X |
| Object.constructor | Property | X | X |
| Object.eval() | Method | X | X |
| Object.prototype | Property | X | X |
| Object.toString() | Method | X | X |
| Object.valueof() | Method | X | X |
| Option | Object | X | X |
| Option.defaultSelected | Property | X | X |
| Option.selected | Property | X | X |
| Option.text | Property | X | X |
| Option.value | Property | X | X |
| Packages | Object | X | X |
| Packages.java | Property | X | X |
| Packages.netscape | Property | X | X |
| Packages.sun | Property | X | X |
| parseFloat() | Method | X | X |
| parseInt() | Method | X | X |
| Password | Object | X | X |
| Password.blur() | Method | X | X |
| Password.defaultValue | Property | X | X |
| Password.focus() | Method | X | X |
| Password.form | Property | X | X |
| Password.name | Property | X | X |
| Password.onBlur | Event | X | X |
| Password.onFocus | Event | X | X |
| Password.select() | Method | X | X |
| Password.type | Property | X | X |

*continues*

| Syntax | Type | 3.0 | 3.5 |
|---|---|---|---|
| Password.value | Property | X | X |
| Plugin | Object | X | X |
| Plugin.description | Property | X | X |
| Plugin.filename | Property | X | X |
| Plugin.length | Property | X | X |
| Plugin.name | Property | X | X |
| Radio | Object | X | X |
| Radio.blur() | Method | X | X |
| Radio.checked | Property | X | X |
| Radio.click() | Method | X | X |
| Radio.defaultChecked | Property | X | X |
| Radio.focus() | Method | X | X |
| Radio.form | Property | X | X |
| Radio.name | Property | X | X |
| Radio.onBlur | Event | X | X |
| Radio.onClick | Event | X | X |
| Radio.onFocus | Event | X | X |
| Radio.type | Property | X | X |
| Radio.value | Property | X | X |
| Reset | Object | X | X |
| Reset.blur() | Method | X | X |
| Reset.click() | Method | X | X |
| Reset.focus() | Method | X | X |
| Reset.form | Property | X | X |
| Reset.name | Property | X | X |
| Reset.onBlur | Event | X | X |
| Reset.onClick | Event | X | X |
| Reset.onFocus | Event | X | X |
| Reset.type | Property | X | X |
| Reset.value | Property | X | X |
| return | Statement | X | X |
| Select | Object | X | X |
| Select.blur() | Method | X | X |
| Select.focus() | Method | X | X |
| Select.form | Property | X | X |
| Select.length | Property | X | X |
| Select.name | Property | X | X |
| Select.onBlur | Event Handler | X | X |
| Select.onChange | Event Handler | X | X |
| Select.onFocus | Event Handler | X | X |
| Select.options | Property | X | X |
| Select.options.length | Property | X | X |
| Select.options.selectedIndex | Property | X | X |

| Syntax | Type | 3.0 | 3.5 |
|---|---|---|---|
| Select.selectedIndex | Property | X | X |
| Select.type | Property | X | X |
| String() | Object | X | X |
| String.anchor() | Method | X | X |
| String.big() | Method | X | X |
| String.blink() | Method | X | X |
| String.bold() | Method | X | X |
| String.charAt() | Method | X | X |
| String.charCodeAt() | Method | X | X |
| String.fixed() | Method | X | X |
| String.fontcolor() | Method | X | X |
| String.fontsize() | Method | X | X |
| String.fromCharCode() | Method | X | X |
| String.indexOf() | Method | X | X |
| String.italics() | Method | X | X |
| String.lastIndexOf() | Method | X | X |
| String.length | Property | X | X |
| String.link() | Method | X | X |
| String.prototype | Property | X | X |
| String.small() | Method | X | X |
| String.split() | Method | X | X |
| String.strike() | Method | X | X |
| String.sub() | Method | X | X |
| String.substring() | Method | X | X |
| String.sup() | Method | X | X |
| String.toLowerCase() | Method | X | X |
| String.toUpperCase() | Method | X | X |
| Submit | Object | X | X |
| Submit.blur() | Method | X | X |
| Submit.click() | Method | X | X |
| Submit.focus() | Method | X | X |
| Submit.form | Property | X | X |
| Submit.name | Property | X | X |
| Submit.onBlur | Event Handler | X | X |
| Submit.onClick | Event Handler | X | X |
| Submit.onFocus | Event Handler | X | X |
| Submit.type | Property | X | X |
| Submit.value | Property | X | X |
| Text | Object | X | X |
| Text.blur() | Method | X | X |
| Text.defaultValue | Property | X | X |
| Text.focus() | Method | X | X |

*continues*

| Syntax | Type | 3.0 | 3.5 |
|---|---|---|---|
| Text.form | Property | X | X |
| Text.name | Property | X | X |
| Text.onBlur | Event Handler | X | X |
| Text.onChange | Event Handler | X | X |
| Text.onFocus | Event Handler | X | X |
| Text.onSelect | Event Handler | X | X |
| Text.select() | Method | X | X |
| Text.type | Property | X | X |
| Text.value | Property | X | X |
| Textarea | Object | X | X |
| Textarea.blur() | Method | X | X |
| Textarea.defaultValue | Property | X | X |
| Textarea.focus() | Method | X | X |
| Textarea.form | Property | X | X |
| Textarea.name | Property | X | X |
| Textarea.onBlur | Event Handler | X | X |
| Textarea.onChange | Event Handler | X | X |
| Textarea.onFocus | Event Handler | X | X |
| Textarea.onSelect | Event Handler | X | X |
| Textarea.select() | Method | X | X |
| Textarea.type | Property | X | X |
| Textarea.value | Property | X | X |
| this | Keyword | X | X |
| typeof | Operator | X | X |
| unescape() | Function | X | X |
| var | Keyword | X | X |
| void | Operator | X | X |
| while | Statement | X | X |
| Window | Object | X | X |
| window.alert() | Method | X | X |
| window.blur() | Method | X | X |
| window.clearTimeout() | Method | X | X |
| window.close() | Method | X | X |
| window.closed | Property | X | X |
| window.confirm() | Method | X | X |
| window.defaultStatus | Property | X | X |
| window.document | Property | X | X |
| window.focus() | Method | X | X |
| window.frames | Property | X | X |
| window.frames.length | Property | X | X |
| window.history | Property | X | X |
| window.length | Property | X | X |
| window.location | Property | X | X |

| Syntax | Type | 3.0 | 3.5 |
|---|---|---|---|
| window.name | Property | X | X |
| window.onBlur | Event Handler | X | X |
| window.onError | Event Handler | X | X |
| window.onFocus | Event Handler | X | X |
| window.onLoad | Event Handler | X | X |
| window.onUnLoad | Event Handler | X | X |
| window.open() | Method | X | X |
| window.opener | Property | X | X |
| window.parent | Property | X | X |
| window.prompt() | Method | X | X |
| window.scroll() | Method | X | X |
| window.self | Property | X | X |
| window.setTimeout() | Method | X | X |
| window.status | Property | X | X |
| window.top | Property | X | X |
| with | Statement | X | X |

# APPENDIX D

## ECMAScript Standard Syntax

The following table contains a list of ECMAScript syntax that is supported in the Netscape, Microsoft, and Opera Software implementations. Note that this only contains the syntax that is supported in the browsers released by these companies. Each supported object, method, property, or event is listed, followed by the version of the standard that supports it.

**NOTE**

At the time of this writing, the ECMAScript 2.0 standard was not finalized. All items contained in the 2.0 version column are proposed.

# ECMAScript Standard Syntax

| Syntax | Type | 1.0 | 2.0 |
|---|---|---|---|
| - | Operator | X | X |
| -- | Operator | X | X |
| -= | Operator | X | X |
| ! | Operator | X | X |
| != | Operator | X | X |
| % | Operator | X | X |
| %= | Operator | X | X |
| & | Operator | X | X |
| && | Operator | X | X |
| &= | Operator | X | X |
| * | Operator | X | X |
| *= | Operator | X | X |
| , | Operator | X | X |
| / | Operator | X | X |
| /**/ | Operator | X | X |
| // | Operator | X | X |
| /= | Operator | X | X |
| ?: | Operator | X | X |
| ^ | Operator | X | X |
| ^= | Operator | X | X |
| ¦ | Operator | X | X |
| ¦¦ | Operator | X | X |
| ¦= | Operator | X | X |
| ~ | Operator | X | X |
| + | Operator | X | X |
| ++ | Operator | X | X |
| += | Operator | X | X |
| < | Operator | X | X |
| << | Operator | X | X |
| <<= | Operator | X | X |
| <= | Operator | X | X |
| = | Operator | X | X |
| == | Operator | X | X |
| > | Operator | X | X |
| >= | Operator | X | X |
| >> | Operator | X | X |
| >>= | Operator | X | X |
| >>> | Operator | X | X |
| >>>= | Operator | X | X |
| Array() | Object | X | X |
| Array.join() | Method | X | X |

| Syntax | Type | 1.0 | 2.0 |
|---|---|---|---|
| Array.length | Property | X | X |
| Array.prototype | Property | X | X |
| Array.reverse() | Method | X | X |
| Array.sort() | Method | X | X |
| Array.toString() | Method | X | X |
| Boolean() | Object | X | X |
| Boolean.prototype | Property | X | X |
| Boolean.toString() | Method | X | X |
| break | Statement | X | X |
| catch | Reserved | X | X |
| class | Reserved | X | X |
| const | Reserved | X | X |
| continue | Statement | X | X |
| Date() | Object | X | X |
| Date.getDate() | Method | X | X |
| Date.getDay() | Method | X | X |
| Date.getFullYear() | Method | X | X |
| Date.getHours() | Method | X | X |
| Date.getMilliseconds() | Method | X | X |
| Date.getMinutes() | Method | X | X |
| Date.getMonth() | Method | X | X |
| Date.getSeconds() | Method | X | X |
| Date.getTime() | Method | X | X |
| Date.get TimezoneOffset() | Method | X | X |
| Date.getUTCDate() | Method | X | X |
| Date.getUTCDay() | Method | X | X |
| Date.getUTCFullYear() | Method | X | X |
| Date.getUTCHours() | Method | X | X |
| Date.getUTC Milliseconds() | Method | X | X |
| Date.getUTCMinutes() | Method | X | X |
| Date.getUTCMonth() | Method | X | X |
| Date.getUTCSeconds() | Method | X | X |
| Date.getYear() | Method | X | X |
| Date.parse() | Method | X | X |
| Date.prototype | Property | X | X |
| Date.setDate() | Method | X | X |
| Date.setFullYear() | Method | X | X |
| Date.setHours() | Method | X | X |
| Date.setMilliseconds() | Method | X | X |
| Date.setMinutes() | Method | X | X |

*continues*

| Syntax | Type | 1.0 | 2.0 |
| --- | --- | --- | --- |
| Date.setMonth() | Method | X | X |
| Date.setSeconds() | Method | X | X |
| Date.setTime() | Method | X | X |
| Date.setUTCDate() | Method | X | X |
| Date.setUTCFullYear() | Method | X | X |
| Date.setUTCHours() | Method | X | X |
| Date.setUTCMilliseconds() | Method | X | X |
| Date.setUTCMinutes() | Method | X | X |
| Date.setUTCMonth() | Method | X | X |
| Date.setUTCSeconds() | Method | X | X |
| Date.setYear() | Method | X | X |
| Date.toGMTString() | Method | X | X |
| Date.toLocaleString() | Method | X | X |
| Date.toSource() | Method | | X |
| Date.toString() | Method | X | X |
| Date.toUTCString() | Method | X | X |
| Date.UTC() | Method | X | X |
| debugger | Reserved | X | X |
| delete | Statement | X | X |
| do...while | Statement | X | X |
| escape() | Method | X | X |
| eval() | Method | X | X |
| export | Keyword | X | X |
| extends | Keyword | X | X |
| finally | Keyword | X | X |
| for | Statement | X | X |
| for...in | Statement | X | X |
| function | Keyword | X | X |
| if...else | Statement | X | X |
| import | Keyword | X | X |
| in | Statement | X | X |
| Infinity | Keyword | X | X |
| isFinite() | Method | X | X |
| isNaN() | Method | X | X |
| Math() | Object | X | X |
| Math.abs() | Method | X | X |
| Math.acos() | Method | X | X |
| Math.asin() | Method | X | X |
| Math.atan() | Method | X | X |
| Math.atan2() | Method | X | X |
| Math.ceil() | Method | X | X |
| Math.cos() | Method | X | X |
| Math.E | Property | X | X |

| Syntax | Type | 1.0 | 2.0 |
|---|---|---|---|
| Math.exp() | Method | X | X |
| Math.floor() | Method | X | X |
| Math.LN10 | Property | X | X |
| Math.LN2 | Property | X | X |
| Math.log() | Method | X | X |
| Math.LOG10E | Property | X | X |
| Math.LOG2E | Property | X | X |
| Math.max() | Method | X | X |
| Math.min() | Method | X | X |
| Math.PI | Property | X | X |
| Math.pow() | Method | X | X |
| Math.random() | Method | X | X |
| Math.round() | Method | X | X |
| Math.sin() | Method | X | X |
| Math.sqrt() | Method | X | X |
| Math.SQRT1_2 | Property | X | X |
| Math.SQRT2 | Property | X | X |
| Math.tan() | Method | X | X |
| Math.toSource() | Method | X | X |
| Math.toString() | Method | X | X |
| NaN | Keyword | X | X |
| new | Keyword | X | X |
| Number() | Object | X | X |
| Number.MAX_VALUE | Property | X | X |
| Number.MIN_VALUE | Property | X | X |
| Number.NaN | Property | X | X |
| Number.NEGATIVE_INFINITY | Property | X | X |
| Number.POSITIVE_INFINITY | Property | X | X |
| Number.prototype | Property | X | X |
| Number.toSource() | Method | X | X |
| Number.toString() | Method | X | X |
| Object() | Object | X | X |
| Object.constructor | Property | X | X |
| Object.prototype | Property | X | X |
| parseFloat() | Method | X | X |
| parseInt() | Method | X | X |
| return | Operator | X | X |
| Select.length | Property | X | X |
| Select.options.length | Property | X | X |
| String() | Object | X | X |
| String.charAt() | Method | X | X |
| String.charCodeAt() | Method | X | X |

*continues*

| Syntax | Type | 1.0 | 2.0 |
|---|---|---|---|
| String.fromCharCode() | Method | X | X |
| String.indexOf() | Method | X | X |
| String.lastIndexOf() | Method | X | X |
| String.length | Property | X | X |
| String.prototype | Property | X | X |
| String.split() | Method | X | X |
| String.toLowerCase() | Method | X | X |
| String.toSource() | Method | X | X |
| String.toString() | Method | X | X |
| String.toUpperCase() | Method | X | X |
| this | Keyword | X | X |
| throw | Statement | X | X |
| try | Statement | X | X |
| typeof | Operator | X | X |
| undefined | Keyword | X | X |
| unescape() | Function | X | X |
| var | Keyword | X | X |
| void | Operator | X | X |
| while | Statement | X | X |
| with | Statement | X | X |

# APPENDIX E

## Server-Side JavaScript Syntax Support

The following table contains a list of Server-Side JavaScript syntax that Netscape Enterprise servers support. Each supported object, method, or property is listed, followed by the version of the server that supports it.

# Server-Side JavaScript-Supported Syntax

| Syntax | Type | NES2.0 | NES3.0 |
|---|---|---|---|
| - | Operator | X | X |
| - - | Operator | X | X |
| ! | Operator | X | X |
| != | Operator | X | X |
| % | Operator | X | X |
| %= | Operator | X | X |
| & | Operator | X | X |
| && | Operator | X | X |
| &= | Operator | X | X |
| * | Operator | X | X |
| *= | Operator | X | X |
| , | Operator | X | X |
| / | Operator | X | X |
| /**/ | Operator | X | X |
| // | Operator | X | X |
| /= | Operator | X | X |
| ?: | Operator | X | X |
| ^ | Operator | X | X |
| ^= | Operator | X | X |
| ¦ | Operator | X | X |
| ¦¦ | Operator | X | X |
| ¦= | Operator | X | X |
| ~ | Operator | X | X |
| + | Operator | X | X |
| ++ | Operator | X | X |
| += | Operator | X | X |
| < | Operator | X | X |
| << | Operator | X | X |
| <<= | Operator | X | X |
| <= | Operator | X | X |
| = | Operator | X | X |
| -= | Operator | X | X |
| == | Operator | X | X |
| > | Operator | X | X |
| >= | Operator | X | X |
| >> | Operator | X | X |
| >>= | Operator | X | X |
| >>> | Operator | X | X |
| >>>= | Operator | X | X |
| addClient() | Function | X | X |
| addResponseHeader() | Function | | X |

| Syntax | Type | NES2.0 | NES3.0 |
|---|---|---|---|
| Array() | Object | X | X |
| Array.concat() | Method | | X |
| Array.join() | Method | X | X |
| Array.length | Property | X | X |
| Array.pop() | Method | | X |
| Array.push() | Method | | X |
| Array.reverse() | Method | X | X |
| Array.shift() | Method | | X |
| Array.slice() | Method | | X |
| Array.sort() | Method | X | X |
| Array.splice() | Method | | X |
| Array.toString() | Method | X | X |
| Array.unshift() | Method | | X |
| blob | Object | X | X |
| blob.blobImage() | Method | X | X |
| blob.blobLink() | Method | X | X |
| Boolean() | Object | X | X |
| Boolean.prototype | Property | X | X |
| Boolean.toString() | Method | X | X |
| break | Keyword | X | X |
| callC() | Function | X | X |
| client | Object | X | X |
| client.destroy() | Method | X | X |
| client.expiration() | Method | X | X |
| Connection | Object | | X |
| Connection.beginTransaction() | Method | | X |
| Connection.commitTransaction() | Method | | X |
| Connection.connected() | Method | | X |
| Connection.cursor() | Method | | X |
| Connection.execute() | Method | | X |
| Connection.majorErrorCode() | Method | | X |
| Connection.majorErrorMessage() | Method | | X |
| Connection.minorErrorCode() | Method | | X |
| Connection.minorErrorMessage() | Method | | X |
| Connection.prototype | Property | | X |
| Connection.release() | Method | | X |
| Connection.rollbackTransaction() | Method | | X |
| Connection.SQLTable() | Method | | X |
| Connection.storedProc() | Method | | X |
| Connection.toString() | Method | | X |
| continue | Statement | X | X |
| Cursor | Object | X | X |

*continues*

| Syntax | Type | NES2.0 | NES3.0 |
|---|---|---|---|
| Cursor.close() | Method | X | X |
| Cursor.columnName() | Method | X | X |
| Cursor.columns() | Method | X | X |
| Cursor.*cursorColumn* | Property | X | X |
| Cursor.deleteRow() | Method | X | X |
| Cursor.insertRow() | Method | X | X |
| Cursor.next() | Method | X | X |
| Cursor.prototype | Property | X | X |
| Cursor.updateRow() | Method | X | X |
| database | Object | X | X |
| database.beginTransaction() | Method | X | X |
| database.commitTransaction() | Method | X | X |
| database.connect() | Method | X | X |
| database.connected() | Method | X | X |
| database.cursor() | Method | X | X |
| database.disconnect() | Method | X | X |
| database.execute() | Method | X | X |
| database.majorErrorCode() | Method | X | X |
| database.majorErrorMessage() | Method | X | X |
| database.minorErrorCode() | Method | X | X |
| database.minorErrorMessage() | Method | X | X |
| database.prototype | Property | X | X |
| database.rollbackTransaction() | Method | X | X |
| database.SQLTable() | Method | X | X |
| database.storedProc() | Method |  | X |
| database.storedProcArgs() | Method |  | X |
| database.toString() | Method | X | X |
| Date() | Object | X | X |
| Date.getDate() | Method | X | X |
| Date.getDay() | Method | X | X |
| Date.getHours() | Method | X | X |
| Date.getMinutes() | Method | X | X |
| Date.getMonth() | Method | X | X |
| Date.getSeconds() | Method | X | X |
| Date.getTime() | Method | X | X |
| Date.getTimezoneOffset() | Method | X | X |
| Date.getYear() | Method | X | X |
| Date.parse() | Method | X | X |
| Date.prototype | Property | X | X |
| Date.setDate() | Method | X | X |
| Date.setHours() | Method | X | X |
| Date.setMinutes() | Method | X | X |
| Date.setMonth() | Method | X | X |

| Syntax | Type | NES2.0 | NES3.0 |
|---|---|---|---|
| Date.setSeconds() | Method | X | X |
| Date.setTime() | Method | X | X |
| Date.setYear() | Method | X | X |
| Date.toGMTString() | Method | X | X |
| Date.toLocaleString() | Method | X | X |
| Date.toString() | Method | X | X |
| Date.UTC() | Method | X | X |
| DbPool() | Object | | X |
| DbPool.connect() | Method | | X |
| DbPool.connected() | Method | | X |
| DbPool.connection() | Method | | X |
| DbPool.DbPool() | Method | | X |
| DbPool.disconnect() | Method | | X |
| DbPool.majorErrorCode() | Method | | X |
| DbPool.majorErrorMessage() | Method | | X |
| DbPool.minorErrorCode() | Method | | X |
| DbPool.minorErrorMessage() | Method | | X |
| DbPool.prototype | Property | | X |
| DbPool.storedProcArgs() | Method | | X |
| DbPool.toString() | Method | | X |
| debug() | Function | x | X |
| delete | Statement | X | X |
| deleteResponseHeader() | Function | | X |
| do...while | Statement | X | X |
| Embed | Object | X | X |
| escape() | Function | X | X |
| export | Statement | | X |
| File() | Object | X | X |
| File.byteToString() | Method | X | X |
| File.clearError() | Method | X | X |
| File.close() | Method | X | X |
| File.eof() | Method | X | X |
| File.error() | Method | X | X |
| File.exists() | Method | X | X |
| File.flush() | Method | X | X |
| File.getLength() | Method | X | X |
| File.getPosition() | Method | X | X |
| File.open() | Method | X | X |
| File.prototype | Property | X | X |
| File.read() | Method | X | X |
| File.readByte() | Method | X | X |
| File.readln() | Method | X | X |

*continues*

| Syntax | Type | NES2.0 | NES3.0 |
|---|---|---|---|
| File.setPosition() | Method | X | X |
| File.stringToByte() | Method | X | X |
| File.write() | Method | X | X |
| File.writeByte() | Method | X | X |
| File.writeln() | Method | X | X |
| flush() | Function | X | X |
| for | Statement | X | X |
| for...in | Statement | X | X |
| function | Statement | X | X |
| Function() | Object | X | X |
| Function.arguments | Property | X | X |
| Function.arity | Property | | X |
| Function.caller | Property | X | X |
| Function.prototype | Property | X | X |
| Function.toString() | Method | X | X |
| getOptionValue() | Method | X | X |
| getOptionValueCount() | Method | X | X |
| if...else | Statement | X | X |
| isNaN() | Function | X | X |
| Lock() | Object | | X |
| Lock.isValid() | Method | | X |
| Lock.lock() | Method | | X |
| Lock.unlock() | Method | | X |
| Math() | Object | X | X |
| Math.abs() | Method | X | X |
| Math.acos() | Method | X | X |
| Math.asin() | Method | X | X |
| Math.atan() | Method | X | X |
| Math.atan2() | Method | X | X |
| Math.ceil() | Method | X | X |
| Math.cos() | Method | X | X |
| Math.E | Property | X | X |
| Math.exp() | Method | X | X |
| Math.floor() | Method | X | X |
| Math.LN10 | Property | X | X |
| Math.LN2 | Property | X | X |
| Math.log() | Method | X | X |
| Math.LOG10E | Property | X | X |
| Math.LOG2E | Property | X | X |
| Math.max() | Method | X | X |
| Math.min() | Method | X | X |
| Math.PI | Property | X | X |
| Math.pow() | Method | X | X |

# O'REILLY BOOK REGISTRATION

Register your book with O'Reilly by completing this card and receive a **FREE** copy of our latest catalog. Or register online at **register.oreilly.com** and, in addition to our catalog, we'll send you email notification of new editions of this book, information about new titles, and special offers available only to registered O'Reilly customers.

Which book(s) are you registering? Please include title and ISBN # (above bar code on back cover)

Title _____ ISBN # _____

Title _____ ISBN # _____

Title _____ ISBN # _____

Name _____ Company/Organization _____

Address _____

City _____ State _____ Zip/Postal Code _____ Country _____

Telephone _____ Email address _____

**www.oreilly.com**

Part #10326

# BUSINESS REPLY MAIL

FIRST CLASS MAIL    PERMIT NO. 80    SEBASTOPOL, CA

Postage will be paid by addressee

**O'Reilly & Associates, Inc.**
BOOK REGISTRATION
1005 GRAVENSTEIN HIGHWAY NORTH
SEBASTOPOL, CA 95472-9910

| Syntax | Type | NES2.0 | NES3.0 |
|--------|------|--------|--------|
| Math.random() | Method | X | X |
| Math.round() | Method | X | X |
| Math.sin() | Method | X | X |
| Math.sqrt() | Method | X | X |
| Math.SQRT1_2 | Property | X | X |
| Math.SQRT2 | Property | X | X |
| Math.tan() | Method | X | X |
| Math.toSource() | Method | X | X |
| Math.toString() | Method | X | X |
| NaN | Keyword | X | X |
| new | Operator | X | X |
| Number() | Object | X | X |
| Number.MAX_VALUE | Property | X | X |
| Number.MIN_VALUE | Property | X | X |
| Number.NaN | Property | X | X |
| Number.NEGATIVE_INFINITY | Property | X | X |
| Number.POSITIVE_INFINITY | Property | X | X |
| Number.prototype | Property | X | X |
| Object() | Object | X | X |
| Object.constructor | Property | X | X |
| Object.eval() | Method | X | X |
| Object.unwatch() | Method | | X |
| Object.valueof() | Method | X | X |
| Object.watch() | Method | | X |
| Option | Object | X | X |
| Option.defaultSelected | Property | X | X |
| Option.selected | Property | X | X |
| Option.text | Property | X | X |
| Option.value | Property | X | X |
| parseFloat() | Function | X | X |
| parseInt() | Function | X | X |
| project | Object | X | X |
| project.lock() | Method | X | X |
| project.unlock() | Method | X | X |
| redirect() | Function | X | X |
| RegExp() | Object | | X |
| RegExp,$* | Property | | X |
| RegExp.$& | Property | | X |
| RegExp.$_ | Property | | X |
| RegExp.$` | Property | | X |
| RegExp.$' | Property | | X |
| RegExp.$+ | Property | | X |

*continues*

| Syntax | Type | NES2.0 | NES3.0 |
|---|---|---|---|
| RegExp.$1,$2,...$9 | Property | | X |
| RegExp.compile() | Method | | X |
| RegExp.exec() | Method | | X |
| RegExp.global | Property | | X |
| RegExp.ignoreCase | Property | | X |
| RegExp.input | Property | | X |
| RegExp.lastIndex | Property | | X |
| RegExp.lastMatch | Property | | X |
| RegExp.lastParen | Property | | X |
| RegExp.leftContext | Property | | X |
| RegExp.multiline | Property | | X |
| RegExp.rightContext | Property | | X |
| RegExp.source | Property | | X |
| RegExp.test() | Method | | X |
| registerCFunction() | Function | X | X |
| request | Object | X | X |
| request.agent | Property | X | X |
| request.imageX | Property | X | X |
| request.imageY | Property | X | X |
| request.*inputName* | Property | X | X |
| request.ip | Property | X | X |
| request.method | Property | X | X |
| request.protocol | Property | X | X |
| Resultset | Object | | X |
| Resultset.close() | Method | | X |
| Resultset.columnName() | Method | | X |
| Resultset.columns() | Method | | X |
| Resultset.next() | Method | | X |
| Resultset.prototype | Property | | X |
| return | Statement | X | X |
| SendMail() | Object | | X |
| SendMail.Bcc | Property | | X |
| SendMail.Body | Property | | X |
| SendMail.Cc | Property | | X |
| SendMail.errorCode() | Method | | X |
| SendMail.errorMessage() | Method | | X |
| SendMail.Errorsto | Property | | X |
| SendMail.From | Property | | X |
| SendMail.Organization | Property | | X |
| SendMail.prototype | Property | | X |
| SendMail.Replyto | Property | | X |
| SendMail.send() | Method | | X |
| SendMail.Smtpserver | Property | | X |

| Syntax | Type | NES2.0 | NES3.0 |
| --- | --- | --- | --- |
| SendMail.Subject | Property | | X |
| SendMail.To | Property | | X |
| server | Object | X | X |
| server.host | Property | X | X |
| server.hostname | Property | X | X |
| server.lock() | Method | X | X |
| server.port | Property | X | X |
| server.protocol | Property | X | X |
| server.unlock() | Method | X | X |
| ssjs_generateClientID() | Function | | X |
| ssjs_getCGIVariable() | Function | | X |
| ssjs_getClientID() | Function | | X |
| Stproc | Object | | X |
| Stproc.close() | Method | | X |
| Stproc.outParamCount() | Method | | X |
| Stproc.outParameters() | Method | | X |
| Stproc.prototype | Property | | X |
| Stproc.resultSet() | Method | | X |
| Stproc.returnValue() | Method | | X |
| String() | Object | X | X |
| String.anchor() | Method | X | X |
| String.big() | Method | X | X |
| String.blink() | Method | X | X |
| String.bold() | Method | X | X |
| String.charAt() | Method | X | X |
| String.charCodeAt() | Method | | X |
| String.concat() | Method | | X |
| String.fixed() | Method | X | X |
| String.fontcolor() | Method | X | X |
| String.fontsize() | Method | X | X |
| String.fromCharCode() | Method | | X |
| String.indexOf() | Method | X | X |
| String.italics() | Method | X | X |
| String.lastIndexOf() | Method | X | X |
| String.length | Property | X | X |
| String.link() | Method | X | X |
| String.prototype | Property | | X |
| String.slice() | Method | X | X |
| String.small() | Method | X | X |
| String.split() | Method | X | X |
| String.strike() | Method | X | X |
| String.sub() | Method | X | X |

*continues*

| Syntax | Type | NES2.0 | NES3.0 |
|---|---|---|---|
| String.substr() | Method | | X |
| String.substring() | Method | X | X |
| String.sup() | Method | X | X |
| String.toLowerCase() | Method | X | X |
| String.toUpperCase() | Method | X | X |
| switch | Statement | | X |
| this | Keyword | X | X |
| var | Keyword | X | X |
| while | Statement | X | X |
| with | Statement | X | X |
| write() | Function | X | X |

# APPENDIX F

## JavaScript Resources

When you program a lot in a particular language, especially one that's Internet related, you come across many resources. This appendix contains everything from general information to core documentation and reference to newsgroups to code snippet sites—all on the JavaScript language and all online.

## General Information

- **Ask the JavaScript Pro**
  http://www.inquiry.com/techtips/js_pro/
- **DevEdge Online—JavaScript**
  http://developer.netscape.com/tech/javascript/index.html
- **Danny Goodman's JavaScript Pages**
  http://www.dannyg.com/javascript
- **javascript.com**  http://www.javascript.com
- **JavaScript Directories**
  http://www.developer.com/directories/pages/dir.javascript.html
- **Doc JavaScript**  http://www.webreference.com/js
- **Focus on JavaScript**
  http://javascript.about.com
- **Java Goodies JavaScript Repository**
  http://www.javagoodies.com
- **The JavaScript Archive**
  http://planetx.bloomu.edu/~mpscho/jsarchive
- **The JavaScript Workshop**  http://www.starlingtech.com/books/javascript
- **JavaScript World**  http://www.jsworld.com
- **Java/JavaScript Resources on the Internet**
  http://www.Web-Hosting.com/javalinks.html
- **Netscape's Core JavaScript 1.4 Guide**
  http://developer.netscape.com/docs/manuals/js/core/jsguide/index.htm

- **Netscape's Server-Side JavaScript 1.2 Guide**
  http://developer.netscape.com/
- **Timothy's JavaScript Examples** http://www.essex1.com/people/
  timothy/js-index.htm
- **Using JavaScript and Graphics**
  http://www.javaworld.com/javaworld/jw-08-1996
  /jw-08-javascript.html
- **Using JavaScript's Built-In Objects** http://www.javaworld.com/
  javaworld/jw-05-1996/jw-05-javascript.html
- **Voodoo's Intro to JavaScript** http://rummelplatz.
  uni-mannheim.de/~skoch/js/script.htm
- **Webcoder.COM** http://webcoder.com
- **Yahoo! Computers and Internet: Programming Languages: JavaScript**
  http://www.yahoo.com/Computers_and_Internet/Programming_Languages/
  JavaScript
- **Open Directory Top: Computers: Programming: Languages: JavaScript**
  http://www.dmoz.org/Computers/Programming/Languages/JavaScript

# Reference

- **Ecma-262** http://www.ecma.ch/stand/ecma-262.htm
- **Microsoft Scripting Technologies** http://msdn.microsoft.com/scripting
- **Netscape's Core JavaScript Reference** http://developer.netscape.com/

# Newsgroups

- **secnews.netscape.com** netscape.public.mozilla.jseng
- **secnews.netscape.com (Secure)** at the following locations:
  netscape.dev.js-debugger
  netscape.dev.livewire
  netscape.dev.livewire.dbconfig
  netscape.dev.livewire.programming
  netscape.dev.visual-javascript
  netscape.devs-javascript
  netscape.devs-livescript
- **Public Newsgroups** at the following locations:
  comp.lang.javascript
  borland.public.intrabuilder.javascript

# Code Snippets

- **Cut-N-Paste JavaScript**
  http://www.infohiway.com/javascript/indexf.htm

# INDEX

## Symbols

# M

# X

# Y - Z